Easy Learning

French

Dictionary

BEGINNER'S FRENCH DICTIONARY

 HarperResource

An Imprint of HarperCollins*Publishers*

Easy Learning
French
Dictionary

HarperCollins*Publishers*

third edition 2004

© HarperCollins Publishers 1996, 1998, 2001, 2004

HarperCollins Publishers
Westerhill Road, Bishopbriggs, Glasgow G64 2QT
Great Britain

www.collinsdictionaries.com

Collins® and Bank of English® are registered trademarks of
HarperCollins Publishers Limited

ISBN 0-00-716345-2

HarperCollins Publishers, Inc
10 East 53rd Street, New York, NY 10022

ISBN 0-06-057579-4

Library of Congress Cataloging-in-Publication Data has been applied for

www.harpercollins.com

project management
Ray Carrick, Michela Clari

general editor
Horst Kopleck

editorial coordination
Vivian Marr, Nicola Cooke
second edition
Sharon J. Hunter, Caitlin McMahon
third edition
Gaëlle Amiot-Cadey

editors
Christine Penman   Daphne Day   Chantal Testa
Harry Campbell   Cécile Aubinière-Robb   Gavin Killip
Hélène Bernaërt   Elspeth Anderson   Caroline Lehni
Joane Siksous   Sabine Citron

computing staff
Ann Rautenbach

our thanks to the following for their help in researching the project
Maree Airlie, Teresa Álvarez, Phyllis Gautier, Janet Gough, Sharon Hunter,
Mary James, Cordelia Lilly, Carol MacLeod, Jill McNair, Janet Chalmers

illustrations   *maps*
Richard Anderson   HarperCollins Cartographic

series editor
Lorna Sinclair Knight

Corpus Acknowledgements

We would like to acknowledge the assistance of the many hundreds of individuals and
companies who have kindly given permission for copyright material to be used in the
Bank of English. The written sources include many national and regional newspapers in
Britain and overseas; magazine and periodical publishers; and book publishers in Britain,
the United States and Australia. Extensive spoken data has been provided by radio and
television broadcasting companies; research workers at many universities and other
institutions; and numerous individual contributors. We are grateful to them all.

Printed in Italy by Amadeus S.p.A.

CONTENTS

INTRODUCTION

Collins Easy Learning French Dictionary is an innovative dictionary designed specifically for anyone starting to learn French. We are grateful to all those teachers who have contributed to its development by advising us on how to tailor it to the needs of their students. We also gratefully acknowledge the help of the examining boards, whom we have consulted throughout this project, and whose word lists and exam papers we carefully studied when compiling this dictionary.

Note on trademarks
Entered words which we have reason to believe constitute trademarks have been designated as such. However, neither the presence nor the absence of such designation should be regarded as affecting the legal status of any trademark.

DICTIONARY SKILLS

Using a dictionary is a skill you can improve with practice and by following some basic guidelines. This section gives you a detailed explanation of how to use the dictionary to ensure you get the most out of it.

The answers to the questions in this section are on page 16.

▶ MAKE SURE YOU LOOK IN THE RIGHT SIDE OF THE DICTIONARY

The French–English side comes first: you look there to find the meaning of a French word. The second part is English–French. That's what you need for translating into French. (To remind yourself which side is which, you could remember the phrase *French first.*) At the top of every page, you will see either **French ~ English** or **English ~ French**, so you can see immediately if you've got the side you want. The middle pages of the book have a blue border so that you can see where one side finishes and the other starts.

> 1 Which side of the dictionary would you need to look up to translate *"le vélo"*?

▶ FINDING THE WORD YOU WANT

When you are looking for a word, for example **nouveau**, look at the first letter – **n** – and find the **N** section in the French–English side. Look at page 186. At the top of the page, you'll find the words **né → nez**. These are the first and last words on that page. So **nouveau** is not going to be on page 186 because its second letter, **o**, comes after **e**, the second letter of **nez**. You have to go past all the words starting with **ne** and all the words starting with **ni** until you get to words starting with **no**. Scan down these until you find the word you want. Remember that even if a letter has an accent on it, it makes no difference to the alphabetical order.

> 2 Which comes first – *"nager"* or *"nécessaire"*?
> 3 Does *"nouveau"* come before or after *"Noël"*?
> 4 Does *"chou–fleur"* come before or after *"chocolat"*?

► MAKE SURE YOU LOOK AT THE RIGHT ENTRY

An entry is made up of a **word**, its <u>translations</u> and, often, example phrases to show you how to use the translations. If there is more than one entry for the same word, then there is a warning box to tell you so. Look at the following example entries:

> **flat** ADJECTIVE
> | see also **flat** NOUN |
> [1] <u>plat</u> ◊ *a flat roof* un toit plat ◊ *flat shoes* des chaussures plates
> [2] <u>crevé</u> (*tyre*) ◊ *I've got a flat tyre.* J'ai un pneu crevé.

> **flat** NOUN
> | see also **flat** ADJECTIVE |
> l' <u>appartement</u> MASC ◊ *She lives in a flat.* Elle habite un appartement.

> 5 Which of the two entries above will help you translate the phrase "My car has a flat tyre"?
> Look for the two clues which are there to help you:
>
> ◇ an example similar to what you want to say
> ◇ the word ADJECTIVE

Always pay attention to information boxes – they tell you if there is more than one entry for the same word, give you guidance on grammatical points, and tell you about differences between French and British life.

► CHOOSING THE RIGHT TRANSLATION

The main translation of a word is shown on a new line and is underlined to make it stand out from the rest of the entry. If there is more than one main translation for a word, each one is numbered. If an entry continues over the page, there is a signpost to indicate this ☞.

Often you will see phrases in *italics*, preceded by a white diamond ◊. These show how the translation they follow can be used. They also help you choose the translation you want because they give you examples of the context in which it can be used.

> **bouillant** ADJECTIVE
> [1] <u>boiling</u> ◊ *Faites cuire les pâtes à l'eau bouillante.* Cook the pasta in boiling water.
> [2] <u>piping hot</u> ◊ *La soupe est servie bouillante.* The soup should be served piping hot.

> to **overlook** VERB
> [1] <u>donner sur</u> (*have view of*) ◊ *The hotel overlooked the beach.* L'hôtel donnait sur la plage.
> [2] <u>négliger</u> (*forget about*) ◊ *He had overlooked one important problem.* Il avait négligé un problème important.

6 Use the dictionary to translate "That's a very hard question".

Words often have more than one meaning and more than one translation: if you don't **get** to the station on time, you don't arrive on time, but if you say "I don't **get** it", you mean you don't understand. When you are translating from English, be careful to choose the French word that has the particular meaning you want. The dictionary offers you a lot of help with this. Look at the following entry:

pool NOUN
1 la flaque (*puddle*)
2 l' étang MASC (*pond*)
3 la piscine (*for swimming*)
4 le billard américain (*game*)

A **pool** can be a puddle, a pond or a swimming pool; **pool** can also be a game. Underlining highlights all the main translations, the numbers tell you that there is more than one possible translation and the words in brackets in *italics* after the translations help you choose the translation you want.

7 How would you translate "I like playing pool"?

Never take the first translation you see without looking at the others. Always look to see if there is more than one translation underlined.

Phrases in **bold type** preceded by a black diamond ♦ are phrases which are particularly common or important. Sometimes the phrases have a completely different translation from the main translation; sometimes the translation is the same. For example:

le **dommage** NOUN
damage ◊ *La tempête a causé d'importants dommages.* The storm caused a lot of damage.
♦**C'est dommage.** It's a shame. ◊ *C'est dommage que tu ne puisses pas venir.* It's a shame you can't come.

to **go out** VERB
1 sortir (*person*) ◊ *Are you going out tonight?* Tu sors ce soir?
♦**to go out with somebody** sortir avec quelqu'un ◊ *Are you going out with him?* Est-ce que tu sors avec lui?
2 s'éteindre (*light, fire, candle*) ◊ *Suddenly the lights went out.* Soudain, les lumières se sont éteintes.

When you look up a word, make sure you look beyond the main translations to see if the entry includes any **bold phrases**.

8 In a job advert you read that applicants "*doivent tous passer une visite médicale*". What must they all do?

Look up "visite" and find the answer as quickly as possible by skimming down the *bold phrases*.

► MAKING USE OF PHRASES IN THE DICTIONARY

Sometimes when you look up a word you will find not only the word, but the exact phrase you want. For example, you might want to say "*What's the date today?*". Look up **date** and you will find:

> **date** NOUN
> 1 la <u>date</u> ◊ *my date of birth* ma date de naissance
> ♦**What's the date today?** Quel jour sommes-nous?

Sometimes you have to adapt what you find in the dictionary. If you want to say "*I play darts*" and look up **dart** you will find:

> **dart** NOUN
> la <u>fléchette</u> ◊ *to play darts* jouer aux fléchettes

You have to substitute *je joue* for the infinitive form *jouer*. You will often have to adapt the infinitive in this way, adding the correct ending for **je**, **tu**, **il** etc and choosing the present, future or past form. For help with this, look at the verb tables. **Jouer** is a verb ending in *–er* so it follows the same pattern as **aimer**, which is set out on page 316.

> **9** How would you say "*We played football*"?

Phrases containing nouns and adjectives also need to be adapted. You may need to make the noun plural, or the adjective feminine or plural. Remember that some nouns and adjectives have irregular feminine or plural forms and that this is shown in the entry.

> **10** How would you say "*The jewels are beautiful*"?

► DON'T OVERUSE THE DICTIONARY

It takes time to look up words so try to avoid using the dictionary unnecessarily, especially in exams. Think carefully about what you want to say and see if you can put it another way, using words you already know. To rephrase things you can:

◇ Use a word with a similar meaning. This is particularly easy with adjectives, as there are a lot of words which mean *good*, *bad*, *big* etc and you're sure to know at least one.

◇ Use negatives: if the cake you made was a total disaster, you could just say it wasn't very good.

◇ Use particular examples instead of general terms. If you are asked to describe the sports facilities in your area, and time is short, don't look up *facilities* - say something like "In our town there is a swimming pool and a football ground."

11 You want to ask "*Have you got any pets?*". How could you avoid using the word "*pet*" if you don't know it?

12 How could you say "*The palace of Versailles is huge*" without looking up the word "*huge*"?

You can also often guess the meaning of a French word by using others to give you a clue. If you see the sentence "*j'écoute de la musique rap*", you may not know the meaning of the word **écoute**, but you do know it's a verb because it's preceded by **j'**. Therefore it must be something you can do to music: **listen**. So the translation is: *I listen to rap music.*

13 In a description of a holiday centre you see a picture of bikes and read "*On peut louer des vélos: 20F la journée*". You may not know the meaning of "*louer*", but you can see that you have to pay 20 francs, which gives you a clue to what it could mean. What can you do – ride bikes, borrow bikes or hire bikes?

PARTS OF SPEECH

There are two entries for **flat** because this word can be a noun or an adjective. It helps to choose correctly between entries if you know how to recognize these different types of words.

▶ NOUNS AND PRONOUNS

Nouns often appear with words like *a, the, this, that, my, your* and *his*. They can be singular (abbreviated to SING in the dictionary):

his **dog**　　　　　her **cat**　　　　　*a* **street**

or plural (abbreviated to PL in the dictionary):

the **facts**　　　*those* **people**　　　*his* **shoes**　　　*our* **holidays**

They can be the subject of a verb:

Vegetables are good for you

or the object of a verb:

I play **tennis**

Words like *I, me, you, he, she, him, her* and *they* are pronouns. They can be used instead of nouns. You can refer to a person as *he* or *she* or to a thing as *it*.

> *I bought my mother a box of chocolates.*
>
> **14** Which three words are nouns in this sentence?
> **15** Which of the nouns is plural?
> **16** Which word is a pronoun?

French nouns are either masculine or feminine (abbreviated to MASC and FEM). Masculine nouns are shown by **le**:

le bateau　　　　　*le* chien　　　　　*le* jardin

Feminine nouns are shown by **la**:

> **la** porte   **la** robe   **la** souris

If a noun starts with a vowel or a vowel sound, then **le** or **la** becomes **l'**:

> **l'**ami   **l'**eau   **l'**orage   **l'**histoire

The plural forms of **le**, **la** and **l'** is **les**. As in English, the plural of most French nouns is made by adding **s**:

> **les** chiens   **les** portes   **les** tables

If the singular form already ends in **s**, or if it ends in **x**, then you don't have to add anything:

> **l'**ananas   **les** ananas
> **la** voix   **les** voix

Sometimes, however, the plural form is irregular and this is shown in the entry:

cheval NOUN (PL les **chevaux**)
  horse

horse NOUN
  le <u>cheval</u>
  (les chevaux PL)

Je me brosse les dents tous les soirs.

17 Two words in this sentence are nouns. Which ones?
18 Are they singular or plural?
19 What is the plural form of *"le choix"*?
20 Look in the dictionary to find the plural form of *"le travail"*.

▶ ADJECTIVES

Flat can be an adjective as well as a noun. Adjectives describe nouns: your tyre can be **flat**, you can have a pair of **flat** shoes.

21 *"Dark"* is an adjective in one of these sentences and a noun in the other. Which is which?

I'm not afraid of the dark.
She's got dark hair.

French adjectives can be masculine or feminine, singular or plural, depending on the noun they describe:

un **petit** garçon (MASC SING)
une **petite** fille (FEM SING = masculine singular + e)
trois **petits** garçons (MASC PL = masculine singular + s)
trois **petites** filles (FEM PL = masculine singular + es)

Only the masculine singular form of regular adjectives is shown in the dictionary.

So if you want to find out what sort of shoes **des chaussures plates** are, look under **plat**.

If the feminine or the plural form of an adjective does *not* follow the above rules, then the irregular form is shown in the dictionary:

frais ADJECTIVE (FEM SING **fraîche**)
| *see also* **frais** NOUN |
1 fresh

fresh ADJECTIVE
frais MASC
fraîche FEM

bon ADJECTIVE, ADVERB (FEM SING **bonne**)
| *see also* **bon** NOUN |
1 good

good ADJECTIVE
1 bon MASC
bonne FEM

If the masculine form ends in **s** or **x**, then you don't need to add **s** to make the masculine plural. And if the masculine form ends in **e**, you don't add anything to form the feminine form. But remember – if the adjective ends in **é**, then it behaves like any regular adjective.

MASC SING	FEM SING	MASC PL	FEM PL
gris	grise	gris	grises
anxieux	anxieuse	anxieux	anxieuses
agréable	agréable	agréables	agréables
passé	passée	passés	passées

Some adjectives remain the same whether they're masculine, feminine or plural. This is also shown in the dictionary:

arrière ADJECTIVE (MASC, FEM, PL)
| *see also* **arrière** NOUN |
back

back ADJECTIVE, ADVERB
| *see also* **back** NOUN, VERB |
arrière MASC, FEM, PL

22 What is the feminine singular form of "*vert*"?
23 What is the masculine plural form of "*aimable*"?
24 What forms can "*heureux*" be?
25 What is the masculine plural form of "*gras*"? And the feminine singular (look in the dictionary for this one)?

She's going to record the programme for me.
His time in the race was a new world record.

Record in the first sentence is a verb. In the second, it is a noun.

One way to recognize a verb is that it frequently comes with a pronoun such as **I**, **you** or **she**, or with somebody's name. Verbs can relate to the present, the past or the future. They have a number of different forms to show this: **I'm going** (present), **he will go** (future), and **Nicola went by herself** (past). Often verbs appear with **to**: **they promised to go**. This basic form of the verb is called the infinitive.

In this dictionary, verbs are preceded by "to", so you can identify them at a glance. No matter which of the four previous examples you want to translate, you should look up to **go**, not **going** or **went**. If you want to translate **I thought**, look up to **think**

---

26 What would you look up to translate the verbs in these phrases?

I **went**	*she's* **crying**	*he was* **lying**
I **did** *it*	*he's* out	*they've* **gone**

Verbs have different endings, depending on whether you are talking about **je**, **tu**, **nous**, **ils** etc: **j'aime**, **tu aimes**, **nous aimons**, **ils aiment** etc. They also have different forms for the present, future, past etc. **Nous mangeons** (*we eat* = present), **nous avons mangé** (*we ate* = past). **manger** is the infinitive and is the form that appears in the dictionary.

Sometimes the verb changes completely between the infinitive form and the **je**, **tu**, **ils** etc form. For example, *I go* is **je vais**, but *to go* is **aller**, and **nous faisons** (*we do*) comes from **faire** (*to do*). **J'ai fait** (*I have done* or *I did*) also comes from **faire**.

On pages 316-329 of the dictionary, you will find tables of the most important forms of 14 French verbs. And on pages 330-332, you will find a list of the main forms of other French irregular verbs.

▶ ADVERBS

An adverb is a word that describes a verb or an adjective:

> Write **soon**.
> They arrived **late**.
>
> Check your work **carefully**.
> The film was **very** good.

In the sentence "*The swimming pool is open daily*", **daily** is an adverb describing the adjective **open**. In the phrase "*my daily routine*", **daily** is an adjective describing the noun **routine**. We use the same word in English but to get the right French translation, it is important to know if it's being used as an adjective or an adverb. When you look up **daily** you find:

> **daily** ADJECTIVE, ADVERB
> [1] quotidien MASC
> quotidienne FEM
> ◊ *It's part of my daily routine.* Ça fait
> partie de mes occupations
> quotidiennes.
> [2] tous les jours ◊ *The pool is open
> daily from 9 a.m. to 6 p.m.* La piscine
> est ouverte tous les jours de neuf
> heures à dix-huit heures.

The examples show you **daily** being used as an adjective and as an adverb and will help you choose the right French translation.

> Take the sentence "The menu changes daily".
>
> 27 Does "daily" go with the noun "menu" or the verb "changes"?
> 28 Is it an adverb or an adjective?
> 29 How would you translate "daily" in this sentence?

▶ PREPOSITIONS

Prepositions are words like **for**, **with** and **across**, which are followed by nouns or pronouns:

*I've got a present **for** David.*   *Come **with** me.*   *He ran **across** the road.*

> *The party's over.*
> *The shop's just over the road.*
>
> 30 In one of these sentences "over" is an adjective describing a noun, in the other it is a preposition followed by a noun. Which is which?

▶ ANSWERS

1 the French side
2 **nager**
3 **nouveau** comes after **Noël**
4 **chou–fleur** comes after **chocolat**
5 the first entry (the ADJECTIVE entry)
6 **C'est une question très difficile.**
7 **J'aime jouer au billard américain.**
8 they must all have a **medical examination**
9 **Nous avons joué au football.**
10 **Les bijoux sont beaux.**
11 you could ask "Have you got a cat or a dog?"
12 you could say "Very big."
13 you can **hire** bikes
14 **mother**, **box** and **chocolates** are nouns
15 **chocolates** is plural
16 **I** is a pronoun
17 **dents** and **soirs** are nouns
18 they are both plural
19 **les choix**
20 **les travaux**
21 **dark** in the first sentence is a noun and in the second, it's an adjective
22 **verte**
23 **aimables**
24 masculine singular or plural
25 the masculine plural form is **gras** and the feminine singular form is **grasse**
26 to **go**, to **cry**, to **lie**, to **do**, to **be**, to **go**
27 **daily** goes with the verb **changes**
28 it is an adverb
29 **tous les jours**
30 in the first sentence, **over** is an adjective and in the second, it's a preposition

A

a VERB *see* **avoir**

> *a should not be confused with the preposition à.*

♦ **Il a beaucoup d'amis.** He has a lot of friends.
♦ **Il a mangé des frites.** He had some chips.
♦ **Il a neigé pendant la nuit.** It snowed during the night.
♦ **il y a (1)** there is ◊ *Il y a un bon film à la télé.* There's a good film on TV.
♦ **il y a (2)** there are ◊ *Il y a beaucoup de monde.* There are lots of people.

à PREPOSITION

> *à should not be confused with the verb form a. See also **au (=à+le)** and **aux (=à+les)**.*

1. at ◊ *être à la maison* to be at home ◊ *à trois heures* at 3 o'clock
2. in ◊ *être à Paris* to be in Paris ◊ *habiter au Portugal* to live in Portugal ◊ *habiter à la campagne* to live in the country ◊ *au printemps* in the spring ◊ *au mois de juin* in June
3. to ◊ *aller à Paris* to go to Paris ◊ *aller au Portugal* to go to Portugal ◊ *aller à la campagne* to go to the country ◊ *donner quelque chose à quelqu'un* to give something to somebody ◊ *Cette veste appartient à Marie.* This jacket belongs to Marie. ◊ *Je n'ai rien à faire.* I've got nothing to do.
♦ **Ce livre est à Paul.** This book is Paul's.
♦ **Cette voiture est à nous.** This car is ours.
4. by ◊ *à bicyclette* by bicycle ◊ *être payé à l'heure* to be paid by the hour
♦ **à pied** on foot
♦ **C'est à côté de chez moi.** It's near my house.
♦ **C'est à dix kilomètres d'ici.** It's 10 kilometres from here.
♦ **C'est à dix minutes d'ici.** It's 10 minutes from here.
♦ **cent kilomètres à l'heure** 100 kilometres an hour
♦ **À bientôt!** See you soon! ◊ *À demain!* See you tomorrow! ◊ *À samedi!* See you on Saturday! ◊ *À tout à l'heure!* See you later!

abandonner VERB

1. to abandon ◊ *Avant les vacances, beaucoup de chiens sont abandonnés par leurs maîtres.* Before the holidays, a lot of dogs are abandoned by their owners.
2. to give up ◊ *J'ai décidé d'abandonner la natation.* I've decided to give up swimming.

l'**abeille** FEM NOUN
bee

abîmer VERB
to damage
♦ **s'abîmer** to get damaged

l'**abonnement** MASC NOUN
1. season ticket
2. subscription (*to magazine*)

s'**abonner** VERB
♦ **s'abonner à une revue** to take out a subscription to a magazine

l'**abord** MASC NOUN
♦ **d'abord** first ◊ *Je vais rentrer chez moi d'abord.* I'll go home first.

aboyer VERB
to bark

l'**abri** MASC NOUN
shelter
♦ **être à l'abri** to be under cover
♦ **se mettre à l'abri** to shelter

l'**abricot** MASC NOUN
apricot

s'**abriter** VERB
to shelter

l'**absence** FEM NOUN
absence
♦ **Il est passé pendant ton absence.** He came while you were away.

absent ADJECTIVE
absent

absolument ADVERB
absolutely

l'**accélérateur** MASC NOUN
accelerator

accélérer VERB
to accelerate

l'**accent** MASC NOUN
accent ◊ *Il a l'accent de Marseille.* He has a Marseilles accent.
♦ **un accent aigu** an acute accent
♦ **un accent grave** a grave accent
♦ **un accent circonflexe** a circumflex

accentuer VERB
to stress

accepter VERB
to accept
♦ **accepter de faire quelque chose** to agree to do something

l' **accès** MASC NOUN
access ◊ *avoir accès à quelque chose*
to have access to something
♦**"Accès aux quais"** "To the trains"

l' **accessoire** MASC NOUN
1 accessory ◊ *les accessoires de
mode* fashion accessories
2 prop

l' **accident** MASC NOUN
accident ◊ *un accident de la route* a
road accident ◊ *Elle a eu un accident
de ski.* She had a skiing accident.
♦**par accident** by chance

accompagner VERB
to accompany

accomplir VERB
to carry out ◊ *Il n'a pas réussi à
accomplir cette tâche.* He didn't
manage to carry out this task.

l' **accord** MASC NOUN
agreement
♦**être d'accord** to agree ◊ *Tu es
d'accord avec moi?* Do you agree
with me?
♦**se mettre d'accord** to come to an
agreement
♦**D'accord!** OK!

l' **accordéon** MASC NOUN
accordion ◊ *Ray joue de l'accordéon.*
Ray plays the accordion.

l' **accoudoir** MASC NOUN
armrest

l' **accrochage** MASC NOUN
collision

accrocher VERB
♦**accrocher quelque chose à (1)** to hang
something on ◊ *Il a accroché sa veste
au portemanteau.* He hung his jacket
on the coat rack.
♦**accrocher quelque chose à (2)** to hitch
something up to ◊ *Ils ont accroché la
remorque à leur voiture.* They hitched
the trailer up to their car.
♦**s'accrocher à quelque chose** to catch
on something ◊ *Sa jupe s'est
accrochée aux ronces.* Her skirt got
caught on the brambles.

s' **accroupir** VERB
to squat down

l' **accueil** MASC NOUN
welcome ◊ *Il nous a remerciés de
notre accueil.* He thanked us for our
welcome.
♦**Elle s'occupe de l'accueil des
visiteurs.** She's in charge of looking
after visitors.
♦**"Accueil"** "Reception"

accueillant ADJECTIVE

welcoming ◊ *Ses parents ont été très
accueillants.* Her parents were very
welcoming.

accueillir VERB
to welcome

accumuler VERB
to accumulate
♦**s'accumuler** to pile up

l' **accusation** FEM NOUN
accusation

l' **accusé** MASC NOUN
accused ◊ *L'accusé a déclaré que ...*
The accused stated that ...
♦**un accusé de réception** an
acknowledgement of receipt

l' **accusée** FEM NOUN
accused

accuser VERB
to accuse ◊ *accuser quelqu'un de
quelque chose* to accuse somebody
of something

l' **achat** MASC NOUN
purchase
♦**faire des achats** to do some shopping

acheter VERB
to buy ◊ *J'ai acheté des gâteaux à la
pâtisserie.* I bought some cakes at the
cake shop.
♦**acheter quelque chose à quelqu'un (1)**
to buy something for somebody
◊ *Qu'est-ce tu lui as acheté pour
son anniversaire?* What did you buy
him for his birthday?
♦**acheter quelque chose à quelqu'un (2)**
to buy something from somebody
◊ *J'ai acheté des œufs au fermier.* I
bought some eggs from the farmer.

acide ADJECTIVE
see also **acide** NOUN
acid ◊ *Ce pamplemousse est trop
acide.* This grapefruit is too acid.

l' **acide** MASC NOUN
see also **acide** ADJECTIVE
acid

l' **acier** MASC NOUN
steel

l' **acné** FEM NOUN
acne ◊ *Il a de l'acné.* He has acne.

acquérir VERB
to acquire

acquis VERB see **acquérir**

acquitter VERB
to acquit ◊ *L'accusé a été acquitté.*
The accused was acquitted.

l' **acte** MASC NOUN
act
♦**un acte de naissance** a birth
certificate

l'**acteur** MASC NOUN
actor ◊ *Il est acteur.* He's an actor.
◊ *un acteur de cinéma* a film actor

actif ADJECTIVE (FEM SING **active**)
active
♦ **la population active** the working
population

l'**action** FEM NOUN
action
♦ **une bonne action** a good deed

s'**activer** VERB
1 to bustle about ◊ *Elle s'activait à
préparer le repas.* She bustled about
preparing the meal.
2 to move oneself ◊ *Allez! Active-
toi!* Come on! Get moving!

l'**activité** FEM NOUN
activity

l'**actrice** FEM NOUN
actress ◊ *Elle est actrice.* She's an
actress. ◊ *une actrice de cinéma* a
film actress

l'**actualité** FEM NOUN
current events
♦ **un problème d'actualité** a topical issue
♦ **les actualités** the news

actuel ADJECTIVE (FEM SING **actuelle**)
present ◊ *le système actuel* the
present system
♦ **à l'heure actuelle** at the present time
*Be careful! **actuel** does not mean
actual.*

actuellement ADVERB
at present
*Be careful! **actuellement** does not
mean **actually**.*

l'**adaptateur** MASC NOUN
adaptor

l'**addition** FEM NOUN
1 addition ◊ *les additions et les
soustractions* additions and
subtractions
2 bill ◊ *L'addition, s'il vous plaît!*
Can we have the bill, please?

additionner VERB
to add up

l'**adhérent** MASC NOUN
member

l'**adhérente** FEM NOUN
member

adhésif ADJECTIVE (FEM SING **adhésive**)
♦ **le ruban adhésif** sticky tape

adieu EXCLAMATION
farewell!

l'**adjectif** MASC NOUN
adjective

admettre VERB
1 to admit ◊ *Il refuse d'admettre
qu'il s'est trompé.* He won't admit
that he made a mistake.
2 to allow ◊ *Les chiens ne sont pas
admis.* Dogs are not allowed.

l'**administration** FEM NOUN
administration
♦ **l'Administration** the Civil Service

admirable ADJECTIVE
wonderful

l'**admirateur** MASC NOUN
admirer

l'**admiratrice** FEM NOUN
admirer

admirer VERB
to admire

admis VERB *see* **admettre**

l'**adolescence** FEM NOUN
adolescence

l'**adolescent** MASC NOUN
teenager

l'**adolescente** FEM NOUN
teenager

adopter VERB
to adopt

adorable ADJECTIVE
lovely

adorer VERB
to love ◊ *Elle adore le chocolat.* She
loves chocolate. ◊ *J'adore jouer au
tennis.* I love playing tennis.

l'**adresse** FEM NOUN
address
♦ **mon adresse électronique** my email
address

adresser VERB
♦ **adresser la parole à quelqu'un** to
speak to someone
♦ **s'adresser à quelqu'un (1)** to speak to
somebody ◊ *C'est à toi que je
m'adresse.* It's you I'm speaking to.
♦ **s'adresser à quelqu'un (2)** to go and
see somebody ◊ *Adressez-vous au
patron.* Go and see the boss.
◊ *Adressez-vous aux renseignements.*
Ask at the enquiry desk.
♦ **s'adresser à quelqu'un (3)** to be
aimed at somebody ◊ *Ce film
s'adresse surtout aux enfants.* This
film is aimed mainly at children.

l'**adulte** MASC/FEM NOUN
adult

l'**adverbe** MASC NOUN
adverb

l'**adversaire** MASC/FEM NOUN
opponent

aérien ADJECTIVE (FEM SING **aérienne**)
♦ **une compagnie aérienne** an airline

l'**aérobic** MASC NOUN

☞

aerobics ◊ *Teresa fait de l'aérobic.* Teresa does aerobics.

l' **aérogare** FEM NOUN
terminal

l' **aéroglisseur** MASC NOUN
hovercraft

l' **aéroport** MASC NOUN
airport

l' **affaire** FEM NOUN
see also **les affaires**
1 case ◊ *une affaire de drogue* a drugs case
2 business ◊ *Son affaire marche bien.* His business is doing well.
◆ **une bonne affaire** a real bargain
◆ **Ça fera l'affaire.** This will do nicely.
◆ **avoir affaire à quelqu'un** to deal with somebody

les **affaires** FEM NOUN
see also **l'affaire**
1 things ◊ *Va chercher tes affaires!* Go and get your things!
2 business ◊ *Les affaires marchent bien en ce moment.* Business is good at the moment. ◊ *Mêle-toi de tes affaires.* (informal) Mind your own business.
◆ **un homme d'affaires** a businessman
◆ **le ministre des Affaires étrangères** the Foreign Secretary

l' **affection** FEM NOUN
affection

affectueusement ADVERB
affectionately

affectueux ADJECTIVE (FEM SING **affectueuse**)
affectionate

l' **affiche** FEM NOUN
poster

afficher VERB
to put up ◊ *Ils ont affiché les résultats dehors.* They've put the results up outside.
◆ **"Défense d'afficher"** "Stick no bills"

affilée
◆ **d'affilée** ADVERB
at a stretch ◊ *Il a travaillé douze heures d'affilée.* He worked 12 hours at a stretch.

l' **affirmation** FEM NOUN
assertion

affirmer VERB
to claim ◊ *Il a affirmé que c'était la vérité.* He claimed it was the truth.
◆ **s'affirmer** to assert yourself ◊ *Il est trop timide, il faut qu'il s'affirme.* He's too shy, he should assert himself.

l' **affluence** FEM NOUN
◆ **les heures d'affluence** the rush hour

s' **affoler** VERB
to panic ◊ *Ne t'affole pas!* Don't panic!

affranchir VERB
to stamp

affreux ADJECTIVE (FEM SING **affreuse**)
awful

affronter VERB
to face ◊ *L'Allemagne affronte l'Italie en finale.* Germany will face Italy in the final.

afin de CONJUNCTION
◆ **afin de faire quelque chose** so as to do something ◊ *Je me suis levé très tôt afin d'être prêt à temps.* I got up very early so as to be ready on time.

afin que CONJUNCTION
so that
afin que is followed by a verb in the subjunctive.
◊ *Il m'a téléphoné afin que je sois prêt à temps.* He phoned me so that I'd be ready on time.

africain ADJECTIVE, NOUN (FEM SING **africaine**)
African
◆ **un Africain** an African (*man*)
◆ **une Africaine** an African (*woman*)

l' **Afrique** FEM NOUN
Africa
◆ **en Afrique (1)** in Africa
◆ **en Afrique (2)** to Africa
◆ **l'Afrique du Sud** South Africa

agacer VERB
to get on somebody's nerves ◊ *Tu m'agaces avec tes questions!* You're getting on my nerves with all your questions!

l' **âge** MASC NOUN
age
◆ **Quel âge as-tu?** How old are you?

âgé ADJECTIVE
old ◊ *Son père est âgé.* His father's old. ◊ *Il est âgé de dix ans.* He's 10 years old.
◆ **les personnes âgées** the elderly

l' **agence** FEM NOUN
1 agency ◊ *l'agence pour l'emploi* the employment agency
◆ **une agence de voyages** a travel agency
2 office ◊ *l'agence de Londres* the London office
◆ **une agence immobilière** an estate agent's

l' **agenda** MASC NOUN
diary ◊ *J'ai perdu mon agenda.* I have lost my diary.
Be careful! The French word **agenda** *does not mean* **agenda**.

s' **agenouiller** VERB
  to kneel down

l' **agent** MASC NOUN
  ♦ **un agent de police** a policeman
  ♦ **un agent d'entretien** a cleaner

l' **agglomération** FEM NOUN
  town
  ♦ **l'agglomération parisienne** Greater
  Paris

aggraver VERB
  to make worse
  ♦ **s'aggraver** to worsen

agir VERB
  to act ◊ *Il a agi par vengeance.* He
  acted out of vengeance.
  ♦ **Il s'agit de ...** It's about ... ◊ *Il s'agit*
  du club de sport. It's about the sports
  club. ◊ *De quoi s'agit-il?* What is it
  about?
  ♦ **Il s'agit de faire attention.** We must
  be careful.

agité ADJECTIVE
  1 restless ◊ *Les élèves sont agités.*
  The pupils are restless.
  2 rough ◊ *La mer est agitée.* The
  sea is rough.
  ♦ **un sommeil agité** broken sleep

agiter VERB
  to shake ◊ *Agitez la bouteille.* Shake
  the bottle.

l' **agneau** MASC NOUN (PL les **agneaux**)
  lamb

l' **agrafe** FEM NOUN
  staple (*for papers*)

l' **agrafeuse** FEM NOUN
  stapler

agrandir VERB
  1 to enlarge ◊ *J'ai fait agrandir mes*
  photos. I've had my photos enlarged.
  2 to extend ◊ *Ils ont agrandi leur*
  jardin. They've extended their garden.
  ♦ **s'agrandir** to expand ◊ *Leur magasin*
  s'est agrandi. Their shop has
  expanded.

agréable ADJECTIVE
  nice

agréer VERB
  ♦ **Veuillez agréer, Monsieur,**
  l'expression de mes sentiments les
  meilleurs. Jean Ormal. Yours
  sincerely, Jean Ormal.

agressif ADJECTIVE (FEM SING **agressive**)
  aggressive

l' **agressivité** FEM NOUN
  aggression
  ♦ **faire preuve d'agressivité envers de**
  quelqu'un to be aggressive to
  somebody
  ♦ **l'agressivité au volant** road rage

agricole ADJECTIVE
  agricultural ◊ *le matériel agricole*
  agricultural machinery
  ♦ **une exploitation agricole** a farm

l' **agriculteur** MASC NOUN
  farmer
  ♦ **Il est agriculteur.** He's a farmer.

l' **agriculture** FEM NOUN
  farming

ai VERB *see* **avoir**
  ♦ **J'ai deux chats.** I have two cats.
  ♦ **J'ai bien dormi.** I slept well.

l' **aide** FEM NOUN
  1 help ◊ *J'ai besoin de ton aide.* I
  need your help. ◊ *appeler quelqu'un*
  à l'aide to call to somebody for help
  ♦ **À l'aide!** Help!
  2 aid ◊ *une aide financière* financial
  aid
  ♦ **à l'aide de** using ◊ *J'ai réussi à ouvrir*
  la boîte à l'aide d'un couteau. I
  managed to open the tin using a
  knife.

aider VERB
  to help

l' **aide-soignant** MASC NOUN (PL les **aides-**
  soignants)
  auxiliary nurse ◊ *Il est aide-soignant.*
  He's an auxiliary nurse.

l' **aide-soignante** FEM NOUN (PL les **aides-**
  soignantes)
  auxiliary nurse ◊ *Françoise est aide-*
  soignante. Françoise is an auxiliary
  nurse.

aie VERB *see* **avoir**

aïe EXCLAMATION
  Ouch!

aigre ADJECTIVE
  sour

aigu ADJECTIVE (FEM SING **aiguë**)
  sharp (*pain*) ◊ *Il a ressenti une*
  douleur aiguë dans le bas du dos. He
  felt a sharp pain in the small of his
  back.
  ♦ **e accent aigu** e acute

l' **aiguille** FEM NOUN
  needle ◊ *une aiguille à tricoter* a
  knitting needle
  ♦ **les aiguilles d'une montre** the hands
  of a watch

l' **ail** MASC NOUN
  garlic

l' **aile** FEM NOUN
  wing

aille VERB *see* **aller**

ailleurs ADVERB
  somewhere else
  ♦ **partout ailleurs** everywhere else

☞

♦ **nulle part ailleurs** nowhere else
♦ **d'ailleurs** besides

aimable ADJECTIVE
kind

l' **aimant** MASC NOUN
magnet

aimer VERB
1 to love ◊ *Elle aime ses enfants.* She loves her children.
2 to like ◊ *Tu aimes le chocolat?* Do you like chocolate? ◊ *J'aime bien ce garçon.* I like this boy. ◊ *J'aime bien jouer au tennis.* I like playing tennis. ◊ *J'aimerais aller en Grèce.* I'd like to go to Greece.
♦ **J'aimerais mieux ne pas y aller.** I'd rather not go.

aîné ADJECTIVE
see also **aîné** NOUN
elder ◊ *mon frère aîné* my big brother

l' **aîné** MASC NOUN
see also **aîné** ADJECTIVE
oldest child ◊ *Il est l'aîné.* He's the oldest child.

l' **aînée** FEM NOUN
oldest child ◊ *Elle est l'aînée.* She's the oldest child.

ainsi ADVERB
in this way ◊ *Il faut faire ainsi.* This is the way to do it.
♦ **C'est ainsi qu'il a réussi.** That's how he succeeded.
♦ **ainsi que** as well as
♦ **et ainsi de suite** and so on

l' **air** MASC NOUN
1 air ◊ *l'air chaud* warm air
♦ **prendre l'air** to get some fresh air
2 tune ◊ *Elle a joué un air au piano.* She played a tune on the piano.
♦ **Elle a l'air fatiguée.** She looks tired.
♦ **Il a l'air d'un clown.** He looks like a clown.

l' **aire de jeux** FEM NOUN
playground

l' **aire de repos** FEM NOUN
rest area (on motorway)

l' **aise** FEM NOUN
♦ **être à l'aise** to be at ease ◊ *Elle est à l'aise avec tout le monde.* She's at ease with everybody.
♦ **être mal à l'aise** to be ill at ease
♦ **se mettre à l'aise** to make oneself comfortable

ait VERB *see* **avoir**

ajouter VERB
to add

l' **alarme** FEM NOUN

alarm ◊ *donner l'alarme* to raise the alarm

l' **Albanie** FEM NOUN
Albania

l' **album** MASC NOUN
album

l' **alcool** MASC NOUN
alcohol ◊ *Je ne bois pas d'alcool.* I don't drink alcohol.
♦ **les alcools forts** spirits

alcoolisé ADJECTIVE
alcoholic
♦ **une boisson non alcoolisée** a soft drink

les **alentours** MASC NOUN
♦ **dans les alentours** in the area
♦ **aux alentours de Paris** in the Paris area
♦ **aux alentours de cinq heures** around 5 o'clock

l' **algèbre** FEM NOUN
algebra

Alger NOUN
Algiers

l' **Algérie** FEM NOUN
Algeria

algérien ADJECTIVE, NOUN (FEM SING **algérienne**)
Algerian
♦ **un Algérien** an Algerian (*man*)
♦ **une Algérienne** an Algerian (*woman*)

l' **algue** FEM NOUN
seaweed

l' **aliment** MASC NOUN
food

l' **alimentation** FEM NOUN
1 groceries ◊ *le rayon alimentation du supermarché* the grocery department in the supermarket
2 diet ◊ *Elle a une alimentation saine.* She has a healthy diet.

l' **allée** FEM NOUN
1 path ◊ *les allées du parc* the paths in the park
2 drive (*in street names*)
♦ **les allées et venues** comings and goings

allégé ADJECTIVE
low-fat ◊ *un yaourt allégé* a low-fat yoghurt

l' **Allemagne** FEM NOUN
Germany
♦ **en Allemagne (1)** in Germany
♦ **en Allemagne (2)** to Germany

allemand ADJECTIVE, NOUN
German ◊ *Elle parle allemand.* She speaks German.
♦ **un Allemand** a German (*man*)

♦ **une Allemande** a German (*woman*)
♦ **les Allemands** the Germans

aller VERB
| see also **aller** NOUN |

Present tense:
je vais	nous allons
tu vas	vous allez
il/elle va	ils/elles vont
Past participle:	
allé	

to go ◊ *Je suis allé à Londres.* I went
to London. ◊ *Je dois y aller.* I've got
to go. ◊ *Elle ira le voir.* She'll go and
see him. ◊ *Je vais me fâcher.* I'm
going to get angry.
♦ **s'en aller** to go away ◊ *Je m'en vais
demain.* I'm going tomorrow.
♦ **aller bien à quelqu'un** to suit
somebody ◊ *Cette robe te va bien.*
This dress suits you.
♦ **Allez! Dépêche-toi!** Come on! Hurry
up!
♦ **Comment allez-vous? – Je vais bien.**
How are you? – I'm fine.
♦ **Comment ça va? – Ça va bien.** How
are you? – I'm fine.
♦ **aller mieux** to be better

l' **aller** MASC NOUN
| see also **aller** VERB |

① outward journey ◊ *L'aller nous a
pris trois heures.* The journey there
took us three hours.
② single (*ticket*) ◊ *Je voudrais un
aller pour Angers.* I'd like a single to
Angers.
♦ **un aller simple** a single
♦ **un aller retour (1)** a return ticket ◊ *Je
voudrais un aller retour pour
Londres.* I'd like a return to London.
♦ **un aller retour (2)** a round trip ◊ *Il a
fait l'aller retour en dix heures.* He
did the round trip in ten hours.

allergique ADJECTIVE
♦ **allergique à** allergic to ◊ *Je suis
allergique aux poils de chat.* I'm
allergic to cat fur.

allô EXCLAMATION
Hello! ◊ *Allô! Je voudrais parler à
Monsieur Simon.* Hello! I'd like to
speak to Mr Simon.

l' **allocation** FEM NOUN
allowance
♦ **les allocations chômage**
unemployment benefit

s' **allonger** VERB
to lie down ◊ *Il s'est allongé sur son
lit.* He lay down on his bed.

allumer VERB

① to put on (*light*) ◊ *Tu peux allumer
la lumière?* Can you put the light on?
② to switch on ◊ *Allume la radio.*
Switch on the radio.
③ to light ◊ *Elle a allumé une
cigarette.* She lit a cigarette.
♦ **s'allumer** (*light*) to come on ◊ *La
lumière s'est allumée.* The light came
on.

l' **allumette** FEM NOUN
match ◊ *une boîte d'allumettes* a box
of matches

l' **allure** FEM NOUN
① speed ◊ *à toute allure* at top speed
② look ◊ *avoir une drôle d'allure* to
look odd

l' **allusion** FEM NOUN
reference

alors ADVERB
① then ◊ *Tu as fini? Alors je m'en
vais.* Have you finished? I'm going
then.
② so ◊ *Alors je lui ai dit de partir.* So
I told him to leave.
♦ **Et alors?** So what?
③ at that time ◊ *Il habitait alors à
Paris.* He was living in Paris at that
time.
♦ **alors que (1)** as ◊ *Il est arrivé alors
que je partais.* He arrived just as I
was leaving.
♦ **alors que (2)** while ◊ *Alors que je
travaillais dur, lui se reposait.* While I
was working hard, he was resting.

les **Alpes** FEM NOUN
Alps ◊ *dans les Alpes* in the Alps

l' **alphabet** MASC NOUN
alphabet

alphabétique ADJECTIVE
alphabetical ◊ *par ordre alphabétique*
in alphabetical order

l' **alpinisme** MASC NOUN
mountaineering

l' **alpiniste** MASC/FEM NOUN
mountaineer

l' **Alsace** FEM NOUN
Alsace

l' **amande** FEM NOUN
almond
♦ **la pâte d'amandes** marzipan

l' **amant** MASC NOUN
lover

amateur ADJECTIVE (FEM SING **amateur**)
| see also **amateur** NOUN |
amateur ◊ *Elle est pianiste amateur.*
She's an amateur pianist.

l' **amateur** MASC NOUN
| see also **amateur** ADJECTIVE |
amateur

☞

♦ **en amateur** as a hobby ◊ *Il fait de la photo en amateur.* He takes photos as a hobby.

♦ **C'est un amateur de musique.** He's a music lover.

l' **ambassade** FEM NOUN
embassy

l' **ambassadeur** MASC NOUN
ambassador

l' **ambiance** FEM NOUN
atmosphere ◊ *Je n'aime pas l'ambiance ici.* I don't like the atmosphere here. ◊ *Il y a de l'ambiance dans ce café.* This café has a lively atmosphere.

♦ **la musique d'ambiance** background music

ambitieux ADJECTIVE (FEM SING **ambitieuse**)
ambitious

l' **ambition** FEM NOUN
ambition ◊ *Il a l'ambition de devenir Premier ministre.* His ambition is to be Prime Minister.

♦ **Il a beaucoup d'ambition.** He's very ambitious.

l' **ambulance** FEM NOUN
ambulance

l' **âme** FEM NOUN
soul

l' **amélioration** FEM NOUN
improvement

améliorer VERB
to improve

♦ **s'améliorer** to improve ◊ *Le temps s'améliore.* The weather's improving.

l' **amende** FEM NOUN
fine ◊ *une amende de cinquante euros* a 50 euro fine

amener VERB
to bring ◊ *Qu'est-ce qui t'amène?* What brings you here? ◊ *Est-ce que je peux amener un ami?* Can I bring a friend?

amer ADJECTIVE (FEM SING **amère**)
bitter

américain ADJECTIVE, NOUN (FEM SING **américaine**)
American

♦ **un Américain** an American (*man*)

♦ **une Américaine** an American (*woman*)

l' **Amérique** FEM NOUN
America

♦ **en Amérique (1)** in America

♦ **en Amérique (2)** to America

♦ **l'Amérique du Nord** North America

♦ **l'Amérique du Sud** South America

l' **ami** MASC NOUN
friend

♦ **C'est son petit ami.** He's her boyfriend.

amical ADJECTIVE (MASC PL **amicaux**)
friendly

amicalement ADVERB
in a friendly way

♦ **amicalement, Pierre** best wishes, Pierre

l' **amie** FEM NOUN
friend

♦ **C'est sa petite amie.** She's his girlfriend.

l' **amitié** FEM NOUN
friendship

♦ **Fais mes amitiés à Paul.** Give my regards to Paul.

♦ **Amitiés, Christèle.** (*in letter*) Best wishes, Christèle.

l' **amour** MASC NOUN
love

♦ **faire l'amour** to make love

amoureux ADJECTIVE (FEM SING **amoureuse**)
in love ◊ *être amoureux de quelqu'un* to be in love with somebody

l' **amour-propre** MASC NOUN
self-esteem

l' **amphithéâtre** MASC NOUN
lecture theatre

amplement ADVERB

♦ **Nous avons amplement le temps.** We have plenty of time.

l' **ampoule** FEM NOUN
① light bulb
② blister ◊ *J'ai une ampoule au pied.* I've got a blister on my foot.

amusant ADJECTIVE
amusing

les **amuse-gueule** MASC NOUN
party nibbles

amuser VERB
to amuse

♦ **s'amuser (1)** to play ◊ *Les enfants s'amusent dehors.* The children are playing outside.

♦ **s'amuser (2)** to enjoy oneself ◊ *On s'est bien amusés à cette soirée.* We really enjoyed ourselves at that party.

l' **an** MASC NOUN
year

♦ **le premier de l'an** New Year's Day

♦ **le nouvel an** New Year

l' **analyse** FEM NOUN
① analysis
② test (*medical*) ◊ *une analyse d'urine* a urine test

l' **ananas** MASC NOUN

A

pineapple

l' **ancêtre** MASC/FEM NOUN
ancestor

l' **anchois** MASC NOUN
anchovy

ancien ADJECTIVE (FEM SING **ancienne**)
[1] former ◊ *C'est une ancienne élève.*
She's a former pupil.
[2] old ◊ *notre ancienne voiture* our
old car
[3] antique ◊ *un fauteuil ancien* an
antique chair

l' **ancre** FEM NOUN
anchor

Andorre FEM NOUN
Andorra

l' **âne** MASC NOUN
donkey

l' **ange** MASC NOUN
angel
♦ **être aux anges** to be over the moon

l' **angine** FEM NOUN
throat infection

anglais ADJECTIVE, NOUN (FEM SING **anglaise**)
English ◊ *Est-ce que vous parlez
anglais?* Do you speak English?
♦ **un Anglais** an Englishman
♦ **une Anglaise** an Englishwoman
♦ **les Anglais** the English

l' **angle** MASC NOUN
[1] angle ◊ *un angle droit* a right
angle
[2] corner ◊ *à l'angle de la rue* at the
corner of the street

l' **Angleterre** FEM NOUN
England
♦ **en Angleterre (1)** in England
◊ *J'habite en Angleterre.* I live in
England.
♦ **en Angleterre (2)** to England ◊ *Je suis
allée en Angleterre le mois dernier.* I
went to England last month.

anglo- PREFIX
anglo-
♦ **les îles Anglo-Normandes** the Channel
Islands

anglophone ADJECTIVE
English-speaking

angoissé ADJECTIVE
stressed ◊ *Il était angoissé à l'idée
de prendre l'avion.* He was stressed
about the idea of taking the plane.

l' **animal** MASC NOUN (PL les **animaux**)
animal

l' **animateur** MASC NOUN
[1] host ◊ *Il est animateur à la télé.*
He's a TV host.

[2] youth leader ◊ *Pierre est
animateur au centre sportif.* Pierre is
a youth leader at the sports centre.

l' **animatrice** FEM NOUN
[1] host ◊ *Elle est animatrice à la télé.*
She's a TV host.
[2] youth leader ◊ *Cécile est
animatrice au centre sportif.* Cécile is
a youth leader at the sports centre.

animé ADJECTIVE
lively ◊ *Cette rue est très animée.*
This is a very lively street.
♦ **un dessin animé** a cartoon

l' **anis** MASC NOUN
aniseed

l' **anneau** MASC NOUN (PL les **anneaux**)
ring

l' **année** FEM NOUN
year ◊ *l'année dernière* last year
◊ *l'année prochaine* next year

l' **anniversaire** MASC NOUN
[1] birthday ◊ *C'est l'anniversaire de
Janet.* It's Janet's birthday.
[2] anniversary ◊ *un anniversaire de
mariage* a wedding anniversary

l' **annonce** FEM NOUN
advert ◊ *J'ai lu votre annonce dans
le journal.* I saw your advert in the
newspaper. ◊ *passer une annonce* to
place an ad
♦ **les petites annonces** the small ads

annoncer VERB
to announce ◊ *Ils ont annoncé leurs
fiançailles.* They've announced their
engagement.

l' **annuaire** MASC NOUN
phone book

annuel ADJECTIVE (FEM SING **annuelle**)
annual

annuler VERB
to cancel

anonyme ADJECTIVE
anonymous

l' **anorak** MASC NOUN
anorak

l' **ANPE** FEM NOUN (= *Agence nationale
pour l'emploi*)
job centre ◊ *Je suis allé à l'ANPE.* I
went to the job centre.

l' **Antarctique** MASC NOUN
Antarctic

l' **antenne** FEM NOUN
[1] aerial
♦ **antenne parabolique** satellite dish
♦ **être à l'antenne** to be on the air
[2] antenna

l' **antibiotique** MASC NOUN
antibiotic

l' **antidépresseur** MASC NOUN
antidepressant ◊ *Elle est sous antidépresseurs depuis un mois.* She's been on antidepressants for a month.

l' **antigel** MASC NOUN
antifreeze

les **Antilles** FEM NOUN
West Indies
♦ **aux Antilles (1)** in the West Indies
♦ **aux Antilles (2)** to the West Indies

antipathique ADJECTIVE
unpleasant ◊ *Je le trouve plutôt antipathique.* I find him rather unpleasant.

antipelliculaire ADJECTIVE
anti-dandruff

l' **antiquaire** MASC/FEM NOUN
antique dealer ◊ *Elle est antiquaire.* She's an antique dealer.

l' **antiquité** FEM NOUN
antique ◊ *un magasin d'antiquités* an antique shop
♦ **pendant l'antiquité** in classical times

antiseptique ADJECTIVE
⏐ *see also* **antiseptique** NOUN ⏐
antiseptic

l' **antiseptique** MASC NOUN
⏐ *see also* **antiseptique** ADJECTIVE ⏐
antiseptic

l' **antivol** MASC NOUN
① lock (*on bike*)
② steering lock (*on car*)

anxieux ADJECTIVE (FEM SING **anxieuse**)
anxious ◊ *Il est anxieux de nature.* He's a born worrier.

août MASC NOUN
August
♦ **en août** in August

apercevoir VERB
to see ◊ *J'aperçois la côte.* I can see the shore.
♦ **s'apercevoir de quelque chose** to notice something
♦ **s'apercevoir que ...** to notice that ...

l' **apéritif** MASC NOUN
aperitif ◊ *Venez donc prendre l'apéritif ce soir!* Come round for drinks this evening!

apparaître VERB
to appear

l' **appareil** MASC NOUN
device
♦ **un appareil dentaire** a brace (*for teeth*)
♦ **les appareils ménagers** domestic appliances
♦ **un appareil photo** a camera

♦ **Qui est à l'appareil?** Who's speaking? (*on phone*)

apparemment ADVERB
apparently

l' **apparence** FEM NOUN
appearance

l' **apparition** FEM NOUN
appearance ◊ *Il n'a fait qu'une brève apparition.* He only appeared briefly.

l' **appartement** MASC NOUN
flat

appartenir VERB
♦ **appartenir à quelqu'un** to belong to somebody

apparu VERB *see* **apparaître**

l' **appel** MASC NOUN
① cry ◊ *un appel au secours* a cry for help
② phone call
♦ **faire appel à quelqu'un** to appeal to somebody
♦ **faire l'appel** to call the register (*in school*)
♦ **faire un appel de phares** to flash one's headlights

appeler VERB
to call ◊ *Elle a appelé le médecin.* She called the doctor. ◊ *J'ai appelé Richard à Londres.* I called Richard in London.
♦ **s'appeler** to be called ◊ *Comment ça s'appelle?* What is it called? ◊ *Elle s'appelle Muriel.* Her name's Muriel. ◊ *Comment tu t'appelles?* What's your name?

l' **appendicite** FEM NOUN
appendicitis

appétissant ADJECTIVE
appetizing

l' **appétit** MASC NOUN
appetite
♦ **Bon appétit!** Enjoy your meal!

applaudir VERB
to clap (*applaud*)

les **applaudissements** MASC NOUN
applause SING

appliquer VERB
① to apply
② to enforce ◊ *appliquer la loi* to enforce the law
♦ **s'appliquer** to apply oneself

apporter VERB
to bring

apprécier VERB
to appreciate

appréhender VERB
to dread ◊ *J'appréhende cette réunion.* I'm dreading this meeting.

apprendre VERB
　☐1 to learn ◇ *apprendre quelque chose par cœur* to learn something by heart
◆ **apprendre à faire quelque chose** to learn to do something ◇ *J'apprends à faire la cuisine.* I'm learning to cook.
　☐2 to hear ◇ *J'ai appris son départ.* I heard that she had left.
◆ **apprendre quelque chose à quelqu'un (1)** to teach somebody something ◇ *Ma mère m'a appris l'anglais.* My mother taught me English. ◇ *Elle lui a appris à conduire.* She taught him to drive.
◆ **apprendre quelque chose à quelqu'un (2)** to tell somebody something ◇ *Jean m'a appris la nouvelle.* Jean told me the news.

l'**apprentissage** MASC NOUN
　learning ◇ *On dit que l'apprentissage de l'arabe est très difficile.* Learning Arabic is said to be very difficult.

appris VERB *see* **apprendre**

l'**approbation** FEM NOUN
　approval ◇ *donner son approbation* to give one's approval

approcher VERB
◆ **approcher de** to approach ◇ *Nous approchons de Paris.* We are approaching Paris.
◆ **s'approcher de** to come closer to ◇ *Ne t'approche pas, j'ai la grippe!* Don't get too close to me, I've got flu!

approprié ADJECTIVE
　suitable ◇ *une tenue appropriée* suitable clothes

approuver VERB
　to approve of ◇ *Je n'approuve pas ses méthodes.* I don't approve of his methods.

approximatif ADJECTIVE (FEM SING **approximative**)
　☐1 approximate ◇ *un prix approximatif* an approximate price
　☐2 rough ◇ *un calcul approximatif* a rough calculation

l'**appui** MASC NOUN
　support ◇ *J'ai besoin de votre appui.* I need your support.

appuyer VERB
　☐1 to press ◇ *appuyer sur un bouton* to press a button
　☐2 to lean ◇ *Elle a appuyé son vélo contre la porte.* She leaned her bike against the door.
◆ **s'appuyer** to lean ◇ *Elle s'est appuyée contre le mur.* She leaned against the wall. ◇ *Il s'est appuyé sur la table.* He leaned on the table.

après PREPOSITION, ADVERB
　☐1 after ◇ *après le déjeuner* after lunch ◇ *après son départ* after he had left ◇ *après qu'il est parti* after he had left ◇ *Nous viendrons après avoir fait la vaisselle.* We'll come after we've done the dishes.
　☐2 afterwards ◇ *aussitôt après* immediately afterwards
◆ **après coup** afterwards ◇ *J'y ai repensé après coup.* I thought about it again afterwards.
◆ **d'après** according to ◇ *D'après lui, c'est une erreur.* According to him, that's a mistake.
◆ **après tout** after all

après-demain ADVERB
　the day after tomorrow

l'**après-midi** MASC OR FEM NOUN
　afternoon

l'**après-rasage** MASC NOUN
　aftershave

l'**aquarium** MASC NOUN
　aquarium

arabe ADJECTIVE, NOUN
　☐1 Arab ◇ *les pays arabes* the Arab countries
　☐2 Arabic ◇ *la littérature arabe* Arabic literature ◇ *Il parle arabe.* He speaks Arabic.
◆ **un Arabe** an Arab (*man*)
◆ **une Arabe** an Arab (*woman*)

l'**Arabie Saoudite** FEM NOUN
　Saudi Arabia

l'**araignée** FEM NOUN
　spider

l'**arbitre** MASC NOUN
　☐1 referee
　☐2 umpire

l'**arbre** MASC NOUN
　tree
◆ **un arbre généalogique** a family tree

l'**arbuste** MASC NOUN
　shrub

l'**arc** MASC NOUN
　bow ◇ *son arc et ses flèches* his bow and arrows

l'**arc-en-ciel** MASC NOUN (PL les **arcs-en-ciel**)
　rainbow

l'**archéologie** FEM NOUN
　archaeology

l'**archéologue** MASC/FEM NOUN
　archaeologist ◇ *Elle est archéologue.* She's an archaeologist.

l'**archipel** MASC NOUN
　archipelago

l'**architecte** MASC NOUN

☞

architect ◊ *Il est architecte.* He's an architect.

l'**architecture** FEM NOUN
architecture

l'**Arctique** MASC NOUN
Arctic

l'**ardoise** FEM NOUN
slate

l'**arène** FEM NOUN
bullring
• **des arènes romaines** a Roman amphitheatre
• **l'arène politique** the political arena

l'**arête** FEM NOUN
fish bone

l'**argent** MASC NOUN
1 silver ◊ *une bague en argent* a silver ring
2 money ◊ *Je n'ai plus d'argent.* I haven't got any more money.
• **l'argent de poche** pocket money
• **l'argent liquide** cash

argentin ADJECTIVE, NOUN (FEM SING **argentine**)
Argentinian
• **un Argentin** an Argentinian (*man*)
• **une Argentine** an Argentinian (*woman*)

l'**Argentine** FEM NOUN
Argentina

l'**argile** FEM NOUN
clay

l'**argot** MASC NOUN
slang

l'**arme** FEM NOUN
weapon
• **une arme à feu** a firearm

l'**armée** FEM NOUN
army
• **l'armée de l'air** the Air Force

l'**armistice** MASC NOUN
armistice

l'**armoire** FEM NOUŃ
wardrobe

l'**armure** FEM NOUN
armour ◊ *un chevalier en armure* a knight in armour

arnaquer VERB (*informal*)
to con

aromatisé ADJECTIVE
flavoured

l'**arôme** MASC NOUN
1 aroma
2 flavouring (*added to food*)

arpenter VERB
to pace up and down ◊ *Il arpentait le couloir.* He was pacing up and down the corridor.

arrache-pied

• **d'arrache-pied** ADVERB
furiously ◊ *travailler d'arrache-pied* to work furiously

arracher VERB
1 to take out ◊ *Le dentiste m'a arraché une dent.* The dentist took one of my teeth out.
2 to tear out ◊ *Arrachez la page.* Tear the page out.
3 to pull up ◊ *Elle a arraché les mauvaises herbes.* She pulled up the weeds.
• **arracher quelque chose à quelqu'un** to snatch something from somebody

arranger .VERB
1 to arrange ◊ *arranger des fleurs dans un vase* to arrange flowers in a vase
2 to suit ◊ *Ça m'arrange de partir plus tôt.* It suits me to leave earlier.
• **s'arranger** to come to an agreement ◊ *Arrangez-vous avec le patron.* You'll have to come to an agreement with the boss.
• **Je vais m'arranger pour venir.** I'll organize things so that I can come.
• **Ça va s'arranger.** Things will work themselves out.

l'**arrestation** FEM NOUN
arrest ◊ *en état d'arrestation* under arrest

l'**arrêt** MASC NOUN
stop ◊ *un arrêt de bus* a bus stop
• **sans arrêt (1)** non-stop ◊ *Elle travaille sans arrêt.* She works non-stop.
• **sans arrêt (2)** continually ◊ *Ils se disputent sans arrêt.* They quarrel continually.

arrêter VERB
1 to stop
• **Arrête!** Stop it!
• **arrêter de faire quelque chose** to stop doing something
2 to switch off ◊ *Il a arrêté le moteur.* He switched the engine off.
3 to arrest ◊ *Mon voisin a été arrêté.* My neighbour's been arrested.
• **s'arrêter** to stop ◊ *Elle s'est arrêtée devant une vitrine.* She stopped in front of a shop window.
• **s'arrêter de faire quelque chose** to stop doing something ◊ *s'arrêter de fumer* to stop smoking

les **arrhes** FEM NOUN
deposit SING ◊ *verser des arrhes* to pay a deposit

l'**arrière** MASC NOUN
see also **arrière** ADJECTIVE

back ◊ *l'arrière de la maison* the back
of the house
♦ **à l'arrière** at the back
♦ **en arrière** behind ◊ *Ils sont restés en
arrière.* They stayed behind.

arrière ADJECTIVE (MASC, FEM, PL)
see also **arrière** NOUN
back ◊ *le siège arrière* the back seat
◊ *les roues arrière* the rear wheels

l' **arrière-grand-mère** FEM NOUN (PL les
arrière-grands-mères)
great-grandmother

l' **arrière-grand-père** MASC NOUN (PL les
arrière-grands-pères)
great-grandfather

l' **arrivée** FEM NOUN
arrival

arriver VERB
1 to arrive ◊ *J'arrive à l'école à huit
heures.* I arrive at school at 8 o'clock.
2 to happen ◊ *Qu'est-ce qui est
arrivée à Ann?* What happened to
Ann?
♦ **arriver à faire quelque chose** to
manage to do something ◊ *J'espère
que je vais y arriver.* I hope I'll
manage it.
♦ **Il m'arrive de dormir jusqu'à midi.** I
sometimes sleep till midday.

arrogant ADJECTIVE
arrogant

l' **arrondissement** MASC NOUN
district

> *🛈 Paris, Lyons and Marseilles are
> divided into numbered districts
> called **arrondissements**.*

arroser VERB
to water ◊ *Daphne arrose ses
tomates.* Daphne is watering her
tomatoes.
♦ **Ils ont arrosé leur victoire.** They had
a drink to celebrate their victory.

l' **arrosoir** MASC NOUN
watering can

l' **art** MASC NOUN
art

l' **artère** FEM NOUN
1 artery
2 thoroughfare ◊ *les grandes artères
de Paris* the main roads of Paris

l' **artichaut** MASC NOUN
artichoke

l' **article** MASC NOUN
1 article ◊ *un article de journal* a
newspaper article
2 item ◊ *les articles en promotion*
items on special offer

l' **articulation** FEM NOUN
joint ◊ *l'articulation du genou* the
knee joint

articuler VERB
to pronounce clearly

artificiel ADJECTIVE (FEM SING **artificielle**)
artificial

l' **artisan** MASC NOUN
self-employed craftsman

l' **artiste** MASC/FEM NOUN
1 artist
2 performer

artistique ADJECTIVE
artistic

as VERB see **avoir**
see also **as** NOUN
♦ **Tu as de beaux cheveux.** You've got
nice hair.

l' **as** MASC NOUN
see also **as** VERB
ace ◊ *l'as de trèfle* the ace of clubs

l' **ascenseur** MASC NOUN
lift

l' **Ascension** FEM NOUN
Ascension

asiatique ADJECTIVE
Asiatic ◊ *la cuisine asiatique* Oriental
cooking ◊ *le Sud-Est asiatique* South
East Asia

l' **Asie** FEM NOUN
Asia
♦ **en Asie (1)** in Asia
♦ **en Asie (2)** to Asia

l' **aspect** MASC NOUN
appearance

l' **asperge** FEM NOUN
asparagus

l' **aspirateur** MASC NOUN
vacuum cleaner
♦ **passer l'aspirateur** to vacuum

l' **aspirine** FEM NOUN
aspirin

assaisonner VERB
to season

l' **assassin** MASC NOUN
murderer

assassiner VERB
to murder

assembler VERB
to assemble
♦ **s'assembler** to gather ◊ *Une foule
énorme s'était assemblée.* A huge
crowd had gathered.

s' **asseoir** VERB
to sit down ◊ *Asseyez-vous!*
Sit down! ◊ *Assieds-toi!* Sit
down!

assez ADVERB

[1] enough ◊ *Nous n'avons pas assez de temps.* We don't have enough time. ◊ *Est-ce qu'il y a assez de pain?* Is there enough bread?

♦ **J'en ai assez!** I've had enough!

[2] quite ◊ *Il faisait assez beau.* The weather was quite nice.

l' **assiette** FEM NOUN

plate ◊ *une assiette creuse* a soup plate ◊ *une assiette à dessert* a dessert plate

♦ **une assiette anglaise** assorted cold meats

assis VERB *see* **asseoir**

assis ADJECTIVE

sitting ◊ *Il est assis par terre.* He's sitting on the floor.

l' **assistance** FEM NOUN

[1] audience ◊ *Y a-t-il un médecin dans l'assistance?* Is there a doctor in the audience?

[2] aid ◊ *l'assistance humanitaire* humanitarian aid

[3] assistance ◊ *avec l'assistance de quelqu'un* with the assistance of somebody

l' **assistant** MASC NOUN

assistant ◊ *Il était assistant d'anglais à Tourcoing.* He was an English assistant in Tourcoing.

♦ **un assistant social** a social worker

l' **assistante** FEM NOUN

assistant ◊ *Elle est assistante de français à Oxford.* She's a French assistant in Oxford.

♦ **une assistante sociale** a social worker

assister VERB

♦ **assister à un accident** to witness an accident

♦ **assister à un cours** to attend a class

♦ **assister à un concert** to be at a concert

l' **association** FEM NOUN

association

l' **associé** MASC NOUN

partner (*in business*)

l' **associée** FEM NOUN

partner (*in business*)

s' **associer** VERB

to go into partnership

assommer VERB

to knock out ◊ *Il l'a assommé avec une bouteille.* He knocked him out with a bottle.

l' **Assomption** FEM NOUN

Assumption

assorti ADJECTIVE

[1] matching ◊ *des couleurs assorties* matching colours

[2] assorted ◊ *des chocolats assortis* assorted chocolates

♦ **être assorti à quelque chose** to match something ◊ *Son sac est assorti à ses chaussures.* Her bag matches her shoes.

l' **assortiment** MASC NOUN

assortment

l' **assurance** FEM NOUN

[1] insurance ◊ *une assurance maladie* medical insurance

[2] confidence ◊ *parler avec assurance* to speak with confidence

assurer VERB

[1] to insure ◊ *La maison est assurée.* The house is insured. ◊ *être assuré contre quelque chose* to be insured against something

[2] to assure ◊ *Je t'assure que c'est vrai!* I assure you it's true!

♦ **s'assurer de quelque chose** to make sure of something ◊ *Il s'est assuré que la porte était fermée.* He made sure the door was shut.

l' **asthme** MASC NOUN

asthma ◊ *une crise d'asthme* an asthma attack

l' **astronaute** MASC/FEM NOUN

astronaut

l' **astronomie** FEM NOUN

astronomy

astucieux ADJECTIVE (FEM SING **astucieuse**)

clever

l' **atelier** MASC NOUN

[1] workshop

[2] studio (*artist's*)

Athènes NOUN

Athens

l' **athlète** MASC/FEM NOUN

athlete

l' **athlétisme** MASC NOUN

athletics ◊ *un championnat d'athlétisme* an athletics championship

l' **Atlantique** MASC NOUN

Atlantic

l' **atlas** MASC NOUN

atlas

l' **atmosphère** FEM NOUN

atmosphere

atomique ADJECTIVE

atomic ◊ *la bombe atomique* the atomic bomb

l' **atout** MASC NOUN

1 asset ◊ *L'atout principal de ce joueur, c'est sa vitesse.* This player's main asset is his speed.
2 trump card ◊ *J'avais quatre atouts dans mon jeu.* I had four trump cards in my hand.

atroce ADJECTIVE
terrible

attachant ADJECTIVE
lovable

attacher VERB
to tie up ◊ *Elle a attaché ses cheveux avec un élastique.* She tied her hair up with an elastic band.
♦ **s'attacher à quelqu'un** to become attached to somebody
♦ **une poêle qui n'attache pas** a non-stick frying pan

attaquer VERB
to attack

atteindre VERB
to reach

attendant
♦ **en attendant** ADVERB
in the meantime

attendre VERB
to wait ◊ *attendre quelqu'un* to wait for someone ◊ *J'attends d'avoir un appartement à moi.* I'm waiting until I've got a flat of my own. ◊ *Attends qu'il ne pleuve plus.* Wait until it's stopped raining.
♦ **attendre un enfant** to be expecting a baby
♦ **s'attendre à** to expect ◊ *Je m'attends à ce qu'il soit en retard.* I expect he'll be late.
Be careful! attendre does not mean to attend.

l'**attentat** MASC NOUN
♦ **un attentat à la bombe** a terrorist bombing

l'**attente** FEM NOUN
wait ◊ *deux heures d'attente* two hours' wait
♦ **la salle d'attente** the waiting room

attentif ADJECTIVE (FEM SING **attentive**)
attentive

l'**attention** FEM NOUN
attention ◊ *à l'attention de* for the attention of
♦ **faire attention** to be careful
♦ **Attention!** Watch out! ◊ *Attention, tu vas te faire écraser!* Watch out, you'll get run over!

attentionné ADJECTIVE
thoughtful

atterrir VERB
to land

l'**atterrissage** MASC NOUN
landing (of plane)

attirant ADJECTIVE
attractive

attirer VERB
to attract ◊ *attirer l'attention de quelqu'un* to attract somebody's attention
♦ **s'attirer des ennuis** to get into trouble ◊ *Si tu continues, tu vas t'attirer des ennuis.* If you keep on like that, you'll get yourself into trouble.

l'**attitude** FEM NOUN
attitude

l'**attraction** FEM NOUN
♦ **un parc d'attractions** an amusement park

attraper VERB
to catch

attrayant ADJECTIVE
attractive

attrister VERB
to sadden

au PREPOSITION see **à**
au is the contracted form of à + le.
♦ **au printemps** in the spring

l'**aube** FEM NOUN
dawn ◊ *à l'aube* at dawn

l'**auberge** FEM NOUN
inn
♦ **une auberge de jeunesse** a youth hostel

l'**aubergine** FEM NOUN
aubergine

aucun ADJECTIVE, PRONOUN
1 no ◊ *Il n'a aucun ami.* He's got no friends. ◊ *Aucun enfant ne pourrait le faire.* No child could do that.
2 none ◊ *Aucun d'entre eux n'est venu.* None of them came. ◊ *Aucune de mes amies n'aime le football.* None of my female friends like football. ◊ *Tu aimes ses films? – Je n'en ai vu aucun.* Do you like his films? – I haven't seen any of them.
♦ **sans aucun doute** without any doubt

au-delà ADVERB
♦ **au-delà de** beyond ◊ *Votre ticket n'est pas valable au-delà de cette limite.* Your ticket is not valid beyond this point.

au-dessous ADVERB
1 downstairs ◊ *Ils habitent au-dessous.* They live downstairs.
2 underneath
♦ **au-dessous de** under ◊ *au-dessous du pont* under the bridge ◊ *dix degrés au-dessous de zéro* ten degrees below zero

au-dessus ADVERB
　1 upstairs ◊ *J'habite au-dessus.* I live upstairs.
　2 above
　♦**au-dessus de** above ◊ *au-dessus de la table* above the table

audiovisuel ADJECTIVE (FEM SING **audiovisuelle**)
　audiovisual

l'**auditeur** MASC NOUN
　listener (to radio)

l'**auditrice** FEM NOUN
　listener (to radio)

l'**augmentation** FEM NOUN
　rise

augmenter VERB
　to increase

aujourd'hui ADVERB
　today

auparavant ADVERB
　first ◊ *Vous pouvez utiliser l'ordinateur mais auparavant vous devez taper le mot de passe.* You can use the computer but first you have to key in the password.

auquel PRONOUN (MASC PL **auxquels**, FEM PL **auxquelles**)
　***auquel** is the contracted form of **à** + **lequel**.*
　◊ *l'homme auquel j'ai parlé* the man I spoke to

aura, aurai, auras, aurez, aurons, auront VERB *see* **avoir**

l'**aurore** FEM NOUN
　daybreak

ausculter VERB
　♦**Le médecin l'a ausculté.** The doctor listened to his chest.

aussi ADVERB
　1 too ◊ *Dors bien. – Toi aussi.* Sleep well. – You too. ◊ *Lui aussi parle espagnol.* He too speaks Spanish.
　2 also ◊ *J'aimerais aussi que tu achètes le journal.* I'd also like you to get the paper. ◊ *Je parle anglais et aussi allemand.* I speak English and also German.
　♦**aussi ... que** as ... as ◊ *aussi grand que moi* as big as me

aussitôt ADVERB
　straight away ◊ *aussitôt après son retour* straight after his return
　♦**aussitôt que** as soon as ◊ *aussitôt que tu auras fini* as soon as you've finished

l'**Australie** FEM NOUN
　Australia
　♦**en Australie (1)** in Australia
　♦**en Australie (2)** to Australia

australien ADJECTIVE, NOUN (FEM SING **australienne**)
　Australian
　♦**un Australien** an Australian (*man*)
　♦**une Australienne** an Australian (*woman*)

autant ADVERB
　♦**autant de (1)** so much ◊ *Je ne veux pas autant de gâteau.* I don't want so much cake.
　♦**autant de (2)** so many ◊ *Je n'ai jamais vu autant de monde.* I've never seen so many people.
　♦**autant ... que (1)** as much ... as ◊ *J'ai autant d'argent que toi.* I've got as much money as you have.
　♦**autant ... que (2)** as many ... as ◊ *J'ai autant d'amis que lui.* I've got as many friends as he has.
　♦**d'autant plus que** all the more since ◊ *Elle est d'autant plus déçue qu'il le lui avait promis.* She's all the more disappointed since he had promised her.
　♦**d'autant moins que** even less since ◊ *C'est d'autant moins pratique pour lui qu'il doit changer deux fois de train.* It's even less convenient for him since he has to change trains twice.

l'**auteur** MASC NOUN
　author

l'**auto** FEM NOUN
　car

l'**autobus** MASC NOUN
　bus ◊ *en autobus* by bus

l'**autocar** MASC NOUN
　coach ◊ *en autocar* by coach

autocollant ADJECTIVE
　see also **autocollant** NOUN
　self-adhesive ◊ *une étiquette autocollante* a self-adhesive label
　♦**une enveloppe autocollante** a self-seal envelope

l'**autocollant** MASC NOUN
　see also **autocollant** ADJECTIVE
　sticker

l'**auto-école** FEM NOUN
　driving school

automatique ADJECTIVE
　automatic

l'**automne** MASC NOUN
　autumn
　♦**en automne** in autumn

automobile ADJECTIVE
　see also **automobile** NOUN
　♦**une course automobile** a motor race

l'**automobile** FEM NOUN
　see also **automobile** ADJECTIVE

car

l' **automobiliste** MASC/FEM NOUN
   motorist

l' **autoradio** MASC NOUN
   car radio

l' **autorisation** FEM NOUN
   1 permission ◊ *Il m'a donné l'autorisation de sortir ce soir.* He's given me permission to go out tonight.
   2 permit ◊ *Il faut une autorisation pour camper ici.* You need a permit to camp here.

   autoriser VERB
   to give permission for ◊ *Il m'a autorisé à en parler.* He's given me permission to talk about it.

   autoritaire ADJECTIVE
   authoritarian

l' **autorité** FEM NOUN
   authority

l' **autoroute** FEM NOUN
   motorway

l' **auto-stop** MASC NOUN
   ♦ **faire de l'auto-stop** to hitchhike

l' **auto-stoppeur** MASC NOUN
   hitchhiker

l' **auto-stoppeuse** FEM NOUN
   hitchhiker

   autour ADVERB
   around ◊ *autour de la maison* around the house

   autre ADJECTIVE, PRONOUN
   other ◊ *Je viendrai un autre jour.* I'll come some other day. ◊ *J'ai d'autres projets.* I've got other plans.
   ♦ **autre chose** something else
   ♦ **autre part** somewhere else
   ♦ **un autre** another ◊ *Tu veux un autre morceau de gâteau?* Would you like another piece of cake?
   ♦ **l'autre** the other ◊ *Non, pas celui-ci, l'autre.* No, not that one, the other one.
   ♦ **d'autres** others ◊ *Je t'en apporterai d'autres.* I'll bring you some others.
   ♦ **les autres** the others ◊ *Les autres sont arrivés plus tard.* The others arrived later.
   ♦ **ni l'un ni l'autre** neither of them
   ♦ **entre autres** among other things ◊ *Nous avons parlé, entre autres, de nos projets de vacances.* We talked about our holiday plans, among other things.

   autrefois ADVERB
   in the old days

   autrement ADVERB
   1 differently ◊ *Il l'a fait autrement.* He did it differently.
   2 otherwise ◊ *Je n'ai pas pu faire autrement.* I couldn't do otherwise.
   ♦ **autrement dit** in other words

l' **Autriche** FEM NOUN
   Austria
   ♦ **en Autriche (1)** in Austria
   ♦ **en Autriche (2)** to Austria

   autrichien ADJECTIVE, NOUN (FEM SING **autrichienne**)
   Austrian
   ♦ **un Autrichien** an Austrian (*man*)
   ♦ **une Autrichienne** an Austrian (*woman*)

l' **autruche** FEM NOUN
   ostrich

   aux PREPOSITION *see* **à**

   aux is the contracted form of à + les.
   ◊ *J'ai dit aux enfants d'aller jouer.* I told the children to go and play.

   auxquelles PRONOUN

   auxquelles is the contracted form of à + lesquelles.
   ◊ *les revues auxquelles il est abonné* the magazines to which he subscribes

   auxquels PRONOUN

   auxquels is the contracted form of à + lesquels.
   ◊ *les enfants auxquels il a parlé* the children he spoke to

   avaient, avais, avait VERB *see* **avoir**
   ♦ **Il y avait beaucoup de monde.** There were lots of people.

l' **avalanche** FEM NOUN
   avalanche

   avaler VERB
   to swallow

l' **avance** FEM NOUN
   ♦ **être en avance** to be early
   ♦ **à l'avance** beforehand ◊ *réserver longtemps à l'avance* to book well beforehand
   ♦ **d'avance** in advance ◊ *payer d'avance* to pay in advance

   avancé ADJECTIVE
   advanced ◊ *à un niveau avancé* at an advanced level
   ♦ **bien avancé** well under way ◊ *Les travaux sont déjà bien avancés.* The work is already well under way.

   avancer VERB
   1 to move forward ◊ *Il avançait prudemment.* He was moving forward cautiously.
   2 to bring forward ◊ *La date de l'examen a été avancée.* The date of the exam has been brought forward.

A

☞

3 to put forward ◊ *Il a avancé sa montre d'une heure.* He put his watch forward an hour.
4 to be fast (*watch*) ◊ *Ma montre avance d'une heure.* My watch is an hour fast.
5 to lend ◊ *Peux-tu m'avancer dix euros?* Can you lend me 10 euros?

avant PREPOSITION, ADJECTIVE
see also **avant** NOUN
1 before ◊ *avant qu'il ne pleuve* before it rains ◊ *avant de partir* before leaving
2 front ◊ *la roue avant* the front wheel ◊ *le siège avant* the front seat
♦ **avant tout** above all

l' **avant** MASC NOUN
see also **avant** PREPOSITION
front ◊ *l'avant de la voiture* the front of the car
♦ **à l'avant** in front
♦ **en avant** forward ◊ *Il a fait un pas en avant.* He took a step forward.

l' **avantage** MASC NOUN
advantage

l' **avant-bras** MASC NOUN (PL les **avant-bras**)
forearm

avant-dernier ADJECTIVE (FEM **avant-dernière**, MASC PL **avant-derniers**)
last but one ◊ *l'avant-dernière page* the last page but one ◊ *Ils sont arrivés avant-derniers.* They arrived last but one.

avant-hier ADVERB
the day before yesterday ◊ *Il est arrivé avant-hier.* He arrived the day before yesterday.

avare ADJECTIVE
see also **avare** NOUN
miserly

l' **avare** MASC/FEM NOUN
see also **avare** ADJECTIVE
miser

avec PREPOSITION
with ◊ *avec mon père* with my father
♦ **Et avec ça?** Anything else? (*in shop*)

l' **avenir** MASC NOUN
future
♦ **à l'avenir** in future ◊ *À l'avenir, essayez d'être à l'heure.* Try to be on time in future.
♦ **dans un proche avenir** in the near future

l' **aventure** FEM NOUN
adventure

l' **avenue** FEM NOUN
avenue

l' **averse** FEM NOUN
shower (*of rain*)

avertir VERB
to warn
♦ **avertir quelqu'un de quelque chose** to warn somebody about something

l' **avertissement** MASC NOUN
warning

aveugle ADJECTIVE
blind

l' **avion** MASC NOUN
plane
♦ **aller en avion** to go by plane ◊ *Il est allé en Italie en avion.* He flew to Italy.
♦ **par avion** by airmail

l' **aviron** MASC NOUN
rowing

l' **avis** MASC NOUN
1 opinion ◊ *J'aimerais avoir ton avis.* I'd like to have your opinion.
♦ **à mon avis** in my opinion
2 notice ◊ *jusqu'à nouvel avis* until further notice
♦ **changer d'avis** to change one's mind ◊ *J'ai changé d'avis.* I've changed my mind.

l' **avocat** MASC NOUN
1 lawyer ◊ *Il est avocat.* He's a lawyer.
2 avocado

l' **avocate** FEM NOUN
lawyer ◊ *Elle est avocate.* She's a lawyer.

l' **avoine** FEM NOUN
oats ◊ *les flocons d'avoine* porridge oats

avoir VERB

Present tense:	
j'ai	*nous avons*
tu as	*vous avez*
il/elle a	*ils/elles ont*
Past participle:	
eu	

1 to have ◊ *Ils ont deux enfants.* They have two children. ◊ *Il a les yeux bleus.* He's got blue eyes. ◊ *J'ai déjà mangé.* I've already eaten. ◊ *Est-ce que tu as vu ce film?* Have you seen this film? ◊ *Je lui ai parlé hier.* I spoke to him yesterday.
♦ **On t'a bien eu!** (*informal*) You've been had!
2 to be ◊ *Il a trois ans.* He's three. ◊ *J'avais dix ans quand je l'ai rencontré.* I was ten when I met him.
♦ **il y a (1)** there is ◊ *Il y a quelqu'un à la porte.* There's somebody at the door.

- **il y a (2)** there are ◊ *Il y a des chocolats sur la table.* There are some chocolates on the table.
- **il y a (3)** ago ◊ *Je l'ai rencontré il y a deux ans.* I met him two years ago.
- **Qu'est-ce qu'il y a?** What's the matter?
- **Il n'y a qu'à partir plus tôt.** We'll just have to leave earlier.

l' **avortement** MASC NOUN
  abortion

avouer VERB
  to admit

avril MASC NOUN
  April
- **en avril** in April

ayez, ayons VERB *see* **avoir**

B

le **baby-foot** NOUN
    table football ◊ *jouer au baby-foot* to play table football

le **baby-sitting** NOUN
    ♦ **faire du baby-sitting** to babysit

le **bac** NOUN = **baccalauréat**

le **baccalauréat** NOUN
    A levels ◊ *Jacqueline a passé son baccalauréat l'année dernière.* Jacqueline did her A levels last year.

> ❶ The French **baccalauréat**, or **bac** for short, is taken at the age of 17 or 18. Students have to sit one of a variety of set subject combinations, rather than being able to choose any combination of subjects they want. If you pass you have the right to a place at university.

bâcler VERB
    to botch up ◊ *Je déteste le travail bâclé!* I hate work that's not done properly!

le **bagage** NOUN
    luggage
    ♦ **faire ses bagages** to pack
    ♦ **les bagages à main** hand luggage ◊ *un bagage à main* a piece of hand luggage

la **bagarre** NOUN
    fight ◊ *Une bagarre a éclaté à la fermeture du pub.* A fight broke out when the pub closed.

se **bagarrer** VERB
    to fight ◊ *Il s'est encore bagarré avec son frère.* He's been fighting with his brother again.

la **bagnole** NOUN (*informal*)
    car

la **bague** NOUN
    ring

la **baguette** NOUN
    ① stick of French bread
    ② chopstick ◊ *manger avec des baguettes* to eat with chopsticks
    ♦ **une baguette magique** a magic wand

la **baie** NOUN
    bay

la **baignade** NOUN
    ♦ **"baignade interdite"** "no swimming"

se **baigner** VERB
    to go swimming ◊ *Si on allait se baigner?* Shall we go swimming?

la **baignoire** NOUN
    bath (*bathtub*)

bâiller VERB
    to yawn

le **bain** NOUN
    bath ◊ *prendre un bain* to take a bath ◊ *prendre un bain de soleil* to sunbathe

le **baiser** NOUN
    kiss

la **baisse** NOUN
    fall ◊ *La baisse du taux de chômage.* The fall in the unemployment rate.
    ♦ **être en baisse** to be falling
    ♦ **revoir les chiffres à la baisse** to revise figures downwards

baisser VERB
    ① to turn down ◊ *Il fait moins froid, tu peux baisser le chauffage.* It's not so cold, you can turn down the heating.
    ② to fall ◊ *Le prix des CD a baissé.* The price of CDs has fallen.
    ♦ **se baisser** to bend down ◊ *Il s'est baissé pour ramasser son mouchoir.* He bent down to pick up his handkerchief.

le **bal** NOUN
    dance ◊ *un bal populaire* a local dance

la **balade** NOUN (*informal*)
    walk ◊ *faire une balade* to go for a walk

se **balader** VERB (*informal*)
    to wander around ◊ *J'adore me balader dans les rues de Paris.* I love to wander around the streets of Paris.

le **baladeur** NOUN
    personal stereo

le **balai** NOUN
    broom ◊ *Je vais donner un coup de balai dans la cuisine.* I'm going to sweep the kitchen.

la **balance** NOUN
    scales PL (*for weighing*)
    ♦ **la Balance** Libra ◊ *Todd est Balance.* Todd is Libra.

se **balancer** VERB
    to swing

la **balançoire** NOUN
    swing

balayer VERB

B

1 to sweep ◊ *Jean-Pierre a balayé la cuisine.* Jean-Pierre swept the kitchen.
2 to sweep up ◊ *Va balayer les feuilles sur la terrasse.* Go and sweep up the leaves on the terrace.

le **balayeur** NOUN
roadsweeper

balbutier VERB
to stammer

le **balcon** NOUN
balcony

la **baleine** NOUN
whale

la **balle** NOUN
1 ball ◊ *une balle de tennis* a tennis ball
2 bullet

la **ballerine** NOUN
1 ballet dancer
2 ballet shoe ◊ *une paire de ballerines rouges* a pair of red ballet shoes

le **ballet** NOUN
ballet

le **ballon** NOUN
1 ball ◊ *lancer le ballon* to throw the ball
♦ **un ballon de football** a football
2 balloon

balnéaire ADJECTIVE
♦ **une station balnéaire** a seaside resort

banal ADJECTIVE (MASC PL **banaux**)
1 commonplace ◊ *La violence est devenue banale à la télévision.* Violence has become commonplace on television.
2 hackneyed ◊ *L'intrigue du film est très banale.* The plot of the film is very hackneyed.

la **banane** NOUN
1 banana ◊ *La banane est un fruit.* Banana is a fruit.
2 bumbag ◊ *Mes clés sont dans ma banane.* My keys are in my bumbag.

le **banc** NOUN
bench

bancaire ADJECTIVE
♦ **une carte bancaire** a bank card

le **bandage** NOUN
bandage

la **bande** NOUN
1 gang ◊ *une bande de voyous* a gang of louts
2 bunch ◊ *C'est une bande d'idiots!* They are a bunch of idiots!
3 bandage ◊ *une bande Velpeau* ® a crepe bandage

♦ **une bande dessinée** a comic strip

> 🛈 Comic strips are very popular in France with people of all ages.

♦ **une bande magnétique** a tape
♦ **la bande sonore** the sound track
♦ **Elle fait toujours bande à part.** She always keeps to herself.

le **bandeau** NOUN (PL les **bandeaux**)
headband

bander VERB
to bandage ◊ *L'infirmière lui a bandé la jambe.* The nurse bandaged his leg.

le **bandit** NOUN
bandit

la **banlieue** NOUN
suburbs ◊ *Christèle habite en banlieue.* Christèle lives in the suburbs.
♦ **les lignes de banlieue** suburban lines
♦ **les trains de banlieue** commuter trains

la **banque** NOUN
bank

le **banquet** NOUN
dinner ◊ *le banquet annuel de l'association* the club's annual dinner

la **banquette** NOUN
seat ◊ *la banquette arrière de la voiture* the back seat of the car

le **banquier** NOUN
banker

le **baptême** NOUN
christening ◊ *le baptême de notre fille* our daughter's christening
♦ **C'était mon baptême de l'air.** It was the first time I had flown.

le **baquet** NOUN
tub

le **bar** NOUN
bar

la **baraque** NOUN (*informal*)
house ◊ *Elle habite dans une belle baraque.* She lives in a beautiful house.

barbant ADJECTIVE (*informal*)
boring ◊ *Il est vraiment barbant!* He's so boring!

barbare ADJECTIVE
barbaric

la **barbe** NOUN
beard ◊ *Il porte la barbe.* He's got a beard.
♦ **Quelle barbe!** (*informal*) What a drag!
♦ **la barbe à papa** candyfloss

le **barbecue** NOUN

☞

barbecue

barbouiller VERB
to daub ◊ *Les murs étaient barbouillés de graffitis.* The walls were daubed with graffiti.
♦ **J'ai l'estomac barbouillé.** (*informal*) I'm feeling queasy.

barbu ADJECTIVE
bearded ◊ *un grand barbu* a big, bearded man

barder VERB (*informal*)
♦ **Ça va barder!** There's going to be trouble!

le **baromètre** NOUN
barometer

la **barque** NOUN
rowing boat ◊ *Ils sont allés faire une promenade en barque.* They've gone for a row.

le **barrage** NOUN
dam
♦ **un barrage de police** a police roadblock

la **barre** NOUN
bar (*metal*) ◊ *une barre de fer* an iron bar

le **barreau** NOUN (PL les **barreaux**)
bar (*on window*) ◊ *Il s'est retrouvé derrière les barreaux.* He ended up behind bars.

barrer VERB
to block ◊ *Il y a un tronc d'arbre qui barre la route.* There's a tree trunk blocking the road.
♦ **se barrer** (*informal*) to clear off ◊ *Barre-toi!* Clear off!

la **barrette** NOUN
hair slide

la **barrière** NOUN
fence

le **bar-tabac** NOUN (PL les **bars-tabacs**)

> ⓘ *A bar-tabac is a bar which also sells cigarettes and stamps; you can tell a bar-tabac by the red diamond-shaped sign outside it.*

le **bas** NOUN
see also **bas** ADJECTIVE
① bottom ◊ *en bas de la page* at the bottom of the page ◊ *en bas de l'escalier* at the bottom of the stairs
② stocking ◊ *une paire de bas* a pair of stockings

bas ADJECTIVE, ADVERB (FEM SING **basse**)
see also **bas** NOUN
low ◊ *parler à voix basse* to speak in a low voice

♦ **en bas (1)** down ◊ *Ça me donne le vertige de regarder en bas.* I get dizzy if I look down.
♦ **en bas (2)** (down) at the bottom ◊ *Son nom est tout en bas.* His name is down at the bottom. ◊ *Il y a un marchand de journaux en bas de la rue.* There's a newsagent's at the bottom of the street.
♦ **en bas (3)** downstairs ◊ *Elle habite en bas.* She lives downstairs.

le **bas-côté** NOUN
verge ◊ *Il s'est garé sur le bas-côté de la route.* He stopped his car on the verge.

la **bascule** NOUN
♦ **un fauteuil à bascule** a rocking chair

la **base** NOUN
base ◊ *la base de la pyramide* the base of the pyramid
♦ **de base** basic ◊ *Le pain et le lait sont des aliments de base.* Bread and milk are basic foods.
♦ **à base de** made from ◊ *des produits de beauté à base de plantes* cosmetics made from plants
♦ **une base de données** a database

le **basilic** NOUN
basil

le **basket** NOUN
basketball ◊ *jouer au basket* to play basketball

les **baskets** FEM NOUN
trainers ◊ *une paire de baskets* a pair of trainers

le/la **Basque** NOUN
Basque (*person, language*)

basque ADJECTIVE
Basque

basse ADJECTIVE see **bas**

la **basse-cour** NOUN (PL les **basses-cours**)
farmyard

le **bassin** NOUN
① pond ◊ *Il y a un bassin à poissons rouges dans le parc.* There's a goldfish pond in the park.
② pelvis ◊ *une fracture du bassin* a fractured pelvis

la **bassine** NOUN
bowl (*for washing*)

le **bas-ventre** NOUN
stomach ◊ *Elle se plaint de douleurs dans le bas-ventre.* She is complaining of pains in her stomach.

la **bataille** NOUN
battle

le **bateau** NOUN (PL les **bateaux**)
boat

B

le **bateau-mouche** NOUN (PL les **bateaux-mouches**)
  pleasure boat

bâti ADJECTIVE
  ◆**bien bâti** well-built

le **bâtiment** NOUN
  building

bâtir VERB
  to build

le **bâton** NOUN
  stick ◊ un coup de bâton a blow with a stick

le **battement** NOUN
  ◆**J'ai dix minutes de battement.** I've got ten minutes free.

la **batterie** NOUN
  1 battery ◊ La batterie est à plat. The battery is flat.
  2 drums ◊ jouer de la batterie to play drums
  ◆**la batterie de cuisine** the pots and pans

le **batteur** NOUN
  drummer

battre VERB
  to beat ◊ Quand je le vois, mon cœur bat plus vite. When I see him, my heart beats faster.
  ◆**se battre** to fight ◊ Je me bats souvent avec mon frère. I fight a lot with my brother.
  ◆**battre les cartes** to shuffle the cards
  ◆**battre les blancs en neige** beat the egg whites until stiff
  ◆**battre son plein** to be in full swing ◊ À minuit, la fête battait son plein. At midnight, the party was in full swing.

bavard ADJECTIVE
  talkative

bavarder VERB
  to chat

baver VERB
  to dribble

baveux ADJECTIVE (FEM SING **baveuse**)
  runny ◊ une omelette baveuse a runny omelette

la **bavure** NOUN
  blunder ◊ une bavure policière a police blunder

le **bazar** NOUN
  general store
  ◆**Quel bazar!** (informal) What a mess!

BCBG ADJECTIVE (= bon chic bon genre)
  posh

la **BD** NOUN (= bande dessinée)
  comic strip ◊ Rose adore les BD. Rose loves comic strips.

béant ADJECTIVE
  gaping ◊ un trou béant a gaping hole

beau ADJECTIVE, ADVERB (MASC SING ALSO **bel**, FEM SING **belle**, MASC PL **beaux**)
  beau changes to bel before a vowel and most words beginning with "h".
  1 lovely ◊ un bel été a lovely summer ◊ une belle journée a fine day
  2 beautiful ◊ C'est une belle femme. She is a beautiful woman.
  3 good-looking ◊ C'est un beau garçon. He is a good-looking boy.
  4 handsome ◊ un bel homme a handsome man
  ◆**Il fait beau aujourd'hui.** It's a nice day today.
  ◆**J'ai beau essayer, je n'y arrive pas.** However hard I try, I just can't do it.

beaucoup ADVERB
  1 a lot ◊ Il boit beaucoup. He drinks a lot.
  2 much ◊ Elle n'a pas beaucoup d'argent. She hasn't got much money. ◊ Janet est beaucoup plus grande que moi. Janet is much taller than me.
  ◆**beaucoup de** a lot of ◊ Il y avait beaucoup de monde au concert. There were a lot of people at the concert. ◊ Elle fait beaucoup de fautes. She makes a lot of mistakes.
  ◆**J'ai eu beaucoup de chance.** I was very lucky.

le **beau-fils** NOUN (PL les **beaux-fils**)
  1 son-in-law
  2 stepson

le **beau-frère** NOUN (PL les **beaux-frères**)
  brother-in-law

le **beau-père** NOUN (PL les **beaux-pères**)
  1 father-in-law
  2 stepfather

la **beauté** NOUN
  beauty

les **beaux-arts** MASC NOUN
  fine arts

les **beaux-parents** MASC NOUN
  in-laws

le **bébé** NOUN
  baby

le **bec** NOUN
  beak

la **bécane** NOUN (informal)
  bike

la **bêche** NOUN
  spade

bêcher VERB
  to dig ◊ Il bêchait son jardin. He was digging the garden.

bégayer VERB
to stammer

beige ADJECTIVE
beige

le **beignet** NOUN
fritter ◊ *les beignets aux pommes*
apple fritters

bel ADJECTIVE *see* **beau**

le/la **Belge** NOUN
Belgian

belge ADJECTIVE
Belgian

la **Belgique** NOUN
Belgium
♦ **en Belgique (1)** in Belgium
♦ **en Belgique (2)** to Belgium

le **bélier** MASC NOUN
ram
♦ **le Bélier** Aries ◊ *Christine est Bélier.*
Christine's Aries.

belle ADJECTIVE *see* **beau**

la **belle-famille** NOUN (PL les **belles-familles**)
in-laws

la **belle-fille** NOUN (PL les **belles-filles**)
① daughter-in-law
② stepdaughter

la **belle-mère** NOUN (PL les **belles-mères**)
① mother-in-law
② stepmother

la **belle-sœur** NOUN (PL les **belles-sœurs**)
sister-in-law

la **bénédiction** NOUN
blessing

le **bénéfice** NOUN
profit ◊ *La société réalise de gros bénéfices.* The company is making big profits.

bénévole ADJECTIVE
voluntary ◊ *du travail bénévole*
voluntary work

bénir VERB
to bless

bénit ADJECTIVE
consecrated ◊ *l'eau bénite* holy water

la **béquille** NOUN
crutch ◊ *Gabriel marche avec des béquilles.* Gabriel walks on crutches.

le **berceau** NOUN (PL les **berceaux**)
cradle

bercer VERB
to rock

la **berceuse** NOUN
lullaby

le **béret** NOUN

le **beret** NOUN

la **berge** NOUN
bank (*of river*)

le **berger** NOUN
shepherd

la **bergère** NOUN
shepherdess

le **besoin** NOUN
need
♦ **avoir besoin de quelque chose** to need something ◊ *J'ai besoin d'argent.* I need some money. ◊ *J'ai besoin d'y réfléchir.* I need to think about it.
♦ **une famille dans le besoin** a needy family

le **bétail** NOUN
livestock

la **bête** NOUN
see also **bête** ADJECTIVE
animal

bête ADJECTIVE
see also **bête** NOUN
stupid

la **bêtise** NOUN
♦ **faire une bêtise** to do something stupid ◊ *Je crois que j'ai fait une bêtise.* I think I've done something stupid.
♦ **dire des bêtises** to talk nonsense ◊ *Tu dis des bêtises!* You're talking nonsense!

le **béton** NOUN
concrete
♦ **un alibi en béton** a cast-iron alibi

la **betterave** NOUN
beetroot ◊ *la salade de betterave*
beetroot salad

le/la **beur** NOUN (*informal*)

> 🅘 *A* **beur** *is a young person of North African origin born in France.*

le **beurre** NOUN
butter ◊ *une sauce au beurre* a sauce made with butter

beurrer VERB
to butter

Beyrouth NOUN
Beirut

le **bibelot** NOUN
ornament

le **biberon** NOUN
baby's bottle

la **Bible** NOUN
Bible

le/la **bibliothécaire** NOUN
librarian

la **bibliothèque** NOUN

[1] library ◊ *emprunter un livre à la bibliothèque* to borrow a book from the library

[2] bookcase ◊ *une bibliothèque en chêne massif* a bookcase made of solid oak

le **bic** ® NOUN

Biro ®

la **biche** NOUN

doe

la **bicyclette** NOUN

bicycle

le **bidet** NOUN

bidet

le **bidon** NOUN

see also **bidon** ADJECTIVE

can ◊ *un bidon d'essence* a can of petrol

bidon ADJECTIVE (*informal*)

see also **bidon** NOUN

phoney ◊ *Son histoire est complètement bidon.* His story is a complete load of rubbish.

le **bidonville** NOUN

shanty town

la **Biélorussie** NOUN

Belarus

le **bien** NOUN

see also **bien** ADJECTIVE

[1] good ◊ *le bien et le mal* good and evil ◊ *Jean m'a dit beaucoup de bien de toi.* Jean told me a lot of good things about you. ◊ *C'est pour son bien.* It's for his own good.

♦**faire du bien à quelqu'un** to do somebody good ◊ *Ses vacances lui ont fait beaucoup de bien.* His holiday has done him a lot of good.

[2] possession ◊ *son bien le plus précieux* his most treasured possession

bien ADJECTIVE, ADVERB

see also **bien** NOUN

[1] well ◊ *Daphne travaille bien.* Daphne works well. ◊ *Je me sens bien.* I feel fine. ◊ *Je ne me sens pas bien.* I don't feel well.

[2] good ◊ *Ce restaurant est vraiment bien.* This restaurant is really good.

[3] quite ◊ *bien assez* quite enough

♦**Je veux bien le faire.** I'm quite willing to do it.

♦**bien mieux** much better

♦**J'espère bien y aller.** I very much hope to go.

[4] right ◊ *Ce n'est pas bien de dire du mal des gens.* It's not right to say nasty things about people. ◊ *Il croyait*

bien faire. He thought he was doing the right thing.

♦**C'est bien fait pour lui!** It serves him right!

le **bien-être** NOUN

well-being ◊ *une sensation de bien-être* a feeling of well-being

la **bienfaisance** NOUN

charity

♦**une œuvre de bienfaisance** a charity

bien que CONJUNCTION

although ◊ *Il fait assez chaud bien qu'il n'y ait pas de soleil.* It's quite warm although there's no sun.

bien sûr ADVERB

of course

bientôt ADVERB

soon ◊ *À bientôt!* See you soon!

le **bienvenu** NOUN

♦**Vous êtes le bienvenu!** You're welcome! ◊ *Vous êtes tous les bienvenus!* You're all welcome!

la **bienvenue** NOUN

welcome ◊ *Bienvenue à Paris!* Welcome to Paris! ◊ *Vous êtes la bienvenue!* You're welcome!

la **bière** NOUN

beer

♦**la bière blonde** lager

♦**la bière brune** brown ale

♦**la bière pression** draught beer

le **bifteck** NOUN

steak

le **bigoudi** NOUN

roller (*in hair*)

le **bijou** NOUN (PL les **bijoux**)

jewel

la **bijouterie** NOUN

jeweller's

le **bijoutier** NOUN

jeweller

la **bijoutière** NOUN

jeweller ◊ *Elle est bijoutière.* She's a jeweller.

le **bilan** NOUN

♦**faire le bilan de quelque chose** to assess something ◊ *Il faut faire le bilan de la situation.* We need to assess the situation.

bilingue ADJECTIVE

bilingual

le **billard** NOUN

billiards

♦**le billard américain** pool

la **bille** NOUN

marble (*toy*) ◊ *jouer aux billes* to play marbles

le **billet** NOUN

B

☞

1 <u>ticket</u> ◊ *un billet d'avion* a plane ticket

2 <u>banknote</u> ◊ *un billet de dix euros* a 10 euro note

le **billion** NOUN
<u>billion</u>

la **biographie** NOUN
<u>biography</u>

la **biologie** NOUN
<u>biology</u>

biologique ADJECTIVE
1 <u>organic</u> ◊ *des légumes biologiques* organic vegetables
2 <u>biological</u> ◊ *des armes biologiques* biological weapons

la **Birmanie** NOUN
<u>Burma</u>

bis ADVERB
see also **bis** NOUN
◊ *Il habite au douze bis rue des Fleurs.* He lives at 12A rue des Fleurs.

le **bis** NOUN
see also **bis** ADVERB
<u>encore</u>

la **biscotte** NOUN
<u>toasted bread</u> (*sold in packets*)

le **biscuit** NOUN
<u>biscuit</u>
♦ **un biscuit de Savoie** a sponge cake

la **bise** NOUN
<u>kiss</u> ◊ *Grosses bises de Bretagne.* Love and kisses from Brittany.
♦ **faire la bise à quelqu'un** (*informal*) to give somebody a peck on the cheek ◊ *Elle m'a fait la bise.* She gave me a peck on the cheek.

> ⓘ *Between girls and boys, and between girls, the normal French way of saying hello and goodbye is with kisses, usually one on each cheek. Boys shake hands with each other instead.*

le **bisou** NOUN (*informal*)
<u>kiss</u> ◊ *Viens faire un bisou à maman!* Come and give Mummy a little kiss!

bissextile ADJECTIVE
♦ **une année bissextile** a leap year

le **bistrot** NOUN (*informal*)
<u>café</u>

> ⓘ *Cafés in France sell both alcoholic and non-alcoholic drinks.*

bizarre ADJECTIVE
<u>strange</u>

la **blague** NOUN (*informal*)
1 <u>joke</u> ◊ *raconter une blague* to tell a joke
♦ **Sans blague!** No kidding!
2 <u>trick</u> ◊ *André nous a encore fait une blague!* André has played a trick on us again!

blaguer VERB (*informal*)
<u>to joke</u>

le **blaireau** NOUN (PL les **blaireaux**)
<u>shaving brush</u>

blâmer VERB
<u>to blame</u>

blanc ADJECTIVE (FEM SING **blanche**)
see also **blanc** NOUN
1 <u>white</u> ◊ *un chemisier blanc* a white blouse
2 <u>blank</u> ◊ *une page blanche* a blank page

le **blanc** NOUN
see also **blanc** ADJECTIVE
1 <u>white</u> ◊ *Colette est habillée tout en blanc.* Colette is dressed all in white.
2 <u>white wine</u> ◊ *un verre de blanc* a glass of white wine
♦ **un blanc d'œuf** an egg white
♦ **un blanc de poulet** a chicken breast

le **Blanc** NOUN
<u>white man</u>

la **Blanche** NOUN
<u>white woman</u>

blanche ADJECTIVE *see* **blanc**

la **blanchisserie** NOUN
<u>laundry</u>

le **blé** NOUN
<u>wheat</u>

blessé ADJECTIVE
see also **blessé** NOUN
<u>injured</u>

le **blessé** NOUN
see also **blessé** ADJECTIVE
<u>injured person</u> ◊ *L'accident a fait trois blessés.* Three people were injured in the accident.

la **blessée** NOUN
<u>injured person</u>

blesser VERB
1 <u>to injure</u> ◊ *Il a été blessé dans un accident de voiture.* He was injured in a car accident.
2 <u>to hurt</u> ◊ *Thérèse a fait exprès de le blesser.* Thérèse hurt him on purpose.
♦ **se blesser** to hurt oneself ◊ *Je me suis blessé au pied.* I've hurt my foot.

la **blessure** NOUN
<u>injury</u>

B

bleu ADJECTIVE
see also **bleu** NOUN
1 blue ◊ *une veste bleue* a blue jacket
♦**bleu marine** navy blue
2 very rare (*steak*)

le **bleu** NOUN
see also **bleu** ADJECTIVE
1 blue ◊ *J'aime le bleu.* I like blue.
2 bruise ◊ *Il a un bleu au front.* He's got a bruise on his forehead.

le **bleuet** NOUN
cornflower

le **bloc** NOUN
pad ◊ *un bloc de papier à lettres* a pad of writing paper
♦**le bloc opératoire** the operating theatre

le **bloc-notes** NOUN (PL les **blocs-notes**)
note pad

blond ADJECTIVE
blond
♦**blond cendré** ash blond ◊ *Andrew a les cheveux blond cendré.* Andrew has ash blond hair.

bloquer VERB
to block ◊ *bloquer le passage* to block the way
♦**être bloqué dans un embouteillage** to be stuck in a traffic jam

se **blottir** VERB
to huddle ◊ *Ils étaient blottis l'un contre l'autre.* They were huddled together.

la **blouse** NOUN
overall

le **blouson** NOUN
jacket ◊ *un blouson en cuir* a leather jacket

le **bob** NOUN
cotton sunhat

la **bobine** NOUN
reel ◊ *une bobine de fil* a reel of thread

le **bocal** NOUN (PL les **bocaux**)
jar

le **bœuf** NOUN
1 ox
2 beef ◊ *un rôti de bœuf* a joint of beef

bof EXCLAMATION (*informal*)
♦**Le film t'a plu? - Bof! C'était pas terrible!** Did you like the film? – Well … it wasn't that great!
♦**Comment ça va? – Bof! Pas terrible.** How is it going? – Oh … not too well actually.

le **bohémien** NOUN
gipsy

la **bohémienne** NOUN
gipsy

boire VERB
to drink
♦**boire un coup** (*informal*) to have a drink

le **bois** NOUN
wood
♦**en bois** wooden ◊ *une table en bois* a wooden table
♦**avoir la gueule de bois** (*informal*) to have a hangover

la **boisson** NOUN
drink ◊ *une boisson chaude* a hot drink ◊ *une boisson non alcoolisée* a soft drink

la **boîte** NOUN
1 box ◊ *une boîte d'allumettes* a box of matches
♦**une boîte aux lettres** a letter box
♦**une boîte postale** a PO Box
2 tin ◊ *une boîte de sardines* a tin of sardines
♦**une boîte de conserve** a tin
♦**en boîte** tinned ◊ *des petits pois en boîte* tinned peas
♦**une boîte de nuit** a night club
♦**sortir en boîte** to go clubbing

boiter VERB
to limp

le **bol** NOUN
bowl
♦**en avoir ras le bol** (*informal*) to be fed up ◊ *J'en ai ras le bol de ce boulot.* I'm fed up with this job.

bombarder VERB
to bomb

la **bombe** NOUN
1 bomb
2 aerosol ◊ *du déodorant en bombe aérosol* aerosol deodorant

bon ADJECTIVE, ADVERB (FEM SING **bonne**)
see also **bon** NOUN
1 good ◊ *un bon restaurant* a good restaurant ◊ *Le tabac n'est pas bon pour la santé.* Smoking isn't good for you.
♦**être bon en maths** to be good at maths
♦**sentir bon** to smell nice
♦**Bon courage!** Good luck!
♦**Bon voyage!** Have a good trip!
♦**Bon week-end!** Have a nice weekend!
♦**Bonne chance!** Good luck!
♦**Bonne journée!** Have a nice day!
♦**Bonne nuit!** Good night!
♦**Bon anniversaire!** Happy birthday!
♦**Bonne année!** Happy New Year!

☞

2 right ◊ *Il est arrivé au bon moment.* He arrived at the right moment. ◊ *Ce n'est pas la bonne réponse.* That's not the right answer.
♦ **Il fait bon aujourd'hui.** It's nice today.
♦ **de bonne heure** early
♦ **bon marché** cheap ◊ *Les fraises ne sont pas bon marché en hiver.* Strawberries aren't cheap in winter.
♦ **Ah bon?** Really? ◊ *Je pars aux États-Unis la semaine prochaine. – Ah bon?* I'm going to the States next week. – Really?
♦ **J'aimerais vraiment que tu viennes! – Bon, d'accord.** I'd really like you to come! – OK then, I will.
♦ **Est-ce que ce yaourt est encore bon?** Is this yoghurt still OK?

le **bon** NOUN
> see also **bon** ADJECTIVE

voucher ◊ *un bon d'achat* a voucher
♦ **pour de bon** for good ◊ *Cette fois, c'est pour de bon.* This time it's for good.

le **bonbon** NOUN
sweet

bondé ADJECTIVE
crowded

bondir VERB
to leap

le **bonheur** NOUN
happiness
♦ **porter bonheur** to bring luck

le **bonhomme** NOUN (PL les **bonshommes**)
♦ **un bonhomme de neige** a snowman

bonjour EXCLAMATION
1 Hello! ◊ *Donne le bonjour à tes parents de ma part.* Say hello to your parents for me.
2 Good morning!
3 Good afternoon!
> *bonjour is used in the morning and afternoon; in the evening **bonsoir** is used instead.*
♦ **C'est simple comme bonjour!** It's easy as pie!

bonne ADJECTIVE see **bon**

le **bonnet** NOUN
hat ◊ *un bonnet de laine* a woolly hat
♦ **un bonnet de bain** a bathing cap

bonsoir EXCLAMATION
Good evening!

la **bonté** NOUN
kindness

le **bord** NOUN
1 edge ◊ *le bord de la table* the edge of the table

2 side ◊ *Jane a garé sa voiture au bord de la route.* Jane parked her car on the side of the road.
♦ **au bord de la mer** at the seaside
♦ **au bord de l'eau** by the water
♦ **monter à bord** to go on board
♦ **être au bord des larmes** to be on the verge of tears

le **bordeaux** NOUN
> see also **bordeaux** ADJECTIVE

Bordeaux wine
♦ **du bordeaux rouge** claret

bordeaux ADJECTIVE
> see also **bordeaux** NOUN

maroon ◊ *une jupe bordeaux* a maroon skirt

le **bordel** NOUN
brothel ◊ *Quel bordel!* (informal) What a bloody mess!

border VERB
1 to line ◊ *une route bordée d'arbres* a tree-lined street
2 to trim ◊ *un col bordé de dentelle* a collar trimmed with lace
3 to tuck up ◊ *Sa mère vient la border tous les soirs.* Her mother comes and tucks her up every night.

la **bordure** NOUN
border
♦ **une villa en bordure de mer** a villa right by the sea

la **borne** NOUN
terminal (*of computer*)

la **Bosnie** NOUN
Bosnia
♦ **la Bosnie-Herzégovine** Bosnia-Herzegovina

la **bosse** NOUN
bump ◊ *Jacques a une grosse bosse au front.* Jacques has got a big bump on his forehead. ◊ *La route est pleine de bosses.* The road is very bumpy.

bosser VERB (informal)
to work
♦ **bosser un examen** to study for an exam

le **bossu** NOUN
hunchback

la **bossue** NOUN
hunchback

botanique ADJECTIVE
> see also **botanique** NOUN

botanic ◊ *les jardins botaniques* the botanic gardens

la **botanique** NOUN
> see also **botanique** ADJECTIVE

botany

la **botte** NOUN

⬚1⬚ boot ◊ *une paire de bottes* a pair of boots
♦ **les bottes de caoutchouc** wellington boots
⬚2⬚ bunch ◊ *une botte de radis* a bunch of radishes

le **bottin** ® NOUN
phone book

le **bouc** NOUN
⬚1⬚ goatee beard
⬚2⬚ billy goat
♦ **un bouc émissaire** a scapegoat

la **bouche** NOUN
mouth
♦ **le bouche à bouche** the kiss of life
♦ **une bouche d'égout** a manhole
♦ **une bouche de métro** an entrance to the underground

la **bouchée** NOUN
mouthful
♦ **une bouchée à la reine** a chicken vol-au-vent

boucher VERB
see also **boucher** NOUN
⬚1⬚ to fill ◊ *boucher un trou* to fill a hole
⬚2⬚ to block ◊ *L'évier est bouché.* The sink is blocked. ◊ *J'ai le nez bouché.* My nose is blocked.

le **boucher** NOUN
see also **boucher** VERB
butcher ◊ *Il est boucher.* He's a butcher.

la **bouchère** NOUN
butcher ◊ *Elle est bouchère.* She's a butcher.

la **boucherie** NOUN
butcher's

le **bouchon** NOUN
⬚1⬚ top (*of plastic bottle*)
⬚2⬚ cork (*of wine bottle*)
⬚3⬚ hold-up ◊ *Il y avait beaucoup de bouchons sur l'autoroute.* There were a lot of hold-ups on the motorway.

la **boucle** NOUN
curl (*of hair*)
♦ **une boucle d'oreille** an earring ◊ *une paire de boucles d'oreilles* a pair of earrings

bouclé ADJECTIVE
curly

le **bouclier** NOUN
shield

le/la **bouddhiste** NOUN
Buddhist

bouder VERB
to sulk

le **boudin** NOUN
♦ **le boudin noir** black pudding

♦ **le boudin blanc** white pudding

la **boue** NOUN
mud

la **bouée** NOUN
buoy
♦ **une bouée de sauvetage** a life buoy

boueux ADJECTIVE (FEM SING **boueuse**)
muddy

la **bouffe** NOUN (*informal*)
food ◊ *La bouffe est infecte à la cantine.* The food in the canteen is revolting.

la **bouffée** NOUN
♦ **une bouffée d'air frais** a breath of fresh air

bouffer VERB (*informal*)
to eat

le **bougeoir** NOUN
candlestick

bouger VERB
to move

la **bougie** NOUN
candle

la **bouillabaisse** NOUN
fish soup

bouillant ADJECTIVE
⬚1⬚ boiling ◊ *Faites cuire les pâtes à l'eau bouillante.* Cook the pasta in boiling water.
⬚2⬚ piping hot ◊ *La soupe est servie bouillante.* The soup should be served piping hot.

bouillir VERB
to boil ◊ *L'eau bout.* The water's boiling.
♦ **Je bous d'impatience.** I'm bursting with impatience.

la **bouilloire** NOUN
kettle

le **bouillon** NOUN
stock ◊ *du bouillon de légumes* vegetable stock

la **bouillotte** NOUN
hot-water bottle

le **boulanger** NOUN
baker ◊ *Il est boulanger.* He's a baker.

la **boulangère** NOUN
baker ◊ *Elle est boulangère.* She's a baker.

la **boulangerie** NOUN
baker's

la **boule** NOUN
ball ◊ *une boule de cristal* a crystal ball
♦ **une boule de neige** a snowball
♦ **jouer aux boules** to play bowls

le **boulevard** NOUN

☞

boulevard

bouleverser VERB
[1] to move deeply ◊ *Cette histoire déchirante m'a bouleversée.* This heartbreaking story moved me deeply.
[2] to shatter ◊ *La mort de son ami l'a bouleversé.* He was shattered by the death of his friend.
[3] to turn upside down ◊ *Cette rencontre a bouleversé sa vie.* This meeting turned his life upside down.

le **boulot** NOUN (*informal*)
[1] job ◊ *Anita a trouvé du boulot.* Anita has found a job.
[2] work ◊ *J'ai beaucoup de boulot en ce moment.* I've got a lot of work to do at the moment.

la **boum** NOUN (*informal*)
party

le **bouquet** NOUN
bunch of flowers ◊ *un bouquet de roses* a bunch of roses

le **bouquin** NOUN (*informal*)
book

bouquiner VERB (*informal*)
to read

bourdonner VERB
to buzz

le **bourg** NOUN
small market town

bourgeois ADJECTIVE
middle-class ◊ *un quartier bourgeois* a posh area

le **bourgeon** NOUN
bud

la **Bourgogne** NOUN
Burgundy

bourré ADJECTIVE
◆ **bourré de** stuffed with ◊ *un portefeuille bourré de billets* a wallet stuffed with banknotes
◆ **être bourré** (*informal*) to be plastered ◊ *Il était complètement bourré.* He was completely plastered.

le **bourreau** NOUN (PL les **bourreaux**)
executioner
◆ **C'est un véritable bourreau de travail.** He's a real workaholic.

bourrer VERB
to stuff ◊ *bourrer une valise de vêtements* to stuff clothes into a case

la **bourse** NOUN
grant
◆ **la Bourse** the Stock Exchange

bous VERB *see* **bouillir**

la **bousculade** NOUN

crush ◊ *la bousculade dans les grands magasins au moment des soldes* the crush in the big stores at sale time

bousculer VERB
[1] to jostle ◊ *être bousculé par la foule* to be jostled by the crowd
[2] to rush ◊ *Je n'aime pas qu'on me bouscule.* I don't like to be rushed.

la **boussole** NOUN
compass

bout VERB *see* **bouillir**

le **bout** NOUN
[1] end ◊ *Elle habite au bout de la rue.* She lives at the end of the street. ◊ *Jane est assise en bout de table.* Jane is sitting at the end of the table.
[2] tip ◊ *le bout du nez* the tip of the nose
[3] bit ◊ *un petit bout de fromage* a bit of cheese
◆ **un bout de papier** a scrap of paper
◆ **au bout de** after ◊ *Au bout d'un moment, il s'est endormi.* After a while he fell asleep.
◆ **Elle est à bout.** She's at the end of her tether.

la **bouteille** NOUN
bottle ◊ *une bouteille de vin rouge* a bottle of red wine
◆ **une bouteille de gaz** a gas cylinder

la **boutique** NOUN
shop

le **bouton** NOUN
[1] button
[2] spot (*on skin*) ◊ *J'ai un bouton sur le nez.* I've got a spot on my nose.
[3] bud ◊ *un bouton de rose* a rosebud
◆ **un bouton d'or** a buttercup

le **bowling** NOUN
[1] tenpin bowling
[2] bowling alley

la **boxe** NOUN
boxing

le **boxeur** NOUN
boxer

le **bracelet** NOUN
bracelet

le **bracelet-montre** NOUN (PL les **bracelets-montres**)
wristwatch

le **brancard** NOUN
stretcher

le **brancardier** NOUN
stretcher-bearer

la **branche** NOUN
branch

branché ADJECTIVE (*informal*)
    trendy ◊ *avoir un look branché* to
    look trendy

brancher VERB
    ☐1 to connect ◊ *Le téléphone est
    branché?* Is the phone connected?
    ☐2 to plug in ◊ *L'aspirateur n'est pas
    branché.* The hoover isn't plugged in.

le **bras** NOUN
    arm

la **brasse** NOUN
    breaststroke ◊ *nager la brasse* to do
    the breaststroke

la **brasserie** NOUN
    café-restaurant

brave ADJECTIVE
    nice ◊ *C'est un brave type.* He's a
    nice enough fellow.

bravo EXCLAMATION
    Bravo!

le **break** NOUN
    estate car

la **brebis** NOUN
    ewe
    ◆ **le fromage de brebis** sheep's cheese

bref ADJECTIVE, ADVERB (FEM SING **brève**)
    short ◊ *Sa lettre était brève.* His letter
    was short.
    ◆ **en bref** in brief ◊ *l'actualité en bref*
    the news in brief
    ◆ **... bref, ça s'est bien terminé.** ... to
    cut a long story short, it turned out
    all right in the end.

le **Brésil** NOUN
    Brazil

la **Bretagne** NOUN
    Brittany

la **bretelle** NOUN
    strap ◊ *La bretelle de son soutien-
    gorge dépasse.* Her bra strap is
    showing.
    ◆ **les bretelles** braces ◊ *Il porte des
    bretelles.* He's wearing braces.

breton ADJECTIVE, NOUN (FEM SING **bretonne**)
    Breton ◊ *Ils parlent breton.* They
    speak Breton.
    ◆ **un Breton** a Breton (*man*)
    ◆ **une Bretonne** a Breton (*woman*)
    ◆ **les Bretons** the Bretons

brève ADJECTIVE see **bref**

le **brevet** NOUN
    certificate

le **brevet des collèges** NOUN

> ⓘ The **brevet des collèges** is an
> exam you take at the end of **collège**,
> at the age of 15.

le **bricolage** NOUN
    do-it-yourself ◊ *Elle aime le
    bricolage.* She likes doing DIY.
    ◊ *un magasin de bricolage* a DIY
    shop

la **bricole** NOUN (*informal*)
    ◆ **J'ai acheté une bricole pour le
    bébé de Sabine.** I've bought a
    little something for Sabine's
    baby.
    ◆ **J'ai encore quelques bricoles à faire
    avant de partir.** I've still got a few
    things to do before I go.

bricoler VERB
    to do DIY ◊ *Pascal aime bricoler.*
    Pascal loves doing DIY.

le **bricoleur** NOUN
    DIY enthusiast

la **bricoleuse** NOUN
    DIY enthusiast

le **bridge** NOUN
    bridge (*game*) ◊ *Horst adore jouer
    au bridge.* Horst loves playing
    bridge.

brièvement ADVERB
    briefly ◊ *Expliquez-moi brièvement ce
    qui s'est passé.* Tell me briefly what
    happened.

la **brigade** NOUN
    squad (*of police*) ◊ *la brigade des
    stups* (*informal*) the drugs squad

brillamment ADVERB
    brilliantly ◊ *Il a réussi brillamment à
    son examen.* He did brilliantly in the
    exam.

brillant ADJECTIVE
    ☐1 brilliant ◊ *une brillante carrière* a
    brilliant career ◊ *Ses notes ne sont
    pas brillantes.* His marks aren't
    brilliant.
    ☐2 shiny ◊ *des cheveux brillants*
    shiny hair

briller VERB
    to shine

le **brin** NOUN
    ◆ **un brin d'herbe** a blade of grass
    ◆ **un brin de muguet** a sprig of lily of
    the valley

la **brindille** NOUN
    twig

la **brioche** NOUN
    brioche bun

la **brique** NOUN
    brick

le **briquet** NOUN
    cigarette lighter

la **brise** NOUN
    breeze

se **briser** VERB
　　to break ◊ *Le vase s'est brisé en
　　mille morceaux.* The vase broke into
　　a thousand pieces.

le/la **Britannique** NOUN
　　Briton
　　♦ **les Britanniques** the British

britannique ADJECTIVE
　　British

la **brocante** NOUN
　　junk ◊ *un magasin de brocante* a
　　junk shop

le **brocanteur** NOUN
　　dealer in second-hand goods

la **brocanteuse** NOUN
　　dealer in second-hand goods

la **broche** NOUN
　　brooch ◊ *une broche en argent* a
　　silver brooch
　　♦ **à la broche** spit-roasted ◊ *un poulet à
　　la broche* a spit-roasted chicken

la **brochette** NOUN
　　skewer
　　♦ **les brochettes d'agneau** lamb kebabs

la **brochure** NOUN
　　brochure

broder VERB
　　to embroider

la **broderie** NOUN
　　embroidery

la **bronchite** NOUN
　　bronchitis ◊ *avoir une bronchite* to
　　have bronchitis

le **bronze** NOUN
　　bronze

bronzer VERB
　　to get a tan ◊ *Il est bien bronzé.*
　　He's got a good tan.
　　♦ **se bronzer** to sunbathe

la **brosse** NOUN
　　brush
　　♦ **une brosse à cheveux** a hairbrush
　　♦ **une brosse à dents** a toothbrush
　　♦ **Il est coiffé en brosse.** He's got a
　　crew cut.

brosser VERB
　　to brush
　　♦ **se brosser les dents** to brush one's
　　teeth ◊ *Je me brosse les dents tous
　　les soirs.* I brush my teeth every
　　night.

la **brouette** NOUN
　　wheelbarrow

le **brouillard** NOUN
　　fog ◊ *Il y a du brouillard.* It's foggy.

le **brouillon** NOUN
　　first draft ◊ *Ce n'est qu'un brouillon.*
　　It's just a first draft.

les **broussailles** FEM NOUN
　　undergrowth SING

brouter VERB
　　to graze (*animals*)

broyer VERB
　　to crush
　　♦ **broyer du noir** to be down in the
　　dumps

le **brugnon** NOUN
　　nectarine

le **bruit** NOUN
　　1 noise ◊ *J'ai entendu un bruit.* I
　　heard a noise. ◊ *faire du bruit* to
　　make a noise
　　♦ **sans bruit** without a sound
　　2 rumour ◊ *Des bruits circulent à
　　son sujet.* There are rumours going
　　round about him.

brûlant ADJECTIVE
　　1 blazing ◊ *un soleil brûlant* a
　　blazing sun
　　2 boiling hot ◊ *Faith boit son café
　　brûlant.* Faith drinks her coffee
　　boiling hot.

le **brûlé** NOUN
　　smell of burning ◊ *Ça sent le brûlé.*
　　There's a smell of burning.

brûler VERB
　　to burn
　　♦ **se brûler** to burn oneself

la **brûlure** NOUN
　　burn
　　♦ **des brûlures d'estomac** heartburn

la **brume** NOUN
　　mist

brumeux ADJECTIVE (FEM SING **brumeuse**)
　　misty

brun ADJECTIVE
　　brown
　　♦ **Elle est brune.** She's got dark hair.

le **brushing** NOUN
　　blow-dry ◊ *une coupe et un brushing*
　　a cut and blow-dry

brusque ADJECTIVE
　　abrupt
　　♦ **d'un ton brusque** brusquely

brusquer VERB
　　to rush ◊ *Il ne faut pas la brusquer.*
　　You mustn't rush her.

brut ADJECTIVE
　　♦ **le champagne brut** dry champagne
　　♦ **le pétrole brut** crude oil
　　♦ **son salaire brut** his gross salary

brutal ADJECTIVE (MASC PL **brutaux**)
　　brutal

brutaliser VERB

to knock about ◊ *Il a été brutalisé par la police.* He was treated roughly by the police.

Bruxelles NOUN
Brussels

bruyamment ADVERB
noisily

bruyant ADJECTIVE
noisy

la **bruyère** NOUN
heather

bu VERB *see* **boire**

la **bûche** NOUN
log
◆ **la bûche de Noël** the Yule log

> *ℹ️ This is what is usually eaten in France instead of Christmas pudding.*

le **bûcheron** NOUN
woodcutter

le **budget** NOUN
budget

le **buffet** NOUN
[1] sideboard ◊ *un buffet en chêne* an oak sideboard
[2] buffet ◊ *un buffet froid* a cold buffet ◊ *un buffet de gare* a station buffet

le **buisson** NOUN
bush

la **Bulgarie** NOUN
Bulgaria

la **bulle** NOUN
bubble ◊ *une bulle de savon* a soap bubble

le **bulletin** NOUN
[1] bulletin
◆ **le bulletin d'informations** the news bulletin
[2] report ◊ *Ton bulletin n'est pas fameux.* Your school report isn't very good.
◆ **le bulletin météorologique** the weather report
◆ **le bulletin de salaire** pay slip
◆ **le bulletin de vote** the ballot paper

le **bureau** NOUN (PL les **bureaux**)
[1] desk ◊ *Posez le dossier sur mon bureau.* Put the file on my desk.
[2] office ◊ *Il vous attend dans son bureau.* He's waiting for you in his office.
◆ **un bureau de change** a bureau de change
◆ **le bureau de poste** the post office
◆ **le bureau de tabac** the tobacconist's
◆ **le bureau de vote** the polling station

bus VERB *see* **boire**

le **bus** NOUN
bus

le **buste** NOUN
bust

but VERB *see* **boire**

le **but** NOUN
[1] aim ◊ *Ils n'ont pas de but dans la vie.* They have no aim in life.
◆ **Quel est le but de votre visite?** What's the reason for your visit?
◆ **dans le but de** with the intention of ◊ *Je suis venue dans le but de vous aider.* I came to help you.
[2] goal ◊ *marquer un but* to score a goal

le **butane** NOUN
Calor gas ®

le **butin** NOUN
loot ◊ *Les cambrioleurs se sont partagé le butin.* The burglars shared the stolen goods.

buvais, buvait VERB *see* **boire**

le **buvard** NOUN
blotter

C

c' PRONOUN *see* **ce**

ça PRONOUN
1. this ◊ *Est-ce que vous pouvez me donner un peu de ça?* Can you give me a bit of this?
2. that ◊ *Est-ce que tu peux prendre ça, là-bas dans le coin?* Can you bring that from over there in the corner?
3. it ◊ *Ça ne fait rien.* It doesn't matter.
   ♦ **Comment ça va?** How are you?
   ♦ **Ça alors!** Well, well!
   ♦ **C'est ça.** That's right.
   ♦ **Ça y est!** That's it!

çà ADVERB
   ♦ **çà et là** here and there

la **cabane** NOUN
   hut

le **cabillaud** NOUN
   cod

la **cabine** NOUN
   cabin (*on a ship*)
   ♦ **une cabine d'essayage** a fitting room
   ♦ **une cabine téléphonique** a phone box

le **cabinet** NOUN
   surgery (*of doctor, of dentist*)
   ♦ **une chambre avec cabinet de toilette** a room with washing facilities

les **cabinets** MASC NOUN
   toilet SING

le **câble** NOUN
   cable
   ♦ **la télévision par câble** cable (*television*)

cabosser VERB
   to dent

la **cacahuète** NOUN
   peanut
   ♦ **le beurre de cacahuète** peanut butter

le **cacao** NOUN
   cocoa
   ♦ **le beurre de cacao** cocoa butter

cache-cache MASC NOUN
   ♦ **jouer à cache-cache** to play hide-and-seek

le **cachemire** NOUN
   cashmere

le **cache-nez** NOUN (PL les **cache-nez**)
   long woollen scarf

cacher VERB
   to hide ◊ *Cache toi sous le lit!* Hide under the bed! ◊ *Tu me caches quelque chose!* You're hiding something!

♦ **se cacher** to hide ◊ *Elle s'est cachée sous la table.* She's hiding under the table.

le **cachet** NOUN
1. tablet
   ♦ **un cachet d'aspirine** an aspirin
2. fee (*for performer*) ◊ *Il a touché un gros cachet pour ce concert.* He got a big fee for the concert.
   ♦ **le cachet de la poste** the postmark

la **cachette** NOUN
   hiding place
   ♦ **en cachette** on the sly ◊ *Il est sorti en cachette sans réveiller ses parents.* He crept out on the sly without waking his parents.

le **cachot** NOUN
   dungeon

le **cactus** NOUN
   cactus

le **cadavre** NOUN
   corpse

le **Caddie** ® NOUN
   supermarket trolley

le **cadeau** NOUN (PL les **cadeaux**)
   present ◊ *un cadeau d'anniversaire* a birthday present ◊ *un cadeau de Noël* a Christmas present
   ♦ **faire un cadeau à quelqu'un** to give somebody a present

le **cadenas** NOUN
   padlock

cadet ADJECTIVE (FEM SING **cadette**)
   see also **cadet** NOUN
1. younger (*brother, sister*) ◊ *ma sœur cadette* my younger sister
2. youngest (*son, daughter*) ◊ *son fils cadet* his youngest son

le **cadet** NOUN
   see also **cadet** ADJECTIVE
   youngest ◊ *C'est le cadet de la famille.* He's the youngest of the family.

la **cadette** NOUN
   youngest ◊ *la cadette de la famille* the youngest of the family

le **cadre** NOUN
1. frame ◊ *un cadre en bois* a wooden frame
2. surroundings ◊ *L'hôtel est situé dans un très beau cadre.* The hotel is set in beautiful surroundings.
3. executive ◊ *un cadre supérieur* a senior executive

C

le **cafard** NOUN
cockroach
 ♦ **avoir le cafard** (*informal*) to be feeling
down ◊ *J'ai le cafard.* I'm feeling
down.

le **café** NOUN
 1 coffee ◊ *un café au lait* a white
coffee ◊ *un café crème* a strong white
coffee
 2 café

> 🛈 *Cafés in France sell both alcoholic
> and non-alcoholic drinks.*

le **café-tabac** NOUN (PL les **cafés-tabacs**)

> 🛈 *A café-tabac is a bar which also
> sells cigarettes and stamps; you can
> tell a café-tabac by the red
> diamond-shaped sign outside it.*

la **cafétéria** NOUN
cafeteria

la **cafetière** NOUN
 1 coffee maker
 2 coffee pot

la **cage** NOUN
cage
 ♦ **la cage d'escalier** the stairwell

la **cagoule** NOUN
balaclava

le **cahier** NOUN
exercise book ◊ *mon cahier de
brouillon* my rough book

la **caille** NOUN
quail

le **caillou** NOUN (PL les **cailloux**)
pebble

la **caisse** NOUN
 1 box ◊ *une caisse à outils* a tool
box
 2 till ◊ *le ticket de caisse* the till
receipt
 3 checkout ◊ *J'ai dû faire la queue à
la caisse.* I had to queue at the
checkout.

le **caissier** NOUN
cashier

la **caissière** NOUN
cashier

le **cake** NOUN
fruit cake

le **calcul** NOUN
 1 calculation ◊ *Je me suis trompé
dans mes calculs.* I made a mistake
in my calculations.
 2 arithmetic ◊ *Je ne suis pas très
bon en calcul.* I'm not very good at
arithmetic.

la **calculatrice** NOUN
calculator

calculer VERB
to work out ◊ *J'ai calculé combien
ça allait coûter.* I worked out how
much it was going to cost.

la **calculette** NOUN
pocket calculator

la **cale** NOUN
wedge

calé ADJECTIVE (*informal*)
 ♦ **Elle est calée en histoire.** She's really
good at history.

le **caleçon** NOUN
 1 boxer shorts
 2 leggings

le **calendrier** NOUN
calendar

le **calepin** NOUN
notebook

caler VERB
to stall ◊ *La voiture a calé dans une
côte.* The car stalled on a hill.

câlin ADJECTIVE
 see also **câlin** NOUN
cuddly

le **câlin** NOUN
 see also **câlin** ADJECTIVE
cuddle ◊ *faire un câlin à quelqu'un* to
give somebody a cuddle

le **calmant** NOUN
tranquillizer

calme ADJECTIVE
 see also **calme** NOUN
 1 quiet ◊ *un endroit calme* a quiet
place
 2 calm ◊ *Caitlin est restée très
calme.* Caitlin stayed very
calm.

le **calme** NOUN
 see also **calme** ADJECTIVE
peace and quiet ◊ *J'ai besoin de
calme pour travailler.* I need peace
and quiet to work.

calmer VERB
to soothe ◊ *Cette pommade calme
les démangeaisons.* This ointment
soothes itching.
 ♦ **se calmer** to calm down ◊ *Calme-toi!*
Calm down!

la **calorie** NOUN
calorie

le/la **camarade** NOUN
friend
 ♦ **un camarade de classe** a school
friend

le **cambriolage** NOUN
burglary

cambrioler VERB
to burgle

le **cambrioleur** NOUN
burglar

la **cambrioleuse** NOUN
burglar

la **camelote** NOUN (*informal*)
junk ◊ *C'est vraiment de la camelote.*
It's absolute junk.

la **caméra** NOUN
camera (*cinema, TV*)
♦ **une caméra numérique** a digital
camera

le **caméscope** ® NOUN
camcorder

le **camion** NOUN
lorry

la **camionnette** NOUN
van

le **camionneur** NOUN
lorry driver

la **camomille** NOUN
camomile tea

le **camp** NOUN
camp ◊ *un camp de prisonniers* a
prison camp ◊ *un camp de vacances*
a holiday camp

la **campagne** NOUN
1 country
♦ **à la campagne** in the country ◊ *Nous*
passons nos vacances à la
campagne. We spend our holidays in
the country.
2 campaign ◊ *une campagne de*
marketing a marketing campaign

camper VERB
to camp

le **campeur** NOUN
camper

la **campeuse** NOUN
camper

le **camping** NOUN
camping ◊ *faire du camping* to go
camping
♦ **un terrain de camping** a campsite

le **Canada** NOUN
Canada
♦ **au Canada (1)** in Canada
♦ **au Canada (2)** to Canada

canadien ADJECTIVE, NOUN (FEM SING
canadienne)
Canadian
♦ **un Canadien** a Canadian (*man*)
♦ **une Canadienne** a Canadian (*woman*)

le **canal** NOUN (PL les **canaux**)
canal

le **canapé** NOUN
1 sofa

2 open sandwich

le **canard** NOUN
duck

le **canari** NOUN
canary

le **cancer** NOUN
cancer ◊ *le cancer du poumon* lung
cancer
♦ **le Cancer** Cancer ◊ *Sabine est Cancer.*
Sabine's Cancer.

le **candidat** NOUN
1 candidate (*in exam, election*)
2 applicant (*for job*)

la **candidate** NOUN
1 candidate (*in exam, election*)
2 applicant (*for job*)

la **candidature** NOUN
♦ **poser sa candidature à un poste** to
apply for a job ◊ *Il a posé sa*
candidature à des dizaines de postes.
He has applied for dozens of jobs.

le **caneton** NOUN
duckling

la **canette** NOUN
♦ **une canette de bière** a small bottle of
beer

le **caniche** NOUN
poodle

la **canicule** NOUN
scorching heat

le **canif** NOUN
penknife

le **caniveau** NOUN (PL les **caniveaux**)
gutter

la **canne** NOUN
walking stick
♦ **une canne à pêche** a fishing rod

la **cannelle** NOUN
cinnamon

le **canoë** NOUN
1 canoe
2 canoeing ◊ *faire du canoë* to go
canoeing

le **canon** NOUN
1 gun
2 cannon

le **canot** NOUN
dinghy ◊ *un canot pneumatique* a
rubber dinghy
♦ **un canot de sauvetage** a lifeboat

la **cantatrice** NOUN
opera singer

la **cantine** NOUN
canteen

le **caoutchouc** NOUN
rubber
♦ **des bottes en caoutchouc** Wellington
boots

le cap NOUN
cape

capable ADJECTIVE
◆**Elle est capable de marcher pendant des heures.** She can walk for hours.
◆**Il est capable de changer d'avis au dernier moment.** He's capable of changing his mind at the last minute.

la cape NOUN
cape

le capitaine NOUN
captain

la capitale NOUN
capital ◊ *la capitale de la France* the capital of France

le capot NOUN
bonnet (*of car*)

la capote NOUN (*informal*)
condom

la câpre NOUN
caper (*food*)

le caprice NOUN
◆**faire des caprices** to make a fuss ◊ *Il n'aime pas les enfants qui font des caprices.* He doesn't like children who make a fuss.

capricieux ADJECTIVE (FEM SING **capricieuse**)
◆**un enfant capricieux** an awkward child

le Capricorne NOUN
Capricorn ◊ *Helen est Capricorne.* Helen's Capricorn.

captivant ADJECTIVE
fascinating

la captivité NOUN
captivity ◊ *en captivité* in captivity

capturer VERB
to capture

la capuche NOUN
hood ◊ *un manteau à capuche* a coat with a hood

le capuchon NOUN
cap (*of pen*)

la capucine NOUN
nasturtium

le car NOUN
see also **car** CONJUNCTION
coach ◊ *un car scolaire* a school bus

car CONJUNCTION
see also **car** NOUN
because ◊ *Nous sommes inquiets car il n'est pas encore rentré.* We're worried because he isn't back yet.

la carabine NOUN
rifle

le caractère NOUN
personality ◊ *Il a le même caractère que son père.* He's got the same personality as his father.
◆**Il a bon caractère.** He's good-natured.
◆**Elle a mauvais caractère.** She's bad-tempered.
◆**Il n'a pas un caractère facile.** He isn't easy to get on with.

caractéristique ADJECTIVE
see also **caractéristique** NOUN
characteristic

la caractéristique NOUN
see also **caractéristique** ADJECTIVE
characteristic

la carafe NOUN
jug ◊ *une carafe d'eau* a jug of water

les Caraïbes FEM NOUN
Caribbean Islands

le caramel NOUN
1 caramel ◊ *la crème caramel* crème caramel
2 toffee

la caravane NOUN
caravan

carbonique ADJECTIVE
◆**le gaz carbonique** carbon dioxide

le carburant NOUN
fuel

cardiaque ADJECTIVE
◆**une crise cardiaque** a heart attack
◆**Ma tante est cardiaque.** My aunt has heart trouble.

le cardigan NOUN
cardigan

le/la cardiologue NOUN
heart specialist

le carême NOUN
Lent

la caresse NOUN
stroke ◊ *faire des caresses à un chat* to stroke a cat

caresser VERB
to stroke

la carie NOUN
tooth decay ◊ *J'ai une carie.* I've got a hole in my tooth.

caritatif ADJECTIVE (FEM SING **caritative**)
◆**une organisation caritative** a charity

le carnaval NOUN
carnival

le carnet NOUN
1 notebook
2 book ◊ *un carnet d'adresses* an address book ◊ *un carnet de chèques* a cheque book ◊ *un carnet de*

☞

timbres a book of stamps ◊ *un carnet de tickets* a book of tickets

> ❶ In the Paris metro it is cheaper to buy tickets in a book of ten, known as a **carnet**.

♦ **mon carnet de notes** my school report

la **carotte** NOUN
   carrot ◊ *les carottes râpées* grated carrots

carré ADJECTIVE
   see also **carré** NOUN
   square
♦ **un mètre carré** a square metre

le **carré** NOUN
   see also **carré** ADJECTIVE
   square

le **carreau** NOUN (PL les **carreaux**)
   ① check ◊ *une chemise à carreaux* a checked shirt
   ② tile (*on floor, wall*) ◊ *Je viens de laver les carreaux de la cuisine.* I've just washed the kitchen floor.
   ③ pane ◊ *Il a cassé un carreau.* He broke a windowpane.
   ④ diamonds (*cards*) ◊ *l'as de carreau* the ace of diamonds

le **carrefour** NOUN
   junction

le **carrelage** NOUN
   tiled floor

carrément ADVERB
   ① completely ◊ *C'est carrément impossible.* It's completely impossible.
   ② straight out ◊ *Dis-lui carrément ce que tu penses.* Tell him straight out what you think.

la **carrière** NOUN
   career
♦ **un militaire de carrière** a professional soldier

la **carrure** NOUN
   build ◊ *Il a une carrure d'athlète.* He has an athletic build.

le **cartable** NOUN
   satchel

la **carte** NOUN
   ① card
♦ **une carte d'anniversaire** a birthday card
♦ **une carte postale** a postcard
♦ **une carte de vœux** a Christmas card

> ❶ The French send greetings cards (**les cartes de vœux**) in January rather than at Christmas, with best wishes for the New Year.

♦ **une carte bancaire** a cash card
♦ **une carte bleue**

> ❶ *Carte bleue* is a major French debit card.

♦ **une carte de crédit** a credit card
♦ **une carte de fidélité** a loyalty card
♦ **une carte d'embarquement** a boarding card
♦ **une carte d'identité** an identity card
♦ **une carte de séjour** a residence permit
♦ **une carte téléphonique** a phonecard
♦ **un jeu de cartes (1)** a pack of cards
♦ **un jeu de cartes (2)** a card game
   ② map ◊ *une carte de France* a map of France ◊ *une carte routière* a road map
   ③ menu ◊ *la carte des vins* the wine list
♦ **manger à la carte** to eat à la carte ◊ *Nous allons manger à la carte.* We'll choose from the à la carte menu.

le **carton** NOUN
   ① cardboard ◊ *un morceau de carton* a piece of cardboard
   ② cardboard box ◊ *un carton à chaussures* a shoe box

la **cartouche** NOUN
   cartridge
♦ **une cartouche de cigarettes** a carton of cigarettes

le **cas** NOUN (PL les **cas**)
   case ◊ *plusieurs cas* several cases
♦ **ne faire aucun cas de** to take no notice of
♦ **en aucun cas** on no account
♦ **en tout cas** at any rate
♦ **au cas où** in case ◊ *Prends un sandwich au cas où la cantine serait fermée.* Take a sandwich in case the canteen's closed.
♦ **en cas de** in case of ◊ *En cas d'incendie, appelez ce numéro.* In case of fire, call this number.

la **cascade** NOUN
   waterfall

le **cascadeur** NOUN
   stuntman

la **case** NOUN
   ① square (*in board game*)
   ② box (*on form*)

la **caserne** NOUN
   barracks

cash ADVERB
♦ **payer cash** to pay cash

le **casier** NOUN
   locker

le **casque** NOUN

1 helmet
2 headphones

la **casquette** NOUN
cap

cassant ADJECTIVE
♦ **Il m'a parlé d'un ton cassant.** He spoke to me curtly.

le **casse-croûte** NOUN (PL les **casse-croûte**)
snack

le **casse-noix** NOUN (PL les **casse-noix**)
nutcrackers

casse-pieds ADJECTIVE (MASC, FEM, PL) (*informal*)
♦ **Il est vraiment casse-pieds!** He's a real pain in the neck!

casser VERB
to break ◊ *J'ai cassé un verre.* I've broken a glass.
♦ **se casser** to break ◊ *Il s'est cassé la jambe au ski.* He broke his leg when he was skiing.
♦ **se casser la tête** (*informal*) to go to a lot of trouble ◊ *Je ne vais pas me casser la tête pour le dîner: je vais ouvrir une boîte de conserve.* I'm not going to go to a whole lot of trouble over dinner: I'll just open a tin.

la **casserole** NOUN
saucepan

le **casse-tête** NOUN (PL les **casse-tête**)
♦ **C'est un vrai casse-tête!** It's a real headache!

la **cassette** NOUN
cassette

le **cassis** NOUN
blackcurrant

le **castor** NOUN
beaver

le **catalogue** NOUN
catalogue

la **catastrophe** NOUN
disaster

le **catch** NOUN
wrestling

le **catéchisme** NOUN
catechism

la **catégorie** NOUN
category

catégorique ADJECTIVE
firm ◊ *un refus catégorique* a flat refusal

la **cathédrale** NOUN
cathedral

catholique ADJECTIVE
see also **catholique** NOUN
Catholic

le/la **catholique** NOUN

see also **catholique** ADJECTIVE
Catholic

le **cauchemar** NOUN
nightmare ◊ *faire un cauchemar* to have a nightmare

la **cause** NOUN
cause
♦ **à cause de** because of ◊ *Nous n'avons pas pu sortir à cause du mauvais temps.* We couldn't go out because of the bad weather.

causer VERB
1 to cause ◊ *La tempête a causé beaucoup de dégâts.* The storm caused a lot of damage.
2 to chat ◊ *Nous n'avons pas beaucoup eu le temps de causer.* We didn't have much time to chat.

la **caution** NOUN
1 bail
2 deposit

le **cavalier** NOUN
1 rider
2 partner (*at dance*)

la **cavalière** NOUN
rider

la **cave** NOUN
cellar

la **caverne** NOUN
cave

le **CD** NOUN (PL les **CD**)
CD

le **CD-ROM** NOUN (PL les **CD-ROM**)
CD-ROM

ce ADJECTIVE (MASC SING **cet**, FEM SING **cette**, PL **ces**)
see also **ce** PRONOUN

*ce changes to **cet** before a vowel and most words beginning with "h".*

1 this ◊ *Tu peux prendre ce livre.* You can take this book. ◊ *cet après-midi* this afternoon ◊ *cet hiver* this winter
♦ **ce livre-ci** this book
♦ **cette voiture-ci** this car
2 that ◊ *Je n'aime pas du tout ce film.* I don't like that film at all.
♦ **ce livre-là** that book
♦ **cette voiture-là** that car

ce PRONOUN
see also **ce** ADJECTIVE

*ce changes to **c'** before the vowel in **est, était** and **étaient**.*

it ◊ *Ce n'est pas facile.* It's not easy.
♦ **c'est (1)** it is ◊ *C'est vraiment trop cher.* It's really too expensive.
◊ *Ouvre, c'est moi!* Open the door, it's me!

☞

♦**c'est (2)** he is ◊ *C'est un peintre du début du siècle.* He's a painter from the turn of the century.

♦**c'est (3)** she is ◊ *C'est une actrice très célèbre.* She's a very famous actress.

♦**ce sont** they are ◊ *Ce sont des amis à mes parents.* They're friends of my parents'.

♦**Qui est-ce?** Who is it?

♦**Qu'est-ce que c'est?** What is it?

♦**ce qui** what ◊ *C'est ce qui compte.* That's what matters.

♦**tout ce qui** everything that ◊ *J'ai rangé tout ce qui traînait par terre.* I've tidied up everything that was on the floor.

♦**ce que** what ◊ *Je vais lui dire ce que je pense.* I'm going to tell him what I think.

♦**tout ce que** everything ◊ *Tu peux avoir tout ce que tu veux.* You can have everything you want.

ceci PRONOUN
this ◊ *Prends ceci, tu en auras besoin.* Take this, you'll need it.

céder VERB
to give in ◊ *Elle a tellement insisté qu'il a fini par céder.* She went on so much that he eventually gave in.

♦**céder à** to give in to ◊ *Je ne veux pas céder à ses caprices.* I'm not going to give in to her whims.

le **cédérom** NOUN
CD-ROM

la **cédille** NOUN
cedilla

la **ceinture** NOUN
belt ◊ *une ceinture en cuir* a leather belt

♦**une ceinture de sauvetage** a lifebelt

♦**votre ceinture de sécurité** your seatbelt

cela PRONOUN
1 it ◊ *Cela dépend.* It depends.
2 that ◊ *Je n'aime pas cela.* I don't like that.

♦**C'est cela.** That's right.

♦**à part cela** apart from that

célèbre ADJECTIVE
famous

célébrer VERB
to celebrate

le **céleri** NOUN
♦**le céleri-rave** celeriac
♦**le céleri en branche** celery

célibataire ADJECTIVE, NOUN
single
♦**un célibataire** a bachelor
♦**une célibataire** a single woman

celle PRONOUN *see* **celui**

celles PRONOUN *see* **ceux**

la **cellule** NOUN
cell

celui PRONOUN (FEM **celle**, MASC PL **ceux**, FEM PL **celles**)
the one ◊ *Prends celui que tu préfères.* Take the one you like best. ◊ *Je n'ai pas d'appareil photo mais je peux emprunter celui de ma sœur.* I haven't got a camera but I can borrow my sister's. ◊ *Je n'ai pas de platine laser mais je peux emprunter celle de mon frère.* I haven't got a CD player but I can borrow my brother's.

♦**celui-ci** this one
♦**celle-ci** this one
♦**celui-là** that one
♦**celle-là** that one

la **cendre** NOUN
ash

le **cendrier** NOUN
ashtray

censé ADJECTIVE
♦**être censé faire quelque chose** to be supposed to do something ◊ *Vous êtes censé arriver à l'heure.* You're supposed to get here on time.

cent NUMBER
a hundred ◊ *cent euros* a hundred euros

> *cent* is spelt with an **-s** when there are two or more hundreds, but not when it is followed by another number, as in "a hundred and two".

◊ *trois cents ans* three hundred years ◊ *cent deux kilomètres* a hundred and two kilometres ◊ *trois cent cinquante kilomètres* three hundred and fifty kilometres ◊ *trois cent mille kilomètres* three hundred thousand kilometres

le **cent** NOUN
cent (*currency*)

la **centaine** NOUN
about a hundred ◊ *Il y avait une centaine de personnes dans la salle.* There were about a hundred people in the hall.

♦**des centaines de** hundreds of ◊ *Des centaines de réfugiés se sont présentés à l'ambassade.* Hundreds of refugees came to the embassy.

le **centenaire** NOUN
centenary

centième ADJECTIVE
hundredth

le **centilitre** NOUN
centilitre

le **centime** NOUN
centime

> *i* The euro is divided into 100 **centimes**.

◊ *une pièce de cinquante centimes* a 50-centime coin

le **centimètre** NOUN
centimetre

central ADJECTIVE (MASC PL **centraux**)
central

la **centrale** NOUN
power station ◊ *une centrale nucléaire* a nuclear power station

le **centre** NOUN
centre
♦ **un centre commercial** a shopping centre
♦ **un centre d'appels** a call centre

le **centre-ville** NOUN (PL les **centres-villes**)
town centre

cependant ADVERB
however

le **cercle** NOUN
circle ◊ *Entourez d'un cercle la bonne réponse.* Put a circle round the right answer.
♦ **un cercle vicieux** a vicious circle

le **cercueil** NOUN
coffin

la **céréale** NOUN
cereal ◊ *un bol de céréales* a bowl of cereal
♦ **un pain aux cinq céréales** a multigrain loaf

la **cérémonie** NOUN
ceremony

le **cerf** NOUN
stag

le **cerf-volant** NOUN (PL les **cerfs-volants**)
kite

la **cerise** NOUN
cherry

le **cerisier** NOUN
cherry tree

cerné ADJECTIVE
♦ **avoir les yeux cernés** to have shadows under one's eyes ◊ *Elle avait les yeux cernés.* She had shadows under her eyes.

cerner VERB
♦ **J'ai du mal à le cerner.** I can't figure him out.

certain ADJECTIVE
[1] certain ◊ *Je suis certain que je l'ai remis en place.* I'm certain that I put

it back. ◊ *Ce n'est pas certain.* It's not certain.
[2] some ◊ *Certaines personnes n'aiment pas la crème.* Some people don't like cream.
♦ **un certain temps** quite some time ◊ *J'ai mis un certain temps à comprendre ce qu'elle disait.* It took me quite some time to understand what she was saying.

certainement ADVERB
[1] definitely ◊ *C'est certainement le meilleur film que j'ai vu cette année.* It's definitely the best film I've seen this year.
[2] of course ◊ *Est-ce que je peux t'emprunter ton stylo? – Mais certainement!* Can I borrow your pen? – Of course!

certains PRONOUN
[1] some ◊ *certains de ses amis* some of his friends ◊ *certains d'entre vous* some of you
[2] some people ◊ *Certains pensent que le film est meilleur que le roman.* Some people think that the film is better than the novel.

certes ADVERB
certainly ◊ *Nous nous connaissons, certes, mais nous ne sommes pas amis.* We know each other, certainly, but we are not friends.

le **certificat** NOUN
certificate

le **cerveau** NOUN (PL les **cerveaux**)
brain

la **cervelle** NOUN
brain
♦ **se creuser la cervelle** (*informal*) to rack one's brains

le **CES** NOUN (= *Collège d'enseignement secondaire*)
secondary school

> *i* In France pupils go to a **CES** between the ages of 11 and 15, and then to a **lycée** until the age of 18.

ces ADJECTIVE
[1] these ◊ *Tu peux prendre ces photos si tu veux.* You can have these photos if you like.
♦ **ces photos-ci** these photos
[2] those ◊ *Ces montagnes sont dangereuses en hiver.* Those mountains are dangerous in winter.
♦ **ces livres-là** those books

cesse
♦ **sans cesse** ADVERB
continually

☞

♦**Elle me dérange sans cesse.** She keeps interrupting me.

cesser VERB
to stop ◊ *cesser de faire quelque chose* to stop doing something

le **cessez-le-feu** NOUN (PL les **cessez-le-feu**)
ceasefire

c'est-à-dire ADVERB
that is ◊ *Est-ce que tu peux venir lundi prochain, c'est-à-dire le quinze?* Can you come next Monday, that's the 15th?

cet ADJECTIVE (FEM SING **cette**)
ce changes to cet before a vowel and most words beginning with "h".
1 this ◊ *cet après-midi* this afternoon ◊ *cet hiver* this winter ◊ *cette année* this year
♦**cette semaine-ci** this week
2 that ◊ *Est-ce que tu peux me passer cette assiette?* Could you pass me that plate?
♦**cet homme-là** that man
♦**cette nuit (1)** tonight ◊ *On prévoit de l'orage pour cette nuit.* A storm is forecast for tonight.
♦**cette nuit (2)** last night ◊ *J'ai très mal dormi cette nuit.* I slept very badly last night.

cette PRONOUN *see* **ce**

ceux PRONOUN (FEM PL **celles**)
the ones ◊ *Prends ceux que tu préfères.* Take the ones you like best. ◊ *Je n'ai pas de skis mais je peux emprunter ceux de ma sœur.* I haven't got any skis but I can borrow my sister's. ◊ *Je n'ai pas de jumelles mais je peux emprunter celles de mon frère.* I haven't got any binoculars but I can borrow my brother's.
♦**ceux-ci** these ones
♦**celles-ci** these ones
♦**ceux-là** those ones
♦**celles-là** those ones

chacun PRONOUN
1 each ◊ *Il nous a donné un cadeau à chacun.* He gave us each a present. ◊ *Nous avons chacun donné dix euros.* We each gave 10 euros.
2 everyone ◊ *Chacun fait ce qu'il veut.* Everyone does what they like.

le **chagrin** NOUN
♦**avoir du chagrin** to be very upset ◊ *Elle a eu beaucoup de chagrin à la mort de sa tante.* She was terribly upset by the death of her aunt.

le **chahut** NOUN

bedlam ◊ *Il y avait du chahut dans la classe.* There was bedlam in the classroom.

la **chaîne** NOUN
1 chain ◊ *une chaîne en or* a gold chain
2 channel (*on TV*) ◊ *Le film passe sur quelle chaîne?* Which channel is the film on?
♦**une chaîne hi-fi** a hi-fi system
♦**une chaîne laser** a CD player
♦**une chaîne stéréo** a music centre
♦**travailler à la chaîne** to work on an assembly line

la **chair** NOUN
flesh
♦**en chair et en os** in the flesh ◊ *J'ai vu Mel Gibson en chair et en os.* I saw Mel Gibson in the flesh.
♦**avoir la chair de poule** to have goose pimples

la **chaise** NOUN
chair
♦**une chaise longue** a deckchair

le **châle** NOUN
shawl

la **chaleur** NOUN
1 heat
2 warmth

chaleureux ADJECTIVE (FEM SING **chaleureuse**)
warm ◊ *un accueil chaleureux* a warm welcome

se **chamailler** VERB (*informal*)
to squabble ◊ *Elle se chamaille sans cesse avec son frère.* She's always squabbling with her brother.

la **chambre** NOUN
room ◊ *C'est la chambre de Camille.* This is Camille's room.
♦**une chambre à coucher** a bedroom
♦**une chambre d'amis** a spare room
♦**une chambre à un lit** a single room
♦**une chambre pour une personne** a single room
♦**une chambre pour deux personnes** a double room
♦**"Chambres d'hôte"** "Bed and Breakfast"

le **chameau** NOUN (PL les **chameaux**)
camel

le **champ** NOUN
field

le **champagne** NOUN
champagne

le **champignon** NOUN
mushroom ◊ *une omelette aux champignons* a mushroom omelette

♦ **un champignon de Paris** a button mushroom

le **champion** NOUN
   champion

le **championnat** NOUN
   championship ◊ *le championnat du monde* the world championship

la **championne** NOUN
   champion

la **chance** NOUN
   [1] luck
   ♦ **Bonne chance!** Good luck!
   ♦ **par chance** luckily
   ♦ **avoir de la chance** to be lucky ◊ *Tu as de la chance de partir au soleil!* You're lucky, going off to the sun!
   [2] chance ◊ *Il n'a aucune chance.* He's got no chance. ◊ *Il a des chances de réussir.* He's got a good chance of passing.

le **change** NOUN
   exchange ◊ *le taux de change* the exchange rate

le **changement** NOUN
   change ◊ *Il n'aime pas le changement.* He doesn't like changes.

changer VERB
   to change ◊ *Il n'a pas beaucoup changé.* He hasn't changed much. ◊ *J'ai changé les draps ce matin.* I changed the sheets this morning. ◊ *J'ai changé trois cents euros.* I changed 300 euros.
   ♦ **se changer** to get changed ◊ *Je vais me changer avant de sortir.* I'm going to get changed before I go out.
   ♦ **changer de** to change ◊ *Je change de chaussures et j'arrive!* I'll change my shoes and then I'll be ready!
   ♦ **changer d'avis** to change one's mind ◊ *Appelle-moi si tu changes d'avis.* Give me a ring if you change your mind.
   ♦ **changer de chaîne** to change the channel

la **chanson** NOUN
   song

le **chant** NOUN
   singing ◊ *des cours de chant* singing lessons
   ♦ **un chant de Noël** a Christmas carol

le **chantage** NOUN
   blackmail ◊ *faire du chantage à quelqu'un* to blackmail somebody

chanter VERB
   to sing

le **chanteur** NOUN
   singer

la **chanteuse** NOUN
   singer

le **chantier** NOUN
   building site

la **Chantilly** NOUN
   whipped cream

chantonner VERB
   to hum

le **chapeau** NOUN (PL les **chapeaux**)
   hat

la **chapelle** NOUN
   chapel

le **chapitre** NOUN
   chapter

chaque ADJECTIVE
   [1] every ◊ *chaque année* every year
   [2] each ◊ *Ces verres coûtent cinq euros chaque.* These glasses cost 5 euros each.

le **char** NOUN
   tank (*military*)

le **charabia** NOUN (*informal*)
   gibberish ◊ *Je n'y comprends rien: c'est du charabia.* I don't understand any of it: it's gibberish.

la **charade** NOUN
   [1] riddle
   [2] charade ◊ *jouer aux charades* to play charades

le **charbon** NOUN
   coal
   ♦ **le charbon de bois** charcoal

la **charcuterie** NOUN
   [1] pork butcher's
   [2] cold meats

> ❶ A **charcuterie** sells cuts of pork and pork products such as sausages, salami and pâté, as well as various cooked dishes and salads; **charcuterie** served at a meal is an assortment of ham, sausage and pâtés.

le **charcutier** NOUN
   pork butcher

la **charcutière** NOUN
   pork butcher

le **chardon** NOUN
   thistle

charger VERB
   to load
   ♦ **charger quelqu'un de faire quelque chose** to tell somebody to do something ◊ *Paul m'a chargé de vous dire que la clé est sous le paillasson.* Paul told me to tell you that the key's under the mat.

le **chariot** NOUN
trolley (at supermarket)

charmant ADJECTIVE
charming

le **charme** NOUN
charm

charmer VERB
to charm

la **charrue** NOUN
plough

la **chasse** NOUN
1 hunting ◊ un chien de chasse a hunting dog
2 shooting ◊ la chasse au canard duck shooting
♦ **tirer la chasse d'eau** to flush the toilet

le **chasse-neige** NOUN (PL les **chasse-neige**)
snowplough

chasser VERB
1 to hunt ◊ Mon père chasse le lapin. My father hunts rabbits.
2 to chase away ◊ Ils ont chassé les cambrioleurs. They chased away the robbers.
3 to get rid of ◊ Ouvre donc la fenêtre pour chasser les odeurs de cuisine. Open the window to get rid of the cooking smells.

le **chasseur** NOUN
hunter

le **chat** NOUN
cat

la **châtaigne** NOUN
chestnut

le **châtaignier** NOUN
chestnut tree

châtain ADJECTIVE (MASC, FEM, PL)
brown ◊ J'ai les cheveux châtain. I've got brown hair.

le **château** NOUN (PL les **châteaux**)
1 castle
♦ **un château fort** a castle
2 palace ◊ le château de Versailles the palace of Versailles

le **chaton** NOUN
kitten

chatouiller VERB
to tickle

chatouilleux ADJECTIVE (FEM SING **chatouilleuse**)
ticklish

la **chatte** NOUN
cat (female)

chaud ADJECTIVE
1 warm ◊ des vêtements chauds warm clothes
♦ **avoir chaud** to be warm ◊ J'ai assez chaud. I'm warm enough.

2 hot ◊ Il fait chaud aujourd'hui. It's hot today. ◊ un plat chaud a hot dish ◊ Attention, c'est chaud! Mind, it's hot! ◊ J'ai trop chaud! I'm too hot!

le **chauffage** NOUN
heating ◊ Le chauffage est en panne. The heating isn't working.
♦ **le chauffage central** central heating

le **chauffe-eau** NOUN (PL les **chauffe-eau**)
water heater

chauffer VERB
to warm ◊ Je vais mettre de l'eau à chauffer pour faire du thé. I'm going to put some water on to make tea.

le **chauffeur** NOUN
driver ◊ un chauffeur de taxi a taxi driver

le **chaume** NOUN
♦ **un toit de chaume** a thatched roof

la **chaussée** NOUN
road surface ◊ "Attention! Chaussée déformée" "Uneven road surface"

chausser VERB
♦ **Vous chaussez du combien?** What size shoe do you take?

la **chaussette** NOUN
sock

le **chausson** NOUN
slipper
♦ **un chausson aux pommes** an apple turnover

la **chaussure** NOUN
shoe
♦ **les chaussures de ski** ski boots

chauve ADJECTIVE
bald

la **chauve-souris** NOUN (PL les **chauves-souris**)
bat (animal)

le **chef** NOUN
1 head ◊ le chef de famille the head of the family
♦ **le chef de l'État** the Head of State
2 boss ◊ Je dois demander la permission à mon chef. I have to get permission from my boss.
♦ **un chef d'entreprise** a company director
3 chef ◊ la spécialité du chef the chef's speciality
♦ **un chef d'orchestre** a conductor

le **chef-d'œuvre** NOUN (PL les **chefs-d'œuvre**)
masterpiece

le **chemin** NOUN

1 path ◊ *Je suis descendu à la plage par un petit chemin.* I went down a little path to the beach.
2 way ◊ *Quel est le chemin le plus court pour aller à l'aéroport?* What's the quickest way to the airport?
♦ **en chemin** on the way ◊ *Je mangerai mon sandwich en chemin.* I'll eat my sandwich on the way.
♦ **le chemin de fer** the railway

la **cheminée** NOUN
1 chimney
2 fireplace

la **chemise** NOUN
1 shirt ◊ *une chemise à carreaux* a checked shirt
♦ **une chemise de nuit** a nightdress
2 folder ◊ *J'ai classé mes cours dans des chemises de couleurs différentes.* I've sorted my notes into different coloured folders.

le **chemisier** NOUN
blouse

le **chêne** NOUN
oak ◊ *une armoire en chêne* an oak wardrobe

le **chenil** NOUN
kennels

la **chenille** NOUN
caterpillar

le **chèque** NOUN
cheque
♦ **les chèques de voyage** traveller's cheques

le **chéquier** NOUN
cheque book

cher ADJECTIVE, ADVERB (FEM SING **chère**)
1 dear ◊ *Chère Mélusine ...* Dear Mélusine ...
2 expensive ◊ *C'est trop cher.* It's too expensive. ◊ *coûter cher* to be expensive

chercher VERB
1 to look for ◊ *Je cherche mes clés.* I'm looking for my keys.
2 to look up ◊ *chercher un mot dans le dictionnaire* to look up a word in the dictionary
♦ **aller chercher (1)** to go to get ◊ *Elle est allée chercher du pain pour ce midi.* She's gone to get some bread for lunch.
♦ **aller chercher (2)** to pick up ◊ *J'irai te chercher à la gare.* I'll pick you up at the station.

le **chercheur** NOUN
scientist

la **chercheuse** NOUN
scientist

chère ADJECTIVE *see* **cher**

chéri ADJECTIVE
see also **chéri** NOUN
darling ◊ *ma petite fille chérie* my darling daughter

le **chéri** NOUN
see also **chéri** ADJECTIVE
darling
♦ **mon chéri** darling

la **chérie** NOUN
darling
♦ **ma chérie** darling

le **cheval** NOUN (PL les **chevaux**)
horse ◊ *un cheval de course* a racehorse
♦ **à cheval** on horseback
♦ **faire du cheval** to go riding

le **chevalier** NOUN
knight

la **chevalière** NOUN
signet ring

chevalin ADJECTIVE
♦ **une boucherie chevaline** a horsemeat butcher's

les **chevaux** MASC NOUN *see* **cheval**

le **chevet** NOUN
♦ **une table de chevet** a bedside table
♦ **une lampe de chevet** a bedside lamp

les **cheveux** MASC NOUN
hair SING ◊ *Elle a les cheveux courts.* She's got short hair.

la **cheville** NOUN
ankle ◊ *se fouler la cheville* to sprain your ankle

la **chèvre** NOUN
goat
♦ **le fromage de chèvre** goat's cheese

le **chevreau** NOUN (PL les **chevreaux**)
kid (*animal, leather*)

le **chèvrefeuille** NOUN
honeysuckle

le **chevreuil** NOUN
1 roe deer
2 venison ◊ *un rôti de chevreuil* roast venison

le **chewing-gum** NOUN
chewing gum

chez PREPOSITION
♦ **chez Pierre (1)** at Pierre's house
♦ **chez Pierre (2)** to Pierre's house
♦ **chez moi (1)** at my house ◊ *Je suis resté chez moi ce week-end.* I stayed at home this weekend.
♦ **chez moi (2)** to my house ◊ *Je vais rentrer chez moi.* I'm going home.
♦ **chez le dentiste (1)** at the dentist's ◊ *J'ai rendez-vous chez le dentiste demain matin.* I've got an

appointment at the dentist's tomorrow morning.
♦ **chez le dentiste (2)** to the dentist's
◊ *Je vais chez le dentiste.* I'm going to the dentist's.

chic ADJECTIVE
1 smart ◊ *une tenue chic* a smart outfit
2 nice ◊ *C'est chic de ta part de m'avoir invité.* (*informal*) It was nice of you to invite me.

la **chicorée** NOUN
endive

le **chien** NOUN
dog
♦ **"Attention, chien méchant"** "Beware of the dog"

la **chienne** NOUN
bitch (*dog*)

le **chiffon** NOUN
cloth

chiffonner VERB
to crease ◊ *Ma robe est toute chiffonnée.* My dress is all creased.

le **chiffre** NOUN
figure ◊ *en chiffres ronds* in round figures
♦ **les chiffres romains** Roman numerals

le **chignon** NOUN
bun (*in hair*) ◊ *Elle s'est fait un chignon.* She put her hair in a bun.

le **Chili** NOUN
Chile

la **chimie** NOUN
chemistry ◊ *un cours de chimie* a chemistry lesson

chimique ADJECTIVE
chemical ◊ *une réaction chimique* a chemical reaction
♦ **les produits chimiques** chemicals

la **Chine** NOUN
China

chinois ADJECTIVE, NOUN
Chinese ◊ *Il apprend le chinois.* He's learning Chinese.
♦ **un Chinois** a Chinese (*man*)
♦ **une Chinoise** a Chinese (*woman*)
♦ **les Chinois** the Chinese

le **chiot** NOUN
puppy

les **chips** FEM NOUN
crisps ◊ *un paquet de chips* a packet of crisps

chirurgical ADJECTIVE (MASC PL **chirurgicaux**)
♦ **une intervention chirurgicale** an operation

la **chirurgie** NOUN
surgery
♦ **la chirurgie esthétique** plastic surgery

le **chirurgien** NOUN
surgeon

le **choc** NOUN
shock ◊ *Ça m'a fait un sacré choc de le voir comme ça.* It gave me a hell of a shock to see him in that state.
♦ **Elle est encore sous le choc.** She's still in shock.

le **chocolat** NOUN
chocolate
♦ **un chocolat chaud** a hot chocolate
♦ **le chocolat à croquer** dark chocolate

le **chœur** NOUN
choir

choisir VERB
to choose

le **choix** NOUN
1 choice
♦ **avoir le choix** to have the choice
2 selection ◊ *Il n'y a pas beaucoup de choix dans ce magasin.* There's not a very wide selection of things in this shop.

le **chômage** NOUN
unemployment
♦ **être au chômage** to be unemployed

le **chômeur** NOUN
unemployed person ◊ *Il est chômeur.* He's unemployed.

la **chômeuse** NOUN
unemployed woman ◊ *Elle est chômeuse.* She's unemployed.

choquer VERB
to shock ◊ *Cette remarque m'a choqué.* I was shocked by that remark.

la **chorale** NOUN
choir

la **chose** NOUN
thing ◊ *J'ai fait des choses intéressantes pendant les vacances.* I did some interesting things during the holidays.
♦ **C'est peu de chose.** It's nothing really.

le **chou** NOUN (PL les **choux**)
cabbage
♦ **les choux de Bruxelles** Brussels sprouts
♦ **un chou à la crème** a choux bun

le **chouchou** NOUN (*informal*)
teacher's pet

la **chouchoute** NOUN (*informal*)
teacher's pet

la **choucroute** NOUN
sauerkraut (*with sausages and ham*)

la **chouette** NOUN
see also **chouette** ADJECTIVE
owl

chouette ADJECTIVE (*informal*)
see also **chouette** NOUN
brilliant ◊ *Chouette alors!* Brilliant!

le **chou-fleur** NOUN (PL les **choux-fleurs**)
cauliflower

chrétien ADJECTIVE (FEM SING **chrétienne**)
Christian ◊ *Il est chrétien.* He's a
Christian.

le **Christ** NOUN
Christ

chronologique ADJECTIVE
chronological

le **chronomètre** NOUN
stopwatch

chronométrer VERB
to time

le **chrysanthème** NOUN
chrysanthemum

*i Chrysanthemums are strongly
associated with funerals in France.*

chuchoter VERB
to whisper

chut EXCLAMATION
Shh!

la **chute** NOUN
fall
♦ **faire une chute** to fall
♦ **une chute d'eau** a waterfall

Chypre NOUN
Cyprus

-ci ADVERB
♦ **ce livre-ci** this book
♦ **ces bottes-ci** these boots

la **cible** NOUN
target

la **ciboulette** NOUN
chives

la **cicatrice** NOUN
scar

se **cicatriser** VERB
to heal up ◊ *Cette plaie s'est vite
cicatrisée.* This wound has healed up
quickly.

ci-contre ADVERB
opposite ◊ *la page ci-contre* the
opposite page

ci-dessous ADVERB
below ◊ *la photo ci-dessous* the
picture below

ci-dessus ADVERB
above

le **cidre** NOUN
cider

le **ciel** NOUN
① sky ◊ *un ciel nuageux* a cloudy
sky
② heaven ◊ *être au ciel* to be in
heaven

le **cierge** NOUN
candle (*in church*)

la **cigale** NOUN
cicada

le **cigare** NOUN
cigar ◊ *Il fume le cigare.* He smokes
cigars.

la **cigarette** NOUN
cigarette

la **cigogne** NOUN
stork

ci-joint ADVERB
enclosed ◊ *Veuillez trouver ci-joint
mon curriculum vitae.* Please find
enclosed my CV.

le **cil** NOUN
eyelash

le **ciment** NOUN
cement

le **cimetière** NOUN
cemetery

le/la **cinéaste** NOUN
film-maker

le **cinéma** NOUN
cinema

cinq NUMBER
five ◊ *Il est cinq heures du matin.* It's
five in the morning. ◊ *Il a cinq ans.*
He's five.
♦ **le cinq février** the fifth of February

la **cinquantaine** NOUN
about fifty ◊ *Il y avait une
cinquantaine de personnes.* There
were about fifty people there.
♦ **Il a la cinquantaine.** He's in his fifties.

cinquante NUMBER
fifty ◊ *Il a cinquante ans.* He's fifty.
♦ **cinquante et un** fifty-one
♦ **cinquante-deux** fifty-two

cinquième ADJECTIVE
see also **cinquième** NOUN
fifth ◊ *au cinquième étage* on the
fifth floor

la **cinquième** NOUN
see also **cinquième** ADJECTIVE
year 8

*i In French secondary schools,
years are counted from the **sixième**
(youngest) to **première** and **terminale**
(oldest).*

◊ *Mon frère est en cinquième.* My brother's in year 8.

le **cintre** NOUN
coat hanger

le **cirage** NOUN
shoe polish

circonflexe ADJECTIVE
♦ **un accent circonflexe** a circumflex

la **circonstance** NOUN
circumstance ◊ *dans les circonstances actuelles* in the present circumstances

la **circulation** NOUN
1 traffic ◊ *Il y avait beaucoup de circulation.* There was a lot of traffic.
2 circulation ◊ *Elle a des problèmes de circulation.* She has bad circulation.

circuler VERB
to run ◊ *Il n'y a qu'un bus sur trois qui circule.* Only one bus in three is running.

la **cire** NOUN
wax

le **ciré** NOUN
oilskin jacket

cirer VERB
to polish (*shoes, floor*)

le **cirque** NOUN
circus

les **ciseaux** MASC NOUN
♦ **une paire de ciseaux** a pair of scissors

le **citadin** NOUN
city dweller

la **citation** NOUN
quotation

la **cité** NOUN
estate ◊ *J'habite dans une cité.* I live on an estate.
♦ **une cité universitaire** halls of residence
♦ **une cité-dortoir** a dormitory town

citer VERB
to quote

le **citoyen** NOUN
citizen

la **citoyenne** NOUN
citizen

la **citoyenneté** NOUN
citizenship

le **citron** NOUN
lemon
♦ **un citron vert** a lime
♦ **un citron pressé** a fresh lemon juice

la **citronnade** NOUN
still lemonade

la **citrouille** NOUN
pumpkin

le **civet** NOUN
stew ◊ *du civet de lapin* rabbit stew

civil ADJECTIVE
civilian
♦ **en civil** in civilian clothes

la **civilisation** NOUN
civilization

civique ADJECTIVE
♦ **l'instruction civique** PSHE

clair ADJECTIVE, ADVERB
1 light ◊ *vert clair* light green ◊ *C'est une pièce très claire.* It's a very light room.
2 clear (*water*)
♦ **voir clair** to see clearly
♦ **le clair de lune** moonlight

clairement ADVERB
clearly

la **clairière** NOUN
clearing

clandestin ADJECTIVE
♦ **un passager clandestin** a stowaway

la **claque** NOUN
slap ◊ *Elle m'a donné une claque.* She gave me a slap.

claquer VERB
1 to bang ◊ *On entend des volets qui claquent.* You can hear shutters banging.
2 to slam ◊ *Elle est partie en claquant la porte.* She left, slamming the door behind her.

les **claquettes** FEM NOUN
♦ **faire des claquettes** to tap-dance

la **clarinette** NOUN
clarinet

la **classe** NOUN
1 class ◊ *C'est la meilleure élève de la classe.* She's the best pupil in the class. ◊ *voyager en première classe* to travel first class
2 classroom

classer VERB
to arrange ◊ *Les livres sont classés par ordre alphabétique.* The books are arranged in alphabetical order.

le **classeur** NOUN
ring binder

classique ADJECTIVE
1 classical ◊ *de la musique classique* classical music
2 classic ◊ *un style classique* a classic style

le **clavier** NOUN
keyboard (*of computer, typewriter*)

la **clé** NOUN

1 key ◊ *une clé de voiture* a car key
2 clef ◊ *la clé de sol* the treble clef
◊ *la clé de fa* the bass clef

la **clef** NOUN = **clé**

le **client** NOUN
  customer

la **cliente** NOUN
  customer

la **clientèle** NOUN
  customers

cligner VERB
  ◆**cligner des yeux** to blink

le **clignotant** NOUN
  indicator ◊ *Il a mis son clignotant à gauche.* He's indicating left.

le **climat** NOUN
  climate

la **climatisation** NOUN
  air conditioning

climatisé ADJECTIVE
  air-conditioned ◊ *L'hôtel est climatisé.* The hotel is air-conditioned.

le **clin d'œil** NOUN (PL les **clins d'œil**)
  wink
  ◆**en un clin d'œil** in a flash

la **clinique** NOUN
  private hospital

cliquer VERB
  to click ◊ *cliquer sur une icône* to click on an icon

le **clochard** NOUN
  tramp

la **cloche** NOUN
  bell

le **clocher** NOUN
  1 church tower
  2 steeple

le **clone** NOUN
  clone

cloner VERB
  to clone

le **clou** NOUN
  nail
  ◆**un clou de girofle** a clove

le **clown** NOUN
  clown

le **club** NOUN
  club

le **cobaye** NOUN
  guinea pig

le **coca** NOUN
  Coke ®

la **cocaïne** NOUN
  cocaine

la **coccinelle** NOUN
  ladybird

cocher VERB
  to tick ◊ *Cochez la bonne réponse.* Tick the right answer.

le **cochon** NOUN
  see also **cochon** ADJECTIVE
  pig
  ◆**un cochon d'Inde** a guinea pig

cochon ADJECTIVE (*informal*)
  see also **cochon** NOUN
  dirty ◊ *une histoire cochonne* a dirty story

le **cocktail** NOUN
  1 cocktail
  2 cocktail party

le **coco** NOUN
  ◆**une noix de coco** a coconut

cocorico EXCLAMATION
  1 Cock-a-doodle-doo!
  2 Three cheers for France!

> ❶ The symbol of France is the cockerel and so **cocorico!** is sometimes used as an expression of French national pride.

la **cocotte** NOUN
  casserole (*pan*)
  ◆**une cocotte-minute** ® a pressure cooker

le **code** NOUN
  code
  ◆**le code de la route** the highway code
  ◆**le code postal** the postcode
  ◆**le code confidentiel** PIN number

le **cœur** NOUN
  heart
  ◆**avoir bon cœur** to be kind-hearted
  ◆**la dame de cœur** the queen of hearts
  ◆**avoir mal au cœur** to feel sick
  ◆**par cœur** by heart ◊ *apprendre quelque chose par cœur* to learn something by heart

le **coffre** NOUN
  1 boot (*of car*)
  2 chest (*furniture*)

le **coffre-fort** NOUN (PL les **coffres-forts**)
  safe

le **coffret** NOUN
  ◆**un coffret à bijoux** a jewellery box

le **cognac** NOUN
  brandy

se **cogner** VERB
  ◆**se cogner à quelque chose** to bang into something ◊ *Je me suis cogné à la table.* I banged into the table. ◊ *Je me suis cogné la tête contre la porte du placard.* I banged my head on the cupboard door.

coiffé ADJECTIVE
♦**Tu es bien coiffée.** Your hair looks nice.
coiffer VERB
♦**se coiffer** to do one's hair
le **coiffeur** NOUN
hairdresser
la **coiffeuse** NOUN
hairdresser
la **coiffure** NOUN
hairstyle ◊ *Cette coiffure te va bien.* That hairstyle suits you.
♦**un salon de coiffure** a hairdresser's
le **coin** NOUN
corner
♦**au coin de la rue** on the corner of the street
♦**Tu habites dans le coin?** Do you live near here?
♦**Je ne suis pas du coin.** I'm not from here.
♦**le bistrot du coin** the local pub
coincé ADJECTIVE
1 stuck ◊ *La clé est coincée dans la serrure.* The key is stuck in the keyhole.
2 stuffy ◊ *Il est un peu coincé.* (*informal*) He's a bit stuffy.
coincer VERB
to jam ◊ *La porte est coincée.* The door's jammed.
la **coïncidence** NOUN
coincidence
le **col** NOUN
1 collar
2 pass (*of mountain*)
la **colère** NOUN
anger
♦**Je suis en colère.** I'm angry.
♦**se mettre en colère** to get angry
le **colin** NOUN
hake
la **colique** NOUN
diarrhoea
le **colis** NOUN
parcel
collaborer VERB
to collaborate
collant ADJECTIVE
see also **collant** NOUN
1 sticky
2 clingy
♦**Je le trouve un peu collant.** (*informal*) He's always hanging around me.
le **collant** NOUN
see also **collant** ADJECTIVE
tights ◊ *un collant en laine* woollen tights

la **colle** NOUN
1 glue ◊ *un tube de colle* a tube of glue
2 detention ◊ *J'ai une heure de colle samedi prochain.* (*informal*) I've got an hour's detention next Saturday.
♦**Je n'en sais rien: tu me poses une colle.** (*informal*) I really don't know: you've got me there.
la **collecte** NOUN
collection (*of money*) ◊ *On a fait une collecte au profit des victimes.* There was a collection for the victims.
la **collection** NOUN
collection ◊ *une collection de timbres* a stamp collection
collectionner VERB
to collect
le **collège** NOUN
secondary school

ⓘ In France pupils go to a **collège** between the ages of 11 and 15, and then to a **lycée** until the age of 18.

le **collégien** NOUN
schoolboy
la **collégienne** NOUN
schoolgirl
le/la **collègue** NOUN
colleague
coller VERB
1 to stick ◊ *Il y a un chewing-gum collé sous la chaise.* There's a bit of chewing gum stuck under the chair.
2 to be sticky ◊ *Ce timbre ne colle plus.* This stamp won't stick on.
3 to press ◊ *J'ai collé mon oreille au mur.* I pressed my ear against the wall.
le **collier** NOUN
1 necklace ◊ *un collier de perles* a pearl necklace
2 collar (*of dog, cat*)
la **colline** NOUN
hill
la **collision** NOUN
crash
la **colombe** NOUN
dove
la **colonie** NOUN
♦**aller en colonie de vacances** to go to summer camp
la **colonne** NOUN
column
♦**la colonne vertébrale** the spine
le **colorant** NOUN
colouring

le **coloris** NOUN
　colour

le **coma** NOUN
　coma ◊ *être dans le coma* to be in a
　coma

le **combat** NOUN
　fighting ◊ *Les combats ont repris ce*
　matin. Fighting started again this
　morning.
◆**un combat de boxe** a boxing match

le **combattant** NOUN
◆**un ancien combattant** a war veteran

combattre VERB
　to fight

combien ADVERB
　[1] how much ◊ *Vous en voulez*
　combien? Un kilo? How much do you
　want? One kilo?
◆**C'est combien?** How much is that?
　◊ *Combien est-ce que ça coûte?* How
　much does it cost? ◊ *Combien ça*
　fait? How much does it come to?
　[2] how many ◊ *Tu en veux*
　combien? Deux? How many do you
　want? Two?
◆**combien de (1)** how much ◊ *Combien*
　de purée est-ce que je vous sers? How
　much mashed potato shall I give you?
◆**combien de (2)** how many ◊ *Combien*
　de personnes as-tu invitées? How
　many people have you invited?
◆**combien de temps** how long
　◊ *Combien de temps est-ce que tu*
　seras absente? How long will you be
　away?
◆**Il y a combien de temps?** How long
　ago? ◊ *Il est parti il y a combien de*
　temps? How long ago did he leave?
◆**On est le combien aujourd'hui? – On**
　est le vingt. What's the date today? –
　It's the 20th.

la **combinaison** NOUN
　[1] combination ◊ *J'ai changé la*
　combinaison de mon antivol. I've
　changed the combination on my bike
　lock.
　[2] slip *(petticoat)*
◆**une combinaison de plongée** a
　wetsuit
◆**une combinaison de ski** a ski suit

le **comble** NOUN
◆**Alors ça, c'est le comble!** That's the
　last straw!

la **comédie** NOUN
　comedy
◆**une comédie musicale** a musical

le **comédien** NOUN
　actor

la **comédienne** NOUN
　actress

comestible ADJECTIVE
　edible

comique ADJECTIVE
　⸢see also **comique** NOUN⸥
　comical

le **comique** NOUN
　⸢see also **comique** ADJECTIVE⸥
　comedian

le **comité** NOUN
　committee

le **commandant** NOUN
　captain *(of ship, plane)*

la **commande** NOUN
　order ◊ *un bon de commande* an
　order form
◆**être aux commandes** to be at the
　controls

commander VERB
　[1] to order ◊ *J'ai commandé une*
　robe par catalogue. I've ordered a
　dress from a catalogue.
　[2] to give orders ◊ *C'est moi qui*
　commande ici, pas vous! I give the
　orders here, not you!

comme CONJUNCTION, ADVERB
　[1] like ◊ *Il est comme son père.* He's
　like his father. ◊ *Je voudrais un*
　manteau comme celui de la photo.
　I'd like a coat like the one in the
　picture.
　[2] for ◊ *Qu'est-ce que tu veux*
　comme dessert? What would you like
　for pudding?
　[3] as ◊ *J'ai travaillé comme serveuse*
　cet été. I worked as a waitress this
　summer. ◊ *Faites comme vous*
　voulez. Do as you like.
◆**comme ça** like this ◊ *Ça se plie*
　comme ça. You fold it like this.
　◊ *C'était un poisson grand comme ça.*
　The fish was this big.
◆**comme il faut** properly ◊ *Mets le*
　couvert comme il faut! Set the table
　properly!
◆**Comme tu as grandi!** How you've
　grown!
◆**Regarde comme c'est beau!** Look,
　isn't it lovely!
◆**comme ci comme ça** SO-SO
　◊ *Comment est-ce que tu as trouvé le*
　film? – Comme ci comme ça. What
　did you think of the film? – So-so.

le **commencement** NOUN
　beginning

commencer VERB
　to start ◊ *Les cours commencent à*
　huit heures. Lessons start at 8
　o'clock. ◊ *Il a commencé à pleuvoir.* It
　started raining. ◊ *J'ai commencé de*

☞

réviser pour les examens. I've started revising for the exams.

comment ADVERB
> how ◇ *Comment arrives-tu à travailler dans ce bruit?* How can you possibly work with this noise?
♦ **Comment allez-vous?** How are you?
♦ **Comment dit-on "pomme" en anglais?** How do you say "pomme" in English?
♦ **Comment s'appelle-t-il?** What's his name?
♦ **Comment?** What did you say?

le commentaire NOUN
> comment

les commérages MASC NOUN
> gossip SING

le commerçant NOUN
> shopkeeper

le commerce NOUN
> [1] trade ◇ *le commerce extérieur* foreign trade
♦ **le commerce électronique** e-commerce
> [2] business ◇ *Il fait des études de commerce.* He's studying business.
> [3] shop ◇ *tenir un commerce* to have a shop
♦ **On trouve ça dans le commerce.** You can find it in the shops.

commercial ADJECTIVE (MASC PL **commerciaux**)
♦ **un centre commercial** a shopping centre

commettre VERB
> to commit ◇ *Il a commis un crime grave.* He has committed a serious crime.

le commissaire NOUN
> police superintendent

le commissariat NOUN
> police station

les commissions FEM NOUN
> shopping SING ◇ *J'ai quelques commissions à faire.* I've got some shopping to do.

commode ADJECTIVE
> see also **commode** NOUN
> handy ◇ *Ce sac est très commode pour les voyages.* This bag is very handy for travelling.
♦ **Son père n'est pas commode.** His father is a difficult character.

la commode NOUN
> see also **commode** ADJECTIVE
> chest of drawers

commun ADJECTIVE
> shared ◇ *une salle de bain commune* a shared bathroom ◇ *Nous avons des*

intérêts communs. We have interests in common.
♦ **en commun** in common ◇ *Ils n'ont rien en commun.* They've got nothing in common.
♦ **les transports en commun** public transport
♦ **mettre quelque chose en commun** to share something ◇ *Nous mettons tous nos livres en commun.* We share all our books.

la communauté NOUN
> community

la communication NOUN
> communication
♦ **une communication téléphonique** a telephone call

la communion NOUN
> communion ◇ *faire sa première communion* to make one's first communion

communiquer VERB
> to communicate

communiste ADJECTIVE
> communist ◇ *le Parti communiste* the Communist Party

compact ADJECTIVE
> compact
♦ **un disque compact** a compact disc

la compagne NOUN
> [1] companion
> [2] partner (*living together*)

la compagnie NOUN
> company ◇ *J'aime avoir de la compagnie.* I like to have company. ◇ *Je viendrai te tenir compagnie.* I'll come to keep you company.
♦ **une compagnie d'assurances** an insurance company
♦ **une compagnie aérienne** an airline

le compagnon NOUN
> [1] companion
> [2] partner (*living together*)

la comparaison NOUN
> comparison ◇ *en comparaison de* in comparison with

comparer VERB
> to compare

le compartiment NOUN
> compartment (*on train*)

le compas NOUN
> compass (*for drawing circles*)

compatible ADJECTIVE
> compatible

la compétence NOUN
> competence

compétent ADJECTIVE
> competent

compétitif ADJECTIVE (FEM SING **compétitive**)
competitive

la **compétition** NOUN
competition
♦ **avoir l'esprit de compétition** to be competitive

complet ADJECTIVE (FEM SING **complète**)
see also **complet** NOUN
1 complete ◊ *les œuvres complètes de Shakespeare* the complete works of Shakespeare
2 full ◊ *L'hôtel est complet.* The hotel is full.
♦ **"complet"** "no vacancies"
♦ **le pain complet** wholemeal bread

le **complet** NOUN
see also **complet** ADJECTIVE
suit (*for man*)

complètement ADVERB
completely ◊ *J'avais complètement oublié que tu venais.* I'd completely forgotten that you were coming.

compléter VERB
to complete ◊ *Complétez les phrases suivantes.* Complete the following phrases.

complexe ADJECTIVE
complex

complexé ADJECTIVE
screwed-up

la **complication** NOUN
complication

le/la **complice** NOUN
accomplice

les **compliments** MASC NOUN
compliment SING
♦ **faire des compliments** to compliment ◊ *Il m'a fait des compliments sur ma robe.* He complimented me on my dress.

compliqué ADJECTIVE
complicated ◊ *C'est une histoire compliquée.* It's a complicated story.

le **complot** NOUN
plot

le **comportement** NOUN
behaviour

comporter VERB
1 to consist of ◊ *Le château comporte trois parties.* The castle consists of three parts.
2 to have ◊ *Ce modèle comporte un écran couleur.* This model has a colour screen.
♦ **se comporter** to behave ◊ *Il s'est comporté de façon odieuse.* He behaved atrociously.

composer VERB

to compose (*music, text*)
♦ **composer un numéro** to dial a number
♦ **se composer de** to consist of ◊ *L'uniforme se compose d'une veste, d'un pantalon et d'une cravate.* The uniform consists of a jacket, trousers and a tie.

le **compositeur** NOUN
composer

la **composition** NOUN
test ◊ *Nous avons une composition de français cet après-midi.* We've got a French test this afternoon.

la **compositrice** NOUN
composer

le **compostage** NOUN
date stamping

composter VERB
to punch ◊ *N'oublie pas de composter ton billet avant de monter dans le train.* Remember to punch your ticket before you get on the train.

> *ⓘ In France you have to punch your ticket on the platform to validate it before getting onto the train.*

la **compote** NOUN
stewed fruit
♦ **la compote de prunes** stewed plums

compréhensible ADJECTIVE
understandable

compréhensif ADJECTIVE (FEM SING **compréhensive**)
understanding
> *Be careful! **compréhensif** does not mean **comprehensive**.*

la **compréhension** NOUN
1 comprehension ◊ *la compréhension orale* listening comprehension
2 sympathy
♦ **Elle a fait preuve de beaucoup de compréhension à mon égard.** She was very sympathetic towards me.

comprendre VERB
1 to understand ◊ *Je ne comprends pas ce que vous dites.* I don't understand what you're saying.
2 to include ◊ *Le forfait ne comprend pas la location des skis.* The price doesn't include ski hire.

le **comprimé** NOUN
tablet ◊ *un comprimé d'aspirine* an aspirin

compris ADJECTIVE
included ◊ *Le service n'est pas compris.* Service is not included.

◆**y compris** including ◊ *Ils ont tout vendu, y compris leur voiture.* They sold everything, including their car.

◆**non compris** excluding ◊ *un menu à vingt euros, vin non compris* a set menu for 20 euros, excluding wine

◆**cent euros tout compris** 100 euros all-inclusive

compromettre VERB
to compromise

le **compromis** NOUN
compromise ◊ *Ils sont parvenus à un compromis.* They came to a compromise.

la **comptabilité** NOUN
accounting ◊ *un cours de comptabilité* a course in accounting

le/la **comptable** NOUN
accountant ◊ *Il est comptable.* He's an accountant.

comptant ADVERB
◆**payer comptant** to pay cash

le **compte** NOUN
account ◊ *J'ai déposé le chèque sur mon compte.* I've paid the cheque into my account.

◆**Le compte est bon.** That's the right amount.

◆**tenir compte de (1)** to take into account ◊ *Ils ont tenu compte de mon expérience.* They took my experience into account.

◆**tenir compte de (2)** to take notice of ◊ *Il n'a pas tenu compte de mes conseils.* He took no notice of my advice.

◆**travailler à son compte** to be self-employed

◆**en fin de compte** all things considered ◊ *Le voyage ne s'est pas mal passé, en fin de compte.* The journey wasn't bad, all things considered.

compter VERB
to count

le **compte rendu** NOUN (PL les **comptes rendus**)
report

le **compteur** NOUN
meter

le **comptoir** NOUN
bar ◊ *au comptoir* at the bar

con ADJECTIVE (FEM SING **conne**) (*rude*)
bloody stupid

se **concentrer** VERB
to concentrate ◊ *J'ai du mal à me concentrer.* I find it hard to concentrate.

la **conception** NOUN
design

concernant PREPOSITION
regarding ◊ *Concernant notre nouveau projet, je voudrais ajouter que ...* Regarding our new project, I would like to add that ...

concerner VERB
to concern ◊ *en ce qui me concerne* as far as I'm concerned

◆**Je ne me sens pas concerné.** I don't feel it's anything to do with me.

le **concert** NOUN
concert

le/la **concierge** NOUN
caretaker

conclure VERB
to conclude

la **conclusion** NOUN
conclusion

le **concombre** NOUN
cucumber

concorder VERB
to tally ◊ *Les dates concordent.* The dates tally.

le **concours** NOUN
① competition ◊ *un concours de chant* a singing competition
② competitive exam

concret ADJECTIVE (FEM SING **concrète**)
concrete

conçu VERB
designed ◊ *Ces appartements sont très mal conçus.* These flats are very badly designed.

la **concurrence** NOUN
competition ◊ *La concurrence est vive sur ce marché.* There's a lot of competition in this market.

le **concurrent** NOUN
competitor

la **concurrente** NOUN
competitor

condamner VERB
① to sentence ◊ *Il a été condamné à deux ans de prison.* He was sentenced to two years in prison. ◊ *condamner à mort* to sentence to death
② to condemn ◊ *Le gouvernement a condamné cette décision.* The government condemned this decision.

la **condition** NOUN
condition ◊ *Je le ferai à une condition ...* I'll do it, on one condition ...

◆**à condition que** provided that ◊ *Je viendrai à condition qu'il me le*

demande. I'll come provided he asks me to.
♦ **les conditions de travail** working conditions

le **conditionnel** NOUN
conditional tense

le **conducteur** NOUN
driver

la **conductrice** NOUN
driver

conduire VERB
to drive ◊ *Est-ce que tu sais conduire?* Can you drive? ◊ *Je te conduirai chez le docteur.* I'll drive you to the doctor's.
♦ **se conduire** to behave ◊ *Il s'est mal conduit.* He behaved badly.

la **conduite** NOUN
behaviour

la **conférence** NOUN
1 lecture ◊ *donner une conférence* to give a lecture
2 conference ◊ *une conférence internationale* an international conference

se **confesser** VERB
to go to confession

les **confettis** MASC NOUN
confetti

la **confiance** NOUN
1 trust
♦ **avoir confiance en quelqu'un** to trust somebody ◊ *Je n'ai pas confiance en lui.* I don't trust him.
2 confidence
♦ **Tu peux avoir confiance. Il sera à l'heure.** You don't need to worry. He'll be on time.
♦ **confiance en soi** self-confidence ◊ *Elle manque de confiance en elle.* She lacks self-confidence.

confiant ADJECTIVE
confident

les **confidences** FEM NOUN
♦ **faire des confidences à quelqu'un** to confide in someone ◊ *Elle me fait quelquefois des confidences.* She sometimes confides in me.

confidentiel ADJECTIVE (FEM SING **confidentielle**)
confidential

confier VERB
♦ **se confier à quelqu'un** to confide in somebody ◊ *Elle s'est confiée à sa meilleure amie.* She confided in her best friend.

confirmer VERB
to confirm

la **confiserie** NOUN

sweet shop

confisquer VERB
to confiscate

confit ADJECTIVE
♦ **des fruits confits** crystallized fruits

la **confiture** NOUN
jam ◊ *la confiture de fraises* strawberry jam
♦ **la confiture d'oranges** marmalade

le **conflit** NOUN
conflict

confondre VERB
to mix up ◊ *On le confond souvent avec son frère.* People often mix him up with his brother.

le **confort** NOUN
comfort
♦ **tout confort** with all mod cons ◊ *un appartement tout confort* a flat with all mod cons

confortable ADJECTIVE
comfortable ◊ *des chaussures confortables* comfortable shoes

confus ADJECTIVE
1 unclear ◊ *J'ai trouvé ses explications confuses.* I thought his explanation was unclear.
2 embarrassed ◊ *Il avait l'air confus.* He looked embarrassed.

la **confusion** NOUN
1 confusion
2 embarrassment ◊ *rougir de confusion* to go red with embarrassment

le **congé** NOUN
holiday ◊ *une semaine de congé* a week's holiday
♦ **en congé** on holiday ◊ *Je serai en congé la semaine prochaine.* I'll be on holiday next week.
♦ **un congé de maladie** sick leave ◊ *Il est en congé de maladie.* He's on sick leave.

le **congélateur** NOUN
freezer

congeler VERB
to freeze

la **conjonction** NOUN
conjunction

la **conjonctivite** NOUN
conjunctivitis

la **conjugaison** NOUN
conjugation

la **connaissance** NOUN
1 knowledge ◊ *... pour approfondir vos connaissances ...* to increase your knowledge

☞

2 acquaintance ◊ *Ce n'est pas vraiment une amie, juste une connaissance.* She's not really a friend, just an acquaintance.
♦ **perdre connaissance** to lose consciousness
♦ **faire la connaissance de quelqu'un** to meet somebody ◊ *J'ai fait la connaissance de son frère.* I met her brother.

connaître VERB
to know ◊ *Je ne connais pas du tout cette région.* I don't know this area at all. ◊ *Je le connais de vue.* I know him by sight.
♦ **Ils se sont connus à Nantes.** They first met in Nantes.
♦ **s'y connaître en quelque chose** to know about something ◊ *Je ne m'y connais pas beaucoup en musique classique.* I don't know much about classical music.

se connecter VERB
to log on ◊ *Je me suis connecté sur Internet il y a dix minutes.* I logged onto the internet ten minutes ago.

la **connerie** NOUN (*rude*)
bloody stupid thing ◊ *faire une connerie* to do something bloody stupid

connu ADJECTIVE
well-known ◊ *C'est un acteur connu.* He's a well-known actor.

conquérir VERB
to conquer

consacrer VERB
to devote ◊ *Il consacre beaucoup de temps à ses enfants.* He devotes a lot of time to his children. ◊ *Je suis désolé, je n'ai pas beaucoup de temps à vous consacrer.* I'm afraid I can't spare much time for you.

la **conscience** NOUN
conscience ◊ *avoir mauvaise conscience* to have a guilty conscience
♦ **prendre conscience de** to become aware of ◊ *Ils ont fini par prendre conscience de la gravité de la situation.* They eventually became aware of the seriousness of the situation.

consciencieux ADJECTIVE (FEM SING **consciencieuse**)
conscientious

conscient ADJECTIVE
conscious

consécutif ADJECTIVE (FEM SING **consécutive**)
consecutive

le **conseil** NOUN
advice ◊ *Est-ce que je peux te demander conseil?* Can I ask you for some advice?
♦ **un conseil** a piece of advice

conseiller VERB
see also **conseiller** NOUN
1 to advise ◊ *Il a été mal conseillé.* He has been badly advised.
2 to recommend ◊ *Il m'a conseillé ce livre.* He recommended this book to me.

le **conseiller** NOUN
see also **conseiller** VERB
1 councillor (*political*) ◊ *un conseiller municipal* a town councillor
2 adviser
♦ **le conseiller d'orientation** the careers adviser

le **consentement** NOUN
consent ◊ *le consentement des parents* the parents' consent

consentir VERB
to agree ◊ *consentir à quelque chose* to agree to something

la **conséquence** NOUN
consequence
♦ **en conséquence** consequently

conséquent ADJECTIVE
♦ **par conséquent** consequently

le **conservatoire** NOUN
school of music ◊ *Elle fait du piano au conservatoire.* She's learning the piano at the school of music.

la **conserve** NOUN
tin ◊ *Je vais ouvrir une conserve.* I'll open a tin.
♦ **une boîte de conserve** a tin
♦ **les conserves** tinned food ◊ *Il n'est pas bon de manger tous les jours des conserves.* It's not healthy to eat tinned food every day.
♦ **en conserve** tinned ◊ *des petits pois en conserve* tinned peas

conserver VERB
to keep ◊ *J'ai conservé toutes ses lettres.* I've kept all her letters.
♦ **se conserver** to keep ◊ *Ce pain se conserve plus d'une semaine.* This bread will keep for more than a week.

considérable ADJECTIVE
considerable ◊ *Il a fait des progrès considérables.* He's made considerable progress.

la **considération** NOUN
♦ **prendre quelque chose en considération** to take something into consideration

considérer VERB
- ♦**considérer que** to believe that ◊ *Je considère que le gouvernement devrait investir davantage dans l'éducation.* I believe that the government should invest more money in education.

la **consigne** NOUN
  left-luggage office
- ♦**une consigne automatique** a left-luggage locker

consistant ADJECTIVE
  substantial ◊ *un petit déjeuner consistant* a substantial breakfast

consister VERB
- ♦**consister à** to consist of ◊ *Mon travail consiste à répondre au téléphone et à recevoir les clients.* My job consists of answering the phone and welcoming the customers. ◊ *En quoi consiste votre travail?* What does your job involve?

la **console de jeu** NOUN
  games console

consoler VERB
  to console

le **consommateur** NOUN
  1 consumer
  2 customer (*in café*)

la **consommation** NOUN
  1 consumption ◊ *la consommation d'électricité* electricity consumption
  2 drink ◊ *Le billet d'entrée donne droit à une consommation gratuite.* The ticket entitles you to one free drink.

la **consommatrice** NOUN
  1 consumer
  2 customer (*in café*)

consommer VERB
  1 to use ◊ *Ces grosses voitures consomment beaucoup d'essence.* These big cars use a lot of petrol.
  2 to have a drink ◊ *Est-ce qu'on peut consommer à la terrasse?* Can we have drinks outside?

la **consonne** NOUN
  consonant

constamment ADVERB
  constantly ◊ *Elle se plaint constamment.* She's constantly complaining.

constant ADJECTIVE
  constant

constater VERB
  to notice

constipé ADJECTIVE
  constipated

constitué ADJECTIVE

- ♦**être constitué de** to consist of

constituer VERB
  to make up ◊ *les États qui constituent la Fédération russe* the states which make up the Russian Federation

la **construction** NOUN
  building ◊ *des matériaux de construction* building materials
- ♦**une maison en construction** a house being built

construire VERB
  to build ◊ *Ils font construire une maison neuve.* They're having a new house built.

le **consulat** NOUN
  consulate ◊ *le consulat de France* the French consulate

la **consultation** NOUN
- ♦**les heures de consultation** surgery hours

consulter VERB
  1 to consult ◊ *Tu devrais consulter un médecin.* You should see a doctor.
  2 to see patients ◊ *Le docteur ne consulte pas le samedi.* The doctor doesn't see patients on Saturdays.

le **contact** NOUN
  contact ◊ *les contacts humains* human contact
- ♦**Il a le contact facile.** He's very approachable.
- ♦**garder le contact avec quelqu'un** to keep in touch with somebody

contacter VERB
  to get in touch with ◊ *Je te contacterai dès que j'aurai des nouvelles.* I'll get in touch with you as soon as I have some news.

contagieux ADJECTIVE (FEM SING **contagieuse**)
  infectious ◊ *une maladie contagieuse* an infectious disease ◊ *Restez chez vous si vous êtes contagieux.* Stay at home if you've got something infectious.

contaminer VERB
  to contaminate

le **conte de fées** NOUN (PL les **contes de fées**)
  fairy tale

contempler VERB
  to gaze at

contemporain ADJECTIVE
  contemporary
- ♦**un auteur contemporain** a modern writer

contenir VERB

to contain ◊ *un portefeuille contenant de l'argent* a wallet containing money

content ADJECTIVE
glad ◊ *Je suis content que tu sois venu.* I'm glad you've come.
♦**content de** pleased with ◊ *Elle m'a dit qu'elle était contente de mon travail.* She told me she was pleased with my work.

contenter VERB
to please ◊ *Il est difficile à contenter.* He's hard to please.
♦**Je me contente de peu.** I can make do with very little.

contesté ADJECTIVE
controversial ◊ *Cette décision est très contestée.* This is a very controversial decision.

le **continent** NOUN
continent

continu ADJECTIVE
continuous
♦**faire la journée continue** to work without taking a full lunch break

continuellement ADVERB
constantly

continuer VERB
to carry on ◊ *Continuez sans moi!* Carry on without me! ◊ *Il ne veut pas continuer ses études.* He doesn't want to go on studying.
♦**continuer à faire quelque chose** to go on doing something ◊ *Ils ont continué à regarder la télé sans me dire bonjour.* They went on watching TV without saying hello to me.
♦**continuer de faire quelque chose** to go on doing something ◊ *Il continue de fumer malgré son asthme.* He keeps on smoking, despite his asthma.

contourner VERB
to go round ◊ *La route contourne la ville.* The road goes round the town.

le **contraceptif** NOUN
contraceptive

la **contraception** NOUN
contraception

le **contractuel** NOUN
traffic warden

la **contractuelle** NOUN
traffic warden

la **contradiction** NOUN
contradiction
♦**par esprit de contradiction** just to be awkward ◊ *Il a refusé de venir par esprit de contradiction.* He refused to come, just to be awkward.

le **contraire** NOUN
opposite ◊ *Il a fait le contraire de ce que je lui avais demandé.* He did the opposite of what I asked him.
♦**au contraire** on the contrary

contrarier VERB
[1] to annoy ◊ *Il avait l'air contrarié.* He looked annoyed.
[2] to upset ◊ *Est-ce que tu serais contrariée si je ne venais pas?* Would you be upset if I didn't come?

le **contraste** NOUN
contrast

le **contrat** NOUN
contract ◊ *un contrat de travail* an employment contract

la **contravention** NOUN
parking ticket

contre PREPOSITION
[1] against ◊ *Ne mets pas ton vélo contre le mur.* Don't put your bike against the wall. ◊ *Tu es pour ou contre ce projet?* Are you for or against this plan?
[2] for ◊ *échanger quelque chose contre quelque chose* to swap something for something
♦**par contre** on the other hand

la **contrebande** NOUN
smuggling
♦**des produits de contrebande** smuggled goods

la **contrebasse** NOUN
double bass

contrecœur
♦**à contrecœur** ADVERB
reluctantly ◊ *Il est venu à contrecœur.* He came reluctantly.

contredire VERB
to contradict ◊ *Il ne supporte pas d'être contredit.* He can't stand being contradicted.

la **contre-indication** NOUN
♦**"Contre-indication en cas d'eczéma"** "Should not be used by people with eczema"

le **contresens** NOUN
mistranslation

le **contretemps** NOUN
♦**Désolé d'être en retard: j'ai eu un contretemps.** Sorry I'm late: I was held up.

contribuer VERB
♦**contribuer à** to contribute to ◊ *Est-ce que tu veux contribuer au cadeau pour Marie?* Do you want to contribute to Marie's present?

le **contrôle** NOUN

C

1 control ◊ *le contrôle des passeports* passport control
2 check
♦ **un contrôle d'identité** an identity check
♦ **le contrôle des billets** ticket inspection
3 test ◊ *un contrôle antidopage* a drugs test
♦ **le contrôle continu** continuous assessment

contrôler VERB
to check ◊ *Personne n'a contrôlé mon billet.* Nobody checked my ticket.

le **contrôleur** NOUN
ticket inspector

la **contrôleuse** NOUN
ticket inspector

controversé ADJECTIVE
controversial

convaincre VERB
1 to persuade ◊ *Il a essayé de me convaincre de rester.* He tried to persuade me to stay.
2 to convince ◊ *Tu n'as pas l'air convaincu.* You don't look convinced.

la **convalescence** NOUN
convalescence

convenable ADJECTIVE
decent ◊ *un hôtel convenable* a decent hotel
♦ **Ce n'est pas convenable.** It's bad manners.

convenir VERB
♦ **convenir à** to suit ◊ *Est-ce que cette date te convient?* Does this date suit you? ◊ *J'espère que cela vous conviendra.* I hope this will suit you.
♦ **convenir de** to agree on ◊ *Nous avons convenu d'une date.* We've agreed on a date.

conventionné ADJECTIVE
♦ **un médecin conventionné** a Health Service doctor

> *ⓘ All doctors in France charge for treatment, but patients of Health Service doctors get their money refunded by the government.*

convenu ADJECTIVE
agreed ◊ *au moment convenu* at the agreed time

la **conversation** NOUN
conversation

la **convocation** NOUN
notification

convoquer VERB

♦ **convoquer quelqu'un à une réunion** to invite somebody to a meeting ◊ *Le directeur a convoqué tous les parents à la réunion.* The headmaster has invited all the parents to the meeting.

cool ADJECTIVE (*informal*)
cool

la **coopération** NOUN
co-operation

coopérer VERB
to co-operate

les **coordonnées** FEM NOUN
contact details ◊ *As-tu ses coordonnées?* Do you have his contact details?

le **copain** NOUN (*informal*)
1 friend ◊ *C'est un bon copain.* He's a good friend.
2 boyfriend ◊ *Je l'ai vue avec son copain hier soir.* I saw her with her boyfriend last night.

la **copie** NOUN
1 copy ◊ *Ce tableau n'est qu'une copie.* This picture is only a copy.
2 paper ◊ *Il a des copies à corriger ce week-end.* He's got some papers to mark this weekend.

copier VERB
to copy
♦ **copier-coller** to copy and paste

copieux ADJECTIVE (FEM SING **copieuse**)
hearty ◊ *un repas copieux* a hearty meal

la **copine** NOUN (*informal*)
1 friend ◊ *Je sors avec une copine ce soir.* I'm going out with a friend tonight.
2 girlfriend ◊ *Je ne savais pas qu'il avait une copine.* I didn't know he had a girlfriend.

le **coq** NOUN
cockerel

la **coque** NOUN
hull (*of boat*)
♦ **un œuf à la coque** a soft-boiled egg

le **coquelicot** NOUN
poppy

la **coqueluche** NOUN
whooping cough

le **coquillage** NOUN
1 shellfish
2 shell ◊ *Nous avons ramassé des coquillages sur la plage.* We picked up some shells on the beach.

la **coquille** NOUN
shell
♦ **une coquille d'œuf** an eggshell
♦ **une coquille Saint-Jacques** a scallop

coquin ADJECTIVE
cheeky ◊ *Il m'a regardé d'un air coquin.* He gave me a cheeky look.

le **cor** NOUN
horn ◊ *Je joue du cor.* I play the horn.

le **corbeau** NOUN (PL les **corbeaux**)
crow

la **corbeille** NOUN
basket ◊ *une corbeille de fruits* a basket of fruit
♦ **une corbeille à papier** a wastepaper basket

la **corde** NOUN
① rope
② string (*of violin, tennis racket*)
♦ **une corde à linge** a clothes line

la **cordonnerie** NOUN
shoe repair shop

le **cordonnier** NOUN
cobbler

coriace ADJECTIVE
tough

la **corne** NOUN
horn

la **cornemuse** NOUN
bagpipes ◊ *jouer de la cornemuse* to play the bagpipes

le **cornet** NOUN
♦ **un cornet de frites** a bag of chips
♦ **un cornet de glace** an ice cream cone

le **cornichon** NOUN
gherkin

la **Cornouailles** NOUN
Cornwall

le **corps** NOUN
body

correct ADJECTIVE
① correct ◊ *Ce n'est pas tout à fait correct.* That's not quite correct.
② reasonable ◊ *un salaire correct* a reasonable salary ◊ *Le repas était tout à fait correct.* The meal was quite reasonable.

la **correction** NOUN
correction

la **correspondance** NOUN
① correspondence
♦ **un cours par correspondance** a correspondence course
② connection (*train, plane*) ◊ *Il y a une correspondance pour Toulouse à dix heures.* There's a connection for Toulouse at ten o'clock.

le **correspondant** NOUN
penfriend

la **correspondante** NOUN
penfriend

correspondre VERB
to correspond
♦ **Faites correspondre les phrases.** Match the sentences together.

le **corridor** NOUN
corridor

corriger VERB
to mark ◊ *Vous pouvez corriger mon test?* Can you mark my test?

le **corsage** NOUN
blouse

corse ADJECTIVE, NOUN
Corsican
♦ **un Corse** a Corsican (*man*)
♦ **une Corse** a Corsican (*woman*)

la **Corse** NOUN
Corsica

la **corvée** NOUN
chore ◊ *Quelle corvée!* What a chore!

costaud ADJECTIVE
brawny

le **costume** NOUN
① suit (*man's*) ◊ *Tu devrais mettre un costume pour l'entretien.* You should wear a suit for the interview.
② costume (*theatre*) ◊ *Nous avons fait nous-mêmes tous les costumes pour la pièce.* We made all the costumes for the play ourselves.

la **côte** NOUN
① coastline ◊ *La route longe la côte.* The road follows the coastline.
♦ **la Côte d'Azur** the French Riviera
② hill ◊ *J'ai grimpé la côte.* I went up the hill.
③ rib ◊ *Il s'est cassé une côte en tombant.* He broke a rib when he fell.
④ chop ◊ *une côte de porc* a pork chop
♦ **une côte de bœuf** a rib of beef
♦ **côte à côte** side by side

le **côté** NOUN
side
♦ **à côté de (1)** next to ◊ *Le café est à côté du sucre.* The coffee's next to the sugar.
♦ **à côté de (2)** next door to ◊ *Il habite à côté de chez moi.* He lives next door to me.
♦ **de l'autre côté** on the other side ◊ *La pharmacie est de l'autre côté de la rue.* The chemist's is on the other side of the street.
♦ **De quel côté est-il parti?** Which way did he go?
♦ **mettre quelque chose de côté** to save something ◊ *J'ai mis de l'argent de côté.* I've saved some money.

la **côtelette** NOUN

chop ◊ *une côtelette d'agneau* a lamb chop

la **cotisation** NOUN
> [1] subscription (*to club, union*)
> [2] contributions (*to pension, national insurance*)
> ◆**cotisations sociales** social security contributions

le **coton** NOUN
> cotton ◊ *une chemise en coton* a cotton shirt
> ◆**le coton hydrophile** cotton wool

le **Coton-tige** ® NOUN
> (PL les **Cotons-tiges**)
> cotton bud

le **cou** NOUN
> neck

couchant ADJECTIVE
> ◆**le soleil couchant** the setting sun

la **couche** NOUN
> [1] layer ◊ *la couche d'ozone* the ozone layer
> [2] coat (*of paint, varnish*)
> [3] nappy

couché ADJECTIVE
> [1] lying down ◊ *Il était couché sur le tapis.* He was lying on the carpet.
> [2] in bed ◊ *Il est déjà couché.* He's already in bed.

le **coucher** NOUN
> see also **coucher** VERB
> ◆**un coucher de soleil** a sunset

se **coucher** VERB
> see also **coucher** NOUN
> [1] to go to bed ◊ *Je me suis couché tard hier soir.* I went to bed late last night.
> [2] to set (*sun*)

la **couchette** NOUN
> [1] couchette (*on train*)
> [2] bunk (*on boat*)

le **coude** NOUN
> elbow

coudre VERB
> [1] to sew ◊ *J'aime coudre.* I like sewing.
> [2] to sew on ◊ *Il ne sait même pas coudre un bouton.* He can't even sew a button on.

la **couette** NOUN
> duvet

les **couettes** FEM NOUN
> bunches ◊ *Quand j'étais petite, ma mère me faisait des couettes.* When I was little, my mother put my hair in bunches.

couler VERB

> [1] to run ◊ *Ne laissez pas couler les robinets.* Don't leave the taps running. ◊ *J'ai le nez qui coule.* My nose is running.
> [2] to flow ◊ *La rivière coulait lentement.* The river was flowing slowly.
> [3] to leak ◊ *Mon stylo coule.* My pen's leaking.
> [4] to sink ◊ *Le bateau a coulé.* The boat sank.

la **couleur** NOUN
> colour ◊ *De quelle couleur est leur voiture?* What colour is their car? ◊ *une pellicule couleur* a colour film
> ◆**Tu as pris des couleurs.** You've got a tan.

la **couleuvre** NOUN
> grass snake

les **coulisses** FEM NOUN
> wings (*in theatre*)
> ◆**dans les coulisses** behind the scenes

le **couloir** NOUN
> corridor

le **coup** NOUN
> [1] knock ◊ *donner un coup à quelque chose* to give something a knock
> [2] blow
> ◆**Il m'a donné un coup!** He hit me!
> ◆**un coup de pied** a kick
> ◆**un coup de poing** a punch
> [3] shock ◊ *Ça m'a fait un coup de le voir comme ça!* (*informal*) It gave me a shock to see him like that!
> ◆**un coup de feu** a shot
> ◆**un coup de fil** (*informal*) a ring ◊ *Je te donnerai un coup de fil demain.* I'll give you a ring tomorrow.
> ◆**donner un coup de main à quelqu'un** to give somebody a hand ◊ *Je viendrai te donner un coup de main.* I'll come and give you a hand.
> ◆**un coup d'œil** a quick look ◊ *jeter un coup d'œil* to have a quick look
> ◆**attraper un coup de soleil** to get sunburnt
> ◆**un coup de téléphone** a phone call
> ◆**un coup de tonnerre** a clap of thunder
> ◆**boire un coup** (*informal*) to have a drink
> ◆**après coup** afterwards ◊ *Après coup j'ai regretté de m'être mis en colère.* Afterwards I was sorry I'd got angry.
> ◆**à tous les coups** (*informal*) every time ◊ *Je me trompe de rue à tous les coups.* I get the street wrong every time.
> ◆**du premier coup** first time ◊ *Il a été reçu au permis du premier coup.* He passed his driving test first time.

☞

♦ **sur le coup** at first ◊ *Sur le coup je ne l'ai pas reconnu.* I didn't recognize him at first.

coupable ADJECTIVE
> *see also* **coupable** NOUN

guilty

le/la **coupable** NOUN
> *see also* **coupable** ADJECTIVE

culprit

la **coupe** NOUN
cup (*sport*) ◊ *la coupe du monde* the World Cup
♦ **une coupe de cheveux** a haircut
♦ **une coupe de champagne** a glass of champagne

le **coupe-ongle** NOUN
nail-clippers

couper VERB
1 to cut
2 to turn off ◊ *couper le courant* to turn off the electricity
3 to take a short-cut ◊ *On peut couper par la forêt.* There's a short-cut through the woods.
♦ **couper l'appétit** to spoil one's appetite
♦ **se couper** to cut oneself ◊ *Je me suis coupé le doigt avec une boîte de conserve.* I cut my finger on a tin.
♦ **couper la parole à quelqu'un** to interrupt somebody

le **couple** NOUN
couple

le **couplet** NOUN
verse ◊ *le premier couplet* the first verse

la **coupure** NOUN
cut
♦ **une coupure de courant** a power cut

la **cour** NOUN
1 yard ◊ *la cour de l'école* the school yard
2 court ◊ *la cour de Louis XIV* the court of Louis XIV ◊ *la cour d'assises* the criminal court

le **courage** NOUN
courage

courageux ADJECTIVE (FEM SING **courageuse**)
brave

couramment ADVERB
1 fluently ◊ *Elle parle couramment japonais.* She speaks Japanese fluently.
2 commonly ◊ *C'est une expression que l'on emploie couramment.* It's a commonly used phrase.

courant ADJECTIVE
> *see also* **courant** NOUN

1 common ◊ *C'est une erreur courante.* It's a common mistake.
2 standard ◊ *C'est un modèle courant.* It's a standard model.

le **courant** NOUN
> *see also* **courant** ADJECTIVE

1 current (*of river*)
♦ **un courant d'air** a draught
2 power ◊ *une panne de courant* a power cut
♦ **Je le ferai dans le courant de la semaine.** I'll do it some time during the week.
♦ **être au courant de quelque chose** to know about something ◊ *Je ne suis pas au courant de ses projets pour l'été.* I don't know about her plans for the summer.
♦ **mettre quelqu'un au courant de quelque chose** to tell somebody about something
♦ **Tu es au courant?** Have you heard about it?
♦ **se tenir au courant de quelque chose** to keep up with something ◊ *J'essaie de me tenir au courant de l'actualité.* I try to keep up with the news.

le **coureur** NOUN
runner
♦ **un coureur à pied** a runner
♦ **un coureur cycliste** a racing cyclist
♦ **un coureur automobile** a racing driver

la **coureuse** NOUN
runner

la **courgette** NOUN
courgette

courir VERB
to run ◊ *Elle a traversé la rue en courant.* She ran across the street.
♦ **courir un risque** to run a risk

la **couronne** NOUN
crown

courons, courez VERB *see* **courir**

le **courrier** NOUN
mail ◊ *Est-ce qu'il y avait du courrier ce matin?* Was there any mail this morning?
♦ **N'oublie pas de poster le courrier.** Don't forget to post the letters.
♦ **le courrier électronique** email
> Be careful! The French word **courrier** does not mean **courier**.

la **courroie** NOUN
♦ **la courroie du ventilateur** fan belt

le **cours** NOUN
1 lesson ◊ *un cours d'espagnol* a Spanish lesson ◊ *des cours particuliers* private lessons
2 course ◊ *un cours intensif* a crash course

[3] rate ◊ *le cours du change* the exchange rate

♦**au cours de** during ◊ *Il a été réveillé trois fois au cours de la nuit.* He was woken up three times during the night.

la **course** NOUN
[1] running ◊ *la course de fond* long-distance running
[2] race ◊ *une course hippique* a horse race
[3] shopping ◊ *J'ai juste une course à faire.* I've just got a bit of shopping to do.

♦**faire les courses** to go shopping ◊ *Elle est partie faire les courses de la semaine.* She's gone to do her weekly shopping.

court ADJECTIVE
see also **court** NOUN
short

le **court** NOUN
see also **court** ADJECTIVE
♦**un court de tennis** a tennis court

couru VERB see **courir**

le **couscous** NOUN
couscous

> ℹ️ *couscous is a spicy North African dish made with meat, vegetables and steamed semolina.*

le **cousin** NOUN
cousin

la **cousine** NOUN
cousin

le **coussin** NOUN
cushion

le **coût** NOUN
cost ◊ *le coût de la vie* the cost of living

le **couteau** NOUN (PL les **couteaux**)
knife

coûter VERB
to cost ◊ *Est-ce que ça coûte cher?* Does it cost a lot?

♦**Combien ça coûte?** How much is it?

coûteux ADJECTIVE (FEM SING **coûteuse**)
expensive

la **coutume** NOUN
custom

la **couture** NOUN
[1] sewing ◊ *Je n'aime pas la couture.* I don't like sewing.
♦**faire de la couture** to sew
[2] seam ◊ *La couture de mon pantalon s'est défaite.* The seam of my trousers has come undone.

le **couturier** NOUN

fashion designer ◊ *un grand couturier* a top designer

la **couturière** NOUN
dressmaker

le **couvercle** NOUN
[1] lid (*of pan*)
[2] top (*of tube, jar, spray can*)

couvert VERB see **couvrir**

couvert ADJECTIVE
see also **couvert** NOUN
overcast (*sky*)
♦**couvert de** covered with ◊ *Cet arbre est couvert de fleurs au printemps.* This tree is covered with blossom in spring.

le **couvert** NOUN
see also **couvert** ADJECTIVE
♦**mettre le couvert** to lay the table

les **couverts** MASC NOUN
cutlery SING ◊ *Les couverts sont dans le tiroir de gauche.* The cutlery is in the left-hand drawer.

la **couverture** NOUN
blanket

le **couvre-lit** NOUN
bedspread

couvrir VERB
to cover ◊ *Le chien est revenu couvert de boue.* The dog came back covered with mud.
♦**se couvrir (1)** to wrap up ◊ *Couvre-toi bien: il fait très froid dehors.* Wrap up well: it's very cold outside.
♦**se couvrir (2)** to cloud over ◊ *Le ciel se couvre.* The sky's clouding over.

le **crabe** NOUN
crab

cracher VERB
to spit

le **crachin** NOUN
drizzle

la **craie** NOUN
chalk

craindre VERB
to fear ◊ *Tu n'as rien à craindre.* You've got nothing to fear.

la **crainte** NOUN
fear
♦**de crainte de** for fear of ◊ *Il n'ose rien dire de crainte de la vexer.* He daren't say anything for fear of upsetting her.

craintif ADJECTIVE (FEM SING **craintive**)
timid

la **crampe** NOUN
cramp ◊ *J'ai une crampe au mollet.* I've got a cramp in my calf.

le **cran** NOUN
hole (*in belt*)

☞

◆ **avoir du cran** (*informal*) to have guts

le **crâne** NOUN
skull

crâner VERB (*informal*)
to show off

le **crapaud** NOUN
toad

craquer VERB
1 to creak ◇ *Le plancher craque.* The floor creaks.
2 to burst ◇ *Ma fermeture éclair a craqué.* My zip's burst.
3 to crack up ◇ *Je vais finir par craquer!* (*informal*) I'm going to crack up at this rate!
◆ **Quand j'ai vu cette robe, j'ai craqué!** (*informal*) When I saw that dress, I couldn't resist it!

la **crasse** NOUN
filth

la **cravate** NOUN
tie

le **crawl** NOUN
crawl ◇ *nager le crawl* to do the crawl

le **crayon** NOUN
pencil ◇ *un crayon de couleur* a coloured pencil
◆ **un crayon feutre** a felt-tip pen

la **création** NOUN
creation

la **crèche** NOUN
1 nursery ◇ *Elle dépose son fils à la crèche à huit heures.* She leaves her son at the nursery at 8 o'clock.
2 nativity scene

le **crédit** NOUN
credit

créer VERB
to create

la **crémaillère** NOUN
◆ **pendre la crémaillère** to have a house-warming party

la **crème** NOUN
see also **le crème**
cream
◆ **la crème anglaise** custard
◆ **la crème Chantilly** whipped cream
◆ **la crème fouettée** whipped cream
◆ **une crème caramel** a crème caramel
◆ **une crème au chocolat** a chocolate dessert

le **crème** NOUN
see also **la crème**
white coffee ◇ *un grand crème* a large white coffee

la **crémerie** NOUN
cheese shop

crémeux ADJECTIVE (FEM SING **crémeuse**)
creamy

la **crêpe** NOUN
pancake

la **crêperie** NOUN
pancake restaurant

le **crépuscule** NOUN
dusk

le **cresson** NOUN
watercress

la **Crète** NOUN
Crete

creuser VERB
to dig (*a hole*)
◆ **Ça creuse!** That gives you a real appetite!
◆ **se creuser la cervelle** (*informal*) to rack one's brains

creux ADJECTIVE (FEM SING **creuse**)
hollow

la **crevaison** NOUN
puncture

crevé ADJECTIVE
1 punctured ◇ *un pneu crevé* a puncture
2 knackered ◇ *Je suis complètement crevé!* (*informal*) I'm knackered!

crever VERB
1 to burst (*balloon*)
2 to have a puncture (*motorist*)
◇ *J'ai crevé sur l'autoroute.* I had a puncture on the motorway.
◆ **Je crève de faim!** (*informal*) I'm starving!
◆ **Je crève de froid!** (*informal*) I'm freezing!

la **crevette** NOUN
prawn
◆ **une crevette rose** a prawn
◆ **une crevette grise** a shrimp

le **cri** NOUN
1 scream ◇ *J'ai entendu un cri.* I heard a scream. ◇ *pousser des cris de douleur* to scream with pain
2 call ◇ *Il sait reconnaître les cris des oiseaux.* He can identify the calls of birds.
◆ **C'est le dernier cri.** It's the latest fashion. ◇ *Ce haut est du dernier cri.* This top is the latest fashion.

criard ADJECTIVE
garish (*colours*)

le **cric** NOUN
jack (*for car*)

crier VERB
to shout
◆ **crier de douleur** to scream with pain

le **crime** NOUN

1 crime ◊ *un crime de guerre* a war crime

2 murder ◊ *Un crime a été commis ici.* There was a murder here.

le **criminel** NOUN
1 criminal ◊ *un criminel de guerre* a war criminal
2 murderer

la **criminelle** NOUN
1 criminal
2 murderer

le **crin** NOUN
horsehair

la **crinière** NOUN
mane

le **criquet** NOUN
grasshopper

la **crise** NOUN
1 crisis
♦ **la crise économique** the recession
2 attack ◊ *une crise d'asthme* an asthma attack ◊ *une crise cardiaque* a heart attack
♦ **une crise de foie** an upset stomach
♦ **piquer une crise de nerfs** to go hysterical
♦ **avoir une crise de fou rire** to have a fit of the giggles

le **cristal** NOUN (PL les **cristaux**)
crystal ◊ *un verre en cristal* a crystal glass

le **critère** NOUN
criterion

critique ADJECTIVE
see also **critique** NOUN
critical

le **critique** NOUN
see also **la critique** AND **critique** ADJECTIVE
critic ◊ *un critique de cinéma* a film critic

la **critique** NOUN
see also **le critique** AND **critique** ADJECTIVE
1 criticism ◊ *Elle ne supporte pas les critiques.* She can't stand being criticized.
2 review ◊ *Le film a reçu de bonnes critiques.* The film's had good reviews.

critiquer VERB
to criticize

la **Croatie** NOUN
Croatia

le **crochet** NOUN
1 hook
2 detour ◊ *faire un crochet* to make a detour
3 crochet ◊ *un pull au crochet* a crocheted sweater

le **crocodile** NOUN
crocodile

croire VERB
to believe ◊ *Il croit tout ce qu'on lui raconte.* He believes everything he's told.
♦ **croire que** to think that ◊ *Tu crois qu'il fera meilleur demain?* Do you think the weather will be better tomorrow?
♦ **croire à quelque chose** to believe in something
♦ **croire en Dieu** to believe in God

crois VERB see **croire**

croîs VERB see **croître**

le **croisement** NOUN
crossroads ◊ *Tournez à gauche au croisement.* Turn left at the crossroads.

croiser VERB
♦ **J'ai croisé Anne-Laure dans la rue.** I bumped into Anne-Laure in the street.
♦ **croiser les bras** to fold one's arms
♦ **croiser les jambes** to cross one's legs
♦ **se croiser** to pass each other ◊ *Nous nous croisons dans l'escalier tous les matins.* We pass each other on the stairs every morning.

la **croisière** NOUN
cruise

la **croissance** NOUN
growth

le **croissant** NOUN
croissant ◊ *un croissant au beurre* a butter croissant

croit VERB see **croire**

croître VERB
to grow

la **croix** NOUN
cross
♦ **la Croix-Rouge** the Red Cross

le **croque-madame** NOUN (PL les **croque-madame**)
toasted ham and cheese sandwich with fried egg on top

le **croque-monsieur** NOUN (PL les **croque-monsieur**)
toasted ham and cheese sandwich

croquer VERB
to munch ◊ *croquer une pomme* to munch an apple
♦ **le chocolat à croquer** plain chocolate

le **croquis** NOUN
sketch

la **crotte** NOUN
♦ **une crotte de chien** dog dirt

le **crottin** NOUN

1 manure ◊ du crottin de cheval horse manure
2 small goat's cheese

croustillant ADJECTIVE
crusty

la **croûte** NOUN
1 crust (of bread)
♦ **en croûte** in pastry
2 rind (of cheese)
3 scab (on skin)

le **croûton** NOUN
1 crust (end of loaf)
2 crouton ◊ des croûtons frottés d'ail garlic croutons

croyons, croyez VERB see **croire**

les **CRS** MASC NOUN
French riot police

cru VERB see **croire**

cru ADJECTIVE
raw ◊ la viande crue raw meat
♦ **le jambon cru** Parma ham

crû VERB see **croître**

la **cruauté** NOUN
cruelty

la **cruche** NOUN
jug

les **crudités** FEM NOUN
assorted raw vegetables

cruel ADJECTIVE (FEM SING **cruelle**)
cruel

les **crustacés** MASC NOUN
shellfish

le **cube** NOUN
cube
♦ **un mètre cube** a cubic metre

la **cueillette** NOUN
picking ◊ la cueillette des champignons mushroom picking

cueillir VERB
to pick (flowers, fruit)

la **cuiller** NOUN
spoon
♦ **une cuiller à café** a teaspoon
♦ **une cuiller à soupe** a soup spoon

la **cuillère** NOUN
spoon
♦ **une cuillère à café** a teaspoon
♦ **une cuillère à soupe** a soup spoon

la **cuillerée** NOUN
spoonful

le **cuir** NOUN
leather ◊ un sac en cuir a leather bag
♦ **le cuir chevelu** the scalp

cuire VERB
to cook ◊ cuire quelque chose à feu vif to cook something on a high heat

♦ **cuire quelque chose au four** to bake something
♦ **cuire quelque chose à la vapeur** to steam something
♦ **faire cuire** to cook ◊ "Faire cuire pendant une heure" "Cook for one hour"
♦ **bien cuit** well done
♦ **trop cuit** overdone

la **cuisine** NOUN
1 kitchen
2 cooking ◊ la cuisine française French cooking
♦ **faire la cuisine** to cook

cuisiné ADJECTIVE
♦ **un plat cuisiné** a ready-made meal

cuisiner VERB
to cook ◊ J'aime beaucoup cuisiner. I love cooking.

le **cuisinier** NOUN
cook

la **cuisinière** NOUN
1 cook
2 cooker ◊ une cuisinière à gaz a gas cooker

la **cuisse** NOUN
thigh
♦ **une cuisse de poulet** a chicken leg

la **cuisson** NOUN
cooking ◊ "une heure de cuisson" "cooking time: one hour"

cuit VERB see **cuire**

le **cuivre** NOUN
copper

le **cul** NOUN (rude)
bum

le **culot** NOUN (informal)
cheek ◊ Quel culot! What a cheek! ◊ Il a un sacré culot! He's got a damn cheek!

la **culotte** NOUN
knickers PL

la **culpabilité** NOUN
guilt

le **cultivateur** NOUN
farmer

la **cultivatrice** NOUN
farmer

cultivé ADJECTIVE
cultured ◊ Il est très cultivé. He's very cultured.

cultiver VERB
to grow ◊ Il cultive la vigne. He grows grapes.
♦ **cultiver la terre** to farm the land

la **culture** NOUN
1 farming ◊ les cultures intensives intensive farming

. 2 education ◊ *Pour cet emploi, on demande une bonne culture générale.* For this job, a good general education is needed.

♦ **la culture physique** physical education

le **culturisme** NOUN
   body-building

le **curé** NOUN
   parish priest

le **cure-dent** NOUN
   toothpick

curieux ADJECTIVE (FEM SING **curieuse**)
   curious

la **curiosité** NOUN
   curiosity

le **curriculum vitae** NOUN
   CV

le **curseur** NOUN
   cursor

la **cuvette** NOUN
   bowl ◊ *une cuvette en plastique* a plastic bowl

le **CV** NOUN (= *curriculum vitae*)
   CV

le **cybercafé** NOUN
   internet café

cyclable ADJECTIVE
   ♦ **une piste cyclable** a cycle track

le **cycle** NOUN
   cycle

le **cyclisme** NOUN
   cycling

le/la **cycliste** NOUN
   cyclist

le **cyclomoteur** NOUN
   moped

le **cyclone** NOUN
   hurricane

le **cygne** NOUN
   swan

C

D

d' PREPOSITION, ARTICLE *see* **de**

la **dactylo** NOUN

    1 typist ◊ *Elle est dactylo.* She's a typist.

    2 typing ◊ *Je prends des cours de dactylo.* I'm doing typing lessons.

le **daim** NOUN

    suede ◊ *une veste en daim* a suede jacket

la **dame** NOUN

    1 lady
    2 queen (*in cards, chess*)

les **dames** FEM NOUN

    draughts

le **Danemark** NOUN

    Denmark

le **danger** NOUN

    danger
    ♦ **être en danger** to be in danger
    ♦ **"Danger de mort"** "Extremely dangerous"

dangereux ADJECTIVE (FEM SING **dangereuse**)

    dangerous

danois ADJECTIVE, NOUN (FEM SING **danoise**)

    Danish ◊ *Il parle danois.* He speaks Danish.
    ♦ **un Danois** a Dane (*man*)
    ♦ **une Danoise** a Dane (*woman*)
    ♦ **les Danois** the Danish

dans PREPOSITION

    1 in ◊ *Il est dans sa chambre.* He's in his bedroom. ◊ *dans deux mois* in two months' time
    2 into ◊ *Il est entré dans mon bureau.* He came into my office.
    3 out of ◊ *On a bu dans des verres en plastique.* We drank out of plastic glasses.

la **danse** NOUN

    1 dance ◊ *la danse moderne* modern dance ◊ *des danses folkloriques* folk dances
    ♦ **la danse classique** ballet
    2 dancing ◊ *des cours de danse* dancing lessons

danser VERB

    to dance

le **danseur** NOUN

    dancer

la **danseuse** NOUN

    dancer

la **date** NOUN

    date ◊ *votre date de naissance* your date of birth ◊ *la date limite de vente* the sell-by date
    ♦ **un ami de longue date** an old friend

dater VERB

    ♦ **dater de** to date from ◊ *Cette coutume date du moyen âge.* This custom dates from the Middle Ages.

la **datte** NOUN

    date (*fruit*)

le **dauphin** NOUN

    dolphin

davantage ADVERB

    ♦ **davantage de** more ◊ *Il faudrait davantage de stages de formation.* There should be more training courses.

de PREPOSITION, ARTICLE

    See also du (=de+le) and des (=de+les). de changes to d' before a vowel and most words beginning with "h".

    1 of ◊ *le toit de la maison* the roof of the house ◊ *la voiture de Paul* Paul's car ◊ *la voiture de mes parents* my parents' car ◊ *la voiture d'Hélène* Hélène's car ◊ *deux bouteilles de vin* two bottles of wine ◊ *un litre d'essence* a litre of petrol
    ♦ **un bébé d'un an** a one-year-old baby
    ♦ **un billet de cinquante euros** a 50-euro note
    2 from ◊ *de Londres à Paris* from London to Paris ◊ *Il vient de Londres.* He comes from London. ◊ *une lettre de Victor* a letter from Victor
    3 by ◊ *augmenter de dix euros* to increase by ten euros
    You use de to form expressions with the meaning of some and any.
    ♦ **Je voudrais de l'eau.** I'd like some water. ◊ *du pain et de la confiture* bread and jam
    ♦ **Il n'a pas de famille.** He hasn't got any family.
    ♦ **Il n'y a plus de biscuits.** There aren't any more biscuits.

le **dé** NOUN

    1 dice
    2 thimble

le **dealer** NOUN (*informal*)

    drug-pusher

déballer VERB

    to unpack

le **débardeur** NOUN

tank top

débarquer VERB
to disembark ◊ *Nous avons dû débarquer à Marseille.* We had to disembark at Marseilles.
♦**débarquer chez quelqu'un** (*informal*) to descend on somebody ◊ *Ils ont débarqué chez nous à dix heures du soir.* They descended on us at ten o'clock at night.

le **débarras** NOUN
junk room
♦**Bon débarras!** Good riddance!

débarrasser VERB
to clear ◊ *Tu peux débarrasser la table, s'il te plaît?* Can you clear the table please?
♦**se débarrasser de quelque chose** to get rid of something ◊ *Je me suis débarrassé de mon vieux frigo.* I got rid of my old fridge.

le **débat** NOUN
debate

se **débattre** VERB
to struggle

débile ADJECTIVE
crazy ◊ *C'est complètement débile!* (*informal*) That's totally crazy!

débordé ADJECTIVE
♦**être débordé** to be snowed under

déborder VERB
to overflow (*river*)
♦**déborder d'énergie** to be full of energy

le **débouché** NOUN
job prospect ◊ *Quels débouchés y a-t-il après ces études?* What sort of job does this course qualify you for?

déboucher VERB
[1] to unblock (*sink, pipe*)
[2] to open (*bottle*)
♦**déboucher sur** to lead into ◊ *La rue débouche sur une place.* The street leads into a square.

debout ADVERB
[1] standing up ◊ *Il a mangé ses céréales debout.* He ate his cereal standing up.
[2] upright ◊ *Mets les livres debout sur l'étagère.* Put the books upright on the shelf.
[3] up ◊ *Tu es déjà debout?* Are you up already?
♦**Debout!** Get up!

déboutonner VERB
to unbutton

débraillé ADJECTIVE
sloppily dressed

débrancher VERB

to unplug

le **débris** NOUN
♦**des débris de verre** bits of glass

débrouillard ADJECTIVE
streetwise

se **débrouiller** VERB
to manage ◊ *C'était difficile, mais je ne me suis pas trop mal débrouillé.* It was difficult, but I managed OK.
♦**Débrouille-toi tout seul.** Sort things out for yourself.

le **début** NOUN
beginning ◊ *au début* at the beginning
♦**début mai** in early May

le **débutant** NOUN
beginner

la **débutante** NOUN
beginner

débuter VERB
to start

décaféiné ADJECTIVE
decaffeinated

le **décalage horaire** NOUN
time difference (*between time zones*)
◊ *Il y a une heure de décalage horaire entre la France et la Grande-Bretagne.* There's an hour's time difference between France and Britain.

décalquer VERB
to trace

décapiter VERB
to behead

décapotable ADJECTIVE
convertible

décapsuler VERB
♦**décapsuler une bouteille** to take the top off a bottle

le **décapsuleur** NOUN
bottle-opener

décéder VERB
to die ◊ *Son père est décédé il y a trois ans.* His father died three years ago.

décembre MASC NOUN
December
♦**en décembre** in December

décemment ADVERB
decently

décent ADJECTIVE
decent

la **déception** NOUN
disappointment

décerner VERB
to award

le **décès** NOUN

death

décevant ADJECTIVE
disappointing ◊ *Ses résultats sont plutôt décevants.* His results are rather disappointing.

décevoir VERB
to disappoint

décharger VERB
to unload

se **déchausser** VERB
to take off one's shoes

les **déchets** MASC NOUN
waste SING ◊ *les déchets nucléaires* nuclear waste ◊ *les déchets toxiques* toxic waste

déchiffrer VERB
to decipher

déchirant ADJECTIVE
heart-rending

déchirer VERB
1 to tear (*clothes*)
2 to tear up ◊ *déchirer une lettre* to tear up a letter
3 to tear out ◊ *déchirer une page d'un livre* to tear a page out of a book
♦ **se déchirer** to tear ◊ *se déchirer un muscle* to tear a muscle

la **déchirure** NOUN
tear (*rip*)
♦ **une déchirure musculaire** a torn muscle

décidé ADJECTIVE
determined
♦ **C'est décidé.** It's decided.

décidément ADVERB
certainly ◊ *Décidément, je n'ai pas de chance aujourd'hui.* I'm certainly not having much luck today.

décider VERB
to decide
♦ **décider de faire quelque chose** to decide to do something ◊ *Ils ont décidé de passer leurs vacances en Normandie.* They decided to go to Normandy for their holiday.
♦ **se décider** to make up one's mind ◊ *Elle n'arrive pas à se décider.* She can't make up her mind.

décisif ADJECTIVE (FEM SING **décisive**)
decisive

la **décision** NOUN
decision

la **déclaration** NOUN
statement ◊ *Je n'ai aucune déclaration à faire.* I have no statement to make.
♦ **faire une déclaration de vol** to report something as stolen

déclarer VERB
to declare ◊ *déclarer la guerre à un pays* to declare war on a country
♦ **se déclarer** to break out ◊ *Le feu s'est déclaré dans la cantine.* The fire broke out in the canteen.

déclencher VERB
to set off (*alarm, explosion*)
♦ **se déclencher** to go off

le **déclic** NOUN
click

décoiffé ADJECTIVE
♦ **Elle était toute décoiffée.** Her hair was in a real mess.

le **décollage** NOUN
takeoff (*of plane*)

décollé ADJECTIVE
♦ **avoir les oreilles décollées** to have sticking-out ears

décoller VERB
1 to unstick ◊ *décoller une étiquette* to unstick a label
♦ **se décoller** to come unstuck
2 to take off ◊ *L'avion a décollé avec dix minutes de retard.* The plane took off ten minutes late.

décolleté ADJECTIVE
see also **décolleté** NOUN
low-cut

le **décolleté** NOUN
see also **décolleté** ADJECTIVE
♦ **un décolleté plongeant** a plunging neckline

se **décolorer** VERB
to fade ◊ *Ce T-shirt s'est décoloré au lavage.* This T-shirt has faded in the wash.
♦ **se faire décolorer les cheveux** to have one's hair bleached

les **décombres** MASC NOUN
rubble SING

se **décommander** VERB
to cry off ◊ *Elle devait venir mais elle s'est décommandée à la dernière minute.* She was supposed to be coming, but she cried off at the last minute.

déconcerté ADJECTIVE
disconcerted

décongeler VERB
to thaw

se **déconnecter** VERB
to log out

déconner VERB (*rude*)
to talk rubbish ◊ *Non mais, sans déconner, c'est vrai?* No kidding, is that true?

déconseiller VERB

◆**déconseiller à quelqu'un de faire quelque chose** to advise somebody not to do something ◊ *Je lui ai déconseillé d'y aller.* I advised him not to go.

◆**C'est déconseillé.** It's not recommended.

décontenancé ADJECTIVE
  disconcerted

décontracté ADJECTIVE
  relaxed
◆**s'habiller décontracté** to dress casually

se **décontracter** VERB
  to relax ◊ *Il est allé faire du footing pour se décontracter.* He went jogging to relax.

le **décor** NOUN
  décor

le **décorateur** NOUN
  interior decorator

la **décoration** NOUN
  decoration

la **décoratrice** NOUN
  interior decorator

décorer VERB
  to decorate

les **décors** MASC NOUN
  ① scenery SING (*in play*)
  ② set SING (*in film*)

décortiquer VERB
  to shell
◆**des crevettes décortiquées** peeled shrimps

découdre VERB
  to unpick
◆**se découdre** to come unstitched

découper VERB
  ① to cut out ◊ *J'ai découpé cet article dans le journal.* I cut this article out of the paper.
  ② to carve (*meat*)

décourageant ADJECTIVE
  discouraging

décourager VERB
  to discourage
◆**se décourager** to get discouraged ◊ *Ne te décourage pas!* Don't give up!

décousu ADJECTIVE
  unstitched ◊ *L'ourlet est décousu.* The hem's come unstitched.

le **découvert** NOUN
  overdraft

la **découverte** NOUN
  discovery

découvrir VERB
  to discover

décrire VERB
  to describe

décrocher VERB
  ① to take down ◊ *Tu peux m'aider à décrocher les rideaux?* Can you help me take down the curtains?
  ② to pick up the phone ◊ *Il a décroché et a composé le numéro.* He picked up the phone and dialled the number.
◆**décrocher le téléphone** to take the phone off the hook

déçu VERB
  disappointed

dédaigneux ADJECTIVE (FEM SING **dédaigneuse**)
  disdainful ◊ *d'un air dédaigneux* disdainfully

le **dédain** NOUN
  disdain ◊ *avec dédain* with disdain

dedans ADVERB
  inside ◊ *C'est une jolie boîte: qu'est-ce qu'il y a dedans?* That's a nice box: what's in it?
◆**là-dedans (1)** in there ◊ *J'ai trouvé les clés là-dedans.* I found the keys in there.
◆**là-dedans (2)** in that ◊ *Il y a du vrai là-dedans.* There's some truth in that.

dédicacé ADJECTIVE
◆**un exemplaire dédicacé** a signed copy

dédier VERB
  to dedicate

déduire VERB
  to take off ◊ *Tu as déduit les vingt euros que je te devais?* Did you take off the twenty euros I owed you?
◆**déduire que** to deduce that ◊ *J'en déduis qu'il m'a menti.* That means he must have been lying.

défaire VERB
  to undo
◆**défaire sa valise** to unpack
◆**se défaire** to come undone

la **défaite** NOUN
  defeat

le **défaut** NOUN
  fault

défavorable ADJECTIVE
  unfavourable

défavorisé ADJECTIVE
  underprivileged

défectueux ADJECTIVE (FEM SING **défectueuse**)
  faulty

défendre VERB
  ① to forbid
◆**défendre à quelqu'un de faire quelque chose** to forbid somebody to do

☞

something ◊ *Sa mère lui a défendu
de le revoir.* Her mother forbade her
to see him again.

2 to defend ◊ *défendre ses idées* to
defend your ideas ◊ *défendre
quelqu'un* to defend somebody

défendu ADJECTIVE
forbidden ◊ *C'est défendu.* It's not
allowed.

la **défense** NOUN

1 defence ◊ *prendre la défense de
quelqu'un* to back somebody up
♦ **"défense de fumer"** "no smoking"

2 tusk (*of elephant*)

le **défi** NOUN
challenge
♦ **d'un air de défi** defiantly
♦ **sur un ton de défi** defiantly

défier VERB

1 to challenge ◊ *Je te défie de
trouver un meilleur exemple.* I
challenge you to find a better
example.

2 to dare ◊ *Il m'a défié d'aller à
l'école en pyjama.* He dared me to go
to school in my pyjamas.

défigurer VERB
to disfigure

le **défilé** NOUN

1 parade
♦ **un défilé de mode** a fashion show

2 march

défiler VERB
to march

définir VERB
to define

définitif ADJECTIVE (FEM SING **définitive**)
final
♦ **en définitive** in the end ◊ *En
définitive, ils ont décidé de rester.* In
the end, they decided to stay.

définitivement ADVERB
for good ◊ *Elle s'est définitivement
installée en Écosse en 1980.* She
settled in Scotland for good in 1980.

déformer VERB
to stretch ◊ *Ne tire pas sur ton pull,
tu vas le déformer.* Don't pull at your
sweater, you'll stretch it.
♦ **se déformer** to stretch ◊ *Ce T-shirt
s'est déformé au lavage.* This T-shirt
has stretched in the wash.

se **défouler** VERB
to unwind ◊ *Je fais de l'aérobic pour
me défouler.* I do aerobics to unwind.

dégagé ADJECTIVE
♦ **d'un air dégagé** casually
♦ **sur un ton dégagé** casually

dégager VERB

1 to free ◊ *Ils ont mis une heure à
dégager les victimes.* They took an
hour to free the victims.

2 to clear ◊ *des gouttes qui
dégagent le nez* drops to clear your
nose
♦ **Ça se dégage.** (*weather*) It's clearing
up.

se **dégarnir** VERB
to go bald

les **dégâts** MASC NOUN
damage

le **dégel** NOUN
thaw

dégeler VERB
to thaw ◊ *faire dégeler un poulet
congelé* to thaw out a frozen chicken

dégivrer VERB

1 to defrost

2 to de-ice

dégonfler VERB
to let down ◊ *Quelqu'un a dégonflé
mes pneus.* Somebody let down my
tyres.
♦ **se dégonfler** (*informal*) to chicken out

dégouliner VERB
to trickle

dégourdi ADJECTIVE
smart ◊ *Il n'est pas très dégourdi.*
He's pretty clueless.

dégourdir VERB
♦ **se dégourdir les jambes** to stretch
one's legs

le **dégoût** NOUN
disgust ◊ *une expression de dégoût*
a disgusted expression
♦ **avec dégoût** disgustedly

dégoûtant ADJECTIVE
disgusting

dégoûté ADJECTIVE
disgusted
♦ **être dégoûté de tout** to be sick of
everything

dégoûter VERB
to disgust ◊ *Ce genre de
comportement me dégoûte.* That kind
of behaviour makes me sick.
♦ **dégoûter quelqu'un de quelque chose**
to put somebody off something ◊ *Ça
m'a dégoûté de la viande.* That put
me off meat.

se **dégrader** VERB
to deteriorate

le **degré** NOUN
degree
♦ **de l'alcool à 90 degrés** surgical spirit

dégringoler VERB

1 to rush down ◊ *Il a dégringolé l'escalier.* He rushed down the stairs.

2 to collapse

♦**Elle a fait dégringoler la pile de livres.** She knocked over the stack of books.

dégueulasse ADJECTIVE (*rude*)
disgusting

le **déguisement** NOUN
disguise

déguiser VERB

♦**se déguiser en quelque chose** to dress up as something ◊ *Elle s'était déguisée en vampire.* She was dressed up as a vampire.

la **dégustation** NOUN
tasting

déguster VERB

1 to taste (*food, wine*)

2 to enjoy

dehors ADVERB
outside ◊ *Je t'attends dehors.* I'll wait for you outside.

♦**jeter quelqu'un dehors** to throw somebody out

♦**en dehors de** apart from ◊ *En dehors de lui, tout le monde était content.* Apart from him, everybody was happy.

déjà ADVERB

1 already ◊ *J'ai déjà fini.* I've already finished.

2 before ◊ *Tu es déjà venu en France?* Have you been to France before?

déjeuner VERB
> see also **déjeuner** NOUN

to have lunch

le **déjeuner** NOUN
> see also **déjeuner** VERB

lunch

le **délai** NOUN

1 extension ◊ *J'ai demandé un délai d'une semaine.* I've asked for a week's extension.

2 time limit ◊ *être dans les délais* to be within the time limit

> Be careful! **délai** does not mean **delay**.

délasser VERB
to relax ◊ *La lecture délasse.* Reading's relaxing.

♦**se délasser** to relax ◊ *J'ai pris un bain pour me délasser.* I had a bath to relax.

délavé ADJECTIVE
faded ◊ *un jean délavé* a pair of faded jeans

le **délégué** NOUN

representative ◊ *les délégués de classe* the class representatives

ⓘ *In French schools, each class elects two representatives or* **délégués de classe**, *one boy and one girl.*

la **déléguée** NOUN
representative

déléguer VERB
to delegate

délibéré ADJECTIVE
deliberate

délicat ADJECTIVE

1 delicate ◊ *avoir la peau délicate* to have delicate skin

2 tricky ◊ *une situation délicate* a tricky situation

3 tactful ◊ *Il est toujours très délicat.* He's always very tactful.

4 thoughtful ◊ *C'est une attention délicate de sa part.* That was a kind thought on his part.

délicatement ADVERB

1 gently

2 tactfully

le **délice** NOUN
delight ◊ *Vivre ici est un vrai délice.* Living here is a real delight. ◊ *Ce gâteau est un vrai délice.* This cake's a real treat.

délicieux ADJECTIVE (FEM SING **délicieuse**)
delicious

la **délinquance** NOUN
crime ◊ *de nouvelles mesures pour combattre la délinquance juvénile* new measures to fight juvenile delinquency

le **délinquant** NOUN
criminal

la **délinquante** NOUN
criminal

délirer VERB
♦**Mais tu délires!** (*informal*) You're crazy!

le **délit** NOUN
criminal offence

délivrer VERB
to set free (*prisoner*)

le **deltaplane** NOUN
hang-glider
♦**faire du deltaplane** to go hang-gliding

demain ADVERB
tomorrow
♦**À demain!** See you tomorrow!

la **demande** NOUN
request

D

☞

◆ **une demande en mariage** an offer of marriage

◆ **"demandes d'emploi"** "situations wanted"

demandé ADJECTIVE

◆ **très demandé** very much in demand

demander VERB

1. to ask for ◊ *J'ai demandé la permission.* I've asked for permission. ◊ *On a demandé notre chemin à un chauffeur de taxi.* We asked a taxi driver the way. ◊ *Je lui ai demandé de m'aider.* I asked him to help me.

2. to require ◊ *un travail qui demande beaucoup de temps* a job that requires a lot of time

◆ **se demander** to wonder ◊ *Je me demande à quelle heure il va venir.* I wonder what time he'll come.

Be careful! **demander** *does not mean* *to demand.*

le **demandeur d'asile** NOUN
asylum seeker

le **demandeur d'emploi** NOUN
job-seeker

la **demandeuse d'asile** NOUN
asylum seeker

la **demandeuse d'emploi** NOUN
job-seeker

la **démangeaison** NOUN
itching

démanger VERB
to itch ◊ *Ça me démange.* It itches.

le **démaquillant** NOUN
make-up remover

démaquiller VERB

◆ **se démaquiller** to remove one's make-up

la **démarche** NOUN

1. walk ◊ *Il a une drôle de démarche.* He's got a funny walk.

2. step ◊ *faire les démarches nécessaires pour obtenir quelque chose* to take the necessary steps to obtain something

démarrer VERB
to start (*car*)

démêler VERB
to untangle

le **déménagement** NOUN
move ◊ *C'était le jour de notre déménagement.* It was the day we moved house.

◆ **un camion de déménagement** a removal van

déménager VERB
to move house

le **déménageur** NOUN
removal man

dément ADJECTIVE
crazy

démentiel ADJECTIVE (FEM SING **démentielle**)
insane

se **démerder** VERB (*rude*)
to get by ◊ *Ne t'inquiète pas, il saura se démerder.* Don't worry, he'll get by.

◆ **Démerde-toi tout seul.** Sort things out for yourself.

demeurer VERB
to live

demi ADJECTIVE, ADVERB
see also **demi** NOUN
half ◊ *Il a trois ans et demi.* He's three and a half.

◆ **Il est trois heures et demie.** It's half past three.

◆ **Il est midi et demi.** It's half past twelve.

◆ **à demi endormi** half-asleep

le **demi** NOUN
see also **demi** ADJECTIVE
half pint of beer

◆ **Un demi, s'il vous plaît!** A beer please!

la **demi-baguette** NOUN
half a baguette

le **demi-cercle** NOUN
semicircle

la **demi-douzaine** NOUN
half-dozen ◊ *une demi-douzaine d'œufs* half a dozen eggs

la **demie** NOUN
half-hour ◊ *Le bus passe à la demie.* The bus comes by on the half-hour.

demi-écrémé ADJECTIVE
semi-skimmed

la **demi-finale** NOUN
semifinal

le **demi-frère** NOUN
half-brother

la **demi-heure** NOUN
half an hour ◊ *dans une demi-heure* in half an hour ◊ *toutes les demi-heures* every half an hour

la **demi-journée** NOUN
half-day ◊ *On peut louer un parasol à la demi-journée.* You can hire a sun umbrella for a half-day.

le **demi-litre** NOUN
half litre ◊ *un demi-litre de lait* half a litre of milk

la **demi-livre** NOUN
half-pound ◊ *une demi-livre de tomates* half a pound of tomatoes

la **demi-pension** NOUN

half board
♦ **Cet hôtel propose des tarifs raisonnables en demi-pension.** This hotel has reasonable rates for half board.

le/la **demi-pensionnaire** NOUN
♦ **être demi-pensionnaire** to take school lunches

demi-sel ADJECTIVE
♦ **du beurre demi-sel** slightly salted butter

la **demi-sœur** NOUN
half-sister

la **démission** NOUN
resignation
♦ **donner sa démission** to resign

démissionner VERB
to resign

le **demi-tarif** NOUN
[1] half-price ◊ *un billet à demi-tarif* a half-price season ticket
[2] half-fare ◊ *voyager à demi-tarif* to travel half-fare

le **demi-tour** NOUN
♦ **faire demi-tour** to turn back ◊ *La nuit commence à tomber; il est temps de faire demi-tour.* It's getting dark; it's time we turned back.

la **démocratie** NOUN
democracy

démocratique ADJECTIVE
democratic

démodé ADJECTIVE
old-fashioned

la **demoiselle** NOUN
young lady
♦ **une demoiselle d'honneur** a bridesmaid

démolir VERB
to demolish

le **démon** NOUN
devil

démonter VERB
[1] to take down (*tent*)
[2] to take apart (*machine*)

démontrer VERB
to show

dénoncer VERB
to denounce
♦ **se dénoncer** to give oneself up ◊ *Il s'est dénoncé à la police.* He gave himself up to the police.

le **dénouement** NOUN
outcome

la **densité** NOUN
density

la **dent** NOUN

tooth ◊ *une dent de lait* a milk tooth
◊ *une dent de sagesse* a wisdom tooth

dentaire ADJECTIVE
dental

la **dentelle** NOUN
lace ◊ *un chemisier en dentelle* a lacy blouse

le **dentier** NOUN
denture

le **dentifrice** NOUN
toothpaste

le/la **dentiste** NOUN
dentist

le **déodorant** NOUN
deodorant

le **dépannage** NOUN
♦ **un service de dépannage** a breakdown service

dépanner VERB
[1] to fix ◊ *Il a dépanné la voiture en cinq minutes.* He fixed the car in five minutes.
[2] to help out ◊ *Il m'a prêté dix euros pour me dépanner.* (*informal*) He lent me 10 euros to help me out.

la **dépanneuse** NOUN
breakdown lorry

le **départ** NOUN
departure ◊ *Le départ est à onze heures.* The departure is at 11.
♦ **Je lui téléphonerai la veille de son départ.** I'll phone him the day before he leaves.

le **département** NOUN
[1] department ◊ *le département d'anglais à l'université* the English department at the university
[2] administrative area

> ℹ *France is divided into 96* **départements**, *administrative areas rather like counties.*

◊ *le département du Vaucluse* the Vaucluse region

dépasser VERB
[1] to overtake ◊ *Il y a une voiture qui essaie de nous dépasser.* There's a car trying to overtake us.
[2] to pass ◊ *Nous avons dépassé Dijon.* We've passed Dijon.
[3] to exceed (*sum, limit*)

dépaysé ADJECTIVE
♦ **se sentir un peu dépaysé** to feel a bit lost

se **dépêcher** VERB
to hurry ◊ *Dépêche-toi!* Hurry up!

dépendre VERB

☞

◆**dépendre de** to depend on ◊ *Ça dépend du temps.* It depends on the weather.

◆**dépendre de quelqu'un** to be dependent on somebody

◆**Ça dépend.** It depends.

dépenser VERB
to spend (*money*)

dépensier ADJECTIVE (FEM SING **dépensière**)

◆**Il est dépensier.** He's a big spender.

◆**Elle n'est pas dépensière.** She's not exactly extravagant.

dépilatoire ADJECTIVE

◆**une crème dépilatoire** a hair-removing cream

le **dépit** NOUN

◆**en dépit de** in spite of ◊ *Il y est allé en dépit de mes conseils.* He went in spite of my advice.

déplacé ADJECTIVE
uncalled-for ◊ *C'était une remarque déplacée.* That remark was uncalled-for.

le **déplacement** NOUN
trip ◊ *Ça vaut le déplacement.* It's worth the trip.

déplacer VERB
[1] to move ◊ *Tu peux m'aider à déplacer la table?* Can you help me move the table?
[2] to put off ◊ *déplacer un rendez-vous* to put off an appointment

◆**se déplacer (1)** to travel around ◊ *Il se déplace beaucoup pour son travail.* He travels around a lot for his work.

◆**se déplacer (2)** to get around ◊ *Il a du mal à se déplacer.* He has difficulty getting around.

◆**se déplacer une vertèbre** to slip a disc

déplaire VERB

◆**Cela me déplaît.** I dislike this.

déplaisant ADJECTIVE
unpleasant

le **dépliant** NOUN
leaflet

déplier VERB
to unfold

déposer VERB
[1] to leave ◊ *J'ai déposé mon sac à la consigne.* I left my bag at the left luggage office.
[2] to put down ◊ *Déposez le paquet sur la table.* Put the parcel down on the table.

◆**déposer quelqu'un** to drop somebody off

dépourvu ADJECTIVE

◆**prendre quelqu'un au dépourvu** to take somebody by surprise ◊ *Sa question m'a pris au dépourvu.* His question took me by surprise.

la **dépression** NOUN
depression

◆**faire de la dépression** to be suffering from depression

◆**faire une dépression** to have a breakdown

déprimant ADJECTIVE
depressing

déprimer VERB
to get depressed ◊ *Il déprime tout le temps.* He gets depressed all the time.

◆**Ce genre de temps me déprime.** This kind of weather makes me depressed.

depuis PREPOSITION, ADVERB
[1] since ◊ *Il habite Paris depuis 1983.* He's been living in Paris since 1983.
◊ *Je ne lui ai pas parlé depuis.* I haven't spoken to him since.

◆**depuis que** since ◊ *Il a plu tous les jours depuis qu'elle est arrivée.* It's rained every day since she arrived.
[2] for ◊ *Il habite Paris depuis cinq ans.* He's been living in Paris for five years.

◆**Depuis combien de temps?** How long? ◊ *Depuis combien de temps est-ce que vous le connaissez?* How long have you known him?

◆**Depuis quand?** How long? ◊ *Depuis quand est-ce que vous le connaissez?* How long have you known him?

le **député** NOUN
Member of Parliament

la **députée** NOUN
Member of Parliament

déraciner VERB
to uproot

le **dérangement** NOUN

◆**en dérangement** out of order ◊ *Le téléphone est en dérangement.* The phone's out of order.

déranger VERB
[1] to bother ◊ *Excusez-moi de vous déranger.* I'm sorry to bother you.

◆**Ne vous dérangez pas, je vais répondre au téléphone.** You stay there, I'll answer the phone.
[2] to disorganize ◊ *Ne dérange pas mes livres, s'il te plaît.* Don't disorganize my books, please.

déraper VERB
to skid

le/la **dermatologue** NOUN

dermatologist ◊ *Elle est dermatologue.* She's a dermatologist.

dernier ADJECTIVE (FEM SING **dernière**)
1. last ◊ *Il est arrivé dernier.* He arrived last. ◊ *la dernière fois* the last time
2. latest ◊ *le dernier film de Spielberg* Spielberg's latest film
♦ **en dernier** last ◊ *Ajoutez le lait en dernier.* Put the milk in last.

dernièrement ADVERB
recently

dérouler VERB
1. to unroll
2. to unwind
♦ **se dérouler** to take place ◊ *L'action se déroule dans les années vingt.* The action takes place in the 1920s.
♦ **Tout s'est déroulé comme prévu.** Everything went as planned.

derrière ADVERB, PREPOSITION

see also **derrière** NOUN

behind

le **derrière** NOUN

see also **derrière** ADVERB

1. back ◊ *la porte de derrière* the back door
2. backside ◊ *un coup de pied dans le derrière* a kick up the backside

des ARTICLE

des is the contracted form of de + les.

1. some ◊ *Tu veux des chips?* Would you like some crisps?
des is sometimes not translated.
◊ *J'ai des cousins en France.* I have cousins in France. ◊ *pendant des mois* for months
2. any ◊ *Tu as des frères?* Have you got any brothers?
3. of the ◊ *la fin des vacances* the end of the holidays ◊ *la voiture des Durand* the Durands' car
♦ **Il arrive des États-Unis.** He's arriving from the United States.

dès PREPOSITION
as early as ◊ *dès le mois de novembre* from November
♦ **dès le début** right from the start
♦ **Il vous appellera dès son retour.** He'll call you as soon as he gets back.
♦ **dès que** as soon as ◊ *Il m'a reconnu dès qu'il m'a vu.* He recognized me as soon as he saw me.

désabusé ADJECTIVE
disillusioned

le **désaccord** NOUN
disagreement

désagréable ADJECTIVE

unpleasant

désaltérer VERB
♦ **L'eau désaltère bien.** Water is very thirst-quenching.
♦ **se désaltérer** to quench one's thirst ◊ *Nous sommes allés dans un café pour nous désaltérer.* We went into a café to have a drink.

désapprobateur ADJECTIVE (FEM SING **désapprobatrice**)
disapproving ◊ *un regard désapprobateur* a disapproving look

le **désastre** NOUN
disaster

le **désavantage** NOUN
disadvantage

désavantager VERB
♦ **désavantager quelqu'un** to put somebody at a disadvantage ◊ *Cette nouvelle loi va désavantager les femmes.* The new law will put women at a disadvantage.

descendre VERB
1. to go down ◊ *Je suis tombé en descendant l'escalier.* I fell as I was going down the stairs.
2. to come down ◊ *Attends en bas; je descends!* Wait downstairs; I'm coming down!
3. to get down ◊ *Vous pouvez descendre ma valise, s'il vous plaît?* Can you get my suitcase down, please?
4. to get off ◊ *Nous descendons à la prochaine station.* We're getting off at the next station.

la **descente** NOUN
way down ◊ *Je t'attendrai au bas de la descente.* I'll wait for you at the bottom of the hill.
♦ **une descente de police** a police raid

la **description** NOUN
description

déséquilibré ADJECTIVE
unbalanced

déséquilibrer VERB
♦ **déséquilibrer quelqu'un** to throw somebody off balance ◊ *Le coup de poing l'a déséquilibré.* The punch threw him off balance.

désert ADJECTIVE

see also **désert** NOUN

deserted ◊ *Le dimanche, le centre commercial est désert.* On Sundays, the shopping centre is deserted.
♦ **une île déserte** a desert island

le **désert** NOUN

see also **désert** ADJECTIVE

desert

déserter VERB
to desert

désertique ADJECTIVE
desert ◊ *une région désertique* a desert region

désespéré ADJECTIVE
desperate

désespérer VERB
to despair ◊ *Il ne faut pas désespérer.* Don't despair.

le **désespoir** NOUN
despair

déshabiller VERB
to undress
♦ **se déshabiller** to get undressed

déshériter VERB
to disinherit
♦ **les déshérités** the underprivileged

déshydraté ADJECTIVE
dehydrated

désigner VERB
to choose ◊ *On l'a désignée pour remettre le prix.* She was chosen to present the prize.
♦ **désigner quelque chose du doigt** to point at something

le **désinfectant** NOUN
disinfectant

désinfecter VERB
to disinfect

désintéressé ADJECTIVE
[1] unselfish ◊ *un acte désintéressé* an unselfish action
[2] impartial ◊ *un conseil désintéressé* impartial advice

désintéresser VERB
♦ **se désintéresser de quelque chose** to lose interest in something

le **désir** NOUN
[1] wish ◊ *Vos désirs sont des ordres.* Your wish is my command.
[2] will ◊ *le désir de réussir* the will to succeed
[3] desire ◊ *Ses yeux brillaient de désir.* Her eyes were shining with desire.

désirer VERB
to want ◊ *Vous désirez?* (*in shop*) What would you like?

désobéir VERB
♦ **désobéir à quelqu'un** to disobey somebody

désobéissant ADJECTIVE
disobedient

désobligeant ADJECTIVE
unpleasant ◊ *faire une remarque désobligeante* to make an unpleasant remark

le **désodorisant** NOUN
air freshener

désolé ADJECTIVE
sorry ◊ *Je suis vraiment désolé.* I'm very sorry.
♦ **Désolé!** Sorry!

désopilant ADJECTIVE
hilarious

désordonné ADJECTIVE
untidy

le **désordre** NOUN
untidiness
♦ **Quel désordre!** What a mess!
♦ **en désordre** untidy ◊ *Sa chambre est toujours en désordre.* His bedroom is always untidy.

désormais ADVERB
from now on ◊ *Désormais, je boirai de l'eau.* From now on I'll drink water.

desquelles PRONOUN
desquelles is the contracted form of **de + lesquelles**.
◊ *des négociations au cours desquelles les patrons ont fait des concessions* negotiations during which the employers made concessions

desquels PRONOUN
desquels is the contracted form of **de + lesquels**.
◊ *les lacs au bord desquels nous avons campé* the lakes on the banks of which we camped

dessécher VERB
to dry out ◊ *Le soleil dessèche la peau.* The sun dries your skin out.

desserrer VERB
to loosen

le **dessert** NOUN
pudding ◊ *Qu'est-ce que vous désirez comme dessert?* What would you like for pudding?

le **dessin** NOUN
drawing ◊ *C'est un dessin de ma petite sœur.* It's a drawing my little sister did.
♦ **un dessin animé** a cartoon (*film*)
♦ **un dessin humoristique** a cartoon (*drawing*)

le **dessinateur** NOUN
♦ **un dessinateur industriel** a draughtsman

dessiner VERB
to draw

dessous ADVERB
see also **dessous** NOUN
underneath

- ♦ **en dessous** underneath ◊ *Soulève le pot de fleurs, la clé est en dessous.* Lift the flowerpot, the key's underneath.
- ♦ **par-dessous** underneath ◊ *Le grillage ne sert à rien, les lapins passent par-dessous.* The fence is useless, the rabbits get in underneath.
- ♦ **là-dessous** under there ◊ *Il s'est caché là-dessous.* He hid under there.
- ♦ **ci-dessous** below ◊ *Complétez les phrases ci-dessous.* Complete the sentences below.
- ♦ **au-dessous de** below ◊ *vingt degrés au-dessous de zéro* 20 degrees below zero

le **dessous** NOUN

> see also **dessous** ADVERB

underneath
- ♦ **les voisins du dessous** the downstairs neighbours
- ♦ **avoir le dessus** to have the upper hand
- ♦ **les dessous** underwear ◊ *des dessous en soie* silk underwear

le **dessous-de-plat** NOUN (PL les **dessous-de-plat**)
tablemat

dessus ADVERB

> see also **dessus** NOUN

on top ◊ *un gâteau avec des bougies dessus* a cake with candles on top
- ♦ **par-dessus** over ◊ *Nous avons sauté par-dessus la barrière.* We jumped over the gate.
- ♦ **au-dessus** above ◊ *la taille au-dessus* the size above ◊ *au-dessus du lit* above the bed
- ♦ **là-dessus (1)** on there ◊ *Tu peux écrire là-dessus.* You can write on there.
- ♦ **là-dessus (2)** with that ◊ *"Je démissionne!" Là-dessus, il est parti.* "I resign!" With that, he left.
- ♦ **ci-dessus** above ◊ *l'exemple ci-dessus* the example above

le **dessus** NOUN

> see also **dessus** ADVERB

top
- ♦ **les voisins du dessus** the upstairs neighbours

le/la **destinataire** NOUN
addressee

la **destination** NOUN
destination
- ♦ **les passagers à destination de Paris** passengers travelling to Paris

destiné ADJECTIVE

intended for ◊ *Ce livre est destiné aux enfants.* This book is intended for children.
- ♦ **Elle était destinée à faire ce métier.** She was destined to go into that job.

la **destruction** NOUN
destruction

le **détachant** NOUN
stain remover

détacher VERB
to undo
- ♦ **se détacher de quelque chose (1)** to come off something ◊ *La poignée de la porte s'est détachée.* The door-handle came off.
- ♦ **se détacher de quelque chose (2)** to break away from something ◊ *Un wagon s'est détaché du reste du train.* A carriage broke away from the rest of the train.

le **détail** NOUN
detail
- ♦ **en détail** in detail

le **détective** NOUN
detective ◊ *un détective privé* a private detective

déteindre VERB
to fade (*in wash*)

détendre VERB
to relax ◊ *La lecture, ça me détend.* I find reading relaxing.
- ♦ **se détendre** to relax ◊ *Il est allé prendre un bain pour se détendre.* He's gone to have a bath to relax.

la **détente** NOUN
relaxation

le **détenu** NOUN
prisoner

la **détenue** NOUN
prisoner

se **détériorer** VERB
to deteriorate

déterminé ADJECTIVE
1 determined ◊ *C'est un homme déterminé.* He's a determined man.
2 specific ◊ *un but déterminé* a specific aim

détestable ADJECTIVE
horrible

détester VERB
to hate

la **détonation** NOUN
bang ◊ *J'ai entendu une détonation.* I heard a bang.

le **détour** NOUN
detour
- ♦ **Ça vaut le détour.** It's worth the trip.

le **détournement** NOUN

♦**un détournement d'avion** a hijacking

détrempé ADJECTIVE
waterlogged

les **détritus** MASC NOUN
litter SING

détruire VERB
to destroy

la **dette** NOUN
debt

le **deuil** NOUN
♦**être en deuil** to be in mourning

deux NUMBER
two ◊ *Il était deux heures.* It was two
o'clock. ◊ *Elle a deux ans.* She's two.
♦**deux fois** twice
♦**deux points** colon
♦**tous les deux** both ◊ *Nous y sommes
allées toutes les deux.* We both went.
♦**le deux février** the second of February

deuxième ADJECTIVE
second ◊ *au deuxième étage* on the
second floor

deuxièmement ADVERB
secondly

devais, devait, devaient VERB *see*
devoir

dévaliser VERB
to rob

devant ADVERB, PREPOSITION
see also **devant** NOUN
1 in front ◊ *Il marchait devant.* He
was walking in front.
2 in front of ◊ *Il était assis devant
moi.* He was sitting in front of me.
♦**passer devant** to go past ◊ *Nous
sommes passés devant chez toi.* We
went past your house.

le **devant** NOUN
see also **devant** ADVERB
front ◊ *le devant de la maison* the
front of the house
♦**les pattes de devant** the front legs

le **développement** NOUN
development
♦**les pays en voie de développement**
developing countries

développer VERB
to develop ◊ *donner une pellicule à
développer* to take a film to be
developed
♦**se développer** to develop

devenir VERB
to become

devez VERB *see* **devoir**

la **déviation** NOUN
diversion

deviez VERB *see* **devoir**

deviner VERB
to guess

la **devinette** NOUN
riddle ◊ *poser une devinette à
quelqu'un* to ask somebody a riddle

devions VERB *see* **devoir**

dévisager VERB
♦**dévisager quelqu'un** to stare at
somebody

la **devise** NOUN
currency ◊ *les devises étrangères*
foreign currency

dévisser VERB
to unscrew

dévoiler VERB
to unveil

devoir VERB
see also **devoir** NOUN

Present tense:
je dois   nous devons
tu dois   vous devez
il/elle doit   ils/elles
                       doivent
Past participle:
dû

1 to have to ◊ *Je dois partir.* I've
got to go.
2 must ◊ *Tu dois être fatigué.* You
must be tired.
3 to be due to ◊ *Le nouveau centre
commercial doit ouvrir en mai.* The
new shopping centre is due to open
in May.
♦**devoir quelque chose à quelqu'un** to
owe somebody something ◊ *Combien
est-ce que je vous dois?* How much
do I owe you?

le **devoir** NOUN
see also **devoir** VERB
1 exercise
♦**les devoirs** homework
♦**un devoir sur table** a written test
2 duty ◊ *Aller voter fait partie des
devoirs du citoyen.* Voting is part of
one's duty as a citizen.

devons VERB *see* **devoir**

dévorer VERB
to devour

dévoué ADJECTIVE
devoted

**devra, devrai, devras, devrez,
devrons, devront** VERB *see* **devoir**

le **diabète** NOUN
diabetes

diabétique ADJECTIVE
diabetic ◊ *Je suis diabétique.* I'm
diabetic.

le **diable** NOUN
devil

le **diabolo** NOUN
  fruit cordial and lemonade
  ♦ **un diabolo menthe** a mint cordial and lemonade

diagonal ADJECTIVE (MASC PL **diagonaux**)
  diagonal

la **diagonale** NOUN
  diagonal
  ♦ **en diagonale** diagonally

le **diagramme** NOUN
  diagram

le **dialecte** NOUN
  dialect

le **dialogue** NOUN
  dialogue

le **diamant** NOUN
  diamond

le **diamètre** NOUN
  diameter

la **diapo** NOUN (*informal*)
  slide
  ♦ **une pellicule diapo** a slide film

la **diapositive** NOUN
  slide ◊ *projeter des diapositives* to show some slides

la **diarrhée** NOUN
  diarrhoea ◊ *avoir la diarrhée* to have diarrhoea

le **dictateur** NOUN
  dictator

la **dictature** NOUN
  dictatorship

la **dictée** NOUN
  dictation

dicter VERB
  to dictate

le **dictionnaire** NOUN
  dictionary

diététique ADJECTIVE
  ♦ **un magasin diététique** a health food shop

le **dieu** NOUN (PL les **dieux**)
  god ◊ *Dieu* God ◊ *Mon Dieu!* Oh my God!

le **différé** NOUN
  ♦ **une émission en différé** a recording

la **différence** NOUN
  difference
  ♦ **la différence d'âge** the age difference
  ♦ **à la différence de** unlike

différent ADJECTIVE
  ① different ◊ *pour des raisons différentes* for different reasons
  ② various ◊ *pour différentes raisons* for various reasons
  ♦ **différent de** different to ◊ *Son point de vue est différent du mien.* His point of view is different to mine.

difficile ADJECTIVE
  difficult ◊ *C'est difficile à comprendre.* It's difficult to understand.

difficilement ADVERB
  ♦ **faire quelque chose difficilement** to have trouble doing something ◊ *Ma grand-mère se déplace difficilement.* My grandmother has trouble getting around.
  ♦ **Je pouvais difficilement refuser.** It was difficult for me to refuse.

la **difficulté** NOUN
  difficulty ◊ *avec difficulté* with difficulty
  ♦ **être en difficulté** to be in difficulties

digérer VERB
  to digest

le **digestif** NOUN
  after-dinner liqueur

digne ADJECTIVE
  ♦ **digne de** worthy of ◊ *digne de confiance* trustworthy

la **dignité** NOUN
  dignity

le **dilemme** NOUN
  dilemma ◊ *être devant un dilemme* to be faced with a dilemma

diluer VERB
  to dilute

le **dimanche** NOUN
  ① Sunday ◊ *Aujourd'hui, on est dimanche.* It's Sunday today.
  ② on Sunday ◊ *Dimanche, nous allons déjeuner chez mes grands-parents.* On Sunday we're having lunch at my grandparents'.
  ♦ **le dimanche** on Sundays ◊ *Le dimanche, je fais la grasse matinée.* I have a lie-in on Sundays.
  ♦ **tous les dimanches** every Sunday
  ♦ **dimanche dernier** last Sunday
  ♦ **dimanche prochain** next Sunday

diminuer VERB
  to decrease ◊ *Est-ce que tu peux diminuer le son?* Could you turn down the sound?

le **diminutif** NOUN
  pet name

la **diminution** NOUN
  ① reduction
  ② decrease

la **dinde** NOUN
  turkey ◊ *la dinde de Noël* the Christmas turkey

le **dindon** NOUN
  turkey

  le dindon refers to a live turkey, whereas **la dinde** refers to the meat.

D

le **dîner** NOUN
> see also **dîner** VERB

dinner (evening meal)

dîner VERB
> see also **dîner** NOUN

to have dinner (evening meal)

dingue ADJECTIVE (informal)
crazy

diplomate ADJECTIVE
> see also **diplomate** NOUN

diplomatic

le **diplomate** NOUN
> see also **diplomate** ADJECTIVE

diplomat

la **diplomatie** NOUN
diplomacy

le **diplôme** NOUN
qualification

diplômé ADJECTIVE
qualified

dire VERB
1 to say ◊ Il a dit qu'il ne viendrait
pas. He said he wouldn't come.
♦ **on dit que ...** they say that ... ◊ On dit
que la nourriture est excellente là-
bas. They say that the food is
excellent there.
2 to tell
♦ **dire quelque chose à quelqu'un** to tell
somebody something ◊ Elle m'a dit la
vérité. She told me the truth. ◊ Il
nous a dit de regarder cette
émission. He told us to watch this
programme.
♦ **On dirait qu'il va pleuvoir.** It looks as
if it's going to rain.
♦ **se dire quelque chose** ◊ Quand je l'ai
vu, je me suis dit qu'avait vieilli.
When I saw him, I thought to myself
that he'd aged.
♦ **Est-ce que ça se dit?** Can you say that?
♦ **Ça ne me dit rien.** That doesn't
appeal to me.

direct ADJECTIVE
direct
♦ **en direct** live ◊ une émission en
direct a live broadcast

directement ADVERB
straight ◊ Il est rentré directement
chez lui. He went straight home.

le **directeur** NOUN
1 headteacher ◊ Il est directeur.
He's a headteacher.
2 manager ◊ Il est directeur du
personnel. He's a personnel manager.

la **direction** NOUN
1 management ◊ la direction et les
ouvriers the management and the
workers

2 direction ◊ "toutes directions" "all
routes"

la **directrice** NOUN
1 headteacher ◊ Elle est directrice.
She's a headteacher.
2 manager ◊ Elle est directrice
commerciale. She's a sales manager.

dirent VERB see **dire**

le **dirigeant** NOUN
leader

la **dirigeante** NOUN
leader

diriger VERB
to manage ◊ Il dirige une petite
entreprise. He manages a small
company.
♦ **se diriger vers** to head for ◊ Il se
dirigeait vers la gare. He was heading
for the station.

dis VERB see **dire**
♦ **Dis-moi la vérité!** Tell me the truth!
♦ **dis donc** hey ◊ Il a drôlement changé,
dis donc! Hey, he's really changed!
◊ Dis donc, tu te souviens de Sam?
Hey, do you remember Sam?

disaient, disais, disait VERB see **dire**

la **discothèque** NOUN
disco (club)

le **discours** NOUN
speech

discret ADJECTIVE (FEM SING **discrète**)
discreet

la **discrimination** NOUN
discrimination ◊ la discrimination
raciale racial discrimination ◊ la
discrimination sexuelle sex
discrimination

la **discussion** NOUN
discussion

discutable ADJECTIVE
debatable

discuter VERB
1 to talk ◊ Nous avons discuté
pendant des heures. We talked for
hours.
2 to argue ◊ C'est ce que j'ai
décidé, alors ne discutez pas! That's
what I've decided, so don't argue!

disent, disiez, disions VERB see **dire**

disons VERB see **dire**
let's say ◊ C'est à, disons, une heure
à pied. It's an hour's walk, say.

disparaître VERB
to disappear
♦ **faire disparaître quelque chose** (1) to
make something disappear ◊ Il a fait
disparaître le lapin dans son chapeau.

He made the rabbit disappear in his hat.
- **faire disparaître quelque chose (2)** to get rid of something ◊ *Ils ont fait disparaître tous les documents compromettants.* They got rid of all the incriminating documents.

la **disparition** NOUN
    disappearance
- **une espèce en voie de disparition** an endangered species

disparu ADJECTIVE
- **être porté disparu** to be reported missing

le **dispensaire** NOUN
    community clinic

dispensé ADJECTIVE
- **être dispensé de quelque chose** to be excused something ◊ *Elle est dispensée de gymnastique.* She's excused gym.

disperser VERB
    to break up ◊ *La police a dispersé les manifestants.* The police broke up the demonstrators.
- **se disperser** to break up ◊ *Une fois l'ambulance partie, la foule s'est dispersée.* Once the ambulance had left, the crowd broke up.

disponible ADJECTIVE
    available

disposé ADJECTIVE
- **être disposé à faire quelque chose** to be willing to do something ◊ *Il était disposé à m'aider.* He was willing to help me.

disposer VERB
- **disposer de quelque chose** to have access to something ◊ *Je dispose d'un ordinateur.* I have access to a computer.

la **disposition** NOUN
- **prendre ses dispositions** to make arrangements ◊ *Est-ce que vous avez pris vos dispositions pour partir en France?* Have you made arrangements to go to France?
- **avoir quelque chose à sa disposition** to have something at one's disposal ◊ *J'ai une voiture à ma disposition pour la semaine.* I have a car at my disposal for the week.
- **Je suis à votre disposition.** I am at your service.
- **Je tiens ces livres à votre disposition.** The books are at your disposal.

la **dispute** NOUN
    argument

se **disputer** VERB

to argue

le **disquaire** NOUN
    record dealer

le **disque** NOUN
    record
- **un disque compact** a compact disc
- **le disque dur** hard disk

la **disquette** NOUN
    floppy disk

disséminé ADJECTIVE
    scattered

disséquer VERB
    to dissect

la **dissertation** NOUN
    essay

dissimuler VERB
    to conceal

se **dissiper** VERB
    to clear ◊ *Le brouillard va se dissiper dans l'après-midi.* The fog will clear during the afternoon.

le **dissolvant** NOUN
    nail polish remover

dissoudre VERB
    to dissolve
- **se dissoudre** to dissolve

dissuader VERB
- **dissuader quelqu'un de faire quelque chose** to dissuade somebody from doing something ◊ *Elle m'a dissuadé d'aller voir ce film.* She dissuaded me from going to see the film.

la **distance** NOUN
    distance

la **distillerie** NOUN
    distillery

distingué ADJECTIVE
    distinguished

distinguer VERB
    to distinguish

la **distraction** NOUN
    entertainment ◊ *Il lit beaucoup: c'est sa seule distraction.* He reads a lot: it's his only form of entertainment.

distraire VERB
- **Va voir un film, ça te distraira.** Go and see a film, it'll take your mind off things.

distrait ADJECTIVE
    absent-minded

distribuer VERB
    ☐1 to give out ◊ *Distribue les livres, s'il te plaît.* Give out the books, please.
    ☐2 to deal (cards)

le **distributeur** NOUN
- **un distributeur automatique** a vending machine

D

♦ **un distributeur de billets** a cash dispenser

dit VERB see **dire**

dit ADJECTIVE
known as ◊ *Pierre, dit Pierrot* Pierre, known as Pierrot

dites VERB see **dire**

♦ **Dites-moi ce que vous pensez.** Tell me what you think.

♦ **dites donc** hey ◊ *Dites donc, vous, là-bas!* Hey, you there!

divers ADJECTIVE
diverse

♦ **pour diverses raisons** for various reasons

se **divertir** VERB
to enjoy oneself

divin ADJECTIVE
divine

diviser VERB
to divide ◊ *Quatre divisé par deux égalent deux.* 4 divided by 2 equals 2.

le **divorcé** NOUN
divorcee

la **divorcée** NOUN
divorcee

divorcer VERB
to get divorced

dix NUMBER
ten ◊ *Elle a dix ans.* She's ten. ◊ *à dix heures* at ten o'clock

♦ **le dix février** the tenth of February

dix-huit NUMBER
eighteen ◊ *Elle a dix-huit ans.* She's eighteen. ◊ *à dix-huit heures* at 6 p.m.

dixième ADJECTIVE
tenth ◊ *au dixième étage* on the tenth floor

dix-neuf NUMBER
nineteen ◊ *Elle a dix-neuf ans.* She's nineteen. ◊ *à dix-neuf heures* at 7 p.m.

dix-sept NUMBER
seventeen ◊ *Elle a dix-sept ans.* She's seventeen. ◊ *à dix-sept heures* at 5 p.m.

la **dizaine** NOUN
about ten ◊ *une dizaine de jours* about ten days

le **do** NOUN
[1] C ◊ *en do majeur* in C major
[2] do ◊ *do, ré, mi …* do, re, mi …

le **docteur** NOUN
doctor ◊ *Elle est docteur.* She's a doctor.

le **document** NOUN
document

le **documentaire** NOUN
documentary

le/la **documentaliste** NOUN
librarian

la **documentation** NOUN
documentation

documenter VERB

♦ **se documenter sur quelque chose** to gather information on something

dodu ADJECTIVE
plump

le **doigt** NOUN
finger

♦ **les doigts de pied** the toes

dois, doit, doivent VERB see **devoir**

le **domaine** NOUN
[1] estate ◊ *Il possède un immense domaine en Normandie.* He owns a huge estate in Normandy.
[2] field ◊ *La chimie n'est pas mon domaine.* Chemistry's not my field.

domestique ADJECTIVE
see also **domestique** NOUN
domestic

♦ **les animaux domestiques** pets

le/la **domestique** NOUN
see also **domestique** ADJECTIVE
servant

le **domicile** NOUN
place of residence

♦ **à domicile** at home ◊ *Il travaille à domicile.* He works at home.

domicilié ADJECTIVE

♦ **"domicilié à: …"** "address: …"

dominer VERB
to dominate

♦ **se dominer** to control oneself

les **dominos** MASC NOUN
dominoes ◊ *jouer aux dominos* to play dominoes

le **dommage** NOUN
damage ◊ *La tempête a causé d'importants dommages.* The storm caused a lot of damage.

♦ **C'est dommage.** It's a shame. ◊ *C'est dommage que tu ne puisses pas venir.* It's a shame you can't come.

dompter VERB
to tame

le **dompteur** NOUN
animal tamer

la **dompteuse** NOUN
animal tamer

le **don** NOUN
[1] donation
[2] gift ◊ *avoir un don pour quelque chose* to have a gift for something

♦ **Elle a le don de m'énerver.** She's got a knack of getting on my nerves.

donc CONJUNCTION

so

le **donjon** NOUN
keep (of castle)

les **données** FEM NOUN
data

donner VERB
[1] to give
♦ **donner quelque chose à quelqu'un** to give somebody something ◊ *Elle m'a donné son adresse.* She gave me her address.
♦ **Ça m'a donné faim.** That made me feel hungry.
[2] to give away ◊ *Tu as toujours ta veste en daim? – Non, je l'ai donnée.* Have you still got your suede jacket? – No, I gave it away.
♦ **donner sur quelque chose** to overlook something ◊ *une fenêtre qui donne sur la mer* a window overlooking the sea

dont PRONOUN
[1] of which ◊ *deux livres, dont l'un est en anglais* two books, one of which is in English ◊ *le prix dont il est si fier* the prize he's so proud of
[2] of whom ◊ *dix blessés, dont deux grièvement* ten people injured, two of them seriously ◊ *la fille dont je t'ai parlé* the girl I told you about

doré ADJECTIVE
golden ◊ *une étoile dorée* a golden star

dorénavant ADVERB
from now on ◊ *Dorénavant, tu feras attention.* From now on, you'll be careful.

dorloter VERB
to pamper

dormir VERB
[1] to sleep ◊ *Tu as bien dormi?* Did you sleep well?
[2] to be asleep ◊ *Ne faites pas de bruit, il dort.* Don't make any noise, he's asleep.

le **dortoir** NOUN
dormitory

le **dos** NOUN
back ◊ *dos à dos* back to back
♦ **faire quelque chose dans le dos de quelqu'un** to do something behind somebody's back ◊ *Elle me critique dans mon dos.* She criticizes me behind my back.
♦ **de dos** from behind
♦ **nager le dos crawlé** to swim backstroke
♦ **"voir au dos"** "see over"

la **dose** NOUN

dose ◊ *Ne pas dépasser la dose prescrite.* Do not exceed the stated dose.

le **dossier** NOUN
[1] file ◊ *une pile de dossiers* a stack of files
[2] report ◊ *un bon dossier scolaire* a good school report
[3] feature (in magazine)
[4] back (of chair)

la **douane** NOUN
customs

le **douanier** NOUN
customs officer

le **double** NOUN
♦ **le double** twice as much ◊ *Il gagne le double.* He earns twice as much. ◊ *le double du prix normal* twice the normal price
♦ **en double** in duplicate ◊ *Garde cette photo, je l'ai en double.* Keep this photo, I've got a copy of it.
♦ **le double messieurs** the men's doubles (tennis)

double-cliquer VERB
to double-click ◊ *double-cliquer sur une icône* to double-click on an icon

doubler VERB
[1] to double ◊ *Le prix a doublé en dix ans.* The price has doubled in 10 years.
[2] to overtake ◊ *Il est dangereux de doubler sur cette route.* It's dangerous to overtake on this road.
♦ **un film doublé** a dubbed film

douce ADJECTIVE see **doux**

doucement ADVERB
[1] gently ◊ *Il a frappé doucement à la porte.* He knocked gently at the door.
[2] slowly ◊ *Roulez doucement!* Drive slowly! ◊ *Je ne comprends pas, parle plus doucement.* I don't understand, speak more slowly.

la **douceur** NOUN
[1] softness ◊ *Cette crème maintient la douceur de votre peau.* This cream keeps your skin soft.
[2] gentleness ◊ *parler avec douceur* to speak gently
♦ **L'avion a atterri en douceur.** The plane made a smooth landing.

la **douche** NOUN
shower
♦ **les douches** the shower room
♦ **prendre une douche** to have a shower

se **doucher** VERB
to have a shower

doué ADJECTIVE

D

talented
+ **être doué en quelque chose** to be
good at something ◊ *Il est doué en
maths.* He's good at maths.

douillet ADJECTIVE (FEM SING **douillette**)
1 cosy ◊ *un anorak douillet* a cosy
anorak
2 soft ◊ *Je ne supporte pas la
douleur: je suis très douillette.* I can't
stand pain: I'm a real softie.

la **douleur** NOUN
pain

douloureux ADJECTIVE (FEM SING
douloureuse)
painful

le **doute** NOUN
doubt
+ **sans doute** probably

douter VERB
to doubt
+ **douter de quelque chose** to doubt
something ◊ *Je doute de sa sincérité.*
I have my doubts about his sincerity.
+ **se douter de quelque chose** to
suspect something ◊ *Je ne me
doutais de rien.* I didn't suspect
anything.
+ **Je m'en doutais.** I suspected as
much.

douteux ADJECTIVE (FEM SING **douteuse**)
1 dubious ◊ *une plaisanterie d'un
goût douteux* a joke in dubious taste
2 suspicious-looking ◊ *un individu
douteux* a suspicious-looking person

Douvres NOUN
Dover

doux ADJECTIVE (FEM SING **douce,** MASC PL
doux)
1 soft ◊ *un tissu doux* soft material
◊ *les drogues douces* soft drugs
2 sweet ◊ *du cidre doux* sweet cider
3 mild ◊ *Il fait doux aujourd'hui.* It's
mild today.
4 gentle ◊ *C'est quelqu'un de très
doux.* He's a very gentle person.
+ **en douce** on the quiet ◊ *Il m'a donné
cinq euros en douce.* He slipped me
5 euros on the quiet.

la **douzaine** NOUN
dozen ◊ *une douzaine d'œufs* a
dozen eggs
+ **une douzaine de personnes** about
twelve people

douze NUMBER
twelve ◊ *Il a douze ans.* He's twelve.
+ **le douze février** the twelfth of
February

douzième ADJECTIVE

twelfth ◊ *au douzième étage* on the
twelfth floor

la **dragée** NOUN
sugared almond

draguer VERB (*informal*)
+ **draguer quelqu'un** to chat somebody
up ◊ *Il est en train de la draguer.*
He's chatting her up.
+ **se faire draguer** to get chatted up
◊ *Marie-Claire aime se faire draguer.*
Marie-Claire likes being chatted
up.

le **dragueur** NOUN (*informal*)
flirt (*person*)

la **dragueuse** NOUN (*informal*)
flirt (*person*)

dramatique ADJECTIVE
tragic ◊ *une situation dramatique* a
tragic situation
+ **l'art dramatique** drama

le **drame** NOUN
drama (*incident*)
+ **Ça n'est pas un drame si tu ne viens
pas.** It's not the end of the world if
you don't come.

le **drap** NOUN
sheet (*for bed*)

le **drapeau** NOUN (PL les **drapeaux**)
flag ◊ *le drapeau français* the French
flag

dressé ADJECTIVE
trained ◊ *un chien bien dressé* a
well-trained dog

dresser VERB
1 to draw up ◊ *dresser une liste* to
draw up a list
2 to train ◊ *dresser un chien* to train
a dog
+ **dresser l'oreille** to prick up one's ears
◊ *Quand elle a dit ça, il a dressé
l'oreille.* When she said that, he
pricked up his ears.

la **drogue** NOUN
drug ◊ *le problème de la drogue* the
drugs problem ◊ *la lutte contre la
drogue* the war against drugs
+ **les drogues douces** soft drugs
+ **les drogues dures** hard drugs

le **drogué** NOUN
drug addict

la **droguée** NOUN
drug addict

droguer VERB
+ **droguer quelqu'un** to drug somebody
+ **se droguer** to take drugs

la **droguerie** NOUN
hardware shop

droit ADJECTIVE, ADVERB

see also **droit** NOUN

[1] right ◊ *le bras droit* the right arm
◊ *le côté droit* the right-hand side
[2] straight ◊ *une ligne droite* a
straight line ◊ *Tiens-toi droite!* Stand
up straight!
♦ **tout droit** straight on

le **droit** NOUN

see also **droit** ADJECTIVE

[1] right ◊ *les droits de l'homme*
human rights
♦ **avoir le droit de faire quelque chose**
to be allowed to do something ◊ *On
n'a pas le droit de fumer à l'école.*
We're not allowed to smoke at
school.
[2] law ◊ *faire son droit* to study law
◊ *un étudiant en droit* a law student

la **droite** NOUN

see also **droit** ADJECTIVE

right ◊ *sur votre droite* on your right
♦ **à droite (1)** on the right ◊ *la troisième
rue à droite* the third street on the
right
♦ **à droite (2)** to the right ◊ *à droite de
la fenêtre* to the right of the window
◊ *Tournez à droite.* Turn right.
♦ **la voie de droite** the right-hand lane
♦ **la droite** the right (*in politics*) ◊ *Elle est
très à droite.* She's very right-wing.

droitier ADJECTIVE (FEM SING **droitière**)

right-handed ◊ *Elle est droitière.*
She's right-handed.

drôle ADJECTIVE

funny ◊ *Ça n'est pas drôle.* It's not
funny.
♦ **un drôle de temps** funny weather

drôlement ADVERB (*informal*)

really ◊ *C'est drôlement bon.* It's
really good.

du ARTICLE

du is the contracted form of *de + le.*

[1] some ◊ *Tu veux du fromage?*
Would you like some cheese?
[2] any ◊ *Tu as du chocolat?* Have
you got any chocolate?
[3] of the ◊ *la porte du garage* the
door of the garage ◊ *la femme du
directeur* the headmaster's wife

dû VERB *see* **devoir**

see also **dû** ADJECTIVE

♦ **Nous avons dû nous arrêter.** We had
to stop.

dû ADJECTIVE (FEM **due**, MASC PL **dus**)

see also **dû** VERB

♦ **dû à** due to ◊ *un retard dû au
mauvais temps* a delay due to bad
weather

le **duc** NOUN

duke

la **duchesse** NOUN

duchess

dupe ADJECTIVE

♦ **Elle me ment mais je ne suis pas
dupe.** She lies to me but I'm not
taken in by that.

duquel PRONOUN (MASC PL **desquels,** FEM PL
desquelles)

duquel is the contracted form of *de
+ lequel.*

◊ *l'homme duquel il parle* the man he
is talking about

dur ADJECTIVE, ADVERB

hard ◊ *travailler dur* to work hard
◊ *être dur avec quelqu'un* to be hard
on somebody

durant PREPOSITION

[1] during ◊ *durant la nuit* during the
night
[2] for ◊ *durant des années* for years
◊ *des mois durant* for months

la **durée** NOUN

length ◊ *Quelle est la durée des
études d'ingénieur?* How long does it
take to train as an engineer?
♦ **pour une durée de quinze jours** for a
period of two weeks
♦ **de courte durée** short ◊ *un séjour de
courte durée* a short stay
♦ **de longue durée** long ◊ *une absence
de longue durée* a long absence

durement ADVERB

harshly

durer VERB

to last

la **dureté** NOUN

harshness ◊ *traiter quelqu'un avec
dureté* to treat somebody harshly

le **DVD** NOUN

DVD

dynamique ADJECTIVE

dynamic

dyslexique ADJECTIVE

dyslexic

D

E

l'**eau** FEM NOUN (PL les **eaux**)
  water
- ◆ **l'eau minérale** mineral water
- ◆ **l'eau plate** still water
- ◆ **tomber à l'eau** to fall through ◊ *Nos projets sont tombés à l'eau.* Our plans have fallen through.

ébahi ADJECTIVE
  amazed

éblouir VERB
  to dazzle

l'**éboueur** MASC NOUN
  dustman

ébouillanter VERB
  to scald

l'**écaille** FEM NOUN
  scale (*of fish*)

s'**écailler** VERB
  to flake

l'**écart** MASC NOUN
  gap
- ◆ **à l'écart de** away from ◊ *Ils se sont assis à l'écart des autres.* They sat down away from the others.

écarté ADJECTIVE
  remote
- ◆ **les bras écartés** arms outstretched
- ◆ **les jambes écartées** legs apart

écarter VERB
  to open wide (*arms, legs*)
- ◆ **s'écarter** to move ◊ *Ils se sont écartés pour le laisser passer.* They moved to let him pass.

l'**échafaudage** MASC NOUN
  scaffolding

l'**échalote** FEM NOUN
  shallot

l'**échange** MASC NOUN
  exchange ◊ *en échange de* in exchange for

échanger VERB
  to swap ◊ *Je t'échange ce timbre contre celui-là.* I'll swap you this stamp for that one.

l'**échantillon** MASC NOUN
  sample

échapper VERB
- ◆ **échapper à** to escape from ◊ *Le prisonnier a réussi à échapper à la police.* The prisoner managed to escape from the police.
- ◆ **s'échapper** to escape ◊ *Il s'est échappé de prison.* He escaped from prison.

- ◆ **l'échapper belle** to have a narrow escape ◊ *Nous l'avons échappé belle.* We had a narrow escape.

l'**écharde** FEM NOUN
  splinter of wood

l'**écharpe** FEM NOUN
  scarf

s'**échauffer** VERB
  to warm up (*before exercise*)

l'**échec** MASC NOUN
  failure

les **échecs** MASC NOUN
  chess SING ◊ *jouer aux échecs* to play chess

l'**échelle** FEM NOUN
  [1] ladder
  [2] scale (*of map*)

échevelé ADJECTIVE
  dishevelled

l'**écho** MASC NOUN
  echo

échouer VERB
- ◆ **échouer à un examen** to fail an exam

éclabousser VERB
  to splash

l'**éclair** MASC NOUN
  flash of lightning
- ◆ **un éclair au chocolat** a chocolate éclair

l'**éclairage** MASC NOUN
  lighting

l'**éclaircie** FEM NOUN
  bright interval

éclairer VERB
- ◆ **Cette lampe éclaire bien.** This lamp gives a good light.

l'**éclat** MASC NOUN
  [1] fragment (*of glass*) ◊ *La vase a volé en éclats.* The vase smashed into pieces.
  [2] brightness (*of sun, colour*)
- ◆ **des éclats de rire** roars of laughter

éclatant ADJECTIVE
  brilliant ◊ *des dents d'une blancheur éclatante* brilliant white teeth

éclater VERB
  [1] to burst (*tyre, balloon*)
- ◆ **éclater de rire** to burst out laughing
- ◆ **éclater en sanglots** to burst into tears
  [2] to break out ◊ *La Seconde Guerre mondiale a éclaté en 1939.* The Second World War broke out in 1939.

écœurant ADJECTIVE

sickly

écœurer VERB
- ◆**Tous ces mensonges m'écœurent.** All these lies make me sick.

l' **école** FEM NOUN
school ◊ *aller à l'école* to go to school ◊ *une école privée* a private school ◊ *une école publique* a state school ◊ *une école maternelle* a nursery school

> ℹ️ The **école maternelle** is a state school for 2-6 year-olds.

l' **écolier** MASC NOUN
schoolboy

l' **écolière** FEM NOUN
schoolgirl

l' **écologie** FEM NOUN
ecology

écologique ADJECTIVE
ecological ◊ *une lessive écologique* an ecological washing powder

l' **économie** FEM NOUN
1 economy ◊ *l'économie de la France* the French economy
2 economics ◊ *un cours d'économie* an economics class

les **économies** FEM NOUN
savings
- ◆**faire des économies** to save up ◊ *Je fais des économies pour partir en vacances.* I'm saving up for my holidays.

économique ADJECTIVE
1 economic ◊ *une crise économique* an economic crisis
2 economical ◊ *Il est plus économique d'acheter une grande boîte de lessive.* It's more economical to buy a big box of washing powder. ◊ *Cette petite voiture est économique.* This little car is cheap to run.

économiser VERB
to save

l' **économiseur d'écran** MASC NOUN
screen saver

l' **écorce** FEM NOUN
1 bark (*of tree*)
2 peel (*of orange, lemon*)

s' **écorcher** VERB
- ◆**Je me suis écorché le genou.** I've grazed my knee.

écossais ADJECTIVE, NOUN (FEM SING **écossaise**)
1 Scottish ◊ *Elle est écossaise.* She's Scottish.
- ◆**un Écossais** a Scot (*man*)
- ◆**une Écossaise** a Scot (*woman*)

- ◆**les Écossais** the Scots
2 tartan ◊ *une jupe écossaise* a tartan skirt

l' **Écosse** FEM NOUN
Scotland
- ◆**en Écosse (1)** in Scotland ◊ *Il a passé une semaine en Écosse.* He spent a week in Scotland.
- ◆**en Écosse (2)** to Scotland ◊ *Nous allons en Écosse l'été prochain.* We're going to Scotland next summer.

s' **écouler** VERB
1 to flow out (*water*)
2 to pass ◊ *Le temps s'écoule trop vite.* Time passes too quickly.

écouter VERB
to listen to ◊ *J'aime écouter de la musique.* I like listening to music.
- ◆**Écoute-moi!** Listen!

l' **écouteur** MASC NOUN
earpiece (*of phone*)

l' **écran** MASC NOUN
screen
- ◆**le petit écran** television
- ◆**l'écran total** sunblock

écraser VERB
1 to crush ◊ *Écrasez une gousse d'ail.* Crush a clove of garlic.
2 to run over ◊ *Regarde bien avant de traverser, sinon tu vas te faire écraser.* Look carefully before you cross or you'll get run over.
- ◆**s'écraser** to crash ◊ *L'avion s'est écrasé dans le désert.* The plane crashed in the desert.

écrémé ADJECTIVE
skimmed ◊ *le lait écrémé* skimmed milk

l' **écrevisse** FEM NOUN
crayfish

écrire VERB
to write ◊ *Nous nous écrivons régulièrement.* We write to each other regularly.
- ◆**Ça s'écrit comment?** How do you spell that?

l' **écrit** MASC NOUN
written paper ◊ *L'écrit d'anglais a lieu la semaine prochaine.* The written paper in English is next week.
- ◆**par écrit** in writing

l' **écriteau** MASC NOUN (PL les **écriteaux**)
notice

l' **écriture** FEM NOUN
writing ◊ *J'ai du mal à lire son écriture.* I can't read his writing.

l' **écrivain** MASC NOUN
writer ◊ *Elle est écrivain.* She's a writer.

E

☞

l'**écrou** MASC NOUN
nut (metal)

s'**écrouler** VERB
to collapse

écru ADJECTIVE
off-white

l'**écureuil** MASC NOUN
squirrel

l'**écurie** FEM NOUN
stable

EDF FEM NOUN (= Électricité de France)
French electricity company

Édimbourg NOUN
Edinburgh

éditer VERB
to publish ◊ On vient d'éditer un nouveau dictionnaire. A new dictionary has just been published.

l'**éditeur** MASC NOUN
publisher

l'**édition** FEM NOUN
1 edition ◊ une édition de poche a paperback edition
2 publishing ◊ Il travaille dans l'édition. He works in publishing.

l'**édredon** MASC NOUN
eiderdown

l'**éducateur** MASC NOUN
teacher (of people with special needs)

éducatif ADJECTIVE (FEM SING **éducative**)
educational ◊ un jeu éducatif an educational game

l'**éducation** FEM NOUN
1 education ◊ l'éducation physique physical education ◊ Il n'a pas beaucoup d'éducation. He's not very well educated.
2 upbringing ◊ Il a reçu une éducation très stricte. He had a very strict upbringing.

l'**éducatrice** FEM NOUN
teacher (of people with special needs)

éduquer VERB
to educate

effacer VERB
to rub out

effarant ADJECTIVE
amazing ◊ Il a mangé une quantité effarante de pain. He ate an amazing amount of bread.

effectivement ADVERB
indeed ◊ Il est effectivement plus rapide de passer par là. It is indeed quicker to go this way. ◊ Oui, effectivement. Yes, indeed.

Be careful! **effectivement** *does not mean* **effectively***.*

effectuer VERB

1 to make ◊ Ils ont effectué de nombreux changements. They have made a lot of changes.
2 to do ◊ On vient d'effectuer des travaux dans le bâtiment. They have just done some work in the building.

effervescent ADJECTIVE
effervescent ◊ un comprimé effervescent an effervescent tablet

l'**effet** MASC NOUN
effect
♦ **faire de l'effet** to take effect ◊ Ce médicament fait rapidement de l'effet. This medicine takes effect quickly.
♦ **Ça m'a fait un drôle d'effet de le revoir.** It gave me a strange feeling to see him again.
♦ **en effet** yes indeed ◊ Je ne me sens pas très bien. – En effet, tu as l'air pâle. I don't feel very well. – Yes, you do look pale.

efficace ADJECTIVE
1 efficient ◊ C'est une femme efficace. She's an efficient woman.
2 effective ◊ un médicament efficace an effective medicine

s'**effondrer** VERB
to collapse

s'**efforcer** VERB
♦ **s'efforcer de faire quelque chose** to try hard to do something ◊ Il s'efforce d'être aimable avec la clientèle. He tries hard to be polite to the customers.

l'**effort** MASC NOUN
effort ◊ faire un effort to make an effort

effrayant ADJECTIVE
frightening

effrayer VERB
to frighten

effronté ADJECTIVE
cheeky ◊ Ce gamin est vraiment effronté. This kid's really cheeky.

effroyable ADJECTIVE
horrifying

égal ADJECTIVE (MASC PL **égaux**)
equal ◊ une quantité égale de farine et de sucre an equal quantity of flour and sugar
♦ **Ça m'est égal. (1)** I don't mind. ◊ Tu préfères du riz ou des pâtes? – Ça m'est égal. Would you rather have rice or pasta? – I don't mind.
♦ **Ça m'est égal. (2)** I don't care. ◊ Fais ce que tu veux, ça m'est égal. Do what you like, I don't care.

également ADVERB
also

égaler VERB
　to equal

l' **égalité** FEM NOUN
　equality
◆**être à égalité** to be level ◊ *Maintenant les deux joueurs sont à égalité.* The two players are now level.

l' **égard** MASC NOUN
◆**à cet égard** in this respect

égarer VERB
　to mislay ◊ *J'ai égaré mes clés.* I've mislaid my keys.
◆**s'égarer** to get lost ◊ *Ils se sont égarés dans la forêt.* They got lost in the forest.

l' **église** FEM NOUN
　church ◊ *aller à l'église* to go to church

l' **égoïsme** MASC NOUN
　selfishness

égoïste ADJECTIVE
　selfish

l' **égout** MASC NOUN
　sewer

l' **égratignure** FEM NOUN
　scratch

l' **Égypte** FEM NOUN
　Egypt

égyptien ADJECTIVE (FEM SING **égyptienne**)
　Egyptian

eh EXCLAMATION
　hey!
◆**eh bien** well

l' **élan** MASC NOUN
◆**prendre de l'élan** to gather speed

s' **élancer** VERB
　to hurl oneself

élargir VERB
　to widen

l' **élastique** MASC NOUN
　rubber band

l' **électeur** MASC NOUN
　voter (*man*)

l' **élection** FEM NOUN
　election ◊ *les élections présidentielles* the presidential election

l' **électrice** FEM NOUN
　voter (*woman*)

l' **électricien** MASC NOUN
　electrician

l' **électricité** FEM NOUN
　electricity ◊ *une facture d'électricité* an electricity bill
◆**allumer l'électricité** to turn on the light
◆**éteindre l'électricité** to turn off the light

l' **électrique** ADJECTIVE
　electric ◊ *le courant électrique* the electric current

l' **électronique** FEM NOUN
　electronics

élégant ADJECTIVE
　smart

élémentaire ADJECTIVE
　elementary

l' **éléphant** MASC NOUN
　elephant

l' **élevage** MASC NOUN
　cattle rearing ◊ *faire de l'élevage* to rear cattle
◆**un élevage de porcs** a pig farm
◆**un élevage de poulets** a chicken farm
◆**les truites d'élevage** farmed trout

élevé ADJECTIVE
　high ◊ *Le prix est trop élevé.* The price is too high.
◆**être bien élevé** to have good manners
◆**être mal élevé** to have bad manners

l' **élève** MASC/FEM NOUN
　pupil

élever VERB
　[1] to bring up ◊ *Il a été élevé par sa grand-mère.* He was brought up by his grandmother.
　[2] to breed ◊ *Son oncle élève des chevaux.* His uncle breeds horses.
◆**élever la voix** to raise one's voice
◆**s'élever à** to come to ◊ *À combien s'élèvent les dégâts?* How much does the damage come to?

l' **éleveur** MASC NOUN
　breeder

éliminatoire ADJECTIVE
◆**une note éliminatoire** a fail mark
◆**une épreuve éliminatoire** a qualifying round (*sport*)

éliminer VERB
　to eliminate

élire VERB
　to elect

elle PRONOUN
　[1] she ◊ *Elle est institutrice.* She is a primary school teacher.
　[2] her ◊ *Vous pouvez avoir confiance en elle.* You can trust her.
　[3] it ◊ *Prends cette chaise: elle est plus confortable.* Take this chair: it's more comfortable.
　elle is also used for emphasis.
◊ *Elle, elle est toujours en retard!* Oh, SHE's always late!
◆**elle-même** herself ◊ *Elle l'a choisi elle-même.* She chose it herself.

elles PRONOUN

E

☞

they ◊ *Où sont Anne et Rachel? – Elles sont allées au cinéma.* Where are Anne and Rachel? – They've gone to the cinema.
♦ **elles-mêmes** themselves

élogieux ADJECTIVE (FEM SING **élogieuse**)
complimentary ◊ *Ton professeur a été très élogieux à propos de ton travail.* Your teacher was very complimentary about your work.

éloigné ADJECTIVE
distant

s'**éloigner** VERB
to go far away ◊ *Ne vous éloignez pas: le dîner est bientôt prêt!* Don't go far away: dinner will soon be ready!
♦ **Vous vous éloignez du sujet.** You are getting off the point.

l'**Élysée** MASC NOUN
Elysée Palace

> *ⓘ The **Élysée** is the residence of the French president.*

l'**e-mail** MASC NOUN
email

l'**emballage** MASC NOUN
♦ **le papier d'emballage** wrapping paper

emballer VERB
to wrap
♦ **s'emballer** (*informal*) to get excited ◊ *Il s'est emballé pour ce projet.* He got really excited about this plan.

l'**embarquement** MASC NOUN
boarding ◊ *"embarquement immédiat"* "now boarding"
◊ *L'embarquement des passagers n'a pas encore été annoncé.* Passenger boarding has not been announced yet.

l'**embarras** MASC NOUN
embarrassment ◊ *Votre question me met dans l'embarras.* It's difficult for me to answer your question.
♦ **Vous n'avez que l'embarras du choix.** The only problem is choosing.

embarrassant ADJECTIVE
embarrassing

embarrasser VERB
to embarrass ◊ *Cela m'embarrasse de vous demander encore un service.* I feel embarrassed to ask you to do something more for me.

embaucher VERB
to take on ◊ *L'entreprise vient d'embaucher cinquante ouvriers.* The firm has just taken on fifty workers.

embêtant ADJECTIVE
annoying

les **embêtements** MASC NOUN
trouble SING

embêter VERB
to bother
♦ **s'embêter** to be bored ◊ *Qu'est-ce qu'on s'embête ici!* Isn't it boring here!

l'**embouteillage** MASC NOUN
traffic jam

embrasser VERB
to kiss ◊ *Ils se sont embrassés.* They kissed each other.

s'**embrouiller** VERB
to get confused ◊ *Il s'embrouille dans ses explications.* He gets confused when he explains things.

émerveiller VERB
to dazzle

l'**émeute** FEM NOUN
riot

émigrer VERB
to emigrate

l'**émission** FEM NOUN
programme ◊ *une émission de télévision* a TV programme

s'**emmêler** VERB
to get tangled ◊ *Ma laine s'est emmêlée.* My wool has got tangled.

emménager VERB
to move in ◊ *Nous venons d'emménager dans une nouvelle maison.* We've just moved into a new house.

emmener VERB
to take ◊ *Ils m'ont emmené au cinéma pour mon anniversaire.* They took me to the cinema for my birthday.

emmerder VERB (*rude*)
♦ **Ça m'emmerde!** It pisses me off!
♦ **Je t'emmerde!** Piss off!
♦ **s'emmerder** to be bored stiff

l'**émoticon** MASC NOUN
smiley (*computing*)

émotif ADJECTIVE (FEM SING **émotive**)
emotional ◊ *Il est très émotif.* He's very emotional.

l'**émotion** FEM NOUN
emotion

émouvoir VERB
to move ◊ *Sa lettre l'a beaucoup émue.* She was deeply moved by his letter.

emparer VERB
♦ **s'emparer de** to grab ◊ *Il s'est emparé de ma valise.* He grabbed my case.

l'**empêchement** MASC NOUN
♦**Nous avons eu un empêchement de dernière minute.** We were held up at the last minute.

empêcher VERB
to prevent ◊ *Le café le soir m'empêche de dormir.* Coffee at night keeps me awake.
♦**Il n'a pas pu s'empêcher de rire.** He couldn't help laughing.

l'**empereur** MASC NOUN
emperor

s'**empiffrer** VERB (*informal*)
to stuff one's face ◊ *Arrête de t'empiffrer!* Stop stuffing your face!

empiler VERB
to pile up

empirer VERB
to worsen ◊ *La situation a encore empiré.* The situation got even worse.

l'**emplacement** MASC NOUN
site ◊ *Un panneau indique l'emplacement du château.* A sign shows the site of the castle.

l'**emploi** MASC NOUN
[1] use ◊ *prêt à l'emploi* ready for use
♦**le mode d'emploi** directions for use
[2] job ◊ *la création d'emplois* job creation
♦**un emploi du temps** a timetable

l'**employé** MASC NOUN
employee
♦**un employé de bureau** an office worker

l'**employée** FEM NOUN
employee
♦**une employée de banque** a bank clerk

employer VERB
[1] to use ◊ *Quelle méthode employez-vous?* What method do you use?
[2] to employ ◊ *L'entreprise emploie dix ingénieurs.* The firm employs ten engineers.

l'**employeur** MASC NOUN
employer

empoisonner VERB
to poison

emporter VERB
to take ◊ *N'emportez que le strict nécessaire.* Only take the bare minimum.
♦**plats à emporter** take-away meals
♦**s'emporter** to lose one's temper ◊ *Je m'emporte facilement.* I'm quick to lose my temper.

l'**empreinte** FEM NOUN

♦**une empreinte digitale** a fingerprint

s'**empresser** VERB
♦**s'empresser de faire quelque chose** to be quick to do something ◊ *Ils se sont empressés de nous annoncer la nouvelle.* They were quick to tell us the news.

emprisonner VERB
to imprison

l'**emprunt** MASC NOUN
loan

emprunter VERB
to borrow
♦**emprunter quelque chose à quelqu'un** to borrow something from somebody ◊ *Je peux t'emprunter dix euros?* Can I borrow ten euros from you?

l'**EMT** ABBREVIATION (= *éducation manuelle et technique*)
design and technology

ému ADJECTIVE
touched ◊ *J'ai été très ému par sa gentillesse.* I was very touched by her kindness.

en PREPOSITION, PRONOUN
[1] in ◊ *Il habite en France.* He lives in France. ◊ *La mariée est en blanc.* The bride is in white. ◊ *Je le verrai en mai.* I'll see him in May.
[2] to ◊ *Je vais en France cet été.* I'm going to France this summer.
[3] by ◊ *C'est plus rapide en voiture.* It's quicker by car.
[4] made of ◊ *C'est en verre.* It's made of glass. ◊ *un collier en argent* a silver necklace
[5] while ◊ *Il s'est coupé le doigt en ouvrant une boîte de conserve.* He cut his finger while opening a tin.
♦**Elle est sortie en courant.** She ran out.

*When **en** is used with **avoir** and **il y a**, it is not translated in English.*
◊ *Est-ce que tu as un dictionnaire? – Oui, j'en ai un.* Have you got a dictionary? – Yes, I've got one.
◊ *Combien d'élèves y a-t-il dans ta classe? – Il y en a trente.* How many pupils are there in your class? – There are 30.

*en is also used with verbs and expressions normally followed by **de** to avoid repeating the same word.*
◊ *Si tu as un problème, tu peux m'en parler.* If you've got a problem, you can talk about it with me. ◊ *Est-ce que tu peux me rendre ce livre? J'en ai besoin.* Can you give me back that book? I need it. ◊ *Il a un beau jardin*

E

☞

et il en est très fier. He's got a beautiful garden and is very proud of it.
◆ **J'en ai assez.** I've had enough.

encaisser VERB
to cash (*money*)

enceinte ADJECTIVE
pregnant ◊ *Elle est enceinte de six mois.* She's 6 months pregnant.

enchanté ADJECTIVE
delighted ◊ *Ma mère est enchantée de sa nouvelle voiture.* My mother's delighted with her new car.
◆ **Enchanté!** Pleased to meet you!

encombrant ADJECTIVE
bulky

encombrer VERB
to clutter

encore ADVERB
1 still ◊ *Il est encore au travail.* He's still at work. ◊ *Il reste encore deux morceaux de gâteau.* There are two bits of cake left.
2 even ◊ *C'est encore mieux.* That's even better.
3 again ◊ *Il m'a encore demandé de l'argent.* He asked me for money again.
◆ **encore une fois** once again
◆ **pas encore** not yet ◊ *Je n'ai pas encore fini.* I haven't finished yet.

encourager VERB
to encourage

l' **encre** FEM NOUN
ink

l' **encyclopédie** FEM NOUN
encyclopaedia

l' **endive** FEM NOUN
chicory

endommager VERB
to damage

endormi ADJECTIVE
asleep

endormir VERB
to deaden ◊ *Cette piqûre sert à endormir le nerf.* This injection is to deaden the nerve.
◆ **s'endormir** to go to sleep

l' **endroit** MASC NOUN
place ◊ *C'est un endroit très tranquille.* It's a very quiet place.
◆ **à l'endroit (1)** the right way out
◆ **à l'endroit (2)** the right way up

endurant ADJECTIVE
tough (*person*)

endurcir VERB
to toughen up ◊ *Ces exercices servent à endurcir les soldats.* These

exercises are to toughen up the soldiers.
◆ **s'endurcir** to become hardened

endurer VERB
to endure

l' **énergie** FEM NOUN
1 energy ◊ *Je n'ai pas beaucoup d'énergie ce matin.* I haven't got much energy this morning.
2 power ◊ *l'énergie nucléaire* nuclear power
◆ **avec énergie** vigorously ◊ *Il a protesté avec énergie.* He protested vigorously.

énergique ADJECTIVE
energetic
◆ **des mesures énergiques** strong measures

énerver VERB
◆ **Il m'énerve!** He gets on my nerves!
◆ **Ce bruit m'énerve.** This noise gets on my nerves.
◆ **s'énerver** to get worked up
◆ **Ne t'énerve pas!** Take it easy!

l' **enfance** FEM NOUN
childhood
◆ **Je le connais depuis l'enfance.** I've known him since I was a child.

l' **enfant** MASC/FEM NOUN
child

l' **enfer** MASC NOUN
hell

s' **enfermer** VERB
◆ **Il s'est enfermé dans sa chambre.** He shut himself up in his bedroom.

enfiler VERB
1 to put on ◊ *J'ai rapidement enfilé un pull avant de sortir.* I quickly put on a sweater before going out.
2 to thread ◊ *J'ai du mal à enfiler cette aiguille.* I am having difficulty threading this needle.

enfin ADVERB
at last ◊ *J'ai enfin réussi à le joindre.* I have at last managed to contact him.

enflé ADJECTIVE
swollen

enfler VERB
to swell

enfoncer VERB
◆ **Il marchait, les mains enfoncées dans les poches.** He was walking with his hands thrust into his pockets.
◆ **s'enfoncer** to sink ◊ *Les roues de la voiture s'enfonçaient dans la boue.* The wheels of the car were sinking into the mud.

s' **enfuir** VERB
to run off

Français ~ Anglais

l'**engagement** MASC NOUN
  commitment

engager VERB
  to take on (*person*) ◊ *engager
  quelqu'un* to take somebody on

s'**engager** VERB
  to commit oneself ◊ *Le Premier
  ministre s'est engagé à combattre le
  chômage.* The Prime Minister has
  committed himself to fighting
  unemployment.
  ◆ **Il s'est engagé dans l'armée à dix-
  huit ans.** He joined the army when
  he was 18.

les **engelures** FEM NOUN
  chilblains

l'**engin** MASC NOUN
  device
  *Be careful! The French word engin
  does not mean engine.*

s'**engourdir** VERB
  to go numb ◊ *Mes doigts se sont
  engourdis avec le froid.* My fingers
  have gone numb with the cold.

engueuler VERB (*informal*)
  ◆ **engueuler quelqu'un** to tell somebody
  off ◊ *Tu vas te faire engueuler!*
  You're going to get a telling-off!

l'**énigme** FEM NOUN
  riddle

s'**enivrer** VERB
  to get drunk

enjamber VERB
  to stride over ◊ *enjamber une
  barrière* to stride over a fence

l'**enlèvement** MASC NOUN
  kidnapping

enlever VERB
  [1] to take off ◊ *Enlève donc ton
  manteau!* Take off your coat!
  [2] to kidnap ◊ *Un groupe terroriste a
  enlevé la femme de l'ambassadeur.* A
  terrorist group has kidnapped the
  ambassador's wife.

enneigé ADJECTIVE
  snowed up ◊ *Les routes sont encore
  enneigées.* The roads are still snowed
  up.

l'**ennemi** MASC NOUN
  enemy

l'**ennemie** FEM NOUN
  enemy

l'**ennui** MASC NOUN
  [1] boredom
  ◆ **C'est à mourir d'ennui.** It's enough to
  bore you to death.
  [2] problem ◊ *avoir des ennuis* to
  have problems

ennuyer VERB

to bother ◊ *J'espère que cela ne
vous ennuie pas trop.* I hope it
doesn't bother you too much.
◆ **s'ennuyer** to be bored

ennuyeux ADJECTIVE (FEM SING **ennuyeuse**)
  [1] boring
  [2] awkward ◊ *Tu ne peux pas venir
  plus tôt? C'est bien ennuyeux.* You
  can't come any earlier? That's rather
  awkward.

énorme ADJECTIVE
  huge

énormément ADVERB
  ◆ **Il a énormément grossi.** He's got
  terribly fat.
  ◆ **Il y a énormément de neige.** There's
  an enormous amount of snow.

l'**enquête** FEM NOUN
  [1] investigation ◊ *La police a ouvert
  une enquête.* The police have begun
  an investigation.
  [2] survey ◊ *une enquête parmi les
  étudiants a montré que ...* a survey of
  students has shown that ...

enquêter VERB
  to investigate ◊ *La police enquête
  actuellement sur le crime.* The police
  are currently investigating the crime.

enrageant ADJECTIVE
  infuriating

enrager VERB
  to be furious ◊ *J'enrage de n'avoir
  pas pu profiter de cette occasion.* I'm
  furious I wasn't able to take
  advantage of this opportunity.

l'**enregistrement** MASC NOUN
  recording
  ◆ **l'enregistrement des bagages**
  baggage check-in

enregistrer VERB
  [1] to record ◊ *Ils viennent
  d'enregistrer un nouvel album.*
  They've just recorded a new album.
  [2] to check in ◊ *Vous pouvez
  enregistrer plusieurs valises.* You can
  check in several cases.

s'**enrhumer** VERB
  to catch a cold ◊ *Je suis enrhumé.*
  I've got a cold.

s'**enrichir** VERB
  to get rich

enrouler VERB
  to wind ◊ *Enroulez le fil autour de la
  bobine.* Wind the thread round the
  bobbin.

l'**enseignant** MASC NOUN
  teacher

l'**enseignante** FEM NOUN
  teacher

E

l'**enseignement** MASC NOUN
[1] education ◊ *les réformes de l'enseignement* education reforms
[2] teaching ◊ *l'enseignement des langues étrangères* the teaching of foreign languages

enseigner VERB
to teach ◊ *Mon père enseigne les maths dans un lycée.* My father teaches maths in a secondary school.

ensemble ADVERB
| see also **ensemble** NOUN |
together ◊ *tous ensemble* all together

l'**ensemble** MASC NOUN
| see also **ensemble** ADVERB |
outfit ◊ *Elle portait un ensemble vert.* She was wearing a green outfit.
♦**l'ensemble de** the whole of ◊ *L'ensemble du personnel est en grève.* The whole workforce is on strike.
♦**dans l'ensemble** on the whole

ensoleillé ADJECTIVE
sunny

ensuite ADVERB
then ◊ *Nous sommes allés au cinéma et ensuite au restaurant.* We went to the cinema and then to a restaurant.

entamer VERB
to start ◊ *Qui a entamé le gâteau?* Who's started the cake?

s'**entasser** VERB
to cram ◊ *Ils se sont tous entassés dans ma voiture.* They all crammed into my car.

entendre VERB
[1] to hear ◊ *Je ne t'entends pas.* I can't hear you.
♦**J'ai entendu dire qu'il est dangereux de nager ici.** I've heard that it's dangerous to swim here.
[2] to mean ◊ *Qu'est-ce que tu entends par là?* What do you mean by that?
♦**s'entendre** to get on ◊ *Il s'entend bien avec sa sœur.* He gets on well with his sister.

entendu ADJECTIVE
♦**C'est entendu!** Agreed! ◊ *Je passerai te prendre à sept heures, c'est entendu.* That's agreed then, I'll pick you up at 7 o'clock.
♦**bien entendu** of course ◊ *Il est bien entendu que je n'en parlerai à personne.* I won't tell anybody about it of course.

l'**enterrement** MASC NOUN
funeral (*burial*)

enterrer VERB

to bury

entêté ADJECTIVE
stubborn

s'**entêter** VERB
to persist ◊ *Il s'entête à refuser de voir le médecin.* He persists in refusing to go to the doctor.

l'**enthousiasme** MASC NOUN
enthusiasm

s'**enthousiasmer** VERB
to get enthusiastic ◊ *Il s'enthousiasme facilement.* He gets very enthusiastic about things.

entier ADJECTIVE (FEM SING **entière**)
whole ◊ *Il a mangé une quiche entière.* He ate a whole quiche. ◊ *Je n'ai pas lu le livre en entier.* I haven't read the whole book.
♦**le lait entier** full fat milk

entièrement ADVERB
completely

l'**entorse** FEM NOUN
sprain ◊ *Il s'est fait une entorse à la cheville.* He's sprained his ankle.

entourer VERB
to surround ◊ *Le jardin est entouré d'un mur de pierres.* The garden is surrounded by a stone wall.

l'**entracte** MASC NOUN
interval

l'**entraînement** MASC NOUN
training

entraîner VERB
[1] to lead ◊ *Il se laisse facilement entraîner par les autres.* He's easily led.
[2] to train ◊ *Il entraîne l'équipe de France depuis cinq ans.* He's been training the French team for five years.
[3] to involve ◊ *Un mariage entraîne beaucoup de dépenses.* A wedding involves a lot of expense.
♦**s'entraîner** to train ◊ *Il s'entraîne au foot tous les samedis matins.* He does football training every Saturday morning.

l'**entraîneur** MASC NOUN
trainer

entre PREPOSITION
between ◊ *Il est assis entre son père et son oncle.* He's sitting between his father and his uncle.
♦**entre eux** among themselves
♦**l'un d'entre eux** one of them

l'**entrecôte** FEM NOUN
rib steak

l'**entrée** FEM NOUN
[1] entrance

E

[2] starter (of meal) ◊ *Qu'est ce que vous prenez comme entrée?* What would you like for the starter?

entreprendre VERB
   to start on ◊ *Elle a entrepris des démarches pour adopter un enfant.* She's started on the procedures for adopting a child.

l'**entrepreneur** MASC NOUN
   contractor

l'**entreprise** FEM NOUN
   firm

entrer VERB
   [1] to come in ◊ *Entrez donc!* Come on in!
   [2] to go in ◊ *Ils sont tous entrés dans la maison.* They all went into the house.
   ♦ **entrer à l'hôpital** to go into hospital
   ♦ **entrer des données** to enter data ◊ *J'ai entré toutes les adresses de mon agenda sur mon ordinateur.* I've entered all the addresses in my diary onto my computer.

entre-temps ADVERB
   meanwhile

l'**entretien** MASC NOUN
   [1] maintenance ◊ *un contrat d'entretien* a maintenance contract
   [2] interview ◊ *On m'a convoqué à un entretien pour un travail.* I've been called for a job interview.

l'**entrevue** FEM NOUN
   interview ◊ *une entrevue avec le ministre* an interview with the minister

entrouvert ADJECTIVE
   half-open ◊ *La porte était entrouverte.* The door was half open.

envahir VERB
   to invade

l'**enveloppe** FEM NOUN
   envelope

envelopper VERB
   to wrap

envers PREPOSITION
   see also **envers** NOUN
   towards ◊ *Il est bien disposé envers elle.* He's well disposed towards her. ◊ *son attitude envers moi* his attitude to me

l'**envers** MASC NOUN
   see also **envers** PREPOSITION
   ♦ **à l'envers** inside out ◊ *Je dois repasser ce chemisier à l'envers.* I have to iron this blouse inside out.

l'**envie** FEM NOUN
   ♦ **avoir envie de faire quelque chose** to feel like doing something ◊ *J'avais*

envie de pleurer. I felt like crying. ◊ *J'ai envie d'aller aux toilettes.* I want to go to the toilet.
   ♦ **Cette glace me fait envie.** I fancy some of that ice cream.

envier VERB
   to envy

environ ADVERB
   about ◊ *C'est à soixante kilomètres environ.* It's about 60 kilometres.

l'**environnement** MASC NOUN
   environment

les **environs** MASC NOUN
   area SING ◊ *les environs de Nantes* the Nantes area ◊ *Il y a beaucoup de choses intéressantes à voir dans les environs.* There are a lot of interesting things to see in the area.
   ♦ **aux environs de dix-neuf heures** around 7 p.m.

envisager VERB
   to consider ◊ *Est-ce que vous envisagez de travailler à l'étranger?* Are you considering working abroad?

s'**envoler** VERB
   [1] to fly away ◊ *Le papillon s'est envolé.* The butterfly flew away.
   [2] to blow away ◊ *Toutes mes feuilles de cours se sont envolées.* All my lecture notes blew away.

envoyer VERB
   to send ◊ *Ma tante m'a envoyé une carte pour mon anniversaire.* My aunt sent me a card for my birthday.
   ♦ **envoyer quelqu'un chercher quelque chose** to send somebody to get something ◊ *Sa mère l'a envoyé chercher du pain.* His mother sent him to get some bread.
   ♦ **envoyer un e-mail à quelqu'un** to send sb an email

épais ADJECTIVE (FEM SING **épaisse**)
   thick

l'**épaisseur** FEM NOUN
   thickness

épatant ADJECTIVE (*informal*)
   great ◊ *C'est un type épatant.* He's a great guy.

l'**épaule** FEM NOUN
   shoulder

l'**épée** FEM NOUN
   sword

épeler VERB
   to spell ◊ *Est-ce que vous pouvez épeler votre nom s'il vous plaît?* Can you spell your name please?

l'**épice** FEM NOUN
   spice

épicé ADJECTIVE

☞

spicy ◊ *Ce n'est pas assez épicé pour moi: je trouve ça trop fade.* It's not spicy enough for me: I think it's too bland.

l' **épicerie** FEM NOUN
grocer's shop

l' **épicier** MASC NOUN
grocer

l' **épicière** FEM NOUN
grocer

l' **épidémie** FEM NOUN
epidemic

épiler VERB
♦ **s'épiler les jambes** to wax one's legs
♦ **s'épiler les sourcils** to pluck one's eyebrows

les **épinards** MASC NOUN
spinach SING

l' **épine** FEM NOUN
thorn

l' **épingle** FEM NOUN
pin
♦ **une épingle de sûreté** a safety pin

l' **épisode** MASC NOUN
episode

éplucher VERB
to peel

l' **éponge** FEM NOUN
sponge

l' **époque** FEM NOUN
time ◊ *à cette époque de l'année* at this time of year
♦ **à l'époque** at that time ◊ *À l'époque, beaucoup de gens n'avaient pas l'eau courante.* At that time a lot of people didn't have running water.

l' **épouse** FEM NOUN
wife

épouser VERB
to marry

épouvantable ADJECTIVE
awful

l' **épouvante** FEM NOUN
terror
♦ **un film d'épouvante** a horror film

épouvanter VERB
to terrify

l' **époux** MASC NOUN
husband
♦ **les nouveaux époux** the newly-weds

l' **épreuve** FEM NOUN
[1] test ◊ *une épreuve orale* an oral test ◊ *une épreuve écrite* a written test
[2] event (*sport*)

éprouver VERB
to feel ◊ *Qu'est-ce que vous avez éprouvé à ce moment-là?* What did you feel at that moment?

l' **EPS** FEM NOUN (= *éducation physique et sportive*)
PE (= *physical education*)

épuisé ADJECTIVE
exhausted

épuiser VERB
to wear out ◊ *Ce travail m'a complètement épuisé.* This job has completely worn me out.
♦ **s'épuiser** to wear oneself out ◊ *Il s'épuise à garder un jardin impeccable.* He wears himself out keeping his garden immaculate.

l' **Équateur** MASC NOUN
Ecuador

l' **équateur** MASC NOUN
equator

l' **équation** FEM NOUN
equation

l' **équerre** FEM NOUN
set square

l' **équilibre** MASC NOUN
balance ◊ *J'ai failli perdre l'équilibre.* I nearly lost my balance.

équilibré ADJECTIVE
well-balanced

l' **équipage** MASC NOUN
crew

l' **équipe** FEM NOUN
team

équipé ADJECTIVE
♦ **bien équipé** well-equipped

l' **équipement** MASC NOUN
equipment

les **équipements** MASC NOUN
facilities ◊ *les équipements sportifs* sports facilities

l' **équitation** FEM NOUN
riding ◊ *faire de l'équitation* to go riding

l' **équivalent** MASC NOUN
equivalent

l' **erreur** FEM NOUN
mistake
♦ **faire erreur** to be mistaken

es VERB see **être**
♦ **Tu es très gentille.** You're very kind.

l' **ESB** FEM NOUN (= *encéphalite spongiforme bovine*)
BSE

l' **escabeau** MASC NOUN (PL les **escabeaux**)
stepladder

l' **escalade** FEM NOUN
climbing ◊ *faire de l'escalade* to go climbing

escalader VERB
to climb

l'**escale** FEM NOUN
♦**faire escale** to stop off

l'**escalier** MASC NOUN
stairs
♦**un escalier roulant** an escalator

l'**escargot** MASC NOUN
snail

l'**esclavage** MASC NOUN
slavery

l'**esclave** MASC/FEM NOUN
slave

l'**escrime** FEM NOUN
fencing

l'**escroc** MASC NOUN
crook

l'**espace** MASC NOUN
space
♦**espace de travail** workspace

s'**espacer** VERB
to become less frequent ◊ *Ses
visites se sont peu à peu espacées.*
His visits became less and less
frequent.

l'**espadrille** FEM NOUN
rope-soled sandal

l'**Espagne** FEM NOUN
Spain
♦**en Espagne (1)** in Spain
♦**en Espagne (2)** to Spain

espagnol ADJECTIVE, NOUN
Spanish ◊ *J'apprends l'espagnol.* I'm
learning Spanish.
♦**un Espagnol** a Spaniard (*man*)
♦**une Espagnole** a Spaniard (*woman*)

l'**espèce** FEM NOUN
① sort ◊ *Elle portait une espèce de
cape en velours.* She was wearing a
sort of velvet cloak.
② species ◊ *une espèce en voie de
disparition* an endangered species
♦**Espèce d'idiot!** You idiot!

les **espèces** FEM NOUN
cash SING ◊ *payer en espèces* to pay
cash

espérer VERB
to hope
♦**J'espère bien.** I hope so. ◊ *Tu penses
avoir réussi? – Oui, j'espère bien.* Do
you think you've passed? – Yes, I
hope so.

espiègle ADJECTIVE
mischievous

l'**espion** MASC NOUN
spy

l'**espionnage** MASC NOUN
spying
♦**un roman d'espionnage** a spy novel

l'**espionne** FEM NOUN
spy

l'**espoir** MASC NOUN
hope

l'**esprit** MASC NOUN
mind ◊ *Ça ne m'est pas venu à
l'esprit.* It didn't cross my mind.
♦**avoir de l'esprit** to be witty ◊ *Il a
beaucoup d'esprit.* He's very witty.

l'**esquimau** ® MASC NOUN (PL les
esquimaux)
ice lolly

l'**Esquimau** MASC NOUN (PL les **Esquimaux**)
Eskimo

l'**Esquimaude** FEM NOUN
Eskimo

l'**essai** MASC NOUN
attempt ◊ *Ce n'est pas mal pour un
coup d'essai.* It's not bad for a first
attempt.
♦**prendre quelqu'un à l'essai** to take
somebody on for a trial period

essayer VERB
① to try ◊ *Essaie de rentrer de
bonne heure.* Try to come home
early.
② to try on ◊ *Essaie ce pull: il
devrait bien t'aller.* Try this sweater
on: it ought to look good on you.

l'**essence** FEM NOUN
petrol

essentiel ADJECTIVE (FEM SING **essentielle**)
essential
♦**Tu es là: c'est l'essentiel.** You're here:
that's the main thing.

s'**essouffler** VERB
to get out of breath

l'**essuie-glace** MASC NOUN
windscreen wiper

essuyer VERB
to wipe
♦**essuyer la vaisselle** to dry the dishes
♦**s'essuyer** to dry oneself ◊ *Vous
pouvez vous essuyer les mains avec
cette serviette.* You can dry your
hands on this towel.

est VERB see **être**
see also **est** ADJECTIVE, NOUN
♦**Elle est merveilleuse.** She's
marvellous.

est ADJECTIVE
see also **est** VERB, NOUN
① east ◊ *la côte est des États-Unis*
the east coast of the United States
② eastern ◊ *dans la partie est du
pays* in the eastern part of the
country

l'**est** MASC NOUN
see also **est** VERB, ADJECTIVE

east ◊ *Je vis dans l'est de la France.* I live in the East of France.
◆ **vers l'est** eastwards
◆ **à l'est de Paris** east of Paris
◆ **l'Europe de l'Est** Eastern Europe
◆ **le vent d'est** the east wind

est-ce que ADVERB
◆ **Est-ce que c'est cher?** Is it expensive?
◆ **Quand est-ce qu'il part?** When is he leaving?

l'**esthéticienne** FEM NOUN
beautician

l'**estime** FEM NOUN
◆ **J'ai beaucoup d'estime pour elle.** I think a lot of her.

estimer VERB
◆ **estimer quelqu'un** to have great respect for somebody ◊ *Mon père l'estime beaucoup.* My father has a lot of respect for him.
◆ **estimer que** to consider that ◊ *J'estime que c'est de sa faute.* I consider that it's his fault.

l'**estivant** MASC NOUN
holiday-maker

l'**estivante** FEM NOUN
holiday-maker

l'**estomac** MASC NOUN
stomach

l'**Estonie** FEM NOUN
Estonia

l'**estrade** FEM NOUN
platform

et CONJUNCTION
and

établir VERB
to establish
◆ **s'établir à son compte** to set up in business

l'**établissement** MASC NOUN
establishment
◆ **un établissement scolaire** a school

l'**étage** MASC NOUN
floor ◊ *au premier étage* on the first floor
◆ **à l'étage** upstairs

l'**étagère** FEM NOUN
shelf

étaient VERB *see* **être**

l'**étain** MASC NOUN
tin

étais, était VERB *see* **être**
◆ **Il était très jeune.** He was very young.

l'**étalage** MASC NOUN
display

étaler VERB

to spread ◊ *Il a étalé la carte sur la table.* He spread the map on the table.

étanche ADJECTIVE
1 watertight ◊ *Le toit n'est pas étanche.* The roof isn't watertight.
2 waterproof (*watch*)

l'**étang** MASC NOUN
pond

étant VERB *see* **être**
◆ **Mes revenus étant limités** ... My income being limited ...

l'**étape** FEM NOUN
stage ◊ *une étape importante de la vie* an important stage in life
◆ **faire étape** to stop off

l'**État** MASC NOUN
state (*nation*) ◊ *un chef d'État* a head of state

l'**état** MASC NOUN
1 state (*country*)
2 condition ◊ *en bon état* in good condition ◊ *en mauvais état* in poor condition
◆ **remettre quelque chose en état** to repair something
◆ **le bureau d'état civil** the registry office

les **États-Unis** MASC NOUN
United States
◆ **aux États-Unis (1)** in the United States
◆ **aux États-Unis (2)** to the United States

été VERB *see* **être**
see also **été** NOUN
◆ **Il a été licencié.** He's been made redundant.

l'**été** MASC NOUN
see also **été** VERB
summer
◆ **en été** in the summer

éteindre VERB
1 to switch off ◊ *N'oubliez pas d'éteindre la lumière en sortant.* Don't forget to switch off the light when you leave.
2 to put out (*cigarette*)

étendre VERB
to spread ◊ *Elle a étendu une nappe propre sur la table.* She spread a clean cloth on the table.
◆ **étendre le linge** to hang out the washing
◆ **s'étendre** to lie down ◊ *Je vais m'étendre cinq minutes.* I'm going to lie down for five minutes.

l'**éternité** FEM NOUN

♦**J'ai attendu une éternité chez le médecin.** I waited for ages at the doctor's.

éternuer VERB
to sneeze

êtes VERB see **être**
♦**Vous êtes en retard.** You're late.

étiez VERB see **être**

étinceler VERB
to sparkle

étions VERB see **être**

l'**étiquette** FEM NOUN
label ◊ *L'étiquette du pot de confiture s'est décollée.* The label has come off the jam pot.

s'**étirer** VERB
to stretch ◊ *Elle s'est étirée paresseusement.* She stretched lazily.

l'**étoile** FEM NOUN
star
♦**une étoile de mer** a starfish
♦**une étoile filante** a shooting star
♦**dormir à la belle étoile** to sleep under the stars

étonnant ADJECTIVE
amazing

étonner VERB
to surprise ◊ *Cela m'étonnerait que le colis soit déjà arrivé.* I'd be surprised if the parcel had arrived yet.

étouffer VERB
♦**On étouffe ici: ouvre donc les fenêtres.** It's stifling in here: open the windows.
♦**s'étouffer** to choke ◊ *Ne mange pas si vite: tu vas t'étouffer!* Don't eat so fast: you'll choke!

l'**étourderie** FEM NOUN
absent-mindedness
♦**une erreur d'étourderie** a slip

étourdi ADJECTIVE
scatterbrained

l'**étourdissement** MASC NOUN
♦**avoir des étourdissements** to feel dizzy

étrange ADJECTIVE
strange

étranger ADJECTIVE (FEM SING **étrangère**)
| see also **étranger** NOUN |
foreign ◊ *un pays étranger* a foreign country
♦**une personne étrangère** a stranger

l'**étranger** MASC NOUN
| see also **étranger** ADJECTIVE |
[1] foreigner
[2] stranger
♦**à l'étranger** abroad

l'**étrangère** FEM NOUN
[1] foreigner
[2] stranger

étrangler VERB
to strangle
♦**s'étrangler** to choke ◊ *s'étrangler avec quelque chose* to choke on something

l'**être** MASC NOUN
| see also **être** VERB |
♦**un être humain** a human being

être VERB
| see also **être** NOUN |

Present tense:	
je suis	nous sommes
tu es	vous êtes
il/elle est	ils/elles sont
Past participle:	
été	

[1] to be ◊ *Je suis heureux.* I'm happy. ◊ *Mon père est instituteur.* My father's a primary school teacher. ◊ *Il est dix heures.* It's 10 o'clock.
[2] to have ◊ *Il n'est pas encore arrivé.* He hasn't arrived yet.

les **étrennes** FEM NOUN
♦**Nous avons donné des étrennes à la gardienne.** We gave the caretaker a New Year gift.

étroit ADJECTIVE
narrow
♦**être à l'étroit** to be cramped ◊ *Nous sommes un peu à l'étroit dans cet appartement.* We're a bit cramped in this flat.

l'**étude** FEM NOUN
study ◊ *une étude de cas* a case study
♦**faire des études** to be studying ◊ *Il fait des études de droit.* He's studying law.

l'**étudiant** MASC NOUN
student

l'**étudiante** FEM NOUN
student

étudier VERB
to study

l'**étui** MASC NOUN
case ◊ *un étui à lunettes* a glasses case

eu VERB see **avoir**
♦**J'ai eu une bonne note.** I got a good mark.

euh EXCLAMATION
er ◊ *Euh ... je ne m'en souviens pas.* Er ... I can't remember.

l'**euro** MASC NOUN
euro (*currency*)

E

l'**Europe** FEM NOUN
Europe
♦ **en Europe (1)** in Europe
♦ **en Europe (2)** to Europe

européen ADJECTIVE (FEM SING **européenne**)
European

eux PRONOUN
them ◊ *Je pense souvent à eux.* I
often think of them.
eux is also used for emphasis.
◊ *Elle a accepté l'invitation, mais eux
ont refusé.* She accepted the
invitation, but THEY refused.

évacuer VERB
to evacuate

s'**évader** VERB
to escape

l'**évangile** MASC NOUN
gospel

s'**évanouir** VERB
to faint

s'**évaporer** VERB
to evaporate

évasif ADJECTIVE (FEM SING **évasive**)
evasive

l'**évasion** FEM NOUN
escape ◊ *Ils ont préparé leur évasion
pendant des mois.* They spent
months planning their escape.

éveillé ADJECTIVE
1 awake ◊ *Il est resté éveillé toute la
nuit.* He stayed awake all night.
2 bright ◊ *C'est un enfant très
éveillé pour son âge.* He's very bright
for his age.

s'**éveiller** VERB
to awaken

l'**événement** MASC NOUN
event

l'**éventail** MASC NOUN
fan (hand-held)
♦ **un large éventail de prix** a wide
range of prices

l'**éventualité** FEM NOUN
♦ **dans l'éventualité d'un retard** in the
event of a delay

éventuel ADJECTIVE (FEM SING **éventuelle**)
possible ◊ *une solution éventuelle* a
possible solution ◊ *les conséquences
éventuelles* the possible
consequences
**Be careful! éventuel does not mean
eventual.**

éventuellement ADVERB
possibly ◊ *Nous pourrions
éventuellement avoir besoin de vous.*
We may need you. ◊ *les difficultés
que vous pourriez éventuellement*

rencontrer the difficulties that you
may have
**Be careful! éventuellement does not
mean eventually.**

l'**évêque** MASC NOUN
bishop

évidemment ADVERB
1 obviously ◊ *Les tomates sont
évidemment chères en cette saison.*
Tomatoes are obviously dear at this
time of year.
2 of course ◊ *Est-ce que je peux
utiliser ton téléphone? – Évidemment,
tu n'as pas besoin de demander.* Can
I use your phone? – Of course, you
don't need to ask.

l'**évidence** FEM NOUN
♦ **C'est une évidence.** It's quite obvious.
♦ **de toute évidence** obviously ◊ *De
toute évidence, il ne veut pas nous
voir.* Obviously he doesn't want to
see us.
♦ **être en évidence** to be clearly visible
◊ *La lettre était en évidence sur la
table.* The letter was clearly visible on
the table.
♦ **mettre en évidence** to reveal

évident ADJECTIVE
obvious

l'**évier** MASC NOUN
sink

éviter VERB
to avoid

évolué ADJECTIVE
advanced

évoluer VERB
to progress ◊ *La chirurgie esthétique
a beaucoup évolué.* Plastic surgery
has progressed a great deal.
♦ **Il a beaucoup évolué.** He has come
on a great deal.

l'**évolution** FEM NOUN
1 development ◊ *une évolution
rapide* rapid development
2 evolution ◊ *la théorie de
l'évolution* the theory of evolution

évoquer VERB
to mention ◊ *Il a évoqué divers
problèmes dans son discours.* He
mentioned various problems in his
speech.

exact ADJECTIVE
1 right ◊ *Avez-vous l'heure exacte?*
Have you got the right time? ◊ *Votre
voiture est garée dehors, n'est-ce
pas? – C'est exact.* Your car's parked
outside, isn't it? – That's right.
2 exact ◊ *Est-ce que vous pouvez
m'indiquer le prix exact du billet?*

Can you tell me the exact price of the ticket?

exactement ADVERB
exactly ◊ *C'est exactement ce que je cherchais.* That's exactly what I was looking for.

ex aequo ADJECTIVE
♦**Ils sont arrivés ex aequo.** They finished neck and neck.

exagérer VERB
[1] to exaggerate ◊ *Vous exagérez!* You're exaggerating!
[2] to go too far ◊ *Ça fait trois fois que tu arrives en retard: tu exagères!* That's three times you've been late: you really go too far sometimes!

l' **examen** MASC NOUN
exam ◊ *Nous allons passer l'examen d'anglais vendredi matin.* We're doing our English exam on Friday morning. ◊ *un examen de français* a French exam
♦**un examen médical** a medical

examiner VERB
to examine

exaspérant ADJECTIVE
infuriating

exaspérer VERB
to infuriate

l' **excédent** MASC NOUN
♦**l' excédent de bagages** excess baggage

excéder VERB
to exceed ◊ *un contrat dont la durée n'excède pas deux ans* a contract for a period not exceeding two years
♦**excéder quelqu'un** to drive somebody mad ◊ *Les cris des enfants l'excédaient.* The noise of the children was driving her mad.

excellent ADJECTIVE
excellent

excentrique ADJECTIVE
eccentric

excepté PREPOSITION
except ◊ *Toutes les chaussures excepté les sandales sont en solde.* All the shoes except sandals are reduced.

l' **exception** FEM NOUN
exception
♦**à l'exception de** except

exceptionnel ADJECTIVE (FEM SING **exceptionnelle**)
exceptional

l' **excès** MASC NOUN
♦**faire des excès** to overindulge ◊ *On fait souvent des excès aux environs*

de Noël. People often overindulge around Christmas.
♦**les excès de vitesse** speeding

excessif ADJECTIVE (FEM SING **excessive**)
excessive

excitant ADJECTIVE
see also **excitant** NOUN
exciting

l' **excitant** MASC NOUN
see also **excitant** ADJECTIVE
stimulant ◊ *Le thé et le café sont des excitants.* Tea and coffee are stimulants.

l' **excitation** FEM NOUN
excitement

exciter VERB
to excite ◊ *Il était tout excité à l'idée de revoir ses cousins.* He was all excited about seeing his cousins again.
♦**s'exciter** (*informal*) to get excited ◊ *Ne t'excite pas trop vite: ça ne va peut-être pas marcher!* Don't get excited too soon: it may not work!

l' **exclamation** FEM NOUN
exclamation

exclu ADJECTIVE
♦**Il n'est pas exclu que ...** It's not impossible that ...

exclusif ADJECTIVE (FEM SING **exclusive**)
exclusive

l' **excursion** FEM NOUN
[1] trip ◊ *faire une excursion* to go on a trip
[2] walk ◊ *une excursion dans la montagne* a walk in the hills

l' **excuse** FEM NOUN
[1] excuse ◊ *Il trouve toujours une bonne excuse pour ne pas faire la vaisselle.* He always finds a good excuse for not doing the washing-up.
[2] apology ◊ *présenter ses excuses* to offer one's apologies
♦**un mot d'excuse** a note ◊ *Vous devez apporter un mot d'excuse signé par vos parents.* You have to bring a note signed by your parents.

excuser VERB
to excuse
♦**Excusez-moi. (1)** Sorry! ◊ *Excusez-moi, je ne vous avais pas vu.* Sorry, I didn't see you.
♦**Excusez-moi. (2)** Excuse me. ◊ *Excusez-moi, est-ce que vous avez l'heure?* Excuse me, have you got the time?
♦**s'excuser** to apologize ◊ *Il s'est excusé de son retard.* He apologized for being late.

E

exécuter VERB
1 to execute ◊ *Le prisonnier a été exécuté à l'aube.* The prisoner was executed at dawn.
2 to perform ◊ *Le pianiste va maintenant exécuter une valse de Chopin.* The pianist is now going to perform a waltz by Chopin.

l' **exemplaire** MASC NOUN
copy

l' **exemple** MASC NOUN
example ◊ *donner l'exemple* to set an example
♦ **par exemple** for example

s' **exercer** VERB
to practise

l' **exercice** MASC NOUN
exercise

exhiber VERB
to show off ◊ *Il aime bien exhiber ses décorations.* He likes showing off his medals.
♦ **s'exhiber** to expose oneself

l' **exhibitionniste** MASC NOUN
flasher

exigeant ADJECTIVE
hard to please ◊ *Elle est vraiment exigeante.* She's really hard to please.

exiger VERB
1 to demand ◊ *Le propriétaire exige d'être payé immédiatement.* The landlord is demanding to be paid immediately.
2 to require ◊ *Ce travail exige beaucoup de patience.* This job requires a lot of patience.

l' **exil** MASC NOUN
exile

exister VERB
to exist ◊ *Ça n'existe pas.* It doesn't exist. ◊ *Ce manteau existe également en rose.* This coat's also available in pink.

exotique ADJECTIVE
exotic ◊ *une plante exotique* an exotic plant ◊ *un yaourt aux fruits exotiques* a tropical fruit yoghurt

expédier VERB
to send ◊ *expédier un colis* to send a parcel

l' **expéditeur** MASC NOUN
sender

l' **expédition** FEM NOUN
expedition
♦ **l'expédition du courrier** the dispatch of the mail

l' **expéditrice** FEM NOUN
sender

l' **expérience** FEM NOUN
1 experience ◊ *Elle a plusieurs années d'expérience.* She's got several years' experience.
2 experiment ◊ *une expérience de chimie* a chemistry experiment

expérimenter VERB
to test ◊ *Ces produits de beauté n'ont pas été expérimentés sur des animaux.* These cosmetics have not been tested on animals.

l' **expert** MASC NOUN
expert

expirer VERB
1 to expire (*document, passport*)
2 to run out (*time allowed*)
3 to breathe out (*person*)

l' **explication** FEM NOUN
explanation
♦ **une explication de texte** a critical analysis (*of a text*)

expliquer VERB
to explain ◊ *Il m'a expliqué comment faire.* He explained to me how to do it.
♦ **ça s'explique** it's understandable

l' **exploit** MASC NOUN
achievement

l' **exploitation** FEM NOUN
exploitation ◊ *Cet organisme lutte contre l'exploitation des femmes.* This organization fights against the exploitation of women.
♦ **une exploitation agricole** a farm

exploiter VERB
to exploit ◊ *Il s'est fait exploiter par le patron du restaurant.* He was exploited by the owner of the restaurant.

explorer VERB
to explore

exploser VERB
to explode ◊ *La bombe a explosé en pleine rue.* The bomb exploded in the middle of the street.

l' **explosif** MASC NOUN
explosive

l' **explosion** FEM NOUN
explosion

l' **exportateur** MASC NOUN
exporter

l' **exportation** FEM NOUN
export

l' **exportatrice** FEM NOUN
exporter

exporter VERB
to export

l' **exposé** MASC NOUN

talk ◊ *On nous a demandé de faire un exposé sur l'environnement.* We were asked to give a talk on the environment.

exposer VERB
 1 to show ◊ *Il expose ses peintures dans une galerie d'art.* He shows his paintings in a private art gallery.
 2 to expose ◊ *N'exposez pas la pellicule à la lumière.* Do not expose the film to light.
 3 to set out ◊ *Il nous a exposé les raisons de son départ.* He set out the reasons for his departure.
 ♦ **s'exposer au soleil** to stay out in the sun ◊ *Ne vous exposez pas trop longtemps au soleil.* Don't stay out too long in the sun.

l' **exposition** FEM NOUN
 exhibition ◊ *une exposition de peinture* an exhibition of paintings

exprès ADVERB
 1 on purpose ◊ *Je suis sûr qu'il l'a fait exprès.* I'm sure he did it on purpose.
 2 specially ◊ *J'ai fait ce gâteau exprès pour toi.* I made this cake specially for you.

l' **express** MASC NOUN
 1 espresso (*coffee*)
 2 fast train ◊ *Il a décidé de prendre l'express de dix heures.* He decided to catch the fast train at 10 o'clock.

l' **expression** FEM NOUN
 1 expression
 2 phrase

exprimer VERB
 to express
 ♦ **s'exprimer** to express oneself ◊ *Il s'exprime très bien pour un enfant de huit ans.* For a child of 8, he expresses himself very well.

exquis ADJECTIVE
 exquisite

extérieur ADJECTIVE
 see also **extérieur** NOUN
 outside

l' **extérieur** MASC NOUN
 see also **extérieur** ADJECTIVE
 outside
 ♦ **à l'extérieur** outside ◊ *Les toilettes sont à l'extérieur.* The toilet is outside.

l' **externat** MASC NOUN
 day school

l' **externe** MASC/FEM NOUN
 day pupil

l' **extincteur** MASC NOUN
 fire extinguisher

extra ADJECTIVE (MASC, FEM, PL)
 excellent ◊ *Ce fromage est extra!* This cheese is excellent!

extraire VERB
 to extract

l' **extrait** MASC NOUN
 extract

extraordinaire ADJECTIVE
 extraordinary

extravagant ADJECTIVE
 extravagant

extrême ADJECTIVE
 see also **extrême** NOUN
 extreme ◊ *l'extrême droite et l'extrême gauche* the far right and the far left

l' **extrême** MASC NOUN
 see also **extrême** ADJECTIVE
 extreme

extrêmement ADVERB
 extremely

l' **Extrême-Orient** MASC NOUN
 the Far East

l' **extrémité** FEM NOUN
 end ◊ *La gare est à l'autre extrémité de la ville.* The station is at the other end of the town.

E

F

F ABBREVIATION
franc

le **fa** NOUN
F

la **fabrication** NOUN
manufacture

fabriquer VERB
to make ◊ *fabriqué en France* made in France
♦ **Qu'est-ce qu'il fabrique?** (*informal*) What's he up to?

la **fac** NOUN (*informal*)
university
♦ **à la fac** at university

la **face** NOUN
♦ **face à face** face to face
♦ **en face de** opposite ◊ *Le bus s'arrête en face de chez moi.* The bus stops opposite my house.
♦ **faire face à quelque chose** to face something
♦ **Pile ou face? – Face.** Heads or tails? – Heads.

fâché ADJECTIVE
angry
♦ **être fâché contre quelqu'un** to be angry with somebody ◊ *Elle est fâchée contre moi.* She's angry with me.
♦ **être fâché avec quelqu'un** to be on bad terms with somebody ◊ *Elle est fâchée avec sa sœur.* She's on bad terms with her sister.

se **fâcher** VERB
♦ **se fâcher contre quelqu'un** to lose one's temper with somebody
♦ **se fâcher avec quelqu'un** to fall out with somebody ◊ *Il s'est fâché avec son frère.* He's fallen out with his brother.

facile ADJECTIVE
easy
♦ **facile à faire** easy to do

facilement ADVERB
easily

la **facilité** NOUN
♦ **un logiciel d'une grande facilité d'utilisation** a very user-friendly piece of software
♦ **Il a des facilités en langues.** He has a gift for languages.
Be careful! **facilité** *does not mean* **facility.**

la **façon** NOUN
way ◊ *De quelle façon?* In what way?

♦ **de toute façon** anyway

le **facteur** NOUN
postman ◊ *Il est facteur.* He's a postman.

la **facture** NOUN
bill ◊ *une facture de gaz* a gas bill

facultatif ADJECTIVE (FEM SING **facultative**)
optional

la **faculté** NOUN
faculty
♦ **avoir une grande faculté de concentration** to have great powers of concentration

fade ADJECTIVE
tasteless ◊ *La soupe est un peu fade.* The soup is a bit tasteless.

faible ADJECTIVE
weak ◊ *Je me sens encore faible.* I still feel a bit weak.
♦ **Il est faible en maths.** He's not very good at maths.

la **faiblesse** NOUN
weakness

la **faïence** NOUN
pottery

faillir VERB
♦ **J'ai failli tomber.** I nearly fell down.

la **faillite** NOUN
bankruptcy
♦ **une entreprise en faillite** a bankrupt business
♦ **faire faillite** to go bankrupt

la **faim** NOUN
hunger
♦ **avoir faim** to be hungry

fainéant ADJECTIVE
lazy

faire VERB

Present tense:	
je fais	nous faisons
tu fais	vous faites
il/elle fait	ils/elles font
Past participle:	
fait	

[1] to make ◊ *Je vais faire un gâteau pour ce soir.* I'm going to make a cake for tonight. ◊ *Ils font trop de bruit.* They're making too much noise. ◊ *Je voudrais me faire de nouveaux amis.* I'd like to make new friends.
[2] to do ◊ *Qu'est-ce que tu fais?* What are you doing? ◊ *Il fait de l'italien.* He's doing Italian. ◊ *Qui veut*

faire la vaisselle? Who'll do the dishes?

③ to play ◊ *Il fait du piano.* He plays the piano.

④ to be ◊ *Qu'est-ce qu'il fait chaud!* Isn't it hot! ◊ *Espérons qu'il fera beau demain.* Let's hope it'll be nice weather tomorrow.

♦ **Ça ne fait rien.** It doesn't matter.

♦ **Ça fait cinquante-trois euros en tout.** That makes fify-three euros in all.

♦ **Ça fait trois ans qu'il habite à Paris.** He's lived in Paris for three years.

♦ **faire tomber** to knock over ◊ *Le chat a fait tomber le vase.* The cat knocked over the vase.

♦ **faire faire quelque chose** to get something done ◊ *Je dois faire réparer ma voiture.* I've got to get my car repaired.

♦ **Je vais me faire couper les cheveux.** I'm going to get my hair cut.

♦ **Ne t'en fais pas!** Don't worry!

fais, faisaient, faisais, faisait VERB *see* **faire**

le **faisan** NOUN
pheasant

faisiez, faisions, faisons, fait VERB *see* **faire**

le **fait** NOUN
fact ◊ *Le fait que ...* The fact that ...

♦ **un fait divers** a news item

♦ **au fait** by the way ◊ *Au fait, tu as aimé le film d'hier?* By the way, did you enjoy the film yesterday?

♦ **en fait** actually ◊ *En fait je n'ai pas beaucoup de temps.* I haven't got much time actually.

faites VERB *see* **faire**

la **falaise** NOUN
cliff

falloir VERB *see* **faut, faudra, faudrait**

famé ADJECTIVE

♦ **un quartier mal famé** a rough area

fameux ADJECTIVE (FEM SING **fameuse**)

♦ **Ce n'est pas fameux.** It's not great.

familial ADJECTIVE (MASC PL **familiaux**)
family ◊ *une atmosphère familiale* a family atmosphere

♦ **les allocations familiales** child benefit

familier ADJECTIVE (FEM SING **familière**)
familiar

la **famille** NOUN
① family ◊ *une famille nombreuse* a big family ◊ *Nous passons Noël en famille.* We have a family Christmas.
② relatives ◊ *Il a de la famille à Paris.* He's got relatives in Paris.

la **famine** NOUN
famine

fanatique ADJECTIVE
⬚ *see also* **fanatique** NOUN
fanatical

le/la **fanatique** NOUN
⬚ *see also* **fanatique** ADJECTIVE
fanatic

la **fanfare** NOUN
brass band

fantaisie ADJECTIVE

♦ **des bijoux fantaisie** costume jewellery

fantastique ADJECTIVE
fantastic

le **fantôme** NOUN
ghost

la **farce** NOUN
① stuffing (*for chicken, turkey*)
② practical joke ◊ *Il aime faire des farces.* He likes to play practical jokes.

farci ADJECTIVE
stuffed ◊ *des tomates farcies* stuffed tomatoes

la **farine** NOUN
flour

fascinant ADJECTIVE
fascinating

fasciner VERB
to fascinate

le **fascisme** NOUN
fascism

fasse, fassent, fasses, fassiez, fassions VERB *see* **faire**

♦ **Pourvu qu'il fasse beau demain!** Let's hope it'll be fine tomorrow!

fatal ADJECTIVE
fatal

♦ **C'était fatal.** It was bound to happen.

la **fatalité** NOUN
fate

fatigant ADJECTIVE
tiring

la **fatigue** NOUN
tiredness

fatigué ADJECTIVE
tired

se **fatiguer** VERB
to get tired

fauché ADJECTIVE (*informal*)
hard up

faudra VERB
faudra is the future tense of falloir.

♦ **Il faudra qu'on soit plus rapide.** We'll have to be quicker.

faudrait VERB
faudrait is the conditional tense of falloir.

♦ **Il faudrait qu'on fasse attention.** We ought to be careful.

F

se **faufiler** VERB
- ♦ **Il s'est faufilé à travers la foule.** He made his way through the crowd.

la **faune** NOUN
wildlife

fausse ADJECTIVE see **faux**

faut VERB
> **faut is the present tense of falloir.**
- ♦ **Il faut faire attention.** You've got to be careful.
- ♦ **Nous n'avons pas le choix, il faut y aller.** We've no choice, we've got to go.
- ♦ **Il faut que je parte.** I've got to go.
- ♦ **Il faut du courage pour faire ce métier.** It takes courage to do that job.
- ♦ **Il me faut de l'argent.** I need money.

la **faute** NOUN
1. mistake ◊ *faire une faute* to make a mistake
2. fault ◊ *Ce n'est pas de ma faute.* It's not my fault.
- ♦ **sans faute** without fail ◊ *Je t'appellerai sans faute.* I'll phone you without fail.

le **fauteuil** NOUN
armchair
- ♦ **un fauteuil roulant** a wheelchair

faux ADJECTIVE, ADVERB (FEM SING **fausse**)
> see also **faux** NOUN
untrue ◊ *C'est entièrement faux.* It's totally untrue.
- ♦ **faire un faux pas** to trip
- ♦ **Il chante faux.** He sings out of tune.

le **faux** NOUN
> see also **faux** ADJECTIVE
fake ◊ *Ce tableau est un faux.* This painting is a fake.

la **faveur** NOUN
favour

favori ADJECTIVE (FEM SING **favorite**)
favourite

favoriser VERB
to favour ◊ *Ce système d'examen favorise ceux qui ont de la mémoire.* This exam system favours people with good memories.

le **fax** NOUN
fax

faxer VERB
to fax
- ♦ **faxer un document à quelqu'un** to fax somebody a document

la **fée** NOUN
fairy

feignant ADJECTIVE (*informal*)
lazy

les **félicitations** FEM NOUN
congratulations

féliciter VERB
to congratulate

la **femelle** NOUN
female (*animal*)

féminin ADJECTIVE
1. female ◊ *les personnages féminins du roman* the female characters in the novel
2. feminine ◊ *Elle est très féminine.* She's very feminine.
3. women's ◊ *Elle joue dans l'équipe féminine de France.* She plays in the French women's team.

féministe ADJECTIVE
feminist

la **femme** NOUN
1. woman
2. wife ◊ *la femme du directeur* the headmaster's wife
- ♦ **une femme au foyer** a housewife
- ♦ **une femme de ménage** a cleaning woman
- ♦ **une femme de chambre** a chambermaid

se **fendre** VERB
to crack

la **fenêtre** NOUN
window

le **fenouil** NOUN
fennel

la **fente** NOUN
slot

le **fer** NOUN
iron
- ♦ **un fer à cheval** a horseshoe
- ♦ **un fer à repasser** an iron

fera, ferai, feras, ferez VERB see **faire**

férié ADJECTIVE
- ♦ **un jour férié** a public holiday

feriez, ferions VERB see **faire**

ferme ADJECTIVE
> see also **ferme** NOUN
firm ◊ *Elle s'est montrée très ferme à mon égard.* She was very firm with me.

la **ferme** NOUN
> see also **ferme** ADJECTIVE
farm

fermé ADJECTIVE
1. closed ◊ *La pharmacie est fermée.* The chemist's is closed.
2. off ◊ *Est-ce que le gaz est fermé?* Is the gas off?

fermer VERB
1. to close ◊ *N'oublie pas de fermer la fenêtre.* Don't forget to close the window.

2 to turn off ◊ *As-tu bien fermé le robinet?* Have you turned the tap off?
◆**fermer à clef** to lock ◊ *N'oublie pas de fermer la porte à clef!* Don't forget to lock the door!

la**fermeture** NOUN
◆**les heures de fermeture** closing times
◆**une fermeture éclair** ® a zip

le**fermier** NOUN
farmer

la**fermière** NOUN
1 woman farmer
2 farmer's wife

féroce ADJECTIVE
fierce

ferons, feront VERB *see* **faire**

les**fesses** FEM NOUN
buttocks

le**festival** NOUN
festival

les**festivités** FEM NOUN
festivities

la**fête** NOUN
1 party ◊ *On organise une petite fête pour son anniversaire.* We're having a little party for his birthday.
◆**faire la fête** to party
2 name day ◊ *C'est sa fête aujourd'hui.* It's his name day today.
◆**une fête foraine** a funfair
◆**la Fête Nationale** Bastille Day
◆**les fêtes de fin d'année** the festive season

fêter VERB
to celebrate

le**feu** NOUN (PL les **feux**)
1 fire ◊ *prendre feu* to catch fire ◊ *faire du feu* to make a fire
◆**Au feu!** Fire!
◆**un feu de joie** a bonfire
2 traffic light ◊ *un feu rouge* a red light ◊ *le feu vert* the green light ◊ *Tournez à gauche aux feux.* Turn left at the lights.
◆**Avez-vous du feu?** Have you got a light?
3 heat ◊ *... mijoter à feu doux* ... simmer over a gentle heat
◆**un feu d'artifice** a firework display

le**feuillage** NOUN
leaves

la**feuille** NOUN
1 leaf ◊ *des feuilles mortes* fallen leaves
2 sheet ◊ *une feuille de papier* a sheet of paper
◆**une feuille de maladie** a claim form for medical expenses

feuilleté ADJECTIVE
◆**de la pâte feuilletée** flaky pastry

feuilleter VERB
to leaf through

le**feuilleton** NOUN
serial

le**feutre** NOUN
felt
◆**un stylo-feutre** a felt-tip pen

la**fève** NOUN
broad bean

février MASC NOUN
February
◆**en février** in February

fiable ADJECTIVE
reliable

les**fiançailles** FEM NOUN
engagement SING

fiancé ADJECTIVE
◆**être fiancé à quelqu'un** to be engaged to somebody

se**fiancer** VERB
to get engaged

la**ficelle** NOUN
1 string ◊ *Passe-moi un bout de ficelle.* Give me a piece of string.
2 thin baguette (*bread*)

la**fiche** NOUN
form ◊ *Remplissez cette fiche s'il vous plaît.* Fill in this form please.

se**ficher** VERB (*informal*)
◆**Je m'en fiche!** I don't care!
◆**Fiche-moi la paix!** Leave me alone!
◆**Quoi, tu n'as fait que ça? Tu te fiches de moi!** You've only done that much? You can't be serious!

le**fichier** NOUN
file

fichu ADJECTIVE (*informal*)
◆**Ce parapluie est fichu.** This umbrella's knackered.

fidèle ADJECTIVE
faithful

fier ADJECTIVE (FEM SING **fière**)
proud

la**fierté** NOUN
pride

la**fièvre** NOUN
fever ◊ *J'ai de la fièvre.* I've got a temperature. ◊ *Il a trente-neuf de fièvre.* He's got a temperature of 39°C.

fiévreux ADJECTIVE (FEM SING **fiévreuse**)
feverish

la**figue** NOUN
fig

la**figure** NOUN

F

1 face ◊ *Il a reçu le ballon en pleine figure.* The ball hit him smack in the face.
2 figure (*illustration*) ◊ *Voir figure 2.1, page 32.* See figure 2.1, page 32.

le **fil** NOUN
thread ◊ *le fil à coudre* sewing thread
♦ **le fil de fer** wire
♦ **un coup de fil** a phone call

la **file** NOUN
line (*of people, objects*)
♦ **une file d'attente** a queue ◊ *se mettre à la file* to join the queue
♦ **à la file** one after the other
♦ **en file indienne** in single file

filer VERB
to speed along ◊ *Les voitures filent sur l'autoroute.* The cars are speeding along the motorway.
♦ **File dans ta chambre!** Off to your room with you!

le **filet** NOUN
net

la **fille** NOUN
1 girl ◊ *C'est une école de filles.* It's a girls' school.
2 daughter ◊ *C'est leur fille aînée.* She's their oldest daughter.

la **fillette** NOUN
little girl

le **filleul** NOUN
godson

la **filleule** NOUN
goddaughter

le **film** NOUN
film
♦ **un film policier** a thriller
♦ **un film d'aventures** an adventure film
♦ **un film d'épouvante** a horror film
♦ **le film alimentaire** Clingfilm ®

le **fils** NOUN
son

la **fin** NOUN
see also **fin** ADJECTIVE
end ◊ *Elle n'a pas regardé la fin du film.* She didn't watch the end of the film.
♦ **"Fin"** "The End"
♦ **À la fin, il a réussi à se décider.** In the end he managed to make up his mind.
♦ **Il sera en vacances fin juin.** He'll be on holiday at the end of June.
♦ **en fin de journée** at the end of the day
♦ **en fin de compte** when all's said and done
♦ **sans fin** endless

fin ADJECTIVE
see also **fin** NOUN
fine
♦ **des fines herbes** mixed herbs

la **finale** NOUN
final ◊ *les quarts de finale* the quarter finals

finalement ADVERB
1 at last ◊ *Nous sommes finalement arrivés.* At last we arrived.
2 after all ◊ *Finalement, tu avais raison.* You were right after all.

fini ADJECTIVE
finished

finir VERB
to finish ◊ *Le cours finit à onze heures.* The lesson finishes at 11 o'clock. ◊ *Je viens de finir ce livre.* I've just finished this book.
♦ **Il a fini par se décider.** He made up his mind in the end.

finlandais ADJECTIVE, NOUN
Finnish ◊ *Ils parlent finlandais.* They speak Finnish.
♦ **un Finlandais** a Finn (*man*)
♦ **une Finlandaise** a Finn (*woman*)
♦ **les Finlandais** the Finns

la **Finlande** NOUN
Finland

la **firme** NOUN
firm

fis VERB see **faire**

la **fissure** NOUN
crack

fit VERB see **faire**

fixe ADJECTIVE
1 steady ◊ *Il n'a pas d'emploi fixe.* He hasn't got a steady job.
2 set ◊ *Il mange toujours à heures fixes.* He always eats at set times.
♦ **un menu à prix fixe** a set menu

fixer VERB
1 to fix ◊ *Les volets sont fixés avec des crochets.* The shutters are fixed with hooks. ◊ *Nous avons fixé une heure pour nous retrouver.* We fixed a time to meet.
2 to stare at ◊ *Ne fixe pas les gens comme ça!* Don't stare at people like that!

le **flacon** NOUN
bottle ◊ *un flacon de parfum* a bottle of perfume

le **flageolet** NOUN
small haricot bean

flamand ADJECTIVE, NOUN (FEM SING **flamande**)
1 Flemish ◊ *Il parle flamand chez lui.* He speaks Flemish at home.

2 Fleming (*Dutch-speaking Belgian*)
♦ **les Flamands** the Dutch-speaking Belgians

flambé ADJECTIVE
♦ **des bananes flambées** flambéed bananas

la **flamme** NOUN
flame
♦ **en flammes** on fire

le **flan** NOUN
baked custard

flâner VERB
to stroll

la **flaque** NOUN
puddle (*of water*)

le **flash** NOUN (PL les **flashes**)
flash (*of camera*)
♦ **un flash d'information** a newsflash

flatter VERB
to flatter

la **flèche** NOUN
arrow

les **fléchettes** FEM NOUN
darts ◊ *jouer aux fléchettes* to play darts

la **fleur** NOUN
flower

fleuri ADJECTIVE
1 full of flowers ◊ *Son jardin était très fleuri.* Her garden was full of flowers.
2 flowery ◊ *un papier peint fleuri* flowery wallpaper

fleurir VERB
to flower ◊ *Cette plante fleurit en automne.* This plant flowers in autumn.

le/la **fleuriste** NOUN
florist

le **fleuve** NOUN
river

le **flic** NOUN (*informal*)
cop

le **flipper** NOUN
pinball machine

flirter VERB
to flirt

le **flocon** NOUN
flake

flotter VERB
to float

flou ADJECTIVE
blurred

le **fluor** NOUN
♦ **le dentifrice au fluor** fluoride toothpaste

la **flûte** NOUN

flute ◊ *Je joue de la flûte.* I play the flute.
♦ **une flûte à bec** a recorder
♦ **Flûte!** (*informal*) Heck!

la **foi** NOUN
faith

le **foie** NOUN
liver
♦ **une crise de foie** a stomach upset

le **foin** NOUN
hay
♦ **un rhume des foins** hay fever

la **foire** NOUN
fair

la **fois** NOUN
time ◊ *la première fois* the first time ◊ *à chaque fois* each time ◊ *À chaque fois que je vais à la bibliothèque, j'oublie ma carte.* Every time I go to the library, I forget my card. ◊ *deux fois deux font quatre* two times two is four
♦ **une fois** once
♦ **deux fois** twice ◊ *deux fois plus de gens* twice as many people
♦ **une fois que** once ◊ *Tu te sentiras mieux une fois que tu auras mangé.* You'll feel better once you've had something to eat.
♦ **à la fois** at once ◊ *Je ne peux pas faire deux choses à la fois.* I can't do two things at once.

la **folie** NOUN
madness ◊ *C'est de la folie pure!* It's absolute madness!
♦ **faire une folie** to be extravagant

folklorique ADJECTIVE
folk ◊ *de la musique folklorique* folk music

folle ADJECTIVE (MASC SING **fou**)
mad

foncé ADJECTIVE
dark ◊ *bleu foncé* dark blue

foncer VERB (*informal*)
♦ **Je vais foncer à la boulangerie.** I'm just going to dash to the baker's.

la **fonction** NOUN
function
♦ **une voiture de fonction** a company car

le/la **fonctionnaire** NOUN
civil servant

fonctionner VERB
to work

le **fond** NOUN
1 bottom ◊ *Mon porte-monnaie est au fond de mon sac.* My purse is at the bottom of my bag.

2 end ◊ *Les toilettes sont au fond du couloir.* The toilets are at the end of the corridor.
- **dans le fond** all things considered ◊ *Dans le fond, ce n'est pas si grave.* All things considered, it's not that bad.

fonder VERB
to found

fondre VERB
to melt ◊ *La tablette de chocolat a fondu dans ma poche.* The bar of chocolate melted in my pocket.
- **fondre en larmes** to burst into tears

fondu ADJECTIVE
- **du beurre fondu** melted butter

font VERB *see* **faire**

la **fontaine** NOUN
fountain

le **foot** NOUN (*informal*)
football

le **football** NOUN
football ◊ *jouer au football* to play football

le **footballeur** NOUN
footballer

le **footing** NOUN
jogging ◊ *faire du footing* to go jogging

forain ADJECTIVE
see also **forain** NOUN
- **une fête foraine** a funfair

le **forain** NOUN
see also **forain** ADJECTIVE
fairground worker

la **force** NOUN
strength ◊ *Je n'ai pas beaucoup de force dans les bras.* I haven't got much strength in my arms.
- **à force de** by ◊ *Il a grossi à force de manger autant.* He got fat by eating so much.
- **de force** by force ◊ *Ils lui ont enlevé son pistolet de force.* They took the gun from him by force.

forcé ADJECTIVE
forced ◊ *un sourire forcé* a forced smile
- **C'est forcé.** (*informal*) It's inevitable.

forcément ADVERB
- **Ça devait forcément arriver.** That was bound to happen.
- **pas forcément** not necessarily

la **forêt** NOUN
forest

le **forfait** NOUN
all-in price

- **C'est compris dans le forfait.** It's included in the price.

le **forgeron** NOUN
blacksmith

la **formalité** NOUN
formality ◊ *Ce n'est qu'une simple formalité.* It's just a formality.

le **format** NOUN
size

la **formation** NOUN
training ◊ *la formation professionnelle* vocational training
- **la formation continue** in-house training
- **Il a une formation d'ingénieur.** He is a trained engineer.

la **forme** NOUN
shape
- **être en forme** to be in good shape
- **Je ne suis pas en forme aujourd'hui.** I'm not feeling too good today.
- **Tu as l'air en forme.** You're looking well.

formellement ADVERB
strictly ◊ *Il est formellement interdit de fumer dans les couloirs.* It is strictly forbidden to smoke in the corridors.

former VERB
to form

formidable ADJECTIVE
great

le **formulaire** NOUN
form

fort ADJECTIVE, ADVERB
1 strong ◊ *Le café est trop fort.* The coffee's too strong.
2 good ◊ *Il est très fort en espagnol.* He's very good at Spanish.
3 loud ◊ *Est-ce vous pouvez parler plus fort?* Can you speak louder?
- **frapper fort** to hit hard

le **fortifiant** NOUN
tonic (*medicine*)

la **fortune** NOUN
fortune
- **de fortune** makeshift ◊ *Il a traversé la rivière sur un radeau de fortune.* He crossed the river on a makeshift raft.

le **forum de discussion** NOUN
chatroom

le **fossé** NOUN
ditch

fou ADJECTIVE (MASC SING ALSO **fol**, FEM SING **folle**)
mad
- **Il y a un monde fou sur la plage!** (*informal*) There are loads of people on the beach!
- **attraper le fou rire** to get the giggles

la **foudre** NOUN
lightning ◊ *Il a été frappé par la foudre.* He was struck by lightning.

foudroyant ADJECTIVE
instant ◊ *un succès foudroyant* an instant hit

le **fouet** NOUN
whisk

la **fougère** NOUN
fern

fouiller VERB
to rummage

le **fouillis** NOUN
mess ◊ *Il y a du fouillis dans sa chambre.* His bedroom is a mess.

le **foulard** NOUN
scarf ◊ *un foulard en soie* a silk scarf

la **foule** NOUN
crowd
♦ **une foule de** masses of ◊ *J'ai une foule de choses à faire demain.* I've got masses of things to do tomorrow.

se **fouler** VERB
♦ **se fouler la cheville** to sprain one's ankle

le **four** NOUN
oven ◊ *un four à micro-ondes* a microwave oven

la **fourchette** NOUN
fork

la **fourmi** NOUN
ant
♦ **avoir des fourmis dans les jambes** to have pins and needles

le **fourneau** NOUN (PL les **fourneaux**)
stove

fourni ADJECTIVE
thick (*beard, hair*)

fournir VERB
to supply

le **fournisseur** NOUN
supplier
♦ **un fournisseur d'accès à Internet** an internet service provider

les **fournitures** FEM NOUN
♦ **les fournitures scolaires** school stationery

fourré ADJECTIVE
filled ◊ *un gâteau fourré à la confiture* a cake filled with jam

fourrer VERB (*informal*)
to put ◊ *Où as-tu fourré mon sac?* Where have you put my bag?

le **fourre-tout** NOUN (PL les **fourre-tout**)
holdall

la **fourrure** NOUN
fur ◊ *un manteau de fourrure* a fur coat

foutre VERB (*rude*)
to do ◊ *Qu'est-ce qu'il fout?* What the hell is he doing?
♦ **Je n'en ai rien à foutre!** I don't give a damn!

foutu ADJECTIVE (*rude*)
1 knackered ◊ *Mon stylo est foutu.* My pen's knackered.
2 bloody ◊ *Qu'est-ce que j'ai fait de ce foutu stylo?* Where did I put that bloody pen?

le **foyer** NOUN
home ◊ *dans la plupart des foyers français* in most French homes
♦ **un foyer de jeunes** a youth club

la **fracture** NOUN
fracture

fragile ADJECTIVE
fragile ◊ *Attention, c'est fragile!* Be careful, it's fragile!

la **fragilité** NOUN
fragility

fraîche ADJECTIVE *see* **frais**

la **fraîcheur** NOUN
1 cool ◊ *la fraîcheur du soir* the cool of the evening
2 freshness ◊ *Je ne suis pas sûre de la fraîcheur du poisson.* I'm not sure about the freshness of the fish.

frais ADJECTIVE (FEM SING **fraîche**)
see also **frais** NOUN
1 fresh ◊ *des œufs frais* fresh eggs ◊ *Cette salade n'est pas très fraîche.* This lettuce isn't very fresh.
2 chilly ◊ *Il fait un peu frais ce soir.* It's a bit chilly this evening.
3 cool ◊ *des boissons fraîches* cool drinks
♦ **"servir frais"** "serve chilled"
♦ **mettre au frais** to put in a cool place

les **frais** MASC NOUN
see also **frais** ADJECTIVE
expenses

la **fraise** NOUN
strawberry

la **framboise** NOUN
raspberry

franc ADJECTIVE (FEM SING **franche**)
see also **franc** NOUN
frank

le **franc** NOUN
see also **franc** ADJECTIVE
franc

> ℹ The **franc** is the unit of currency in Switzerland and many former French colonies.

français ADJECTIVE, NOUN (FEM SING **française**)
French ◊ *Il parle français couramment.* He speaks French fluently.
♦**un Français** a Frenchman
♦**une Française** a Frenchwoman
♦**les Français** the French

la **France** NOUN
France
♦**en France (1)** in France ◊ *Je suis né en France.* I was born in France.
♦**en France (2)** to France ◊ *Je pars en France pour Noël.* I'm going to France for Christmas.

franche ADJECTIVE *see* **franc**

franchement ADVERB
[1] frankly ◊ *Il m'a parlé franchement.* He spoke to me frankly.
[2] really ◊ *C'est franchement mauvais.* It's really bad.

franchir VERB
to get over

la **franchise** NOUN
frankness

francophone ADJECTIVE
French-speaking

la **frange** NOUN
fringe

la **frangipane** NOUN
almond cream

frapper VERB
to strike ◊ *Il l'a frappée au visage.* He struck her in the face. ◊ *Son air fatigué m'a frappé.* I was struck by how tired she looked.

fredonner VERB
to hum

le **freezer** NOUN
freezing compartment

le **frein** NOUN
brake
♦**le frein à main** handbrake

freiner VERB
to brake

frêle ADJECTIVE
frail

le **frelon** NOUN
hornet

frémir VERB
shudder ◊ *Cette idée me fait frémir.* The idea makes me shudder.

fréquemment ADVERB
frequently

fréquent ADJECTIVE
frequent

fréquenté ADJECTIVE

busy ◊ *une rue très fréquentée* a very busy street
♦**un bar mal fréquenté** a rough pub

fréquenter VERB
to see (*person*) ◊ *Je ne le fréquente pas beaucoup.* I don't see him often.

le **frère** NOUN
brother

le **friand** NOUN
♦**un friand au fromage** a cheese puff

la **friandise** NOUN
sweet

le **fric** NOUN (*informal*)
cash

le **frigidaire** ® NOUN
refrigerator

le **frigo** NOUN (*informal*)
fridge

frileux ADJECTIVE (FEM SING **frileuse**)
♦**être frileux** to feel the cold ◊ *Elle est très frileuse.* She really feels the cold.

frimer VERB (*informal*)
to show off

les **fringues** FEM NOUN (*informal*)
clothes

fripé ADJECTIVE
crumpled

frire VERB
♦**faire frire** to fry ◊ *Faites frire les boulettes dans de l'huile très chaude.* Fry the meatballs in very hot oil.

frisé ADJECTIVE
curly ◊ *Elle est très frisée.* She's got very curly hair.

le **frisson** NOUN
shiver

frissonner VERB
to shiver

frit ADJECTIVE
fried ◊ *du poisson frit* fried fish

les **frites** FEM NOUN
chips

la **friture** NOUN
[1] fried food ◊ *On lui a conseillé d'éviter les fritures.* He's been advised to avoid fried food.
[2] fried fish ◊ *Nous allons faire une friture ce soir.* We are going to have fried fish tonight.

froid ADJECTIVE
see also **froid** NOUN
cold ◊ *Ça me laisse froid.* It leaves me cold. ◊ *de la viande froide* cold meat

le **froid** NOUN
> see also **froid** ADJECTIVE

cold
♦ **Il fait froid.** It's cold.
♦ **avoir froid** to be cold ◇ *Est-ce que tu as froid?* Are you cold?

se **froisser** VERB
1 to crease ◇ *Ce tissu se froisse très facilement.* This material creases very easily.
2 to take offence ◇ *Paul se froisse très facilement.* Paul's very quick to take offence.
♦ **se froisser un muscle** to strain a muscle

frôler VERB
1 to brush against ◇ *Le chat m'a frôlé au passage.* The cat brushed against me as it went past.
2 to narrowly avoid ◇ *Nous avons frôlé la catastrophe.* We narrowly avoided disaster.

le **fromage** NOUN
cheese
♦ **du fromage blanc** soft white cheese

le **froment** NOUN
wheat
♦ **une crêpe de froment** a pancake (*made with wheat flour*)

froncer VERB
♦ **froncer les sourcils** to frown

le **front** NOUN
forehead

la **frontière** NOUN
border

frotter VERB
to rub ◇ *se frotter les yeux* to rub one's eyes
♦ **frotter une allumette** to strike a match

le **fruit** NOUN
fruit
♦ **un fruit** a piece of fruit ◇ *Est-ce que vous voulez manger un fruit?* Would you like some fruit?
♦ **les fruits de mer** seafood

fruité ADJECTIVE
fruity

frustrer VERB
to frustrate

la **fugue** NOUN
♦ **faire une fugue** to run away

fuir VERB
1 to flee ◇ *fuir devant un danger* to flee from danger
2 to drip ◇ *Le robinet fuit.* The tap's dripping.

la **fuite** NOUN
1 leak ◇ *Il y a une fuite de gaz.* There is a gas leak.
2 flight (*escape*)
♦ **être en fuite** to be on the run

fumé ADJECTIVE
smoked ◇ *du saumon fumé* smoked salmon

la **fumée** NOUN
smoke

fumer VERB
to smoke

le **fumeur** NOUN
smoker

la **fumeuse** NOUN
smoker

fur
♦ **au fur et à mesure** ADVERB
as you go along ◇ *Je vérifie mon travail au fur et à mesure.* I check my work as I go along.
♦ **au fur et à mesure que** as ◇ *Je réponds à mon courrier au fur et à mesure que je le reçois.* I answer my mail as I receive it.

le **furet** NOUN
ferret

la **fureur** NOUN
fury
♦ **faire fureur** to be all the rage ◇ *Ce genre de sac fait fureur actuellement.* This sort of bag is all the rage at the moment.

furieux ADJECTIVE (FEM SING **furieuse**)
furious

le **furoncle** NOUN
boil (*on skin*)

fus VERB *see* **être**

le **fuseau** NOUN (PL les **fuseaux**)
ski pants

la **fusée** NOUN
rocket

le **fusil** NOUN
gun

fut VERB *see* **être**

futé ADJECTIVE
crafty

le **futur** NOUN
future

F

G

gâcher VERB
to waste ◊ *Je n'aime pas gâcher la nourriture.* I don't like to waste food.

le **gâchis** NOUN
waste

la **gaffe** NOUN
- **faire une gaffe** to do something stupid
- **Fais gaffe!** (*informal*) Watch out! ◊ *Fais gaffe: la peinture est encore humide!* Watch out: the paint's still wet!

le **gage** NOUN
forfeit (*in a game*) ◊ *recevoir un gage* to pay a forfeit

le **gagnant** NOUN
winner

la **gagnante** NOUN
winner

gagner VERB
to win ◊ *Qui a gagné?* Who won?
- **gagner du temps** to gain time
- **Il gagne bien sa vie.** He makes a good living.

gai ADJECTIVE
cheerful ◊ *Elle est très gaie.* She's very cheerful.

la **gaieté** NOUN
cheerfulness

la **galerie** NOUN
gallery ◊ *une galerie de peinture* an art gallery
- **une galerie marchande** a shopping arcade
- **une galerie de jeux d'arcade** an amusement arcade

le **galet** NOUN
pebble

la **galette** NOUN
1 round flat cake ◊ *une galette de blé noir* a buckwheat pancake
2 biscuit ◊ *des galettes pur beurre* shortbread biscuits
- **la galette des Rois**

> ❶ A **galette des Rois** is a cake eaten on Twelfth Night containing a figurine. The person who finds it is the king (or queen) and gets a paper crown. They then choose someone else to be their queen (or king).

Galles FEM NOUN
- **le pays de Galles** Wales
- **le prince de Galles** the Prince of Wales

gallois ADJECTIVE, NOUN
Welsh ◊ *un peintre gallois* a Welsh painter
- **un Gallois** a Welshman
- **une Galloise** a Welshwoman
- **les Gallois** the Welsh

le **galop** NOUN
gallop

galoper VERB
to gallop

le **gamin** NOUN (*informal*)
kid

la **gamine** NOUN (*informal*)
kid

la **gamme** NOUN
scale (*in music*) ◊ *Je dois faire des gammes tous les soirs.* I have to do my scales every night.
- **une gamme de produits** a range of products

gammée ADJECTIVE
- **la croix gammée** the swastika

le **gant** NOUN
glove ◊ *des gants en laine* woollen gloves
- **un gant de toilette** a face cloth

le **garage** NOUN
garage

le/la **garagiste** NOUN
1 garage owner
2 mechanic

la **garantie** NOUN
guarantee

garantir VERB
to guarantee

le **garçon** NOUN
1 boy
2 waiter (*in a café*) ◊ *Garçon!* Waiter!
- **un vieux garçon** a bachelor

le **garde** NOUN
see also **la garde**
1 warder (*in prison*)
2 security man
- **un garde du corps** a bodyguard

la **garde** NOUN
see also **le garde**
1 guarding ◊ *Il est chargé de la garde des prisonniers.* He's responsible for guarding the prisoners.
2 guard ◊ *la relève de la garde* the changing of the guard
- **être de garde** to be on duty ◊ *Mon père est de garde ce soir.* My father

is on duty tonight. ◊ *La pharmacie de garde ce week-end est ...* The duty chemist this weekend is ...
♦ **mettre en garde** to warn ◊ *Elle m'a mis en garde contre les pickpockets.* She warned me about pickpockets.

le **garde-côte** NOUN (PL les **garde-côtes**)
   coastguard

garder VERB
   1 to keep ◊ *Tu as gardé toutes ses lettres?* Have you kept all his letters?
   2 to look after ◊ *Je garde ma nièce samedi après-midi.* I'm looking after my niece on Saturday afternoon.
   3 to guard ◊ *Ils ont pris un gros chien pour garder la maison.* They got a big dog to guard the house.
♦ **garder le lit** to stay in bed
♦ **se garder** to keep ◊ *Ces crêpes se gardent bien.* These pancakes keep well.

la **garderie** NOUN
   nursery

la **garde-robe** NOUN
   wardrobe (*clothes*) ◊ *Elle a une garde-robe bien fournie.* She's got an extensive wardrobe.

le **gardien** NOUN
   1 caretaker
   2 attendant (*in a museum*)
♦ **un gardien de but** a goalkeeper
♦ **un gardien de la paix** a police officer

la **gardienne** NOUN
   1 caretaker
   2 attendant (*in a museum*)

la **gare** NOUN
   | see also **gare** EXCLAMATION |
   station ◊ *la gare routière* the bus station

gare EXCLAMATION
   | see also **gare** NOUN |
♦ **Gare aux serpents!** Watch out for snakes!

garer VERB
   to park
♦ **se garer** to park ◊ *Où t'es-tu garé?* Where are you parked?

garni ADJECTIVE
♦ **un plat garni** a dish served with accompaniments (*vegetables, chips, rice etc*)

le **gars** NOUN (*informal*)
   guy

gaspiller VERB
   to waste

le **gâteau** NOUN (PL les **gâteaux**)
   cake
♦ **les gâteaux secs** biscuits

gâter VERB

to spoil ◊ *Il aime gâter ses petits enfants.* He likes to spoil his grandchildren.
♦ **se gâter** to go bad ◊ *Le temps va se gâter.* The weather's going to break.

gauche ADJECTIVE
   | see also **gauche** NOUN |
   left ◊ *le bras gauche* the left arm ◊ *le côté gauche* the left-hand side

la **gauche** NOUN
   | see also **gauche** ADJECTIVE |
   left ◊ *sur votre gauche* on your left
♦ **à gauche (1)** on the left ◊ *la deuxième rue à gauche* the second street on the left
♦ **à gauche (2)** to the left ◊ *à gauche de l'armoire* to the left of the cupboard ◊ *Tournez à gauche.* Turn left.
♦ **la voie de gauche** the left-hand lane
♦ **la gauche** the left (*in politics*) ◊ *Il est de gauche.* He's left-wing.

gaucher ADJECTIVE (FEM SING **gauchère**)
   left-handed

la **gaufre** NOUN
   waffle

la **gaufrette** NOUN
   wafer

le **Gaulois** NOUN
   Gaul ◊ *Astérix le Gaulois* Asterix the Gaul

gaulois ADJECTIVE
   Gallic

le **gaz** NOUN
   gas

gazeux ADJECTIVE (FEM SING **gazeuse**)
♦ **une boisson gazeuse** a fizzy drink
♦ **de l'eau gazeuse** sparkling water

le **gazole** NOUN
   diesel (*fuel*)

le **gazon** NOUN
   lawn

le **GDF** NOUN (= *Gaz de France*)
   French gas company

le **géant** NOUN
   giant

le **gel** NOUN
   frost

la **gelée** NOUN
   jelly

geler VERB
   to freeze ◊ *Il a gelé cette nuit.* There was a frost last night.

la **gélule** NOUN
   capsule (*containing medicine*)

les **Gémeaux** MASC NOUN
   Gemini ◊ *Henry est Gémeaux.* Henry's Gemini.

gémir VERB

☞

to moan

gênant ADJECTIVE
awkward ◊ *un silence gênant* an
awkward silence

la **gencive** NOUN
gum (*in mouth*)

le **gendarme** NOUN
policeman

la **gendarmerie** NOUN
1 police force
2 police station ◊ *Vous devriez
porter plainte à la gendarmerie.* You
should go to the police station and
report it.

le **gendre** NOUN
son-in-law

gêné ADJECTIVE
embarrassed

gêner VERB
1 to bother ◊ *Je ne voudrais pas
vous gêner.* I don't want to bother
you.
2 to feel awkward ◊ *Son regard la
gênait.* The way he was looking at
her made her feel awkward.

général ADJECTIVE (MASC PL **généraux**)
see also **général** NOUN
general
♦ **en général** usually

le **général** NOUN (PL les **généraux**)
see also **général** ADJECTIVE
general

généralement ADVERB
generally

le/la **généraliste** NOUN
family doctor

la **génération** NOUN
generation

généreux ADJECTIVE (FEM SING **généreuse**)
generous

la **générosité** NOUN
generosity

le **genêt** NOUN
broom (*bush*)

la **génétique** NOUN
genetics

génétiquement ADVERB
genetically ◊ *génétiquement modifié*
genetically-modified ◊ *les aliments
génétiquement modifiés* GM foods
◊ *un organisme génétiquement
modifié* a genetically-modified
organism

Genève NOUN
Geneva

génial ADJECTIVE (MASC PL **géniaux**)
(*informal*)
great ◊ *Le film d'hier soir*

était génial. The film last night was
great.

le **genou** NOUN (PL les **genoux**)
knee ◊ *Elle est à genoux.* She's on
her knees. ◊ *se mettre à genoux* to
kneel down

le **genre** NOUN
kind ◊ *C'est un genre de gâteau à la
crème.* It's a kind of cream cake.

les **gens** MASC NOUN
people

gentil ADJECTIVE (FEM SING **gentille**)
1 nice ◊ *Nos voisins sont très
gentils.* Our neighbours are very nice.
2 kind ◊ *C'était très gentil de votre
part.* It was very kind of you.

la **gentillesse** NOUN
kindness ◊ *Je l'ai remerciée de sa
gentillesse.* I thanked her for her
kindness. ◊ *C'est un homme d'une
grande gentillesse.* He is a very nice
man.

gentiment ADVERB
1 nicely ◊ *Demande-le lui gentiment.*
Ask him nicely.
2 kindly ◊ *Ils nous ont gentiment
proposé de rester dîner.* They kindly
invited us to stay for dinner.

la **géographie** NOUN
geography

la **géométrie** NOUN
geometry

le **gérant** NOUN
manager

la **gérante** NOUN
manager

gérer VERB
to manage

germain ADJECTIVE
♦ **un cousin germain** a first cousin

le **geste** NOUN
gesture ◊ *Il a voulu faire un geste.*
He wanted to make a gesture.
♦ **Ne faites pas un geste!** Don't move!

la **gestion** NOUN
management

le/la **gestionnaire de site** NOUN
webmaster

la **gifle** NOUN
slap across the face

gifler VERB
to slap across the face

gigantesque ADJECTIVE
gigantic

le **gigot** NOUN
leg of lamb

le **gilet** NOUN

① waistcoat ◊ *un gilet en cuir* a leather waistcoat
② cardigan ◊ *un gilet tricoté main* a hand-knitted cardigan
♦ **un gilet de sauvetage** a life jacket

le **gingembre** NOUN
ginger

la **girafe** NOUN
giraffe

le **gitan** NOUN
gipsy

la **gitane** NOUN
gipsy

le **gîte** NOUN
♦ **un gîte rural** a holiday house

la **glace** NOUN
① ice ◊ *L'étang est recouvert de glace.* The pond is covered with ice.
② ice cream ◊ *une glace à la fraise* a strawberry ice cream
③ mirror ◊ *Il se regarde souvent dans la glace.* He often looks at himself in the mirror.

glacé ADJECTIVE
① icy ◊ *Il soufflait un vent glacé.* An icy wind was blowing.
② iced ◊ *un thé glacé* an iced tea

glacial ADJECTIVE (MASC PL **glaciaux**)
icy

le **glaçon** NOUN
ice cube

glissant ADJECTIVE
slippery

glisser VERB
① to slip ◊ *Il a glissé sur une peau de banane.* He slipped on a banana skin.
② to be slippery ◊ *Attention, ça glisse!* Watch out, it's slippery!

global ADJECTIVE (MASC PL **globaux**)
total ◊ *la somme globale* the total amount

la **gloire** NOUN
glory

la **godasse** NOUN (*informal*)
shoe

le **goéland** NOUN
seagull

le **golf** NOUN
① golf ◊ *Il joue au golf.* He plays golf.
② golf course ◊ *un golf dix-huit trous* an 18-hole golf course

le **golfe** NOUN
gulf
♦ **le golfe de Gascogne** the Bay of Biscay

la **gomme** NOUN
rubber

gommer VERB
to rub out

gonflé ADJECTIVE
① swollen (*arm, finger, stomach*) ◊ *Elle a les pieds gonflés.* Her feet are swollen.
② inflated (*ball, tyre*) ◊ *Le ballon de foot était mal gonflé.* The football wasn't properly inflated.
♦ **Il est gonflé!** He's got a nerve!

gonfler VERB
① to blow up ◊ *gonfler un ballon* to blow up a balloon
② to pump up ◊ *Tu devrais gonfler ton pneu arrière.* You should pump up your back tyre.

la **gorge** NOUN
① throat ◊ *J'ai mal à la gorge.* I've got a sore throat.
② gorge ◊ *les gorges du Tarn* the Tarn gorges

la **gorgée** NOUN
sip ◊ *une gorgée d'eau* a sip of water

le **gorille** NOUN
gorilla

le/la **gosse** NOUN (*informal*)
kid

le **goudron** NOUN
tar

le **gouffre** NOUN
chasm
♦ **Cette voiture est un vrai gouffre!** This car eats up money!

la **gourde** NOUN
water bottle

gourmand ADJECTIVE
greedy

la **gourmandise** NOUN
greed

la **gousse** NOUN
♦ **une gousse d'ail** a clove of garlic

le **goût** NOUN
taste ◊ *Ça n'a pas de goût.* It's got no taste. ◊ *Elle a très bon goût.* She's got very good taste.

goûter VERB
⏵ see also **goûter** NOUN
① to taste ◊ *Goûte donc ce fromage: tu verras comme il est bon!* Have a taste of this cheese: you'll see how nice it is!
② to have a snack (*in the afternoon*) ◊ *Les enfants goûtent généralement vers quatre heures.* The children usually have a snack around 4 o'clock.

le **goûter** NOUN

☞

see also **goûter** VERB
afternoon snack

la **goutte** NOUN
drop

le **gouvernement** NOUN
government

gouverner VERB
to govern

la **grâce** NOUN
♦ **grâce à** thanks to ◊ *Je suis arrivé à l'heure grâce à toi.* I arrived on time thanks to you.

gracieux ADJECTIVE (FEM SING **gracieuse**)
graceful

les **gradins** MASC NOUN
terraces (*in stadium*)

graduel ADJECTIVE (FEM SING **graduelle**)
gradual

les **graffiti** MASC NOUN
graffiti SING

le **grain** NOUN
grain ◊ *un grain de sable* a grain of sand
♦ **un grain de beauté** a beauty spot
♦ **un grain de café** a coffee bean
♦ **un grain de raisin** a grape

la **graine** NOUN
seed

la **graisse** NOUN
fat

la **grammaire** NOUN
grammar

le **gramme** NOUN
gramme

grand ADJECTIVE, ADVERB
[1] **tall** ◊ *Il est grand pour son âge.* He's tall for his age.
[2] **big** ◊ *une grande valise* a big suitcase ◊ *C'est sa grande sœur.* She's his big sister.
♦ **une grande personne** a grown-up
[3] **long** ◊ *un grand voyage* a long journey
♦ **les grandes vacances** the summer holidays
[4] **great** ◊ *C'est un grand ami à moi.* He's a great friend of mine.
♦ **un grand magasin** a department store
♦ **une grande surface** a hypermarket
♦ **les grandes écoles** top ranking colleges (*at university level*)
♦ **au grand air** out in the open air ◊ *Ça te fera beaucoup de bien d'être au grand air.* It'll be very good for you to be out in the open air.
♦ **grand ouvert** wide open

grand-chose NOUN
♦ **pas grand-chose** not much ◊ *Je n'ai pas acheté grand-chose au marché.* I

didn't buy much at the market.
◊ *Voici un petit cadeau: ce n'est pas grand-chose.* Here's a little present: it's nothing much.

la **Grande-Bretagne** NOUN
Britain

la **grandeur** NOUN
size

grandir VERB
to grow ◊ *Il a beaucoup grandi.* He's grown a lot.

la **grand-mère** NOUN (PL les **grands-mères**)
grandmother

grand-peine
♦ **à grand-peine** ADVERB
with great difficulty

le **grand-père** NOUN (PL les **grands-pères**)
grandfather

les **grands-parents** MASC NOUN
grandparents

la **grange** NOUN
barn

la **grappe** NOUN
♦ **une grappe de raisin** a bunch of grapes

gras ADJECTIVE (FEM SING **grasse**)
[1] **fatty** (*food*) ◊ *Évitez les aliments gras.* Avoid fatty foods.
[2] **greasy** ◊ *des cheveux gras* greasy hair
[3] **oily** ◊ *une peau grasse* oily skin
♦ **faire la grasse matinée** to have a lie-in

gratis ADJECTIVE, ADVERB
free ◊ *J'ai eu ce stylo gratis.* I got this pen free.

le **gratte-ciel** NOUN (PL les **gratte-ciel**)
skyscraper

gratter VERB
[1] **to scratch** ◊ *Ne gratte pas tes piqûres de moustiques!* Don't scratch your mosquito bites!
[2] **to be itchy** ◊ *C'est épouvantable comme ça gratte!* It's terribly itchy!

gratuit ADJECTIVE
free ◊ *entrée gratuite* entrance free ◊ *J'ai deux places gratuites pour le film.* I've got two complimentary tickets for the film.

grave ADJECTIVE
[1] **serious** ◊ *une maladie grave* a serious illness ◊ *Il avait l'air grave.* He was looking serious.
[2] **deep** ◊ *Il a une voix grave.* He's got a deep voice.
♦ **Ce n'est pas grave.** It doesn't matter. ◊ *J'ai oublié ma clé. – Ce n'est pas grave, j'ai la mienne.* I've forgotten

my key. – It doesn't matter, I've got
mine.

gravement ADVERB
    seriously ◊ *Il a été gravement blessé.*
    He was seriously injured.

le **graveur** NOUN
    ◆**un graveur de CD** a CD burner

grec ADJECTIVE, NOUN (FEM SING **grecque**)
    Greek
    ◆**J'apprends le grec.** I'm learning
    Greek.
    ◆**un Grec** a Greek (*man*)
    ◆**une Grecque** a Greek (*woman*)
    ◆**les Grecs** the Greeks

la **Grèce** NOUN
    Greece
    ◆**en Grèce (1)** in Greece
    ◆**en Grèce (2)** to Greece

la **grêle** NOUN
    hail

grêler VERB
    ◆**Il grêle.** It's hailing.

grelotter VERB
    to shiver

la **grenade** NOUN
    ⨻ pomegranate
    ⨻ grenade

le **grenier** NOUN
    attic

la **grenouille** NOUN
    frog

la **grève** NOUN
    ⨻ strike
    ◆**en grève** on strike ◊ *Ils sont en grève
    depuis dix jours.* They have been on
    strike for ten days.
    ◆**faire grève** to be on strike
    ⨻ shore ◊ *Nous nous sommes
    promenés le long de la grève.* We
    went for a walk along the shore.

le/la **gréviste** NOUN
    striker

grièvement ADVERB
    ◆**grièvement blessé** seriously injured

la **griffe** NOUN
    ⨻ claw ◊ *Le chat m'a donné un coup
    de griffe.* The cat scratched me.
    ⨻ label ◊ *la griffe d'un grand
    couturier* the label of a top designer

griffer VERB
    to scratch ◊ *Le chat m'a griffé.* The
    cat scratched me.

grignoter VERB
    to nibble

la **grillade** NOUN
    grilled food ◊ *une grillade d'agneau*
    grilled lamb

la **grille** NOUN

⨻ wire fence ◊ *L'usine est entourée
d'une haute grille.* The factory is
surrounded by a high wire fence.
⨻ metal gate ◊ *Le facteur a sonné à
la grille du jardin.* The postman rang
at the garden gate.

le **grille-pain** NOUN (PL les **grille-pain**)
    toaster

griller VERB
    ⨻ to toast
    ◆**du pain grillé** toast
    ⨻ to grill ◊ *des saucisses grillées*
    grilled sausages

la **grimace** NOUN
    ◆**faire des grimaces** to make faces

grimper VERB
    to climb

grincer VERB
    to creak

grincheux ADJECTIVE (FEM SING **grincheuse**)
    grumpy

la **grippe** NOUN
    flu
    ◆**avoir la grippe** to have flu ◊ *J'ai eu
    une mauvaise grippe l'hiver dernier.* I
    had a bad attack of flu last winter.

grippé ADJECTIVE
    ◆**être grippé** to have flu

gris ADJECTIVE
    grey

le **Groenland** NOUN
    Greenland

grogner VERB
    ⨻ to growl ◊ *Le chien a grogné
    quand je me suis approché de lui.*
    The dog growled when I went near it.
    ⨻ to complain ◊ *Arrête donc de
    grogner!* Stop complaining!

gronder VERB
    ◆**se faire gronder** to get a telling off
    ◊ *Tu vas te faire gronder par ton
    père!* You're going to get a telling off
    from your father!

gros ADJECTIVE (FEM SING **grosse**)
    ⨻ big ◊ *une grosse pomme* a big
    apple
    ⨻ fat ◊ *Je suis trop grosse pour
    porter ça!* I'm too fat to wear that!

la **groseille** NOUN
    ◆**la groseille rouge** redcurrant
    ◆**la groseille à maquereau** gooseberry

la **grossesse** NOUN
    pregnancy

grossier ADJECTIVE (FEM SING **grossière**)
    rude ◊ *Ne sois pas si grossier!* Don't
    be so rude!
    ◆**une erreur grossière** a bad mistake

grossir VERB

G

☞

to put on weight ◊ *Il a beaucoup grossi.* He's put on a lot of weight.

grosso modo ADVERB
roughly ◊ *Dis-moi grosso modo ce que tu en penses.* Give me a rough idea what you think of it.

la **grotte** NOUN
cave

le **groupe** NOUN
group ◊ *votre groupe sanguin* your blood group

grouper VERB
to group ◊ *On nous a groupés dans différentes classes selon notre niveau.* We were grouped in different classes according to our level.
♦ **se grouper** to gather ◊ *Nous nous sommes groupés autour du feu.* We gathered round the fire.

le **guépard** NOUN
cheetah

la **guêpe** NOUN
wasp

guérir VERB
to recover ◊ *Il est maintenant complètement guéri.* He's now completely recovered.

la **guérison** NOUN
recovery

la **guerre** NOUN
war ◊ *en guerre* at war ◊ *une guerre civile* a civil war ◊ *la Deuxième Guerre mondiale* the Second World War

guetter VERB
to look out for ◊ *Elle guette l'arrivée du facteur tous les matins.* She looks out for the postman every morning.

la **gueule** NOUN

mouth (*rude when used for people*) ◊ *Le chat a ramené une souris dans sa gueule.* The cat brought in a mouse in its mouth.
♦ **Ta gueule!** (*rude*) Shut your face!
♦ **avoir la gueule de bois** (*informal*) to have a hangover

gueuler VERB (*informal*)
to bawl

le **guichet** NOUN
counter (*in bank, booking office*)

le **guide** NOUN
guide

guider VERB
to guide

le **guidon** NOUN
handlebars

les **guillemets** MASC NOUN
inverted commas ◊ *entre guillemets* in inverted commas

la **guirlande** NOUN
tinsel ◊ *Nous avons décoré le sapin de Noël avec des guirlandes.* We decorated the Christmas tree with tinsel.
♦ **des guirlandes en papier** paper chains

la **guitare** NOUN
guitar ◊ *Sais-tu jouer de la guitare?* Can you play the guitar?

la **gym** NOUN (*informal*)
PE

le **gymnase** NOUN
gym ◊ *Le lycée a un nouveau gymnase.* The school's got a new gym.

la **gymnastique** NOUN
gymnastics ◊ *faire de la gymnastique* to do one's exercises

H

habile ADJECTIVE
  skilful ◊ *Il est très habile de ses mains.*
  He is very clever with his hands.

habillé ADJECTIVE
  1 dressed ◊ *Il n'est pas encore
  habillé.* He's not dressed yet.
  2 smart ◊ *Cette robe fait très habillé.*
  This dress looks very smart.

s'**habiller** VERB
  1 to get dressed ◊ *Je me suis
  rapidement habillé.* I got dressed
  quickly.
  2 to dress up ◊ *Est-ce qu'il faut
  s'habiller pour la réception?* Do you
  have to dress up to go to the party?

l'**habitant** MASC NOUN
  inhabitant ◊ *Les habitants du quartier
  sont contre ce projet.* The local
  people are against this plan.

l'**habitante** FEM NOUN
  inhabitant

habiter VERB
  to live ◊ *Il habite à Montpellier.* He
  lives in Montpellier.

les **habits** MASC NOUN
  clothes

l'**habitude** FEM NOUN
  habit ◊ *une mauvaise habitude* a bad
  habit
  ◆ **avoir l'habitude de quelque chose** to
  be used to something ◊ *Elle a
  l'habitude des enfants.* She's used to
  children. ◊ *Je n'ai pas l'habitude de
  parler en public.* I'm not used to
  speaking in public.
  ◆ **d'habitude** usually
  ◆ **comme d'habitude** as usual

habituel ADJECTIVE (FEM SING **habituelle**)
  usual

s'**habituer** VERB
  ◆ **s'habituer à quelque chose** to get
  used to something ◊ *Il faudra que tu
  t'habitues à te lever tôt.* You'll have
  to get used to getting up early.

le **hachis** NOUN
  mince
  ◆ **le hachis Parmentier** shepherd's pie

la **haie** NOUN
  hedge

la **haine** NOUN
  hatred

haïr VERB
  to hate

l'**haleine** FEM NOUN

breath ◊ *avoir mauvaise haleine* to
have bad breath ◊ *être hors d'haleine*
to be out of breath

les **halles** FEM NOUN
  covered market SING

la **halte** NOUN
  stop ◊ *faire halte* to make a stop
  ◆ **Halte!** Stop!

l'**haltérophilie** FEM NOUN
  weightlifting

le **hamburger** NOUN
  hamburger

l'**hameçon** MASC NOUN
  fish hook

le **hamster** NOUN
  hamster

la **hanche** NOUN
  hip

le **handball** NOUN
  handball ◊ *jouer au handball* to play
  handball

le **handicapé** NOUN
  handicapped man

la **handicapée** NOUN
  handicapped woman

le **harcèlement** NOUN
  harassment ◊ *le harcèlement sexuel*
  sexual harassment

le **hareng** NOUN
  herring
  ◆ **un hareng saur** a kipper

le **haricot** NOUN
  bean
  ◆ **les haricots verts** runner beans
  ◆ **les haricots blancs** haricot beans

l'**harmonica** MASC NOUN
  mouth organ

la **harpe** NOUN
  harp

le **hasard** NOUN
  coincidence ◊ *C'était un pur hasard.*
  It was pure coincidence.
  ◆ **au hasard** at random ◊ *Choisis un
  numéro au hasard.* Choose a number
  at random.
  ◆ **par hasard** by chance ◊ *Je l'ai
  rencontrée tout à fait par hasard au
  supermarché.* I met her at the
  supermarket quite by chance.
  ◆ **à tout hasard (1)** just in case ◊ *Prends
  un parapluie à tout hasard.* Take an
  umbrella just in case.
  ◆ **à tout hasard (2)** on the off chance
  ◊ *Je ne sais pas s'il est chez lui, mais*

je vais l'appeler à tout hasard. I don't know if he's at home, but I'll phone on the off chance.

la **hâte** NOUN
- ◆**à la hâte** hurriedly ◇ *Elle s'est habillée à la hâte.* She got dressed hurriedly.
- ◆**J'ai hâte de te voir.** I can't wait to see you.

la **hausse** NOUN
  1. increase ◇ *la hausse des prix* price increase
  2. rise ◇ *On annonce une légère hausse de température.* The forecast is for a slight rise in temperature.

hausser VERB
- ◆**hausser les épaules** to shrug one's shoulders

haut ADJECTIVE, ADVERB
  see also **haut** NOUN
  1. high ◇ *une haute montagne* a high mountain
  2. aloud ◇ *penser tout haut* to think aloud

le **haut** NOUN
  see also **haut** ADJECTIVE
  top
- ◆**un mur de trois mètres de haut** a wall 3 metres high
- ◆**en haut (1)** upstairs ◇ *La salle de bain est en haut.* The bathroom is upstairs.
- ◆**en haut (2)** at the top ◇ *Le nid est tout en haut de l'arbre.* The nest is right at the top of the tree.

la **hauteur** NOUN
  height

le **haut-parleur** NOUN
  loudspeaker

l' **hebdomadaire** MASC NOUN
  weekly (*magazine*)

l' **hébergement** MASC NOUN
  accommodation

héberger VERB
  to put up ◇ *Mon cousin a dit qu'il nous hébergerait.* My cousin said he would put us up.

hein? EXCLAMATION
  eh?
- ◆**Hein? Qu'est-ce que tu dis?** Eh? What did you say?

hélas ADVERB
  unfortunately ◇ *Hélas, il ne restait plus de billets.* Unfortunately there were no tickets left.

l' **hélicoptère** MASC NOUN
  helicopter

l' **hémorragie** FEM NOUN
  haemorrhage

l' **herbe** FEM NOUN

grass
- ◆**les herbes de Provence** mixed herbs

le **hérisson** NOUN
  hedgehog

hériter VERB
  to inherit

l' **héritier** MASC NOUN
  heir

l' **héritière** FEM NOUN
  heiress

hermétique ADJECTIVE
  airtight

l' **héroïne** FEM NOUN
  1. heroine ◇ *l'héroïne du roman* the heroine of the novel
  2. heroin (*drug*)

le **héros** NOUN
  hero

l' **hésitation** FEM NOUN
  hesitation

hésiter VERB
  to hesitate ◇ *Il n'a pas hésité à nous aider.* He didn't hesitate to help us. ◇ *J'ai hésité entre le pull vert et le cardigan jaune.* I couldn't decide between the green pullover and the yellow cardigan. ◇ *Est-ce que tu viens ce soir? – J'hésite ...* Are you coming this evening? – I'm not sure ...
- ◆**sans hésiter** without hesitating

l' **heure** FEM NOUN
  1. hour ◇ *Le trajet dure six heures.* The journey lasts six hours.
  2. time ◇ *Vous avez l'heure?* Have you got the time?
- ◆**Quelle heure est-il?** What time is it?
- ◆**À quelle heure?** What time? ◇ *À quelle heure arrivons-nous?* What time do we arrive?
- ◆**deux heures du matin** 2 o'clock in the morning
- ◆**être à l'heure** to be on time
- ◆**une heure de français** a period of French

heureusement ADVERB
  luckily ◇ *Heureusement qu'il n'a pas été blessé.* Luckily he wasn't hurt.

heureux ADJECTIVE (FEM SING **heureuse**)
  happy

heurter VERB
  to hit

l' **hexagone** MASC NOUN
  hexagon
- ◆**l'Hexagone** France

  ⓘ *France is often referred to as **l'Hexagone** because of its six-sided shape.*

le **hibou** NOUN (PL les **hiboux**)
  owl

hier ADVERB
  yesterday
  ♦ **avant-hier** the day before yesterday

la **hi-fi** NOUN
  stereo
  ♦ **une chaîne hi-fi** a stereo system

hippique ADJECTIVE
  ♦ **un club hippique** a riding centre
  ♦ **un concours hippique** a horse show

l' **hippopotame** MASC NOUN
  hippopotamus

l' **hirondelle** FEM NOUN
  swallow (*bird*)

l' **histoire** FEM NOUN
  ① history ◊ *un cours d'histoire* a
  history lesson
  ② story ◊ *Ce roman raconte l'histoire
  de deux enfants.* This novel tells the
  story of two children.
  ♦ **Ne fais pas d'histoires!** Don't make a
  fuss!

historique ADJECTIVE
  historic ◊ *un monument historique* a
  historic monument

l' **hiver** MASC NOUN
  winter
  ♦ **en hiver** in winter

la **HLM** NOUN (= *habitation à loyer modéré*)
  council flat
  ♦ **des HLM** council housing

le **hockey** NOUN
  hockey
  ♦ **le hockey sur glace** ice hockey

hollandais ADJECTIVE, NOUN
  Dutch
  ♦ **J'apprends le hollandais.** I'm learning
  Dutch.
  ♦ **un Hollandais** a Dutch man
  ♦ **une Hollandaise** a Dutch woman
  ♦ **les Hollandais** the Dutch

la **Hollande** NOUN
  Holland
  ♦ **en Hollande (1)** in Holland
  ♦ **en Hollande (2)** to Holland

le **homard** NOUN
  lobster

homéopathique ADJECTIVE
  homeopathic

l' **hommage** MASC NOUN
  tribute

l' **homme** MASC NOUN
  man
  ♦ **un homme d'affaires** a businessman

homosexuel ADJECTIVE (FEM SING
  homosexuelle)
  homosexual

la **Hongrie** NOUN
  Hungary

hongrois ADJECTIVE
  Hungarian

honnête ADJECTIVE
  honest

l' **honnêteté** FEM NOUN
  honesty

l' **honneur** MASC NOUN
  honour

la **honte** NOUN
  shame ◊ *avoir honte de quelque
  chose* to be ashamed of something

l' **hôpital** MASC NOUN (PL les **hôpitaux**)
  hospital

le **hoquet** NOUN
  ♦ **avoir le hoquet** to have hiccups

l' **horaire** MASC NOUN
  timetable
  ♦ **les horaires de train** the train
  timetable

l' **horizon** MASC NOUN
  horizon

horizontal ADJECTIVE (MASC PL
  horizontaux)
  horizontal

l' **horloge** FEM NOUN
  clock

l' **horreur** FEM NOUN
  horror ◊ *un film d'horreur* a horror
  film
  ♦ **avoir horreur de** to hate ◊ *J'ai horreur
  du chou.* I hate cabbage.

horrible ADJECTIVE
  horrible

hors PREPOSITION
  ♦ **hors de** out of ◊ *Elle est hors de
  danger maintenant.* She's out of
  danger now.
  ♦ **hors taxes** duty-free

le **hors-d'œuvre** NOUN (PL les **hors-
  d'œuvre**)
  starter (*food*)

hospitalier ADJECTIVE (FEM SING
  hospitalière)
  hospitable ◊ *Ils sont très hospitaliers.*
  They're very hospitable.
  ♦ **les services hospitaliers** hospital
  services

l' **hospitalité** FEM NOUN
  hospitality

hostile ADJECTIVE
  hostile

l' **hôte** MASC/FEM NOUN
  ① host ◊ *N'oubliez pas de remercier
  vos hôtes.* Don't forget to thank your
  hosts.

H

☞

[2] guest ◊ *Cette ferme accueille des hôtes payants.* This farm takes paying guests.

l' **hôtel** MASC NOUN
hotel
♦ **l'hôtel de ville** the town hall

l' **hôtesse** FEM NOUN
hostess
♦ **une hôtesse de l'air** a stewardess

la **housse** NOUN
cover ◊ *une housse de couette* a quilt cover ◊ *une housse de téléphone* a phone cover

le **houx** NOUN
holly

l' **huile** FEM NOUN
oil
♦ **l'huile solaire** suntan oil

huit NUMBER
eight ◊ *Il est huit heures du matin.* It's eight in the morning. ◊ *Il a huit ans.* He's eight.
♦ **le huit février** the eighth of February
♦ **dans huit jours** in a week's time

la **huitaine** NOUN
♦ **une huitaine de jours** about a week ◊ *Nous serons de retour dans une huitaine de jours.* We'll be back in about a week.

huitième ADJECTIVE
eighth ◊ *au huitième étage* on the eighth floor

l' **huître** FEM NOUN
oyster

humain ADJECTIVE
see also **humain** NOUN
human

l' **humain** MASC NOUN
see also **humain** ADJECTIVE
human being

l' **humeur** FEM NOUN
mood ◊ *Il est de bonne humeur.* He's

in a good mood. ◊ *Elle était de mauvaise humeur.* She was in a bad mood.

humide ADJECTIVE
damp ◊ *L'herbe est humide.* The grass is damp. ◊ *un climat humide* a damp climate

humilier VERB
to humiliate

humoristique ADJECTIVE
humorous
♦ **des dessins humoristiques** cartoons

l' **humour** MASC NOUN
humour ◊ *Il n'a pas beaucoup d'humour.* He hasn't got much sense of humour.

hurler VERB
to howl

la **hutte** NOUN
hut

hydratant ADJECTIVE
♦ **une crème hydratante** a moisturizing cream

l' **hygiène** FEM NOUN
hygiene

hygiénique ADJECTIVE
hygienic
♦ **une serviette hygiénique** a sanitary towel
♦ **le papier hygiénique** toilet paper

l' **hymne** MASC NOUN
♦ **l'hymne national** the national anthem

l' **hypermarché** MASC NOUN
hypermarket

hypermétrope ADJECTIVE
long-sighted

hypocrite ADJECTIVE
hypocritical ◊ *Il est hypocrite.* He's a hypocrite.

l' **hypothèse** FEM NOUN
hypothesis

I

l' **iceberg** MASC NOUN
  iceberg

ici ADVERB
  here ◊ *Les assiettes sont ici.* The
  plates are here.
  ◆ **La mer monte parfois jusqu'ici.** The
  sea sometimes comes in as far as
  this.
  ◆ **Jusqu'ici nous n'avons eu aucun
  problème avec la voiture.** So far we
  haven't had any problems with the
  car.

l' **icône** FEM NOUN
  icon

idéal ADJECTIVE (MASC PL **idéaux**)
  ideal ◊ *C'est l'endroit idéal pour faire
  un pique-nique.* It's an ideal place to
  have a picnic.

l' **idée** FEM NOUN
  idea ◊ *C'est une bonne idée.* It's a
  good idea.

identifier VERB
  to identify ◊ *La police a identifié le
  meurtrier.* The police have identified
  the murderer.

identique ADJECTIVE
  identical ◊ *Ils ont obtenu des
  résultats identiques.* They obtained
  identical results.

l' **identité** FEM NOUN
  identity
  ◆ **une pièce d'identité** a form of
  identification ◊ *Avez-vous une pièce
  d'identité?* Have you got any form of
  identification?

idiot ADJECTIVE
  see also **idiot** NOUN
  [1] stupid ◊ *une plaisanterie idiote* a
  stupid joke
  [2] silly ◊ *Ne sois pas idiot!* Don't be
  silly!

l' **idiot** MASC NOUN
  see also **idiot** ADJECTIVE
  idiot

l' **idiote** FEM NOUN
  idiot

ignoble ADJECTIVE
  horrible ◊ *Il a été ignoble avec elle.*
  He was horrible to her.

ignorant ADJECTIVE
  ignorant

ignorer VERB
  [1] not to know ◊ *J'ignore son nom.* I
  don't know his name.

  [2] to ignore ◊ *Il m'a complètement
  ignoré.* He completely ignored me.

il PRONOUN
  [1] he ◊ *Il est parti ce matin de bonne
  heure.* He left early this morning.
  [2] it ◊ *Méfie-toi de ce chien: il mord.*
  Be careful of that dog: it bites. ◊ *Il
  pleut.* It's raining.

l' **île** FEM NOUN
  island
  ◆ **les îles Anglo-Normandes** the Channel
  Islands
  ◆ **les îles Britanniques** the British Isles
  ◆ **les îles Féroé** the Faroe Islands

illégal ADJECTIVE (MASC PL **illégaux**)
  illegal

illimité ADJECTIVE
  unlimited

illisible ADJECTIVE
  illegible ◊ *une écriture illisible*
  illegible handwriting

illuminer VERB
  to floodlight ◊ *Le château est
  illuminé tous les soirs pendant l'été.*
  The castle is floodlit every night in
  the summer.

l' **illusion** FEM NOUN
  illusion ◊ *Tu te fais des illusions!*
  You're deluding yourself!

l' **illustration** FEM NOUN
  illustration

illustré ADJECTIVE
  see also **illustré** NOUN
  illustrated

l' **illustré** MASC NOUN
  see also **illustré** ADJECTIVE
  comic

illustrer VERB
  to illustrate ◊ *Vous pouvez illustrer
  votre rédaction avec des exemples.*
  You may illustrate your essay with
  examples.

ils PRONOUN
  they ◊ *Ils nous ont appelés hier soir.*
  They phoned us last night.

l' **image** FEM NOUN
  picture ◊ *Les films donnent une
  fausse image de l'Amérique.* Films
  give a false picture of America.

l' **imagination** FEM NOUN
  imagination ◊ *Elle a beaucoup
  d'imagination.* She's got a vivid
  imagination.

imaginer VERB

to imagine

l'**imbécile** MASC/FEM NOUN
idiot

l'**imitation** FEM NOUN
imitation

imiter VERB
to imitate

l'**immatriculation** FEM NOUN
♦**une plaque d'immatriculation** a numberplate (of car)

l'**immédiat** MASC NOUN
♦**dans l'immédiat** for the moment ◊ *Je n'ai pas besoin de ce livre dans l'immédiat.* I don't need this book for the moment.

immédiatement ADVERB
immediately

immense ADJECTIVE
[1] huge ◊ *une immense fortune* a huge fortune
[2] tremendous ◊ *un immense soulagement* a tremendous relief

l'**immeuble** MASC NOUN
block of flats

l'**immigration** FEM NOUN
immigration

l'**immigré** MASC NOUN
immigrant

l'**immigrée** FEM NOUN
immigrant

immobile ADJECTIVE
motionless

immobilier ADJECTIVE (FEM SING **immobilière**)
♦**une agence immobilière** an estate agent's

immobiliser VERB
to immobilize

immunisé ADJECTIVE
immunized

l'**impact** MASC NOUN
impact

impair ADJECTIVE
odd ◊ *un nombre impair* an odd number

impardonnable ADJECTIVE
unforgivable

l'**impasse** FEM NOUN
cul-de-sac

l'**impatience** FEM NOUN
impatience

impatient ADJECTIVE
impatient

impeccable ADJECTIVE
[1] immaculate ◊ *Elle est toujours impeccable.* She's always immaculate.
[2] perfect ◊ *Il a fait un travail impeccable.* He's done a perfect job. ◊ *C'est impeccable!* That's perfect!

l'**imper** MASC NOUN (*informal*)
mac

l'**impératif** MASC NOUN
imperative

l'**impératrice** FEM NOUN
empress

l'**imperméable** MASC NOUN
raincoat

impertinent ADJECTIVE
cheeky ◊ *Ne sois pas impertinent!* Don't be cheeky!

impitoyable ADJECTIVE
merciless

impliquer VERB
to mean ◊ *Si tu vas à l'université, ça implique que tu vas devoir nous quitter.* If you go to university, it'll mean that you have to leave us.
♦**être impliqué dans** to be involved in ◊ *Il est impliqué dans un scandale financier.* He's involved in a financial scandal.

impoli ADJECTIVE
rude

l'**importance** FEM NOUN
importance ◊ *C'est sans importance.* It doesn't matter.

important ADJECTIVE
[1] important ◊ *un rôle important* an important role
[2] considerable ◊ *une somme importante* a considerable sum

l'**importation** FEM NOUN
import ◊ *Les importations de pétrole ont baissé.* Oil imports have fallen.

importer VERB
see also **n'importe**
[1] to import (*goods*)
[2] to matter ◊ *Peu importe.* It doesn't matter.

imposant ADJECTIVE
imposing

imposer VERB
to impose
♦**imposer quelque chose à quelqu'un** to make somebody do something

impossible ADJECTIVE
see also **impossible** NOUN
impossible

l'**impossible** MASC NOUN
see also **impossible** ADJECTIVE
♦**Nous ferons l'impossible pour finir à temps.** We'll do our utmost to finish on time.

l'**impôt** MASC NOUN

tax

imprécis ADJECTIVE
imprecise

l'**impression** FEM NOUN
impression ◊ *Il a fait bonne impression à ma mère.* He made a good impression on my mother.

impressionnant ADJECTIVE
impressive

impressionner VERB
to impress

imprévisible ADJECTIVE
unpredictable

imprévu ADJECTIVE
unexpected

l'**imprimante** FEM NOUN
printer (*for computer*)

imprimé ADJECTIVE
printed ◊ *un tissu imprimé* a printed fabric ◊ *C'est imprimé en grandes lettres.* It's printed in large letters.

imprimer VERB
to print

impropre ADJECTIVE
♦**impropre à la consommation** unfit for human consumption

improviser VERB
to improvise

improviste ADVERB
♦**arriver à l'improviste** to arrive unexpectedly

l'**imprudence** FEM NOUN
carelessness
♦**Ne fais pas d'imprudences!** Don't do anything silly!

imprudent ADJECTIVE
① unwise ◊ *Il serait imprudent de prendre la voiture aujourd'hui.* It would be unwise to take the car today.
② careless ◊ *un conducteur imprudent* a careless driver

impuissant ADJECTIVE
helpless ◊ *Elle se sentait complètement impuissante.* She felt completely helpless.

impulsif ADJECTIVE (FEM SING **impulsive**)
impulsive

inabordable ADJECTIVE
prohibitive ◊ *des prix inabordables* prohibitive prices

inaccessible ADJECTIVE
inaccessible ◊ *Cette plage est inaccessible par la route.* This beach is inaccessible by road.

inachevé ADJECTIVE
unfinished

inadmissible ADJECTIVE
intolerable ◊ *Ce type de comportement est inadmissible!* This sort of behaviour is intolerable!

inanimé ADJECTIVE
unconscious ◊ *On l'a retrouvé inanimé sur la route.* He was found unconscious on the road.

inaperçu ADJECTIVE
♦**passer inaperçu** to go unnoticed

inattendu ADJECTIVE
unexpected

l'**inattention** FEM NOUN
♦**une faute d'inattention** a careless mistake

inaugurer VERB
to open (*an exhibition*)

incapable ADJECTIVE
incapable ◊ *être incapable de faire quelque chose* to be incapable of doing something

incassable ADJECTIVE
unbreakable

l'**incendie** MASC NOUN
fire ◊ *un incendie de forêt* a forest fire

incertain ADJECTIVE
① uncertain ◊ *Son avenir est encore incertain.* His future is still uncertain.
② unsettled ◊ *Le temps est incertain.* The weather is unsettled.

l'**incident** MASC NOUN
incident

inciter VERB
♦**inciter quelqu'un à faire quelque chose** to encourage somebody to do something ◊ *J'ai incité mes parents à partir en voyage.* I encouraged my parents to go on a trip.

inclure VERB
to enclose ◊ *Veuillez inclure une enveloppe timbrée libellée à votre adresse.* Please enclose a stamped addressed envelope.
♦**jusqu'au dix mars inclus** until 10th March inclusive

incohérent ADJECTIVE
incoherent

incollable ADJECTIVE
♦**être incollable sur quelque chose** (*informal*) to know everything there is to know about something
♦**le riz incollable** non-stick rice

incolore ADJECTIVE
colourless

incompétent ADJECTIVE
incompetent

incompris ADJECTIVE
misunderstood

I

l' **inconnu** MASC NOUN
  stranger ◊ *Ne parle pas à des
  inconnus.* Don't speak to strangers.
  ♦ **l'inconnu** the unknown ◊ *la peur de
  l'inconnu* the fear of the unknown

l' **inconnue** FEM NOUN
  stranger

inconsciemment ADVERB
  unconsciously

inconscient ADJECTIVE
  unconscious ◊ *Il est resté inconscient
  quelques minutes.* He was
  unconscious for several minutes.

incontestable ADJECTIVE
  indisputable

incontournable ADJECTIVE
  inevitable ◊ *l'incontournable petite
  robe noire* the inevitable little black
  dress

l' **inconvénient** MASC NOUN
  disadvantage
  ♦ **si vous n'y voyez pas d'inconvénient**
  if you have no objection

incorrect ADJECTIVE
  ① incorrect ◊ *une réponse incorrecte*
  an incorrect answer
  ② rude ◊ *Il a été incorrect avec la
  voisine.* He was rude to the woman
  next door.

incroyable ADJECTIVE
  incredible

inculper VERB
  ♦ **inculper de** to charge with ◊ *Il a été
  inculpé de meurtre.* He was charged
  with murder.

l' **Inde** FEM NOUN
  India

indécis ADJECTIVE
  ① indecisive ◊ *Il est constamment
  indécis.* He's always indecisive.
  ② undecided ◊ *Je suis encore
  indécis.* I'm still undecided.

indéfiniment ADVERB
  indefinitely

indélicat ADJECTIVE
  tactless

indemne ADJECTIVE
  unharmed ◊ *Il s'en est sorti
  indemne.* He escaped unharmed.

indemniser VERB
  to compensate ◊ *Les victimes
  demandent maintenant à être
  indemnisées.* The victims are now
  demanding compensation.

indépendamment ADVERB
  independently
  ♦ **indépendamment de** irrespective of
  ◊ *Les allocations familiales sont
  versées indépendamment des
  revenus.* Child benefit is given
  irrespective of income.

l' **indépendance** FEM NOUN
  independence

indépendant ADJECTIVE
  independent

l' **index** MASC NOUN
  ① index finger
  ② index (*in book*)

indicatif ADJECTIVE (FEM SING **indicative**)
  │ see also **indicatif** NOUN │
  ♦ **à titre indicatif** for your information

l' **indicatif** MASC NOUN
  │ see also **indicatif** ADJECTIVE │
  ① dialling code
  ② indicative (*of verb*)
  ③ theme tune (*of TV programme*)

les **indications** FEM NOUN
  instructions ◊ *Il suffit de suivre les
  indications.* You just have to follow
  the instructions.

l' **indice** MASC NOUN
  clue ◊ *La police cherche des indices.*
  The police are looking for clues.

indien ADJECTIVE, NOUN (FEM SING **indienne**)
  Indian
  ♦ **un Indien** an Indian (*man*)
  ♦ **une Indienne** an Indian (*woman*)

l' **indifférence** FEM NOUN
  indifference

indifférent ADJECTIVE
  indifferent

l' **indigène** MASC/FEM NOUN
  native

indigeste ADJECTIVE
  indigestible

l' **indigestion** FEM NOUN
  indigestion

indigne ADJECTIVE
  unworthy

indigner VERB
  ♦ **s'indigner de quelque chose** to get
  indignant about something

indiqué ADJECTIVE
  advisable ◊ *Ce n'est pas très indiqué.*
  It's not really advisable.

indiquer VERB
  to point out ◊ *Il m'a indiqué la
  mairie.* He pointed out the town hall.

indirect ADJECTIVE
  indirect

indiscipliné ADJECTIVE
  unruly

indiscret ADJECTIVE (FEM SING **indiscrète**)
  indiscreet

indispensable ADJECTIVE

indispensable

indisposé ADJECTIVE
indisposed
♦ **être indisposée** to be having one's period

l' **individu** MASC NOUN
individual

individuel ADJECTIVE (FEM SING **individuelle**)
individual ◇ *servi en portions individuelles* served in individual portions
♦ **Vous aurez une chambre individuelle.** You'll have a room of your own.

indolore ADJECTIVE
painless

l' **Indonésie** FEM NOUN
Indonesia

indulgent ADJECTIVE
indulgent
♦ **Elle est trop indulgente avec son fils.** She's not firm enough with her son.

l' **industrie** FEM NOUN
industry

industriel ADJECTIVE (FEM SING **industrielle**)
see also **industriel** NOUN
industrial

l' **industriel** MASC NOUN
see also **industriel** ADJECTIVE
industrialist

inédit ADJECTIVE
unpublished

inefficace ADJECTIVE
[1] ineffective (*treatment*)
[2] inefficient ◇ *un service de transports publics inefficace* an inefficient public transport system

inégal ADJECTIVE (MASC PL **inégaux**)
[1] unequal ◇ *un combat inégal* an unequal struggle
[2] uneven ◇ *la qualité est inégale* the quality varies

inévitable ADJECTIVE
unavoidable
♦ **C'était inévitable!** That was bound to happen!

inexact ADJECTIVE
inaccurate

in extremis ADVERB
♦ **Il a réussi à attraper son train in extremis.** He just managed to catch his train.
♦ **Ils ont évité un accident in extremis.** They avoided an accident by the skin of their teeth.

l' **infarctus** MASC NOUN
coronary

infatigable ADJECTIVE

indefatigable ◇ *Il est infatigable.* He's indefatigable.

infect ADJECTIVE
revolting (*meal*)

s' **infecter** VERB
to go septic ◇ *La plaie s'est infectée.* The wound has gone septic.

l' **infection** FEM NOUN
infection

inférieur ADJECTIVE
lower ◇ *les membres inférieurs* the lower limbs ◇ *C'est moins cher, mais de qualité inférieure.* It's cheaper but of lower quality.

infernal ADJECTIVE (MASC PL **infernaux**)
terrible ◇ *Ils faisaient un bruit infernal.* They were making a terrible noise.

l' **infini** MASC NOUN
♦ **à l'infini** indefinitely ◇ *On pourrait en parler à l'infini.* We could discuss this indefinitely.

l' **infinitif** MASC NOUN
infinitive

l' **infirme** MASC/FEM NOUN
disabled person

l' **infirmerie** FEM NOUN
medical room ◇ *Elle est à l'infirmerie.* She's in the medical room.

l' **infirmier** MASC NOUN
nurse

l' **infirmière** FEM NOUN
nurse

inflammable ADJECTIVE
inflammable

l' **influence** FEM NOUN
influence

influencer VERB
to influence

l' **informaticien** MASC NOUN
computer scientist

l' **informaticienne** FEM NOUN
computer scientist

les **informations** FEM NOUN
[1] news (*on TV*) ◇ *les informations de vingt heures* the 8 o'clock news
[2] information ◇ *Je voudrais quelques informations, s'il vous plaît.* I'd like some information, please.
♦ **une information** a piece of information

l' **informatique** FEM NOUN
computing

informer VERB
to inform
♦ **s'informer** to find out ◇ *Je ne connais pas les heures de fermeture, mais je*

☞

vais m'informer. I don't know when they close, but I'm going to find out.

infuser VERB
[1] to brew (*tea*)
[2] to infuse (*herbal tea*)

l' **infusion** FEM NOUN
herbal tea

l' **ingénieur** MASC NOUN
engineer

ingrat ADJECTIVE
ungrateful

l' **ingrédient** MASC NOUN
ingredient

inhabituel ADJECTIVE (FEM SING **inhabituelle**)
unusual

inhumain ADJECTIVE
inhuman

initial ADJECTIVE (MASC PL **initiaux**)
initial

l' **initiale** FEM NOUN
initial

l' **initiation** FEM NOUN
introduction ◊ *un stage d'initiation à la planche à voile* an introductory course in windsurfing

l' **initiative** FEM NOUN
initiative ◊ *avoir de l'initiative* to have initiative

injecter VERB
to inject

l' **injection** FEM NOUN
injection

l' **injure** FEM NOUN
[1] insult ◊ *Il a pris ça comme une injure.* He took this as an insult.
[2] abuse ◊ *lancer des injures à quelqu'un* to hurl abuse at somebody

injurier VERB
to insult

injurieux ADJECTIVE (FEM SING **injurieuse**)
abusive (*language*)

injuste ADJECTIVE
unfair

innocent ADJECTIVE
innocent

innombrable ADJECTIVE
innumerable

innover VERB
to break new ground

inoccupé ADJECTIVE
empty ◊ *un appartement inoccupé* an empty flat

inoffensif ADJECTIVE (FEM SING **inoffensive**)
harmless

l' **inondation** FEM NOUN
flood

inoubliable ADJECTIVE
unforgettable

inoxydable ADJECTIVE
♦*l'acier inoxydable* stainless steel

inquiet ADJECTIVE (FEM SING **inquiète**)
worried

inquiétant ADJECTIVE
worrying

s' **inquiéter** VERB
to worry ◊ *Ne t'inquiète pas!* Don't worry!

l' **inquiétude** FEM NOUN
anxiety

insatisfait ADJECTIVE
dissatisfied

l' **inscription** FEM NOUN
registration (*for school, course*)

s' **inscrire** VERB
♦*s'inscrire à* (1) to join ◊ *Je me suis inscrit au club de tennis.* I've joined the tennis club.
♦*s'inscrire à* (2) to register ◊ *N'attends pas trop pour t'inscrire à la fac.* Don't leave it too long to register at the university.

l' **insecte** MASC NOUN
insect

insensible ADJECTIVE
insensitive ◊ *Il la trouve insensible.* He thinks she's insensitive.

l' **insigne** MASC NOUN
badge

insignifiant ADJECTIVE
insignificant

insister VERB
to insist
♦*N'insiste pas!* Don't keep on!

l' **insolation** FEM NOUN
sunstroke

insolent ADJECTIVE
cheeky

insouciant ADJECTIVE
carefree

insoutenable ADJECTIVE
unbearable ◊ *une douleur insoutenable* an unbearable pain

inspecter VERB
to inspect

l' **inspecteur** MASC NOUN
inspector

l' **inspection** FEM NOUN
inspection

l' **inspectrice** FEM NOUN
inspector

inspirer VERB
[1] to inspire

♦ **s'inspirer de** to take one's inspiration from ◊ *Le peintre s'est inspiré d'un poème.* The painter took his inspiration from a poem.
[2] to breathe in ◊ *Inspirez! Expirez!* Breathe in! Breathe out!

instable ADJECTIVE
[1] unsteady (*piece of furniture*)
[2] unstable (*person*)

les **installations** FEM NOUN
facilities ◊ *Cet appartement est pourvu de toutes les installations modernes.* This flat has all modern facilities.

installer VERB
[1] to put up (*shelves*)
[2] to install (*gas, telephone*)
♦ **s'installer** to settle in ◊ *Nous nous sommes installés dans notre nouvel appartement.* We've settled into our new flat.
♦ **Installez-vous, je vous en prie.** Have a seat please.

l'**instant** MASC NOUN
moment ◊ *dans un instant* in a moment ◊ *Le dîner sera prêt dans un instant.* Dinner will be ready in a moment. ◊ *pour l'instant* for the moment

instantané ADJECTIVE
instant ◊ *du café instantané* instant coffee

l'**instinct** MASC NOUN
instinct

l'**institut** MASC NOUN
institute

l'**instituteur** MASC NOUN
primary school teacher

l'**institution** FEM NOUN
institution

l'**institutrice** FEM NOUN
primary school teacher

l'**instruction** FEM NOUN
[1] instruction ◊ *J'ai suivi ses instructions.* I followed his instructions.
[2] education ◊ *Il n'a pas beaucoup d'instruction.* He's not very well-educated.

s'**instruire** VERB
to educate oneself

instruit ADJECTIVE
educated

l'**instrument** MASC NOUN
instrument ◊ *un instrument de musique* a musical instrument

insuffisant ADJECTIVE
insufficient

♦ **"travail insuffisant"** (*on school report*) "must make more effort"

l'**insuline** FEM NOUN
insulin

insultant ADJECTIVE
insulting ◊ *Il s'est montré insultant avec elle.* He was insulting to her.

l'**insulte** FEM NOUN
insult

insulter VERB
to insult

insupportable ADJECTIVE
unbearable

intact ADJECTIVE
intact

intégral ADJECTIVE (MASC PL **intégraux**)
♦ **le texte intégral** unabridged version
♦ **un remboursement intégral** a full refund

l'**intégrisme** MASC NOUN
fundamentalism

l'**intelligence** FEM NOUN
intelligence

intelligent ADJECTIVE
intelligent

intense ADJECTIVE
intense

intensif ADJECTIVE (FEM SING **intensive**)
intensive
♦ **un cours intensif** a crash course

l'**intention** FEM NOUN
intention
♦ **avoir l'intention de faire quelque chose** to intend to do something ◊ *J'ai l'intention de lui en parler.* I intend to speak to him about it.

l'**interdiction** FEM NOUN
♦ **"interdiction de stationner"** "no parking"
♦ **"interdiction de fumer"** "no smoking"

interdire VERB
to forbid ◊ *Ses parents lui ont interdit de sortir.* His parents have forbidden him to go out.

interdit ADJECTIVE
forbidden ◊ *Il est interdit de fumer dans les couloirs.* Smoking in the corridors is forbidden.

intéressant ADJECTIVE
interesting ◊ *un livre intéressant* an interesting book
♦ **On lui a fait une offre intéressante.** They made him an attractive offer.
♦ **On trouve des CD à des prix très intéressants dans ce magasin.** You can get very cheap CDs in this shop.

intéresser VERB
to interest

♦ **s'intéresser à** to be interested in ◊ *Est-ce que vous vous intéressez à la politique?* Are you interested in politics?

l' **intérêt** MASC NOUN
interest
♦ **avoir intérêt à faire quelque chose** to do well to do something ◊ *Tu as intérêt à te dépêcher si tu veux prendre le train de dix heures.* You'd better hurry up if you want to catch the 10 o'clock train.

l' **intérieur** MASC NOUN
inside ◊ *Il fait plus frais à l'intérieur de la maison.* It's cooler inside the house.

l' **interlocuteur** MASC NOUN
♦ **son interlocuteur** the man he's speaking to

l' **interlocutrice** FEM NOUN
♦ **son interlocutrice** the woman he's speaking to

l' **intermédiaire** MASC NOUN
intermediary
♦ **par l'intermédiaire de** through ◊ *Je l'ai rencontré par l'intermédiaire de sa sœur.* I met him through his sister.

l' **internat** MASC NOUN
boarding school

international ADJECTIVE (MASC PL **internationaux**)
international

l' **internaute** MASC/FEM NOUN
internet user

l' **interne** MASC/FEM NOUN
boarder

l' **Internet** MASC NOUN
internet ◊ *sur Internet* on the internet

l' **interphone** MASC NOUN
intercom

l' **interprète** MASC/FEM NOUN
interpreter

interpréter VERB
to interpret

interrogatif ADJECTIVE (FEM SING **interrogative**)
interrogative

l' **interrogation** FEM NOUN
1 question
2 test ◊ *une interrogation écrite* a written test ◊ *une interrogation orale* an oral test

l' **interrogatoire** MASC NOUN
questioning
♦ **C'est un interrogatoire ou quoi?** Am I being cross-examined?

interroger VERB
to question

interrompre VERB
to interrupt

l' **interrupteur** MASC NOUN
switch

l' **interruption** FEM NOUN
interruption
♦ **sans interruption** without stopping ◊ *Il a parlé pendant deux heures sans interruption.* He spoke for two hours without stopping.

l' **intervalle** MASC NOUN
interval
♦ **dans l'intervalle** in the meantime

intervenir VERB
1 to intervene
2 to take action ◊ *La police est intervenue.* The police took action.

l' **intervention** FEM NOUN
intervention ◊ *une intervention militaire* a military intervention
♦ **une intervention chirurgicale** a surgical operation

l' **interview** FEM NOUN
interview (*on radio, TV*)

l' **intestin** MASC NOUN
intestine

intime ADJECTIVE
intimate
♦ **un journal intime** a diary

intimider VERB
to intimidate

l' **intimité** FEM NOUN
♦ **dans l'intimité** in private ◊ *Ce que vous faites dans l'intimité ne m'intéresse pas.* What you do in private doesn't interest me.
♦ **Le mariage a eu lieu dans l'intimité.** The wedding ceremony was private.

intitulé ADJECTIVE
entitled

intolérable ADJECTIVE
intolerable

l' **intoxication** FEM NOUN
♦ **une intoxication alimentaire** food poisoning

l' **Intranet** MASC NOUN
Intranet

intransigeant ADJECTIVE
uncompromising

l' **intrigue** FEM NOUN
plot (*of book, film*)

l' **introduction** FEM NOUN
introduction

introduire VERB
to introduce

l' **intuition** FEM NOUN
intuition

inusable ADJECTIVE

hard-wearing

inutile ADJECTIVE
useless

l' **invalide** MASC/FEM NOUN
disabled person

l' **invasion** FEM NOUN
invasion

inventer VERB
1 to invent
2 to make up ◊ *inventer une excuse*
to make up an excuse

l' **inventeur** MASC NOUN
inventor

l' **invention** FEM NOUN
invention

inverse ADJECTIVE
see also **inverse** NOUN
◆ dans l'ordre inverse in reverse order
◆ en sens inverse in the opposite
direction

l' **inverse** MASC NOUN
see also **inverse** ADJECTIVE
reverse
◆ Tu t'es trompé, c'est l'inverse. You've
got it wrong, it's the other way
round.

l' **investissement** MASC NOUN
investment

invisible ADJECTIVE
invisible

l' **invitation** FEM NOUN
invitation

l' **invité** MASC NOUN
guest

l' **invitée** FEM NOUN
guest

inviter VERB
to invite

involontaire ADJECTIVE
unintentional ◊ *C'était tout à fait
involontaire.* It was quite
unintentional.

invraisemblable ADJECTIVE
unlikely ◊ *une histoire
invraisemblable* an implausible
story

ira, irai, iraient, irais VERB see **aller**
◆ J'irai demain au supermarché. I'll go
to the supermarket tomorrow.

l' **Irak** MASC NOUN
Iraq

l' **Iran** MASC NOUN
Iran

iras, irez VERB see **aller**

irlandais ADJECTIVE, NOUN (FEM SING
irlandaise)
Irish

◆ un Irlandais an Irishman
◆ une Irlandaise an Irishwoman
◆ les Irlandais the Irish

l' **Irlande** FEM NOUN
Ireland
◆ en Irlande (1) in Ireland
◆ en Irlande (2) to Ireland
◆ la République d'Irlande the Irish
Republic
◆ l'Irlande du Nord Northern Ireland

l' **ironie** FEM NOUN
irony

ironique ADJECTIVE
ironical

irons, iront VERB see **aller**
◆ Nous irons à la plage cet après-midi.
We'll go to the beach this afternoon.

irrationnel ADJECTIVE (FEM SING
irrationnelle)
irrational

irréel ADJECTIVE (FEM SING **irréelle**)
unreal

irrégulier ADJECTIVE (FEM SING **irrégulière**)
irregular

irrésistible ADJECTIVE
irresistible

irritable ADJECTIVE
irritable

irriter VERB
to irritate

islamique ADJECTIVE
Islamic

l' **Islande** FEM NOUN
Iceland

isolé ADJECTIVE
isolated ◊ *une ferme isolée* an
isolated farm

Israël MASC NOUN
Israel

israélien ADJECTIVE, NOUN (FEM SING
israélienne)
Israeli
◆ un Israélien an Israeli (*man*)
◆ une Israélienne an Israeli (*woman*)
◆ les Israéliens the Israelis

israélite ADJECTIVE
Jewish

l' **issue** FEM NOUN
◆ une voie sans issue a dead end
◆ l'issue de secours emergency exit

l' **Italie** FEM NOUN
Italy
◆ en Italie (1) in Italy
◆ en Italie (2) to Italy

italien ADJECTIVE, NOUN (FEM SING **italienne**)
Italian ◊ *J'apprends l'italien.* I'm
learning Italian.
◆ un Italien an Italian (*man*)

♦ **une Italienne** an Italian (*woman*)
♦ **les Italiens** the Italians

l'**itinéraire** MASC NOUN
route

l'**IUT** MASC NOUN (= *Institut universitaire de technologie*)

institute of technology (*at university level*)

ivre ADJECTIVE
drunk

l'**ivrogne** MASC/FEM NOUN
drunkard

J

j' PRONOUN *see* **je**

la **jalousie** NOUN
　jealousy

jaloux ADJECTIVE (FEM SING **jalouse**)
　jealous

jamais ADVERB
　1 never ◇ *Tu vas souvent au cinéma?
　– Non, jamais.* Do you go to the cinema
　often? – No, never. ◇ *Il ne boit jamais
　d'alcool.* He never drinks alcohol.
　2 ever

> *Phrases with **jamais** meaning **ever**
> are used with a verb in the
> subjunctive.*

　◇ *C'est la plus belle chose que j'aie
　jamais vue.* It's the most beautiful
　thing I've ever seen.

la **jambe** NOUN
　leg

le **jambon** NOUN
　ham
　♦ **le jambon cru** Parma ham

le **jambonneau** NOUN (PL les **jambonneaux**)
　knuckle of ham

janvier MASC NOUN
　January
　♦ **en janvier** in January

le **Japon** NOUN
　Japan
　♦ **au Japon (1)** in Japan
　♦ **au Japon (2)** to Japan

japonais ADJECTIVE, NOUN (FEM SING
　japonaise)
　Japanese ◇ *Elle parle japonais.* She
　speaks Japanese.
　♦ **un Japonais** a Japanese (*man*)
　♦ **une Japonaise** a Japanese (*woman*)
　♦ **les Japonais** the Japanese

le **jardin** NOUN
　garden ◇ *un jardin potager* a
　vegetable garden

le **jardinage** NOUN
　gardening

le **jardinier** NOUN
　gardener

la **jardinière** NOUN
　gardener

jaune ADJECTIVE
　| *see also* **jaune** NOUN |
　yellow

le **jaune** NOUN
　| *see also* **jaune** ADJECTIVE |
　yellow
　♦ **un jaune d'œuf** an egg yolk

jaunir VERB
　to turn yellow

la **jaunisse** NOUN
　jaundice

Javel NOUN
　♦ **l'eau de Javel** bleach

le **jazz** NOUN
　jazz

J.-C. ABBREVIATION (= *Jésus-Christ*)
　♦ **44 avant J.-C.** 44 BC
　♦ **115 après J.-C.** 115 AD

je PRONOUN

> **je** *changes to **j'** before a vowel and
> most words beginning with "h".*

　I ◇ *Je t'appellerai ce soir.* I'll phone
　you this evening. ◇ *J'arrive!* I'm
　coming! ◇ *J'hésite.* I'm not sure.

le **jean** NOUN
　jeans PL

la **jeannette** NOUN
　Brownie ◇ *Elle est jeannette.* She's a
　Brownie.

Jésus-Christ MASC NOUN
　Jesus Christ

le **jet** NOUN
　1 jet (*of water*)
　♦ **un jet d'eau** a fountain
　2 jet plane

jetable ADJECTIVE
　disposable

la **jetée** NOUN
　jetty

jeter VERB
　1 to throw ◇ *Il a jeté son sac sur le
　lit.* He threw his bag onto the bed.
　2 to throw away ◇ *Ils ne jettent
　jamais rien.* They never throw
　anything away.
　♦ **jeter un coup d'œil** to have a look

le **jeton** NOUN
　counter (*in board game*)

le **jeu** NOUN (PL les **jeux**)
　game ◇ *Je n'aime pas les jeux de
　société.* I don't like board games.
　♦ **un jeu d'arcade** a video game
　♦ **un jeu de cartes (1)** a pack of cards
　♦ **un jeu de cartes (2)** a card game
　♦ **un jeu de mots** a pun
　♦ **un jeu électronique** an electronic
　game
　♦ **les jeux vidéo** video games
　♦ **en jeu** at stake ◇ *Des vies humaines
　sont en jeu.* Human lives are at stake.

le **jeudi** NOUN

☞

[1] Thursday ◊ *Aujourd'hui, nous sommes jeudi.* It's Thursday today.
[2] on Thursday ◊ *Il arrivera jeudi matin.* He's arriving on Thursday morning.
- **le jeudi** on Thursdays ◊ *Le musée est fermé le jeudi.* The museum is closed on Thursdays.
- **tous les jeudis** every Thursday
- **jeudi dernier** last Thursday
- **jeudi prochain** next Thursday

jeun
- **à jeun** ADVERB
on an empty stomach ◊ *à prendre à jeun* to be taken on an empty stomach ◊ *Il faut être à jeun pour la prise de sang.* You mustn't have eaten anything before giving a blood sample.

jeune ADJECTIVE
see also **jeune** NOUN
young ◊ *un jeune homme* a young man ◊ *une jeune femme* a young woman
- **une jeune fille** a girl

jeune NOUN
see also **jeune** ADJECTIVE
young person ◊ *les jeunes* young people

la **jeunesse** NOUN
youth

le **job** NOUN (*informal*)
job

le **jogging** NOUN
[1] jogging ◊ *Il fait du jogging.* He goes jogging.
[2] tracksuit ◊ *Je me suis acheté un jogging rose.* I bought myself a pink tracksuit.

la **joie** NOUN
joy

joindre VERB
[1] to put together ◊ *On va joindre les deux tables.* We're going to put the two tables together.
[2] to contact ◊ *Vous pouvez le joindre chez lui.* You can contact him at home.

joint ADJECTIVE
- **une pièce jointe** an enclosure (*in letter*)

joli ADJECTIVE
pretty

le **jonc** NOUN
rush

la **jonquille** NOUN
daffodil

la **joue** NOUN
cheek

jouer VERB
[1] to play ◊ *Elle est allée jouer avec les petits voisins.* She's gone to play with the children next door.
- **jouer de** to play (*instrument*) ◊ *Il joue de la guitare et du piano.* He plays the guitar and the piano.
- **jouer à** to play (*sport, game*) ◊ *Elle joue au tennis.* She plays tennis. ◊ *jouer aux cartes* to play cards
[2] to act ◊ *Je trouve qu'il joue très bien dans ce film.* I think he acts very well in this film.
- **On joue Hamlet au Théâtre de la Ville.** Hamlet is on at the Théâtre de la Ville.

le **jouet** NOUN
toy

le **joueur** NOUN
player
- **être mauvais joueur** to be a bad loser

la **joueuse** NOUN
player

le **jour** NOUN
day ◊ *J'ai passé trois jours chez mes cousins.* I stayed with my cousins for three days.
- **Il fait jour.** It's daylight.
- **mettre quelque chose à jour** to update something
- **le jour de l'An** New Year's Day
- **un jour de congé** a day off
- **un jour férié** a public holiday
- **dans huit jours** in a week
- **dans quinze jours** in a fortnight

le **journal** NOUN (PL les **journaux**)
[1] newspaper
- **le journal télévisé** the television news
[2] diary ◊ *Elle tient un journal depuis l'âge de douze ans.* She has been keeping a diary since she was 12.

journalier ADJECTIVE (FEM SING **journalière**)
daily

le **journalisme** NOUN
journalism

le/la **journaliste** NOUN
journalist ◊ *Elle est journaliste.* She's a journalist.

la **journée** NOUN
day

joyeux ADJECTIVE (FEM SING **joyeuse**)
happy
- **Joyeux anniversaire!** Happy birthday!
- **Joyeux Noël!** Merry Christmas!

le **judo** NOUN
judo

le **juge** NOUN
judge

juger VERB

to judge

juif ADJECTIVE (FEM SING **juive**)
  Jewish ◊ *la cuisine juive* Jewish
  cooking
♦ **un juif** a Jew (*man*)
♦ **une juive** a Jew (*woman*)

juillet MASC NOUN
  July
♦ **en juillet** in July

juin MASC NOUN
  June
♦ **en juin** in June

le **jumeau** NOUN (PL les **jumeaux**)
  twin

jumeler VERB
  to twin ◊ *Saint-Brieuc est jumelée
  avec Aberystwyth.* Saint-Brieuc is
  twinned with Aberystwyth.

la **jumelle** NOUN
  twin

les **jumelles** FEM NOUN
  binoculars

la **jument** NOUN
  mare

la **jungle** NOUN
  jungle

la **jupe** NOUN
  skirt

jurer VERB
  to swear ◊ *Je jure que c'est vrai!* I
  swear it's true!

juridique ADJECTIVE
  legal

le **jury** NOUN
  jury

le **jus** NOUN
  juice
♦ **un jus de fruit** a fruit juice

jusqu'à PREPOSITION
  1 as far as ◊ *Nous avons marché
  jusqu'au village.* We walked as far as
  the village.
  2 until ◊ *Il fait généralement chaud
  jusqu'à la mi-août.* It's usually hot
  until mid-August.
♦ **jusqu'à ce que** until ◊ *Tu peux rester
  ici jusqu'à ce qu'il cesse de pleuvoir.*
  You can stay here until it stops
  raining.
♦ **jusqu'à présent** so far

jusque PREPOSITION
  as far as ◊ *Je l'ai raccompagnée
  jusque chez elle.* I went with her as
  far as her house. ◊ *Jusqu'ici nous
  n'avons pas eu de problèmes.* Up to
  now we've had no problems.
  ◊ *Jusqu'où es-tu allé?* How far did
  you go?

juste ADJECTIVE, ADVERB
  1 fair ◊ *Il est sévère, mais juste.*
  He's strict but fair.
  2 tight ◊ *Cette veste est un peu
  juste.* This jacket is a bit tight.
♦ **juste assez** just enough
♦ **chanter juste** to sing in tune

justement ADVERB
  just ◊ *C'est justement pour cela qu'il
  est parti!* That's just the reason why
  he left!

la **justesse** NOUN
♦ **de justesse** only just ◊ *Il a eu son
  permis de justesse.* He only just
  passed his driving test.

la **justice** NOUN
  justice

justifier VERB
  to justify

juteux ADJECTIVE (FEM SING **juteuse**)
  juicy

juvénile ADJECTIVE
  youthful

J

K

la **K7** NOUN (= *cassette*)
  cassette

kaki ADJECTIVE
  khaki

le **kangourou** NOUN
  kangaroo

le **karaté** NOUN
  karate

la **kermesse** NOUN
  fair

kidnapper VERB
  to kidnap

le **kilo** NOUN
  kilo

le **kilogramme** NOUN
  kilogramme

le **kilomètre** NOUN
  kilometre

le/la **kinésithérapeute** NOUN
  physiotherapist

le **kiosque** NOUN

♦ **un kiosque à journaux** a news stand

le **kit** NOUN kit ◊ *en kit* in kit form ◊ *un kit mains libres* a hands-free kit ◊ *un kit piéton* a hands-free kit

le **klaxon** NOUN
  horn (*of car*)

klaxonner VERB
  to sound the horn

km ABBREVIATION (= *kilomètre*)
♦ **km/h** kph (= kilometres per hour)

KO ADJECTIVE
  knocked out
♦ **mettre quelqu'un KO** to knock somebody out ◊ *Il l'a mis KO au troisième round.* He knocked him out in the third round.
♦ **Je suis complètement KO** (*informal*) I'm knackered.

le **K-way** ® NOUN
  cagoule

L

l' ARTICLE, PRONOUN *see* **la, le**

la ARTICLE, PRONOUN

> *see also* **la** NOUN

la changes to l' before a vowel and most words beginning with "h".

[1] the ◊ *la maison* the house ◊ *l'actrice* the actress ◊ *l'herbe* the grass

[2] her ◊ *Je la connais depuis longtemps.* I've known her for a long time. ◊ *C'est une femme intelligente: je l'admire beaucoup.* She's an intelligent woman: I admire her very much.

[3] it ◊ *C'est une bonne émission: je la regarde tous les jours.* It's a good programme: I watch it every day.

[4] one's

♦ **se mordre la langue** to bite one's tongue ◊ *Je me suis mordu la langue.* I've bitten my tongue.

♦ **six euros la douzaine** six euros a dozen

le la NOUN

> *see also* **la** ARTICLE

[1] A ◊ *en la bémol* in A flat

[2] la ◊ *sol, la, si, do* so, la, ti, do

là ADVERB

[1] there ◊ *Ton livre est là, sur la table.* Your book's there, on the table.

[2] here ◊ *Elle n'est pas là.* She isn't here.

♦ **C'est là que ...** (1) That's where ... ◊ *C'est là que je suis né.* That's where I was born.

♦ **C'est là que ...** (2) That's when ... ◊ *C'est là que j'ai réalisé que je m'étais trompé.* That's when I realized that I had made a mistake.

là-bas ADVERB

over there

le labo NOUN (*informal*)

lab

le laboratoire NOUN

laboratory

labourer VERB

to plough

le labyrinthe NOUN

maze

le lac NOUN

lake

lacer VERB

to do up (*shoes*)

le lacet NOUN

lace

♦ **des chaussures à lacets** lace-up shoes

lâche ADJECTIVE

> *see also* **lâche** NOUN

[1] loose ◊ *Le nœud est trop lâche.* The knot's too loose.

[2] cowardly

♦ **Il est lâche.** He's a coward.

le lâche NOUN

> *see also* **lâche** ADJECTIVE

coward

lâcher VERB

[1] to let go of ◊ *Il n'a pas lâché ma main de tout le film.* He didn't let go of my hand until the end of the film.

[2] to drop ◊ *Il a été tellement surpris qu'il a lâché son verre.* He was so surprised that he dropped his glass.

[3] to fail ◊ *Les freins ont lâché.* The brakes failed.

la lâcheté NOUN

cowardice

lacrymogène ADJECTIVE

♦ **le gaz lacrymogène** tear gas

la lacune NOUN

gap

là-dedans ADVERB

in there ◊ *Qu'est-ce qu'il y a là-dedans?* What's in there?

là-dessous ADVERB

[1] under there ◊ *Mon carnet d'adresses est quelque part là-dessous.* My address book is under there somewhere.

[2] behind it ◊ *Il y a quelque chose de louche là-dessous.* There's something fishy behind it.

là-dessus ADVERB

on there

là-haut ADVERB

up there

laid ADJECTIVE

ugly

la laideur NOUN

ugliness

le lainage NOUN

woollen garment

la laine NOUN

wool ◊ *un pull en laine* a wool jumper

♦ **une laine polaire** a fleece (*jacket*)

laïque ADJECTIVE

♦ **une école laïque** a state school

la laisse NOUN

☞

<u>lead</u> ◊ *Tenez votre chien en laisse.*
Keep your dog on a lead.

laisser VERB
1 to leave ◊ *J'ai laissé mon
parapluie à la maison.* I've left my
umbrella at home.
2 to let ◊ *Laisse-le parler.* Let him
speak.
◆**Elle se laisse aller.** She's letting
herself go.

le **laisser-aller** NOUN
<u>carelessness</u>

le **lait** NOUN
<u>milk</u>
◆**un café au lait** a white coffee

la **laitue** NOUN
<u>lettuce</u>

les **lambeaux** MASC NOUN
◆**en lambeaux** tattered

la **lame** NOUN
<u>blade</u> ◊ *une lame de rasoir* a razor
blade

la **lamelle** NOUN
<u>thin strip</u>

lamentable ADJECTIVE
<u>appalling</u>

se **lamenter** VERB
<u>to moan</u>

le **lampadaire** NOUN
<u>standard lamp</u>

la **lampe** NOUN
<u>lamp</u>
◆**une lampe de poche** a torch

la **lance** NOUN
<u>spear</u>

le **lancement** NOUN
<u>launch</u>

lancer VERB
　see also **lancer** NOUN
1 to throw ◊ *Lance-moi le ballon!*
Throw me the ball!
2 to launch ◊ *Ils viennent de lancer
un nouveau modèle.* They've just
launched a new model.
◆**se lancer dans** to embark on ◊ *Il s'est
lancé là-dedans sans bien réfléchir.*
He embarked on it without thinking
properly.

le **lancer** NOUN
　see also **lancer** VERB
◆**le lancer de poids** putting the shot

lancinant ADJECTIVE
◆**une douleur lancinante** a shooting
pain

le **landau** NOUN
<u>pram</u>

la **lande** NOUN
<u>moor</u>

le **langage** NOUN
<u>language</u>

la **langouste** NOUN
<u>crayfish</u>

la **langue** NOUN
1 tongue ◊ *Un petit garçon m'a tiré
la langue.* A little boy stuck out his
tongue at me.
◆**sa langue maternelle** his mother
tongue
2 language ◊ *une langue étrangère*
a foreign language ◊ *une langue
vivante* a modern language

la **lanière** NOUN
<u>strap</u>

le **lapin** NOUN
<u>rabbit</u>

le **laps** NOUN
◆**un laps de temps** a space of time

la **laque** NOUN
<u>hair spray</u>

laquelle PRONOUN (PL **lesquelles**)
1 which ◊ *Laquelle de ces photos
préfères-tu?* Which of these photos
do you prefer? ◊ *À laquelle de tes
sœurs ressembles-tu?* Which of your
sisters do you look like?
2 whom ◊ *la personne à laquelle
vous faites référence* the person to
whom you are referring
*laquelle is often not translated in
English.*
◊ *la personne à laquelle je pense* the
person I'm thinking of

le **lard** NOUN
<u>streaky bacon</u>

les **lardons** MASC NOUN
<u>chunks of bacon</u>

large ADJECTIVE, ADVERB
　see also **large** NOUN
<u>wide</u>
◆**voir large** to allow a bit extra
◊ *Achète un autre pain: il vaut mieux
voir large.* Buy another loaf of bread:
it's better to have a bit extra.

le **large** NOUN
　see also **large** ADJECTIVE
◆**cinq mètres de large** 5 m wide
◆**le large** the open sea
◆**au large de** off the coast of ◊ *Le
bateau est actuellement au large du
Portugal.* The boat is off the coast of
Portugal at the moment.

largement ADVERB
◆**Vous avez largement le temps.** You
have plenty of time.
◆**C'est largement suffisant.** That's
ample.

la **largeur** NOUN

width

la **larme** NOUN
   tear ◊ *être en larmes* to be in tears

la **laryngite** NOUN
   laryngitis

le **laser** NOUN
   laser
   ♦ **une chaîne laser** a compact disc
   player
   ♦ **un disque laser** a compact disc

lasser VERB
   ♦ **se lasser de** to get tired of ◊ *Il s'est
   lassé de la tapisserie à fleurs du
   salon.* He's got tired of the flowery
   wallpaper in the sitting room.

le **latin** NOUN
   Latin

le **laurier** NOUN
   laurel tree ◊ *une feuille de laurier* a
   bay leaf

lavable ADJECTIVE
   washable

le **lavabo** NOUN
   washbasin

le **lavage** NOUN
   wash ◊ *Ce pull a rétréci au lavage.*
   This jumper has shrunk in the wash.

la **lavande** NOUN
   lavender

le **lave-linge** NOUN (PL les **lave-linge**)
   washing machine

laver VERB
   to wash
   ♦ **se laver** to wash ◊ *se laver les mains*
   to wash one's hands

la **laverie** NOUN
   ♦ **une laverie automatique** a launderette

le **lave-vaisselle** NOUN (PL les **lave-
   vaisselle**)
   dishwasher

le ARTICLE, PRONOUN

   *le changes to l' before a vowel and
   most words beginning with "h".*

   [1] the ◊ *le livre* the book ◊ *l'arbre* the
   tree ◊ *l'hélicoptère* the helicopter
   [2] him ◊ *Daniel est un vieil ami: je le
   connais depuis plus de vingt ans.*
   Daniel is an old friend: I've known
   him for over 20 years.
   [3] it ◊ *Où est mon stylo? Je ne le
   trouve plus.* Where's my pen? I can't
   find it. ◊ *Où est le fromage? – Je l'ai
   mis au frigo.* Where's the cheese? –
   I've put it in the fridge.
   [4] one's
   ♦ **se laver le visage** to wash one's face
   ◊ *Évitez de vous laver le visage avec
   du savon.* Avoid washing your face
   with soap.

♦ **dix euros le kilo** 10 euros a kilo
♦ **Il est arrivé le douze mai.** He arrived
   on 12 May.

lécher VERB
   to lick

le **lèche-vitrine** NOUN
   ♦ **faire du lèche-vitrine** to go window-
   shopping

la **leçon** NOUN
   lesson

le **lecteur** NOUN
   [1] reader
   [2] foreign language assistant (*at a
   university*)
   ♦ **un lecteur de cassettes** a cassette
   player
   ♦ **un lecteur de CD** a CD player

la **lectrice** NOUN
   [1] reader
   [2] foreign language assistant (*at a
   university*)

la **lecture** NOUN
   reading

   *Be careful! The French word **lecture**
   does not mean **lecture**.*

légal ADJECTIVE (MASC PL **légaux**)
   legal

la **légende** NOUN
   [1] legend
   [2] key (*of map*)
   [3] caption (*of picture*)

léger ADJECTIVE (FEM SING **légère**)
   [1] light
   [2] slight ◊ *un léger retard* a slight
   delay
   ♦ **à la légère** thoughtlessly ◊ *Il a agi à
   la légère.* He acted thoughtlessly.

légèrement ADVERB
   [1] lightly ◊ *Habille-toi légèrement: il
   va faire chaud.* Wear light clothes: it's
   going to be hot.
   [2] slightly ◊ *Il est légèrement plus
   grand que son frère.* He's slightly
   taller than his brother.

les **législatives** FEM NOUN
   general election SING

le **légume** NOUN
   vegetable

le **lendemain** NOUN
   next day ◊ *le lendemain de son
   arrivée* the day after he arrived
   ♦ **le lendemain matin** the next morning

lent ADJECTIVE
   slow

lentement ADVERB
   slowly

la **lenteur** NOUN
   slowness

L

la **lentille** NOUN
   1 contact lens ◊ *Est-ce que tu portes des lentilles?* Do you wear contact lenses?
   2 lentil ◊ *un rôti de porc aux lentilles* roast pork with lentils

le **léopard** NOUN
   leopard

lequel PRONOUN (FEM SING **laquelle**, MASC PL **lesquels**, FEM PL **lesquelles**)
   1 which ◊ *Lequel de ces films as-tu préféré?* Which of the films did you prefer?
   2 whom ◊ *l'homme avec lequel elle a été vue pour la dernière fois* the man with whom she was last seen
   lequel is often not translated in English.
   ◊ *le garçon avec lequel elle est sortie* the boy she went out with

les ARTICLE, PRONOUN
   1 the ◊ *les arbres* the trees
   2 them ◊ *Elle les a invités à dîner.* She invited them to dinner.
   3 one's
  ◆ **se brosser les dents** to brush one's teeth ◊ *Elle s'est brossé les dents.* She brushed her teeth.
  ◆ **dix euros les cinq** 10 euros for 5

la **lesbienne** NOUN
   lesbian

lesquels PRONOUN (FEM **lesquelles**)
   1 which ◊ *Lesquelles de ces photos préfères-tu?* Which of the photos do you prefer?
   2 whom ◊ *les personnes avec lesquelles il est associé* the people with whom he is in partnership
   lesquels is often not translated in English.
   ◊ *les gens chez lesquels nous avons dîné* the people we had dinner with

la **lessive** NOUN
   1 washing powder ◊ *une marque de lessive* a brand of washing powder
   2 wash ◊ *Est-ce que vous avez quelque chose à mettre à la lessive?* Have you got anything to go in the wash?
  ◆ **faire la lessive** to do the washing

leste ADJECTIVE
   nimble

la **Lettonie** NOUN
   Latvia

la **lettre** NOUN
   letter ◊ *écrire une lettre* to write a lettre

les **lettres** FEM NOUN
   arts ◊ *la faculté de lettres* the Faculty of Arts

leur ADJECTIVE, PRONOUN
   1 their ◊ *leur ami* their friend
   2 them ◊ *Je leur ai dit la vérité.* I told them the truth.
  ◆ **le leur** theirs ◊ *mon camion et le leur* my truck and theirs ◊ *Ma voiture est rouge, la leur est bleue.* My car's red, theirs is blue.

leurs ADJECTIVE, PRONOUN
   their ◊ *leurs amis* their friends
  ◆ **les leurs** theirs ◊ *tes livres et les leurs* your books and theirs

levé ADJECTIVE
  ◆ **être levé** to be up ◊ *Est-ce qu'il est levé?* Is he up?

la **levée** NOUN
   collection (*of mail*) ◊ *Prochaine levée: 17 heures* Next collection: 5 p.m.

lever VERB
   see also **lever** NOUN
   to raise ◊ *Levez vos verres!* Raise your glasses! ◊ *Levez la main si vous connaissez la réponse.* Put your hand up if you know the answer.
  ◆ **lever les yeux** to look up
  ◆ **se lever (1)** to get up ◊ *Il se lève tous les jours à six heures.* He gets up at 6 o'clock every day. ◊ *Lève-toi!* Get up!
  ◆ **se lever (2)** to rise ◊ *Le soleil se lève actuellement à cinq heures.* At the moment the sun rises at 5 o'clock.
  ◆ **se lever (3)** to stand up ◊ *Levez-vous!* Stand up!

le **lever** NOUN
   see also **lever** VERB
  ◆ **le lever du soleil** sunrise

le **levier** NOUN
   lever

la **lèvre** NOUN
   lip

le **lévrier** NOUN
   greyhound

la **levure** NOUN
   yeast
  ◆ **la levure chimique** baking powder

le **lexique** NOUN
   word list

le **lézard** NOUN
   lizard

la **liaison** NOUN
   affair ◊ *Ils ont eu une liaison dans leur jeunesse.* They had an affair when they were younger.

la **libellule** NOUN
   dragonfly

libérer VERB

to free ◊ *Les otages ont été libérés.*
The hostages were freed.
♦ **se libérer** to find time ◊ *J'essaierai de me libérer cet après-midi.* I'll try to find time this afternoon.

la **liberté** NOUN
freedom
♦ **mettre en liberté** to release ◊ *Il a été mis en liberté au bout d'un an de prison.* He was released after a year in prison.

le/la **libraire** NOUN
bookseller

la **librairie** NOUN
bookshop

> Be careful! *librairie* does not mean *library*.

libre ADJECTIVE
1 free ◊ *Tu es libre de faire ce que tu veux.* You are free to do as you wish. ◊ *Est-ce que cette place est libre?* Is this seat free?
♦ **Avez-vous une chambre de libre?** Have you got a free room?
2 clear ◊ *La route est libre: vous pouvez traverser.* The road is clear: you can cross.
♦ **une école libre** a private school

le **libre-service** NOUN (PL les **libres-services**)
self-service store

la **Libye** NOUN
Libya

la **licence** NOUN
1 degree ◊ *une licence de droit* a law degree
2 licence ◊ *une licence d'exportation* an export licence

le **licencié** NOUN
graduate

la **licenciée** NOUN
graduate

le **licenciement** NOUN
redundancy

licencier VERB
to make redundant ◊ *Ils viennent de licencier sept employés.* They've just made 7 employees redundant.

le **liège** NOUN
cork ◊ *des sets en liège* cork mats
♦ **un bouchon en liège** a cork (*for bottle*)

le **lien** NOUN
1 connection ◊ *Il n'y a aucun lien entre ces deux événements.* There's no connection between these two events.
♦ **un lien de parenté** a family tie
2 link (*in computing*)

lier VERB

♦ **lier conversation avec quelqu'un** to get into conversation with somebody
♦ **se lier avec quelqu'un** to make friends with somebody ◊ *Je ne me lie pas facilement.* I don't make friends easily.

le **lierre** NOUN
ivy

le **lieu** NOUN (PL les **lieux**)
place ◊ *votre lieu de travail* your place of work
♦ **avoir lieu** to take place ◊ *La cérémonie a eu lieu dans la salle des fêtes.* The ceremony took place in the village hall.
♦ **au lieu de** instead of ◊ *J'aimerais une pomme au lieu de la glace.* I'd like an apple instead of ice cream.

le **lièvre** NOUN
hare

la **ligne** NOUN
1 line (*phone, train*) ◊ *La ligne est mauvaise.* It's a bad line. ◊ *la ligne de bus numéro six* the number 6 bus
♦ **en ligne** (*computing*) on-line
2 figure ◊ *C'est mauvais pour la ligne.* It's bad for your figure.

ligoter VERB
to tie up

la **ligue** NOUN
league

le **lilas** NOUN
lilac

la **limace** NOUN
slug

la **lime** NOUN
♦ **une lime à ongles** a nail file

la **limitation** NOUN
♦ **la limitation de vitesse** the speed limit

la **limite** NOUN
1 boundary (*of property, football pitch*)
2 limit ◊ *Est-ce qu'il y a une limite d'âge?* Is there an age limit?
♦ **À la limite, on pourrait prendre le bus.** At a pinch we could go by bus.
♦ **la date limite** the deadline
♦ **la date limite de vente** the sell-by date

limiter VERB
to limit ◊ *Le nombre de billets est limité à deux par personne.* The number of tickets is limited to two per person.

la **limonade** NOUN
lemonade

le **lin** NOUN
linen ◊ *une veste en lin* a linen jacket

L

le **linge** NOUN
1 linen ◊ *le linge sale* dirty linen
2 washing ◊ *laver le linge* to do the washing
♦**du linge de corps** underwear

la **lingerie** NOUN
underwear (*women's*)

le **lion** NOUN
lion
♦**le Lion** Leo ◊ *Il est Lion.* He is Leo.

la **lionne** NOUN
lioness

la **liqueur** NOUN
liqueur

liquide ADJECTIVE
see also **liquide** NOUN
liquid

le **liquide** NOUN
see also **liquide** ADJECTIVE
liquid
♦**payer quelque chose en liquide** to pay cash for something

lire VERB
to read ◊ *Tu as lu "Madame Bovary"?* Have you read "Madame Bovary"?

lis, lisent, lisez VERB *see* **lire**
♦**Je lis beaucoup.** I read a lot.

lisible ADJECTIVE
legible

lisse ADJECTIVE
smooth

la **liste** NOUN
list
♦**faire la liste de** to make a list of ◊ *J'ai fait la liste de tout ce dont j'ai besoin.* I've made a list of all the things I need.

lit VERB *see* **lire**
see also **lit** NOUN

le **lit** NOUN
see also **lit** VERB
bed ◊ *un grand lit* a double bed ◊ *aller au lit* to go to bed
♦**faire son lit** to make one's bed ◊ *Je n'ai pas eu le temps de faire mon lit ce matin.* I haven't had time to make my bed this morning.
♦**un lit de camp** a campbed

la **literie** NOUN
bedding

la **litière** NOUN
1 litter (*for cat*)
2 bedding (*of caged pet*)

le **litre** NOUN
litre

littéraire ADJECTIVE
♦**une œuvre littéraire** a work of literature

la **littérature** NOUN
literature

le **littoral** NOUN (PL les **littoraux**)
coast

la **Lituanie** NOUN
Lithuania

la **livraison** NOUN
delivery
♦**la livraison des bagages** baggage reclaim

le **livre** NOUN
see also **la livre**
book
♦**un livre de poche** a paperback

la **livre** NOUN
see also **le livre**
pound

> ℹ The French **livre** is 500 grams.

◊ *une livre de beurre* a pound of butter
♦**la livre sterling** the pound sterling
◊ *Le guide coûte trois livres.* The guide book costs £3.

livrer VERB
to deliver

le **livret** NOUN
booklet
♦**le livret scolaire** the school report book

le **livreur** NOUN
delivery man

local ADJECTIVE (MASC PL **locaux**)
see also **local** NOUN
local

le **local** NOUN (PL les **locaux**)
see also **local** ADJECTIVE
premises ◊ *Nous cherchons un local pour les répétitions.* We are looking for premises to rehearse in.

le/la **locataire** NOUN
1 tenant
2 lodger ◊ *Ils ont décidé de prendre un locataire.* They have decided to take a lodger.

la **location** NOUN
♦**location de voitures** car rental
♦**location de skis** ski hire
> Be careful! The French word **location** does not mean **location**.

locaux ADJECTIVE, NOUN *see* **local**

la **locomotive** NOUN
locomotive

la **loge** NOUN
dressing room

le **logement** NOUN
1 housing
2 accommodation

loger VERB

to stay ◊ *Elle loge chez sa cousine quand elle revient dans la région.* She stays with her cousin when she comes back to the area.

♦**trouver à se loger** to find somewhere to live ◊ *J'ai eu du mal à trouver à me loger.* I had difficulty finding somewhere to live.

le **logiciel** NOUN

software

logique ADJECTIVE

see also **logique** NOUN

logical

la **logique** NOUN

see also **logique** ADJECTIVE

logic

la **loi** NOUN

law

loin ADVERB

1 far ◊ *La gare n'est pas très loin d'ici.* The station is not very far from here.

2 far off ◊ *Noël n'est plus tellement loin.* Christmas isn't far off now.

3 a long time ago ◊ *Les vacances paraissent déjà tellement loin!* The holidays already seem such a long time ago!

♦**au loin** in the distance ◊ *On aperçoit la mer au loin.* You can see the sea in the distance.

♦**de loin (1)** from a long way away ◊ *On voit l'église de loin.* You can see the church from a long way away.

♦**de loin (2)** by far ◊ *C'est de loin l'élève la plus brillante.* She is by far the brightest pupil.

♦**C'est plus loin que la gare.** It's further on than the station.

lointain ADJECTIVE

see also **lointain** NOUN

distant ◊ *un pays lointain* a distant country ◊ *C'est un parent lointain de ma mère.* He's a distant relation of my mother.

le **lointain** NOUN

see also **lointain** ADJECTIVE

♦**dans le lointain** in the distance

le **loir** NOUN

dormouse

♦**dormir comme un loir** to sleep like a log

les **loisirs** MASC NOUN

1 free time SING ◊ *Qu'est-ce que vous faites pendant vos loisirs?* What do you do in your free time?

2 hobby ◊ *Le ski et l'équitation sont des loisirs coûteux.* Skiing and riding are expensive hobbies.

le **Londonien** NOUN

Londoner

la **Londonienne** NOUN

Londoner

Londres NOUN

London ◊ *le métro de Londres* the London underground

♦**à Londres (1)** in London

♦**à Londres (2)** to London

long ADJECTIVE (FEM SING **longue**)

see also **long** NOUN

long

le **long** NOUN

see also **long** ADJECTIVE

♦**un bateau de trois mètres de long** a boat 3 m long

♦**tout le long de** all along ◊ *Il y a des chemins de randonnée tout le long de la côte.* There are footpaths all along the coast.

♦**marcher de long en large** to walk up and down

longer VERB

♦**La route longe la forêt.** The road runs along the edge of the forest.

♦**Nous avons longé la Seine à pied.** We walked along the Seine.

longtemps ADVERB

a long time ◊ *J'ai attendu longtemps chez le dentiste.* I waited a long time at the dentist's.

♦**pendant longtemps** for a long time ◊ *On a cru pendant longtemps que la Terre était plate.* For a long time people thought the Earth was flat.

♦**mettre longtemps à faire quelque chose** to take a long time to do something ◊ *Il a mis longtemps à répondre à ma lettre.* He took a long time to answer my letter.

longue ADJECTIVE see **long**

la **longue** NOUN

♦**à la longue** in the end ◊ *Elle a fini par agacer tout le monde à la longue.* In the end she got on everybody's nerves.

longuement ADVERB

at length ◊ *Elle m'a longuement parlé de ses projets d'avenir.* She talked to me at length about her plans for the future.

la **longueur** NOUN

length

♦**à longueur de journée** all day long ◊ *Elle mâche du chewing-gum à*

☞

longueur de journée. She chews gum all day long.

le **look** NOUN
look ◊ *Il a un look d'enfer.* He looks so cool.

les **loques** FEM NOUN
♦ **être en loques** to be torn to bits ◊ *Sa chemise était en loques.* His shirt was torn to bits.

lors de PREPOSITION
during ◊ *Je l'ai rencontré lors de mon stage en entreprise.* I met him during my work placement.

lorsque CONJUNCTION
when ◊ *J'allais composer ton numéro lorsque tu as appelé.* I was about to dial your number when you called.

le **lot** NOUN
prize
♦ **le gros lot** the jackpot

la **loterie** NOUN
[1] lottery ◊ *la loterie nationale* the National Lottery
[2] raffle ◊ *J'ai gagné cet ours en peluche dans une loterie.* I won this teddy in a raffle.

la **lotion** NOUN
lotion ◊ *une bouteille de lotion solaire* a bottle of suntan lotion
♦ **une lotion après-rasage** an aftershave
♦ **une lotion démaquillante** cleansing milk

le **lotissement** NOUN
housing estate

le **loto** NOUN
lottery
♦ **le loto sportif** the pools

le **loubard** NOUN (*informal*)
lout

louche ADJECTIVE
see also **louche** NOUN
fishy ◊ *une histoire louche* a fishy story

la **louche** NOUN
see also **louche** ADJECTIVE
ladle

loucher VERB
to squint

louer VERB
[1] to let ◊ *Ils louent des chambres à des étudiants.* They let rooms to students.
♦ **"à louer"** "to let"
[2] to rent ◊ *Je loue un petit appartement au centre-ville.* I rent a little flat in the centre of town.
[3] to hire ◊ *Est-ce que vous louez des vélos?* Do you hire bikes? ◊ *Nous*

allons louer une voiture pour le week-end. We're going to hire a car for the weekend.
[4] to praise ◊ *Les journaux ont loué le courage des pompiers.* The newspapers praised the courage of the firefighters.

le **loup** NOUN
wolf

la **loupe** NOUN
magnifying glass

louper VERB (*informal*)
to miss ◊ *Dépêche-toi, tu vas louper ton train!* Hurry up, you'll miss your train!

lourd ADJECTIVE
see also **lourd** ADVERB
heavy ◊ *Mon sac est très lourd.* My bag's very heavy.

lourd ADVERB
see also **lourd** ADJECTIVE
close (*weather*) ◊ *Il fait très lourd aujourd'hui.* It's very close today.

la **loutre** NOUN
otter

la **loyauté** NOUN
loyalty

le **loyer** NOUN
rent

lu VERB see **lire**

la **lucarne** NOUN
skylight

la **luge** NOUN
sledge

lugubre ADJECTIVE
gloomy

lui PRONOUN
[1] him ◊ *Il a été très content du cadeau que je lui ai offert.* He was very pleased with the present I gave him. ◊ *C'est bien lui!* It's definitely him! ◊ *J'ai pensé à lui toute la journée.* I thought about him all day long.
[2] to him ◊ *Mon père est d'accord: je lui ai parlé ce matin.* My father said yes: I spoke to him this morning.
[3] her ◊ *Elle a été très contente du cadeau que je lui ai offert.* She was very pleased with the present I gave her.
[4] to her ◊ *Ma mère est d'accord: je lui ai parlé ce matin.* My mother said yes: I spoke to her this morning.
[5] it ◊ *Qu'est-ce que tu donnes à ton chat? – Je lui donne de la viande crue.* What do you give your cat? – I give it raw meat.

lui is also used for emphasis.
◊ *Lui, il est toujours en retard!* Oh him, he's always late!
♦ **lui-même** himself ◊ *Il a construit son bateau lui-même.* He built his boat himself.

la **lumière** NOUN
light
♦ **la lumière du jour** daylight

lumineux ADJECTIVE (FEM SING **lumineuse**)
♦ **une enseigne lumineuse** a neon sign

lunatique ADJECTIVE
temperamental ◊ *Il est plutôt lunatique.* He's rather temperamental.

le **lundi** NOUN
☐1 Monday ◊ *Aujourd'hui, nous sommes lundi.* It's Monday today.
☐2 on Monday ◊ *Ils sont arrivés lundi.* They arrived on Monday.
♦ **le lundi** on Mondays ◊ *Le lundi, je vais à la piscine.* I go swimming on Mondays.
♦ **tous les lundis** every Monday
♦ **lundi dernier** last Monday
♦ **lundi prochain** next Monday
♦ **le lundi de Pâques** Easter Monday

la **lune** NOUN
moon
♦ **la lune de miel** honeymoon

les **lunettes** FEM NOUN
glasses
♦ **des lunettes de soleil** sunglasses
♦ **des lunettes de plongée** swimming goggles

la **lutte** NOUN
☐1 fight ◊ *la lutte contre le racisme* the fight against racism
☐2 wrestling ◊ *une épreuve de lutte* a wrestling bout

lutter VERB
to fight

le **luxe** NOUN
luxury
♦ **de luxe** luxury ◊ *un hôtel de luxe* a luxury hotel

luxueux ADJECTIVE (FEM SING **luxueuse**)
luxurious

le **lycée** NOUN
secondary school
♦ **lycée technique** technical college

> ⓘ In France pupils go to a **collège** between the ages of 11 and 15, and then to a **lycée** until the age of 18.

le **lycéen** NOUN
secondary school pupil

la **lycéenne** NOUN
secondary school pupil

L

M

M. ABBREVIATION (= *Monsieur*)
    Mr ◊ *M. Bernard* Mr Bernard

m' PRONOUN *see* **me**

ma ADJECTIVE
    my ◊ *ma mère* my mother ◊ *ma montre* my watch

les **macaronis** MASC NOUN
    macaroni SING

la **Macédoine** NOUN
    Macedonia

la **macédoine** NOUN
    ♦**la macédoine de fruits** fruit salad
    ♦**la macédoine de légumes** mixed vegetables

mâcher VERB
    to chew

le **machin** NOUN (*informal*)
    thingy ◊ *Passe-moi le machin pour râper les carottes.* Pass me the thingy for grating carrots. ◊ *Qu'est-ce que c'est que ce vieux machin?* What's this old thing?

machinalement ADVERB
    ♦**Elle a regardé sa montre machinalement.** She looked at her watch without thinking.

la **machine** NOUN
    machine
    ♦**une machine à laver** a washing machine
    ♦**une machine à écrire** a typewriter
    ♦**une machine à coudre** a sewing machine
    ♦**une machine à sous** a fruit machine

le **machiste** NOUN
    male chauvinist

le **macho** NOUN (*informal*)
    male chauvinist pig

la **mâchoire** NOUN
    jaw

mâchonner VERB
    to chew

le **maçon** NOUN
    bricklayer

Madame FEM NOUN (PL **Mesdames**)
    1 Mrs ◊ *Madame Legall* Mrs Legall
    2 lady ◊ *Occupez-vous de Madame.* Could you look after this lady?
    3 Madam ◊ *Madame, ...* Dear Madam, ... (*in letter*) ◊ *Madame! Vous avez oublié votre parapluie!* Excuse me! You've forgotten your umbrella!

Mademoiselle FEM NOUN (PL **Mesdemoiselles**)

    1 Miss ◊ *Mademoiselle Martin* Miss Martin
    2 Madam ◊ *Mademoiselle, ...* Dear Madam, ... (*in letter*)

le **magasin** NOUN
    shop ◊ *Les magasins ouvrent à huit heures.* The shops open at 8 o'clock.
    ♦**faire les magasins** to go shopping

le **magazine** NOUN
    magazine

le **magicien** NOUN
    magician

la **magicienne** NOUN
    magician

la **magie** NOUN
    magic ◊ *un tour de magie* a magic trick

magique ADJECTIVE
    magic ◊ *une baguette magique* a magic wand

magistral ADJECTIVE (MASC PL **magistraux**)
    ♦**un cours magistral** a lecture (*at university*)

magnétique ADJECTIVE
    magnetic

le **magnétophone** NOUN
    tape recorder
    ♦**un magnétophone à cassettes** a cassette recorder

le **magnétoscope** NOUN
    video recorder

magnifique ADJECTIVE
    superb

mai MASC NOUN
    May
    ♦**en mai** in May

maigre ADJECTIVE
    1 skinny ◊ *Ma mère me trouve trop maigre.* My mother says I'm too skinny.
    2 lean (*meat*)
    3 low-fat (*cheese, yoghurt*)

maigrir VERB
    to lose weight ◊ *Il fait un régime pour essayer de maigrir.* He's on a diet, to try to lose weight. ◊ *Elle a maigri de deux kilos en un mois.* She's lost two kilos in a month.

le **maillot de bain** NOUN
    1 swimsuit
    2 swimming trunks

la **main** NOUN
    hand ◊ *Donne-moi la main!* Give me your hand!

◆**serrer la main à quelqu'un** to shake hands with somebody
◆**se serrer la main** to shake hands ◊ *Les deux présidents se sont serré la main.* The two presidents shook hands.
◆**sous la main** to hand ◊ *Est-ce que tu as son adresse sous la main?* Have you got his address to hand?

la **main-d'œuvre** NOUN
 workforce ◊ *la main-d'œuvre de l'usine* the workforce of the factory
◆**la main-d'œuvre immigrée** immigrant labour

maintenant ADVERB
 1 now ◊ *Qu'est-ce que tu veux faire maintenant?* What do you want to do now? ◊ *C'est maintenant ou jamais.* It's now or never.
 2 nowadays ◊ *Maintenant la plupart des gens font leurs courses au supermarché.* Nowadays most people do their shopping at the supermarket.

maintenir VERB
 to maintain ◊ *Il maintient qu'il n'était pas là le jour du crime.* He maintains he wasn't there on the day of the crime.
◆**se maintenir** to hold ◊ *Espérons que le beau temps va se maintenir pour le week-end!* Let's hope the good weather will hold over the weekend!

le **maire** NOUN
 mayor

la **mairie** NOUN
 town hall

mais CONJUNCTION
 but ◊ *C'est cher mais de très bonne qualité.* It's expensive, but very good quality.

le **maïs** NOUN
 1 maize
 2 sweetcorn

la **maison** NOUN
 see also **maison** ADJECTIVE
 house ◊ *Ils habitent dans la maison qui est au bout de la rue.* They live in the house at the end of the street.
◆**une maison des jeunes** a youth club
◆**des maisons mitoyennes (1)** semi-detached houses
◆**des maisons mitoyennes (2)** terraced houses
◆**à la maison (1)** at home ◊ *Je serai à la maison cet après-midi.* I'll be at home this afternoon.
◆**à la maison (2)** home ◊ *Elle est rentrée à la maison.* She's gone home.

maison ADJECTIVE (MASC, FEM, PL)

 see also **maison** NOUN
 home-made ◊ *Je préfère les tartes maison à celles qui sont achetées.* I prefer home-made pies to bought ones.

le **maître** NOUN
 1 teacher (*in primary school*)
 2 master (*of dog*)
◆**un maître d'hôtel** a head waiter (*in restaurant*)
◆**un maître nageur** a lifeguard

la **maîtresse** NOUN
 1 teacher (*in primary school*)
 2 mistress ◊ *Il paraît qu'il a une maîtresse.* They say he's got a mistress.

la **maîtrise** NOUN
 master's degree ◊ *Elle a une maîtrise d'anglais.* She's got a master's degree in English.
◆**la maîtrise de soi** self-control

maîtriser VERB
◆**se maîtriser** to control oneself ◊ *Il se met facilement en colère et a du mal à se maîtriser.* He loses his temper easily and finds it hard to control himself.

majestueux ADJECTIVE (FEM SING **majestueuse**)
 majestic

majeur ADJECTIVE
◆**être majeur** to be 18 ◊ *Tu feras ce que tu voudras quand tu seras majeure.* You can do what you like once you're 18. ◊ *Elle sera majeure en août.* She comes of age in August.
◆**la majeure partie** most ◊ *la majeure partie de mon salaire* most of my salary

la **majorité** NOUN
 majority ◊ *dans la majorité des cas* in the majority of cases
◆**la majorité et l'opposition** the government and the opposition

Majorque FEM NOUN
 Majorca

la **majuscule** NOUN
 capital letter ◊ *un M majuscule* a capital M

mal ADVERB, ADJECTIVE (MASC, FEM, PL)
 see also **mal** NOUN
 1 badly ◊ *Ce travail a été mal fait.* The work was badly done. ◊ *Il a mal compris.* He misunderstood.
 2 wrong ◊ *C'est mal de mentir.* It's wrong to tell lies.
◆**aller mal** to be ill ◊ *Son grand-père va très mal.* His grandfather is very ill.

M

☞

◆**pas mal** quite good ◊ *Je te trouve pas mal sur cette photo.* I think you look quite good in this photo.

le **mal** NOUN (PL les **maux**)

see also **mal** ADVERB

1 ache ◊ *J'ai mal à la tête.* I've got a headache. ◊ *J'ai mal aux dents.* I've got toothache. ◊ *J'ai mal au dos.* My back hurts. ◊ *Est-ce que vous avez mal à la gorge?* Have you got a sore throat?

◆**Ça fait mal.** It hurts.

◆**Où est-ce que tu as mal?** Where does it hurt?

◆**faire mal à quelqu'un** to hurt somebody ◊ *Attention, tu me fais mal!* Be careful, you're hurting me!

◆**se faire mal** to hurt oneself ◊ *Je me suis fait mal au bras.* I hurt my arm.

◆**se donner du mal pour faire quelque chose** to go to a lot of trouble to do something ◊ *Il s'est donné beaucoup de mal pour que cette soirée soit réussie.* He went to a lot of trouble to make the party a success.

◆**avoir le mal de mer** to be seasick

◆**avoir le mal du pays** to be homesick

2 evil ◊ *le bien et le mal* good and evil

◆**dire du mal de quelqu'un** to speak ill of somebody

malade ADJECTIVE

see also **malade** NOUN

ill

◆**tomber malade** to fall ill

le/la **malade** NOUN

see also **malade** ADJECTIVE

patient

la **maladie** NOUN

illness

maladif ADJECTIVE (FEM SING **maladive**)

sickly ◊ *C'est un enfant maladif.* He's a sickly child.

la **maladresse** NOUN

clumsiness

maladroit ADJECTIVE

clumsy

le **malaise** NOUN

◆**avoir un malaise** to feel faint ◊ *Elle a eu un malaise après le déjeuner.* She felt faint after lunch.

◆**Son arrivée a créé un malaise parmi les invités.** Her arrival made the guests feel uncomfortable.

la **malchance** NOUN

bad luck

mâle ADJECTIVE

male

la **malédiction** NOUN

curse

mal en point ADJECTIVE (MASC, FEM, PL)

◆**Il avait l'air mal en point quand je l'ai vu hier soir.** He didn't look too good when I saw him last night.

le **malentendu** NOUN

misunderstanding

le **malfaiteur** NOUN

criminal

mal famé ADJECTIVE (FEM **mal famée**, MASC PL **mal famés**)

◆**un quartier mal famé** a seedy area

malgache ADJECTIVE

from Madagascar ◊ *Sa mère est malgache.* His mother's from Madagascar.

malgré PREPOSITION

in spite of ◊ *Il est toujours généreux malgré ses problèmes d'argent.* He's always generous in spite of his financial problems.

◆**malgré tout** all the same ◊ *Il faisait mauvais mais nous sommes sortis malgré tout.* The weather was bad but we went out all the same.

le **malheur** NOUN

tragedy ◊ *Elle a eu beaucoup de malheurs dans sa vie.* She's had a lot of tragedy in her life.

◆**faire un malheur** (*informal*) to be a smash hit ◊ *Leur dernier album a fait un malheur.* Their latest album was a smash hit.

malheureusement ADVERB

unfortunately

malheureux ADJECTIVE (FEM SING **malheureuse**)

miserable ◊ *Qu'est-ce que tu as? Tu as l'air malheureux.* What's wrong with you? You look miserable.

malhonnête ADJECTIVE

dishonest

la **malice** NOUN

mischief ◊ *Son regard était plein de malice.* His eyes were full of mischief.

malicieux ADJECTIVE (FEM SING **malicieuse**)

mischievous

Be careful! **malicieux** *does not mean* **malicious***.*

malin ADJECTIVE (FEM SING **maligne**)

crafty

◆**C'est malin!** (*informal*) That's clever! ◊ *Ah c'est malin! Nous voilà enfermés à cause de toi!* That's clever! You've got us locked in!

la **malle** NOUN

trunk

malodorant ADJECTIVE

foul-smelling

malpropre ADJECTIVE
dirty

malsain ADJECTIVE
unhealthy

Malte MASC NOUN
Malta

maltraiter VERB
to ill-treat ◊ *Il maltraite son chien.* He
ill-treats his dog.
♦ **des enfants maltraités** abused
children

malveillant ADJECTIVE
malicious ◊ *des rumeurs
malveillantes* malicious rumours

la **maman** NOUN
mum

la **mamie** NOUN
granny

le **mammifère** NOUN
mammal

la **manche** NOUN
see also **le manche**
[1] sleeve (*of clothes*)
[2] leg (*of game*) ◊ *Ils ont gagné la
première manche du match.* They
won the first leg of the match.
♦ **la Manche** the Channel

le **manche** NOUN
see also **la manche**
handle (*of pan*)

la **mandarine** NOUN
mandarin orange

le **manège** NOUN
merry-go-round

la **manette** NOUN
lever

mangeable ADJECTIVE
edible ◊ *C'est à peine mangeable!*
It's practically inedible!

manger VERB
to eat

la **mangue** NOUN
mango

maniaque ADJECTIVE
fussy

la **manie** NOUN
[1] obsession
♦ **avoir la manie de** to be obsessive
about ◊ *Il a la manie du rangement.*
He's obsessive about tidying up.
[2] habit ◊ *J'essaie de respecter ses
petites manies.* I try to go along with
her little ways.

manier VERB
to handle

la **manière** NOUN
see also **les manières**
way

♦ **de manière à** so as to ◊ *Nous
sommes partis tôt de manière à
éviter la circulation.* We left early so
as to avoid the traffic.
♦ **de toute manière** in any case ◊ *Je
n'aurais pas pu venir de toute
manière.* I couldn't have come in any
case.

maniéré ADJECTIVE
affected

les **manières** FEM NOUN
see also **la manière**
[1] manners ◊ *apprendre les bonnes
manières* to learn good manners
[2] fuss ◊ *Ne fais pas de manières:
mange ta soupe!* Don't make a fuss:
eat your soup!

le **manifestant** NOUN
demonstrator

la **manifestante** NOUN
demonstrator

la **manifestation** NOUN
demonstration ◊ *une manifestation
pour la paix* a peace demonstration

manifester VERB
to demonstrate

manipuler VERB
[1] to handle ◊ *Ce vase doit être
manipulé avec soin.* This vase must
be handled with care.
[2] to manipulate ◊ *Tous les partis
essaient de manipuler l'opinion
publique.* All the parties are trying to
manipulate public opinion.

le **mannequin** NOUN
model ◊ *Elle est mannequin.* She's a
model.

manœuvrer VERB
to manœuvre

le **manque** NOUN
withdrawal ◊ *un drogué en état de
manque* a drug addict suffering
withdrawal symptoms
♦ **le manque de** lack of ◊ *Le manque de
sommeil peut provoquer toutes
sortes de troubles.* Lack of sleep can
cause all sorts of problems.

manqué ADJECTIVE
♦ **un garçon manqué** a tomboy

manquer VERB
to miss ◊ *Tu n'as rien manqué: le
film n'était pas très bon.* You didn't
miss anything: the film wasn't very
good. ◊ *Il manque des pages à ce
livre.* There are some pages missing
from this book.
♦ **Mes parents me manquent.** I miss my
parents.

M

♦**Ma sœur me manque.** I miss my sister.

♦**Il manque encore dix euros.** We are still 10 euros short.

♦**manquer de** to lack ◊ *La quiche manque de sel.* The quiche hasn't got enough salt in it. ◊ *Je trouve qu'il a manqué de tact.* I don't think he was very tactful.

♦**Il a manqué se tuer.** He nearly got killed.

le **manteau** NOUN (PL les **manteaux**)
coat

manuel ADJECTIVE (FEM SING **manuelle**)
see also **manuel** NOUN
manual

le **manuel** NOUN
see also **manuel** ADJECTIVE
1 textbook
2 handbook

le **maquereau** NOUN (PL les **maquereaux**)
mackerel

la **maquette** NOUN
model ◊ *une maquette de bateau* a model boat

le **maquillage** NOUN
make-up

se **maquiller** VERB
to put on one's make-up ◊ *Je vais me maquiller en vitesse.* I'll just quickly put on my make-up.

le **marais** NOUN
marsh

le **marbre** NOUN
marble ◊ *une statue en marbre* a marble statue

le **marchand** NOUN
1 shopkeeper
♦**un marchand de journaux** a newsagent
2 stallholder (*in market*)

la **marchande** NOUN
1 shopkeeper
♦**une marchande de fruits et de légumes** a greengrocer
2 stallholder (*in market*)

marchander VERB
to haggle

la **marchandise** NOUN
goods

la **marche** NOUN
1 step ◊ *Fais attention à la marche!* Mind the step!
2 walking ◊ *La marche me fait du bien.* Walking does me good.
♦**être en état de marche** to be in working order ◊ *Cette voiture est en parfait état de marche.* This car is in perfect running order.

♦**Ne montez jamais dans un train en marche.** Never try to get into a moving train.

♦**mettre en marche** to start ◊ *Comment est-ce qu'on met la machine à laver en marche?* How do you start the washing machine?

♦**la marche arrière** reverse gear

♦**faire marche arrière** to reverse
3 march ◊ *une marche militaire* a military march

le **marché** NOUN
market
♦**un marché aux puces** a flea market
♦**le marché noir** the black market

marcher VERB
1 to walk ◊ *Elle marche cinq kilomètres par jour.* She walks 5 kilometres every day.
2 to run ◊ *Le métro marche normalement aujourd'hui.* The underground is running normally today.
3 to work ◊ *Est-ce que l'ascenseur marche?* Is the lift working?
4 to go well ◊ *Est-ce que les affaires marchent actuellement?* Is business going well at the moment?
♦**Alors les études, ça marche?** (*informal*) How are you getting on at school?
♦**faire marcher quelqu'un** to pull somebody's leg ◊ *Il essaie de te faire marcher.* He's pulling your leg.

le **marcheur** NOUN
walker

la **marcheuse** NOUN
walker

le **mardi** NOUN
1 Tuesday ◊ *Aujourd'hui, nous sommes mardi.* It's Tuesday today.
2 on Tuesday ◊ *Ils reviennent mardi.* They're coming back on Tuesday.
♦**le mardi** on Tuesdays ◊ *Le mardi, je vais à la gym.* I go to the gym on Tuesdays.
♦**tous les mardis** every Tuesday
♦**mardi dernier** last Tuesday
♦**mardi prochain** next Tuesday
♦**Mardi gras** Shrove Tuesday

la **mare** NOUN
pond

le **marécage** NOUN
marsh

la **marée** NOUN
tide ◊ *la marée haute* high tide ◊ *la marée basse* low tide ◊ *la marée montante* the rising tide ◊ *la marée descendante* the ebb tide
♦**une marée noire** an oil slick

la **margarine** NOUN
margarine

la **marge** NOUN
margin

le **mari** NOUN
husband ◊ *son mari* her husband

le **mariage** NOUN
1 marriage
2 wedding ◊ *un mariage civil* a
registry office wedding ◊ *un mariage
religieux* a church wedding

marié ADJECTIVE
see also **marié** NOUN
married

le **marié** NOUN
see also **marié** ADJECTIVE
bridegroom
♦ **les mariés** the bride and groom

la **mariée** NOUN
bride

se **marier** VERB
to marry ◊ *Elle s'est mariée avec un
ami d'enfance.* She married a
childhood friend.

marin ADJECTIVE
see also **marin** NOUN
sea ◊ *l'air marin* the sea air
♦ **un pull marin** a sailor's jersey

le **marin** NOUN
see also **marin** ADJECTIVE
sailor

marine ADJECTIVE (MASC, FEM, PL)
see also **marine** NOUN
♦ **bleu marine** navy-blue ◊ *un pull bleu
marine* a navy-blue sweater

la **marine** NOUN
see also **marine** ADJECTIVE
navy
♦ **la marine nationale** the French navy

la **marionnette** NOUN
puppet

le **marketing** NOUN
marketing

la **marmelade** NOUN
stewed fruit
♦ **la marmelade de pommes** stewed
apple
♦ **la marmelade d'oranges** marmalade

la **marmite** NOUN
cooking pot

marmonner VERB
to mumble

le **Maroc** NOUN
Morocco

marocain ADJECTIVE
Moroccan

la **maroquinerie** NOUN
leather goods shop

marquant ADJECTIVE
significant ◊ *un événement marquant*
a significant event

la **marque** NOUN
1 mark ◊ *des marques de doigts*
fingermarks
2 make ◊ *De quelle marque est ton
jean?* What make are your jeans?
3 brand ◊ *une grande marque de
cognac* a well-known brand of cognac
♦ **l'image de marque** the public image
◊ *Le ministre tient à son image de
marque.* The minister cares about his
public image.
♦ **une marque déposée** a registered
trademark
♦ **A vos marques! prêts! partez!** Ready,
steady, go!

marquer VERB
1 to mark ◊ *Peux-tu marquer sur la
carte où se trouve le village?* Can
you mark where the village is on the
map?
2 to score ◊ *L'équipe irlandaise a
marqué dix points.* The Irish team
scored ten points.
3 to celebrate ◊ *On va sortir au
restaurant pour marquer ton
anniversaire.* We'll eat out to
celebrate your birthday.

la **marraine** NOUN
godmother

marrant ADJECTIVE (*informal*)
funny

marre ADVERB (*informal*)
♦ **en avoir marre de quelque chose** to
be fed up with something ◊ *J'en ai
marre de faire la vaisselle.* I'm fed up
with doing the dishes.

se **marrer** VERB (*informal*)
to have a good laugh ◊ *On
s'est bien marrés.* We had a good
laugh.

le **marron** NOUN
see also **marron** ADJECTIVE
chestnut ◊ *la crème de marrons*
chestnut purée

marron ADJECTIVE (MASC, FEM, PL)
see also **marron** NOUN
brown ◊ *des chaussures marron*
brown shoes

le **marronnier** NOUN
chestnut tree

mars MASC NOUN
March
♦ **en mars** in March

le **marteau** NOUN (PL les **marteaux**)
hammer

M

martyriser VERB
to batter ◊ *des enfants martyrisés* battered children

masculin ADJECTIVE
1 men's ◊ *la mode masculine* men's fashion
2 masculine ◊ *"chat" est un nom masculin.* "chat" is a masculine noun. ◊ *Elle a une allure assez masculine.* She looks rather masculine.

le **masque** NOUN
mask

le **massacre** NOUN
massacre

massacrer VERB
to massacre

le **massage** NOUN
massage

la **masse** NOUN
♦ **une masse de** (*informal*) masses of ◊ *J'ai une masse de choses à faire.* I've got masses of things to do.
♦ **produire en masse** to mass-produce ◊ *Ces jouets sont produits en masse en Chine.* These toys are mass-produced in China.
♦ **venir en masse** to come en masse ◊ *Les gens sont venus en masse pour accueillir Nelson Mandela.* People came en masse to welcome Nelson Mandela.

masser VERB
to massage
♦ **se masser** to gather ◊ *Les manifestants se sont massés devant l'ambassade.* The demonstrators gathered in front of the embassy.

massif ADJECTIVE (FEM SING **massive**)
1 solid (*gold, silver, wood*) ◊ *un bracelet en or massif* a solid gold bracelet
2 massive ◊ *une dose massive d'antibiotiques* a massive dose of antibiotics
3 mass ◊ *des départs massifs* a mass exodus

mat ADJECTIVE
matt ◊ *blanc mat* matt white ◊ *Je voudrais mes photos en mat.* I would like my photos matt.
♦ **être mat** to be checkmate (*chess*)

le **match** NOUN
match ◊ *un match de football* a football match
♦ **le match aller** the first leg
♦ **le match retour** the second leg
♦ **faire match nul** to draw

le **matelas** NOUN
mattress

♦ **un matelas pneumatique** an air bed

matelassé ADJECTIVE
quilted ◊ *une veste matelassée* a quilted jacket

le **matelot** NOUN
sailor

les **matériaux** MASC NOUN
materials

le **matériel** NOUN
1 equipment ◊ *du matériel de laboratoire* laboratory equipment
2 gear ◊ *Il a pris tout son matériel de pêche avec lui.* He took all his fishing gear with him.

maternel ADJECTIVE (FEM SING **maternelle**)
motherly ◊ *Elle est très maternelle.* She's very motherly.
♦ **ma grand-mère maternelle** my mother's mother
♦ **mon oncle maternel** my mother's brother

la **maternelle** NOUN
nursery school

> *ⓘ The **maternelle** is a state school for 2-6 year-olds.*

la **maternité** NOUN
♦ **le congé de maternité** maternity leave ◊ *Notre professeur de musique est en congé de maternité.* Our music teacher is on maternity leave.

les **mathématiques** FEM NOUN
mathematics

les **maths** FEM NOUN (*informal*)
maths

la **matière** NOUN
subject ◊ *Le latin est une matière facultative.* Latin is an optional subject.
♦ **sans matières grasses** fat-free
♦ **les matières premières** raw materials

le **matin** NOUN
morning ◊ *à trois heures du matin* at 3 o'clock in the morning ◊ *du matin au soir* from morning till night
♦ **Je suis du matin.** I'm at my best in the morning.
♦ **de bon matin** early in the morning

matinal ADJECTIVE (MASC PL **matinaux**)
morning ◊ *Je fais ma gymnastique matinale avant de déjeuner.* I do my morning exercises before breakfast.
♦ **être matinal** to be up early ◊ *Tu es bien matinal aujourd'hui!* You're up early today!

la **matinée** NOUN
morning ◊ *Je t'appellerai demain dans la matinée.* I'll call you

sometime tomorrow morning. ◊ *en début de matinée* early in the morning

le **matou** NOUN
tomcat

matrimonial ADJECTIVE (MASC PL **matrimoniaux**)

♦ *une agence matrimoniale* a marriage bureau

maudire VERB
to curse

maudit ADJECTIVE (*informal*)
blasted ◊ *Où est passé ce maudit parapluie?* Where's that blasted umbrella got to?

maussade ADJECTIVE
sullen

mauvais ADJECTIVE, ADVERB

① bad ◊ *une mauvaise note* a bad mark ◊ *Tu arrives au mauvais moment.* You've come at a bad time.

♦ *Il fait mauvais.* The weather's bad.

♦ *être mauvais en* to be bad at ◊ *Je suis mauvais en allemand.* I'm bad at German.

② poor ◊ *J'ai trouvé que le film était mauvais.* I thought the film was poor. ◊ *Il est en mauvaise santé.* His health is poor.

♦ *Tu as mauvaise mine.* You don't look well.

③ wrong ◊ *Vous avez fait le mauvais numéro.* You've dialled the wrong number.

♦ *des mauvaises herbes* weeds

♦ *sentir mauvais* to smell

les **maux** MASC NOUN

♦ *des maux de ventre* stomachache SING

♦ *des maux de tête* headache SING

maximal ADJECTIVE (MASC PL **maximaux**)
maximum

le **maximum** NOUN
maximum

♦ *au maximum* (1) as much as one can ◊ *Remplis le seau au maximum.* Fill the bucket as full as you can.

♦ *au maximum* (2) at the very most ◊ *Ça va vous coûter deux cents euros au maximum.* It'll cost you 200 euros at the very most.

la **mayonnaise** NOUN
mayonnaise

le **mazout** NOUN
fuel oil

me PRONOUN

> *me changes to m' before a vowel and most words beginning with "h".*

① me ◊ *Elle me téléphone tous les jours.* She phones me every day. ◊ *Il*

m'attend depuis une heure. He's been waiting for me for an hour.

② to me ◊ *Il me parle en allemand.* He talks to me in German. ◊ *Elle m'a expliqué la situation.* She explained the situation to me.

③ myself ◊ *Je vais me préparer quelque chose à manger.* I'm going to make myself something to eat.

> *With reflexive verbs, **me** is often not translated.*

◊ *Je me lève à sept heures tous les matins.* I get up at 7 every morning.

le **mec** NOUN (*informal*)
guy

le **mécanicien** NOUN
mechanic

la **mécanique** NOUN

① mechanics

② mechanism (*of watch, clock*)

le **mécanisme** NOUN
mechanism

méchamment ADVERB
nastily ◊ *Il lui a répondu méchamment.* He answered him nastily.

la **méchanceté** NOUN
nastiness

méchant ADJECTIVE
nasty ◊ *C'est un homme méchant.* He's a nasty man. ◊ *Ne sois pas méchant avec ton petit frère.* Don't be nasty to your little brother.

♦ *"Attention, chien méchant"* "Beware of the dog"

la **mèche** NOUN
lock (*of hair*)

mécontent ADJECTIVE

♦ *mécontent de* unhappy with ◊ *Elle est mécontente de sa coupe de cheveux.* She's unhappy with her haircut.

le **mécontentement** NOUN
displeasure ◊ *Il a exprimé son mécontentement.* He expressed his displeasure.

la **médaille** NOUN
medal

le **médecin** NOUN
doctor ◊ *aller chez le médecin* to go to the doctor

la **médecine** NOUN
medicine (*subject*) ◊ *Il fait médecine.* He's studying medicine.

les **médias** MASC NOUN
media SING

médical ADJECTIVE (MASC PL **médicaux**)
medical ◊ *la recherche médicale* medical research

M

◆**passer une visite médicale** to have a medical

le **médicament** NOUN
medicine (*drug*)

médiéval ADJECTIVE (MASC PL **médiévaux**)
medieval

médiocre ADJECTIVE
poor ◇ *des notes médiocres* poor marks

la **Méditerranée** NOUN
Mediterranean

méditerranéen ADJECTIVE (FEM SING **méditerranéenne**)
Mediterranean

la **méduse** NOUN
jellyfish

la **méfiance** NOUN
mistrust

méfiant ADJECTIVE
mistrustful

se **méfier** VERB
◆**se méfier de quelqu'un** to distrust somebody ◇ *Si j'étais toi, je me méfierais de lui.* If I were you, I wouldn't trust him.

la **mégarde** NOUN
◆**par mégarde** by mistake ◇ *J'ai emporté son livre par mégarde.* I took his book by mistake.

le **mégot** NOUN
cigarette end

meilleur ADJECTIVE, ADVERB, NOUN
better ◇ *Ce serait meilleur avec du fromage râpé.* It would be better with grated cheese. ◇ *Il paraît que le film est meilleur que le livre.* They say that the film is better than the book.
◆**le meilleur** the best ◇ *C'est elle qui est la meilleure en sport.* She's the best at sport. ◇ *Je préfère garder le meilleur pour la fin.* I like to keep the best for last.
◆**le meilleur des deux** the better of the two
◆**meilleur marché** cheaper ◇ *La bière est meilleur marché en France.* Beer's cheaper in France.

le **mél** NOUN
email

mélancolique ADJECTIVE
melancholy

le **mélange** NOUN
mixture

mélanger VERB
① to mix ◇ *Mélangez le tout.* Mix everything together.
② to muddle up ◇ *Tu mélanges tout!* You're muddling everything up!

la **mêlée** NOUN
scrum

mêler VERB
◆**se mêler** to mix ◇ *Il ne cherche pas à se mêler aux autres.* He doesn't try to mix with the others.
◆**Mêle-toi de ce qui te regarde!** (*informal*) Mind your own business!

la **mélodie** NOUN
melody

le **melon** NOUN
melon

le **membre** NOUN
① limb
② member ◇ *un membre de la famille* a member of the family ◇ *les pays membres de l'Union européenne* the member countries of the European Union

la **mémé** NOUN (*informal*)
granny

même ADJECTIVE, ADVERB, PRONOUN
① same ◇ *J'ai le même manteau.* I've got the same coat. ◇ *Tiens, c'est curieux j'ai le même!* That's strange, I've got the same one!
◆**en même temps** at the same time
◆**moi-même** myself ◇ *Je l'ai fait moi-même.* I did it myself.
◆**toi-même** yourself ◇ *Est-ce que tu vas faire les travaux toi-même?* Are you going to do the work yourself?
◆**eux-mêmes** themselves
② even ◇ *Il n'a même pas pleuré.* He didn't even cry.

la **mémoire** NOUN
memory

la **menace** NOUN
threat

menacer VERB
to threaten

le **ménage** NOUN
housework ◇ *faire le ménage* to do the housework
◆**une femme de ménage** a cleaning woman

ménager ADJECTIVE (FEM SING **ménagère**)
◆**les travaux ménagers** housework

la **ménagère** NOUN
housewife

le **mendiant** NOUN
beggar

la **mendiante** NOUN
beggar

mendier VERB
to beg

mener VERB
to lead ◇ *Cette rue mène directement à la gare.* This street leads straight to the station.
♦**Cela ne vous mènera à rien!** That will get you nowhere!

la **méningite** NOUN
meningitis

les **menottes** FEM NOUN
handcuffs

le **mensonge** NOUN
lie

la **mensualité** NOUN
monthly payment ◇ *en dix mensualités* in ten monthly payments

mensuel ADJECTIVE (FEM SING **mensuelle**)
monthly

les **mensurations** FEM NOUN
measurements

la **mentalité** NOUN
mentality

le **menteur** NOUN
liar

la **menteuse** NOUN
liar

la **menthe** NOUN
mint

la **mention** NOUN
grade ◇ *Il a été reçu avec mention bien.* He got a grade B pass.

mentionner VERB
to mention

mentir VERB
to lie ◇ *Tu mens!* You're lying!

le **menton** NOUN
chin

menu ADJECTIVE, ADVERB
see also **menu** NOUN
1 slim ◇ *Elle est menue.* She's slim. ◇ *Elle est petite et menue.* She's petite.
2 very fine ◇ *Les oignons doivent être coupés menu.* The onions have to be cut up very fine.

le **menu** NOUN
see also **menu** ADJECTIVE
menu ◇ *le menu du jour* today's menu ◇ *le menu touristique* the tourist menu ◇ *le menu d'aide* the help menu

la **menuiserie** NOUN
woodwork

le **menuisier** NOUN
joiner

le **mépris** NOUN
contempt ◇ *Il nous a traités avec mépris.* He treated us with contempt.

méprisant ADJECTIVE

contemptuous

mépriser VERB
to despise

la **mer** NOUN
1 sea ◇ *en mer* at sea
♦**au bord de la mer** at the seaside
♦**la mer du Nord** the North Sea
2 tide ◇ *La mer est basse.* The tide is out. ◇ *La mer sera haute à sept heures.* It'll be high tide at 7 o'clock.

la **mercerie** NOUN
1 haberdashery
2 haberdasher's shop

merci EXCLAMATION
thank you ◇ *Merci de m'avoir raccompagné.* Thank you for taking me home.
♦**merci beaucoup** thank you very much

le **mercredi** NOUN
1 Wednesday ◇ *Aujourd'hui, nous sommes mercredi.* It's Wednesday today.
2 on Wednesday ◇ *Nous comptons partir mercredi.* We plan to leave on Wednesday.
♦**le mercredi** on Wednesdays ◇ *Le musée est fermé le mercredi.* The museum is shut on Wednesdays.
♦**tous les mercredis** every Wednesday
♦**mercredi dernier** last Wednesday
♦**mercredi prochain** next Wednesday

la **merde** NOUN (*rude*)
shit ◇ *Merde!* Shit!

la **mère** NOUN
mother

la **merguez** NOUN
spicy sausage

méridional ADJECTIVE (MASC PL **méridionaux**)
southern ◇ *Il a un accent méridional.* He's got a southern accent.

la **meringue** NOUN
meringue

mériter VERB
to deserve

le **merlan** NOUN
whiting

le **merle** NOUN
blackbird

la **merveille** NOUN
♦**Cet ordinateur est une vraie merveille!** This computer's really wonderful!
♦**à merveille** wonderfully ◇ *Elle se porte à merveille depuis son opération.* She's been wonderfully well since the operation.

merveilleux ADJECTIVE (FEM SING **merveilleuse**)

M

☞

marvellous

mes ADJECTIVE
my ◊ *mes parents* my parents

Mesdames FEM NOUN
ladies ◊ *Bonjour, Mesdames.* Good
morning, ladies.

Mesdemoiselles FEM NOUN
ladies ◊ *Bonjour, Mesdemoiselles.*
Good morning, ladies.

mesquin ADJECTIVE
mean

le **message** NOUN
message

la **messagerie** NOUN
◆**une messagerie vocale** voice mail
◆**la messagerie électronique** email

la **messe** NOUN
mass ◊ *aller à la messe* to go to
mass ◊ *la messe de minuit* midnight
mass

messieurs MASC NOUN
gentlemen ◊ *Que puis-je faire pour
vous, Messieurs?* What can I do for
you, gentlemen?
◆**Messieurs, ...** Dear Sirs, ... (*in letter*)

la **mesure** NOUN
[1] measurement ◊ *J'ai pris les
mesures de la fenêtre.* I took the
measurements of the window.
◆**sur mesure** tailor-made ◊ *un costume
sur mesure* a tailor-made suit
[2] measure ◊ *L'établissement a pris
des mesures pour lutter contre le
vandalisme.* The school has taken
measures to combat vandalism.
◆**au fur et à mesure** as one goes along
◊ *Quand je cuisine, je préfère faire la
vaisselle au fur et à mesure.* When
I'm cooking, I prefer to wash up as I
go along.
◆**être en mesure de faire quelque
chose** to be in a position to do
something ◊ *Nous ne sommes pas en
mesure de vous renseigner.* We are
not in a position to give you any
information.

mesurer VERB
to measure ◊ *Mesurez la longueur et
la largeur.* Measure the length and
the width.
◆**Il mesure un mètre quatre-vingts.**
He's 1 m 80 tall.

met VERB *see* **mettre**

le **métal** NOUN (PL les **métaux**)
metal

métallique ADJECTIVE
metallic

la **météo** NOUN

weather forecast ◊ *Qu'est-ce que dit
la météo pour cet après-midi?* What's
the weather forecast for this
afternoon?

la **méthode** NOUN
[1] method ◊ *des méthodes
d'enseignement modernes* modern
teaching methods
[2] tutor (*manual*) ◊ *une méthode de
guitare* a guitar tutor

le **métier** NOUN
job ◊ *Tu aimerais faire quel métier
plus tard?* What job would you like to
do when you're older?

le **mètre** NOUN
metre
◆**un mètre ruban** a tape measure

le **métro** NOUN
underground ◊ *prendre le métro* to
go by underground

mets VERB *see* **mettre**

le **metteur en scène** NOUN (PL les
metteurs en scène)
[1] producer (*of play*)
[2] director (*of film*)

mettre VERB

Present tense:	
je mets	nous mettons
tu mets	vous mettez
il/elle met	ils/elles mettent
Past participle:	
mis	

[1] to put ◊ *Où est-ce que tu as mis
les clés?* Where have you put the
keys?
[2] to put on ◊ *Je mets mon manteau
et j'arrive.* I'll put on my coat and
then I'll be ready. ◊ *Il fait froid, je
vais mettre le chauffage.* It's cold, I'm
going to put the heating on.
[3] to wear ◊ *Marie-Claire ne met pas
souvent de jupe.* Marie-Claire doesn't
often wear a skirt. ◊ *Je n'ai rien à me
mettre!* I've got nothing to wear!
[4] to take ◊ *Combien de temps as-tu
mis pour aller à Lille?* How long did
it take you to get to Lille? ◊ *Elle met
des heures à se préparer.* She takes
hours getting ready.
◆**mettre en marche** to start ◊ *Comment
met-on la machine à laver en
marche?* How do you start the
washing machine?
◆**Vous pouvez vous mettre là.** You
can sit there.
◆**se mettre au lit** to get into bed
◆**se mettre en maillot de bain** to put
on one's swimsuit

M

♦ **se mettre à** to start ◊ *Il s'est mis à la peinture à cinquante ans.* He started painting when he was 50. ◊ *Il est temps de se mettre au travail.* It's time to start work. ◊ *Elle s'est mise à pleurer.* She started crying.

le **meuble** NOUN
  piece of furniture ◊ *Je me suis cogné contre un meuble.* I bumped into a piece of furniture. ◊ *Ce magasin vend de beaux meubles.* This shop sells nice furniture.

le **meublé** NOUN
  1 furnished flat
  2 furnished room

meubler VERB
  to furnish

le **meurtre** NOUN
  murder

le **meurtrier** NOUN
  murderer

la **meurtrière** NOUN
  murderess

Mexico NOUN
  Mexico City

le **Mexique** NOUN
  Mexico

le **mi** NOUN
  1 E ◊ *mi bémol* E flat
  2 mi ◊ *do, ré, mi ...* do, re, mi ...

mi- PREFIX
  1 half- ◊ *mi-clos* half-shut
  2 mid- ◊ *à la mi-janvier* in mid-January

miauler VERB
  to mew

la **miche** NOUN
  loaf

mi-chemin
♦ **à mi-chemin** ADVERB
  halfway

le **micro** NOUN
  microphone

le **microbe** NOUN
  germ

le **micro-ondes** NOUN
  microwave oven

le **micro-ordinateur** NOUN
  microcomputer

le **microscope** NOUN
  microscope

le **midi** NOUN
  1 midday ◊ *à midi* at midday
♦ **midi et demi** half past twelve
  2 lunchtime ◊ *On a bien mangé à midi.* We had a good meal at lunchtime.
♦ **le Midi** the South of France

la **mie** NOUN
  breadcrumbs

le **miel** NOUN
  honey

mien PRONOUN
♦ **le mien** mine ◊ *Ce vélo-là, c'est le mien.* That bike's mine.

mienne PRONOUN
♦ **la mienne** mine ◊ *Cette valise-là, c'est la mienne.* That case is mine.

miennes PRONOUN
♦ **les miennes** mine ◊ *Heureusement que tu as tes clés: j'ai oublié les miennes.* It's lucky you've got your keys: I forgot mine.

miens PRONOUN
♦ **les miens** mine ◊ *Ces CD-là, ce sont les miens.* Those CDs are mine.

la **miette** NOUN
  crumb (*of bread, cake*)

mieux ADVERB, ADJECTIVE, NOUN
  better ◊ *Je la connais mieux que son frère.* I know her better than her brother. ◊ *Elle va mieux.* She's better. ◊ *Les cheveux courts lui vont mieux.* She looks better with short hair.
♦ **Il vaut mieux que tu appelles ta mère.** You'd better phone your mother.
♦ **le mieux** the best ◊ *C'est la région que je connais le mieux.* It's the region I know best.
♦ **faire de son mieux** to do one's best ◊ *Essaie de faire de ton mieux.* Try to do your best.
♦ **de mieux en mieux** better and better
♦ **au mieux** at best

mignon ADJECTIVE (FEM SING **mignonne**)
  sweet ◊ *Qu'est-ce qu'il est mignon!* Isn't he sweet!

la **migraine** NOUN
  migraine ◊ *J'ai la migraine.* I've got a migraine.

mijoter VERB
  to simmer

le **milieu** NOUN (PL les **milieux**)
  1 middle
♦ **au milieu de** in the middle of ◊ *Place le vase au milieu de la table.* Put the vase in the middle of the table.
♦ **au beau milieu de** in the middle of ◊ *Quelqu'un a sonné à la porte au beau milieu de la nuit.* Somebody rang the bell in the middle of the night.
  2 background ◊ *le milieu familial* the family background ◊ *Il vient d'un milieu modeste.* He comes from a modest background.

☞

③ environment ◊ *le milieu marin* the marine environment

militaire ADJECTIVE

see also **militaire** NOUN

military ◊ *faire son service militaire* to do one's military service

le **militaire** NOUN

see also **militaire** ADJECTIVE

serviceman ◊ *Son père est militaire.* His father is in the services.
♦ **un militaire de carrière** a professional soldier

mille NUMBER

a thousand ◊ *mille euros* a thousand euros ◊ *deux mille personnes* two thousand people

le **millénaire** NOUN

millennium ◊ *le troisième millénaire* the third millennium

le **millefeuille** NOUN

vanilla slice

le **millénium** NOUN

millennium

le **milliard** NOUN

thousand million ◊ *cinq milliards d'euros* five thousand million euros

le/la **milliardaire** NOUN

multimillionaire

le **millier** NOUN

thousand ◊ *des milliers de personnes* thousands of people
♦ **par milliers** by the thousand

le **milligramme** NOUN

milligramme

le **millimètre** NOUN

millimetre

le **million** NOUN

million ◊ *deux millions de personnes* two million people

le/la **millionnaire** NOUN

millionaire

le/la **mime** NOUN

mime artist

mimer VERB

to mimic

minable ADJECTIVE

① shabby ◊ *un imperméable minable* a shabby raincoat
② pathetic

mince ADJECTIVE

① thin ◊ *une mince tranche de jambon* a thin slice of ham
② slim ◊ *Il est grand et mince.* He's tall and slim.
♦ **Mince alors!** (*informal*) Oh bother!

la **minceur** NOUN

① thinness ◊ *la minceur des murs* the thinness of the walls

② slimness ◊ *Elle enviait la minceur de sa sœur.* She envied her sister's slimness.

la **mine** NOUN

① expression
② look ◊ *Tu as bonne mine.* You look well. ◊ *Il a mauvaise mine.* He doesn't look well. ◊ *Elle avait une mine fatiguée.* She was looking tired.
③ appearance ◊ *Il ne faut pas juger les gens d'après leur mine.* You shouldn't judge people by their appearance.
④ lead (*of pencil*)
⑤ mine ◊ *une mine de charbon* a coal mine
♦ **faire mine de faire quelque chose** to pretend to do something ◊ *Elle a fait mine de le croire.* She pretended to believe him.
♦ **mine de rien** somehow or other ◊ *Elle a réussi mine de rien à le faire parler de lui.* Somehow or other she got him to talk about himself.

minéral ADJECTIVE (MASC PL **minéraux**)

mineral ◊ *l'eau minérale* mineral water

minéralogique ADJECTIVE

♦ **une plaque minéralogique** a number plate

le **minet** NOUN

pussycat

la **minette** NOUN

pussycat (*female*)

mineur ADJECTIVE

see also **mineur** NOUN

minor

le **mineur** NOUN

see also **mineur** ADJECTIVE

① boy under 18
♦ **les mineurs** the under-18s
② miner ◊ *Mon grand-père était mineur.* My grandfather was a miner.

la **mineure** NOUN

girl under 18

le **minidisque** NOUN

Minidisc ®

la **minijupe** NOUN

miniskirt

minimal ADJECTIVE (MASC PL **minimaux**)

minimum

le **minimum** NOUN

minimum ◊ *Il en fait le minimum.* He does the absolute minimum.
♦ **au minimum** at the very least

le **ministère** NOUN

ministry ◊ *le ministère des Affaires étrangères* the Foreign Office

le **ministre** NOUN

minister ◊ *le ministre des Affaires étrangères* the Foreign Secretary

le **Minitel** ® NOUN

> ❶ *Minitel* is France Telecom's online data service. You can use it instead of a phone directory, and to make bookings for transport, exhibitions etc.

la **minorité** NOUN
minority

Minorque FEM NOUN
Minorca

le **minuit** NOUN
midnight ◊ *à minuit et quart* at a quarter past midnight

minuscule ADJECTIVE
> see also **minuscule** NOUN

tiny

la **minuscule** NOUN
> see also **minuscule** ADJECTIVE

small letter

la **minute** NOUN
minute
♦ **à la minute** just this minute ◊ *Je viens de l'appeler à la minute.* I've just this minute called him.

minutieux ADJECTIVE (FEM SING **minutieuse**)
meticulous
♦ **C'est un travail minutieux.** It's a fiddly job.

la **mirabelle** NOUN
small yellow plum

le **miracle** NOUN
miracle

le **miroir** NOUN
mirror

mis VERB *see* **mettre**

mis ADJECTIVE
♦ **bien mis** well turned out ◊ *Elle est toujours bien mise.* She's always well turned out.

miser VERB (*informal*)
to bank on ◊ *On ne peut pas miser là-dessus.* We can't bank on it.

misérable ADJECTIVE
shabby-looking ◊ *une femme d'aspect misérable* a shabby-looking woman

la **misère** NOUN
extreme poverty
♦ **un salaire de misère** starvation wages

le/la **missionnaire** NOUN
missionary

mit VERB *see* **mettre**

la **mi-temps** NOUN
> ① half (*of match*) ◊ *la première mi-temps* the first half ◊ *la deuxième mi-temps* the second half
> ② half-time ◊ *Je lui parlerai à la mi-temps.* I'll speak to him at half-time.
♦ **travailler à mi-temps** to work part-time

la **mitraillette** NOUN
submachine gun

mixte ADJECTIVE
♦ **une école mixte** a mixed school

Mlle ABBREVIATION (PL **Mlles**)
(= *Mademoiselle*)
Miss ◊ *Mlle Renoir* Miss Renoir

Mme ABBREVIATION (PL **Mmes**)
(= *Madame*)
Mrs ◊ *Mme Leroy* Mrs Leroy

le **mobile** NOUN
motive ◊ *Quel était le mobile du crime?* What was the motive for the crime?

le **mobilier** NOUN
furniture

la **mobylette** ® NOUN
moped

moche ADJECTIVE (*informal*)
> ① awful ◊ *Cette couleur est vraiment moche.* That colour's really awful. ◊ *Je me trouve moche!* I think I look awful!
> ② rotten ◊ *Il a la grippe, c'est moche pour lui.* He's got flu, that's rotten for him.

la **mode** NOUN
> see also **le mode**

fashion ◊ *être à la mode* to be fashionable

le **mode** NOUN
> see also **la mode**

♦ **le mode d'emploi** directions for use
♦ **le mode de vie** the way of life

le **modèle** NOUN
> ① model ◊ *Le nouveau modèle sort en septembre.* The new model is coming out in September.
> ② style (*of clothes*) ◊ *Est-ce que vous avez le même modèle en plus grand?* Have you got the same style in a bigger size?

modéré ADJECTIVE
moderate

moderne ADJECTIVE
modern

moderniser VERB
to modernize

modeste ADJECTIVE

M

☞

modest ◊ *Ne sois pas si modeste!*
Don't be so modest!

la **modestie** NOUN
modesty

moelleux ADJECTIVE (FEM SING **moelleuse**)
soft ◊ *un coussin moelleux* a soft
cushion

les **mœurs** FEM NOUN
social attitudes
♦**l'évolution des mœurs** changing
attitudes

moi PRONOUN
me ◊ *Coucou, c'est moi!* Hello, it's
me!
♦**Moi, je pense que tu as tort.** I
personally think you're wrong.
♦**à moi** mine ◊ *Ce livre n'est pas à
moi.* This book isn't mine. ◊ *un ami à
moi* a friend of mine

moi-même PRONOUN
myself ◊ *J'ai tricoté ce pull moi-
même.* I knitted this jumper myself.

moindre ADJECTIVE
♦**le moindre** the slightest ◊ *Il ne fait
pas le moindre effort.* He doesn't
make the slightest effort. ◊ *Je n'en ai
pas la moindre idée.* I haven't the
slightest idea.

le **moine** NOUN
monk

le **moineau** NOUN (PL les **moineaux**)
sparrow

moins ADVERB, PREPOSITION
1 less ◊ *Ça coûte moins de deux
cents euros.* It costs less than 200
euros.
2 fewer ◊ *Il y a moins de gens
aujourd'hui.* There are fewer people
today.
♦**Il est cinq heures moins dix.** It's 10 to
5.
3 minus ◊ *quatre moins trois* 4
minus 3 ◊ *Il a fait moins cinq la nuit
dernière.* It was minus five last night.
♦**le moins** the least ◊ *C'est le modèle
le moins cher.* It's the least expensive
model. ◊ *Ce sont les plages qui sont
les moins polluées.* These are the
least polluted beaches. ◊ *C'est
l'album que j'aime le moins.* This is
the album I like the least.
♦**de moins en moins** less and less ◊ *Il
vient nous voir de moins en moins.*
He comes to see us less and less
often.
♦**Il a trois ans de moins que moi.** He's
three years younger than me.
♦**au moins** at least ◊ *Ne te plains pas:
au moins il ne pleut pas!* Don't
complain: at least it's not raining!

♦**à moins que** unless
*à moins que is followed by a verb in
the subjunctive.*
◊ *Je te retrouverai à dix heures à
moins que le train n'ait du retard.* I'll
meet you at 10 o'clock unless the
train's late.

le **mois** NOUN
month

le **moisi** NOUN
♦**Ça sent le moisi.** It smells musty.

moisir VERB
to go mouldy ◊ *Le pain a moisi.* The
bread's gone mouldy.

la **moisson** NOUN
harvest

moite ADJECTIVE
sweaty ◊ *J'ai toujours les mains
moites.* My hands are always sweaty.

la **moitié** NOUN
half ◊ *Il a mangé la moitié du gâteau
à lui seul.* He ate half the cake all by
himself.
♦**la moitié du temps** half the time
♦**à la moitié de** halfway through ◊ *Elle
est partie à la moitié du film.* She left
halfway through the film.
♦**à moitié** half ◊ *Ton verre est encore à
moitié plein.* Your glass is still half-
full. ◊ *Ce sac était à moitié prix.* This
bag was half-price.
♦**partager moitié moitié** to go halves
◊ *On partage moitié moitié, d'accord?*
We'll go halves, OK?

la **molaire** NOUN
back tooth

la **Moldavie** NOUN
Moldova

molle ADJECTIVE
lethargic ◊ *Je la trouve un peu
molle.* I find her a bit lethargic.

le **mollet** NOUN
see also **mollet** ADJECTIVE
calf (of leg)

mollet ADJECTIVE
see also **mollet** NOUN
♦**un œuf mollet** a soft-boiled egg

le/la **môme** NOUN (*informal*)
kid

le **moment** NOUN
moment
♦**en ce moment** at the moment ◊ *Nous
avons beaucoup de travail en ce
moment.* We have a lot of work at
the moment.
♦**pour le moment** for the moment
◊ *Nous ne pensons pas déménager
pour le moment.* We're not thinking
of moving for the moment.

◆**au moment où** just as ◊ *Il est arrivé au moment où j'allais partir.* He turned up just as I was leaving.

◆**à ce moment-là (1)** at that point ◊ *À ce moment-là, on a vu arriver la police.* At that point, we saw the police coming.

◆**à ce moment-là (2)** in that case ◊ *À ce moment-là, je devrai partir plus tôt.* In that case I'll have to leave earlier.

◆**à tout moment (1)** at any moment ◊ *Elle peut arriver à tout moment.* She could arrive at any moment.

◆**à tout moment (2)** constantly ◊ *Il nous dérange à tout moment pour des riens.* He's constantly bothering us about silly little things.

◆**sur le moment** at the time ◊ *Sur le moment je n'ai rien dit.* At the time I didn't say anything.

◆**par moments** at times ◊ *Elle se sent seule par moments.* She feels lonely at times.

momentané ADJECTIVE
<u>momentary</u>

la **momie** NOUN
<u>mummy</u> (*Egyptian*)

mon ADJECTIVE (FEM SING **ma**, PL **mes**)
<u>my</u> ◊ *mon frère* my brother ◊ *mon ami* my friend

la **monarchie** NOUN
<u>monarchy</u>

le **monastère** NOUN
<u>monastery</u>

le **monde** NOUN
<u>world</u> ◊ *faire le tour du monde* to go round the world

◆**Il y a du monde.** There are a lot of people.

◆**beaucoup de monde** a lot of people ◊ *Il y avait beaucoup de monde au concert.* There were a lot of people at the concert.

◆**peu de monde** not many people

mondial ADJECTIVE (MASC PL **mondiaux**)
⑴ <u>world</u> ◊ *la population mondiale* the world population
⑵ <u>world-wide</u> ◊ *une crise mondiale* a world-wide crisis

le **moniteur** NOUN
⑴ <u>instructor</u> ◊ *un moniteur de voile* a sailing instructor
⑵ <u>monitor</u> ◊ *le moniteur de mon ordinateur* my computer monitor

la **monitrice** NOUN
<u>instructor</u> ◊ *une monitrice de ski* a ski instructor

la **monnaie** NOUN
◆**une pièce de monnaie** a coin

◆**avoir de la monnaie** to have change ◊ *Est-ce que tu as de la monnaie?* Have you got any change? ◊ *Est-ce que vous avez la monnaie de dix euros?* Do you have change for 10 euros?

◆**rendre la monnaie à quelqu'un** to give somebody their change

monotone ADJECTIVE
<u>monotonous</u>

Monsieur MASC NOUN (PL **Messieurs**)
⑴ <u>Mr</u> ◊ *Monsieur Dupont* Mr Dupont
⑵ <u>man</u> ◊ *Il y a un monsieur qui veut te voir.* There's a man to see you.
⑶ <u>Sir</u> ◊ *Monsieur, ...* Dear Sir, ... (*in letter*) ◊ *Monsieur! Vous avez oublié votre parapluie!* Excuse me! You've forgotten your umbrella!

le **monstre** NOUN
see also **monstre** ADJECTIVE
<u>monster</u>

monstre ADJECTIVE
see also **monstre** NOUN
◆**Nous avons un travail monstre.** We've got a terrific amount of work.

le **mont** NOUN
<u>mount</u>
◆**le mont Everest** Mount Everest
◆**le mont Blanc** Mont Blanc

M

la **montagne** NOUN
<u>mountain</u> ◊ *de hautes montagnes* high mountains ◊ *Nous passons tous les ans un mois à la montagne.* We spend a month in the mountains every year.

◆**les montagnes russes** roller coaster

montagneux ADJECTIVE (FEM SING **montagneuse**)
<u>mountainous</u> ◊ *une région montagneuse* a mountainous area

montant ADJECTIVE
⑴ <u>rising</u> ◊ *la marée montante* the rising tide
⑵ <u>high</u> ◊ *un pull à col montant* a high-necked jumper

monter VERB
⑴ <u>to go up</u> ◊ *Elle a du mal à monter les escaliers.* She has difficulty going upstairs. ◊ *Les prix ont encore monté.* Prices have gone up again.
⑵ <u>to assemble</u> ◊ *Est-ce que ces étagères sont difficiles à monter?* Are these shelves difficult to assemble?

◆**monter dans** to get on ◊ *Il est temps de monter dans l'avion.* It's time to get on the plane.

◆**monter sur** to stand on ◊ *Tu vas devoir monter sur une chaise pour changer l'ampoule.* You'll have to

☞

stand on a chair to change the light
bulb.
♦ **monter à cheval** to ride

la **montre** NOUN
watch

montrer VERB
to show ◊ *Est-ce que vous pouvez
me montrer la gare sur le plan?* Can
you show me the station on the
map?

la **monture** NOUN
frames (*of glasses*)

le **monument** NOUN
monument

se **moquer** VERB
♦ **se moquer de (1)** to make fun of ◊ *Ils
se sont moqués de mes chaussures
jaunes.* They made fun of my yellow
shoes.
♦ **se moquer de (2)** (*informal*) not to
care about ◊ *Il se moque
complètement de la mode.* He
couldn't care less about fashion.

la **moquette** NOUN
fitted carpet

moqueur ADJECTIVE (FEM SING **moqueuse**)
mocking

le **moral** NOUN
♦ **Elle a le moral.** She's in good spirits.
♦ **J'ai le moral à zéro.** I'm feeling really
down.

la **morale** NOUN
moral ◊ *La morale de cette histoire
est ...* The moral of the story is ...
♦ **faire la morale à quelqu'un** to lecture
somebody

le **morceau** NOUN (PL les **morceaux**)
piece ◊ *un morceau de pain* a piece
of bread

mordre VERB
to bite

mordu ADJECTIVE
♦ **Il est mordu de jazz.** (*informal*) He's
crazy about jazz.

la **morgue** NOUN
mortuary

le **morse** NOUN
walrus

la **morsure** NOUN
bite

la **mort** NOUN
see also **mort** ADJECTIVE
death

mort ADJECTIVE
see also **mort** NOUN
dead ◊ *Nous avons trouvé un oiseau
mort.* We found a dead bird.

◊ *Napoléon est mort en 1821.*
Napoleon died in 1821.
♦ **Il était mort de peur.** He was scared
to death.
♦ **Je suis morte de fatigue.** I'm dead
tired.

mortel ADJECTIVE (FEM SING **mortelle**)
[1] deadly ◊ *un poison mortel* a
deadly poison ◊ *Ces réunions de
famille sont mortelles!* (*informal*)
These family gatherings are deadly!
[2] fatal ◊ *une chute mortelle* a fatal
fall

la **morue** NOUN
cod

Moscou NOUN
Moscow

la **mosquée** NOUN
mosque

le **mot** NOUN
[1] word ◊ *mot à mot* word for word
♦ **des mots croisés** a crossword
♦ **le mot de passe** the password
[2] note ◊ *Je vais lui écrire un mot
pour lui dire qu'on arrive.* I'll write
her a note to say we're coming.

le **motard** NOUN
[1] biker
[2] motorcycle cop (*informal*) ◊ *Il s'est
fait arrêter par un motard pour excès
de vitesse.* He was stopped for
speeding by a motorcycle cop.

le **moteur** NOUN
engine
♦ **un bateau à moteur** a motor boat
♦ **un moteur de recherche** a search
engine

le **motif** NOUN
pattern ◊ *des rideaux avec un motif
d'oiseaux* curtains with a bird pattern
♦ **sans motif** for no reason ◊ *Il s'est
fâché sans motif.* He got angry for no
reason.

motivé ADJECTIVE
motivated

la **moto** NOUN
motorbike

le/la **motocycliste** NOUN
motorcyclist

mou ADJECTIVE (FEM SING **molle**)
[1] soft ◊ *Mon matelas est trop mou.*
My mattress is too soft.
[2] lethargic ◊ *Je le trouve un peu
mou.* I find him a bit lethargic.

la **mouche** NOUN
fly
♦ **prendre la mouche** to get into a huff

se **moucher** VERB
to blow one's nose

le **moucheron** NOUN
  midge

le **mouchoir** NOUN
  handkerchief
  ♦ **un mouchoir en papier** a tissue

moudre VERB
  to grind

la **moue** NOUN
  pout
  ♦ **faire la moue** to pout

la **mouette** NOUN
  seagull

la **moufle** NOUN
  mitt

mouillé ADJECTIVE
  wet

mouiller VERB
  to get wet ◊ *J'ai mouillé les manches de mon pull.* I got the sleeves of my jumper wet.
  ♦ **se mouiller** to get wet ◊ *Attention, tu vas te mouiller!* Careful, you'll get wet!

moulant ADJECTIVE
  figure-hugging ◊ *une robe moulante* a figure-hugging dress

la **moule** NOUN
  see also **le moule**
  mussel

le **moule** NOUN
  see also **la moule**
  ♦ **un moule à gâteaux** a cake tin

le **moulin** NOUN
  mill

moulu VERB see **moudre**

mourir VERB
  to die
  ♦ **mourir de faim** to starve ◊ *Des centaines de personnes sont mortes de faim.* Hundreds of people starved to death.
  ♦ **Je meurs de faim!** I'm starving!
  ♦ **mourir de froid** to die of exposure
  ♦ **Je meurs de froid!** I'm freezing!
  ♦ **mourir d'envie de faire quelque chose** to be dying to do something ◊ *Je meurs d'envie d'aller me baigner.* I'm dying to go for a swim.

la **mousse** NOUN
  1 moss ◊ *un rocher recouvert de mousse* a rock covered with moss
  2 froth (*on beer*)
  3 lather (*of soap, shampoo*)
  4 mousse ◊ *une mousse au chocolat* a chocolate mousse ◊ *une mousse de poisson* a fish mousse
  ♦ **la mousse à raser** shaving foam

mousseux ADJECTIVE (FEM SING **mousseuse**)

  ♦ **un vin mousseux** a sparkling wine

la **moustache** NOUN
  moustache
  ♦ **les moustaches** whiskers

le **moustique** NOUN
  mosquito

la **moutarde** NOUN
  mustard

le **mouton** NOUN
  1 sheep ◊ *une peau de mouton* a sheepskin
  2 mutton ◊ *un gigot de mouton* a leg of mutton

le **mouvement** NOUN
  movement

mouvementé ADJECTIVE
  eventful ◊ *des vacances mouvementées* eventful holidays

moyen ADJECTIVE (FEM SING **moyenne**)
  see also **moyen** NOUN
  1 average ◊ *Je suis plutôt moyenne en langues.* I'm just average at languages.
  2 medium ◊ *Elle est de taille moyenne.* She's of medium height.
  ♦ **le moyen âge** the Middle Ages

le **moyen** NOUN
  see also **moyen** ADJECTIVE
  way ◊ *Quel est le meilleur moyen de le convaincre?* What's the best way of convincing him?
  ♦ **Je n'en ai pas les moyens.** I can't afford it.
  ♦ **Ils n'ont pas les moyens de s'acheter une voiture.** They can't afford to buy a car.
  ♦ **un moyen de transport** a means of transport
  ♦ **par tous les moyens** by every possible means

la **moyenne** NOUN
  ♦ **avoir la moyenne** to get a pass mark ◊ *J'espère avoir la moyenne en maths.* I hope to get a pass mark in maths.
  ♦ **en moyenne** on average
  ♦ **la moyenne d'âge** the average age

le **Moyen-Orient** NOUN
  Middle East

muet ADJECTIVE (FEM SING **muette**)
  dumb
  ♦ **un film muet** a silent film

le **muguet** NOUN
  lily of the valley

multiple ADJECTIVE
  numerous ◊ *en de multiples occasions* on numerous occasions

multiplier VERB
  to multiply

M

municipal ADJECTIVE (MASC PL **municipaux**)
- **la bibliothèque municipale** the public library

la **municipalité** NOUN
    town council

munir VERB
- **munir quelqu'un de** to equip someone with
- **se munir de** to equip oneself with

les **munitions** FEM NOUN
    ammunition SING

le **mur** NOUN
    wall

mûr ADJECTIVE
    1 ripe (*fruit*)
    2 mature (*person*)

la **mûre** NOUN
    bramble

mûrir VERB
    1 to ripen ◊ *Les fraises ont mis du temps à mûrir.* The strawberries took a while to ripen.
    2 to make mature ◊ *Cette expérience l'a beaucoup mûrie.* That experience has made her much more mature.

murmurer VERB
    to whisper ◊ *Il m'a murmuré à l'oreille qu'il allait partir.* He whispered in my ear that he was going to go.

la **muscade** NOUN
    nutmeg

le **muscat** NOUN
    1 muscat grape
    2 muscatel (*wine*) ◊ *un verre de muscat* a glass of muscatel

le **muscle** NOUN

muscle NOUN

musclé ADJECTIVE
    muscular

le **museau** NOUN (PL les **museaux**)
    muzzle

le **musée** NOUN
    museum

musical ADJECTIVE (MASC PL **musicaux**)
    musical
- **avoir l'oreille musicale** to be musical

le **music-hall** NOUN
    variety ◊ *une chanteuse de music-hall* a variety singer

le **musicien** NOUN
    musician

la **musicienne** NOUN
    musician

la **musique** NOUN
    music

musulman ADJECTIVE, NOUN
    Muslim
- **un musulman** a Muslim (*man*)
- **une musulmane** a Muslim (*woman*)

la **mutation** NOUN
    transfer ◊ *Il a demandé sa mutation à Paris.* He asked for a transfer to Paris.

myope ADJECTIVE
    short-sighted

le **mystère** NOUN
    mystery

mystérieux ADJECTIVE (FEM SING **mystérieuse**)
    mysterious

le **mythe** NOUN
    myth

N

n' PRONOUN *see* **ne**

la **nage** NOUN
- ◆**traverser une rivière à la nage** to swim across a river
- ◆**être en nage** to be sweating profusely

la **nageoire** NOUN
fin

nager VERB
to swim

le **nageur** NOUN
swimmer

la **nageuse** NOUN
swimmer

naïf ADJECTIVE (FEM SING **naïve**)
naïve

le **nain** NOUN
dwarf

la **naissance** NOUN
birth
- ◆**votre date de naissance** your date of birth

naître VERB
to be born
- ◆**Il est né en 1992.** He was born in 1992.

naïve ADJECTIVE *see* **naïf**

la **nana** NOUN (*informal*)
girl

la **nappe** NOUN
tablecloth

la **narine** NOUN
nostril

natal ADJECTIVE
native ◊ *mon pays natal* my native country

la **natation** NOUN
swimming ◊ *La natation est mon sport favori.* Swimming's my favourite sport.
- ◆**faire de la natation** to go swimming

la **nation** NOUN
nation
- ◆**les Nations unies** the United Nations

national ADJECTIVE (MASC PL **nationaux**)
national
- ◆**la fête nationale espagnole** the national day of Spain

la **nationale** NOUN
main road ◊ *En vélo, il vaut mieux éviter les nationales.* When on a bike it's better to avoid main roads.

la **nationalité** NOUN
nationality

la **natte** NOUN

plait ◊ *Cécile avait des nattes.* Cécile had plaits.

la **nature** NOUN
see also **nature** ADJECTIVE
nature

nature ADJECTIVE
see also **nature** NOUN
plain ◊ *un yaourt nature* a plain yoghurt

naturel ADJECTIVE (FEM SING **naturelle**)
natural

naturellement ADVERB
of course ◊ *Vous viendrez à notre fête? – Naturellement!* Are you coming to our party? – Of course! ◊ *Naturellement, il est encore en retard.* Of course, he's late again.

le **naufrage** NOUN
shipwreck

nautique ADJECTIVE
water
- ◆**les sports nautiques** water sports
- ◆**le ski nautique** water-skiing

le **navet** NOUN
turnip

la **navette** NOUN
shuttle ◊ *la navette entre la gare et l'aéroport* the shuttle between the station and the airport
- ◆**faire la navette** to commute ◊ *Je fais la navette entre Paris et Ivry.* I commute between Paris and Ivry.

le **navigateur** NOUN
browser (*on computer*)

la **navigation** NOUN
- ◆**La navigation est interdite ici.** Boats are not allowed here.

naviguer VERB
to sail

le **navire** NOUN
ship

ne ADVERB
ne is combined with words such as **pas, personne, plus** *and* **jamais** *to form negative phrases.*
◊ *Je ne peux pas venir.* I can't come. ◊ *Ils ne vont jamais en boîte.* They never go to discos. ◊ *Je ne connais personne.* I don't know anyone.
ne changes to n' before a vowel and most words beginning with "h".
◊ *Je n'ai pas d'argent.* I haven't got any money. ◊ *Il n'habite plus à Paris.* He doesn't live in Paris any more.

☞

ne is sometimes not translated.
◊ *C'est plus loin que je ne le croyais.*
It's further than I thought.

né VERB *see* **naître**
born ◊ *Elle est née en 1990.* She was
born in 1990.

néanmoins ADVERB
nevertheless

nécessaire ADJECTIVE
necessary ◊ *Il est nécessaire de
réserver.* It's necessary to book.

le **nectar** NOUN
♦ **le nectar d'abricot** apricot drink

néerlandais ADJECTIVE, NOUN (FEM SING
néerlandaise)
Dutch ◊ *Manon parle néerlandais.*
Manon speaks Dutch.
♦ **un Néerlandais** a Dutchman
♦ **une Néerlandaise** a Dutchwoman
♦ **les Néerlandais** the Dutch

négatif ADJECTIVE (FEM SING **négative**)
| *see also* **négatif** NOUN |
negative

le **négatif** NOUN
| *see also* **négatif** ADJECTIVE |
negative (*of photo*)

négligé ADJECTIVE
scruffy ◊ *une tenue négligée* scruffy
clothes

négliger VERB
to neglect ◊ *Ces derniers temps il a
négligé son travail.* He's been
neglecting his work recently.

négocier VERB
to negotiate

la **neige** NOUN
snow
♦ **un bonhomme de neige** a snowman

neiger VERB
to snow

le **nénuphar** NOUN
water lily

le **néon** NOUN
neon ◊ *une lampe au néon* a neon
light ◊ *La cuisine est éclairée au
néon.* The kitchen has a neon light.

néo-zélandais ADJECTIVE, NOUN (FEM SING
néo-zélandaise)
New Zealand ◊ *Le champion néo-
zélandais a gagné la course.* The New
Zealand champion won the race.
♦ **un Néo-Zélandais** a New Zealander
(*man*)
♦ **une Néo-Zélandaise** a New Zealander
(*woman*)

le **nerf** NOUN
nerve

♦ **taper sur les nerfs de quelqu'un** to
get on somebody's nerves ◊ *Il me
tape sur les nerfs.* He's getting on my
nerves.

nerveux ADJECTIVE (FEM SING **nerveuse**)
nervous

la **nervosité** NOUN
nervousness

n'est-ce pas ADVERB
n'est-ce pas is used to check that
something is true.
◊ *Nous sommes le douze aujourd'hui,
n'est-ce pas?* It's the 12th today, isn't
it? ◊ *Ils sont venus l'an dernier,
n'est-ce pas?* They came last year,
didn't they? ◊ *Elle aura dix-huit ans
en octobre, n'est-ce pas?* She'll be 18
in October, won't she?

le **Net** NOUN
the Net

net ADJECTIVE, ADVERB (FEM SING **nette**)
[1] clear ◊ *L'image n'est pas nette.*
The picture isn't very clear.
[2] net ◊ *Poids net: 500 g.* Net weight:
500 g.
[3] flatly ◊ *Il a refusé net de nous
aider.* He flatly refused to help us.
♦ **s'arrêter net** to stop dead

nettement ADVERB
much ◊ *Ce magasin est nettement
plus cher.* This shop is much more
expensive.

le **nettoyage** NOUN
cleaning
♦ **le nettoyage à sec** dry cleaning

nettoyer VERB
to clean

neuf NUMBER
| *see also* **neuf** ADJECTIVE |
nine ◊ *Claire a neuf ans.* Claire's
nine. ◊ *Il est neuf heures du matin.*
It's nine in the morning.
♦ **le neuf février** the ninth of February

neuf ADJECTIVE (FEM SING **neuve**)
| *see also* **neuf** NUMBER |
new ◊ *des chaussures neuves* new
shoes

neutre ADJECTIVE
neutral

neuve ADJECTIVE *see* **neuf**

neuvième ADJECTIVE
ninth ◊ *au neuvième étage* on the
ninth floor

le **neveu** NOUN (PL les **neveux**)
nephew

le **nez** NOUN
nose

♦ **se trouver nez à nez avec quelqu'un** to come face to face with somebody

ni CONJUNCTION
♦ **ni ... ni ...** neither ... nor ... ◊ *Je n'aime ni les lentilles ni les épinards.* I like neither lentils nor spinach. ◊ *Elles ne sont venues ni l'une ni l'autre.* Neither of them came.

la **niche** NOUN
kennel

le **nid** NOUN
nest

la **nièce** NOUN
niece

nier VERB
to deny

n'importe ADVERB
♦ **n'importe quel** any old ◊ *N'importe quel stylo fera l'affaire.* Any old pen will do.
♦ **n'importe qui** anybody ◊ *N'ouvre pas la porte à n'importe qui.* Don't open the door to just anybody.
♦ **n'importe quoi** anything ◊ *Je ferais n'importe quoi pour elle.* I'd do anything for her.
♦ **Tu dis n'importe quoi.** You're talking rubbish.
♦ **n'importe où** anywhere ◊ *On trouve ces fleurs n'importe où.* You can find these flowers anywhere.
♦ **Ne laisse pas tes affaires n'importe où.** Don't leave your things lying everywhere.
♦ **n'importe quand** any time ◊ *Tu peux venir n'importe quand.* You can come any time.
♦ **n'importe comment** any old how ◊ *Ces livres sont rangés n'importe comment.* These books have been put away any old how.

le **niveau** NOUN (PL les **niveaux**)
[1] level ◊ *le niveau de l'eau* the water level
[2] standard ◊ *Ces deux enfants n'ont pas le même niveau.* These two children aren't at the same level.
♦ **le niveau de vie** the standard of living

noble ADJECTIVE
noble

la **noblesse** NOUN
nobility

la **noce** NOUN
wedding
♦ **un repas de noce** a wedding reception
♦ **Leurs noces d'or.** Their golden wedding anniversary.

nocif ADJECTIVE (FEM SING **nocive**)

harmful ◊ *une substance nocive* a harmful substance

nocturne ADJECTIVE
see also **nocturne** NOUN
[1] nocturnal ◊ *un oiseau nocturne* a nocturnal bird
[2] by night ◊ *Découvrez le Paris nocturne!* Discover Paris by night!

la **nocturne** NOUN
see also **nocturne** ADJECTIVE
late-night opening ◊ *Nocturne le vendredi jusqu'à vingt-trois heures.* Late-night opening until 11 p.m. on Fridays.

le **Noël** NOUN
Christmas ◊ *Qu'est-ce que tu as eu pour Noël?* What did you get for Christmas?
♦ **Joyeux Noël!** Merry Christmas!

le **nœud** NOUN
[1] knot ◊ *Il a fait un nœud à la corde.* He tied a knot in the rope.
[2] bow ◊ *Janet avait un nœud dans les cheveux.* Janet had a bow in her hair.
♦ **un nœud papillon** a bow tie

noir ADJECTIVE
see also **noir** NOUN
[1] black ◊ *Elle porte une robe noire.* She's wearing a black dress. ◊ *Elle est noire.* She's black.
[2] dark ◊ *Il fait noir dehors.* It's dark outside.

le **noir** NOUN
see also **noir** ADJECTIVE
dark ◊ *J'ai peur du noir.* I'm afraid of the dark.
♦ **le travail au noir** moonlighting

le **Noir** NOUN
black man
♦ **les Noirs** black people

la **Noire** NOUN
black woman

la **noisette** NOUN
hazelnut

la **noix** NOUN (PL les **noix**)
walnut
♦ **une noix de coco** a coconut
♦ **les noix de cajou** cashew nuts
♦ **une noix de beurre** a knob of butter

le **nom** NOUN
[1] name ◊ *votre nom* your name
♦ **mon nom de famille** my surname
♦ **son nom de jeune fille** her maiden name
[2] noun (*in grammar*) ◊ *un nom commun* a common noun ◊ *un nom propre* a proper noun

le **nombre** NOUN

N

number ◇ *Treize est un nombre impair.* Thirteen is an odd number. ◇ *un grand nombre d'amis* a large number of friends

nombreux ADJECTIVE (FEM SING **nombreuse**)

[1] many ◇ *Il a gagné de nombreux matchs.* He's won many matches.

[2] large ◇ *une famille nombreuse* a large family

◆**peu nombreux** few ◇ *Nous étions peu nombreux à la réunion.* There were few of us at the meeting.

le **nombril** NOUN

navel

nommer VERB

[1] to name ◇ *Il n'a voulu nommer personne.* He didn't want to name anybody.

[2] to appoint ◇ *Il a été nommé directeur.* He was appointed director.

non ADVERB

no ◇ *Tu as vu Jean-Pierre? – Non.* Have you seen Jean-Pierre? – No.

◆**non seulement** not only ◇ *Il est non seulement intelligent, mais aussi très gentil.* Not only is he intelligent, he's also very nice.

◆**moi non plus** Neither do I. ◇ *Je n'aime pas les hamburgers. – Moi non plus.* I don't like hamburgers. – Neither do I. ◇ *Il n'y est pas allé et moi non plus.* He didn't go and neither did I.

non alcoolisé ADJECTIVE

non-alcoholic ◇ *les boissons non alcoolisées* non-alcoholic drinks

le **non-fumeur** NOUN

non-smoker ◇ *Gavin est un non-fumeur.* Gavin's a non-smoker.

◆**une voiture non-fumeurs** a no-smoking carriage

le **nord** NOUN

see also **nord** ADJECTIVE

north ◇ *Ils vivent dans le nord de l'île.* They live in the north of the island.

◆**vers le nord** northwards

◆**au nord de Paris** north of Paris

◆**l'Afrique du Nord** North Africa

◆**le vent du nord** the north wind

nord ADJECTIVE

see also **nord** NOUN

[1] north ◇ *la face nord du Mont-Blanc* the north face of Mont-Blanc

◆**le pôle Nord** the North Pole

[2] northern ◇ *Nous avons visité la partie nord de l'île.* We visited the northern part of the island.

le **nord-est** NOUN

north-east ◇ *les régions du nord-est* north-eastern regions

le **nord-ouest** NOUN

north-west

◆**l'Europe du nord-ouest** north-west Europe

normal ADJECTIVE (MASC PL **normaux**)

[1] normal ◇ *un bébé normal* a normal baby

[2] natural ◇ *C'est tout à fait normal.* It's perfectly natural.

◆**Vous trouvez que c'est normal?** Does that seem right to you?

normalement ADVERB

normally ◇ *Les aéroports fonctionnent tous normalement.* The airports are all working normally.

◆**Normalement, elle doit arriver à huit heures.** She's supposed to arrive at 8 o'clock.

◆**Tu es libre ce week-end? – Oui, normalement.** Are you free this weekend? – Yes, I should be.

normand ADJECTIVE

◆**un village normand** a village in Normandy

◆**la côte normande** the coast of Normandy

la **Normandie** NOUN

Normandy

la **Norvège** NOUN

Norway

norvégien ADJECTIVE, NOUN (FEM SING **norvégienne**)

Norwegian

◆**Elle parle norvégien.** She speaks Norwegian.

◆**un Norvégien** a Norwegian (*man*)

◆**une Norvégienne** a Norwegian (*woman*)

nos ADJECTIVE

our ◇ *Où sont nos affaires?* Where are our things?

le **notaire** NOUN

solicitor ◇ *Son père est notaire.* His father's a solicitor.

la **note** NOUN

[1] note ◇ *J'ai pris des notes pendant la conférence.* I took notes at the lecture. ◇ *Il a joué quelques notes au piano.* He played a few notes on the piano.

[2] mark ◇ *Vincent a de bonnes notes en maths.* Vincent's got good marks in maths.

[3] bill ◇ *Il n'a pas payé sa note.* He didn't pay his bill.

noter VERB

to make a note of ◊ *Tu as noté leur adresse?* Did you make a note of their address?

les **notions** FEM NOUN
basics ◊ *Il faut avoir des notions d'anglais.* You have to have some basic English. ◊ *Elle a des notions de comptabilité.* She knows the basics of accounting.

notre ADJECTIVE (PL **nos**)
our ◊ *Voici notre maison.* Here's our house.

nôtre PRONOUN
◆ **le nôtre** ours ◊ *À qui est ce chien? – C'est le nôtre.* Whose dog is it? – It's ours. ◊ *Leur voiture est rouge, la nôtre est bleue.* Their car is red, ours is blue.

nôtres PRONOUN
◆ **les nôtres** ours ◊ *Ces places-là sont les nôtres.* Those seats are ours.

nouer VERB
to tie

les **nouilles** FEM NOUN
noodles

le **nounours** NOUN
teddy bear

nourrir VERB
to feed

la **nourriture** NOUN
food

nous PRONOUN
1 we ◊ *Nous avons deux enfants.* We have two children.
2 us ◊ *Viens avec nous.* Come with us.
◆ **nous-mêmes** ourselves

nouveau ADJECTIVE (MASC SING ALSO **nouvel**, FEM SING **nouvelle**, MASC PL **nouveaux**)
see also **nouveau** NOUN
new ◊ *Il me faut un nouveau pantalon.* I need some new trousers. ◊ *Elle a une nouvelle voiture.* She's got a new car.

nouveau changes to nouvel before a vowel and most words beginning with "h".

◊ *le nouvel élève dans ma classe* the new boy in my class
◆ **le nouvel an** New Year

le **nouveau** NOUN (PL les **nouveaux**)
see also **nouveau** ADJECTIVE
new pupil ◊ *Il y a plusieurs nouveaux dans la classe.* There are several new pupils in the class.
◆ **de nouveau** again ◊ *Il pleut de nouveau.* It's raining again.

le **nouveau-né** NOUN

newborn child

la **nouveauté** NOUN
novelty

nouvel, nouvelle ADJECTIVE see **nouveau**

la **nouvelle** NOUN
1 news ◊ *Tu connais la nouvelle? Teresa a gagné au loto.* Have you heard the news? Teresa won the lottery. ◊ *C'est une bonne nouvelle.* That's good news.
2 short story ◊ *une nouvelle de Balzac* a short story by Balzac
◆ **les nouvelles** the news ◊ *J'ai écouté les nouvelles à la radio.* I listened to the news on the radio.
◆ **avoir des nouvelles de quelqu'un** to hear from somebody ◊ *Je n'ai pas eu de nouvelles de lui.* I haven't heard from him.

la **Nouvelle-Zélande** NOUN
New Zealand

novembre MASC NOUN
November
◆ **en novembre** in November

le **noyau** NOUN (PL les **noyaux**)
stone (*of fruit*) ◊ *un noyau d'abricot* an apricot stone

le **noyer** NOUN
see also **noyer** VERB
walnut tree

se **noyer** VERB
see also **noyer** NOUN
to drown ◊ *Il s'est noyé dans la rivière.* He drowned in the river.

nu ADJECTIVE
1 naked ◊ *Ils se sont baignés nus.* They went for a swim naked. ◊ *tout nus* stark naked
2 bare ◊ *Elle avait les bras nus.* Her arms were bare. ◊ *Les murs étaient nus.* The walls were bare.

le **nuage** NOUN
cloud
◆ **un nuage de lait** a drop of milk

nuageux ADJECTIVE (FEM SING **nuageuse**)
cloudy

nucléaire ADJECTIVE
nuclear ◊ *l'énergie nucléaire* nuclear power

le/la **nudiste** NOUN
nudist

la **nuit** NOUN
night ◊ *Ils ont fait du bruit toute la nuit.* They were noisy all night.
◆ **Il fait nuit.** It's dark.
◆ **cette nuit** tonight ◊ *Il va rentrer cette nuit.* He'll be back tonight.
◆ **Bonne nuit!** Good night!
◆ **de nuit** by night

N

nul ADJECTIVE (FEM SING **nulle**)
<u>rubbish</u>
♦ **Ce film est nul.** (*informal*) This film's rubbish.
♦ **être nul** to be no good ◊ *Je suis nul en maths.* I'm no good at maths.
♦ **un match nul** a draw (*in sport*) ◊ *Ils ont fait match nul.* It was a draw.
♦ **nulle part** nowhere ◊ *Je ne le vois nulle part.* I can't see it anywhere.

numérique ADJECTIVE
<u>digital</u> ◊ *un appareil photo numérique* a digital camera

le **numéro** NOUN
<u>number</u> ◊ *J'habite au numéro trois.* I live at number 3.
♦ **mon numéro de téléphone** my phone number
♦ **le numéro de compte** the account number

nu-pieds ADJECTIVE, ADVERB
<u>barefoot</u> ◊ *Il se promenait nu-pieds.* He was walking barefoot.

la **nuque** NOUN
<u>nape of the neck</u>

le **nylon** NOUN
<u>nylon</u>

O

obéir VERB
to obey
♦ **obéir à quelqu'un** to obey somebody ◊ *Elle refuse d'obéir à ses parents.* She refuses to obey her parents.

obéissant ADJECTIVE
obedient

l' **objet** MASC NOUN
object
♦ **les objets de valeur** valuables
♦ **les objets trouvés** the lost property office

obligatoire ADJECTIVE
compulsory

obliger VERB
♦ **obliger quelqu'un à faire quelque chose** to force somebody to do something
♦ **Je suis bien obligé d'accepter.** I can't really refuse.

obscur ADJECTIVE
dark

l' **obscurité** FEM NOUN
darkness ◊ *dans l'obscurité* in the dark

l' **obsédé** MASC NOUN
sex maniac
♦ **un obsédé sexuel** a sex maniac

obséder VERB
to obsess ◊ *Il est obsédé par le travail.* He's obsessed by work.

l' **observation** FEM NOUN
comment ◊ *J'ai une ou deux observations à faire.* I've got one or two comments to make.

observer VERB
1 to watch ◊ *Il observait les canards sur le lac.* He watched the ducks on the lake.
2 to observe ◊ *Ils observent le règlement.* They observe the rules.

l' **obstacle** MASC NOUN
1 obstacle ◊ *surmonter un obstacle* to overcome an obstacle
2 fence (*in show jumping*)
♦ **une course d'obstacles** an obstacle race

obstiné ADJECTIVE
stubborn

obtenir VERB
1 to get ◊ *Ils ont obtenu cinquante pour cent des voix.* They got 50% of the votes.
2 to achieve ◊ *Nous avons obtenu de bons résultats.* We achieved good results.

l' **occasion** FEM NOUN
1 opportunity ◊ *C'est une occasion à ne pas manquer.* It's an opportunity not to be missed.
2 occasion ◊ *à l'occasion de son anniversaire* on the occasion of his birthday ◊ *à plusieurs occasions* on several occasions
3 bargain ◊ *Cet ordinateur est une bonne occasion.* This computer's a real bargain.
♦ **d'occasion** second-hand ◊ *une voiture d'occasion* a second-hand car

l' **Occident** MASC NOUN
West
♦ **en Occident** in the West

occidental ADJECTIVE (MASC PL **occidentaux**)
western
♦ **les pays occidentaux** the West

l' **occupation** FEM NOUN
occupation ◊ *la France sous l'Occupation* France during the Occupation

occupé ADJECTIVE
1 busy ◊ *Le directeur est très occupé.* The director's very busy.
2 taken ◊ *Est-ce que cette place est occupée?* Is this seat taken?
3 engaged ◊ *Les toilettes sont occupées.* The toilet's engaged. ◊ *La ligne est occupée.* The line's engaged.

occuper VERB
to occupy ◊ *Les enfants ne sont pas faciles à occuper quand il pleut.* Children aren't easy to keep occupied when it rains.
♦ **s'occuper de quelque chose (1)** to be in charge of something ◊ *Elle s'occupe d'un club de sport.* She's in charge of a sports club.
♦ **s'occuper de quelque chose (2)** to deal with something ◊ *Je vais m'occuper de ce dossier.* I'm going to deal with this file.
♦ **On s'occupe de vous?** (*in a shop*) Are you being attended to?

l' **océan** MASC NOUN
ocean ◊ *l'océan Indien* the Indian Ocean

octobre MASC NOUN

October
♦ **en octobre** in October

l' **odeur** FEM NOUN
smell ◊ *Il y a une drôle d'odeur ici.*
There's a funny smell round here.

odieux ADJECTIVE (FEM SING **odieuse**)
horrible ◊ *Elle a été odieuse avec
nous.* She was horrible to us.

l' **œil** MASC NOUN (PL les **yeux**)
eye ◊ *J'ai quelque chose dans l'œil.*
I've got something in my eye.
♦ **à l'œil** (*informal*) for free ◊ *Il est entré
à l'œil.* He got in for free.

l' **œillet** MASC NOUN
carnation

l' **œuf** MASC NOUN
egg
♦ **un œuf à la coque** a soft-boiled egg
♦ **un œuf dur** a hard-boiled egg
♦ **un œuf au plat** a fried egg
♦ **les œufs brouillés** scrambled eggs
♦ **un œuf de Pâques** an Easter egg

l' **œuvre** FEM NOUN
work ◊ *J'étudie une œuvre de
Molière.* I'm studying one of
Molière's works.
♦ **une œuvre d'art** a work of art

offert VERB *see* **offrir**

l' **office** MASC NOUN
♦ **un office du tourisme** a tourist office

officiel ADJECTIVE (FEM SING **officielle**)
official

l' **officier** MASC NOUN
officer ◊ *Il est officier de marine.*
He's a naval officer.

l' **offre** FEM NOUN
offer ◊ *une offre spéciale* a special
offer
♦ **"offres d'emploi"** "situations vacant"

offrir VERB
♦ **offrir quelque chose (1)** to offer
something ◊ *On lui a offert un poste
de secrétaire.* They offered her a
secretarial post. ◊ *Elle lui a offert à
boire.* She offered him a drink.
♦ **offrir quelque chose (2)** to give
something ◊ *Il lui a offert des roses.*
He gave her roses.
♦ **s'offrir quelque chose** to treat oneself
to something ◊ *Je me suis offert un
nouveau sac.* I treated myself to a
new bag.

l' **oie** FEM NOUN
goose

l' **oignon** MASC NOUN
onion

l' **oiseau** MASC NOUN (PL les **oiseaux**)
bird

l' **olive** FEM NOUN
olive ◊ *l'huile d'olive* olive oil

olympique ADJECTIVE
♦ **les Jeux olympiques** the Olympic
Games

l' **ombre** FEM NOUN
1 shade ◊ *Je vais me mettre à
l'ombre.* I'm going to sit in the shade.
2 shadow
♦ **l'ombre à paupières** eye shadow

l' **omelette** FEM NOUN
omelette

l' **omnibus** MASC NOUN
local train

on PRONOUN
1 we ◊ *On va à la plage demain.*
We're going to the beach tomorrow.
◊ *On a pensé que ça te ferait plaisir.*
We thought you'd be pleased.
2 someone ◊ *On m'a volé mon sac.*
Someone has stolen my bag.
♦ **On m'a dit d'attendre.** I was told to
wait.
♦ **On vous demande au téléphone.**
There's a phone call for you.
3 you ◊ *On peut visiter le château
en été.* You can visit the castle in
the summer. ◊ *D'ici on peut voir la
côte française.* From here you can
see the French coast.

l' **oncle** MASC NOUN
uncle

l' **onde** FEM NOUN
wave (on radio) ◊ *sur les grandes
ondes* on long wave

l' **ongle** MASC NOUN
nail
♦ **se couper les ongles** to cut one's
nails ◊ *Elle s'est coupé les ongles.*
She cut her nails.

ont VERB *see* **avoir**
♦ **Ils ont beaucoup d'argent.** They've
got lots of money.
♦ **Elles ont passé de bonnes vacances.**
They had a good holiday.

l' **ONU** FEM NOUN (= *Organisation des
Nations unies*)
UN (= United Nations)

onze NUMBER
eleven ◊ *Elle a onze ans.* She's eleven.
◊ *à onze heures* at eleven o'clock
♦ **le onze juin** the eleventh of June

onzième ADJECTIVE
eleventh ◊ *au onzième étage* on the
eleventh floor

l' **opéra** MASC NOUN
opera

l' **opération** FEM NOUN
operation

opérer VERB
to operate on ◊ *Elle a été opérée de l'appendicite.* She was operated on for appendicitis.
♦ **se faire opérer** to have an operation ◊ *Elle s'est fait opérer.* She's had an operation.

l' **opinion** FEM NOUN
opinion

opposé ADJECTIVE
see also **opposé** NOUN
opposite ◊ *Elle est partie dans la direction opposée.* She went off in the opposite direction.
♦ **être opposé à quelque chose** to be opposed to something

l' **opposé** MASC NOUN
see also **opposé** ADJECTIVE
the opposite

opposer VERB
♦ **opposer quelqu'un à quelqu'un** to pit somebody against somebody ◊ *Ce match oppose les Français aux Allemands.* This match pits the French against the Germans.
♦ **s'opposer** to conflict ◊ *Ces deux points de vue s'opposent.* These two points of view conflict.
♦ **s'opposer à quelque chose** to oppose something ◊ *Son père s'oppose à son mariage.* Her father's against her marriage.

l' **opposition** FEM NOUN
opposition
♦ **par opposition à** as opposed to ◊ *la littérature contemporaine par opposition à la littérature classique* modern literature, as opposed to classics
♦ **faire opposition à un chèque** to stop a cheque

l' **opticien** MASC NOUN
optician ◊ *Il est opticien.* He's an optician.

l' **opticienne** FEM NOUN
optician ◊ *Elle est opticienne.* She's an optician.

optimiste ADJECTIVE
optimistic

l' **option** FEM NOUN
option
♦ **une matière à option** an optional subject

l' **or** MASC NOUN
see also **or** CONJUNCTION
gold ◊ *un bracelet en or* a gold bracelet

or CONJUNCTION
see also **or** NOUN

and yet ◊ *Il était sûr de gagner, or il a perdu.* He was sure he would win, and yet he lost.

l' **orage** MASC NOUN
thunderstorm

orageux ADJECTIVE (FEM SING **orageuse**)
stormy

oral ADJECTIVE (MASC PL **oraux**)
see also **oral** NOUN
♦ **une épreuve orale** an oral exam
♦ **à prendre par voie orale** to be taken orally

l' **oral** MASC NOUN (PL les **oraux**)
see also **oral** ADJECTIVE
oral (*exam*) ◊ *un oral de français* a French oral

l' **orange** FEM NOUN
see also **orange** ADJECTIVE
orange (*fruit*)

orange ADJECTIVE (MASC, FEM, PL)
see also **orange** NOUN
orange (*in colour*) ◊ *des fleurs orange* orange flowers

l' **orchestre** MASC NOUN
1 orchestra ◊ *un orchestre symphonique* a symphony orchestra
2 band ◊ *un orchestre de jazz* a jazz band

l' **ordi** MASC NOUN (*informal*)
computer

ordinaire ADJECTIVE
see also **ordinaire** NOUN
1 ordinary ◊ *des gens ordinaires* ordinary people
2 standard ◊ *un format ordinaire* a standard size

l' **ordinaire** MASC NOUN
see also **ordinaire** ADJECTIVE
♦ **sortir de l'ordinaire** to be out of the ordinary

l' **ordinateur** MASC NOUN
computer

l' **ordonnance** FEM NOUN
prescription

ordonné ADJECTIVE
tidy

ordonner VERB
♦ **ordonner à quelqu'un de faire quelque chose** to order somebody to do something

l' **ordre** MASC NOUN
order ◊ *par ordre alphabétique* in alphabetical order
♦ **dans l'ordre** in order ◊ *dans le bon ordre* in the right order
♦ **mettre en ordre** to tidy up
♦ **jusqu'à nouvel ordre** until further notice

O

les **ordures** FEM NOUN
　　rubbish SING
　◆**jeter quelque chose aux ordures** to
　　throw something in the bin

l'**oreille** FEM NOUN
　　ear

l'**oreiller** MASC NOUN
　　pillow

les **oreillons** MASC NOUN
　　mumps

l'**organe** MASC NOUN
　　organ (*in body*)

l'**organisateur** MASC NOUN
　　organizer

l'**organisation** FEM NOUN
　　organization

l'**organisatrice** FEM NOUN
　　organizer

　organiser VERB
　　to organize
　◆**s'organiser** to get organized ◇ *Il ne*
　　sait pas s'organiser. He can't get
　　himself organized.

l'**organisme** MASC NOUN
　　body (*organization*)

l'**orgue** MASC NOUN
　　organ ◇ *Carl joue de l'orgue.* Carl
　　plays the organ.

　orgueilleux ADJECTIVE (FEM SING
　　orgueilleuse)
　　proud

l'**Orient** MASC NOUN
　　East
　◆**en Orient** in the East

　oriental ADJECTIVE (MASC PL **orientaux**)
　　[1] oriental ◇ *un palais oriental* an
　　oriental palace
　　[2] eastern ◇ *la frontière orientale de*
　　la Pologne Poland's eastern border

l'**orientation** FEM NOUN
　　orientation
　◆**avoir le sens de l'orientation** to have
　　a good sense of direction
　◆**l'orientation professionnelle** careers
　　advice

　originaire ADJECTIVE
　◆**Elle est originaire de Paris.** She's
　　from Paris.

　original ADJECTIVE (MASC PL **originaux**)
　　see also **original** NOUN
　　original ◇ *un film en version*
　　originale a film in the original
　　language

l'**original** MASC NOUN (PL les **originaux**)
　　see also **original** ADJECTIVE
　　original ◇ *L'original est au Louvre.*
　　The original is in the Louvre.
　◆**un vieil original** an old eccentric

l'**origine** FEM NOUN
　　origin
　◆**à l'origine** originally

l'**orphelin** MASC NOUN
　　orphan

l'**orpheline** FEM NOUN
　　orphan

l'**orteil** MASC NOUN
　　toe

l'**orthographe** FEM NOUN
　　spelling

l'**os** MASC NOUN
　　bone

　oser VERB
　　to dare
　◆**oser faire quelque chose** to dare to
　　do something

l'**otage** MASC NOUN
　　hostage

　ôter VERB
　　[1] to take off ◇ *Elle a ôté son*
　　manteau. She took off her coat.
　　[2] to take away

　ou CONJUNCTION
　　or
　◆**ou ... ou ...** either ... or ...
　◆**ou bien** or else ◇ *On pourrait aller au*
　　cinéma ou bien rentrer directement.
　　We could go to the cinema or else
　　go straight home.

　où PRONOUN, ADVERB
　　[1] where ◇ *Où est Nick?* Where's
　　Nick? ◇ *Où allez-vous?* Where are you
　　going? ◇ *Je sais où il est.* I know
　　where he is. ◇ *C'est la maison où je*
　　suis né. That's the house where I
　　was born. ◇ *la ville d'où je viens* the
　　town I come from
　　[2] that ◇ *Le jour où il est parti, tout*
　　le monde a pleuré. The day that he
　　left, everyone cried.
　◆**Par où allons-nous passer?** Which
　　way are we going to go?

l'**ouate** FEM NOUN
　　cotton wool

　oublier VERB
　　[1] to forget ◇ *N'oublie pas de fermer*
　　la porte. Don't forget to shut the
　　door.
　　[2] to leave ◇ *J'ai oublié mon sac*
　　chez Sabine. I left my bag at
　　Sabine's.

l'**ouest** MASC NOUN
　　see also **ouest** ADJECTIVE
　　west ◇ *Elle vit dans l'ouest de*
　　l'Angleterre. She lives in the West of
　　England.
　◆**à l'ouest de Paris** west of Paris
　◆**vers l'ouest** westwards

◆**l'Europe de l'Ouest** Western Europe
◆**le vent d'ouest** the west wind

ouest ADJECTIVE (MASC, FEM, PL)
see also **ouest** NOUN
1 west ◇ *la côte ouest de l'Écosse*
the west coast of Scotland
2 western ◇ *la partie ouest du pays*
the western part of the country

ouf EXCLAMATION
phew!

oui ADVERB
yes

l'**ouragan** MASC NOUN
hurricane

l'**ourlet** MASC NOUN
seam

l'**ours** MASC NOUN
bear
◆**un ours en peluche** a teddy bear

l'**outil** MASC NOUN
tool

outré ADJECTIVE
outraged ◇ *Il a été outré de son
insolence.* He was outraged at her
cheek.

ouvert VERB see **ouvrir**

ouvert ADJECTIVE
1 open ◇ *Le magasin est ouvert.* The
shop's open.
2 on ◇ *Il a laissé le robinet ouvert.*
He left the tap on.
◆**avoir l'esprit ouvert** to be open-
minded

l'**ouverture** FEM NOUN
opening ◇ *les heures d'ouverture*
opening hours

l'**ouvre-boîte** MASC NOUN
tin opener

l'**ouvre-bouteille** MASC NOUN
bottle-opener

l'**ouvreuse** FEM NOUN
usherette

l'**ouvrier** MASC NOUN
worker ◇ *Son père est ouvrier dans
une usine.* His father's a factory
worker.

l'**ouvrière** FEM NOUN
worker ·

ouvrir VERB
to open ◇ *Ouvrez!* Open up! ◇ *Elle
a ouvert la porte.* She opened the
door.
◆**s'ouvrir** to open ◇ *La porte s'est
ouverte.* The door opened.

ovale ADJECTIVE
oval

l'**ovni** MASC NOUN (= *objet volant non
identifié*)
UFO

l'**oxygène** MASC NOUN
oxygen

l'**ozone** MASC NOUN
ozone

O

P

le **Pacifique** NOUN
Pacific ◊ *l'océan Pacifique* the Pacific Ocean

le **pacifiste** NOUN
pacifist

la **pagaille** NOUN
mess SING ◊ *Quelle pagaille!* What a mess!

la **page** NOUN
page ◊ *Tournez la page.* Turn the page.
♦ **la page d'accueil** the home page

la **paie** NOUN
wages

le **paiement** NOUN
payment

le **paillasson** NOUN
doormat

la **paille** NOUN
straw

le **pain** NOUN
1 bread ◊ *un morceau de pain* a piece of bread ◊ *une tranche de pain* a slice of bread
2 loaf ◊ *J'ai acheté un pain.* I bought a loaf of bread.
♦ **le pain complet** wholemeal bread
♦ **le pain d'épice** gingerbread
♦ **le pain de mie** sandwich loaf
♦ **le pain grillé** toast

pair ADJECTIVE
even ◊ *un nombre pair* an even number
♦ **une jeune fille au pair** an au pair

la **paire** NOUN
pair ◊ *une paire de chaussures* a pair of shoes

paisible ADJECTIVE
peaceful ◊ *un village paisible* a peaceful village

la **paix** NOUN
peace
♦ **faire la paix (1)** to make peace ◊ *Les deux pays ont fait la paix.* The two countries have made peace with each other.
♦ **faire la paix (2)** to make it up ◊ *Laure a fait la paix avec son frère.* Laure made it up with her brother.
♦ **avoir la paix** to have peace and quiet ◊ *J'aimerais bien avoir la paix.* I'd like to have a bit of peace and quiet.
♦ **Fiche-lui la paix!** (*informal*) Leave him alone!

le **palais** NOUN
1 palace ◊ *le palais de Buckingham* Buckingham Palace
2 palate (*in mouth*)

pâle ADJECTIVE
pale ◊ *bleu pâle* pale blue

la **Palestine** NOUN
Palestine

la **pâleur** NOUN
paleness

le **palier** NOUN
landing ◊ *Il m'attendait sur le palier.* He was waiting for me on the landing.

pâlir VERB
to go pale

la **palme** NOUN
flipper (*for swimming*)

palmé ADJECTIVE
webbed ◊ *Les canards ont les pieds palmés.* Ducks have webbed feet.

le **palmier** NOUN
palm tree

palpitant ADJECTIVE
thrilling ◊ *un roman palpitant* a thrilling novel

le **pamplemousse** NOUN
grapefruit

le **panaché** NOUN
shandy

la **pancarte** NOUN
sign ◊ *Il y a une pancarte dans la vitrine.* There's a sign in the window.

pané ADJECTIVE
fried in breadcrumbs ◊ *du poisson pané* fish in breadcrumbs

le **panier** NOUN
basket

la **panique** NOUN
panic

paniquer VERB
to panic

la **panne** NOUN
breakdown
♦ **être en panne** to have broken down ◊ *L'ascenseur est en panne.* The lift's not working.
♦ **tomber en panne** to break down ◊ *Nous sommes tombés en panne sur l'autoroute.* We broke down on the motorway. ◊ *Nous sommes tombés en panne d'essence.* We've run out of petrol.
♦ **une panne de courant** a power cut

le **panneau** NOUN (PL les **panneaux**)
  sign ◊ *Ce panneau dit que la maison est à vendre.* This sign says that the house is for sale.
  ◆ **panneau d'affichage (1)** billboard
  ◆ **panneau d'affichage (2)** bulletin board (*on internet*)

le **panorama** NOUN
  panorama

le **pansement** NOUN
  1 dressing (*bandage*)
  2 sticking plaster

le **pantalon** NOUN
  trousers PL ◊ *Son pantalon est trop court.* His trousers are too short.
  ◆ **un pantalon de ski** a pair of ski pants

la **pantoufle** NOUN
  slipper

la **PAO** ABBREVIATION (= *publication assistée par ordinateur*)
  DTP (= desktop publishing)

le **paon** NOUN
  peacock

le **papa** NOUN
  dad

le **pape** NOUN
  pope

la **papeterie** NOUN
  stationer's

le **papi** NOUN (*informal*)
  granddad

le **papier** NOUN
  paper ◊ *une feuille de papier* a sheet of paper
  ◆ **Vos papiers, s'il vous plaît.** Your identity papers, please.
  ◆ **les papiers d'identité** identity papers
  ◆ **le papier à lettres** writing paper
  ◆ **le papier hygiénique** toilet paper
  ◆ **le papier peint** wallpaper

le **papillon** NOUN
  butterfly

le **paquebot** NOUN
  liner

la **pâquerette** NOUN
  daisy

Pâques MASC NOUN
  Easter ◊ *Je viendrai te voir à Pâques.* I'll come and see you at Easter.
  ◆ **les œufs de Pâques** Easter eggs

> 🛈 In France, Easter eggs are said to be brought by the Easter bells or **cloches de Pâques** which fly from Rome and drop them in people's gardens.

---

le **paquet** NOUN

  1 packet ◊ *Je voudrais un paquet de cigarettes.* I'd like a packet of cigarettes.
  2 parcel ◊ *Sa mère lui a envoyé un paquet.* His mother sent him a parcel.

le **paquet-cadeau** NOUN (PL les **paquets-cadeaux**)
  gift-wrapped parcel ◊ *La vendeuse m'a fait un paquet-cadeau.* The shop assistant gift-wrapped it for me.

par PREPOSITION
  1 by ◊ *L'Amérique a été découverte par Christophe Colomb.* America was discovered by Christopher Columbus.
  ◆ **deux par deux** two by two ◊ *Les élèves sont entrés deux par deux.* The pupils went in two by two.
  2 with ◊ *Son nom commence par un H.* His name begins with H.
  3 out of ◊ *Elle regardait par la fenêtre.* She was looking out of the window. ◊ *par habitude* out of habit
  4 via ◊ *Nous sommes passés par Lyon pour aller à Grenoble.* We went via Lyons to Grenoble.
  5 through ◊ *Il faut passer par la douane avant de prendre l'avion.* You have to go through customs before boarding the plane.
  6 per ◊ *Prenez trois cachets par jour.* Take three tablets per day. ◊ *Le voyage coûte deux mille euros par personne.* The trip costs two thousand euros per person.
  ◆ **par ici (1)** this way ◊ *Il faut passer par ici pour y arriver.* You have to go this way to get there.
  ◆ **par ici (2)** round here ◊ *Il y a beaucoup de touristes par ici.* There are lots of tourists round here.
  ◆ **par-ci, par-là** here and there

le **parachute** NOUN
  parachute

le/la **parachutiste** NOUN
  parachutist

le **paradis** NOUN
  heaven

les **parages** MASC NOUN
  ◆ **dans les parages** in the area ◊ *Il n'y a pas d'hôtel dans les parages.* There are no hotels in the area.

le **paragraphe** NOUN
  paragraph

paraître VERB
  1 to seem ◊ *Ça paraît incroyable.* It seems unbelievable.

☞

[2] to look ◊ *Elle paraît plus jeune que son frère.* She looks younger than her brother.

◆**il paraît que** it seems that ◊ *Il paraît que c'est la faute de la direction.* It seems that it's the management's fault.

le **parallèle** NOUN

see also **la parallèle**

parallel ◊ *Il a fait un parallèle entre ces deux événements.* He drew a parallel between the two events.

la **parallèle** NOUN

see also **le parallèle**

parallel line

paralysé ADJECTIVE
paralysed

le **parapluie** NOUN
umbrella

le **parasol** NOUN
parasol

le **parc** NOUN

[1] park ◊ *Le dimanche, Chantal va se promener au parc.* On Sundays Chantal goes for a walk in the park.

◆**un parc d'attractions** an amusement park

[2] grounds ◊ *Le château est situé au milieu d'un grand parc.* The castle is surrounded by extensive grounds.

parce que CONJUNCTION
because ◊ *Il n'est pas venu parce qu'il n'avait pas de voiture.* He didn't come because he didn't have a car.

le **parcmètre** NOUN
parking meter

parcourir VERB

[1] to cover ◊ *Gavin a parcouru cinquante kilomètres à vélo.* Gavin covered 50 kilometres on his bike.

[2] to glance through ◊ *J'ai parcouru le journal d'aujourd'hui.* I glanced through today's newspaper.

le **parcours** NOUN
journey

par-dessous ADVERB
underneath ◊ *Il portait un pull et une chemise par-dessous.* He was wearing a jumper with a shirt underneath.

le **pardessus** NOUN
overcoat

par-dessus ADVERB, PREPOSITION

[1] on top ◊ *Elle porte un chemisier et un pull rouge par-dessus.* She's wearing a blouse with a red jumper on top.

[2] over ◊ *Elle a sauté par-dessus le mur.* She jumped over the wall.

◆**en avoir par-dessus la tête** to have had enough ◊ *J'en ai par-dessus la tête de tous ces problèmes.* I've had enough of all these problems.

le **pardon** NOUN

see also **pardon** EXCLAMATION

forgiveness

pardon EXCLAMATION

see also **pardon** NOUN

[1] sorry! ◊ *Oh, pardon! J'espère que je ne vous ai pas fait mal.* Oh, sorry! I hope I didn't hurt you.

◆**demander pardon à quelqu'un** to apologize to somebody ◊ *Il leur a demandé pardon.* He apologized to them.

◆**Je vous demande pardon.** I'm sorry.

[2] excuse me! ◊ *Pardon, madame! Pouvez-vous me dire où se trouve la poste?* Excuse me! Could you tell me where the post office is?

[3] pardon? ◊ *Pardon? Je n'ai pas compris ce que vous avez dit.* Pardon? I didn't understand what you said.

pardonner VERB
to forgive ◊ *Nous lui avons pardonné de nous avoir menti.* We forgave him for lying to us.

le **pare-brise** NOUN (PL les **pare-brise**)
windscreen

le **pare-chocs** NOUN
bumper

pareil ADJECTIVE (FEM SING **pareille**)

[1] the same ◊ *Ces deux maisons ne sont pas pareilles.* These two houses aren't the same.

[2] like that ◊ *J'aime bien sa voiture. J'en voudrais une pareille.* I like his car. I'd like one like that.

[3] such ◊ *Je refuse d'écouter des bêtises pareilles.* I won't listen to such nonsense.

◆**sans pareil** unequalled ◊ *Il a joué cette symphonie avec un talent sans pareil.* He played this symphony with unequalled talent.

la **parenthèse** NOUN
bracket ◊ *entre parenthèses* in brackets

les **parents** MASC NOUN

[1] parents (*mother and father*)
[2] relatives ◊ *parents et amis* friends and relatives

la **paresse** NOUN
laziness

paresseux ADJECTIVE (FEM SING **paresseuse**)

lazy

parfait ADJECTIVE
perfect

parfaitement ADVERB
perfectly ◇ *Il parle parfaitement l'arabe.* He speaks perfect Arabic.

parfois ADVERB
sometimes

le **parfum** NOUN
1 perfume
2 flavour ◇ *Je voudrais une glace. – Quel parfum veux-tu?* I'd like an ice cream. – What flavour would you like?

parfumé ADJECTIVE
1 fragrant ◇ *une rose très parfumée* a very fragrant rose
2 flavoured ◇ *des biscuits parfumés au café* coffee-flavoured biscuits

la **parfumerie** NOUN
perfume shop

le **pari** NOUN
bet

parier VERB
to bet

Paris NOUN
Paris
♦ **à Paris (1)** in Paris
♦ **à Paris (2)** to Paris

parisien ADJECTIVE, NOUN (FEM SING **parisienne**)
1 Parisian ◇ *un célèbre couturier parisien* a famous Parisian designer
2 Paris ◇ *le métro parisien* the Paris metro
♦ **un Parisien** a Parisian (*man*)
♦ **une Parisienne** a Parisian (*woman*)

le **parking** NOUN
car park

> Be careful! The French word **parking** does not mean **parking**.

le **parlement** NOUN
parliament

parler VERB
1 to speak ◇ *Vous parlez français?* Do you speak French?
2 to talk ◇ *Nous étions en train de parler quand le directeur est entré.* We were talking when the headmaster came in.
♦ **parler de quelque chose à quelqu'un** to tell somebody about something ◇ *Il m'a parlé de sa nouvelle voiture.* He told me about his new car.

parmi PREPOSITION
among ◇ *Ils étaient parmi les meilleurs de la classe.* They were among the best pupils in the class.

la **paroi** NOUN

wall

la **paroisse** NOUN
parish

la **parole** NOUN
1 speech ◇ *l'usage de la parole* the power of speech
2 word ◇ *Il m'a donné sa parole.* He gave me his word. ◇ *Elle a tenu parole.* She kept her word.
♦ **les paroles** lyrics ◇ *J'aime les paroles de cette chanson.* I like the lyrics of this song.

le **parquet** NOUN
floor (*wooden*)

le **parrain** NOUN
godfather

parrainer VERB
to sponsor ◇ *Cette entreprise parraine notre équipe de rugby.* This firm is sponsoring our rugby team.

pars VERB *see* **partir**

la **part** NOUN
1 share ◇ *Vous n'avez pas eu votre part.* You haven't had your share.
2 piece ◇ *une part de gâteau* a piece of cake
♦ **prendre part à quelque chose** to take part in something ◇ *Il va prendre part à la réunion.* He's going to take part in the meeting.
♦ **de la part de (1)** on behalf of ◇ *Je dois vous remercier de la part de mon frère.* I must thank you on behalf of my brother.
♦ **de la part de (2)** from ◇ *C'est un cadeau pour toi, de la part de Françoise.* It's a present for you, from Françoise.
♦ **à part** except ◇ *Ils sont tous venus, à part Christian.* They all came, except Christian.

partager VERB
1 to share ◇ *Ils partagent un appartement.* They share a flat.
2 to divide ◇ *Janet a partagé le gâteau en quatre.* Janet divided the cake into four.

le/la **partenaire** NOUN
partner

le **parti** NOUN
party ◇ *le Parti socialiste* the Socialist Party

le **participant** NOUN
participant

la **participante** NOUN
participant

la **participation** NOUN
participation

le **participe** NOUN

P

participle
+ **le participe passé** the past participle
+ **le participe présent** the present participle

participer VERB
+ **participer à quelque chose (1)** to take part in something ◊ *André va participer à la course.* André is going to take part in the race.
+ **participer à quelque chose (2)** to contribute to something ◊ *Je voudrais participer aux frais.* I would like to contribute to the cost.

la **particularité** NOUN
characteristic

particulier ADJECTIVE (FEM SING **particulière**)
1 private ◊ *une maison particulière* a private house
2 distinctive ◊ *Ce vin a un arôme particulier.* This wine has a distinctive flavour.
3 particular ◊ *Dans ce cas particulier, je ne peux rien faire.* In this particular case, I can't do anything.
+ **en particulier (1)** particularly ◊ *J'aime les fruits, en particulier les fraises.* I like fruit, particularly strawberries.
+ **en particulier (2)** in private ◊ *Est-ce que je peux vous parler en particulier?* Can I speak to you in private?

particulièrement ADVERB
particularly

la **partie** NOUN
1 part ◊ *Une partie du groupe partira en Italie.* Part of the group will go to Italy.
2 game ◊ *Nous avons fait une partie de tennis.* We played a game of tennis. ◊ *une partie de cartes* a game of cards
+ **en partie** partly ◊ *Cela explique en partie le problème.* That partly explains the problem.
+ **en grande partie** largely ◊ *Son histoire est en grande partie vraie.* His story is largely true.
+ **faire partie de** to be part of ◊ *Ce tableau fait partie d'une très belle collection.* This picture is part of a very beautiful collection.

partiel ADJECTIVE (FEM SING **partielle**)
partial

partir VERB
to go ◊ *Je lui ai téléphoné mais il était déjà parti.* I phoned him but he'd already gone.
+ **partir en vacances** to go on holiday

+ **partir de** to leave ◊ *Il est parti de Nice à sept heures.* He left Nice at 7.
+ **à partir de** from ◊ *Je serai chez moi à partir de huit heures.* I'll be at home from eight o'clock onwards.

la **partition** NOUN
score (*in music*) ◊ *une partition de piano* a piano score

partout ADVERB
everywhere

paru VERB *see* **paraître**

la **parution** NOUN
publication ◊ *Ce roman a eu beaucoup de succès dès sa parution.* This novel was very successful from the moment it came out.

parvenir VERB
+ **parvenir à faire quelque chose** to manage to do something ◊ *Elle est finalement parvenue à ouvrir la porte.* She finally managed to open the door.
+ **faire parvenir quelque chose à quelqu'un** to send something to somebody ◊ *Je vous ferai parvenir le colis avant lundi.* I'll send you the parcel before Monday.

pas ADVERB
see also **pas** NOUN
+ **ne ... pas** not ◊ *Il ne pleut pas.* It's not raining. ◊ *Elle n'est pas venue.* She didn't come. ◊ *Ils n'ont pas de voiture.* They haven't got a car.
+ **Vous viendrez à notre soirée, n'est-ce pas?** You're coming to our party, aren't you?
+ **C'est Harry qui a gagné, n'est-ce pas?** Harry won, didn't he?
+ **pas moi** not me ◊ *Elle veut aller au cinéma, pas moi.* She wants to go to the cinema, but I don't.
+ **pas du tout** not at all ◊ *Je n'aime pas du tout ça.* I don't like that at all.
+ **pas mal** not bad ◊ *Ce n'est pas mal pour un début.* That's not bad for a first attempt. ◊ *Comment allez-vous? – Pas mal.* How are you? – Not bad.
+ **pas mal de** quite a lot of ◊ *Il y avait pas mal de monde au concert.* There were quite a lot of people at the concert.

le **pas** NOUN
see also **pas** ADVERB
1 pace ◊ *Il marchait d'un pas rapide.* He walked at a fast pace.
2 step ◊ *Faites trois pas en avant.* Take three steps forward. ◊ *un pas en arrière* a step backwards

3 footstep ◊ *J'entends des pas dans l'escalier.* I can hear footsteps on the stairs.

♦ **au pas** at walking pace ◊ *Le cheval est parti au pas.* The horse set off at walking pace.

♦ **faire les cent pas** to pace up and down ◊ *Il faisait les cent pas dans le corridor.* He was pacing up and down the corridor.

le **passage** NOUN

passage ◊ *J'ai traduit un passage de ce livre.* I translated a passage from this book.

♦ **Il a été éclaboussé au passage de la voiture.** He was soaked by a passing car.

♦ **de passage** passing through ◊ *Nous sommes de passage à Toulouse.* We're just passing through Toulouse.

♦ **un passage à niveau** a level crossing

♦ **un passage clouté** a pedestrian crossing

♦ **un passage protégé** a pedestrian crossing

♦ **un passage souterrain** a subway

passager ADJECTIVE (FEM SING **passagère**)

see also **passager** NOUN

temporary

le **passager** NOUN

see also **passager** ADJECTIVE

passenger

♦ **un passager clandestin** a stowaway

la **passagère** NOUN

passenger

le **passant** NOUN

passer-by

la **passante** NOUN

passer-by

passé ADJECTIVE

see also **passé** NOUN

1 last ◊ *Je l'ai vu la semaine passée.* I saw him last week.

2 past ◊ *Il est minuit passé.* It's past midnight.

le **passé** NOUN

see also **passé** ADJECTIVE

1 past ◊ *dans le passé* in the past

2 past tense ◊ *Mettez ce verbe au passé.* Put this verb into the past tense.

♦ **le passé composé** the perfect tense

♦ **le passé simple** the past historic

le **passeport** NOUN

passport

passer VERB

1 to cross ◊ *Nous avons passé la frontière belge.* We crossed the Belgian border.

2 to go through ◊ *Il faut passer la douane en sortant.* You have to go through customs on the way out.

3 to take ◊ *Gordon a passé ses examens la semaine dernière.* Gordon took his exams last week.

> Be careful! **passer un examen** does not mean **to pass an exam**.

4 to spend ◊ *Elle a passé la journée à ne rien faire.* She spent the day doing nothing. ◊ *Ils passent toujours leurs vacances au Danemark.* They always spend their holidays in Denmark.

5 to pass ◊ *Passe-moi le sel, s'il te plaît.* Pass me the salt, please.

6 to show ◊ *On passe "Le Kid" au cinéma cette semaine.* They're showing "The Kid" at the cinema this week.

7 to call in ◊ *Je passerai chez vous ce soir.* I'll call in this evening.

♦ **passer à la radio** to be on the radio ◊ *Mon père passe à la radio demain soir.* My father's on the radio tomorrow night.

♦ **passer à la télévision** to be on the television ◊ *"Titanic" passe à la télé ce soir.* "Titanic" is on TV tonight.

♦ **Ne quittez pas, je vous passe Madame Chevalier.** Hold on please, I'm putting you through to Mrs Chevalier.

♦ **passer par** to go through ◊ *Ils sont passés par Paris pour aller à Tours.* They went through Paris to get to Tours.

♦ **en passant** in passing ◊ *Je lui ai dit en passant que j'allais me marier.* I told him in passing that I was getting married.

♦ **laisser passer** to let through ◊ *Il m'a laissé passer.* He let me through.

♦ **se passer (1)** to take place ◊ *Cette histoire se passe au moyen âge.* This story takes place in the Middle Ages.

♦ **se passer (2)** to go ◊ *Comment se sont passés tes examens?* How did your exams go?

♦ **se passer (3)** to happen ◊ *Que s'est-il passé? Un accident?* What happened? Was there an accident?

♦ **Qu'est-ce qui se passe? Pourquoi est-ce qu'elle pleure?** What's the matter? Why is she crying?

♦ **se passer de** to do without ◊ *Je me passerai de café ce matin.* I'll do without coffee this morning.

la **passerelle** NOUN

1 footbridge (*over river*)

2 gangway (*onto plane, boat*)

P

le **passe-temps** NOUN
   pastime

passif ADJECTIVE (FEM SING **passive**)
   see also **passif** NOUN
   passive

le **passif** NOUN
   see also **passif** ADJECTIVE
   passive ◊ *Mettez ce verbe au passif.*
   Put this verb into the passive.

la **passion** NOUN
   passion

passionnant ADJECTIVE
   fascinating

passionné ADJECTIVE
   keen ◊ *Donald est un lecteur*
   passionné. Donald is a keen reader.
   ◆ **Il est passionné de voile.** He's a
   sailing fanatic.

passionner VERB
   ◆ **Son travail le passionne.** He's
   passionate about his work.
   ◆ **se passionner pour quelque chose** to
   have a passion for something ◊ *Harry*
   se passionne pour les perroquets.
   Harry has a passion for parrots.

la **passoire** NOUN
   sieve

la **pastèque** NOUN
   watermelon

le **pasteur** NOUN
   minister (*priest*)

la **pastille** NOUN
   cough sweet

la **patate** NOUN (*informal*)
   potato
   ◆ **une patate douce** a sweet potato

la **pâte** NOUN
   1 pastry
   2 dough
   3 cake mixture
   ◆ **la pâte à crêpes** pancake batter
   ◆ **la pâte à modeler** Plasticine ®
   ◆ **la pâte d'amandes** marzipan

le **pâté** NOUN
   pâté ◊ *Nous avons mangé du pâté*
   en entrée. We had pâté as a starter.
   ◆ **un pâté de maisons** a block (*of*
   houses)

paternel ADJECTIVE (FEM SING **paternelle**)
   ◆ **ma grand-mère paternelle** my father's
   mother
   ◆ **mon oncle paternel** my father's
   brother

les **pâtes** FEM NOUN
   pasta SING

la **patience** NOUN
   patience

patient ADJECTIVE

   see also **patient** NOUN
   patient

le **patient** NOUN
   see also **patient** ADJECTIVE
   patient

la **patiente** NOUN
   patient

patienter VERB
   to wait ◊ *Veuillez patienter un*
   instant, s'il vous plaît. Please wait a
   moment.

le **patin** NOUN
   1 skate ◊ *Nic a enfilé ses patins.* Nic
   put her skates on.
   2 skating ◊ *Ils font du patin tous les*
   mercredis. They go skating every
   Wednesday.
   ◆ **les patins à glace** ice skates
   ◆ **les patins en ligne** Rollerblades ®
   ◆ **les patins à roulettes** roller skates

le **patinage** NOUN
   skating
   ◆ **le patinage artistique** figure skating

patiner VERB
   to skate

le **patineur** NOUN
   skater

la **patineuse** NOUN
   skater

la **patinoire** NOUN
   ice rink

la **pâtisserie** NOUN
   cake shop
   ◆ **faire de la pâtisserie** to bake
   ◊ *J'adore faire de la pâtisserie.* I love
   baking.
   ◆ **les pâtisseries** cakes

le **pâtissier** NOUN
   confectioner

la **pâtissière** NOUN
   confectioner

la **patrie** NOUN
   homeland

le **patron** NOUN
   1 boss
   2 pattern (*for dressmaking*)

la **patronne** NOUN
   boss
   ◆ **Elle est patronne de café.** She runs a
   café.

patronner VERB
   to sponsor ◊ *Le festival est patronné*
   par des entreprises locales. The
   festival is sponsored by local
   businesses.

la **patrouille** NOUN
   patrol

la **patte** NOUN

1 paw (*of dog, cat*)
2 leg (*of bird, animal*)

paumer VERB (*informal*)
to lose ◊ *J'ai paumé mes clefs.* I've lost my keys.

la **paupière** NOUN
eyelid

la **pause** NOUN
1 break ◊ *Ils font une pause.* They're having a break. ◊ *une pause de midi* a lunch break
2 pause ◊ *Il y a eu une pause dans la conversation.* There was a pause in the conversation.

pauvre ADJECTIVE
poor ◊ *Sa famille est pauvre.* His family is poor. ◊ *Pauvre Jean-Pierre! Il n'a pas eu de chance!* Poor Jean-Pierre! He was unlucky!

la **pauvreté** NOUN
poverty

pavé ADJECTIVE
cobbled ◊ *Les rues étaient pavées.* The streets were cobbled.

le **pavillon** NOUN
house ◊ *Ils habitent un pavillon de banlieue.* They've got a house in the suburbs.

payant ADJECTIVE
paying ◊ *Ce sont des hôtes payants.* They're paying guests.
♦**C'est payant.** You have to pay. ◊ *L'entrée de la boîte est payante.* You have to pay to get into the nightclub.

la **paye** NOUN
wages

payer VERB
1 to pay for ◊ *Combien as-tu payé ta voiture?* How much did you pay for your car?
♦**J'ai payé ce T-shirt vingt euros.** I paid 20 euros for this T-shirt.
2 to pay ◊ *Elle a été payée aujourd'hui.* She got paid today. ◊ *Son métier paye bien.* His job pays good money. ◊ *Elle est mal payée.* She is badly paid.
♦**faire payer quelque chose à quelqu'un** to charge somebody for something ◊ *Il me l'a fait payer dix euros.* He charged me 10 euros for it.
♦**payer quelque chose à quelqu'un** to buy somebody something ◊ *Allez, je vous paye un verre.* Come on, I'll buy you a drink.

le **pays** NOUN
country
♦**du pays** local ◊ *le vin du pays* the local wine

le **paysage** NOUN
landscape

le **paysan** NOUN
farmer

la **paysanne** NOUN
farmer

les **Pays-Bas** MASC NOUN
Netherlands
♦**aux Pays-Bas (1)** in the Netherlands
♦**aux Pays-Bas (2)** to the Netherlands

le **pays de Galles** NOUN
Wales
♦**au pays de Galles (1)** in Wales ◊ *Daphne habite au pays de Galles.* Daphne lives in Wales.
♦**au pays de Galles (2)** to Wales ◊ *Elle part au pays de Galles la semaine prochaine.* She is going to Wales next week.

le **PC** NOUN
see also **PC** ABBREVIATION
PC (= personal computer) ◊ *Il a tapé le rapport sur son PC.* He typed the report on his PC.

PC ABBREVIATION (= *Parti communiste*)
see also **PC** NOUN
Communist Party

le **PDG** NOUN (= *président-directeur général*)
MD (= managing director)

le **péage** NOUN
1 toll ◊ *Nous avons payé vingt euros de péage.* We paid a toll of 20 euros.
2 tollbooth ◊ *Sabine s'est arrêtée au péage de l'autoroute.* Sabine stopped at the motorway tollbooth.

ℹ *French motorways charge a toll.*

la **peau** NOUN (PL les **peaux**)
skin ◊ *Elle a la peau douce.* She's got soft skin.

le/la **Peau-Rouge** NOUN (PL les **Peaux-Rouges**)
Red Indian

la **pêche** NOUN
1 peach
2 fishing
♦**aller à la pêche** to go fishing
♦**la pêche à la ligne** angling

le **péché** NOUN
sin

pêcher VERB
1 to fish for ◊ *Ils sont partis pêcher la truite.* They've gone fishing for trout.

P

2 to catch ◊ *Jacques a pêché deux saumons.* Jacques caught two salmon.

le **pêcheur** NOUN
fisherman ◊ *Son père est pêcheur.* His father's a fisherman.
♦ **un pêcheur à la ligne** an angler

pédagogique ADJECTIVE
educational

la **pédale** NOUN
pedal

le **pédalo** NOUN
pedalo

pédestre ADJECTIVE
♦ **une randonnée pédestre** a ramble

le **peigne** NOUN
comb

peigner VERB
to comb ◊ *Elle peigne sa poupée.* She's combing her doll's hair.
♦ **se peigner** to comb one's hair ◊ *Il faut que je me peigne.* I must comb my hair.

le **peignoir** NOUN
dressing gown
♦ **un peignoir de bain** a bathrobe

peindre VERB
to paint

la **peine** NOUN
trouble
♦ **avoir de la peine à faire quelque chose** to have trouble doing something ◊ *J'ai eu beaucoup de peine à la convaincre.* I had a lot of trouble convincing her.
♦ **se donner de la peine** to make a real effort ◊ *Il s'est donné beaucoup de peine pour obtenir ces renseignements.* He made a real effort to get this information.
♦ **prendre la peine de faire quelque chose** to go to the trouble of doing something ◊ *Il a pris la peine de me rapporter ma valise.* He went to the trouble of returning my case to me.
♦ **faire de la peine à quelqu'un** to upset somebody ◊ *Ça me fait de la peine de la voir pleurer.* It upsets me to see her crying.
♦ **ce n'est pas la peine** there's no point ◊ *Ce n'est pas la peine de téléphoner.* There's no point in phoning.
♦ **à peine (1)** hardly ◊ *J'ai à peine eu le temps de me changer.* I hardly had time to get changed.
♦ **à peine (2)** only just ◊ *Elle vient à peine de se lever.* She's only just got up.

le **peintre** NOUN
painter

la **peinture** NOUN
1 painting ◊ *On expose des peintures de Gautier au musée.* There's an exhibition of Gautier's paintings at the museum.
2 paint ◊ *J'ai acheté de la peinture verte.* I bought some green paint.
♦ **"peinture fraîche"** "wet paint"

pêle-mêle ADVERB
higgledy-piggledy

peler VERB
to peel

la **pelle** NOUN
1 shovel
2 spade

la **pellicule** NOUN
film ◊ *une pellicule couleur* a colour film

les **pellicules** FEM NOUN
dandruff SING

la **pelote** NOUN
ball ◊ *une pelote de laine* a ball of wool

la **pelouse** NOUN
lawn

la **peluche** NOUN
♦ **un animal en peluche** a soft toy

le **penchant** NOUN
♦ **avoir un penchant pour quelque chose** to have a liking for something

pencher VERB
to tilt ◊ *Ce tableau penche vers la droite.* The picture's tilting to the right.
♦ **se pencher (1)** to lean over ◊ *Françoise s'est penchée sur son cahier.* Françoise leant over her exercise book.
♦ **se pencher (2)** to bend down ◊ *Il s'est penché pour ramasser sa casquette.* He bent down to pick his cap up.
♦ **se pencher (3)** to lean out ◊ *Annick s'est penchée par la fenêtre.* Annick leant out of the window.

pendant PREPOSITION
during ◊ *Ça s'est passé pendant l'été.* It happened during the summer.
♦ **pendant que** while ◊ *Christian a téléphoné pendant que Chantal prenait son bain.* Christian phoned while Chantal was having a bath.

le **pendentif** NOUN
pendant

la **penderie** NOUN
wardrobe (for hanging clothes)

pendre VERB

to hang ◊ *Il a pendu sa veste dans l'armoire.* He hung his jacket in the wardrobe.
- **pendre quelqu'un** to hang somebody ◊ *L'assassin a été pendu.* The murderer was hanged.

la **pendule** NOUN
clock

pénétrer VERB
1 to enter ◊ *Ils ont pénétré dans la maison en passant par le jardin.* They entered the house through the garden.
2 to penetrate ◊ *L'armée a pénétré sur le territoire ennemi.* The army penetrated enemy territory.

pénible ADJECTIVE
hard ◊ *Travailler sur un chantier est pénible.* Working on a building site is hard.
- **Il est vraiment pénible.** He's a real nuisance.

péniblement ADVERB
with difficulty

la **péniche** NOUN
barge

le **pénis** NOUN
penis

la **pénombre** NOUN
half-light

la **pensée** NOUN
thought ◊ *Il était perdu dans ses pensées.* He was lost in thought.

penser VERB
to think ◊ *Je pense que Yann a eu raison de partir.* I think Yann was right to leave.
- **penser à quelque chose** to think about something ◊ *Je pense à mes vacances.* I'm thinking about my holidays. ◊ *Pensez-y.* Think about it.
- **faire penser quelqu'un à quelque chose** to remind someone of something ◊ *Cette photo me fait penser à la Grèce.* This photo reminds me of Greece.
- **faire penser quelqu'un à faire quelque chose** to remind someone to do something ◊ *Fais-moi penser à téléphoner à Claire.* Remind me to phone Claire.
- **penser faire quelque chose** to be planning to do something ◊ *Ils pensent partir en Espagne en juillet.* They're planning to go to Spain in July.

la **pension** NOUN
1 boarding school ◊ *Leur fille est en pension.* Their daughter is at boarding school.
2 pension ◊ *Ma grand-mère reçoit sa pension tous les mois.* My grandma gets her pension every month.
3 boarding house
- **la pension complète** full board

le/la **pensionnaire** NOUN
boarder

le **pensionnat** NOUN
boarding school

la **pente** NOUN
slope ◊ *une pente raide* a steep slop
- **en pente** sloping ◊ *Le toit de cette maison est en pente.* This house has a sloping roof.

la **Pentecôte** NOUN
Whitsun

le **pépin** NOUN
1 pip ◊ *Cette orange est pleine de pépins.* This orange is full of pips.
2 problem ◊ *avoir un pépin* (*informal*) to have a slight problem

perçant ADJECTIVE
1 sharp ◊ *Il a une vue perçante.* He has very sharp eyes.
2 piercing ◊ *un cri perçant* a piercing cry

percer VERB
to pierce ◊ *Elle s'est fait percer les oreilles.* She's had her ears pierced.

percuter VERB
to smash into

le **perdant** NOUN
loser

la **perdante** NOUN
loser

perdre VERB
to lose ◊ *Cécile a perdu ses clés.* Cécile's lost her keys.
- **J'ai perdu mon chemin.** I've lost my way.
- **perdre un match** to lose a match
- **perdre du temps** to waste time ◊ *J'ai perdu beaucoup de temps ce matin.* I've wasted a lot of time this morning. ◊ *Nous avons perdu notre temps à cette réunion.* That meeting was a waste of time.
- **se perdre** to get lost ◊ *Je me suis perdu en route.* I got lost on the way here.

perdu VERB *see* **perdre**

le **père** NOUN
father
- **le père Noël** Father Christmas

perfectionné ADJECTIVE
sophisticated

perfectionner VERB

P

to improve ◊ *Elle a besoin de perfectionner son anglais.* She needs to improve her English.

périmé ADJECTIVE
out-of-date ◊ *Mon passeport est périmé.* My passport's out of date.
♦ *Ces yaourts sont périmés.* These yoghurts are past their use-by date.

la **période** NOUN
period

périodique ADJECTIVE
periodic

périphérique ADJECTIVE
see also **périphérique** NOUN
outlying ◊ *un quartier périphérique* an outlying district

le **périphérique** NOUN
see also **périphérique** ADJECTIVE
ring road

la **perle** NOUN
pearl

la **permanence** NOUN
♦ *assurer une permanence* to operate a basic service ◊ *Ma banque assure une permanence le samedi matin.* My bank operates a basic service on Saturday mornings.
♦ *être de permanence* to be on duty ◊ *Sophie ne peut pas venir, elle est de permanence ce soir.* Sophie can't come, she's on duty tonight.
♦ *en permanence* permanently ◊ *Elle se plaint en permanence.* She's always complaining.

permanent ADJECTIVE
1 permanent ◊ *Il a un poste permanent.* He has a permanent job.
2 continuous ◊ *J'en ai assez de tes critiques permanentes.* I've had enough of your constant criticism.

la **permanente** NOUN
perm

permettre VERB
to allow
♦ *permettre à quelqu'un de faire quelque chose* to allow somebody to do something ◊ *Sa mère lui permet de sortir le soir.* His mother allows him to go out at night.

le **permis** NOUN
permit ◊ *Il vous faut un permis pour camper ici.* You need a permit to camp here.
♦ *le permis de conduire* driving licence
♦ *un permis de séjour* a residence permit
♦ *un permis de travail* a work permit

la **permission** NOUN

permission ◊ *Qui t'a donné la permission d'entrer?* Who gave you permission to come in?
♦ *avoir la permission de faire quelque chose* to have permission to do something ◊ *J'ai la permission d'utiliser sa chaîne hi-fi.* I've got his permission to use his hi-fi.
♦ *être en permission* to be on leave (*from the army*)

le **Pérou** NOUN
Peru

perpétuel ADJECTIVE (FEM SING **perpétuelle**)
perpetual

perplexe ADJECTIVE
puzzled ◊ *Ma question l'a laissé perplexe.* She was puzzled by my question.

le **perroquet** NOUN
parrot

la **perruche** NOUN
budgie

la **perruque** NOUN
wig

le **persil** NOUN
parsley

le **personnage** NOUN
1 figure ◊ *les grands personnages de l'histoire de France* the important figures in French history
2 character ◊ *le personnage principal du film* the main character in the film

la **personnalité** NOUN
1 personality ◊ *Ray a une personnalité forte.* Ray has a strong personality.
2 prominent figure ◊ *Il y avait beaucoup de personnalités politiques à ce dîner.* There were lots of prominent political figures at the dinner.

la **personne** NOUN
see also **personne** PRONOUN
person ◊ *Il y avait une trentaine de personnes dans la pièce.* There were about 30 people in the room. ◊ *une personne âgée* an elderly person
♦ *en personne* in person

personne PRONOUN
see also **personne** NOUN
1 nobody ◊ *Il n'y a personne à la maison.* There's nobody at home. ◊ *Personne n'est venu le chercher.* Nobody came to fetch him.
2 anybody ◊ *Elle ne veut voir personne.* She doesn't want to see anybody.

personnel ADJECTIVE (FEM SING
personnelle)

see also **personnel** NOUN

personal

le **personnel** NOUN

see also **personnel** ADJECTIVE

staff ◊ *Il nous faut plus de personnel.*
We need more staff.
♦**le service du personnel** the personnel
department

personnellement ADVERB

personally ◊ *Personnellement, je ne
suis pas d'accord.* Personally, I don't
agree.

la **perspective** NOUN

prospect ◊ *Les perspectives sont
bonnes.* The prospects are good.
♦**perspectives d'avenir** prospects ◊ *Il y
a des perspectives d'avenir dans ce
métier.* This job has good prospects.
♦**en perspective (1)** in prospect ◊ *Il y a
des changements en perspective.*
Changes in prospect.
♦**en perspective (2)** in perspective ◊ *Il a
dessiné la maison en perspective.* He
drew the house in perspective.

persuader VERB

to persuade
♦**persuader quelqu'un de faire quelque
chose** to persuade somebody to do
something ◊ *Elle m'a persuadé de
l'accompagner.* She persuaded me to
go with her.

la **perte** NOUN

1 loss ◊ *des pertes d'emploi* job
losses
2 waste ◊ *Cette réunion a été une
perte de temps.* The meeting was a
waste of time.

perturber VERB

to disrupt ◊ *Un car en panne
perturbait la circulation.* A coach had
broken down and was disrupting the
traffic.

le **pèse-personne** NOUN

bathroom scales PL

peser VERB

to weigh ◊ *Elle pèse cent kilos.* She
weighs 100 kilos.

pessimiste ADJECTIVE

pessimistic

le **pétale** NOUN

petal

la **pétanque** NOUN

*ⓘ pétanque is a type of bowls
played in France, especially in the
south.*

le **pétard** NOUN

firecracker

péter VERB (*rude*)

to fart

pétillant ADJECTIVE

sparkling

petit ADJECTIVE

1 small ◊ *Sonia habite une petite
ville.* Sonia lives in a small town.
2 little ◊ *Elle a une jolie petite
maison.* She has a nice little house.
♦**petit à petit** bit by bit
♦**un petit ami** a boyfriend
♦**une petite amie** a girlfriend
♦**le petit déjeuner** breakfast ◊ *prendre
le petit déjeuner* to have breakfast
♦**un petit pain** a bread roll
♦**les petites annonces** the small ads
♦**des petits pois** garden peas
♦**les petits** young (*of animal*) ◊ *la lionne
et ses petits* the lioness and her
young

la **petite-fille** NOUN (PL les **petites-filles**)

granddaughter

le **petit-fils** NOUN (PL les **petits-fils**)

grandson

les **petits-enfants** MASC NOUN

grandchildren

le **pétrole** NOUN

oil ◊ *une lampe à pétrole* an oil lamp
*Be careful! pétrole does not mean
petrol.*

peu ADVERB, NOUN

not much ◊ *J'ai peu mangé à midi.* I
didn't eat much for lunch. ◊ *Il voyage
peu.* He doesn't travel much.
♦**un peu** a bit ◊ *Elle est un peu timide.*
She's a bit shy. ◊ *un peu de gâteau* a
bit of cake
♦**un petit peu** a little bit ◊ *un petit peu
de crème* a little bit of cream
♦**peu de (1)** not many ◊ *Il y a peu de
bons films au cinéma.* There aren't
very many good films on at the
cinema. ◊ *Elle a peu d'amis.* She
hasn't got many friends.
♦**peu de (2)** not much ◊ *Il a peu
d'espoir de réussir.* He doesn't have
much hope of succeeding. ◊ *Il lui
reste peu d'argent.* He hasn't got
much money left.
♦**à peu près (1)** more or less ◊ *J'ai à
peu près fini.* I've more or less
finished.
♦**à peu près (2)** about ◊ *Le voyage
prend à peu près deux heures et
demie.* The journey takes about two
and a half hours.
♦**peu à peu** little by little
♦**peu avant** shortly before

P

☞

◆**peu après** shortly afterwards
◆**de peu** only just ◊ *Chantal a manqué son train de peu.* Chantal only just missed her train.

le**peuple** NOUN
people ◊ *le peuple français* the French people

la**peur** NOUN
fear
◆**avoir peur de** to be afraid of ◊ *Il a peur du noir.* He's afraid of the dark.
◆**avoir peur de faire quelque chose** to be frightened of doing something ◊ *Elle a peur d'y aller toute seule.* She's frightened of going on her own.
◆**faire peur à quelqu'un** to frighten somebody ◊ *Cet homme-là me fait peur.* That man frightens me.

peureux ADJECTIVE (FEM SING **peureuse**)
fearful

peut VERB *see* **pouvoir**
◆**Il ne peut pas venir.** He can't come.

peut-être ADVERB
perhaps ◊ *Je l'ai peut-être oublié à la maison.* Perhaps I've left it at home.
◆**peut-être que** perhaps ◊ *Peut-être qu'ils n'ont pas pu téléphoner.* Perhaps they weren't able to phone.

peuvent, peux VERB *see* **pouvoir**
◆**Je ne peux pas le faire.** I can't do it.

p. ex. ABBREVIATION (= *par exemple*)
e.g.

le**phare** NOUN
[1] **lighthouse** ◊ *On voit le phare depuis le pont du bateau.* You can see the lighthouse from the ship's deck.
[2] **headlight** ◊ *Il a laissé les phares de sa voiture allumés.* He left his headlights on.

la**pharmacie** NOUN
chemist's

> ❶ *Chemist's shops in France are identified by a special green cross outside the shop.*

le**pharmacien** NOUN
pharmacist

le**phasme** NOUN
stick insect

la**pharmacienne** NOUN
pharmacist

le**phénomène** NOUN
phenomenon

la**philosophie** NOUN
philosophy

le**phoque** NOUN

seal (*animal*)

la**photo** NOUN
photograph ◊ *Elle a fait développer ses photos.* She's had her photographs developed.
◆**en photo** in photographs ◊ *Je n'ai vu Venise qu'en photo.* I've only seen Venice in photographs.
◆**prendre quelqu'un en photo** to take a photo of somebody ◊ *Claire nous a pris en photo.* Claire took a photo of us.
◆**une photo d'identité** a passport photograph

la**photocopie** NOUN
photocopy

photocopier VERB
to photocopy

la**photocopieuse** NOUN
photocopier

le/la**photographe** NOUN
photographer

la**photographie** NOUN
[1] **photography**
[2] **photograph**

photographier VERB
to photograph

la**phrase** NOUN
sentence

physique ADJECTIVE
> *see also* **physique** NOUN

physical

le**physique** NOUN
> *see also* **la physique, physique** ADJECTIVE
◆**Il a un physique agréable.** He's quite good-looking.

la**physique** NOUN
> *see also* **le physique, physique** ADJECTIVE
physics ◊ *Il est professeur de physique.* He is a physics teacher.

le/la**pianiste** NOUN
pianist ◊ *Elle est pianiste.* She's a pianist.

le**piano** NOUN
piano

le**pic** NOUN
peak ◊ *les pics enneigés des Alpes* the snowy peaks of the Alps
◆**à pic (1)** vertically ◊ *La falaise tombe à pic dans la mer.* The cliff drops vertically into the sea.
◆**à pic (1)** just at the right time ◊ *Tu es arrivé à pic.* You arrived just at the right time.

la**pièce** NOUN
[1] **room** ◊ *Mon lit est au centre de la pièce.* My bed is in the middle of the room.

♦ **un cinq-pièces** a five-roomed flat

2 play ◊ *On joue une pièce de Shakespeare au théâtre.* There's a play by Shakespeare on at the theatre.

3 part ◊ *Il faut changer une pièce du moteur.* There's an engine part which needs changing.

4 coin ◊ *des pièces d'un euro* some one-euro coins

♦ **cinquante euros pièce** 50 euros each ◊ *J'ai acheté ces T-shirts dix euros pièce.* I bought these T-shirts for ten euros each.

♦ **un maillot une pièce** a one-piece swimsuit

♦ **un maillot deux-pièces** a bikini

♦ **Avez-vous une pièce d'identité?** Have you got any identification?

♦ **une pièce jointe** an email attachment

le **pied** NOUN

foot ◊ *J'ai mal aux pieds.* My feet are hurting.

♦ **à pied** on foot

♦ **avoir pied** to be able to touch the bottom ◊ *Justine n'aime pas nager là où elle n'a pas pied.* Justine doesn't like swimming where she can't touch the bottom.

le **pied-noir** NOUN (PL les **pieds-noirs**)

> **ⓘ** A **pied-noir** is a French person born in Algeria; most of them moved to France during the Algerian war in the 1950s.

◊ *Sa grand-mère est pied-noir.* His grandmother was born in Algeria.

le **piège** NOUN

trap

♦ **prendre quelqu'un au piège** to trap somebody

piéger VERB

to trap

♦ **un colis piégé** a parcel bomb

♦ **une voiture piégée** a car bomb

la **pierre** NOUN

stone

♦ **une pierre précieuse** a precious stone

le **piéton** NOUN

pedestrian

la **piétonne** NOUN

pedestrian

piétonnier ADJECTIVE (FEM SING **piétonnière**)

♦ **une rue piétonnière** a pedestrianized street

♦ **un quartier piétonnier** a pedestrianized area

la **pieuvre** NOUN

octopus

le **pigeon** NOUN

pigeon

piger VERB (*informal*)

to understand

la **pile** NOUN

> see also **pile** ADVERB

1 pile ◊ *Il y a une pile de disques sur la table.* There's a pile of records on the table.

2 battery ◊ *La pile de ma montre est usée.* The battery in my watch has run out.

pile ADVERB

> see also **pile** NOUN

♦ **à deux heures pile** at two on the dot

♦ **jouer à pile ou face** to toss up

♦ **Pile ou face?** Heads or tails?

le **pilote** NOUN

pilot

♦ **un pilote de course** a racing driver

♦ **un pilote de ligne** an airline pilot

piloter VERB

to fly (*a plane*)

la **pilule** NOUN

pill

♦ **prendre la pilule** to be on the pill

le **piment** NOUN

chilli

le **pin** NOUN

pine

le **pinard** NOUN (*informal*)

wine

la **pince** NOUN

1 pliers PL (*tool*)

2 pincer (*of crab*)

♦ **une pince à épiler** tweezers

♦ **une pince à linge** a clothes peg

le **pinceau** NOUN (PL les **pinceaux**)

paintbrush

la **pincée** NOUN

♦ **une pincée de sel** a pinch of salt

pincer VERB

to pinch ◊ *Elle m'a pincé le bras.* She pinched my arm.

le **pingouin** NOUN

penguin

le **ping-pong** NOUN

table tennis ◊ *jouer au ping-pong* to play table tennis

la **pintade** NOUN

guinea fowl

le **pion** NOUN

1 pawn (*in chess*)

2 piece (*in draughts*)

3 supervisor (*man*)

P

☞

i *In French secondary schools, the teachers are not responsible for supervising the pupils outside class. This job is done by people called **pions** or **surveillants**.*

la **pionne** NOUN
  supervisor (*woman*)

la **pipe** NOUN
  pipe ◊ *Mon grand-père fume la pipe.* My granddad smokes a pipe.

piquant ADJECTIVE
  1 prickly
  2 spicy

le **pique** NOUN
  see also **la pique**
  spades PL ◊ *l'as de pique* the ace of spades

la **pique** NOUN
  see also **le pique**
  cutting remark ◊ *envoyer des piques à quelqu'un* to make cutting remarks to somebody

le **pique-nique** NOUN
  picnic

piquer VERB
  1 to bite ◊ *Nous avons été piqués par les moustiques.* We were bitten by mosquitoes.
  2 to burn ◊ *Cette sauce me pique la langue.* This sauce is burning my tongue.
  3 to steal ◊ *On m'a piqué mon porte-monnaie.* (*informal*) I've had my purse stolen.
  ◆ **se piquer** to prick oneself ◊ *Il s'est piqué avec une aiguille.* He pricked himself with a needle.

le **piquet** NOUN
  1 post ◊ *Le chien est attaché à un piquet.* The dog is tied to a post.
  2 peg ◊ *Il nous manque un des piquets de la tente.* One of our tent pegs is missing.

la **piqûre** NOUN
  1 injection ◊ *Le médecin lui a fait une piqûre.* The doctor gave him an injection.
  2 bite ◊ *une piqûre de moustique* a mosquito bite
  3 sting ◊ *une piqûre d'abeille* a bee sting

le **pirate** NOUN
  pirate
  ◆ **un pirate informatique** a hacker

pire ADJECTIVE, NOUN
  worse ◊ *C'est encore pire qu'avant.* It's even worse than before.

◆ **le pire** the worst ◊ *C'est la pire journée que j'aie jamais passée.* That's the worst day I've ever had. ◊ *Ce gamin est le pire de la bande.* That boy is the worst in the group.
◆ **le pire de** the worst of ◊ *Le pire de tout, c'est qu'on s'ennuie tout le temps.* The worst of it is that we're always bored.

la **piscine** NOUN
  swimming pool

pisser VERB (*informal*)
  to have a pee

la **pistache** NOUN
  pistachio ◊ *une glace à la pistache* a pistachio ice cream

la **piste** NOUN
  1 lead ◊ *La police est sur une piste.* The police are following a lead.
  2 runway ◊ *L'avion s'est posé sur la piste.* The plane landed on the runway.
  3 ski run ◊ *Le skieur a descendu la piste.* The skier came down the ski run.
  ◆ **une piste artificielle** a dry ski slope
  ◆ **la piste de danse** the dance floor
  ◆ **une piste cyclable** a cycle lane

le **pistolet** NOUN
  pistol

pistonner VERB
  ◆ **Il a été pistonné pour avoir ce travail.** They pulled some strings to get him this job.

la **pitié** NOUN
  pity
  ◆ **Il me fait pitié.** I feel sorry for him.
  ◆ **avoir pitié de quelqu'un** to feel sorry for somebody

pittoresque ADJECTIVE
  picturesque

la **pizza** NOUN
  pizza

le **placard** NOUN
  cupboard

la **place** NOUN
  1 place ◊ *Vincent a eu la troisième place au concours.* Vincent got third place in the competition.
  2 square ◊ *la place du village* the village square
  3 space ◊ *Il ne reste plus de place pour se garer.* There's no more space to park. ◊ *Ça prend de la place.* It takes up a lot of room.
  4 seat ◊ *Toutes les places ont été vendues.* All the seats have been sold. ◊ *remettre quelque chose en place* to put something back in its place

♦**sur place** on the spot

♦**à la place** instead ◊ *Il ne reste plus de tarte; désirez-vous quelque chose d'autre à la place?* There's no pie left; would you like something else instead?

♦**à la place de** instead of

placer VERB

[1] to seat ◊ *Nous étions placés à côté du directeur.* We were seated next to the manager.

[2] to invest ◊ *Il a placé ses économies en Bourse.* He invested his money on the Stock Exchange.

le **plafond** NOUN
ceiling

la **plage** NOUN
beach

la **plaie** NOUN
wound

plaindre VERB

♦**plaindre quelqu'un** to feel sorry for somebody ◊ *Je te plains.* I feel sorry for you.

♦**se plaindre** to complain ◊ *Il n'arrête pas de se plaindre.* He never stops complaining.

♦**se plaindre à quelqu'un** to complain to somebody ◊ *Ils se sont plaints au directeur.* They complained to the manager.

♦**se plaindre de quelque chose** to complain about something ◊ *Elle s'est plainte du bruit.* She complained about the noise.

la **plaine** NOUN
plain (*level area*)

la **plainte** NOUN
complaint

♦**porter plainte** to lodge a complaint

plaire VERB

♦**Ce cadeau me plaît beaucoup.** I like this present a lot.

♦**Ce film plaît beaucoup aux jeunes.** The film is very popular with young people.

♦**Ça t'a plu d'aller en Italie?** Did you enjoy going to Italy?

♦**Elle lui plaît.** He fancies her.

♦**s'il te plaît** please

♦**s'il vous plaît** please

plaisanter VERB
to joke

la **plaisanterie** NOUN
joke

le **plaisir** NOUN
pleasure

♦**faire plaisir à quelqu'un** to please somebody ◊ *J'y suis allé pour lui faire plaisir.* I went there to please him. ◊ *Ce cadeau me fait très plaisir.* I'm very pleased with this present.

plaît VERB *see* **plaire**

le **plan** NOUN
plan

♦**un plan de la ville** a street map

♦**au premier plan** in the foreground

la **planche** NOUN
plank

♦**une planche à repasser** an ironing board

♦**une planche à roulettes** a skateboard

♦**une planche à voile** a sailboard

le **plancher** NOUN
floor

planer VERB

[1] to glide ◊ *L'avion planait dans le ciel.* The plane was gliding in the sky.

[2] to have one's head in the clouds ◊ *Ce garçon plane complètement.* (*informal*) He's not with us at all.

la **planète** NOUN
planet

la **plante** NOUN
plant

planter VERB

[1] to plant ◊ *Daphné a planté des tomates.* Daphne planted some tomatoes.

[2] to hammer in ◊ *Jean-Pierre a planté un clou dans le mur.* Jean-Pierre hammered a nail into the wall.

[3] to pitch ◊ *André a planté sa tente au bord du lac.* André pitched his tent next to the lake.

♦**Ne reste pas planté là!** Don't just stand there!

♦**se planter** (*informal*) to fail ◊ *Je me suis planté en maths.* I failed maths.

la **plaque** NOUN
(metal) plate

♦**une plaque de verglas** a patch of ice

♦**une plaque de chocolat** a bar of chocolate

plaqué ADJECTIVE

♦**plaqué or** gold-plated

♦**plaqué argent** silver-plated

plaquer VERB (*informal*)

[1] to ditch ◊ *Elle a plaqué son copain.* She ditched her boyfriend.

[2] to pack in ◊ *Il a plaqué son boulot.* He packed in his job.

la **plaquette** NOUN

♦**une plaquette de chocolat** a bar of chocolate

♦**une plaquette de beurre** a pack of butter

P

le **plastique** NOUN
plastic

plat ADJECTIVE
see also **plat** NOUN
flat
◆ **être à plat ventre** to be lying face down
◆ **l'eau plate** still water

le **plat** NOUN
see also **plat** ADJECTIVE
1 dish
2 course ◊ *le plat principal* the main course
◆ **un plat cuisiné** a pre-cooked meal
◆ **le plat de résistance** the main course
◆ **le plat du jour** the dish of the day

le **platane** NOUN
plane tree

le **plateau** NOUN (PL les **plateaux**)
1 tray
◆ **un plateau de fromages** a selection of cheeses
2 plateau

le **platine** NOUN
see also **la platine**
platinum

la **platine** NOUN
see also **le platine**
turntable (*of record player*)
◆ **une platine laser** a CD player

le **plâtre** NOUN
plaster ◊ *une statue en plâtre* a statue made of plaster ◊ *avoir un bras dans le plâtre* to have an arm in plaster

plein ADJECTIVE
see also **plein** NOUN
full
◆ **à plein temps** full-time ◊ *Elle travaille à plein temps.* She works full-time.
◆ **plein de** (*informal*) lots of ◊ *un gâteau avec plein de crème* a cake with lots of cream
◆ **Il y a plein de gens dans la rue.** The street is full of people.
◆ **en plein air** in the open air
◆ **en pleine nuit** in the middle of the night
◆ **en plein jour** in broad daylight

le **plein** NOUN
see also **plein** ADJECTIVE
◆ **faire le plein** to fill up (*petrol tank*) ◊ *Faites le plein, s'il vous plaît.* Fill it up, please.

pleurer VERB
to cry

pleut VERB see **pleuvoir**

pleuvoir VERB
to rain ◊ *Il pleut.* It's raining.

le **pli** NOUN
1 fold
2 pleat ◊ *Elle a repassé les plis de sa jupe.* She ironed the pleats of her skirt.
3 crease ◊ *Il y a un pli sur la manche de ta chemise.* There's a crease in the sleeve of your shirt.

pliant ADJECTIVE
folding ◊ *un lit pliant* a folding bed

plier VERB
1 to fold ◊ *Elle a plié sa serviette.* She folded her towel.
2 to bend ◊ *Elle a plié le bras.* She bent her arm.

le **plomb** NOUN
1 lead ◊ *Ces jouets sont en plomb.* These toys are made of lead.
2 fuse ◊ *Les plombs ont sauté.* The fuses have blown.
◆ **l'essence sans plomb** unleaded petrol

le **plombier** NOUN
plumber
◆ **Il est plombier.** He's a plumber.

la **plongée** NOUN
diving ◊ *faire de la plongée* to go diving

le **plongeoir** NOUN
diving board

le **plongeon** NOUN
dive

plonger VERB
to dive ◊ *Jean a plongé dans la piscine.* Jean dived into the swimming pool.
◆ **J'ai plongé ma main dans l'eau.** I plunged my hand into the water.
◆ **être plongé dans son travail** to be absorbed in your work
◆ **se plonger dans un livre** to get absorbed in a book

plu VERB see **plaire, pleuvoir**

la **pluie** NOUN
rain ◊ *sous la pluie* in the rain

la **plume** NOUN
feather ◊ *une plume d'oiseau* a bird's feather
◆ **un stylo à plume** a fountain pen

plupart
◆ **la plupart** PRONOUN
most (of them) ◊ *La plupart ont moins de quinze ans.* Most of them are under 15.
◆ **la plupart des** most ◊ *La plupart des gens ont vu ce film.* Most people have seen this film.
◆ **la plupart du temps** most of the time

le **pluriel** NOUN
plural
◆ **au pluriel** in the plural

plus ADVERB, PREPOSITION

♦ **ne ... plus (1)** not ... any more ◊ *Je ne veux plus le voir.* I don't want to see him any more.

♦ **ne ... plus (2)** no longer ◊ *Il ne travaille plus ici.* He's no longer working here.

♦ **Je n'ai plus de pain.** I've got no bread left.

♦ **plus ... que** more ... than ◊ *Il est plus intelligent que son frère.* He's more intelligent than his brother. ◊ *Il travaille plus que moi.* He works more than me. ◊ *Elle est plus grande que moi.* She's bigger than me.

♦ **C'est le plus grand de la famille.** He's the tallest in his family.

♦ **plus ... plus ...** the more ... the more ... ◊ *Plus il gagne d'argent, plus il en veut.* The more money he earns, the more he wants.

♦ **plus de (1)** more ◊ *Il nous faut plus de pain.* We need more bread.

♦ **plus de (2)** more than ◊ *Il y avait plus de dix personnes.* There were more than 10 people.

♦ **de plus** more ◊ *Il nous faut un joueur de plus.* We need one more player. ◊ *Le voyage a pris trois heures de plus que prévu.* The journey took 3 hours more than planned.

♦ **en plus** more ◊ *J'ai apporté quelques gâteaux en plus.* I brought a few more cakes.

♦ **de plus en plus** more and more ◊ *Il y a de plus en plus de touristes par ici.* There are more and more tourists round here. ◊ *Il fait de plus en plus chaud.* It's getting hotter and hotter.

♦ **un peu plus difficile** a bit more difficult ◊ *Il fait un peu plus froid qu'hier.* It's a bit colder than yesterday.

♦ **plus ou moins** more or less

♦ **Quatre plus deux égalent six.** 4 plus 2 is 6.

plusieurs PRONOUN
several ◊ *Gaëlle a acheté plusieurs chemises.* Gaëlle bought several shirts. ◊ *Il y en a plusieurs.* There are several of them.

le plus-que-parfait NOUN
pluperfect

plutôt ADVERB
1 quite ◊ *Elle est plutôt jolie.* She's quite pretty.
2 rather ◊ *L'eau est plutôt froide.* The water's rather cold.
3 instead ◊ *Demande-leur plutôt de venir avec toi.* Ask them to come with you instead.

♦ **plutôt que** rather than ◊ *Invite Marie plutôt que Nathalie.* Invite Marie rather than Nathalie.

pluvieux ADJECTIVE (FEM SING **pluvieuse**)
rainy

le pneu NOUN
tyre

la pneumonie NOUN
pneumonia

la poche NOUN
pocket
♦ **l'argent de poche** pocket money
♦ **un livre de poche** a paperback

la poêle NOUN
frying pan
♦ **une poêle à frire** a frying pan

le poème NOUN
poem

la poésie NOUN
1 poetry
2 poem

le poète NOUN
poet

le poids NOUN
weight ◊ *vendre quelque chose au poids* to sell something by weight
♦ **prendre du poids** to put on weight ◊ *Il a pris du poids.* He's put on weight.
♦ **perdre du poids** to lose weight ◊ *Elle a perdu du poids.* She's lost weight.
♦ **un poids lourd** a lorry

la poignée NOUN
1 handful ◊ *une poignée de sel* a handful of salt
2 handle ◊ *la poignée de la porte* the door handle
♦ **une poignée de main** a handshake

le poignet NOUN
1 wrist ◊ *Je me suis fait mal au poignet.* I've hurt my wrist.
2 cuff (*of shirt*)

le poil NOUN
1 hair ◊ *Il y a des poils de chat partout sur la moquette.* There are cat hairs all over the carpet.
2 fur ◊ *Ton chien a un beau poil.* Your dog's got lovely fur.
♦ **à poil** (*informal*) stark naked

poilu ADJECTIVE
hairy

poinçonner VERB
to punch ◊ *Le contrôleur a poinçonné les billets.* The conductor punched the tickets.

le poing NOUN
fist
♦ **un coup de poing** a punch

P

le **point** NOUN

[1] point ◊ *Je ne suis pas d'accord sur ce point.* I don't agree with this point. ◊ *Son point faible, c'est qu'elle est trop gentille.* Her weak point is she's too nice.

◆ **point de vue** point of view

[2] full stop

◆ **être sur le point de faire quelque chose** to be just about to do something ◊ *J'étais sur le point de te téléphoner.* I was just about to phone you.

◆ **mettre au point** to finalize

◆ **Ce n'est pas encore au point.** It's not finalized yet.

◆ **à point** medium ◊ *Comment voulez-vous votre steak? – À point.* How would you like your steak? – Medium.

◆ **un point d'exclamation** an exclamation mark

◆ **un point d'interrogation** a question mark

◆ **un point noir** a blackhead

la **pointe** NOUN

point ◊ *la pointe d'un couteau* the point of a knife

◆ **être à la pointe du progrès** to be in the forefront of progress

◆ **sur la pointe des pieds** on tiptoe

◆ **les heures de pointe** peak hours

le **pointillé** NOUN

dotted line

pointu ADJECTIVE

pointed ◊ *un chapeau pointu* a pointed hat

la **pointure** NOUN

size (*of shoes*) ◊ *Quelle est votre pointure?* What size shoes do you take?

le **point-virgule** NOUN (PL **points-virgules**)

semicolon

la **poire** NOUN

pear

le **poireau** NOUN (PL les **poireaux**)

leek ◊ *la soupe aux poireaux* leek soup

le **pois** NOUN

pea

◆ **les petits pois** peas

◆ **les pois chiches** chickpeas

◆ **à pois** spotted ◊ *une robe à pois* a spotted dress

le **poison** NOUN

poison

le **poisson** NOUN

fish ◊ *Je n'aime pas le poisson.* I don't like fish. ◊ *André a pêché deux poissons.* André caught two fish.

◆ **les Poissons** Pisces ◊ *Monique est Poissons.* Monique is Pisces.

◆ **Poisson d'avril!** April fool!

ⓘ Pinning a paper fish to somebody's back is a traditional April fool joke in France.

◆ **un poisson rouge** a goldfish

la **poissonnerie** NOUN

fish shop

le **poissonnier** NOUN

fishmonger

la **poitrine** NOUN

[1] chest ◊ *J'ai mal à la poitrine.* My chest hurts.

[2] bust ◊ *Quel est votre tour de poitrine?* What's your bust size?

le **poivre** NOUN

pepper (*spice*)

le **poivron** NOUN

pepper (*vegetable*)

le **pôle** NOUN

pole

◆ **le pôle Nord** the North Pole

◆ **le pôle Sud** the South Pole

poli ADJECTIVE

polite

la **police** NOUN

police ◊ *La police recherche le voleur.* The police are looking for the thief.

◆ **police secours** emergency services ◊ *Ils ont appelé police secours.* They phoned the emergency services.

◆ **une police d'assurance** an insurance policy

policier ADJECTIVE (FEM SING **policière**)

see also **policier** NOUN

◆ **un roman policier** a detective novel

le **policier** NOUN

see also **policier** ADJECTIVE

policeman ◊ *Il est policier.* He's a policeman.

la **politesse** NOUN

politeness

la **politique** NOUN

politics ◊ *La politique ne l'intéresse pas du tout.* He's not at all interested in politics.

◆ **un homme politique** a politician

pollué ADJECTIVE

polluted

polluer VERB

to pollute

la **pollution** NOUN

pollution

le **polo** NOUN

polo shirt

la **Pologne** NOUN
　Poland

　polonais ADJECTIVE, NOUN (FEM SING
　polonaise)
　Polish ◊ *Elle parle polonais.* She
　speaks Polish.
　♦ **un Polonais** a Pole (*man*)
　♦ **une Polonaise** a Pole (*woman*)
　♦ **les Polonais** the Poles

la **Polynésie** NOUN
　Polynesia

la **pommade** NOUN
　ointment

la **pomme** NOUN
　apple
　♦ **les pommes de terre** potatoes
　♦ **les pommes frites** chips
　♦ **les pommes vapeur** boiled potatoes

la **pompe** NOUN
　pump
　♦ **une pompe à essence** a petrol pump
　♦ **les pompes funèbres** undertakers

le **pompier** NOUN
　fireman

le **pompiste** NOUN
　petrol pump attendant

　ponctuel ADJECTIVE (FEM SING **ponctuelle**)
　[1] punctual ◊ *Elle est toujours très
　ponctuelle.* She's always very punctual.
　[2] occasional ◊ *On a rencontré
　quelques problèmes ponctuels.* We've
　had the occasional problem.

　pondre VERB
　to lay (*eggs*)

le **poney** NOUN
　pony

le **pont** NOUN
　[1] bridge
　[2] deck (*of ship*)
　♦ **faire le pont** to take a long weekend
　◊ *Nous faisons le pont pour la
　Pentecôte.* We're taking a long
　weekend for Whitsun.

　populaire ADJECTIVE
　[1] popular ◊ *Ce chanteur est très
　populaire en France.* This singer's
　very popular in France.
　[2] working-class ◊ *un quartier
　populaire de la ville* a working-class
　area of town

la **population** NOUN
　population

le **porc** NOUN
　[1] pig ◊ *Ils élèvent des porcs.* They
　breed pigs.
　[2] pork ◊ *du rôti de porc* roast pork

la **porcelaine** NOUN

china ◊ *une tasse en porcelaine* a
china cup

le **port** NOUN
　[1] harbour
　[2] port

le **portable** NOUN
　mobile phone ◊ *Je vais appeler
　Marie sur mon portable.* I'll phone
　Marie on my mobile.

le **portail** NOUN
　gate

　portatif ADJECTIVE (FEM SING **portative**)
　portable

la **porte** NOUN
　[1] door ◊ *Ferme la porte, s'il te plaît.*
　Close the door, please.
　♦ **la porte d'entrée** the front door
　[2] gate ◊ *Vol 432 à destination de
　Paris: porte numéro trois.* Flight 432
　to Paris: gate 3.
　♦ **mettre quelqu'un à la porte** to sack
　somebody

le **porte-bagages** NOUN
　luggage rack

le **porte-clés** NOUN
　key ring

la **portée** NOUN
　♦ **à portée de la main** within arm's
　reach
　♦ **hors de portée** out of reach

le **portefeuille** NOUN
　wallet

le **portemanteau** NOUN (PL les
　portemanteaux)
　[1] coat hanger
　[2] coat rack

le **porte-monnaie** NOUN (PL les **porte-
　monnaie**)
　purse

　porter VERB
　[1] to carry ◊ *Il portait une valise.* He
　was carrying a suitcase.
　[2] to wear ◊ *Elle porte une robe
　bleue.* She's wearing a blue dress.
　♦ **se porter bien** to be well
　♦ **se porter mal** to be unwell

le **porteur** NOUN
　porter

la **portière** NOUN
　door (*of car*)

la **portion** NOUN
　portion

le **porto** NOUN
　port (*wine*)

le **portrait** NOUN
　portrait

　portugais ADJECTIVE, NOUN (FEM SING
　portugaise)

P

☞

Portuguese ◊ *Il parle portugais.* He speaks Portuguese.

◆ **un Portugais** a Portuguese (*man*)
◆ **une Portugaise** a Portuguese (*woman*)
◆ **les Portugais** the Portuguese

le **Portugal** NOUN
Portugal

◆ **au Portugal (1)** in Portugal
◆ **au Portugal (2)** to Portugal

poser VERB

1 to put down ◊ *J'ai posé la cafetière sur la table.* I put the coffee pot down on the table.
2 to pose ◊ *Cela pose un problème.* That poses a problem.

◆ **poser une question à quelqu'un** to ask somebody a question
◆ **se poser** to land ◊ *L'avion s'est posé à huit heures.* The plane landed at 8 o'clock.

positif ADJECTIVE (FEM SING **positive**)
positive

la **position** NOUN
position

posséder VERB
to own ◊ *Ils possèdent une jolie maison.* They own a lovely house.

la **possibilité** NOUN
possibility

possible ADJECTIVE
possible ◊ *Alain leur a dit que ce n'était pas possible.* Alain told them it wasn't possible.

◆ **le plus de gens possible** as many people as possible
◆ **le plus tôt possible** as early as possible
◆ **le moins d'argent possible** as little money as possible
◆ **Il travaille le moins possible.** He works as little as possible.
◆ **dès que possible** as soon as possible
◆ **faire son possible** to do all one can ◊ *Je ferai tout mon possible.* I'll do all I can.

la **poste** NOUN

see also **le poste**

1 post ◊ *Je vais l'envoyer par la poste.* I'm going to send it by post.
2 post office ◊ *Je vais à la poste pour acheter des timbres.* I'm going to the post office to buy some stamps.

◆ **mettre une lettre à la poste** to post a letter

le **poste** NOUN

see also **la poste**

1 post ◊ *Jean-Pierre a trouvé un poste de professeur.* Jean-Pierre has found a teaching post.

2 extension (*phone*) ◊ *Pouvez-vous me passer le poste de M. Salzedo?* Can you put me through to Mr Salzedo's extension?
3 set ◊ *un poste de radio* a radio set

◆ **un poste de police** a police station

poster VERB

see also **poster** NOUN

to post ◊ *Je vais poster ce colis.* I'm going to post this parcel.

le **poster** NOUN

see also **poster** VERB

poster ◊ *un poster de la Grèce* a poster of Greece

postérieur ADJECTIVE

1 later ◊ *Ce document est postérieur à 1314.* This document is from later than 1314.
2 back ◊ *la partie postérieure de ma jambe* the back of my leg

le **pot** NOUN
jar ◊ *J'ai fait trois pots de confiture.* I've made three jars of jam.

◆ **prendre un pot** (*informal*) to have a drink ◊ *On va prendre un pot ce soir.* We're going for a drink tonight.
◆ **un pot de fleurs** a plant pot

potable ADJECTIVE

◆ **eau potable** drinking water
◆ **"eau non potable"** "not drinking water"

le **potage** NOUN
soup

le **potager** NOUN
vegetable garden

le **pot-au-feu** NOUN (PL les **pot-au-feu**)
beef stew

le **pot-de-vin** NOUN (PL les **pots-de-vin**)
bribe

le **pote** NOUN (*informal*)
mate ◊ *Je sors avec mes potes ce soir.* I'm going out with my mates tonight.

le **poteau** NOUN (PL les **poteaux**)
post ◊ *Il s'est appuyé contre un poteau.* He leant against a post.

◆ **un poteau indicateur** a signpost

potentiel ADJECTIVE (FEM SING **potentielle**)
potential

la **poterie** NOUN

1 pottery ◊ *Elle fait de la poterie à l'école.* She does pottery at school.
2 piece of pottery ◊ *J'ai acheté deux poteries.* I bought two pieces of pottery.

le **potier** NOUN
potter

le **pou** NOUN (PL les **poux**)
louse

la **poubelle** NOUN
   dustbin

le **pouce** NOUN
   [1] thumb ◊ *Je me suis coincé le pouce dans la porte.* I trapped my thumb in the door.
   [2] inch ◊ *Un pouce fait à peu près deux virgule cinq centimètres.* 1 inch equals roughly 2.5 centimetres.
   ♦ **manger sur le pouce** to have a quick snack

la **poudre** NOUN
   [1] powder
   [2] face powder
   ♦ **la poudre à laver** washing powder
   ♦ **le lait en poudre** powdered milk
   ♦ **le café en poudre** instant coffee

le **poulain** NOUN
   foal

la **poule** NOUN
   hen

le **poulet** NOUN
   [1] chicken ◊ *J'adore le poulet.* I love chicken. ◊ *un poulet rôti* a roast chicken
   [2] cop ◊ *Il s'est fait attraper par les poulets.* (*informal*) He got caught by the cops.

le **pouls** NOUN
   pulse ◊ *Il m'a pris le pouls.* He took my pulse.

le **poumon** NOUN
   lung

la **poupée** NOUN
   doll

pour PREPOSITION
   for ◊ *C'est un cadeau pour toi.* It's a present for you. ◊ *Qu'est-ce que tu veux pour ton petit déjeuner?* What would you like for breakfast?
   ♦ **pour faire quelque chose** to do something ◊ *Je lui ai téléphoné pour l'inviter.* I phoned him to invite him.
   ♦ **Pour aller à Strasbourg, s'il vous plaît?** Which way is it to Strasbourg, please?
   ♦ **pour que** so that
   pour que is followed by a verb in the subjunctive.
   ◊ *Je lui ai prêté mon pull pour qu'elle n'ait pas froid.* I lent her my jumper so that she wouldn't be cold.
   ♦ **pour cent** per cent

le **pourboire** NOUN
   tip ◊ *Il a donné un pourboire au garçon.* He gave the waiter a tip.

le **pourcentage** NOUN
   percentage

pourquoi ADVERB, CONJUNCTION
   why ◊ *Pourquoi est-ce qu'il ne vient pas avec nous?* Why isn't he coming with us? ◊ *Elle ne m'a pas dit pourquoi.* She didn't tell me why.

pourra, pourrai, pourras, pourrez VERB *see* **pouvoir**

pourri ADJECTIVE
   rotten

pourrir VERB
   to go bad ◊ *Ces poires ont pourri.* These pears have gone bad.

pourrons, pourront VERB *see* **pouvoir**

la **poursuite** NOUN
   chase
   ♦ **se lancer à la poursuite de quelqu'un** to chase after somebody

poursuivre VERB
   to carry on with ◊ *Ils ont poursuivi leur travail.* They carried on with their work.
   ♦ **se poursuivre** to go on ◊ *Le concert s'est poursuivi très tard.* The concert went on very late.

pourtant ADVERB
   yet ◊ *Il a raté son examen. Pourtant, il n'est pas bête.* He failed his exam, yet he's not stupid.
   ♦ **C'est pourtant facile!** But it's easy!

pourvu ADJECTIVE
   ♦ **pourvu que ...** let's hope that ...
   pourvu que is followed by a verb in the subjunctive.
   ◊ *Pourvu qu'il ne pleuve pas!* Let's hope it doesn't rain!

pousser VERB
   [1] to push ◊ *Ils ont dû pousser la voiture.* They had to push the car.
   [2] to grow ◊ *Mes cheveux poussent vite.* My hair grows quickly.
   ♦ **pousser un cri** to give a cry
   ♦ **se pousser** to move over ◊ *Pousse-toi, je ne vois rien.* Move over, I can't see a thing.

la **poussette** NOUN
   pushchair

la **poussière** NOUN
   [1] dust ◊ *La table est couverte de poussière.* The table's covered in dust.
   [2] speck of dust ◊ *J'ai une poussière dans l'œil.* I've got a speck of dust in my eye.

poussiéreux ADJECTIVE (FEM SING **poussiéreuse**)
   dusty

le **poussin** NOUN
   chick

le **pouvoir** NOUN
   see also **pouvoir** VERB

P

☞

power ◊ *Le Premier ministre a beaucoup de pouvoir.* The Prime Minister has a lot of power.

pouvoir VERB

see also **pouvoir** NOUN

Present tense:

je peux	nous pouvons
tu peux	vous pouvez
il/elle peut	ils/elles peuvent

Past participle:
pu

can ◊ *Je peux lui téléphoner si tu veux.* I can phone her if you want.
◊ *Puis-je venir vous voir samedi?* May I come and see you on Saturday?
◊ *Je ne pourrai pas venir samedi.* I can't come on Saturday. ◊ *J'ai fait tout ce que j'ai pu.* I did all I could.
♦ **Je n'en peux plus.** I'm exhausted.
♦ **Il se peut que ...** It's possible that ...
il se peut que is followed by a verb in the subjunctive.
◊ *Il se peut qu'elle ait déménagé.* It's possible that she's moved house. ◊ *Il se peut que j'y aille.* I might go.

la **prairie** NOUN
meadow

la **pratique** NOUN

see also **pratique** ADJECTIVE

practice ◊ *Je manque de pratique.* I'm out of practice.

pratique ADJECTIVE

see also **pratique** NOUN

practical ◊ *Ce sac est très pratique.* This bag's very practical.

pratiquement ADVERB
virtually ◊ *J'ai pratiquement fini.* I've virtually finished.

pratiquer VERB
to practise ◊ *Je dois pratiquer mon espagnol.* I need to practise my Spanish.
♦ **Pratiquez-vous un sport?** Do you do any sport?

le **pré** NOUN
meadow

la **précaution** NOUN
precaution ◊ *prendre ses précautions* to take precautions
♦ **par précaution** as a precaution ◊ *Il a pris une assurance par précaution.* He took out insurance as a precaution.
♦ **avec précaution** cautiously
♦ **"à manipuler avec précaution"** "handle with care"

précédemment ADVERB
previously

précédent ADJECTIVE
previous

précieux ADJECTIVE (FEM SING **précieuse**)
precious
♦ **une pierre précieuse** a precious stone
♦ **de précieux conseils** invaluable advice

le **précipice** NOUN
ravine ◊ *Leur voiture est tombée dans un précipice.* Their car fell into a ravine.

précipitamment ADVERB
hurriedly ◊ *Chantal est partie précipitamment.* Chantal left hurriedly.

la **précipitation** NOUN
haste ◊ *Il a agi avec précipitation.* He acted hastily.

se **précipiter** VERB
to rush

précis ADJECTIVE
precise
♦ **à huit heures précises** at exactly eight o'clock

précisément ADVERB
precisely

préciser VERB
[1] to be more specific about ◊ *Pouvez-vous préciser ce que vous voulez dire?* Can you be more specific about what you want to say?
[2] to specify ◊ *Pouvez-vous préciser les raisons de ce changement?* Can you specify the reasons for this change?

la **précision** NOUN
[1] precision
[2] detail ◊ *Je vais vous donner quelques précisions.* I'm going to give you some details.

la **préfecture** NOUN

ⓘ A **préfecture** is the headquarters of a **département**, one of the 96 administrative areas of France.

♦ **la préfecture de police** the police headquarters

préférable ADJECTIVE
preferable

préféré ADJECTIVE
favourite

la **préférence** NOUN
preference ◊ *Je n'ai pas de préférence.* I've no preference.
♦ **de préférence** preferably

préférer VERB
to prefer ◊ *Je préfère la cuisine de Teresa.* I prefer Teresa's cooking. ◊ *Je*

préfère manger à la cantine. I prefer to eat in the canteen.
- **Je préférerais du thé.** I'd rather have tea.
- **préférer quelqu'un à quelqu'un** to prefer somebody to somebody ◊ *Je le préfère à son frère.* I prefer him to his brother.

préhistorique ADJECTIVE
prehistoric

le **préjugé** NOUN
prejudice ◊ *avoir des préjugés contre quelqu'un* to be prejudiced against somebody

premier ADJECTIVE (FEM SING **première**)
see also **première** NOUN
first ◊ *au premier étage* on the first floor ◊ *C'est notre premier jour de vacances.* It's the first day of our holiday. ◊ *C'est la première fois que je viens ici.* It's the first time I've been here. ◊ *le premier mai* the first of May ◊ *Il est arrivé premier.* He came first.
- **le Premier ministre** the Prime Minister

la **première** NOUN
see also **premier** ADJECTIVE
1 first class ◊ *Nous avons voyagé en première.* We travelled first class.
2 first gear ◊ *Passe en première pour prendre ce virage.* Change into first to go round this bend.
3 lower sixth form

*ⓘ In French secondary schools, years are counted from the **sixième** (youngest) to **première** and **terminale** (oldest).*

◊ *Ma sœur est en première.* My sister's in the lower sixth.

premièrement ADVERB
firstly

prendre VERB
to take ◊ *Prends tes affaires et viens avec moi.* Take your things and come with me.
- **prendre quelque chose à quelqu'un** to take something from somebody ◊ *Il m'a pris mon stylo!* He's taken my pen!
- **Nous avons pris le train de huit heures.** We took the eight o'clock train.
- **Je prends toujours le train pour aller à Paris.** I always go to Paris by train.
- **passer prendre** to pick up ◊ *Je dois passer prendre Richard.* I have to pick up Richard.

- **prendre à gauche** to turn left ◊ *Prenez à gauche en arrivant au rond-point.* Turn left at the roundabout.
- **Il se prend pour Napoléon.** He thinks he's Napoleon.
- **s'en prendre à quelqu'un** to lay into somebody (*verbally*) ◊ *Il s'en est pris à moi.* He laid into me.
- **s'y prendre** to set about it ◊ *Tu t'y prends mal!* You're setting about it the wrong way!

le **prénom** NOUN
first name ◊ *Quel est votre prénom?* What's your first name?

préoccupé ADJECTIVE
worried

la **préparation** NOUN
preparation

préparer VERB
1 to prepare ◊ *Elle prépare le dîner.* She's preparing dinner.
2 to make ◊ *Je vais préparer le café.* I'm going to make the coffee.
3 to prepare for ◊ *Laure prépare son examen d'économie.* Laure's preparing for her economics exam.
- **se préparer** to get ready ◊ *Ils se préparent à partir.* They're getting ready to go.

la **préposition** NOUN
preposition

près ADVERB
- **tout près** nearby ◊ *J'habite tout près.* I live nearby.
- **près de (1)** near (to) ◊ *Est-ce que c'est près d'ici?* Is it near here?
- **près de (2)** next to ◊ *Assieds-toi près de moi.* Sit down next to me.
- **près de (3)** nearly ◊ *Il y avait près de cinq cents spectateurs.* There were nearly 500 spectators.
- **de près** closely ◊ *Il a regardé la photo de près.* He looked closely at the photo.
- **à peu de chose près** more or less

la **présence** NOUN
1 presence ◊ *Sa présence est rassurante.* His presence is reassuring.
2 attendance ◊ *La présence aux cours est obligatoire.* Attendance at lessons is compulsory.

présent ADJECTIVE
see also **présent** NOUN
present

le **présent** NOUN
see also **présent** ADJECTIVE
present tense
- **à présent** now

P

la **présentation** NOUN
  presentation
  ◆ **faire les présentations** to do the introductions

présenter VERB
  to present ◊ *Il présentait le spectacle.* He presented the show.
  ◆ **présenter quelqu'un à quelqu'un** to introduce somebody to somebody ◊ *Il m'a présenté à sa sœur.* He introduced me to his sister.
  ◆ **Marc, je te présente Anaïs.** Marc, this is Anaïs.
  ◆ **se présenter (1)** to introduce oneself ◊ *Elle s'est présentée à ses collègues.* She introduced herself to her colleagues.
  ◆ **se présenter (2)** to arise ◊ *Si l'occasion se présente, nous irons en Écosse.* If the chance arises, we'll go to Scotland.
  ◆ **se présenter (3)** to stand ◊ *Monsieur Legros se présente encore aux élections.* Mr Legros is standing for election again.

le **préservatif** NOUN
  condom

préserver VERB
  to protect ◊ *préserver du froid* to protect from the cold

le **président** NOUN
  1 president ◊ *le président des États-Unis* the president of the United States
  2 chairman ◊ *le président du conseil d'administration* the chairman of the board of directors
  ◆ **le président directeur général** the chairman and managing director

présider VERB
  1 to chair ◊ *Duncan a présidé la réunion.* Duncan chaired the meeting.
  2 to be the guest of honour ◊ *Il présidait à table.* He was the guest of honour at the table.

presque ADVERB
  nearly ◊ *Il est presque six heures.* It's nearly 6 o'clock. ◊ *Nous sommes presque arrivés.* We're nearly there.
  ◆ **presque rien** hardly anything ◊ *Elle n'a presque rien mangé.* She's hardly eaten anything.
  ◆ **presque pas** hardly at all ◊ *Il ne dort presque pas.* He hardly sleeps at all.
  ◆ **presque pas de** hardly any ◊ *Il n'y a presque pas de place.* There's hardly any space.

la **presqu'île** NOUN
  peninsula

la **presse** NOUN

press ◊ *les représentants de la presse* representatives of the press

pressé ADJECTIVE
  1 in a hurry ◊ *Je ne peux pas rester, je suis pressé.* I can't stay, I'm in a hurry.
  2 urgent ◊ *Ce n'est pas très pressé.* It's not very urgent.
  ◆ **une orange pressée** a fresh orange juice

presser VERB
  1 to squeeze ◊ *Tu peux me presser un citron?* Can you squeeze me a lemon?
  2 to be urgent ◊ *Est-ce que ça presse?* Is it urgent?
  ◆ **se presser** to hurry up ◊ *Allez, presse-toi, on va être en retard!* Come on, hurry up, we're going to be late!
  ◆ **Rien ne presse.** There's no hurry.

le **pressing** NOUN
  dry-cleaner's

la **pression** NOUN
  1 pressure
  ◆ **faire pression sur quelqu'un** to put pressure on somebody
  2 draught beer (*informal*)

prêt ADJECTIVE
  see also **prêt** NOUN
  ready ◊ *Le déjeuner est prêt.* Lunch is ready. ◊ *Tu es prête?* Are you ready?

le **prêt** NOUN
  see also **prêt** ADJECTIVE
  loan

le **prêt-à-porter** NOUN
  ready-to-wear clothes PL

prétendre VERB
  ◆ **prétendre que** to claim that ◊ *Il prétend qu'il ne la connaît pas.* He claims he doesn't know her.
  Be careful! **prétendre** *does not mean* ***to pretend.***

prétendu ADJECTIVE
  so-called ◊ *un prétendu expert* a so-called expert

prétentieux ADJECTIVE (FEM SING **prétentieuse**)
  pretentious

prêter VERB
  ◆ **prêter quelque chose à quelqu'un** to lend something to someone ◊ *Il m'a prêté sa voiture.* He lent me his car.
  ◆ **prêter attention à quelque chose** to pay attention to something

le **prétexte** NOUN

excuse ◇ *Il avait un prétexte pour ne pas venir.* He had an excuse for not coming.

♦**sous aucun prétexte** on no account ◇ *Ne le dérangez sous aucun prétexte.* On no account must you disturb him.

prétexter VERB
to give as an excuse ◇ *Elle a prétexté une réunion.* She gave a meeting as her excuse. ◇ *Il a prétexté qu'il avait un rendez-vous.* He gave the excuse that he had an appointment.

le **prêtre** NOUN
priest

la **preuve** NOUN
[1] evidence ◇ *Il y a des preuves contre lui.* There's evidence against him.
[2] proof ◇ *Vous n'avez aucune preuve.* You haven't got any proof.
♦**faire preuve de courage** to show courage
♦**faire ses preuves** to prove oneself ◇ *Pour être embauché ici, il faut faire ses preuves.* To be employed here, you need to prove yourself.

prévenir VERB
♦**prévenir quelqu'un** to warn somebody ◇ *Je te préviens, il est de mauvaise humeur.* I'm warning you, he's in a bad mood.

la **prévention** NOUN
prevention
♦**des mesures de prévention** preventative measures
♦**la prévention routière** road safety

la **prévision** NOUN
♦**les prévisions météorologiques** the weather forecast
♦**en prévision de quelque chose** in anticipation of something

prévoir VERB
[1] to plan ◇ *Nous prévoyons un pique-nique pour dimanche.* We're planning to have a picnic on Sunday.
♦**Le départ est prévu pour dix heures.** The departure's scheduled for 10 o'clock.
[2] to allow ◇ *J'ai prévu assez à manger pour quatre.* I allowed enough food for four.
[3] to foresee ◇ *J'avais prévu qu'il serait en retard.* I'd foreseen that he'd be late.
♦**Je prévois qu'il me faudra une heure de plus.** I reckon on it taking me another hour.

prier VERB

to pray to ◇ *Les Grecs priaient Dionysos.* The Greeks prayed to Dionysos.
♦**prier quelqu'un de faire quelque chose** to ask somebody to do something ◇ *Elle l'a prié de sortir.* She asked him to leave.
♦**je vous en prie (1)** please do ◇ *Je peux m'asseoir? – Je vous en prie.* May I sit down? – Please do.
♦**je vous en prie (2)** please ◇ *Je vous en prie, ne me laissez pas seule.* Please, don't leave me alone.
♦**je vous en prie (3)** don't mention it ◇ *Merci pour votre aide. – Je vous en prie.* Thanks for your help. – Don't mention it.

la **prière** NOUN
prayer ◇ *faire ses prières* to say one's prayers
♦**"prière de ne pas fumer"** "no smoking please"

le **primaire** NOUN
primary education ◇ *Ses enfants sont encore en primaire.* His children are still in primary education.
♦**l'école primaire** primary school

la **prime** NOUN
[1] bonus ◇ *Il a eu une prime en récompense de son travail.* He received a bonus for his work.
[2] free gift ◇ *J'ai eu ce stylo en prime avec l'agenda.* I got this pen as a free gift with the diary.
[3] premium ◇ *une prime d'assurance* an insurance premium

la **primevère** NOUN
primrose

le **prince** NOUN
prince ◇ *le prince Charles* Prince Charles

la **princesse** NOUN
princess ◇ *la princesse Diana* Princess Diana

principal ADJECTIVE (MASC PL **principaux**)
see also **principal** NOUN
main ◇ *le rôle principal* the main role

le **principal** NOUN (PL les **principaux**)
see also **principal** ADJECTIVE
[1] headmaster ◇ *le principal du collège* the headmaster of the school
[2] main thing ◇ *Personne n'a été blessé; c'est le principal.* Nobody was injured; that's the main thing.

le **principe** NOUN
principle
♦**pour le principe** on principle

P

☞

◆ **en principe (1)** as a rule ◇ *Il déjeune en principe à midi et demi.* As a rule he has lunch at 12.30.

◆ **en principe (2)** in theory ◇ *En principe Anne doit arriver lundi.* In theory, Anne should arrive on Monday.

le **printemps** NOUN
spring

◆ **au printemps** in spring

la **priorité** NOUN
1 priority ◇ *C'est à faire en priorité.* It needs to be done as a priority.
2 right of way ◇ *Tu n'as pas la priorité.* You haven't got right of way.

pris VERB *see* **prendre**

pris ADJECTIVE
1 taken ◇ *Est-ce que cette place est prise?* Is this seat taken?
2 busy ◇ *Je serai très pris la semaine prochaine.* I'll be very busy next week.

◆ **avoir le nez pris** to have a stuffy nose

◆ **être pris de panique** to be panic-stricken

la **prise** NOUN
1 plug
2 socket

◆ **une prise de courant** a power point

◆ **une prise multiple** an adaptor

◆ **une prise de sang** a blood test

la **prison** NOUN
prison ◇ *aller en prison* to go to prison ◇ *être en prison* to be in prison

prisonnier ADJECTIVE
see also **prisonnier** NOUN
captive

le **prisonnier** NOUN
see also **prisonnier** ADJECTIVE
prisoner

la **prisonnière** NOUN
prisoner

prit VERB *see* **prendre**

privé ADJECTIVE
private ◇ *la propriété privée* private property ◇ *ma vie privée* my private life

◆ **en privé** in private

priver VERB

◆ **priver quelqu'un de quelque chose** to deprive somebody of something ◇ *Le prisonnier a été privé de nourriture.* The prisoner was deprived of food.

◆ **Tu seras privé de dessert!** You won't get any pudding!

le **prix** NOUN
1 price ◇ *Je n'arrive pas à lire le prix de ce livre.* I can't see the price of this book.

2 prize ◇ *Cécile a eu le prix de la meilleure actrice.* Cécile got the prize for best actress.

◆ **hors de prix** exorbitantly priced ◇ *Les repas sont hors de prix ici!* The price of meals here is exorbitant!

◆ **à aucun prix** not at any price ◇ *Je n'irai là-bas à aucun prix.* I'm not going there, not at any price.

◆ **à tout prix** at all costs ◇ *Je veux à tout prix voir ce film.* I want to see this film at all costs.

probable ADJECTIVE
likely ◇ *Il est probable qu'elle viendra.* It's likely she'll come.

◆ **C'est peu probable.** That's unlikely.

probablement ADVERB
probably

le **problème** NOUN
problem

le **procédé** NOUN
process

le **procès** NOUN
trial ◇ *Le procès du meurtrier commence mardi.* The murder trial starts on Tuesday.

◆ **Il est en procès avec son employeur.** He's involved in a lawsuit with his employer.

prochain ADJECTIVE
next ◇ *Nous descendons au prochain arrêt.* We're getting off at the next stop.

◆ **la prochaine fois** next time

◆ **la semaine prochaine** next week

◆ **À la prochaine!** See you!

prochainement ADVERB
soon

proche ADJECTIVE
1 near ◇ *Les magasins les plus proches étaient à trois kilomètres.* The nearest shops were 3 kilometres away. ◇ *dans un proche avenir* in the near future
2 close ◇ *un ami proche* a close friend

◆ **proche de** near to ◇ *La cathédrale est proche du château.* The cathedral is near the castle.

◆ **le Proche-Orient** the Middle East

les **proches** MASC NOUN
close relatives

proclamer VERB
to proclaim

procurer VERB

◆ **procurer quelque chose à quelqu'un** to get something for somebody ◇ *C'est lui qui m'a procuré ce travail.* He got me this job.

◆ **se procurer quelque chose** to get something ◊ *Je me suis procuré leur dernier catalogue.* I got their latest catalogue.

le **producteur** NOUN
producer

la **production** NOUN
production

la **productrice** NOUN
producer

produire VERB
to produce
◆ **se produire** to take place ◊ *Ces changements se sont produits l'an dernier.* The changes took place last year.

le **produit** NOUN
product ◊ *les produits de beauté* beauty products

le **prof** NOUN (*informal*)
teacher ◊ *Elle est prof de maths.* She's a maths teacher.

le **professeur** NOUN
1 teacher ◊ *Philippe est professeur d'histoire.* Philippe's a history teacher.
2 professor ◊ *le professeur Dupont* Professor Dupont
◆ **un professeur de faculté** a university lecturer

la **profession** NOUN
profession ◊ *Quelle est votre profession?* What's your profession?
◆ **"sans profession"** "unemployed"

professionnel ADJECTIVE (FEM SING **professionnelle**)
professional

le **profil** NOUN
1 profile (*of person*) ◊ *de profil* in profile
2 contours (*of object*)

le **profit** NOUN
profit ◊ *La société a fait des profits importants.* The company made significant profits.
◆ **tirer profit de quelque chose** to profit from something
◆ **au profit de** in aid of ◊ *un spectacle au profit de l'UNICEF* a show in aid of UNICEF

profiter VERB
◆ **profiter de quelque chose** to take advantage of something ◊ *Profitez du beau temps pour aller faire du vélo.* Take advantage of the good weather and go cycling.
◆ **Profitez-en bien!** Make the most of it!

profond ADJECTIVE
deep
◆ **peu profond** shallow

la **profondeur** NOUN
depth

le **programme** NOUN
1 programme ◊ *le programme du festival* the festival programme
2 syllabus ◊ *le programme de maths* the maths syllabus
3 program ◊ *un programme informatique* a computer program

programmer VERB
1 to show ◊ *Ce film est programmé dimanche soir.* The film is scheduled for Sunday evening.
2 to program ◊ *Mon ordinateur n'est pas programmé pour ça.* My computer isn't programmed to do that.

le **programmeur** NOUN
programmer ◊ *Marc est programmeur.* Marc is a programmer.

la **programmeuse** NOUN
programmer ◊ *Elle est programmeuse.* She's a programmer.

le **progrès** NOUN
progress ◊ *faire des progrès* to make progress

progresser VERB
to progress

progressif ADJECTIVE (FEM SING **progressive**)
progressive

le **projecteur** NOUN
1 projector ◊ *Le projecteur de diapositives est en panne.* The slide projector is broken.
2 spotlight ◊ *sous les projecteurs* under the spotlight

le **projet** NOUN
1 plan ◊ *des projets de vacances* holiday plans
2 draft ◊ *le projet de construction d'un musée* the draft for the construction of a museum
◆ **un projet de loi** a bill (*in parliament*)

projeter VERB
1 to plan ◊ *Ils projettent d'acheter une maison.* They're planning to buy a house.
2 to cast ◊ *une ombre projetée sur le mur* a shadow cast onto the wall
◆ **Elle a été projetée hors de la voiture.** She was thrown out of the car.

prolonger VERB
1 to prolong ◊ *Je vais prolonger mes vacances en Espagne.* I'm going to prolong my holidays in Spain.
2 to extend ◊ *Je vais prolonger mon abonnement.* I'm going to extend my subscription.

P

☞

♦**se prolonger** to go on ◊ *La réunion s'est prolongée tard.* The meeting went on late.

la **promenade** NOUN
walk ◊ *Il y a de belles promenades par ici.* There are some nice walks round here.
♦**faire une promenade** to go for a walk
♦**faire une promenade en voiture** to go for a drive
♦**faire une promenade à vélo** to go for a bike ride

promener VERB
to take for a walk ◊ *Cordelia promène son chien tous les jours.* Cordelia takes her dog for a walk every day.
♦**se promener** to go for a walk ◊ *Chantal est partie se promener.* Chantal has gone for a walk.

la **promesse** NOUN
promise ◊ *faire une promesse* to make a promise ◊ *tenir sa promesse* to keep one's promise

promettre VERB
to promise ◊ *On m'a promis une augmentation.* They promised me a pay rise. ◊ *Elle m'a promis de me téléphoner.* She promised to phone me.

la **promotion** NOUN
promotion ◊ *Il espère avoir bientôt une promotion.* He's hoping to get promotion soon.
♦**être en promotion** to be on special offer ◊ *Les côtes de porc sont en promotion.* Pork chops are on special offer.

le **pronom** NOUN
pronoun

prononcer VERB
1 to pronounce ◊ *Le russe est difficile à prononcer.* Russian is difficult to pronounce.
2 to deliver ◊ *prononcer un discours* to deliver a speech
♦**se prononcer** to be pronounced ◊ *Le "e" final ne se prononce pas.* The final "e" isn't pronounced.

la **prononciation** NOUN
pronunciation

la **propagande** NOUN
propaganda

se **propager** VERB
to spread ◊ *Le feu s'est propagé rapidement.* The fire spread quickly.

la **proportion** NOUN
proportion

le **propos** NOUN

♦**à propos** by the way ◊ *À propos, quand est-ce que tu viens?* By the way, when are you coming?
♦**à propos de quelque chose** about something ◊ *C'est à propos de la soirée de vendredi.* It's about the party on Friday.

proposer VERB
♦**proposer quelque chose à quelqu'un (1)** to suggest something to somebody ◊ *Nous lui avons proposé une promenade en bateau.* We suggested going on a boat ride to him.
♦**proposer quelque chose à quelqu'un (2)** to offer somebody something ◊ *Ils m'ont proposé des chocolats.* They offered me some chocolates.

la **proposition** NOUN
offer ◊ *J'accepte ta proposition avec plaisir.* I'll be pleased to accept your offer.

propre ADJECTIVE
see also **propre** NOUN
1 clean ◊ *Ce mouchoir n'est pas propre.* This handkerchief isn't clean.
2 own ◊ *Gordon l'a fabriqué de ses propres mains.* Gordon made it with his own hands.
♦**propre à** characteristic of ◊ *C'est une coutume propre au Berry.* It's a custom you find in the Berry region.

le **propre** NOUN
see also **propre** ADJECTIVE
♦**recopier quelque chose au propre** to make a fair copy of something

proprement ADVERB
properly ◊ *Mange proprement!* Eat properly!
♦**le village proprement dit** the village itself
♦**à proprement parler** strictly speaking

la **propreté** NOUN
cleanliness

le **propriétaire** NOUN
see also **la propriétaire**
1 owner
2 landlord

la **propriétaire** NOUN
see also **le propriétaire**
1 owner
2 landlady

la **propriété** NOUN
property ◊ *la propriété privée* private property

le **prospectus** NOUN
leaflet

prospère ADJECTIVE
prosperous

la **prostituée** NOUN
   prostitute

protecteur ADJECTIVE (FEM SING **protectrice**)
   [1] protective ◊ *un vernis protecteur* a protective varnish
   [2] patronizing ◊ *un ton protecteur* a patronizing tone

la **protection** NOUN
   protection

protéger VERB
   to protect

la **protéine** NOUN
   protein

protestant ADJECTIVE (FEM SING **protestante**)
   Protestant ◊ *une église protestante* a Protestant church
   ♦ **Robert est protestant.** Robert is a Protestant.

la **protestation** NOUN
   protest

protester VERB
   to protest ◊ *Ils protestent contre leurs conditions de travail.* They're protesting about their working conditions.

prouver VERB
   to prove

la **provenance** NOUN
   origin
   ♦ **un avion en provenance de Berlin** a plane arriving from Berlin

provenir VERB
   ♦ **provenir de (1)** to come from ◊ *Ces tomates proviennent d'Espagne.* These tomatoes come from Spain.
   ♦ **provenir de (2)** to be the result of ◊ *Cela provient d'un manque d'organisation.* This is the result of a lack of organization.

le **proverbe** NOUN
   proverb

la **province** NOUN
   province
   ♦ **en province** in the provinces ◊ *Ils habitent en province.* They live in the provinces.

le **proviseur** NOUN
   headteacher (*of state secondary school*) ◊ *Elle est proviseur.* She's a headteacher.

la **provision** NOUN
   supply ◊ *une provision de pommes de terre* a supply of potatoes

les **provisions** FEM NOUN
   food ◊ *Nous n'avons plus beaucoup de provisions.* We haven't got much food left.

provisoire ADJECTIVE
   temporary ◊ *un emploi provisoire* a temporary job

provoquer VERB
   [1] to provoke ◊ *Il l'a provoquée en la traitant d'imbécile.* He provoked her by calling her stupid.
   [2] to cause ◊ *Cet accident a provoqué la mort de quarante personnes.* The accident caused the death of 40 people.

la **proximité** NOUN
   proximity
   ♦ **à proximité** nearby ◊ *Sabine habite à proximité.* Sabine lives nearby.

prudemment ADVERB
   [1] carefully ◊ *Conduisez prudemment!* Drive carefully!
   [2] wisely ◊ *Prudemment, il a fait des économies.* Wisely, he saved some money.
   [3] cautiously ◊ *Le gouvernement a réagi prudemment.* The government reacted cautiously.

la **prudence** NOUN
   caution
   ♦ **avec prudence** carefully ◊ *Ils ont conduit avec prudence.* They drove carefully.

prudent ADJECTIVE
   [1] careful ◊ *Soyez prudents!* Be careful!
   [2] wise ◊ *Laisse ton passeport à la maison, c'est plus prudent.* It would be wiser to leave your passport at home.

la **prune** NOUN
   plum

le **pruneau** NOUN (PL les **pruneaux**)
   prune

le/la **psychiatre** NOUN
   psychiatrist

la **psychologie** NOUN
   psychology

psychologique ADJECTIVE
   psychological

le/la **psychologue** NOUN
   psychologist

pu VERB *see* **pouvoir**
   ♦ **Je n'ai pas pu venir hier.** I couldn't come yesterday.

la **pub** NOUN (*informal*)
   [1] advertising ◊ *Il y a trop de pub à la télé.* There's too much advertising on TV.
   [2] adverts ◊ *Le film a été coupé par la pub.* The film was interrupted by adverts.

public ADJECTIVE (FEM SING **publique**)

P

☞

see also **public** NOUN

public ◇ *un jardin public* a public park

♦ **une école publique** a state school

le **public** NOUN

see also **public** ADJECTIVE

1 public ◇ *Ce parc est ouvert au public.* The park's open to the public.
2 audience ◇ *Le public a applaudi le chanteur.* The audience applauded the singer.

♦ **en public** in public ◇ *Je déteste parler en public.* I hate speaking in public.

publicitaire ADJECTIVE

♦ **une agence publicitaire** an advertising agency

♦ **un film publicitaire** a publicity film

la **publicité** NOUN

1 advertising ◇ *Muriel travaille dans la publicité.* Muriel works in advertising.
2 advert ◇ *Il y a trop de publicités dans ce journal.* There are too many adverts in this newspaper.

♦ **faire de la publicité pour quelque chose** to publicize something

publier VERB

to publish ◇ *Bob vient de publier son nouveau roman.* Bob has just published his new novel.

publique ADJECTIVE see **public**

la **puce** NOUN

1 flea ◇ *Ce chien a des puces.* This dog has fleas.
2 chip ◇ *une puce électronique* a microchip

♦ **une carte à puce** a smart card

les **puces** FEM NOUN

flea market SING

puer VERB

to stink ◇ *Ça pue le tabac ici!* It stinks of tobacco round here!

puéril ADJECTIVE

childish

puis VERB

see also **puis** ADVERB

see **pouvoir**

♦ **Puis-je venir vous voir samedi?** May I come and see you on Saturday?

puis ADVERB

see also **puis** VERB

then ◇ *Faites dorer le poulet, puis ajoutez le vin blanc.* Fry the chicken till golden, then add white wine.

puisque CONJUNCTION

since ◇ *Puisque c'est si cher, nous irons manger ailleurs.* Since it's so expensive, we'll eat elsewhere.

la **puissance** NOUN

power

puissant ADJECTIVE

powerful

le **puits** NOUN

well ◇ *Il a un puits dans son jardin.* He's got a well in his garden.

le **pull** NOUN

jumper

le **pull-over** NOUN

jumper

le **pulvérisateur** NOUN

spray ◇ *un pulvérisateur de parfum* a perfume spray

pulvériser VERB

1 to pulverize ◇ *L'explosion a pulvérisé le bâtiment.* The explosion pulverized the building.
2 to spray ◇ *Il a pulvérisé de l'insecticide sur ses plantes.* He sprayed insecticide on his plants.

la **punaise** NOUN

drawing pin

punir VERB

to punish ◇ *Il a été puni pour avoir menti.* He was punished for lying.

la **punition** NOUN

punishment

le **pupitre** NOUN

desk (for pupil)

pur ADJECTIVE

1 pure ◇ *L'eau de cette source est très pure.* The water from this spring is very pure.
2 neat (undiluted) ◇ *du whisky pur* neat whisky ◇ *de l'eau de Javel pure* concentrated bleach

♦ **c'est de la folie pure** it's sheer madness

la **purée** NOUN

mashed potatoes

♦ **la purée de marrons** chestnut purée

la **putain** NOUN (rude)

whore

le **puzzle** NOUN

jigsaw puzzle

le **PV** NOUN (= *procès-verbal*)

parking ticket

le **pyjama** NOUN

pyjamas PL

la **pyramide** NOUN

pyramid

les **Pyrénées** FEM NOUN

Pyrenees

♦ **dans les Pyrénées** in the Pyrenees

Q

le **QI** NOUN (= *quotient intellectuel*)
  IQ

le **quai** NOUN
  [1] quay ◊ *être à quai* to be alongside
  the quay
  [2] platform ◊ *Le train partira du quai
  numéro quatre.* The train will leave
  from platform 4.

qualifié ADJECTIVE
  qualified

qualifier VERB
  ◆ **se qualifier** to qualify ◊ *Bob s'est
  qualifié pour la demi-finale.* Bob has
  qualified for the semifinal.

la **qualité** NOUN
  quality ◊ *Ces outils sont de très
  bonne qualité.* These are very good
  quality tools.

quand CONJUNCTION, ADVERB
  when ◊ *Quand est-ce que tu pars en
  vacances?* When are you going on
  holiday? ◊ *Quand je serai riche,
  j'achèterai une belle maison.* When
  I'm rich, I'll buy a nice house.
  ◆ **quand même** all the same ◊ *Je ne
  voulais pas de dessert, mais j'en ai
  mangé quand même.* I didn't want
  any dessert, but I had some all the
  same.

quant à PREPOSITION
  regarding ◊ *Quant au problème de
  chauffage ...* Regarding the problem
  with the heating ... ◊ *Quant à moi, je
  n'arriverai qu'à dix heures.* As for
  me, I won't be arriving till 10 o'clock.

la **quantité** NOUN
  amount
  ◆ **des quantités de** a great deal of

la **quarantaine** NOUN
  about forty ◊ *une quarantaine de
  personnes* about forty people
  ◆ **Elle a la quarantaine.** She's in her
  forties.

quarante NUMBER
  forty ◊ *Elle a quarante ans.* She's
  forty.
  ◆ **quarante et un** forty-one
  ◆ **quarante-deux** forty-two

le **quart** NOUN
  quarter
  ◆ **le quart de** a quarter of ◊ *Elle a
  mangé le quart du gâteau.* She ate a
  quarter of the cake.
  ◆ **trois quarts** three quarters
  ◆ **un quart d'heure** a quarter of an hour

  ◆ **deux heures et quart** a quarter past
  two
  ◆ **dix heures moins le quart** a quarter
  to ten
  ◆ **Un quart d'eau minérale, s'il vous
  plaît.** A small bottle of mineral water,
  please.

le **quartier** NOUN
  [1] area (of town) ◊ *un quartier
  tranquille* a quiet area
  ◆ **un cinéma de quartier** a local cinema
  [2] piece ◊ *un quartier d'orange* a
  piece of orange

le **quartz** NOUN
  ◆ **une montre à quartz** a quartz watch

quasi ADVERB
  nearly ◊ *La quasi-totalité des récoltes
  a été détruite.* Nearly all of the crop
  was destroyed.

quasiment ADVERB
  nearly ◊ *Le film est quasiment fini.*
  The film's nearly finished.
  ◆ **quasiment jamais** hardly ever ◊ *Ils ne
  vont quasiment jamais en boîte.* They
  hardly ever go clubbing.

quatorze NUMBER
  fourteen ◊ *Mon frère a quatorze ans.*
  My brother's fourteen. ◊ *à quatorze
  heures* at 2 p.m.
  ◆ **le quatorze février** the fourteenth of
  February

quatre NUMBER
  four ◊ *Il est quatre heures du matin.*
  It's four in the morning. ◊ *Il a quatre
  ans.* He's four.
  ◆ **le quatre mars** the fourth of March
  ◆ **faire les quatre cents coups** to be a
  bit wild ◊ *Todd a fait les quatre cents
  coups dans sa jeunesse.* Todd was a
  bit wild in his youth.

quatre-vingts NUMBER
  eighty

  *quatre-vingts is spelt with an -s
  when it is followed by a noun, but
  not when it is followed by another
  number.*

  ◊ *quatre-vingts euros* eighty euros
  ◊ *Elle a quatre-vingt-deux ans.* She's
  eighty-two.
  ◆ **quatre-vingt-dix** ninety
  ◆ **quatre-vingt-onze** ninety-one
  ◆ **quatre-vingt-quinze** ninety-five
  ◆ **quatre-vingt-dix-huit** ninety-eight

quatrième ADJECTIVE
  see also **quatrième** NOUN

☞

fourth ◇ *au quatrième étage* on the fourth floor

la **quatrième** NOUN

see also **quatrième** ADJECTIVE

year 9

> *In French secondary schools, years are counted from the **sixième** (youngest) to **première** and **terminale** (oldest).*

◇ *Mon frère est en quatrième.* My brother's in year 9.

que CONJUNCTION, PRONOUN, ADVERB

1 that ◇ *Il sait que tu es là.* He knows that you're here. ◇ *la dame que j'ai rencontrée hier* the lady that I met yesterday ◇ *Le gâteau qu'elle a fait est délicieux.* The cake she's made is delicious.

♦ **Je veux que tu viennes.** I want you to come.

2 what ◇ *Que fais-tu?* What are you doing? ◇ *Que vas-tu lui dire?* What are you going to tell him?

♦ **Qu'est-ce que ...?** What ...? ◇ *Qu'est-ce que tu fais?* What are you doing? ◇ *Qu'est-ce que c'est?* What's that?

♦ **plus ... que** more ... than ◇ *C'est plus difficile que je ne le pensais.* It's more difficult than I thought. ◇ *Il est plus grand que moi.* He's bigger than me.

♦ **aussi ... que** as ... as ◇ *Elle est aussi jolie que sa sœur.* She's as pretty as her sister. ◇ *Le train est aussi cher que l'avion.* The train is as expensive as the plane.

♦ **ne ... que** only ◇ *Il ne boit que de l'eau.* He only drinks water. ◇ *Je ne l'ai vu qu'une fois.* I've only seen him once.

♦ **Qu'il est bête!** He's so silly!

quel ADJECTIVE (FEM SING **quelle**)

1 who ◇ *Quel est ton chanteur préféré?* Who's your favourite singer?

2 what ◇ *Quelle est ta couleur préférée?* What's your favourite colour? ◇ *Quelle heure est-il?* What time is it? ◇ *Quelle bonne surprise!* What a surprise!

3 which ◇ *Quel groupe préfères-tu?* Which band do you like best?

♦ **quel que soit (1)** whoever ◇ *quel que soit le coupable* whoever is guilty

♦ **quel que soit (2)** whatever ◇ *quel que soit votre avis* whatever your opinion

quelle ADJECTIVE see **quel**

quelque ADJECTIVE, ADVERB

1 some ◇ *Il a quelques amis à Paris.* He has some friends in Paris. ◇ *J'ai acheté quelques disques.* I bought some records.

2 a few ◇ *Il reste quelques bouteilles.* There are a few bottles left.

3 few ◇ *Ils ont fini les quelques bouteilles qui restaient.* They finished the few bottles that were left.

♦ **quelque chose (1)** something ◇ *J'ai quelque chose pour toi.* I've got something for you. ◇ *Je voudrais quelque chose de moins cher.* I'd like something cheaper.

♦ **quelque chose (2)** anything ◇ *Avez-vous quelque chose à déclarer?* Have you got anything to declare? ◇ *Tu as pensé à quelque chose d'autre?* Did you think of anything else?

♦ **quelque part (1)** somewhere ◇ *J'ai oublié mon sac quelque part.* I've left my bag somewhere.

♦ **quelque part (2)** anywhere ◇ *Vous allez quelque part ce week-end?* Are you going anywhere this weekend?

quelquefois ADVERB

sometimes

quelques-uns PRONOUN (FEM **quelques-unes**)

some ◇ *As-tu vu ses films? J'en ai vu quelques-uns.* Have you seen his films? I've seen some of them.

quelqu'un PRONOUN

1 somebody ◇ *Quelqu'un t'a appelé.* Somebody phoned you. ◇ *Il y a quelqu'un à la porte.* There's somebody at the door.

2 anybody ◇ *Est-ce que quelqu'un a vu mon parapluie?* Has anybody seen my umbrella? ◇ *Il y a quelqu'un?* Is there anybody there?

la **querelle** NOUN

quarrel

qu'est-ce que see **que**

qu'est-ce qui see **qui**

la **question** NOUN

1 question ◇ *Je t'ai posé une question.* I asked you a question.

2 matter ◇ *Ils se sont disputés pour des questions d'argent.* They argued over money matters.

♦ **Il n'en est pas question.** There's no question of it. ◇ *Il n'est pas question que je paye.* There's no question of me paying.

♦ **De quoi est-il question?** What's it about?

◆ **Il est question de l'organisation du concert.** It's about the organization of the concert.

◆ **hors de question** out of the question ◊ *Il est hors de question que nous restions ici.* It's out of the question that we stay here.

le **questionnaire** NOUN
questionnaire

questionner VERB
to question

la **queue** NOUN
[1] tail ◊ *Le chien a agité la queue.* The dog wagged its tail.
◆ **faire la queue** to queue
◆ **une queue de cheval** a ponytail
[2] rear ◊ *en queue du train* at the rear of the train
[3] bottom ◊ *en queue de liste* at the bottom of the list
[4] stalk (of fruit, leaf) ◊ *la queue d'une cerise* a cherry stalk

qui PRONOUN
[1] who ◊ *Qui a téléphoné?* Who phoned? ◊ *Einstein était un génie.* Einstein was a genius.
[2] whom ◊ *C'est la personne à qui j'ai parlé hier.* It's the person whom I spoke to yesterday.
[3] that ◊ *Donne-moi la veste qui est sur la chaise.* Give me the jacket that's on the chair.
◆ **Qui est-ce qui ...?** Who ...? ◊ *Qui est-ce qui t'emmène au spectacle?* Who's taking you to the show?
◆ **Qui est-ce que ...?** Who ...? ◊ *Qui est-ce que tu as vu à cette soirée?* Who did you see at the party?
◆ **Qu'est-ce qui ...?** What ...? ◊ *Qu'est-ce qui est sur la table?* What's on the table? ◊ *Qu'est-ce qui te prend?* What's the matter with you?
◆ **À qui est ce sac?** Whose bag is this?
◆ **À qui parlais-tu?** Who were you talking to?

la **quille** NOUN
◆ **un jeu de quilles** skittles

la **quincaillerie** NOUN
ironmonger's (shop)

la **quinzaine** NOUN
about fifteen ◊ *Il y avait une quinzaine de personnes.* There were about fifteen people there.
◆ **une quinzaine de jours** a fortnight

quinze NUMBER
fifteen ◊ *Anaïs a quinze ans.* Anaïs is fifteen. ◊ *à quinze heures* at 3 p.m.
◆ **le quinze février** the fifteenth of February
◆ **dans quinze jours** in a fortnight's time

la **quittance** NOUN
[1] receipt
[2] bill

quitter VERB
to leave ◊ *J'ai quitté la maison à huit heures.* I left the house at 8 o'clock.
◆ **se quitter** to part ◊ *Les deux amis se sont quittés devant le café.* The two friends parted in front of the café.
◆ **Ne quittez pas.** (on telephone) Hold the line. ◊ *Ne quittez pas, je vous passe Monsieur Divan.* Hold the line, I'll put you through to Monsieur Divan.

quoi PRONOUN
what? ◊ *À quoi penses-tu?* What are you thinking about? ◊ *C'est quoi, ce truc?* What's this thing?
◆ **Quoi de neuf?** What's new?
◆ **As-tu de quoi écrire?** Have you got anything to write with?
◆ **Je n'ai pas de quoi acheter une voiture.** I can't afford to buy a car.
◆ **Quoi qu'il arrive.** Whatever happens.
◆ **Il n'y a pas de quoi.** Don't mention it.
◆ **Il n'y a pas de quoi s'énerver.** There's no reason for getting worked up.
◆ **En quoi puis-je vous aider?** How may I help you?

quoique CONJUNCTION
even though ◊ *Il va l'acheter quoique ce soit cher.* He's going to buy it even though it's expensive.

quotidien ADJECTIVE (FEM SING **quotidienne**)
see also **quotidien** NOUN
daily ◊ *Il est parti faire sa promenade quotidienne.* He's gone for his daily walk.
◆ **la vie quotidienne** everyday life

le **quotidien** NOUN
see also **quotidien** ADJECTIVE
daily paper ◊ *"Le Monde" est un quotidien.* "Le Monde" is a daily paper.

R

le **rab** NOUN (*informal*)
 seconds (*of meal*) ◇ *Il y a du rab?* Are there any seconds?

le **rabais** NOUN
 reduction (*in price*)
 ◆**au rabais** at a discount

la **racaille** NOUN
 riff-raff

raccompagner VERB
 to take home ◇ *Tu peux me raccompagner?* Can you take me home?

le **raccourci** NOUN
 shortcut

raccrocher VERB
 to hang up (*telephone*)

la **race** NOUN
 ⓵ race ◇ *la race humaine* the human race
 ⓶ breed ◇ *De quelle race est ton chat?* What breed is your cat?
 ◆**de race** pedigree ◇ *un chien de race* a pedigree dog

racheter VERB
 ⓵ to buy another ◇ *J'ai racheté un portefeuille.* I've bought another wallet. ◇ *racheter du lait* to buy more milk
 ⓶ to buy ◇ *Il m'a racheté ma moto.* He bought my bike from me.

la **racine** NOUN
 root

le **racisme** NOUN
 racism

raciste ADJECTIVE
 racist

raconter VERB
 ◆**raconter quelque chose à quelqu'un** to tell somebody about something ◇ *Raconte-moi ce qui s'est passé.* Tell me what happened. ◇ *Raconte-moi une histoire.* Tell me a story.
 ◆**Qu'est-ce que tu racontes?** What are you talking about?

le **radar** NOUN
 radar

le **radiateur** NOUN
 radiator
 ◆**un radiateur électrique** an electric heater

radin ADJECTIVE (*informal*)
 stingy

la **radio** NOUN
 ⓵ radio ◇ *à la radio* on the radio
 ⓶ X-ray
 ◆**passer une radio** to have an X-ray ◇ *Elle a passé une radio des poumons.* She had a chest X-ray.

le **radio-réveil** NOUN (PL les **radios-réveils**)
 clock radio

le **radis** NOUN
 radish

raffoler VERB
 ◆**raffoler de** to be crazy about ◇ *Elle raffole de la tarte aux pommes.* She really loves apple tart.

rafraîchir VERB
 to cool down
 ◆**se rafraîchir (1)** to get cooler ◇ *Le temps se rafraîchit.* The weather's getting cooler.
 ◆**se rafraîchir (2)** to freshen up ◇ *Il a pris une douche pour se rafraîchir.* He had a shower to freshen up.

rafraîchissant ADJECTIVE
 refreshing

la **rage** NOUN
 rabies
 ◆**une rage de dents** raging toothache

le **ragoût** NOUN
 stew

raide ADJECTIVE
 ⓵ steep ◇ *Cette pente est raide.* This is a steep slope.
 ⓶ straight ◇ *Laure a les cheveux raides.* Laure has straight hair.
 ⓷ stiff ◇ *Son bras est encore raide.* His arm's still stiff.
 ⓸ flat broke ◇ *Je suis raide ce mois-ci.* (*informal*) I'm flat broke this month.

la **raie** NOUN
 ⓵ skate (*fish*)
 ⓶ parting (*in hair*)

le **rail** NOUN
 rail ◇ *par rail* by rail

le **raisin** NOUN
 grapes ◇ *le raisin blanc* green grapes
 ◆**des raisins secs** raisins

la **raison** NOUN
 reason ◇ *sans raison* for no reason ◇ *Raison de plus pour y aller.* All the more reason for going.
 ◆**Ce n'est pas une raison.** That's no excuse.
 ◆**avoir raison** to be right ◇ *Tu as raison.* You're right.
 ◆**en raison de** because of ◇ *en raison d'une grève* because of a strike

raisonnable ADJECTIVE
sensible ◊ *Elle est très raisonnable pour son âge.* She's very sensible for her age.

le **raisonnement** NOUN
reasoning ◊ *J'ai du mal à suivre son raisonnement.* I have difficulty following his reasoning.

rajouter VERB
to add

ralentir VERB
to slow down

râler VERB (*informal*)
to moan

le **ramassage** NOUN
♦**le ramassage scolaire** the school bus service

ramasser VERB
1 to pick up ◊ *Il a ramassé son crayon.* He picked up his pencil.
2 to take in ◊ *Il a ramassé les copies.* He took in the exam papers.

la **rame** NOUN
1 oar (*of boat*)
2 train (*on the underground*)

le **rameau** NOUN (PL les **rameaux**)
branch
♦**le dimanche des Rameaux** Palm Sunday

ramener VERB
1 to bring back ◊ *Je t'ai ramené un souvenir de Grèce.* I've brought you back a present from Greece.
2 to take home ◊ *Tu me ramènes?* Will you take me home?

ramer VERB
to row ◊ *C'est Jean-Pierre qui ramait.* Jean-Pierre was rowing.

la **rampe** NOUN
banister

la **rancune** NOUN
♦**garder rancune à quelqu'un** to bear somebody a grudge
♦**Sans rancune!** No hard feelings!

rancunier ADJECTIVE (FEM SING **rancunière**)
vindictive

la **randonnée** NOUN
♦**une randonnée à vélo** a bike ride
♦**une randonnée pédestre** a ramble
♦**faire de la randonnée** to go hiking

le **randonneur** NOUN
hiker

la **randonneuse** NOUN
hiker

le **rang** NOUN
row (*line*) ◊ *au premier rang* in the front row ◊ *se mettre en rangs* to get into rows

la **rangée** NOUN
row (*line*) ◊ *une rangée de chaises* a row of chairs

ranger VERB
1 to put away ◊ *J'ai rangé tes affaires.* I've put your things away.
2 to tidy up ◊ *Va ranger ta chambre.* Go and tidy up your room.

le **rap** NOUN
rap ◊ *Robert est chanteur de rap.* Robert's a rap singer.

râper VERB
to grate ◊ *le fromage râpé* grated cheese

rapide ADJECTIVE
1 fast ◊ *Cette voiture est très rapide.* This is a very fast car.
2 quick ◊ *J'ai jeté un coup d'œil rapide sur ton travail.* I had a quick glance at your work.

rapidement ADVERB
quickly

le **rappel** NOUN
1 booster (*vaccination*)
2 curtain call

rappeler VERB
to call back ◊ *Je te rappelle dans cinq minutes.* I'll call you back in 5 minutes.
♦**rappeler quelque chose à quelqu'un** to remind somebody of something ◊ *Cette odeur me rappelle mon enfance.* This smell reminds me of my childhood.
♦**rappeler à quelqu'un de faire quelque chose** to remind somebody to do something ◊ *Rappelle-moi d'acheter des billets.* Remind me to get tickets.
♦**se rappeler** to remember ◊ *Il s'est rappelé qu'il avait une course à faire.* He remembered he had some shopping to do.

le **rapport** NOUN
see also **les rapports**
1 report ◊ *Il a écrit un rapport.* He wrote a report.
2 connection ◊ *Je ne vois pas le rapport.* I can't see the connection.
♦**par rapport à** in comparison with

rapporter VERB
to bring back ◊ *Je leur ai rapporté un cadeau.* I brought them back a present.

le **rapporteur** NOUN
telltale

la **rapporteuse** NOUN
telltale

les **rapports** MASC NOUN
see also **le rapport**

R

☞

relations ◊ *Leurs rapports avec leurs voisins se sont améliorés.* Their relations with their neighbours have improved.
♦ **les rapports sexuels** sexual intercourse

rapprocher VERB
1 to bring together ◊ *Cet accident a rapproché les deux frères.* The accident brought the two brothers together.
2 to bring closer ◊ *Il a rapproché le fauteuil de la télé.* He brought the armchair closer to the TV.
♦ **se rapprocher** to come closer ◊ *Rapproche-toi, tu verras mieux.* Come closer, you'll see better.

la **raquette** NOUN
1 racket (*tennis*)
2 bat (*table tennis*)

rare ADJECTIVE
rare ◊ *une plante rare* a rare plant

rarement ADVERB
rarely

ras ADJECTIVE, ADVERB
short ◊ *un chien à poil ras* a short-haired dog
♦ **à ras bords** to the brim ◊ *Il a rempli son verre à ras bords.* He filled his glass to the brim.
♦ **en avoir ras le bol de quelque chose** (*informal*) to be fed up with something
♦ **un pull ras du cou** a crew-neck jumper

raser VERB
to shave off ◊ *Ray a rasé sa barbe.* Ray has shaved off his beard.
♦ **se raser** to shave

le **rasoir** NOUN
see also **rasoir** ADJECTIVE
razor

rasoir ADJECTIVE (MASC, FEM, PL) (*informal*)
see also **rasoir** NOUN
dead boring

rassembler VERB
to assemble ◊ *Il a rassemblé les enfants dans la cour.* He assembled the children in the playground.
♦ **se rassembler** to gather together ◊ *Les passagers se sont rassemblés près du car.* The passengers gathered near the coach.

rassurer VERB
to reassure
♦ **Je suis rassuré.** I don't need to worry any more.
♦ **se rassurer** to be reassured ◊ *Rassure-toi!* Don't worry!

le **rat** NOUN
rat

raté ADJECTIVE
unsuccessful ◊ *Le gâteau est raté.* The cake hasn't turned out well.

le **râteau** NOUN (PL les **râteaux**)
rake

rater VERB
1 to miss ◊ *Chantal a raté son train.* Chantal missed her train.
2 to fail ◊ *J'ai raté mon examen de maths.* I failed my maths exam. ◊ *Elle a raté sa pizza.* Her pizza didn't turn out right.

la **RATP** NOUN
Paris transport authority

rattacher VERB
to tie up again ◊ *rattacher ses lacets* to tie up one's laces

rattraper VERB
1 to recapture ◊ *La police a rattrapé le voleur.* The police recaptured the thief.
2 to catch up with ◊ *Je vais rattraper Cécile.* I'll catch up with Cécile.
3 to make up for ◊ *Il faut rattraper le temps perdu.* We must make up for lost time.
♦ **se rattraper** to make up for it ◊ *Je n'ai pas le temps de sortir mais je me rattraperai après les examens.* I haven't got time to go out, but I'll make up for it after the exams.

la **rature** NOUN
correction ◊ *un texte sans ratures* a text with no corrections

ravi ADJECTIVE
♦ **être ravi** to be delighted ◊ *Ils étaient ravis de nous voir.* They were delighted to see us. ◊ *Je suis ravi que vous puissiez venir.* I'm delighted that you can come.

se **raviser** VERB
to change your mind ◊ *Il allait accepter, mais il s'est ravisé.* He was going to accept, but he changed his mind.

ravissant ADJECTIVE
lovely

rayé ADJECTIVE
striped ◊ *une chemise rayée* a striped shirt

rayer VERB
1 to scratch ◊ *Il a rayé la peinture de sa voiture.* He scratched the paintwork of his car.

[2] to cross off ◊ *Son nom a été rayé de la liste.* His name has been crossed off the list.

le **rayon** NOUN

[1] ray ◊ *un rayon de soleil* a ray of sunshine

[2] radius ◊ *le rayon d'un cercle* the radius of a circle

[3] shelf ◊ *les rayons d'une bibliothèque* the shelves of a bookcase

[4] department ◊ *le rayon hi-fi vidéo* the hi-fi and video department

♦ **les rayons X** X-rays

la **rayure** NOUN
stripe

le **ré** NOUN

[1] D ◊ *en ré majeur* in D major

[2] re ◊ *do, ré, mi ...* do, re, mi ...

la **réaction** NOUN
reaction

réagir VERB
to react

le **réalisateur** NOUN
director (*of film*) ◊ *Spielberg est réalisateur.* Spielberg is a film director.

la **réalisatrice** NOUN
director (*of film*) ◊ *Elle est réalisatrice.* She's a film director.

réaliser VERB

[1] to carry out ◊ *Ils ont réalisé leur projet.* They carried out their plan.

[2] to fulfil ◊ *Il a réalisé son rêve.* He has fulfilled his dream.

[3] to realize ◊ *Tu réalises ce que tu dis?* Do you realize what you're saying?

[4] to make ◊ *réaliser un film* to make a film

♦ **se réaliser** to come true ◊ *Mon rêve s'est réalisé.* My dream has come true.

réaliste ADJECTIVE
realistic

la **réalité** NOUN
reality

♦ **en réalité** in fact

le **rebelle** NOUN
rebel

rebondir VERB
to bounce

le **rebord** NOUN
edge ◊ *le rebord du lavabo* the edge of the washbasin

♦ **le rebord de la fenêtre** the window ledge

recaler VERB (*informal*)

♦ **J'ai été recalé en maths.** I failed maths.

récemment ADVERB
recently

récent ADJECTIVE
recent

le **récepteur** NOUN
receiver

la **réception** NOUN
reception desk

le/la **réceptionniste** NOUN
receptionist ◊ *Elle est réceptionniste.* She's a receptionist.

la **recette** NOUN
recipe

recevoir VERB

[1] to receive ◊ *J'ai reçu une lettre.* I received a letter.

[2] to see ◊ *Il a déjà reçu trois clients.* He has already seen three clients.

[3] to have round ◊ *Je reçois des amis à dîner.* I'm having friends round for dinner.

♦ **être reçu à un examen** to pass an exam

le **rechange** NOUN

♦ **de rechange** spare (*battery, bulb*) ◊ *des vêtements de rechange* a change of clothes

la **recharge** NOUN
refill

le **réchaud** NOUN
stove

réchauffer VERB

[1] to reheat ◊ *Je vais réchauffer les légumes.* I'll reheat the vegetables.

[2] to warm up ◊ *Un bon café va te réchauffer.* A nice cup of coffee will warm you up.

♦ **se réchauffer** to warm oneself ◊ *Je vais me réchauffer près du feu.* I'll go and warm myself by the fire.

la **recherche** NOUN
research ◊ *Je voudrais faire de la recherche.* I'd like to do research.

♦ **être à la recherche de quelque chose** to be looking for something ◊ *Je suis à la recherche d'un emploi.* I'm looking for a job.

♦ **les recherches** search ◊ *La police a interrompu les recherches.* The police called off the search.

recherché ADJECTIVE
much sought-after

rechercher VERB
to look for ◊ *La police recherche l'assassin.* The police are looking for the killer.

la **rechute** NOUN
relapse

R

le **récipient** NOUN
  container

le **récit** NOUN
  story

réciter VERB
  to recite

la **réclamation** NOUN
  complaint ◊ *J'ai une réclamation à faire.* I want to make a complaint.
  ◆**les réclamations** the complaints department

la **réclame** NOUN
  advert ◊ *une réclame de lessive* an advert for washing powder
  ◆**en réclame** on special offer ◊ *Le saumon était en réclame au supermarché.* Salmon was on special offer at the supermarket.

réclamer VERB
  [1] to demand ◊ *Nous réclamons la semaine de trente heures.* We demand a 30-hour week.
  [2] to complain ◊ *Elles sont toujours en train de réclamer.* They're always complaining about something.

reçois VERB *see* **recevoir**

la **récolte** NOUN
  harvest

récolter VERB
  [1] to harvest ◊ *Ils ont récolté le blé.* They harvested the wheat.
  [2] to collect ◊ *Ils ont récolté deux cents euros.* They collected 200 euros.
  [3] to get ◊ *Il a récolté une amende.* (*informal*) He got a fine.

le **recommandé** NOUN
  ◆**en recommandé** by registered mail ◊ *Je voudrais envoyer ce paquet en recommandé.* I'd like to send this parcel registered.

recommander VERB
  to recommend ◊ *Je vous recommande ce restaurant.* I recommend this restaurant.

recommencer VERB
  [1] to start again ◊ *Il a recommencé à pleuvoir.* It's started raining again.
  [2] to do again ◊ *S'il n'est pas puni, il va recommencer.* If he's not punished he'll do it again.

la **récompense** NOUN
  reward

récompenser VERB
  to reward ◊ *Il m'a récompensée de mes efforts.* He rewarded me for my efforts.

réconcilier VERB

◆**se réconcilier avec quelqu'un** to be make it up with somebody ◊ *Il s'est réconcilié avec sa sœur.* He has made it up with his sister.

reconnaissant ADJECTIVE
  grateful

reconnaître VERB
  [1] to recognize ◊ *Je ne l'ai pas reconnu.* I didn't recognize him.
  [2] to admit ◊ *Je reconnais que j'ai eu tort.* I admit I was wrong.

reconstruire VERB
  to rebuild

le **record** NOUN
  record ◊ *battre un record* to break a record

recouvrir VERB
  to cover ◊ *La neige recouvre le sol.* The ground is covered in snow.

la **récréation** NOUN
  break ◊ *Les élèves sont en récréation.* The pupils are having their break.
  ◆**la cour de récréation** the playground (*of school*)

le **rectangle** NOUN
  rectangle

rectangulaire ADJECTIVE
  rectangular

rectifier VERB
  to correct

le **reçu** NOUN
  see also **reçu** VERB
  receipt

reçu VERB *see* **recevoir**
  see also **reçu** NOUN
  ◆**J'ai reçu un colis ce matin.** I received a parcel this morning.
  ◆**être reçu à un examen** to pass an exam

reculer VERB
  [1] to step back ◊ *Il a reculé pour la laisser entrer.* He stepped back to let her in.
  [2] to reverse ◊ *J'ai reculé pour laisser passer le camion.* I reversed to let the lorry past.
  [3] to postpone ◊ *Ils ont reculé la date du spectacle.* They postponed the show.

reculons
  ◆**à reculons** ADVERB
  backwards ◊ *Elle est entrée à reculons.* She came in backwards.

récupérer VERB
  [1] to get back ◊ *Je vais récupérer ma voiture au garage.* I'm going to get my car back from the garage.

2 **to make up** ◊ *J'ai des heures à récupérer.* I've got time to make up.
3 **to recover** ◊ *J'ai besoin de récupérer.* I need to recover.

recycler VERB
to recycle
♦ **se recycler** to retrain ◊ *Il a décidé de se recycler en informatique.* He decided to retrain as a computer programmer.

la **rédaction** NOUN
essay

redemander VERB
1 **to ask again for** ◊ *Je vais lui redemander son adresse.* I'll ask him for his address again.
2 **to ask for more** ◊ *Je vais redemander des carottes.* I'm going to ask for more carrots.

redescendre VERB
to go back down ◊ *Il est redescendu au premier étage.* He went back down to the first floor. ◊ *Elle a redescendu l'escalier.* She went back down the stairs.

rédiger VERB
to write (*an essay*)

redoubler VERB
to repeat a year ◊ *Il a raté son examen et doit redoubler.* He's failed his exam and will have to repeat the year.

la **réduction** NOUN
1 **reduction** ◊ *une réduction du nombre des touristes* a reduction in the number of tourists
2 **discount** ◊ *une réduction de vingt euros* a 20 euro discount

réduire VERB
to cut ◊ *Ils ont réduit leurs prix.* They've cut their prices. ◊ *Il a réduit de moitié ses dépenses.* He has cut his spending by half.

réel ADJECTIVE (FEM SING **réelle**)
real

réellement ADVERB
really

refaire VERB
1 **to do again** ◊ *Je dois refaire ce rapport.* I've got to do this report again.
2 **to take up again** ◊ *Je voudrais refaire de la gym.* I'd like to take up gymnastics again.

le **réfectoire** NOUN
refectory

la **référence** NOUN
reference

♦ **faire référence à quelque chose** to refer to something
♦ **Ce n'est pas une référence!** That's no recommendation!

réfléchi ADJECTIVE
reflexive (*verb*)
♦ **C'est tout réfléchi.** My mind's made up.

réfléchir VERB
to think ◊ *Il est en train de réfléchir.* He's thinking.
♦ **réfléchir à quelque chose** to think about something ◊ *Je vais réfléchir à ta proposition.* I'll think about your suggestion.

le **reflet** NOUN
reflection ◊ *les reflets du soleil sur la mer* the reflection of the sun on the sea

refléter VERB
to reflect

le **réflexe** NOUN
reflex ◊ *avoir de bons réflexes* to have good reflexes

la **réflexion** NOUN
1 **thought** ◊ *Elle est en pleine réflexion.* She's deep in thought.
2 **remark** ◊ *faire des réflexions désagréables* to make nasty remarks
♦ **réflexion faite** on reflection

le **refrain** NOUN
chorus (*of song*)

le **réfrigérateur** NOUN
refrigerator

refroidir VERB
to cool ◊ *Laissez le gâteau refroidir.* Leave the cake to cool.
♦ **se refroidir** to get colder ◊ *Le temps se refroidit.* It's getting colder.

se **réfugier** VERB
to take shelter ◊ *Je me suis réfugié sous un arbre.* I took shelter under a tree.

le **refus** NOUN
refusal
♦ **Ce n'est pas de refus.** I wouldn't say no. ◊ *Voulez-vous une bière? – Ce n'est pas de refus.* Would you like a beer? – I wouldn't say no.

refuser VERB
to refuse ◊ *Il a refusé de payer sa part.* He refused to pay his share. ◊ *On lui a refusé une augmentation.* He was refused a pay rise.
♦ **Je refuse qu'on me parle ainsi!** I won't let anybody talk to me like that!

se **régaler** VERB

R

♦**Merci beaucoup: je me suis régalé!** Thank you very much: it was absolutely delicious!

le **regard** NOUN
look ◊ *Il lui a jeté un regard méfiant.* He gave him a mistrustful look. ◊ *On voyait à son regard qu'elle était contrariée.* You could tell from the look in her eyes that she was upset.
♦**Tous les regards se sont tournés vers lui.** All eyes turned towards him.

regarder VERB
1 to look at ◊ *Il regardait ses photos de vacances.* He was looking at his holiday photos. ◊ *Regarde! J'ai presque fini.* Look! I've nearly finished.
2 to watch ◊ *Je regarde la télévision.* I'm watching television. ◊ *Regarde où tu mets les pieds!* Watch where you put your feet!
3 to concern ◊ *Ça ne nous regarde pas.* It doesn't concern us.
♦**ne pas regarder à la dépense** to spare no expense

le **régime** NOUN
1 régime (*of a country*)
2 diet ◊ *un régime sans sel* a salt-free diet ◊ *se mettre au régime* to go on a diet ◊ *suivre un régime* to be on a diet
♦**un régime de bananes** a bunch of bananas

la **région** NOUN
region

régional ADJECTIVE (MASC PL **régionaux**)
regional

le **registre** NOUN
register

la **règle** NOUN
1 ruler ◊ *Il a souligné son nom avec une règle.* He underlined his name with a ruler.
2 rule ◊ *C'est la règle.* That's the rule. ◊ *en règle générale* as a general rule
♦**être en règle** to be in order ◊ *Mes papiers sont en règle.* My papers are in order.
♦**les règles** period (*menstruation*)

le **règlement** NOUN
rules ◊ *Le règlement est affiché à l'entrée.* The rules are up on the wall by the entrance.

régler VERB
1 to adjust ◊ *Il faut que je règle mon rétroviseur.* I'll have to adjust my rear-view mirror.
2 to tune ◊ *J'ai réglé ma radio sur 476 FM.* I tuned my radio to 476 FM.

3 to set ◊ *J'ai réglé le thermostat à vingt degrés.* I've set the thermostat to 20 degrees.
4 to solve ◊ *Le problème est réglé.* The problem's solved.
5 to settle ◊ *Elle a réglé sa facture.* She's settled her bill. ◊ *J'ai réglé Jean-Pierre pour l'essence.* I've settled up with Jean-Pierre for the petrol.

la **réglisse** NOUN
liquorice

le **règne** NOUN
reign ◊ *sous le règne de Henri IV* in the reign of Henry IV

régner VERB
to reign

le **regret** NOUN
regret
♦**à regret** reluctantly

regretter VERB
1 to regret ◊ *Elle regrette ce qu'elle a dit.* She regrets saying what she did.
♦**Je regrette.** I'm sorry. ◊ *Je regrette, je ne peux pas vous aider.* I'm sorry, I can't help you.
2 to miss ◊ *Je regrette mon ancien travail.* I miss my old job.

regrouper VERB
to group together ◊ *Nous avons regroupé les enfants suivant leur âge.* We grouped the children together according to age.
♦**se regrouper** to gather together ◊ *Les agriculteurs se sont regroupés pour constituer un syndicat.* The farmers joined together to form a union.

régulier ADJECTIVE (FEM SING **régulière**)
1 regular ◊ *des livraisons régulières* regular deliveries ◊ *des bus réguliers* a regular bus service
2 steady ◊ *à un rythme régulier* at a steady rate
3 scheduled ◊ *des vols réguliers pour Marseille* scheduled flights to Marseilles

régulièrement ADVERB
regularly

le **rein** NOUN
kidney
♦**les reins** back (*of body*) ◊ *J'ai mal aux reins.* My back hurts.

la **reine** NOUN
queen

rejoindre VERB
to go back to ◊ *J'ai rejoint mes amis.* I went back to my friends.

♦**Je te rejoins au café**. I'll see you at the café.

♦**se rejoindre** to meet up ◊ *Elles se sont rejointes une heure après.* They met up an hour later.

relâcher VERB
to release (*prisoner, animal*)
♦**se relâcher** to get slack ◊ *Il se relâche dans son travail.* His work is getting careless.

le **relais** NOUN
relay race ◊ *le relais quatre fois cent mètres* the 4 x 100 metre relay
♦**prendre le relais** to take over

la **relation** NOUN
relationship
♦**les relations franco-britanniques** Anglo-French relations

se **relaxer** VERB
to relax

se **relayer** VERB
♦**se relayer pour faire quelque chose** to take it in turns to do something

le **relevé** NOUN
♦**un relevé de compte** a bank statement

relever VERB
⒈ to collect ◊ *Je relève les copies dans cinq minutes.* I'll collect the papers in five minutes.
⒉ to react to ◊ *Je n'ai pas relevé sa réflexion.* I didn't react to his remark.
♦**relever la tête** to look up
♦**se relever** to get up ◊ *Il est tombé mais s'est relevé aussitôt.* He fell, but got up immediately.

la **religieuse** NOUN
⒈ nun
⒉ choux cream bun ◊ *des religieuses au chocolat* choux buns with chocolate cream and icing

religieux ADJECTIVE (FEM **religieuse**)
religious

la **religion** NOUN
religion

relire VERB
⒈ to read over ◊ *Il a relu sa copie avant de la rendre.* He read his exam paper over before handing it in.
⒉ to read again ◊ *Je voudrais relire ce roman.* I'd like to read this novel again.

remarquable ADJECTIVE
remarkable

la **remarque** NOUN
⒈ remark ◊ *Il a fait une remarque désagréable.* He made a nasty remark.
⒉ comment ◊ *Avez-vous des remarques à faire?* Have you any comments to make?

remarquer VERB
to notice ◊ *J'ai remarqué qu'elle avait l'air triste.* I noticed she was looking sad.
♦**faire remarquer quelque chose à quelqu'un** to point something out to somebody ◊ *Je lui ai fait remarquer que c'était un peu cher.* I pointed out to him that it was rather expensive.
♦**Remarquez, il n'est pas si bête que ça.** Mind you, he's not as stupid as all that.
♦**se remarquer** to be noticeable ◊ *David ne s'est pas rasé ce matin. Ça se remarque.* It's obvious David didn't shave this morning.
♦**se faire remarquer** to call attention to oneself

le **remboursement** NOUN
refund

rembourser VERB
to pay back ◊ *Il m'a remboursé l'argent qu'il me devait.* He paid me back the money he owed me.
♦**"satisfait ou remboursé"** "satisfaction or your money back"

le **remède** NOUN
⒈ medicine
⒉ cure

remercier VERB
to thank ◊ *Je te remercie pour ton cadeau.* Thank you for your present.
♦**remercier quelqu'un d'avoir fait quelque chose** to thank somebody for doing something ◊ *Je vous remercie de m'avoir invité.* Thank you for inviting me.

remettre VERB
⒈ to put back on ◊ *Il a remis son pull.* He put his sweater back on.
⒉ to put back ◊ *Il a remis sa veste dans l'armoire.* He put his jacket back in the wardrobe.
⒊ to put off ◊ *J'ai dû remettre mon rendez-vous.* I've had to put my appointment off.
♦**se remettre** to recover (*from illness*) ◊ *Mélusine s'est bien remise de son opération.* Mélusine has fully recovered from her operation.

le **remonte-pente** NOUN
ski-lift

remonter VERB
⒈ to go back up ◊ *Il est remonté au premier étage.* He has gone back up to the first floor.
⒉ to go up ◊ *Ils ont remonté la pente.* They went up the hill.

R

☞

3 to buck up ◊ *Cette nouvelle m'a un peu remontée.* The news bucked me up a bit.
♦ **remonter le moral à quelqu'un** to cheer somebody up

le **remords** NOUN
♦ **avoir des remords** to feel remorse

la **remorque** NOUN
trailer (*of car*)

les **remparts** MASC NOUN
city walls

le **remplaçant** NOUN
supply teacher

la **remplaçante** NOUN
supply teacher

remplacer VERB
to replace ◊ *Il faut remplacer cette ampoule.* We need to replace this bulb. ◊ *Il remplace le prof de maths.* He's replacing the maths teacher.
♦ **remplacer par** to replace with

rempli ADJECTIVE
busy ◊ *une journée bien remplie* a very busy day
♦ **rempli de** full of ◊ *La salle était remplie de monde.* The room was full of people.

remplir VERB
1 to fill up ◊ *Elle a rempli son verre de vin.* She filled her glass with wine.
2 to fill in ◊ *Tu as rempli ton formulaire?* Have you filled in your form?
♦ **se remplir** to fill up ◊ *La salle s'est remplie de monde.* The room filled up with people.

remuer VERB
1 to move ◊ *Elle a remué le bras.* She moved her arm.
2 to stir ◊ *Remuez la sauce pendant deux minutes.* Stir the sauce for two minutes.
♦ **se remuer** (*informal*) to go to a lot of trouble ◊ *Ils se sont beaucoup remués pour organiser cette soirée.* They went to a lot of trouble organizing this party.

le **renard** NOUN
fox

la **rencontre** NOUN
♦ **faire la rencontre de quelqu'un** to meet somebody ◊ *J'ai fait la rencontre de personnes intéressantes ce soir.* I met some interesting people this evening.
♦ **aller à la rencontre de quelqu'un** to go and meet somebody ◊ *Je viendrai à ta rencontre.* I'll come and meet you.

rencontrer VERB
to meet
♦ **se rencontrer** to meet ◊ *Ils se sont rencontrés il y a deux ans.* They met two years ago.

le **rendez-vous** NOUN
1 appointment ◊ *J'ai rendez-vous chez le coiffeur.* I've got an appointment at the hairdresser's.
◊ *prendre rendez-vous avec quelqu'un* to make an appointment with somebody
2 date ◊ *Tu sors ce soir? – Oui, j'ai un rendez-vous.* Are you going out tonight? – Yes, I've got a date.
♦ **donner rendez-vous à quelqu'un** to arrange to meet somebody

rendre VERB
1 to give back ◊ *J'ai rendu ses disques à Christine.* I've given Christine her records back.
2 to take back ◊ *J'ai rendu mes livres à la bibliothèque.* I've taken my books back to the library.
♦ **rendre quelqu'un célèbre** to make somebody famous
♦ **se rendre** to give oneself up ◊ *Le meurtrier s'est rendu à la police.* The murderer gave himself up to the police.
♦ **se rendre compte de quelque chose** to realize something

le **renfermé** NOUN
♦ **sentir le renfermé** to smell stuffy

renifler VERB
to sniff

le **renne** NOUN
reindeer

renommé ADJECTIVE
renowned ◊ *La Bretagne est renommée pour ses plages.* Brittany is renowned for its beaches.

renoncer VERB
♦ **renoncer à** to give up ◊ *Ils ont renoncé à leur projet.* They've given up their plan.
♦ **renoncer à faire quelque chose** to give up the idea of doing something

renouveler VERB
to renew (*passport, contract*)
♦ **se renouveler** to happen again ◊ *J'espère que ça ne se renouvellera pas.* I hope that won't happen again.

le **renseignement** NOUN
piece of information ◊ *Il me manque un renseignement.* There's one piece of information I still need.
♦ **les renseignements (1)** information ◊ *Il m'a donné des renseignements.* He gave me some information.

♦ **les renseignements (2)** information desk

♦ **les renseignements (3)** directory inquiries

renseigner VERB

♦ **renseigner quelqu'un sur quelque chose** to give somebody information about something

♦ **Est-ce que je peux vous renseigner?** Can I help you?

♦ **se renseigner** to find out ◊ *Je vais me renseigner pour voir s'il n'y a pas un vol direct.* I'm going to find out if there's a direct flight.

rentable ADJECTIVE
profitable

la **rentrée** NOUN

♦ **la rentrée (des classes)** the start of the new school year

rentrer VERB

[1] to come in ◊ *Rentre, tu vas prendre froid.* Come in, you'll catch cold.

[2] to go in ◊ *Elle est rentrée dans le magasin.* She went into the shop.

[3] to get home ◊ *Je suis rentré à sept heures hier soir.* I got home at 7 o'clock last night.

[4] to put away ◊ *Tu as rentré la voiture?* Have you put the car away?

♦ **rentrer dans** to crash into ◊ *Sa voiture est rentrée dans un arbre.* He crashed into a tree.

♦ **rentrer dans l'ordre** to get back to normal

la **renverse** NOUN

♦ **tomber à la renverse** to fall backwards

renverser VERB

[1] to knock over ◊ *J'ai renversé mon verre.* I knocked my glass over.

[2] to knock down ◊ *Elle a été renversée par une voiture.* She was knocked down by a car.

[3] to spill ◊ *Il a renversé de l'eau partout.* He has spilt water everywhere.

♦ **se renverser** to fall over (*glass, vase*)

renvoyer VERB

[1] to send back ◊ *Je t'ai renvoyé ton courrier.* I've sent your mail back to you.

[2] to dismiss ◊ *On a renvoyé deux employés.* Two employees have been dismissed.

répandu ADJECTIVE
common ◊ *C'est un préjugé très répandu.* It's a very common prejudice.

♦ **du vin répandu sur la table** wine spilt on the table

♦ **des papiers répandus sur le sol** papers scattered over the floor

le **réparateur** NOUN
repairman

la **réparation** NOUN
repair

réparer VERB
to repair

repartir VERB
to set off again ◊ *Il s'est arrêté pour déjeuner avant de repartir.* He stopped for lunch before setting off again. ◊ *Il était là tout à l'heure, mais il est reparti.* He was here a moment ago, but he's gone again.

♦ **repartir à zéro** to start again from scratch

le **repas** NOUN
meal

♦ **le repas de midi** lunch

♦ **le repas du soir** dinner

le **repassage** NOUN
ironing ◊ *Je déteste le repassage.* I hate ironing.

repasser VERB

[1] to come back ◊ *Je repasserai demain.* I'll come back tomorrow.

[2] to go back ◊ *Je dois repasser au magasin.* I've got to go back to the shop.

[3] to iron ◊ *J'ai repassé ma chemise.* I've ironed my shirt.

[4] to resit ◊ *Elle doit repasser son examen.* She's got to resit her exam.

repérer VERB
to spot ◊ *J'ai repéré deux fautes.* I spotted two mistakes.

♦ **se repérer** to find one's way around ◊ *J'ai du mal à me repérer de nuit.* I have difficulty finding my way around when it's dark.

le **répertoire** NOUN
directory

répéter VERB

[1] to repeat ◊ *Elle répète toujours la même chose.* She keeps repeating the same thing.

[2] to rehearse ◊ *Les acteurs répètent une scène.* The actors are rehearsing a scene.

♦ **se répéter** to happen again ◊ *J'espère que cela ne se répétera pas!* I hope this won't happen again!

la **répétition** NOUN

[1] repetition ◊ *Il y a beaucoup de répétitions dans ce texte.* There's a lot of repetition in this text.

R

♦ **des grèves à répétition** repeated
strikes

2 rehearsal ◊ *Ils ont une répétition
cet après-midi.* They've got a
rehearsal this afternoon.

♦ **la répétition générale** the dress
rehearsal

le **répondeur** NOUN
answering machine

répondre VERB
to answer ◊ *répondre à quelqu'un* to
answer somebody

la **réponse** NOUN
answer ◊ *C'est la bonne réponse.*
That's the right answer.

le **reportage** NOUN
1 report ◊ *J'ai vu ce reportage aux
informations.* I saw that report on the
news.
2 story ◊ *J'ai lu ce reportage dans
"La Gazette".* I read that story in "La
Gazette".

le **reporter** NOUN
reporter ◊ *Christian est reporter.*
Christian is a reporter.

le **repos** NOUN
rest

reposer VERB
to put back down ◊ *Elle a reposé
son verre sur la table.* She put her
glass back down on the table.
♦ **se reposer** to have a rest ◊ *Tu
pourras te reposer demain.* You'll be
able to have a rest tomorrow.
♦ **se reposer sur quelqu'un** to rely on
somebody

repousser VERB
1 to grow again ◊ *Ses cheveux ont
repoussé.* Her hair has grown again.
2 to postpone ◊ *Le voyage est
repoussé.* The trip's been postponed.

reprendre VERB
1 to take back ◊ *Il a repris son livre.*
He's taken his book back.
2 to go back to ◊ *Elle a repris le
travail.* She went back to work.
3 to start again ◊ *La réunion
reprendra à deux heures.* The
meeting will start again at 2 o'clock.
♦ **reprendre du pain** to take more bread
♦ **reprendre la route** to set off again
♦ **reprendre son souffle** to get one's
breath back

le **représentant** NOUN
rep ◊ *Il est représentant chez Harper
Collins.* He's a rep for Harper Collins.

la **représentante** NOUN
rep ◊ *Elle est représentante.* She's a
sales rep.

la **représentation** NOUN
performance ◊ *la dernière
représentation d'une pièce* the final
performance of a play

représenter VERB
to show ◊ *Le tableau représente un
enfant et un chat.* The picture shows
a child with a cat.
♦ **se représenter** to arise again ◊ *Cette
occasion ne se représentera pas.* This
opportunity won't arise again.

le **reproche** NOUN
♦ **faire des reproches à quelqu'un** to
reproach somebody

reprocher VERB
♦ **reprocher quelque chose à quelqu'un**
to reproach somebody for something
◊ *Il m'a reproché mon retard.* He
reproached me for being late.
♦ **Qu'est-ce que tu lui reproches?** What
have you got against him?

la **reproduction** NOUN
reproduction

reproduire VERB
to reproduce
♦ **se reproduire** to happen again ◊ *Je te
promets que ça ne se reproduira pas!*
I promise it won't happen again!

républicain ADJECTIVE
republican

la **république** NOUN
republic ◊ *la République française*
the French Republic

répugnant ADJECTIVE
repulsive

la **réputation** NOUN
reputation

le **requin** NOUN
shark

le **RER** NOUN
Greater Paris high-speed train
service

le **réseau** NOUN (PL les **réseaux**)
network

la **réservation** NOUN
reservation

la **réserve** NOUN
stock ◊ *avoir quelque chose en
réserve* to have a stock of something
♦ **mettre quelque chose en réserve** to
put something aside

réservé ADJECTIVE
reserved ◊ *Cette table est réservée.*
This table's reservee.

réserver VERB
1 to reserve ◊ *Cette table est
réservée.* This table is reserved.

2 to book ◊ *Nous avons réservé une chambre.* We've booked a room.

3 to save ◊ *Je t'ai réservé une part de gâteau.* I've saved you a piece of cake.

le **réservoir** NOUN
    petrol tank

la **résidence** NOUN
    block of flats
 ♦ **une résidence secondaire** a second home

résistant ADJECTIVE
    1 hard-wearing ◊ *Ce tissu est résistant.* This fabric is hard-wearing.
    2 robust ◊ *Il est très résistant.* He's very robust.

résister VERB
    to resist

résolu ADJECTIVE
 ♦ **Le problème est résolu.** The problem's solved.

résoudre VERB
    to solve

le **respect** NOUN
    respect

respecter VERB
    to respect

la **respiration** NOUN
    breathing

respirer VERB
    to breathe

la **responsabilité** NOUN
    responsibility

responsable ADJECTIVE
    see also **responsable** NOUN
    responsible ◊ *être responsable de quelque chose* to be responsible for something

le/la **responsable** NOUN
    see also **responsable** ADJECTIVE
    1 person in charge ◊ *Je voudrais parler au responsable.* I'd like to speak to the person in charge.
    2 person responsible ◊ *Il faut punir les responsables.* Those responsible must be punished.

ressembler VERB
 ♦ **ressembler à (1)** to look like ◊ *Elle ne ressemble pas à sa sœur.* She doesn't look like her sister.
 ♦ **ressembler à (2)** to be like ◊ *Ça ressemble à un conte de fées.* It's like a fairy tale.
 ♦ **se ressembler (1)** to look alike ◊ *Les deux frères ne se ressemblent pas.* The two brothers don't look alike.
 ♦ **se rassembler (2)** to be alike ◊ *Ces deux pays ne se ressemblent pas.* These two countries aren't alike.

le **ressort** NOUN
    spring (*metal*) ◊ *Le ressort est cassé.* The spring is broken.

ressortir VERB
    to go out again

le **restaurant** NOUN
    restaurant

le **reste** NOUN
    rest
 ♦ **un reste de poulet** some left-over chicken
 ♦ **les restes** the left-overs

rester VERB
    1 to stay ◊ *Je reste à la maison ce week-end.* I'm staying at home this weekend.
    2 to be left ◊ *Il reste du pain.* There's some bread left. ◊ *Il me reste assez de temps.* I still have enough time.
 ♦ **Il ne me reste plus qu'à ...** I've just got to ... ◊ *Il ne me reste plus qu'à ranger mes affaires.* I've just got to put my things away.
 ♦ **Restons-en là.** Let's leave it at that.

le **résultat** NOUN
    result ◊ *le résultat des examens* the exam results

le **résumé** NOUN
    summary

résumer VERB
    to summarize
    *Be careful! **résumer** does not mean **to resume**.*

se **rétablir** VERB
    to get well

le **retard** NOUN
    delay ◊ *un retard de livraison* a delay in delivery
 ♦ **avoir du retard** to be late
 ♦ **être en retard de deux heures** to be two hours late
 ♦ **prendre du retard** to be delayed

retarder VERB
    1 to be slow ◊ *Ma montre retarde.* My watch is slow.
    2 to put back ◊ *Je dois retarder la pendule d'une heure.* I've got to put the clock back an hour.
 ♦ **être retardé** to be delayed ◊ *J'ai été retardé par un coup de téléphone.* I was held up by a phone call.

retenir VERB
    1 to remember ◊ *Tu as retenu leur adresse?* Do you remember their address?
    2 to book ◊ *J'ai retenu une chambre à l'hôtel.* I've booked a room at the hotel.

R

☞

◆**retenir son souffle** to hold one's breath

retenu ADJECTIVE
1 reserved ◊ *Cette place est retenue.* This seat is reserved.
2 held up ◊ *J'ai été retenu par un coup de téléphone.* I was held up by a phone call.

la **retenue** NOUN
detention ◊ *Gerry est en retenue.* Gerry's in detention.

retirer VERB
1 to withdraw ◊ *Elle a retiré de l'argent.* She withdrew some money.
2 to take off ◊ *Il a retiré son pull.* He took off his sweater.

le **retour** NOUN
return
◆**être de retour** to be back ◊ *Je serai de retour la semaine prochaine.* I'll be back next week.

retourner VERB
1 to go back ◊ *Est-ce que tu es retourné à Londres?* Have you been back to London?
2 to turn over ◊ *Elle a retourné la crêpe.* She turned the pancake over. ◊ *Il a retourné la poubelle.* He turned the bin upside down.
◆**se retourner (1)** to turn round ◊ *Janet s'est retournée.* Janet turned round.
◆**se retourner (2)** to turn over ◊ *La voiture s'est retournée.* The car turned over.

la **retraite** NOUN
◆**être à la retraite** to be retired
◆**prendre sa retraite** to retire

retraité ADJECTIVE
see also **retraité** NOUN
retired ◊ *Mon oncle est maintenant retraité.* My uncle's now retired.

le **retraité** NOUN
see also **retraité** ADJECTIVE
pensioner

la **retraitée** NOUN
pensioner

rétrécir VERB
to shrink ◊ *Son pull a rétréci au lavage.* Her sweater shrank in the wash.
◆**se rétrécir** to get narrower ◊ *La rue se rétrécit.* The street gets narrower.

retrouver VERB
1 to find ◊ *J'ai retrouvé mon portefeuille.* I've found my wallet.
2 to meet up with ◊ *Je te retrouve au café à trois heures.* I'll meet you at the café at 3 o'clock.

◆**se retrouver (1)** to meet up ◊ *Ils se sont retrouvés devant le cinéma.* They met up in front of the cinema.
◆**se retrouver (2)** to find one's way around ◊ *Je n'arrive pas à me retrouver.* I can't find my way around.

le **rétroviseur** NOUN
rear-view mirror

la **réunion** NOUN
meeting

se **réunir** VERB
to meet ◊ *Ils se sont réunis à cinq heures.* They met at 5 o'clock.

réussi ADJECTIVE
successful ◊ *une soirée très réussie* a very successful party
◆**être réussi** to be a success ◊ *Le repas était très réussi.* The meal was delicious.

réussir VERB
to be successful ◊ *Tous ses enfants ont très bien réussi.* All her children are very successful.
◆**réussir à faire quelque chose** to succeed in doing something
◆**réussir à un examen** to pass an exam

la **réussite** NOUN
success

la **revanche** NOUN
return match
◆**prendre sa revanche** to get one's own back ◊ *Il a pris sa revanche en refusant de lui prêter son vélo.* He got his own back by refusing to lend him his bike.
◆**en revanche** on the other hand ◊ *C'est cher mais en revanche c'est de la bonne qualité.* It is dear but on the other hand it's good quality.

le **rêve** NOUN
dream
◆**de rêve** fantastic ◊ *des vacances de rêve* fantastic holidays

le **réveil** NOUN
alarm clock
◆**mettre le réveil à huit heures** to set the alarm for eight o'clock

le **réveille-matin** NOUN (PL les **réveille-matin**)
alarm clock

réveiller VERB
to wake up ◊ *réveiller quelqu'un* to wake somebody up
◆**se réveiller** to wake up

le **réveillon** NOUN
◆**le réveillon du premier de l'an** New Year's Eve celebrations

◆**le réveillon de Noël** Christmas Eve celebrations

réveillonner VERB
1 to celebrate New Year's Eve
2 to celebrate Christmas Eve

revenir VERB
to come back ◊ *Reviens vite!* Come back soon! ◊ *Son nom m'est revenu cinq minutes après.* His name came back to me five minutes later.
◆**Ça revient au même.** It comes to the same thing.
◆**Ça revient cher.** It costs a lot.
◆**Je n'en reviens pas!** I can't get over it!
◆**revenir sur ses pas** to retrace one's steps

le **revenu** NOUN
income

rêver VERB
to dream
◆**rêver de quelque chose** to dream of something ◊ *J'ai rêvé de mes vacances cette nuit.* I dreamt about my holidays last night.

le **réverbère** NOUN
street lamp

le **revers** NOUN
1 backhand ◊ *Becker a un excellent revers.* Becker has an excellent backhand.
2 lapel (*of jacket*)
◆**le revers de la médaille** the other side of the coin

revient VERB *see* **revenir**

réviser VERB
1 to revise ◊ *Je dois réviser mon anglais.* I've got to revise my English.
2 to service ◊ *Je dois faire réviser ma voiture.* I must get my car serviced.

la **révision** NOUN
revision

revoir VERB
1 to see again ◊ *J'ai revu Sophie hier soir.* I saw Sophie again last night.
2 to revise ◊ *Il est en train de revoir sa géographie.* He's revising his geography.
◆**au revoir** goodbye

la **révolution** NOUN
revolution ◊ *la Révolution française* the French Revolution

le **revolver** NOUN
revolver

la **revue** NOUN
magazine

le **rez-de-chaussée** NOUN

ground floor ◊ *au rez-de-chaussée* on the ground floor

le **Rhin** NOUN
Rhine

le **rhinocéros** NOUN
rhinoceros

le **Rhône** NOUN
Rhone

la **rhubarbe** NOUN
rhubarb

le **rhum** NOUN
rum

le **rhume** NOUN
cold ◊ *J'ai attrapé un rhume.* I've caught a cold.
◆**un rhume de cerveau** a head cold
◆**le rhume des foins** hay fever

ri VERB *see* **rire**
◆**Nous avons bien ri.** We had a good laugh.

riche ADJECTIVE
1 well-off ◊ *Sa famille est très riche.* His family's very well-off.
2 rich ◊ *riche en vitamines* rich in vitamins

le **rideau** NOUN (PL les **rideaux**)
curtain ◊ *tirer les rideaux* to draw the curtains

ridicule ADJECTIVE
ridiculous ◊ *Je trouve ça complètement ridicule.* I think that's absolutely ridiculous.

rien PRONOUN
see also **rien** NOUN
1 nothing ◊ *Qu'est-ce que tu as acheté? – Rien.* What have you bought? – Nothing. ◊ *Ça n'a rien à voir.* It has nothing to do with it.
◆**rien d'intéressant** nothing interesting
◆**rien d'autre** nothing else
◆**rien du tout** nothing at all
2 anything ◊ *Il n'a rien dit.* He didn't say anything.
◆**rien que (1)** just ◊ *rien que pour lui faire plaisir* just to please him ◊ *Rien que la voiture coûte un million.* The car alone costs a million.
◆**rien que (2)** nothing but ◊ *rien que la vérité* nothing but the truth
◆**De rien!** Not at all! ◊ *Merci beaucoup! – De rien!* Thank you very much! – Not at all!

le **rien** NOUN
see also **rien** PRONOUN
◆**pour un rien** at the slightest thing ◊ *Il se met en colère pour un rien.* He loses his temper over the slightest thing.
◆**en un rien de temps** in no time at all

R

rigoler VERB (*informal*)
1 to laugh ◊ *Elle a rigolé en le voyant tomber.* She laughed when she saw him fall.
2 to have fun ◊ *On a bien rigolé hier soir.* We had good fun last night.
3 to be joking ◊ *Ne te fâche pas, je rigolais.* Don't get upset, I was only joking.
♦ **pour rigoler** for a laugh

rigolo ADJECTIVE (FEM SING **rigolote**) (*informal*)
funny

rincer VERB
to rinse

rire VERB
see also **rire** NOUN
to laugh ◊ *Ce film m'a vraiment fait rire.* That film really made me laugh. ◊ *Nous avons bien ri.* We had a good laugh.
♦ **pour rire** for a laugh

le **rire** NOUN
see also **rire** VERB
laughter ◊ *Il a un rire bruyant.* He has a loud laugh.

le **risque** NOUN
1 risk ◊ *prendre des risques* to take risks ◊ *à tes risques et périls* at your own risk
2 danger ◊ *Il n'y a pas de risque qu'il l'apprenne.* There's no danger of him finding out.

risqué ADJECTIVE
risky

risquer VERB
to risk
♦ **Ça ne risque rien.** It's quite safe.
♦ **Il risque de se tuer.** He could get himself killed.
♦ **C'est ce qui risque de se passer.** That's what might well happen.

le **rivage** NOUN
shore

la **rivière** NOUN
river

le **riz** NOUN
rice

le **RMI** NOUN
Income Support ◊ *Il touche le RMI.* He's on Income Support.

la **RN** NOUN (= *route nationale*)
A road

la **robe** NOUN
dress
♦ **une robe de soirée** an evening dress
♦ **une robe de mariée** a wedding dress
♦ **une robe de chambre** a dressing gown

le **robinet** NOUN
tap

le **robot** NOUN
robot

la **roche** NOUN
rock (*stone*)

le **rocher** NOUN
rock

le **rock** NOUN
rock (*music*) ◊ *un chanteur de rock* a rock singer

rôder VERB
to loiter ◊ *Il y a un homme louche qui rôde autour de l'école.* There's a suspicious man loitering around the school.

les **rognons** MASC NOUN
kidneys (*in cooking*)

le **roi** NOUN
king
♦ **le jour des Rois** Twelfth Night

le **rôle** NOUN
role

les **rollers** MASC NOUN
Rollerblades ®

romain ADJECTIVE
Roman ◊ *des ruines romaines* Roman remains

le **roman** NOUN
novel
♦ **un roman policier** a detective story
♦ **un roman d'espionnage** a spy story

le **romancier** NOUN
novelist

romantique ADJECTIVE
romantic

rompre VERB
1 to split up ◊ *Paul et Justine ont rompu.* Paul and Justine have split up.
2 to break off ◊ *Ils ont rompu leurs fiançailles.* They've broken off their engagement.

les **ronces** FEM NOUN
brambles

ronchonner VERB (*informal*)
to grouse

rond ADJECTIVE
see also **rond** NOUN
1 round ◊ *La Terre est ronde.* The earth is round.
♦ **ouvrir des yeux ronds** to stare in amazement
2 chubby ◊ *Il a les joues rondes.* He has chubby cheeks.
3 drunk ◊ *Il est complètement rond.* (*informal*) He's completely drunk.

le **rond** NOUN
see also **rond** ADJECTIVE

circle ◇ *Elle a dessiné un rond sur le sable.* She drew a circle in the sand.
- **en rond** in a circle ◇ *Ils se sont assis en rond.* They sat down in a circle.
- **tourner en rond** to go round in circles
- **Je n'ai plus un rond.** (*informal*) I haven't a penny left.

la **rondelle** NOUN
slice ◇ *une rondelle de citron* a slice of lemon

le **rond-point** NOUN (PL les **ronds-points**)
roundabout ◇ *La voiture s'est arrêtée au rond-point.* The car stopped at the roundabout.

ronfler VERB
to snore

le **rosbif** NOUN
roast beef

la **rose** NOUN
see also **rose** ADJECTIVE
rose

rose ADJECTIVE
see also **rose** NOUN
pink

le **rosé** NOUN
rosé (wine) ◇ *Je prendrai un verre de rosé.* I'll have a glass of rosé.

le **rosier** NOUN
rosebush

le **rôti** NOUN
roast meat
- **un rôti de bœuf** a joint of beef

rôtir VERB
to roast ◇ *faire rôtir quelque chose* to roast something

la **roue** NOUN
wheel ◇ *une roue de secours* a spare wheel

rouge ADJECTIVE
see also **rouge** NOUN
red

le **rouge** NOUN
see also **rouge** ADJECTIVE
1 red ◇ *Le rouge est ma couleur préférée.* Red is my favourite colour.
2 red wine ◇ *un verre de rouge* a glass of red wine
- **passer au rouge (1)** to change to red ◇ *Le feu est passé au rouge.* The light changed to red.
- **passer au rouge (2)** to go through a red light ◇ *Jean-Pierre est passé au rouge.* Jean-Pierre went through a red light.
- **un rouge à lèvres** a lipstick

la **rougeole** NOUN
measles

rougir VERB

1 to blush ◇ *Il a rougi en me voyant.* He blushed when he saw me.
2 to flush ◇ *Il a rougi de colère.* He flushed with anger.

la **rouille** NOUN
rust

rouillé ADJECTIVE
rusty

rouiller VERB
to go rusty

roulant ADJECTIVE
- **un fauteuil roulant** a wheelchair
- **une table roulante** a trolley

le **rouleau** NOUN (PL les **rouleaux**)
roll ◇ *un rouleau de papier peint* a roll of wallpaper
- **un rouleau à pâtisserie** a rolling pin

rouler VERB
1 to go ◇ *Le train roulait à 250 km/h.* The train was going at 250 km an hour.
2 to drive ◇ *Il a roulé sans s'arrêter.* He drove without stopping.
3 to roll ◇ *Gilles a roulé une cigarette.* Gilles rolled a cigarette.
4 to roll up ◇ *Il a roulé le tapis.* He rolled the carpet up.
5 to con ◇ *Ils se sont fait rouler.* (*informal*) They were conned.
- **Alors, ça roule?** (*informal*) How's it going?

la **Roumanie** NOUN
Romania

le **rouquin** NOUN (*informal*)
redhead

la **rouquine** NOUN (*informal*)
redhead

rousse ADJECTIVE see **roux**

la **rousse** NOUN
redhead

la **route** NOUN
1 road ◇ *au bord de la route* at the roadside
- **une route nationale** an A road
2 way ◇ *Je ne connais pas la route.* I don't know the way.
- **Il y a trois heures de route.** It's a 3-hour journey.
- **en route** on the way ◇ *Ils se sont arrêtés en route.* They stopped on the way.
- **mettre en route** to start up ◇ *Il a mis le moteur en route.* He started the engine up.
- **se mettre en route** to set off ◇ *Il s'est mis en route à cinq heures.* He set off at 5 o'clock.

le **routier** NOUN

R

☞

1 lorry driver ◊ *Son père est routier.* His father's a lorry driver.
2 transport café ◊ *Nous avons mangé dans un routier.* We ate in a transport café.

la **routine** NOUN
routine

roux ADJECTIVE (FEM SING **rousse**)
see also **roux** NOUN
1 red ◊ *Harry a les cheveux roux.* Harry has red hair.
2 red-haired ◊ *Isobel est rousse.* Isobel's red-haired.

le **roux** NOUN
see also **roux** ADJECTIVE
redhead

royal ADJECTIVE (MASC PL **royaux**)
royal

le **royaume** NOUN
kingdom
♦ **le Royaume-Uni** the United Kingdom

le **ruban** NOUN
ribbon
♦ **le ruban adhésif** adhesive tape

la **rubéole** NOUN
German measles

la **ruche** NOUN
hive

rudement ADVERB (*informal*)
terribly ◊ *C'était rudement bon.* It was terribly good.

la **rue** NOUN
street

la **ruelle** NOUN
alley

le **rugby** NOUN
rugby ◊ *Yann joue au rugby.* Yann plays rugby.

rugueux ADJECTIVE (FEM SING **rugueuse**)
rough

la **ruine** NOUN
ruin ◊ *les ruines de la cathédrale* the ruins of the cathedral

ruiner VERB
to ruin

le **ruisseau** NOUN (PL les **ruisseaux**)
stream

la **rumeur** NOUN
rumour

la **rupture** NOUN
break-up

la **ruse** NOUN
trickery ◊ *une ruse* a trick

rusé ADJECTIVE
cunning

russe ADJECTIVE, NOUN
Russian ◊ *Il parle russe.* He speaks Russian.
♦ **un Russe** a Russian (*man*)
♦ **une Russe** a Russian (*woman*)
♦ **les Russes** the Russians

la **Russie** NOUN
Russia

le **rythme** NOUN
1 rhythm ◊ *J'aime le rythme de cette musique.* I like the beat of this music.
2 pace ◊ *Il marche à un bon rythme.* He walks at a good pace.

S

s' PRONOUN see se

sa ADJECTIVE
1. his ◊ *Paul est allé voir sa grand-mère.* Paul's gone to see his grandmother.
2. her ◊ *Elle a embrassé sa mère.* She kissed her mother.

le sable NOUN
sand
• des sables mouvants quicksand

le sablé NOUN
shortbread biscuit

le sabot NOUN
1. clog
2. hoof (of horse)

le sac NOUN
bag
• un sac de voyage a travel bag
• un sac de couchage a sleeping bag
• un sac à main a handbag
• un sac à dos a rucksack
• voyager sac au dos to go backpacking

le sachet NOUN
sachet (of sugar, coffee)
• du potage en sachet packet soup
• un sachet de thé a tea bag

la sacoche NOUN
bag
• une sacoche de bicyclette a saddlebag

sacré ADJECTIVE
sacred

sage ADJECTIVE
1. good (well-behaved) ◊ *Sois sage.* Be good.
2. wise (sensible) ◊ *Il serait plus sage d'attendre.* It would be wiser to wait.

la sagesse NOUN
wisdom ◊ *Il a eu la sagesse de ne pas y aller.* He wisely didn't go.
• une dent de sagesse a wisdom tooth

le Sagittaire NOUN
Sagittarius ◊ *Michèle est Sagittaire.* Michèle is Sagittarius.

saignant ADJECTIVE
rare (meat)

saigner VERB
to bleed
• saigner du nez to have a nosebleed

sain ADJECTIVE
healthy
• sain et sauf safe and sound

saint ADJECTIVE
see also **saint** NOUN

holy ◊ *la semaine sainte* Holy Week ◊ *le Saint-Esprit* the Holy Spirit
• la Sainte Vierge the Blessed Virgin
• le vendredi saint Good Friday
• la Saint-Sylvestre New Year's Eve

le saint NOUN
see also **saint** ADJECTIVE
saint

la sainte NOUN
saint

sais VERB see savoir
• Je ne sais pas. I don't know.

saisir VERB
to take hold of
• saisir l'occasion de faire quelque chose to seize the opportunity to do something

la saison NOUN
season ◊ *Ce n'est pas la saison des fraises.* Strawberries are out of season. ◊ *un temps de saison* seasonable weather
• la saison des vendanges harvest time

sait VERB see savoir
• Il sait que ... He knows that ...
• On ne sait jamais! You never know!

la salade NOUN
1. lettuce
2. salad ◊ *une salade composée* a mixed salad ◊ *une salade de fruits* a fruit salad

le saladier NOUN
salad bowl

le salaire NOUN
salary

le salami NOUN
salami

le salarié NOUN
salaried employee

la salariée NOUN
salaried employee

le salaud NOUN (rude)
bastard

sale ADJECTIVE
dirty

salé ADJECTIVE
1. salty ◊ *La soupe est trop salée.* The soup's too salty.
2. salted ◊ *du beurre salé* salted butter
3. savoury ◊ *des biscuits salés* savoury biscuits

saler VERB

☞

to put salt in ◊ *J'ai oublié de saler la soupe.* I forgot to put salt in the soup.

la **saleté** NOUN

dirt ◊ *J'ai horreur de la saleté.* I hate dirt. ◊ *Il y a une saleté sur ta chemise.* There's some dirt on your shirt.

◆ **faire des saletés** to make a mess

salir VERB

◆ **salir quelque chose** to get something dirty

◆ **se salir** to get oneself dirty ◊ *Mets un tablier, sinon tu vas te salir.* Put on an apron or you'll get yourself dirty.

la **salle** NOUN

1 room
2 audience ◊ *Toute la salle l'a applaudi.* The whole audience applauded him.
3 ward (*in hospital*) ◊ *Il est à la salle douze.* He's in Ward 12.

◆ **la salle à manger** the dining room
◆ **la salle de séjour** the living room
◆ **la salle de bains** the bathroom
◆ **la salle d'attente** the waiting room
◆ **une salle de classe** a classroom
◆ **la salle des professeurs** the staffroom
◆ **une salle de concert** a concert hall
◆ **la salle d'embarquement** the departure lounge

le **salon** NOUN

lounge

◆ **un salon de thé** a tearoom
◆ **un salon de coiffure** a hair salon
◆ **un salon de beauté** a beauty salon

la **salope** NOUN (*rude*)

bitch

la **salopette** NOUN

1 dungarees
2 overalls

saluer VERB

◆ **saluer quelqu'un (1)** to say hello to somebody ◊ *Je l'ai croisé dans la rue et il m'a salué.* I met him in the street and he said hello.

◆ **saluer quelqu'un (2)** to say goodbye to somebody ◊ *Il nous a salués et il est parti.* He said goodbye and left.

salut EXCLAMATION (*informal*)

Hi!

la **salutation** NOUN

greeting

le **samedi** NOUN

1 Saturday ◊ *Aujourd'hui, nous sommes samedi.* It's Saturday today.
2 on Saturday ◊ *Nous sommes allés au cinéma samedi.* We went to the cinema on Saturday.

◆ **le samedi** on Saturdays ◊ *Le magasin ferme à dix-huit heures le samedi.* The shop closes at 6 p.m. on Saturdays.

◆ **tous les samedis** every Saturday
◆ **samedi dernier** last Saturday
◆ **samedi prochain** next Saturday

le **SAMU** NOUN

ambulance service

la **sandale** NOUN

sandal

le **sandwich** NOUN

sandwich

le **sang** NOUN

blood

◆ **en sang** covered in blood

le **sang-froid** NOUN

◆ **garder son sang-froid** to keep calm
◆ **perdre son sang-froid** to lose one's cool
◆ **faire quelque chose de sang-froid** to do something in cold blood

le **sanglier** NOUN

wild boar

le **sanglot** NOUN

◆ **éclater en sanglots** to burst into tears

sans PREPOSITION

without ◊ *Elle est venue sans son frère.* She came without her brother.

◆ **un pull sans manches** a sleeveless sweater

le/la **sans-abri** NOUN (PL les **sans-abri**)

homeless person ◊ *les sans-abri* the homeless

sans-gêne ADJECTIVE

inconsiderate

la **santé** NOUN

health ◊ *en bonne santé* in good health

◆ **Santé!** Cheers!

saoudien ADJECTIVE, NOUN (FEM SING **saoudienne**)

Saudi Arabian

◆ **un Saoudien** a Saudi Arabian (*man*)
◆ **une Saoudienne** a Saudi Arabian (*woman*)

le **sapeur-pompier** NOUN (PL les **sapeurs-pompiers**)

fireman

◆ **les sapeurs-pompiers** the fire brigade

le **sapin** NOUN

fir tree

◆ **un sapin de Noël** a Christmas tree

la **Sardaigne** NOUN

Sardinia

la **sardine** NOUN

sardine

le **satellite** NOUN

satellite ◊ *la télévision par satellite*
satellite TV

satisfaire VERB
to satisfy

satisfaisant ADJECTIVE
satisfactory

satisfait ADJECTIVE
satisfied ◊ *être satisfait de quelque chose* to be satisfied with something

la **sauce** NOUN
1 sauce
2 gravy

la **saucisse** NOUN
sausage

le **saucisson** NOUN
salami

sauf PREPOSITION
except ◊ *Tout le monde est venu sauf lui.* Everyone came except him.
◆ **sauf si** unless ◊ *On ira se promener, sauf s'il fait mauvais.* We'll go for a walk, unless the weather's bad.
◆ **sauf que** except that ◊ *Tout s'est bien passé, sauf que nous sommes arrivés en retard.* Everything went OK, except that we arrived late.

le **saumon** NOUN
salmon

saur ADJECTIVE
◆ **un hareng saur** a kipper

le **saut** NOUN
jump
◆ **le saut en longueur** the long jump
◆ **le saut en hauteur** the high jump
◆ **le saut à la perche** the pole vault
◆ **le saut à l'élastique** bungee jumping
◆ **un saut périlleux** a somersault

sauter VERB
to jump ◊ *Nous avons sauté par-dessus la barrière.* We jumped over the gate.
◆ **sauter à la corde** to skip (*with a rope*)
◆ **faire sauter quelque chose** to blow something up ◊ *On a fait sauter le commissariat de police la nuit dernière.* The police station was blown up last night.

la **sauterelle** NOUN
grasshopper

sauvage ADJECTIVE
1 wild ◊ *les animaux sauvages* wild animals ◊ *faire du camping sauvage* to camp in the wild
◆ **une région sauvage** an unspoiled area
2 shy ◊ *Il est sauvage.* He's shy.

sauvegarder VERB
to save (*file on computer*)

sauver VERB
to save

◆ **se sauver (1)** to run away ◊ *Il s'est sauvé à toutes jambes.* He ran away as fast as he could.
◆ **se sauver (2)** (*informal*) to be off ◊ *Allez, je me sauve!* Right, I'm off.

le **sauvetage** NOUN
rescue

le **sauveur** NOUN
saviour

savais, savait VERB *see* **savoir**
◆ **Je ne savais pas qu'il devait venir.** I didn't know he was going to come.

le **savant** NOUN
scientist

savent VERB *see* **savoir**
◆ **Ils ne savent pas ce qu'ils veulent.** They don't know what they want.

la **saveur** NOUN
flavour

savez VERB *see* **savoir**
◆ **Est-ce que vous savez où elle habite?** Do you know where she lives?

savoir VERB
to know ◊ *Je ne sais pas où il est allé.* I don't know where he's gone. ◊ *Nous ne savons pas s'il est bien arrivé.* We don't know if he's arrived safely. ◊ *Tu savais que Canberra était la capitale de l'Australie?* Did you know that Canberra was the capital of Australia? ◊ *Il ne sait pas ce qu'il va faire ce week-end.* He doesn't know what he's going to do this weekend.
◆ **Tu sais nager?** Can you swim?

le **savon** NOUN
soap

la **savonnette** NOUN
bar of soap

savons VERB *see* **savoir**

savoureux ADJECTIVE (FEM SING
savoureuse)
tasty

le **saxo** NOUN (*informal*)
see also **la saxo**
1 sax
2 sax player

la **saxo** NOUN (*informal*)
see also **le saxo**
sax player

le **scandale** NOUN
scandal
◆ **faire scandale** to cause a scandal ◊ *Ce film a fait scandale.* The film caused a scandal.

scandaleux ADJECTIVE (FEM SING
scandaleuse)
outrageous

S

le/la **Scandinave** NOUN
Scandinavian

scandinave ADJECTIVE
Scandinavian

la **Scandinavie** NOUN
Scandinavia

le **scarabée** NOUN
beetle

la **scène** NOUN
scene ◊ *une scène d'amour* a love
scene ◊ *la scène du crime* the scene
of the crime ◊ *Il m'a fait une scène.*
He made a scene.
♦ *une scène de ménage* a domestic row

sceptique ADJECTIVE
sceptical

le **schéma** NOUN
diagram

schématique ADJECTIVE
♦ *l'explication schématique d'une
théorie* the broad outline of a theory
♦ *Cette interprétation est un peu trop
schématique.* This interpretation is a
bit oversimplified.

la **scie** NOUN
saw
♦ *une scie à métaux* a hacksaw

la **science** NOUN
science
♦ *Elle est forte en sciences.* She is
good at science.
♦ *les sciences physiques* physics
♦ *les sciences naturelles* biology
♦ *les sciences économiques* economics
♦ *sciences po* (*informal*) politics ◊ *Mon
frère fait sciences po à Paris.* My
brother is studying politics in Paris.

la **science-fiction** NOUN
science fiction

scientifique ADJECTIVE
see also **scientifique** NOUN
scientific

le/la **scientifique** NOUN
see also **scientifique** ADJECTIVE
1 scientist
2 science student

scier VERB
to saw

scolaire ADJECTIVE
school ◊ *l'année scolaire* the school
year ◊ *les vacances scolaires* the
school holidays ◊ *mon livret scolaire*
my school report

le **Scorpion** NOUN
Scorpio ◊ *Catherine est Scorpion.*
Catherine is Scorpio.

le **Scotch** ® NOUN
adhesive tape

le **scrupule** NOUN
scruple

sculpter VERB
to sculpt

le **sculpteur** NOUN
sculptor

la **sculpture** NOUN
sculpture

le/la **SDF** NOUN (= *sans domicile fixe*)
homeless person
♦ *les SDF* the homeless

se PRONOUN

*se forms part of reflexive
constructions.*

1 himself ◊ *Il se regarde dans la
glace.* He's looking at himself in the
mirror.
2 herself ◊ *Elle se regarde dans la
glace.* She's looking at herself in the
mirror.
3 itself ◊ *Le chien s'est fait mal.* The
dog hurt itself.
4 oneself ◊ *se regarder dans une
glace* to look at oneself in a mirror
5 themselves ◊ *Ils se sont regardés
dans la glace.* They looked at
themselves in the mirror.

*se changes to s' before a vowel and
most words beginning with "h".*

◊ *Elle s'admire dans sa nouvelle robe.*
She's admiring herself in her new
dress.
6 each other ◊ *Ils s'aiment.* They
love each other.

la **séance** NOUN
1 session ◊ *une séance de
rééducation* a physiotherapy session
2 showing (*at the cinema*) ◊ *La
prochaine séance est à dix-neuf
heures.* The next showing is at 7 p.m.

le **seau** NOUN (PL les **seaux**)
bucket

sec ADJECTIVE (FEM SING **sèche**)
1 dry ◊ *Mon jean n'est pas encore
sec.* My jeans aren't dry yet.
2 dried ◊ *des figues sèches* dried
figs

le **sèche-cheveux** NOUN (PL les **sèche-
cheveux**)
hair dryer

le **sèche-linge** NOUN (PL les **sèche-linge**)
tumble dryer

sécher VERB
1 to dry
2 to be stumped ◊ *J'ai
complètement séché à l'interrogation
de maths.* (*informal*) I was completely
stumped in the maths test.

♦**se sécher** to dry oneself ◊ *Sèche-toi avec cette serviette.* Dry yourself with this towel.

la **sécheresse** NOUN
drought ◊ *une terrible sécheresse* a terrible drought

le **séchoir** NOUN
dryer

second ADJECTIVE
see also **second** NOUN
second ◊ *Il est arrivé second.* He came second.

le **second** NOUN
see also **second** ADJECTIVE
second floor ◊ *Elle habite au second.* She lives on the second floor.

secondaire ADJECTIVE
secondary ◊ *l'enseignement secondaire* secondary education
♦**des effets secondaires** side effects

la **seconde** NOUN
① second ◊ *Attends une seconde!* Wait a second!
② year 11

> ⓘ In French secondary schools, years are counted from the **sixième** (youngest) to **première** and **terminale** (oldest).

◊ *Ma sœur est en seconde.* My sister's in year 11.
③ second class ◊ *voyager en seconde* to travel second-class

secouer VERB
to shake ◊ *secouer la tête* to shake one's head

secourir VERB
to rescue

le **secourisme** NOUN
first aid ◊ *J'ai un brevet de secourisme.* I've got a first aid qualification.

le **secours** NOUN
help ◊ *Il est allé chercher du secours.* He went to get help. ◊ *Au secours!* Help!
♦**les premiers secours** first aid
♦**une sortie de secours** an emergency exit
♦**la roue de secours** the spare wheel

le **secret** NOUN
see also **secret** ADJECTIVE
secret

secret ADJECTIVE (FEM SING **secrète**)
see also **secret** NOUN
secret

le **secrétaire** NOUN
see also **la secrétaire**

① secretary
② writing desk

la **secrétaire** NOUN
see also **le secrétaire**
secretary

le **secrétariat** NOUN
secretary's office

le **secteur** NOUN
sector ◊ *le secteur public* the public sector ◊ *le secteur privé* the private sector

la **section** NOUN
department (*of school*)

la **sécu** NOUN (*informal*)
Social Security

la **sécurité** NOUN
① safety
♦**être en sécurité** to be safe ◊ *On ne se sent pas en sécurité dans ce quartier.* You don't feel safe in this neighbourhood.
♦**la sécurité routière** road safety
♦**une ceinture de sécurité** a seatbelt
② security ◊ *par mesure de sécurité* as a security measure
♦**la sécurité sociale** Social Security
♦**la sécurité de l'emploi** job security

séduisant ADJECTIVE
attractive

le **seigle** NOUN
rye ◊ *un pain de seigle* a loaf of rye bread

le **seigneur** NOUN
lord
♦**le Seigneur** the Lord

le **sein** NOUN
breast
♦**au sein de** within ◊ *Chaque pays est autonome au sein de l'Europe.* Each country is independent within Europe.

seize NUMBER
sixteen ◊ *Elle a seize ans.* She's sixteen. ◊ *à seize heures* at 4 p.m.
♦**le seize février** the sixteenth of February

seizième ADJECTIVE
sixteenth

le **séjour** NOUN
stay ◊ *J'ai fait un séjour d'une semaine en Italie.* I stayed in Italy for a week.

le **sel** NOUN
salt

sélectionner VERB
to select

le **self** NOUN (*informal*)
self-service restaurant

le **self-service** NOUN

S

☞

self-service restaurant

la **selle** NOUN
saddle

selon PREPOSITION
according to ◇ *selon lui* according to him ◇ *selon mon humeur* according to what mood I'm in ◇ *Ils sont répartis selon leur âge.* They're divided up according to age.

la **semaine** NOUN
week
♦ **en semaine** on weekdays

semblable ADJECTIVE
similar

le **semblant** NOUN
♦ **faire semblant de faire quelque chose** to pretend to do something ◇ *Il fait semblant de dormir.* He's pretending to be asleep.

sembler VERB
to seem ◇ *Le temps semble s'améliorer.* The weather seems to be improving. ◇ *Il me semble inutile de s'en inquiéter.* It seems pointless to me to worry about it.

la **semelle** NOUN
1 sole
2 insole

la **semoule** NOUN
semolina

le **sens** NOUN
1 sense ◇ *avoir le sens de l'humour* to have a sense of humour ◇ *Je n'ai pas le sens de l'orientation.* I've got no sense of direction. ◇ *avoir le sens du rythme* to have a sense of rhythm ◇ *Ça n'a pas de sens.* It doesn't make sense.
♦ **le bon sens** common sense
2 direction ◇ *Tu tournes la poignée dans le mauvais sens.* You're turning the handle in the wrong direction.
♦ **sens dessus dessous** upside down
♦ **un sens interdit** a one-way street ◇ *J'ai pris un sens interdit.* I went the wrong way down a one-way street.
♦ **un sens unique** a one-way street

la **sensation** NOUN
feeling

sensationnel ADJECTIVE (FEM SING **sensationnelle**)
sensational

sensé ADJECTIVE
sensible

sensible ADJECTIVE
1 sensitive ◇ *Il est très sensible.* He's very sensitive.
2 visible ◇ *une amélioration sensible* a visible improvement

Be careful! The French word **sensible** *does not mean* **sensible**.

sensiblement ADVERB
1 visibly ◇ *Elle a sensiblement progressé.* She made visible progress.
2 approximately ◇ *Elles sont sensiblement de la même taille.* They are approximately the same height.

la **sentence** NOUN
sentence (*judgement*)

le **sentier** NOUN
path

le **sentiment** NOUN
feeling

sentimental ADJECTIVE (MASC PL **sentimentaux**)
sentimental

sentir VERB
1 to smell ◇ *Ça sent bon.* That smells good. ◇ *Ça sent mauvais.* It smells bad.
2 to smell of ◇ *Ça sent les frites ici.* It smells of chips in here.
3 to taste ◇ *Tu sens l'ail dans le rôti?* Can you taste the garlic in the roast?
4 to feel ◇ *Ça t'a fait mal? – Non, je n'ai rien senti.* Did it hurt? – No, I didn't feel a thing. ◇ *Je ne me sens pas bien.* I don't feel well.
♦ **Il ne peut pas la sentir.** (*informal*) He can't stand her.

séparé ADJECTIVE
separated ◇ *Mes parents sont séparés.* My parents are separated.

séparément ADVERB
separately

séparer VERB
to separate ◇ *Séparez le blanc du jaune.* Separate the yolk from the white.
♦ **se séparer** to separate ◇ *Mes parents se sont séparés l'année dernière.* My parents separated last year.

sept NUMBER
seven ◇ *Il est arrivé à sept heures.* He arrived at seven o'clock. ◇ *Elle a sept ans.* She's seven.
♦ **le sept décembre** the seventh of December

septembre MASC NOUN
September
♦ **en septembre** in September

le **septennat** NOUN

🛈 **le septennat** is the seven-year term of office of the French President.

septième ADJECTIVE
seventh ◊ *au septième étage* on the
seventh floor

sera, serai, seras, serez VERB *see* **être**
♦ **Je serai de retour à dix heures.** I'll be
back at 10 o'clock.

la **série** NOUN
series

sérieusement ADVERB
seriously

sérieux ADJECTIVE (FEM SING **sérieuse**)
see also **sérieux** NOUN
1 serious ◊ *Il plaisantait? – Non, il
était sérieux.* Was he joking? – No, he
was serious.
2 responsible ◊ *C'est un employé
très sérieux.* He's a very responsible
employee.

le **sérieux** NOUN
see also **sérieux** ADJECTIVE
♦ **garder son sérieux** to keep a straight
face ◊ *J'ai eu du mal à garder mon
sérieux.* I had trouble keeping a
straight face.
♦ **prendre quelque chose au sérieux** to
take something seriously
♦ **prendre quelqu'un au sérieux** to take
somebody seriously
♦ **Il manque un peu de sérieux.** He's
not very responsible.

la **seringue** NOUN
syringe

séronégatif ADJECTIVE (FEM SING
séronégative)
HIV-negative

serons, seront VERB *see* **être**

séropositif ADJECTIVE (FEM SING
séropositive)
HIV-positive

le **serpent** NOUN
snake

la **serre** NOUN
greenhouse
♦ **l'effet de serre** the greenhouse
effect

serré ADJECTIVE
1 tight ◊ *Mon pantalon est trop
serré.* My trousers are too tight.
2 close-fought ◊ *Ça a été un
match serré.* It was a close-fought
game.

serrer VERB
♦ **Ce pantalon me serre trop.** These
trousers are too tight for me.
♦ **serrer la main à quelqu'un** to shake
hands with somebody
♦ **se serrer** to squeeze up ◊ *Serrez-vous
un peu pour que je puisse m'asseoir.*
Squeeze up a bit so I can sit down.

♦ **serrer quelqu'un dans ses bras** to hug
somebody
♦ **"Serrer à droite"** "Keep right"

la **serrure** NOUN
lock

sers, sert VERB *see* **servir**

le **serveur** NOUN
1 waiter (*in café*)
2 server (*computer*)

la **serveuse** NOUN
waitress

serviable ADJECTIVE
helpful

le **service** NOUN
1 service (*in restaurant*) ◊ *Le
service est compris.* Service is
included.
♦ **être de service** to be on duty
♦ **hors service** out of order
♦ **faire le service** to serve (*at table*) ◊ *Tu
peux faire le service s'il te plaît?*
Could you serve please?
2 favour ◊ *rendre service à
quelqu'un* to do somebody a favour
◊ *Est-ce que je peux te demander un
service?* Can I ask you a favour?
3 serve (*sport*) ◊ *Il a un bon service.*
He's got a good serve.
♦ **le service militaire** military service
♦ **les services sociaux** the social
services
♦ **les services secrets** the secret
service

la **serviette** NOUN
1 towel ◊ *une serviette de bain* a
bath towel
♦ **une serviette hygiénique** a sanitary
towel
2 serviette (*napkin*)
3 briefcase

servir VERB
to serve ◊ *On vous sert?* Are you
being served?
♦ **À toi de servir.** (*tennis*) It's your
serve.
♦ **se servir** to help oneself ◊ *Servez-vous.* Help yourself.
♦ **se servir de** to use ◊ *Tu te sers
souvent de ton vélo?* Do you use
your bike a lot?
♦ **servir à quelqu'un** to be of use to
somebody ◊ *Ça m'a beaucoup servi.*
It was very useful.
♦ **À quoi ça sert?** What's it for?
♦ **Ça ne sert à rien.** It's no use. ◊ *Ça ne
sert à rien d'insister.* It's no use
insisting.

ses ADJECTIVE
1 his ◊ *Il est parti voir ses*

S

grands-parents. He's gone to see his grandparents.
2 her ◊ *Delphine a oublié ses baskets.* Delphine's forgotten her trainers.
3 its ◊ *la ville et ses alentours* the town and its surroundings

le **set** NOUN
1 tablemat (*on table*)
2 set (*in tennis*)

le **seuil** NOUN
doorstep

seul ADJECTIVE, ADVERB
1 alone ◊ *vivre seul* to live alone
2 by oneself ◊ *Elle est venue seule.* She came by herself.
◆**faire quelque chose tout seul** to do something by oneself ◊ *Elle a fait ça toute seule?* Did she do it by herself?
◆**se sentir seul** to feel lonely
◆**un seul livre** one book only ◊ *Vous avez droit à un seul livre.* You're entitled to one book only.
◆**Il reste une seule nectarine.** There's only one nectarine left.
◆**le seul livre que ...** the only book that ... ◊ *C'est le seul Agatha Christie que je n'aie pas lu.* That's the only Agatha Christie I haven't read.
◆**le seul** the only one ◊ *C'est la seule que je ne connaisse pas.* She's the only one I don't know.

seulement ADVERB
only
◆**non seulement ... mais** not only ... but ◊ *Non seulement il a plu, mais en plus il a fait froid.* Not only did it rain, but it was cold as well.

sévère ADJECTIVE
strict ◊ *Mon prof de maths est très sévère.* My maths teacher is very strict.

le **sexe** NOUN
sex

sexuel ADJECTIVE (FEM SING **sexuelle**)
sexual ◊ *l'éducation sexuelle* sex education

le **shampooing** NOUN
shampoo
◆**se faire un shampooing** to wash one's hair

le **short** NOUN
shorts ◊ *Il était en short.* He was wearing shorts.

le **si** NOUN
see also **si** CONJUNCTION
1 B ◊ *en si bémol* in B flat
2 ti ◊ *la, si, do* la, ti, do

si CONJUNCTION, ADVERB
see also **si** NOUN

1 if ◊ *si tu veux* if you like ◊ *Je me demande si elle va venir.* I wonder if she'll come. ◊ *si seulement* if only
2 so ◊ *Elle est si gentille.* She's so kind. ◊ *Tout s'est passé si vite.* Everything happened so fast.
3 yes ◊ *Tu n'es pas allé à l'école habillé comme ça? – Si.* You didn't go to school dressed like that? – Yes I did.

la **Sicile** NOUN
Sicily

le **sida** NOUN
AIDS ◊ *Il a le sida.* He's got AIDS.

le **siècle** NOUN
century ◊ *le vingtième siècle* the twentieth century

le **siège** NOUN
1 seat (*in vehicle*)
2 head office

sien PRONOUN
◆**le sien (1)** his ◊ *C'est le vélo de Paul? – Oui, c'est le sien.* Is this Paul's bike? – Yes, it's his.
◆**le sien (2)** hers ◊ *C'est le vélo d'Isabelle? – Oui, c'est le sien.* Is this Isabelle's bike? – Yes, it's hers.

sienne PRONOUN
◆**la sienne (1)** his ◊ *C'est la montre de Paul? – Oui, c'est la sienne.* Is this Paul's watch? – Yes, it's his.
◆**la sienne (2)** hers ◊ *C'est la montre d'Isabelle? – Oui, c'est la sienne.* Is this Isabelle's watch? – Yes, it's hers.

siennes PRONOUN
◆**les siennes (1)** his ◊ *Ce sont les cassettes de Christian? – Oui, ce sont les siennes.* Are these Christian's cassettes? – Yes, they're his.
◆**les siennes (2)** hers ◊ *Ce sont les lunettes de Daphne? – Oui, ce sont les siennes.* Are these Daphne's glasses? – Yes, they're hers.

siens PRONOUN
◆**les siens (1)** his ◊ *Ce sont les sandwichs de Pierre? – Oui, ce sont les siens.* Are these Pierre's sandwiches? – Yes, they're his.
◆**les siens (2)** hers ◊ *Ce sont les sandwichs de Justine? – Oui, ce sont les siens.* Are these Justine's sandwiches? – Yes, they're hers.

la **sieste** NOUN
nap ◊ *faire la sieste* to have a nap

siffler VERB
to whistle

le **sifflet** NOUN
whistle

le **sigle** NOUN

acronym

le **signal** NOUN (PL les **signaux**)
   signal

la **signature** NOUN
   signature

le **signe** NOUN
   sign
◆**faire un signe de la main** to wave
◆**faire signe à quelqu'un d'entrer** to
   beckon to somebody to come in
◆**les signes du zodiaque** the signs of
   the zodiac

signer VERB
   to sign

le **signet** NOUN
   bookmark

la **signification** NOUN
   meaning

signifier VERB
   to mean ◊ *Que signifie ce mot?* What
   does this word mean?

le **silence** NOUN
   silence
◆**Silence!** Be quiet!

silencieux ADJECTIVE (FEM SING **silencieuse**)
   ⓵ silent ◊ *Elle est restée silencieuse.*
   She remained silent.
   ⓶ quiet ◊ *C'est très silencieux ici.* It's
   very quiet here.

la **silhouette** NOUN
   figure ◊ *J'ai vu une silhouette dans
   le brouillard.* I saw a figure in the
   mist.

similaire ADJECTIVE
   similar

le **simple** NOUN
   see also **simple** ADJECTIVE
   singles (*tennis*) ◊ *le simple messieurs*
   the men's singles ◊ *le simple dames*
   the ladies' singles

simple ADJECTIVE
   see also **simple** NOUN
   simple

simplement ADVERB
   simply ◊ *C'est tout simplement
   inadmissible.* It's quite simply
   unacceptable.

simuler VERB
   to simulate

simultané ADJECTIVE
   simultaneous

sincère ADJECTIVE
   sincere

sincèrement ADVERB
   sincerely

la **sincérité** NOUN
   sincerity

le **singe** NOUN
   monkey

le **singulier** NOUN
   singular ◊ *au féminin singulier* in the
   feminine singular

sinistre ADJECTIVE
   sinister

sinon CONJUNCTION
   otherwise ◊ *Dépêche-toi, sinon je
   pars sans toi.* Hurry up, otherwise I'll
   leave without you.

la **sirène** NOUN
   mermaid
◆**la sirène d'alarme** the fire alarm

le **sirop** NOUN
   syrup
◆**le sirop contre la toux** cough mixture

le **site** NOUN
   setting ◊ *un site très sauvage* a
   totally unspoiled setting
◆**un site pittoresque** a beauty spot
◆**un site touristique** a tourist attraction
◆**un site archéologique** an
   archaeological site
◆**un site Web** a website

sitôt ADVERB
◆**sitôt dit, sitôt fait** no sooner said
   than done
◆**pas de sitôt** not for a long time ◊ *On
   ne le reverra pas de sitôt.* We won't
   see him again for a long time.

la **situation** NOUN
   ⓵ situation
◆**la situation de famille** marital status
   ⓶ job ◊ *Il a une belle situation.* He's
   got a good job.

se **situer** VERB
   to be situated ◊ *Versailles se situe à
   l'ouest de Paris.* Versailles is situated
   to the west of Paris.
◆**bien situé** well situated

six NUMBER
   six ◊ *Il est rentré à six heures.* He
   got back at six o'clock. ◊ *Il a six ans.*
   He's six.
◆**le six février** the sixth of February

sixième ADJECTIVE
   see also **sixième** NOUN
   sixth ◊ *au sixième étage* on the sixth
   floor

la **sixième** NOUN
   see also **sixième** ADJECTIVE
   year 7

> ⓘ In French secondary schools,
> years are counted from the *sixième*
> (youngest) to *première* and *terminale*
> (oldest).

S

◊ *Mon frère est en sixième.* My brother's in year 7.

le **ski** NOUN
  1 ski ◊ *J'ai loué des skis.* I hired skis.
  2 skiing ◊ *J'adore le ski.* I love skiing. ◊ *faire du ski* to go skiing
  ◆ **le ski de fond** cross-country skiing
  ◆ **le ski nautique** water-skiing
  ◆ **le ski de piste** downhill skiing
  ◆ **le ski de randonnée** cross-country skiing

skier VERB
  to ski

le **skieur** NOUN
  skier

la **skieuse** NOUN
  skier

le **slip** NOUN
  pants
  ◆ **un slip de bain** swimming trunks

la **Slovaquie** NOUN
  Slovakia

la **Slovénie** NOUN
  Slovenia

le **SMIC** NOUN
  guaranteed minimum wage ◊ *Il touche le SMIC.* He's on the legal minimum wage.

le **smoking** NOUN
  dinner suit

la **SNCF** NOUN (= *Société nationale des chemins de fer français*)
  French railways

snob ADJECTIVE (FEM SING **snob**)
  snobbish

sobre ADJECTIVE
  1 sober
  2 plain ◊ *C'est une veste très sobre.* It's a very plain jacket.

social ADJECTIVE (MASC PL **sociaux**)
  social

le/la **socialiste** NOUN
  socialist

la **société** NOUN
  1 society
  2 company ◊ *une société financière* an finance company

la **sociologie** NOUN
  sociology

la **socquette** NOUN
  ankle sock

la **sœur** NOUN
  sister
  ◆ **une bonne sœur** (*informal*) a nun

soi PRONOUN
  oneself ◊ *avoir confiance en soi* to have confidence in oneself

◆ **rester chez soi** to stay at home
◆ **Ça va de soi.** It goes without saying.

soi-disant ADVERB, ADJECTIVE
  supposedly ◊ *Il était soi-disant parti à Paris.* He had supposedly left for Paris.
  ◆ **un soi-disant poète** a so-called poet

la **soie** NOUN
  silk

la **soif** NOUN
  thirst
  ◆ **avoir soif** to be thirsty

soigner VERB
  to look after (*ill person, animal*) ◊ *Soigne-toi bien ce week-end!* Take good care of yourself this weekend!

soigneux ADJECTIVE (FEM SING **soigneuse**)
  careful ◊ *Tu devrais être plus soigneux avec tes livres.* You should be more careful with your books.

soi-même PRONOUN
  oneself ◊ *Il vaut mieux le faire soi-même.* It's better to do it oneself.

le **soin** NOUN
  care
  ◆ **prendre soin de quelque chose** to take care of something ◊ *Prends bien soin de ce livre.* Take good care of this book.

les **soins** MASC NOUN
  treatment SING
  ◆ **les premiers soins** first aid
  ◆ **"aux bons soins de Madame Martin"** (*on letter*) "c/o Mrs Martin"

le **soir** NOUN
  evening ◊ *ce soir* this evening
  ◆ **à sept heures du soir** at 7 p.m.
  ◆ **demain soir** tomorrow night
  ◆ **hier soir** last night

la **soirée** NOUN
  evening ◊ *en tenue de soirée* in evening dress

sois VERB see **être**
  ◆ **Sois tranquille!** Be quiet!

soit CONJUNCTION
  ◆ **soit ..., soit ...** either ... or ... ◊ *soit lundi, soit mardi* either Monday or Tuesday

la **soixantaine** NOUN
  about sixty ◊ *une soixantaine de personnes* about sixty people
  ◆ **Elle a la soixantaine.** She's in her sixties.

soixante NUMBER
  sixty ◊ *Il a soixante ans.* He's sixty.
  ◊ *soixante et un* sixty-one
  ◊ *soixante-deux* sixty-two

♦ **soixante et onze** seventy-one
♦ **soixante-quinze** seventy-five
soixante-dix NUMBER
  seventy ◊ *Il a soixante-dix ans.* He's
  seventy.
le **soja** NOUN
  soya
♦ **des germes de soja** beansprouts
le **sol** NOUN
  1 floor ◊ *un sol carrelé* a tiled floor
♦ **à même le sol** on the floor
  2 soil ◊ *sur le sol français* on French
  soil
  3 G ◊ *sol dièse* G sharp
  4 so ◊ *do, ré, mi, fa, sol ...* do, re,
  mi, fa, so ...
solaire ADJECTIVE
  solar ◊ *le système solaire* the solar
  system
♦ **la crème solaire** sun cream
le **soldat** NOUN
  soldier
le **solde** NOUN
♦ **être en solde** to be reduced ◊ *Les
  chemisiers sont en solde.* The
  blouses are reduced.
♦ **les soldes** the sales ◊ *faire les soldes*
  to go round the sales ◊ *les soldes de
  janvier* the January sales
soldé ADJECTIVE
♦ **être soldé** to be reduced ◊ *un article
  soldé à dix euros* an item reduced to
  10 euros
la **sole** NOUN
  sole (*fish*)
le **soleil** NOUN
  sun ◊ *au soleil* in the sun
♦ **Il y a du soleil.** It's sunny.
le **solfège** NOUN
  musical theory ◊ *Il joue du violon
  sans connaître le solfège.* He plays
  the violin but he can't read music.
solidaire ADJECTIVE
♦ **être solidaire de quelqu'un** to back
  somebody up
solide ADJECTIVE
  1 strong (*person*)
  2 solid (*object*)
solitaire ADJECTIVE
  see also **solitaire** NOUN
  solitary
le/la **solitaire** NOUN
  see also **solitaire** ADJECTIVE
  loner
la **solitude** NOUN
  loneliness
la **solution** NOUN
  solution

♦ **une solution de facilité** an easy way
  out
sombre ADJECTIVE
  dark
le **sommaire** NOUN
  summary
la **somme** NOUN
  see also **le somme**
  sum
le **somme** NOUN
  see also **la somme**
  nap ◊ *faire un somme* to take a nap
le **sommeil** NOUN
  sleep
♦ **avoir sommeil** to be sleepy
sommes VERB see **être**
♦ **Nous sommes en vacances.** We're on
  holiday.
le **sommet** NOUN
  summit
le **somnifère** NOUN
  sleeping pill
somptueux ADJECTIVE (FEM SING
  somptueuse)
  sumptuous
son ADJECTIVE (FEM SING **sa**, PL **ses**)
  see also **son** NOUN
  1 his ◊ *son père* his father ◊ *Il a
  perdu son portefeuille.* He's lost his
  wallet.
  2 her ◊ *son père* her father ◊ *Elle a
  perdu son sac.* She's lost her bag.
le **son** NOUN
  see also **son** ADJECTIVE
  1 sound ◊ *Le son n'est pas très bon.*
  The sound's not very good. ◊ *baisser
  le son* to turn the sound down
  2 bran
♦ **le pain de son** brown bread
le **sondage** NOUN
  survey
♦ **un sondage d'opinion** an opinion poll
sonner VERB
  to ring ◊ *On a sonné.* Somebody
  rang the doorbell. ◊ *Le téléphone a
  sonné.* The phone rang.
la **sonnerie** NOUN
  bell (*electric*) ◊ *La sonnerie du
  téléphone l'a réveillé.* He was woken
  by the phone ringing.
la **sonnette** NOUN
  bell ◊ *la sonnette d'alarme* the alarm
  bell
la **sono** NOUN (*informal*)
  sound system
sont VERB see **être**
♦ **Ils sont en vacances.** They're on
  holiday.

S

sophistiqué ADJECTIVE
<u>sophisticated</u>

la **sorcière** NOUN
<u>witch</u>

le **sort** NOUN
1 <u>spell</u> ◊ *jeter un sort à quelqu'un* to cast a spell on somebody
♦ **un mauvais sort** a curse
2 <u>fate</u> ◊ *abandonner quelqu'un à son triste sort* to leave somebody to their fate
♦ **tirer au sort** to draw lots

la **sorte** NOUN
<u>sort</u> ◊ *C'est une sorte de gâteau.* It's a sort of cake. ◊ *toutes sortes de choses* all sorts of things

la **sortie** NOUN
<u>way out</u> ◊ *Où est la sortie?* Where's the way out?
♦ **la sortie de secours** the emergency exit
♦ **Attends-moi à la sortie de l'école.** Meet me after school.

sortir VERB
1 <u>to go out</u> ◊ *Il est sorti sans rien dire.* He went out without saying a word. ◊ *Il est sorti acheter un journal.* He's gone out to buy a newspaper. ◊ *J'aime sortir.* I like going out.
2 <u>to come out</u> ◊ *Elle sort de l'hôpital demain.* She's coming out of hospital tomorrow. ◊ *Je l'ai rencontré en sortant de la pharmacie.* I met him coming out of the chemist's. ◊ *Ce modèle vient juste de sortir.* This model has just come out.
3 <u>to take out</u> ◊ *Elle a sorti son porte-monnaie de son sac.* She took her purse out of her handbag. ◊ *Je vais sortir la voiture du garage.* I'll get the car out of the garage.
♦ **sortir avec quelqu'un** to be going out with somebody ◊ *Tu sors avec lui?* Are you going out with him?
♦ **s'en sortir** to manage ◊ *Ne t'en fais pas, tu t'en sortiras.* Don't worry, you'll manage OK.

la **sottise** NOUN
♦ **Ne fais pas de sottises.** Don't do anything silly.
♦ **Ne dis pas de sottises.** Don't talk nonsense.

le **sou** NOUN
♦ **une machine à sous** a fruit machine
♦ **Je n'ai pas un sou sur moi.** I haven't got a penny on me.
♦ **être près de ses sous** (*informal*) to be tight-fisted

le **souci** NOUN
<u>worry</u>

♦ **se faire du souci** to worry

soucieux ADJECTIVE (FEM SING **soucieuse**)
<u>worried</u> ◊ *Tu as l'air soucieux.* You look worried.

la **soucoupe** NOUN
<u>saucer</u>
♦ **une soucoupe volante** a flying saucer

soudain ADJECTIVE, ADVERB
1 <u>sudden</u> ◊ *une douleur soudaine* a sudden pain
2 <u>suddenly</u> ◊ *Soudain, il s'est fâché.* Suddenly, he got angry.

le **souffle** NOUN
<u>breath</u>
♦ **à bout de souffle** out of breath

le **soufflé** NOUN
<u>soufflé</u> ◊ *un soufflé au fromage* a cheese soufflé

souffler VERB
1 <u>to blow</u> ◊ *Le vent soufflait fort.* The wind was blowing hard.
2 <u>to blow out</u> ◊ *Souffle les bougies!* Blow out the candles!

la **souffrance** NOUN
<u>suffering</u>

souffrant ADJECTIVE
<u>unwell</u>

souffrir VERB
<u>to be in pain</u> ◊ *Il souffre beaucoup.* He's in a lot of pain.

le **souhait** NOUN
<u>wish</u> ◊ *faire un souhait* to make a wish ◊ *Tous nos souhaits de réussite.* All our best wishes for your success. ◊ *les souhaits de bonne année* New Year's wishes
♦ **Atchoum! – À tes souhaits!** Atchoo! – Bless you!

souhaiter VERB
<u>to wish</u> ◊ *Il souhaite aller à l'université.* He wishes to go to university. ◊ *Nous vous souhaitons une bonne année.* We wish you a happy New Year.

soûl ADJECTIVE (*informal*)
<u>drunk</u>

soulager VERB
<u>to relieve</u>

soulever VERB
1 <u>to lift</u> ◊ *Je n'arrive pas à soulever cette valise.* I can't lift this suitcase.
2 <u>to raise</u> ◊ *Il faudra soulever la question lors de la réunion.* We'll have to raise the matter at the meeting.

le **soulier** NOUN
<u>shoe</u>

souligner VERB
<u>to underline</u>

le **soupçon** NOUN
　suspicion
　♦ **un soupçon de** a dash of ◊ *Ajoutez un soupçon de rhum.* Add a dash of rum.

soupçonner VERB
　to suspect

la **soupe** NOUN
　soup

souper VERB
　to have supper

le **soupir** NOUN
　sigh

soupirer VERB
　to sigh

souple ADJECTIVE
　[1] supple (*person*)
　[2] flexible (*system*)

la **source** NOUN
　spring ◊ *l'eau de source* spring water

le **sourcil** NOUN
　eyebrow

sourd ADJECTIVE
　deaf

souriant ADJECTIVE
　cheerful

le **sourire** NOUN
　　see also **sourire** VERB
　smile

sourire VERB
　　see also **sourire** NOUN
　to smile ◊ *sourire à quelqu'un* to smile at somebody

la **souris** NOUN
　mouse

sournois ADJECTIVE
　sly

sous PREPOSITION
　under
　♦ **sous terre** underground
　♦ **sous la pluie** in the rain

sous-entendu ADJECTIVE
　　see also **sous-entendu** NOUN
　implied

le **sous-entendu** NOUN
　　see also **sous-entendu** ADJECTIVE
　insinuation

sous-marin ADJECTIVE
　　see also **sous-marin** NOUN
　underwater

le **sous-marin** NOUN
　　see also **sous-marin** ADJECTIVE
　submarine

le **sous-sol** NOUN
　basement

le **sous-titre** NOUN
　subtitle

sous-titré ADJECTIVE
　with subtitles

la **soustraction** NOUN
　subtraction

les **sous-vêtements** MASC NOUN
　underwear SING

soutenir VERB
　to support ◊ *Il m'a toujours soutenu contre elle.* He's always supported me against her.
　♦ **soutenir que** to maintain that ◊ *Elle soutenait que c'était impossible.* She maintained that it was impossible.
　♦ **soutenir l'allure** to keep up ◊ *Il marchait trop vite et je n'arrivais pas à soutenir l'allure.* He was walking too fast and I couldn't keep up.

souterrain ADJECTIVE
　　see also **souterrain** NOUN
　underground

le **souterrain** NOUN
　　see also **souterrain** ADJECTIVE
　underground passage

le **soutien** NOUN
　support

le **soutien-gorge** NOUN (PL les **soutiens-gorge**)
　bra

le **souvenir** NOUN
　　see also **se souvenir** VERB
　[1] memory ◊ *garder un bon souvenir de quelque chose* to have happy memories of something
　[2] souvenir
　♦ **Garde ce livre en souvenir de moi.** Keep the book: it'll remind you of me.

se **souvenir** VERB
　　see also **souvenir** NOUN
　♦ **se souvenir de quelque chose** to remember something ◊ *Je ne me souviens pas de son adresse.* I can't remember his address.
　♦ **se souvenir que** to remember that ◊ *Je me souviens qu'il neigeait.* I remember it was snowing.

souvent ADVERB
　often

soyez, soyons VERB *see* **être**
　♦ **Soyons clairs!** Let's be clear about this!

la **SPA** NOUN (= *Société protectrice des animaux*)
　RSPCA

spacieux ADJECTIVE (FEM SING **spacieuse**)
　spacious

les **spaghettis** MASC NOUN
　spaghetti SING

le **sparadrap** NOUN
　sticking plaster

S

le **speaker** NOUN
announcer

la **speakerine** NOUN
announcer

spécial ADJECTIVE (MASC PL **spéciaux**)
1 special ◊ *Qu'est-ce que tu fais ce week-end? – Rien de spécial.* What are you doing this weekend? – Nothing special.
♦ **les effets spéciaux** special effects
2 peculiar ◊ *Elle a des goûts un peu spéciaux.* She has rather peculiar tastes.

spécialement ADVERB
1 specially ◊ *Il est venu spécialement pour te parler.* He came specially to speak to you.
2 particularly ◊ *Ce n'est pas spécialement difficile.* It's not particularly difficult.

se **spécialiser** VERB
♦ **se spécialiser dans quelque chose** to specialize in something ◊ *Je me suis spécialisé en histoire contemporaine.* I specialized in modern history.

le/la **spécialiste** NOUN
specialist

la **spécialité** NOUN
speciality

spécifier VERB
to specify

le **spectacle** NOUN
show

spectaculaire ADJECTIVE
spectacular

le **spectateur** NOUN
1 member of the audience
2 spectator

la **spectatrice** NOUN
1 member of the audience
2 spectator

la **spéléologie** NOUN
potholing

spirituel ADJECTIVE (FEM SING **spirituelle**)
1 spiritual
2 witty

splendide ADJECTIVE
magnificent

spontané ADJECTIVE
spontaneous

le **sport** NOUN
see also **sport** ADJECTIVE
sport ◊ *faire du sport* to do sport
♦ **les sports d'hiver** winter sports

sport ADJECTIVE (MASC, FEM, PL)
see also **sport** NOUN
casual ◊ *une veste sport* a casual jacket

sportif ADJECTIVE (FEM SING **sportive**)
see also **sportif** NOUN
1 sporty ◊ *Elle est très sportive.* She's very sporty.
2 sports ◊ *un club sportif* a sports club

le **sportif** NOUN
see also **sportif** ADJECTIVE
sportsman

la **sportive** NOUN
sportswoman

le **spot** NOUN
spotlight
♦ **un spot publicitaire** a commercial break

le **square** NOUN
public gardens

le **squelette** NOUN
skeleton

stable ADJECTIVE
stable
♦ **un emploi stable** a steady job

le **stade** NOUN
stadium

le **stage** NOUN
1 training course ◊ *faire un stage de formation professionnelle* to go on a vocational training course
2 work experience ◊ *Caroline a fait un stage chez Collins.* Caroline did work experience at Collins.
♦ **faire un stage en entreprise** to do a work placement
*Be careful! The French word **stage** does not mean **stage**.*

le/la **stagiaire** NOUN
see also **stagiaire** ADJECTIVE
trainee

stagiaire ADJECTIVE
see also **stagiaire** NOUN
trainee ◊ *un professeur stagiaire* a trainee teacher

le **stand** NOUN
1 stand (*at exhibition*)
2 stall (*at fair*)

le/la **standardiste** NOUN
operator

la **station** NOUN
♦ **une station de métro** an underground station
♦ **une station de taxis** a taxi rank
♦ **une station de ski** a ski resort

le **stationnement** NOUN
parking
♦ **"stationnement interdit"** "no parking"

stationner VERB
to park

la **station-service** NOUN (PL les **stations-service**)
service station

la **statistique** NOUN
statistic

le **steak** NOUN
steak
  ◆ **un steak frites** steak and chips
  ◆ **un steak haché** a hamburger

la **sténo** NOUN
shorthand ◇ *un cours de sténo* a shorthand course

la **sténodactylo** NOUN
shorthand typist

stérile ADJECTIVE
sterile

stimulant ADJECTIVE
stimulating

stimuler VERB
to stimulate

le **stop** NOUN
stop sign
  ◆ **faire du stop** to hitchhike

stopper VERB
to stop

le **store** NOUN
  1 blind (*on window*)
  2 awning

le **strapontin** NOUN
foldaway seat

la **stratégie** NOUN
strategy

stratégique ADJECTIVE
strategic

stressant ADJECTIVE
stressful

stressé ADJECTIVE
stressed out

strict ADJECTIVE
  1 strict (*person*) ◇ *Ma prof de français est très stricte.* My French teacher's very strict.
  2 severe (*clothes*) ◇ *une tenue très stricte* a very severe outfit
  ◆ **le strict minimum** the bare minimum

la **strophe** NOUN
stanza

studieux ADJECTIVE (FEM SING **studieuse**)
studious

le **studio** NOUN
  1 studio flat
  2 studio ◇ *un studio de télévision* a television studio

stupéfait ADJECTIVE
astonished

les **stupéfiants** MASC NOUN
narcotics

stupéfier VERB
to astonish ◇ *Sa réponse m'a stupéfié.* I was astonished by his answer.

stupide ADJECTIVE
stupid

le **style** NOUN
style

le/la **styliste** NOUN
designer

le **stylo** NOUN
pen
  ◆ **un stylo plume** a fountain pen
  ◆ **un stylo bille** a ballpoint pen
  ◆ **un stylo-feutre** a felt-tip pen

su VERB *see* **savoir**
  ◆ **Si j'avais su ...** If I'd known ...

subir VERB
to suffer (*defeat*)
  ◆ **subir une opération** to have an operation

subit ADJECTIVE
sudden

subitement ADVERB
suddenly

subjectif ADJECTIVE (FEM SING **subjective**)
subjective

le **subjonctif** NOUN
subjunctive

substituer VERB
to substitute ◇ *substituer un mot à un autre* to substitute one word for another

subtil ADJECTIVE
subtle

la **subvention** NOUN
subsidy

subventionner VERB
to subsidize

le **succès** NOUN
success ◇ *avoir du succès* to be successful

le **successeur** NOUN
successor

la **succursale** NOUN
branch (*of company*)

sucer VERB
to suck

la **sucette** NOUN
lollipop

le **sucre** NOUN
sugar
  ◆ **un sucre** a sugar-lump ◇ *Je prends deux sucres dans mon café.* I take two lumps of sugar in my coffee.
  ◆ **du sucre en morceaux** lump sugar
  ◆ **un sucre d'orge** a barley sugar
  ◆ **du sucre en poudre** caster sugar
  ◆ **du sucre glace** icing sugar

S

sucré ADJECTIVE
[1] sweet ◊ *Ce gâteau est un peu trop sucré.* This cake is a bit too sweet.
[2] sweetened ◊ *du lait concentré sucré* sweetened condensed milk

les **sucreries** FEM NOUN
sweet things

le **sucrier** NOUN
sugar bowl

le **sud** NOUN
see also **sud** ADJECTIVE
south ◊ *Ils vivent dans le sud de la France.* They live in the South of France.
♦ **vers le sud** southwards
♦ **au sud de Paris** south of Paris
♦ **l'Amérique du Sud** South America
♦ **le vent du sud** the south wind

sud ADJECTIVE
see also **sud** NOUN
[1] south ◊ *la côte sud de l'Espagne* the south coast of Spain
♦ **le pôle sud** the South Pole
[2] southern ◊ *Nous avons visité la partie sud du pays.* We visited the southern part of the country.

sud-africain ADJECTIVE
South African

sud-américain ADJECTIVE
South American

le **sud-est** NOUN
south-east ◊ *au sud-est* in the south-east

le **sud-ouest** NOUN
south-west ◊ *au sud-ouest* in the south-west

la **Suède** NOUN
Sweden

suédois ADJECTIVE, NOUN (FEM SING **suédoise**)
Swedish ◊ *Ils parlent suédois.* They speak Swedish.
♦ **un Suédois** a Swede (*man*)
♦ **une Suédoise** a Swede (*woman*)
♦ **les Suédois** the Swedes

suer VERB
to sweat

la **sueur** NOUN
sweat
♦ **en sueur** sweating

suffire VERB
to be enough ◊ *Tiens, voilà dix euros. Ça te suffit?* Here's 10 euros. Is that enough for you?
♦ **Ça suffit!** That's enough!

suffisamment ADVERB
enough ◊ *Ça n'est pas suffisamment grand.* It's not big enough. ◊ *Il n'y a*

pas suffisamment de chaises. There aren't enough chairs.

suffisant ADJECTIVE
[1] sufficient ◊ *Ça n'est pas une raison suffisante.* That's not sufficient reason.
[2] smug ◊ *Il est un peu trop suffisant.* He's rather smug.

suffoquer VERB
to suffocate

suggérer VERB
to suggest

se **suicider** VERB
to commit suicide

suis VERB see **être, suivre**
♦ **Je suis écossais.** I'm Scottish.
♦ **Suis-moi.** Follow me.

suisse ADJECTIVE, NOUN
see also **la Suisse**
Swiss ◊ *le franc suisse* the Swiss franc
♦ **un Suisse** a Swiss man
♦ **une Suisse** a Swiss woman
♦ **les Suisses** the Swiss

la **Suisse** NOUN
see also **suisse** ADJECTIVE
Switzerland ◊ *la Suisse allemande* German-speaking Switzerland ◊ *la Suisse romande* French-speaking Switzerland

la **suite** NOUN
[1] rest ◊ *Je vous raconterai la suite de l'histoire demain.* I'll tell you the rest of the story tomorrow.
[2] sequel (*to book, film*)
♦ **tout de suite** straightaway ◊ *J'y vais tout de suite.* I'll go straightaway.
♦ **de suite** in succession ◊ *Il a commis la même erreur trois fois de suite.* He made the same mistake three times in succession.
♦ **par la suite** subsequently ◊ *Il s'est avéré par la suite qu'il était coupable.* He subsequently turned out to be guilty.

suivant ADJECTIVE
following ◊ *le jour suivant* the following day ◊ *l'exercice suivant* the following exercise
♦ **Au suivant!** Next!

suivre VERB
[1] to follow ◊ *Il m'a suivie jusque chez moi.* He followed me home. ◊ *Vous me suivez ou est-ce que je parle trop vite?* Are you following me or am I speaking too fast?
[2] to do ◊ *Je suis un cours d'anglais à la fac.* I'm doing an English course at college.

③ to keep up ◊ *Il n'arrive pas à
suivre en maths.* He can't keep up in
maths. ◊ *J'aime suivre l'actualité.* I
like to keep up with the news.
♦ **"à suivre"** "to be continued"
♦ **suivre un régime** to be on a diet

sujet ADJECTIVE (FEM SING **sujette**)
see also **sujet** NOUN
♦ **être sujet à** to be prone to ◊ *Il est
sujet au vertige.* He suffers from
vertigo.

le **sujet** NOUN
see also **sujet** ADJECTIVE
subject
♦ **au sujet de** about ◊ *C'est à quel
sujet? – C'est au sujet de l'annonce
parue dans "Le Monde" d'aujourd'hui.*
What's it about? – It's about the
advertisement in today's "Le Monde".
♦ **un sujet de conversation** a topic of
conversation
♦ **un sujet d'examen** an examination
question
♦ **un sujet de plaisanterie** something to
joke about

super ADJECTIVE (MASC, FEM, PL)
see also **super** NOUN
great

le **super** NOUN
see also **super** ADJECTIVE
super (*petrol*)

superficiel ADJECTIVE (FEM SING
superficielle)
superficial

superflu ADJECTIVE
superfluous

supérieur ADJECTIVE
see also **supérieur** NOUN
① upper ◊ *la lèvre supérieure* the
upper lip
② superior ◊ *qualité supérieure*
superior quality ◊ *Il a toujours l'air
tellement supérieur!* He always looks
so superior!
♦ **supérieur à** greater than ◊ *Choisissez
un nombre supérieur à cent.* Choose
a number greater than 100.

le **supérieur** NOUN
see also **supérieur** ADJECTIVE
superior ◊ *mon supérieur
hiérarchique* my immediate superior

le **supermarché** NOUN
supermarket

superposé ADJECTIVE
♦ **des lits superposés** bunk beds

superstitieux ADJECTIVE (FEM SING
superstitieuse)
superstitious

le **suppléant** NOUN

supply teacher

la **suppléante** NOUN
supply teacher

le **supplément** NOUN
♦ **payer un supplément** to pay an
additional charge
♦ **Le vin est en supplément.** Wine is
extra.
♦ **un supplément de travail** extra work

supplémentaire ADJECTIVE
additional ◊ *Voici quelques exercices
supplémentaires.* Here are some
additional exercises.
♦ **faire des heures supplémentaires** to
do overtime

le **supplice** NOUN
torture ◊ *C'était un supplice.* It was
torture.

supplier VERB
♦ **supplier quelqu'un de faire quelque
chose** to beg somebody to do
something ◊ *Je t'en supplie!* I'm
begging you!

supportable ADJECTIVE
bearable

supporter VERB
to stand (*tolerate*) ◊ *Je ne supporte
pas l'hypocrisie.* I can't stand
hypocrisy. ◊ *Elle ne supporte pas
qu'on la critique.* She can't stand
being criticized. ◊ *Je ne peux pas la
supporter.* I can't stand her. ◊ *Je
supporte mal la chaleur.* I can't stand
hot weather.
*Be careful! **supporter** does not mean
to support.*

supposer VERB
to suppose

supprimer VERB
① to cut ◊ *Deux mille emplois ont
été supprimés.* Two thousand jobs
have been cut.
② to cancel ◊ *Le train de Londres a
été supprimé.* The train to London
has been cancelled.
③ to get rid of ◊ *Ils ont supprimé
les témoins gênants.* They got rid of
the awkward witnesses.

sur PREPOSITION
① on ◊ *Pose-le sur la table.* Put it
down on the table. ◊ *Vous verrez
l'hôpital sur votre droite.* You'll see
the hospital on your right. ◊ *une
conférence sur Balzac* a lecture on
Balzac
② in ◊ *une personne sur dix* 1
person in 10
③ out of ◊ *J'ai eu onze sur vingt en
maths.* I got 11 out of 20 in maths.

S

☞

④ <u>by</u> ◊ *quatre mètres sur deux* 4 metres by 2

sûr ADJECTIVE
① <u>sure</u> ◊ *Tu es sûr?* Are you sure?
♦ **sûr et certain** absolutely certain
② <u>reliable</u> ◊ *C'est quelqu'un de très sûr.* He's a very reliable person.
③ <u>safe</u> ◊ *Ce quartier n'est pas très sûr la nuit.* This neighbourhood isn't very safe at night.
♦ **sûr de soi** self-confident ◊ *Elle est très sûre d'elle.* She's very self-confident.

sûrement ADVERB
<u>certainly</u> ◊ *Sûrement pas!* Certainly not! ◊ *Il est sûrement déjà parti.* He's sure to have already left.

la **sûreté** NOUN
♦ **mettre quelque chose en sûreté** to put something in a safe place

le **surf** NOUN
<u>surfing</u>

la **surface** NOUN
<u>surface</u>
♦ **les grandes surfaces** the supermarkets

surfer VERB
<u>to go surfing</u>
♦ **surfer sur le Net** to surf the Net

surgelé ADJECTIVE
<u>frozen</u> ◊ *des frites surgelées* frozen chips

les **surgelés** MASC NOUN
<u>frozen food</u> SING

surhumain ADJECTIVE
<u>superhuman</u>

sur-le-champ ADVERB
<u>immediately</u>

le **surlendemain** NOUN
♦ **le surlendemain de son arrivée** two days after he arrived
♦ **le surlendemain dans la matinée** two days later, in the morning

se **surmener** VERB
<u>to work too hard</u> ◊ *Ne te surmène pas trop pendant le week-end.* Don't work too hard over the weekend.

surmonter VERB
<u>to overcome</u> ◊ *Il nous reste de nombreux obstacles à surmonter.* We still have many obstacles to overcome.

surnaturel ADJECTIVE (FEM SING **surnaturelle**)
<u>supernatural</u>

le **surnom** NOUN
<u>nickname</u>

surnommer NOUN
<u>to nickname</u> ◊ *On l'a surnommé "Kiki".* We nicknamed him "Kiki".

surpeuplé ADJECTIVE
<u>overpopulated</u>

surprenant ADJECTIVE
<u>surprising</u>

surprendre VERB
<u>to surprise</u> ◊ *Ça me surprendrait beaucoup qu'il arrive à l'heure.* I'd be very surprised if he arrived on time.
♦ **surprendre quelqu'un en train de faire quelque chose** to catch somebody doing something ◊ *Je l'ai surpris en train de fouiller dans mon placard.* I caught him rummaging in my cupboard.

surpris ADJECTIVE
<u>surprised</u> ◊ *Il était surpris de me voir.* He was surprised to see me.

la **surprise** NOUN
<u>surprise</u> ◊ *faire une surprise à quelqu'un* to give somebody a surprise

sursauter VERB
<u>to jump</u> ◊ *J'ai sursauté en entendant mon nom.* I jumped when I heard my name.

surtout ADVERB
① <u>especially</u> ◊ *Il est assez timide, surtout avec les filles.* He's rather shy, especially with girls.
② <u>above all</u> ◊ *Ce canapé est joli et surtout, il n'est pas salissant.* This sofa is pretty, and even more important, it doesn't show the dirt. ◊ *Surtout, ne répète pas ce que je t'ai dit!* Whatever you do, don't repeat what I told you!

le **surveillant** NOUN
<u>supervisor</u> (*man*)

ⓘ *In French secondary schools, the teachers are not responsible for supervising the pupils outside class. This job is done by people called* **surveillants** *or* **pions**.

la **surveillante** NOUN
<u>supervisor</u> (*woman*)

surveiller VERB
① <u>to keep an eye on</u> ◊ *Tu peux surveiller mes bagages?* Can you keep an eye on my luggage?
② <u>to keep a watch on</u> ◊ *La police a surveillé la maison pendant une semaine.* The police kept the house under surveillance for a week.
③ <u>to supervise</u> ◊ *Nous sommes toujours surveillés pendant la récréation.* We're always supervised during break.

♦**surveiller un examen** to invigilate an exam

♦**surveiller sa ligne** to watch one's figure

le **survêtement** NOUN
tracksuit ◊ *un haut de survêtement* a tracksuit top ◊ *un pantalon de survêtement* tracksuit bottoms

la **survie** NOUN
survival

le **survivant** NOUN
survivor

la **survivante** NOUN
survivor

survivre VERB
to survive ◊ *survivre à un accident* to survive an accident

survoler VERB
to fly over

sus ADVERB
♦**en sus** in addition

susceptible ADJECTIVE
touchy

suspect ADJECTIVE
suspicious ◊ *dans des circonstances suspectes* under suspicious circumstances

suspecter VERB
to suspect

le **suspense** NOUN
suspense
♦**un film à suspense** a thriller

la **suture** NOUN
♦**un point de suture** a stitch

svelte ADJECTIVE
slender

SVP ABBREVIATION (= *s'il vous plaît*)
please

le **sweat** NOUN
sweatshirt

la **syllabe** NOUN
syllable

le **symbole** NOUN
symbol

symbolique ADJECTIVE
symbolic

symboliser VERB
to symbolize

symétrique ADJECTIVE
symmetrical

sympa ADJECTIVE (*informal*)
nice ◊ *Elle est très sympa.* She's a really nice person.

la **sympathie** NOUN
♦**J'ai beaucoup de sympathie pour lui.** I like him a lot.

sympathique ADJECTIVE
nice ◊ *Ce sont des gens très sympathiques.* They're very nice people.

Be careful! **sympathique** does not mean **sympathetic**.

sympathiser VERB
to get on well ◊ *Nous avons immédiatement sympathisé avec nos voisins.* We got on well with our neighbours straight away.

le **symptôme** NOUN
symptom

la **synagogue** NOUN
synagogue

le **syndicat** NOUN
trade union
♦**le syndicat d'initiative** the tourist information office

synonyme ADJECTIVE
see also **synonyme** NOUN
synonymous ◊ *être synonyme de* to be synonymous with

le **synonyme** NOUN
see also **synonyme** ADJECTIVE
synonym

synthétique ADJECTIVE
synthetic

la **Syrie** NOUN
Syria

syrien ADJECTIVE (FEM SING **syrienne**)
Syrian

systématique ADJECTIVE
systematic

le **système** NOUN
system

S

T

t' PRONOUN *see* **te**

ta ADJECTIVE
 your ◊ *J'ai vu ta sœur hier.* I saw your sister yesterday.

le **tabac** NOUN
 1 tobacco ◊ *le tabac blond* light tobacco ◊ *le tabac brun* dark tobacco
 2 smoking ◊ *Le tabac est mauvais pour la santé.* Smoking is bad for you.

la **table** NOUN
 table
 ♦ **mettre la table** to lay the table
 ♦ **se mettre à table** to sit down to eat
 ♦ **À table!** Dinner's ready!
 ♦ **une table de nuit** a bedside table
 ♦ **"table des matières"** "contents"

le **tableau** NOUN (PL les **tableaux**)
 painting ◊ *un tableau de Monet* a painting by Monet
 ♦ **le tableau d'affichage** the notice board
 ♦ **le tableau noir** the blackboard

la **tablette** NOUN
 ♦ **une tablette de chocolat** a bar of chocolate

le **tableur** NOUN
 speadsheet

le **tablier** NOUN
 apron

le **tabouret** NOUN
 stool

la **tache** NOUN
 mark (*stain*)
 ♦ **des taches de rousseur** freckles

la **tâche** NOUN
 task

tacher VERB
 to leave a stain

tâcher VERB
 ♦ **tâcher de faire quelque chose** to try to do something ◊ *Tâche d'être à l'heure!* Try to be on time!

le **tact** NOUN
 tact ◊ *avoir du tact* to be tactful

la **tactique** NOUN
 tactics
 ♦ **changer de tactique** to try something different

la **taie** NOUN
 ♦ **une taie d'oreiller** a pillowcase

la **taille** NOUN
 1 waist ◊ *Elle a la taille fine.* She has a slim waist.

 2 height ◊ *un homme de taille moyenne* a man of average height
 3 size ◊ *Avez-vous ma taille?* Have you got my size?

le **taille-crayon** NOUN
 pencil sharpener

le **tailleur** NOUN
 1 tailor
 2 suit (*lady's*)
 ♦ **Il est assis en tailleur.** He's sitting cross-legged.

se **taire** VERB
 to stop talking
 ♦ **Taisez-vous!** Be quiet!

le **talon** NOUN
 heel

le **tambour** NOUN
 drum

la **Tamise** NOUN
 Thames

le **tampon** NOUN
 pad ◊ *un tampon à récurer* a scouring pad
 ♦ **un tampon hygiénique** a tampon

tamponneuse ADJECTIVE
 ♦ **les autos tamponneuses** dodgems

tandis que CONJUNCTION
 while ◊ *Il a toujours de bonnes notes, tandis que les miennes sont mauvaises.* He always gets good marks, while mine are poor.

tant ADVERB
 so much ◊ *Je l'aime tant!* I love him so much!
 ♦ **tant de (1)** so much ◊ *tant de nourriture* so much food
 ♦ **tant de (2)** so many ◊ *tant de livres* so many books
 ♦ **tant que (1)** until ◊ *Tu ne sortiras pas tant que tu n'auras pas fini tes devoirs.* You're not going out until you've finished your homework.
 ♦ **tant que (2)** while ◊ *Profites-en tant que tu peux.* Make the most of it while you can.
 ♦ **tant mieux** so much the better
 ♦ **tant pis** never mind

la **tante** NOUN
 aunt

tantôt ADVERB
 sometimes ◊ *Nous venons tantôt à pied, tantôt en bus.* Sometimes we walk, sometimes we come by bus.

le **tapage** NOUN

1 racket ◊ *Ils ont fait du tapage toute la nuit.* They made a racket all night long.

2 fuss ◊ *On a fait beaucoup de tapage autour de cette affaire.* There was a lot of fuss about that business.

taper VERB
to beat down ◊ *Le soleil tape.* The sun's really beating down.
♦ **taper quelqu'un** to hit somebody ◊ *Papa, il m'a tapé!* Dad, he hit me!
♦ **taper sur quelque chose** to bang on something
♦ **taper des pieds** to stamp one's feet
♦ **taper des mains** to clap one's hands
♦ **taper à la machine** to type ◊ *Tu sais taper à la machine?* Can you type? ◊ *Je vais taper cette lettre.* I'm going to type this letter.

le **tapis** NOUN
1 carpet
♦ **le tapis roulant (1)** the Travelator ® (*for people*)
♦ **le tapis roulant (2)** the conveyor belt (*in factory*)
♦ **le tapis roulant (3)** the carousel (*at baggage reclaim*)
♦ **un tapis de souris** a mouse mat

tapisser VERB
to paper

la **tapisserie** NOUN
1 wallpaper ◊ *Tu aimes la tapisserie de ma chambre?* Do you like the wallpaper in my bedroom?
2 tapestry

taquiner VERB
to tease

tard ADVERB
late ◊ *Il est tard.* It's late.
♦ **plus tard** later on
♦ **au plus tard** at the latest

tardif ADJECTIVE (FEM SING **tardive**)
late ◊ *un déjeuner tardif* a late lunch

le **tarif** NOUN
♦ **le tarif des consommations** the price list (*in café*)
♦ **une communication à tarif réduit** an off-peak phone call
♦ **un billet de train à tarif réduit** a concessionary train ticket
♦ **un billet de train à plein tarif** a full-price train ticket
♦ **Est-ce que vous faites un tarif de groupe?** Is there a reduction for groups?

la **tarte** NOUN
tart

la **tartine** NOUN

slice of bread ◊ *une tartine de confiture* a slice of bread and jam

tartiner VERB
to spread
♦ **le fromage à tartiner** cheese spread

le **tas** NOUN
heap ◊ *un tas de charbon* a heap of coal
♦ **un tas de** (*informal*) loads of ◊ *J'ai lu un tas de livres pendant les vacances.* I read loads of books in the holidays.

la **tasse** NOUN
cup

le **taureau** NOUN (PL les **taureaux**)
bull
♦ **le Taureau** Taurus ◊ *Ils sont tous les deux Taureau.* They're both Taurus.

le **taux** NOUN
rate ◊ *le taux de change* the exchange rate

la **taxe** NOUN
tax
♦ **la boutique hors taxes** the duty-free shop

le **taxi** NOUN
taxi

tchèque ADJECTIVE
Czech
♦ **la République tchèque** the Czech Republic

te PRONOUN

*te changes to **t'** before a vowel and most words beginning with "h".*

1 you ◊ *Je te vois.* I can see you. ◊ *Il t'a vu?* Did he see you?
2 to you ◊ *Est-ce qu'il te parle en français?* Does he talk to you in French? ◊ *Elle t'a parlé?* Did she speak to you?
3 yourself ◊ *Tu vas te rendre malade.* You'll make yourself sick.
*With reflexive verbs, **te** is often not translated.*
◊ *Comment tu t'appelles?* What's your name?

le **technicien** NOUN
technician

la **technicienne** NOUN
technician

technique ADJECTIVE
see also **technique** NOUN
technical

la **technique** NOUN
see also **technique** ADJECTIVE
technique

la **techno** NOUN
techno music

T

la **technologie** NOUN
technology

le **teint** NOUN
complexion ◊ *Elle a le teint clair.*
She's got a fair complexion.

la **teinte** NOUN
shade (*colour*)

le **teinturier** NOUN
dry cleaner's ◊ *Je vais porter ce
manteau chez le teinturier.* I'm going
to take this coat to the dry cleaner's.

tel ADJECTIVE (FEM SING **telle**)
♦ **Il a un tel enthousiasme!** He's got
such enthusiasm!
♦ **rien de tel** nothing like ◊ *Il n'y a rien
de tel qu'une bonne nuit de sommeil.*
There's nothing like a good night's
sleep.
♦ **J'ai tout laissé tel quel.** I left
everything as it was.
♦ **tel que** such as

la **télé** NOUN
telly ◊ *à la télé* on telly

la **télécarte** NOUN
phonecard

télécharger VERB
to download

la **télécommande** NOUN
remote control

la **téléconférence** NOUN
video conference

la **télécopie** NOUN
fax

le **télégramme** NOUN
telegram

le **téléphérique** NOUN
cable car

le **téléphone** NOUN
telephone ◊ *Elle est au téléphone.*
She's on the phone.

téléphoner VERB
to phone ◊ *Je vais téléphoner à
Claire.* I'll phone Claire. ◊ *Je peux
téléphoner?* Can I make a phone call?

le **télésiège** NOUN
chairlift

le **téléski** NOUN
ski-tow

le **téléspectateur** NOUN
viewer (*TV*)

la **téléspectatrice** NOUN
viewer (*TV*)

le **téléviseur** NOUN
television set

la **télévision** NOUN
television ◊ *à la télévision* on
television
♦ **la télévision en circuit fermé** CCTV

♦ **la télévision numérique** digital TV

telle ADJECTIVE
♦ **Je n'ai jamais eu une telle peur.** I've
never had such a fright.
♦ **telle que** such as

tellement ADVERB
1 so ◊ *Andrew est tellement gentil.*
Andrew's so nice. ◊ *Il travaille
tellement.* He works so hard.
2 so much ◊ *Il a tellement mangé
que ...* He ate so much that ...
3 so many ◊ *Il y avait tellement de
monde.* There were so many people.

telles ADJECTIVE
such ◊ *Je n'ai jamais entendu de
telles bêtises!* I've never heard such
nonsense!

tels ADJECTIVE
such ◊ *Nous n'avons pas de tels
orages chez nous.* We don't have
such storms back home.

le **témoignage** NOUN
testimony

témoigner VERB
to testify

le **témoin** NOUN
witness

la **température** NOUN
temperature ◊ *avoir de la
température* to have a temperature

la **tempête** NOUN
storm

le **temple** NOUN
1 church (*Protestant*)
2 temple (*Hindu, Sikh, Buddhist*)

temporaire ADJECTIVE
temporary

le **temps** NOUN
1 weather ◊ *Quel temps fait-il?*
What's the weather like?
2 time ◊ *Je n'ai pas le temps.* I
haven't got time. ◊ *Prends ton temps.*
Take your time. ◊ *Il est temps de
partir.* It's time to go.
♦ **juste à temps** just in time
♦ **de temps en temps** from time to time
♦ **en même temps** at the same time
♦ **à temps** in time ◊ *Il est arrivé à
temps pour le match.* He arrived in
time for the match.
♦ **à plein temps** full time ◊ *Elle travaille
à plein temps.* She works full time.
♦ **à temps complet** full time
♦ **à temps partiel** part time ◊ *le travail à
temps partiel* part-time work
♦ **dans le temps** at one time ◊ *Dans le
temps, on pouvait circuler en vélo
sans danger.* At one time, it was safe
to go around by bike.

3 tense (of verb)

tenais, tenait VERB see **tenir**

la **tendance** NOUN
 ♦ **avoir tendance à faire quelque chose** to tend to do something ◊ *Il a tendance à exagérer.* He tends to exaggerate.

tendre ADJECTIVE
 see also **tendre** VERB
 tender

tendre VERB
 see also **tendre** ADJECTIVE
 to stretch out ◊ *Ils ont tendu une corde entre deux arbres.* They stretched out a rope between two trees.
 ♦ **tendre quelque chose à quelqu'un** to hold something out to somebody ◊ *Il lui a tendu les clés.* He held out the keys to her.
 ♦ **tendre la main** to hold out one's hand
 ♦ **tendre le bras** to reach out
 ♦ **tendre un piège à quelqu'un** to set a trap for someone

tendrement ADVERB
 tenderly

la **tendresse** NOUN
 tenderness

tendu ADJECTIVE
 tense ◊ *Il était très tendu aujourd'hui.* He was very tense today.

tenir VERB
 to hold ◊ *Tu peux tenir la lampe, s'il te plaît?* Can you hold the torch, please? ◊ *Il tenait un enfant par la main.* He was holding a child by the hand.
 ♦ **Tenez votre chien en laisse.** Keep your dog on the lead.
 ♦ **tenir à quelqu'un** to be attached to somebody ◊ *Il tient beaucoup à elle.* He's very attached to her.
 ♦ **tenir à faire quelque chose** to be determined to do something ◊ *Elle tient à y aller.* She's determined to go.
 ♦ **tenir de quelqu'un** to take after somebody ◊ *Il tient de son père.* He takes after his father.
 ♦ **Tiens, voilà un stylo.** Here's a pen.
 ♦ **Tiens, c'est Alain là-bas!** Look, that's Alain over there!
 ♦ **Tiens?** Really?
 ♦ **se tenir (1)** to stand ◊ *Il se tenait près de la porte.* He was standing by the door.
 ♦ **se tenir (2)** to be held ◊ *La foire va se tenir place du marché.* The fair will be held in the market place.
 ♦ **se tenir droit (1)** to stand up straight ◊ *Tiens-toi droit!* Stand up straight!

♦ **se tenir droit (2)** to sit up straight ◊ *Arrête de manger le nez dans ton assiette, tiens-toi droit.* Don't slouch while you're eating, sit up straight.
 ♦ **Tiens-toi bien!** Behave yourself!

le **tennis** NOUN
 1 tennis ◊ *Elle joue au tennis.* She plays tennis.
 ♦ **le tennis de table** table tennis
 2 tennis court ◊ *Il est au tennis.* He's at the tennis court.
 ♦ **les tennis** trainers

tentant ADJECTIVE
 tempting

la **tentation** NOUN
 temptation

la **tentative** NOUN
 attempt

la **tente** NOUN
 tent

tenter VERB
 to tempt ◊ *J'ai été tenté de tout abandonner.* I was tempted to give up. ◊ *Ça ne me tente vraiment pas d'aller à la piscine.* I don't really fancy going to the swimming pool.
 ♦ **tenter de faire quelque chose** to try to do something ◊ *Il a tenté plusieurs fois de s'évader.* He tried several times to escape.

tenu VERB see **tenir**

la **tenue** NOUN
 clothes
 ♦ **en tenue de soirée** in evening dress

le **terme** NOUN
 ♦ **à court terme** short-term
 ♦ **à long terme** long-term

la **terminale** NOUN
 upper sixth ◊ *Je suis en terminale.* I'm in the upper sixth.

> ⓘ In French secondary schools, years are counted from the **sixième** (youngest) to **première** and **terminale** (oldest).

terminer VERB
 to finish
 ♦ **se terminer** to end ◊ *Les vacances se terminent demain.* The holidays end tomorrow.

le **terminus** NOUN
 terminus

le **terrain** NOUN
 land ◊ *Il veut acheter un terrain en Normandie.* He wants to buy some land in Normandy.
 ♦ **un terrain de camping** a campsite
 ♦ **un terrain de football** a football pitch

◆ **un terrain de golf** a golf course
◆ **un terrain de jeu** a playground
◆ **un terrain de sport** a sports ground
◆ **un terrain vague** a piece of waste ground

la **terrasse** NOUN
terrace
◆ **Si on s'asseyait en terrasse?** Shall we sit outside? (*at café*)

la **terre** NOUN
earth
◆ **la Terre** the Earth
◆ **Elle s'est assise par terre.** She sat on the floor.
◆ **Il est tombé par terre.** He fell down.
◆ **la terre cuite** terracotta ◊ *un pot en terre cuite* a terracotta pot
◆ **la terre glaise** clay

terrible ADJECTIVE
terrible ◊ *Quelque chose de terrible est arrivé.* Something terrible has happened.
◆ **pas terrible** (*informal*) nothing special ◊ *Ce film n'est pas terrible.* The film's nothing special.

la **terrine** NOUN
pâté

le **territoire** NOUN
territory

terrorisé ADJECTIVE
terrified

le **terrorisme** NOUN
terrorism

le/la **terroriste** NOUN
terrorist

tes ADJECTIVE
your ◊ *J'aime bien tes baskets.* I like your trainers.

le **test** NOUN
test

le **testament** NOUN
will ◊ *Il est mort sans testament.* He died without leaving a will.

tester VERB
to test

le **tétanos** NOUN
tetanus

le **têtard** NOUN
tadpole

la **tête** NOUN
head ◊ *de la tête aux pieds* from head to foot
◆ **se laver la tête** to wash one's hair
◆ **la tête la première** headfirst
◆ **tenir tête à quelqu'un** to stand up to somebody
◆ **faire la tête** to sulk
◆ **en avoir par-dessus la tête** to be fed up

têtu ADJECTIVE
stubborn

le **texte** NOUN
text

le **TGV** NOUN (= *train à grande vitesse*)
high-speed train

le **thé** NOUN
tea ◊ *Je vous offre un thé?* Would you like a cup of tea? ◊ *un thé au lait* a white tea

le **théâtre** NOUN
theatre
◆ **faire du théâtre** to act ◊ *Est-ce que tu as déjà fait du théâtre?* Have you ever acted?

la **théière** NOUN
teapot

le **thème** NOUN
1 subject ◊ *Quel est le thème de l'émission?* What's the programme about?
2 prose (*translation into the foreign language*)

la **théorie** NOUN
theory

le **thermomètre** NOUN
thermometer

le **thon** NOUN
tuna

la **thune** NOUN (*informal*)
dosh

le **tibia** NOUN
1 shinbone ◊ *une fracture du tibia* a broken shinbone
2 shin ◊ *Il m'a donné un coup de pied dans le tibia.* He kicked me in the shin.

le **tic** NOUN
nervous twitch

le **ticket** NOUN
ticket ◊ *un ticket de métro* an underground ticket
◆ **le ticket de caisse** the till receipt

tiède ADJECTIVE
1 warm (*water, air*)
2 lukewarm (*food, drink*)

tien PRONOUN
◆ **le tien** yours ◊ *J'ai oublié mon stylo. Tu peux me prêter le tien?* I've forgotten my pen. Can you lend me yours?

tienne PRONOUN
◆ **la tienne** yours ◊ *Ce n'est pas ma raquette, c'est la tienne.* It's not my racket, it's yours.
◆ **À la tienne!** Cheers!

tiennes PRONOUN

♦**les tiennes** yours ◊ *J'ai pris mes baskets, mais j'ai oublié les tiennes.* I've brought my trainers, but I've forgotten yours.

tiens PRONOUN
♦**les tiens** yours ◊ *Je ne trouve pas mes feutres. Je peux utiliser les tiens?* I can't find my felt pens. Can I use yours?

tiens, tient VERB *see* **tenir**

le **tiers** NOUN
third ◊ *Un tiers de la classe était pour.* A third of the class were in favour.
♦**le tiers monde** the Third World

la **tige** NOUN
stem

le **tigre** NOUN
tiger

le **tilleul** NOUN
lime tea

le **timbre** NOUN
stamp

le **timbre-poste** NOUN
postage stamp

timide ADJECTIVE
shy

timidement ADVERB
shyly

la **timidité** NOUN
shyness

le **tir** NOUN
shooting
♦**le tir à l'arc** archery

le **tirage** NOUN
♦**par tirage au sort** by drawing lots ◊ *Les prix seront attribués par tirage au sort.* The prizes will be awarded by drawing lots.

le **tire-bouchon** NOUN
corkscrew

la **tirelire** NOUN
money box

tirer VERB
1 to pull ◊ *Elle a tiré un mouchoir de son sac.* She pulled a handkerchief out of her bag. ◊ *Il m'a tiré les cheveux.* He pulled my hair. ◊ *"Tirer"* "Pull"
2 to draw ◊ *tirer les rideaux* to draw the curtains ◊ *tirer un trait* to draw a line ◊ *tirer des conclusions* to draw conclusions
♦**tirer au sort** to draw lots
3 to fire ◊ *Il a tiré plusieurs coups de feu.* He fired several shots. ◊ *Il a tiré sur les policiers.* He fired at the police.

♦**Tu t'en tires bien.** You're doing well.

le **tiret** NOUN
dash (*hyphen*)

le **tiroir** NOUN
drawer

la **tisane** NOUN
herbal tea

tisser VERB
to weave

le **tissu** NOUN
material
♦**un sac en tissu** a cloth bag

le **titre** NOUN
title
♦**les gros titres** the headlines
♦**un titre de transport** a travel ticket

tituber VERB
to stagger

le **toast** NOUN
1 piece of toast
2 toast ◊ *porter un toast à quelqu'un* to drink a toast to somebody

le **toboggan** NOUN
slide

toi PRONOUN
you ◊ *Ça va? – Oui, et toi?* How are you? – Fine, and you? ◊ *J'ai faim, pas toi?* I'm hungry, aren't you?
♦**Assieds-toi.** Sit down.
♦**C'est à toi de jouer.** It's your turn to play.
♦**Est-ce que ce stylo est à toi?** Is this pen yours?

la **toile** NOUN
♦**un pantalon de toile** cotton trousers
♦**un sac de toile** a canvas bag
♦**une toile cirée** an oilcloth
♦**une toile d'araignée** a cobweb

la **toilette** NOUN
1 wash ◊ *faire sa toilette* to have a wash
2 outfit ◊ *une toilette élégante* an elegant outfit

les **toilettes** FEM NOUN
toilet SING

toi-même PRONOUN
yourself ◊ *Tu as fait ça toi-même?* Did you do it yourself?

le **toit** NOUN
roof
♦**un toit ouvrant** a sunroof

tolérant ADJECTIVE
tolerant

tolérer VERB
to tolerate

la **tomate** NOUN
tomato

la **tombe** NOUN

T

grave

le **tombeau** NOUN (PL les **tombeaux**)
tomb

la **tombée** NOUN
◆**à la tombée de la nuit** at nightfall

tomber VERB
to fall ◊ *Attention, tu vas tomber!* Be careful, you'll fall!
◆**laisser tomber (1)** to drop ◊ *Elle a laissé tomber son stylo.* She dropped her pen.
◆**laisser tomber (2)** to give up ◊ *Il a laissé tomber le piano.* He gave up the piano.
◆**laisser tomber (3)** to let down ◊ *Il ne laisse jamais tomber ses amis.* He never lets his friends down.
◆**tomber sur quelqu'un** to bump into someone ◊ *Je suis tombé sur lui en sortant de chez Pierre.* I bumped into him coming out of Pierre's place.
◆**Ça tombe bien.** That's lucky.
◆**Il tombe de sommeil.** He's asleep on his feet.

ton ADJECTIVE (FEM SING **ta**, PL **tes**)
see also **ton** NOUN
your ◊ *C'est ton stylo?* Is this your pen?

le **ton** NOUN
see also **ton** ADJECTIVE
1 tone of voice ◊ *Ne me parle pas sur ce ton.* Don't speak to me in that tone of voice.
2 colour ◊ *J'adore les tons pastel.* I love pastel colours.

la **tonalité** NOUN
dialling tone

la **tondeuse** NOUN
lawnmower

tondre VERB
to mow

tonique ADJECTIVE
fortifying

la **tonne** NOUN
tonne

le **tonneau** NOUN (PL les **tonneaux**)
barrel

le **tonnerre** NOUN
thunder

le **tonus** NOUN
◆**avoir du tonus** to be energetic

le **torchon** NOUN
tea towel

tordre VERB
◆**se tordre la cheville** to twist one's ankle

tordu ADJECTIVE

1 bent ◊ *Ce clou est un peu tordu.* This nail's a bit bent.
2 crazy ◊ *une histoire complètement tordue* a crazy story

le **torrent** NOUN
mountain stream

le **torse** NOUN
chest ◊ *Il était torse nu.* He was bare-chested.

le **tort** NOUN
◆**avoir tort** to be wrong
◆**donner tort à quelqu'un** to lay the blame on somebody

le **torticolis** NOUN
stiff neck ◊ *J'ai le torticolis.* I've got a stiff neck.

la **tortue** NOUN
tortoise

la **torture** NOUN
torture

torturer VERB
to torture

tôt ADVERB
early
◆**au plus tôt** at the earliest
◆**tôt ou tard** sooner or later

total ADJECTIVE (MASC PL **totaux**)
see also **total** NOUN
total

le **total** NOUN (PL les **totaux**)
see also **total** ADJECTIVE
total ◊ *faire le total* to work out the total
◆**au total** in total

totalement ADVERB
totally

la **totalité** NOUN
◆**la totalité des profs** all the teachers
◆**la totalité du personnel** the entire staff

touchant ADJECTIVE
touching

toucher VERB
1 to touch ◊ *Ne touche pas à mes livres!* Don't touch my books!
◆**Nos deux jardins se touchent.** Our gardens are next to each other.
2 to feel ◊ *Ce pull a l'air doux. Je peux toucher?* That sweater looks soft. Can I feel it?
3 to hit ◊ *La balle l'a touché en pleine poitrine.* The bullet hit him right in the chest.
4 to affect ◊ *Ces nouvelles réformes ne nous touchent pas.* The new reforms don't affect us.
5 to receive ◊ *Il a touché une grosse somme d'argent.* He received a large sum of money.

toujours ADVERB
  1 always ◊ *Il est toujours très gentil.*
  He's always very nice.
  ♦ **pour toujours** forever
  2 still ◊ *Quand on est revenus,*
  Pierre était toujours là. When we got
  back Pierre was still there.

le **toupet** NOUN (*informal*)
  ♦ **avoir du toupet** to have a nerve

la **tour** NOUN
  | *see also* **le tour** |
  1 tower ◊ *la Tour Eiffel* the Eiffel
  Tower
  2 tower block ◊ *Il y a beaucoup de*
  tours dans ce quartier. There are a
  lot of tower blocks in this area.

le **tour** NOUN
  | *see also* **la tour** |
  turn ◊ *C'est ton tour de jouer.* It's
  your turn to play.
  ♦ **faire un tour** to go for a walk ◊ *Allons*
  faire un tour dans le parc. Let's go
  for a walk in the park.
  ♦ **faire un tour en voiture** to go for a
  drive
  ♦ **faire un tour à vélo** to go for a ride
  ◊ *Tu veux aller faire un tour à vélo?*
  Do you want to go for a bike ride?
  ♦ **faire le tour du monde** to travel
  round the world
  ♦ **à tour de rôle** alternately

le **tourbillon** NOUN
  whirlpool

le **tourisme** NOUN
  tourism

le/la **touriste** NOUN
  tourist

  touristique ADJECTIVE
  tourist

se **tourmenter** VERB
  to fret ◊ *Ne te tourmente pas, ça*
  s'arrangera. Don't fret about it, it'll be
  all right.

le **tournant** NOUN
  1 bend ◊ *Il y a beaucoup de*
  tournants dangereux sur cette route.
  There are a lot of dangerous bends
  on this road.
  2 turning point ◊ *Ça a été un*
  tournant dans sa vie. It was a turning
  point in his life.

la **tournée** NOUN
  1 round ◊ *Le facteur commence sa*
  tournée à sept heures du matin. The
  postman starts his round at 7 o'clock
  in the morning. ◊ *Allez, qu'est-ce que*
  vous voulez boire? C'est ma tournée.
  Right, what are you drinking? It's my
  round.
  2 tour ◊ *Il est en tournée aux États-*
  Unis. He's on tour in the United
  States.

tourner VERB
  1 to turn ◊ *Tournez à droite au*
  prochain feu. Turn right at the lights.
  ◊ *Tourne-toi un peu plus vers moi, et*
  souris! Turn towards me a bit more,
  and smile!
  2 to go sour ◊ *Le lait a tourné.* The
  milk's gone sour.
  ♦ **mal tourner** to go wrong ◊ *Ça a mal*
  tourné. It all went wrong.
  ♦ **tourner le dos à quelqu'un** to have
  one's back to somebody
  ♦ **tourner un film** to make a film

le **tournesol** NOUN
  sunflower

le **tournevis** NOUN
  screwdriver

le **tournoi** NOUN
  tournament

la **tourte** NOUN
  pie ◊ *une tourte aux poireaux* a leek
  pie

tous ADJECTIVE, PRONOUN *see* **tout**

la **Toussaint** NOUN
  All Saints' Day

tousser VERB
  to cough

tout ADJECTIVE, ADVERB, PRONOUN (MASC PL
  tous, FEM PL **toutes**)
  1 all ◊ *tout le lait* all the milk ◊ *toute*
  la nuit all night ◊ *tous les livres* all
  the books ◊ *toutes les filles* all the
  girls ◊ *toute la journée* all day ◊ *tout*
  le temps all the time ◊ *C'est tout.*
  That's all. ◊ *Je les connais tous.* I
  know them all. ◊ *Nous y sommes*
  toutes allées. We all went. ◊ *Ça fait*
  combien en tout? How much is that
  all together?
  ♦ **Il est tout seul.** He's all alone.
  ♦ **pas du tout** not at all
  ♦ **tout de même** all the same
  2 every ◊ *tous les jours* every day
  ◊ *tous les deux jours* every two days
  ♦ **tout le monde** everybody
  ♦ **tous les deux** both ◊ *Nous y sommes*
  allés tous les deux. We both went.
  ♦ **tous les trois** all three ◊ *Je les ai*
  invités tous les trois. I invited all
  three of them.
  3 everything ◊ *Il a tout organisé.*
  He organized everything.
  4 very ◊ *Elle habite tout près.* She
  lives very close.
  ♦ **tout en haut** right at the top
  ♦ **tout droit** straight ahead
  ♦ **tout d'abord** first of all

T

☞

◆**tout à coup** suddenly

◆**tout à fait** absolutely

◆**tout à l'heure (1)** just now ◊ *Je l'ai vu tout à l'heure.* I saw him just now.

◆**tout à l'heure (2)** in a moment ◊ *Je finirai ça tout à l'heure.* I'll finish it in a moment.

◆**À tout à l'heure!** See you later!

◆**tout de suite** straight away

◆**Il a fait son travail tout en chantant.** He sang as he worked.

toutefois ADVERB
however

toutes ADJECTIVE, PRONOUN *see* **tout**

la **toux** NOUN
cough

le/la **toxicomane** NOUN
drug addict

la **toxicomanie** NOUN
drug addiction

le **TP** NOUN (= *travaux pratiques*)
practical class ◊ *J'ai un TP de biologie à deux heures.* I've got a biology practical at two o'clock.

le **trac** NOUN

◆**avoir le trac** to be feeling nervous

tracasser VERB
to worry ◊ *La santé de mon père me tracasse.* My dad's health worries me.

◆**se tracasser** to worry ◊ *Arrête de te tracasser pour rien!* Stop worrying about nothing!

la **trace** NOUN
[1] trace ◊ *Le voleur n'a pas laissé de traces.* The thief left no traces.
[2] mark ◊ *des traces de doigts* finger marks

◆**des traces de pas** footprints

tracer VERB
to draw ◊ *tracer un trait* to draw a line

le **tracteur** NOUN
tractor

la **tradition** NOUN
tradition

traditionnel ADJECTIVE (FEM SING **traditionnelle**)
traditional

le **traducteur** NOUN
translator

la **traduction** NOUN
translation

la **traductrice** NOUN
translator

traduire VERB
to translate

le **trafic** NOUN
traffic

◆**le trafic de drogue** drug trafficking

le **trafiquant** NOUN

◆**un trafiquant de drogue** a drug trafficker

tragique ADJECTIVE
tragic

trahir VERB
to betray

la **trahison** NOUN
betrayal

le **train** NOUN
train

◆**un train électrique** a train set

◆**Il est en train de manger.** He's eating.

le **traîneau** NOUN (PL les **traîneaux**)
sledge

traîner VERB
[1] to wander around ◊ *J'ai vu des jeunes qui traînaient en ville.* I saw some young people wandering around town.
[2] to hang about ◊ *Dépêche-toi, ne traîne pas!* Hurry up, don't hang about!
[3] to drag on ◊ *La réunion a traîné jusqu'à midi.* The meeting dragged on till 12 o'clock.

◆**traîner des pieds** to drag one's feet

◆**laisser traîner qch** to leave sth lying around ◊ *Ne laisse pas traîner tes affaires.* Don't leave your things lying around.

le **train-train** NOUN
humdrum routine

traire VERB
to milk

le **trait** NOUN
[1] line ◊ *Tracez un trait.* Draw a line.
[2] feature ◊ *Elle a les traits fins.* She has delicate features.

◆**boire quelque chose d'un trait** to drink something down in one gulp

◆**un trait d'union** a hyphen

le **traitement** NOUN
treatment

◆**le traitement de texte** word processing

traiter VERB
to treat ◊ *Elle le traite comme un chien.* She treats him like a dog.

◆**Il m'a traité d'imbécile.** He called me an idiot.

◆**traiter de** to be about ◊ *Cet article traite des sans-abri.* This article is about the homeless.

le **traiteur** NOUN
caterer

le **trajet** NOUN

① journey ◊ *Il n'a pas arrêté de parler pendant tout le trajet.* He talked for the whole journey. ◊ *J'ai une heure de trajet pour aller au travail.* My journey to work takes an hour.
② route ◊ *C'est le trajet le plus court.* It's the shortest route.

le **tramway** NOUN
tram

tranchant ADJECTIVE
sharp (*knife*)

la **tranche** NOUN
slice

tranquille ADJECTIVE
quiet ◊ *Cette rue est très tranquille.* This is a very quiet street.
♦ **Sois tranquille, il ne va rien lui arriver.** Don't worry, nothing will happen to him.
♦ **Tiens-toi tranquille!** Be quiet!
♦ **Laisse-moi tranquille.** Leave me alone.
♦ **Laisse ça tranquille.** Leave it alone.

tranquillement ADVERB
quietly ◊ *Nous étions tranquillement installés dans le salon.* We were just sitting quietly in the living room.
♦ **Je peux travailler tranquillement cinq minutes?** Can I have five minutes to myself to work in peace?

la **tranquillité** NOUN
peace and quiet

transférer VERB
to transfer

transformer VERB
① to transform ◊ *Son séjour en France l'a transformé.* His stay in France has transformed him.
② to convert ◊ *Ils ont transformé la grange en garage.* They've converted the barn into a garage.
♦ **se transformer en** to turn into ◊ *La chenille se transforme en papillon.* The caterpillar turns into a butterfly.

la **transfusion** NOUN
♦ **une transfusion sanguine** a blood transfusion

transiger VERB
to compromise

transmettre VERB
♦ **transmettre quelque chose à quelqu'un** to pass something on to somebody

transpercer VERB
to go through ◊ *La pluie a transpercé mes vêtements.* The rain went through my clothes.

la **transpiration** NOUN
perspiration

transpirer VERB
to perspire

le **transport** NOUN
transport
♦ **les transports en commun** public transport

transporter VERB
① to carry ◊ *Le train transportait des marchandises.* The train was carrying freight.
② to move ◊ *Je ne sais pas comment je vais transporter mes affaires.* I don't know how I'm going to move my stuff.

traumatiser VERB
to traumatize

le **travail** NOUN (PL les **travaux**)
① work ◊ *J'ai beaucoup de travail.* I've got a lot of work.
② job ◊ *Il a un travail intéressant.* He's got an interesting job.
♦ **Il est sans travail depuis un an.** He has been out of work for a year.
♦ **le travail au noir** moonlighting

travailler VERB
to work

travailleur ADJECTIVE (FEM SING **travailleuse**)
see also **travailleur** NOUN
hard-working

le **travailleur** NOUN
see also **travailleur** ADJECTIVE
worker

la **travailleuse** NOUN
worker

les **travaillistes** MASC NOUN
the Labour Party SING

les **travaux** MASC NOUN
① work SING ◊ *des travaux de construction* building work
② roadworks ◊ *Il y a beaucoup de bruit à cause des travaux dans la rue.* There's a lot of noise from the roadworks.
♦ **être en travaux** to be undergoing alterations
♦ **les travaux dirigés** supervised practical work
♦ **les travaux manuels** handicrafts
♦ **les travaux ménagers** housework
♦ **les travaux pratiques** practical work

le **travers** NOUN
♦ **en travers de** across ◊ *Il y avait un arbre en travers de la route.* There was a tree lying across the road.
♦ **de travers** crooked ◊ *Son chapeau était de travers.* His hat was crooked.
♦ **comprendre de travers** to misunderstand ◊ *Elle comprend*

T

toujours tout de travers. She always gets the wrong idea.

♦ **J'ai avalé de travers.** Something went down the wrong way.

♦ **à travers** through ◊ *Cette vitre est tellement sale qu'on ne voit rien à travers.* This window is so dirty you can't see anything through it.

la **traversée** NOUN
  crossing

traverser VERB
  1 to cross ◊ *Traversez la rue.* Cross the street.
  2 to go through ◊ *Nous avons traversé la France pour aller en Espagne.* We went through France on the way to Spain. ◊ *La pluie a traversé mon manteau.* The rain went through my coat.

le **traversin** NOUN
  bolster

trébucher VERB
  to trip up

le **trèfle** NOUN
  1 clover
  2 clubs (*at cards*) ◊ *le roi de trèfle* the king of clubs

treize NUMBER
  thirteen ◊ *Il a treize ans.* He's thirteen. ◊ *à treize heures* at 1 p.m.
  ♦ **le treize février** the thirteenth of February

treizième ADJECTIVE
  thirteenth

le **tréma** NOUN
  diaeresis

le **tremblement de terre** NOUN
  earthquake

trembler VERB
  to shake ◊ *trembler de peur* to shake with fear
  ♦ **trembler de froid** to shiver

trempé ADJECTIVE
  soaking wet
  ♦ **trempé jusqu'aux os** soaked to the skin

tremper VERB
  to soak
  ♦ **tremper sa main dans l'eau** to dip one's hand in the water

le **tremplin** NOUN
  springboard

la **trentaine** NOUN
  about thirty ◊ *une trentaine de personnes* about thirty people
  ♦ **Il a la trentaine.** He's in his thirties.

trente NUMBER
  thirty ◊ *Elle a trente ans.* She's thirty.

♦ **le trente janvier** the thirtieth of January
♦ **trente et un** thirty-one
♦ **trente-deux** thirty-two

trentième ADJECTIVE
  thirtieth

très ADVERB
  very

le **trésor** NOUN
  treasure

la **tresse** NOUN
  plait

le **triangle** NOUN
  triangle

la **tribu** NOUN
  tribe

le **tribunal** NOUN (PL les **tribunaux**)
  court

tricher VERB
  to cheat

tricolore ADJECTIVE
  three-coloured
  ♦ **le drapeau tricolore** the French tricolour

> **ⓘ** *le drapeau tricolore* is the French flag which is blue, white and red.

le **tricot** NOUN
  1 knitting ◊ *On fait du tricot à l'école.* We do knitting at school.
  2 sweater ◊ *Mets un tricot, il fait froid.* Put a sweater on, it's cold.

tricoter VERB
  to knit

trier VERB
  to sort out ◊ *Je vais trier mes papiers avant de partir en vacances.* I'm going to sort out my papers before I go on holiday.

le **trimestre** NOUN
  term

trinquer VERB
  to clink glasses

le **triomphe** NOUN
  triumph

triompher VERB
  to triumph

les **tripes** FEM NOUN
  tripe

le **triple** NOUN
  ♦ **Ça m'a coûté le triple.** It cost me three times as much.
  ♦ **Il gagne le triple de mon salaire.** He earns three times my salary.

tripler VERB
  to treble

les **triplés** MASC NOUN

triplets

triste ADJECTIVE
<u>sad</u>

la **tristesse** NOUN
<u>sadness</u>

le **trognon** NOUN
<u>core</u> ◊ *un trognon de pomme* an apple core

trois NUMBER
<u>three</u> ◊ *à trois heures du matin* at three in the morning ◊ *Elle a trois ans.* She's three. ◊ *trois fois* three times
♦ **le trois février** the third of February

troisième ADJECTIVE
> see also **troisième** NOUN

<u>third</u> ◊ *au troisième étage* on the third floor

la **troisième** NOUN
> see also **troisième** ADJECTIVE

<u>year 10</u>

> ⓘ *In French secondary schools, years are counted from the* **sixième** *(youngest) to* **première** *and* **terminale** *(oldest).*

◊ *Mon frère est en troisième.* My brother's in year 10.

les **trois-quarts** MASC NOUN
<u>three-quarters</u> ◊ *les trois-quarts de la classe* three-quarters of the class

le **trombone** NOUN
1 <u>trombone</u> ◊ *Il joue du trombone.* He plays the trombone.
2 <u>paper clip</u>

la **trompe** NOUN
<u>trunk</u> ◊ *la trompe d'un éléphant* an elephant's trunk

tromper VERB
<u>to deceive</u>
♦ **se tromper** to make a mistake ◊ *Tout le monde peut se tromper.* Anyone can make a mistake.
♦ **se tromper de jour** to get the wrong day
♦ **Vous vous êtes trompé de numéro.** You've got the wrong number.

la **trompette** NOUN
<u>trumpet</u> ◊ *Il joue de la trompette.* He plays the trumpet.
♦ **Il a le nez en trompette.** He's got a turned-up nose.

le **tronc** NOUN
<u>trunk</u> ◊ *un tronc d'arbre* a tree trunk

trop ADVERB
1 <u>too</u> ◊ *Il conduit trop vite.* He drives too fast.

2 <u>too much</u> ◊ *J'ai trop mangé.* I've eaten too much.
♦ **trop de (1)** too much ◊ *J'ai acheté trop de pain.* I bought too much bread. ◊ *trois euros de trop* 3 euros too much
♦ **trop de (2)** too many ◊ *J'ai apporté trop de vêtements.* I've brought too many clothes.
♦ **trois personnes de trop** 3 people too many

le **tropique** NOUN
<u>tropic</u>

le **trottoir** NOUN
<u>pavement</u>

le **trou** NOUN
<u>hole</u>
♦ **J'ai eu un trou de mémoire.** My mind went blank.

trouble ADJECTIVE, ADVERB
<u>cloudy</u> ◊ *L'eau est trouble.* The water's cloudy.
♦ **Sans mes lunettes je vois trouble.** Without my glasses I can't see properly.

les **troubles** MASC NOUN
♦ **une période de troubles politiques** a period of political instability

trouer VERB
<u>to make a hole in</u> ◊ *Il a troué la moquette avec sa cigarette.* He made a hole in the carpet with his cigarette.

la **trouille** NOUN
♦ **avoir la trouille** (*informal*) to be scared to death

la **troupe** NOUN
<u>troop</u>
♦ **une troupe de théâtre** a theatre company

le **troupeau** NOUN (PL les **troupeaux**)
♦ **un troupeau de moutons** a flock of sheep
♦ **un troupeau de vaches** a herd of cows

la **trousse** NOUN
<u>pencil case</u>
♦ **une trousse de secours** a first-aid kit
♦ **une trousse de toilette** a toilet bag

trouver VERB
1 <u>to find</u> ◊ *Je ne trouve pas mes lunettes.* I can't find my glasses.
2 <u>to think</u> ◊ *Je trouve que c'est bête.* I think it's stupid.
♦ **se trouver** to be ◊ *Où se trouve la poste?* Where is the post office? ◊ *Nice se trouve dans le sud de la France.* Nice is in the South of France.
♦ **se trouver mal** to pass out

T

le **truc** NOUN (*informal*)
⊡ thing ◊ *un truc en plastique* a thing made of plastic ◊ *J'ai plein de trucs à faire ce week-end.* I've got loads of things to do this weekend.
② trick ◊ *Je vais te montrer un truc qui réussit à tous les coups.* I'll show you a trick that never fails.

la **truite** NOUN
trout

le **T-shirt** NOUN
T-shirt

TSVP ABBREVIATION (= *tournez s'il vous plaît*)
PTO (= please turn over)

tu PRONOUN
you ◊ *Est-ce que tu as un animal familier?* Have you got a pet?

le **tuba** NOUN
⊡ tuba ◊ *Je joue du tuba.* I play the tuba.
② snorkel

le **tube** NOUN
⊡ tube ◊ *un tube de dentifrice* a tube of toothpaste
◆ **un tube de rouge à lèvres** a lipstick
② hit ◊ *Ça va être le tube de l'été.* It's going to be this summer's hit.

tuer VERB
to kill
◆ **se tuer** to get killed ◊ *Il s'est tué dans un accident de voiture.* He got killed in a car accident.

tue-tête
◆ **à tue-tête** ADVERB
at the top of one's voice ◊ *crier à tue-tête* to shout at the top of one's voice ◊ *Il chantait à tue-tête.* He was singing at the top of his voice.

la **tuile** NOUN
tile ◊ *un toit en tuiles* a tiled roof

la **tunique** NOUN
tunic

la **Tunisie** NOUN
Tunisia

tunisien ADJECTIVE (FEM SING **tunisienne**)
Tunisian

le **tunnel** NOUN
tunnel
◆ **le tunnel sous la Manche** the Channel Tunnel

turbulent ADJECTIVE
boisterous

turc ADJECTIVE, NOUN (FEM SING **turque**)
Turkish ◊ *Il parle turc.* He speaks Turkish.
◆ **un Turc** a Turk (*man*)
◆ **une Turque** a Turk (*woman*)

la **Turquie** NOUN
Turkey

tutoyer VERB
◆ **tutoyer quelqu'un** to address somebody as "tu"

ⓘ **tutoyer quelqu'un** means to use **tu** when speaking to someone, rather than **vous**. Use **tu** only when talking to one person and when that person is someone of your own age or younger or whom you know well; use **vous** to everyone else. If in doubt use **vous**.

◆ **On se tutoie?** Shall we use "tu" to each other?

le **tuyau** NOUN (PL les **tuyaux**)
⊡ pipe
◆ **un tuyau d'arrosage** a hosepipe
② tip ◊ *Il m'a donné un bon tuyau.* (*informal*) He gave me a handy tip.

la **TVA** NOUN (= *taxe sur la valeur ajoutée*)
VAT

le **tympan** NOUN
eardrum

le **type** NOUN (*informal*)
guy ◊ *C'est un type formidable.* He's a great guy.

typique ADJECTIVE
typical

le **tyran** NOUN
tyrant ◊ *C'est un vrai tyran.* He's a real tyrant.

le/la **tzigane** NOUN
gipsy

U

l' **UE** FEM NOUN (= *Union européenne*)
the EU (= European Union)

un ARTICLE, PRONOUN, ADJECTIVE

1 a ◊ *un garçon* a boy
an ◊ *un œuf* an egg

2 one ◊ *l'un des meilleurs* one of
the best ◊ *un citron et deux oranges*
one lemon and two oranges
◊ *Combien de timbres? – Un.* How
many stamps? – One. ◊ *Elle a un an.*
She's one year old.

♦ **l'un ..., l'autre ...** one ..., the other ...
◊ *L'un est grand, l'autre est petit.* One
is tall, the other is short.

♦ **les uns ..., les autres ...** some ...,
others ... ◊ *Les uns marchaient, les
autres couraient.* Some were walking,
others were running.

♦ **l'un ou l'autre** either of them ◊ *Prends
l'un ou l'autre, ça m'est égal.* Take
either of them, I don't mind.

♦ **un par un** one by one ◊ *Ils entraient
un par un.* They went in one by one.

unanime ADJECTIVE
unanimous

l' **unanimité** FEM NOUN
♦ **à l'unanimité** unanimously

une ARTICLE, PRONOUN, ADJECTIVE

1 a ◊ *une fille* a girl
an ◊ *une pomme* an apple

2 one ◊ *une pomme et deux
bananes* one apple and two bananas
◊ *Combien de cartes postales? – Une.*
How many postcards? – One. ◊ *à une
heure du matin* at one in the
morning ◊ *l'une des meilleures* one
of the best

♦ **l'une ..., l'autre ...** one ..., the other ...
◊ *L'une est grande, l'autre est petite.*
One is tall, the other is short.

♦ **les unes..., les autres...** some ...,
others ... ◊ *Les unes marchaient, les
autres couraient.* Some were walking,
others were running.

♦ **l'une ou l'autre** either of them
◊ *Prends l'une ou l'autre, ça m'est
égal.* Take either of them, I don't
mind.

♦ **une par une** one by one ◊ *Elles
entraient une par une.* They went in
one by one.

uni ADJECTIVE

1 plain ◊ *un tissu uni* a plain fabric
2 close-knit ◊ *une famille unie* a
close-knit family

l' **uniforme** MASC NOUN
uniform

l' **union** FEM NOUN
union

♦ **l'Union européenne** the European
Union

♦ **l'ex-Union soviétique** the former
Soviet Union

unique ADJECTIVE
unique ◊ *Tout individu a des
empreintes uniques.* Everyone's
fingerprints are unique. ◊ *C'est une
occasion unique.* It's a unique
opportunity.

♦ **Il est fils unique.** He's an only child.

♦ **Elle est fille unique.** She's an only
child.

uniquement ADVERB
only

l' **unité** FEM NOUN

1 unity ◊ *l'unité européenne*
European unity
2 unit ◊ *une unité de mesure* a unit
of measurement

l' **univers** MASC NOUN
universe

universitaire ADJECTIVE
university ◊ *un diplôme universitaire*
a university degree

♦ **faire des études universitaires** to
study at university

l' **université** FEM NOUN
university ◊ *aller à l'université* to go
to university

l' **urgence** FEM NOUN
♦ **C'est une urgence.** It's urgent.

♦ **Il n'y a pas urgence.** It's not urgent.

♦ **le service des urgences** the accident
and emergency department

♦ **Il a été transporté d'urgence à
l'hôpital.** He was rushed to hospital.

♦ **Téléphonez d'urgence.** Phone as soon
as possible.

urgent ADJECTIVE
urgent

l' **urine** FEM NOUN
urine

les **USA** MASC NOUN
USA

♦ **aux USA (1)** in the USA
♦ **aux USA (2)** to the USA

l' **usage** MASC NOUN
use ◊ *à usage interne* for internal use
◊ *à usage externe* for external use
only

☞

◆**hors d'usage** out of action ◊ *Cet appareil est hors d'usage.* That machine's out of action.

usagé ADJECTIVE
1 <u>old</u> ◊ *un manteau usagé* an old coat
2 <u>used</u> ◊ *une seringue usagée* a used syringe

l'**usager** MASC NOUN
<u>user</u> ◊ *les usagers de la route* road users

usé ADJECTIVE
<u>worn</u> ◊ *Mon jean est un peu usé.* My jeans are a bit worn.

s'**user** VERB
<u>to wear out</u> ◊ *Mes baskets se sont usées en quinze jours.* My trainers wore out in two weeks.

l'**usine** FEM NOUN
<u>factory</u> ◊ *une usine de sardines* a sardine factory

l'**ustensile** MASC NOUN
◆**un ustensile de cuisine** a kitchen utensil

usuel ADJECTIVE (FEM SING **usuelle**)
<u>everyday</u> ◊ *la langue usuelle* everyday language

utile ADJECTIVE
<u>useful</u>

l'**utilisation** FEM NOUN
<u>use</u> ◊ *L'utilisation des calculatrices est interdite.* It is forbidden to use calculators.

utiliser VERB
<u>to use</u>

l'**utilité** FEM NOUN
<u>use</u> ◊ *Cet objet n'est pas d'une grande utilité.* This object isn't much use.

V

va VERB *see* **aller**

les **vacances** FEM NOUN
holidays ◊ *aller en vacances* to go on
holiday ◊ *être en vacances* to be on
holiday
 ◆ **les vacances de Noël** the Christmas
holidays
 ◆ **les vacances de Pâques** the Easter
holidays
 ◆ **les grandes vacances** the summer
holidays

le **vacancier** NOUN
holiday-maker

la **vacancière** NOUN
holiday-maker

le **vacarme** NOUN
racket ◊ *Qu'est-ce que c'est que ce
vacarme?* What's all this racket?

le **vaccin** NOUN
vaccination

la **vaccination** NOUN
vaccination ◊ *La vaccination est
obligatoire.* Vaccination is
compulsory.

vacciner VERB
to vaccinate ◊ *se faire vacciner
contre la rubéole* to be vaccinated
against German measles

la **vache** NOUN
| *see also* **vache** ADJECTIVE |
cow

vache ADJECTIVE (*informal*)
| *see also* **vache** NOUN |
mean ◊ *C'est vraiment vache, ce qu'il
a dit.* What he said was really mean.
◊ *Il est vache.* He's a mean sod.

vachement ADVERB (*informal*)
really ◊ *Viens te baigner, l'eau est
vachement chaude.* Come in the
water, it's really warm.

le **vagabond** NOUN
tramp

le **vagin** NOUN
vagina

la **vague** NOUN
| *see also* **vague** ADJECTIVE |
wave (*in sea*)
 ◆ **une vague de chaleur** a heat wave

vague ADJECTIVE
| *see also* **vague** NOUN |
vague ◊ *J'ai un vague souvenir de
lui.* I vaguely remember him.

vain ADJECTIVE
 ◆ **en vain** in vain

vaincre VERB
1 to defeat ◊ *L'armée a été vaincue.*
The army was defeated.
2 to overcome ◊ *Il a réussi à
vaincre sa timidité.* He managed to
overcome his shyness.

le **vainqueur** NOUN
winner

vais VERB *see* **aller**
 ◆ **Je vais écrire à mes cousins.** I'm
going to write to my cousins.

le **vaisseau** NOUN (PL les **vaisseaux**)
 ◆ **un vaisseau spatial** a spaceship
 ◆ **un vaisseau sanguin** a blood vessel

la **vaisselle** NOUN
1 washing-up ◊ *Je vais faire la
vaisselle.* I'll do the washing-up.
2 dishes ◊ *Tu peux ranger la
vaisselle s'il te plaît?* Can you put the
dishes away please?

valable ADJECTIVE
valid ◊ *Ce billet d'avion est valable
un an.* This plane ticket is valid for
one year.

le **valet** NOUN
jack (*in card games*) ◊ *le valet de
carreau* the jack of diamonds

la **valeur** NOUN
value ◊ *sans valeur* of no value
 ◆ **des objets de valeur** valuables ◊ *Ne
laissez pas d'objets de valeur dans
votre chambre.* Don't leave any
valuables in your room.

valider VERB
to stamp ◊ *Vous devez faire valider
votre billet avant votre départ.* You
must get your ticket stamped before
you leave.

la **valise** NOUN
suitcase
 ◆ **faire sa valise** to pack

la **vallée** NOUN
valley

valoir VERB
to be worth ◊ *Ça vaut combien?*
How much is it worth? ◊ *Cette voiture
vaut très cher.* This car's worth a lot
of money.
 ◆ **Ça vaut mieux.** That would be better.
◊ *Il vaut mieux ne rien dire.* It would
be better to say nothing.
 ◆ **valoir la peine** to be worth it ◊ *Ça
vaudrait la peine d'essayer.* It would
be worth a try.

le **vampire** NOUN

☞

vampire

le **vandalisme** NOUN
vandalism

la **vanille** NOUN
vanilla ◊ *une glace à la vanille* a vanilla ice cream

la **vanité** NOUN
vanity

vaniteux ADJECTIVE (FEM SING **vaniteuse**)
conceited

se **vanter** VERB
to boast

la **vapeur** NOUN
steam ◊ *des légumes cuits à la vapeur* steamed vegetables

la **varappe** NOUN
rock climbing ◊ *faire de la varappe* to go rock climbing

variable ADJECTIVE
changeable (*weather*)

la **varicelle** NOUN
chickenpox ◊ *Elle a la varicelle.* She's got chickenpox.

varié ADJECTIVE
varied ◊ *Son travail est très varié.* His job is very varied.

varier VERB
to vary
♦ *Le menu varie tous les jours.* The menu changes every day.

la **variété** NOUN
variety ◊ *Il n'y a pas beaucoup de variété.* There isn't much variety.
♦ *une émission de variétés* a television variety show

vas VERB *see* **aller**

le **vase** NOUN
see also **la vase**
vase

la **vase** NOUN
see also **le vase**
mud

vaste ADJECTIVE
vast

vaudrait, vaut VERB *see* **valoir**

le **vautour** NOUN
vulture

le **veau** NOUN (PL les **veaux**)
1 calf (*animal*)
2 veal (*meat*)

vécu VERB *see* **vivre**
♦ *Il a vécu à Paris pendant dix ans.* He lived in Paris for ten years.

la **vedette** NOUN
1 star ◊ *une vedette de cinéma* a film star
2 motor boat

♦ *une vedette de police* a police launch

végétal ADJECTIVE (MASC PL **végétaux**)
vegetable ◊ *l'huile végétale* vegetable oil

végétarien ADJECTIVE (FEM SING **végétarienne**)
vegetarian ◊ *Je suis végétarien.* I'm a vegetarian.

la **végétation** NOUN
vegetation

le **véhicule** NOUN
vehicle

la **veille** NOUN
the day before ◊ *la veille de son départ* the day before he left ◊ *la veille au soir* the previous evening
♦ *la veille de Noël* Christmas Eve
♦ *la veille du jour de l'An* New Year's Eve

veiller VERB
to stay up
♦ *veiller sur quelqu'un* to watch over somebody

veinard ADJECTIVE (*informal*)
♦ *Qu'est-ce qu'il est veinard!* He's such a lucky devil!

la **veine** NOUN
vein
♦ *avoir de la veine* (*informal*) to be lucky

le/la **véliplanchiste** NOUN
windsurfer

le **vélo** NOUN
bike ◊ *faire du vélo* to go cycling
♦ *un vélo tout-terrain* a mountain bike

le **vélomoteur** NOUN
moped

le **velours** NOUN
velvet ◊ *une robe en velours* a velvet dress
♦ *le velours côtelé* corduroy ◊ *un pantalon en velours côtelé* corduroy trousers

les **vendanges** FEM NOUN
grape harvest SING ◊ *On fait les vendanges en septembre.* The grape harvest is in September.

le **vendeur** NOUN
shop assistant

la **vendeuse** NOUN
shop assistant

vendre VERB
to sell
♦ *vendre quelque chose à quelqu'un* to sell somebody something ◊ *Il m'a vendu son vélo.* He sold me his bike.
♦ "*à vendre*" "for sale"

le **vendredi** NOUN

⓵ Friday ◊ *Aujourd'hui, nous
sommes vendredi.* It's Friday today.
⓶ on Friday ◊ *Il est venu vendredi.*
He came on Friday.
♦ **le vendredi** on Fridays ◊ *Je joue au
foot le vendredi.* I play football on
Fridays.
♦ **tous les vendredis** every Friday
♦ **vendredi dernier** last Friday
♦ **vendredi prochain** next Friday
♦ **le Vendredi saint** Good Friday

vénéneux ADJECTIVE (FEM SING **vénéneuse**)
poisonous (*plant*) ◊ *un champignon
vénéneux* a poisonous mushroom

la **vengeance** NOUN
revenge

se **venger** VERB
to get revenge

venimeux ADJECTIVE (FEM SING **venimeuse**)
poisonous (*animal*) ◊ *un serpent
venimeux* a poisonous snake

le **venin** NOUN
poison

venir VERB
to come ◊ *Il viendra demain.* He'll
come tomorrow. ◊ *Il est venu nous
voir.* He came to see us.
♦ **venir de** to have just ◊ *Je viens de le
voir.* I've just seen him. ◊ *Je viens de
lui téléphoner.* I've just phoned him.
♦ **faire venir quelqu'un** to call
somebody out ◊ *faire venir le
médecin* to call the doctor out

le **vent** NOUN
wind ◊ *Il y a du vent.* It's windy.

la **vente** NOUN
sale
♦ **en vente** on sale ◊ *Ce modèle est en
vente dans les grands magasins.* This
model is on sale in the department
stores.
♦ **la vente par téléphone** telesales
♦ **une vente aux enchères** an auction

le **ventilateur** NOUN
fan (*for cooling*)

le **ventre** NOUN
stomach ◊ *avoir mal au ventre* to
have stomachache

venu VERB *see* **venir**

le **ver** NOUN
worm
♦ **un ver de terre** an earthworm

le **verbe** NOUN
verb

le **verdict** NOUN
verdict

le **verger** NOUN
orchard

verglacé ADJECTIVE
icy ◊ *La route était verglacée.* The
road was icy.

le **verglas** NOUN
black ice

véridique ADJECTIVE
truthful

la **vérification** NOUN
check ◊ *une vérification d'identité* an
identity check

vérifier VERB
to check

véritable ADJECTIVE
real ◊ *C'était un véritable cauchemar.*
It was a real nightmare.
♦ **en cuir véritable** made of real leather

la **vérité** NOUN
truth ◊ *dire la vérité* to tell the truth

verni ADJECTIVE
varnished
♦ **des chaussures vernies** patent leather
shoes

vernir VERB
to varnish

le **vernis** NOUN
varnish ◊ *le vernis à ongles* nail
varnish

verra, verrai, verras VERB *see* **voir**
♦ **on verra ...** we'll see ...

le **verre** NOUN
⓵ glass ◊ *une table en verre* a glass
table ◊ *un verre d'eau* a glass of
water
♦ **boire un verre** to have a drink
⓶ lens (*of spectacles*) ◊ *des verres de
contact* contact lenses

verrez, verrons, verront VERB *see* **voir**

le **verrou** NOUN
bolt (*on door*)

verrouiller VERB
to bolt ◊ *N'oublie pas de verrouiller
la porte du garage.* Don't forget to
bolt the garage door.

la **verrue** NOUN
wart

le **vers** NOUN
~~see also **vers** PREPOSITION~~
line (*of poetry*) ◊ *au troisième vers* in
the third line

vers PREPOSITION
~~see also **vers** NOUN~~
⓵ towards ◊ *Il allait vers la gare.* He
was going towards the station.
⓶ at about ◊ *Il est rentré chez lui
vers cinq heures.* He went home at
about 5 o'clock.

verse
♦ **à verse** ADVERB

V

◊ *Il pleut à verse.* It's pouring with rain.

le **Verseau** NOUN
Aquarius ◊ *Georges est Verseau.* Georges is Aquarius.

le **versement** NOUN
instalment ◊ *en cinq versements* in 5 instalments

verser VERB
to pour ◊ *Est-ce que tu peux me verser un verre d'eau?* Could you pour me a glass of water?

la **version** NOUN
1 version
2 translation (*from the foreign language*)
♦ **un film en version originale** a film in the original language

le **verso** NOUN
back (*of sheet of paper*)
♦ **voir au verso** see overleaf

vert ADJECTIVE
green

la **vertèbre** NOUN
vertebra

vertical ADJECTIVE (MASC PL **verticaux**)
vertical

le **vertige** NOUN
vertigo ◊ *avoir le vertige* to have vertigo

la **verveine** NOUN
verbena tea

la **vessie** NOUN
bladder

la **veste** NOUN
jacket

le **vestiaire** NOUN
1 cloakroom (*in theatre, museum*)
2 changing room (*at sports ground*)

le **vestibule** NOUN
hall

le **vêtement** NOUN
garment
♦ **les vêtements** clothes

le/la **vétérinaire** NOUN
vet ◊ *Elle est vétérinaire.* She's a vet.

le **veuf** NOUN
widower ◊ *Il est veuf.* He's a widower.

veuille, veuillez, veuillons, veulent, veut VERB *see* **vouloir**
♦ **Veuillez fermer la porte en sortant.** Please shut the door when you go out.

la **veuve** NOUN
widow ◊ *Elle est veuve.* She's a widow.

veux VERB *see* **vouloir**

vexer VERB
♦ **vexer quelqu'un** to hurt somebody's feelings
♦ **se vexer** to be offended

la **viande** NOUN
meat
♦ **la viande hachée** mince

vibrer VERB
to vibrate

le **vice** NOUN
vice

vicieux ADJECTIVE (FEM SING **vicieuse**)
lecherous ◊ *Il est un peu vicieux.* He's a bit of a lecher.

la **victime** NOUN
victim

la **victoire** NOUN
victory

vide ADJECTIVE
see also **vide** NOUN
empty

le **vide** NOUN
see also **vide** ADJECTIVE
vacuum ◊ *emballé sous vide* vacuum-packed
♦ **avoir peur du vide** to be afraid of heights

la **vidéo** NOUN
see also **vidéo** ADJECTIVE
video

vidéo ADJECTIVE (MASC, FEM, PL)
see also **vidéo** NOUN
video ◊ *une cassette vidéo* a video cassette ◊ *un jeu vidéo* a video game ◊ *une caméra vidéo* a video camera

le **vidéoclip** NOUN
music video

le **vidéoclub** NOUN
video shop

vider VERB
to empty

la **vie** NOUN
life
♦ **être en vie** to be alive

vieil ADJECTIVE
*vieil is used with a masculine singular noun in place of **vieux** when the noun begins with a vowel sound.*
old ◊ *un vieil arbre* an old tree ◊ *un vieil homme* an old man

le **vieillard** NOUN
old man

vieille ADJECTIVE (MASC SING **vieux**)
see also **vieille** NOUN
old ◊ *une vieille dame* an old lady
♦ **une vieille fille** an old maid

la **vieille** NOUN
see also **vieille** ADJECTIVE

old woman

♦ **Eh bien, ma vieille ...** (*informal*) Well, my dear ...

la **vieillesse** NOUN
old age

vieillir VERB
to age ◊ *Il a beaucoup vieilli depuis la dernière fois que je l'ai vu.* He's aged a lot since I last saw him.

viendrai, vienne, viens VERB *see* **venir**
♦ **Je viendrai dès que possible.** I'll come as soon as possible.
♦ **Je voudrais que tu viennes.** I'd like you to come.
♦ **Viens ici!** Come here!

la **Vierge** NOUN
> *see also* **vierge** ADJECTIVE

Virgo ◊ *Pascal est Vierge.* Pascal is Virgo.
♦ **la Vierge** the Virgin Mary

vierge ADJECTIVE
> *see also* **Vierge** NOUN

[1] virgin ◊ *Il est vierge.* He's a virgin.
[2] blank ◊ *une cassette vierge* a blank cassette

le **Viêt-Nam** NOUN
Vietnam

vietnamien ADJECTIVE, NOUN (FEM SING **vietnamienne**)
Vietnamese
♦ **un Vietnamien** a Vietnamese (*man*)
♦ **une Vietnamienne** a Vietnamese (*woman*)
♦ **les Vietnamiens** the Vietnamese

vieux ADJECTIVE (FEM SING **vieille**)
> *see also* **vieux** NOUN

old ◊ *Il fait plus vieux que son âge.* He looks older than he is.
♦ **un vieux garçon** a bachelor

le **vieux** NOUN
> *see also* **vieux** ADJECTIVE

old man ◊ *Eh bien, mon vieux ...* (*informal*) Well, my old mate ...
♦ **les vieux** old people

vieux jeu ADJECTIVE (MASC, FEM, PL)
old-fashioned ◊ *Il est un peu vieux jeu.* He's a bit old-fashioned.

vif ADJECTIVE (FEM SING **vive**)
[1] sharp (*mentally*) ◊ *Il est très vif.* He's very sharp.
♦ **avoir l'esprit vif** to be quick-witted
[2] crisp ◊ *L'air est plus vif à la campagne qu'en ville.* The air is crisper in the country than in the town.
[3] bright (*colour*) ◊ *un bleu vif* a bright blue

la **vigne** NOUN
vine

♦ **des champs de vigne** vineyards

le **vigneron** NOUN
wine grower

la **vignette** NOUN
tax disc

le **vignoble** NOUN
vineyard

vilain ADJECTIVE
[1] naughty ◊ *C'est très vilain de dire des mensonges.* It's very naughty to tell lies.
[2] ugly ◊ *Il n'est pas vilain.* He's not bad-looking.

la **villa** NOUN
villa ◊ *une villa en multipropriété* a time-share villa

le **village** NOUN
village

le **villageois** NOUN
villager

la **villageoise** NOUN
villager

la **ville** NOUN
town ◊ *Je vais en ville.* I'm going into town.
♦ **une grande ville** a city

le **vin** NOUN
wine ◊ *le vin blanc* white wine ◊ *le vin rouge* red wine ◊ *le vin de pays* the local wine ◊ *le vin ordinaire* table wine

le **vinaigre** NOUN
vinegar

la **vinaigrette** NOUN
French dressing

vingt NUMBER
twenty ◊ *Elle a vingt ans.* She's twenty. ◊ *à vingt heures* at 8 p.m.
♦ **le vingt février** the twentieth of February
♦ **vingt et un** twenty-one
♦ **vingt-deux** twenty-two

la **vingtaine** NOUN
about twenty ◊ *une vingtaine de personnes* about twenty people
♦ **Il a une vingtaine d'années.** He's about twenty.

vingtième ADJECTIVE
twentieth

le **viol** NOUN
rape

violemment ADVERB
violently

la **violence** NOUN
violence

violent ADJECTIVE
violent

violer VERB

☞

to rape

violet ADJECTIVE (FEM SING **violette**)
purple

la **violette** NOUN
violet (*flower*)

le **violon** NOUN
violin ◊ *Je joue du violon.* I play the violin.

le **violoncelle** NOUN
cello ◊ *Elle joue du violoncelle.* She plays the cello.

le/la **violoniste** NOUN
violinist

la **vipère** NOUN
viper

le **virage** NOUN
bend ◊ *une route pleine de virages dangereux* a road full of dangerous bends

la **virgule** NOUN
[1] comma
[2] decimal point ◊ *trois virgule cinq* three point five

le **virus** NOUN
virus

vis VERB *see* **vivre**
see also **vis** NOUN

◆**Je vis en Écosse.** I live in Scotland.

la **vis** NOUN
see also **vis** VERB
screw

le **visa** NOUN
visa

le **visage** NOUN
face ◊ *Elle a le visage rond.* She's got a round face.

vis-à-vis de PREPOSITION
with regard to ◊ *Ce n'est pas très juste vis-à-vis de lui.* It's not very fair to him.

viser VERB
to aim at ◊ *Il faut viser la cible.* You have to aim at the target.

la **visibilité** NOUN
visibility

visible ADJECTIVE
visible

la **visière** NOUN
peak (*of cap*)

la **visite** NOUN
visit
◆**rendre visite à quelqu'un** to visit somebody ◊ *Je vais rendre visite à mon grand-père.* I'm going to visit my grandfather.
◆**avoir de la visite** to have visitors ◊ *Nous avons de la visite aujourd'hui.* We've got visitors today.

◆**une visite guidée** a guided tour
◆**une visite médicale** a medical examination

visiter VERB
to visit

le **visiteur** NOUN
visitor

la **visiteuse** NOUN
visitor

le **vison** NOUN
mink (*fur*) ◊ *un manteau en vison* a mink coat

vit VERB *see* **vivre**
◆**Il vit chez ses parents.** He lives with his parents.

vital ADJECTIVE (MASC PL **vitaux**)
vital ◊ *C'est une question vitale.* It's of vital importance.

la **vitamine** NOUN
vitamin

vite ADVERB
[1] quick ◊ *Vite, ils arrivent!* Quick, they're coming! ◊ *Je peux aller dire au revoir à Claire? – Oui, mais fais vite!* Can I go and say goodbye to Claire? – Yes, but be quick! ◊ *Prenons la voiture, ça ira plus vite.* Let's take the car, it'll be quicker.
◆**Le temps passe vite.** Time flies.
[2] fast ◊ *Il roule trop vite.* He drives too fast.
[3] soon ◊ *Il va vite oublier.* He'll soon forget.
◆**Il a vite compris.** He understood immediately.

la **vitesse** NOUN
[1] speed ◊ *à toute vitesse* at top speed ◊ *Nous sommes rentrés à toute vitesse.* We rushed back home.
[2] gear ◊ *en première vitesse* in first gear

le **viticulteur** NOUN
wine grower ◊ *Mon oncle est viticulteur.* My uncle is a wine grower.

le **vitrail** NOUN (PL les **vitraux**)
stained-glass window

la **vitre** NOUN
window ◊ *Il a cassé une vitre.* He broke a window.

la **vitrine** NOUN
shop window

vivant ADJECTIVE
[1] living ◊ *les êtres vivants* living creatures ◊ *les expériences sur les animaux vivants* experiments on live animals
[2] lively ◊ *Elle est très vivante.* She's very lively.

vive ADJECTIVE (MASC SING **vif**)
> see also **vive** EXCLAMATION

[1] sharp (*mentally*) ◊ *Elle est très vive.* She's very sharp.
[2] bright (*colour*)
♦ **à vive allure** at a brisk pace
♦ **de vive voix** in person ◊ *Je te le dirai de vive voix.* I'll tell you about it when I see you.

vive EXCLAMATION
> see also **vive** ADJECTIVE

♦ **Vive le roi!** Long live the king!

vivement EXCLAMATION
♦ **Vivement les vacances!** Roll on the holidays!

vivre VERB
to live ◊ *J'aimerais vivre à l'étranger.* I'd like to live abroad. ◊ *Et ton grand-père? Il vit encore?* What about your grandfather? Is he still alive?

vlan EXCLAMATION
wham!

la **VO** NOUN
♦ **un film en VO** a film in the original language

le **vocabulaire** NOUN
vocabulary

la **vocation** NOUN
vocation

le **vœu** NOUN (PL les **vœux**)
wish ◊ *faire un vœu* to make a wish ◊ *Meilleurs vœux de bonne année!* Best wishes for the New Year!

la **vogue** NOUN
fashion ◊ *C'est très en vogue en ce moment.* It's very fashionable at the moment.

voici PREPOSITION
[1] this is ◊ *Voici mon frère et voilà ma sœur.* This is my brother and that's my sister.
[2] here is ◊ *Tu as perdu ton stylo? Tiens, en voici un autre.* Have you lost your pen? Here's another one.
♦ **Le voici!** Here he is! ◊ *Tu veux tes clés? Tiens, les voici!* You want your keys? Here you are!

la **voie** NOUN
lane ◊ *une route à trois voies* a 3-lane road
♦ **par voie buccale** orally ◊ *à prendre par voie buccale* to be taken orally
♦ **la voie ferrée** the railway track

voilà PREPOSITION
[1] there is ◊ *Tiens! Voilà Paul.* Look! There's Paul. ◊ *Tu as perdu ton stylo? Tiens, en voilà un autre.* Have you lost your pen? There's another one.
♦ **Les voilà!** There they are!

[2] that is ◊ *Voilà ma sœur.* That's my sister.

le **voile** NOUN
> see also **la voile**

veil ◊ *un voile de mariée* a wedding veil

la **voile** NOUN
> see also **le voile**

[1] sail
[2] sailing ◊ *faire de la voile* to go sailing
♦ **un bateau à voiles** a sailing boat

le **voilier** NOUN
sailing boat

voir VERB

Present tense:	
je vois	nous voyons
tu vois	vous voyez
il/elle voit	ils/elles voient
Past participle:	
vu	

to see ◊ *Venez me voir quand vous serez à Paris.* Come and see me when you're in Paris. ◊ *Je ne vois pas pourquoi il a fait ça.* I can't see why he did that.
♦ **faire voir quelque chose à quelqu'un** to show somebody something ◊ *Il m'a fait voir sa collection de timbres.* He showed me his stamp collection.
♦ **se voir** to be obvious ◊ *Est-ce que cette tache se voit?* Does that stain show? ◊ *Ça fait des années qu'elle n'a pas joué au tennis – Oui, ça se voit!* She hasn't played tennis for years – Yes, you can tell!
♦ **avoir quelque chose à voir avec** to have something to do with ◊ *Ça n'a rien à voir avec lui, c'est entre toi et moi.* It's nothing to do with him, it's between you and me.
♦ **Je ne peux vraiment pas la voir.** (*informal*) I really can't stand her.

le **voisin** NOUN
neighbour

le **voisinage** NOUN
♦ **dans le voisinage** in the vicinity

la **voisine** NOUN
neighbour

la **voiture** NOUN
car ◊ *une voiture de sport* a sports car

la **voix** NOUN (PL les **voix**)
[1] voice ◊ *à voix basse* in a low voice
♦ **à haute voix** aloud

V

2 vote ◊ *Il a obtenu cinquante pour cent des voix.* He got 50% of the votes.

le **vol** NOUN
1 flight
♦**à vol d'oiseau** as the crow flies
♦**le vol à voile** gliding
2 theft ◊ *un vol à main armée* an armed robbery

la **volaille** NOUN
poultry

le **volant** NOUN
1 steering wheel
2 shuttlecock

le **volcan** NOUN
volcano

la **volée** NOUN
volley (*in tennis*)
♦**rattraper une balle à la volée** to catch a ball in mid-air

voler VERB
1 to fly ◊ *J'aimerais savoir voler.* I'd like to be able to fly.
2 to steal ◊ *On a volé mon appareil photo.* My camera's been stolen.
♦**voler quelque chose à quelqu'un** to steal something from somebody ◊ *Ça n'est pas son stylo, il me l'a volé.* That's not his pen, he stole it from me.
♦**voler quelqu'un** to rob somebody

le **volet** NOUN
shutter

le **voleur** NOUN
thief
♦**Au voleur !** Stop thief!

la **voleuse** NOUN
thief

le **volley** NOUN
volleyball ◊ *jouer au volley* to play volleyball

le/la **volontaire** NOUN
volunteer

la **volonté** NOUN
willpower ◊ *Il a beaucoup de volonté.* He's got a lot of willpower.
♦**la bonne volonté** goodwill
♦**la mauvaise volonté** lack of goodwill

volontiers ADVERB
1 gladly ◊ *Je l'aiderais volontiers s'il me le demandait.* I'd gladly help him if he asked me.
2 please ◊ *Voulez-vous boire quelque chose? – Volontiers!* Would you like something to drink? – Yes, please!

le **volume** NOUN
volume ◊ *un dictionnaire en deux volumes* a two-volume dictionary

volumineux ADJECTIVE (FEM SING **volumineuse**)
bulky

vomir VERB
to vomit ◊ *Il a vomi toute la nuit.* He was vomiting all night.

vont VERB *see* **aller**

vos ADJECTIVE
your ◊ *Rangez vos jouets, les enfants!* Children, put your toys away! ◊ *Merci pour vos fleurs, M. Durand.* Thanks for your flowers, Mr Durand.

le **vote** NOUN
vote

voter VERB
to vote

votre ADJECTIVE (PL **vos**)
your ◊ *C'est votre manteau?* Is this your coat?

vôtre PRONOUN
♦**le vôtre** yours ◊ *J'aime bien notre prof de maths, mais le vôtre est plus patient.* I like our maths teacher, but yours is more patient. ◊ *À qui est cette écharpe? C'est la vôtre?* Whose is this scarf? Is it yours?
♦**À la vôtre!** Cheers!

vôtres PRONOUN
♦**les vôtres** yours ◊ *J'ai oublié mes lunettes de soleil. Vous avez apporté les vôtres?* I've forgotten my sunglasses. Have you brought yours?

voudra, voudrai, voudrais, voudras, voudrez, voudrons, voudront VERB *see* **vouloir**
♦**Je voudrais ...** I'd like ... ◊ *Je voudrais deux litres de lait, s'il vous plaît.* I'd like two litres of milk, please.

vouloir VERB

Present tense:	
je veux	nous voulons
tu veux	vous voulez
il/elle veut	ils/elles veulent
Past participle:	
voulu	

to want ◊ *Elle veut un vélo pour Noël.* She wants a bike for Christmas. ◊ *Je ne veux pas de dessert.* I don't want any pudding. ◊ *Il ne veut pas venir.* He doesn't want to come. ◊ *On va au cinéma? – Si tu veux.* Shall we go to the cinema? – If you like.
♦**Je veux bien.** I'll be happy to. ◊ *Je veux bien le faire à ta place si ça t'arrange.* I don't mind doing it for you if you prefer.

♦**Voulez-vous une tasse de thé? – Je veux bien.** Would you like a cup of tea? – Yes please.

♦**sans le vouloir** without meaning to ◇ *Je l'ai vexé sans le vouloir.* I upset him without meaning to.

♦**en vouloir à quelqu'un** to be angry at somebody ◇ *Il m'en veut de ne pas l'avoir invité à mon anniversaire.* He's angry at me for not inviting him to my birthday party.

♦**vouloir dire** to mean ◇ *Qu'est-ce que ça veut dire?* What does that mean?

voulu VERB *see* **vouloir**

vous PRONOUN

1 you ◇ *Vous aimez la pizza?* Do you like pizza?

2 to you ◇ *Je vous écrirai bientôt.* I'll write to you soon.

3 yourself ◇ *Vous vous êtes fait mal?* Have you hurt yourself?

♦**vous-même** yourself ◇ *Vous l'avez fait vous-même?* Did you do it yourself?

vouvoyer VERB

♦**vouvoyer quelqu'un** to address somebody as "vous"

> ⓘ **vouvoyer quelqu'un** means to use **vous** when speaking to someone, rather than **tu**. Use **tu** only when talking to one person and when that person is someone of your own age or younger or whom you know well; use **vous** to everyone else. If in doubt use **vous**.

♦**Est-ce que je dois vouvoyer ta sœur?** Should I use "vous" to your sister?

le voyage NOUN

journey ◇ *Avez-vous fait bon voyage?* Did you have a good journey?

♦**Bon voyage!** Have a good trip!

voyager VERB

to travel

le voyageur NOUN

passenger

la voyageuse NOUN

passenger

voyaient, voyais, voyait VERB *see* **voir**

la voyelle NOUN

vowel

voyez, voyiez, voyions VERB *see* **voir**

voyons VERB *see* **voir**

1 let's see ◇ *Voyons ce qu'on peut faire.* Let's see what we can do.

2 come on ◇ *Voyons, sois raisonnable!* Come on, be reasonable!

le voyou NOUN

hooligan

vrac

♦**en vrac** ADVERB

loose ◇ *du thé en vrac* loose tea

vrai ADJECTIVE

true ◇ *une histoire vraie* a true story ◇ *C'est vrai?* Is that true?

♦**à vrai dire** to tell the truth

vraiment ADVERB

really

vraisemblable ADJECTIVE

likely ◇ *C'est peu vraisemblable.* That's not very likely. ◇ *Il va falloir trouver une excuse vraisemblable.* We'll have to find a convincing excuse.

le VTT NOUN (= *vélo tout-terrain*)

mountain bike

vu VERB *see* **voir**

♦**être bien vu** to be popular (*person*) ◇ *Est-ce qu'il est bien vu à l'école?* Is he popular at school?

♦**être mal vu** to be disapproved of ◇ *C'est mal vu de fumer ici.* They don't like people smoking here.

la vue NOUN

1 eyesight ◇ *J'ai une mauvaise vue.* I've got bad eyesight.

2 view ◇ *Il y a une belle vue d'ici.* There's a lovely view from here.

♦**à vue d'œil** visibly ◇ *Elle grandit à vue d'œil.* Every time you see her, she's got taller.

vulgaire ADJECTIVE

vulgar ◇ *Ne dit pas ça, c'est très vulgaire.* Don't say that, it's very vulgar.

V

W

le **wagon** NOUN
  railway carriage

le **wagon-lit** NOUN (PL les **wagons-lits**)
  sleeper (*on train*)

le **wagon-restaurant** NOUN (PL les **wagons-restaurants**)
  restaurant car

le **walkman** ® NOUN
  Walkman ®

wallon ADJECTIVE, NOUN (FEM SING **wallonne**)
  Walloon (*French-speaking Belgian*)
  ◆ **les Wallons** the French-speaking Belgians

la **Wallonie** NOUN
  French-speaking Belgium

les **W.-C.** MASC NOUN
  toilet SING

le **Web** NOUN
  Web

le **webmaster** NOUN
  webmaster

le **webzine** NOUN
  webzine

le **week-end** NOUN
  weekend

le **western** NOUN
  western (*film*)

le **whisky** NOUN (PL les **whiskies**)
  whisky

X

xénophobe ADJECTIVE
prejudiced against foreigners
la **xénophobie** NOUN

prejudice against foreigners
le **xylophone** NOUN
xylophone

Y

y PRONOUN
there ◊ *Nous y sommes allés l'été dernier.* We went there last summer. ◊ *Regarde dans le tiroir: je pense que les clés y sont.* Look in the drawer: I think the keys are in there.
y replaces phrases with à in constructions like the ones below:
♦ **Je pensais à l'examen. – Mais arrête d'y penser!** I was thinking about the exam. – Well, stop thinking about it!
♦ **Je ne m'attendais pas à ça. – Moi, je m'y attendais.** I wasn't expecting that. – I was expecting it.
le **yaourt** NOUN
yoghurt ◊ *un yaourt nature* a plain yoghurt ◊ *un yaourt aux fruits* a fruit

yoghurt
les **yeux** MASC NOUN (SING **œil**)
eyes ◊ *Elle a les yeux bleus.* She's got blue eyes.
le **yoga** NOUN
yoga
le **yoghourt** NOUN
yoghurt
la **Yougoslavie** NOUN
Yugoslavia
♦ **l'ex-Yougoslavie** the former Yugoslavia
youpi EXCLAMATION
Yippee!
le **yoyo** NOUN
yo-yo

Z

zapper VERB
to channel hop
le **zèbre** NOUN
zebra
le **zéro** NOUN
zero
♦ **Ils ont gagné trois à zéro.** They won three-nil.
zézayer VERB
to lisp ◊ *Il zézaie.* He's got a lisp.
le **zigzag** NOUN
♦ **faire des zigzags** to zigzag
la **zone** NOUN

zone
♦ **une zone industrielle** an industrial estate
♦ **une zone piétonne** a pedestrian precinct
le **zoo** NOUN
zoo
zoologique ADJECTIVE
zoological ◊ *un jardin zoologique* zoological gardens
zut EXCLAMATION
Oh heck!

FRENCH IN ACTION

PUZZLES AND WORDGAMES

The puzzles and wordgames on the following pages have been designed to give you practice in using your dictionary. Make sure you read the "Dictionary Skills" section at the front of this book before you start. Don't worry, there are answers at the end of the wordgames in case you get really stuck!

WORDGAME 1

► CHOOSING THE RIGHT TRANSLATION ◄

Complete the crossword below by looking up the English words in the list and finding the correct French translations. There is a slight catch, however! All the English words have more than one French translation, but only one will fit correctly into each part of the crossword.

1. CLASS	7. CALF
2. THROW	8. PLACE
3. KNOW	9. DINNER
4. FIND	10. STAY
5. NUT	11. HARD
6. TAKE	12. LATE

WORDGAME 2

▶ PARTS OF SPEECH ◀

In each sentence below a word has been shaded. Put a tick in the appropriate box to show whether it's a **noun**, **adjective**, **adverb** or **verb** each time. Look in the section "Dictionary Skills" at the front of the book to remind you what nouns, adjectives, adverbs and verbs are. Remember, there may be more than one entry for each word.

SENTENCE	NOUN	ADJ	ADV	VERB
1. La ferme de mes parents est en Alsace.				
2. Il n'est pas franc.				
3. Le magasin ferme dans deux minutes.				
4. Le dîner est à 20 heures.				
5. Tu veux goûter ma mousse au chocolat?				
6. Je n'aime pas la bière.				
7. C'est un faux passeport.				
8. J'entends des pas dans l'escalier.				
9. Ce film nous a fait rire.				
10. Cette voiture est mal garée.				

▶ NOUNS ◀

a. This list contains the feminine form of some French nouns. Use your dictionary to find the **masculine** form. Remember, the masculine form usually appears in a separate entry.

b. Use your dictionary to find the **plural** of the following nouns. Remember, the plural form appears in brackets and in bold after the singular form.

MASCULINE	FEMININE
	danseuse
	boulangère
	Américaine
	animatrice
	avocate
	Parisienne
	libraire
	téléspectatrice
	pionne
	veuve

SINGULAR	PLURAL
chou	
canal	
bateau	
sapeur-pompier	
neveu	
travail	
vœu	
voix	
œil	
croque-monsieur	

WORDGAME 4

► ADJECTIVES ◄

Use the French-English side of your dictionary to find the **feminine singular** form of these adjectives. Remember, the feminine singular form appears in brackets and in bold after the masculine form.

MASCULINE	FEMININE
1. naturel	
2. beau	
3. heureux	
4. américain	
5. gros	
6. blanc	
7. faux	
8. sec	
9. favori	
10. frais	
11. bon	
12. fou	
13. public	
14. naïf	

WORDGAME 5

▶ VERB TENSES ◀

Use the verb tables on pages 316 to 329 to help you fill in the blanks in the table below.

INFINITIVE	PRESENT	IMPERFECT	FUTURE
faire		je	
se laver	il		
voir			nous
finir			elle
avoir		il	
aller	vous		
être	elles		
vouloir		ils	
devoir	tu		
mettre			je
dire		il	
pouvoir			nous

298

WORDGAME 6

► «MOTS CODÉS» ◄

In the boxes below, the letters of eight French words have been replaced by numbers. A number represents the same letter each time.

Try to crack the code and find the eight words. If you need help, use your dictionary.

Here is a clue: all the words you are looking for have something to do with CLOTHES.

1. | P¹ | 2 | 3 | 4 | 2 | 5 | 6 | 3 |

2. | 7 | 8 | P¹ | E⁹ |

3. | 10 | 11 | 3 | 11 | 7 | 8 | P¹ | 9 |

4. | 10 | 2 | 3 | 4 | 9 | 2 | 8 |

5. | P¹ | 8 | 5 | 5 |

6. | 12 | 13 | 2 | P¹ | 9 | 2 | 8 |

7. | 12 | 13 | 2 | 8 | 14 | 14 | 9 | 4 | 4 | 9 |

8. | 12 | 13 | 2 | 8 | 14 | 14 | 8 | 15 | 9 |

299

WORDGAME 7

► «MOTS CUISINÉS» ◄

Here is a list of French words for things you will find in the kitchen. Unfortunately, they have all been jumbled up. Try to work out what each word is and put the word in the boxes on the right. You will see there are five shaded boxes below. The five letters in the shaded boxes make up *another* French word for an object you can find in the kitchen.

1. féac   Tu prends du sucre
dans ton _____ ?

2. rever   Encore un _____
de vin?

3. lesvisale   je déteste faire
la _____.

4. rascosele   Elle a fait cuire les pâtes
dans une grande _____.

5. grifo   Le fromage est
dans le _____.

The word you are looking for is:

WORDGAME 1

1. classe
2. lancer
3. connaître
4. trouver
5. noisette
6. emmener
7. mollet
8. endroit
9. dîner
10. rester
11. dur
12. tard

WORDGAME 2

1. noun
2. adjective
3. verb
4. noun
5. verb
6. adverb
7. adjective
8. noun
9. verb
10. adverb

WORDGAME 3a

Masculine forms
1. danseur
2. boulanger
3. Américain
4. animateur
5. avocat
6. Parisien
7. libraire
8. téléspectateur
9. pion
10. veuf

WORDGAME 3b

Plural forms
1. choux
2. canaux
3. bateaux
4. sapeurs-pompiers
5. neveux
6. travaux
7. vœux
8. voix
9. yeux
10. croque-monsieur

WORDGAME 4

1. naturelle
2. belle
3. heureuse
4. américaine
5. grosse
6. blanche
7. fausse
8. sèche
9. favorite
10. fraîche
11. bonne
12. folle
13. publique
14. naïve

WORDGAME 5

1. je faisais
2. il se lave
3. nous verrons
4. elle finira
5. il avait
6. vous allez
7. elles sont
8. ils voulaient
9. tu dois
10. je mettrai
11. il disait
12. nous pourrons

WORDGAME 6

1. pantalon
2. jupe
3. minijupe
4. manteau
5. pull
6. chapeau
7. chaussette
8. chaussure

WORDGAME 7

1. café
2. verre
3. vaisselle
4. casserole
5. frigo

Missing word – évier

CORRESPONDENCE

▶ LETTER

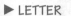

Address of sender

Nathalie Leduc
18 rue des Tulipes
65004 Gervais

Place & Date

Gervais, le 14 février 2001

Chers Grand-maman et Grand-papa

Merci beaucoup pour les CD que vous m'avez envoyés. Vous avez vraiment bien choisi puisqu'il s'agit de mes deux chanteurs préférés: je n'arrête pas de les écouter!

Sinon, rien de nouveau ici. Je passe presque tout mon temps à préparer mes examens, qui commencent dans quinze jours. J'espère que je les réussirai tous, mais j'ai le trac pour mon examen de maths: c'est la matière que j'aime le moins.

Maman m'a dit que vous partiez en Crète la semaine prochaine. Je vous souhaite de très bonnes vacances, et je suis sûre que vous reviendrez tout bronzés.

Grosses bises

Or:
Affectueusement
Amicalement

Nathalie

STARTING A PERSONAL LETTER

Merci pour ta lettre.
Ça m'a fait plaisir d'avoir de tes nouvelles.
Je suis désolé de ne pas t'avoir écrit plus tôt.

Thank you for your letter.
It was lovely to hear from you.
I'm sorry I didn't write sooner.

ENDING A PERSONAL LETTER

Écris-moi bientôt!
Embrasse Sophie pour moi.
Paul te fait ses amitiés.

Write soon!
Give my love to Sophie.
Paul sends his best wishes.

CORRESPONDENCE

► EMAIL

To give your email address to
someone in French, say:
"Alice at n t net point co point f r"

	Nouveau Message
A:	alice@ntnet.co.fr
De:	patrick@onemo.net
Objet:	show
Cc:	antoine@blt.com
Copie cachée:	

Fichier joint   Envoyer

Salut!

Je viens d'acheter le nouvel album de Rockstar. Il est génial!

J'ai trois billets gratuits pour leur show à Orléans samedi
prochain, et j'espère que vous pourrez venir avec moi tous
les deux!

À bientôt!

Nouveau message	New message
A	To
De	From
Objet	Subject
Cc	cc
Copie cachée	bcc
Fichier joint	Attachment
Envoyer	Send

TELEPHONE

▶ WHEN YOUR NUMBER ANSWERS

– **Bonjour! J'aimerais parler à Valérie.**
– Hello! Could I speak to Valérie, please?

– **Pourriez-vous lui demander de me rappeler, s'il vous plaît?**
– Would you ask him/her to call me back, please?

– **Je rappellerai dans une demi-heure.**
– I'll call back in half an hour.

▶ ANSWERING THE TELEPHONE

– **Bonjour! C'est Marc à l'appareil.** – Hello! It's Marc speaking.

– **C'est moi.** – Speaking.

– **Qui est à l'appareil?** – Who's speaking?

▶ WHEN THE SWITCHBOARD ANSWERS

– **C'est de la part de qui?** – Who shall I say is calling?

– **Je vous le/la passe.** – I'm putting you through.

– **Ne quittez pas.** – Please hold.

– **Voulez-vous laisser un message?** – Would you like to leave a message?

▶ DIFFICULTIES

– **Je n'arrive pas à avoir le numéro.**
– I can't get through.

– **Je suis désolé, j'ai dû faire un faux numéro.**
– I'm sorry, I dialled the wrong number.

– **La ligne est très mauvaise.**
– This is a very bad line.

– **Leur téléphone est en dérangement.**
– Their phone is out of order.

NUMBERS

1	un(e)	13	treize	50	cinquante
2	deux	14	quatorze	60	soixante
3	trois	15	quinze	70	soixante-dix
4	quatre	16	seize	71	soixante et onze
5	cinq	17	dix-sept	72	soixante-douze
6	six	18	dix-huit	80	quatre-vingts
7	sept	19	dix-neuf	81	quatre-vingt-un(e)
8	huit	20	vingt	90	quatre-vingt-dix
9	neuf	21	vingt et un(e)	91	quatre-vingt-onze
10	dix	22	vingt-deux	100	cent
11	onze	30	trente		
12	douze	40	quarante		

101	cent un(e)	1,000	mille
300	trois cents	2,000	deux mille
301	trois cent un(e)	1,000,000	un million

▶ FRACTIONS etc

1/2	un demi
1/3	un tiers
2/3	deux tiers
1/4	un quart
1/5	un cinquième
0.5	zéro virgule cinq (0,5)
3.4	trois virgule quatre (3,4)
10%	dix pour cent
100%	cent pour cent

▶ EXAMPLES

il habite au dix — he lives at number ten
à la page dix-neuf — on page nineteen
au chapitre sept — in chapter seven

NUMBERS

1st	premier (1ᵉʳ), première (1ʳᵉ)	14th	quatorzième (14ᵉ)
2nd	deuxième (2ᵉ)	15th	quinzième (15ᵉ)
3rd	troisième (3ᵉ)	16th	seizième (16ᵉ)
4th	quatrième (4ᵉ)	17th	dix-septième (17ᵉ)
5th	cinquième (5ᵉ)	18th	dix-huitième (18ᵉ)
6th	sixième (6ᵉ)	19th	dix-neuvième (19ᵉ)
7th	septième (7ᵉ)	20th	vingtième (20ᵉ)
8th	huitième (8ᵉ)	21st	vingt et unième (21ᵉ)
9th	neuvième (9ᵉ)	22nd	vingt-deuxième (22ᵉ)
10th	dixième (10ᵉ)	30th	trentième (30ᵉ)
11th	onzième (11ᵉ)	100th	centième (100ᵉ)
12th	douzième (12ᵉ)	101st	cent unième (101ᵉ)
13th	treizième (13ᵉ)	1000th	millième (1000ᵉ)

Pierre est arrivé premier

▶ EXAMPLES

il habite au cinquième (étage)	he lives on the fifth floor
il est arrivé troisième	he came in third
échelle au vingt-cinq millième	scale one to twenty-five thousand

DATE

▶ LES JOURS DE LA SEMAINE

lundi
mardi
mercredi
jeudi
vendredi
samedi
dimanche

Quand?
lundi
le lundi
tous les lundis
mardi dernier
vendredi prochain
samedi en huit
samedi en quinze

▶ LES MOIS

janvier
février
mars
avril
mai
juin
juillet
août
septembre
octobre
novembre
décembre

Quand?
en février
le 1er décembre
le premier décembre
en 2001
en deux mille un

Quel jour sommes-nous?
Nous sommes le...
dimanche 1er octobre or
  dimanche premier octobre
lundi 26 février or
  lundi vingt-six février

▶ DAYS OF THE WEEK

Monday
Tuesday
Wednesday
Thursday
Friday
Saturday
Sunday

When?
on Monday
on Mondays
every Monday
last Tuesday
next Friday
a week on Saturday
two weeks on Saturday

▶ MONTHS OF THE YEAR

January
February
March
April
May
June
July
August
September
October
November
December

When?
in February
on 1 December
on the first of December
in 2001
in two thousand and one

What day is it?
It's...
Sunday, 1 October or
  Sunday, the first of October
Monday, 26 February or
  Monday, the twenty-sixth of February

TIME

Quelle heure est-il? What time is it?
Il est... It's...

À quelle heure? At what time?

une heure

une heure dix

une heure et quart

une heure et demie

deux heures moins vingt

deux heures moins le quart

à minuit

à midi

à une heure (de l'après-midi)

à huit heures (du soir)

In France times are often given in the twenty-four hour clock.

à 11.15
or
onze heures quinze

à 20.45
or
vingt heures quarante-cinq

FALSE FRIENDS

French ≠ English

actuel ≠ actual

le système actuel   →   the present system

The film is based on   →   Le film repose sur des faits réels.
actual events.

actuellement ≠ actually

Elle enseigne actuellement   →   She is currently teaching in Toulouse.
à Toulouse.

Did it actually happen?   →   Est-ce que c'est vraiment arrivé?

agenda ≠ agenda

J'ai perdu mon agenda.   →   I've lost my diary.

on the agenda   →   à l'ordre du jour

attendre ≠ attend

J'attends d'avoir un   →   I'm waiting until I've got a flat of
appartement à moi.   my own.

They attended the meeting.   →   Ils ont assisté à la réunion.

compréhensif ≠ comprehensive

Mon patron s'est montré   →   My boss was very understanding.
très compréhensif

a comprehensive list   →   une liste complète

courrier ≠ courier

Est-ce qu'il y avait du courrier   →   Was there any post this morning?
ce matin?

They sent it by courier.   →   Ils l'ont envoyé par coursier.

délai ≠ delay

J'ai demandé un **délai** d'une semaine. $\longrightarrow$ I've asked for a week's **extension**.

There will be **delays** to trains on the London-Brighton line. $\longrightarrow$ Il y aura des **retards** sur la ligne Londres-Brighton.

demander ≠ demand

J'ai **demandé** la permission. $\longrightarrow$ I've **asked for** permission.

I **demand** to see your superior. $\longrightarrow$ J'**exige de** voir votre chef.

effectivement ≠ effectively

Oui, **effectivement** $\longrightarrow$ Yes, **indeed**.

to use sth **effectively** $\longrightarrow$ utiliser **efficacement** qch

engin ≠ engine

un **engin** thermonucléaire $\longrightarrow$ a thermonuclear **device**

My car has a 1.6 litre **engine**. $\longrightarrow$ Ma voiture a un **moteur** de 1,6 litres.

éventuel ≠ eventual

une solution **éventuelle** $\longrightarrow$ a **possible** solution

The **eventual** winner of the election. $\longrightarrow$ Le candidat **qui a finalement** remporté les élections.

éventuellement ≠ eventually

Nous pourrions **éventuelle-ment** y aller en voiture. $\longrightarrow$ We could **possibly** go by car.

He **eventually** became Prime Minister. $\longrightarrow$ Il est **finalement** devenu Premier ministre.

lecture ≠ lecture

La **lecture** est mon → **Reading** is my favourite hobby.
passe-temps favori.

He's giving a **lecture** on → Il donne une **conférence** sur les
crocodiles. crocodiles.

librairie ≠ library

On trouve cette BD dans la → You can buy this comic in most
plupart des **librairies**. **bookshops**.

the public **library** → la **bibliothèque** municipale

location ≠ location

location de voitures → car **rental**

A hotel set in a beautiful → Un hôtel situé dans un **endroit**
location. magnifique.

malicieux ≠ malicious

un sourire **malicieux** → a **mischievous** smile

a **malicious** rumour → une rumeur **malveillante**

parking ≠ parking

un **parking** souterrain → an underground **car park**

"no **parking**" → "**stationnement** interdit"

passer un examen ≠ to pass an exam

Je **passe** mon examen de → I'm **sitting** my maths exam tomorrow.
maths demain.

I've **passed** my maths exam. → J'ai **réussi** mon examen de maths.

pétrole ≠ petrol

le **pétrole** de la mer du Nord → North Sea **oil**

This car uses too much **petrol**. → Cette voiture consomme trop d'**essence**.

résumer ≠ resume

Pouvez-vous **résumer** cet article? → Could you **summarize** this article?

They've **resumed** work. → Ils ont **repris** le travail.

sensible ≠ sensible

Elle est très **sensible** → She's very **sensitive**.

Be **sensible**! → Sois **raisonnable**!

stage ≠ stage

Caroline a fait un **stage** chez Collins. → Caroline did **work experience** at Collins.

on **stage** → sur **scène**

the first **stage** of the operation → la première **phase** de l'opération

supporter ≠ support

Elle ne **supporte** pas qu'on la critique → She can't **stand** being criticized.

My mum has always **supported** me. → Ma mère m'a toujours **soutenu**.

sympathique ≠ sympathetic

Ce sont des gens très **sympathiques**. → They're very **nice** people.

She was very **sympathetic** when I told her what had happened. → Elle s'est montrée très **compatissante** quand je lui ai expliqué ce qui s'était passé.

FRENCH VERB TABLES

▶ CONTENTS

FRENCH VERB TABLES

This section contains fourteen important French verbs that you need to learn. All French verbs fall into two main categories – **regular** and **irregular** – and it is important to learn which verbs fall into which category.

The tables are arranged in the following order:

1. Regular verbs – **aimer**, **finir**, **attendre** and **se laver**
2. Very important irregular verbs – **avoir** and **être**
3. Other common irregular verbs – **aller**, **devoir**, **dire**, **faire**, **mettre**, **pouvoir**, **voir** and **vouloir**

At the top of each table you will find the infinitive, the imperative and the past participle. The lower section of the table shows you how to form six tenses of the verb:

PRESENT	e.g. je fais = **I do** *or* **I am doing**
*PRESENT SUBJUNCTIVE**	e.g. je fasse = **I do**
IMPERFECT	e.g. je faisais = **I was doing** or **I did**
PERFECT	e.g. j'ai fait = **I did** or **I have done**
FUTURE	e.g. je ferai = **I will do**
CONDITIONAL	e.g. je ferais = **I would do**

*The French side of your dictionary will tell you which words must be followed by the subjunctive.

▶ REGULAR VERBS

There are three groups of regular verbs:

1. "-ER" verbs = verbs that end in -**er** like **aimer** on p316
2. "-IR" verbs = verbs that end in -**ir** like **finir** on p317
3. "-RE" verbs = verbs that end in -**re** like **attendre** on p318

They are called regular verbs because they follow one of three set patterns. When you have learnt these patterns, you will be able to form *any* regular verb.

HOW TO FORM A REGULAR VERB

i. a) To form the present, imperfect or present subjunctive tense, take the infinitive minus the last two letters. This is called the stem e.g. *aimer* → **aim-**, *finir* → **fin-**, and *attendre* → **attend-**

   b) To form the future or conditional tense, the stem is the whole infinitive for "-ER" and "-IR" verbs and the infinitive minus its final "E" for "-RE" verbs e.g. *aimer* → **aimer**, *finir* → **finir** and *attendre* → **attendr-**

ii. Next add the appropriate **ending**. You need to ask yourself three questions:

   a) **What sort of** verb am I using (-ER, -IR, -RE)?
   b) **Who** is doing the verb? (je, tu, il *etc*)?
   c) **When** are they doing it (in the present, the past or the future)?

Look at the verb tables for **aimer**, **finir** and **attendre**. The verb endings are underlined. These endings can be tagged onto the stem of *any* regular verb.

▶ AVOIR AND ÊTRE

Avoir (to have) and **être** (to be) are very important verbs which **must** be learnt. You use them when you want to say "**I have**" *etc* or "**I am**" *etc*. The present tense of **avoir** or **être** is also used to form the **perfect tense**. In most cases, **avoir** is used to form the perfect, but reflexive verbs like **se laver** (to wash oneself) and verbs of movement like **aller** (to go) and **venir** (to come) use **être** – e.g. the French for both "he's gone" and "he went" is **il est allé**, not **il a allé**. The following verbs use **être**:

aller	mourir	retourner
arriver	naître	revenir
descendre	partir	sortir
devenir	passer	tomber
entrer	rentrer	venir
monter	rester	

HOW TO FORM THE PERFECT TENSE

a) Take the infinitive of a French verb e.g. **donner**
b) Check if the verb uses **avoir** or **être** to form the perfect tense. e.g. **donner** uses **avoir**
c) If the person involved is **il** (he), take the appropriate present form of **avoir** – **il a**
d) Add the **past participle** – **il a donné**. The past participle is shown near the top of each verb table. If you want to form the past participle of *any* regular verb, simply take the infinitive of the verb, knock off the last two letters and add the following endings:

"-ER" verbs add **é** – e.g. aimer → aim**é**
"-IR" verbs add **i** – e.g. finir → fin**i**
"-RE" verbs add **u** – e.g. attendre → attend**u**

e) **il a donné** means "he gave" or "he has given"

▶ IRREGULAR VERBS

Many French verbs are irregular and this means you have to learn them individually. There are tables of the most important irregular verbs such as **avoir** (to have), **être** (to be) and **faire** (to do) in this section. When you are translating from French and meet an unfamiliar verb form, you may be able to guess from the context that it comes from one of these verbs, and you can use the verb table to check. The most common irregular verb parts are listed on the French side of the dictionary, so you could also look there.

HOW TO USE THE VERB TABLES

You will find some useful example phrases at the top of each verb table, but if you can't find what you need to say or write in French there, use the verb table itself to help you. Imagine that you want to find the French for "he wants". Here's how to do it:

a) Look up **want** on the English-French side of the dictionary to find the French translation
b) French translation = **vouloir**
c) Turn to the verb tables section of your dictionary and find **vouloir**
d) When does he want it? He wants it **now**, so look for the heading *PRESENT*
e) Who wants it? **He** does. The French for "he" is **il** so look for **il** under the *PRESENT* heading
f) The French for "he wants" is "**il veut**"

FRENCH VERB TABLES

▶ aimer

to like *or* to love

IMPERATIVE

aime
aimons
aimez

EXAMPLE PHRASES

Tu **aimes** le chocolat? Do you like
  chocolate?
Je t'**aime**. I love you.
J'**aimerais** aller en Grèce. I'd like to
  go to Greece.

PAST PARTICIPLE

aimé

PRESENT

j'	aime
tu	aimes
il	aime
nous	aimons
vous	aimez
ils	aiment

PERFECT

j'	ai aimé
tu	as aimé
il	a aimé
nous	avons aimé
vous	avez aimé
ils	ont aimé

FUTURE

j'	aimerai
tu	aimeras
il	aimera
nous	aimerons
vous	aimerez
ils	aimeront

PRESENT SUBJUNCTIVE

j'	aime
tu	aimes
il	aime
nous	aimions
vous	aimiez
ils	aiment

IMPERFECT

j'	aimais
tu	aimais
il	aimait
nous	aimions
vous	aimiez
ils	aimaient

CONDITIONAL

j'	aimerais
tu	aimerais
il	aimerait
nous	aimerions
vous	aimeriez
ils	aimeraient

FRENCH VERB TABLES

▶ finir

to finish

EXAMPLE PHRASES

Finis *ta soupe!* Finish your soup!
J'**ai fini!** I've finished!
Je **finirai** *mes devoirs demain.* I'll
  finish my homework tomorrow.

IMPERATIVE

finis
finissons
finissez

PAST PARTICIPLE

fini

PRESENT

je	finis
tu	finis
il	finit
nous	finissons
vous	finissez
ils	finissent

PERFECT

j'	ai fini
tu	as fini
il	a fini
nous	avons fini
vous	avez fini
ils	ont fini

FUTURE

je	finirai
tu	finiras
il	finira
nous	finirons
vous	finirez
ils	finiront

PRESENT SUBJUNCTIVE

je	finisse
tu	finisses
il	finisse
nous	finissions
vous	finissiez
ils	finissent

IMPERFECT

je	finissais
tu	finissais
il	finissait
nous	finissions
vous	finissiez
ils	finissaient

CONDITIONAL

je	finirais
tu	finirais
il	finirait
nous	finirions
vous	finiriez
ils	finiraient

FRENCH VERB TABLES

▶ attendre

to wait

attends
attendons
attendez

Attends–moi! Wait for me!
*Tu **attends** depuis longtemps?* Have you been waiting long?
*Je l'**ai attendu** à la poste.* I waited for him at the post office.

PAST PARTICIPLE

attendu

PRESENT

j'	attends
tu	attends
il	attend
nous	attendons
vous	attendez
ils	attendent

PERFECT

j'	ai attendu
tu	as attendu
il	a attendu
nous	avons attendu
vous	avez attendu
ils	ont attendu

FUTURE

j'	attendrai
tu	attendras
il	attendra
nous	attendrons
vous	attendrez
ils	attendront

PRESENT SUBJUNCTIVE

j'	attende
tu	attendes
il	attende
nous	attendions
vous	attendiez
ils	attendent

IMPERFECT

j'	attendais
tu	attendais
il	attendait
nous	attendions
vous	attendiez
ils	attendaient

CONDITIONAL

j'	attendrais
tu	attendrais
il	attendrait
nous	attendrions
vous	attendriez
ils	attendraient

FRENCH VERB TABLES

▶ se laver

to wash (oneself)

EXAMPLE PHRASES

Je **me lave** chaque matin. I have a
wash every morning.
Il **s'est lavé** les mains. He washed
his hands.
Elle va **se laver** les cheveux. She's going
to wash her hair.

IMPERATIVE

lave-toi
lavons-nous
lavez-vous

PAST PARTICIPLE

lavé

PRESENT

je	me lave
tu	te laves
il	se lave
nous	nous lavons
vous	vous lavez
ils	se lavent

PRESENT SUBJUNCTIVE

je	me lave
tu	te laves
il	se lave
nous	nous lavions
vous	vous laviez
ils	se lavent

PERFECT

je	me suis lavé
tu	t'es lavé
il	s'est lavé
nous	nous sommes lavés
vous	vous êtes lavés
ils	se sont lavés

IMPERFECT

je	me lavais
tu	te lavais
il	se lavait
nous	nous lavions
vous	vous laviez
ils	se lavaient

FUTURE

je	me laverai
tu	te laveras
il	se lavera
nous	nous laverons
vous	vous laverez
ils	se laveront

CONDITIONAL

je	me laverais
tu	te laverais
il	se laverait
nous	nous laverions
vous	vous laveriez
ils	se laveraient

FRENCH VERB TABLES

▶ avoir

to have

IMPERATIVE

aie
ayons
ayez

EXAMPLE PHRASES

Il **a** les yeux bleus. He's got blue eyes
Quel âge **as**-tu? How old are you?
Il **a eu** un accident. He's had an
  accident.
J'**avais** faim. I was hungry.

PAST PARTICIPLE

eu

PRESENT

j' ai
tu as
il a
nous avons
vous avez
ils ont

PERFECT

j' ai eu
tu as eu
il a eu
nous avons eu
vous avez eu
ils ont eu

FUTURE

j' aurai
tu auras
il aura
nous aurons
vous aurez
ils auront

PRESENT SUBJUNCTIVE

j' aie
tu aies
il ait
nous ayons
vous ayez
ils aient

IMPERFECT

j' avais
tu avais
il avait
nous avions
vous aviez
ils avaient

CONDITIONAL

j' aurais
tu aurais
il aurait
nous aurions
vous auriez
ils auraient

FRENCH VERB TABLES

▶ être

to be

EXAMPLE PHRASES

*Mon père **est** professeur.* My father's
  a teacher.
*Quelle heure **est**-il? Il **est** 10 heures.*
  What time is it? – It's 10 o'clock
*Ils ne **sont** pas encore arrivés.*
  They haven't arrived yet.

IMPERATIVE

sois
soyons
soyez

PAST PARTICIPLE

été

PRESENT		PRESENT SUBJUNCTIVE	
je	suis	je	sois
tu	es	tu	sois
il	est	il	soit
nous	sommes	nous	soyons
vous	êtes	vous	soyez
ils	sont	ils	soient

PERFECT		IMPERFECT	
j'	ai été	j'	étais
tu	as été	tu	étais
il	a été	il	était
nous	avons été	nous	étions
vous	avez été	vous	étiez
ils	ont été	ils	étaient

FUTURE		CONDITIONAL	
je	serai	je	serais
tu	seras	tu	serais
il	sera	il	serait
nous	serons	nous	serions
vous	serez	vous	seriez
ils	seront	ils	seraient

FRENCH VERB TABLES

▶ aller

to go

IMPERATIVE

va
allons
allez

EXAMPLE PHRASES

*Vous **allez** au cinéma?* Are you going
to the cinema?
*Je **suis allé** à Londres.* I went to
London.
*Est-ce que tu **es** déjà **allé** en
Allemagne?* Have you ever been
to Germany?

PAST PARTICIPLE

allé

PRESENT

je	vais
tu	vas
il	va
nous	allons
vous	allez
ils	vont

PERFECT

je	suis allé
tu	es allé
il	est allé
nous	sommes allés
vous	êtes allés
ils	sont allés

FUTURE

j'	irai
tu	iras
il	ira
nous	irons
vous	irez
ils	iront

PRESENT SUBJUNCTIVE

j'	aille
tu	ailles
il	aille
nous	allions
vous	alliez
ils	aillent

IMPERFECT

j'	allais
tu	allais
il	allait
nous	allions
vous	alliez
ils	allaient

CONDITIONAL

j'	irais
tu	irais
il	irait
nous	irions
vous	iriez
ils	iraient

FRENCH VERB TABLES

▶ devoir

to have to

EXAMPLE PHRASES

Je **dois** aller faire les courses ce matin.
  I have to do the shopping this morning.
Il **a dû** faire ses devoirs hier soir. He had
  to do his homework last night.
Il **devait** prendre le train pour aller
  travailler. He had to go to work by train.

IMPERATIVE

dois
devons
devez

PAST PARTICIPLE

dû, due, dus

PRESENT

je	dois
tu	dois
il	doit
nous	devons
vous	devez
ils	doivent

PERFECT

j'	ai dû
tu	as dû
il	a dû
nous	avons dû
vous	avez dû
ils	ont dû

FUTURE

je	devrai
tu	devras
il	devra
nous	devrons
vous	devrez
ils	devront

PRESENT SUBJUNCTIVE

je	doive
tu	doives
il	doive
nous	devions
vous	deviez
ils	doivent

IMPERFECT

je	devais
tu	devais
il	devait
nous	devions
vous	deviez
ils	devaient

CONDITIONAL

je	devrais
tu	devrais
il	devrait
nous	devrions
vous	devriez
ils	devraient

FRENCH VERB TABLES

▶ dire

to say

IMPERATIVE

dis
disons
dites

EXAMPLE PHRASES

*Qu'est-ce qu'elle **dit**?* What is she
  saying?
*"Bonjour!" **a**-t-il **dit**.* "Hello!" he said.
*Il m'**a dit** que le film était nul.* He
  told me that the film was rubbish.

PAST PARTICIPLE

dit

PRESENT		*PRESENT SUBJUNCTIVE*	
je	dis	je	dise
tu	dis	tu	dises
il	dit	il	dise
nous	disons	nous	disions
vous	dites	vous	disiez
ils	disent	ils	disent

PERFECT		*IMPERFECT*	
j'	ai dit	je	disais
tu	as dit	tu	disais
il	a dit	il	disait
nous	avons dit	nous	disions
vous	avez dit	vous	disiez
ils	ont dit	ils	disaient

FUTURE		*CONDITIONAL*	
je	dirai	je	dirais
tu	diras	tu	dirais
il	dira	il	dirait
nous	dirons	nous	dirions
vous	direz	vous	diriez
ils	diront	ils	diraient

FRENCH VERB TABLES

▶ faire

to do *or* to make

*Qu'est-ce que tu **fais**?* What are
  you doing?
*Qu'est-ce qu'il **a fait**?* What has he
  done? *or* What did he do?
*J'**ai fait** un gâteau.* I've made a cake *or*
  I made a cake.

IMPERATIVE

fais
faisons
faites

PAST PARTICIPLE

fait

PRESENT

je	fais
tu	fais
il	fait
nous	faisons
vous	faites
ils	font

PERFECT

j'	ai fait
tu	as fait
il	a fait
nous	avons fait
vous	avez fait
ils	ont fait

FUTURE

je	ferai
tu	feras
il	fera
nous	ferons
vous	ferez
ils	feront

PRESENT SUBJUNCTIVE

je	fasse
tu	fasses
il	fasse
nous	fassions
vous	fassiez
ils	fassent

IMPERFECT

je	faisais
tu	faisais
il	faisait
nous	faisions
vous	faisiez
ils	faisaient

CONDITIONAL

je	ferais
tu	ferais
il	ferait
nous	ferions
vous	feriez
ils	feraient

FRENCH VERB TABLES

▶ mettre

to put

IMPERATIVE

mets
mettons
mettez

EXAMPLE PHRASES

Mets ton manteau! Put your coat on!
*Où est-ce que tu **as mis** les clés?*
  Where have you put the keys?
*J'**ai mis** le livre sur la table.* I put
  the book on the table.

PAST PARTICIPLE

mis

PRESENT

je	mets
tu	mets
il	met
nous	mettons
vous	mettez
ils	mettent

PERFECT

j'	ai mis
tu	as mis
il	a mis
nous	avons mis
vous	avez mis
ils	ont mis

FUTURE

je	mettrai
tu	mettras
il	mettra
nous	mettrons
vous	mettrez
ils	mettront

PRESENT SUBJUNCTIVE

je	mette
tu	mettes
il	mette
nous	mettions
vous	mettiez
ils	mettent

IMPERFECT

je	mettais
tu	mettais
il	mettait
nous	mettions
vous	mettiez
ils	mettaient

CONDITIONAL

je	mettrais
tu	mettrais
il	mettrait
nous	mettrions
vous	mettriez
ils	mettraient

FRENCH VERB TABLES

► pouvoir

to be able

EXAMPLE PHRASES

*Je **peux** t'aider, si tu veux.* I can help you if you like.
*J'ai fait tout ce que j'**ai pu**.* I did all I could.
*Je ne **pourrai** pas venir samedi.* I won't be able to come on Saturday.

IMPERATIVE

the imperative of **pouvoir** is not used

PAST PARTICIPLE

pu

PRESENT

je	peux
tu	peux
il	peut
nous	pouvons
vous	pouvez
ils	peuvent

PERFECT

j'	ai pu
tu	as pu
il	a pu
nous	avons pu
vous	avez pu
ils	ont pu

FUTURE

je	pourrai
tu	pourras
il	pourra
nous	pourrons
vous	pourrez
ils	pourront

PRESENT SUBJUNCTIVE

je	puisse
tu	puisses
il	puisse
nous	puissions
vous	puissiez
ils	puissent

IMPERFECT

je	pouvais
tu	pouvais
il	pouvait
nous	pouvions
vous	pouviez
ils	pouvaient

CONDITIONAL

je	pourrais
tu	pourrais
il	pourrait
nous	pourrions
vous	pourriez
ils	pourraient

FRENCH VERB TABLES

▶ voir

to see

vois
voyons
voyez

*Venez me **voir** quand vous serez à Paris.*
  Come and see me when you're in Paris.
*Je ne **vois** rien sans mes lunettes.*
  I can't see anything without my glasses.
*Est-ce que tu l'**as vu**?* Did you see
  him? or Have you seen him?

PAST PARTICIPLE

vu

PRESENT

je	vois
tu	vois
il	voit
nous	voyons
vous	voyez
ils	voient

PERFECT

j'	ai vu
tu	as vu
il	a vu
nous	avons vu
vous	avez vu
ils	ont vu

FUTURE

je	verrai
tu	verras
il	verra
nous	verrons
vous	verrez
ils	verront

PRESENT SUBJUNCTIVE

je	voie
tu	voies
il	voie
nous	voyions
vous	voyiez
ils	voient

IMPERFECT

je	voyais
tu	voyais
il	voyait
nous	voyions
vous	voyiez
ils	voyaient

CONDITIONAL

je	verrais
tu	verrais
il	verrait
nous	verrions
vous	verriez
ils	verraient

FRENCH VERB TABLES

▶ vouloir

to want

EXAMPLE PHRASES

*Elle **veut** un vélo pour Noël.*
  She wants a bike for Christmas.
*Ils **voulaient** aller au cinéma.*
  They wanted to go to the cinema.
*Tu **voudrais** une tasse de thé?*
  Would you like a cup of tea?

IMPERATIVE

veuille
veuillons
veuillez

PAST PARTICIPLE

voulu

PRESENT		*PRESENT SUBJUNCTIVE*	
je	veux	je	veuille
tu	veux	tu	veuilles
il	veut	il	veuille
nous	voulons	nous	voulions
vous	voulez	vous	vouliez
ils	veulent	ils	veuillent

PERFECT		*IMPERFECT*	
j'	ai voulu	je	voulais
tu	as voulu	tu	voulais
il	a voulu	il	voulait
nous	avons voulu	nous	voulions
vous	avez voulu	vous	vouliez
ils	ont voulu	ils	voulaient

FUTURE		*CONDITIONAL*	
je	voudrai	je	voudrais
tu	voudras	tu	voudrais
il	voudra	il	voudrait
nous	voudrons	nous	voudrions
vous	voudrez	vous	voudriez
ils	voudront	ils	voudraient

FRENCH IRREGULAR VERB FORMS

The following list is a summary of the main forms of other irregular verbs that you are likely to come across. For the present tense, all **je** and **nous** forms are shown. The **il**, **vous** and **ils** forms are also included wherever the part of the verb that goes with them follows an unusual pattern. For the imperfect, future and present subjunctive tenses, only the **je** form is given.

INFINITIVE	PRESENT	PAST PARTICIPLE	IMPERFECT	FUTURE	PRESENT SUBJUNCTIVE
acheter	j'achète nous achetons ils achètent	acheté	j'achetais	j'achèterai	j'achète
appeler	j'appelle il appelle nous appelons	appelé	j'appelais	j'appellerai	j'appelle
apprendre	j'apprends nous apprenons vous apprenez ils apprennent	appris	j'apprenais	j'apprendrai	j'apprenne
s'asseoir	je m'assieds nous nous asseyons vous vous asseyez ils s'asseyent	assis	je m'asseyais	je m'assiérai	je m'asseye
battre	je bats il bat nous battons	battu	je battais	je battrai	je batte
boire	je bois nous buvons ils boivent	bu	je buvais	je boirai	je boive
bouillir	je bous nous bouillons	bouilli	je bouillais	je bouillirai	je bouille
conclure	je conclus nous concluons	conclu	je concluais	je conclurai	je conclue
conduire	je conduis nous conduisons	conduit	je conduisais	je conduirai	je conduise
connaître	je connais il connaît nous connaissons	connu	je connaissais	je connaîtrai	je connaisse
coudre	je couds nous cousons vous cousez ils cousent	cousu	je cousais	je coudrai	je couse
courir	je cours nous courons	couru	je courais	je courrai	je coure
couvrir	je couvre nous couvrons	couvert	je couvrais	je couvrirai	je couvre
craindre	je crains nous craignons	craint	je craignais	je craindrai	je craigne

INFINITIVE	PRESENT	PAST PARTICIPLE	IMPERFECT	FUTURE	PRESENT SUBJUNCTIVE
créer	je crée nous créons	créé	je créais	je créerai	je crée
croire	je crois nous croyons ils croient	cru	je croyais	je croirai	je croie
croître	je croîs nous croissons	crû crue crus crues	je croissais	je croîtrai	je croisse
cueillir	je cueille nous cueillons	cueilli	je cueillais	je cueillerai	je cueille
cuire	je cuis nous cuisons ils cuisent	cuit	je cuisais	je cuirai	je cuise
dormir	je dors nous dormons	dormi	je dormais	je dormirai	je dorme
écrire	j'écris nous écrivons	écrit	j'écrivais	j'écrirai	j'écrive
falloir	il faut	fallu	il fallait	il faudra	il faille
fuir	je fuis nous fuyons ils fuient	fui	je fuyais	je fuirai	je fuie
haïr	je hais nous haïssons ils haïssent	haï	je haïssais	je haïrai	je haïsse
jeter	je jette nous jetons ils jettent	jeté	je jetais	je jetterai	je jette
joindre	je joins nous joignons	joint	je joignais	je joindrai	je joigne
lever	je lève nous levons ils lèvent	levé	je levais	je lèverai	je lève
lire	je lis nous lisons	lu	je lisais	je lirai	je lise
manger	je mange nous mangeons	mangé	je mangeais	je mangerai	je mange
mentir	je mens nous mentons	menti	je mentais	je mentirai	je mente
mourir	je meurs nous mourons ils meurent	mort	je mourais	je mourrai	je meure
naître	je nais il naît nous naissons	né	je naissais	je naîtrai	je naisse
offrir	j'offre nous offrons	offert	j'offrais	j'offrirai	j'offre

INFINITIVE	PRESENT	PAST PARTICIPLE	IMPERFECT	FUTURE	PRESENT SUBJUNCTIVE
paraître	je parais il paraît nous paraissons	paru	je paraissais	je paraîtrai	je paraisse
partir	je pars nous partons	parti	je partais	je partirai	je parte
plaire	je plais il plaît nous plaisons	plu	je plaisais	je plairai	je plaise
pleuvoir	il pleut	plu	il pleuvait	il pleuvra	il pleuve
prendre	je prends nous prenons ils prennent	pris	je prenais	je prendrai	je prenne
recevoir	je reçois il reçoit ils reçoivent	reçu	je recevais	je recevrai	je reçoive
rire	je ris nous rions	ri	je riais	je rirai	je rie
savoir	je sais nous savons ils savent	su	je savais	je saurai	je sache
servir	je sers nous servons	servi	je servais	je servirai	je serve
sortir	je sors nous sortons	sorti	je sortais	je sortirai	je sorte
souffrir	je souffre nous souffrons	souffert	je souffrais	je souffrirai	je souffre
suffire	je suffis nous suffisons	suffi	je suffisais	je suffirai	je suffise
suivre	je suis nous suivons	suivi	je suivais	je suivrai	je suive
se taire	je me tais nous nous taisons	tu	je me taisais	je me tairai	je me taise
tenir	je tiens nous tenons ils tiennent	tenu	je tenais	je tiendrai	je tienne
vaincre	je vaincs il vainc nous vainquons	vaincu	je vainquais	je vaincrai	je vainque
valoir	je vaux il vaut nous valons	valu	je valais	je vaudrai	je vaille
venir	je viens nous venons ils viennent	venu	je venais	je viendrai	je vienne
vivre	je vis nous vivons	vécu	je vivais	je vivrai	je vive

A

a ARTICLE

*Use **un** for masculine nouns, **une** for feminine nouns.*

un MASC ◊ *a book* un livre ◊ *a year ago* il y a un an
une FEM ◊ *an apple* une pomme

*You do not translate **a** when you want to describe somebody's job in French.*

◊ *He's a butcher.* Il est boucher.
◊ *She's a doctor.* Elle est médecin.
♦ **once a week** une fois par semaine
♦ **10 km an hour** dix kilomètres à l'heure
♦ **30 pence a kilo** trente pence le kilo
♦ **a hundred pounds** cent livres

AA NOUN (= *Automobile Association*)
la société de dépannage

aback ADVERB
♦ **to be taken aback** être décontenancé
◊ *I was taken aback by his reaction.* Sa réaction m'a décontenancé.

to **abandon** VERB
abandonner

abbey NOUN
l' abbaye FEM

abbreviation NOUN
l' abréviation FEM

ability NOUN
♦ **to have the ability to do something** être capable de faire quelque chose

able ADJECTIVE
♦ **to be able to do something** être capable de faire quelque chose

to **abolish** VERB
abolir

abortion NOUN
l' avortement MASC
♦ **She had an abortion.** Elle s'est fait avorter.

about PREPOSITION, ADVERB
1 à propos de (*concerning*) ◊ *I'm phoning you about tomorrow's meeting.* Je vous appelle à propos de la réunion de demain.
2 environ (*approximately*) ◊ *It takes about 10 hours.* Ça prend dix heures environ.
♦ **about a hundred pounds** une centaine de livres
♦ **at about 11 o'clock** vers onze heures
3 dans (*around*) ◊ *to walk about the town* se promener dans la ville
4 sur ◊ *a book about London* un livre sur Londres

♦ **to be about to do something** être sur le point de faire quelque chose ◊ *I was about to go out.* J'étais sur le point de sortir.
♦ **to talk about something** parler de quelque chose
♦ **What's it about?** De quoi s'agit-il?
♦ **How about going to the cinema?** Et si nous allions au cinéma?

above PREPOSITION, ADVERB
1 au-dessus de (*higher than*) ◊ *He put his hands above his head.* Il a mis ses mains au-dessus de sa tête.
♦ **the flat above** l'appartement du dessus
♦ **mentioned above** mentionné ci-dessus
♦ **above all** par-dessus tout
2 plus de (*more than*) ◊ *above 40 degrees* plus de quarante degrés

abroad ADVERB
à l'étranger ◊ *to go abroad* partir à l'étranger

abrupt ADJECTIVE
brusque ◊ *He was a bit abrupt with me.* Il s'est montré un peu brusque avec moi.

abruptly ADVERB
brusquement ◊ *He got up abruptly.* Il s'est levé brusquement.

absence NOUN
l' absence FEM

absent ADJECTIVE
absent

absent-minded ADJECTIVE
distrait ◊ *She's a bit absent-minded.* Elle est un peu distraite.

absolutely ADVERB
1 tout à fait (*completely*) ◊ *Chantal's absolutely right.* Chantal a tout à fait raison.
2 absolument ◊ *Do you think it's a good idea? – Absolutely!* Tu trouves que c'est une bonne idée? – Absolument!

absorbed ADJECTIVE
♦ **to be absorbed in something** être absorbé par quelque chose
♦ **to be absorbed in a book** être plongé dans un livre

absurd ADJECTIVE
absurde ◊ *That's absurd!* C'est absurde!

abuse NOUN
see also **abuse** VERB
l' abus MASC (*misuse*)

♦ **to shout abuse at somebody** insulter quelqu'un
♦ **the issue of child abuse** la question des enfants maltraités
♦ **the problem of drug abuse** le problème de la drogue

to **abuse** VERB
see also **abuse** NOUN
1 maltraiter ◊ abused children les enfants maltraités MASC PL
♦ **to be abused** être maltraité (child, woman)
2 injurier (insult)
♦ **to abuse drugs** se droguer

abusive ADJECTIVE
insultant (insulting) ◊ abusive behaviour un comportement insultant
♦ **When I refused, he became abusive.** Quand j'ai refusé, il s'est mis à m'injurier.
♦ **children with abusive parents** les enfants maltraités par leurs parents

academic ADJECTIVE
universitaire ◊ the academic year l'année universitaire FEM

academy NOUN
le collège ◊ a military academy un collège militaire

to **accelerate** VERB
accélérer

accelerator NOUN
l' accélérateur MASC

accent NOUN
l' accent MASC ◊ He's got a French accent. Il a l'accent français.

to **accept** VERB
accepter

acceptable ADJECTIVE
acceptable

access NOUN
1 l' accès MASC ◊ He has access to confidential information. Il a accès à des renseignements confidentiels.
2 le droit de visite ◊ Her ex-husband has access to the children. Son ex-mari a le droit de visite.

accessible ADJECTIVE
accessible

accessory NOUN
l' accessoire MASC ◊ fashion accessories les accessoires de mode

accident NOUN
l' accident MASC ◊ to have an accident avoir un accident
♦ **by accident (1)** (by mistake) accidentellement ◊ The burglar killed him by accident. Le cambrioleur l'a tué accidentellement.

♦ **by accident (2)** (by chance) par hasard ◊ She met him by accident. Elle l'a rencontré par hasard.

accidental ADJECTIVE
accidentel MASC
accidentelle FEM

to **accommodate** VERB
recevoir ◊ The hotel can accommodate 50 people. L'hôtel peut recevoir cinquante personnes.

accommodation NOUN
le logement

to **accompany** VERB
accompagner

accord NOUN
♦ **of his own accord** de son plein gré ◊ He left of his own accord. Il est parti de son plein gré.

accordingly ADVERB
en conséquence

according to PREPOSITION
selon ◊ According to him, everyone had gone. Selon lui, tout le monde était parti.

accordion NOUN
l' accordéon MASC

account NOUN
1 le compte ◊ a bank account un compte en banque
♦ **to do the accounts** tenir la comptabilité
2 (report)
le compte rendu
(PL les comptes rendus)
◊ He gave a detailed account of what happened. Il a donné un compte rendu détaillé des événements.
♦ **to take something into account** tenir compte de quelque chose
♦ **on account of** à cause de ◊ We couldn't go out on account of the bad weather. Nous n'avons pas pu sortir à cause du mauvais temps.

to **account for** VERB
expliquer ◊ If she was ill, that would account for her poor results. Si elle était malade, cela expliquerait ses résultats médiocres.

accountable ADJECTIVE
♦ **to be accountable to someone for something** être responsable de quelque chose devant quelqu'un

accountancy NOUN
la comptabilité

accountant NOUN
le/la comptable ◊ She's an accountant. Elle est comptable.

accuracy NOUN
l' exactitude FEM

A

accurate ADJECTIVE
précis ◊ *accurate information* les renseignements précis MASC

accurately ADVERB
avec précision

accusation NOUN
l' accusation FEM

to accuse VERB
♦**to accuse somebody of something** accuser quelqu'un de quelque chose ◊ *The police are accusing her of murder.* La police l'accuse de meurtre.

ace NOUN
l' as MASC ◊ *the ace of hearts* l'as de cœur

ache NOUN
see also **ache** VERB
la douleur

to ache VERB
see also **ache** NOUN
♦**My leg's aching.** J'ai mal à la jambe.

to achieve VERB
1 atteindre (*an aim*)
2 remporter (*victory*)

achievement NOUN
l' exploit MASC ◊ *That was quite an achievement.* C'était un véritable exploit.

acid NOUN
l' acide MASC

acid rain NOUN
les pluies acides FEM PL

acne NOUN
l' acné FEM

acre NOUN
le demi-hectare

ℹ️ *In France, land is measured in hectares. One acre is about 0.4 hectares.*

acrobat NOUN
l' acrobate MASC/FEM ◊ *He's an acrobat.* Il est acrobate.

across PREPOSITION, ADVERB
de l'autre côté de ◊ *the shop across the road* la boutique de l'autre côté de la rue
♦**to walk across the road** traverser la rue
♦**to run across the road** traverser la rue en courant
♦**across from** (*opposite*) en face de ◊ *He sat down across from her.* Il s'est assis en face d'elle.

to act VERB
see also **act** NOUN

1 jouer (*in play, film*) ◊ *He acts really well.* Il joue vraiment bien. ◊ *She's acting the part of Juliet.* Elle joue le rôle de Juliette.
2 agir (*take action*) ◊ *The police acted quickly.* La police a agi rapidement.
♦**She acts as his interpreter.** Elle lui sert d'interprète.

act NOUN
see also **act** VERB
l' acte MASC (*in play*) ◊ *in the first act* au premier acte

action NOUN
l' action FEM ◊ *The film was full of action.* Il y avait beaucoup d'action dans le film.
♦**to take firm action against** prendre des mesures énergiques contre

active ADJECTIVE
actif MASC
active FEM
◊ *He's a very active person.* Il est très actif.
♦**an active volcano** un volcan en activité

activity NOUN
l' activité FEM ◊ *outdoor activities* les activités de plein air

actor NOUN
l' acteur MASC ◊ *Brad Pitt is a well-known actor.* Brad Pitt est un acteur connu.

actress NOUN
l' actrice FEM ◊ *Julia Roberts is a well-known actress.* Julia Roberts est une actrice connue.

actual ADJECTIVE
réel MASC
réelle FEM
◊ *The film is based on actual events.* Le film repose sur des faits réels.
♦**What's the actual amount?** Quel est le montant exact?
*Be careful not to translate **actual** by **actuel**.*

actually ADVERB
1 vraiment (*really*) ◊ *Did it actually happen?* Est-ce que c'est vraiment arrivé?
2 en fait (*in fact*) ◊ *Actually, I don't know him at all.* En fait, je ne le connais pas du tout.
*Be careful not to translate **actually** by **actuellement**.*

acupuncture NOUN
l' acuponcture FEM

ad NOUN
1 l' annonce FEM (*in paper*)
2 la pub (*on TV, radio*)

AD ABBREVIATION

☞

ap. J.-C. (= après Jésus-Christ) ◊ *in 800 AD* en huit cents après Jésus-Christ

to **adapt** VERB
adapter ◊ *His novel was adapted for television.* Son roman a été adapté pour la télévision.
♦**to adapt to something** (*get used to*) s'adapter à quelque chose ◊ *He adapted to his new school very quickly.* Il s'est adapté très vite à sa nouvelle école.

adaptor NOUN
l' adaptateur MASC

to **add** VERB
ajouter ◊ *Add two eggs to the mixture.* Ajoutez deux œufs au mélange.
♦**to add up** additionner ◊ *Add the figures up.* Additionnez les chiffres.

addict NOUN
(*drug addict*)
le drogué
la droguée
♦**Jean-Pierre's a football addict.** Jean-Pierre est un mordu de football.

addicted ADJECTIVE
♦**to be addicted to** (*drug*) s'adonner à ◊ *She's addicted to heroin.* Elle s'adonne à l'héroïne.
♦**She's addicted to soap operas.** C'est une mordue des soaps.

addition NOUN
♦**in addition** en plus ◊ *He's broken his leg and, in addition, he's caught a cold.* Il s'est cassé la jambe et en plus, il a attrapé un rhume.
♦**in addition to** en plus de ◊ *In addition to the price of the cassette, there's a charge for postage.* En plus du prix de la cassette, il y a des frais de port.

address NOUN
l' adresse FEM ◊ *What's your address?* Quelle est votre adresse?

adjective NOUN
l' adjectif MASC

to **adjust** VERB
régler ◊ *You can adjust the height of the chair.* Tu peux régler la hauteur de la chaise.
♦**to adjust to something** (*get used to*) s'adapter à quelque chose ◊ *He adjusted to his new school very quickly.* Il s'est adapté très vite à sa nouvelle école.

adjustable ADJECTIVE
réglable

administration NOUN

l' administration FEM

admiral NOUN
l' amiral MASC

to **admire** VERB
admirer

admission NOUN
l' entrée FEM ◊ *"admission free"* "entrée gratuite"

to **admit** VERB
① admettre (*agree*) ◊ *I must admit that ...* Je dois admettre que ...
② reconnaître (*confess*) ◊ *He admitted that he'd done it.* Il a reconnu qu'il l'avait fait.

admittance NOUN
♦**"no admittance"** "accès interdit"

adolescence NOUN
l' adolescence FEM

adolescent NOUN
l' adolescent MASC
l' adolescente FEM

to **adopt** VERB
adopter ◊ *Phil was adopted.* Phil a été adopté.

adopted ADJECTIVE
adoptif MASC
adoptive FEM
◊ *an adopted son* un fils adoptif

adoption NOUN
l' adoption FEM

to **adore** VERB
adorer

Adriatic Sea NOUN
la mer Adriatique

adult NOUN
l' adulte MASC/FEM
♦**adult education** l'enseignement pour adultes MASC

to **advance** VERB
see also **advance** NOUN
① avancer (*move forward*) ◊ *The troops are advancing.* Les troupes avancent.
② progresser (*progress*) ◊ *Technology has advanced a lot.* La technologie a beaucoup progressé.

advance NOUN
see also **advance** VERB
♦**in advance** à l'avance ◊ *They bought the tickets in advance.* Ils ont acheté les billets à l'avance.

advance booking NOUN
♦**Advance booking is essential.** Il est indispensable de réserver.

advanced ADJECTIVE
avancé

advantage NOUN

l' <u>avantage</u> MASC ◊ *Going to university has many advantages.* Aller à l'université présente de nombreux avantages.
♦**to take advantage of something** profiter de quelque chose ◊ *He took advantage of the good weather to go for a walk.* Il a profité du beau temps pour faire une promenade.
♦**to take advantage of somebody** exploiter quelqu'un ◊ *The company was taking advantage of its employees.* La société exploitait ses employés.

adventure NOUN
l' <u>aventure</u> FEM

adverb NOUN
l' <u>adverbe</u> MASC

advert, advertisement NOUN
1 la <u>publicité</u> (*on TV*)
2 l' <u>annonce</u> FEM (*in newspaper*)

to **advertise** VERB
faire de la <u>publicité</u> pour ◊ *They're advertising the new model.* Ils font de la publicité pour leur nouveau modèle.
♦**Jobs are advertised in the paper.** Le journal publie des annonces d'emplois.

advertising NOUN
la <u>publicité</u>

advice NOUN
les <u>conseils</u> MASC PL ◊ *to give somebody advice* donner des conseils à quelqu'un
♦**a piece of advice** un conseil ◊ *He gave me a good piece of advice.* Il m'a donné un bon conseil.

to **advise** VERB
<u>conseiller</u> ◊ *He advised me to wait.* Il m'a conseillé d'attendre. ◊ *He advised me not to go there.* Il m'a conseillé de ne pas y aller.

aerial NOUN
l' <u>antenne</u> FEM

aerobics PL NOUN
l' <u>aérobic</u> FEM SING ◊ *I'm going to aerobics tonight.* Je vais au cours d'aérobic ce soir.

aeroplane NOUN
l' <u>avion</u> MASC

aerosol NOUN
la <u>bombe</u>

affair NOUN
1 l' <u>aventure</u> FEM (*romantic*) ◊ *to have an affair with somebody* avoir une aventure avec quelqu'un
2 l' <u>affaire</u> FEM (*event*)

to **affect** VERB

affecter

affectionate ADJECTIVE
<u>affectueux</u> MASC
<u>affectueuse</u> FEM

to **afford** VERB
<u>avoir les moyens d'acheter</u> ◊ *I can't afford a new pair of jeans.* Je n'ai pas les moyens d'acheter un nouveau jean.
♦**We can't afford to go on holiday.** Nous n'avons pas les moyens de partir en vacances.

afraid ADJECTIVE
♦**to be afraid of something** avoir peur de quelque chose ◊ *I'm afraid of spiders.* J'ai peur des araignées.
♦**I'm afraid I can't come.** Je crains de ne pouvoir venir.
♦**I'm afraid so.** Hélas oui.
♦**I'm afraid not.** Hélas non.

Africa NOUN
l' <u>Afrique</u> FEM
♦**in Africa** en Afrique

African ADJECTIVE
see also **African** NOUN
<u>africain</u> MASC
<u>africaine</u> FEM

African NOUN
see also **African** ADJECTIVE
l' <u>Africain</u> MASC
l' <u>Africaine</u> FEM

after PREPOSITION, ADVERB, CONJUNCTION
<u>après</u> ◊ *after dinner* après le dîner ◊ *He ran after me.* Il a couru après moi. ◊ *soon after* peu après
♦**after I'd had a rest** après m'être reposé
♦**after having asked** après avoir demandé
♦**after all** après tout

afternoon NOUN
l' <u>après-midi</u> MASC/FEM ◊ *3 o'clock in the afternoon* trois heures de l'après-midi ◊ *this afternoon* cet après-midi ◊ *on Saturday afternoon* samedi après-midi

afters NOUN
le <u>dessert</u>

aftershave NOUN
l' <u>après-rasage</u> MASC

afterwards ADVERB
<u>après</u> ◊ *She left not long afterwards.* Elle est partie peu de temps après.

again ADVERB
1 <u>de nouveau</u> (*once more*) ◊ *They're friends again.* Ils sont de nouveau amis.

☞

2 encore une fois (*one more time*)
◊ *Can you tell me again?* Tu peux me le dire encore une fois?
♦ **not ... again** ne ... plus ◊ *I won't go there again.* Je n'y retournerai plus.
♦ **Do it again!** Refais-le!
♦ **again and again** à plusieurs reprises

against PREPOSITION
contre ◊ *He leant against the wall.* Il s'est appuyé contre le mur. ◊ *I'm against nuclear testing.* Je suis contre les essais nucléaires.

age NOUN
l' âge MASC ◊ *at the age of 16* à l'âge de seize ans ◊ *an age limit* une limite d'âge
♦ **I haven't been to the cinema for ages.** Ça fait une éternité que je ne suis pas allé au cinéma.

aged ADJECTIVE
♦ **aged 10** âgé de dix ans

agenda NOUN
l' ordre du jour MASC ◊ *on the agenda* à l'ordre du jour ◊ *the agenda for today's meeting* l'ordre du jour de la réunion d'aujourd'hui

*Be careful not to translate **agenda** by the French word **agenda**.*

agent NOUN
l' agent MASC ◊ *an estate agent* un agent immobilier ◊ *a travel agent* un agent de voyage

aggressive ADJECTIVE
agressif MASC
agressive FEM

ago ADVERB
♦ **two days ago** il y a deux jours
♦ **two years ago** il y a deux ans
♦ **not long ago** il n'y a pas longtemps
♦ **How long ago did it happen?** Il y a combien de temps que c'est arrivé?

agony NOUN
♦ **to be in agony** souffrir le martyre ◊ *He was in agony.* Il souffrait le martyre.

to **agree** VERB
♦ **to agree with** être d'accord avec ◊ *I agree with Carol.* Je suis d'accord avec Carol.
♦ **to agree to do something** accepter de faire quelque chose ◊ *He agreed to go and pick her up.* Il a accepté d'aller la chercher.
♦ **to agree that ...** admettre que ... ◊ *I agree that it's difficult.* J'admets que c'est difficile.
♦ **Garlic doesn't agree with me.** Je ne supporte pas l'ail.

agreed ADJECTIVE

convenu ◊ *at the agreed time* au moment convenu

agreement NOUN
l' accord MASC
♦ **to be in agreement** être d'accord ◊ *Everybody was in agreement with Ray.* Tout le monde était d'accord avec Ray.

agricultural ADJECTIVE
agricole

agriculture NOUN
l' agriculture FEM

ahead ADVERB
devant ◊ *She looked straight ahead.* Elle regardait droit devant elle.
♦ **ahead of time** en avance
♦ **to plan ahead** organiser à l'avance
♦ **The French are 5 points ahead.** Les Français ont cinq points d'avance.
♦ **Go ahead!** Allez-y!

aid NOUN
♦ **in aid of charity** au profit d'associations caritatives

AIDS NOUN
le sida

to **aim** VERB
see also **aim** NOUN
♦ **to aim at** braquer sur ◊ *He aimed a gun at me.* Il a braqué un revolver sur moi.
♦ **The film is aimed at children.** Le film est destiné aux enfants.
♦ **to aim to do something** avoir l'intention de faire quelque chose ◊ *Janice aimed to leave at 5 o'clock.* Janice avait l'intention de partir à cinq heures.

aim NOUN
see also **aim** VERB
l' objectif MASC ◊ *The aim of the festival is to raise money.* L'objectif du festival est de collecter des fonds.

air NOUN
l' air MASC ◊ *to get some fresh air* prendre l'air
♦ **by air** en avion ◊ *I prefer to travel by air.* Je préfère voyager en avion.

air-conditioned ADJECTIVE
climatisé

air conditioning NOUN
la climatisation

Air Force NOUN
l' armée de l'air FEM

air hostess NOUN
l' hôtesse de l'air FEM ◊ *She's an air hostess.* Elle est hôtesse de l'air.

airline NOUN
la compagnie aérienne

airmail NOUN
♦**by airmail** par avion

airplane NOUN [US]
l' avion MASC

airport NOUN
l' aéroport MASC

aisle NOUN
l' allée centrale FEM

alarm NOUN
l' alarme FEM (*warning*)
♦**a fire alarm** un avertisseur d'incendie

alarm clock NOUN
le réveil

album NOUN
l' album MASC

alcohol NOUN
l' alcool MASC

alcoholic NOUN
see also **alcoholic** ADJECTIVE
l' alcoolique MASC/FEM ◊ *He's an alcoholic.* C'est un alcoolique.

alcoholic ADJECTIVE
see also **alcoholic** NOUN
alcoolisé ◊ *alcoholic drinks* des boissons alcoolisées

alert ADJECTIVE
[1] (*bright*)
vif MASC
vive FEM
◊ *a very alert baby* un bébé très vif
[2] (*paying attention*)
vigilant ◊ *We must stay alert.* Nous devons rester vigilants.

A levels PL NOUN
le baccalauréat SING

ⓘ The **baccalauréat** (or **bac** for short) is taken at the age of 17 or 18. Students have to sit one of a variety of set subject combinations, rather than being able to choose any combination of subjects they want. If you pass you have the right to a place at university.

Algeria NOUN
l' Algérie FEM
♦**in Algeria** en Algérie

alien NOUN
l' extra-terrestre MASC/FEM (*from outer space*)

alike ADVERB
♦**to look alike** se ressembler ◊ *The two sisters look alike.* Les deux sœurs se ressemblent.

alive ADJECTIVE
vivant

all ADJECTIVE, PRONOUN, ADVERB

tout
(MASC PL tous)
◊ *all the time* tout le temps ◊ *I ate all of it.* J'ai tout mangé. ◊ *all day* toute la journée ◊ *all the books* tous les livres ◊ *all the girls* toutes les filles
♦**All of us went.** Nous y sommes tous allés.
♦**after all** après tout ◊ *After all, nobody can make us go.* Après tout, personne ne peut nous obliger à y aller.
♦**all alone** tout seul ◊ *She's all alone.* Elle est toute seule.
♦**not at all** pas du tout ◊ *I'm not tired at all.* Je ne suis pas du tout fatigué.
♦**The score is 5 all.** Le score est de cinq partout.

allergic ADJECTIVE
allergique
♦**to be allergic to something** être allergique à quelque chose ◊ *I'm allergic to cats' hair.* Je suis allergique aux poils de chat.

alley NOUN
la ruelle

to **allow** VERB
♦**to be allowed to do something** être autorisé à faire quelque chose ◊ *He's not allowed to go out at night.* Il n'est pas autorisé à sortir le soir.
♦**to allow somebody to do something** permettre à quelqu'un de faire quelque chose ◊ *His mum allowed him to go out.* Sa mère lui a permis de sortir.

all right ADVERB
[1] bien (*okay*) ◊ *Everything turned out all right.* Tout s'est bien terminé.
♦**Are you all right?** Ça va?
[2] pas mal (*not bad*) ◊ *The film was all right.* Le film n'était pas mal.
[3] d'accord (*when agreeing*) ◊ *We'll talk about it later. – All right.* On en reparlera plus tard. – D'accord.
♦**Is that all right with you?** Tu es d'accord?

almond NOUN
l' amande FEM

almost ADVERB
presque ◊ *I've almost finished.* J'ai presque fini.

alone ADJECTIVE, ADVERB
seul ◊ *She lives alone.* Elle habite seule.
♦**to leave somebody alone** laisser quelqu'un tranquille ◊ *Leave her alone!* Laisse-la tranquille!
♦**to leave something alone** ne pas toucher à quelque chose ◊ *Leave my*

☞

things alone! Ne touche pas à mes affaires!

along PREPOSITION, ADVERB
le long de ◊ *Chris was walking along the beach.* Chris se promenait le long de la plage.
♦**all along** depuis le début ◊ *He was lying to me all along.* Il m'a menti depuis le début.

aloud ADVERB
à haute voix ◊ *He read the poem aloud.* Il a lu le poème à haute voix.

alphabet NOUN
l' alphabet MASC

Alps PL NOUN
les Alpes FEM PL

already ADVERB
déjà ◊ *Liz had already gone.* Liz était déjà partie.

also ADVERB
aussi

altar NOUN
l' autel MASC

to **alter** VERB
changer

alternate ADJECTIVE
♦**on alternate days** tous les deux jours

alternative NOUN
see also **alternative** ADJECTIVE
le choix ◊ *You have no alternative.* Tu n'as pas le choix.
♦**Fruit is a healthy alternative to chocolate.** Les fruits sont plus sains que le chocolat.
♦**There are several alternatives.** Il y a plusieurs possibilités.

alternative ADJECTIVE
see also **alternative** NOUN
autre ◊ *They made alternative plans.* Ils ont pris d'autres dispositions.
♦**an alternative solution** une solution de rechange
♦**alternative medicine** la médecine douce

alternatively ADVERB
♦**Alternatively, we could just stay at home.** On pourrait aussi rester à la maison.

although CONJUNCTION
bien que
bien que has to be followed by a verb in the subjunctive.
◊ *Although she was tired, she stayed up late.* Bien qu'elle soit fatiguée, elle s'est couchée tard.

altogether ADVERB
[1] en tout (*in total*) ◊ *You owe me £20 altogether.* Tu me dois vingt livres en tout.

[2] tout à fait (*completely*) ◊ *I'm not altogether happy with your work.* Je ne suis pas tout à fait satisfait de votre travail.

aluminium NOUN (US **aluminum**)
l' aluminium MASC

always ADVERB
toujours ◊ *He's always moaning.* Il est toujours en train de ronchonner.

am VERB see **be**

a.m. ABBREVIATION
du matin ◊ *at 4 a.m.* à quatre heures du matin

amateur NOUN
l' amateur MASC

to **amaze** VERB
♦**to be amazed** être stupéfait ◊ *I was amazed that I managed to do it.* J'étais stupéfait d'avoir réussi.

amazed ADJECTIVE
stupéfait ◊ *I was amazed that I managed to do it.* J'étais stupéfait d'y être arrivé.

amazing ADJECTIVE
[1] (*surprising*)
stupéfiant ◊ *That's amazing news!* C'est une nouvelle stupéfiante!
[2] (*excellent*)
exceptionnel MASC
exceptionnelle FEM
◊ *Vivian's an amazing cook.* Vivian est une cuisinière exceptionnelle.

ambassador NOUN
l' ambassadeur MASC
l' ambassadrice FEM

amber ADJECTIVE
♦**an amber light** un feu orange

ambition NOUN
l' ambition FEM

ambitious ADJECTIVE
ambitieux MASC
ambitieuse FEM
◊ *She's very ambitious.* Elle est très ambitieuse.

ambulance NOUN
l' ambulance FEM

amenities PL NOUN
les aménagements MASC PL
♦**The hotel has very good amenities.** L'hôtel est très bien aménagé.

America NOUN
l' Amérique FEM
♦**in America** en Amérique
♦**to America** en Amérique

American ADJECTIVE
see also **American** NOUN

américain ◊ *He's American.* Il est
américain. ◊ *She's American.* Elle est
américaine.

American NOUN

see also **American** ADJECTIVE

l' Américain MASC
l' Américaine FEM
♦**the Americans** les Américains

among PREPOSITION
parmi ◊ *There were six children
among them.* Il y avait six enfants
parmi eux.
♦**We were among friends.** Nous étions
entre amis.
♦**among other things** entre autres

amount NOUN
1 la somme ◊ *a large amount of
money* une grosse somme d'argent
2 la quantité
♦**a huge amount of rice** une énorme
quantité de riz

amp NOUN
1 l' ampère MASC (*of electricity*)
2 l' ampli MASC (*for hi-fi*)

amplifier NOUN
l' amplificateur MASC (*for hi-fi*)

to **amuse** VERB
amuser ◊ *He was most amused by
the story.* L'histoire l'a beaucoup
amusé.

amusement arcade NOUN
la salle de jeux électroniques

an ARTICLE *see* **a**

to **analyse** VERB
analyser

analysis NOUN
l' analyse FEM

to **analyze** VERB US
analyser

ancestor NOUN
l' ancêtre MASC/FEM

anchor NOUN
l' ancre FEM

ancient ADJECTIVE
1 (*civilization*)
antique ◊ *ancient Greece* la Grèce
antique
2 (*custom, building*)
ancien MASC
ancienne FEM
◊ *an ancient monument* un
monument ancien

and CONJUNCTION
et ◊ *you and me* toi et moi ◊ *2 and 2
are 4* deux et deux font quatre
♦**Please try and come!** Essaie de venir!
♦**He talked and talked.** Il n'a pas arrêté
de parler.
♦**better and better** de mieux en mieux

angel NOUN
l' ange MASC

anger NOUN
la colère

angle NOUN
l' angle MASC

angler NOUN
le pêcheur à la ligne
la pêcheuse à la ligne

angling NOUN
la pêche à la ligne

angry ADJECTIVE
en colère ◊ *Dad looks very angry.*
Papa a l'air très en colère.
♦**to be angry with somebody** être
furieux contre quelqu'un ◊ *Mum's
really angry with you.* Maman est
vraiment furieuse contre toi.
♦**to get angry** se fâcher

animal NOUN
l' animal MASC
(PL les animaux)

ankle NOUN
la cheville

anniversary NOUN
l' anniversaire MASC ◊ *a wedding
anniversary* un anniversaire de
mariage

to **announce** VERB
annoncer

announcement NOUN
l' annonce FEM

to **annoy** VERB
agacer ◊ *He's really annoying me.* Il
m'agace vraiment.
♦**to get annoyed** se fâcher ◊ *Don't get
so annoyed!* Ne vous fâchez pas!

annoying ADJECTIVE
agaçant ◊ *It's really annoying.* C'est
vraiment agaçant.

annual ADJECTIVE
annuel MASC
annuelle FEM
◊ *an annual meeting* une réunion
annuelle

anorak NOUN
l' anorak MASC

another ADJECTIVE
un autre
une autre
◊ *Would you like another piece of
cake?* Tu veux un autre morceau de
gâteau? ◊ *Have you got another skirt?*
Tu as une autre jupe?

to **answer** VERB

see also **answer** NOUN

répondre à ◊ *Can you answer my
question?* Peux-tu répondre à ma

☞

question? ◊ *to answer the phone* répondre au téléphone

♦**to answer the door** aller ouvrir ◊ *Can you answer the door please?* Tu peux aller ouvrir s'il te plaît?

answer NOUN

see also **answer** VERB

1 la réponse (*to question*)
2 la solution (*to problem*)

answering machine NOUN
le répondeur

ant NOUN
la fourmi

to **antagonize** VERB
contrarier ◊ *He didn't want to antagonize her.* Il ne voulait pas la contrarier.

Antarctic NOUN
l' Antarctique FEM

anthem NOUN
♦**the national anthem** l'hymne national MASC

antibiotic NOUN
l' antibiotique MASC

antidepressant NOUN
l' antidépresseur MASC

antique NOUN
le meuble ancien (*furniture*)

antique shop NOUN
le magasin d'antiquités

antiseptic NOUN
l' antiseptique MASC

any ADJECTIVE, PRONOUN, ADVERB

*Use **du**, **de la** or **des** to translate **any** according to the gender of the French noun that follows it. **du** and **de la** become **de l'** when they're followed by a noun starting with a vowel.*

1 du ◊ *Would you like any bread?* Voulez-vous du pain?
de la ◊ *Would you like any beer?* Voulez-vous de la bière?
de l' ◊ *Have you got any mineral water?* Avez-vous de l'eau minérale?
des ◊ *Have you got any Blur CDs?* Avez-vous des CD de Blur?

*If you want to say you haven't got any of something, use **de** whatever the gender of the following noun is. **de** becomes **d'** when it comes before a noun starting with a vowel.*

2 de ◊ *I haven't got any books.* Je n'ai pas de livres.
d' ◊ *I haven't got any money.* Je n'ai pas d'argent.

*Use **en** where there is no noun after **any**.*

3 en ◊ *Sorry, I haven't got any.* Désolé, je n'en ai pas.

♦**any more (1)** (*additional*) encore de ◊ *Would you like any more coffee?* Est-ce que tu veux encore du café?

♦**any more (2)** (*no longer*) ne ... plus ◊ *I don't love him any more.* Je ne l'aime plus.

anybody PRONOUN

1 quelqu'un (*in question*) ◊ *Has anybody got a pen?* Est-ce que quelqu'un a un stylo?
2 n'importe qui (*no matter who*) ◊ *Anybody can learn to swim.* N'importe qui peut apprendre à nager.

*Use **ne ... personne** in a negative sentence. **ne** comes before the verb, **personne** after it.*

3 ne ... personne ◊ *I can't see anybody.* Je ne vois personne.

anyhow ADVERB
de toute façon ◊ *He doesn't want to go out and anyhow he's not allowed.* Il ne veut pas sortir et de toute façon il n'y est pas autorisé.

anyone PRONOUN

1 quelqu'un (*in question*) ◊ *Has anyone got a pen?* Est-ce que quelqu'un a un stylo?
2 n'importe qui (*no matter who*) ◊ *Anyone can learn to swim.* N'importe qui peut apprendre à nager.

*Use **ne ... personne** in a negative sentence. **ne** comes before the verb, **personne** after it.*

3 ne ... personne ◊ *I can't see anyone.* Je ne vois personne.

anything PRONOUN

1 quelque chose (*in question*) ◊ *Would you like anything to eat?* Tu veux manger quelque chose?
2 n'importe quoi (*no matter what*) ◊ *Anything could happen.* Il pourrait arriver n'importe quoi.

*Use **ne ... rien** in a negative sentence. **ne** comes before the verb, **rien** after it.*

3 ne ... rien ◊ *I can't hear anything.* Je n'entends rien.

anyway ADVERB
de toute façon ◊ *He doesn't want to go out and anyway he's not allowed.* Il ne veut pas sortir et de toute façon il n'y est pas autorisé.

anywhere ADVERB

1 quelque part (*in question*) ◊ *Have you seen my coat anywhere?* Est-ce

que tu as vu mon manteau quelque part?

2 n'importe où ◊ *You can buy stamps almost anywhere.* On peut acheter des timbres presque n'importe où.

Use *ne ... nulle part* in a negative sentence. *ne* comes before the verb, *nulle part* after it.

3 ne ... nulle part ◊ *I can't find it anywhere.* Je ne le trouve nulle part.

apart ADVERB
♦**The two towns are 10 kilometres apart.** Les deux villes sont à dix kilomètres l'une de l'autre.
♦**apart from** à part ◊ *Apart from that, everything's fine.* À part ça, tout va bien.

apartment NOUN
l' appartement MASC

to **apologize** VERB
s'excuser ◊ *He apologized for being late.* Il s'est excusé de son retard.
♦**I apologize!** Je vous prie de m'excuser.

apology NOUN
les excuses FEM PL

apostrophe NOUN
l' apostrophe FEM

apparatus NOUN
1 le matériel (*in* lab)
2 les agrès MASC PL (*in* gym)

apparent ADJECTIVE
apparent

apparently ADVERB
apparemment

to **appeal** VERB
see also **appeal** NOUN
lancer un appel ◊ *They appealed for help.* Ils ont lancé un appel au secours.
♦**Greece doesn't appeal to me.** Ça ne me tente pas d'aller en Grèce.
♦**Does that appeal to you?** Ça te tente?

appeal NOUN
see also **appeal** VERB
l' appel MASC ◊ *They have launched an appeal.* Ils ont lancé un appel.

to **appear** VERB
1 apparaître (*come into view*) ◊ *The bus appeared around the corner.* Le bus est apparu au coin de la rue.
♦**to appear on TV** passer à la télé
2 paraître (*seem*) ◊ *She appeared to be asleep.* Elle paraissait dormir.

appearance NOUN
l' apparence FEM (*looks*) ◊ *She takes great care over her appearance.* Elle prend grand soin de son apparence.

appendicitis NOUN
l' appendicite FEM

appetite NOUN
l' appétit MASC

to **applaud** VERB
applaudir

applause NOUN
les applaudissements MASC PL

apple NOUN
la pomme
♦**an apple tree** un pommier

applicant NOUN
le candidat
la candidate
◊ *There were a hundred applicants for the job.* Il y avait cent candidats pour ce poste.

application NOUN
♦**a job application** une candidature

application form NOUN
1 le dossier de candidature (*for job*)
2 le dossier d'inscription (*for university*)

to **apply** VERB
♦**to apply for a job** poser sa candidature à un poste
♦**to apply to** (*be relevant*) s'appliquer à ◊ *This rule doesn't apply to us.* Ce règlement ne s'applique pas à nous.

appointment NOUN
le rendez-vous ◊ *I've got a dental appointment.* J'ai rendez-vous chez le dentiste.

to **appreciate** VERB
être reconnaissant de ◊ *I really appreciate your help.* Je vous suis extrêmement reconnaissant de votre aide.

apprentice NOUN
l' apprenti MASC
l' apprentie FEM

to **approach** VERB
1 s'approcher de (*get nearer to*) ◊ *He approached the house.* Il s'est approché de la maison.
2 aborder (*tackle*) ◊ *to approach a problem* aborder un problème

appropriate ADJECTIVE
approprié ◊ *That dress isn't very appropriate for an interview.* Cette robe n'est pas très appropriée pour un entretien.

approval NOUN
l' approbation FEM

to **approve** VERB
♦**to approve of** approuver ◊ *I don't approve of his choice.* Je n'approuve pas son choix.

☞

♦**They didn't approve of his girlfriend.**
Sa copine ne leur a pas plu.

approximate ADJECTIVE
approximatif MASC
approximative FEM

apricot NOUN
l' abricot MASC

April NOUN
avril MASC
♦**in April** en avril
♦**April Fool's Day** le premier avril

apron NOUN
le tablier

Aquarius NOUN
le Verseau ◊ *I'm Aquarius.* Je suis
Verseau.

Arab ADJECTIVE
see also **Arab** NOUN
arabe ◊ *the Arab countries* les pays
arabes

Arab NOUN
see also **Arab** ADJECTIVE
l' Arabe MASC/FEM

Arabic NOUN
l' arabe MASC

arch NOUN
l' arc MASC

archaeologist NOUN
l' archéologue MASC/FEM ◊ *He's an
archaeologist.* Il est archéologue.

archaeology NOUN
l' archéologie FEM

archbishop NOUN
l' archevêque MASC

archeologist NOUN US
l' archéologue MASC/FEM ◊ *He's an
archeologist.* Il est archéologue.

archeology NOUN US
l' archéologie FEM

architect NOUN
l' architecte MASC/FEM ◊ *She's an
architect.* Elle est architecte.

architecture NOUN
l' architecture FEM

Arctic NOUN
l' Arctique MASC

are VERB *see* **be**

area NOUN
[1] la région ◊ *She lives in the Paris
area.* Elle habite dans la région
parisienne.
[2] le quartier ◊ *My favourite area of
Paris is Montmartre.* Montmartre est
le quartier de Paris que je préfère.
[3] la superficie ◊ *The field has an
area of 1500m².* Le champ a une
superficie de mille cinq cent mètres
carrés.

Argentina NOUN
l' Argentine FEM
♦**in Argentina** en Argentine

Argentinian ADJECTIVE
argentin

to **argue** VERB
se disputer ◊ *They never stop
arguing.* Ils n'arrêtent pas de se
disputer.

argument NOUN
♦**to have an argument** se disputer
◊ *They had an argument.* Ils se sont
disputés.

Aries NOUN
le Bélier ◊ *I'm Aries.* Je suis Bélier.

arm NOUN
le bras

armchair NOUN
le fauteuil

armour NOUN (US **armor**)
l' armure FEM

army NOUN
l' armée FEM

around PREPOSITION, ADVERB
[1] autour de ◊ *She wore a scarf
around her neck.* Elle portait une
écharpe autour du cou.
[2] environ (*approximately*) ◊ *It costs
around £100.* Cela coûte environ cent
livres.
[3] vers (*date, time*) ◊ *Let's meet at
around 8 p.m.* Retrouvons-nous vers
vingt heures.
♦**around here (1)** (*nearby*) près d'ici ◊ *Is
there a chemist's around here?* Est-ce
qu'il y a une pharmacie près d'ici?
♦**around here (2)** (*in this area*) dans les
parages ◊ *He lives around here.* Il
habite dans les parages.

to **arrange** VERB
♦**to arrange to do something** prévoir
de faire quelque chose ◊ *They
arranged to go out together on
Friday.* Ils ont prévu de sortir
ensemble vendredi.
♦**to arrange a meeting** convenir d'un
rendez-vous ◊ *Can we arrange a
meeting?* Pouvons-nous convenir d'un
rendez-vous?
♦**to arrange a party** organiser une fête

arrangement NOUN
l' arrangement MASC (*plan*)
♦**They made arrangements to go out
on Friday night.** Ils ont organisé une
sortie vendredi soir.

to **arrest** VERB
see also **arrest** NOUN

A

arrêter ◊ *The police have arrested 5 people.* La police a arrêté cinq personnes.

arrest NOUN
see also **arrest** VERB
l' arrestation FEM ◊ *You're under arrest!* Vous êtes en état d'arrestation!

arrival NOUN
l' arrivée FEM

to **arrive** VERB
arriver ◊ *I arrived at 5 o'clock.* Je suis arrivé à cinq heures.

arrow NOUN
la flèche

art NOUN
l' art MASC

artery NOUN
l' artère FEM

art gallery NOUN
le musée

article NOUN
l' article MASC ◊ *a newspaper article* un article de journal

artificial ADJECTIVE
artificiel MASC
artificielle FEM

artist NOUN
l' artiste MASC/FEM ◊ *She's an artist.* C'est une artiste.

artistic ADJECTIVE
artistique

as CONJUNCTION, ADVERB
1 au moment où (*while*) ◊ *He came in as I was leaving.* Il est arrivé au moment où je partais.
2 puisque (*since*) ◊ *As it's Sunday, you can have a lie-in.* Tu peux faire la grasse matinée, puisque c'est dimanche.
♦**as ... as** aussi ... que ◊ *Pierre's as tall as Michel.* Pierre est aussi grand que Michel.
♦**twice as ... as** deux fois plus ... que ◊ *Her coat cost twice as much as mine.* Son manteau a coûté deux fois plus cher que le mien.
♦**as much ... as** autant ... que ◊ *I haven't got as much money as you.* Je n'ai pas autant d'argent que toi.
♦**as soon as possible** dès que possible ◊ *I'll do it as soon as possible.* Je le ferai dès que possible.
♦**as from tomorrow** à partir de demain ◊ *As from tomorrow, the shop will stay open until 10 p.m.* À partir de demain, le magasin restera ouvert jusqu'à vingt-deux heures.

♦**as though** comme si ◊ *She acted as though she hadn't seen me.* Elle a fait comme si elle ne m'avait pas vu.
♦**as if** comme si
♦**He works as a waiter in the holidays.** Il travaille comme serveur pendant les vacances.

asap ABBREVIATION (= *as soon as possible*)
dès que possible

ashamed ADJECTIVE
♦**to be ashamed** avoir honte ◊ *You should be ashamed of yourself!* Tu devrais avoir honte!

ashtray NOUN
le cendrier

Asia NOUN
l' Asie FEM
♦**in Asia** en Asie

Asian ADJECTIVE
see also **Asian** NOUN
asiatique ◊ *He's Asian.* C'est un Asiatique. ◊ *She's Asian.* C'est une Asiatique.

Asian NOUN
see also **Asian** ADJECTIVE
l' Asiatique MASC/FEM

to **ask** VERB
1 demander (*inquire, request*) ◊ *"Have you finished?" she asked.* "Tu as fini?" a-t-elle demandé.
♦**to ask somebody something** demander quelque chose à quelqu'un ◊ *He asked her how old she was.* Il lui a demandé quel âge elle avait.
♦**to ask for something** demander quelque chose ◊ *He asked for a cup of tea.* Il a demandé une tasse de thé.
♦**to ask somebody to do something** demander à quelqu'un de faire quelque chose ◊ *She asked him to do the shopping.* Elle lui a demandé de faire les courses.
♦**to ask about something** se renseigner sur quelque chose ◊ *I asked about train times to Leeds.* Je me suis renseigné sur les horaires des trains pour Leeds.
♦**to ask somebody a question** poser une question à quelqu'un
2 inviter ◊ *Have you asked Matthew to the party?* Est-ce que tu as invité Matthew à la fête?
♦**He asked her out.** (*on a date*) Il lui a demandé de sortir avec lui.

asleep ADJECTIVE
♦**to be asleep** dormir ◊ *He's asleep.* Il dort.

☞

♦**to fall asleep** s'endormir ◊ *I fell asleep in front of the TV.* Je me suis endormi devant la télé.

asparagus NOUN
les <u>asperges</u> FEM PL

aspect NOUN
l' <u>aspect</u> MASC

aspirin NOUN
l' <u>aspirine</u> FEM

asset NOUN
l' <u>atout</u> MASC ◊ *Her experience will be an asset to the firm.* Son expérience sera un atout pour l'entreprise.

assignment NOUN
le <u>devoir</u> (*in school*)

assistance NOUN
l' <u>aide</u> FEM

assistant NOUN
1 (*in shop*)
le <u>vendeur</u>
la <u>vendeuse</u>
2 (*helper*)
l' <u>assistant</u> MASC
l' <u>assistante</u> FEM

association NOUN
l' <u>association</u> FEM

assortment NOUN
l' <u>assortiment</u> MASC

to **assume** VERB
<u>supposer</u> ◊ *I assume she won't be coming.* Je suppose qu'elle ne viendra pas.

to **assure** VERB
<u>assurer</u> ◊ *He assured me he was coming.* Il m'a assuré qu'il viendrait.

asthma NOUN
l' <u>asthme</u> MASC ◊ *I've got asthma.* J'ai de l'asthme.

to **astonish** VERB
<u>étonner</u>

astonished ADJECTIVE
<u>étonné</u>

astonishing ADJECTIVE
<u>étonnant</u>

astrology NOUN
l' <u>astrologie</u> FEM

astronaut NOUN
l' <u>astronaute</u> MASC/FEM

astronomy NOUN
l' <u>astronomie</u> FEM

asylum seeker NOUN
le <u>demandeur d'asile</u>
la <u>demandeuse d'asile</u>

at PREPOSITION

> à + *le* becomes *au*, à + *les* becomes *aux*.

<u>à</u> ◊ *at 4 o'clock* à quatre heures ◊ *at Christmas* à Noël ◊ *at 50 km/h* à

cinquante km/h ◊ *at home* à la maison ◊ *two at a time* deux à la fois ◊ *at school* à l'école
<u>au</u> ◊ *at the office* au bureau
<u>aux</u> ◊ *at the races* aux courses
♦**at night** la nuit
♦**What are you doing at the weekend?** Qu'est-ce que tu fais ce week-end?

ate VERB *see* **eat**

Athens NOUN
<u>Athènes</u>
♦**in Athens** à Athènes

athlete NOUN
l' <u>athlète</u> MASC/FEM

athletic ADJECTIVE
<u>athlétique</u>

athletics NOUN
l' <u>athlétisme</u> MASC ◊ *I like watching the athletics on TV.* J'aime bien regarder les épreuves d'athlétisme à la télé.

Atlantic NOUN
l' <u>océan Atlantique</u> MASC

atlas NOUN
l' <u>atlas</u> MASC

atmosphere NOUN
l' <u>atmosphère</u> FEM

atom NOUN
l' <u>atome</u> MASC

atomic ADJECTIVE
<u>atomique</u>

to **attach** VERB
<u>fixer</u> ◊ *He attached a rope to the car.* Il a fixé une corde à la voiture.
♦**Please find attached** ... Veuillez trouver ci-joint ...

attached ADJECTIVE
♦**to be attached to** être attaché à ◊ *He's very attached to his family.* Il est très attaché à sa famille.

attachment NOUN
la <u>pièce jointe</u> (*email*)

to **attack** VERB
> *see also* **attack** NOUN

<u>attaquer</u> ◊ *The dog attacked her.* Le chien l'a attaquée.

attack NOUN
> *see also* **attack** VERB

l' <u>attaque</u> FEM

attempt NOUN
> *see also* **attempt** VERB

la <u>tentative</u> ◊ *She gave up after several attempts.* Elle y a renoncé après plusieurs tentatives.

to **attempt** VERB
> *see also* **attempt** NOUN

♦**to attempt to do something** essayer de faire quelque chose ◊ *I attempted* *to write a song.* J'ai essayé d'écrire une chanson.

to **attend** VERB
assister à ◊ *to attend a meeting* assister à une réunion
> *Be careful not to translate* **to attend** *by* **attendre.**

attention NOUN
l' attention FEM
♦**to pay attention to** faire attention à ◊ *He didn't pay attention to what I was saying.* Il ne faisait pas attention à ce que je disais.

attic NOUN
le grenier

attitude NOUN
l' attitude FEM (*way of thinking*) ◊ *I really don't like your attitude!* Je n'aime pas du tout ton attitude!

attorney NOUN US
l' avocat MASC
l' avocate FEM

to **attract** VERB
attirer ◊ *The Lake District attracts lots of tourists.* La région des lacs attire de nombreux touristes.

attraction NOUN
l' attraction FEM ◊ *a tourist attraction* une attraction touristique

attractive ADJECTIVE
séduisant ◊ *She's very attractive.* Elle est très séduisante.

aubergine NOUN
l' aubergine FEM

auction NOUN
la vente aux enchères

audience NOUN
les spectateurs MASC PL (*in theatre*)

audition NOUN
l' audition FEM

August NOUN
août MASC
♦**in August** en août

aunt, aunty NOUN
la tante ◊ *my aunt* ma tante

au pair NOUN
la jeune fille au pair ◊ *She's an au pair.* Elle est jeune fille au pair.

Australia NOUN
l' Australie FEM
♦**in Australia** en Australie
♦**to Australia** en Australie

Australian ADJECTIVE
> see also **Australian** NOUN
australien MASC
australienne FEM
◊ *He's Australian.* Il est australien.

Australian NOUN

> see also **Australian** ADJECTIVE
l' Australien MASC
l' Australienne FEM
♦**the Australians** les Australiens

Austria NOUN
l' Autriche FEM
♦**in Austria** en Autriche

Austrian ADJECTIVE
> see also **Austrian** NOUN
autrichien MASC
autrichienne FEM
◊ *She's Austrian.* Elle est autrichienne.

Austrian NOUN
> see also **Austrian** ADJECTIVE
l' Autrichien MASC
l' Autrichienne FEM
♦**the Austrians** les Autrichiens

author NOUN
l' auteur MASC ◊ *She's a famous author.* C'est un auteur connu.

autobiography NOUN
l' autobiographie FEM

autograph NOUN
l' autographe MASC

automatic ADJECTIVE
automatique ◊ *an automatic door* une porte automatique

automatically ADVERB
automatiquement

autumn NOUN
l' automne MASC
♦**in autumn** en automne

availability NOUN
la disponibilité

available ADJECTIVE
disponible ◊ *Free brochures are available on request.* Des brochures gratuites sont disponibles sur demande. ◊ *Is Mr Cooke available today?* Est-ce que Monsieur Cooke est disponible aujourd'hui?

avalanche NOUN
l' avalanche FEM

avenue NOUN
l' avenue FEM

average NOUN
> see also **average** ADJECTIVE
la moyenne ◊ *on average* en moyenne

average ADJECTIVE
> see also **average** NOUN
moyen MASC
moyenne FEM
◊ *the average price* le prix moyen

avocado NOUN
l' avocat MASC

to **avoid** VERB

éviter ◊ *He avoids her when she's in a bad mood.* Il l'évite lorsqu'elle est de mauvaise humeur.
♦ **to avoid doing something** éviter de faire quelque chose ◊ *Avoid going out on your own at night.* Évite de sortir seul le soir.

awake ADJECTIVE
♦ **to be awake** être réveillé ◊ *Is she awake?* Elle est réveillée?
♦ **He was still awake.** Il ne dormait pas encore.

award NOUN
le prix ◊ *He's won an award.* Il a remporté un prix. ◊ *the award for the best actor* le prix du meilleur acteur

aware ADJECTIVE
♦ **to be aware of something** être conscient de quelque chose

away ADJECTIVE, ADVERB
absent (*not here*) ◊ *André's away today.* André est absent aujourd'hui.
♦ **He's away for a week.** Il est parti pour une semaine.
♦ **The town's 2 kilometres away.** La ville est à deux kilomètres d'ici.
♦ **The coast is 2 hours away by car.** La côte est à deux heures de route.
♦ **Go away!** Va-t'en!

♦ **to put something away** ranger quelque chose ◊ *He put his toys away in the cupboard.* Il a rangé ses jouets dans le placard.

away match NOUN
le match à l'extérieur
(PL les matchs à l'extérieur)

awful ADJECTIVE
affreux MASC
affreuse FEM
◊ *That's awful!* C'est affreux!
♦ **an awful lot of …** énormément de …

awfully ADVERB
♦ **I'm awfully sorry.** Je suis vraiment désolé.

awkward ADJECTIVE
[1] délicat (*difficult to deal with*) ◊ *an awkward situation* une situation délicate
[2] gênant (*embarrassing*) ◊ *an awkward question* une question gênante
♦ **It's a bit awkward for me to come and see you.** Ce n'est pas très pratique pour moi de venir vous voir.

axe NOUN
la hache

B

BA NOUN
la licence
♦ **a BA in French** une licence de
français

baby NOUN
le bébé

baby carriage NOUN US
le landau

to **babysit** VERB
faire du baby-sitting

babysitter NOUN
le/la baby-sitter

babysitting NOUN
le baby-sitting

bachelor NOUN
le célibataire ◊ *He's a bachelor.* Il est
célibataire.

back NOUN
⎡ *see also* **back** ADJECTIVE, VERB ⎤
1 le dos (*of person, horse, book*)
2 l' arrière MASC (*of car, house*) ◊ *in
the back* à l'arrière
3 le verso (*of page*) ◊ *on the back* au
verso
4 le fond (*of room, garden*) ◊ *at the
back* au fond

back ADJECTIVE, ADVERB
⎡ *see also* **back** NOUN, VERB ⎤
arrière MASC, FEM, PL ◊ *the back seat* le
siège arrière ◊ *the back wheel of my
bike* la roue arrière de mon vélo
♦ **the back door** la porte de derrière
♦ **to get back** rentrer ◊ *What time did
you get back?* À quelle heure est-ce
que tu es rentré?
♦ **We went there by bus and walked
back.** Nous y sommes allés en bus et
nous sommes rentrés à pied.
♦ **He's not back yet.** Il n'est pas encore
rentré.
♦ **to call somebody back** rappeler
quelqu'un ◊ *I'll call back later.* Je
rappellerai plus tard.

to **back** VERB
⎡ *see also* **back** NOUN, ADJECTIVE ⎤
soutenir (*support*) ◊ *I'm backing Tony
Blair.* Je soutiens Tony Blair.
♦ **to back a horse** parier sur un cheval
♦ **to back out** se désister ◊ *They
promised to help and then backed
out.* Ils avaient promis de nous aider
et ils se sont désistés.
♦ **to back somebody up** soutenir
quelqu'un

backache NOUN

le mal au dos ◊ *to have backache*
avoir mal au dos

backbone NOUN
la colonne vertébrale

to **backfire** VERB
échouer (*go wrong*)

background NOUN
1 l' arrière-plan MASC ◊ *a house in the
background* une maison à l'arrière-
plan
♦ **background noise** les bruits de fond
MASC PL
2 le milieu
(les milieux PL)
◊ *his family background* son milieu
familial

backhand NOUN
le revers

backing NOUN
le soutien (*support*)

backpack NOUN
le sac à dos

backpacker NOUN
1 (*globe-trotter*)
le routard
la routarde
2 (*hill-walker*)
le randonneur
la randonneuse

backpacking NOUN
♦ **to go backpacking** voyager sac au
dos

back pain NOUN
le mal au dos ◊ *to have back pain*
avoir mal au dos

backside NOUN
le derrière

backstroke NOUN
le dos crawlé

backup NOUN
le soutien (*support*)
♦ **a backup file** une sauvegarde

backwards ADVERB
en arrière ◊ *to take a step backwards*
faire un pas en arrière
♦ **to fall backwards** tomber à la
renverse

back yard NOUN
la cour

bacon NOUN
1 le lard (*French type*)
2 le bacon (*British type*) ◊ *bacon and
eggs* des œufs au bacon

bad ADJECTIVE

[1] mauvais ◊ *a bad film* un mauvais film ◊ *the bad weather* le mauvais temps ◊ *to be in a bad mood* être de mauvaise humeur
♦ **to be bad at something** être mauvais en quelque chose ◊ *I'm really bad at maths.* Je suis vraiment mauvais en maths.

[2] grave (*serious*) ◊ *a bad accident* un accident grave

[3] vilain (*naughty*) ◊ *You bad boy!* Vilain!
♦ **to go bad** (*food*) se gâter
♦ **I feel bad about it.** Ça m'ennuie.
♦ **not bad** pas mal ◊ *That's not bad at all.* Ce n'est pas mal du tout.

badge NOUN
le badge

badly ADVERB
mal ◊ *badly paid* mal payé
♦ **badly wounded** grièvement blessé
♦ **He badly needs a rest.** Il a sérieusement besoin de se reposer.

badminton NOUN
le badminton ◊ *to play badminton* jouer au badminton

bad-tempered ADJECTIVE
♦ **to be bad-tempered (1)** (*by nature*) avoir mauvais caractère ◊ *He's a really bad-tempered person.* Il a vraiment mauvais caractère.
♦ **to be bad-tempered (2)** (*temporarily*) être de mauvaise humeur ◊ *He was really bad-tempered yesterday.* Il était vraiment de mauvaise humeur hier.

baffled ADJECTIVE
déconcerté

bag NOUN
le sac
♦ **an old bag** (*person*) une vieille peau

baggage NOUN
les bagages MASC PL

baggage reclaim NOUN
la livraison des bagages

baggy ADJECTIVE
ample

bagpipes PL NOUN
la cornemuse SING ◊ *Ed plays the bagpipes.* Ed joue de la cornemuse.

to **bake** VERB
♦ **to bake a cake** faire un gâteau

baked ADJECTIVE
cuit au four MASC
cuite au four FEM
◊ *baked potatoes* les pommes de terre cuites au four FEM
♦ **baked beans** les haricots blancs à la sauce tomate MASC

baker NOUN
le boulanger
la boulangère
◊ *He's a baker.* Il est boulanger.

bakery NOUN
la boulangerie

baking ADJECTIVE
♦ **It's baking in here!** Il fait une chaleur torride ici!

balance NOUN
l' équilibre MASC ◊ *to lose one's balance* perdre l'équilibre

balanced ADJECTIVE
équilibré

balcony NOUN
le balcon

bald ADJECTIVE
chauve

ball NOUN
[1] la balle (*tennis, golf, cricket*)
[2] le ballon (*football, rugby*)

ballet NOUN
le ballet ◊ *We went to a ballet.* Nous sommes allés voir un ballet.
♦ **ballet lessons** les cours de danse MASC

ballet dancer NOUN
le danseur classique
la danseuse classique

ballet shoes PL NOUN
les chaussons de danse MASC PL

balloon NOUN
le ballon (*for parties*)
♦ **a hot-air balloon** une montgolfière

ballpoint pen NOUN
le stylo à bille

ballroom dancing NOUN
la danse de salon

ban NOUN
see also **ban** VERB
l' interdiction FEM

to **ban** VERB
see also **ban** NOUN
interdire

banana NOUN
la banane ◊ *a banana skin* une peau de banane

band NOUN
[1] le groupe (*rock band*)
[2] la fanfare (*brass band*)

bandage NOUN
see also **bandage** VERB
le bandage

to **bandage** VERB
see also **bandage** NOUN
mettre un bandage à ◊ *The nurse bandaged his arm.* L'infirmière lui a mis un bandage au bras.

Band-Aid ® NOUN US
le pansement adhésif

bandit NOUN
le bandit

bang NOUN
see also **bang** VERB
[1] la détonation ◇ *I heard a loud bang.* J'ai entendu une forte détonation.
[2] le coup ◇ *a bang on the head* un coup sur la tête
◆ **Bang!** Pan!

to **bang** VERB
see also **bang** NOUN
se cogner (*part of body*) ◇ *I banged my head.* Je me suis cogné la tête.
◆ **to bang the door** claquer la porte
◆ **to bang on the door** cogner à la porte

banger NOUN
[1] le tacot (*old car*) ◇ *His car's an old banger.* Sa voiture est un vieux tacot.
[2] la saucisse (*sausage*) ◇ *bangers and mash* les saucisses à la purée

Bangladesh NOUN
le Bangladesh
◆ **from Bangladesh** du Bangladesh

bank NOUN
[1] la banque (*financial*)
[2] le bord (*of river, lake*)

bank account NOUN
le compte en banque

banker NOUN
le banquier

bank holiday NOUN
le jour férié

banknote NOUN
le billet de banque

banned ADJECTIVE
interdit

bar NOUN
[1] le bar (*pub*)
[2] le comptoir (*counter*)
◆ **a bar of chocolate** une tablette de chocolat
◆ **a bar of soap** une savonnette

barbaric ADJECTIVE
barbare

barbecue NOUN
le barbecue

barber NOUN
le coiffeur pour hommes

bare ADJECTIVE
nu

barefoot ADJECTIVE, ADVERB
nu-pieds MASC, FEM, PL ◇ *The children go around barefoot.* Les enfants se promènent nu-pieds.

◆ **to be barefoot** avoir les pieds nus ◇ *She was barefoot.* Elle avait les pieds nus.

barely ADVERB
à peine ◇ *I could barely hear what she was saying.* J'entendais à peine ce qu'elle disait.

bargain NOUN
l' affaire FEM ◇ *It was a bargain!* C'était une affaire!

barge NOUN
la péniche

to **bark** VERB
aboyer

barmaid NOUN
la barmaid ◇ *She's a barmaid.* Elle est barmaid.

barman NOUN
le barman ◇ *He's a barman.* Il est barman.

barn NOUN
la grange

barrel NOUN
le tonneau
(les tonneaux PL)

barrier NOUN
la barrière

bartender NOUN US
le barman ◇ *He's a bartender.* Il est barman.

base NOUN
la base

baseball NOUN
le base-ball
◆ **a baseball cap** une casquette de base-ball

based ADJECTIVE
◆ **based on** fondé sur

basement NOUN
le sous-sol

to **bash** VERB
see also **bash** NOUN
◆ **to bash something** taper sur quelque chose

bash NOUN
see also **bash** VERB
◆ **I'll have a bash.** Je vais essayer.

basic ADJECTIVE
[1] de base ◇ *It's a basic model.* C'est un modèle de base.
[2] rudimentaire ◇ *The accommodation is pretty basic.* Le logement est plutôt rudimentaire.

basically ADVERB
tout simplement ◇ *Basically, I just don't like him.* Tout simplement, je ne l'aime pas.

basics PL NOUN

☞

les <u>rudiments</u> MASC PL

basil NOUN
le <u>basilic</u>

basin NOUN
le <u>lavabo</u> (*washbasin*)

basis NOUN
♦**on a daily basis** quotidiennement
♦**on a regular basis** régulièrement

basket NOUN
le <u>panier</u>

basketball NOUN
le <u>basket</u>

bass NOUN
1 la <u>basse</u> (*guitar, singer*) ◊ *He plays the bass.* Il joue de la basse. ◊ *He's a bass.* Il est basse.
♦**a bass guitar** une guitare basse
♦**a double bass** une contrebasse
2 les <u>graves</u> MASC PL (*on hi-fi*)

bass drum NOUN
la <u>grosse caisse</u>

bassoon NOUN
le <u>basson</u> ◊ *I play the bassoon.* Je joue du basson.

bastard NOUN
le <u>salaud</u> (*rude*) ◊ *You bastard!* Salaud!

bat NOUN
1 (*for cricket, rounders*)
la <u>batte</u>
2 (*for table tennis*)
la <u>raquette</u>
3 (*animal*)
la <u>chauve-souris</u>
(les chauves-souris PL)

bath NOUN
1 le <u>bain</u> ◊ *to have a bath* prendre un bain
♦**a hot bath** un bain chaud
2 la <u>baignoire</u> (*bathtub*) ◊ *There's a spider in the bath.* Il y a une araignée dans la baignoire.

to **bathe** VERB
se <u>baigner</u>

bathing suit NOUN US
le <u>maillot de bain</u>

bathroom NOUN
la <u>salle de bains</u>

baths PL NOUN
la <u>piscine</u> SING

bath towel NOUN
la <u>serviette de bain</u>

batter NOUN
la <u>pâte à frire</u>

battery NOUN
1 la <u>pile</u> (*for torch, toy*)
2 la <u>batterie</u> (*of car*)

battle NOUN

la <u>bataille</u> ◊ *the Battle of Hastings* la bataille de Hastings
♦**It was a battle, but we managed in the end.** Il a fallu se battre, mais on a fini par y arriver.

battleship NOUN
le <u>cuirassé</u>

bay NOUN
la <u>baie</u>

BC ABBREVIATION (= *before Christ*)
<u>av. J.-C.</u> (= *avant Jésus-Christ*) ◊ *in 200 BC* en deux cents avant Jésus-Christ

to **be** VERB
<u>être</u> ◊ *I'm tired.* Je suis fatigué.
◊ *You're late.* Tu es en retard. ◊ *She's English.* Elle est anglaise. ◊ *Edinburgh is in Scotland.* Édimbourg est en Écosse. ◊ *It's 4 o'clock.* Il est quatre heures. ◊ *We are all happy.* Nous sommes tous heureux. ◊ *They are in Paris at the moment.* Ils sont à Paris en ce moment. ◊ *I've been ill.* J'ai été malade.
♦**It's the 28th of October today.** Nous sommes le vingt-huit octobre.
♦**Have you been to Greece before?** Est-ce que tu es déjà allé en Grèce?
♦**I've never been to Paris.** Je ne suis jamais allé à Paris.
♦**to be killed** être tué
When you are saying what somebody's occupation is, you leave out the "a" in French.
◊ *She's a doctor.* Elle est médecin.
◊ *He's a student.* Il est étudiant.
*With certain adjectives, such as "cold", "hot", "hungry" and "thirsty", use **avoir** instead of **être**.*
♦**I'm cold.** J'ai froid.
♦**I'm hungry.** J'ai faim.
*When saying how old somebody is, use **avoir** not **être**.*
♦**I'm fourteen.** J'ai quatorze ans.
♦**How old are you?** Quel âge as-tu?
*When referring to the weather, use **faire**.*
♦**It's cold.** Il fait froid.
♦**It's too hot.** Il fait trop chaud.
♦**It's a nice day.** Il fait beau.

beach NOUN
la <u>plage</u>

bead NOUN
la <u>perle</u>

beak NOUN
le <u>bec</u>

beam NOUN
le <u>rayon</u>

beans PL NOUN
1 les <u>haricots</u> MASC PL

② les haricots blancs à la sauce tomate MASC PL (*baked beans*) ◊ *I had beans on toast.* J'ai mangé des haricots blancs à la sauce tomate sur du pain grillé.
- **broad beans** les fèves FEM
- **green beans** les haricots verts MASC
- **kidney beans** les haricots rouges MASC

bear NOUN
> see also **bear** VERB

l' ours MASC

to **bear** VERB
> see also **bear** NOUN

- **I can't bear it!** C'est insupportable!
- **to bear up** tenir le coup
- **Bear up!** Tiens bon!

beard NOUN
la barbe
- **He's got a beard.** Il est barbu.
- **a man with a beard** un barbu

bearded ADJECTIVE
barbu

beat NOUN
> see also **beat** VERB

le rythme

to **beat** VERB
> see also **beat** NOUN

battre ◊ *We beat them 3-0.* On les a battus trois à zéro.
- **Beat it!** Fiche le camp! (*informal*)
- **to beat somebody up** tabasser quelqu'un (*informal*)

beautiful ADJECTIVE
beau MASC
belle FEM
(beaux MASC PL)

beautifully ADVERB
admirablement

beauty NOUN
la beauté

beauty spot NOUN
le site pittoresque

became VERB *see* **become**

because CONJUNCTION
parce que ◊ *I did it because ...* Je l'ai fait parce que ...
- **because of** à cause de ◊ *because of the weather* à cause du temps

to **become** VERB
devenir ◊ *He became a famous writer.* Il est devenu un grand écrivain.

bed NOUN
le lit ◊ *in bed* au lit
- **to go to bed** aller se coucher
- **to go to bed with somebody** coucher avec quelqu'un

bed and breakfast NOUN

la chambre d'hôte ◊ *We stayed in a bed and breakfast.* Nous avons logé dans une chambre d'hôte.
- **How much is it for bed and breakfast?** C'est combien pour la chambre et le petit déjeuner?

bedclothes PL NOUN
les draps et les couvertures MASC PL

bedding NOUN
la literie

bedroom NOUN
la chambre

bedsit NOUN
la chambre meublée

bedspread NOUN
le dessus-de-lit
(les dessus-de-lit PL)

bedtime NOUN
- **Ten o'clock is my usual bedtime.** Je me couche généralement à dix heures.
- **Bedtime!** Au lit!

bee NOUN
l' abeille FEM

beef NOUN
le bœuf
- **roast beef** le rosbif

beefburger NOUN
le hamburger

been VERB *see* **be**

beer NOUN
la bière

beetle NOUN
le scarabée

beetroot NOUN
la betterave rouge

before PREPOSITION, CONJUNCTION, ADVERB
① avant ◊ *before Tuesday* avant mardi
② avant de ◊ *before going* avant de partir ◊ *Before opening the packet, read the instructions.* Avant d'ouvrir le paquet, lisez le mode d'emploi. ◊ *I'll phone before I leave.* J'appellerai avant de partir.
③ déjà (*already*) ◊ *I've seen this film before.* J'ai déjà vu ce film. ◊ *Have you been to Scotland before?* Vous êtes déjà venu en Écosse?
- **the day before** la veille
- **the week before** la semaine précédente

beforehand ADVERB
à l'avance

to **beg** VERB
① mendier (*for money*)
② supplier ◊ *He begged me to stop.* Il m'a supplié d'arrêter.

☞

began VERB see **begin**

beggar NOUN
le mendiant
la mendiante

to **begin** VERB
commencer
♦**to begin doing something** commencer
à faire quelque chose

beginner NOUN
le débutant
la débutante
◊ *I'm just a beginner.* Je ne suis
qu'un débutant.

beginning NOUN
le début ◊ *in the beginning* au début

begun VERB see **begin**

behalf NOUN
♦**on behalf of somebody** pour
quelqu'un

to **behave** VERB
se comporter ◊ *He behaved like an
idiot.* Il s'est comporté comme un
idiot. ◊ *She behaved very badly.* Elle
s'est très mal comportée.
♦**to behave oneself** être sage ◊ *Did the
children behave themselves?* Est-ce
que les enfants ont été sages?
♦**Behave!** Sois sage!

behaviour NOUN (US **behavior**)
le comportement

behind PREPOSITION, ADVERB
see also **behind** NOUN
derrière ◊ *behind the television*
derrière la télévision
♦**to be behind** (*late*) avoir du retard
◊ *I'm behind with my revision.* J'ai
du retard dans mes révisions.

behind NOUN
see also **behind** PREPOSITION, ADVERB
le derrière

beige ADJECTIVE
beige

Belgian ADJECTIVE
see also **Belgian** NOUN
belge ◊ *Belgian chocolate* le chocolat
belge ◊ *She's Belgian.* Elle est belge.

Belgian NOUN
see also **Belgian** ADJECTIVE
le/la Belge
♦**the Belgians** les Belges

Belgium NOUN
la Belgique
♦**in Belgium** en Belgique

to **believe** VERB
croire ◊ *I don't believe you.* Je ne te
crois pas.

♦**to believe in something** croire à
quelque chose ◊ *Do you believe in
ghosts?* Tu crois aux fantômes?
♦**to believe in God** croire en Dieu

bell NOUN
1 la sonnette (*doorbell*)
♦**to ring the bell** sonner à la porte
2 la cloche (*in church*)
3 la sonnerie (*in school*)
4 la clochette ◊ *Our cat has a bell
on its neck.* Notre chat a une
clochette sur son collier.

belly NOUN
le ventre

to **belong** VERB
♦**to belong to somebody** être à
quelqu'un ◊ *Who does it belong to?*
C'est à qui? ◊ *That belongs to me.*
C'est à moi.
♦**Do you belong to any clubs?** Est-ce
que tu es membre d'un club?
♦**Where does this belong?** Où est-ce
que ça va?

belongings PL NOUN
les affaires FEM PL

below PREPOSITION, ADVERB
1 au-dessous de ◊ *below the castle*
au-dessous du château
2 en dessous ◊ *on the floor below* à
l'étage en dessous
♦**10 degrees below freezing** moins dix

belt NOUN
la ceinture

beltway NOUN US
le périphérique

bench NOUN
1 le banc (*seat*)
2 l' établi MASC (*for woodwork*)

bend NOUN
see also **bend** VERB
1 le virage (*in road*)
2 le coude (*in river*)

to **bend** VERB
see also **bend** NOUN
1 courber (*back*)
2 plier (*leg, arm*) ◊ *I can't bend my
arm.* Je n'arrive pas à plier le bras.
♦**"do not bend"** "ne pas plier"
3 tordre (*object*) ◊ *You've bent it.* Tu
l'as tordu.
4 se tordre ◊ *It bends easily.* Ça se
tord facilement.
♦**to bend down** se baisser
♦**to bend over** se pencher

beneath PREPOSITION
sous

benefit NOUN
see also **benefit** VERB
l' avantage MASC (*advantage*)

B

♦ **unemployment benefit** les allocations de chômage FEM PL

to **benefit** VERB

see also **benefit** NOUN

♦ **He'll benefit from the change.** Le changement lui fera du bien.

bent VERB see **bend**

bent ADJECTIVE
  tordu ◊ *a bent fork* une fourchette tordue

beret NOUN
  le béret

berserk ADJECTIVE
♦ **to go berserk** devenir fou furieux ◊ *She went berserk.* Elle est devenue folle furieuse.

berth NOUN
  la couchette

beside PREPOSITION
  à côté de ◊ *beside the television* à côté de la télévision
♦ **He was beside himself.** Il était hors de lui.
♦ **That's beside the point.** Cela n'a rien à voir.

besides ADVERB
  en plus ◊ *Besides, it's too expensive.* En plus, c'est trop cher.

best ADJECTIVE, ADVERB
  [1] meilleur ◊ *He's the best player in the team.* Il est le meilleur joueur de l'équipe. ◊ *Janet's the best at maths.* Janet est la meilleure en maths.
  [2] le mieux ◊ *Emma sings best.* C'est Emma qui chante le mieux. ◊ *That's the best I can do.* Je ne peux pas faire mieux.
♦ **to do one's best** faire de son mieux ◊ *It's not perfect, but I did my best.* Ça n'est pas parfait, mais j'ai fait de mon mieux.
♦ **to make the best of it** s'en contenter ◊ *We'll have to make the best of it.* Il va falloir nous en contenter.

best man NOUN
  le garçon d'honneur

bet NOUN

see also **bet** VERB

  le pari ◊ *to make a bet* faire un pari

to **bet** VERB

see also **bet** NOUN

  parier ◊ *I bet you he won't come.* Je te parie qu'il ne viendra pas. ◊ *I bet he forgot.* Je parie qu'il a oublié.

to **betray** VERB
  trahir

better ADJECTIVE, ADVERB
  [1] meilleur ◊ *This one's better than that one.* Celui-ci est meilleur que

celui-là. ◊ *a better way to do it* une meilleure façon de le faire
  [2] mieux ◊ *That's better!* C'est mieux comme ça.
♦ **better still** encore mieux ◊ *Go and see her tomorrow, or better still, go today.* Va la voir demain, ou encore mieux, vas-y aujourd'hui.
♦ **to get better (1)** (*improve*) s'améliorer ◊ *I hope the weather gets better soon.* J'espère que le temps va s'améliorer bientôt. ◊ *My French is getting better.* Mon français s'améliore.
♦ **to get better (2)** (*from illness*) se remettre ◊ *I hope you get better soon.* J'espère que tu vas vite te remettre.
♦ **to feel better** se sentir mieux ◊ *Are you feeling better now?* Tu te sens mieux maintenant?
♦ **You'd better do it straight away.** Vous feriez mieux de le faire immédiatement.
♦ **I'd better go home.** Je ferais mieux de rentrer.

betting shop NOUN
  le bureau de paris

between PREPOSITION
  entre ◊ *Stroud is between Oxford and Bristol.* Stroud est entre Oxford et Bristol. ◊ *between 15 and 20 minutes* entre quinze et vingt minutes.

bewildered ADJECTIVE
♦ **He looked bewildered.** Il avait l'air perplexe.

beyond PREPOSITION
  au-delà de ◊ *There was a lake beyond the mountain.* Il y avait un lac au-delà de la montagne.
♦ **beyond belief** incroyable
♦ **beyond repair** irréparable

biased ADJECTIVE
  partial

Bible NOUN
  la Bible

bicycle NOUN
  le vélo

bifocals PL NOUN
  les verres à double foyer MASC PL

big ADJECTIVE
  [1] grand ◊ *a big house* une grande maison ◊ *my big brother* mon grand frère ◊ *her big sister* sa grande sœur
♦ **He's a big guy.** C'est un grand gaillard.
  [2] (*car, animal, book, parcel*)
  gros MASC
  grosse FEM

☞

◊ *a big car* une grosse voiture

bigheaded ADJECTIVE
♦**to be bigheaded** avoir la grosse tête

bike NOUN
le <u>vélo</u> ◊ *by bike* en vélo

bikini NOUN
le <u>bikini</u>

bilingual ADJECTIVE
<u>bilingue</u>

bill NOUN
[1] l' <u>addition</u> FEM (*in restaurant*) ◊ *Can we have the bill, please?* L'addition, s'il vous plaît.
[2] la <u>facture</u> (*for gas, electricity*)
[3] le <u>billet</u> [US] ◊ *a five-dollar bill* un billet de cinq dollars

billiards NOUN
le <u>billard</u> ◊ *to play billiards* jouer au billard

billion NOUN
le <u>milliard</u>

bin NOUN
la <u>poubelle</u>

bingo NOUN
le <u>bingo</u>

binoculars PL NOUN
les <u>jumelles</u> FEM PL
♦**a pair of binoculars** des jumelles

biochemistry NOUN
la <u>biochimie</u>

biography NOUN
la <u>biographie</u>

biology NOUN
la <u>biologie</u>

bird NOUN
l' <u>oiseau</u> MASC
(les oiseaux PL)

birdwatching NOUN
♦**My hobby's birdwatching.** Mon passe-temps favori est d'observer les oiseaux.
♦**to go birdwatching** aller observer les oiseaux

Biro ® NOUN
le <u>bic</u> ®

birth NOUN
la <u>naissance</u> ◊ *date of birth* la date de naissance

birth certificate NOUN
l' <u>acte de naissance</u> MASC

birth control NOUN
la <u>contraception</u>

birthday NOUN
l' <u>anniversaire</u> MASC ◊ *When's your birthday?* Quelle est la date de ton anniversaire?
♦**a birthday cake** un gâteau d'anniversaire

♦**a birthday card** une carte d'anniversaire
♦**I'm going to have a birthday party.** Je vais faire une fête pour mon anniversaire.

biscuit NOUN
le <u>gâteau sec</u>

bishop NOUN
l' <u>évêque</u> MASC

bit VERB *see* **bite**

bit NOUN
le <u>morceau</u>
(les morceaux PL)
◊ *Would you like another bit?* Est-ce que tu en veux un autre morceau?
♦**a bit of (1)** (*piece of*) un morceau de ◊ *a bit of cake* un morceau de gâteau
♦**a bit of (2)** (*a little*) un peu de ◊ *a bit of music* un peu de musique
♦**It's a bit of a nuisance.** C'est ennuyeux.
♦**a bit** un peu ◊ *He's a bit mad.* Il est un peu fou. ◊ *a bit too hot* un peu trop chaud ◊ *Wait a bit!* Attends un peu! ◊ *Do you play football? – A bit.* Tu joues au football? – Un peu.
♦**to fall to bits** se désintégrer
♦**to take something to bits** démonter quelque chose
♦**bit by bit** petit à petit

bitch NOUN
[1] la <u>garce</u> (*person*)
[2] la <u>chienne</u> (*female dog*)

to **bite** VERB
[see also **bite** NOUN]
[1] <u>mordre</u> (*person, dog*)
[2] <u>piquer</u> (*insect*) ◊ *I got bitten by mosquitoes.* Je me suis fait piquer par des moustiques.
♦**to bite one's nails** se ronger les ongles

bite NOUN
[see also **bite** VERB]
[1] la <u>piqûre</u> (*insect bite*)
[2] la <u>morsure</u> (*animal bite*)
♦**to have a bite to eat** manger un morceau

bitten VERB *see* **bite**

bitter ADJECTIVE
[see also **bitter** NOUN]
[1] <u>amer</u> MASC
<u>amère</u> FEM
[2] (*weather, wind*)
<u>glacial</u>
(glaciaux MASC PL)
◊ *It's bitter today.* Il fait un froid glacial aujourd'hui.

bitter NOUN
see also **bitter** ADJECTIVE
la bière brune

black ADJECTIVE
noir ◊ *a black jacket* une veste noire
◊ *She's black.* Elle est noire.

blackberry NOUN
la mûre

blackbird NOUN
le merle

blackboard NOUN
le tableau noir

black coffee NOUN
le café

blackcurrant NOUN
le cassis

blackmail NOUN
see also **blackmail** VERB
le chantage ◊ *That's blackmail!* C'est
du chantage!

to **blackmail** VERB
see also **blackmail** NOUN
♦**to blackmail somebody** faire chanter
quelqu'un ◊ *He blackmailed her.* Il l'a
fait chanter.

blackout NOUN
la panne d'électricité (*power cut*)
♦**to have a blackout** (*faint*) s'évanouir

black pudding NOUN
le boudin

blade NOUN
la lame

to **blame** VERB
♦**Don't blame me!** Ça n'est pas ma
faute!
♦**I blame the police.** À mon avis, c'est
la faute de la police.
♦**He blamed it on my sister.** Il a dit
que c'était la faute de ma sœur.

blank ADJECTIVE
see also **blank** NOUN
① (*paper*)
blanc MASC
blanche FEM
② (*cassette, video, page*)
vierge
♦**My mind went blank.** J'ai eu un trou.

blank NOUN
see also **blank** ADJECTIVE
le blanc ◊ *Fill in the blanks.*
Remplissez les blancs.

blank cheque NOUN
le chèque en blanc

blanket NOUN
la couverture

blast NOUN
♦**a bomb blast** une explosion

blatant ADJECTIVE

flagrant

blaze NOUN
l' incendie MASC

blazer NOUN
le blazer

bleach NOUN
l' eau de Javel FEM

bleached ADJECTIVE
décoloré ◊ *bleached hair* les cheveux
décolorés MASC PL

bleak ADJECTIVE
désolé (*place*)
♦**The future looks bleak.** L'avenir
semble peu prometteur.

to **bleed** VERB
saigner ◊ *My nose is bleeding.* Je
saigne du nez.

bleeper NOUN
le bip

blender NOUN
le mixer

to **bless** VERB
bénir (*religiously*)
♦**Bless you!** (*after sneezing*) À tes
souhaits!

blew VERB *see* **blow**

blind ADJECTIVE
see also **blind** NOUN
aveugle

blind NOUN
see also **blind** ADJECTIVE
le store (*for window*)

blindfold NOUN
see also **blindfold** VERB
le bandeau
(les bandeaux PL)

to **blindfold** VERB
see also **blindfold** NOUN
♦**to blindfold somebody** bander les
yeux à quelqu'un

to **blink** VERB
cligner des yeux

bliss NOUN
♦**It was bliss!** C'était merveilleux!

blister NOUN
l' ampoule FEM

blizzard NOUN
la tempête de neige

blob NOUN
la goutte ◊ *a blob of glue* une goutte
de colle

block NOUN
see also **block** VERB
l' immeuble MASC ◊ *He lives in our
block.* Il habite dans notre immeuble.
♦**a block of flats** un immeuble

to **block** VERB

☞

see also **block** NOUN
bloquer

blockage NOUN
l' obstruction FEM

bloke NOUN
le mec (*informal*)

blonde ADJECTIVE
blond ◊ *She's got blonde hair.* Elle a
les cheveux blonds.

blood NOUN
le sang

blood pressure NOUN
◆**to have high blood pressure** faire de
la tension

blood sports NOUN
les sports sanguinaires MASC PL

blood test NOUN
la prise de sang

bloody ADJECTIVE
◆**bloody difficult** sacrément difficile
◆**that bloody television** cette putain de
télévision
◆**Bloody hell!** Merde!

blouse NOUN
le chemisier

blow NOUN
see also **blow** VERB
le coup

to **blow** VERB
see also **blow** NOUN
souffler (*wind, person*)
◆**to blow one's nose** se moucher
◆**to blow a whistle** siffler
◆**to blow out a candle** éteindre une
bougie
◆**to blow up (1)** faire sauter ◊ *The
terrorists blew up a police station.*
Les terroristes ont fait sauter un
commissariat de police.
◆**to blow up (2)** gonfler ◊ *to blow up a
balloon* gonfler un ballon
◆**The house blew up.** La maison a
sauté.

blow-dry NOUN
le brushing
◆**A cut and blow-dry, please.** Une
coupe brushing, s'il vous plaît.

blown VERB *see* **blow**

blue ADJECTIVE
bleu ◊ *a blue dress* une robe bleue
◆**a blue film** un film pornographique
◆**It came out of the blue.** C'était
complètement inattendu.

blues PL NOUN
le blues SING

to **bluff** VERB
see also **bluff** NOUN
bluffer

bluff NOUN
see also **bluff** VERB
le bluff ◊ *It's just a bluff.* C'est du
bluff.

blunder NOUN
la gaffe

blunt ADJECTIVE
1 brusque (*person*)
2 émoussé (*knife*)

to **blush** VERB
rougir

board NOUN
1 (*wooden*)
la planche
2 (*blackboard*)
le tableau
(les tableaux PL)
◊ *on the board* au tableau
3 (*noticeboard*)
le panneau
(les panneaux PL)
4 (*for board games*)
le jeu
(les jeux PL)
5 (*for chess*)
l' échiquier MASC
◆**on board** à bord
◆**"full board"** "pension complète"

boarder NOUN
l' interne MASC/FEM

board game NOUN
le jeu de société
(les jeux de société PL)

boarding card NOUN
la carte d'embarquement

boarding school NOUN
le pensionnat
◆**I go to boarding school.** Je suis
interne.

to **boast** VERB
se vanter ◊ *Stop boasting!* Arrête de
te vanter!
◆**to boast about something** se vanter
de quelque chose

boat NOUN
le bateau
(les bateaux PL)

body NOUN
le corps

bodybuilding NOUN
le culturisme

bodyguard NOUN
le garde du corps

bog NOUN
la tourbière (*marsh*)

boil NOUN
see also **boil** VERB
le furoncle

to **boil** VERB

B

see also **boil** NOUN
1. faire bouillir ◊ *to boil some water* faire bouillir de l'eau
♦**to boil an egg** faire cuire un œuf
2. bouillir ◊ *The water's boiling.* L'eau bout. ◊ *The water's boiled.* L'eau a bouilli.
♦**to boil over** déborder

boiled ADJECTIVE
à l'eau ◊ *boiled potatoes* des pommes de terre à l'eau
♦**a boiled egg** un œuf à la coque

boiling ADJECTIVE
♦**It's boiling in here!** Il fait une chaleur torride ici!
♦**boiling hot** torride ◊ *a boiling hot day* une journée torride

bolt NOUN
1. le verrou (*on door*)
2. le boulon (*with nut*)

bomb NOUN
see also **bomb** VERB
la bombe

to **bomb** VERB
see also **bomb** NOUN
bombarder

bomber NOUN
le bombardier

bombing NOUN
l' attentat à la bombe MASC

bond NOUN
le lien

bone NOUN
1. l' os MASC (*of human, animal*)
2. l' arête FEM (*of fish*)

bone dry ADJECTIVE
complètement sec MASC
complètement sèche FEM

bonfire NOUN
le feu
(les feux PL)

bonnet NOUN
le capot (*of car*)

bonus NOUN
1. la prime (*extra payment*)
2. le plus (*added advantage*)

book NOUN
see also **book** VERB
le livre

to **book** VERB
see also **book** NOUN
réserver ◊ *We haven't booked.* Nous n'avons pas réservé.

bookcase NOUN
la bibliothèque

booklet NOUN
la brochure

bookmark NOUN

le signet (*computing*)

bookshelf NOUN
l' étagère à livres FEM

bookshop NOUN
la librairie

to **boost** VERB
stimuler ◊ *to boost the economy* stimuler l'économie
♦**The win boosted the team's morale.** La victoire a remonté le moral de l'équipe.

boot NOUN
1. le coffre (*of car*)
2. la botte (*fashion boot*)
3. la chaussure de marche (*for hiking*)
♦**football boots** des chaussures de foot

booze NOUN
l' alcool MASC

border NOUN
la frontière

bore VERB *see* **bear**

bored ADJECTIVE
♦**to be bored** s'ennuyer ◊ *I was bored.* Je m'ennuyais.
♦**to get bored** s'ennuyer

boredom NOUN
l' ennui MASC

boring ADJECTIVE
ennuyeux MASC
ennuyeuse FEM

born ADJECTIVE
♦**to be born** naître ◊ *I was born in 1982.* Je suis né en mille neuf cent quatre-vingt-deux.

to **borrow** VERB
emprunter ◊ *Can I borrow your pen?* Je peux emprunter ton stylo?
♦**to borrow something from somebody** emprunter quelque chose à quelqu'un ◊ *I borrowed some money from a friend.* J'ai emprunté de l'argent à un ami.

Bosnia NOUN
la Bosnie

Bosnian ADJECTIVE
bosniaque

boss NOUN
le patron
la patronne

to **boss around** VERB
♦**to boss somebody around** donner des ordres à quelqu'un

bossy ADJECTIVE
autoritaire

both ADJECTIVE, PRONOUN
tous les deux MASC PL
toutes les deux FEM PL

☞

◊ *We both went.* Nous y sommes allés tous les deux. ◊ *Emma and Jane both went.* Emma et Jane y sont allées toutes les deux. ◊ *Both of your answers are wrong.* Vos réponses sont toutes les deux mauvaises. ◊ *Both of them have left.* Ils sont partis tous les deux. ◊ *Both of us went.* Nous y sommes allés tous les deux. ◊ *Both Maggie and John are against it.* Maggie et John sont tous les deux contre.
♦ **He speaks both German and Italian.** Il parle allemand et italien.

to **bother** VERB
  1 tracasser (*worry*) ◊ *What's bothering you?* Qu'est-ce qui te tracasse?
  2 déranger (*disturb*) ◊ *I'm sorry to bother you.* Je suis désolé de vous déranger.
♦ **no bother** aucun problème
♦ **Don't bother!** Ça n'est pas la peine!
♦ **to bother to do something** prendre la peine de faire quelque chose ◊ *He didn't bother to tell me about it.* Il n'a pas pris la peine de m'en parler.

bottle NOUN
  la bouteille

bottle bank NOUN
  le conteneur à verre

bottle-opener NOUN
  l' ouvre-bouteille MASC

bottom NOUN
  see also **bottom** ADJECTIVE
  1 le fond (*of container, bag, sea*)
  2 le derrière (*buttocks*)
  3 le bas (*of page, list*)

bottom ADJECTIVE
  see also **bottom** NOUN
  inférieur ◊ *the bottom shelf* l'étagère inférieure
♦ **the bottom sheet** le drap de dessous

bought VERB see **buy**

to **bounce** VERB
  rebondir

bouncer NOUN
  le videur

bound ADJECTIVE
♦ **He's bound to fail.** Il va sûrement échouer.

boundary NOUN
  la frontière

bow NOUN
  see also **bow** VERB
  1 le nœud (*knot*) ◊ *to tie a bow* faire un nœud
  2 l' arc MASC ◊ *a bow and arrows* un arc et des flèches

to **bow** VERB
  see also **bow** NOUN
  faire une révérence

bowels PL NOUN
  les intestins MASC PL

bowl NOUN
  see also **bowl** VERB
  le bol (*for soup, cereal*)

to **bowl** VERB
  see also **bowl** NOUN
  lancer la balle (*in cricket*)

bowler NOUN
  le lanceur (*in cricket*)

bowling NOUN
  le bowling
♦ **to go bowling** jouer au bowling
♦ **a bowling alley** un bowling

bowls NOUN
  les boules FEM PL ◊ *to play bowls* jouer aux boules

bow tie NOUN
  le nœud papillon

box NOUN
  la boîte ◊ *a box of matches* une boîte d'allumettes
♦ **a cardboard box** un carton

boxer NOUN
  le boxeur

boxer shorts PL NOUN
  le caleçon SING

boxing NOUN
  la boxe

Boxing Day NOUN
  le lendemain de Noël ◊ *on Boxing Day* le lendemain de Noël

boy NOUN
  le garçon

boyfriend NOUN
  le copain ◊ *Have you got a boyfriend?* Est-ce que tu as un copain?

bra NOUN
  le soutien-gorge
  (les soutiens-gorge PL)

brace NOUN
  l' appareil MASC (*on teeth*) ◊ *She wears a brace.* Elle a un appareil.

bracelet NOUN
  le bracelet

brackets PL NOUN
♦ **in brackets** entre parenthèses

brain NOUN
  le cerveau
  (les cerveaux PL)

brainy ADJECTIVE
  intelligent

brake NOUN
  see also **brake** VERB

le <u>frein</u>

to **brake** VERB

> *see also* **brake** NOUN

<u>freiner</u>

branch NOUN

1 la <u>branche</u> (*of tree*)
2 l' <u>agence</u> FEM (*of bank*)

brand NOUN

la <u>marque</u> ◇ *a well-known brand of coffee* une marque de café bien connue

brand name NOUN

la <u>marque</u>

brand-new ADJECTIVE

<u>tout neuf</u> MASC
<u>toute neuve</u> FEM

brandy NOUN

le <u>cognac</u>

brass NOUN

le <u>cuivre</u>

♦ **the brass section** les cuivres

brass band NOUN

la <u>fanfare</u>

brat NOUN

♦ **He's a spoiled brat.** C'est un enfant gâté.

brave ADJECTIVE

<u>courageux</u> MASC
<u>courageuse</u> FEM

Brazil NOUN

le <u>Brésil</u>

♦ **in Brazil** au Brésil

bread NOUN

le <u>pain</u> ◇ *brown bread* le pain complet ◇ *white bread* le pain blanc

♦ **bread and butter** les tartines de pain beurrées FEM PL

break NOUN

> *see also* **break** VERB

1 la <u>pause</u> (*rest*) ◇ *to take a break* faire une pause
2 la <u>récréation</u> (*at school*) ◇ *during morning break* pendant la récréation du matin

♦ **the Christmas break** les vacances de Noël FEM PL

♦ **Give me a break!** Laisse-moi tranquille!

to **break** VERB

> *see also* **break** NOUN

1 <u>casser</u> ◇ *Careful, you'll break something!* Attention, tu vas casser quelque chose!
2 <u>se casser</u> (*get broken*) ◇ *Careful, it'll break!* Attention, ça va se casser!

♦ **to break one's leg** se casser la jambe ◇ *I broke my leg.* Je me suis cassé la jambe.

♦ **He broke his arm.** Il s'est cassé le bras.

♦ **to break a promise** rompre une promesse

♦ **to break a record** battre un record

♦ **to break the law** violer la loi

to **break down** VERB

<u>tomber en panne</u> ◇ *The car broke down.* La voiture est tombée en panne.

to **break in** VERB

<u>entrer par effraction</u>

to **break off** VERB

1 <u>casser</u> ◇ *He broke off a piece of chocolate.* Il a cassé un bout de chocolat.
2 <u>se casser</u> ◇ *The branch broke off when she sat on it.* La branche s'est cassée quand elle s'est assise dessus.

to **break open** VERB

<u>forcer</u> (*door, cupboard*)

to **break out** VERB

1 <u>se déclarer</u> (*fire*)
2 <u>éclater</u> (*war*)
3 <u>s'évader</u> (*prisoner*)

♦ **to break out in a rash** être couvert de boutons

to **break up** VERB

1 <u>se disperser</u> (*crowd*)
2 <u>se terminer</u> (*meeting, party*)
3 <u>se séparer</u> (*couple*)

♦ **to break up a fight** mettre fin à une bagarre

♦ **We break up next Wednesday.** Nos vacances commencent mercredi.

breakdown NOUN

1 la <u>panne</u> (*in vehicle*) ◇ *to have a breakdown* tomber en panne
2 la <u>dépression</u> (*mental*) ◇ *to have a breakdown* faire une dépression

breakdown van NOUN

la <u>dépanneuse</u>

breakfast NOUN

le <u>petit déjeuner</u> ◇ *What would you like for breakfast?* Qu'est-ce vous voulez pour le petit déjeuner?

break-in NOUN

le <u>cambriolage</u>

breast NOUN

le <u>sein</u> (*of woman*)

♦ **chicken breast** le blanc de poulet

to **breast-feed** VERB

<u>allaiter</u>

breaststroke NOUN

la <u>brasse</u>

breath NOUN

l' <u>haleine</u> FEM ◇ *to have bad breath* avoir mauvaise haleine

♦ **to be out of breath** être essoufflé

☞

♦**to get one's breath back** reprendre son souffle

to **breathe** VERB
respirer

to **breathe in** VERB
inspirer

to **breathe out** VERB
expirer

to **breed** VERB
see also **breed** NOUN
se reproduire (*reproduce*)
♦**to breed dogs** faire de l'élevage de chiens

breed NOUN
see also **breed** VERB
la race

breeze NOUN
la brise

brewery NOUN
la brasserie

to **bribe** VERB
soudoyer

brick NOUN
la brique
♦**a brick wall** un mur en brique

bricklayer NOUN
le maçon

bride NOUN
la mariée

bridegroom NOUN
le marié

bridesmaid NOUN
la demoiselle d'honneur

bridge NOUN
1 le pont ◊ *a suspension bridge* un pont suspendu
2 le bridge ◊ *to play bridge* jouer au bridge

brief ADJECTIVE
bref MASC
brève FEM

briefcase NOUN
la serviette

briefly ADVERB
brièvement

briefs PL NOUN
le slip SING
♦**a pair of briefs** un slip

bright ADJECTIVE
1 (*colour, light*)
vif MASC
vive FEM
◊ *a bright colour* une couleur vive
♦**bright blue** bleu vif ◊ *a bright blue car* une voiture bleu vif
2 intelligent ◊ *He's not very bright.* Il n'est pas très intelligent.

brilliant ADJECTIVE

1 (*wonderful*)
génial
(géniaux MASC PL)
◊ *Brilliant!* Génial!
2 (*clever*)
brillant ◊ *a brilliant scientist* un savant brillant

to **bring** VERB
1 apporter ◊ *Bring warm clothes.* Apportez des vêtements chauds.
◊ *Could you bring me my trainers?* Tu peux m'apporter mes baskets?
2 amener (*person*) ◊ *Can I bring a friend?* Est-ce que je peux amener un ami?

to **bring about** VERB
provoquer ◊ *The war brought about a change in people's attitudes.* La guerre a provoqué un changement dans l'attitude des gens.

to **bring back** VERB
rapporter

to **bring forward** VERB
avancer ◊ *The meeting was brought forward.* On a avancé la réunion.

to **bring up** VERB
élever ◊ *She brought up 5 children on her own.* Elle a élevé cinq enfants toute seule.

Britain NOUN
la Grande-Bretagne
♦**in Britain** en Grande-Bretagne
♦**to Britain** en Grande-Bretagne
♦**I'm from Britain.** Je suis britannique.
♦**Great Britain** la Grande-Bretagne

British ADJECTIVE
britannique
♦**the British** les Britanniques MASC PL
♦**the British Isles** les îles Britanniques FEM PL

Brittany NOUN
la Bretagne
♦**in Brittany** en Bretagne
♦**to Brittany** en Bretagne
♦**She's from Brittany.** Elle est bretonne.

broad ADJECTIVE
large (*wide*)
♦**in broad daylight** en plein jour

broadcast NOUN
see also **broadcast** VERB
l' émission FEM

to **broadcast** VERB
see also **broadcast** NOUN
diffuser ◊ *The interview was broadcast all over the world.* L'interview a été diffusé dans le monde entier.
♦**to broadcast live** retransmettre en direct

B

broad-minded ADJECTIVE
large d'esprit

broccoli NOUN
les brocolis MASC PL

brochure NOUN
la brochure

to **broil** VERB US
♦ **to broil something** faire griller quelque chose

broke VERB see **break**

broke ADJECTIVE
♦ **to be broke** (without money) être fauché

broken ADJECTIVE
cassé ◊ It's broken. C'est cassé. ◊ a broken leg une jambe cassée ◊ He's got a broken arm. Il a le bras cassé.

bronchitis NOUN
la bronchite

bronze NOUN
le bronze ◊ the bronze medal la médaille de bronze

brooch NOUN
la broche

broom NOUN
le balai

brother NOUN
le frère ◊ my brother mon frère ◊ my big brother mon grand frère

brother-in-law NOUN
le beau-frère
(les beaux-frères PL)

brought VERB see **bring**

brown ADJECTIVE
[1] (clothes)
marron MASC, FEM, PL
[2] (hair)
brun
[3] (tanned)
bronzé
♦ **brown bread** le pain complet

Brownie NOUN
la jeannette

to **browse** VERB
parcourir le Net (on internet)

browser NOUN
le navigateur (for internet)

bruise NOUN
le bleu

brush NOUN
see also **brush** VERB
[1] la brosse
[2] (paintbrush)
le pinceau
(les pinceaux PL)

to **brush** VERB
see also **brush** NOUN
brosser

♦ **to brush one's hair** se brosser les cheveux ◊ I brushed my hair. Je me suis brossé les cheveux.

♦ **to brush one's teeth** se brosser les dents ◊ I brush my teeth every night. Je me brosse les dents tous les soirs.

Brussels NOUN
Bruxelles

♦ **in Brussels** à Bruxelles

♦ **to Brussels** à Bruxelles

Brussels sprouts PL NOUN
les choux de Bruxelles MASC PL

brutal ADJECTIVE
brutal
(brutaux MASC PL)

BSc NOUN (= Bachelor of Science)
la licence

♦ **a BSc in Mathematics** une licence de mathématiques

BSE NOUN (= bovine spongiform encephalopathy)
l' ESB FEM (= l'encéphalite spongiforme bovine)

bubble NOUN
la bulle

bubble bath NOUN
le bain moussant

bubble gum NOUN
le chewing-gum

bucket NOUN
le seau
(les seaux PL)

buckle NOUN
la boucle (on belt, watch, shoe)

Buddhism NOUN
le bouddhisme

Buddhist ADJECTIVE
bouddhiste

buddy NOUN US
le copain
la copine

budget NOUN
le budget

budgie NOUN
la perruche

buffet NOUN
le buffet

buffet car NOUN
la voiture-bar

bug NOUN
[1] l' insecte MASC (insect)
[2] le microbe (infection) ◊ There's a bug going round. Il y a un microbe qui traîne.
♦ **a stomach bug** une gastroentérite
[3] le bug (in computer)

bugged ADJECTIVE

☞

sur écoute ◊ *The room was bugged.*
La pièce était sur écoute.

to **build** VERB
construire ◊ *He's building a garage.*
Il construit un garage.
- **to build up** (*increase*) s'accumuler

builder NOUN
1 l' entrepreneur MASC (*owner of firm*)
2 le maçon (*worker*)

building NOUN
le bâtiment

built VERB *see* **build**

bulb NOUN
l' ampoule FEM (*electric*)

Bulgaria NOUN
la Bulgarie

bull NOUN
le taureau
(les taureaux PL)

bullet NOUN
la balle

bulletin board NOUN
le panneau d'affichage électronique
(*computer*)

bullfighting NOUN
la tauromachie

bully NOUN
see also **bully** VERB
la brute ◊ *He's a big bully.* C'est une
brute.

to **bully** VERB
see also **bully** NOUN
tyranniser

bum NOUN
le derrière (*bottom*)

bum bag NOUN
la banane

bump NOUN
see also **bump** VERB
1 la bosse (*lump*)
2 l' accrochage MASC (*minor accident*)
◊ *We had a bump.* Nous avons eu un
accrochage.

to **bump** VERB
see also **bump** NOUN
- **to bump into something** rentrer dans
quelque chose ◊ *We bumped into his
car.* Nous sommes rentrés dans sa
voiture.
- **to bump into somebody (1)** (*literally*)
rentrer dans quelqu'un ◊ *He stopped
suddenly and I bumped into him.* Il
s'est arrêté subitement et je lui suis
rentré dedans.
- **to bump into somebody (2)** (*meet by
chance*) rencontrer par hasard
- **I bumped into Jane in the**

supermarket. J'ai rencontré Jane par
hasard au supermarché.

bumper NOUN
le pare-chocs
(les pare-chocs PL)

bumpy ADJECTIVE
cahoteux MASC
cahoteuse FEM

bun NOUN
le petit pain au lait

bunch NOUN
- **a bunch of flowers** un bouquet de
fleurs
- **a bunch of grapes** une grappe de
raisin
- **a bunch of keys** un trousseau de clés

bunches PL NOUN
les couettes FEM PL ◊ *She has her hair
in bunches.* Elle a des couettes.

bungalow NOUN
le bungalow

bunk NOUN
la couchette
- **bunk beds** les lits superposés

burger NOUN
le hamburger

burglar NOUN
le cambrioleur
la cambrioleuse

to **burglarize** VERB US
cambrioler

burglary NOUN
le cambriolage

to **burgle** VERB
cambrioler ◊ *Her house was burgled.*
Sa maison a été cambriolée.

burn NOUN
see also **burn** VERB
la brûlure

to **burn** VERB
see also **burn** NOUN
1 brûler (*rubbish, documents*)
2 faire brûler (*food*) ◊ *I burned the
cake.* J'ai fait brûler le gâteau.
- **to burn oneself** se brûler ◊ *I burned
myself on the oven door.* Je me suis
brûlé sur la porte du four.
- **I've burned my hand.** Je me suis
brûlé la main.
- **to burn down** brûler ◊ *The factory
burned down.* L'usine a brûlé.

to **burst** VERB
éclater ◊ *The balloon burst.* Le ballon
a éclaté.
- **to burst a balloon** faire éclater un
ballon
- **to burst out laughing** éclater de rire
- **to burst into flames** prendre feu
- **to burst into tears** fondre en larmes

B

to **bury** VERB
  enterrer

bus NOUN
  l' autobus MASC ◊ *the bus driver* le conducteur d'autobus ◊ *a bus stop* un arrêt d'autobus
  ♦ **the school bus** le car scolaire
  ♦ **a bus pass** une carte d'abonnement pour le bus
  ♦ **a bus station** une gare routière
  ♦ **a bus ticket** un ticket de bus

bush NOUN
  le buisson

business NOUN
  ① l' entreprise FEM (*firm*) ◊ *He's got his own business.* Il a sa propre entreprise.
  ② les affaires FEM PL (*commerce*) ◊ *He's away on business.* Il est en voyage d'affaires.
  ♦ **a business trip** un voyage d'affaires
  ♦ **It's none of my business.** Ça ne me regarde pas.

businessman NOUN
  l' homme d'affaires MASC

businesswoman NOUN
  la femme d'affaires

busker NOUN
  le musicien de rue
  la musicienne de rue

bust NOUN
  la poitrine (*chest*)

busy ADJECTIVE
  ① occupé (*person, phone line*)
  ② chargé (*day, schedule*)
  ③ très fréquenté (*shop, street*)

busy signal NOUN [US]
  la tonalité "occupé"

but CONJUNCTION
  mais ◊ *I'd like to come, but I'm busy.* J'aimerais venir mais je suis occupé.

butcher NOUN
  le boucher ◊ *He's a butcher.* Il est boucher.

butcher's NOUN
  la boucherie

butter NOUN
  le beurre

butterfly NOUN
  le papillon

buttocks PL NOUN
  les fesses FEM PL

button NOUN
  le bouton

to **buy** VERB
  see also **buy** NOUN
  acheter ◊ *He bought me an ice cream.* Il m'a acheté une glace. ◊ *I bought him an ice cream.* Je lui ai acheté une glace.
  ♦ **to buy something from somebody** acheter quelque chose à quelqu'un ◊ *I bought a watch from him.* Je lui ai acheté une montre.

buy NOUN
  see also **buy** VERB
  ♦ **It was a good buy.** C'était une bonne affaire.

by PREPOSITION
  ① par ◊ *The thieves were caught by the police.* Les voleurs ont été arrêtés par la police.
  ② de ◊ *a painting by Picasso* un tableau de Picasso ◊ *a book by Balzac* un livre de Balzac
  ③ en ◊ *by car* en voiture ◊ *by train* en train ◊ *by bus* en autobus
  ④ à côté de (*close to*) ◊ *Where's the bank? – It's by the post office.* Où est la banque? – Elle est à côté de la poste.
  ⑤ avant (*not later than*) ◊ *We have to be there by 4 o'clock.* Nous devons y être avant quatre heures.
  ♦ **by the time** ... quand ... ◊ *By the time I got there it was too late.* Quand je suis arrivé il était déjà trop tard. ◊ *It'll be ready by the time you get back.* Ça sera prêt quand vous reviendrez.
  ♦ **That's fine by me.** Ça me va.
  ♦ **all by himself** tout seul
  ♦ **all by herself** toute seule
  ♦ **I did it all by myself.** Je l'ai fait tout seul.
  ♦ **by the way** au fait

bye EXCLAMATION
  salut!

bypass NOUN
  la route de contournement

C

cab NOUN
le taxi

cabbage NOUN
le chou
(les choux PL)

cabin NOUN
la cabine (on ship)

cabinet NOUN
♦ **a bathroom cabinet** une armoire de
salle de bain
♦ **a drinks cabinet** un bar

cable NOUN
le câble

cable car NOUN
le téléphérique

cable television NOUN
la télévision par câble

cactus NOUN
le cactus

cadet NOUN
♦ **a police cadet** un élève policier
♦ **a cadet officer** un élève officier

café NOUN
le café

> ❶ Cafés in France sell both alcoholic
> and non-alcoholic drinks.

cafeteria NOUN
la cafétéria

cage NOUN
la cage

cagoule NOUN
le K-way ®

cake NOUN
le gâteau
(les gâteaux PL)

to **calculate** VERB
calculer

calculation NOUN
le calcul

calculator NOUN
la machine à calculer

calendar NOUN
le calendrier

calf NOUN
1 (of cow)
le veau
(les veaux PL)
2 (of leg)
le mollet

call NOUN
see also **call** VERB

l' appel MASC (by phone) ◊ Thanks for
your call. Merci de votre appel.
♦ **a phone call** un coup de téléphone
♦ **to be on call** (doctor) être de
permanence ◊ He's on call this
evening. Il est de permanence ce
soir.

to **call** VERB
see also **call** NOUN
appeler ◊ I'll tell him you called. Je
lui dirai que vous avez appelé. ◊ This
is the number to call. C'est le
numéro à appeler. ◊ We called the
police. Nous avons appelé la police.
◊ Everyone calls him Jimmy. Tout le
monde l'appelle Jimmy.
♦ **to be called** s'appeler ◊ He's called
Fluffy. Il s'appelle Fluffy. ◊ What's she
called? Elle s'appelle comment?
♦ **to call somebody names** insulter
quelqu'un
♦ **He called me an idiot.** Il m'a traité
d'idiot.

to **call back** VERB
rappeler (phone again) ◊ I'll call back
at 6 o'clock. Je rappellerai à six
heures.

to **call for** VERB
passer prendre ◊ I'll call for you at
2.30. Je passerai te prendre à deux
heures et demie.

to **call off** VERB
annuler ◊ The match was called off.
Le match a été annulé.

call box NOUN
la cabine téléphonique

call centre NOUN
le centre d'appels

calm ADJECTIVE
calme

to **calm down** VERB
se calmer ◊ Calm down! Calme-toi!

Calor gas ® NOUN
le butane

calorie NOUN
la calorie

calves PL NOUN see **calf**

Cambodia NOUN
le Cambodge
♦ **in Cambodia** au Cambodge

camcorder NOUN
le caméscope

came VERB see **come**

camel NOUN

le <u>chameau</u>
(les chameaux PL)

camera NOUN
[1] (*for photos*)
l' <u>appareil photo</u> MASC
(les appareils photo PL)
[2] (*for filming, TV*)
la <u>caméra</u>

cameraman NOUN
le <u>caméraman</u>

to **camp** VERB
> see also **camp** NOUN

<u>camper</u>

camp NOUN
> see also **camp** VERB

le <u>camp</u>
♦ **a camp bed** un lit de camp

campaign NOUN
la <u>campagne</u>

camper NOUN
[1] (*person*)
le <u>campeur</u>
la <u>campeuse</u>
[2] (*van*)
le <u>camping-car</u>

camping NOUN
le <u>camping</u>
♦ **to go camping** faire du camping ◊ *We went camping in Cornwall.* Nous avons fait du camping en Cornouailles.

camping gas ® NOUN
le <u>butane</u>

campsite NOUN
le <u>terrain de camping</u>

campus NOUN
le <u>campus</u>

can NOUN
> see also **can** VERB

[1] la <u>boîte</u> (*tin*) ◊ *a can of sweetcorn* une boîte de maïs ◊ *a can of beer* une boîte de bière
[2] le <u>bidon</u> (*jerry can*) ◊ *a can of petrol* un bidon d'essence

can VERB
> see also **can** NOUN

[1] <u>pouvoir</u> (*be able to, be allowed to*)
◊ *I can't come.* Je ne peux pas venir.
◊ *Can I help you?* Est-ce que je peux vous aider? ◊ *Can I use your phone?* Est-ce que je peux me servir de votre téléphone? ◊ *You could hire a bike.* Tu pourrais louer un vélo. ◊ *I couldn't sleep because of the noise.* Je ne pouvais pas dormir à cause du bruit.

can is sometimes not translated.
◊ *I can't hear you.* Je ne t'entends pas. ◊ *I can't remember.* Je ne m'en

souviens pas. ◊ *Can you speak French?* Parlez-vous français?
[2] <u>savoir</u> (*have learnt how to*) ◊ *I can swim.* Je sais nager. ◊ *He can't drive.* Il ne sait pas conduire.
♦ **That can't be true!** Ce n'est pas possible!
♦ **You could be right.** Vous avez peut-être raison.

Canada NOUN
le <u>Canada</u>
♦ **in Canada** au Canada
♦ **to Canada** au Canada

Canadian ADJECTIVE
> see also **Canadian** NOUN

<u>canadien</u> MASC
<u>canadienne</u> FEM

Canadian NOUN
> see also **Canadian** ADJECTIVE

le <u>Canadien</u>
la <u>Canadienne</u>

canal NOUN
le <u>canal</u>
(les canaux PL)

Canaries PL NOUN
♦ **the Canaries** les îles Canaries FEM PL

canary NOUN
le <u>canari</u>

to **cancel** VERB
<u>annuler</u> ◊ *The match was cancelled.* Le match a été annulé.

cancellation NOUN
l' <u>annulation</u> FEM

cancer NOUN
[1] le <u>cancer</u> ◊ *He's got cancer.* Il a le cancer.
[2] le <u>Cancer</u> ◊ *I'm Cancer.* Je suis Cancer.

candidate NOUN
le <u>candidat</u>
la <u>candidate</u>

candle NOUN
la <u>bougie</u>

candy NOUN US
les <u>bonbons</u> MASC PL
♦ **a candy** un bonbon

candyfloss NOUN
la <u>barbe à papa</u>

cannabis NOUN
le <u>cannabis</u>

canned ADJECTIVE
<u>en conserve</u> (*food*)

cannot VERB *see* **can**

canoe NOUN
le <u>canoë</u>

canoeing NOUN

♦**to go canoeing** faire du canoë ◊ *We went canoeing.* Nous avons fait du canoë.

can-opener NOUN
l' ouvre-boîte MASC

can't VERB *see* can

canteen NOUN
la cantine

to **canter** VERB
aller au petit galop

canvas NOUN
la toile

cap NOUN
1 la casquette (*hat*)
2 le bouchon (*of bottle, tube*)

capable ADJECTIVE
capable

capacity NOUN
la capacité

capital NOUN
1 la capitale ◊ *Cardiff is the capital of Wales.* Cardiff est la capitale du pays de Galles.
2 la majuscule (*letter*) ◊ *Write your address in capitals.* Écris ton adresse en majuscules.

capitalism NOUN
le capitalisme

capital punishment NOUN
la peine capitale

Capricorn NOUN
le Capricorne ◊ *I'm Capricorn.* Je suis Capricorne.

to **capsize** VERB
chavirer

captain NOUN
le capitaine ◊ *She's captain of the hockey team.* Elle est capitaine de l'équipe de hockey.

caption NOUN
la légende

to **capture** VERB
capturer

car NOUN
la voiture
♦**to go by car** aller en voiture ◊ *We went by car.* Nous y sommes allés en voiture.
♦**a car crash** un accident de voiture

caramel NOUN
le caramel

caravan NOUN
la caravane ◊ *a caravan site* un camping pour caravanes

card NOUN
la carte
♦**a card game** un jeu de cartes

cardboard NOUN
le carton

cardigan NOUN
le cardigan

cardphone NOUN
le téléphone à carte

care NOUN
see also **care** VERB
le soin ◊ *with care* avec soin
♦**to take care of** s'occuper de ◊ *I take care of the children on Saturdays.* Le samedi, je m'occupe des enfants.
♦**Take care! (1)** (*Be careful!*) Fais attention!
♦**Take care! (2)** (*Look after yourself!*) Prends bien soin de toi!

to **care** VERB
see also **care** NOUN
♦**to care about** se soucier de ◊ *They don't care about their image.* Ils se soucient peu de leur image.
♦**I don't care!** Ça m'est égal! ◊ *She doesn't care.* Ça lui est égal.
♦**to care for somebody** (*patients, old people*) s'occuper de quelqu'un

career NOUN
la carrière
♦**a careers adviser** un conseiller d'orientation

careful ADJECTIVE
♦**Be careful!** Fais attention!

carefully ADVERB
1 soigneusement ◊ *She carefully avoided talking about it.* Elle évitait soigneusement d'en parler.
2 prudemment (*safely*) ◊ *Drive carefully!* Conduisez prudemment!
♦**Think carefully!** Réfléchis bien!

careless ADJECTIVE
1 (*work*)
peu soigné
♦**a careless mistake** une faute d'inattention
2 (*person*)
peu soigneux MASC
peu soigneuse FEM
◊ *She's very careless.* Elle est bien peu soigneuse.
3 imprudent ◊ *a careless driver* un conducteur imprudent

caretaker NOUN
le gardien
la gardienne

car-ferry NOUN
le ferry

cargo NOUN
la cargaison

car hire NOUN
la location de voitures

Caribbean ADJECTIVE
| see also **Caribbean** NOUN |

antillais ◊ *Caribbean food* la cuisine
antillaise

Caribbean NOUN
| see also **Caribbean** ADJECTIVE |

1 les Caraïbes FEM PL (*islands*) ◊ *We're
going to the Caribbean.* Nous allons
aux Caraïbes.
♦ He's from the Caribbean. Il est
antillais.
2 la mer des Caraïbes (*sea*)

caring ADJECTIVE
♦ She's a very caring teacher. C'est un
professeur qui se préoccupe du bien-
être de ses élèves.
♦ She has very caring parents. Ses
parents sont très affectueux.

carnation NOUN
l' œillet MASC

carnival NOUN
le carnaval

carol NOUN
♦ a Christmas carol un chant de Noël

car park NOUN
le parking

carpenter NOUN
le charpentier ◊ *He's a carpenter.* Il
est charpentier.

carpentry NOUN
la menuiserie

carpet NOUN
1 le tapis ◊ *a Persian carpet* un
tapis persan
2 la moquette (*fitted*)

car phone NOUN
le téléphone de voiture

car rental NOUN US
la location de voitures

carriage NOUN
la voiture

carrier bag NOUN
le sac en plastique

carrot NOUN
la carotte

to **carry** VERB
1 porter ◊ *I'll carry your bag.* Je vais
porter ton sac.
2 transporter ◊ *a plane carrying 100
passengers* un avion transportant
cent passagers

to **carry on** VERB
continuer ◊ *Carry on!* Continue!
◊ *She carried on talking.* Elle a
continué à parler.

to **carry out** VERB
exécuter (*orders*)

carrycot NOUN
le porte-bébé

cart NOUN
la charrette

carton NOUN
la brique (*of milk, juice*)

cartoon NOUN
1 le dessin animé (*film*)
2 le dessin humoristique (*in
newspaper*)
♦ a strip cartoon une bande dessinée

cartridge NOUN
la cartouche

to **carve** VERB
découper (*meat*)

case NOUN
1 la valise ◊ *I've packed my case.*
J'ai fait ma valise.
2 le cas
(les cas PL)
◊ *in some cases* dans certains cas
♦ in that case dans ce cas ◊ *I don't
want it. – In that case, I'll take it.* Je
n'en veux pas. – Dans ce cas, je le
prends.
♦ in case au cas où ◊ *in case it rains* au
cas où il pleuvrait
♦ just in case à tout hasard ◊ *Take
some money, just in case.* Prends de
l'argent à tout hasard.

cash NOUN
l' argent MASC ◊ *I'm a bit short of
cash.* Je suis un peu à court d'argent.
♦ in cash en liquide ◊ *£2000 in cash*
deux mille livres en liquide
♦ to pay cash payer comptant
♦ a cash card une carte de retrait
♦ the cash desk la caisse
♦ a cash dispenser un distributeur
automatique de billets
♦ a cash register une caisse

cashew NOUN
la noix de cajou

cashier NOUN
le caissier
la caissière

cashmere NOUN
le cachemire ◊ *a cashmere sweater*
un pull en cachemire

casino NOUN
le casino

casserole NOUN
le ragoût ◊ *I'm going to make a
casserole.* Je vais faire un ragoût.
♦ a casserole dish une cocotte

cassette NOUN
la cassette
♦ a cassette player un lecteur de
cassettes
♦ a cassette recorder un magnétophone

cast NOUN
les acteurs MASC PL ◊ *After the play, we met the cast.* Après la représentation, nous avons rencontré les acteurs.

castle NOUN
le château
(les châteaux PL)

casual ADJECTIVE
1 décontracté ◊ *casual clothes* les vêtements décontractés
2 désinvolte ◊ *a casual attitude* une attitude désinvolte
3 en passant ◊ *It was just a casual remark.* C'était juste une remarque en passant.

casually ADVERB
♦**to dress casually** s'habiller de façon décontractée

casualty NOUN
les urgences FEM PL (*in hospital*)

cat NOUN
le chat
la chatte
◊ *Have you got a cat?* Est-ce que tu as un chat?

catalogue NOUN
le catalogue

catalytic converter NOUN
le catalyseur

catarrh NOUN
le rhume chronique

catastrophe NOUN
la catastrophe

to **catch** VERB
1 attraper ◊ *to catch a thief* attraper un voleur ◊ *My cat catches birds.* Mon chat attrape des oiseaux.
♦**to catch somebody doing something** attraper quelqu'un en train de faire quelque chose ◊ *If they catch you smoking ...* S'ils t'attrapent en train de fumer ...
♦**to catch a cold** attraper un rhume
2 prendre (*bus, train*) ◊ *We caught the last bus.* On a pris le dernier bus.
3 saisir (*hear*) ◊ *I didn't catch his name.* Je n'ai pas saisi son nom.
♦**to catch up** rattraper son retard ◊ *I've got to catch up: I was away last week.* Je dois rattraper mon retard: j'étais absent la semaine dernière.

catching ADJECTIVE
contagieux MASC
contagieuse FEM
◊ *It's not catching.* Ce n'est pas contagieux.

catering NOUN
la restauration

cathedral NOUN

la cathédrale

Catholic ADJECTIVE
see also **Catholic** NOUN
catholique

Catholic NOUN
see also **Catholic** ADJECTIVE
le/la catholique ◊ *I'm a Catholic.* Je suis catholique.

cattle PL NOUN
le bétail SING

caught VERB see **catch**

cauliflower NOUN
le chou-fleur
(les choux-fleurs PL)

cause NOUN
see also **cause** VERB
la cause

to **cause** VERB
see also **cause** NOUN
provoquer ◊ *to cause an accident* provoquer un accident

cautious ADJECTIVE
prudent

cautiously ADVERB
avec précaution ◊ *She cautiously opened the door.* Elle a ouvert la porte avec précaution.
♦**He reacted cautiously.** Il a réagi prudemment.

cave NOUN
la grotte

CCTV (= *closed-circuit television*) NOUN
la télévision en circuit fermé

CD NOUN
le CD
(les CD PL)

CD burner NOUN
le graveur de CD

CD player NOUN
la platine laser

CD-ROM NOUN
le CD-ROM
(les CD-ROM PL)

ceasefire NOUN
le cessez-le-feu
(les cessez-le-feu PL)

ceiling NOUN
le plafond

to **celebrate** VERB
fêter (*birthday*)

celebration NOUN
la fête

celebrity NOUN
la célébrité

celery NOUN
le céleri

cell NOUN
la cellule

C

cellar NOUN
la <u>cave</u> ◊ *a wine cellar* une cave à vins

cello NOUN
le <u>violoncelle</u> ◊ *I play the cello.* Je joue du violoncelle.

cement NOUN
le <u>ciment</u>

cemetery NOUN
le <u>cimetière</u>

cent NOUN
le <u>cent</u> ◊ *twenty cents* vingt cents

centenary NOUN
le <u>centenaire</u>

center NOUN US
le <u>centre</u>

centigrade ADJECTIVE
<u>centigrade</u> ◊ *20 degrees centigrade* vingt degrés centigrade

centimetre NOUN (US **centimeter**)
le <u>centimètre</u>

central ADJECTIVE
<u>central</u>
(centraux MASC PL)

central heating NOUN
le <u>chauffage central</u>

centre NOUN
le <u>centre</u> ◊ *a sports centre* un centre sportif

century NOUN
le <u>siècle</u> ◊ *the 20th century* le vingtième siècle ◊ *the 21st century* le vingt et unième siècle

cereal NOUN
les <u>céréales</u> FEM PL ◊ *I have cereal for breakfast.* Je prends des céréales au petit déjeuner.

ceremony NOUN
la <u>cérémonie</u>

certain ADJECTIVE
<u>certain</u> ◊ *a certain person* une certaine personne ◊ *I'm absolutely certain it was him.* Je suis absolument certain que c'était lui.
♦**I don't know for certain.** Je n'en suis pas certain.
♦**to make certain** s'assurer ◊ *I made certain the door was locked.* Je me suis assuré que la porte était fermée à clé.

certainly ADVERB
<u>vraiment</u> ◊ *I certainly expected something better.* Je m'attendais vraiment à quelque chose de mieux.
♦**Certainly not!** Certainement pas!
♦**So it was a surprise? – It certainly was!** C'était donc une surprise? – Ça oui alors!

certificate NOUN
le <u>certificat</u>

CFCs PL NOUN
les <u>CFC</u> MASC PL

chain NOUN
la <u>chaîne</u>

chair NOUN
[1] la <u>chaise</u> ◊ *a table and 4 chairs* une table et quatre chaises
[2] le <u>fauteuil</u> (*armchair*)

chairlift NOUN
le <u>télésiège</u>

chairman NOUN
le <u>président</u>

chalet NOUN
le <u>chalet</u>

chalk NOUN
la <u>craie</u>

challenge NOUN
see also **challenge** VERB
le <u>défi</u>

to **challenge** VERB
see also **challenge** NOUN
♦**She challenged me to a race.** Elle m'a proposé de faire la course avec elle.

challenging ADJECTIVE
<u>stimulant</u> ◊ *a challenging job* un travail stimulant

chambermaid NOUN
la <u>femme de chambre</u>

champagne NOUN
le <u>champagne</u>

champion NOUN
le <u>champion</u>
la <u>championne</u>

championship NOUN
le <u>championnat</u>

chance NOUN
[1] la <u>chance</u> ◊ *Do you think I've got any chance?* Tu crois que j'ai une chance? ◊ *Their chances of winning are very good.* Ils ont de fortes chances de gagner.
♦**No chance!** Pas question!
[2] l' <u>occasion</u> FEM ◊ *I'd like to have a chance to travel.* J'aimerais avoir l'occasion de voyager.
♦**I'll write when I get the chance.** J'écrirai quand j'aurai un moment.
♦**by chance** par hasard ◊ *We met by chance.* Nous nous sommes rencontrés par hasard.
♦**to take a chance** prendre un risque ◊ *I'm taking no chances!* Je ne veux prendre aucun risque!

Chancellor of the Exchequer NOUN
le <u>chancelier de l'Échiquier</u>

to **change** VERB

☞

see also **change** NOUN

1 changer ◊ *The town has changed a lot.* La ville a beaucoup changé. ◊ *I'd like to change £50.* Je voudrais changer cinquante livres.

> Use **changer de** when you change one thing for another.

2 changer de ◊ *You have to change trains in Paris.* Il faut changer de train à Paris. ◊ *I'm going to change my shoes.* Je vais changer de chaussures. ◊ *He wants to change his job.* Il veut changer d'emploi.

♦**to change one's mind** changer d'avis ◊ *I've changed my mind.* J'ai changé d'avis.

♦**to change gear** changer de vitesse

3 se changer ◊ *She's changing to go out.* Elle est en train de se changer pour sortir.

♦**to get changed** se changer ◊ *I'm going to get changed.* Je vais me changer.

4 échanger (*swap*) ◊ *Can I change this sweater? It's too small.* Est-ce que je peux échanger ce pull? Il est trop petit.

change NOUN

see also **change** VERB

1 le changement ◊ *There's been a change of plan.* Il y a eu un changement de programme.

2 la monnaie (*money*) ◊ *I haven't got any change.* Je n'ai pas de monnaie.

♦**a change of clothes** des vêtements de rechange

♦**for a change** pour changer ◊ *Let's play tennis for a change.* Si on jouait au tennis pour changer?

changeable ADJECTIVE
variable

changing room NOUN
1 le salon d'essayage (*in shop*)
2 le vestiaire (*for sport*)

channel NOUN
la chaîne (*TV*) ◊ *There's football on the other channel.* Il y a du football sur l'autre chaîne.

♦**the Channel** la Manche

♦**the Channel Islands** les îles Anglo-Normandes FEM PL

♦**the Channel Tunnel** le tunnel sous la Manche

chaos NOUN
le chaos

chap NOUN
le type ◊ *He's a nice chap.* C'est un type sympa.

chapel NOUN

la chapelle (*part of church*)

chapter NOUN
le chapitre

character NOUN
1 le caractère ◊ *Give me some idea of his character.* Décris-moi un peu son caractère.

♦**She's quite a character.** C'est un drôle de numéro.

2 le personnage (*in play, film*) ◊ *The character played by Depardieu ...* Le personnage joué par Depardieu ...

characteristic NOUN
la caractéristique

charcoal NOUN
le charbon de bois

charge NOUN

see also **charge** VERB

les frais MASC PL ◊ *Is there a charge for delivery?* Est-ce qu'il y a des frais de livraison?

♦**an extra charge** un supplément

♦**free of charge** gratuit

♦**to reverse the charges** appeler en P.C.V. ◊ *I'd like to reverse the charges.* Je voudrais appeler en P.C.V.

♦**to be on a charge** être inculpé ◊ *He's on a charge of murder.* Il est inculpé de meurtre.

♦**to be in charge** être responsable ◊ *Mrs Munday was in charge of the group.* Madame Munday était responsable du groupe.

to **charge** VERB

see also **charge** NOUN

1 prendre (*money*) ◊ *How much did he charge you?* Combien est-ce qu'il vous a pris? ◊ *They charge £10 an hour.* Ils prennent dix livres de l'heure.

2 inculper (*with crime*) ◊ *The police have charged him with murder.* La police l'a inculpé de meurtre.

charity NOUN
l' association caritative FEM ◊ *He gave the money to charity.* Il a donné l'argent à une association caritative.

charm NOUN
le charme ◊ *He's got a lot of charm.* Il a beaucoup de charme.

charming ADJECTIVE
charmant

chart NOUN
le tableau
(les tableaux PL)
◊ *The chart shows the rise of unemployment.* Le tableau indique la progression du chômage.

♦the charts le hit-parade ◊ *This album is number one in the charts.* Cet album est numéro un au hit-parade.

charter flight NOUN
le charter

to **chase** VERB

> *see also* **chase** NOUN

pourchasser

chase NOUN

> *see also* **chase** VERB

la poursuite ◊ *a car chase* une poursuite en voiture

chat NOUN

> *see also* **chat** VERB

♦**to have a chat** bavarder

to **chat** VERB

> *see also* **chat** NOUN

bavarder
♦**to chat somebody up** draguer quelqu'un (*informal*) ◊ *Gabriel's not very good at chatting up girls.* Gabriel n'est pas très doué pour draguer les filles.

chatroom NOUN
le forum de discussion

chat show NOUN
le talk-show

chauvinist NOUN
♦**a male chauvinist** un machiste

cheap ADJECTIVE
bon marché MASC, FEM, PL
◊ *a cheap T-shirt* un T-shirt bon marché

cheaper ADJECTIVE
moins cher MASC
moins chère FEM
◊ *It's cheaper by bus.* C'est moins cher en bus.

to **cheat** VERB

> *see also* **cheat** NOUN

tricher ◊ *You're cheating!* Tu triches!

cheat NOUN

> *see also* **cheat** VERB

le tricheur
la tricheuse

check NOUN

> *see also* **check** VERB

1 le contrôle ◊ *a security check* un contrôle de sécurité
2 le chèque US ◊ *to write a check* faire un chèque
3 l' addition FEM US ◊ *Can we have the check, please?* L'addition, s'il vous plaît.

to **check** VERB

> *see also* **check** NOUN

vérifier ◊ *I'll check the time of the train.* Je vais vérifier l'heure du train.

◊ *Could you check the oil, please?* Pourriez-vous vérifier le niveau d'huile, s'il vous plaît?

♦**to check in (1)** (*at airport*) se présenter à l'enregistrement ◊ *What time do I have to check in?* À quelle heure est-ce que je dois me présenter à l'enregistrement?
♦**to check in (2)** (*in hotel*) se présenter à la réception
♦**to check out** (*from hotel*) régler sa note

checked ADJECTIVE
à carreaux (*fabric*)

checkers NOUN US
les dames FEM PL ◊ *to play checkers* jouer aux dames

check-in NOUN
l' enregistrement MASC

checking account NOUN US
le compte courant

checkout NOUN
la caisse

check-up NOUN
l' examen de routine MASC

cheek NOUN
1 la joue ◊ *He kissed her on the cheek.* Il l'a embrassée sur la joue.
2 le culot ◊ *What a cheek!* Quel culot!

cheeky ADJECTIVE
effronté ◊ *Don't be cheeky!* Ne sois pas effronté!
♦**a cheeky smile** un sourire malicieux

cheer NOUN

> *see also* **cheer** VERB

les hourras MASC PL
♦**to give a cheer** pousser des hourras
♦**Cheers! (1)** (*good health*) À la vôtre!
♦**Cheers! (2)** (*thanks*) Merci!

to **cheer** VERB

> *see also* **cheer** NOUN

applaudir
♦**to cheer somebody up** remonter le moral à quelqu'un ◊ *I was trying to cheer him up.* J'essayais de lui remonter le moral.
♦**Cheer up!** Ne te laisse pas abattre!

cheerful ADJECTIVE
gai

cheerio EXCLAMATION
salut!

cheese NOUN
le fromage

chef NOUN
le chef

chemical NOUN
le produit chimique

chemist NOUN

1 (*dispenser*)

le pharmacien

la pharmacienne

2 (*shop*)

la pharmacie ◊ *You get it from the chemist.* C'est vendu en pharmacie.

> ❶ *Chemist's shops in France are identified by a special green cross outside the shop.*

3 (*scientist*)

le/la chimiste

chemistry NOUN

la chimie ◊ *the chemistry lab* le laboratoire de chimie

cheque NOUN

le chèque ◊ *to write a cheque* faire un chèque ◊ *to pay by cheque* payer par chèque

chequebook NOUN

le carnet de chèques

cherry NOUN

la cerise

chess NOUN

les échecs MASC PL ◊ *to play chess* jouer aux échecs

chessboard NOUN

l' échiquier MASC

chest NOUN

la poitrine (*of person*) ◊ *his chest measurement* son tour de poitrine

♦ **a chest of drawers** une commode

chestnut NOUN

le marron ◊ *We have turkey with chestnuts.* Nous mangeons de la dinde aux marrons.

to **chew** VERB

mâcher

chewing gum NOUN

le chewing-gum

chick NOUN

le poussin ◊ *a hen and her chicks* une poule et ses poussins

chicken NOUN

le poulet

chickenpox NOUN

la varicelle

chickpeas PL NOUN

les pois chiches MASC PL

chief NOUN

see also **chief** ADJECTIVE

le chef ◊ *the chief of security* le chef de la sécurité

chief ADJECTIVE

see also **chief** NOUN

principal ◊ *His chief reason for resigning was the low pay.* La principale raison de sa démission était son mauvais salaire.

child NOUN

l' enfant MASC/FEM ◊ *all the children* tous les enfants

childish ADJECTIVE

puéril

child minder NOUN

la nourrice

children PL NOUN *see* **child**

Chile NOUN

le Chili

♦ **in Chile** au Chili

to **chill** VERB

mettre au frais ◊ *Put the wine in the fridge to chill.* Mets le vin au frais dans le réfrigérateur.

chilli NOUN

le piment

chilly ADJECTIVE

froid

chimney NOUN

la cheminée

chin NOUN

le menton

china NOUN

la porcelaine ◊ *a china plate* une assiette en porcelaine

China NOUN

la Chine

♦ **in China** en Chine

Chinese ADJECTIVE

see also **Chinese** NOUN

chinois ◊ *a Chinese restaurant* un restaurant chinois

♦ **a Chinese man** un Chinois

♦ **a Chinese woman** une Chinoise

Chinese NOUN

see also **Chinese** ADJECTIVE

le chinois (*language*)

♦ **the Chinese** (*people*) les Chinois

chip NOUN

1 la frite (*food*) ◊ *We bought some chips.* Nous avons acheté des frites.

2 la puce (*in computer*)

chiropodist NOUN

le/la pédicure ◊ *He's a chiropodist.* Il est pédicure.

chives PL NOUN

la ciboulette SING

chocolate NOUN

le chocolat ◊ *a chocolate cake* un gâteau au chocolat

♦ **hot chocolate** le chocolat chaud

choice NOUN

le choix ◊ *I had no choice.* Je n'avais pas le choix.

choir NOUN
la chorale ◊ *I sing in the school choir.* Je chante dans la chorale de l'école.

to **choke** VERB
s'étrangler
♦ **He choked on a fishbone.** Il s'est étranglé avec une arête de poisson.

to **choose** VERB
choisir ◊ *It's difficult to choose.* C'est difficile de choisir.

to **chop** VERB
see also **chop** NOUN
émincer ◊ *Chop the onions.* Émincez les oignons.

chop NOUN
see also **chop** VERB
la côte ◊ *a pork chop* une côte de porc

chopsticks PL NOUN
les baguettes FEM PL

chose, chosen VERB *see* **choose**

Christ NOUN
le Christ

christening NOUN
le baptême

Christian NOUN
see also **Christian** ADJECTIVE
le chrétien
la chrétienne

Christian ADJECTIVE
see also **Christian** NOUN
chrétien MASC
chrétienne FEM

Christian name NOUN
le prénom

Christmas NOUN
Noël MASC ◊ *Happy Christmas!* Joyeux Noël!
♦ **Christmas Day** le jour de Noël
♦ **Christmas Eve** la veille de Noël
♦ **a Christmas tree** un arbre de Noël
♦ **a Christmas card** une carte de Noël

> ❶ *The French more often send greetings cards (**une carte de vœux**) in January rather than at Christmas, with best wishes for the New Year.*

♦ **Christmas dinner** le repas de Noël

> ❶ *Most French people have their Christmas meal (**réveillon de Noël**) on the evening of Christmas Eve, though some have a **repas de Noël** on Christmas Day.*

♦ **Christmas pudding**

> ❶ *The French usually have a Yule log (**une bûche de Noël**) for pudding at the Christmas meal. You could explain what Christmas pudding is using the example given.*

◊ *Christmas pudding is made with dried fruit and spices, and steamed.* Le "Christmas pudding" est un gâteau avec des raisins secs, parfumé avec des épices et cuit à la vapeur.

chunk NOUN
le gros morceau
(les gros morceaux PL)
◊ *Cut the meat into chunks.* Coupez la viande en gros morceaux.

church NOUN
l' église FEM ◊ *James doesn't go to church every Sunday.* James ne va pas à l'église tous les dimanches.
♦ **the Church of England** l'Église anglicane

cider NOUN
le cidre

cigar NOUN
le cigare

cigarette NOUN
la cigarette

cigarette lighter NOUN
le briquet

cinema NOUN
le cinéma ◊ *I'm going to the cinema this evening.* Je vais au cinéma ce soir.

cinnamon NOUN
la cannelle

circle NOUN
le cercle ◊ *to stand in a circle* faire cercle.

circular ADJECTIVE
circulaire

circulation NOUN
1 la circulation (*of blood*)
2 le tirage (*of newspaper*)

circumflex NOUN
l' accent circonflexe MASC

circumstances PL NOUN
les circonstances FEM PL

circus NOUN
le cirque

citizen NOUN
le citoyen
la citoyenne
◊ *a French citizen* un citoyen français

citizenship NOUN

☞

la citoyenneté

City NOUN
♦**the City** la City de Londres

city NOUN
la ville
♦**the city centre** le centre-ville ◊ *It's in the city centre.* C'est au centre-ville.

city technology college NOUN
le collège technique

civilization NOUN
la civilisation

civil servant NOUN
le/la fonctionnaire

civil war NOUN
la guerre civile

to **claim** VERB
see also **claim** NOUN
1 prétendre ◊ *He claims to have found the money.* Il prétend avoir trouvé l'argent.
2 percevoir (*receive*) ◊ *She's claiming unemployment benefit.* Elle perçoit des allocations chômage.
♦**She can't claim unemployment benefit.** Elle n'a pas droit aux allocations chômage.
♦**to claim on one's insurance** se faire rembourser par son assurance ◊ *We claimed on our insurance.* On s'est fait rembourser par notre assurance.

claim NOUN
see also **claim** VERB
la demande d'indemnité (*on insurance policy*) ◊ *to make a claim* faire une demande d'indemnité

to **clap** VERB
applaudir (*applaud*)
♦**to clap one's hands** frapper dans ses mains ◊ *I've trained my dog to sit when I clap my hands.* J'ai dressé mon chien à s'asseoir quand je frappe dans mes mains.

clarinet NOUN
la clarinette ◊ *I play the clarinet.* Je joue de la clarinette.

to **clash** VERB
1 jurer (*colours*) ◊ *These two colours clash.* Ces deux couleurs jurent.
2 tomber en même temps (*events*) ◊ *The concert clashes with Ann's party.* Le concert tombe en même temps que la soirée d'Ann.

clasp NOUN
le fermoir (*of necklace*)

class NOUN
1 la classe (*group*) ◊ *We're in the same class.* Nous sommes dans la même classe.

2 le cours (*lesson*) ◊ *I go to dancing classes.* Je vais à des cours de danse.

classic ADJECTIVE
see also **classic** NOUN
classique ◊ *a classic example* un cas classique

classic NOUN
see also **classic** ADJECTIVE
le classique (*book, film*)

classical ADJECTIVE
classique ◊ *I like classical music.* J'aime la musique classique.

classmate NOUN
le camarade de classe
la camarade de classe

classroom NOUN
la classe

classroom assistant NOUN
l' aide-éducateur MASC
l' aide-éducatrice FEM

claw NOUN
1 la griffe (*of cat, dog*)
2 la serre (*of bird*)
3 la pince (*of crab, lobster*)

clean ADJECTIVE
see also **clean** VERB
propre ◊ *a clean shirt* une chemise propre

to **clean** VERB
see also **clean** ADJECTIVE
nettoyer

cleaner NOUN
1 la femme de ménage (*woman*)
2 l' agent d'entretien MASC (*man*)

cleaner's NOUN
la teinturerie

cleaning lady NOUN
la femme de ménage

cleansing lotion NOUN
la lotion démaquillante

clear ADJECTIVE
see also **clear** VERB
1 clair ◊ *a clear explanation* une explication claire ◊ *It's clear you don't believe me.* Il est clair que tu ne me crois pas.
2 libre (*road, way*) ◊ *The road's clear now.* La route est libre maintenant.

to **clear** VERB
see also **clear** ADJECTIVE
1 dégager ◊ *The police are clearing the road after the accident.* La police dégage la route après l'accident.
2 se dissiper (*fog, mist*) ◊ *The mist cleared.* La brume s'est dissipée.
♦**to be cleared of a crime** être reconnu non coupable d'un crime ◊ *She was*

cleared of murder. Elle a été reconnue non coupable du meurtre.
◆**to clear the table** débarrasser la table ◇ *I'll clear the table.* Je vais débarrasser la table.
◆**to clear up** ranger ◇ *Who's going to clear all this up?* Qui va ranger tout ça?
◆**I think it's going to clear up.** (*weather*) Je pense que le temps va se lever.

to **clear off** VERB
filer ◇ *Clear off and leave me alone!* File et laisse-moi tranquille!

clearly ADVERB
1 clairement ◇ *She explained it very clearly.* Elle l'a expliqué très clairement.
2 nettement ◇ *The French coast was clearly visible.* On distinguait nettement la côte française.
3 distinctement ◇ *to speak clearly* parler distinctement

clementine NOUN
la clémentine

clever ADJECTIVE
1 intelligent ◇ *She's very clever.* Elle est très intelligente.
2 (*ingenious*)
astucieux MASC
astucieuse FEM
◇ *a clever system* un système astucieux
◆**What a clever idea!** Quelle bonne idée!

click NOUN
see also **click** VERB
le petit bruit (*of door, camera*)

to **click** VERB
see also **click** NOUN
cliquer (*with mouse*)
◆**to click on an icon** cliquer sur une icône

client NOUN
le client
la cliente

cliff NOUN
la falaise

climate NOUN
le climat

to **climb** VERB
1 escalader ◇ *We're going to climb Snowdon.* Nous allons escalader le Snowdon.
2 monter (*stairs*)

climber NOUN
le grimpeur
la grimpeuse

climbing NOUN
l' escalade FEM

◆**to go climbing** faire de l'escalade ◇ *We're going climbing in Scotland.* Nous allons faire de l'escalade en Écosse.

Clingfilm ® NOUN
le film alimentaire

clinic NOUN
le centre médical
(les centres médicaux PL)

clip NOUN
1 la barrette (*for hair*)
2 le court extrait (*film*) ◇ *some clips from Kevin Costner's latest film* quelques courts extraits du dernier film de Kevin Costner

clippers PL NOUN
◆**nail clippers** le coupe-ongle SING
(les coupe-ongles PL)

cloakroom NOUN
1 le vestiaire (*for coats*)
2 les toilettes FEM PL (*toilet*)

clock NOUN
1 l' horloge FEM ◇ *the church clock* l'horloge de l'église
2 la pendule (*smaller*)
◆**an alarm clock** un réveil
◆**a clock-radio** un radio-réveil

clockwork NOUN
◆**Everything went like clockwork.** Tout a marché comme sur des roulettes.

clog NOUN
le sabot

clone NOUN
see also **clone** VERB
le clone (*animal, plant*)

to **clone** VERB
see also **clone** NOUN
cloner ◇ *a cloned sheep* un mouton cloné

close ADJECTIVE, ADVERB
see also **close** VERB
1 près (*near*) ◇ *The shops are very close.* Les magasins sont tout près.
◆**close to** près de ◇ *The youth hostel is close to the station.* L'auberge de jeunesse est près de la gare.
◆**Come closer.** Rapproche-toi.
2 proche (*in relationship*) ◇ *We're just inviting close relations.* Nous n'invitons que les parents proches. ◇ *She's a close friend of mine.* C'est une proche amie. ◇ *I'm very close to my sister.* Je suis très proche de ma sœur.
3 très serré (*contest*) ◇ *It's going to be very close.* Ça va être très serré.
4 lourd (*weather*) ◇ *It's close this afternoon.* Il fait lourd cet après-midi.

to **close** VERB

☞

see also **close** ADJECTIVE

[1] fermer ◊ What time does the pool close? La piscine ferme à quelle heure? ◊ The shops close at 5.30. Les magasins ferment à cinq heures et demie. ◊ Please close the door. Fermez la porte, s'il vous plaît.

[2] se fermer ◊ The doors close automatically. Les portes se ferment automatiquement.

closed ADJECTIVE
fermé ◊ The bank's closed. La banque est fermée.

closely ADVERB
de près (look, examine)

cloth NOUN
le tissu (material)
♦a cloth un chiffon ◊ Wipe it with a damp cloth. Nettoyez-le avec un chiffon humide.

clothes PL NOUN
les vêtements MASC PL ◊ new clothes des vêtements neufs
♦a clothes line un fil à linge
♦a clothes peg une pince à linge

cloud NOUN
le nuage

cloudy ADJECTIVE
nuageux MASC
nuageuse FEM

clove NOUN
♦a clove of garlic une gousse d'ail

clown NOUN
le clown

club NOUN
le club ◊ a golf club (society and for playing golf) un club de golf
♦the youth club la maison des jeunes
♦clubs (in cards) le trèfle ◊ the ace of clubs l'as de trèfle

to **club together** VERB
se cotiser ◊ We clubbed together to buy her a present. Nous nous sommes cotisés pour lui acheter un cadeau.

clubbing NOUN
♦to go clubbing sortir en boîte

clue NOUN
l' indice MASC ◊ an important clue un indice important
♦I haven't a clue. Je n'en ai pas la moindre idée.

clumsy ADJECTIVE
maladroit

clutch NOUN
la pédale d'embrayage (of car)

clutter NOUN

le désordre ◊ There's too much clutter in here. Il y a trop de désordre ici.

coach NOUN
[1] le car MASC ◊ We went there by coach. Nous y sommes allés en car.
♦the coach station la gare routière
♦a coach trip une excursion en car
[2] l' entraîneur MASC (trainer) ◊ the French coach l'entraîneur de l'équipe de France

coal NOUN
le charbon
♦a coal mine une mine de charbon
♦a coal miner un mineur

coarse ADJECTIVE
[1] (surface, fabric)
rugueux MASC
rugueuse FEM
◊ The bag was made of coarse cloth. Le sac était fait d'un tissu rugueux.
[2] (vulgar)
grossier MASC
grossière FEM
◊ coarse language un langage grossier

coast NOUN
la côte ◊ It's on the west coast of Scotland. C'est sur la côte ouest de l'Écosse.

coastguard NOUN
le garde-côte
(les garde-côtes PL)

coat NOUN
le manteau
(les manteaux PL)
◊ a warm coat un manteau chaud
♦a coat of paint une couche de peinture

coat hanger NOUN
le cintre

cobweb NOUN
la toile d'araignée

cocaine NOUN
la cocaïne

cock NOUN
le coq (cockerel)

cockerel NOUN
le coq

cockney NOUN
le cockney ◊ I'm a cockney. Je suis cockney.

cocoa NOUN
le cacao ◊ a cup of cocoa une tasse de cacao

coconut NOUN
la noix de coco

cod NOUN
le cabillaud

C

code NOUN
le code

coffee NOUN
le café
♦ **A cup of coffee, please.** Un café, s'il vous plaît.

coffeepot NOUN
la cafetière

coffee table NOUN
la table basse

coffin NOUN
le cercueil

coin NOUN
la pièce de monnaie
♦ **a 2 euro coin** une pièce de deux euros

coincidence NOUN
la coïncidence

coinphone NOUN
le téléphone à pièces

Coke ® NOUN
le coca ◊ *a can of Coke* ® une boîte de coca

colander NOUN
la passoire

cold ADJECTIVE
see also **cold** NOUN
froid ◊ *The water's cold.* L'eau est froide.
♦ **It's cold today.** Il fait froid aujourd'hui.
♦ **to be cold** (*person*) avoir froid ◊ *I'm cold.* J'ai froid. ◊ *Are you cold?* Est-ce que tu as froid?

cold NOUN
see also **cold** ADJECTIVE
[1] le froid ◊ *I can't stand the cold.* Je ne supporte pas le froid.
[2] le rhume ◊ *to catch a cold* attraper un rhume
♦ **to have a cold** avoir un rhume ◊ *I've got a bad cold.* J'ai un gros rhume.
♦ **a cold sore** un bouton de fièvre

coleslaw NOUN
la salade de chou cru à la mayonnaise

to **collapse** VERB
s'effondrer ◊ *He collapsed.* Il s'est effondré.

collar NOUN
[1] le col (*of coat, shirt*)
[2] le collier (*for animal*)

collarbone NOUN
la clavicule ◊ *I broke my collarbone.* Je me suis cassé la clavicule.

colleague NOUN
le/la collègue

to **collect** VERB
[1] ramasser ◊ *The teacher collected the exercise books.* Le professeur a ramassé les cahiers. ◊ *They collect the rubbish twice a week.* Ils ramassent les ordures deux fois par semaine.
[2] faire collection de ◊ *I collect stamps.* Je fais collection de timbres.
[3] aller chercher ◊ *Their mother collects them from school.* Leur mère va les chercher à l'école.
[4] faire une collecte ◊ *They're collecting for charity.* Ils font une collecte pour une association caritative.

collect call NOUN US
la communication en PCV

collection NOUN
[1] la collection ◊ *my CD collection* ma collection de CD
[2] la collecte ◊ *a collection for charity* une collecte pour une association caritative
[3] la levée (*of mail*) ◊ *Next collection: 5 p.m.* Prochaine levée: 17 heures

collector NOUN
le collectionneur
la collectionneuse

college NOUN
le collège ◊ *a technical college* un collège d'enseignement technique

to **collide** VERB
entrer en collision

collie NOUN
le colley

colliery NOUN
la houillère

collision NOUN
la collision

colon NOUN
les deux points MASC PL (*punctuation mark*)

colonel NOUN
le colonel

colour NOUN (US **color**)
la couleur ◊ *What colour is it?* C'est de quelle couleur?
♦ **a colour film** (*for camera*) une pellicule en couleur

colourful ADJECTIVE (US **colorful**)
coloré

colouring NOUN (US **coloring**)
le colorant (*for food*)

comb NOUN
see also **comb** VERB
le peigne

to **comb** VERB
see also **comb** NOUN

☞

♦to comb one's hair se peigner ◊ *You haven't combed your hair.* Tu ne t'es pas peigné.

combination NOUN
la combinaison

to **combine** VERB
[1] allier ◊ *The film combines humour with suspense.* Le film allie l'humour au suspense.
[2] concilier ◊ *It's difficult to combine a career with a family.* Il est difficile de concilier carrière et vie de famille.

to **come** VERB
[1] venir ◊ *Can I come too?* Est-ce que je peux venir aussi? ◊ *Some friends came to see us.* Quelques amis sont venus nous voir. ◊ *I'll come with you.* Je viens avec toi.
[2] arriver (*arrive*) ◊ *I'm coming!* J'arrive! ◊ *They came late.* Ils sont arrivés en retard. ◊ *The letter came this morning.* La lettre est arrivée ce matin.
♦to come back revenir ◊ *Come back!* Reviens!
♦to come down (1) (*person, lift*) descendre
♦to come down (2) (*prices*) baisser
♦to come from venir de ◊ *Where do you come from?* Tu viens d'où?
♦to come in entrer ◊ *Come in!* Entrez!
♦Come on! Allez!
♦to come out sortir ◊ *when we came out of the cinema* quand nous sommes sortis du cinéma ◊ *It's just come out on video.* Ça vient de sortir en vidéo.
♦None of my photos came out. Mes photos n'ont rien donné.
♦to come round reprendre connaissance (*after faint, operation*)
♦to come up monter ◊ *Come up here!* Monte!
♦to come up to somebody (1) s'approcher de quelqu'un ◊ *She came up to me and kissed me.* Elle s'est approchée de moi et m'a embrassé.
♦to come up to somebody (2) (*to speak to them*) aborder quelqu'un ◊ *A man came up to me and said ...* Un homme m'a abordé et m'a dit ...

comedian NOUN
le comique

comedy NOUN
la comédie

comfortable ADJECTIVE
[1] confortable (*bed, chair*)
[2] à l'aise (*person*) ◊ *I'm very comfortable, thanks.* Je suis parfaitement à l'aise, merci.

comic NOUN
l' illustré MASC (*magazine*)

comic strip NOUN
la bande dessinée

coming ADJECTIVE
prochain ◊ *in the coming months* au cours des prochains mois

comma NOUN
la virgule

command NOUN
l' ordre MASC

comment NOUN
see also **comment** VERB
le commentaire ◊ *He made no comment.* Il n'a fait aucun commentaire.
♦No comment! Je n'ai rien à dire!

to **comment** VERB
see also **comment** NOUN
♦to comment on something faire des commentaires sur quelque chose

commentary NOUN
le reportage en direct (*on TV, radio*)

commentator NOUN
le commentateur sportif
la commentatrice sportive

commercial NOUN
le spot publicitaire

commission NOUN
la commission ◊ *Salesmen work on commission.* Les représentants travaillent à la commission.

to **commit** VERB
♦to commit a crime commettre un crime
♦to commit oneself s'engager ◊ *I don't want to commit myself.* Je ne veux pas m'engager.
♦to commit suicide se suicider ◊ *He committed suicide.* Il s'est suicidé.

committee NOUN
le comité

common ADJECTIVE
see also **common** NOUN
courant ◊ *"Smith" is a very common surname.* "Smith" est un nom de famille très courant.
♦in common en commun ◊ *We've got a lot in common.* Nous avons beaucoup de choses en commun.

common NOUN
see also **common** ADJECTIVE
le terrain communal ◊ *We went for a walk on the common.* Nous sommes allés nous promener sur le terrain communal.

Commons PL NOUN

C

◆**the House of Commons** la Chambre
des communes

common sense NOUN
le <u>bon sens</u> ◊ *Use your common
sense!* Sers-toi de ton bon sens!

to **communicate** VERB
<u>communiquer</u>

communication NOUN
la <u>communication</u>

communion NOUN
la <u>communion</u> ◊ *my First
Communion* ma première
communion

communism NOUN
le <u>communisme</u>

communist NOUN
see also **communist** ADJECTIVE
le/la <u>communiste</u>

communist ADJECTIVE
see also **communist** NOUN
<u>communiste</u>
◆**the Communist Party** le Parti
communiste

community NOUN
la <u>communauté</u>

to **commute** VERB
<u>faire la navette</u> ◊ *She commutes
between Liss and London.* Elle fait la
navette entre Liss et Londres.

compact disc NOUN
le <u>disque compact</u>
◆**a compact disc player** une platine
laser

companion NOUN
le <u>compagnon</u>
la <u>compagne</u>

company NOUN
⬚1⬚ la <u>société</u> ◊ *He works for a big
company.* Il travaille pour une grosse
société.
⬚2⬚ la <u>compagnie</u> ◊ *an insurance
company* une compagnie d'assurance
◊ *a theatre company* une compagnie
théâtrale
◆**to keep somebody company** tenir
compagnie à quelqu'un ◊ *I'll keep
you company.* Je vais te tenir
compagnie.

comparatively ADVERB
<u>relativement</u>

to **compare** VERB
<u>comparer</u> ◊ *People always compare
him with his brother.* On le compare
toujours à son frère.
◆**compared with** en comparaison de
◊ *Oxford is small compared with
London.* Oxford est une petite ville en
comparaison de Londres.

comparison NOUN
la <u>comparaison</u>

compartment NOUN
le <u>compartiment</u>

compass NOUN
la <u>boussole</u>

compelling ADJECTIVE
<u>fascinant</u> (*gripping*) ◊ *It's a violent yet
compelling film.* C'est un film violent
mais fascinant.

compensation NOUN
l' <u>indemnité</u> FEM ◊ *They got £2000
compensation.* Ils ont reçu une
indemnité de deux mille livres.

compere NOUN
l' <u>animateur</u> MASC
l' <u>animatrice</u> FEM

to **compete** VERB
<u>participer</u> ◊ *I'm competing in the
marathon.* Je participe au marathon.
◆**to compete for something** se disputer
quelque chose ◊ *There are 50 students
competing for 6 places.* Ils sont
cinquante étudiants à se disputer six
places.

competent ADJECTIVE
<u>compétent</u>

competition NOUN
le <u>concours</u> ◊ *a singing competition*
un concours de chant

competitive ADJECTIVE
<u>compétitif</u> MASC
<u>compétitive</u> FEM
◊ *a very competitive price* un prix très
compétitif
◆**to be competitive** (*person*) avoir
l'esprit de compétition ◊ *He's a very
competitive person.* Il a vraiment
l'esprit de compétition.

competitor NOUN
le <u>concurrent</u>
la <u>concurrente</u>

to **complain** VERB
<u>se plaindre</u> ◊ *I'm going to complain
to the manager.* Je vais me plaindre
au directeur. ◊ *We complained about
the noise.* Nous nous sommes plaints
du bruit.

complaint NOUN
la <u>plainte</u> ◊ *There were lots of
complaints about the food.* Il y a eu
beaucoup de plaintes à propos de la
nourriture.

complete ADJECTIVE
<u>complet</u> MASC
<u>complète</u> FEM

completely ADVERB
<u>complètement</u>

complexion NOUN

☞

le teint

complicated ADJECTIVE
compliqué

compliment NOUN
see also **compliment** VERB
le compliment

to **compliment** VERB
see also **compliment** NOUN
complimenter ◊ *They complimented me on my French.* Ils m'ont complimenté sur mon français.

complimentary ADJECTIVE
[1] élogieux (*flattering*) ◊ *He was very complimentary about my garden.* Il a été très élogieux à propos de mon jardin.
[2] gratuit (*free*)
♦ **I've got two complimentary tickets for tonight.** J'ai deux places gratuites pour ce soir.

composer NOUN
le compositeur
la compositrice

comprehension NOUN
[1] la compréhension (*understanding*)
[2] l' exercice de compréhension MASC (*school exercise*)

comprehensive ADJECTIVE
complet MASC
complète FEM
◊ *a comprehensive guide* un guide complet

Be careful not to translate **comprehensive** *by* **compréhensif.**

comprehensive school NOUN
[1] le collège
[2] le lycée

ⓘ *In France pupils go to a* **collège** *between the ages of 11 and 15, and then to a* **lycée** *until the age of 18.*

compromise NOUN
see also **compromise** VERB
le compromis ◊ *We reached a compromise.* Nous sommes parvenus à un compromis.

to **compromise** VERB
see also **compromise** NOUN
♦ **Let's compromise.** Essayons de trouver un compromis.

compulsory ADJECTIVE
obligatoire

computer NOUN
l' ordinateur MASC

computer game NOUN
le jeu électronique
(les jeux électroniques PL)

computer programmer NOUN

le programmeur
la programmeuse
◊ *She's a computer programmer.* Elle est programmeuse.

computer room NOUN
la salle d'informatique

computer science NOUN
l' informatique FEM

computing NOUN
l' informatique FEM

to **concentrate** VERB
se concentrer ◊ *I couldn't concentrate.* Je n'arrivais pas à me concentrer.

concentration NOUN
la concentration

concern NOUN
l' inquiétude FEM (*preoccupation*)
◊ *They expressed concern about the image of the school.* Ils ont exprimé leur inquiétude concernant l'image de l'école.

concerned ADJECTIVE
♦ **to be concerned** s'inquiéter ◊ *His mother is concerned about him.* Sa mère s'inquiète à son sujet.
♦ **as far as I'm concerned** en ce qui me concerne

concerning PREPOSITION
concernant ◊ *For further information concerning the job, contact Mr Ross Hutchinson.* Pour plus d'informations concernant cet emploi, contacter M. Ross Hutchinson.

concert NOUN
le concert

concrete NOUN
le béton

to **condemn** VERB
condamner ◊ *The government has condemned the decision.* Le gouvernement a condamné cette décision.

condition NOUN
[1] la condition ◊ *I'll do it, on one condition ...* Je veux bien le faire, à une condition ...
[2] l' état MASC ◊ *in bad condition* en mauvais état ◊ *in good condition* en bon état

conditional NOUN
le conditionnel

conditioner NOUN
le baume démêlant (*for hair*)

condom NOUN
le préservatif

to **conduct** VERB
diriger (*orchestra*)

conductor NOUN
le chef d'orchestre

cone NOUN
le cornet ◊ *an ice-cream cone* un cornet de glace

conference NOUN
la conférence

to **confess** VERB
avouer ◊ *He finally confessed.* Il a fini par avouer. ◊ *He confessed to the murder.* Il a avoué avoir commis le meurtre.

confession NOUN
la confession

confetti NOUN
les confettis MASC PL

confidence NOUN
[1] la confiance ◊ *I've got confidence in you.* J'ai confiance en toi.
[2] l' assurance FEM ◊ *She lacks confidence.* Elle manque d'assurance.

confident ADJECTIVE
sûr ◊ *I'm confident everything will be okay.* Je suis sûr que tout ira bien.
♦**She's seems quite confident.** Elle a l'air sûre d'elle.

confidential ADJECTIVE
confidentiel MASC
confidentielle FEM

to **confirm** VERB
confirmer (*booking*)

confirmation NOUN
la confirmation

conflict NOUN
le conflit

to **confuse** VERB
♦**to confuse somebody** embrouiller les idées de quelqu'un ◊ *Don't confuse me!* Ne m'embrouille pas les idées!

confused ADJECTIVE
désorienté

confusing ADJECTIVE
♦**The traffic signs are confusing.** Les panneaux de signalisation ne sont pas clairs.

confusion NOUN
la confusion

to **congratulate** VERB
féliciter ◊ *My friends congratulated me on passing the test.* Mes amis m'ont félicité d'avoir réussi à l'examen.

congratulations PL NOUN
les félicitations FEM PL
◊ *Congratulations on your new job!* Félicitations pour votre nouveau poste!

conjunction NOUN

la conjonction

conjurer NOUN
le prestidigitateur

connection NOUN
[1] le rapport ◊ *There's no connection between the two events.* Il n'y a aucun rapport entre les deux événements.
[2] le contact (*electrical*) ◊ *There's a loose connection.* Il y a un mauvais contact.
[3] la correspondance (*of trains, planes*) ◊ *We missed our connection.* Nous avons raté la correspondance.

to **conquer** VERB
conquérir

conscience NOUN
la conscience

conscious ADJECTIVE
conscient

consciousness NOUN
la connaissance
♦**to lose consciousness** perdre connaissance ◊ *I lost consciousness.* J'ai perdu connaissance.

consequence NOUN
la conséquence ◊ *What are the consequences for the environment?* Quelles sont les conséquences pour l'environnement?
♦**as a consequence** en conséquence

consequently ADVERB
par conséquent

conservation NOUN
la protection

conservative ADJECTIVE
see also **conservative** NOUN
conservateur MASC
conservatrice FEM
♦**the Conservative Party** le Parti conservateur

Conservative NOUN
see also **conservative** ADJECTIVE
le conservateur
la conservatrice
♦**to vote Conservative** voter conservateur
♦**the Conservatives** les conservateurs

conservatory NOUN
le jardin d'hiver

to **consider** VERB
[1] considérer ◊ *He considers it a waste of time.* Il considère que c'est une perte de temps.
[2] envisager ◊ *We considered cancelling our holiday.* Nous avons envisagé d'annuler nos vacances.
♦**I'm considering the idea.** J'y songe.

considerate ADJECTIVE

☞

délicat

considering PREPOSITION
[1] étant donné ◊ *Considering we were there for a month ...* Étant donné que nous étions là pour un mois ...
[2] tout compte fait ◊ *I got a good mark, considering.* J'ai eu une bonne note, tout compte fait.

to **consist** VERB
♦ **to consist of** être composé de ◊ *The band consists of three guitarists, a saxophonist and a drummer.* Le groupe est composé de trois guitaristes, un saxophoniste et un batteur.

consonant NOUN
la consonne

constant ADJECTIVE
constant

constantly ADVERB
constamment

constipated ADJECTIVE
constipé

to **construct** VERB
construire

construction NOUN
la construction

to **consult** VERB
consulter

consumer NOUN
le consommateur
la consommatrice

contact NOUN
see also **contact** VERB
le contact ◊ *I'm in contact with her.* Je suis en contact avec elle.

to **contact** VERB
see also **contact** NOUN
joindre ◊ *Where can we contact you?* Où pouvons-nous vous joindre?

contact lenses PL NOUN
les verres de contact MASC PL

to **contain** VERB
contenir

container NOUN
le récipient

contempt NOUN
le mépris

contents PL NOUN
[1] le contenu SING (*of container*)
[2] la table des matières SING (*of book*)

contest NOUN
le concours

contestant NOUN
le concurrent
la concurrente

context NOUN
le contexte

continent NOUN
le continent ◊ *How many continents are there?* Combien y a-t-il de continents?
♦ **the Continent** l'Europe FEM ◊ *I've never been to the Continent.* Je ne suis jamais allé en Europe.

continental breakfast NOUN
le petit déjeuner à la française

to **continue** VERB
[1] continuer ◊ *She continued talking to her friend.* Elle a continué à parler à son amie.
[2] reprendre (*after interruption*) ◊ *We continued working after lunch.* Nous avons repris le travail après le déjeuner.

continuous ADJECTIVE
continu
♦ **continuous assessment** le contrôle continu

contraceptive NOUN
le contraceptif

contract NOUN
le contrat

to **contradict** VERB
contredire

contrary NOUN
le contraire
♦ **on the contrary** au contraire

contrast NOUN
le contraste

to **contribute** VERB
[1] contribuer (*to success, achievement*) ◊ *The treaty will contribute to world peace.* Le traité va contribuer à la paix dans le monde.
[2] participer (*share in*) ◊ *He didn't contribute to the discussion.* Il n'a pas participé à la discussion.
[3] donner (*give*) ◊ *She contributed £10.* Elle a donné dix livres.

contribution NOUN
[1] la contribution
[2] la cotisation (*to pension, national insurance*)

control NOUN
see also **control** VERB
le contrôle
♦ **to lose control** (*of vehicle*) perdre le contrôle ◊ *He lost control of the car.* Il a perdu le contrôle de son véhicule.
♦ **the controls** les commandes FEM (*of machine*)
♦ **to be in control** être maître de la situation
♦ **to keep control** (*of people*) se faire obéir ◊ *He can't keep control of the*

class. Il n'arrive pas à se faire obéir
de sa classe.
♦ **out of control** (*child, class*) déchaîné

to **control** VERB
> *see also* **control** NOUN

[1] diriger (*country, organization*)
[2] se faire obéir de ◊ *He can't
control the class.* Il n'arrive pas à se
faire obéir de sa classe.
[3] maîtriser ◊ *I couldn't control the
horse.* Je ne suis pas arrivé à
maîtriser le cheval.
♦ **to control oneself** se contrôler

controversial ADJECTIVE
controversé ◊ *a controversial book*
un livre controversé

convenient ADJECTIVE
bien situé (*place*) ◊ *The hotel's
convenient for the airport.* L'hôtel est
bien situé par rapport à l'aéroport.
♦ **It's not a convenient time for me.**
C'est une heure qui ne m'arrange
pas.
♦ **Would Monday be convenient for
you?** Est-ce que lundi vous
conviendrait?

conventional ADJECTIVE
conventionnel MASC
conventionnelle FEM

convent school NOUN
le couvent ◊ *She goes to convent
school.* Elle va au couvent.

conversation NOUN
la conversation ◊ *a French
conversation class* un cours de
conversation française

to **convert** VERB
transformer ◊ *We've converted the
loft into a spare room.* Nous avons
transformé le grenier en chambre
d'amis.

to **convict** VERB
reconnaître coupable ◊ *He was
convicted of the murder.* Il a été
reconnu coupable du meurtre.

to **convince** VERB
persuader ◊ *I'm not convinced.* Je
n'en suis pas persuadé.

to **cook** VERB
> *see also* **cook** NOUN

[1] faire la cuisine ◊ *I can't cook.* Je
ne sais pas faire la cuisine.
[2] préparer ◊ *She's cooking lunch.*
Elle est en train de préparer le
déjeuner.
[3] faire cuire ◊ *Cook the pasta for 10
minutes.* Faites cuire les pâtes
pendant dix minutes.

♦ **to be cooked** être cuit ◊ *When the
potatoes are cooked ...* Lorsque les
pommes de terre sont cuites ...

cook NOUN
> *see also* **cook** VERB

le cuisinier
la cuisinière
◊ *Matthew's an excellent cook.*
Matthew est un excellent cuisinier.

cookbook NOUN
le livre de cuisine

cooker NOUN
la cuisinière ◊ *a gas cooker* une
cuisinière à gaz

cookery NOUN
la cuisine

cookie NOUN [US]
le gâteau sec

cooking NOUN
la cuisine ◊ *I like cooking.* J'aime
bien faire la cuisine.

cool ADJECTIVE
frais MASC
fraîche FEM
◊ *a cool place* un endroit frais
♦ **to stay cool** (*keep calm*) garder son
calme ◊ *He stayed cool.* Il a gardé
son calme.
♦ **keep cool!** du calme!

cooperation NOUN
la coopération

cop NOUN
le flic (*informal*)

to **cope** VERB
se débrouiller ◊ *It was hard, but we
coped.* C'était dur, mais nous nous
sommes débrouillés.
♦ **to cope with** faire face à ◊ *She's got
a lot of problems to cope with.* Elle
doit faire face à de nombreux
problèmes.

copper NOUN
[1] le cuivre ◊ *a copper bracelet* un
bracelet en cuivre
[2] le flic (*informal: policeman*)

copy NOUN
> *see also* **copy** VERB

[1] la copie (*of letter, document*)
[2] l' exemplaire MASC (*of book*)

to **copy** VERB
> *see also* **copy** NOUN

copier ◊ *The teacher accused him of
copying.* Le professeur l'a accusé
d'avoir copié.
♦ **to copy and paste** copier-coller

core NOUN
le trognon (*of fruit*) ◊ *an apple core*
un trognon de pomme

cork NOUN
1 le bouchon (of bottle)
2 le liège (material) ◊ a cork table
mat un set de table en liège

corkscrew NOUN
le tire-bouchon

corn NOUN
1 le blé (wheat)
2 le maïs (sweetcorn)
♦**corn on the cob** l'épi de maïs MASC

corner NOUN
1 le coin ◊ in a corner of the room
dans un coin de la pièce
♦**the shop on the corner** la boutique
au coin de la rue
♦**He lives just round the corner.** Il
habite tout près d'ici.
2 le corner (in football)

cornet NOUN
1 le cornet à pistons ◊ He plays the
cornet. Il joue du cornet à pistons.
2 le cornet (ice cream)

cornflakes PL NOUN
les corn-flakes MASC PL

cornstarch NOUN US
la farine de maïs

Cornwall NOUN
la Cornouailles
♦**in Cornwall** en Cornouailles

corporal NOUN
le caporal

corporal punishment NOUN
le châtiment corporel

corpse NOUN
le cadavre

correct ADJECTIVE
see also **correct** VERB
exact ◊ That's correct. C'est exact.
♦**the correct choice** le bon choix
♦**the correct answer** la bonne réponse

to **correct** VERB
see also **correct** ADJECTIVE
corriger

correction NOUN
la correction

correctly ADVERB
correctement

correspondent NOUN
le correspondant
la correspondante
◊ our foreign correspondent notre
correspondant à l'étranger

corridor NOUN
le couloir

corruption NOUN
la corruption

Corsica NOUN
la Corse

♦**in Corsica** en Corse

cosmetics PL NOUN
les produits de beauté MASC PL

cosmetic surgery NOUN
la chirurgie esthétique

to **cost** VERB
see also **cost** NOUN
coûter ◊ The meal costs a hundred
euros. Le repas coûte cent euros.
◊ How much does it cost? Combien
est-ce que ça coûte? ◊ It costs too
much. Ça coûte trop cher.

cost NOUN
see also **cost** VERB
le coût
♦**the cost of living** le coût de la vie
♦**at all costs** à tout prix

costume NOUN
le costume

cosy ADJECTIVE
douillet MASC
douillette FEM

cot NOUN
le lit d'enfant

cottage NOUN
le cottage
♦**a thatched cottage** une chaumière

cottage cheese NOUN
le cottage cheese

cotton NOUN
le coton ◊ a cotton shirt une chemise
en coton
♦**cotton wool** le coton hydrophile

couch NOUN
le canapé

couchette NOUN
la couchette

to **cough** VERB
see also **cough** NOUN
tousser

cough NOUN
see also **cough** VERB
la toux ◊ a bad cough une mauvaise
toux
♦**I've got a cough.** Je tousse.
♦**a cough sweet** une pastille

could VERB see **can**

council NOUN
le conseil

> ❶ The nearest French equivalent of
> a local council would be a **conseil
> municipal**, which administers a
> **commune**.

♦**He's on the council.** Il fait partie du
conseil municipal.
♦**a council estate** une cité HLM

♦ **a council house** une HLM

> ℹ️ *HLM stands for* **habitation à loyer modéré** *which means "low-rent home".*

councillor NOUN
♦ **She's a local councillor.** Elle fait partie du conseil municipal.

to **count** VERB
compter
♦ **to count on** compter sur ◇ *You can count on me.* Tu peux compter sur moi.

counter NOUN
[1] le comptoir (*in shop*)
[2] le guichet (*in post office, bank*)
[3] le jeton (*in game*)

country NOUN
[1] le pays ◇ *the border between the two countries* la frontière entre les deux pays
[2] la campagne ◇ *I live in the country.* J'habite à la campagne.
♦ **country dancing** la danse folklorique

countryside NOUN
la campagne

county NOUN
le comté

> ℹ️ *The nearest French equivalent of a county would be a* **département**.

♦ **the county council**

> ℹ️ *The nearest French equivalent of a county council would be a* **conseil général**, *which administers a* **département**.

couple NOUN
le couple ◇ *the couple who live next door* le couple qui habite à côté
♦ **a couple** deux ◇ *a couple of hours* deux heures
♦ **Could you wait a couple of minutes?** Pourriez-vous attendre quelques minutes?

courage NOUN
le courage

courgette NOUN
la courgette

courier NOUN
[1] (*for tourists*)
l' accompagnateur MASC
l' accompagnatrice FEM
[2] (*delivery service*)
le coursier ◇ *They sent it by courier.* Ils l'ont envoyé par coursier.

> ℹ️ *Be careful not to translate* **courier** *by the French word* **courrier**.

course NOUN
[1] le cours ◇ *a French course* un cours de français ◇ *to go on a course* suivre un cours
[2] le plat ◇ *the main course* le plat principal
♦ **the first course** l'entrée FEM
[3] le terrain ◇ *a golf course* un terrain de golf
♦ **of course** bien sûr ◇ *Do you love me? – Of course I do!* Tu m'aimes? – Bien sûr que oui!

court NOUN
[1] (*of law*)
le tribunal
(les tribunaux PL)
◇ *He was in court last week.* Il est passé devant le tribunal la semaine dernière.
[2] (*tennis*)
le court ◇ *There are tennis and squash courts.* Il y a des courts de tennis et de squash.

courtyard NOUN
la cour

cousin NOUN
le cousin
la cousine

cover NOUN
see also **cover** VERB
[1] la couverture (*of book*)
[2] la housse (*of duvet*)

to **cover** VERB
see also **cover** NOUN
[1] couvrir ◇ *My face was covered with mosquito bites.* J'avais le visage couvert de piqûres de moustique.
[2] prendre en charge ◇ *Our insurance didn't cover it.* Notre assurance ne l'a pas pris en charge.
♦ **to cover up a scandal** étouffer un scandale

cow NOUN
la vache

coward NOUN
le lâche ◇ *She's a coward.* Elle est lâche.

cowardly ADJECTIVE
lâche

cowboy NOUN
le cow-boy

crab NOUN
le crabe

crack NOUN
see also **crack** VERB
[1] la fissure (*in wall*)
[2] la fêlure (*in cup, window*)

☞

3 le crack (*drug*)
♦**I'll have a crack at it**. Je vais tenter le coup.

to **crack** VERB
> see also **crack** NOUN

casser (*nut, egg*)
♦**to crack a joke** sortir une blague

to **crack down on** VERB
être ferme avec ◇ *The police are cracking down on motorists who drive too fast*. La police va être ferme avec les automobilistes qui roulent trop vite.

cracked ADJECTIVE
fêlé (*cup, window*)

cracker NOUN
1 le cracker (*biscuit*)
2 le diablotin (*Christmas cracker*)

cradle NOUN
le berceau
(les berceaux PL)

craft NOUN
les travaux manuels MASC PL ◇ *We do craft at school*. Nous avons des cours de travaux manuels à l'école.
♦**a craft centre** un centre artisanal

craftsman NOUN
l' artisan MASC

to **cram** VERB
1 entasser ◇ *We crammed our stuff into the boot*. Nous avons entassé nos affaires dans le coffre.
2 bachoter (*for exams*)

crammed ADJECTIVE
♦**crammed with** bourré de ◇ *Her bag was crammed with books*. Son sac était bourré de livres.

crane NOUN
la grue (*machine*)

to **crash** VERB
> see also **crash** NOUN

avoir un accident ◇ *He's crashed his car*. Il a eu un accident de voiture.
♦**The plane crashed**. L'avion s'est écrasé.

crash NOUN
> see also **crash** VERB

1 la collision (*of car*)
2 l' accident MASC (*of plane*)
♦**a crash helmet** un casque
♦**a crash course** un cours intensif

to **crawl** VERB
> see also **crawl** NOUN

marcher à quatre pattes (*baby*)

crawl NOUN
> see also **crawl** VERB

le crawl ◇ *to do the crawl* nager le crawl

crazy ADJECTIVE

fou MASC
folle FEM

cream ADJECTIVE
> see also **cream** NOUN

crème MASC, FEM, PL (*colour*)

cream NOUN
> see also **cream** ADJECTIVE

la crème ◇ *strawberries and cream* les fraises à la crème
♦**a cream cake** un gâteau à la crème
♦**cream cheese** le fromage à la crème
♦**sun cream** la crème solaire

crease NOUN
le pli

creased ADJECTIVE
froissé

to **create** VERB
créer

creation NOUN
la création

creative ADJECTIVE
créatif MASC
créative FEM

creature NOUN
la créature

crèche NOUN
la crèche

credit NOUN
le crédit ◇ *on credit* à crédit

credit card NOUN
la carte de crédit

creeps PL NOUN
♦**It gives me the creeps**. Ça me donne la chair de poule.

to **creep up** VERB
s'approcher à pas de loup
♦**to creep up on somebody** s'approcher de quelqu'un à pas de loup

crept VERB *see* **creep up**

cress NOUN
le cresson

crew NOUN
1 l' équipage MASC (*of ship, plane*)
2 l' équipe FEM ◇ *a film crew* une équipe de tournage

crew cut NOUN
les cheveux en brosse MASC PL

cricket NOUN
1 le cricket ◇ *I play cricket*. Je joue au cricket.
♦**a cricket bat** une batte de cricket
2 le grillon (*insect*)

crime NOUN
1 le délit ◇ *Murder is a crime*. Le meurtre est un délit.
2 la criminalité (*lawlessness*)
♦**Crime is rising**. La criminalité augmente.

criminal NOUN
> see also **criminal** ADJECTIVE

le criminel
la criminelle

criminal ADJECTIVE
> see also **criminal** NOUN

criminel MASC
criminelle FEM
◊ *It's criminal!* C'est criminel!
♦ **It's a criminal offence.** C'est un crime puni par la loi.
♦ **to have a criminal record** avoir un casier judiciaire

crisis NOUN
la crise

crisp ADJECTIVE
croquant (*food*)

crisps PL NOUN
les chips FEM PL ◊ *a bag of crisps* un paquet de chips

criterion NOUN
le critère

critic NOUN
le critique

critical ADJECTIVE
critique
♦ **a critical remark** une critique

criticism NOUN
la critique

to **criticize** VERB
critiquer

Croatia NOUN
la Croatie
♦ **in Croatia** en Croatie

to **crochet** VERB
crocheter

crocodile NOUN
le crocodile

crook NOUN
l' escroc MASC (*criminal*)

crop NOUN
la récolte ◊ *a good crop of apples* une bonne récolte de pommes

cross NOUN
> see also **cross** ADJECTIVE, VERB

la croix

cross ADJECTIVE
> see also **cross** NOUN, VERB

fâché ◊ *to be cross about something* être fâché à propos de quelque chose

to **cross** VERB
> see also **cross** ADJECTIVE, NOUN

traverser (*street, bridge*)
♦ **to cross out** barrer
♦ **to cross over** traverser

cross-country NOUN
le cross (*race*)

♦ **cross-country skiing** le ski de fond

crossing NOUN
1. la traversée (*by boat*) ◊ *the crossing from Dover to Calais* la traversée de Douvres à Calais
2. le passage clouté (*for pedestrians*)

crossroads NOUN
le carrefour

crossword NOUN
les mots croisés MASC PL ◊ *I like doing crosswords.* J'aime faire les mots croisés.

to **crouch down** VERB
s'accroupir

crow NOUN
le corbeau
(les corbeaux PL)

crowd NOUN
la foule
♦ **the crowd** (*at sports match*) les spectateurs MASC PL

crowded ADJECTIVE
bondé

crown NOUN
la couronne

crucifix NOUN
le crucifix

crude ADJECTIVE (*vulgar*)
grossier MASC
grossière FEM

cruel ADJECTIVE
cruel MASC
cruelle FEM

cruise NOUN
la croisière ◊ *to go on a cruise* faire une croisière

crumb NOUN
la miette

to **crush** VERB
écraser

crutch NOUN
la béquille

cry NOUN
> see also **cry** VERB

le cri ◊ *He gave a cry of surprise.* Il a poussé un cri de surprise.
♦ **Go on, have a good cry!** Vas-y, pleure un bon coup!

to **cry** VERB
> see also **cry** NOUN

pleurer ◊ *The baby's crying.* Le bébé pleure.

crystal NOUN
le cristal
(les cristaux PL)

CTC NOUN (= *city technology college*)
le collège technique

cub NOUN

C

1 (animal)
le petit
2 (scout)
le louveteau
(les louveteaux PL)

cube NOUN
le cube

cubic ADJECTIVE
♦a cubic metre un mètre cube

cucumber NOUN
le concombre

cuddle NOUN
le câlin ◊ Come and give me a cuddle. Viens me faire un câlin.

cue NOUN
la queue de billard (for snooker, pool)

culottes PL NOUN
la jupe-culotte SING

culture NOUN
la culture

cunning ADJECTIVE
1 (person)
rusé
2 (plan, idea)
astucieux MASC
astucieuse FEM

cup NOUN
1 la tasse ◊ a china cup une tasse en porcelaine
♦a cup of coffee un café
2 la coupe (trophy)

cupboard NOUN
le placard

to **cure** VERB
see also **cure** NOUN
guérir

cure NOUN
see also **cure** VERB
le remède

curious ADJECTIVE
curieux MASC
curieuse FEM

curl NOUN
la boucle (in hair)

curly ADJECTIVE
1 bouclé (loosely curled)
2 frisé (tightly curled)

currant NOUN
le raisin de Corinthe (dried fruit)

currency NOUN
la devise ◊ foreign currency les devises étrangères FEM PL

current NOUN
see also **current** ADJECTIVE
le courant ◊ The current is very strong. Le courant est très fort.

current ADJECTIVE
see also **current** NOUN

actuel MASC
actuelle FEM
◊ the current situation la situation actuelle

current account NOUN
le compte courant

current affairs PL NOUN
l' actualité FEM SING

curriculum NOUN
le programme

curriculum vitae NOUN
le curriculum vitae

curry NOUN
le curry

curse NOUN
la malédiction (spell)

curtain NOUN
le rideau
(les rideaux PL)
♦to draw the curtains tirer les rideaux

cushion NOUN
le coussin

custard NOUN
la crème anglaise (for pouring)

custody NOUN
la garde (of child)

custom NOUN
la coutume MASC ◊ It's an old custom. C'est une ancienne coutume.

customer NOUN
le client
la cliente

customs PL NOUN
la douane SING

customs officer NOUN
le douanier
la douanière

cut NOUN
see also **cut** VERB
1 la coupure ◊ He's got a cut on his forehead. Il a une coupure au front.
2 la coupe ◊ a cut and blow-dry une coupe brushing
3 la réduction (in price, spending)

to **cut** VERB
see also **cut** NOUN
1 couper ◊ I'll cut some bread. Je vais couper du pain.
♦to cut oneself se couper ◊ I cut my foot on a piece of glass. Je me suis coupé au pied avec un morceau de verre.
2 réduire (price, spending)
♦to cut down abattre (tree)
♦to cut off couper ◊ The electricity was cut off. L'électricité a été coupée.
♦to cut up hacher (vegetables, meat)

cutback NOUN

la <u>réduction</u> ◊ *staff cutbacks* des réductions de personnel

cute ADJECTIVE
<u>mignon</u>

cutlery NOUN
les <u>couverts</u> MASC PL

cutting NOUN
la <u>coupure de presse</u> (*from newspaper*)

CV NOUN
le <u>C.V.</u>

cybercafé NOUN
le <u>cybercafé</u>

to **cycle** VERB
   see also **cycle** NOUN
<u>faire de la bicyclette</u> ◊ *I like cycling.* J'aime faire de la bicyclette.
♦ **I cycle to school.** Je vais à l'école à bicyclette.

cycle NOUN
   see also **cycle** VERB
la <u>bicyclette</u>
♦ **a cycle ride** une promenade à bicyclette
♦ **a cycle lane** une piste cyclable

cycling NOUN
le <u>cyclisme</u>

cyclist NOUN
le/la <u>cycliste</u>

cylinder NOUN
le <u>cylindre</u>

Cyprus NOUN
<u>Chypre</u>
♦ **in Cyprus** à Chypre
♦ **We went to Cyprus.** Nous sommes allés à Chypre.

Czech ADJECTIVE
   see also **Czech** NOUN
<u>tchèque</u>
♦ **the Czech Republic** la République tchèque

Czech NOUN
   see also **Czech** ADJECTIVE
1 le/la <u>Tchèque</u> (*person*)
2 le <u>tchèque</u> (*language*)

C

D

dad NOUN
1 le <u>père</u> ◊ *my dad* mon père ◊ *his dad* son père
2 le <u>papa</u>
Use ***papa*** *only when you are talking to your father or using it as his name; otherwise use* ***père***.
♦**Dad!** Papa! ◊ *I'll ask Dad.* Je vais demander à papa.

daddy NOUN
le <u>papa</u> ◊ *Say hello to your daddy!* Dis bonjour à ton papa! ◊ *Hello Daddy!* Bonjour Papa!

daffodil NOUN
la <u>jonquille</u>

daft ADJECTIVE
<u>idiot</u>

daily ADJECTIVE, ADVERB
1 <u>quotidien</u> MASC
<u>quotidienne</u> FEM
◊ *It's part of my daily routine.* Ça fait partie de mes occupations quotidiennes.
2 <u>tous les jours</u> ◊ *The pool is open daily from 9 a.m. to 6 p.m.* La piscine est ouverte tous les jours de neuf heures à dix-huit heures.

dairy NOUN
la <u>crémerie</u> (*shop*)

dairy products PL NOUN
les <u>produits laitiers</u> MASC PL

daisy NOUN
la <u>pâquerette</u>

dam NOUN
le <u>barrage</u>

damage NOUN
see also **damage** VERB
les <u>dégâts</u> MASC PL ◊ *The storm did a lot of damage.* La tempête a fait beaucoup de dégâts.

to **damage** VERB
see also **damage** NOUN
<u>endommager</u>

damn NOUN
see also **damn** ADJECTIVE
♦**I don't give a damn!** Je m'en fiche! (*informal*)
♦**Damn!** Zut! (*informal*)

damn ADJECTIVE, ADVERB
see also **damn** NOUN
♦**It's a damn nuisance!** Quelle barbe!

damp ADJECTIVE
<u>humide</u>

dance NOUN

see also **dance** VERB
1 la <u>danse</u> ◊ *The last dance was a waltz.* La dernière danse était une valse.
2 le <u>bal</u> ◊ *Are you going to the dance tonight?* Tu vas au bal ce soir?

to **dance** VERB
see also **dance** NOUN
<u>danser</u>
♦**to go dancing** aller danser ◊ *Let's go dancing!* Si on allait danser?

dancer NOUN
le <u>danseur</u>
la <u>danseuse</u>

dandruff NOUN
les <u>pellicules</u> FEM PL

Dane NOUN
le <u>Danois</u>
la <u>Danoise</u>

danger NOUN
le <u>danger</u>
♦**in danger** en danger ◊ *His life is in danger.* Sa vie est en danger.
♦**to be in danger of** risquer de ◊ *We were in danger of missing the plane.* Nous risquions de rater l'avion.

dangerous ADJECTIVE
<u>dangereux</u> MASC
<u>dangereuse</u> FEM

Danish ADJECTIVE
see also **Danish** NOUN
<u>danois</u>

Danish NOUN
see also **Danish** ADJECTIVE
le <u>danois</u> (*language*)

to **dare** VERB
<u>oser</u>
♦**to dare to do something** oser faire quelque chose ◊ *I didn't dare to tell my parents.* Je n'ai pas osé le dire à mes parents.
♦**I dare say it'll be okay.** Je suppose que ça va aller.

daring ADJECTIVE
<u>audacieux</u> MASC
<u>audacieuse</u> FEM

dark ADJECTIVE
see also **dark** NOUN
1 <u>sombre</u> (*room*) ◊ *It's dark.* (*inside*) Il fait sombre.
♦**It's dark outside.** Il fait nuit dehors.
♦**It's getting dark.** La nuit tombe.
2 <u>foncé</u> (*colour*) ◊ *She's got dark hair.* Elle a les cheveux foncés. ◊ *a dark green sweater* un pull vert foncé

dark NOUN
> see also **dark** ADJECTIVE

le noir ◊ *I'm afraid of the dark.* J'ai peur du noir.
- **after dark** après la tombée de la nuit

darkness NOUN
l' obscurité FEM ◊ *The room was in darkness.* La chambre était dans l'obscurité.

darling NOUN
le chéri
la chérie
◊ *Thank you, darling!* Merci, chéri!

dart NOUN
la fléchette ◊ *to play darts* jouer aux fléchettes

to **dash** VERB
> see also **dash** NOUN

se précipiter ◊ *Everyone dashed to the window to look.* Tout le monde s'est précipité vers la fenêtre pour regarder.
- **I must dash!** Il faut que je me sauve!

dash NOUN
> see also **dash** VERB

le tiret (*punctuation mark*)

data PL NOUN
les données FEM PL

database NOUN
la base de données (*on computer*)

date NOUN
1 la date ◊ *my date of birth* ma date de naissance
- **What's the date today?** Quel jour sommes-nous?
- **to have a date with somebody** sortir avec quelqu'un ◊ *She's got a date with Ian tonight.* Elle sort avec Ian ce soir.
- **out of date (1)** (*passport*) périmé
- **out of date (2)** (*technology*) dépassé
- **out of date (3)** (*clothes*) démodé
2 la datte (*fruit*)

daughter NOUN
la fille

daughter-in-law NOUN
la belle-fille
(les belles-filles PL)

dawn NOUN
l' aube FEM ◊ *at dawn* à l'aube

day NOUN
> Use **jour** to refer to the whole 24-hour period. **journée** only refers to the time when you are awake.

1 le jour ◊ *We stayed in Nice for three days.* Nous sommes restés trois jours à Nice.
- **every day** tous les jours

2 la journée ◊ *during the day* dans la journée ◊ *I stayed at home all day.* Je suis resté à la maison toute la journée.
- **the day before** la veille ◊ *the day before my birthday* la veille de mon anniversaire
- **the day after** le lendemain
- **the day after tomorrow** après-demain ◊ *We're leaving the day after tomorrow.* Nous partons après-demain.
- **the day before yesterday** avant-hier ◊ *He arrived the day before yesterday.* Il est arrivé avant-hier.

dead ADJECTIVE, ADVERB
1 mort ◊ *He was already dead when the doctor came.* Il était déjà mort quand le docteur est arrivé.
- **He was shot dead.** Il a été abattu.
2 absolument (*totally*) ◊ *You're dead right!* Tu as absolument raison!
- **dead on time** à l'heure pile ◊ *The train arrived dead on time.* Le train est arrivé à l'heure pile.

dead end NOUN
l' impasse FEM

deadline NOUN
la date limite ◊ *The deadline for entries is May 2nd.* La date limite d'inscription est le deux mai.

deaf ADJECTIVE
sourd

deafening ADJECTIVE
assourdissant

deal NOUN
> see also **deal** VERB

le marché
- **It's a deal!** Marché conclu!
- **a great deal** beaucoup ◊ *a great deal of money* beaucoup d'argent

to **deal** VERB
> see also **deal** NOUN

donner (*cards*) ◊ *It's your turn to deal.* C'est à toi de donner.
- **to deal with something** s'occuper de quelque chose ◊ *He promised to deal with it immediately.* Il a promis de s'en occuper immédiatement.

dealer NOUN
1 (*of goods*)
le marchand
la marchande
2 (*of drugs*)
le dealer

dealt VERB *see* **deal**

dear ADJECTIVE
1 cher MASC
chère FEM

D

☞

◊ *Dear Mrs Duval* Chère Madame Duval
♦ **Dear Sir/Madam** (*in a circular*) Madame, Monsieur
  2 (*expensive*)
  coûteux MASC
  coûteuse FEM

death NOUN
la mort ◊ *after his death* après sa mort
♦ **I was bored to death.** Je me suis ennuyé à mourir.

debate NOUN
  see also **debate** VERB
le débat

to **debate** VERB
  see also **debate** NOUN
débattre

debt NOUN
la dette ◊ *He's got a lot of debts.* Il a beaucoup de dettes.
♦ **to be in debt** avoir des dettes

decade NOUN
la décennie

decaffeinated ADJECTIVE
décaféiné

to **decay** VERB
se délabrer (*building*) ◊ *a decaying mansion* un manoir qui se délabre

to **deceive** VERB
tromper

December NOUN
décembre MASC
♦ **in December** en décembre

decent ADJECTIVE
convenable ◊ *a decent education* une éducation convenable

to **decide** VERB
  1 décider ◊ *I decided to write to her.* J'ai décidé de lui écrire. ◊ *I decided not to go.* J'ai décidé de ne pas y aller.
  2 se décider ◊ *I can't decide.* Je n'arrive pas à me décider. ◊ *Haven't you decided yet?* Tu ne t'es pas encore décidé?
♦ **to decide on something** se mettre d'accord sur quelque chose ◊ *They haven't decided on a name yet.* Ils ne se sont pas encore mis d'accord sur un nom.

decimal ADJECTIVE
décimal ◊ *the decimal system* le système décimal

decision NOUN
la décision
♦ **to make a decision** prendre une décision

decisive ADJECTIVE

décidé (*person*)

deck NOUN
  1 (*of ship*)
  le pont
♦ **on deck** sur le pont
  2 (*of cards*)
  le jeu
  (les jeux PL)

deckchair NOUN
la chaise longue

to **declare** VERB
déclarer

to **decorate** VERB
  1 décorer ◊ *I decorated the cake with glacé cherries.* J'ai décoré le gâteau avec des cerises confites.
  2 peindre (*paint*)
  3 tapisser (*wallpaper*)

decorations PL NOUN
les décorations FEM PL

decrease NOUN
  see also **decrease** VERB
la diminution ◊ *a decrease in the number of unemployed people* une diminution du nombre de chômeurs

to **decrease** VERB
  see also **decrease** NOUN
diminuer

dedicated ADJECTIVE
dévoué ◊ *a very dedicated teacher* un professeur très dévoué
♦ **dedicated to (1)** consacré à ◊ *a museum dedicated to Napoleon* un musée consacré à Napoléon
♦ **dedicated to (2)** dédicacé à ◊ *The book is dedicated "to Emma, with love from Harry".* Le livre est dédicacé "à Emma, avec tout mon amour, Harry".

dedication NOUN
  1 le dévouement (*commitment*)
  2 la dédicace (*in book, on radio*)

to **deduct** VERB
déduire

deep ADJECTIVE
  1 (*water, hole, cut*)
  profond ◊ *Is it deep?* Est-ce que c'est profond?
♦ **How deep is the lake?** Quelle est la profondeur du lac?
♦ **a hole 4 metres deep** un trou de quatre mètres de profondeur
  2 (*layer*)
  épais MASC
  épaisse FEM
  ◊ *a deep layer of snow* une épaisse couche de neige ◊ *The snow was really deep.* Il y avait une épaisse couche de neige.

- **He's got a deep voice.** Il a la voix grave.
- **to take a deep breath** respirer à fond

deeply ADVERB
  profondément (*depressed*)

deer NOUN
  1 le cerf (*red deer*)
  2 le daim (*fallow deer*)
  3 le chevreuil (*roe deer*)

defeat NOUN
  see also **defeat** VERB
  la défaite

to **defeat** VERB
  see also **defeat** NOUN
  battre

defect NOUN
  le défaut

defence NOUN
  la défense

to **defend** VERB
  défendre

defender NOUN
  le défenseur

to **define** VERB
  définir

definite ADJECTIVE
  1 précis ◊ *I haven't got any definite plans.* Je n'ai pas de projets précis.
  2 net MASC
  nette FEM
  ◊ *It's a definite improvement.* Cela constitue une nette amélioration.
  3 sûr ◊ *Perhaps we'll go to Spain, but it's not definite.* Nous irons peut-être en Espagne, mais ce n'est pas sûr.
- **He was definite about it.** Il a été catégorique.

definitely ADVERB
  vraiment ◊ *He's definitely the best player.* C'est vraiment lui le meilleur joueur.
- **He's the best player. – Definitely!** C'est le meilleur joueur. – C'est sûr!
- **I definitely think he'll come.** Je suis sûr qu'il va venir.

definition NOUN
  la définition

degree NOUN
  1 le degré ◊ *a temperature of 30 degrees* une température de trente degrés
  2 la licence ◊ *a degree in English* une licence d'anglais

to **delay** VERB
  see also **delay** NOUN
  1 retarder ◊ *We decided to delay our departure.* Nous avons décidé de retarder notre départ.

  2 tarder ◊ *Don't delay!* Ne tarde pas!
- **to be delayed** être retardé ◊ *Our flight was delayed.* Notre vol a été retardé.

delay NOUN
  see also **delay** VERB
  le retard ◊ *There will be delays to trains on the London-Brighton line.* Il y aura des retards sur la ligne Londres-Brighton.
  *Be careful not to translate **delay** by délai.*

to **delete** VERB
  effacer (*on computer, tape*)

deliberate ADJECTIVE
  délibéré

deliberately ADVERB
  exprès ◊ *She did it deliberately.* Elle l'a fait exprès.

delicate ADJECTIVE
  délicat

delicatessen NOUN
  l' épicerie fine FEM

delicious ADJECTIVE
  délicieux MASC
  délicieuse FEM

delight NOUN
- **to her delight** à sa plus grande joie

delighted ADJECTIVE
  ravi ◊ *He'll be delighted to see you.* Il sera ravi de vous voir.

delightful ADJECTIVE
  (*meal, evening*)
  délicieux MASC
  délicieuse FEM

to **deliver** VERB
  1 livrer ◊ *I deliver newspapers.* Je livre les journaux.
  2 distribuer (*mail*)

delivery NOUN
  la livraison

to **demand** VERB
  see also **demand** NOUN
  exiger
  Be careful not to translate to demand by demander.

demand NOUN
  see also **demand** VERB
  la demande (*for product*)

demanding ADJECTIVE
  astreignant ◊ *It's a very demanding job.* C'est un travail très astreignant.

demo NOUN
  la manif (*protest*)

democracy NOUN
  la démocratie

democratic ADJECTIVE
  démocratique

to **demolish** VERB
démolir

to **demonstrate** VERB
[1] faire une démonstration de
(show) ◊ She demonstrated the
technique. Elle a fait une
démonstration de la technique.
[2] manifester (protest)
♦ **to demonstrate against something**
manifester contre quelque chose

demonstration NOUN
[1] la démonstration (of method,
technique)
[2] la manifestation (protest)

demonstrator NOUN
(protester)
le manifestant
la manifestante

denim NOUN
le jean ◊ a denim jacket une veste en
jean

denims PL NOUN
le jean SING (jeans)

Denmark NOUN
le Danemark
♦ **in Denmark** au Danemark
♦ **to Denmark** au Danemark

dense ADJECTIVE
[1] (crowd, fog)
dense
[2] (smoke)
épais MASC
épaisse FEM
♦ **He's so dense!** Il est vraiment
bouché!

dent NOUN
see also **dent** VERB
la bosse

to **dent** VERB
see also **dent** NOUN
cabosser

dental ADJECTIVE
dentaire
♦ **dental floss** le fil dentaire

dentist NOUN
le/la dentiste ◊ Catherine is a dentist.
Catherine est dentiste.

to **deny** VERB
nier ◊ She denied everything. Elle a
tout nié.

deodorant NOUN
le déodorant

to **depart** VERB
partir

department NOUN
[1] le rayon (in shop) ◊ the shoe
department le rayon chaussures
[2] le département (university, school)
◊ the English department le
département d'anglais

department store NOUN
le grand magasin

departure NOUN
le départ

departure lounge NOUN
le hall des départs

to **depend** VERB
♦ **to depend on** dépendre de ◊ The
price depends on the quality. Le prix
dépend de la qualité.
♦ **depending on the weather** selon le
temps
♦ **It depends.** Ça dépend.

to **deport** VERB
expulser

deposit NOUN
[1] les arrhes FEM PL (part payment)
◊ You have to pay a deposit when
you book. Il faut verser des arrhes
lors de la réservation.
[2] la caution (when hiring something)
◊ You get the deposit back when you
return the bike. On vous remboursera
la caution quand vous ramènerez le
vélo.
[3] la consigne (on bottle)

depressed ADJECTIVE
déprimé ◊ I'm feeling depressed. Je
suis déprimé.

depressing ADJECTIVE
déprimant

depth NOUN
la profondeur

deputy head NOUN
le directeur adjoint
la directrice adjointe

to **descend** VERB
descendre

to **describe** VERB
décrire

description NOUN
la description

desert NOUN
le désert

desert island NOUN
l' île déserte FEM

to **deserve** VERB
mériter

design NOUN
see also **design** VERB
[1] la conception ◊ It's a completely
new design. C'est une conception
entièrement nouvelle.
[2] le motif ◊ a geometric design un
motif géométrique

D

♦**fashion design** le stylisme

to **design** VERB
> *see also* **design** NOUN

dessiner (*clothes, furniture*)

designer NOUN
le/la styliste (*of clothes*)

♦**designer clothes** les vêtements griffés MASC

desire NOUN
> *see also* **desire** VERB

le désir

to **desire** VERB
> *see also* **desire** NOUN

désirer

desk NOUN
1 (*in office*)
le bureau
(les bureaux PL)
2 (*for pupil*)
le pupitre
3 (*in hotel*)
la réception
4 (*at airport*)
le comptoir

despair NOUN
le désespoir
♦**I was in despair.** J'étais désespéré.

desperate ADJECTIVE
désespéré ◊ *a desperate situation*
une situation désespérée
♦**to get desperate** désespérer ◊ *I was
getting desperate.* Je commençais à
désespérer.

desperately ADVERB
1 terriblement ◊ *We're desperately
worried.* Nous sommes terriblement
inquiets.
2 désespérément ◊ *He was
desperately trying to persuade her.* Il
essayait désespérément de la
persuader.

to **despise** VERB
mépriser

despite PREPOSITION
malgré

dessert NOUN
le dessert ◊ *for dessert* comme
dessert

destination NOUN
la destination

to **destroy** VERB
détruire

destruction NOUN
la destruction

detached house NOUN
le pavillon

detail NOUN
le détail ◊ *in detail* en détail

detailed ADJECTIVE
détaillé

detective NOUN
l' inspecteur de police MASC
♦**a private detective** un détective privé
♦**a detective story** un roman policier

detention NOUN
♦**to get a detention** être consigné

detergent NOUN
1 le détergent
2 la lessive US

determined ADJECTIVE
déterminé
♦**to be determined to do something**
être déterminé à faire quelque chose
◊ *She's determined to succeed.* Elle
est déterminée à réussir.

detour NOUN
le détour

devaluation NOUN
la dévaluation

devastated ADJECTIVE
anéanti ◊ *I was devastated.* J'étais
anéanti.

devastating ADJECTIVE
1 (*upsetting*)
accablant
2 (*flood, storm*)
dévastateur MASC
dévastatrice FEM

to **develop** VERB
1 développer ◊ *to get a film
developed* faire développer un film
2 se développer ◊ *Girls develop
faster than boys.* Les filles se
développent plus vite que les
garçons.
♦**to develop into** se transformer en
◊ *The argument developed into a
fight.* La dispute s'est transformée en
bagarre.
♦**a developing country** un pays en voie
de développement

development NOUN
le développement ◊ *the latest
developments* les derniers
développements

device NOUN
l' appareil MASC

devil NOUN
le diable ◊ *Poor devil!* Pauvre diable!

to **devise** VERB
concevoir

devoted ADJECTIVE
dévoué ◊ *He's completely devoted to
her.* Il lui est très dévoué.

diabetes NOUN
le diabète

diabetic NOUN

☞

le/la diabétique ◊ *I'm a diabetic.* Je
suis diabétique.

diagonal ADJECTIVE
diagonal
(diagonaux MASC PL)

diagram NOUN
le diagramme

to **dial** VERB
composer (*number*)

dialling tone NOUN
la tonalité

dialogue NOUN
le dialogue

diamond NOUN
le diamant ◊ *a diamond ring* une
bague en diamant
♦**diamonds** (*at cards*) le carreau SING

diaper NOUN US
la couche

diarrhoea NOUN
la diarrhée ◊ *I've got diarrhoea.* J'ai
la diarrhée.

diary NOUN
1 l' agenda MASC ◊ *I've got her phone
number in my diary.* J'ai son numéro
de téléphone dans mon agenda.
2 le journal
(les journaux PL)
◊ *I keep a diary.* Je tiens un journal.

dice NOUN
le dé

dictation NOUN
la dictée

dictionary NOUN
le dictionnaire

did VERB *see* **do**

to **die** VERB
mourir ◊ *He died last year.* Il est
mort l'année dernière.
♦**to be dying to do something** mourir
d'envie de faire quelque chose ◊ *I'm
dying to see you.* Je meurs d'envie
de te voir.

diesel NOUN
1 le gazole (*fuel*) ◊ *30 litres of diesel*
trente litres de gazole
2 la voiture diesel (*car*) ◊ *My car's a
diesel.* J'ai une voiture diesel.

diet NOUN
see also **diet** VERB
1 l' alimentation FEM ◊ *a healthy diet*
une alimentation saine
2 le régime (*for slimming*) ◊ *I'm on a
diet.* Je suis au régime.

to **diet** VERB
see also **diet** NOUN
faire un régime ◊ *I've been dieting
for two months.* Je fais un régime

depuis deux mois.

difference NOUN
la différence ◊ *There's not much
difference in age between us.* Il n'y a
pas une grande différence d'âge
entre nous.
♦**It makes no difference.** Ça revient au
même.

different ADJECTIVE
différent ◊ *We are very different.*
Nous sommes très différents. ◊ *Paris
is different from London.* Paris est
différent de Londres.

difficult ADJECTIVE
difficile ◊ *It's difficult to choose.* C'est
difficile de choisir.

difficulty NOUN
la difficulté ◊ *without difficulty* sans
difficulté
♦**to have difficulty doing something**
avoir du mal à faire quelque chose

to **dig** VERB
1 creuser (*hole*)
2 bêcher (*garden*)
♦**to dig something up** déterrer quelque
chose

digestion NOUN
la digestion

digger NOUN
la pelleteuse (*machine*)

digital camera NOUN
l' appareil photo numérique MASC

digital television NOUN
la télévision numérique

digital watch NOUN
la montre à affichage numérique

dim ADJECTIVE
1 faible (*light*)
2 limité (*stupid*)

dimension NOUN
la dimension

to **diminish** VERB
diminuer

din NOUN
le vacarme

diner NOUN US
le snack

dinghy NOUN
♦**a rubber dinghy** un canot
pneumatique
♦**a sailing dinghy** un dériveur

dining car NOUN
le wagon-restaurant
(les wagons-restaurants PL)

dining room NOUN
la salle à manger

dinner NOUN
1 le déjeuner (*at midday*)

D

2 le dîner (in the evening)

dinner jacket NOUN
le smoking

dinner lady NOUN
la dame de service

dinner party NOUN
le dîner

dinner time NOUN
1 l' heure du déjeuner FEM (midday)
2 l' heure du dîner FEM (evening)

dinosaur NOUN
le dinosaure

dip NOUN
see also **dip** VERB
♦ to go for a dip aller se baigner

to **dip** VERB
see also **dip** NOUN
tremper ◊ He dipped a biscuit into his tea. Il a trempé un biscuit dans son thé.

diploma NOUN
le diplôme ◊ a diploma in social work un diplôme d'assistante sociale

diplomat NOUN
le/la diplomate

diplomatic ADJECTIVE
diplomatique

direct ADJECTIVE, ADVERB
see also **direct** VERB
direct ◊ the most direct route le chemin le plus direct ◊ You can't fly to Nice direct from Cork. Il n'y a pas de vols directs de Cork à Nice.

to **direct** VERB
see also **direct** ADJECTIVE
1 réaliser (film, programme)
2 mettre en scène (play, show)

direction NOUN
la direction ◊ We're going in the wrong direction. Nous allons dans la mauvaise direction.
♦ to ask somebody for directions demander son chemin à quelqu'un

director NOUN
1 (of company)
le directeur
la directrice
2 (of play)
le metteur en scène
(les metteurs en scène PL)
3 (of film, programme)
le réalisateur
la réalisatrice

directory NOUN
1 l' annuaire MASC (phone book)
2 le répertoire (computing)

dirt NOUN
la saleté

dirty ADJECTIVE
sale
♦ to get dirty se salir
♦ to get something dirty salir quelque chose

disabled ADJECTIVE
handicapé
♦ the disabled les handicapés

disadvantage NOUN
le désavantage

to **disagree** VERB
♦ We always disagree. Nous ne sommes jamais d'accord.
♦ I disagree! Je ne suis pas d'accord!
♦ He disagrees with me. Il n'est pas d'accord avec moi.

disagreement NOUN
le désaccord

to **disappear** VERB
disparaître

disappearance NOUN
la disparition

disappointed ADJECTIVE
déçu

disappointing ADJECTIVE
décevant

disappointment NOUN
la déception

disaster NOUN
le désastre

disastrous ADJECTIVE
désastreux MASC
désastreuse FEM

disc NOUN
le disque

discipline NOUN
la discipline

disc jockey NOUN
le disc-jockey

disco NOUN
la soirée disco ◊ There's a disco at the school tonight. Il y a une soirée disco à l'école ce soir.

to **disconnect** VERB
1 débrancher (electrical equipment)
2 couper (telephone, water supply)

discount NOUN
la réduction ◊ a discount for students une réduction pour les étudiants

to **discourage** VERB
décourager
♦ to get discouraged se décourager ◊ Don't get discouraged! Ne te décourage pas!

to **discover** VERB
découvrir

discrimination NOUN

☞

la discrimination ◊ *racial
discrimination* la discrimination
raciale

to **discuss** VERB
1 discuter de ◊ *I'll discuss it with
my parents.* Je vais en discuter avec
mes parents.
2 discuter sur (*topic*) ◊ *We discussed
the problem of pollution.* Nous avons
discuté du problème de la pollution.

discussion NOUN
la discussion

disease NOUN
la maladie

disgraceful ADJECTIVE
scandaleux MASC
scandaleuse FEM

to **disguise** VERB
déguiser ◊ *He was disguised as a
policeman.* Il était déguisé en policier.

disgusted ADJECTIVE
dégoûté ◊ *I was absolutely
disgusted.* J'étais complètement
dégoûté.

disgusting ADJECTIVE
1 dégoûtant (*food, smell*) ◊ *It looks
disgusting.* Ça a l'air dégoûtant.
2 honteux (*disgraceful*) ◊ *That's
disgusting!* C'est honteux!

dish NOUN
le plat ◊ *a china dish* un plat en
porcelaine ◊ *a vegetarian dish* un plat
végétarien
♦**to do the dishes** faire la vaisselle
◊ *He never does the dishes.* Il ne fait
jamais la vaisselle.

dishonest ADJECTIVE
malhonnête

dish soap NOUN US
le produit à vaisselle

dish towel NOUN US
le torchon

dishwasher NOUN
le lave-vaisselle
(les lave-vaisselle PL)

disinfectant NOUN
le désinfectant

disk NOUN
le disque
♦**a floppy disk** une disquette
♦**the hard disk** le disque dur

diskette NOUN
la disquette

to **dislike** VERB
see also **dislike** NOUN
ne pas aimer ◊ *I really dislike
cabbage.* Je n'aime vraiment pas le
chou.

dislike NOUN
see also **dislike** VERB
♦**my likes and dislikes** ce que j'aime et
ce que je n'aime pas

dismal ADJECTIVE
lugubre

to **dismiss** VERB
renvoyer (*employee*)

disobedient ADJECTIVE
désobéissant

display NOUN
see also **display** VERB
l' étalage MASC ◊ *There was a lovely
display of fruit in the window.* Il y
avait un superbe étalage de fruits en
vitrine.
♦**to be on display** être exposé ◊ *Her
best paintings were on display.* Ses
meilleurs tableaux étaient exposés.
♦**a firework display** un feu d'artifice

to **display** VERB
see also **display** NOUN
1 montrer ◊ *She proudly displayed
her medal.* Elle a montré sa médaille
avec fierté.
2 exposer (*in shop window*)

disposable ADJECTIVE
jetable

to **disqualify** VERB
disqualifier
♦**to be disqualified** être disqualifié ◊ *He
was disqualified.* Il a été disqualifié.

to **disrupt** VERB
perturber ◊ *Protesters disrupted the
meeting.* Des manifestants ont
perturbé la réunion. ◊ *Train services
are being disrupted by the strike.* Les
horaires de train sont perturbés par
la grève.

dissatisfied ADJECTIVE
♦**We were dissatisfied with the service.**
Nous n'étions pas satisfaits du
service.

to **dissolve** VERB
dissoudre

distance NOUN
la distance ◊ *a distance of 40
kilometres* une distance de quarante
kilomètres
♦**It's within walking distance.** On peut
y aller à pied.
♦**in the distance** au loin

distant ADJECTIVE
lointain ◊ *in the distant future* dans
un avenir lointain

distillery NOUN
la distillerie ◊ *a whisky distillery* une
distillerie de whisky

distinction NOUN

1 la distinction ◊ *to make a distinction between ...* faire la distinction entre ...
2 la mention très bien ◊ *I got a distinction in my piano exam.* J'ai eu la mention très bien à mon examen de piano.

distinctive ADJECTIVE
distinctif MASC
distinctive FEM

to **distract** VERB
distraire

to **distribute** VERB
distribuer

district NOUN
1 le quartier (*of town*)
2 la région (*of country*)

to **disturb** VERB
déranger ◊ *I'm sorry to disturb you.* Je suis désolé de vous déranger.

ditch NOUN
see also **ditch** VERB
le fossé

to **ditch** VERB
see also **ditch** NOUN
plaquer (*informal*) ◊ *She's just ditched her boyfriend.* Elle vient de plaquer son copain.

dive NOUN
see also **dive** VERB
le plongeon

to **dive** VERB
see also **dive** NOUN
plonger

diver NOUN
le plongeur
la plongeuse

diversion NOUN
la déviation (*for traffic*)

to **divide** VERB
1 diviser ◊ *Divide the pastry in half.* Divisez la pâte en deux. ◊ *12 divided by 3 is 4.* Douze divisé par trois égalent quatre.
2 se diviser ◊ *We divided into two groups.* Nous nous sommes divisés en deux groupes.

diving NOUN
la plongée
♦ **a diving board** un plongeoir

division NOUN
la division

divorce NOUN
le divorce

divorced ADJECTIVE
divorcé ◊ *My parents are divorced.* Mes parents sont divorcés.

DIY NOUN

le bricolage ◊ *to do DIY* faire du bricolage ◊ *a DIY shop* un magasin de bricolage

dizzy ADJECTIVE
♦ **to feel dizzy** avoir la tête qui tourne ◊ *I feel dizzy.* J'ai la tête qui tourne.

DJ NOUN
le disc-jockey

to **do** VERB
1 faire ◊ *What are you doing this evening?* Qu'est-ce que tu fais ce soir? ◊ *I do a lot of cycling.* Je fais beaucoup de vélo. ◊ *I haven't done my homework.* Je n'ai pas fait mes devoirs. ◊ *She did it by herself.* Elle l'a fait toute seule. ◊ *I'll do my best.* Je ferai de mon mieux.
♦ **to do well** marcher bien ◊ *The firm is doing well.* L'entreprise marche bien. ◊ *She's doing well at school.* Ses études marchent bien.
2 aller (*be enough*) ◊ *It's not very good, but it'll do.* Ce n'est pas très bon, mais ça ira.
♦ **That'll do, thanks.** Ça ira, merci.

In English **do** *is used to make questions. In French questions are made either with* **est-ce que** *or by reversing the order of verb and subject.*

◊ *Do you like French food?* Est-ce que vous aimez la cuisine française? ◊ *Where does he live?* Où est-ce qu'il habite? ◊ *Do you speak English?* Parlez-vous anglais? ◊ *What do you do in your free time?* Qu'est-ce que vous faites pendant vos loisirs? ◊ *Where did you go for your holidays?* Où es-tu allé pendant tes vacances?

Use **ne ... pas** *in negative sentences for* **don't***.*

◊ *I don't understand.* Je ne comprends pas. ◊ *Why didn't you come?* Pourquoi n'êtes-vous pas venus?

do *is not translated when it is used in place of another verb.*

◊ *I hate maths. – So do I.* Je déteste les maths. – Moi aussi. ◊ *I didn't like the film. – Neither did I.* Je n'ai pas aimé le film. – Moi non plus. ◊ *Do you like horses? – No I don't.* Est-ce que tu aimes les chevaux? – Non.

Use **n'est-ce pas** *to check information.*

◊ *You go swimming on Fridays, don't you?* Tu fais de la natation le vendredi, n'est-ce pas? ◊ *The bus stops at the youth hostel, doesn't it?*

☞

Le bus s'arrête à l'auberge de jeunesse, n'est-ce pas?
- **How do you do?** Enchanté!
- **to do up (1)** (*shoes*) lacer ◊ *Do up your shoes!* Lace tes chaussures!
- **to do up (2)** (*renovate*) retaper ◊ *They're doing up an old cottage.* Ils retapent une vieille maison.
- **to do up (3)** (*shirt, cardigan*) boutonner
- **Do up your zip!** (*on trousers*) Ferme ta braguette!
- **to do without** se passer de ◊ *I couldn't do without my computer.* Je ne pourrais pas me passer de mon ordinateur.

dock NOUN
le dock (*for ships*)

doctor NOUN
le médecin ◊ *She's a doctor.* Elle est médecin. ◊ *I'd like to be a doctor.* Je voudrais être médecin.

document NOUN
le document

documentary NOUN
le documentaire

to **dodge** VERB
échapper à (*attacker*)

dodgems PL NOUN
les autos tamponneuses FEM PL ◊ *to go on the dodgems* aller faire un tour d'autos tamponneuses

does VERB *see* **do**

doesn't = **does not**

dog NOUN
le chien
la chienne
◊ *Have you got a dog?* Est-ce que tu as un chien?

do-it-yourself NOUN
le bricolage

dole NOUN
les allocations chômage FEM PL
- **to be on the dole** toucher le chômage ◊ *A lot of people are on the dole.* Beaucoup de gens touchent le chômage.
- **to go on the dole** s'inscrire au chômage

doll NOUN
la poupée

dollar NOUN
le dollar

dolphin NOUN
le dauphin

domestic ADJECTIVE
- **a domestic flight** un vol intérieur

dominoes PL NOUN

- **to have a game of dominoes** faire une partie de dominos

to **donate** VERB
donner

done VERB *see* **do**

donkey NOUN
l' âne MASC

donor NOUN
1 (*to charity*)
le donateur
la donatrice
2 (*of blood, organ for transplant*)
le donneur
la donneuse

don't = **do not**

door NOUN
1 la porte ◊ *the first door on the right* la première porte à droite
2 la portière (*of car, train*)

doorbell NOUN
la sonnette
- **to ring the doorbell** sonner
- **Suddenly the doorbell rang.** Soudain, on a sonné.

doorman NOUN
le portier

doorstep NOUN
le pas de la porte

dormitory NOUN
le dortoir

dose NOUN
la dose

dosh NOUN
le fric (*informal: money*)

dot NOUN
le point (*on letter "i", in email address*)
- **on the dot** à l'heure pile ◊ *He arrived at 9 o'clock on the dot.* Il est arrivé à neuf heures pile.

to **double** VERB
see also **double** ADJECTIVE
doubler ◊ *The number of attacks has doubled.* Le nombre d'agressions a doublé.

double ADJECTIVE, ADVERB
see also **double** VERB
double ◊ *a double helping* une double portion
- **to cost double** coûter le double ◊ *First-class tickets cost double.* Les billets de première classe coûtent le double.
- **a double bed** un grand lit
- **a double room** une chambre pour deux personnes
- **a double-decker bus** un autobus à impériale

double bass NOUN

la <u>contrebasse</u> ◊ *I play the double bass.* Je joue de la contrebasse.

to **double-click** VERB
<u>double-cliquer</u> ◊ *to double-click on an icon* double-cliquer sur une icône

double glazing NOUN
le <u>double vitrage</u>

doubles PL NOUN
le <u>double</u> SING (*in tennis*) ◊ *to play mixed doubles* jouer en double mixte

doubt NOUN
see also **doubt** VERB
le <u>doute</u> ◊ *I have my doubts.* J'ai des doutes.

to **doubt** VERB
see also **doubt** NOUN
<u>douter de</u>
♦**I doubt it.** J'en doute.
♦**to doubt that** douter que
douter que has to be followed by a verb in the subjunctive.
◊ *I doubt he'll agree.* Je doute qu'il soit d'accord.

doubtful ADJECTIVE
♦**to be doubtful about doing something** hésiter à faire quelque chose ◊ *I'm doubtful about going by myself.* J'hésite à y aller tout seul.
♦**It's doubtful.** Ce n'est pas sûr.
♦**You sound doubtful.** Tu n'as pas l'air sûr.

dough NOUN
la <u>pâte</u>

doughnut NOUN
le <u>beignet</u> ◊ *a jam doughnut* un beignet à la confiture

Dover NOUN
<u>Douvres</u> ◊ *We went from Dover to Boulogne.* Nous sommes allés de Douvres à Boulogne.
♦**in Dover** à Douvres

down ADVERB, ADJECTIVE, PREPOSITION
①<u>en bas</u> (*below*) ◊ *His office is down on the first floor.* Son bureau est en bas, au premier étage. ◊ *It's down there.* C'est là-bas.
②<u>à terre</u> (*to the ground*) ◊ *He threw down his racket.* Il a jeté sa raquette à terre.
♦**They live just down the road.** Ils habitent tout à côté.
♦**to come down** descendre ◊ *Come down here!* Descends!
♦**to go down** descendre ◊ *The rabbit went down the hole.* Le lapin est descendu dans le terrier.
♦**to sit down** s'asseoir ◊ *Sit down!* Asseyez-vous!

♦**to feel down** avoir le cafard ◊ *I'm feeling a bit down.* J'ai un peu le cafard.
♦**The computer's down.** L'ordinateur est en panne.

to **download** VERB
<u>télécharger</u> ◊ *to download a file* télécharger un fichier

downpour NOUN
la <u>pluie torrentielle</u> ◊ *a sudden downpour* une pluie soudaine et torrentielle

downstairs ADVERB, ADJECTIVE
①<u>au rez-de-chaussée</u> ◊ *The bathroom's downstairs.* La salle de bain est au rez-de-chaussée.
②<u>du rez-de-chaussée</u> ◊ *the downstairs bathroom* la salle de bain du rez-de-chaussée
♦**the people downstairs** les voisins du dessous

downtown ADJECTIVE US
<u>dans le centre</u>

to **doze** VERB
<u>sommeiller</u>
♦**to doze off** s'assoupir

dozen NOUN
la <u>douzaine</u> ◊ *two dozen* deux douzaines ◊ *a dozen eggs* une douzaine d'œufs
♦**I've told you that dozens of times.** Je t'ai dit ça des centaines de fois.

drab ADJECTIVE
<u>terne</u> (*clothes*)

draft NOUN US
le <u>courant d'air</u>

to **drag** VERB
see also **drag** NOUN
<u>traîner</u> (*thing, person*)

drag NOUN
see also **drag** VERB
♦**It's a real drag!** C'est la barbe! (*informal*)
♦**in drag** travesti ◊ *He was in drag.* Il était travesti.

dragon NOUN
le <u>dragon</u>

drain NOUN
see also **drain** VERB
l' <u>égout</u> MASC ◊ *The drains are blocked.* Les égouts sont bouchés.

to **drain** VERB
see also **drain** NOUN
<u>égoutter</u> (*vegetables, pasta*)

draining board NOUN
l' <u>égouttoir</u> MASC

drainpipe NOUN
le <u>tuyau d'écoulement</u>

D

drama NOUN
l' <u>art dramatique</u> MASC ◇ *Drama is my favourite subject.* L'art dramatique est ma matière préférée.
♦ **drama school** l'école d'art dramatique ◇ *I'd like to go to drama school.* J'aimerais entrer dans une école d'art dramatique.
♦ **Greek drama** le théâtre grec

dramatic ADJECTIVE
<u>spectaculaire</u> ◇ *It was really dramatic!* C'était vraiment spectaculaire! ◇ *a dramatic improvement* une amélioration spectaculaire
♦ **dramatic news** une nouvelle extraordinaire

drank VERB *see* **drink**

drapes PL NOUN [US]
les <u>rideaux</u> MASC PL

drastic ADJECTIVE
(*change*)
<u>radical</u>
(radicaux MASC PL)
♦ **to take drastic action** prendre des mesures énergiques

draught NOUN
le <u>courant d'air</u>

draughts NOUN
les <u>dames</u> FEM PL ◇ *to play draughts* jouer aux dames

to **draw** VERB
see also **draw** NOUN
[1] <u>dessiner</u> ◇ *He's good at drawing.* Il dessine bien.
♦ **to draw a picture** faire un dessin
♦ **to draw a picture of somebody** faire le portrait de quelqu'un
♦ **to draw a line** tirer un trait
[2] <u>faire match nul</u> (*sport*) ◇ *We drew 2-2.* Nous avons fait match nul deux à deux.
♦ **to draw the curtains** tirer les rideaux
♦ **to draw lots** tirer au sort

draw NOUN
see also **draw** VERB
[1] le <u>match nul</u> (*sport*) ◇ *The game ended in a draw.* La partie s'est soldée par un match nul.
[2] le <u>tirage au sort</u> (*in lottery*) ◇ *The draw takes place on Saturday.* Le tirage au sort a lieu samedi.

drawback NOUN
l' <u>inconvénient</u> MASC

drawer NOUN
le <u>tiroir</u>

drawing NOUN
le <u>dessin</u>

drawing pin NOUN
la <u>punaise</u>

drawn VERB *see* **draw**

dreadful ADJECTIVE
[1] <u>terrible</u> ◇ *a dreadful mistake* une terrible erreur
[2] <u>affreux</u> MASC
<u>affreuse</u> FEM
◇ *The weather was dreadful.* Il a fait un temps affreux.
♦ **I feel dreadful.** Je ne me sens vraiment pas bien.
♦ **You look dreadful.** (*ill*) Tu as une mine affreuse.

to **dream** VERB
see also **dream** NOUN
<u>rêver</u> ◇ *I dreamed I was in Belgium.* J'ai rêvé que j'étais en Belgique.

dream NOUN
see also **dream** VERB
le <u>rêve</u> ◇ *It was just a dream.* Ce n'était qu'un rêve.
♦ **a bad dream** un cauchemar

to **drench** VERB
♦ **to get drenched** se faire tremper ◇ *We got drenched.* Nous nous sommes fait tremper.

dress NOUN
see also **dress** VERB
la <u>robe</u>

to **dress** VERB
see also **dress** NOUN
<u>s'habiller</u> ◇ *I got up, dressed, and went downstairs.* Je me suis levé, je me suis habillé et je suis descendu.
♦ **to dress somebody** habiller quelqu'un ◇ *She dressed the children.* Elle a habillé les enfants.
♦ **to get dressed** s'habiller ◇ *I got dressed quickly.* Je me suis habillé rapidement.
♦ **to dress up** se déguiser ◇ *I dressed up as a ghost.* Je me suis déguisé en fantôme.

dressed ADJECTIVE
<u>habillé</u> ◇ *I'm not dressed yet.* Je ne suis pas encore habillé. ◇ *How was she dressed?* Comment est-ce qu'elle était habillée?
♦ **She was dressed in a green sweater and jeans.** Elle portait un pull vert et un jean.

dresser NOUN
le <u>vaisselier</u> (*furniture*)

dressing gown NOUN
la <u>robe de chambre</u>

dressing table NOUN
la <u>coiffeuse</u>

drew VERB *see* **draw**

dried VERB *see* **dry**

drier NOUN
le séchoir

drift NOUN
see also **drift** VERB
♦ **a snow drift** une congère

to **drift** VERB
see also **drift** NOUN
[1] aller à la dérive (boat)
[2] s'amonceler (snow)

drill NOUN
see also **drill** VERB
la perceuse

to **drill** VERB
see also **drill** NOUN
percer

to **drink** VERB
see also **drink** NOUN
boire ◊ What would you like to drink? Qu'est-ce que vous voulez boire? ◊ She drank three cups of tea. Elle a bu trois tasses de thé. ◊ He'd been drinking. Il avait bu.
♦ **I don't drink.** Je ne bois pas d'alcool.

drink NOUN
see also **drink** VERB
[1] la boisson ◊ a cold drink une boisson fraîche ◊ a hot drink une boisson chaude
[2] le verre (alcoholic) ◊ They've gone out for a drink. Ils sont allés prendre un verre.
♦ **to have a drink** prendre un verre

drinking water NOUN
l' eau potable FEM

drive NOUN
see also **drive** VERB
[1] le tour en voiture
♦ **to go for a drive** aller faire un tour en voiture ◊ We went for a drive in the country. Nous sommes allés faire un tour à la campagne.
♦ **We've got a long drive tomorrow.** Nous avons une longue route à faire demain.
[2] l' allée FEM (of house) ◊ He parked his car in the drive. Il a garé sa voiture dans l'allée.

to **drive** VERB
see also **drive** NOUN
[1] conduire (a car) ◊ She's learning to drive. Elle apprend à conduire. ◊ Can you drive? Tu sais conduire?
[2] aller en voiture (go by car) ◊ Did you go by train? – No, we drove. Vous êtes partis en train? – Non, nous y sommes allés en voiture.
[3] emmener en voiture ◊ My mother drives me to school. Ma mère m'emmène à l'école en voiture.

♦ **to drive somebody home** raccompagner quelqu'un ◊ He offered to drive me home. Il m'a proposé de me raccompagner.
♦ **to drive somebody mad** rendre quelqu'un fou ◊ He drives her mad. Il la rend folle.

driver NOUN
[1] le conducteur
la conductrice
◊ She's an excellent driver. C'est une excellente conductrice.
[2] (of taxi, bus)
le chauffeur ◊ He's a bus driver. Il est chauffeur d'autobus.

driver's license NOUN US
le permis de conduire

driving instructor NOUN
le moniteur d'auto-école ◊ He's a driving instructor. Il est moniteur d'auto-école.

driving lesson NOUN
la leçon de conduite

driving licence NOUN
le permis de conduire

driving test NOUN
♦ **to take one's driving test** passer son permis de conduire ◊ He's taking his driving test tomorrow. Il passe son permis de conduire demain.
♦ **She's just passed her driving test.** Elle vient d'avoir son permis.

drizzle NOUN
la bruine

drop NOUN
see also **drop** VERB
la goutte ◊ a drop of water une goutte d'eau.

to **drop** VERB
see also **drop** NOUN
[1] laisser tomber ◊ I dropped the glass and it broke. J'ai laissé tomber le verre et il s'est cassé. ◊ I'm going to drop chemistry. Je vais laisser tomber la chimie.
[2] déposer ◊ Could you drop me at the station? Pouvez-vous me déposer à la gare?

drought NOUN
la sécheresse

drove VERB see **drive**

to **drown** VERB
se noyer ◊ A boy drowned here yesterday. Un jeune garçon s'est noyé ici hier.

drug NOUN
[1] le médicament (medicine) ◊ They need food and drugs. Ils ont besoin de nourriture et de médicaments.

☞

2 la <u>drogue</u> (*illegal*) ◊ *hard drugs* les drogues dures ◊ *soft drugs* les drogues douces
♦ **to take drugs** se droguer
♦ **a drug addict** un drogué ◊ *She's a drug addict.* C'est une droguée.
♦ **a drug pusher** un dealer
♦ **a drug smuggler** un trafiquant de drogue
♦ **the drugs squad** la brigade antidrogue

drugstore NOUN US
le <u>drugstore</u>

drum NOUN
le <u>tambour</u> ◊ *an African drum* un tambour africain
♦ **a drum kit** une batterie
♦ **drums** la batterie SING ◊ *I play drums.* Je joue de la batterie.

drummer NOUN
(*in rock group*)
le <u>batteur</u>
la <u>batteuse</u>

drunk ADJECTIVE
see also **drunk** NOUN
<u>ivre</u> ◊ *He was drunk.* Il était ivre.

drunk NOUN
see also **drunk** ADJECTIVE
l' <u>ivrogne</u> MASC/FEM ◊ *The streets were full of drunks.* Les rues étaient pleines d'ivrognes.

dry ADJECTIVE
see also **dry** VERB
1 <u>sec</u> MASC
<u>sèche</u> FEM
◊ *The paint isn't dry yet.* La peinture n'est pas encore sèche.
2 (*weather*)
<u>sans pluie</u> ◊ *a long dry period* une longue période sans pluie

to **dry** VERB
see also **dry** ADJECTIVE
1 <u>sécher</u> ◊ *The washing will dry quickly in the sun.* Le linge va sécher vite au soleil. ◊ *some dried flowers* des fleurs séchées
♦ **to dry one's hair** se sécher les cheveux ◊ *I haven't dried my hair yet.* Je ne me suis pas encore séché les cheveux.
2 <u>faire sécher</u> (*clothes*) ◊ *There's nowhere to dry clothes here.* Il n'y a pas d'endroit où faire sécher les vêtements ici.
♦ **to dry the dishes** essuyer la vaisselle

dry-cleaner's NOUN
la <u>teinturerie</u>

dryer NOUN
le <u>séchoir</u> (*for clothes*)

♦ **a tumble dryer** un séchoir à linge
♦ **a hair dryer** un sèche-cheveux

DTP NOUN (= *desktop publishing*)
la <u>PAO</u> (= publication assistée par ordinateur)

dubbed ADJECTIVE
<u>doublé</u> ◊ *The film was dubbed into French.* Le film était doublé en français.

dubious ADJECTIVE
<u>réticent</u> ◊ *My parents were a bit dubious about it.* Mes parents étaient un peu réticents à ce sujet.

duck NOUN
le <u>canard</u>

due ADJECTIVE, ADVERB
♦ **to be due to do something** devoir faire quelque chose ◊ *He's due to arrive tomorrow.* Il doit arriver demain.
♦ **The plane's due in half an hour.** L'avion doit arriver dans une demi-heure.
♦ **When's the baby due?** Le bébé est prévu pour quand?
♦ **due to** à cause de ◊ *The trip was cancelled due to bad weather.* Le voyage a été annulé à cause du mauvais temps.

dug VERB *see* **dig**

dull ADJECTIVE
1 <u>ennuyeux</u> MASC
<u>ennuyeuse</u> FEM
◊ *He's nice, but a bit dull.* Il est sympathique, mais un peu ennuyeux.
2 (*weather, day*)
<u>maussade</u>

dumb ADJECTIVE
1 <u>muet</u> MASC
<u>muette</u> FEM
♦ **She's deaf and dumb.** Elle est sourde-muette.
2 (*stupid*)
<u>bête</u> ◊ *That was a really dumb thing I did!* C'était vraiment bête de ma part!

dummy NOUN
la <u>tétine</u> (*for baby*)

dump NOUN
see also **dump** VERB
♦ **It's a real dump!** C'est un endroit minable!
♦ **a rubbish dump** une décharge

to **dump** VERB
see also **dump** NOUN
1 <u>déposer</u> (*waste*) ◊ *"no dumping"* "défense de déposer des ordures"
2 <u>plaquer</u> (*informal*) ◊ *He's just dumped his girlfriend.* Il vient de plaquer sa copine.

dungarees PL NOUN
la salopette SING
dungeon NOUN
le cachot
duration NOUN
la durée
during PREPOSITION
pendant ◊ *during the day* pendant la journée
dusk NOUN
le crépuscule ◊ *at dusk* au crépuscule
dust NOUN
see also **dust** VERB
la poussière
to **dust** VERB
see also **dust** NOUN
épousseter ◊ *I dusted the shelves.* J'ai épousseté les étagères.
♦ I hate dusting! Je déteste faire les poussières!
dustbin NOUN
la poubelle
dustman NOUN
l' éboueur MASC ◊ *He's a dustman.* Il est éboueur.
dusty ADJECTIVE
poussiéreux MASC
poussiéreuse FEM
Dutch ADJECTIVE
see also **Dutch** NOUN
hollandais ◊ *She's Dutch.* Elle est hollandaise.
Dutch NOUN
see also **Dutch** ADJECTIVE

le hollandais (*language*)
♦ the Dutch les Hollandais
Dutchman NOUN
le Hollandais
Dutchwoman NOUN
la Hollandaise
duty NOUN
le devoir ◊ *It was his duty to tell the police.* C'était son devoir de prévenir la police.
♦ to be on duty (1) (*policeman*) être de service
♦ to be on duty (2) (*doctor, nurse*) être de garde
duty-free ADJECTIVE
hors taxes MASC, FEM, PL
♦ the duty-free shop la boutique hors taxes
duvet NOUN
la couette
DVD NOUN
le DVD
(les DVD PL)
◊ *I've got that film on DVD.* J'ai ce film en DVD.
DVD player NOUN
le lecteur de DVD
dwarf NOUN
le nain
la naine
dying VERB see **die**
dynamic ADJECTIVE
dynamique
dyslexia NOUN
la dyslexie

D

E

each ADJECTIVE, PRONOUN

① chaque ◊ *each day* chaque jour
◊ *Each house in our street has its own garden.* Chaque maison dans notre rue a son propre jardin.

② chacun MASC
chacune FEM
◊ *The girls each have their own bedroom.* Les filles ont chacune leur chambre. ◊ *They have 10 points each.* Ils ont dix points chacun. ◊ *The plates cost £5 each.* Les assiettes coûtent cinq livres chacune. ◊ *He gave each of us £10.* Il nous a donné dix livres à chacun.

Use a reflexive verb to translate each other.

♦ **They hate each other.** Ils se détestent.
♦ **We wrote to each other.** Nous nous sommes écrit.
♦ **They don't know each other.** Ils ne se connaissent pas.

eager ADJECTIVE
♦ **to be eager to do something** être impatient de faire quelque chose

ear NOUN
l' oreille FEM

earache NOUN
♦ **to have earache** avoir mal aux oreilles

earlier ADVERB

① tout à l'heure ◊ *I saw him earlier.* Je l'ai vu tout à l'heure.

② plus tôt (*in the morning*) ◊ *I ought to get up earlier.* Je devrais me lever plus tôt.

early ADVERB, ADJECTIVE

① tôt (*early in the day*) ◊ *I have to get up early.* Je dois me lever tôt.
♦ **to have an early night** se coucher tôt

② en avance (*ahead of time*) ◊ *I came early to get a good seat.* Je suis venu en avance pour avoir une bonne place.

to **earn** VERB
gagner ◊ *She earns £5 an hour.* Elle gagne cinq livres de l'heure.

earnings PL NOUN
le salaire SING

earring NOUN
la boucle d'oreille

earth NOUN
la terre

earthquake NOUN
le tremblement de terre

easily ADVERB

facilement

east ADJECTIVE, ADVERB
see also **east** NOUN

① est MASC, FEM, PL ◊ *the east coast* la côte est
♦ **an east wind** un vent d'est
♦ **east of** à l'est de ◊ *It's east of London.* C'est à l'est de Londres.
② vers l'est ◊ *We were travelling east.* Nous allions vers l'est.

east NOUN
see also **east** ADJECTIVE
l' est MASC ◊ *in the east* dans l'est

eastbound ADJECTIVE
♦ **The car was eastbound on the M25.** Le voiture se trouvait sur la M25 en direction de l'est.
♦ **Eastbound traffic is moving very slowly.** La circulation vers l'est avance très lentement.

Easter NOUN
Pâques FEM ◊ *at Easter* à Pâques ◊ *We went to my grandparents' for Easter.* Nous sommes allés chez mes grands-parents à Pâques.

Easter egg NOUN
l' œuf de Pâques MASC

eastern ADJECTIVE
♦ **the eastern part of the island** la partie est de l'île
♦ **Eastern Europe** l'Europe de l'Est

easy ADJECTIVE
facile

easy chair NOUN
le fauteuil

easy-going ADJECTIVE
facile à vivre
(faciles à vivre PL)
◊ *She's very easy-going.* Elle est très facile à vivre.

to **eat** VERB
manger
♦ **Would you like something to eat?** Est-ce que tu veux manger quelque chose?

EC NOUN (= *European Community*)
la CE (= Communauté européenne)

eccentric ADJECTIVE
excentrique

echo NOUN
l' écho MASC

eco-friendly ADJECTIVE
respectueux de l'environnement
MASC

respectueuse de l'environnement
FEM

ecological ADJECTIVE
écologique

ecology NOUN
l' écologie FEM

e-commerce NOUN
le commerce électronique

economic ADJECTIVE
rentable (*profitable*)

economical ADJECTIVE
1 économe (*person*)
2 économique (*method, car*)

economics NOUN
l' économie FEM
♦**He's studying economics.** Il étudie les
sciences économiques.

to **economize** VERB
faire des économies ◊ *to economize
on something* faire des économies
sur quelque chose

economy NOUN
l' économie FEM

ecstasy NOUN
l' ecstasy FEM (*drug*)
♦**to be in ecstasy** s'extasier

ecu NOUN (= *European Currency Unit*)
l' écu MASC

eczema NOUN
l' eczéma MASC

edge NOUN
le bord

edgy ADJECTIVE
tendu

Edinburgh NOUN
Édimbourg

editor NOUN
(*of newspaper*)
le rédacteur en chef
la rédactrice en chef

educated ADJECTIVE
cultivé

education NOUN
1 l' éducation FEM ◊ *There should be
more investment in education.* On
devrait investir plus dans l'éducation.
2 l' enseignement MASC (*teaching*)
◊ *She works in education.* Elle
travaille dans l'enseignement.

educational ADJECTIVE
(*experience, toy*)
éducatif MASC
éducative FEM
◊ *It was very educational.* C'était très
éducatif.

effect NOUN
l' effet MASC ◊ *special effects* les effets
spéciaux

effective ADJECTIVE
efficace

effectively ADVERB
efficacement
*Be careful not to translate **effectively**
by **effectivement**.*

efficient ADJECTIVE
efficace

effort NOUN
l' effort MASC

e.g. ABBREVIATION
p. ex. (= *par exemple*)

egg NOUN
l' œuf MASC ◊ *a hard-boiled egg* un
œuf dur ◊ *a soft-boiled egg* un œuf à
la coque ◊ *a fried egg* un œuf sur le
plat
♦**scrambled eggs** les œufs brouillés

egg cup NOUN
le coquetier

eggplant NOUN US
l' aubergine FEM

Egypt NOUN
l' Égypte FEM
♦**in Egypt** en Égypte

Eiffel Tower NOUN
la tour Eiffel

eight NUMBER
huit ◊ *She's eight.* Elle a huit ans.

eighteen NUMBER
dix-huit ◊ *She's eighteen.* Elle a dix-
huit ans.

eighteenth ADJECTIVE
dix-huitième ◊ *her eighteenth
birthday* son dix-huitième
anniversaire ◊ *the eighteenth floor* le
dix-huitième étage
♦**the eighteenth of August** le dix-huit
août

eighth ADJECTIVE
huitième ◊ *the eighth floor* le
huitième étage
♦**the eighth of August** le huit août

eighty NUMBER
quatre-vingts

Eire NOUN
la République d'Irlande
♦**in Eire** en République d'Irlande

either ADVERB, CONJUNCTION, PRONOUN
non plus ◊ *I don't like milk, and I
don't like eggs either.* Je n'aime pas
le lait, et je n'aime pas les œufs non
plus. ◊ *I've never been to Spain. – I
haven't either.* Je ne suis jamais allé
en Espagne. – Moi non plus.
♦**either ... or ...** soit ... soit ... ◊ *You can
have either ice cream or yoghurt.* Tu
peux prendre soit une glace soit un
yaourt.

☞

♦**either of them** l'un ou l'autre ◊ *Take either of them.* Prends l'un ou l'autre.

♦**I don't like either of them.** Je n'aime ni l'un ni l'autre.

elastic NOUN
l' élastique MASC

elastic band NOUN
l' élastique MASC

elbow NOUN
le coude

elder ADJECTIVE
aîné ◊ *my elder sister* ma sœur aînée

elderly ADJECTIVE
âgé

♦**the elderly** les personnes âgées FEM

eldest ADJECTIVE
aîné ◊ *my eldest sister* ma sœur aînée ◊ *He's the eldest.* C'est l'aîné.

to **elect** VERB
élire

election NOUN
l' élection FEM

electric ADJECTIVE
électrique ◊ *an electric fire* un radiateur électrique ◊ *an electric guitar* une guitare électrique

♦**an electric blanket** une couverture chauffante

electrical ADJECTIVE
électrique

♦**an electrical engineer** un ingénieur électricien

electrician NOUN
l' électricien MASC ◊ *He's an electrician.* Il est électricien.

electricity NOUN
l' électricité FEM

electronic ADJECTIVE
électronique

electronics NOUN
l' électronique FEM ◊ *My hobby is electronics.* Ma passion, c'est l'électronique.

elegant ADJECTIVE
élégant

elementary school NOUN US
l' école primaire FEM

elephant NOUN
l' éléphant MASC

elevator NOUN US
l' ascenseur MASC

eleven NUMBER
onze ◊ *She's eleven.* Elle a onze ans.

eleventh ADJECTIVE
onzième ◊ *the eleventh floor* le onzième étage ◊ *the eleventh of August* le onze août

else ADVERB
d'autre ◊ *somebody else* quelqu'un d'autre ◊ *nobody else* personne d'autre ◊ *nothing else* rien d'autre

♦**something else** autre chose

♦**anything else** autre chose ◊ *Would you like anything else?* Désirez-vous autre chose?

♦**I don't want anything else.** Je ne veux rien d'autre.

♦**somewhere else** ailleurs

♦**anywhere else** autre part

email NOUN
⸢see also **email** VERB⸣
le courrier électronique

♦**email address** l'adresse e-mail FEM ◊ *My email address is: ...* Mon adresse e-mail, c'est: ...

to **email** VERB
⸢see also **email** NOUN⸣

♦**to email somebody** envoyer un e-mail à quelqu'un

embankment NOUN
le talus

embarrassed ADJECTIVE
gêné ◊ *I was really embarrassed.* J'étais vraiment gêné.

embarrassing ADJECTIVE
gênant ◊ *It was so embarrassing.* C'était tellement gênant.

embassy NOUN
l' ambassade FEM ◊ *the British Embassy* l'ambassade de Grande-Bretagne ◊ *the French Embassy* l'ambassade de France

to **embroider** VERB
broder

embroidery NOUN
la broderie ◊ *I do embroidery.* Je fais de la broderie.

emergency NOUN
l' urgence FEM ◊ *This is an emergency!* C'est une urgence!

♦**in an emergency** en cas d'urgence

♦**an emergency exit** une sortie de secours

♦**an emergency landing** un atterrissage forcé

♦**the emergency services** les services d'urgence MASC

to **emigrate** VERB
émigrer

emotion NOUN
l' émotion FEM

emotional ADJECTIVE
(*person*)
émotif MASC
émotive FEM

emperor NOUN

l' empereur MASC

to **emphasize** VERB
- **to emphasize something** insister sur quelque chose
- **to emphasize that ...** souligner que ...

empire NOUN
l' empire MASC

to **employ** VERB
employer ◊ *The factory employs 600 people.* L'usine emploie six cents personnes.

employee NOUN
l' employé MASC
l' employée FEM

employer NOUN
l' employeur MASC

employment NOUN
l' emploi MASC

empty ADJECTIVE
see also **empty** VERB
vide

to **empty** VERB
see also **empty** ADJECTIVE
vider
- **to empty something out** vider quelque chose

to **encourage** VERB
encourager
- **to encourage somebody to do something** encourager quelqu'un à faire quelque chose

encouragement NOUN
l' encouragement MASC

encyclopedia NOUN
l' encyclopédie FEM

end NOUN
see also **end** VERB
1 la fin ◊ *the end of the film* la fin du film ◊ *the end of the holidays* la fin des vacances
- **in the end** en fin de compte ◊ *In the end I decided to stay at home.* En fin de compte j'ai décidé de rester à la maison.
- **It turned out all right in the end.** Ça s'est bien terminé.
2 le bout ◊ *at the end of the street* au bout de la rue ◊ *at the other end of the table* à l'autre bout de la table
- **for hours on end** des heures entières

to **end** VERB
see also **end** NOUN
finir ◊ *What time does the film end?* À quelle heure est-ce que le film finit?
- **to end up doing something** finir par faire quelque chose ◊ *I ended up walking home.* J'ai fini par rentrer chez moi à pied.

ending NOUN
la fin ◊ *It was an exciting film, especially the ending.* C'était un film passionnant, surtout la fin.

endless ADJECTIVE
interminable ◊ *The journey seemed endless.* Le voyage a paru interminable.

enemy NOUN
l' ennemi MASC
l' ennemie FEM

energetic ADJECTIVE
énergique (*person*)

energy NOUN
l' énergie FEM

engaged ADJECTIVE
1 occupé (*busy, in use*) ◊ *I phoned, but it was engaged.* J'ai téléphoné, mais c'était occupé.
2 fiancé (*to be married*) ◊ *She's engaged to Brian.* Elle est fiancée à Brian.
- **to get engaged** se fiancer

engaged tone NOUN
la tonalité "occupé"

engagement NOUN
les fiançailles FEM PL ◊ *an engagement ring* une bague de fiançailles

engine NOUN
le moteur
*Be careful not to translate **engine** by the French word **engin**.*

engineer NOUN
l' ingénieur MASC ◊ *He's an engineer.* Il est ingénieur.

engineering NOUN
l' ingénierie FEM

England NOUN
l' Angleterre FEM
- **in England** en Angleterre
- **to England** en Angleterre
- **I'm from England.** Je suis anglais.

English ADJECTIVE
see also **English** NOUN
anglais ◊ *I'm English.* Je suis anglais.
- **English people** les Anglais

English NOUN
see also **English** ADJECTIVE
l' anglais MASC (*language*) ◊ *Do you speak English?* Est-ce que vous parlez anglais?
- **the English** les Anglais

Englishman NOUN
l' Anglais MASC

Englishwoman NOUN
l' Anglaise FEM

to **enjoy** VERB

☞

aimer ◊ *Did you enjoy the film?* Est-ce que vous avez aimé le film?
- **to enjoy oneself** s'amuser ◊ *I really enjoyed myself.* Je me suis vraiment bien amusé. ◊ *Did you enjoy yourselves at the party?* Est-ce vous vous êtes bien amusés à la fête?

enjoyable ADJECTIVE
agréable

enlargement NOUN
l' agrandissement MASC (*of photo*)

enormous ADJECTIVE
énorme

enough PRONOUN, ADJECTIVE
assez de ◊ *enough time* assez de temps ◊ *I didn't have enough money.* Je n'avais pas assez d'argent. ◊ *Have you got enough?* Tu en as assez? ◊ *I've had enough!* J'en ai assez!
- **big enough** suffisamment grand
- **warm enough** suffisamment chaud
- **That's enough.** Ça suffit.

to **enquire** VERB
- **to enquire about something** se renseigner sur quelque chose ◊ *I am going to enquire about train times.* Je vais me renseigner sur les horaires de trains.

enquiry NOUN
- **to make enquiries (about something)** se renseigner (sur quelque chose)
- **"enquiries"** "renseignements"

to **enter** VERB
entrer
- **to enter a room** entrer dans une pièce
- **to enter a competition** s'inscrire à une compétition

to **entertain** VERB
recevoir (*guests*)

entertainer NOUN
l' artiste de variétés MASC/FEM

entertaining ADJECTIVE
amusant

enthusiasm NOUN
l' enthousiasme MASC

enthusiast NOUN
- **a railway enthusiast** un passionné des trains
- **She's a DIY enthusiast.** C'est une passionnée de bricolage.

enthusiastic ADJECTIVE
enthousiaste

entire ADJECTIVE
entier MASC
entière FEM
◊ *the entire world* le monde entier

entirely ADVERB
entièrement

entrance NOUN
l' entrée FEM
- **an entrance exam** un concours d'entrée
- **entrance fee** le prix d'entrée

entry NOUN
l' entrée FEM
- **"no entry" (1)** (*on door*) "défense d'entrer"
- **"no entry" (2)** (*on road sign*) "sens interdit"
- **an entry form** une feuille d'inscription

entry phone NOUN
l' interphone MASC

envelope NOUN
l' enveloppe FEM

envious ADJECTIVE
envieux MASC
envieuse FEM

environment NOUN
l' environnement MASC

environmental ADJECTIVE
écologique

environment-friendly ADJECTIVE
écologique

envy NOUN
| see also **envy** VERB |
l' envie FEM

to **envy** VERB
| see also **envy** NOUN |
envier ◊ *I don't envy you!* Je ne t'envie pas!

epileptic NOUN
l' épileptique MASC/FEM

episode NOUN
l' épisode MASC (*of TV programme, story*)

equal ADJECTIVE
| see also **equal** VERB |
égal
(égaux MASC PL)

to **equal** VERB
| see also **equal** ADJECTIVE |
égaler

equality NOUN
l' égalité FEM

to **equalize** VERB
égaliser (*in sport*)

equator NOUN
l' équateur MASC

equipment NOUN
l' équipement MASC ◊ *fishing equipment* l'équipement de pêche ◊ *skiing equipment* l'équipement de ski

equipped ADJECTIVE
- **equipped with** équipé de
- **to be well equipped** être bien équipé

equivalent NOUN
l' équivalent MASC
♦**equivalent to** équivalent à

error NOUN
l' erreur FEM

escalator NOUN
l' escalier roulant MASC

escape NOUN
| see also **escape** VERB |
l' évasion FEM (*from prison*)

to **escape** VERB
| see also **escape** NOUN |
s'échapper ◊ *A lion has escaped.* Un
lion s'est échappé.
♦**to escape from prison** s'évader de
prison

escort NOUN
l' escorte FEM ◊ *a police escort* une
escorte de police

Eskimo NOUN
l' Esquimau MASC
l' Esquimaude FEM
♦**the Eskimos** les Esquimaux

especially ADVERB
surtout ◊ *It's very hot there,*
especially in the summer. Il fait très
chaud là-bas, surtout en été.

essay NOUN
la dissertation ◊ *a history essay* une
dissertation d'histoire

essential ADJECTIVE
essentiel MASC
essentielle FEM
◊ *It's essential to bring warm clothes.*
Il est essentiel d'apporter des
vêtements chauds.

estate NOUN
la cité (*housing estate*) ◊ *I live on an*
estate. J'habite dans une cité.

estate agent NOUN
l' agent immobilier MASC

estate car NOUN
le break

to **estimate** VERB
estimer ◊ *They estimated it would*
take three weeks. Ils ont estimé que
cela prendrait trois semaines.

etc ABBREVIATION (= *et cetera*)
etc.

Ethiopia NOUN
l' Éthiopie FEM
♦**in Ethiopia** en Éthiopie

ethnic ADJECTIVE
[1] ethnique (*racial*) ◊ *an ethnic*
minority une minorité ethnique
[2] folklorique (*clothes, music*)

EU NOUN (= *European Union*)
l' Union européenne FEM

euro NOUN
l' euro MASC ◊ *50 euros* 50 euros

Eurocheque NOUN
l' eurochèque MASC

Europe NOUN
l' Europe FEM
♦**in Europe** en Europe
♦**to Europe** en Europe

European ADJECTIVE
| see also **European** NOUN |
européen MASC
européenne FEM

European NOUN
| see also **European** ADJECTIVE |
(*person*)
l' Européen MASC
l' Européenne FEM

to **evacuate** VERB
évacuer

eve NOUN
♦**Christmas Eve** la veille de Noël
♦**New Year's Eve** la Saint-Sylvestre

even ADVERB
| see also **even** ADJECTIVE |
même ◊ *I like all animals, even*
snakes. J'aime tous les animaux,
même les serpents.
♦**even if** même si ◊ *I'd never do that,*
even if you asked me. Je ne ferais
jamais ça, même si tu me le
demandais.
♦**not even** même pas ◊ *He never stops*
working, not even at the weekend. Il
n'arrête jamais de travailler, même
pas le week-end.
♦**even though** bien que
bien que has to be followed by a
verb in the subjunctive.
◊ *He's never got any money, even*
though his parents are quite rich. Il
n'a jamais d'argent, bien que ses
parents soient assez riches.
♦**even more** encore plus ◊ *I liked*
Boulogne even more than Paris. J'ai
encore plus aimé Boulogne que Paris.

even ADJECTIVE
| see also **even** ADVERB |
régulier MASC
régulière FEM
◊ *an even layer of snow* une couche
régulière de neige
♦**an even number** un nombre pair
♦**to get even with somebody** prendre
sa revanche sur quelqu'un ◊ *He*
wanted to get even with her. Il
voulait prendre sa revanche sur elle.

evening NOUN
le soir ◊ *in the evening* le soir
◊ *yesterday evening* hier soir
◊ *tomorrow evening* demain soir

E

☞

♦ **all evening** toute la soirée
♦ **Good evening!** Bonsoir!

evening class NOUN
le <u>cours du soir</u>
(les cours du soir PL)

event NOUN
l' <u>événement</u> MASC
♦ **a sporting event** une épreuve sportive

eventful ADJECTIVE
<u>mouvementé</u>

eventual ADJECTIVE
<u>final</u>
> Be careful not to translate **eventual** by **éventuel**.

eventually ADVERB
<u>finalement</u>
> Be careful not to translate **eventually** by **éventuellement**.

ever ADVERB
♦ **Have you ever been to Germany?** Est-ce que tu es déjà allé en Allemagne?
♦ **Have you ever seen her?** Vous l'avez déjà vue?
♦ **I haven't ever done that.** Je ne l'ai jamais fait.
♦ **the best I've ever seen** le meilleur que j'aie jamais vu
♦ **for the first time ever** pour la première fois
♦ **ever since** depuis que ◊ *ever since I met him* depuis que je l'ai rencontré
♦ **ever since then** depuis ce moment-là

every ADJECTIVE
<u>chaque</u> ◊ *every pupil* chaque élève
♦ **every time** chaque fois ◊ *Every time I see him he's depressed.* Chaque fois que je le vois il est déprimé.
♦ **every day** tous les jours
♦ **every week** toutes les semaines
♦ **every now and then** de temps en temps

everybody PRONOUN
<u>tout le monde</u> ◊ *Everybody had a good time.* Tout le monde s'est bien amusé. ◊ *Everybody makes mistakes.* Tout le monde peut se tromper.

everyone PRONOUN
<u>tout le monde</u> ◊ *Everyone opened their presents.* Tout le monde a ouvert ses cadeaux. ◊ *Everyone should have a hobby.* Tout le monde devrait avoir un passe-temps.

everything PRONOUN
<u>tout</u> ◊ *You've thought of everything!* Tu as pensé à tout!
♦ **Have you remembered everything?** Est-ce que tu n'as rien oublié?
♦ **Money isn't everything.** L'argent ne fait pas le bonheur.

everywhere ADVERB
<u>partout</u> ◊ *I looked everywhere, but I couldn't find it.* J'ai regardé partout, mais je n'ai pas pu le trouver.
◊ *There were policemen everywhere.* Il y avait des policiers partout.

evil ADJECTIVE
<u>mauvais</u>

ex- PREFIX
<u>ex-</u> ◊ *his ex-wife* son ex-femme

exact ADJECTIVE
<u>exact</u>

exactly ADVERB
<u>exactement</u> ◊ *exactly the same* exactement le même ◊ *not exactly* pas exactement
♦ **It's exactly 10 o'clock.** Il est dix heures précises.

to **exaggerate** VERB
<u>exagérer</u>

exaggeration NOUN
l' <u>exagération</u> FEM

exam NOUN
l' <u>examen</u> MASC ◊ *a French exam* un examen de français ◊ *the exam results* les résultats des examens MASC

examination NOUN
l' <u>examen</u> MASC

to **examine** VERB
<u>examiner</u> ◊ *He examined her passport.* Il a examiné son passeport. ◊ *The doctor examined him.* Le docteur l'a examiné.

examiner NOUN
l' <u>examinateur</u> MASC
l' <u>examinatrice</u> FEM

example NOUN
l' <u>exemple</u> MASC
♦ **for example** par exemple

excellent ADJECTIVE
<u>excellent</u> ◊ *Her results were excellent.* Elle a eu d'excellents résultats.
♦ **It was excellent fun.** C'était vraiment super.

except PREPOSITION
<u>sauf</u> ◊ *everyone except me* tout le monde sauf moi
♦ **except for** sauf
♦ **except that** sauf que ◊ *The weather was great, except that it was a bit cold.* Il a fait un temps superbe, sauf qu'il a fait un peu froid.

exception NOUN
l' <u>exception</u> FEM
♦ **to make an exception** faire une exception

exceptional ADJECTIVE
<u>exceptionnel</u> MASC

E

exceptionnelle FEM

excess baggage NOUN
l' excédent de bagages MASC

to **exchange** VERB
échanger ◇ *I exchanged the book for a video.* J'ai échangé le livre contre une vidéo.

exchange rate NOUN
le taux de change

excited ADJECTIVE
excité

exciting ADJECTIVE
passionnant

exclamation mark NOUN
le point d'exclamation

excuse NOUN
see also **excuse** VERB
l' excuse FEM

to **excuse** VERB
see also **excuse** NOUN
♦**Excuse me!** Pardon!

ex-directory ADJECTIVE
♦**to be ex-directory** être sur liste rouge
♦**to go ex-directory** se mettre sur liste rouge

to **execute** VERB
exécuter

execution NOUN
l' exécution FEM

executive NOUN
le cadre (*in business*) ◇ *He's an executive.* Il est cadre.

exercise NOUN
l' exercice MASC
♦**an exercise bike** un vélo d'appartement
♦**an exercise book** un cahier

exhausted ADJECTIVE
épuisé

exhaust fumes PL NOUN
les gaz d'échappement MASC PL

exhaust pipe NOUN
le tuyau d'échappement

exhibition NOUN
l' exposition FEM

ex-husband NOUN
l' ex-mari MASC

to **exist** VERB
exister

exit NOUN
la sortie

exotic ADJECTIVE
exotique

to **expect** VERB
1 attendre ◇ *I'm expecting him for dinner.* Je l'attends pour dîner.

◇ *She's expecting a baby.* Elle attend un enfant.
2 s'attendre à ◇ *I was expecting the worst.* Je m'attendais au pire.
3 supposer ◇ *I expect it's a mistake.* Je suppose qu'il s'agit d'une erreur.

expedition NOUN
l' expédition FEM

to **expel** VERB
♦**to get expelled** (*from school*) se faire renvoyer

expenses PL NOUN
les frais MASC PL

expensive ADJECTIVE
cher MASC
chère FEM

experience NOUN
l' expérience FEM

experienced ADJECTIVE
expérimenté

experiment NOUN
l' expérience FEM

expert NOUN
le/la spécialiste ◇ *He's a computer expert.* C'est un spécialiste en informatique.
♦**He's an expert cook.** Il cuisine très bien.

to **expire** VERB
expirer

to **explain** VERB
expliquer

explanation NOUN
l' explication FEM

to **explode** VERB
exploser

to **exploit** VERB
exploiter

exploitation NOUN
l' exploitation FEM

to **explore** VERB
explorer (*place*)

explorer NOUN
l' explorateur MASC
l' exploratrice FEM

explosion NOUN
l' explosion FEM

explosive ADJECTIVE
see also **explosive** NOUN
explosif MASC
explosive FEM

explosive NOUN
see also **explosive** ADJECTIVE
l' explosif MASC

to **express** VERB
exprimer
♦**to express oneself** s'exprimer ◇ *It's not easy to express oneself in a*

☞

foreign language. Ce n'est pas facile de s'exprimer dans une langue étrangère.

expression NOUN
l' expression FEM ◊ *It's an English expression.* C'est une expression anglaise.

expressway NOUN US
l' autoroute urbaine FEM

extension NOUN
1 l' annexe FEM (*of building*)
2 le poste (*telephone*)
In France phone numbers are broken into groups of two digits where possible.
♦**Extension 3137, please.** Poste trente et un trente-sept, s'il vous plaît.

extensive ADJECTIVE
1 vaste (*knowledge, range*) ◊ *The castle is set in extensive grounds.* Le château est situé au cœur d'un vaste domaine.
2 considérable (*damage, alterations*) ◊ *The earthquake caused extensive damage.* Le tremblement de terre a causé des dommages considérables.

extensively ADVERB
♦**He has travelled extensively in Europe.** Il a beaucoup voyagé en Europe.
♦**The building was extensively renovated last year.** Le bâtiment a été entièrement rénové l'année dernière.

extent NOUN
♦**to some extent** dans une certaine mesure

exterior ADJECTIVE
extérieur

extinct ADJECTIVE
♦**to become extinct** disparaître
♦**to be extinct** avoir disparu ◊ *The species is almost extinct.* Cette espèce a presque disparu.

extinguisher NOUN
l' extincteur MASC (*fire extinguisher*)

extortionate ADJECTIVE
exorbitant

extra ADJECTIVE, ADVERB
supplémentaire ◊ *an extra blanket* une couverture supplémentaire
♦**to pay extra** payer un supplément
♦**Breakfast is extra.** Il y a un supplément pour le petit déjeuner.
♦**It costs extra.** Il y a un supplément.

extraordinary ADJECTIVE
extraordinaire

extravagant ADJECTIVE
(*person*)
dépensier MASC
dépensière FEM

extreme ADJECTIVE
extrême

extremely ADVERB
extrêmement

extremist NOUN
l' extrémiste MASC/FEM

eye NOUN
l' œil MASC
(les yeux PL)
◊ *I've got green eyes.* J'ai les yeux verts.
♦**to keep an eye on something** surveiller quelque chose

eyebrow NOUN
le sourcil

eyelash NOUN
le cil

eyelid NOUN
la paupière

eyeliner NOUN
l' eye-liner MASC

eye shadow NOUN
l' ombre à paupières FEM

eyesight NOUN
la vue

F

fabric NOUN
le tissu

fabulous ADJECTIVE
formidable ◇ *The show was fabulous.* Le spectacle était formidable.

face NOUN

see also **face** VERB

[1] le visage (*of person*)
[2] le cadran (*of clock*)
[3] la paroi (*of cliff*)
♦ **on the face of it** à première vue
♦ **in the face of these difficulties** face à ces difficultés
♦ **face to face** face à face
♦ **a face cloth** un gant de toilette

to **face** VERB

see also **face** NOUN

faire face à (*place, problem*)
♦ **to face up to something** faire face à quelque chose ◇ *You must face up to your responsibilities.* Vous devez faire face à vos responsabilités.

face cloth NOUN
le gant de toilette

> *ℹ The French traditionally wash with a towelling glove rather than a flannel.*

facilities PL NOUN
l' équipement MASC SING ◇ *This school has excellent facilities.* Cette école dispose d'un excellent équipement.
♦ **toilet facilities** les toilettes FEM
♦ **cooking facilities** la cuisine équipée SING

fact NOUN
le fait
♦ **in fact** en fait

factory NOUN
l' usine FEM

to **fade** VERB
[1] passer (*colour*) ◇ *The colour has faded in the sun.* La couleur a passé au soleil.
♦ **My jeans have faded.** Mon jean est délavé.
[2] baisser ◇ *The light was fading fast.* La lumière baissait rapidement.
[3] diminuer ◇ *The noise gradually faded.* Le bruit a diminué peu à peu.

fag NOUN
la clope (*cigarette*)

to **fail** VERB

see also **fail** NOUN

[1] rater ◇ *I failed the history exam.* J'ai raté l'examen d'histoire.
[2] échouer ◇ *In our class, no one failed.* Dans notre classe, personne n'a échoué.
[3] lâcher ◇ *My brakes failed.* Mes freins ont lâché.
♦ **to fail to do something** ne pas faire quelque chose ◇ *She failed to return her library books.* Elle n'a pas rendu ses livres à la bibliothèque.

fail NOUN

see also **fail** VERB

♦ **without fail** sans faute

failure NOUN
[1] l' échec MASC ◇ *feelings of failure* un sentiment d'échec SING
[2] le raté
la ratée
◇ *He's a failure.* C'est un raté.
[3] la défaillance ◇ *a mechanical failure* une défaillance mécanique

faint ADJECTIVE

see also **faint** VERB

faible ◇ *His voice was very faint.* Sa voix était très faible.
♦ **to feel faint** se trouver mal

to **faint** VERB

see also **faint** ADJECTIVE

s'évanouir ◇ *All of a sudden she fainted.* Tout à coup elle s'est évanouie.

fair ADJECTIVE

see also **fair** NOUN

[1] juste ◇ *That's not fair.* Ce n'est pas juste.
[2] (*hair*)
blond ◇ *He's got fair hair.* Il a les cheveux blonds.
[3] (*skin*)
clair ◇ *people with fair skin* les gens qui ont la peau claire
[4] (*weather*)
beau MASC
belle FEM
◇ *The weather was fair.* Il faisait beau.
[5] (*good enough*)
assez bon MASC
assez bonne FEM
◇ *I have a fair chance of winning.* J'ai d'assez bonnes chances de gagner.
[6] (*sizeable*)
considérable ◇ *That's a fair distance.* Ça représente une distance considérable.

fair NOUN

see also **fair** ADJECTIVE

la foire ◊ *They went to the fair.* Ils sont allés à la foire.

♦**a trade fair** une foire commerciale

fairground NOUN

le champ de foire

fair-haired ADJECTIVE

♦**My mother is fair-haired.** Ma mère a les cheveux blonds.

fairly ADVERB

[1] équitablement ◊ *The cake was divided fairly.* Le gâteau a été partagé équitablement.

[2] assez (*quite*) ◊ *That's fairly good.* C'est assez bien.

fairness NOUN

la justice

fairy NOUN

la fée

fairy tale NOUN

le conte de fées
(les contes de fées PL)

faith NOUN

[1] la foi ◊ *the Catholic faith* la foi catholique

[2] la confiance ◊ *People have lost faith in the government.* Les gens ont perdu confiance dans le gouvernement.

faithful ADJECTIVE

fidèle

faithfully ADVERB

♦**Yours faithfully ...** (*in letter*) Veuillez agréer mes salutations distinguées ...

fake NOUN

see also **fake** ADJECTIVE

le faux ◊ *The painting was a fake.* Le tableau était un faux.

fake ADJECTIVE

see also **fake** NOUN

faux MASC

fausse FEM

◊ *She wore fake fur.* Elle portait une fausse fourrure.

fall NOUN

see also **fall** VERB

[1] la chute ◊ *a fall of snow* une chute de neige ◊ *She had a nasty fall.* Elle a fait une mauvaise chute.

♦**the Niagara Falls** les chutes du Niagara

[2] l' automne MASC (*autumn*) US

to **fall** VERB

see also **fall** NOUN

[1] tomber ◊ *He tripped and fell.* Il a trébuché et il est tombé.

[2] baisser ◊ *Prices are falling.* Les prix baissent. ·

♦**to fall down (1)** (*person*) tomber ◊ *She's fallen down.* Elle est tombée.

♦**to fall down (2)** (*building*) s'écrouler ◊ *The house is slowly falling down.* La maison est en train de s'écrouler.

♦**to fall for (1)** se laisser prendre à ◊ *They fell for it.* Ils s'y sont laissé prendre.

♦**to fall for (2)** tomber amoureux de ◊ *She's falling for him.* Elle est en train de tomber amoureuse de lui.

♦**to fall off** tomber de ◊ *The book fell off the shelf.* Le livre est tombé de l'étagère.

♦**to fall out with somebody** se fâcher avec quelqu'un ◊ *Sarah's fallen out with her boyfriend.* Sarah s'est fâchée avec son copain.

♦**to fall through** tomber à l'eau ◊ *Our plans have fallen through.* Nos projets sont tombés à l'eau.

fallen VERB *see* **fall**

false ADJECTIVE

faux MASC

fausse FEM

♦**a false alarm** une fausse alerte

♦**false teeth** les fausses dents FEM

fame NOUN

la renommée

familiar ADJECTIVE

familier MASC

familière FEM

◊ *a familiar face* un visage familier

♦**to be familiar with something** bien connaître quelque chose ◊ *I'm familiar with his work.* Je connais bien ses œuvres.

family NOUN

la famille

♦**the Cooke family** la famille Cooke

famine NOUN

la famine

famous ADJECTIVE

célèbre

fan NOUN

[1] l' éventail MASC (*hand-held*)

[2] le ventilateur (*electric*)

[3] le/la fan (*of person, band*) ◊ *I'm a fan of Take That.* Je suis une fan de Take That.

[4] le/la supporter (*of sport*) ◊ *football fans* les supporters de football

fanatic NOUN

le/la fanatique

to **fancy** VERB

♦**to fancy something** avoir envie de quelque chose ◊ *I fancy an ice cream.* J'ai envie d'une glace.

♦**to fancy doing something** avoir envie de faire quelque chose

◆**He fancies her.** Elle lui plaît.

fancy dress NOUN
le déguisement ◊ *He was wearing fancy dress.* Il portait un déguisement.
◆**a fancy-dress ball** un bal costumé

fantastic ADJECTIVE
fantastique

far ADJECTIVE, ADVERB
loin ◊ *Is it far?* Est-ce que c'est loin?
◆**far from** loin de ◊ *It's not far from London.* Ce n'est pas loin de Londres. ◊ *It's far from easy.* C'est loin d'être facile.
◆**How far is it?** C'est à quelle distance?
◆**How far is it to Geneva?** Combien y a-t-il jusqu'à Genève?
◆**How far have you got?** (*with a task*) Où en êtes-vous?
◆**at the far end** à l'autre bout ◊ *at the far end of the room* à l'autre bout de la pièce
◆**far better** beaucoup mieux
◆**as far as I know** pour autant que je sache

fare NOUN
1 le prix du billet (*on trains, buses*)
2 le prix de la course (*in taxi*)
◆**half fare** le demi-tarif
◆**full fare** le plein tarif

Far East NOUN
l' Extrême-Orient MASC
◆**in the Far East** en Extrême-Orient

farm NOUN
la ferme

farmer NOUN
l' agriculteur MASC
l' agricultrice FEM
◊ *He's a farmer.* Il est agriculteur.

farmhouse NOUN
la ferme

farming NOUN
l' agriculture FEM
◆**dairy farming** l'industrie laitière

fascinating ADJECTIVE
fascinant

fashion NOUN
la mode ◊ *a fashion show* un défilé de mode
◆**in fashion** à la mode

fashionable ADJECTIVE
à la mode ◊ *Jane wears very fashionable clothes.* Jane porte des vêtements très à la mode. ◊ *a fashionable restaurant* un restaurant à la mode

fast ADJECTIVE, ADVERB
1 vite ◊ *He can run fast.* Il sait courir vite.

2 rapide ◊ *a fast car* une voiture rapide
◆**That clock's fast.** Cette pendule avance.
◆**He's fast asleep.** Il est profondément endormi.

fat ADJECTIVE
see also **fat** NOUN
gros MASC
grosse FEM

fat NOUN
see also **fat** ADJECTIVE
1 le gras (*on meat, in food*) ◊ *It's very high in fat.* C'est très gras.
2 la matière grasse (*for cooking*)

fatal ADJECTIVE
1 (*causing death*)
mortel MASC
mortelle FEM
◊ *a fatal accident* un accident mortel
2 (*disastrous*)
fatal ◊ *He made a fatal mistake.* Il a fait une erreur fatale.

father NOUN
le père ◊ *my father* mon père

father-in-law NOUN
le beau-père
(les beaux-pères PL)

faucet NOUN US
le robinet

fault NOUN
1 la faute (*mistake*) ◊ *It's my fault.* C'est de ma faute.
2 le défaut (*defect*) ◊ *There's a fault in this material.* Ce tissu a un défaut.
◆**a mechanical fault** une défaillance mécanique

faulty ADJECTIVE
défectueux MASC
défectueuse FEM
◊ *This machine is faulty.* Cette machine est défectueuse.

favour NOUN (US **favor**)
le service
◆**to do somebody a favour** rendre service à quelqu'un ◊ *Could you do me a favour?* Tu peux me rendre service?
◆**to be in favour of something** être pour quelque chose ◊ *I'm in favour of nuclear disarmament.* Je suis pour le désarmement nucléaire.

favourite ADJECTIVE (US **favorite**)
see also **favourite** NOUN
favori MASC
favorite FEM
◊ *Blue's my favourite colour.* Le bleu est ma couleur favorite.

favourite NOUN (US **favorite**)

F

see also **favourite** ADJECTIVE
le favori
la favorite ◇ *Liverpool are favourites to win the Cup.* L'équipe de Liverpool est favorite pour la coupe.

fax NOUN
see also **fax** VERB
le fax
♦**to send somebody a fax** envoyer un fax à quelqu'un

to **fax** VERB
see also **fax** NOUN
♦**to fax somebody** envoyer un fax à quelqu'un

fear NOUN
see also **fear** VERB
la peur

to **fear** VERB
see also **fear** NOUN
craindre ◇ *You have nothing to fear.* Vous n'avez rien à craindre.

feather NOUN
la plume

feature NOUN
la caractéristique (*of person, object*) ◇ *an important feature* une caractéristique essentielle

February NOUN
février MASC
♦**in February** en février

fed VERB *see* **feed**

fed up ADJECTIVE
♦**to be fed up with something** en avoir marre de quelque chose ◇ *I'm fed up of waiting for him.* J'en ai marre de l'attendre.

to **feed** VERB
donner à manger à ◇ *Have you fed the cat?* Est-ce que tu as donné à manger au chat?
♦**He worked hard to feed his family.** Il travaillait dur pour nourrir sa famille.

to **feel** VERB
1 se sentir ◇ *I don't feel well.* Je ne me sens pas bien. ◇ *I feel a bit lonely.* Je me sens un peu seul.
2 sentir ◇ *I didn't feel much pain.* Je n'ai presque rien senti.
3 toucher ◇ *The doctor felt his forehead.* Le docteur lui a touché le front.
♦**I was feeling hungry.** J'avais faim.
♦**I was feeling cold, so I went inside.** J'avais froid, alors je suis rentré.
♦**I feel like ...** (*want*) J'ai envie de ... ◇ *Do you feel like an ice cream?* Tu as envie d'une glace?

feeling NOUN

1 la sensation (*physical*) ◇ *a burning feeling* une sensation de brûlure
2 le sentiment (*emotional*) ◇ *a feeling of satisfaction* un sentiment de satisfaction

feet PL NOUN *see* **foot**

fell VERB *see* **fall**

felt VERB *see* **feel**

felt-tip pen NOUN
le stylo-feutre

female ADJECTIVE
see also **female** NOUN
1 femelle ◇ *a female animal* un animal femelle
2 féminin ◇ *the female sex* le sexe féminin

female NOUN
see also **female** ADJECTIVE
la femelle (*animal*)

feminine ADJECTIVE
féminin

feminist NOUN
le/la féministe

fence NOUN
la barrière

fern NOUN
la fougère

ferret NOUN
le furet

ferry NOUN
le ferry

fertile ADJECTIVE
fertile

fertilizer NOUN
l' engrais MASC

festival NOUN
le festival ◇ *a jazz festival* un festival de jazz

to **fetch** VERB
1 aller chercher ◇ *Fetch the bucket.* Va chercher le seau.
2 se vendre (*sell for*) ◇ *His painting fetched £5000.* Son tableau s'est vendu cinq mille livres.

fever NOUN
la fièvre (*temperature*)

few ADJECTIVE, PRONOUN
peu de (*not many*) ◇ *few books* peu de livres
♦**a few (1)** quelques ◇ *a few hours* quelques heures
♦**a few (2)** quelques-uns ◇ *How many apples do you want? – A few.* Tu veux combien de pommes? – Quelques-unes.
♦**quite a few people** pas mal de monde

fewer ADJECTIVE

moins de ◊ *There are fewer people than there were yesterday.* Il y a moins de monde qu'hier. ◊ *There are fewer pupils in this class.* Il y a moins d'élèves dans cette classe.

fiancé NOUN
le fiancé ◊ *He's my fiancé.* C'est mon fiancé.

fiancée NOUN
la fiancée ◊ *She's my fiancée.* C'est ma fiancée.

fiction NOUN
les romans MASC PL (*novels*)

field NOUN
1 le champ (*in countryside*) ◊ *a field of wheat* un champ de blé
2 le terrain (*for sport*) ◊ *a football field* un terrain de football
3 le domaine (*subject*) ◊ *He's an expert in his field.* C'est un expert dans son domaine.

fierce ADJECTIVE
1 féroce ◊ *The dog looked very fierce.* Le chien avait l'air très féroce.
2 violent ◊ *The wind was very fierce.* Le vent était très violent. ◊ *a fierce attack* une attaque violente

fifteen NUMBER
quinze ◊ *I'm fifteen.* J'ai quinze ans.

fifteenth ADJECTIVE
quinzième ◊ *the fifteenth floor* le quinzième étage
♦ **the fifteenth of August** le quinze août

fifth ADJECTIVE
cinquième ◊ *the fifth floor* le cinquième étage
♦ **the fifth of August** le cinq août

fifty NUMBER
cinquante ◊ *He's fifty.* Il a cinquante ans.

fifty-fifty ADJECTIVE, ADVERB
moitié-moitié ◊ *They split the prize money fifty-fifty.* Ils ont partagé l'argent du prix moitié-moitié.
♦ **a fifty-fifty chance** une chance sur deux

fight NOUN
see also **fight** VERB
1 la bagarre ◊ *There was a fight in the pub.* Il y a eu une bagarre au pub.
2 la lutte ◊ *the fight against cancer* la lutte contre le cancer

to **fight** VERB
see also **fight** NOUN
1 se battre ◊ *They were fighting.* Ils se battaient.
2 lutter contre ◊ *The doctors tried to fight the disease.* Les médecins

ont essayé de lutter contre la maladie. ◊ *He fought against the urge to smoke.* Il a lutté contre son envie de fumer.

fighting NOUN
les bagarres FEM PL ◊ *Fighting broke out outside the pub.* Des bagarres ont éclaté devant le pub.

figure NOUN
1 le chiffre (*number*) ◊ *Can you give me the exact figures?* Pouvez-vous me donner les chiffres exacts?
2 la silhouette (*outline of person*) ◊ *Hélène saw the figure of a man on the bridge.* Hélène a vu la silhouette d'un homme sur le pont.
♦ **She's got a good figure.** Elle est bien faite.
♦ **I have to watch my figure.** Je dois faire attention à ma ligne.
3 le personnage (*personality*) ◊ *She's an important political figure.* C'est un personnage politique important.

to **figure out** VERB
1 calculer ◊ *I'll try to figure out how much it'll cost.* Je vais essayer de calculer combien ça va coûter.
2 voir ◊ *I couldn't figure out what it meant.* Je n'arrivais pas à voir ce que ça voulait dire.
3 cerner ◊ *I can't figure him out at all.* Je n'arrive pas du tout à le cerner.

file NOUN
see also **file** VERB
1 le dossier (*document*) ◊ *Have we got a file on the suspect?* Est-ce que nous avons un dossier sur le suspect?
2 la chemise (*folder*) ◊ *She keeps all her letters in a cardboard file.* Elle garde toutes ses lettres dans une chemise en carton.
3 le classeur (*ring binder*)
4 le fichier (*on computer*)
5 la lime (*for nails, metal*)

to **file** VERB
see also **file** NOUN
1 classer (*papers*)
2 limer (*nails, metal*) ◊ *to file one's nails* se limer les ongles

to **fill** VERB
remplir ◊ *She filled the glass with water.* Elle a rempli le verre d'eau.
♦ **to fill in (1)** remplir ◊ *Can you fill this form in please?* Est-ce que vous pouvez remplir ce formulaire s'il vous plaît?

◆**to fill in (2)** boucher ◊ *He filled the hole in with soil.* Il a bouché le trou avec de la terre.

◆**to fill up** remplir ◊ *He filled the cup up to the brim.* Il a rempli la tasse à ras bords.

◆**Fill it up, please.** (*at petrol station*) Le plein, s'il vous plaît.

film NOUN
[1] le film (*movie*)
[2] la pellicule (*for camera*)

film star NOUN
la vedette de cinéma ◊ *He's a film star.* C'est une vedette de cinéma.

filthy ADJECTIVE
dégoûtant

final ADJECTIVE
see also **final** NOUN
[1] (*last*)
dernier MASC
dernière FEM
◊ *our final farewells* nos derniers adieux
[2] (*definite*)
définitif MASC
définitive FEM
◊ *a final decision* une décision définitive

◆**I'm not going and that's final.** Je n'y vais pas, un point c'est tout.

final NOUN
see also **final** ADJECTIVE
la finale ◊ *Boris Becker is in the final.* Boris Becker va disputer la finale.

finally ADVERB
[1] enfin (*lastly*) ◊ *Finally, I would like to say ...* Enfin, je voudrais dire ...
[2] finalement (*eventually*) ◊ *They finally decided to leave on Saturday instead of Friday.* Ils ont finalement décidé de partir samedi au lieu de vendredi.

to **find** VERB
[1] trouver ◊ *I can't find the exit.* Je ne trouve pas la sortie.
[2] retrouver (*something lost*) ◊ *Did you find your pen?* Est-ce que tu as retrouvé ton crayon?

◆**to find something out** découvrir quelque chose ◊ *I'm determined to find out the truth.* Je suis décidé à découvrir la vérité.

◆**to find out about (1)** (*make enquiries*) se renseigner sur ◊ *Try to find out about the cost of a hotel.* Essaye de te renseigner sur le prix d'un hôtel.

◆**to find out about (2)** (*by chance*) apprendre ◊ *I found out about their affair.* J'ai appris leur liaison.

fine ADJECTIVE, ADVERB
see also **fine** NOUN
[1] excellent (*very good*) ◊ *He's a fine musician.* C'est un excellent musicien.

◆**to be fine** aller bien ◊ *How are you? – I'm fine.* Comment ça va? – Ça va bien.

◆**I feel fine.** Je me sens bien.

◆**The weather is fine today.** Il fait beau aujourd'hui.
[2] fin (*not coarse*) ◊ *She's got very fine hair.* Elle a les cheveux très fins.

fine NOUN
see also **fine** ADJECTIVE
[1] l' amende FEM ◊ *She got a £50 fine.* Elle a eu une amende de cinquante livres.
[2] la contravention (*for traffic offence*) ◊ *I got a fine for driving through a red light.* J'ai eu une contravention pour avoir grillé un feu rouge.

finger NOUN
le doigt

◆**my little finger** mon petit doigt

fingernail NOUN
l' ongle MASC

finish NOUN
see also **finish** VERB
l' arrivée FEM (*of race*) ◊ *We saw the finish of the London Marathon.* Nous avons vu l'arrivée du marathon de Londres.

to **finish** VERB
see also **finish** NOUN
[1] finir ◊ *I've finished!* J'ai fini!

◆**to finish doing something** finir de faire quelque chose
[2] terminer ◊ *I've finished the book.* J'ai terminé ce livre. ◊ *The film has finished.* Le film est terminé.

Finland NOUN
la Finlande
◆**in Finland** en Finlande
◆**to Finland** en Finlande

Finn NOUN
le Finlandais
la Finlandaise

Finnish ADJECTIVE
see also **Finnish** NOUN
finlandais

Finnish NOUN
see also **Finnish** ADJECTIVE
le finnois (*language*)

fire NOUN
see also **fire** VERB
[1] le feu
(les feux PL)
◊ *He made a fire to warm himself up.* Il a fait du feu pour se réchauffer.

♦**to be on fire** être en feu
[2] (*accidental*)
l' <u>incendie</u> MASC ◊ *The house was destroyed by fire.* La maison a été détruite par un incendie.
[3] (*heater*)
le <u>radiateur</u> ◊ *Turn the fire on.* Allume le radiateur.

♦**the fire brigade** les pompiers MASC PL
♦**a fire alarm** un avertisseur d'incendie
♦**a fire engine** une voiture de pompiers
♦**a fire escape** un escalier de secours
♦**a fire extinguisher** un extincteur
♦**a fire station** une caserne de pompiers

to **fire** VERB
see also **fire** NOUN
<u>tirer</u> (*shoot*) ◊ *She fired twice.* Elle a tiré deux fois.

♦**to fire at somebody** tirer sur quelqu'un ◊ *The terrorist fired at the crowd.* Le terroriste a tiré sur la foule.
♦**to fire a gun** tirer un coup de feu
♦**to fire somebody** mettre quelqu'un à la porte ◊ *He was fired from his job.* Il a été mis à la porte.

fireman NOUN
le <u>pompier</u> ◊ *He's a fireman.* Il est pompier.

fireplace NOUN
la <u>cheminée</u>

fire station NOUN
la <u>caserne de pompiers</u>

fireworks PL NOUN
le <u>feu d'artifice</u> SING ◊ *Are you going to see the fireworks?* Est-ce que tu vas voir le feu d'artifice?

firm ADJECTIVE
see also **firm** NOUN
<u>ferme</u> ◊ *to be firm with somebody* se montrer ferme avec quelqu'un

firm NOUN
see also **firm** ADJECTIVE
l' <u>entreprise</u> FEM ◊ *He works for a large firm in London.* Il travaille pour une grande entreprise à Londres.

first ADJECTIVE, ADVERB
see also **first** NOUN
[1] <u>premier</u> MASC
<u>première</u> FEM
◊ *the first of September* le premier septembre ◊ *the first time* la première fois

♦**to come first** (*in exam, race*) arriver premier ◊ *Rachel came first.* Rachel est arrivée première.
[2] <u>d'abord</u> ◊ *I want to get a job, but first I have to pass my exams.* Je

veux trouver du travail, mais d'abord je dois réussir à mes examens.
♦**first of all** tout d'abord

first NOUN
see also **first** ADJECTIVE
le <u>premier</u>
la <u>première</u>
◊ *She was the first to arrive.* Elle est arrivée la première.
♦**at first** au début

first aid NOUN
les <u>premiers secours</u> MASC PL
♦**a first aid kit** une trousse de secours

first-class ADJECTIVE
[1] <u>de première classe</u> ◊ *She has booked a first-class ticket.* Elle a réservé un billet de première classe.
[2] <u>excellent</u> ◊ *a first-class meal* un excellent repas
♦**a first-class stamp**

> ❶ *In France there is no first-class or second-class postage. However letters cost more to send than postcards, so you have to remember to say what you are sending when buying stamps.*

firstly ADVERB
<u>premièrement</u> ◊ *Firstly, let's see what the book is about.* Premièrement, voyons de quoi parle ce livre.

fir tree NOUN
le <u>sapin</u>

fish NOUN
see also **fish** VERB
le <u>poisson</u> ◊ *I caught three fish.* J'ai pêché trois poissons. ◊ *I don't like fish.* Je n'aime pas le poisson.

to **fish** VERB
see also **fish** NOUN
<u>pêcher</u>
♦**to go fishing** aller à la pêche ◊ *We went fishing in the River Dee.* Nous sommes allés à la pêche sur la Dee.

fisherman NOUN
le <u>pêcheur</u> ◊ *He's a fisherman.* Il est pêcheur.

fish fingers PL NOUN
les <u>bâtonnets de poisson</u> MASC PL

fishing NOUN
la <u>pêche</u> ◊ *My hobby is fishing.* La pêche est mon passe-temps favori.

fishing boat NOUN
le <u>bateau de pêche</u>

fishing rod NOUN
la <u>canne à pêche</u>

fishing tackle NOUN

F

☞

le matériel de pêche

fish sticks PL NOUN US
les bâtonnets de poisson MASC PL

fist NOUN
le poing

to **fit** VERB
> see also **fit** ADJECTIVE, NOUN

[1] être la bonne taille (be the right size) ◊ Does it fit? Est-ce que c'est la bonne taille?

> In French you usually specify whether something is too big, small, tight etc.

◆**These trousers don't fit me. (1)** (too big) Ce pantalon est trop grand pour moi.
◆**These trousers don't fit me. (2)** (too small) Ce pantalon est trop petit pour moi.
[2] installer (fix up) ◊ He fitted an alarm in his car. Il a installé une alarme dans sa voiture.
[3] adapter (attach) ◊ She fitted a plug to the hair dryer. Elle a adapté une prise au sèche-cheveux.
◆**to fit in (1)** (match up) correspondre ◊ That story doesn't fit in with what he told us. Cette histoire ne correspond pas à ce qu'il nous a dit.
◆**to fit in (2)** (person) s'adapter ◊ She fitted in well at her new school. Elle s'est bien adaptée à sa nouvelle école.

fit ADJECTIVE
> see also **fit** VERB, NOUN

en forme (in condition) ◊ He felt relaxed and fit after his holiday. Il se sentait détendu et en forme après ses vacances.

fit NOUN
> see also **fit** ADJECTIVE, VERB

◆**to have a fit (1)** (epileptic) avoir une crise d'épilepsie
◆**to have a fit (2)** (be angry) piquer une crise de nerfs ◊ My Mum will have a fit when she sees the carpet! Ma mère va piquer une crise de nerfs quand elle va voir la moquette!

fitted carpet NOUN
la moquette

fitted kitchen NOUN
la cuisine aménagée

fitting room NOUN
la cabine d'essayage

five NUMBER
cinq ◊ He's five. Il a cinq ans.

to **fix** VERB

[1] réparer (mend) ◊ Can you fix my bike? Est-ce que tu peux réparer mon vélo?
[2] fixer (decide) ◊ Let's fix a date for the party. Fixons une date pour la soirée. ◊ They fixed a price for the car. Ils ont fixé un prix pour la voiture.
[3] préparer ◊ Janice fixed some food for us. Janice nous a préparé à manger.

fixed ADJECTIVE
fixe ◊ at a fixed time à une heure fixe ◊ at a fixed price à un prix fixe ◊ a fixed-price menu un menu à prix fixe
◆**My parents have very fixed ideas.** Mes parents ont des idées très arrêtées.

fizzy ADJECTIVE
gazeux MASC
gazeuse FEM
◊ I don't like fizzy drinks. Je n'aime pas les boissons gazeuses.

flabby ADJECTIVE
flasque

flag NOUN
le drapeau
(les drapeaux PL)

flame NOUN
la flamme

flamingo NOUN
le flamant rose

flan NOUN
[1] la tarte (sweet) ◊ a raspberry flan une tarte aux framboises
[2] la quiche (savoury) ◊ a cheese and onion flan une quiche au fromage et aux oignons

flannel NOUN
le gant de toilette (for face)

to **flap** VERB
battre de ◊ The bird flapped its wings. L'oiseau battait des ailes.

flash NOUN
> see also **flash** VERB

le flash
(les flashes PL)
◊ Has your camera got a flash? Est-ce que ton appareil photo a un flash?
◆**a flash of lightning** un éclair
◆**in a flash** en un clin d'œil

to **flash** VERB
> see also **flash** NOUN

[1] clignoter ◊ The police car's blue light was flashing. Le gyrophare de la voiture de police clignotait.

2 projeter ◊ *They flashed a torch in his face.* Ils lui ont projeté la lumière d'une torche en plein visage.
♦**She flashed her headlights.** Elle a fait un appel de phares.

flask NOUN
le thermos (*vacuum flask*)

flat ADJECTIVE
see also **flat** NOUN
1 plat ◊ *a flat roof* un toit plat ◊ *flat shoes* des chaussures plates
2 crevé (*tyre*) ◊ *I've got a flat tyre.* J'ai un pneu crevé.

flat NOUN
see also **flat** ADJECTIVE
l' appartement MASC ◊ *She lives in a flat.* Elle habite un appartement.

to **flatter** VERB
flatter

flattered ADJECTIVE
flatté

flavour NOUN
1 le goût (*taste*) ◊ *It has a very strong flavour.* Ça a un goût très fort.
2 le parfum (*variety*) ◊ *Which flavour of ice cream would you like?* Quel parfum de glace est-ce que tu veux?

flavouring NOUN
le parfum

flew VERB see **fly**

flexible ADJECTIVE
flexible ◊ *flexible working hours* les horaires flexibles MASC

to **flick** VERB
appuyer sur ◊ *She flicked the switch to turn the light on.* Elle a appuyé sur le bouton pour allumer la lumière.
♦**to flick through a book** feuilleter un livre

to **flicker** VERB
trembloter ◊ *The light flickered.* La lumière a trembloté.

flight NOUN
le vol ◊ *What time is the flight to Paris?* À quelle heure est le vol pour Paris?
♦**a flight of stairs** un escalier

flight attendant NOUN
1 l' hôtesse de l'air FEM (*woman*)
2 le steward (*man*)

to **fling** VERB
jeter ◊ *He flung the book onto the floor.* Il a jeté le livre par terre.

flippers NOUN
les palmes FEM PL

to **float** VERB
flotter ◊ *A leaf was floating on the water.* Une feuille flottait sur l'eau.

flock NOUN
♦**a flock of sheep** un troupeau de moutons
♦**a flock of birds** un vol d'oiseaux

flood NOUN
see also **flood** VERB
1 l' inondation FEM ◊ *The rain has caused many floods.* La pluie a provoqué de nombreuses inondations.
2 le flot ◊ *He received a flood of letters.* Il a reçu un flot de lettres.

to **flood** VERB
see also **flood** NOUN
inonder ◊ *The river has flooded the village.* La rivière a inondé le village.

flooding NOUN
les inondations FEM PL

floor NOUN
1 le sol ◊ *a tiled floor* un sol carrelé
♦**on the floor** par terre
2 l' étage MASC (*storey*) ◊ *the first floor* le premier étage
♦**the ground floor** le rez-de-chaussée
♦**on the third floor** au troisième étage

flop NOUN
le fiasco ◊ *The film was a flop.* Le film a été un fiasco.

floppy disk NOUN
la disquette

florist NOUN
le/la fleuriste

flour NOUN
la farine

to **flow** VERB
1 couler (*river*)
2 s'écouler (*flow out*) ◊ *Water was flowing from the pipe.* De l'eau s'écoulait du tuyau.

flower NOUN
see also **flower** VERB
la fleur

to **flower** VERB
see also **flower** NOUN
fleurir

flown VERB see **fly**

flu NOUN
la grippe ◊ *She's got flu.* Elle a la grippe.

fluent ADJECTIVE
♦**He speaks fluent French.** Il parle couramment le français.

flung VERB see **fling**

flush NOUN
see also **flush** VERB
la chasse d'eau (*of toilet*)

to **flush** VERB
see also **flush** NOUN

F

☞

♦ **to flush the toilet** tirer la chasse

flute NOUN
la flûte ◊ *I play the flute.* Je joue de la flûte.

fly NOUN
see also **fly** VERB
la mouche (*insect*)

to **fly** VERB
see also **fly** NOUN
[1] voler ◊ *The plane flies at a speed of 400 km per hour.* L'avion vole à quatre cents kilomètres à l'heure.
[2] aller en avion (*passenger*) ◊ *He flew from Paris to New York.* Il est allé de Paris à New York en avion.
♦ **to fly away** s'envoler ◊ *The bird flew away.* L'oiseau s'est envolé.

foal NOUN
le poulain

focus NOUN
see also **focus** VERB
♦ **to be out of focus** être flou ◊ *The house is out of focus in this photo.* La maison est floue sur cette photo.

to **focus** VERB
see also **focus** NOUN
mettre au point ◊ *Try to focus the binoculars.* Essaye de mettre les jumelles au point.
♦ **to focus on something (1)** (*with camera, telescope*) régler la mise au point sur quelque chose ◊ *The cameraman focused on the bird.* Le caméraman a réglé la mise au point sur l'oiseau.
♦ **to focus on something (2)** (*concentrate*) se concentrer sur quelque chose ◊ *Let's focus on the plot of the play.* Concentrons-nous sur l'intrigue de la pièce.

fog NOUN
le brouillard

foggy ADJECTIVE
♦ **It's foggy.** Il y a du brouillard.
♦ **a foggy day** un jour de brouillard

foil NOUN
le papier d'aluminium (*kitchen foil*) ◊ *She wrapped the meat in foil.* Elle a enveloppé la viande dans du papier d'aluminium.

fold NOUN
see also **fold** VERB
le pli

to **fold** VERB
see also **fold** NOUN
plier ◊ *He folded the newspaper in half.* Il a plié le journal en deux.
♦ **to fold something up** plier quelque chose

♦ **to fold one's arms** croiser ses bras ◊ *She folded her arms.* Elle a croisé les bras.

folder NOUN
[1] la chemise ◊ *She kept all her letters in a folder.* Elle gardait toutes ses lettres dans une chemise.
[2] le classeur (*ring binder*)

folding ADJECTIVE
♦ **a folding chair** une chaise pliante
♦ **a folding bed** un lit pliant

to **follow** VERB
suivre ◊ *She followed him.* Elle l'a suivi. ◊ *You go first and I'll follow.* Va devant, je te suis.

following ADJECTIVE
suivant ◊ *the following day* le jour suivant

fond ADJECTIVE
♦ **to be fond of somebody** aimer beaucoup quelqu'un ◊ *I'm very fond of her.* Je l'aime beaucoup.

food NOUN
la nourriture
♦ **We need to buy some food.** Nous devons acheter à manger.
♦ **cat food** la nourriture pour chat
♦ **dog food** la nourriture pour chien

food processor NOUN
le robot

fool NOUN
l' idiot MASC
l' idiote FEM

foot NOUN
[1] le pied (*of person*) ◊ *My feet are aching.* J'ai mal aux pieds.
[2] la patte (*of animal*) ◊ *The dog's foot was injured.* Le chien était blessé à la patte.
♦ **on foot** à pied
[3] le pied (*12 inches*)

> ⓘ In France measurements are in metres and centimetres rather than feet and inches. A foot is about 30 centimetres.

♦ **Dave is 6 foot tall.** Dave mesure un mètre quatre-vingt.
♦ **That mountain is 5000 feet high.** Cette montagne fait mille six cents mètres de haut.

football NOUN
[1] le football (*game*) ◊ *I like playing football.* J'aime jouer au football.
[2] le ballon (*ball*) ◊ *Paul threw the football over the fence.* Paul a envoyé le ballon par dessus la clôture.

footballer NOUN

le <u>footballeur</u>
la <u>footballeuse</u>

football player NOUN
　le <u>joueur de football</u>
　la <u>joueuse de football</u>
　◊ *He's a famous football player.* C'est
　un joueur de football célèbre.

footie NOUN
　le <u>foot</u>

footpath NOUN
　le <u>sentier</u> ◊ *Jane followed the
　footpath through the forest.* Jane a
　suivi le sentier à travers la forêt.

footprint NOUN
　la <u>trace de pas</u> ◊ *He saw some
　footprints in the sand.* Il a vu des
　traces de pas sur le sable.

footstep NOUN
　le <u>pas</u> ◊ *I can hear footsteps on the
　stairs.* J'entends des pas dans
　l'escalier.

for PREPOSITION
　　*There are several ways of translating
　　for. Scan the examples to find one
　　that is similar to what you want to
　　say.*
　⬚1 <u>pour</u> ◊ *a present for me* un
　cadeau pour moi ◊ *the train for
　London* le train pour Londres ◊ *He
　works for the government.* Il travaille
　pour le gouvernement. ◊ *I'll do it for
　you.* Je vais le faire pour toi. ◊ *Can
　you do it for tomorrow?* Est-ce que
　vous pouvez le faire pour demain?
　◊ *Are you for or against the idea?*
　Êtes-vous pour ou contre cette idée?
　◊ *Oxford is famous for its university.*
　Oxford est célèbre pour son
　université.
　　*When referring to periods of time,
　　use **pendant** for the future and
　　completed actions in the past, and
　　depuis (with the French verb in the
　　present tense) for something that
　　started in the past and is still going
　　on.*
　⬚2 <u>pendant</u> ◊ *He worked in France
　for two years.* Il a travaillé en France
　pendant deux ans. ◊ *She will be
　away for a month.* Elle sera absente
　pendant un mois. ◊ *There are road
　works for three kilometres.* Il y a des
　travaux pendant trois kilomètres.
　⬚3 <u>depuis</u> ◊ *He's been learning
　French for two years.* Il apprend le
　français depuis deux ans. ◊ *She's
　been away for a month.* Elle est
　absente depuis un mois.
　　*When talking about amounts of
　　money, you do not translate for.*

◊ *I sold it for £5.* Je l'ai vendu cinq
livres. ◊ *He paid fifty pence for his
ticket.* Il a payé son billet cinquante
pence.
　♦**What's the French for "lion"?**
　Comment dit-on "lion" en français?
　♦**It's time for lunch.** C'est l'heure du
　déjeuner.
　♦**What for?** Pour quoi faire? ◊ *Give me
　some money! – What for?* Donne-moi
　de l'argent! – Pour quoi faire?
　♦**What's it for?** Ça sert à quoi?
　♦**for sale** à vendre ◊ *The factory's for
　sale.* L'usine est en vente.

to **forbid** VERB
　<u>défendre</u>
　♦**to forbid somebody to do something**
　défendre à quelqu'un de faire
　quelque chose ◊ *I forbid you to go
　out tonight!* Je te défends de sortir
　ce soir.

forbidden ADJECTIVE
　<u>défendu</u> ◊ *Smoking is strictly
　forbidden.* Il est strictement défendu
　de fumer.

force NOUN
　`see also` **force** VERB
　la <u>force</u> ◊ *the force of the explosion*
　la force de l'explosion
　♦**in force** en vigueur ◊ *No-smoking
　rules are now in force.* Un règlement
　qui interdit de fumer est maintenant
　en vigueur.

to **force** VERB
　`see also` **force** NOUN
　<u>forcer</u> ◊ *They forced him to open the
　safe.* Ils l'ont obligé à ouvrir le
　coffre-fort.

forecast NOUN
　♦**the weather forecast** la météo

foreground NOUN
　le <u>premier plan</u> ◊ *in the foreground*
　au premier plan

forehead NOUN
　le <u>front</u>

foreign ADJECTIVE
　<u>étranger</u> MASC
　<u>étrangère</u> FEM

foreigner NOUN
　l' <u>étranger</u> MASC
　l' <u>étrangère</u> FEM

to **foresee** VERB
　<u>prévoir</u> ◊ *He had foreseen the
　problem.* Il avait prévu ce problème.

forest NOUN
　la <u>forêt</u>

forever ADVERB
　⬚1 <u>pour toujours</u> ◊ *He's gone
　forever.* Il est parti pour toujours.

F

[2] toujours (*always*) ◊ *She's forever complaining.* Elle est toujours en train de se plaindre.

forgave VERB *see* **forgive**

to **forge** VERB
contrefaire ◊ *She tried to forge his signature.* Elle a essayé de contrefaire sa signature.

forged ADJECTIVE
faux MASC
fausse FEM
◊ *forged banknotes* des faux billets

to **forget** VERB
oublier ◊ *I've forgotten his name.* J'ai oublié son nom. ◊ *I'm sorry, I completely forgot!* Je suis désolé, j'ai complètement oublié!

to **forgive** VERB
♦ **to forgive somebody** pardonner à quelqu'un ◊ *I forgive you.* Je te pardonne.
♦ **to forgive somebody for doing something** pardonner à quelqu'un d'avoir fait quelque chose ◊ *She forgave him for forgetting her birthday.* Elle lui a pardonné d'avoir oublié son anniversaire.

forgot, forgotten VERB *see* **forget**

fork NOUN
[1] la fourchette (*for eating*)
[2] la fourche (*for gardening*)
[3] la bifurcation (*in road*)

form NOUN
[1] le formulaire (*paper*) ◊ *to fill in a form* remplir un formulaire
[2] la forme (*type*) ◊ *I'm against hunting in any form.* Je suis contre la chasse sous toutes ses formes.
♦ **in top form** en pleine forme
♦ **She's in the fourth form.** Elle est en troisième.

formal ADJECTIVE
[1] (*occasion*)
officiel MASC
officielle FEM
◊ *a formal dinner* un dîner officiel
[2] (*person*)
guindé
[3] (*language*)
soutenu ◊ *In English, "residence" is a formal term.* En anglais, "residence" est un terme soutenu.
♦ **formal clothes** une tenue habillée
♦ **He's got no formal education.** Il n'a pas fait beaucoup d'études.

former ADJECTIVE
ancien MASC
ancienne FEM

◊ *a former pupil* un ancien élève
◊ *the former Prime Minister* l'ancien Premier ministre

formerly ADVERB
autrefois

fort NOUN
le fort

forth ADVERB
♦ **to go back and forth** aller et venir
♦ **and so forth** et ainsi de suite

fortnight NOUN
♦ **a fortnight** quinze jours ◊ *I'm going on holiday for a fortnight.* Je pars en vacances pendant quinze jours.

fortunate ADJECTIVE
♦ **to be fortunate** avoir de la chance
◊ *He was extremely fortunate to survive.* Il a eu énormément de chance de survivre.
♦ **It's fortunate that I remembered the map.** C'est une chance que j'aie pris la carte.

fortunately ADVERB
heureusement ◊ *Fortunately, it didn't rain.* Heureusement, il n'a pas plu.

fortune NOUN
la fortune ◊ *Kate earns a fortune!* Kate gagne une fortune!
♦ **to tell somebody's fortune** dire la bonne aventure à quelqu'un

forty NUMBER
quarante ◊ *He's forty.* Il a quarante ans.

forward ADVERB
see also **forward** VERB
♦ **to move forward** avancer

to **forward** VERB
see also **forward** ADVERB
faire suivre ◊ *He forwarded all Janette's letters.* Il a fait suivre toutes les lettres de Janette.

forward slash NOUN
la barre oblique

to **foster** VERB
♦ **She has fostered more than fifteen children.** Plus de quinze enfants ont été placés chez elle.

foster child NOUN
l' enfant adoptif MASC
l' enfant adoptive FEM

fought VERB *see* **fight**

foul ADJECTIVE
see also **foul** NOUN
infect ◊ *The weather was foul.* Le temps était infect. ◊ *What a foul smell!* Quelle odeur infecte!

foul NOUN
see also **foul** ADJECTIVE

la <u>faute</u> ◇ *Ferguson committed a foul.* Ferguson a fait une faute.

found VERB *see* **find**

to **found** VERB
<u>fonder</u> ◇ *Baden Powell founded the Scout Movement.* Baden Powell a fondé le mouvement scout.

foundations PL NOUN
les <u>fondations</u> FEM PL

fountain NOUN
la <u>fontaine</u>

fountain pen NOUN
le <u>stylo à encre</u>

four NUMBER
<u>quatre</u> ◇ *She's four.* Elle a quatre ans.

fourteen NUMBER
<u>quatorze</u> ◇ *I'm fourteen.* J'ai quatorze ans.

fourteenth ADJECTIVE
<u>quatorzième</u> ◇ *the fourteenth floor* le quatorzième étage
♦**the fourteenth of August** le quatorze août

fourth ADJECTIVE
<u>quatrième</u> ◇ *the fourth floor* le quatrième étage
♦**the fourth of July** le quatre juillet

fox NOUN
le <u>renard</u>

fragile ADJECTIVE
<u>fragile</u>

frame NOUN
le <u>cadre</u> (*for picture*)

France NOUN
la <u>France</u>
♦**in France** en France
♦**to France** en France
♦**He's from France.** Il est français.

frantic ADJECTIVE
♦**I was going frantic.** J'étais dans tous mes états.
♦**to be frantic with worry** être folle d'inquiétude

fraud NOUN
① la <u>fraude</u> (*crime*) ◇ *He was jailed for fraud.* On l'a mis en prison pour fraude.
② l' <u>imposteur</u> MASC (*person*) ◇ *He's not a real doctor, he's a fraud.* Ce n'est pas un vrai médecin, c'est un imposteur.

freckles PL NOUN
les <u>taches de rousseur</u> FEM PL

free ADJECTIVE
see also **free** VERB
① <u>gratuit</u> (*free of charge*) ◇ *a free brochure* une brochure gratuite

② <u>libre</u> (*not busy, not taken*) ◇ *Is this seat free?* Est-ce que cette place est libre? ◇ *Are you free after school?* Tu es libre après l'école?

to **free** VERB
see also **free** ADJECTIVE
<u>libérer</u>

freedom NOUN
la <u>liberté</u>

freeway NOUN US
l' <u>autoroute</u> FEM

to **freeze** VERB
① <u>geler</u> ◇ *The water had frozen.* L'eau avait gelé.
② <u>congeler</u> (*food*) ◇ *She froze the rest of the raspberries.* Elle a congelé le reste des framboises.

freezer NOUN
le <u>congélateur</u>

freezing ADJECTIVE
♦**It's freezing!** Il fait un froid de canard! (*informal*)
♦**I'm freezing!** Je suis gelé! (*informal*)
♦**3 degrees below freezing** moins trois

freight NOUN
la <u>cargaison</u> (*goods*)
♦**a freight train** un train de marchandises

French ADJECTIVE
see also **French** NOUN
<u>français</u> ◇ *He's French.* Il est français. ◇ *She's French.* Elle est française.

French NOUN
see also **French** ADJECTIVE
le <u>français</u> (*language*) ◇ *Do you speak French?* Est-ce que tu parles français?
♦**the French** (*people*) les Français

French beans PL NOUN
les <u>haricots verts</u> MASC PL

French fries PL NOUN
les <u>frites</u> FEM PL

French horn NOUN
le <u>cor (d'harmonie)</u> ◇ *I play the French horn.* Je joue du cor.

French kiss NOUN
le <u>baiser profond</u>

French loaf NOUN
la <u>baguette</u>

Frenchman NOUN
le <u>Français</u>

French windows PL NOUN
la <u>porte-fenêtre</u> SING
(les portes-fenêtres PL)

Frenchwoman NOUN
la <u>Française</u>

frequent ADJECTIVE
<u>fréquent</u> ◇ *frequent showers* des averses fréquentes

F

♦**There are frequent buses to the town centre.** Il y a beaucoup de bus pour le centre ville.

fresh ADJECTIVE
<u>frais</u> MASC
<u>fraîche</u> FEM
♦**I need some fresh air.** J'ai besoin de prendre l'air.

to **freshen up** VERB
<u>faire un brin de toilette</u> ◊ *I'd like to go and freshen up.* Je voudrais faire un brin de toilette.

to **fret** VERB
<u>se tracasser</u> ◊ *Philip was fretting about his exams.* Philip se tracassait au sujet de ses examens.

Friday NOUN
le <u>vendredi</u> ◊ *on Friday* vendredi ◊ *on Fridays* le vendredi ◊ *every Friday* tous les vendredis ◊ *last Friday* vendredi dernier ◊ *next Friday* vendredi prochain

fridge NOUN
le <u>frigo</u>

fried ADJECTIVE
<u>frit</u> ◊ *fried vegetables* des légumes frits
♦**a fried egg** un œuf sur le plat

friend NOUN
l' <u>ami</u> MASC
l' <u>amie</u> FEM

friendly ADJECTIVE
1 <u>gentil</u> MASC
<u>gentille</u> FEM
◊ *She's really friendly.* Elle est vraiment gentille.
2 <u>accueillant</u> ◊ *Liverpool is a very friendly city.* Liverpool est une ville très accueillante.

friendship NOUN
l' <u>amitié</u> FEM

fright NOUN
la <u>peur</u> ◊ *I got a terrible fright!* Ça m'a fait une peur terrible!

to **frighten** VERB
<u>faire peur à</u> ◊ *Horror films frighten him.* Les films d'horreur lui font peur.

frightened ADJECTIVE
♦**to be frightened** avoir peur ◊ *I'm frightened!* J'ai peur!
♦**to be frightened of something** avoir peur de quelque chose ◊ *Anna's frightened of spiders.* Anna a peur des araignées.

frightening ADJECTIVE
<u>effrayant</u>

fringe NOUN
la <u>frange</u> (*of hair*) ◊ *She's got a fringe.* Elle a une frange.

Frisbee ® NOUN
le <u>Frisbee</u> ® ◊ *to play Frisbee* jouer au Frisbee

fro ADVERB
♦**to go to and fro** aller et venir

frog NOUN
la <u>grenouille</u>
♦**frogs' legs** les cuisses de grenouille FEM

from PREPOSITION
<u>de</u> ◊ *Where do you come from?* D'où venez-vous? ◊ *I come from Perth.* Je viens de Perth. ◊ *a letter from my sister* une lettre de ma sœur ◊ *The hotel is one kilometre from the beach.* L'hôtel est à un kilomètre de la plage.
♦**from ... to ...** de ... à ... ◊ *He flew from London to Paris.* Il a pris l'avion de Londres à Paris. ◊ *from 1 o'clock to 2* d'une heure à deux heures ◊ *The price was reduced from £10 to £5.* Ils ont réduit le prix de dix livres à cinq.
♦**from ... onwards ...** à partir de ... ◊ *We'll be at home from 7 o'clock onwards.* Nous serons chez nous à partir de sept heures.

front NOUN
see also **front** ADJECTIVE
le <u>devant</u> ◊ *the front of the house* le devant de la maison
♦**in front** devant ◊ *a house with a car in front* une maison avec une voiture devant ◊ *the car in front* la voiture de devant
♦**in front of** devant ◊ *in front of the house* devant la maison ◊ *the car in front of us* la voiture devant nous
♦**in the front** (*of car*) à l'avant ◊ *I was sitting in the front.* J'étais assis à l'avant.
♦**at the front of the train** à l'avant du train

front ADJECTIVE
see also **front** NOUN
1 <u>de devant</u> ◊ *the front row* la rangée de devant
2 <u>avant</u> ◊ *the front seats of the car* les sièges avant de la voiture
♦**the front door** la porte d'entrée

frontier NOUN
la <u>frontière</u>

frost NOUN
le <u>gel</u>

frosting NOUN US
le <u>glaçage</u> (*on cake*)

frosty ADJECTIVE
♦**It's frosty today.** Il gèle aujourd'hui.

to **frown** VERB

froncer les sourcils ◊ *He frowned.* Il a froncé les sourcils.

froze VERB *see* **freeze**

frozen ADJECTIVE
see also **freeze**
surgelé (*food*) ◊ *frozen chips* des frites surgelées

fruit NOUN
le fruit
◆**fruit juice** le jus de fruits
◆**a fruit salad** une salade de fruits

fruit machine NOUN
la machine à sous

frustrated ADJECTIVE
frustré

to **fry** VERB
faire frire ◊ *Fry the onions for 5 minutes.* Faites frire les oignons pendant cinq minutes.

frying pan NOUN
la poêle

fuel NOUN
le carburant (*for car, aeroplane*) ◊ *to run out of fuel* avoir une panne de carburant

to **fulfil** VERB
réaliser ◊ *Robert fulfilled his dream to visit China.* Robert a réalisé son rêve de visiter la Chine.

full ADJECTIVE, ADVERB
1 plein ◊ *The tank's full.* Le réservoir est plein.
2 complet MASC
complète FEM
◊ *He asked for full information on the job.* Il a demandé des renseignements complets sur le poste.
◆**your full name** vos nom et prénoms ◊ *My full name is Ian John Marr.* Je m'appelle Ian John Marr.
◆**I'm full.** (*after meal*) J'ai bien mangé.
◆**at full speed** à toute vitesse ◊ *He drove at full speed.* Il conduisait à toute vitesse.
◆**There was a full moon.** C'était la pleine lune.

full stop NOUN
le point

full-time ADJECTIVE, ADVERB
à plein temps ◊ *Gillian has got a full-time job.* Gillian a un travail à plein temps. ◊ *Gillian works full-time.* Gillian travaille à plein temps.

fully ADVERB
complètement ◊ *He hasn't fully recovered from his illness.* Il n'est pas complètement remis de sa maladie.

fumes PL NOUN
les fumées FEM PL ◊ *The factory gave out dangerous fumes.* L'usine rejetait des fumées dangereuses.
◆**exhaust fumes** les gaz d'échappement MASC

fun ADJECTIVE
see also **fun** NOUN
marrant ◊ *She's a fun person.* Elle est marrante.

fun NOUN
see also **fun** ADJECTIVE
◆**to have fun** s'amuser ◊ *We had great fun playing in the snow.* Nous nous sommes bien amusés à jouer dans la neige.
◆**for fun** pour rire ◊ *He entered the competition just for fun.* Il a participé à la compétition juste pour rire.
◆**to make fun of somebody** se moquer de quelqu'un ◊ *They made fun of him.* Ils se sont moqués de lui.
◆**It's fun!** C'est chouette!
◆**Have fun!** Amuse-toi bien!

funds PL NOUN
les fonds MASC PL ◊ *to raise funds* collecter des fonds

funeral NOUN
l' enterrement MASC

funfair NOUN
la fête foraine

funny ADJECTIVE
1 drôle (*amusing*) ◊ *It was really funny.* C'était vraiment drôle.
2 bizarre (*strange*) ◊ *There's something funny about him.* Il est un peu bizarre.

fur NOUN
1 la fourrure ◊ *a fur coat* un manteau de fourrure
2 le poil ◊ *the dog's fur* le poil du chien

furious ADJECTIVE
furieux MASC
furieuse FEM
◊ *Dad was furious with me.* Papa était furieux contre moi.

furniture NOUN
les meubles MASC PL ◊ *a piece of furniture* un meuble

further ADVERB, ADJECTIVE
plus loin ◊ *London is further from Manchester than Leeds is.* Londres est plus loin de Manchester que Leeds.
◆**How much further is it?** C'est encore loin?

further education NOUN
l' enseignement postscolaire MASC

F

fuse NOUN

le <u>fusible</u> ◇ *The fuse has blown.* Le fusible a sauté.

fuss NOUN

l' <u>agitation</u> FEM ◇ *What's all the fuss about?* Qu'est-ce que c'est que toute cette agitation?

◆**to make a fuss** faire des histoires ◇ *He's always making a fuss about nothing.* Il fait toujours des histoires pour rien.

fussy ADJECTIVE

<u>difficile</u> ◇ *She is very fussy about her food.* Elle est très difficile sur la nourriture.

future NOUN

1 l' <u>avenir</u> MASC ◇ *What are your plans for the future?* Quels sont vos projets pour l'avenir?

◆**in future** à l'avenir ◇ *Be more careful in future.* Sois plus prudent à l'avenir.

2 le <u>futur</u> (*in grammar*) ◇ *Put this sentence into the future.* Mettez cette phrase au futur.

G

to **gain** VERB
- ◆**to gain weight** prendre du poids
- ◆**to gain speed** prendre de la vitesse

gallery NOUN
le <u>musée</u> ◊ *an art gallery* un musée d'art

to **gamble** VERB
<u>jouer</u> ◊ *He gambled £100 at the casino.* Il a joué cent livres au casino.

gambler NOUN
le <u>joueur</u>

gambling NOUN
le <u>jeu</u> ◊ *He likes gambling.* Il aime le jeu.

game NOUN
1 le <u>jeu</u>
(les jeux PL)
◊ *The children were playing a game.* Les enfants jouaient à un jeu.
2 (*sport*)
le <u>match</u> ◊ *a game of football* un match de football
- ◆**a game of cards** une partie de cartes

gang NOUN
la <u>bande</u>

gangster NOUN
le <u>gangster</u>

gap NOUN
1 le <u>trou</u> ◊ *There's a gap in the hedge.* Il y a un trou dans la haie.
2 l' <u>intervalle</u> MASC ◊ *a gap of four years* un intervalle de quatre ans

garage NOUN
le <u>garage</u>

garbage NOUN
les <u>ordures</u> FEM PL

garden NOUN
le <u>jardin</u>

gardener NOUN
le <u>jardinier</u> ◊ *He's a gardener.* Il est jardinier.

gardening NOUN
le <u>jardinage</u> ◊ *Margaret loves gardening.* Margaret aime le jardinage.

gardens PL NOUN
le <u>jardin public</u> SING

garlic NOUN
l' <u>ail</u> MASC

garment NOUN
le <u>vêtement</u>

gas NOUN
1 le <u>gaz</u>
- ◆**a gas cooker** une cuisinière à gaz

- ◆**a gas cylinder** une bouteille de gaz
- ◆**a gas fire** un radiateur à gaz
- ◆**a gas leak** une fuite de gaz
2 l' <u>essence</u> FEM (*petrol*) US

gasoline NOUN US
l' <u>essence</u> FEM

gate NOUN
1 le <u>portail</u> (*of garden*)
2 la <u>barrière</u> (*of field*)
3 la <u>porte</u> (*at airport*)

gateau NOUN
le <u>gâteau à la crème</u>

to **gather** VERB
<u>se rassembler</u> (*assemble*) ◊ *People gathered in front of Buckingham Palace.* Les gens se sont rassemblés devant Buckingham Palace.
- ◆**to gather speed** prendre de la vitesse ◊ *The train gathered speed.* Le train a pris de la vitesse.

gave VERB *see* **give**

gay ADJECTIVE
<u>homosexuel</u> MASC
<u>homosexuelle</u> FEM

to **gaze** VERB
- ◆**to gaze at something** fixer quelque chose du regard ◊ *He gazed at her.* Il l'a fixée du regard.

GCSE NOUN
le <u>brevet des collèges</u>

gear NOUN
1 la <u>vitesse</u> (*in car*) ◊ *in first gear* en première vitesse ◊ *to change gear* changer de vitesse
2 le <u>matériel</u> ◊ *camping gear* le matériel de camping
- ◆**your sports gear** (*clothes*) tes affaires de sport

gear lever NOUN
le <u>levier de vitesse</u>

gearshift NOUN US
le <u>levier de vitesse</u>

geese PL NOUN *see* **goose**

gel NOUN
le <u>gel</u>
- ◆**hair gel** le gel pour les cheveux

gem NOUN
la <u>pierre précieuse</u>

Gemini NOUN
les <u>Gémeaux</u> MASC PL ◊ *I'm Gemini.* Je suis Gémeaux.

gender NOUN
1 le <u>sexe</u> (*of person*)
2 le <u>genre</u> (*of noun*)

gene NOUN
le gène

general NOUN
see also **general** ADJECTIVE
le général
(les généraux PL)

general ADJECTIVE
see also **general** NOUN
général
(généraux MASC PL)
♦in general en général

general election NOUN
les élections législatives FEM PL

general knowledge NOUN
les connaissances générales FEM PL

generally ADVERB
généralement ◊ I generally go
shopping on Saturday. Généralement,
je fais mes courses le samedi.

generation NOUN
la génération ◊ the younger
generation la nouvelle génération

generator NOUN
le générateur

generous ADJECTIVE
généreux MASC
généreuse FEM
◊ That's very generous of you. C'est
très généreux de votre part.

genetic ADJECTIVE
génétique

genetically-modified ADJECTIVE
génétiquement modifié

genetics NOUN
la génétique

Geneva NOUN
Genève
♦in Geneva à Genève
♦to Geneva à Genève
♦Lake Geneva le lac Léman

genius NOUN
le génie ◊ She's a genius! C'est un
génie!

gentle ADJECTIVE
doux MASC
douce FEM

gentleman NOUN
le monsieur
(les messieurs PL)
◊ Good morning, gentlemen. Bonjour
messieurs.

gently ADVERB
doucement

gents NOUN
les toilettes pour hommes FEM PL
◊ Can you tell me where the gents is,
please? Pouvez-vous me dire où sont
les toilettes, s'il vous plaît?

♦"gents" (on sign) "messieurs"

genuine ADJECTIVE
1 véritable (real) ◊ These are
genuine diamonds. Ce sont de
véritables diamants.
2 sincère (sincere) ◊ She's a very
genuine person. C'est quelqu'un de
très sincère.

geography NOUN
la géographie

gerbil NOUN
la gerbille

germ NOUN
le microbe

German ADJECTIVE
see also **German** NOUN
allemand

German NOUN
see also **German** ADJECTIVE
1 (person)
l' Allemand MASC
l' Allemande FEM
2 (language)
l' allemand ◊ Do you speak German?
Parlez-vous allemand?

German measles NOUN
la rubéole

Germany NOUN
l' Allemagne FEM
♦in Germany en Allemagne
♦to Germany en Allemagne

gesture NOUN
le geste

to **get** VERB

> There are several ways of translating
> get. Scan the examples to find one
> that is similar to what you want to
> say.

1 avoir (have, receive) ◊ I got lots of
presents. J'ai eu beaucoup de
cadeaux. ◊ He got first prize. Il a eu
le premier prix. ◊ He got good exam
results. Il a eu de bons résultats aux
examens. ◊ How many have you got?
Combien en avez-vous?
2 aller chercher (fetch) ◊ Quick, get
help! Allez vite chercher de l'aide!
3 attraper (catch) ◊ They've got the
thief. Ils ont attrapé le voleur.
4 prendre (train, bus) ◊ I'm getting
the bus into town. Je prends le bus
pour aller en ville.
5 comprendre (understand) ◊ I don't
get it. Je ne comprends pas.
6 aller (go) ◊ How do you get to the
castle? Comment est-ce qu'on va au
château?
7 arriver (arrive) ◊ He should get
here soon. Il devrait arriver bientôt.

⑧ <u>devenir</u> (*become*) ◊ *to get old*
devenir vieux

♦**to get something done** faire faire
quelque chose ◊ *to get one's hair cut*
se faire couper les cheveux

♦**to get something for somebody**
trouver quelque chose pour
quelqu'un ◊ *The librarian got the
book for me.* Le bibliothécaire m'a
trouvé le livre.

♦**to have got to do something** devoir
faire quelque chose ◊ *I've got to tell
him.* Je dois le lui dire.

♦**to get away** s'échapper ◊ *One of the
burglars got away.* L'un des
cambrioleurs s'est échappé.

♦**to get back (1)** rentrer ◊ *What time
did you get back?* Tu es rentré à
quelle heure?

♦**to get back (2)** récupérer ◊ *He got his
money back.* Il a récupéré son argent.

♦**to get in** rentrer ◊ *What time did you
get in last night?* Tu es rentré à
quelle heure hier soir?

♦**to get into** monter dans ◊ *Sharon got
into the car.* Sharon est montée dans
la voiture.

♦**to get off** descendre de (*vehicle, bike*)
◊ *Isobel got off the train.* Isobel est
descendue du train.

♦**to get on (1)** (*vehicle*) monter dans
◊ *Phyllis got on the bus.* Phyllis est
montée dans le bus.

♦**to get on (2)** (*bike*) enfourcher ◊ *Carol
got on her bike.* Carol a enfourché
son vélo.

♦**to get on with somebody** s'entendre
avec quelqu'un ◊ *He doesn't get on
with his parents.* Il ne s'entend pas
avec ses parents. ◊ *We got on really
well.* Nous nous sommes très bien
entendus.

♦**to get out** sortir ◊ *Hélène got out of
the car.* Hélène est sortie de la
voiture. ◊ *Get out!* Sortez!

♦**to get something out** sortir quelque
chose ◊ *She got the map out.* Elle a
sorti la carte.

♦**to get over (1)** se remettre ◊ *It took
her a long time to get over the
illness.* Il lui a fallu longtemps pour
se remettre de sa maladie.

♦**to get over (2)** surmonter ◊ *He
managed to get over the problem.* Il
a réussi à résoudre le problème.

♦**to get together** se retrouver ◊ *Could
we get together this evening?*
Pourrait-on se retrouver ce soir?

♦**to get up** se lever ◊ *What time do
you get up?* Tu te lèves à quelle
heure?

ghetto blaster NOUN
le <u>radiocassette portable</u>

ghost NOUN
le <u>fantôme</u>

giant ADJECTIVE
> see also **giant** NOUN

<u>énorme</u> ◊ *They ate a giant meal.* Ils
ont mangé un énorme repas.

giant NOUN
> see also **giant** ADJECTIVE

le <u>géant</u>
la <u>géante</u>

gift NOUN
① (*present*)
le <u>cadeau</u>
(les cadeaux PL)
② (*talent*)
le <u>don</u>

♦**to have a gift for something** être
doué pour quelque chose ◊ *Dave has
a gift for painting.* Dave est doué
pour la peinture.

gifted ADJECTIVE
<u>doué</u> ◊ *Janice is a gifted dancer.*
Janice est douée pour la danse.

gift shop NOUN
la <u>boutique de cadeaux</u>

gigantic ADJECTIVE
<u>gigantesque</u>

gin NOUN
le <u>gin</u>

ginger NOUN
> see also **ginger** ADJECTIVE

le <u>gingembre</u> ◊ *Add a teaspoon of
ginger.* Ajoutez une cuillère à café de
gingembre.

ginger ADJECTIVE
> see also **ginger** NOUN

<u>roux</u> MASC
<u>rousse</u> FEM
◊ *Chris has ginger hair.* Chris a les
cheveux roux.

giraffe NOUN
la <u>girafe</u>

girl NOUN
① la <u>fille</u> ◊ *They've got a girl and
two boys.* Ils ont une fille et deux
garçons.
② la <u>petite fille</u> (*young*) ◊ *a five-
year-old girl* une petite fille de cinq
ans
③ la <u>jeune fille</u> (*older*) ◊ *a sixteen-
year-old girl* une jeune fille de seize
ans ◊ *an English girl* une jeune
Anglaise

girlfriend NOUN
① la <u>copine</u> (*lover*) ◊ *Damon's
girlfriend is called Justine.* La copine
de Damon s'appelle Justine.

2 l' <u>amie</u> FEM (*friend*) ◊ *She often went out with her girlfriends.* Elle sortait souvent avec ses amies.

to **give** VERB
<u>donner</u>

♦**to give something to somebody** donner quelque chose à quelqu'un ◊ *He gave me £10.* Il m'a donné dix livres.

♦**to give something back to somebody** rendre quelque chose à quelqu'un ◊ *I gave the book back to him.* Je lui ai rendu le livre.

♦**to give something out** distribuer quelque chose ◊ *The teacher gave out the books.* Le professeur a distribué les livres.

♦**to give in** céder ◊ *His Mum gave in and let him go out.* Sa mère a cédé et l'a laissé sortir.

♦**to give out** distribuer ◊ *He gave out the exam papers.* Il a distribué les sujets d'examen.

♦**to give up** laisser tomber ◊ *I couldn't do it, so I gave up.* Je n'arrivais pas à le faire, alors j'ai laissé tomber.

♦**to give up doing something** arrêter de faire quelque chose ◊ *He gave up smoking.* Il a arrêté de fumer.

♦**to give oneself up** se rendre ◊ *The thief gave himself up.* Le voleur s'est rendu.

♦**to give way** céder la priorité (*in traffic*)

glad ADJECTIVE
<u>content</u> ◊ *She's glad she's done it.* Elle est contente de l'avoir fait.

glamorous ADJECTIVE
1 (*person*)
<u>glamour</u> MASC, FEM, PL ◊ *She's very glamourous.* Elle est très glamour.
2 (*job*)
<u>prestigieux</u> MASC
<u>prestigieuse</u> FEM

♦**to have a glamorous lifestyle** vivre comme une star

to **glance** VERB
see also **glance** NOUN

♦**to glance at something** jeter un coup d'œil à quelque chose ◊ *Peter glanced at his watch.* Peter a jeté un coup d'œil à sa montre.

glance NOUN
see also **glance** VERB
le <u>coup d'œil</u> ◊ *at first glance* au premier coup d'œil

to **glare** VERB

♦**to glare at somebody** lancer un regard furieux à quelqu'un ◊ *He glared at me.* Il m'a lancé un regard furieux.

glaring ADJECTIVE

♦**a glaring mistake** une erreur qui saute aux yeux

glass NOUN
le <u>verre</u> ◊ *a glass of milk* un verre de lait

glasses PL NOUN
les <u>lunettes</u> FEM PL ◊ *Jean-Pierre wears glasses.* Jean-Pierre porte des lunettes.

glider NOUN
le <u>planeur</u>

gliding NOUN
le <u>vol à voile</u> ◊ *My hobby is gliding.* Je fais du vol à voile.

global ADJECTIVE
<u>mondial</u>
(mondiaux MASC PL)

♦**on a global scale** à l'échelle mondiale

global warming NOUN
le <u>réchauffement de la planète</u>

globe NOUN
le <u>globe</u>

gloomy ADJECTIVE
1 <u>morose</u> ◊ *She's been feeling very gloomy recently.* Elle se sent très morose ces derniers temps.
2 <u>lugubre</u> ◊ *He lives in a small gloomy flat.* Il habite un petit appartement lugubre.

glorious ADJECTIVE
<u>magnifique</u>

glove NOUN
le <u>gant</u>

glove compartment NOUN
la <u>boîte à gants</u>

glue NOUN
see also **glue** VERB
la <u>colle</u>

to **glue** VERB
see also **glue** NOUN
<u>coller</u>

GM ADJECTIVE (= *genetically modified*)
<u>génétiquement modifié</u> ◊ *GM foods* les aliments génétiquement modifiés MASC

GMO ABBREVIATION (= *genetically-modified organism*)
l' <u>OGM</u> MASC (= l'organisme génétiquement modifié)

go NOUN
see also **go** VERB

♦**to have a go at doing something** essayer de faire quelque chose ◊ *He had a go at making a cake.* Il a essayé de faire un gâteau.

♦**Whose go is it?** À qui le tour?

to **go** VERB

see also **go** NOUN

[1] aller ◊ *I'm going to the cinema tonight.* Je vais au cinéma ce soir.

[2] partir (*leave*) ◊ *Where's Pierre? – He's gone.* Où est Pierre? – Il est parti.

[3] s'en aller (*go away*) ◊ *I'm going now.* Je m'en vais.

[4] marcher (*vehicle*) ◊ *My car won't go.* Ma voiture ne marche pas.

♦**to go home** rentrer à la maison ◊ *I go home at about 4 o'clock.* Je rentre à la maison vers quatre heures.

♦**to go for a walk** aller se promener ◊ *Shall we go for a walk?* Si on allait se promener?

♦**How did it go?** Comment est-ce que ça s'est passé?

♦**I'm going to do it tomorrow.** Je vais le faire demain.

♦**It's going to be difficult.** Ça va être difficile.

to **go after** VERB
suivre ◊ *Quick, go after them!* Vite, suivez-les!

to **go ahead** VERB
♦**The meeting will go ahead as planned.** La réunion aura bien lieu comme prévu.

♦**We'll go ahead with your plan.** Nous allons mettre votre projet à exécution.

♦**Go ahead!** Vas-y!

to **go away** VERB
s'en aller ◊ *Go away!* Allez-vous-en!

to **go back** VERB

*Use **rentrer** only when you are entering a building, usually your home; otherwise use **retourner**.*

[1] retourner ◊ *We went back to the same place.* Nous sommes retournés au même endroit.

[2] rentrer ◊ *Is he still here? – No, he's gone back home.* Est-ce qu'il est encore là? – Non, il est rentré chez lui.

to **go by** VERB
passer ◊ *Two policemen went by.* Deux policiers sont passés.

to **go down** VERB

[1] descendre (*person*) ◊ *to go down the stairs* descendre l'escalier

[2] baisser (*decrease*) ◊ *The price of computers has gone down.* Le prix des ordinateurs a baissé.

[3] se dégonfler (*deflate*) ◊ *My airbed kept going down.* Mon matelas pneumatique se dégonflait constamment.

♦**My brother's gone down with flu.** Mon frère a attrapé la grippe.

to **go for** VERB
attaquer (*attack*) ◊ *Suddenly the dog went for me.* Soudain, le chien m'a attaqué.

♦**Go for it!** (*go on!*) Vas-y, fonce!

to **go in** VERB
entrer ◊ *He knocked on the door and went in.* Il a frappé à la porte et il est entré.

to **go off** VERB

[1] exploser (*bomb*) ◊ *The bomb went off.* La bombe a explosé.

[2] se déclencher (*alarm, gun*) ◊ *The fire alarm went off.* L'avertisseur d'incendie s'est déclenché.

[3] sonner (*alarm clock*) ◊ *My alarm clock goes off at seven every morning.* Mon réveil sonne à sept heures tous les matins.

[4] tourner (*food*) ◊ *The milk's gone off.* Le lait a tourné.

[5] partir (*go away*) ◊ *Patrick went off in a huff.* Patrick est parti de mauvaise humeur.

to **go on** VERB

[1] se passer (*happen*) ◊ *What's going on?* Qu'est-ce qui se passe?

[2] continuer (*carry on*) ◊ *The concert went on until 11 o'clock at night.* Le concert a continué jusqu'à onze heures du soir.

♦**to go on doing something** continuer à faire quelque chose ◊ *He went on reading.* Il a continué à lire.

♦**to go on at somebody** être sur le dos de quelqu'un ◊ *My parents always go on at me.* Mes parents sont toujours sur mon dos.

♦**Go on!** Allez! ◊ *Go on, tell me what the problem is!* Allez, dis-moi quel est le problème!

to **go out** VERB

[1] sortir (*person*) ◊ *Are you going out tonight?* Tu sors ce soir?

♦**to go out with somebody** sortir avec quelqu'un ◊ *Are you going out with him?* Est-ce que tu sors avec lui?

[2] s'éteindre (*light, fire, candle*) ◊ *Suddenly the lights went out.* Soudain, les lumières se sont éteintes.

to **go past** VERB
♦**to go past something** passer devant quelque chose ◊ *He went past the shop.* Il est passé devant la boutique.

to **go round** VERB
♦**to go round a corner** prendre un tournant

♦**to go round to somebody's house** aller chez quelqu'un

G

☞

♦**to go round a museum** visiter un musée

♦**to go round the shops** faire les boutiques

♦**There's a bug going round.** Il y a un microbe qui circule.

to **go through** VERB
traverser ◊ *We went through Paris to get to Rennes.* Nous avons traversé Paris pour aller à Rennes.

to **go up** VERB
[1] monter (*person*) ◊ *to go up the stairs* monter l'escalier
[2] augmenter (*increase*) ◊ *The price has gone up.* Le prix a augmenté.

♦**to go up in flames** s'embraser ◊ *The whole factory went up in flames.* L'usine toute entière s'est embrasée.

to **go with** VERB
aller avec ◊ *Does this blouse go with that skirt?* Est-ce que ce chemisier va avec cette jupe?

goal NOUN
le but ◊ *to score a goal* marquer un but ◊ *His goal is to become the world champion.* Son but est de devenir champion du monde.

goalkeeper NOUN
le gardien de but

goat NOUN
la chèvre
♦**goat's cheese** le fromage de chèvre

god NOUN
le dieu
(les dieux PL)
◊ *I believe in God.* Je crois en Dieu.

goddaughter NOUN
la filleule

godfather NOUN
le parrain

godmother NOUN
la marraine

godson NOUN
le filleul

goggles PL NOUN
[1] les lunettes de protection FEM PL (*of welder, mechanic etc*)
[2] les lunettes de plongée FEM PL (*of swimmer*)

gold NOUN
l' or MASC ◊ *They found some gold.* Ils ont trouvé de l'or. ◊ *a gold necklace* un collier en or

goldfish NOUN
le poisson rouge ◊ *I've got five goldfish.* J'ai cinq poissons rouges.

gold-plated ADJECTIVE
plaqué or MASC
plaquée or FEM

golf NOUN
le golf ◊ *My dad plays golf.* Mon père joue au golf.
♦**a golf club** un club de golf

golf course NOUN
le terrain de golf

gone VERB *see* **go**

good ADJECTIVE
[1] bon MASC
bonne FEM
◊ *It's a very good film.* C'est un très bon film. ◊ *Vegetables are good for you.* Les légumes sont bons pour la santé.
♦**to be good at something** être bon en quelque chose ◊ *Jane's very good at maths.* Jane est très bonne en maths.
[2] (*kind*)
gentil MASC
gentille FEM
◊ *They were very good to me.* Ils ont été très gentils avec moi. ◊ *That's very good of you.* C'est très gentil de votre part.
[3] (*not naughty*)
sage ◊ *Be good!* Sois sage!
♦**for good** pour de bon ◊ *One day he left for good.* Un jour il est parti pour de bon.
♦**Good morning!** Bonjour!
♦**Good afternoon!** Bonjour!
♦**Good evening!** Bonsoir!
♦**Good night!** Bonne nuit!
♦**It's no good complaining.** Cela ne sert à rien de se plaindre.

goodbye EXCLAMATION
au revoir!

Good Friday NOUN
le Vendredi saint

good-looking ADJECTIVE
beau MASC
belle FEM
(beaux MASC PL)
◊ *He's very good-looking.* Il est très beau.

good-natured ADJECTIVE
facile à vivre (*person*)

goods PL NOUN
les marchandises FEM PL (*in shop*)
♦**a goods train** un train de marchandises

goose NOUN
l' oie FEM

gooseberry NOUN
la groseille à maquereau

gorgeous ADJECTIVE
[1] superbe ◊ *She's gorgeous!* Elle est superbe!

2 splendide ◊ *The weather was gorgeous.* Il a fait un temps, splendide.

gorilla NOUN
le gorille

gospel NOUN
le gospel (*music*)

gossip NOUN
  see also **gossip** VERB
1 les cancans MASC PL (*rumours*) ◊ *Tell me the gossip!* Raconte-moi les cancans!
2 la commère (*woman*) ◊ *She's such a gossip!* C'est une vraie commère!
3 le bavard (*man*) ◊ *What a gossip!* Quel bavard!

to **gossip** VERB
  see also **gossip** NOUN
1 bavarder (*chat*) ◊ *They were always gossiping.* Elles étaient tout le temps en train de bavarder.
2 faire des commérages (*about somebody*) ◊ *They gossiped about her.* Elles faisaient des commérages à son sujet.

got VERB *see* **get**

gotten VERB US *see* **get**

government NOUN
le gouvernement

GP NOUN
le médecin généraliste

to **grab** VERB
saisir

graceful ADJECTIVE
élégant

grade NOUN
la note (*at school*) ◊ *He got good grades in his exams this year.* Il a eu de bonnes notes à ses examens cette année.

grade school NOUN US
l' école primaire FEM

gradual ADJECTIVE
progressif MASC
progressive FEM

gradually ADVERB
peu à peu ◊ *We gradually got used to it.* Nous nous y sommes habitués peu à peu.

graduate NOUN
1 (*from university*)
le diplômé
la diplômée
2 (*from US high school*)
le bachelier
la bachelière

graffiti PL NOUN
les graffiti MASC PL

grain NOUN
le grain

gram NOUN
le gramme

grammar NOUN
la grammaire

grammar school NOUN
1 le collège
2 le lycée

ⓘ *In France pupils go to a **collège** between the ages of 11 and 15, and then to a **lycée** until the age of 18. French schools are mostly non-selective.*

G

grammatical ADJECTIVE
grammatical
(grammaticaux MASC PL)

gramme NOUN
le gramme ◊ *500 grammes of cheese* cinq cents grammes de fromage

grand ADJECTIVE
somptueux MASC
somptueuse FEM
◊ *Samantha lives in a very grand house.* Samantha habite une maison somptueuse.

grandchild NOUN
le petit-fils
la petite-fille
♦ **my grandchildren** mes petits-enfants MASC

granddad NOUN
le papi ◊ *my granddad* mon papi

granddaughter NOUN
la petite-fille
(les petites-filles PL)

grandfather NOUN
le grand-père
(les grands-pères PL)
◊ *my grandfather* mon grand-père

grandma NOUN
la mamie ◊ *my grandma* ma mamie

grandmother NOUN
la grand-mère
(les grands-mères PL)
◊ *my grandmother* ma grand-mère

grandpa NOUN
le papi ◊ *my grandpa* mon papi

grandparents PL NOUN
les grands-parents MASC PL ◊ *my grandparents* mes grands-parents

grandson NOUN
le petit-fils
(les petits-fils PL)

granny NOUN
la mamie ◊ *my granny* ma mamie

grant NOUN

☞

la bourse

grape NOUN
le raisin

grapefruit NOUN
le pamplemousse

graph NOUN
le graphique

graphics PL NOUN
les images de synthèse FEM PL ◇ *I designed the graphics, she wrote the text.* J'ai conçu les images de synthèse, elle a écrit le texte.
♦**He works in computer graphics.** Il fait de l'infographie.

to **grasp** VERB
saisir

grass NOUN
l' herbe FEM ◇ *The grass is long.* L'herbe est haute.
♦**to cut the grass** tondre le gazon

grasshopper NOUN
la sauterelle

to **grate** VERB
râper ◇ *to grate some cheese* râper du fromage

grateful ADJECTIVE
reconnaissant

grave NOUN
la tombe

gravel NOUN
le gravier

graveyard NOUN
le cimetière

gravy NOUN
la sauce au jus de viande

grease NOUN
le lubrifiant

greasy ADJECTIVE
gras MASC
grasse FEM
◇ *He has greasy hair.* Il a les cheveux gras. ◇ *The food was very greasy.* la nourriture était très grasse.

great ADJECTIVE
1 génial
(géniaux MASC PL)
◇ *That's great!* C'est génial!
2 grand ◇ *a great mansion* un grand manoir

Great Britain NOUN
la Grande-Bretagne
♦**in Great Britain** en Grande-Bretagne
♦**to Great Britain** en Grande-Bretagne
♦**I'm from Great Britain.** Je suis britannique.

great-grandfather NOUN
l' arrière-grand-père MASC
(les arrière-grands-pères PL)

great-grandmother NOUN
l' arrière-grand-mère FEM
(les arrière-grands-mères PL)

Greece NOUN
la Grèce
♦**in Greece** en Grèce
♦**to Greece** en Grèce

greedy ADJECTIVE
1 gourmand (*for food*) ◇ *I want some more cake. – Don't be so greedy!* Je veux encore du gâteau. – Ne sois pas si gourmand!
2 avide (*for money*)

Greek ADJECTIVE
see also **Greek** NOUN
grec MASC
grecque FEM
◇ *Dionysis is Greek.* Dionysis est grec.
◇ *She's Greek.* Elle est grecque.

Greek NOUN
see also **Greek** ADJECTIVE
1 (*person*)
le Grec
la Grecque
2 (*language*)
le grec

green ADJECTIVE
see also **green** NOUN
1 vert ◇ *a green car* une voiture verte ◇ *a green light* un feu vert ◇ *a green salad* une salade verte
2 écologiste (*movement, candidate*)
◇ *the Green Party* le parti écologiste

green NOUN
see also **green** ADJECTIVE
le vert ◇ *a dark green* un vert foncé
♦**greens** (*vegetables*) les légumes verts MASC
♦**the Greens** (*party*) les Verts MASC

greengrocer's NOUN
le marchand de fruits et légumes

greenhouse NOUN
la serre
♦**the greenhouse effect** l'effet de serre MASC

Greenland NOUN
le Groenland

to **greet** VERB
accueillir ◇ *He greeted me with a kiss.* Il m'a accueillie en me donnant un baiser.

greeting NOUN
♦**Greetings from Bangor!** Bonjour de Bangor!
♦**"Season's greetings"** "Meilleurs vœux pour les fêtes de fin d'année"

greetings card NOUN
la carte de vœux

grew VERB see **grow**

grey ADJECTIVE
gris ◊ *She's got grey hair.* Elle a les cheveux gris.
♦**He's going grey.** Il grisonne.

grey-haired ADJECTIVE
grisonnant

grid NOUN
1 (*in road*)
la grille
2 (*of electricity*)
le réseau
(les réseaux PL)

grief NOUN
le chagrin

grill NOUN
see also **grill** VERB
le gril (*of cooker*)
♦**a mixed grill** les grillades FEM PL

to **grill** VERB
see also **grill** NOUN
♦**to grill something** faire griller quelque chose

grim ADJECTIVE
sinistre

to **grin** VERB
see also **grin** NOUN
sourire ◊ *Dave grinned at me.* Dave m'a souri.

grin NOUN
see also **grin** VERB
le large sourire

to **grind** VERB
moudre (*coffee, pepper*)

to **grip** VERB
saisir

gripping ADJECTIVE
palpitant (*exciting*)

grit NOUN
le gravillon

to **groan** VERB
see also **groan** NOUN
gémir ◊ *He groaned with pain.* Il a gémi sous l'effet de la douleur.

groan NOUN
see also **groan** VERB
le gémissement (*of pain*)

grocer NOUN
l' épicier MASC ◊ *He's a grocer.* Il est épicier.

groceries PL NOUN
les provisions FEM PL

grocer's (shop) NOUN
l' épicerie FEM

grocery store NOUN US
l' épicerie FEM

groom NOUN

le marié (*bridegroom*) ◊ *the groom and his best man* le marié et son témoin

to **grope** VERB
♦**to grope for something** chercher quelque chose à tâtons ◊ *He groped for the light switch.* Il a cherché à tâtons l'interrupteur.

gross ADJECTIVE
dégoûtant (*revolting*) ◊ *It was really gross!* C'était vraiment dégoûtant!

grossly ADVERB
largement ◊ *We're grossly underpaid.* Nous sommes largement sous-payés.

ground NOUN
see also **ground** VERB
1 le sol (*earth*) ◊ *The ground's wet.* Le sol est mouillé.
2 le terrain (*for sport*) ◊ *a football ground* un terrain de football
3 la raison (*reason*) ◊ *We've got grounds for complaint.* Nous avons des raisons de nous plaindre.
♦**on the ground** par terre ◊ *We sat on the ground.* Nous nous sommes assis par terre.

ground VERB see **grind**
see also **ground** NOUN
♦**ground coffee** le café moulu

ground floor NOUN
le rez-de-chaussée
♦**on the ground floor** au rez-de-chaussée

group NOUN
le groupe

to **grow** VERB
1 pousser (*plant*) ◊ *Grass grows quickly.* L'herbe pousse vite.
2 grandir (*person, animal*) ◊ *Haven't you grown!* Comme tu as grandi!
3 augmenter (*increase*) ◊ *The number of unemployed people has grown.* Le nombre de chômeurs a augmenté.
4 faire pousser (*cultivate*) ◊ *My Dad grows potatoes.* Mon père fait pousser des pommes de terre.
♦**to grow a beard** se laisser pousser la barbe
♦**to grow up** grandir ◊ *Oh, grow up!* Ne fais pas l'enfant!
♦**He's grown out of his jacket.** Sa veste est devenue trop petite pour lui.

to **growl** VERB
grogner

grown VERB see **grow**

growth NOUN

G

la croissance ◊ economic growth la
croissance économique

grub NOUN
la bouffe (informal)

grudge NOUN
la rancune
♦ **to bear a grudge against somebody**
garder rancune à quelqu'un

gruesome ADJECTIVE
horrible

guarantee NOUN
see also **guarantee** VERB
la garantie
♦ **a five-year guarantee** une garantie de
cinq ans

to **guarantee** VERB
see also **guarantee** NOUN
garantir ◊ I can't guarantee he'll
come. Je ne peux pas garantir qu'il
viendra.

to **guard** VERB
see also **guard** NOUN
garder ◊ They guarded the palace. Ils
gardaient le palais.
♦ **to guard against something** protéger
contre quelque chose

guard NOUN
see also **guard** VERB
le chef de train (of train)
♦ **a security guard** un vigile
♦ **a guard dog** un chien de garde

to **guess** VERB
see also **guess** NOUN
deviner ◊ Can you guess what it is?
Devine ce que c'est!
♦ **to guess wrong** se tromper ◊ Janice
guessed wrong. Janice s'est trompée.

guess NOUN
see also **guess** VERB
la supposition ◊ It's just a guess.
C'est une simple supposition.
♦ **Have a guess!** Devine!

guest NOUN
1 l' invité MASC
l' invitée FEM
◊ We have guests staying with us.
Nous avons des invités.
2 (of hotel)
le client
la cliente

guesthouse NOUN

le petit hôtel

guide NOUN
1 le guide (book, person) ◊ We
bought a guide to Paris. Nous avons
acheté un guide sur Paris. ◊ The
guide showed us round the castle. Le
guide nous a fait visiter le château.
2 l' éclaireuse FEM (girl guide)
♦ **the Guides** les Éclaireuses

guidebook NOUN
le guide

guide dog NOUN
le chien d'aveugle

guilty ADJECTIVE
coupable ◊ to feel guilty se sentir
coupable ◊ She was found guilty. Elle
a été reconnue coupable.

guinea pig NOUN
le cobaye

guitar NOUN
la guitare ◊ I play the guitar. Je joue
de la guitare.

gum NOUN
le chewing-gum (sweet)
♦ **gums** (in mouth) les gencives FEM

gun NOUN
1 le revolver (small)
2 le fusil (rifle)

gunpoint NOUN
♦ **at gunpoint** sous la menace d'une
arme

gust NOUN
♦ **a gust of wind** une rafale de vent

guy NOUN
le type ◊ Who's that guy? C'est qui
ce type? ◊ He's a nice guy. C'est un
type sympa.

gym NOUN
la gym ◊ Emma goes to the gym
every day. Emma va tous les jours à
la gym.
♦ **gym classes** les cours de gym MASC

gymnast NOUN
le/la gymnaste ◊ She's a gymnast.
Elle est gymnaste.

gymnastics NOUN
la gymnastique ◊ to do gymnastics
faire de la gymnastique

gypsy NOUN
le/la Tzigane

H

habit NOUN
l' habitude FEM ◊ *a bad habit* une
mauvaise habitude

to **hack** VERB
◆**to hack into a system** s'introduire
dans un système

hacker NOUN
le/la pirate informatique

had VERB *see* **have**

haddock NOUN
l' églefin MASC

hadn't = **had not**

hail NOUN
see also **hail** VERB
la grêle

to **hail** VERB
see also **hail** NOUN
grêler ◊ *It's hailing.* Il grêle.

hair NOUN
1 les cheveux MASC PL ◊ *She's got
long hair.* Elle a les cheveux longs.
◊ *He's got black hair.* Il a les cheveux
noirs. ◊ *He's losing his hair.* Il perd
ses cheveux.
◆**to brush one's hair** se brosser les
cheveux ◊ *I'm brushing my hair.* Je
me brosse les cheveux.
◆**to wash one's hair** se laver les
cheveux ◊ *I need to wash my hair.* Il
faut que je me lave les cheveux.
◆**to have one's hair cut** se faire couper
les cheveux ◊ *I've just had my hair
cut.* Je viens de me faire couper les
cheveux.
◆**a hair (1)** (*from head*) un cheveu
◆**a hair (2)** (*from body*) un poil
2 le pelage (*fur of animal*)

hairbrush NOUN
la brosse à cheveux

haircut NOUN
la coupe
◆**to have a haircut** se faire couper les
cheveux ◊ *I've just had a haircut.* Je
viens de me faire couper les cheveux.

hairdresser NOUN
le coiffeur
la coiffeuse
◊ *He's a hairdresser.* Il est coiffeur.

hairdresser's NOUN
le coiffeur ◊ *at the hairdresser's* chez
le coiffeur

hair dryer NOUN
le sèche-cheveux
(les sèche-cheveux PL)

hair gel NOUN
le gel pour les cheveux

hairgrip NOUN
la pince à cheveux

hair spray NOUN
la laque

hairstyle NOUN
la coiffure

hairy ADJECTIVE
poilu ◊ *He's got hairy legs.* Il a les
jambes poilues.

half NOUN
see also **half** ADJECTIVE
1 la moitié ◊ *half of the cake* la
moitié du gâteau
2 le billet demi-tarif (*ticket*) ◊ *A half
to York, please.* Un billet demi-tarif
pour York, s'il vous plaît.
◆**two and a half** deux et demi
◆**half an hour** une demi-heure
◆**half past ten** dix heures et demie
◆**half a kilo** cinq cents grammes
◆**to cut something in half** couper
quelque chose en deux

half ADJECTIVE, ADVERB
see also **half** NOUN
1 demi ◊ *a half chicken* un demi-
poulet
2 à moitié ◊ *He was half asleep.* Il
était à moitié endormi.

half-brother NOUN
le demi-frère

half-hour NOUN
la demi-heure

half-price ADJECTIVE, ADVERB
◆**at half-price** à moitié prix

half-sister NOUN
la demi-sœur

half-term NOUN
les petites vacances FEM PL

half-time NOUN
la mi-temps

halfway ADVERB
1 à mi-chemin ◊ *halfway between
Oxford and London* à mi-chemin
entre Oxford et Londres
2 à la moitié ◊ *halfway through the
chapter* à la moitié du chapitre

hall NOUN
1 l' entrée FEM (*in house*)
2 la salle ◊ *the village hall* la salle
des fêtes

Hallowe'en NOUN
la veille de la Toussaint

hallway NOUN
le <u>vestibule</u>

halt NOUN
♦**to come to a halt** s'arrêter

ham NOUN
le <u>jambon</u>
♦**a ham sandwich** un sandwich au jambon

hamburger NOUN
le <u>hamburger</u>

hammer NOUN
le <u>marteau</u>
(les marteaux PL)

hamster NOUN
le <u>hamster</u>

hand NOUN
see also **hand** VERB
1 la <u>main</u> (of person)
♦**to give somebody a hand** donner un coup de main à quelqu'un ◇ *Can you give me a hand?* Tu peux me donner un coup de main?
♦**on the one hand ..., on the other hand ...** d'une part ..., d'autre part ...
2 l' <u>aiguille</u> FEM (of clock)

to **hand** VERB
see also **hand** NOUN
<u>passer</u> ◇ *He handed me the book.* Il m'a passé le livre.
♦**to hand something in** rendre quelque chose ◇ *He handed his exam paper in.* Il a rendu sa copie d'examen.
♦**to hand something out** distribuer quelque chose ◇ *The teacher handed out the books.* Le professeur a distribué les livres.
♦**to hand something over** remettre quelque chose ◇ *She handed the keys over to me.* Elle m'a remis les clés.

handbag NOUN
le <u>sac à main</u>
(les sacs à main PL)

handball NOUN
le <u>handball</u> (game)
♦**to play handball** jouer au handball

handbook NOUN
le <u>manuel</u>

handcuffs PL NOUN
les <u>menottes</u> FEM PL

handkerchief NOUN
le <u>mouchoir</u>

handle NOUN
see also **handle** VERB
1 la <u>poignée</u> (of door)
2 l' <u>anse</u> FEM (of cup)
3 le <u>manche</u> (of knife)
4 la <u>queue</u> (of saucepan)

to **handle** VERB
see also **handle** NOUN

♦**He handled it well.** Il s'en est bien tiré.
♦**Kath handled the travel arrangements.** Kath s'est occupée de l'organisation du voyage.
♦**She's good at handling children.** Elle sait bien s'y prendre avec les enfants.

handlebars PL NOUN
le <u>guidon</u> SING

handmade ADJECTIVE
<u>fait à la main</u>

hands-free kit NOUN
le <u>kit mains libres</u> (phone)

handsome ADJECTIVE
<u>beau</u> MASC
<u>belle</u> FEM
◇ *He's handsome.* Il est beau.

handwriting NOUN
l' <u>écriture</u> FEM

handy ADJECTIVE
1 <u>pratique</u> ◇ *This knife's very handy.* Ce couteau est très pratique.
2 <u>sous la main</u> ◇ *Have you got a pen handy?* Est-ce que tu as un stylo sous la main?

to **hang** VERB
1 <u>accrocher</u> ◇ *Mike hung the painting on the wall.* Mike a accroché le tableau au mur.
2 <u>pendre</u> ◇ *They hanged the criminal.* Ils ont pendu le criminel.
♦**to hang around** traîner ◇ *On Saturdays we hang around in the park.* Le samedi nous traînons dans le parc.
♦**to hang on** patienter ◇ *Hang on a minute please.* Patientez une minute s'il vous plaît.
♦**to hang up (1)** (clothes) accrocher ◇ *Hang your jacket up on the hook.* Accrochez votre veste au portemanteau.
♦**to hang up (2)** (phone) raccrocher ◇ *I tried to phone him but he hung up on me.* J'ai essayé de l'appeler, mais il m'a raccroché au nez.

hanger NOUN
le <u>cintre</u> (coat hanger)

hang-gliding NOUN
le <u>deltaplane</u>
♦**to go hang-gliding** faire du deltaplane

hangover NOUN
la <u>gueule de bois</u> ◇ *to have a hangover* avoir la gueule de bois

to **happen** VERB
<u>se passer</u> ◇ *What's happened?* Qu'est-ce qui s'est passé?

♦ **as it happens** justement ◊ *As it happens, I don't want to go.* Justement, je ne veux pas y aller.

happily ADVERB
[1] joyeusement ◊ *"Don't worry!" he said happily.* "Ne te fais pas de souci!" dit-il joyeusement.
[2] heureusement (*fortunately*) ◊ *Happily, everything went well.* Heureusement, tout s'est bien passé.

happiness NOUN
le bonheur

happy ADJECTIVE
heureux MASC
heureuse FEM
◊ *Janet looks happy.* Janet a l'air heureuse.
♦ **I'm very happy with your work.** Je suis très satisfait de ton travail.
♦ **Happy birthday!** Bon anniversaire!

harassment NOUN
le harcèlement ◊ *police harassment* le harcèlement policier

harbour NOUN (US **harbor**)
le port

hard ADJECTIVE, ADVERB
[1] dur ◊ *This cheese is very hard.* Ce fromage est très dur. ◊ *He's worked very hard.* Il a travaillé très dur.
[2] difficile ◊ *This question's too hard for me.* Cette question est trop difficile pour moi.

hard disk NOUN
le disque dur (*of computer*)

hardly ADVERB
♦ **I've hardly got any money.** Je n'ai presque pas d'argent.
♦ **I hardly know you.** Je te connais à peine.
♦ **hardly ever** presque jamais

hard up ADJECTIVE
fauché

hardware NOUN
le hardware (*computing*)

hare NOUN
le lièvre

to **harm** VERB
♦ **to harm somebody** faire du mal à quelqu'un ◊ *I didn't mean to harm you.* Je ne voulais pas te faire de mal.
♦ **to harm something** nuire à quelque chose ◊ *Chemicals harm the environment.* Les produits chimiques nuisent à l'environnement.

harmful ADJECTIVE
nuisible ◊ *harmful chemicals* des produits chimiques nuisibles

harmless ADJECTIVE

inoffensif MASC
inoffensive FEM
◊ *Most spiders are harmless.* La plupart des araignées sont inoffensives.

harsh ADJECTIVE
dur

has VERB *see* **have**

hasn't = **has not**

hat NOUN
le chapeau (les chapeaux PL)

to **hate** VERB
détester ◊ *I hate maths.* Je déteste les maths.

hatred NOUN
la haine

haunted ADJECTIVE
hanté
♦ **a haunted house** une maison hantée

to **have** VERB
[1] avoir ◊ *Have you got a sister?* Tu as une sœur? ◊ *He's got blue eyes.* Il a les yeux bleus. ◊ *I've got a cold.* J'ai un rhume. ◊ *He's done it, hasn't he?* Il l'a fait, non? ◊ *Have you got any money? – No, I haven't!* Est-ce que tu as de l'argent? – Non, je n'en ai pas!
The perfect tense of some verbs is formed with **être.**
[2] être ◊ *They have arrived.* Ils sont arrivés. ◊ *Has he gone?* Est-ce qu'il est parti?
[3] prendre ◊ *He had his breakfast.* Il a pris son petit déjeuner. ◊ *to have a shower* prendre une douche
♦ **to have got to do something** devoir faire quelque chose ◊ *She's got to do it.* Elle doit le faire.
♦ **to have a party** faire une fête
♦ **to have one's hair cut** se faire couper les cheveux

haven't = **have not**

hay NOUN
le foin

hay fever NOUN
le rhume des foins ◊ *Do you get hay fever?* Est-ce que vous êtes sujet au rhume des foins?

hazelnut NOUN
la noisette

he PRONOUN
il ◊ *He loves dogs.* Il aime les chiens.

head NOUN
see also **head** VERB
[1] (*of person*)
la tête ◊ *The wine went to my head.* Le vin m'est monté à la tête.

☞

2 (*of private or primary school*)
le <u>directeur</u>
la <u>directrice</u>
3 (*of state secondary school*)
le <u>proviseur</u>
4 (*leader*)
le <u>chef</u> ◊ *a head of state* un chef d'État
♦ **to have a head for figures** être doué pour les chiffres
♦ **Heads or tails? – Heads.** Pile ou face? – Face.

to **head** VERB

> see also **head** NOUN

♦ **to head for something** se diriger vers quelque chose ◊ *They headed for the church.* Ils se sont dirigés vers l'église.

headache NOUN
♦ **I've got a headache.** J'ai mal à la tête.

headlight NOUN
le <u>phare</u>

headline NOUN
le <u>titre</u>

headmaster NOUN
1 le <u>directeur</u> (*of private or primary school*)
2 le <u>proviseur</u> (*of state secondary school*)

headmistress NOUN
1 la <u>directrice</u> (*of private or primary school*)
2 le <u>proviseur</u> (*of state secondary school*)

headphones PL NOUN
les <u>écouteurs</u> MASC PL

headquarters PL NOUN
le <u>siège</u> SING (*of organization*)

headteacher NOUN
1 (*of private or primary school*)
le <u>directeur</u>
la <u>directrice</u>
2 (*of state secondary school*)
le <u>proviseur</u>
◊ *She's a headteacher.* Elle est proviseur.

to **heal** VERB
<u>cicatriser</u> ◊ *The wound soon healed.* La blessure a vite cicatrisé.

health NOUN
la <u>santé</u>

healthy ADJECTIVE
1 <u>en bonne santé</u> (*person*) ◊ *Lesley's a healthy person.* Lesley est en bonne santé.
2 <u>sain</u> (*climate, food*) ◊ *a healthy diet* une alimentation saine

heap NOUN

le <u>tas</u> ◊ *a rubbish heap* un tas d'ordures

to **hear** VERB
1 <u>entendre</u> ◊ *He heard the dog bark.* Il a entendu le chien aboyer. ◊ *She can't hear very well.* Elle entend mal. ◊ *I heard that she was ill.* J'ai entendu dire qu'elle était malade.
♦ **to hear about something** entendre parler de quelque chose
2 <u>apprendre</u> (*news*) ◊ *Did you hear the good news?* Est-ce que tu as appris la bonne nouvelle?
♦ **to hear from somebody** avoir des nouvelles de quelqu'un ◊ *I haven't heard from him recently.* Je n'ai pas eu de ses nouvelles récemment.

heart NOUN
le <u>cœur</u>
♦ **to learn something by heart** apprendre quelque chose par cœur
♦ **the ace of hearts** l'as de cœur

heart attack NOUN
la <u>crise cardiaque</u>

heartbroken ADJECTIVE
♦ **to be heartbroken** avoir le cœur brisé

heat NOUN

> see also **heat** VERB

la <u>chaleur</u>

to **heat** VERB

> see also **heat** NOUN

<u>faire chauffer</u> ◊ *Heat gently for 5 minutes.* Faire chauffer à feu doux pendant cinq minutes.
♦ **to heat up (1)** (*cooked food*) faire réchauffer ◊ *He heated the soup up.* Il a fait réchauffer la soupe.
♦ **to heat up (2)** (*water, oven*) chauffer ◊ *The water is heating up.* L'eau chauffe.

heater NOUN
le <u>radiateur</u> ◊ *an electric heater* un radiateur électrique

heather NOUN
la <u>bruyère</u>

heating NOUN
le <u>chauffage</u>

heaven NOUN
le <u>paradis</u>

heavily ADVERB
<u>lourdement</u> ◊ *The car was heavily loaded.* La voiture était lourdement chargée.
♦ **He drinks heavily.** C'est un gros buveur.

heavy ADJECTIVE
1 <u>lourd</u> ◊ *This bag's very heavy.* Ce sac est très lourd.
♦ **heavy rain** une grosse averse

2 chargé (*busy*) ◊ *I've got a very heavy week ahead.* Je vais avoir une semaine très chargée.
♦**to be a heavy drinker** être un gros buveur

he'd = **he would**, = **he had**

hedge NOUN
la haie

hedgehog NOUN
le hérisson

heel NOUN
le talon

height NOUN
1 la taille (*of person*)
2 la hauteur (*of object*)
3 l' altitude FEM (*of mountain*)

heir NOUN
l' héritier MASC

heiress NOUN
l' héritière FEM

held VERB *see* **hold**

helicopter NOUN
l' hélicoptère MASC

hell NOUN
l' enfer MASC
♦**Hell!** merde! (*rude*)

he'll = **he will**, = **he shall**

hello EXCLAMATION
bonjour!

helmet NOUN
le casque

to **help** VERB

  see also **help** NOUN

aider ◊ *Can you help me?* Est-ce que vous pouvez m'aider?
♦**Help!** Au secours!
♦**Help yourself!** Servez-vous!
♦**He can't help it.** Il n'y peut rien.

help NOUN

  see also **help** VERB

l' aide FEM ◊ *Do you need any help?* Vous avez besoin d'aide?

helpful ADJECTIVE
serviable ◊ *He was very helpful.* Il a été très serviable.

hen NOUN
la poule

her ADJECTIVE

  see also **her** PRONOUN

son MASC ◊ *her father* son père
sa FEM ◊ *her mother* sa mère
ses PL ◊ *her parents* ses parents
  *sa becomes **son** before a vowel sound.*
♦**her friend (1)** (*male*) son ami
♦**her friend (2)** (*female*) son amie
  *Do not use **son/sa/ses** with parts of the body.*

◊ *She's going to wash her hair.* Elle va se laver les cheveux. ◊ *She's cleaning her teeth.* Elle se brosse les dents. ◊ *She's hurt her foot.* Elle s'est fait mal au pied.

her PRONOUN

  see also **her** ADJECTIVE

  *la becomes **l'** before a vowel sound.*
1 la ◊ *I can see her.* Je la vois.
◊ *Look at her!* Regarde-la!
l' ◊ *I saw her.* Je l'ai vue.
  *Use **lui** when **her** means **to her**.*
2 lui ◊ *I gave her a book.* Je lui ai donné un livre. ◊ *I told her the truth.* Je lui ai dit la vérité.
  *Use **elle** after prepositions.*
3 elle ◊ *I'm going with her.* Je vais avec elle. ◊ *He sat next to her.* Il s'est assis à côté d'elle.
  ***elle** is also used in comparisons.*
◊ *I'm older than her.* Je suis plus âgé qu'elle.

herb NOUN
l' herbe FEM
♦**herbs** les fines herbes ◊ *What herbs do you use in this sauce?* Quelles fines herbes utilise-t-on pour cette sauce?

here ADVERB
ici ◊ *I live here.* J'habite ici.
♦**here is ...** voici ... ◊ *Here's Helen.* Voici Helen. ◊ *Here he is!* Le voici!
♦**here are ...** voici ... ◊ *Here are the books.* Voici les livres.

heritage NOUN
le patrimoine

hero NOUN
le héros ◊ *He's a real hero!* C'est un véritable héros!

heroin NOUN
l' héroïne FEM ◊ *Heroin is a hard drug.* L'héroïne est une drogue dure.
♦**a heroin addict** un héroïnomane
◊ *She's a heroin addict.* C'est une héroïnomane.

heroine NOUN
l' héroïne FEM ◊ *the heroine of the novel* l'héroïne du roman

hers PRONOUN
le sien + MASC NOUN ◊ *Is this her coat?* – *No, hers is black.* C'est son manteau? – Non, le sien est noir.
la sienne + FEM NOUN ◊ *Is this her car?* – *No, hers is white.* C'est sa voiture? – Non, la sienne est blanche.
les siens + MASC PL NOUN ◊ *my parents and hers* mes parents et les siens
les siennes + FEM PL NOUN ◊ *my reasons and hers* mes raisons et les siennes

H

☞

◆**Is this hers?** C'est à elle? ◊ *This book is hers.* Ce livre est à elle. ◊ *Whose is this? – It's hers.* C'est à qui? – À elle.

herself PRONOUN
1 se ◊ *She's hurt herself.* Elle s'est blessée.
2 elle (*after preposition*) ◊ *She talked mainly about herself.* Elle a surtout parlé d'elle.
3 elle-même ◊ *She did it herself.* Elle l'a fait elle-même.
◆**by herself** toute seule ◊ *She doesn't like travelling by herself.* Elle n'aime pas voyager toute seule.

he's = **he is**, = **he has**

to **hesitate** VERB
hésiter

heterosexual ADJECTIVE
hétérosexuel MASC
hétérosexuelle FEM

hi EXCLAMATION
salut!

hiccups PL NOUN
◆**to have hiccups** avoir le hoquet

to **hide** VERB
se cacher ◊ *He hid behind a bush.* Il s'est caché derrière un buisson.
◆**to hide something** cacher quelque chose ◊ *Paula hid the present.* Paula a caché le cadeau.

hide-and-seek NOUN
◆**to play hide-and-seek** jouer à cache-cache

hideous ADJECTIVE
hideux MASC
hideuse FEM

hi-fi NOUN
la chaîne hi-fi
(les chaînes hi-fi PL)

high ADJECTIVE, ADVERB
1 haut ◊ *It's too high.* C'est trop haut.
◆**How high is the wall?** Quelle est la hauteur du mur?
◆**The wall's 2 metres high.** Le mur fait deux mètres de haut.
2 élevé ◊ *a high price* un prix élevé ◊ *a high temperature* une température élevée
◆**at high speed** à grande vitesse
◆**It's very high in fat.** C'est très gras.
◆**She's got a very high voice.** Elle a la voix très aiguë.
◆**to be high** (*on drugs*) être défoncé (*informal*)
◆**to get high** se défoncer (*informal*) ◊ *to get high on crack* se défoncer au crack

higher education NOUN

l' enseignement supérieur MASC

high-heeled ADJECTIVE
à hauts talons
◆**high-heeled shoes** des chaussures à hauts talons

high jump NOUN
le saut en hauteur (*sport*)

highlight NOUN
see also **highlight** VERB
le clou ◊ *the highlight of the evening* le clou de la soirée

to **highlight** VERB
see also **highlight** NOUN
1 souligner (*underline*)
2 surligner (*with highlighter pen*)

highlighter NOUN
le surligneur

high-rise NOUN
la tour ◊ *I live in a high-rise.* J'habite dans une tour.

high school NOUN
le lycée

to **hijack** VERB
détourner

hijacker NOUN
le pirate de l'air

hike NOUN
la randonnée

hiking NOUN
◆**to go hiking** faire une randonnée

hilarious ADJECTIVE
hilarant ◊ *It was hilarious!* C'était hilarant!

hill NOUN
la colline ◊ *She walked up the hill.* Elle a gravi la colline.

hill-walking NOUN
la randonnée de basse montagne ◊ *to go hill-walking* faire de la randonnée de basse montagne

him PRONOUN
le becomes l' before a vowel sound.
1 le ◊ *I can see him.* Je le vois.
◊ *Look at him!* Regarde-le!
l' ◊ *I saw him.* Je l'ai vu.
Use lui when him means to him, and after prepositions.
2 lui ◊ *I gave him a book.* Je lui ai donné un livre. ◊ *I told him the truth.* Je lui ai dit la vérité. ◊ *I'm going with him.* Je vais avec lui. ◊ *She sat next to him.* Elle s'est assise à côté de lui.
lui is also used in comparisons.
◊ *I'm older than him.* Je suis plus âgé que lui.

himself PRONOUN

⬚1 se ◊ *He's hurt himself.* Il s'est blessé.
⬚2 lui ◊ *He talked mainly about himself.* Il a surtout parlé de lui.
⬚3 lui-même ◊ *He did it himself.* Il l'a fait lui-même.
♦**by himself** tout seul ◊ *He was travelling by himself.* Il voyageait tout seul.

Hindu ADJECTIVE
hindou ◊ *a Hindu temple* un temple hindou

hint NOUN
see also **hint** VERB
l' allusion FEM
♦**to drop a hint** faire une allusion

to **hint** VERB
see also **hint** NOUN
laisser entendre ◊ *He hinted that I had a good chance of getting the job.* Il m'a laissé entendre que j'avais de grandes chances d'avoir ce travail.
♦**What are you hinting at?** Qu'est-ce que vous voulez dire par là ?

hip NOUN
la hanche

hippie NOUN
le hippie
la hippie

hippo NOUN
l' hippopotame MASC

to **hire** VERB
see also **hire** NOUN
⬚1 louer ◊ *to hire a car* louer une voiture
⬚2 engager (*person*) ◊ *They hired a cleaner.* Ils ont engagé une femme de ménage.

hire NOUN
see also **hire** VERB
la location
♦**car hire** location de voitures
♦**for hire** à louer

hire car NOUN
la voiture de location

his ADJECTIVE
see also **his** PRONOUN
son MASC ◊ *his father* son père
sa FEM SING ◊ *his mother* sa mère
ses PL ◊ *his parents* ses parents
sa becomes son before a vowel sound.
♦**his friend (1)** (*male*) son ami
♦**his friend (2)** (*female*) son amie
Do not use son/sa/ses with parts of the body.
◊ *He's going to wash his hair.* Il va se laver les cheveux. ◊ *He's cleaning his*

teeth. Il se brosse les dents. ◊ *He's hurt his foot.* Il s'est fait mal au pied.

his PRONOUN
see also **his** ADJECTIVE
le sien + MASC NOUN ◊ *Is this his coat? – No, his is black.* C'est son manteau? – Non, le sien est noir.
la sienne + FEM NOUN ◊ *Is this his car? – No, his is white.* C'est sa voiture? – Non, la sienne est blanche.
les siens + MASC PL NOUN ◊ *my parents and his* mes parents et les siens
les siennes + FEM PL NOUN ◊ *my reasons and his* mes raisons et les siennes
♦**Is this his?** C'est à lui ? ◊ *This book is his.* Ce livre est à lui. ◊ *Whose is this? – It's his.* C'est à qui? – À lui.

history NOUN
l' histoire FEM

to **hit** VERB
see also **hit** NOUN
⬚1 frapper ◊ *Andrew hit him.* Andrew l'a frappé.
⬚2 renverser ◊ *He was hit by a car.* Il a été renversé par une voiture.
⬚3 toucher ◊ *The arrow hit the target.* La flèche a touché la cible.
♦**to hit it off with somebody** bien s'entendre avec quelqu'un ◊ *She hit it off with his parents.* Elle s'est bien entendue avec ses parents.

hit NOUN
see also **hit** VERB
⬚1 le tube (*song*) ◊ *Blur's latest hit* le dernier tube de Blur
⬚2 le succès (*success*) ◊ *The film was a massive hit.* Le film a eu un immense succès.

hitch NOUN
le contretemps ◊ *There's been a slight hitch.* Il y a eu un léger contretemps.

to **hitchhike** VERB
faire de l'auto-stop

hitchhiker NOUN
l' auto-stoppeur MASC
l' auto-stoppeuse FEM

hitchhiking NOUN
l' auto-stop MASC ◊ *Hitchhiking can be dangerous.* Il peut être dangereux de faire de l'auto-stop.

hit man NOUN
le tueur à gages

HIV-negative ADJECTIVE
séronégatif MASC
séronégative FEM

HIV-positive ADJECTIVE
séropositif MASC
séropositive FEM

hobby NOUN
le passe-temps favori ◊ *What are your hobbies?* Quels sont tes passe-temps favoris?

hockey NOUN
le hockey ◊ *I play hockey.* Je joue au hockey.

to **hold** VERB
1 tenir (*hold on to*) ◊ *She held the baby.* Elle tenait le bébé.
2 contenir (*contain*) ◊ *This bottle holds one litre.* Cette bouteille contient un litre.
♦ **to hold a meeting** avoir une réunion
♦ **Hold the line!** (*on telephone*) Ne quittez pas!
♦ **Hold it!** (*wait*) Attends!
♦ **to get hold of something** (*obtain*) trouver quelque chose ◊ *I couldn't get hold of it.* Je n'ai pas réussi à en trouver.

to **hold on** VERB
1 tenir bon (*keep hold*) ◊ *The cliff was slippery but he managed to hold on.* La falaise était glissante, mais il est parvenu à tenir bon.
♦ **to hold on to something** se cramponner à quelque chose ◊ *He held on to the chair.* Il se cramponnait à la chaise.
2 attendre (*wait*) ◊ *Hold on, I'm coming!* Attends, je viens!
♦ **Hold on!** (*on telephone*) Ne quittez pas!

to **hold up** VERB
♦ **to hold up one's hand** lever la main ◊ *Pierre held up his hand.* Pierre a levé la main.
♦ **to hold somebody up** (*delay*) retenir quelqu'un ◊ *I was held up at the office.* J'ai été retenu au bureau.
♦ **to hold up a bank** (*rob*) braquer une banque (*informal*)

hold-up NOUN
1 le hold-up (*at bank*)
2 le retard (*delay*)
3 le bouchon (*traffic jam*)

hole NOUN
le trou

holiday NOUN
1 les vacances FEM PL ◊ *Did you have a good holiday?* Tu as passé de bonnes vacances? ◊ *our holidays in France* nos vacances en France
♦ **on holiday** en vacances ◊ *to go on holiday* partir en vacances ◊ *We are on holiday.* Nous sommes en vacances.
♦ **the school holidays** les vacances scolaires

2 le jour férié (*public holiday*) ◊ *Next Wednesday is a holiday.* Mercredi prochain est un jour férié.
3 le jour de congé (*day off*) ◊ *He took a day's holiday.* Il a pris un jour de congé.
♦ **a holiday camp** un camp de vacances

Holland NOUN
la Hollande
♦ **in Holland** en Hollande
♦ **to Holland** en Hollande

hollow ADJECTIVE
creux MASC
creuse FEM

holly NOUN
le houx ◊ *a sprig of holly* un brin de houx

holy ADJECTIVE
saint

home NOUN
see also **home** ADVERB
la maison
♦ **at home** à la maison
♦ **Make yourself at home.** Faites comme chez vous.

home ADVERB
see also **home** NOUN
à la maison ◊ *I'll be home at 5 o'clock.* Je serai à la maison à cinq heures.
♦ **to get home** rentrer ◊ *What time did he get home?* Il est rentré à quelle heure?

home address NOUN
l' adresse FEM ◊ *What's your home address?* Quelle est votre adresse?

homeland NOUN
la patrie

homeless ADJECTIVE
sans abri MASC, FEM, PL
♦ **the homeless** les sans-abri

home match NOUN
le match à domicile

homeopathy NOUN
l' homéopathie FEM

home page NOUN
la page d'accueil

homesick ADJECTIVE
♦ **to be homesick** avoir le mal du pays

homework NOUN
les devoirs MASC PL ◊ *Have you done your homework?* Est-ce que tu as fait tes devoirs? ◊ *my geography homework* mes devoirs de géographie

homosexual ADJECTIVE
see also **homosexual** NOUN
homosexuel MASC

homosexuelle FEM

homosexual NOUN
> *see also* **homosexual** ADJECTIVE

l' homosexuel MASC
l' homosexuelle FEM

honest ADJECTIVE
1 (*trustworthy*)
honnête ◊ *She's a very honest person.* Elle est très honnête.
2 (*sincere*)
franc MASC
franche FEM
◊ *He was very honest with her.* Il a été très franc avec elle.

honestly ADVERB
franchement ◊ *I honestly don't know.* Franchement, je n'en sais rien.

honesty NOUN
l' honnêteté FEM

honey NOUN
le miel

honeymoon NOUN
la lune de miel

honour NOUN (US **honor**)
l' honneur MASC

hood NOUN
1 la capuche (*on coat*)
2 le capot (*of car*) US

hook NOUN
le crochet ◊ *He hung the painting on the hook.* Il a suspendu le tableau au crochet.
♦ **to take the phone off the hook** décrocher le téléphone
♦ **a fish-hook** un hameçon

hooligan NOUN
le voyou
(les voyous PL)

hooray EXCLAMATION
hourra!

Hoover ® NOUN
l' aspirateur MASC

to **hoover** VERB
passer l'aspirateur ◊ *to hoover the lounge* passer l'aspirateur dans le salon

to **hope** VERB
> *see also* **hope** NOUN

espérer ◊ *I hope he comes.* J'espère qu'il va venir. ◊ *I'm hoping for good results.* J'espère avoir de bons résultats.
♦ **I hope so.** Je l'espère.
♦ **I hope not.** J'espère que non.

hope NOUN
> *see also* **hope** VERB

l' espoir MASC

♦ **to give up hope** perdre espoir ◊ *Don't give up hope!* Ne perds pas espoir!

hopeful ADJECTIVE
1 plein d'espoir ◊ *I'm hopeful.* Je suis plein d'espoir.
♦ **He's hopeful of winning.** Il a bon espoir de gagner.
2 (*situation*)
prometteur MASC
prometteuse FEM
◊ *The prospects look hopeful.* Les perspectives semblent prometteuses.

hopefully ADVERB
avec un peu de chance ◊ *Hopefully he'll make it in time.* Avec un peu de chance, il arrivera à temps.

hopeless ADJECTIVE
nul MASC
nulle FEM
◊ *I'm hopeless at maths.* Je suis nul en maths.

horizon NOUN
l' horizon MASC

horizontal ADJECTIVE
horizontal
(horizontaux MASC PL)

horn NOUN
1 le klaxon ◊ *He sounded his horn.* Il a klaxonné.
2 le cor ◊ *I play the horn.* Je joue du cor.

horoscope NOUN
l' horoscope MASC

horrible ADJECTIVE
horrible ◊ *What a horrible dress!* Quelle robe horrible!

horrifying ADJECTIVE
effrayant

horror NOUN
l' horreur FEM

horror film NOUN
le film d'horreur

horse NOUN
le cheval
(les chevaux PL)

horse-racing NOUN
les courses de chevaux FEM PL

horseshoe NOUN
le fer à cheval

hose NOUN
le tuyau
(les tuyaux PL)
◊ *a garden hose* un tuyau d'arrosage

hosepipe NOUN
le tuyau d'arrosage

hospital NOUN
l' hôpital MASC
(les hôpitaux PL)

☞

◊ *Take me to the hospital!* Emmenez-moi à l'hôpital! ◊ *in hospital* à l'hôpital

hospitality NOUN
l' hospitalité FEM

host NOUN
l' hôte MASC
l' hôtesse FEM
◊ *Don't forget to write and thank your hosts.* N'oublie pas d'écrire à tes hôtes pour les remercier.

hostage NOUN
l' otage MASC
♦ **to take somebody hostage** prendre quelqu'un en otage

hostel NOUN
le foyer (*for refugees, homeless people*)
♦ **a youth hostel** une auberge de jeunesse

hostile ADJECTIVE
hostile

hot ADJECTIVE
1 chaud (*warm*) ◊ *a hot bath* un bain chaud ◊ *a hot country* un pays chaud
　*When you are talking about a person being hot, you use **avoir chaud**.*
◊ *I'm hot.* J'ai chaud. ◊ *I'm too hot.* J'ai trop chaud.
　*When you mean that the weather is hot, you use **faire chaud**.*
◊ *It's hot.* Il fait chaud. ◊ *It's very hot today.* Il fait très chaud aujourd'hui.
2 épicé (*spicy*) ◊ *a very hot curry* un curry très épicé

hot dog NOUN
le hot-dog

hotel NOUN
l' hôtel MASC ◊ *We stayed in a hotel.* Nous avons logé à l'hôtel.

hour NOUN
l' heure FEM ◊ *She always takes hours to get ready.* Elle passe toujours des heures à se préparer.
♦ **a quarter of an hour** un quart d'heure
♦ **half an hour** une demi-heure
♦ **two and a half hours** deux heures et demie

hourly ADJECTIVE, ADVERB
toutes les heures ◊ *There are hourly buses.* Il y a des bus toutes les heures.
♦ **to be paid hourly** être payé à l'heure

house NOUN
la maison
♦ **at his house** chez lui
♦ **We stayed at their house.** Nous avons séjourné chez eux.

housewife NOUN
la femme au foyer ◊ *She's a housewife.* Elle est femme au foyer.

housework NOUN
le ménage
♦ **to do the housework** faire le ménage

hovercraft NOUN
l' aéroglisseur MASC

how ADVERB
comment ◊ *How are you?* Comment allez-vous?
♦ **How many?** Combien?
♦ **How many ...?** Combien de ...? ◊ *How many pupils are there in the class?* Combien d'élèves y a-t-il dans la classe?
♦ **How much?** Combien?
♦ **How much ...?** Combien de ...? ◊ *How much sugar do you want?* Combien de sucres voulez-vous?
♦ **How old are you?** Quel âge as-tu?
♦ **How far is it to Edinburgh?** Combien y a-t-il de kilomètres d'ici à Édimbourg?
♦ **How long have you been here?** Depuis combien de temps êtes-vous là?
♦ **How do you say "apple" in French?** Comment dit-on "apple" en français?

however CONJUNCTION
pourtant ◊ *This, however, isn't true.* Pourtant, ce n'est pas vrai.

to **howl** VERB
hurler

HTML NOUN
le langage HTML ◊ *an HTML document* un document en langage HTML

to **hug** VERB
　see also **hug** NOUN
serrer dans ses bras ◊ *He hugged her.* Il l'a serrée dans ses bras.

hug NOUN
　see also **hug** VERB
♦ **to give somebody a hug** serrer quelqu'un dans ses bras ◊ *She gave them a hug.* Elle les a serrés dans ses bras.

huge ADJECTIVE
immense

to **hum** VERB
fredonner

human ADJECTIVE
humain ◊ *the human body* le corps humain

human being NOUN
l' être humain MASC

humble ADJECTIVE
humble

humour NOUN (US **humor**)
l' humour MASC

♦**to have a sense of humour** avoir le sens de l'humour

hundred NUMBER
♦**a hundred** cent ◊ *a hundred euros* cent euros
♦**five hundred** cinq cents
♦**five hundred and one** cinq cent un
♦**hundreds of people** des centaines de personnes

hung VERB *see* **hang**

Hungarian NOUN
see also **Hungarian** ADJECTIVE
[1] (*person*)
le Hongrois
la Hongroise
[2] (*language*)
le hongrois

Hungarian ADJECTIVE
see also **Hungarian** NOUN
hongrois ◊ *She's Hungarian.* Elle est hongroise.

Hungary NOUN
la Hongrie
♦**in Hungary** en Hongrie
♦**to Hungary** en Hongrie

hunger NOUN
la faim

hungry ADJECTIVE
♦**to be hungry** avoir faim ◊ *I'm hungry.* J'ai faim.

to **hunt** VERB
[1] chasser (*animal*) ◊ *People used to hunt wild boar.* On chassait le sanglier autrefois.
♦**to go hunting** aller à la chasse
[2] pourchasser (*criminal*) ◊ *The police are hunting the killer.* La police pourchasse le criminel.
♦**to hunt for something** (*search*) chercher quelque chose partout ◊ *I hunted everywhere for that book.* J'ai cherché ce livre partout.

hunting NOUN
la chasse ◊ *I'm against hunting.* Je suis contre la chasse.
♦**fox-hunting** la chasse au renard

hurdle NOUN
l' obstacle MASC

hurricane NOUN

l' ouragan MASC

to **hurry** VERB
see also **hurry** NOUN
se dépêcher ◊ *Sharon hurried back home.* Sharon s'est dépêchée de rentrer chez elle.
♦**Hurry up!** Dépêche-toi!

hurry NOUN
see also **hurry** VERB
♦**to be in a hurry** être pressé
♦**to do something in a hurry** faire quelque chose en vitesse
♦**There's no hurry.** Rien ne presse.

to **hurt** VERB
see also **hurt** ADJECTIVE
♦**to hurt somebody (1)** (*physically*) faire mal à quelqu'un ◊ *You're hurting me!* Tu me fais mal!
♦**to hurt somebody (2)** (*emotionally*) blesser quelqu'un ◊ *His remarks really hurt me.* Ses remarques m'ont vraiment blessé.
♦**to hurt oneself** se faire mal ◊ *I fell over and hurt myself.* Je me suis fait mal en tombant.
♦**That hurts.** Ça fait mal. ◊ *It hurts to have a tooth out.* Ça fait mal de se faire arracher une dent.
♦**My leg hurts.** J'ai mal à la jambe.

hurt ADJECTIVE
see also **hurt** VERB
blessé ◊ *Is he badly hurt?* Est-ce qu'il est grièvement blessé? ◊ *He was hurt in the leg.* Il a été blessé à la jambe. ◊ *I was hurt by what he said.* J'ai été blessé par ce qu'il a dit.
♦**Luckily, nobody got hurt.** Heureusement, il n'y a pas eu de blessés.

husband NOUN
le mari

hut NOUN
la hutte

hymn NOUN
le cantique

hypermarket NOUN
l' hypermarché MASC

hyphen NOUN
le trait d'union

H

I

I PRONOUN
- **1** je ◇ *I speak French.* Je parle français.

  je changes to j' before a vowel and most words beginning with "h".
  ◇ *I love cats.* J'aime les chats.
- **2** moi ◇ *Ann and I* Ann et moi

ice NOUN
- **1** la glace ◇ *There was ice on the lake.* Il y avait de la glace sur le lac.
- **2** le verglas (*on road*)

iceberg NOUN
   l' iceberg MASC

icebox NOUN US
   le frigo

ice cream NOUN
   la glace ◇ *vanilla ice cream* la glace à la vanille

ice cube NOUN
   le glaçon

ice hockey NOUN
   le hockey sur glace

Iceland NOUN
   l' Islande FEM
- ◆**in Iceland** en Islande
- ◆**to Iceland** en Islande

ice lolly NOUN
   la glace à l'eau

ice rink NOUN
   la patinoire

ice-skating NOUN
   le patinage sur glace
- ◆**to go ice-skating** faire du patin à glace

icing NOUN
   le glaçage (*on cake*)
- ◆**icing sugar** le sucre glace

icon NOUN
   l' icône FEM

ICT NOUN
   l' informatique FEM

icy ADJECTIVE
   glacial
   (glaciaux MASC PL)
   ◇ *There was an icy wind.* Il y avait un vent glacial.
- ◆**The roads are icy.** Il y a du verglas sur les routes.

I'd = **I had**, = **I would**

idea NOUN
   l' idée FEM ◇ *Good idea!* Bonne idée!

ideal ADJECTIVE
   idéal
   (idéaux MASC PL)

identical ADJECTIVE
   identique

identification NOUN
   l' identification FEM

to **identify** VERB
   identifier

identity card NOUN
   la carte d'identité

idiot NOUN
   l' idiot MASC
   l' idiote FEM

idiotic ADJECTIVE
   stupide

idle ADJECTIVE
   fainéant (*lazy*)

i.e. ABBREVIATION
   c.-à-d. (= c'est-à-dire)

if CONJUNCTION
   si ◇ *You can have it if you like.* Tu peux le prendre si tu veux.

   si changes to s' before il and ils.
   ◇ *Do you know if he's there?* Savez-vous s'il est là?
- ◆**if only** si seulement ◇ *If only I had more money!* Si seulement j'avais plus d'argent!
- ◆**if not** sinon ◇ *Are you coming? If not, I'll go with Mark.* Est-ce que tu viens? Sinon, j'irai avec Mark.

ignorant ADJECTIVE
   ignorant

to **ignore** VERB
- ◆**to ignore something** ne tenir aucun compte de quelque chose ◇ *She ignored my advice.* Elle n'a tenu aucun compte de mes conseils.
- ◆**to ignore somebody** ignorer quelqu'un ◇ *She saw me, but she ignored me.* Elle m'a vu, mais elle m'a ignoré.
- ◆**Just ignore him!** Ne fais pas attention à lui!

ill ADJECTIVE
   malade (*sick*)
- ◆**to be taken ill** tomber malade ◇ *She was taken ill while on holiday.* Elle est tombée malade pendant qu'elle était en vacances.

I'll = **I will**

illegal ADJECTIVE
   illégal
   (illégaux MASC PL)

illegible ADJECTIVE
   illisible

illness NOUN
  la <u>maladie</u>
to **ill-treat** VERB
  <u>maltraiter</u>
illusion NOUN
  l' <u>illusion</u> FEM
illustration NOUN
  l' <u>illustration</u> FEM
image NOUN
  l' <u>image</u> FEM ◊ *The company has changed its image.* La société a changé d'image.
imagination NOUN
  l' <u>imagination</u> FEM
to **imagine** VERB
  <u>imaginer</u> ◊ *You can imagine how I felt!* Tu peux imaginer ce que j'ai ressenti! ◊ *Is he angry? – I imagine so.* Est-ce qu'il est en colère? – J'imagine que oui.
to **imitate** VERB
  <u>imiter</u>
imitation NOUN
  l' <u>imitation</u> FEM
immediate ADJECTIVE
  <u>immédiat</u>
immediately ADVERB
  <u>immédiatement</u> ◊ *I'll do it immediately.* Je vais le faire immédiatement.
immigrant NOUN
  l' <u>immigré</u> MASC
  l' <u>immigrée</u> FEM
immigration NOUN
  l' <u>immigration</u> FEM
immoral ADJECTIVE
  <u>immoral</u>
  (immoraux MASC PL)
impartial ADJECTIVE
  <u>impartial</u>
  (impartiaux MASC PL)
impatience NOUN
  l' <u>impatience</u> FEM
impatient ADJECTIVE
  <u>impatient</u>
  ♦ **to get impatient** s'impatienter ◊ *People are getting impatient.* Les gens commencent à s'impatienter.
impatiently ADVERB
  <u>avec impatience</u> ◊ *We waited impatiently.* Nous avons attendu avec impatience.
impersonal ADJECTIVE
  <u>impersonnel</u> MASC
  <u>impersonnelle</u> FEM
importance NOUN
  l' <u>importance</u> FEM
important ADJECTIVE

important
impossible ADJECTIVE
  <u>impossible</u>
to **impress** VERB
  <u>impressionner</u> ◊ *She's trying to impress you.* Elle essaie de t'impressionner.
impressed ADJECTIVE
  <u>impressionné</u> ◊ *I'm very impressed!* Je suis très impressionné!
impression NOUN
  l' <u>impression</u> FEM ◊ *I was under the impression that ...* J'avais l'impression que ...
impressive ADJECTIVE
  <u>impressionnant</u>
to **improve** VERB
  [1] <u>améliorer</u> (*make better*) ◊ *They have improved the service.* Ils ont amélioré le service.
  [2] <u>s'améliorer</u> (*get better*) ◊ *The weather is improving.* Le temps s'améliore. ◊ *My French has improved.* Mon français s'est amélioré.
improvement NOUN
  [1] l' <u>amélioration</u> FEM (*of condition*) ◊ *It's a great improvement.* C'est une nette amélioration.
  [2] le <u>progrès</u> (*of learner*) ◊ *There's been an improvement in his French.* Il a fait des progrès en français.
in PREPOSITION, ADVERB

There are several ways of translating in. Scan the examples to find one that is similar to what you want to say. For other expressions with in, see the verbs go, come, get, give etc.

  [1] <u>dans</u> ◊ *in the house* dans la maison ◊ *in my bag* dans mon sac ◊ *in the sixties* dans les années soixante ◊ *I'll see you in three weeks.* Je te verrai dans trois semaines.
  [2] <u>à</u> ◊ *in the country* à la campagne ◊ *in school* à l'école ◊ *in hospital* à l'hôpital ◊ *in London* à Londres ◊ *in spring* au printemps ◊ *in the sun* au soleil ◊ *in the shade* à l'ombre ◊ *in a loud voice* à voix haute ◊ *the boy in the blue shirt* le garçon à la chemise bleue ◊ *It was written in pencil.* C'était écrit au crayon.
  [3] <u>en</u> ◊ *in French* en français ◊ *in summer* en été ◊ *in May* en mai ◊ *in 1996* en dix-neuf cent quatre-vingt seize ◊ *I did it in 3 hours.* Je l'ai fait en trois heures. ◊ *in town* en ville ◊ *in prison* en prison ◊ *in tears* en

I

☞

larmes ◊ *in good condition* en bon
état

*When **in** refers to a country which is
feminine, use **en**; when the country
is masculine, use **au**; when the
country is plural, use **aux**.*

◊ *in France* en France ◊ *in Portugal*
au Portugal ◊ *in the United States*
aux États-Unis

[4] de ◊ *the best pupil in the class* le
meilleur élève de la classe ◊ *the best
team in the world* la meilleure équipe
du monde ◊ *the tallest person in the
family* le plus grand de la famille ◊ *at
4 o'clock in the afternoon* à quatre
heures de l'après-midi ◊ *at 6 in the
morning* à six heures du matin

♦**in the afternoon** l'après-midi
♦**You look good in that dress.** Tu es
jolie avec cette robe.
♦**in time** à temps ◊ *We arrived in time
for dinner.* Nous sommes arrivés à
temps pour le dîner.
♦**in here** ici ◊ *It's hot in here.* Il fait
chaud ici.
♦**in the rain** sous la pluie
♦**one person in ten** une personne sur
dix
♦**to be in** (*at home, work*) être là ◊ *He
wasn't in.* Il n'était pas là.
♦**to ask somebody in** inviter quelqu'un
à entrer

inaccurate ADJECTIVE
inexact

inadequate ADJECTIVE
inadéquat (*measures, resources*)
♦**I felt completely inadequate.** Je ne
me sentais absolument pas à la
hauteur.

incentive NOUN
♦**There is no incentive to work.** Il n'y a
rien qui incite à travailler.

inch NOUN
le pouce

ⓘ *In France measurements are in
metres and centimetres rather than
feet and inches. An inch is about 2.5
centimetres.*

♦**6 inches** quinze centimètres

incident NOUN
l' incident MASC

inclined ADJECTIVE
♦**to be inclined to do something** avoir
tendance à faire quelque chose ◊ *He's
inclined to arrive late.* Il a tendance à
arriver en retard.

to **include** VERB

comprendre ◊ *Service is not
included.* Le service n'est pas
compris.

including PREPOSITION
compris ◊ *It will be 200 euros,
including tax.* Ça coûtera deux cents
euros, toutes taxes comprises.

inclusive ADJECTIVE
compris ◊ *The inclusive price is 200
euros.* Ça coûte deux cents euros
tout compris.
♦**inclusive of tax** taxes comprises

income NOUN
le revenu

income tax NOUN
l' impôt sur le revenu MASC

incompetent ADJECTIVE
incompétent

incomplete ADJECTIVE
incomplet MASC
incomplète FEM

inconsistent ADJECTIVE
incohérent

inconvenience NOUN
♦**I don't want to cause any
inconvenience.** Je ne veux pas vous
déranger.

inconvenient ADJECTIVE
♦**That's very inconvenient for me.** Ça
ne m'arrange pas du tout.

incorrect ADJECTIVE
incorrect

increase NOUN
see also **increase** VERB
l' augmentation FEM ◊ *an increase in
road accidents* une augmentation des
accidents de la route

to **increase** VERB
see also **increase** NOUN
augmenter

incredible ADJECTIVE
incroyable

indecisive ADJECTIVE
indécis (*person*)

indeed ADVERB
vraiment ◊ *It's very hard indeed.*
C'est vraiment très difficile.
♦**Know what I mean? – Indeed I do.** Tu
vois ce que je veux dire? – Oui, tout
à fait.
♦**Thank you very much indeed!** Merci
beaucoup!

independence NOUN
l' indépendance FEM

independent ADJECTIVE
indépendant
♦**an independent school** une école
privée

index NOUN
l' index MASC (*in book*)

index finger NOUN
l' index MASC

India NOUN
l' Inde FEM
♦**in India** en Inde
♦**to India** en Inde

Indian ADJECTIVE
see also **Indian** NOUN
indien MASC
indienne FEM

Indian NOUN
see also **Indian** ADJECTIVE
(*person*)
l' Indien MASC
l' Indienne FEM
♦**an American Indian** un Indien d'Amérique

to **indicate** VERB
indiquer

indicator NOUN
le clignotant (*on car*) ◊ *Put your indicators on.* Mets tes clignotants.

indigestion NOUN
l' indigestion FEM
♦**I've got indigestion.** J'ai une indigestion.

individual ADJECTIVE
individuel MASC
individuelle FEM

indoor ADJECTIVE
♦**an indoor swimming pool** une piscine couverte

indoors ADVERB
à l'intérieur ◊ *They're indoors.* Ils sont à l'intérieur.
♦**to go indoors** rentrer ◊ *We'd better go indoors.* Nous ferions mieux de rentrer.

industrial ADJECTIVE
industriel MASC
industrielle FEM

industrial estate NOUN
la zone industrielle

industry NOUN
l' industrie FEM ◊ *the tourist industry* l'industrie du tourisme ◊ *the oil industry* l'industrie pétrolière ◊ *I'd like to work in industry.* J'aimerais travailler dans l'industrie.

inefficient ADJECTIVE
inefficace

inevitable ADJECTIVE
inévitable

inexpensive ADJECTIVE
bon marché MASC, FEM, PL ◊ *an inexpensive hotel* un hôtel bon marché ◊ *inexpensive holidays* des vacances bon marché

inexperienced ADJECTIVE
inexpérimenté

infant school NOUN

> ⓘ *CP (cours préparatoire) is the equivalent of first-year infants, and CE1 (cours élémentaire première année) the equivalent of second-year infants.*

◊ *He's just started at infant school.* Il vient d'entrer au cours préparatoire.

infection NOUN
l' infection FEM ◊ *an ear infection* une infection de l'oreille
♦**a throat infection** une angine

infectious ADJECTIVE
contagieux MASC
contagieuse FEM
◊ *It's not infectious.* Ce n'est pas contagieux.

infinitive NOUN
l' infinitif MASC

infirmary NOUN
l' hôpital MASC
(les hôpitaux PL)

inflatable ADJECTIVE
gonflable (*mattress, dinghy*)

inflation NOUN
l' inflation FEM

influence NOUN
see also **influence** VERB
l' influence FEM ◊ *He's a bad influence on her.* Il a mauvaise influence sur elle.

to **influence** VERB
see also **influence** NOUN
influencer

influenza NOUN
la grippe

to **inform** VERB
informer
♦**to inform somebody of something** informer quelqu'un de quelque chose ◊ *Nobody informed me of the new plan.* Personne ne m'a informé de ce nouveau projet.

informal ADJECTIVE
1 (*person, party*)
décontracté ◊ *"informal dress"* "tenue décontractée"
2 (*colloquial*)
familier MASC
familière FEM
◊ *informal language* le langage familier

I

◆**an informal visit** une visite non officielle

information NOUN
les <u>renseignements</u> MASC PL
◇ *important information* les renseignements importants
◆**a piece of information** un renseignement
◆**Could you give me some information about trains to Paris?** Pourriez-vous me renseigner sur les trains pour Paris?

information office NOUN
le <u>bureau des renseignements</u>

infuriating ADJECTIVE
<u>exaspérant</u>

ingenious ADJECTIVE
<u>ingénieux</u> MASC
<u>ingénieuse</u> FEM

ingredient NOUN
l' <u>ingrédient</u> MASC

inhabitant NOUN
l' <u>habitant</u> MASC
l' <u>habitante</u> FEM

to **inherit** VERB
<u>hériter de</u> ◇ *She inherited her father's house.* Elle a hérité de la maison de son père.

initials PL NOUN
les <u>initiales</u> FEM PL ◇ *Her initials are CDT.* Ses initiales sont CDT.

initiative NOUN
l' <u>initiative</u> FEM

to **inject** VERB
<u>injecter</u> (*drug*)

injection NOUN
la <u>piqûre</u>

to **injure** VERB
<u>blesser</u>

injured ADJECTIVE
<u>blessé</u>

injury NOUN
la <u>blessure</u>

injury time NOUN
les <u>arrêts de jeu</u> MASC PL

injustice NOUN
l' <u>injustice</u> FEM

ink NOUN
l' <u>encre</u> FEM

in-laws PL NOUN
les <u>beaux-parents</u> MASC PL

inn NOUN
l' <u>auberge</u> FEM

inner ADJECTIVE
<u>intérieur</u>
◆**the inner city** les quartiers déshérités du centre ville MASC PL

inner tube NOUN
la <u>chambre à air</u>

innocent ADJECTIVE
<u>innocent</u>

inquest NOUN
l' <u>enquête</u> FEM

to **inquire** VERB
◆**to inquire about something** se renseigner sur quelque chose ◇ *I'm going to inquire about train times.* Je vais me renseigner sur les horaires des trains.

inquiries office NOUN
le <u>bureau des renseignements</u>

inquiry NOUN
◆**to make inquiries about something** faire des demandes de renseignement ◇ *"inquiries"* "renseignements"

inquisitive ADJECTIVE
<u>curieux</u> MASC
<u>curieuse</u> FEM

insane ADJECTIVE
<u>fou</u> MASC
<u>folle</u> FEM

inscription NOUN
l' <u>inscription</u> FEM

insect NOUN
l' <u>insecte</u> MASC

insect repellent NOUN
l' <u>insectifuge</u> MASC

insensitive ADJECTIVE
<u>indélicat</u> ◇ *That was a bit insensitive of you.* C'était un peu indélicat de ta part.

inside NOUN
see also **inside** ADVERB
l' <u>intérieur</u> MASC

inside ADVERB, PREPOSITION
see also **inside** NOUN
à l'intérieur ◇ *They're inside.* Ils sont à l'intérieur. ◇ *inside the house* à l'intérieur de la maison
◆**to go inside** rentrer
◆**Come inside!** Rentrez!

insincere ADJECTIVE
<u>peu sincère</u>

to **insist** VERB
<u>insister</u> ◇ *I didn't want to, but he insisted.* Je ne voulais pas, mais il a insisté.
◆**to insist on doing something** insister pour faire quelque chose ◇ *She insisted on paying.* Elle a insisté pour payer.
◆**He insisted he was innocent.** Il affirmait qu'il était innocent.

to **inspect** VERB
<u>inspecter</u>

inspector NOUN
l' inspecteur MASC (police) ◊ *Inspector Jill Brown* l'inspecteur Jill Brown
♦**ticket inspector** (*on buses*) le contrôleur

instalment NOUN
1 le versement (*payment*) ◊ *to pay in instalments* payer en plusieurs versements
2 l' épisode MASC (*episode*)

instance NOUN
♦**for instance** par exemple

instant ADJECTIVE
immédiat ◊ *It was an instant success.* Ça a été un succès immédiat.
♦**instant coffee** le café instantané

instantly ADVERB
tout de suite

instead ADVERB
♦**instead of (1)** (*followed by noun*) à la place de ◊ *He went instead of Peter.* Il y est allé à la place de Peter.
♦**instead of (2)** (*followed by verb*) au lieu de ◊ *We played tennis instead of going swimming.* Nous avons joué au tennis au lieu d'aller nager.
♦**The pool was closed, so we played tennis instead.** La piscine était fermée, alors nous avons joué au tennis.

instinct NOUN
l' instinct MASC

institute NOUN
l' institut MASC

institution NOUN
l' institution FEM

to **instruct** VERB
♦**to instruct somebody to do something** donner l'ordre à quelqu'un de faire quelque chose ◊ *She instructed us to wait outside.* Elle nous a donné l'ordre d'attendre dehors.

instructions PL NOUN
1 les instructions FEM PL ◊ *Follow the instructions carefully.* Suivez soigneusement les instructions.
2 le mode d'emploi SING (*booklet*) ◊ *Where are the instructions?* Où est le mode d'emploi?

instructor NOUN
le moniteur
la monitrice
◊ *a skiing instructor* un moniteur de ski ◊ *a driving instructor* un moniteur d'auto-école

instrument NOUN

l' instrument MASC ◊ *Do you play an instrument?* Est-ce que tu joues d'un instrument?

insufficient ADJECTIVE
insuffisant

insulin NOUN
l' insuline FEM

insult NOUN
see also **insult** VERB
l' insulte FEM

to **insult** VERB
see also **insult** NOUN
insulter

insurance NOUN
l' assurance FEM ◊ *his car insurance* son assurance automobile
♦**an insurance policy** une police d'assurance

intelligent ADJECTIVE
intelligent

to **intend** VERB
♦**to intend to do something** avoir l'intention de faire quelque chose ◊ *I intend to do French at university.* J'ai l'intention d'étudier le français à l'université.

intense ADJECTIVE
intense

intensive ADJECTIVE
intensif MASC
intensive FEM

intention NOUN
l' intention FEM

intercom NOUN
l' interphone MASC

interest NOUN
see also **interest** VERB
l' intérêt MASC ◊ *to show an interest in something* manifester de l'intérêt pour quelque chose
♦**What interests do you have?** Quels sont tes centres d'intérêt?
♦**My main interest is music.** Ce qui m'intéresse le plus c'est la musique.

to **interest** VERB
see also **interest** NOUN
intéresser ◊ *It doesn't interest me.* Ça ne m'intéresse pas.
♦**to be interested in something** s'intéresser à quelque chose ◊ *I'm not interested in politics.* Je ne m'intéresse pas à la politique.

interesting ADJECTIVE
intéressant

interior NOUN
l' intérieur MASC

interior designer NOUN
le/la designer

intermediate ADJECTIVE
(*course, level*)
moyen MASC
moyenne FEM

internal ADJECTIVE
interne

international ADJECTIVE
international
(internationaux MASC PL)

internet NOUN
l' Internet MASC ◊ *on the internet* sur Internet

internet café NOUN
le cybercafé

internet user NOUN
l' internaute MASC/FEM

to **interpret** VERB
servir d'interprète ◊ *Steve couldn't speak French, so his friend interpreted.* Comme Steve ne savait pas le français, son ami a servi d'interprète.

interpreter NOUN
l' interprète MASC/FEM

to **interrupt** VERB
interrompre

interruption NOUN
l' interruption FEM

interval NOUN
l' entracte MASC (*in play, concert*)

interview NOUN
see also **interview** VERB
1 l' interview FEM (*on TV, radio*)
2 l' entretien MASC (*for job*)

to **interview** VERB
see also **interview** NOUN
interviewer (*on TV, radio*) ◊ *I was interviewed on the radio.* J'ai été interviewé à la radio.

interviewer NOUN
l' interviewer MASC (*on TV, radio*)

intimate ADJECTIVE
intime

into PREPOSITION
1 dans ◊ *He got into the car.* Il est monté dans la voiture.
2 en ◊ *I'm going into town.* Je vais en ville. ◊ *Translate it into French.* Traduisez ça en français. ◊ *Divide into two groups.* Répartissez-vous en deux groupes.

to **introduce** VERB
présenter ◊ *I'd like to introduce Michelle Davies.* Je vous présente Michelle Davies. ◊ *He introduced me to his parents.* Il m'a présenté à ses parents.

introduction NOUN

l' introduction FEM (*in book*)

intruder NOUN
l' intrus MASC
l' intruse FEM

intuition NOUN
l' intuition FEM

to **invade** VERB
envahir

invalid NOUN
le/la malade

to **invent** VERB
inventer

invention NOUN
l' invention FEM

inventor NOUN
l' inventeur MASC
l' inventrice FEM

investigation NOUN
l' enquête FEM (*police*)

investment NOUN
l' investissement MASC ◊ *The railway system is suffering from a lack of investment.* Le réseau ferroviaire souffre d'un manque d'investissement.

invigilator NOUN
le surveillant
la surveillante

invisible ADJECTIVE
invisible

invitation NOUN
l' invitation FEM

to **invite** VERB
inviter ◊ *He's not invited.* Il n'est pas invité.
♦ **to invite somebody to a party** inviter quelqu'un à une fête

to **involve** VERB
nécessiter ◊ *His job involves a lot of travelling.* Son travail nécessite de nombreux déplacements.
♦ **to be involved in something** (*crime, drugs*) être impliqué dans quelque chose
♦ **to be involved with somebody** (*in relationship*) avoir une relation avec quelqu'un

IQ NOUN (= *intelligence quotient*)
le Q.I. (= quotient intellectuel)

Iran NOUN
l' Iran MASC
♦ **in Iran** en Iran

Iraq NOUN
l' Iraq MASC
♦ **in Iraq** en Iraq

Iraqi ADJECTIVE
see also **Iraqi** NOUN
irakien MASC

irakienne FEM
◊ *the Iraqi government* le
gouvernement irakien

Iraqi NOUN
see also **Iraqi** ADJECTIVE
l' Irakien MASC
l' Irakienne FEM
◆**the Iraqis** les Irakiens

Ireland NOUN
l' Irlande FEM
◆**in Ireland** en Irlande
◆**to Ireland** en Irlande
◆**I'm from Ireland.** Je suis irlandais.

Irish ADJECTIVE
see also **Irish** NOUN
irlandais ◊ *Irish music* la musique
irlandaise

Irish NOUN
see also **Irish** ADJECTIVE
l' irlandais MASC (*language*)
◆**the Irish** (*people*) les Irlandais

Irishman NOUN
l' Irlandais MASC

Irishwoman NOUN
l' Irlandaise FEM

iron NOUN
see also **iron** VERB
1 le fer (*metal*)
2 le fer à repasser (*for clothes*)

to **iron** VERB
see also **iron** NOUN
repasser

ironic ADJECTIVE
ironique

ironing NOUN
le repassage ◊ *to do the ironing*
faire le repassage

ironing board NOUN
la planche à repasser

ironmonger's (shop) NOUN
la quincaillerie

irrelevant ADJECTIVE
hors de propos ◊ *That's irrelevant.*
C'est hors de propos.

irresponsible ADJECTIVE
irresponsable (*person*) ◊ *That was
irresponsible of him.* C'était
irresponsable de sa part.

irritating ADJECTIVE
irritant

is VERB *see* **be**

Islam NOUN
l' Islam MASC

Islamic ADJECTIVE
islamique ◊ *Islamic law* la loi
islamique
◆**Islamic fundamentalists** les intégristes
musulmans MASC

island NOUN
l' île FEM

isle NOUN
◆**the Isle of Man** l'île de Man
◆**the Isle of Wight** l'île de Wight

isolated ADJECTIVE
isolé

ISP NOUN (= *internet service provider*)
le fournisseur d'accès à Internet

Israel NOUN
Israël MASC
◆**in Israel** en Israël

Israeli ADJECTIVE
see also **Israeli** NOUN
israélien MASC
israélienne FEM

Israeli NOUN
see also **Israeli** ADJECTIVE
l' Israélien MASC
l' Israélienne FEM

issue NOUN
see also **issue** VERB
1 la question (*matter*) ◊ *a
controversial issue* une question
controversée
2 le numéro (*of magazine*)

to **issue** VERB
see also **issue** NOUN
distribuer (*equipment, supplies*)

it PRONOUN
Remember to check if **it** *stands for a
masculine or feminine noun.*
1 il ◊ *Where's my book? – It's on the
table.* Où est mon livre? – Il est sur la
table.
elle ◊ *When does the pool close? – It
closes at 8.* La piscine ferme à quelle
heure? – Elle ferme à vingt heures.
Use **le** *or* **la** *when* **it** *is the object of
the sentence.* **le** *and* **la** *change to* **l'**
*before a vowel and most words
beginning with "h".*
2 le ◊ *There's a croissant left. Do
you want it?* Il reste un croissant. Tu
le veux?
l' ◊ *It's a good film. Did you see it?*
C'est un bon film. L'as-tu vu?
la ◊ *I don't want this apple. Take it.*
Je ne veux pas de cette pomme.
Prends-la.
l' ◊ *He's got a new car. – Yes, I saw
it.* Il a une nouvelle voiture. – Oui, je
l'ai vue.
◆**It's raining.** Il pleut.
◆**It's 6 o'clock.** Il est six heures.
◆**It's Friday tomorrow.** Demain c'est
vendredi.
◆**Who is it? – It's me.** Qui est-ce? –
C'est moi.
◆**It's expensive.** C'est cher.

Italian ADJECTIVE

see also **Italian** NOUN

italien MASC
italienne FEM

Italian NOUN

see also **Italian** ADJECTIVE

1 (person)
l' Italien MASC
l' Italienne FEM
2 (language)
l' italien MASC

Italy NOUN
l' Italie FEM
♦in **Italy** en Italie
♦to **Italy** en Italie

to **itch** VERB
♦It itches. Ça me démange.
♦My head's itching. J'ai des
démangeaisons à la tête.

itchy ADJECTIVE
♦My arm is itchy. J'ai des fourmis
dans le bras.

it'd = it had, = it would

item NOUN
l' article MASC (object)

itinerary NOUN
l' itinéraire MASC

it'll = it will

its ADJECTIVE

Remember to check if **its** refers to a
masculine, feminine or plural noun.

son MASC ◊ What's its name? Quel est
son nom?
sa FEM ◊ Every thing in its place.
Chaque chose à sa place.
ses PL ◊ The dog is losing its hair. Le
chien perd ses poils.

it's = it is, = it has

itself PRONOUN

se

se changes to **s'** before a vowel and
most words beginning with "h".

◊ The heating switches itself off. Le
chauffage s'arrête automatiquement.

I've = I have

J

jab NOUN
la piqûre (*injection*)

jack NOUN
1 le cric (*for car*)
2 le valet (*playing card*)

jacket NOUN
la veste
♦ **jacket potatoes** les pommes de terre
en robe des champs FEM

jackpot NOUN
le gros lot
♦ **to win the jackpot** gagner le gros lot

jail NOUN
see also **jail** VERB
la prison
♦ **to go to jail** aller en prison

to **jail** VERB
see also **jail** NOUN
emprisonner

jam NOUN
la confiture ◊ *strawberry jam* la
confiture de fraises
♦ **a traffic jam** un embouteillage

jam jar NOUN
le pot à confiture

jammed ADJECTIVE
coincé ◊ *The window's jammed.* La
fenêtre est coincée.

jam-packed ADJECTIVE
bondé ◊ *The room was jam-packed.*
La salle était bondée.

janitor NOUN
le concierge ◊ *He's a janitor.* Il est
concierge.

January NOUN
janvier MASC
♦ **in January** en janvier

Japan NOUN
le Japon
♦ **in Japan** au Japon
♦ **from Japan** du Japon

Japanese ADJECTIVE
see also **Japanese** NOUN
japonais

Japanese NOUN
see also **Japanese** ADJECTIVE
1 (*person*)
le Japonais
la Japonaise
♦ **the Japanese** les Japonais
2 (*language*)
le japonais

jar NOUN
le bocal

(les bocaux PL)
◊ *an empty jar* un bocal vide
♦ **a jar of honey** un pot de miel

jaundice NOUN
la jaunisse

javelin NOUN
le javelot

jaw NOUN
la mâchoire

jazz NOUN
le jazz

jealous ADJECTIVE
jaloux MASC
jalouse FEM

jeans PL NOUN
le jean SING

Jehovah's Witness NOUN
le témoin de Jéhovah ◊ *She's a
Jehovah's Witness.* Elle est témoin de
Jéhovah.

Jello ® NOUN US
la gelée

jelly NOUN
la gelée

jellyfish NOUN
la méduse

jersey NOUN
le pull-over (*pullover*)

Jesus NOUN
Jésus MASC

jet NOUN
le jet (*plane*)

jetlag NOUN
♦ **to be suffering from jetlag** être sous
le coup du décalage horaire

jetty NOUN
la jetée

Jew NOUN
le Juif
la Juive

jewel NOUN
le bijou
(les bijoux PL)

jeweller NOUN (US **jeweler**)
le bijoutier
la bijoutière
◊ *He's a jeweller.* Il est bijoutier.

jeweller's shop NOUN (US **jeweler's
shop**)
la bijouterie

jewellery NOUN (US **jewelry**)
les bijoux MASC PL

Jewish ADJECTIVE

☞

juif MASC
juive FEM

jigsaw NOUN
le **puzzle**

job NOUN
[1] l' **emploi** MASC ◇ *He's lost his job.* Il a perdu son emploi.
♦**I've got a Saturday job.** Je travaille le samedi.
[2] (*chore, task*)
le **travail**
(les travaux PL)
◇ *That was a difficult job.* C'était un travail difficile.

job centre NOUN
l' **agence pour l'emploi** FEM

jobless ADJECTIVE
sans emploi

jockey NOUN
le **jockey**

to **jog** VERB
faire du jogging

jogging NOUN
le **jogging**
♦**to go jogging** faire du jogging

john NOUN US
les **toilettes** FEM PL

to **join** VERB
[1] **s'inscrire à** (*become member of*)
◇ *I'm going to join the ski club.* Je vais m'inscrire au club de ski.
[2] **se joindre à** ◇ *Do you mind if I join you?* Puis-je me joindre à vous?

joiner NOUN
le **menuisier** ◇ *He's a joiner.* Il est menuisier.

joint NOUN
[1] l' **articulation** FEM (*in body*)
[2] le **rôti** (*of meat*)
[3] le **joint** (*drugs*)

joke NOUN
see also **joke** VERB
la **plaisanterie**
♦**to tell a joke** raconter une plaisanterie

to **joke** VERB
see also **joke** NOUN
plaisanter ◇ *I'm only joking.* Je plaisante.

jolly ADJECTIVE
jovial
(joviaux MASC PL)

Jordan NOUN
la **Jordanie** (*country*)
♦**in Jordan** en Jordanie

to **jot down** VERB
noter

jotter NOUN
(*pad*)

bloc-notes
le **bloc-notes**
(les blocs-notes PL)

journalism NOUN
le **journalisme**

journalist NOUN
le/la **journaliste** ◇ *She's a journalist.* Elle est journaliste.

journey NOUN
[1] le **voyage** ◇ *I don't like long journeys.* Je n'aime pas les longs voyages.
♦**to go on a journey** faire un voyage
[2] le **trajet** (*to school, work*) ◇ *The journey to school takes about half an hour.* Il y a une demi-heure de trajet pour aller à l'école.
♦**a bus journey** un trajet en autobus

joy NOUN
la **joie**

joystick NOUN
le **manette de jeu** (*for computer game*)

judge NOUN
see also **judge** VERB
le **juge** ◇ *She's a judge.* Elle est juge.

to **judge** VERB
see also **judge** NOUN
juger

judo NOUN
le **judo** ◇ *My hobby is judo.* Je fais du judo.

jug NOUN
le **pot**

juggler NOUN
le **jongleur**
la **jongleuse**

juice NOUN
le **jus** ◇ *orange juice* le jus d'orange

July NOUN
juillet MASC
♦**in July** en juillet

jumble sale NOUN
la **vente de charité**

to **jump** VERB
sauter
♦**to jump over something** sauter par-dessus quelque chose
♦**to jump out of the window** sauter par la fenêtre
♦**to jump off the roof** sauter du toit

jumper NOUN
le **pull-over** (*pullover*)

junction NOUN
le **carrefour** (*of roads*)

June NOUN
juin MASC
♦**in June** en juin

jungle NOUN

la <u>jungle</u>

junior NOUN
- **the juniors** (*in school*) les élèves des petites classes

junior school NOUN
l' <u>école primaire</u> FEM

junk NOUN
le <u>bric-à-brac</u> NO PL (*old things*) ◊ *The attic's full of junk.* Le grenier est rempli de bric-à-brac.
- **to eat junk food** manger n'importe comment
- **a junk shop** un magasin de brocante

jury NOUN
le <u>jury</u>

just ADVERB

<u>juste</u> ◊ *just after Christmas* juste après Noël ◊ *We had just enough money.* Nous avions juste assez d'argent. ◊ *just in time* juste à temps
- **just here** ici
- **I'm rather busy just now.** Je suis assez occupé en ce moment.
- **I did it just now.** Je viens de le faire.
- **He's just arrived.** Il vient d'arriver.
- **I'm just coming!** J'arrive!
- **It's just a suggestion.** Ce n'est qu'une suggestion.

justice NOUN
la <u>justice</u>

to **justify** VERB
<u>justifier</u>

J

K

kangaroo NOUN
le kangourou

karaoke NOUN
le karaoké

karate NOUN
le karaté

kebab NOUN
1 la brochette (*shish kebab*)
2 le doner kebab (*doner kebab*)

keen ADJECTIVE
enthousiaste ◊ *He doesn't seem very keen.* Il n'a pas l'air très enthousiaste.
♦**She's a keen student.** C'est une étudiante assidue.
♦**to be keen on something** aimer quelque chose ◊ *I'm keen on maths.* J'aime les maths. ◊ *I'm not very keen on maths.* Je n'aime pas trop les maths.
♦**to be keen on somebody** (*fancy them*) être très attiré par quelqu'un ◊ *He's keen on her.* Il est très attiré par elle.
♦**to be keen on doing something** avoir très envie de faire quelque chose ◊ *I'm not very keen on going.* Je n'ai pas très envie d'y aller.

to **keep** VERB
1 garder (*retain*) ◊ *You can keep it.* Tu peux le garder.
2 rester (*remain*) ◊ *Keep still!* Reste tranquille!
♦**Keep quiet!** Tais-toi!
♦**I keep forgetting my keys.** J'oublie tout le temps mes clés.
♦**to keep on doing something (1)** (*continue*) continuer à faire quelque chose ◊ *He kept on reading.* Il a continué à lire.
♦**to keep on doing something (2)** (*repeatedly*) ne pas arrêter de faire quelque chose ◊ *The car keeps on breaking down.* La voiture n'arrête pas de tomber en panne.
♦**"keep out"** "défense d'entrer"

to **keep up** VERB
se maintenir à la hauteur de quelqu'un ◊ *Matthew walks so fast I can't keep up.* Matthew marche tellement vite que je n'arrive pas à me maintenir à sa hauteur.
♦**I can't keep up with the rest of the class.** Je n'arrive pas à suivre le reste de la classe.

keep-fit NOUN
la gymnastique d'entretien

♦**I go to keep-fit classes.** Je vais à des cours de gymnastique.

kennel NOUN
la niche

kept VERB *see* **keep**

kerosene NOUN [US]
le pétrole

kettle NOUN
la bouilloire

key NOUN
la clé

keyboard NOUN
le clavier ◊ *... with Mike Moran on keyboards* ... avec Mike Moran aux claviers

keyring NOUN
le porte-clés

kick NOUN
see also **kick** VERB
le coup de pied

to **kick** VERB
see also **kick** NOUN
♦**to kick somebody** donner un coup de pied à quelqu'un ◊ *He kicked me.* Il m'a donné un coup de pied. ◊ *He kicked the ball hard.* Il a donné un bon coup de pied dans le ballon.
♦**to kick off** (*in football*) donner le coup d'envoi

kick-off NOUN
le coup d'envoi ◊ *The kick-off is at 10 o'clock.* Le coup d'envoi sera donné à dix heures.

kid NOUN
see also **kid** VERB
le/la gosse (*child*)

to **kid** VERB
see also **kid** NOUN
plaisanter ◊ *I'm just kidding.* Je plaisante.

to **kidnap** VERB
kidnapper

kidney NOUN
1 le rein (*human*) ◊ *He's got kidney trouble.* Il a des problèmes de reins.
2 le rognon (*to eat*) ◊ *I don't like kidneys.* Je n'aime pas les rognons.

to **kill** VERB
tuer ◊ *He was killed in a car accident.* Il a été tué dans un accident de voiture.
♦**Luckily, nobody was killed.** Il n'y a heureusement pas eu de victimes.

♦**Six people were killed in the accident.** L'accident a fait six morts.
♦**to kill oneself** se suicider ◊ *He killed himself.* Il s'est suicidé.

killer NOUN
　1 (*murderer*)
　le meurtrier
　la meurtrière
　◊ *The police are searching for the killer.* La police recherche le meurtrier.
　2 (*hit man*)
　le tueur
　la tueuse
　◊ *a hired killer* un tueur à gages
♦**Meningitis can be a killer.** La méningite peut être mortelle.

kilo NOUN
　le kilo ◊ *10 euros a kilo* dix euros le kilo

kilometre NOUN (US **kilometer**)
　le kilomètre

kilt NOUN
　le kilt

kind ADJECTIVE
　see also **kind** NOUN
　gentil MASC
　gentille FEM
♦**to be kind to somebody** être gentil avec quelqu'un
♦**Thank you for being so kind.** Merci pour votre gentillesse.

kind NOUN
　see also **kind** ADJECTIVE
　la sorte ◊ *It's a kind of sausage.* C'est une sorte de saucisse.

kindergarten NOUN
　l' école maternelle FEM

kindly ADVERB
　gentiment ◊ *"Don't worry," she said kindly.* "Ne t'en fais pas", m'a-t-elle dit gentiment.
♦**Kindly refrain from smoking.** Veuillez vous abstenir de fumer.

kindness NOUN
　la gentillesse

king NOUN
　le roi

kingdom NOUN
　le royaume

kiosk NOUN
　la cabine téléphonique (*phone box*)

kipper NOUN
　le hareng fumé

kiss NOUN
　see also **kiss** VERB
　le baiser ◊ *a passionate kiss* un baiser passionné

to **kiss** VERB
　see also **kiss** NOUN
　1 embrasser ◊ *He kissed her passionately.* Il l'a embrassée passionnément.
　2 s'embrasser ◊ *They kissed.* Ils se sont embrassés.

kit NOUN
　1 les affaires FEM PL (*clothes for sport*) ◊ *I've forgotten my gym kit.* J'ai oublié mes affaires de gym.
　2 la trousse ◊ *a tool kit* une trousse à outils ◊ *a first aid kit* une trousse de secours ◊ *a puncture repair kit* une trousse de réparations
♦**a drum kit** une batterie
♦**a sewing kit** un nécessaire à couture

kitchen NOUN
　la cuisine ◊ *a fitted kitchen* une cuisine aménagée
♦**the kitchen units** les éléments de cuisine MASC
♦**a kitchen knife** un couteau de cuisine

kite NOUN
　le cerf-volant
　(les cerfs-volants PL)

kitten NOUN
　le chaton

knee NOUN
　le genou
　(les genoux PL)
♦**He was on his knees.** Il était à genoux.

to **kneel (down)** VERB
　s'agenouiller

knew VERB see **know**

knickers PL NOUN
　la culotte SING
♦**a pair of knickers** une culotte

knife NOUN
　le couteau
　(les couteaux PL)
♦**a kitchen knife** un couteau de cuisine
♦**a sheath knife** un couteau à gaine
♦**a penknife** un canif

to **knit** VERB
　tricoter

knitting NOUN
　le tricot ◊ *I like knitting.* J'aime faire du tricot.

knives PL NOUN see **knife**

knob NOUN
　le bouton (*on door, radio, TV, radiator*)

to **knock** VERB
　see also **knock** NOUN
　frapper ◊ *Someone's knocking at the door.* Quelqu'un frappe à la porte.
♦**to knock somebody down** renverser quelqu'un ◊ *She was knocked down*

K

☞

by a car. Elle a été renversée par une voiture.

◆**to knock somebody out (1)** (*defeat*) éliminer ◊ *They were knocked out early in the tournament.* Ils ont été éliminés au début du tournoi.

◆**to knock somebody out (2)** (*stun*) assommer ◊ *They knocked out the watchman.* Ils ont assommé le gardien.

knock NOUN

> *see also* **knock** VERB

le <u>coup</u>

knot NOUN

le <u>nœud</u>

◆**to tie a knot in something** faire un nœud à quelque chose

to **know** VERB

> Use **savoir** for knowing facts, **connaître** for knowing people and places.

⒈ <u>savoir</u> ◊ *It's a long way. – Yes, I know.* C'est loin. – Oui, je sais. ◊ *I don't know.* Je ne sais pas. ◊ *I don't know what to do.* Je ne sais pas quoi faire. ◊ *I don't know how to do it.* Je ne sais pas comment faire.

⒉ <u>connaître</u> ◊ *I know her.* Je la connais. ◊ *I know Paris well.* Je connais bien Paris.

◆**I don't know any German.** Je ne parle pas du tout allemand.

◆**to know that ...** savoir que ... ◊ *I know that you like chocolate.* Je sais que tu aimes le chocolat. ◊ *I didn't know that your Dad was a policeman.* Je ne savais pas que ton père était policier.

◆**to know about something (1)** (*be aware of*) être au courant de quelque chose ◊ *Do you know about the meeting this afternoon?* Tu es au courant de la réunion de cet après-midi?

◆**to know about something (2)** (*be knowledgeable about*) s'y connaître en quelque chose ◊ *He knows a lot about cars.* Il s'y connaît en voitures. ◊ *I don't know much about computers.* Je ne m'y connais pas bien en informatique.

◆**to get to know somebody** apprendre à connaître quelqu'un

◆**How should I know?** (*I don't know!*) Comment veux-tu que je le sache?

◆**You never know!** On ne sait jamais!

know-all NOUN

le/la <u>je-sais-tout</u> ◊ *He's such a know-all!* C'est Monsieur je-sais-tout!

know-how NOUN

le <u>savoir-faire</u>

knowledge NOUN

la <u>connaissance</u>

knowledgeable ADJECTIVE

◆**to be knowledgeable about something** s'y connaître en quelque chose ◊ *She's very knowledgeable about computers.* Elle s'y connaît bien en informatique.

known VERB *see* **know**

Koran NOUN

le <u>Coran</u>

Korea NOUN

la <u>Corée</u>

◆**in Korea** en Corée

kosher ADJECTIVE

<u>kascher</u> MASC, FEM, PL

L

lab NOUN (= *laboratory*)
le labo
- **a lab technician** un laborantin

label NOUN
l' étiquette FEM

labor NOUN US
- **to be in labor** être en train
d'accoucher
- **the labor market** le marché du travail
- **a labor union** un syndicat

laboratory NOUN
le laboratoire

Labour NOUN
les travaillistes MASC PL ◊ *My parents
vote Labour.* Mes parents votent pour
les travaillistes.
- **the Labour Party** le parti travailliste

labour NOUN
- **to be in labour** être en train
d'accoucher
- **the labour market** le marché du
travail

labourer NOUN
le manœuvre
- **a farm labourer** un ouvrier agricole

lace NOUN
1 le lacet (*of shoe*)
2 la dentelle ◊ *a lace collar* un col
en dentelle

lack NOUN
le manque ◊ *He got the job despite
his lack of experience.* Il a obtenu le
poste en dépit de son manque
d'expérience.
- **There was no lack of volunteers.** Les
volontaires ne manquaient pas.

lacquer NOUN
la laque

lad NOUN
le gars

ladder NOUN
l' échelle FEM

lady NOUN
la dame
- **a young lady** une jeune fille
- **Ladies and gentlemen ...** Mesdames,
Messieurs ...
- **the ladies'** les toilettes pour dames FEM

ladybird NOUN
la coccinelle

to **lag behind** VERB
rester en arrière

lager NOUN
la bière blonde

laid VERB *see* **lay**

laid-back ADJECTIVE
relaxe

lain VERB *see* **lie**

lake NOUN
le lac
- **Lake Geneva** le lac Léman

lamb NOUN
l' agneau MASC
(les agneaux PL)
- **a lamb chop** une côtelette d'agneau

lame ADJECTIVE
boiteux ◊ *My pony is lame.* Mon
poney boîte.

lamp NOUN
la lampe

lamppost NOUN
le réverbère

lampshade NOUN
l' abat-jour MASC
(les abat-jour PL)

land NOUN
see also **land** VERB
la terre
- **a piece of land** un terrain

to **land** VERB
see also **land** NOUN
atterrir (*plane, passenger*)

landing NOUN
1 l' atterrissage MASC (*of plane*)
2 le palier (*of staircase*)

landlady NOUN
la propriétaire

landlord NOUN
le propriétaire

landmark NOUN
le point de repère (*for finding your
way*)
- **Big Ben is one of London's most
famous landmarks.** Big Ben est l'un
des sites les plus célèbres du paysage
londonien.

landowner NOUN
le propriétaire terrien

landscape NOUN
le paysage

lane NOUN
1 le chemin (*in country*)
2 la voie (*on motorway*)

language NOUN
la langue ◊ *French isn't a difficult
language.* Le français n'est pas une
langue difficile.

☞

◆**to use bad language** dire des grossièretés

language laboratory NOUN
le laboratoire de langues

lap NOUN
le tour de piste (*sport*) ◊ *I ran ten laps.* J'ai fait dix tours de piste en courant.

◆**on my lap** sur mes genoux

laptop NOUN
le portable (*computer*)

larder NOUN
le garde-manger
(les garde-manger PL)

large ADJECTIVE
1 grand ◊ *a large house* une grande maison
2 (*person, animal*)
gros MASC
grosse FEM
◊ *a large dog* un gros chien

largely ADVERB
en grande partie ◊ *It's largely the fault of the government.* C'est en grande partie la faute du gouvernement.

laser NOUN
le laser

lass NOUN
la jeune fille

last ADJECTIVE, ADVERB
see also **last** VERB
1 dernier MASC
dernière FEM
◊ *last Friday* vendredi dernier ◊ *last week* la semaine dernière ◊ *last summer* l'été dernier
2 en dernier ◊ *He arrived last.* Il est arrivé en dernier.
3 pour la dernière fois ◊ *I've lost my bag. – When did you see it last?* J'ai perdu mon sac. – Quand est-ce que tu l'as vu pour la dernière fois? ◊ *When I last saw him, he was wearing a blue shirt.* La dernière fois que je l'ai vu, il portait une chemise bleue.
◆**the last time** la dernière fois ◊ *the last time I saw her* la dernière fois que je l'ai vue ◊ *That's the last time I take your advice!* C'est la dernière fois que je suis tes conseils!
◆**last night (1)** (*evening*) hier soir ◊ *I got home at midnight last night.* Je suis rentré à minuit hier soir.
◆**last night (2)** (*sleeping hours*) la nuit dernière ◊ *I couldn't sleep last night.* J'ai eu du mal à dormir la nuit dernière.
◆**at last** enfin

to **last** VERB
see also **last** ADJECTIVE
durer ◊ *The concert lasts two hours.* Le concert dure deux heures.

lastly ADVERB
finalement ◊ *Lastly, what time do you arrive?* Finalement, à quelle heure arrives-tu?

late ADJECTIVE, ADVERB
1 en retard ◊ *Hurry up or you'll be late!* Dépêche-toi, sinon tu vas être en retard! ◊ *I'm often late for school.* J'arrive souvent en retard à l'école.
◆**to arrive late** arriver en retard ◊ *She arrived late.* Elle est arrivée en retard.
2 tard ◊ *I went to bed late.* Je me suis couché tard.
◆**in the late afternoon** en fin d'après-midi
◆**in late May** fin mai

lately ADVERB
ces derniers temps ◊ *I haven't seen him lately.* Je ne l'ai pas vu ces derniers temps.

later ADVERB
plus tard ◊ *I'll do it later.* Je ferai ça plus tard.
◆**See you later!** À tout à l'heure!

latest ADJECTIVE
dernier MASC
dernière FEM
◊ *their latest album* leur dernier album
◆**at the latest** au plus tard ◊ *by 10 o'clock at the latest* à dix heures au plus tard

Latin NOUN
le latin ◊ *I do Latin.* Je fais du latin.

Latin America NOUN
l' Amérique latine FEM
◆**in Latin America** en Amérique latine

Latin American ADJECTIVE
latino-américain

latter NOUN
le second
la seconde
◆**the former ..., the latter ...** le premier ..., le second ... ◊ *The former lives in the US, the latter in Australia.* Le premier habite aux États-Unis, le second en Australie.
◆**The latter is the more expensive of the two systems.** Ce dernier système est le plus coûteux des deux.

laugh NOUN
see also **laugh** VERB
le rire
◆**It was a good laugh.** (*it was fun*) On s'est bien amusés.

to **laugh** VERB

> see also **laugh** NOUN

rire
* **to laugh at something** se moquer de quelque chose ◊ *They laughed at her.* Ils se sont moqués d'elle.

to **launch** VERB
lancer (*product, rocket, boat*) ◊ *They're going to launch a new model.* Ils vont lancer un nouveau modèle.

Launderette ® NOUN
la laverie

Laundromat ® NOUN US
la laverie

laundry NOUN
le linge (*clothes*)

lavatory NOUN
les toilettes FEM PL

lavender NOUN
la lavande

law NOUN
[1] la loi ◊ *The laws are very strict.* Les lois sont très sévères.
* **It's against the law.** C'est illégal.
[2] le droit (*subject*) ◊ *My sister's studying law.* Ma sœur fait des études de droit.

lawn NOUN
la pelouse

lawnmower NOUN
la tondeuse à gazon

law school NOUN US
la faculté de droit

lawyer NOUN
l' avocat MASC
l' avocate FEM
◊ *My mother's a lawyer.* Ma mère est avocate.

to **lay** VERB

> *lay is also a form of **lie** VERB.*

mettre ◊ *She laid the baby in her cot.* Elle a mis le bébé dans son lit.
* **to lay the table** mettre la table
* **to lay something on (1)** (*provide*) organiser quelque chose ◊ *They laid on extra buses.* Ils ont organisé un service de bus supplémentaire.
* **to lay something on (2)** (*prepare*) préparer quelque chose ◊ *They laid on a special meal.* Ils ont préparé un repas soigné.

to **lay off** VERB
licencier ◊ *My father's been laid off.* Mon père a été licencié.

lay-by NOUN
l' aire de stationnement FEM

layer NOUN

la couche ◊ *the ozone layer* la couche d'ozone

layout NOUN
[1] la mise en page (*of newspaper article*)
[2] la disposition (*of house, buildings*) ◊ *It took me some time to get familiar with the layout of the school.* J'ai mis un certain temps à me familiariser avec la disposition de l'école.

lazy ADJECTIVE
paresseux MASC
paresseuse FEM

lead NOUN

> *This word has two pronunciations. Make sure you choose the right translation.*
> see also **lead** VERB

[1] le fil (*cable*)
[2] la laisse (*for dog*)
* **to be in the lead** être en tête ◊ *Our team is in the lead.* Notre équipe est en tête.
[3] le plomb (*metal*)

to **lead** VERB

> see also **lead** NOUN

mener ◊ *the street that leads to the station* la rue qui mène à la gare
* **to lead the way** montrer le chemin
* **to lead somebody away** emmener quelqu'un ◊ *The police led the man away.* La police a emmené l'homme.

leaded petrol NOUN
l' essence au plomb FEM

leader NOUN
[1] (*of expedition, gang*)
le chef
[2] (*of political party*)
le dirigeant
la dirigeante

lead-free ADJECTIVE
* **lead-free petrol** de l'essence sans plomb

lead singer NOUN
le chanteur principal
la chanteuse principale

leaf NOUN
la feuille

leaflet NOUN
la brochure

league NOUN
le championnat ◊ *They are at the top of the league.* Ils sont en tête du championnat.
* **the Premier League** la première division

leak NOUN

> see also **leak** VERB

L

☞

la <u>fuite</u> ◇ *a gas leak* une fuite de gaz

to **leak** VERB

| see also **leak** NOUN |

<u>fuir</u> (*pipe, water, gas*)

to **lean** VERB

<u>se pencher</u> ◇ *Don't lean over too far.* Ne te penche pas trop. ◇ *She leant out of the window.* Elle s'est penchée par la fenêtre.

♦**to lean forward** se pencher en avant

♦**to lean on something** s'appuyer contre quelque chose ◇ *He leant on the wall.* Il s'est appuyé contre le mur.

♦**to be leaning against something** être appuyé contre quelque chose ◇ *The ladder was leaning against the wall.* L'échelle était appuyée contre le mur.

♦**to lean something against a wall** appuyer quelque chose contre un mur ◇ *He leant his bike against the wall.* Il a appuyé son vélo contre le mur.

to **lean out** VERB

<u>se pencher au dehors</u>

♦**She leant out of the window.** Elle s'est penché par la fenêtre.

to **lean over** VERB

<u>se pencher</u> ◇ *Don't lean over too far.* Ne te penche pas trop loin.

to **leap** VERB

<u>sauter</u> ◇ *They lept over the stream.* Ils ont sauté pour traverser la rivière.

♦**He leapt out of his chair when his team scored.** Il s'est levé d'un bond lorsque son équipe a marqué.

leap year NOUN

l' <u>année bissextile</u> FEM

to **learn** VERB

<u>apprendre</u> ◇ *I'm learning to ski.* J'apprends à skier.

learner NOUN

♦**She's a quick learner.** Elle apprend vite.

♦**French learners** (*people learning French*) ceux qui apprennent le français

learner driver NOUN

le <u>conducteur débutant</u>
la <u>conductrice débutante</u>

learnt VERB *see* **learn**

least ADVERB, ADJECTIVE, PRONOUN

♦**the least (1)** (*followed by noun*) le moins ◇ *It takes the least time.* C'est ce qui prend le moins de temps.

♦**the least (2)** (*after a verb*) le moins ◇ *Maths is the subject I like the least.* Les maths sont la matière que j'aime le moins.

When least is followed by an adjective, the translation depends on whether the noun referred to is masculine, feminine or plural.

♦**the least ... (1)** le moins ... ◇ *the least expensive hotel* l'hôtel le moins cher

♦**the least ... (2)** la moins ... ◇ *the least expensive seat* la place la moins chère

♦**the least ... (3)** les moins ... ◇ *the least expensive hotels* les hôtels les moins chers ◇ *the least expensive seats* les places les moins chères

♦**It's the least I can do.** C'est le moins que je puisse faire.

♦**at least (1)** au moins ◇ *It'll cost at least £200.* Ça va coûter au moins deux cents livres.

♦**at least (2)** du moins ◇ *... but at least nobody was hurt.* ... mais au moins personne n'a été blessé. ◇ *It's totally unfair – at least, that's my opinion.* C'est vraiment injuste – du moins c'est ce que je pense.

leather NOUN

le <u>cuir</u> ◇ *a black leather jacket* un blouson en cuir noir

leave NOUN

| see also **leave** VERB |

1 le <u>congé</u> (*from job*)

2 la <u>permission</u> (*from army*) ◇ *He is on leave for a week.* Il est en permission pendant une semaine.

to **leave** VERB

| see also **leave** NOUN |

1 <u>laisser</u> (*deliberately*) ◇ *Don't leave your camera in the car.* Ne laisse pas ton appareil-photo dans la voiture.

2 <u>oublier</u> (*by mistake*) ◇ *I've left my book at home.* J'ai oublié mon livre à la maison. ◇ *Make sure you haven't left anything behind.* Vérifiez bien que vous n'avez rien oublié.

3 <u>partir</u> (*go*) ◇ *The bus leaves at 8.* Le car part à huit heures. ◇ *She's just left.* Elle vient de partir.

4 <u>quitter</u> (*go away from*) ◇ *We leave London at six o'clock.* Nous quittons Londres à six heures. ◇ *My sister left home last year.* Ma sœur a quitté la maison l'an dernier.

♦**to leave somebody alone** laisser quelqu'un tranquille ◇ *Leave me alone!* Laisse-moi tranquille!

to **leave out** VERB

<u>mettre à l'écart</u> ◇ *Not knowing the language I felt really left out.* Comme je ne connaissais pas la langue, je me suis vraiment senti à l'écart.

leaves PL NOUN *see* **leaf**

Lebanon NOUN

le Liban
◆**in Lebanon** au Liban

lecture NOUN
⎡*see also* **lecture** VERB⎤
[1] (*public*)
la conférence
[2] (*at university*)
le cours magistral
(les cours magistraux PL)
*Be careful not to translate **lecture** by the French word **lecture**.*

to **lecture** VERB
⎡*see also* **lecture** NOUN⎤
[1] enseigner ◇ *She lectures at the technical college.* Elle enseigne au collège technique.
[2] faire la morale ◇ *He's always lecturing us.* Il n'arrête pas de nous faire la morale.

lecturer NOUN
le professeur d'université ◇ *She's a lecturer.* Elle est professeur d'université.

led VERB *see* **lead**

leek NOUN
le poireau
(les poireaux PL)

leek VERB *see* **leave**

left ADJECTIVE, ADVERB
⎡*see also* **left** NOUN⎤
[1] gauche (*not right*) ◇ *my left hand* ma main gauche ◇ *on the left side of the road* sur le côté gauche de la route
[2] à gauche ◇ *Turn left at the traffic lights.* Tournez à gauche aux prochains feux.
◆**I haven't got any money left.** Il ne me reste plus d'argent.

left NOUN
⎡*see also* **left** ADJECTIVE⎤
la gauche
◆**on the left** à gauche ◇ *Remember to drive on the left.* N'oubliez pas de conduire à gauche.

left-hand ADJECTIVE
◆**the left-hand side** la gauche ◇ *It's on the left-hand side.* C'est à gauche.

left-handed ADJECTIVE
gaucher MASC
gauchère FEM

left-luggage office NOUN
la consigne

leg NOUN
la jambe ◇ *She's broken her leg.* Elle s'est cassé la jambe.
◆**a chicken leg** une cuisse de poulet
◆**a leg of lamb** un gigot d'agneau

legal ADJECTIVE
légal

(légaux MASC PL)

leggings NOUN
le caleçon SING

leisure NOUN
les loisirs MASC PL ◇ *What do you do in your leisure time?* Qu'est-ce que tu fais pendant tes loisirs?

leisure centre NOUN
le centre de loisirs

lemon NOUN
le citron

lemonade NOUN
la limonade

to **lend** VERB
prêter ◇ *I can lend you some money.* Je peux te prêter de l'argent.

length NOUN
la longueur
◆**It's about a metre in length.** Ça fait environ un mètre de long.

lens NOUN
[1] la lentille (*contact lens*)
[2] le verre (*of spectacles*)
[3] l' objectif MASC (*of camera*)

Lent NOUN
le carême

lent VERB *see* **lend**

lentil NOUN
la lentille

Leo NOUN
le Lion ◇ *I'm Leo.* Je suis Lion.

leotard NOUN
le justaucorps

lesbian NOUN
la lesbienne

less PRONOUN, ADVERB, ADJECTIVE
[1] moins ◇ *He's less intelligent than her.* Il est moins intelligent qu'elle. ◇ *A bit less, please.* Un peu moins, s'il vous plaît.
[2] moins de ◇ *I've got less time for hobbies now.* J'ai moins de temps pour les loisirs maintenant.
◆**less than (1)** (*with amounts*) moins de ◇ *It's less than a kilometre from here.* C'est à moins d'un kilomètre d'ici. ◇ *It costs less than 100 euros.* Ça coûte moins de cent euros. ◇ *less than half* moins de la moitié
◆**less than (2)** (*in comparisons*) moins que ◇ *He spent less than me.* Il a dépensé moins que moi. ◇ *I've got less than you.* J'en ai moins que toi. ◇ *It cost less than we thought.* Ça a coûté moins cher que nous ne le pensions.

lesson NOUN
[1] la leçon ◇ *a French lesson* une leçon de français

L

☞

② le <u>cours</u> (*class*) ◊ *The lessons last
forty minutes each.* Chaque cours
dure quarante minutes.

to **let** VERB
　①<u>laisser</u> (*allow*)
◆ **to let somebody do something** laisser
quelqu'un faire quelque chose ◊ *Let
me have a look.* Laisse-moi voir.
◊ *My parents won't let me stay out
that late.* Mes parents ne me laissent
pas sortir aussi tard.
◆ **to let somebody know** faire savoir à
quelqu'un ◊ *I'll let you know as soon
as possible.* Je vous le ferai savoir
dès que possible.
◆ **to let down** décevoir ◊ *I won't let you
down.* Je ne vous décevrai pas.
◆ **to let somebody go** lâcher quelqu'un
◊ *Let me go!* Lâche-moi!
◆ **to let in** laisser entrer ◊ *They
wouldn't let me in because I was
under 18.* Ils ne m'ont pas laissé
entrer parce que j'avais moins de
dix-huit ans.

> *To make suggestions using **let's**, you
> can ask questions beginning **si on**.*

◊ *Let's go to the cinema!* Si on allait
au cinéma?
◆ **Let's go!** Allons-y!
　②<u>louer</u> (*hire out*) ◊ *"to let"* "à louer"

letter NOUN
　la <u>lettre</u>

letterbox NOUN
　la <u>boîte à lettres</u>

lettuce NOUN
　la <u>salade</u>

leukaemia NOUN
　la <u>leucémie</u>

level ADJECTIVE
　see also **level** NOUN
<u>plan</u> ◊ *A snooker table must be
perfectly level.* Un billard doit être
parfaitement plan.

level NOUN
　see also **level** ADJECTIVE
le <u>niveau</u>
(les niveaux PL)
◊ *The level of the river is rising.* Le
niveau de la rivière monte.
◆ **"A" levels** le baccalauréat

> ❶ *The French **baccalauréat** (or **bac**
> for short) is taken at the age of 17
> or 18. Students have to sit one of a
> variety of set subject combinations,
> rather than being able to choose any
> combination of subjects they want. If
> you pass you have the right to a
> place at university.*

level crossing NOUN
　le <u>passage à niveau</u>

lever NOUN
　le <u>levier</u>

liable ADJECTIVE
◆ **He's liable to lose his temper.** Il se
met facilement en colère.

liar NOUN
　le <u>menteur</u>
　la <u>menteuse</u>

liberal ADJECTIVE
(*opinions*)
<u>libéral</u>
(libéraux MASC PL)
◆ **the Liberal Democrats** le parti
libéral-démocrate

liberation NOUN
　la <u>libération</u>

liberty NOUN
　la <u>liberté</u>

Libra NOUN
　la <u>Balance</u> ◊ *I'm Libra.* Je suis
Balance.

librarian NOUN
　le/la <u>bibliothécaire</u> ◊ *My mother is
a librarian.* Ma mère est
bibliothécaire.

library NOUN
　la <u>bibliothèque</u>
◆ **a library book** un livre de
bibliothèque

> *Be careful not to translate **library** by
> **librairie**.*

Libya NOUN
　la <u>Libye</u>
◆ **in Libya** en Libye

licence NOUN (US **license**)
　le <u>permis</u>
◆ **a driving licence** un permis de
conduire

to **lick** VERB
　<u>lécher</u>

lid NOUN
　le <u>couvercle</u>

to **lie** VERB
　see also **lie** NOUN
<u>mentir</u> (*not tell the truth*) ◊ *I know
she's lying.* Je sais qu'elle ment.
◆ **to lie down** s'allonger
◆ **to be lying down** être allongé ◊ *He
was lying on the sofa.* Il était allongé
sur le canapé. ◊ *When I'm on holiday
I lie on the beach all day.* Quand je
suis en vacances, je reste allongé sur
la plage toute la journée.

lie NOUN
　see also **lie** VERB
le <u>mensonge</u>
◆ **to tell a lie** mentir

♦**That's a lie!** Ce n'est pas vrai!

lie-in NOUN
♦**to have a lie-in** faire la grasse matinée ◊ *I have a lie-in on Sundays.* Je fais la grasse matinée le dimanche.

lieutenant NOUN
le <u>lieutenant</u>

life NOUN
la <u>vie</u>

lifebelt NOUN
la <u>bouée de sauvetage</u>

lifeboat NOUN
le <u>canot de sauvetage</u>

lifeguard NOUN
le <u>maître nageur</u>

life jacket NOUN
le <u>gilet de sauvetage</u>

life-saving NOUN
le <u>sauvetage</u> ◊ *I've done a course in life-saving.* J'ai pris des cours de sauvetage.

lifestyle NOUN
le <u>style de vie</u>

to **lift** VERB
see also **lift** NOUN
<u>soulever</u> ◊ *It's too heavy, I can't lift it.* C'est trop lourd, je ne peux pas le soulever.

lift NOUN
see also **lift** VERB
l' <u>ascenseur</u> MASC ◊ *The lift isn't working.* L'ascenseur est en panne.
♦**He gave me a lift to the cinema.** Il m'a emmené au cinéma en voiture.
♦**Would you like a lift?** Est-ce que je peux vous déposer quelque part?

light ADJECTIVE
see also **light** NOUN, VERB
1 (*not heavy*)
<u>léger</u> MASC
<u>légère</u> FEM
◊ *a light jacket* une veste légère ◊ *a light meal* un repas léger
2 (*colour*)
<u>clair</u> ◊ *a light blue sweater* un pull bleu clair

light NOUN
see also **light** ADJECTIVE, VERB
1 la <u>lumière</u> ◊ *to switch on the light* allumer la lumière ◊ *to switch off the light* éteindre la lumière
2 la <u>lampe</u> ◊ *There's a light by my bed.* Il y a une lampe près de mon lit.
♦**the traffic lights** les feux MASC
♦**Have you got a light?** (*for cigarette*) Avez-vous du feu?

to **light** VERB
see also **light** ADJECTIVE, NOUN
<u>allumer</u> (*candle, cigarette, fire*)

light bulb NOUN
l' <u>ampoule</u> FEM

lighter NOUN
le <u>briquet</u> (*for cigarettes*)

lighthouse NOUN
le <u>phare</u>

lightning NOUN
les <u>éclairs</u> MASC PL
♦**a flash of lightning** un éclair

to **like** VERB
see also **like** PREPOSITION
1 <u>aimer</u> ◊ *I don't like mustard.* Je n'aime pas la moutarde. ◊ *I like riding.* J'aime monter à cheval.
*Note that **aimer** also means to love, so make sure you use **aimer bien** for just liking somebody.*
2 <u>aimer bien</u> ◊ *I like Paul, but I don't want to go out with him.* J'aime bien Paul, mais je ne veux pas sortir avec lui.
♦**I'd like ...** Je voudrais ... ◊ *I'd like an orange juice, please.* Je voudrais un jus d'orange, s'il vous plaît. ◊ *Would you like some coffee?* Voulez-vous du café?
♦**I'd like to ...** J'aimerais ... ◊ *I'd like to go to Russia one day.* J'aimerais aller en Russie un jour. ◊ *I'd like to wash my hands.* J'aimerais me laver les mains.
♦**Would you like to go for a walk?** Tu veux aller faire une promenade?
♦**... if you like ...** si tu veux

like PREPOSITION
see also **like** VERB
<u>comme</u> ◊ *It's fine like that.* C'est bien comme ça. ◊ *Do it like this.* Fais-le comme ça. ◊ *a city like Paris* une ville comme Paris ◊ *It's a bit like salmon.* C'est un peu comme du saumon.
♦**What's the weather like?** Quel temps fait-il?
♦**to look like somebody** ressembler à quelqu'un ◊ *You look like my brother.* Tu ressembles à mon frère.

likely ADJECTIVE
<u>probable</u> ◊ *That's not very likely.* C'est peu probable.
♦**She's likely to come.** Elle viendra probablement.
♦**She's not likely to come.** Elle ne viendra probablement pas.

Lilo ® NOUN
le <u>matelas pneumatique</u>

lily of the valley NOUN
le <u>muguet</u>

L

lime NOUN
le citron vert (fruit)

limit NOUN
la limite ◊ The speed limit is 70 mph.
La vitesse est limitée à cent dix
kilomètres à l'heure.

limousine NOUN
la limousine

to **limp** VERB
boiter

line NOUN
1 la ligne ◊ a straight line une ligne
droite
2 le trait (to divide, cancel) ◊ Draw a
line under each answer. Tirez un trait
après chaque réponse.
3 la voie (railway track)
♦ Hold the line, please. Ne quittez pas.
♦ It's a very bad line. La ligne est très
mauvaise.
♦ on line (computing) en ligne

linen NOUN
le lin ◊ a linen jacket une veste en lin

liner NOUN
le paquebot (ship)

linguist NOUN
♦ to be a good linguist être doué pour
les langues ◊ She's a good linguist.
Elle est douée pour les langues.

lining NOUN
la doublure (of jacket, skirt etc)

link NOUN
see also **link** VERB
1 le rapport ◊ the link between
smoking and cancer le rapport entre
le tabagisme et le cancer
2 le lien (computing)

to **link** VERB
see also **link** NOUN
relier

lino NOUN
le linoléum

lion NOUN
le lion

lioness NOUN
la lionne

lip NOUN
la lèvre

to **lip-read** VERB
lire sur les lèvres

lip salve NOUN
la pommade pour les lèvres

lipstick NOUN
le rouge à lèvres

liqueur NOUN
la liqueur

liquid NOUN
le liquide

liquidizer NOUN
le mixer

list NOUN
see also **list** VERB
la liste

to **list** VERB
see also **list** NOUN
faire une liste de ◊ List your
hobbies! Fais une liste de tes
hobbies!

to **listen** VERB
écouter ◊ Listen to this! Écoutez ceci!
◊ Listen to me! Écoutez-moi!

listener NOUN
l' auditeur MASC
l' auditrice FEM

lit VERB see **light**

liter NOUN US
le litre

literally ADVERB
vraiment (completely) ◊ It was literally
impossible to find a seat. Il était
vraiment impossible de trouver une
place.
♦ to translate literally faire une
traduction littérale

literature NOUN
la littérature ◊ I'm studying English
Literature. J'étudie la littérature
anglaise.

litre NOUN
le litre

litter NOUN
les ordures FEM PL

litter bin NOUN
la poubelle

little ADJECTIVE
petit ◊ a little girl une petite fille
♦ a little un peu ◊ How much would
you like? – Just a little. Combien en
voulez-vous? – Juste un peu.
♦ very little très peu ◊ We've got very
little time. Nous avons très peu de
temps.
♦ little by little petit à petit

live ADJECTIVE
see also **live** VERB
1 vivant (animal)
2 en direct (broadcast)
♦ There's live music on Fridays. Il y a
des musiciens qui jouent le vendredi.

to **live** VERB
see also **live** ADJECTIVE
1 vivre ◊ I live with my
grandmother. Je vis avec ma
grand-mère.
♦ to live on something vivre de
quelque chose ◊ He lives on benefit.
Il vit de ses indemnités.

[2] **habiter** (*reside*) ◊ *Where do you live?* Où est-ce que tu habites? ◊ *I live in Edinburgh.* J'habite à Édimbourg.

♦**She's living with two Greek students.** Elle partage un appartement avec deux étudiants grecs.

♦**to live together** vivre ensemble ◊ *My parents aren't living together any more.* Mes parents ne vivent plus ensemble.

♦**They're not married, they're living together.** Ils ne sont pas mariés, ils vivent en concubinage.

lively ADJECTIVE
animé ◊ *It was a lively party.* C'était une soirée animée.

♦**She's got a lively personality.** Elle est pleine de vitalité.

liver NOUN
le foie

lives PL NOUN
les vies FEM PL

living NOUN
♦**to make a living** gagner sa vie
♦**What does she do for a living?** Qu'est-ce qu'elle fait dans la vie?

living room NOUN
la salle de séjour

lizard NOUN
le lézard

load NOUN
see also **load** VERB
♦**loads of** un tas de ◊ *loads of people* un tas de gens ◊ *loads of money* un tas d'argent
♦**You're talking a load of rubbish!** Tu ne dis que des bêtises!

to **load** VERB
see also **load** NOUN
charger ◊ *a trolley loaded with luggage* un chariot chargé de bagages

loaf NOUN
le pain
♦**a loaf of bread** un pain

loan NOUN
see also **loan** VERB
le prêt

to **loan** VERB
see also **loan** NOUN
prêter

to **loathe** VERB
détester ◊ *I loathe her.* Je la déteste.

loaves PL NOUN see **loaf**

lobster NOUN
le homard

local ADJECTIVE

local
(locaux MASC PL)
◊ *the local paper* le journal local
♦**a local call** une communication urbaine

location NOUN
l' endroit MASC ◊ *A hotel set in a beautiful location.* Un hôtel situé dans un endroit magnifique.

> Be careful not to translate **location** by the French word **location**.

loch NOUN
le loch

lock NOUN
see also **lock** VERB
la serrure ◊ *The lock is broken.* La serrure est cassée.

to **lock** VERB
see also **lock** NOUN
fermer à clé ◊ *Make sure you lock your door.* N'oubliez pas de fermer votre porte à clé.

to **lock out** VERB
♦**The door slammed and I was locked out.** La porte a claqué et je me suis retrouvé à la porte.

locker NOUN
le casier
♦**the locker room** le vestiaire
♦**the left-luggage lockers** la consigne automatique

locket NOUN
le médaillon

lodger NOUN
le/la locataire

loft NOUN
le grenier

log NOUN
la bûche (*of wood*)

to **log in** VERB
se connecter

to **log off** NOUN
se déconnecter

to **log on** VERB
se connecter

to **log out** VERB
se déconnecter

logical ADJECTIVE
logique

lollipop NOUN
la sucette

lolly NOUN
la glace à l'eau (*ice lolly*)

London NOUN
Londres
♦**in London** à Londres
♦**to London** à Londres
♦**I'm from London.** Je suis de Londres.

L

Londoner NOUN
le <u>Londonien</u>
la <u>Londonienne</u>

loneliness NOUN
la <u>solitude</u>

lonely ADJECTIVE
<u>seul</u>
♦**to feel lonely** se sentir seul ◊ *She feels a bit lonely.* Elle se sent un peu seule.

lonesome ADJECTIVE
♦**to feel lonesome** se sentir seul

long ADJECTIVE, ADVERB
see also **long** VERB
<u>long</u> MASC
<u>longue</u> FEM
◊ *She's got long hair.* Elle a les cheveux longs. ◊ *The room is 6 metres long.* La pièce fait six mètres de long.
♦**how long?** (*time*) combien de temps? ◊ *How long did you stay there?* Combien de temps êtes-vous resté là-bas? ◊ *How long have you been here?* Depuis combien de temps êtes-vous ici? ◊ *How long is the flight?* Combien de temps dure le vol?
♦**I've been waiting a long time.** J'attends depuis longtemps.
♦**It takes a long time.** Ça prend du temps.
♦**as long as** si ◊ *I'll come as long as it's not too expensive.* Je viendrai si ce n'est pas trop cher.

to **long** VERB
see also **long** ADJECTIVE
♦**to long to do something** attendre avec impatience de faire quelque chose
♦**I'm longing to see my boyfriend again.** J'attends avec impatience de revoir mon copain.

long-distance ADJECTIVE
♦**a long-distance call** une communication interurbaine

longer ADVERB
see also **long** ADJECTIVE
♦**They're no longer going out together.** Ils ne sortent plus ensemble.
♦**I can't stand it any longer.** Je ne peux plus le supporter.

long jump NOUN
le <u>saut en longueur</u>

loo NOUN
les <u>toilettes</u> FEM PL ◊ *Where's the loo?* Où sont les toilettes?

look NOUN
see also **look** VERB

♦**to have a look** regarder ◊ *Have a look at this!* Regardez ceci!
♦**I don't like the look of it.** Ça ne me dit rien.

to **look** VERB
see also **look** NOUN
1 <u>regarder</u> ◊ *Look!* Regardez!
♦**to look at something** regarder quelque chose ◊ *Look at the picture.* Regardez cette image.
2 <u>avoir l'air</u> (*seem*) ◊ *She looks surprised.* Elle a l'air surprise. ◊ *That cake looks nice.* Ce gâteau a l'air bon. ◊ *It looks fine.* Ça a l'air bien.
♦**to look like somebody** ressembler à quelqu'un ◊ *He looks like his brother.* Il ressemble à son frère.
♦**What does she look like?** Comment est-elle physiquement?
♦**Look out!** Attention!
♦**to look after** s'occuper de ◊ *I look after my little sister.* Je m'occupe de ma petite sœur.
♦**to look for** chercher ◊ *I'm looking for my passport.* Je cherche mon passeport.
♦**to look forward to something** attendre quelque chose avec impatience ◊ *I'm looking forward to the holidays.* J'attends les vacances avec impatience.
♦**Looking forward to hearing from you.** J'espère avoir bientôt de tes nouvelles.
♦**to look round (1)** (*look behind*) se retourner ◊ *I shouted and he looked round.* J'ai crié et il s'est retourné.
♦**to look round (2)** (*have a look*) jeter un coup d'œil ◊ *I'm just looking round.* Je jette simplement un coup d'œil.
♦**to look round a museum** visiter un musée
♦**I like looking round the shops.** J'aime faire les boutiques.
♦**to look up** (*word, name*) chercher ◊ *If you don't know a word, look it up in the dictionary.* Si vous ne connaissez pas un mot, cherchez-le dans le dictionnaire.

loose ADJECTIVE
<u>ample</u> (*clothes*)
♦**loose change** la petite monnaie

lord NOUN
le <u>seigneur</u> (*feudal*)
♦**the House of Lords** la Chambre des lords
♦**good Lord!** mon Dieu!

lorry NOUN
le <u>camion</u>

lorry driver NOUN

le routier ◊ *He's a lorry driver.* Il est routier.

to **lose** VERB
perdre ◊ *I've lost my purse.* J'ai perdu mon porte-monnaie.
♦**to get lost** se perdre ◊ *I was afraid of getting lost.* J'avais peur de me perdre.

loser NOUN
1 le perdant
la perdante
♦**to be a bad loser** être mauvais perdant
2 (*pathetic person*)
le loser ◊ *He's such a loser!* C'est un vrai loser!

loss NOUN
la perte

lost VERB *see* **lose**

lost ADJECTIVE
perdu

lost-and-found NOUN US
les objets trouvés MASC PL

lost property office NOUN
les objets trouvés MASC PL

lot NOUN
♦**a lot** beaucoup
♦**a lot of** beaucoup de ◊ *We saw a lot of interesting things.* Nous avons vu beaucoup de choses intéressantes.
♦**lots of** un tas de ◊ *She's got lots of money.* Elle a un tas d'argent. ◊ *He's got lots of friends.* Il a un tas d'amis.
♦**What did you do at the weekend? – Not a lot.** Qu'as-tu fait ce week-end? – Pas grand-chose.
♦**Do you like football? – Not a lot.** Tu aimes le football? – Pas tellement.
♦**That's the lot.** C'est tout.

lottery NOUN
la loterie
♦**to win the lottery** gagner à la loterie

loud ADJECTIVE
fort ◊ *The television is too loud.* La télévision est trop forte.

loudly ADVERB
fort

loudspeaker NOUN
le haut-parleur

lounge NOUN
le salon

lousy ADJECTIVE
infect ◊ *The food in the canteen is lousy.* La nourriture de la cantine est infecte.
♦**I feel lousy.** Je suis mal fichu.
(*informal*)

love NOUN
see also **love** VERB

l' amour MASC
♦**to be in love** être amoureux ◊ *She's in love with Paul.* Elle est amoureuse de Paul.
♦**to make love** faire l'amour
♦**Give Delphine my love.** Embrasse Delphine pour moi.
♦**Love, Rosemary.** Amitiés, Rosemary.

to **love** VERB
see also **love** NOUN

1 aimer (*be in love with*) ◊ *I love you.* Je t'aime.
2 aimer beaucoup (*like a lot*)
◊ *Everybody loves her.* Tout le monde l'aime beaucoup. ◊ *I'd love to come.* J'aimerais beaucoup venir.
3 adorer (*things*) ◊ *I love chocolate.* J'adore le chocolat. ◊ *I love skiing.* J'adore le ski.

lovely ADJECTIVE
charmant ◊ *What a lovely surprise!* Quelle charmante surprise! ◊ *She's a lovely person.* Elle est charmante.
♦**It's a lovely day.** Il fait très beau aujourd'hui.
♦**Is your meal OK? – Yes, it's lovely.** Est-ce que c'est bon? – Oui, c'est délicieux.
♦**They've got a lovely house.** Ils ont une très belle maison.
♦**Have a lovely time!** Amusez-vous bien!

lover NOUN
1 (*in relationship*)
l' amant MASC
la maîtresse
2 (*of hobby, wine*)
l' amateur MASC ◊ *an art lover* un amateur d'art ◊ *She is a lover of good food.* Elle est amateur de bonne cuisine.

low ADJECTIVE, ADVERB
(*price, level*)
bas MASC
basse FEM
◊ *That plane is flying very low.* Cet avion vole très bas.
♦**the low season** la basse saison ◊ *in the low season* en basse saison

lower ADJECTIVE
see also **lower** VERB
inférieur ◊ *on the lower floor* a l'étage inférieur

to **lower** VERB
see also **lower** ADJECTIVE
baisser

lower sixth NOUN
la première ◊ *He's in the lower sixth.* Il est en première.

low-fat ADJECTIVE

☞

allégé ◊ *a low-fat yoghurt* un yaourt allégé

loyalty NOUN
la fidélité

loyalty card NOUN
la carte de fidélité

lozenge NOUN
la pastille (*sweet*)

L-plates PL NOUN
les plaques de conducteur débutant FEM PL

luck NOUN
la chance ◊ *She hasn't had much luck.* Elle n'a pas eu beaucoup de chance.
♦**Good luck!** Bonne chance!
♦**Bad luck!** Pas de chance!

luckily ADVERB
heureusement

lucky ADJECTIVE
♦**to be lucky (1)** (*be fortunate*) avoir de la chance ◊ *He's lucky, he's got a job.* Il a de la chance, il a un emploi. ◊ *He wasn't hurt. – That was lucky!* Il n'a pas été blessé. – C'est une chance!
♦**to be lucky (2)** (*bring luck*) porter bonheur ◊ *Black cats are lucky in Britain.* Les chats noirs portent bonheur en Grande-Bretagne.
♦**a lucky horseshoe** un fer à cheval porte-bonheur

luggage NOUN
les bagages MASC PL

lukewarm ADJECTIVE
tiède (*water, food*)
♦**The response was lukewarm.** Sa réaction a été peu enthousiaste.

lump NOUN
1 le morceau
(les morceaux PL)
◊ *a lump of butter* un morceau de beurre

2 (*swelling*)
la bosse ◊ *He's got a lump on his forehead.* Il a une bosse sur le front.

lunatic NOUN
le fou
la folle
◊ *He's an absolute lunatic.* Il est complètement fou.

lunch NOUN
le déjeuner
♦**to have lunch** déjeuner ◊ *We have lunch at 12.30.* Nous déjeunons à midi et demie.

luncheon voucher NOUN
le ticket-restaurant

lung NOUN
le poumon
♦**lung cancer** le cancer du poumon

luscious ADJECTIVE
délicieux MASC
délicieuse FEM

lush ADJECTIVE
luxuriant

lust NOUN
le désir

Luxembourg NOUN
1 le Luxembourg (*country*)
♦**in Luxembourg** au Luxembourg
♦**to Luxembourg** au Luxembourg
2 Luxembourg (*city*)
♦**in Luxembourg** à Luxembourg

luxurious ADJECTIVE
luxueux MASC
luxueuse FEM

luxury NOUN
le luxe ◊ *It was luxury!* C'était un vrai luxe!
♦**a luxury hotel** un hôtel de luxe

lying VERB *see* **lie**

lyrics PL NOUN
les paroles FEM PL (*of song*)

M

mac NOUN
l' <u>imper</u> MASC

macaroni NOUN
les <u>macaronis</u> MASC PL

machine NOUN
la <u>machine</u>

machine gun NOUN
la <u>mitrailleuse</u>

machinery NOUN
les <u>machines</u> FEM PL

mackerel NOUN
le <u>maquereau</u>
(les maquereaux PL)

mad ADJECTIVE
[1] (*insane*)
<u>fou</u> MASC
<u>folle</u> FEM
◊ *You're mad!* Tu es fou!
[2] (*angry*)
<u>furieux</u> MASC
<u>furieuse</u> FEM
◊ *She'll be mad when she finds out.*
Elle sera furieuse quand elle va s'en
apercevoir.
♦ **to be mad about (1)** (*sport, activity*)
être enragé de ◊ *He's mad about
football.* Il est enragé de foot.
♦ **to be mad about (2)** (*person, animal*)
adorer ◊ *She's mad about horses.*
Elle adore les chevaux.

madam NOUN
<u>madame</u> FEM ◊ *Would you like to
order, Madam?* Désirez-vous
commander, Madame?

made VERB *see* **make**

madly ADVERB
♦ **They're madly in love.** Ils sont
éperdument amoureux.

madman NOUN
le <u>fou</u>

madness NOUN
la <u>folie</u> ◊ *It's absolute madness.* C'est
de la pure folie.

magazine NOUN
le <u>magazine</u>

maggot NOUN
l' <u>asticot</u> MASC

magic ADJECTIVE
see also **magic** NOUN
[1] <u>magique</u> (*magical*) ◊ *a magic wand*
une baguette magique
[2] <u>super</u> (*brilliant*)
♦ **It was magic!** C'était super!

magic NOUN

see also **magic** ADJECTIVE
la <u>magie</u>
♦ **a magic trick** un tour de magie
♦ **My hobby is magic.** Je fais des tours
de magie.

magician NOUN
le <u>prestidigitateur</u> (*conjurer*)

magnet NOUN
l' <u>aimant</u> MASC

magnificent ADJECTIVE
[1] <u>magnifique</u> (*beautiful*) ◊ *a
magnificent view* une vue magnifique
[2] <u>superbe</u> (*outstanding*) ◊ *It was a
magnificent effort.* Ils ont fait un
superbe effort.

magnifying glass NOUN
la <u>loupe</u>

maid NOUN
la <u>domestique</u> (*servant*)
♦ **an old maid** (*spinster*) une vieille fille

maiden name NOUN
le <u>nom de jeune fille</u>

mail NOUN
le <u>courrier</u> ◊ *Here's your mail.* Voici
ton courrier.
♦ **email** (*electronic mail*) le courrier
électronique
♦ **by mail** par la poste

mailbox NOUN US
la <u>boîte à lettres</u>

mailing list NOUN
la <u>liste d'adresses</u>

mailman NOUN US
le <u>facteur</u>

main ADJECTIVE
<u>principal</u>
(principaux MASC PL)
◊ *the main problem* le principal
problème
♦ **the main thing is to ...** l'essentiel est
de ...

mainly ADVERB
<u>principalement</u>

main road NOUN
la <u>grande route</u> ◊ *I don't like cycling
on main roads.* Je n'aime pas faire
du vélo sur les grandes routes.

to **maintain** VERB
<u>entretenir</u> (*machine, building*)

maintenance NOUN
l' <u>entretien</u> MASC (*of machine, building*)

maize NOUN
le <u>maïs</u>

majesty NOUN

☞

la majesté
♦**Your Majesty** Votre Majesté

major ADJECTIVE
majeur ◊ *a major problem* un problème majeur
♦**in C major** en do majeur

Majorca NOUN
Majorque FEM ◊ *We went to Majorca in August.* Nous sommes allés à Majorque en août.

majority NOUN
la majorité

make NOUN
see also **make** VERB
la marque ◊ *What make is that car?* De quelle marque est cette voiture?

to **make** VERB
see also **make** NOUN
1 faire ◊ *I'm going to make a cake.* Je vais faire un gâteau. ◊ *He made it himself.* Il l'a fait lui-même. ◊ *I make my bed every morning.* Je fais mon lit tous les matins. ◊ *2 and 2 make 4.* Deux et deux font quatre.
2 fabriquer (*manufacture*) ◊ *made in France* fabriqué en France
3 gagner (*earn*) ◊ *He makes a lot of money.* Il gagne beaucoup d'argent.
♦**to make somebody do something** obliger quelqu'un à faire quelque chose ◊ *My mother makes me do my homework.* Ma mère m'oblige à faire mes devoirs.
♦**to make lunch** préparer le repas ◊ *She's making lunch.* Elle prépare le repas.
♦**to make a phone call** donner un coup de téléphone ◊ *I'd like to make a phone call.* J'aimerais donner un coup de téléphone.
♦**to make fun of somebody** se moquer de quelqu'un ◊ *They made fun of him.* Ils se sont moqués de lui.
♦**What time do you make it?** Quelle heure avez-vous?

to **make out** VERB
1 déchiffrer (*read*) ◊ *I can't make out the address on the label.* Je n'arrive pas à déchiffrer l'adresse sur l'étiquette.
2 comprendre (*understand*) ◊ *I can't make her out at all.* Je n'arrive pas du tout à la comprendre.
3 prétendre (*claim, pretend*) ◊ *They're making out it was my fault.* Ils prétendent que c'était ma faute.
♦**to make a cheque out to somebody** libeller un chèque à l'ordre de quelqu'un

to **make up** VERB

1 inventer (*invent*) ◊ *He made up the whole story.* Il a inventé cette histoire de toutes pièces.
2 se réconcilier (*after argument*) ◊ *They had a quarrel, but soon made up.* Ils se sont disputés, mais se sont vite réconciliés.
♦**to make oneself up** se maquiller ◊ *She spends hours making herself up.* Elle passe des heures à se maquiller.

maker NOUN
le fabriquant ◊ *Europe's biggest car maker* le plus grand fabriquant de voitures d'Europe
♦**a film maker** un cinéaste

make-up NOUN
le maquillage

Malaysia NOUN
la Malaisie
♦**in Malaysia** en Malaisie

male ADJECTIVE
1 mâle (*animals, plants*) ◊ *a male kitten* un chaton mâle
2 masculin (*person, on official forms*) ◊ *Sex: male.* Sexe : masculin.
♦**Most football players are male.** La plupart des joueurs de football sont des hommes.
♦**a male chauvinist** un macho
♦**a male nurse** un infirmier

malicious ADJECTIVE
malveillant ◊ *a malicious rumour* une rumeur malveillante
*Be careful not to translate **malicious** by **malicieux**.*

mall NOUN
le centre commercial

Malta NOUN
Malte
♦**in Malta** à Malte
♦**to Malta** à Malte

mammoth NOUN
see also **mammoth** ADJECTIVE
le mammouth

mammoth ADJECTIVE
see also **mammoth** NOUN
monstre ◊ *a mammoth task* un travail monstre

man NOUN
l' homme MASC ◊ *an old man* un vieil homme

to **manage** VERB
1 diriger (*be in charge of*) ◊ *She manages a big store.* Elle dirige un grand magasin. ◊ *He manages our football team.* Il dirige notre équipe de foot.

2 se débrouiller (get by) ◊ We haven't got much money, but we manage. Nous n'avons pas beaucoup d'argent, mais nous nous débrouillons. ◊ It's okay, I can manage. Ça va, je me débrouille.

◆ **Can you manage okay?** Tu y arrives?

◆ **to manage to do something** réussir à faire quelque chose ◊ Luckily I managed to pass the exam. J'ai heureusement réussi à avoir mon examen.

◆ **I can't manage all that.** (food) C'est trop pour moi.

manageable ADJECTIVE
faisable (task)

management NOUN
1 la gestion (organization) ◊ He's responsible for the management of the company. Il est responsable de la gestion de la société.
2 la direction (people in charge) ◊ "under new management" "changement de direction"

manager NOUN
1 (of company)
le directeur
la directrice
2 (of shop, restaurant)
le gérant
la gérante
3 (of team, performer)
le manager

manageress NOUN
la gérante

mandarin NOUN
la mandarine (fruit)

mango NOUN
la mangue

mania NOUN
la manie

maniac NOUN
le fou
la folle
◊ He drives like a maniac. Il conduit comme un fou.

◆ **a religious maniac** un fanatique religieux

to **manipulate** VERB
manipuler

mankind NOUN
l' humanité FEM

man-made ADJECTIVE
synthétique (fibre)

manner NOUN
la façon

◆ **She behaves in an odd manner.** Elle se comporte de façon étrange.

◆ **He has a confident manner.** Il a de l'assurance.

manners PL NOUN
les manières FEM PL ◊ good manners les bonnes manières ◊ Her manners are appalling. Elle a de très mauvaises manières.

◆ **It's bad manners to speak with your mouth full.** Ce n'est pas poli de parler la bouche pleine.

manpower NOUN
la main-d'œuvre

mansion NOUN
le manoir

mantelpiece NOUN
la cheminée

manual NOUN
le manuel

to **manufacture** VERB
fabriquer

manufacturer NOUN
le fabricant

manure NOUN
le fumier

manuscript NOUN
le manuscrit

many ADJECTIVE, PRONOUN
beaucoup de ◊ The film has many special effects. Le film a beaucoup d'effets spéciaux. ◊ He hasn't got many friends. Il n'a pas beaucoup d'amis. ◊ Were there many people at the concert? Est-ce qu'il y avait beaucoup de gens au concert?

◆ **very many** beaucoup de ◊ I haven't got very many CDs. Je n'ai pas beaucoup de CD.

◆ **not many** pas beaucoup

◆ **How many?** Combien? ◊ How many do you want? Combien en veux-tu?

◆ **how many ...?** combien de ...? ◊ How many euros do you get for £1? Combien d'euros a-t-on pour une livre?

◆ **too many** trop ◊ That's too many. C'est trop.

◆ **too many ...** trop de ... ◊ She makes too many mistakes. Elle fait trop d'erreurs.

◆ **so many** autant ◊ I didn't know there would be so many. Je ne pensais pas qu'il y en aurait autant.

◆ **so many ...** autant de ... ◊ I've never seen so many policemen. Je n'ai jamais vu autant de policiers.

map NOUN
1 la carte (of country, area)
2 le plan (of town)

marathon NOUN

M

☞

le marathon ◇ *the London marathon*
le marathon de Londres

marble NOUN
le marbre ◇ *a marble statue* une
statue en marbre
♦**to play marbles** jouer aux billes

March NOUN
mars MASC
♦**in March** en mars

march NOUN
see also **march** VERB
la manifestation (*demonstration*)

to **march** VERB
see also **march** NOUN
1 marcher au pas (*soldiers*)
2 défiler (*protesters*)

mare NOUN
la jument

margarine NOUN
la margarine

margin NOUN
la marge ◇ *Write notes in the margin.*
Écrivez vos notes dans la marge.

marijuana NOUN
la marijuana

marina NOUN
la marina

marital status NOUN
la situation de famille

mark NOUN
see also **mark** VERB
1 la note (*in school*) ◇ *I get good
marks for French.* J'ai de bonnes
notes en français.
2 la tache (*stain*) ◇ *You've got a
mark on your skirt.* Tu as une tache
sur ta jupe.
3 le mark (*German currency*)

to **mark** VERB
see also **mark** NOUN
corriger ◇ *The teacher hasn't marked
my homework yet.* Le professeur n'a
pas encore corrigé mon devoir.

market NOUN
le marché

marketing NOUN
le marketing

marketplace NOUN
la place du marché

marmalade NOUN
la confiture d'oranges

maroon ADJECTIVE
bordeaux MASC, FEM, PL (*colour*)

marriage NOUN
le mariage

married ADJECTIVE

marié ◇ *They are not married.* Ils ne
sont pas mariés. ◇ *They have been
married for 15 years.* Ils sont mariés
depuis quinze ans. ◇ *a married couple*
un couple marié

marrow NOUN
la courge (*vegetable*)
♦**bone marrow** la moelle

to **marry** VERB
épouser ◇ *He wants to marry her.* Il
veut l'épouser.
♦**to get married** se marier ◇ *My sister's
getting married in June.* Ma sœur se
marie en juin.

marvellous ADJECTIVE (US **marvelous**)
1 excellent ◇ *She's a marvellous
cook.* C'est une excellente cuisinière.
2 superbe ◇ *The weather was
marvellous.* Il a fait un temps
superbe.

marzipan NOUN
la pâte d'amandes

mascara NOUN
le mascara

masculine ADJECTIVE
masculin

mashed potatoes PL NOUN
la purée ◇ *sausages and mashed
potatoes* des saucisses avec de la
purée

mask NOUN
le masque

masked ADJECTIVE
masqué

mass NOUN
1 la multitude ◇ *a mass of books
and papers* une multitude de livres et
de papiers
2 la messe (*in church*) ◇ *We go to
mass on Sunday.* Nous allons à la
messe le dimanche.
♦**the mass media** les médias MASC PL

massage NOUN
le massage

massive ADJECTIVE
énorme

to **master** VERB
maîtriser

masterpiece NOUN
le chef-d'œuvre
(les chefs-d'œuvre PL)

mat NOUN
le paillasson (*doormat*)
♦**a table mat** un set de table
♦**a beach mat** un tapis de plage

match NOUN
see also **match** VERB
1 l' allumette FEM ◇ *a box of matches*
une boîte d'allumettes

② (sport)
le match
(les matchs PL)
◊ a football match un match de foot

to **match** VERB
> see also **match** NOUN

être assorti à ◊ The jacket matches
the trousers. La veste est assortie au
pantalon.
♦ **These colours don't match.** Ces
couleurs ne vont pas ensemble.

matching ADJECTIVE
assorti ◊ My bedroom has matching
wallpaper and curtains. Ma chambre
a du papier peint et des rideaux
assortis.

mate NOUN
le pote (informal) ◊ On Friday night I
go out with my mates. Vendredi soir,
je sors avec mes potes.

material NOUN
① le tissu (cloth)
② la documentation (information,
data) ◊ I'm collecting material for
my project. Je rassemble une
documentation pour mon dossier.
♦ **raw materials** les matières premières
FEM

mathematics NOUN
les mathématiques FEM PL

maths NOUN
les maths FEM PL

matron NOUN
l' infirmière-chef FEM (in hospital)

matter NOUN
> see also **matter** VERB

la question ◊ It's a matter of life and
death. C'est une question de vie ou
de mort.
♦ **What's the matter?** Qu'est-ce qui ne
va pas?
♦ **as a matter of fact** en fait

to **matter** VERB
> see also **matter** NOUN

♦ **it doesn't matter (1)** (I don't mind) ça
ne fait rien ◊ I can't give you the
money today. – It doesn't matter. Je
ne peux pas te donner l'argent
aujourd'hui. – Ça ne fait rien.
♦ **it doesn't matter (2)** (it makes no
difference) ça n'a pas d'importance
◊ Shall I phone today or tomorrow? –
Whenever, it doesn't matter. Est-ce
que j'appelle aujourd'hui ou demain?
– Quand tu veux, ça n'a pas
d'importance.
♦ **It matters a lot to me.** C'est très
important pour moi.

mattress NOUN

le matelas

mature ADJECTIVE
mûr ◊ She's quite mature for her
age. Elle est très mûre pour son âge.

maximum NOUN
> see also **maximum** ADJECTIVE

le maximum

maximum ADJECTIVE
> see also **maximum** NOUN

maximum MASC, FEM, PL ◊ The maximum
speed is 100 km/h. La vitesse
maximum autorisée est de cent
kilomètres à l'heure.
♦ **the maximum amount** le maximum

May NOUN
mai MASC
♦ **in May** en mai
♦ **May Day** le Premier Mai

may VERB
♦ **He may come.** Il va peut-être venir.
◊ It may rain. Il va peut-être pleuvoir.
♦ **Are you going to the party? – I don't
know, I may.** Est-ce que tu vas à la
soirée? – Je ne sais pas, peut-être.
♦ **May I smoke?** Est-ce que je peux
fumer?

maybe ADVERB
peut-être ◊ maybe not peut-être pas
◊ a bit boring, maybe peut-être un
peu ennuyeux ◊ Maybe she's at
home. Elle est peut-être chez elle.
◊ Maybe he'll change his mind. Il va
peut-être changer d'avis.

mayonnaise NOUN
la mayonnaise

mayor NOUN
le maire

maze NOUN
le labyrinthe

me PRONOUN

> *me* becomes *m'* before a vowel
> sound.

① me ◊ Could you lend me your
pen? Est-ce que tu peux me prêter
ton stylo?
m' ◊ Can you tell me the way to the
station? Est-ce que vous pouvez
m'indiquer le chemin de la gare?
◊ Can you help me? Est-ce que tu
peux m'aider? ◊ He heard me. Il m'a
entendu.

> *moi* is used in exclamations.

② moi ◊ Me too! Moi aussi! ◊ Excuse
me! Excusez-moi! ◊ Look at me!
Regarde-moi! ◊ Wait for me!
Attends-moi! ◊ Come with me!
Suivez-moi!

> *moi* is also used after prepositions
> and in comparisons.

M

◇ *You're after me.* Tu es après moi.
◇ *Is it for me?* C'est pour moi?
◇ *She's older than me.* Elle est plus âgée que moi.

meal NOUN
le repas

mealtime NOUN
♦**at mealtimes** aux heures des repas

to **mean** VERB

see also **mean** ADJECTIVE AND **means** NOUN

vouloir dire ◇ *What does "complet" mean?* Qu'est-ce que "complet" veut dire? ◇ *I don't know what it means.* Je ne sais pas ce que ça veut dire. ◇ *What do you mean?* Qu'est que vous voulez dire? ◇ *That's not what I meant.* Ce n'est pas ce que je voulais dire.
♦**Which one do you mean?** Duquel veux-tu parler?
♦**Do you really mean it?** Tu es sérieux?
♦**to mean to do something** avoir l'intention de faire quelque chose ◇ *I didn't mean to offend you.* Je n'avais pas l'intention de vous blesser.

mean ADJECTIVE

see also **mean** VERB AND **means** NOUN

[1] radin (with money) ◇ *He's too mean to buy Christmas presents.* Il est trop radin pour acheter des cadeaux de Noël.
[2] méchant (unkind) ◇ *You're being mean to me.* Tu es méchant avec moi.
♦**That's a really mean thing to say!** Ce n'est vraiment pas gentil de dire ça!

meaning NOUN
le sens

means NOUN

see also **mean** VERB AND ADJECTIVE

le moyen ◇ *He'll do it by any possible means.* Il le fera par tous les moyens. ◇ *a means of transport* un moyen de transport
♦**by means of** au moyen de ◇ *He got in by means of a stolen key.* Il est entré au moyen d'une clé volée.
♦**by all means** bien sûr ◇ *Can I come? – By all means!* Est-ce que je peux venir? – Bien sûr!

meant VERB *see* **mean**

meanwhile ADVERB
pendant ce temps

measles NOUN
la rougeole

to **measure** VERB
[1] mesurer ◇ *I measured the page.* J'ai mesuré la page.

[2] faire ◇ *The room measures 3 metres by 4.* La pièce fait trois mètres sur quatre.

measurements PL NOUN
[1] les dimensions FEM PL (of object) ◇ *What are the measurements of the room?* Quelles sont les dimensions de la pièce?
[2] les mensurations FEM PL (of body) ◇ *What are your measurements?* Quelles sont tes mensurations?
♦**my waist measurement** mon tour de taille
♦**What's your neck measurement?** Quel est votre tour de cou?

meat NOUN
la viande ◇ *I don't eat meat.* Je ne mange pas de viande.

Mecca NOUN
La Mecque

mechanic NOUN
le mécanicien ◇ *He's a mechanic.* Il est mécanicien.

mechanical ADJECTIVE
mécanique

medal NOUN
la médaille
♦**the gold medal** la médaille d'or

medallion NOUN
le médaillon

media PL NOUN
les médias MASC PL

median strip NOUN [US]
le terre-plein central

medical ADJECTIVE

see also **medical** NOUN

médical
(médicaux MASC PL)
◇ *medical treatment* les soins médicaux
♦**medical insurance** l'assurance maladie FEM
♦**to have medical problems** avoir des problèmes de santé
♦**She's a medical student.** Elle est étudiante en médecine.

medical NOUN

see also **medical** ADJECTIVE

♦**to have a medical** passer une visite médicale

medicine NOUN
[1] la médecine (subject) ◇ *I want to study medicine.* Je veux faire médecine.
♦**alternative medicine** la médecine douce
[2] le médicament (medication) ◇ *I need some medicine.* J'ai besoin d'un médicament.

Mediterranean ADJECTIVE
méditerranéen MASC
méditerranéenne FEM
♦the Mediterranean la Méditerranée

medium ADJECTIVE
moyen MASC
moyenne FEM
◊ a man of medium height un
homme de taille moyenne

medium-sized ADJECTIVE
de taille moyenne ◊ a medium-sized
town une ville de taille moyenne

to **meet** VERB
1 rencontrer (by chance) ◊ I met Paul
in the street. J'ai rencontré Paul dans
la rue. ◊ Have you met him before?
Tu l'as déjà rencontré?
2 se rencontrer ◊ We met by
chance in the shopping centre. Nous
nous sommes rencontrés par hasard
dans le centre commercial.
3 retrouver (by arrangement) ◊ I'm
going to meet my friends. Je vais
retrouver mes amis.
4 se retrouver ◊ Let's meet in front
of the tourist office. Retrouvons-nous
devant l'office de tourisme.
♦I like meeting new people. J'aime
faire de nouvelles connaissances.
5 aller chercher (pick up) ◊ I'll meet
you at the station. J'irai te chercher à
la gare.
♦to meet up se retrouver ◊ What time
shall we meet up? On se retrouve à
quelle heure?

meeting NOUN
1 la réunion (for work) ◊ a business
meeting une réunion d'affaires
2 la rencontre (socially) ◊ their first
meeting leur première rencontre

mega ADJECTIVE
♦He's mega rich. Il est hyper-riche.
(informal)

melody NOUN
la mélodie

melon NOUN
le melon

to **melt** VERB
fondre ◊ The snow is melting. La
neige est en train de fondre.

member NOUN
le membre
♦a Member of Parliament un député

membership NOUN
l' adhésion FEM (of party, union) ◊ to
apply for membership faire une
demande d'adhésion

membership card NOUN
la carte de membre

memento NOUN
le souvenir

memorial NOUN
le monument ◊ a war memorial un
monument aux morts

to **memorize** VERB
apprendre par cœur

memory NOUN
1 la mémoire (also for computer) ◊ I
haven't got a good memory. Je n'ai
pas une bonne mémoire.
2 le souvenir (recollection) ◊ to bring
back memories rappeler des
souvenirs

men PL NOUN see **man**
les hommes MASC PL

to **mend** VERB
réparer

meningitis NOUN
la méningite

mental ADJECTIVE
1 mental
(mentaux MASC PL)
◊ a mental illness une maladie
mentale
2 (mad)
fou MASC
folle FEM
◊ You're mental! Tu es fou!
♦a mental hospital un hôpital
psychiatrique

mentality NOUN
la mentalité

to **mention** VERB
mentionner
♦Thank you! – Don't mention it!
Merci! – Il n'y a pas de quoi!

menu NOUN
le menu ◊ Could I have the menu
please? Est-ce que je pourrais avoir
le menu s'il vous plaît?

merchant NOUN
le marchand ◊ a wine merchant un
marchand de vin

mercy NOUN
la pitié

mere ADJECTIVE
♦a mere five percent à peine cinq pour
cent
♦It's a mere formality. C'est une
simple formalité.
♦the merest hint of criticism la
moindre petite critique

meringue NOUN
la meringue

merry ADJECTIVE
♦Merry Christmas! Joyeux Noël!

merry-go-round NOUN

M

☞

le manège

mess NOUN
le fouillis ◊ *My bedroom's usually in a mess.* Il y a généralement du fouillis dans ma chambre.

to **mess about** VERB
♦**to mess about with something** (*interfere with*) tripoter quelque chose ◊ *Stop messing about with my computer!* Arrête de tripoter mon ordinateur!
♦**Don't mess about with my things!** Ne touche pas à mes affaires!

to **mess up** VERB
♦**to mess something up** mettre la pagaille dans quelque chose ◊ *My little brother has messed up my cassettes.* Mon petit frère a mis la pagaille dans mes cassettes.

message NOUN
le message

messenger NOUN
le messager

messy ADJECTIVE
1 salissant (*dirty*) ◊ *a messy job* un travail salissant
2 en désordre (*untidy*) ◊ *Your desk is really messy.* Ton bureau est vraiment en désordre.
3 désordonnée (*person*) ◊ *She's so messy!* Elle est tellement désordonnée!
♦**My writing is terribly messy.** J'ai une écriture de cochon.

met VERB *see* **meet**

metal NOUN
le métal
(les métaux PL)

meter NOUN
1 le compteur (*for gas, electricity, taxi*)
2 le parcmètre (*parking meter*)
3 le mètre (*unit of measurement*) US

method NOUN
la méthode

Methodist NOUN
le/la méthodiste ◊ *I'm a Methodist.* Je suis méthodiste.

metre NOUN
le mètre

metric ADJECTIVE
métrique

Mexico NOUN
le Mexique
♦**in Mexico** au Mexique
♦**to Mexico** au Mexique

to **miaow** VERB
miauler

mice PL NOUN *see* **mouse**

microchip NOUN
la puce

microphone NOUN
le microphone

microscope NOUN
le microscope

microwave oven NOUN
le four à micro-ondes

mid ADJECTIVE
♦**in mid May** à la mi-mai

midday NOUN
le midi
♦**at midday** à midi

middle NOUN
le milieu ◊ *in the middle of the road* au milieu de la route ◊ *in the middle of the night* au milieu de la nuit ◊ *the middle seat* la place du milieu

middle-aged ADJECTIVE
d'un certain âge ◊ *a middle-aged man* un homme d'un certain âge
♦**to be middle-aged** avoir la cinquantaine
♦**She's middle-aged.** Elle a la cinquantaine.

Middle Ages PL NOUN
♦**the Middle Ages** le Moyen Âge SING

middle-class ADJECTIVE
de la classe moyenne ◊ *a middle-class family* une famille de la classe moyenne

Middle East NOUN
le Moyen-Orient
♦**in the Middle East** au Moyen-Orient

middle name NOUN
le deuxième nom

midge NOUN
le moucheron

midnight NOUN
minuit MASC
♦**at midnight** à minuit

midwife NOUN
la sage-femme
(les sages-femmes PL)
◊ *She's a midwife.* Elle est sage-femme.

might VERB
*Use **peut-être** to express possibility.*
◊ *He might come later.* Il va peut-être venir plus tard. ◊ *We might go to Spain next year.* Nous irons peut-être en Espagne l'an prochain. ◊ *She might not have understood.* Elle n'a peut-être pas compris.

migraine NOUN
la migraine ◊ *I've got a migraine.* J'ai la migraine.

mike NOUN

le <u>micro</u>

mild ADJECTIVE
  <u>doux</u> MASC
  <u>douce</u> FEM
  ◊ *The winters are quite mild.* Les hivers sont assez doux.

mile NOUN
  le <u>mille</u>

> *ⓘ In France distances are expressed in kilometres. A mile is about 1.6 kilometres.*

  ◊ *It's 5 miles from here.* C'est à huit kilomètres d'ici.
  ◆ **We walked miles!** Nous avons fait des kilomètres à pied!

military ADJECTIVE
  <u>militaire</u>

milk NOUN
  see also **milk** VERB
  le <u>lait</u> ◊ *tea with milk* du thé au lait

to **milk** VERB
  see also **milk** NOUN
  <u>traire</u>

milk chocolate NOUN
  le <u>chocolat au lait</u>

milkman NOUN

> *ⓘ In France milk is not delivered to people's homes.*

  ◊ *He's a milkman.* Il livre le lait à domicile.

milk shake NOUN
  le <u>milk-shake</u>

mill NOUN
  le <u>moulin</u> (*for grain*)

millennium NOUN
  le <u>millénaire</u> ◊ *the third millennium* le troisième millénaire
  ◆ **the millennium** le millénium

millimetre NOUN (US **millimeter**)
  le <u>millimètre</u>

million NOUN
  le <u>million</u>

millionaire NOUN
  le <u>millionnaire</u>

to **mimic** VERB
  <u>imiter</u>

mince NOUN
  la <u>viande hachée</u>

mince pie NOUN
  la <u>tartelette de Noël</u>

to **mind** VERB
  see also **mind** NOUN

  ① <u>garder</u> ◊ *Could you mind the baby this afternoon?* Est-ce que tu pourrais garder le bébé cet après-midi?
  ② <u>surveiller</u> (*keep an eye on*) ◊ *Could you mind my bags for a few minutes?* Est-ce que vous pourriez surveiller mes bagages pendant quelques minutes?
  ◆ **Do you mind if I open the window?** Est-ce que je pourrais ouvrir la fenêtre?
  ◆ **I don't mind.** Ça ne me dérange pas. ◊ *I don't mind the noise.* Le bruit ne me dérange pas.
  ◆ **Never mind!** Ça ne fait rien!
  ◆ **Mind that bike!** Attention au vélo!
  ◆ **Mind the step!** Attention à la marche!

mind NOUN
  see also **mind** VERB
  ◆ **to make up one's mind** se décider ◊ *I haven't made up my mind yet.* Je ne me suis pas encore décidé.
  ◆ **to change one's mind** changer d'avis ◊ *He's changed his mind.* Il a changé d'avis.
  ◆ **Are you out of your mind?** Tu as perdu la tête?

mine PRONOUN
  see also **mine** NOUN
  le <u>mien</u> + MASC NOUN ◊ *Is this your coat? – No, mine's black.* C'est ton manteau? – Non, le mien est noir.
  la <u>mienne</u> + FEM NOUN ◊ *Is this your car? – No, mine's green.* C'est ta voiture? – Non, la mienne est verte.
  les <u>miens</u> + MASC PL NOUN ◊ *her parents and mine* ses parents et les miens
  les <u>miennes</u> + FEM PL NOUN ◊ *Your hands are dirty, mine are clean.* Tes mains sont sales, les miennes sont propres.
  ◆ **It's mine.** C'est à moi. ◊ *This book is mine.* Ce livre est à moi. ◊ *Whose is this? – It's mine.* C'est à qui? – À moi.

mine NOUN
  see also **mine** PRONOUN
  la <u>mine</u> ◊ *a coal mine* une mine de charbon ◊ *a land mine* une mine terrestre

miner NOUN
  le <u>mineur</u>

mineral water NOUN
  l' <u>eau minérale</u> FEM

miniature ADJECTIVE
  see also **miniature** NOUN
  <u>miniature</u> ◊ *a miniature version* une version miniature

miniature NOUN
  see also **miniature** ADJECTIVE
  la <u>miniature</u>

M

minibus NOUN
le minibus

minicab NOUN
le taxi

> **ⓘ** In France the distinction between black taxis and minicabs does not exist.

Minidisc ® NOUN
le minidisque

minimum NOUN
> see also **minimum** ADJECTIVE

le minimum

minimum ADJECTIVE
> see also **minimum** NOUN

minimum MASC, FEM, PL ◊ The minimum wage in Britain is .... Le salaire minimum en Grande-Bretagne est ... ◊ The minimum age for driving is 17. L'âge minimum pour conduire est dix-sept ans.
◆ **the minimum amount** le minimum

miniskirt NOUN
la mini-jupe

minister NOUN
1 le ministre (in government)
2 le pasteur (of church)

ministry NOUN
le ministère (in government) ◊ The Ministry of Culture Le Ministère de la Culture

mink NOUN
le vison ◊ a mink coat un manteau en vison

minor ADJECTIVE
mineur ◊ a minor problem un problème mineur
◆ **in D minor** en ré mineur
◆ **a minor operation** une opération bénigne

minority NOUN
la minorité

mint NOUN
1 la menthe (plant) ◊ mint sauce la sauce à la menthe
2 le bonbon à la menthe (sweet)

minus PREPOSITION
moins ◊ 16 minus 3 is 13. Seize moins trois égale treize. ◊ It's minus two degrees outside. Il fait moins deux dehors. ◊ I got a B minus. J'ai eu un B moins.

minute NOUN
> see also **minute** ADJECTIVE

la minute ◊ Wait a minute! Attends une minute!

minute ADJECTIVE
> see also **minute** NOUN

minuscule ◊ Her flat is minute. Son appartement est minuscule.

miracle NOUN
le miracle

mirror NOUN
1 la glace (on wall)
2 le rétroviseur (in car)

to **misbehave** VERB
se conduire mal

miscellaneous ADJECTIVE
divers

mischief NOUN
les bêtises FEM PL ◊ My little sister's always up to mischief. Ma petite sœur fait constamment des bêtises.

mischievous ADJECTIVE
coquin

miser NOUN
l' avare MASC/FEM

miserable ADJECTIVE
1 (person)
malheureux MASC
malheureuse FEM
◊ You're looking miserable. Tu as l'air malheureux.
2 (weather)
épouvantable ◊ The weather was miserable. Il faisait un temps épouvantable.
◆ **to feel miserable** ne pas avoir le moral ◊ I'm feeling miserable. Je n'ai pas le moral.

misery NOUN
1 (unhappiness)
la tristesse ◊ All that money brought nothing but misery. Tout cet argent n'a apporté que de la tristesse.
2 (unhappy person)
le pleurnicheur
la pleurnicheuse
◊ She's a real misery. C'est une vraie pleurnicheuse.

misfortune NOUN
le malheur

mishap NOUN
la mésaventure

to **misjudge** VERB
mal juger (person) ◊ I've misjudged her. Je l'ai mal jugée.
◆ **He misjudged the bend.** Il a mal pris le virage.

to **mislay** VERB
égarer ◊ I've mislaid my passport. J'ai égaré mon passeport.

misleading ADJECTIVE
trompeur MASC
trompeuse FEM

Miss NOUN
1 Mademoiselle

(Mesdemoiselles PL)

2 (*in address*)
Mlle
(Mlles PL)

to **miss** VERB

1 rater ◇ *Hurry or you'll miss the bus.* Dépêche-toi ou tu vas rater le bus. ◇ *He missed the target.* Il a raté la cible.

2 manquer ◇ *to miss an opportunity* manquer une occasion

♦ **I miss you.** Tu me manques. ◇ *I'm missing my family.* Ma famille me manque. ◇ *I miss him.* Il me manque. ◇ *I miss them.* Ils me manquent.

missing ADJECTIVE

manquant ◇ *the missing part* la pièce manquante

♦ **to be missing** avoir disparu ◇ *My rucksack is missing.* Mon sac à dos a disparu. ◇ *Two members of the group are missing.* Deux membres du groupe ont disparu.

missionary NOUN
le/la missionnaire

mist NOUN
la brume

mistake NOUN

see also **mistake** VERB

1 la faute (*slip*) ◇ *a spelling mistake* une faute d'orthographe

♦ **to make a mistake (1)** (*in writing, speaking*) faire une faute

♦ **to make a mistake (2)** (*get mixed up*) se tromper ◇ *I'm sorry, I made a mistake.* Je suis désolé, je me suis trompé.

2 l' erreur FEM (*misjudgement*) ◇ *It was a mistake to buy those yellow shoes.* J'ai fait une erreur en achetant ces chaussures jaunes.

♦ **by mistake** par erreur ◇ *I took his bag by mistake.* J'ai pris son sac par erreur.

to **mistake** VERB

see also **mistake** NOUN

♦ **He mistook me for my sister.** Il m'a prise pour ma sœur.

mistaken ADJECTIVE

♦ **to be mistaken** se tromper ◇ *If you think I'm going to get up at 6 o'clock, you're mistaken.* Si tu penses que je vais me lever à six heures, tu te trompes.

mistakenly ADVERB
à tort

mistletoe NOUN
le gui

mistook VERB *see* **mistake**

mistress NOUN

1 le professeur (*teacher*) ◇ *our French mistress* notre professeur de français

2 la maîtresse (*lover*) ◇ *He's got a mistress.* Il a une maîtresse.

to **mistrust** VERB
se méfier de

misty ADJECTIVE
brumeux MASC
brumeuse FEM
◇ *a misty morning* un matin brumeux

to **misunderstand** VERB
mal comprendre ◇ *Sorry, I misunderstood you.* Je suis désolé, je t'avais mal compris.

misunderstanding NOUN
le malentendu

misunderstood VERB *see* **misunderstand**

mix NOUN

see also **mix** VERB

le mélange ◇ *It's a mix of science fiction and comedy.* C'est un mélange de science-fiction et de comédie.

♦ **a cake mix** une préparation pour gâteau

to **mix** VERB

see also **mix** NOUN

1 mélanger ◇ *Mix the flour with the sugar.* Mélangez la farine au sucre.

2 combiner ◇ *He's mixing business with pleasure.* Il combine les affaires et le plaisir.

♦ **to mix with somebody** (*associate*) fréquenter quelqu'un

♦ **He doesn't mix much.** Il se tient à l'écart.

♦ **to mix up** (*people*) confondre ◇ *He always mixes me up with my sister.* Il me confond toujours avec ma sœur.

♦ **The travel agent mixed up the bookings.** L'agence de voyage s'est embrouillée dans les réservations.

♦ **I'm getting mixed up.** Je ne m'y retrouve plus.

mixed ADJECTIVE

♦ **a mixed salad** une salade composée

♦ **a mixed school** une école mixte

♦ **a mixed grill** un assortiment de grillades

mixer NOUN

♦ **She's a good mixer.** Elle est très sociable.

mixture NOUN

le mélange ◇ *a mixture of spices* un mélange d'épices

♦ **cough mixture** le sirop pour la toux

mix-up NOUN
la confusion

to **moan** VERB
râler ◊ *She's always moaning.* Elle
est toujours en train de râler.

mobile home NOUN
le mobile home

mobile phone NOUN
le portable

to **mock** VERB
| see also **mock** ADJECTIVE |
ridiculiser

mock ADJECTIVE
| see also **mock** VERB |
♦ **a mock exam** un examen blanc

mod cons PL NOUN
♦ **"all mod cons"** "tout confort"

model NOUN
| see also **model** ADJECTIVE |
[1] le modèle (*type*) ◊ *His car is the
latest model.* Sa voiture est le tout
dernier modèle.
[2] la maquette (*mock-up*) ◊ *a model
of the castle* une maquette du
château
[3] le mannequin (*fashion*) ◊ *She's a
famous model.* C'est un mannequin
célèbre.

model ADJECTIVE
| see also **model** NOUN |
♦ **a model plane** un modèle réduit
d'avion
♦ **a model railway** un modèle réduit de
voie ferrée
♦ **He's a model pupil.** C'est un élève
modèle.

to **model** VERB
| see also **model** NOUN |
♦ **She was modelling a Lorna Bailey
outfit.** Elle présentait une tenue de la
collection Lorna Bailey.

modem NOUN
le modem

moderate ADJECTIVE
modéré ◊ *His views are quite
moderate.* Ses opinions sont assez
modérées.
♦ **a moderate amount of** un peu de
♦ **a moderate price** un prix raisonnable

modern ADJECTIVE
moderne

to **modernize** VERB
moderniser

modest ADJECTIVE
modeste

to **modify** VERB
modifier

moist ADJECTIVE

humide (*skin, soil*) ◊ *Make sure the
soil is moist.* Assurez-vous que la
terre est humide.

moisture NOUN
l' humidité FEM

moisturizer NOUN
[1] la crème hydratante (*cream*)
[2] le lait hydratant (*lotion*)

moldy ADJECTIVE [US]
moisi

mole NOUN
[1] la taupe (*animal*)
[2] le grain de beauté (*on skin*)

moment NOUN
l' instant MASC ◊ *Could you wait a
moment?* Pouvez-vous attendre un
instant? ◊ *in a moment* dans un
instant ◊ *Just a moment!* Un instant!
♦ **at the moment** en ce moment
♦ **any moment now** d'un moment à
l'autre ◊ *They'll be arriving any
moment now.* Ils vont arriver d'un
moment à l'autre.

momentous ADJECTIVE
capital (*event*)

Monaco NOUN
Monaco
♦ **in Monaco** à Monaco

monarch NOUN
le monarque

monarchy NOUN
la monarchie

monastery NOUN
le monastère

Monday NOUN
le lundi ◊ *on Monday* lundi ◊ *on
Mondays* le lundi ◊ *every Monday*
tous les lundis ◊ *last Monday* lundi
dernier ◊ *next Monday* lundi prochain

money NOUN
l' argent MASC ◊ *I need to change
some money.* J'ai besoin de changer
de l'argent.
♦ **to make money** gagner de l'argent

mongrel NOUN
le bâtard ◊ *My dog's a mongrel.*
Mon chien est un bâtard.

monitor NOUN
le moniteur (*of computer*)

monk NOUN
le moine

monkey NOUN
le singe

monotonous ADJECTIVE
monotone

monster NOUN
le monstre

month NOUN

le <u>mois</u> ◊ *this month* ce mois-ci
◊ *next month* le mois prochain ◊ *last month* le mois dernier ◊ *every month* tous les mois ◊ *at the end of the month* à la fin du mois

monthly ADJECTIVE
<u>mensuel</u> MASC
<u>mensuelle</u> FEM

monument NOUN
le <u>monument</u>

mood NOUN
l' <u>humeur</u> FEM
♦**to be in a bad mood** être de mauvaise humeur
♦**to be in a good mood** être de bonne humeur

moody ADJECTIVE
① <u>lunatique</u> (*temperamental*)
② <u>maussade</u> (*in a bad mood*)

moon NOUN
la <u>lune</u> ◊ *There's a full moon tonight.* Il y a pleine lune ce soir.
♦**to be over the moon** (*happy*) être aux anges

moor NOUN
| *see also* **moor** VERB |
la <u>lande</u>

to **moor** VERB
| *see also* **moor** NOUN |
<u>amarrer</u> (*boat*)

mop NOUN
le <u>balai laveur</u> (*for floor*)

moped NOUN
le <u>cyclomoteur</u>

moral ADJECTIVE
| *see also* **moral** NOUN |
<u>moral</u>
(moraux MASC PL)

moral NOUN
| *see also* **moral** ADJECTIVE |
la <u>morale</u> ◊ *the moral of the story* la morale de l'histoire
♦**morals** la moralité

morale NOUN
le <u>moral</u> ◊ *Their morale is very low.* Leur moral est très bas.

more ADJECTIVE, PRONOUN, ADVERB
*When comparing one amount with another, you usually use **plus**.*
① <u>plus</u> ◊ *Beer is more expensive in Britain.* La bière est plus chère en Grande-Bretagne. ◊ *Could you speak more slowly?* Est-ce que vous pourriez parler plus lentement? ◊ *a bit more* un peu plus ◊ *There isn't any more.* Il n'y en a plus.
♦**more ... than** plus ... que ◊ *He's more intelligent than me.* Il est plus intelligent que moi. ◊ *She practises*

more than I do. Elle s'entraîne plus que moi. ◊ *More girls than boys do French.* Il y a plus de filles que de garçons qui font du français.
② <u>plus de</u> (*followed by noun*) ◊ *There are more girls in the class.* Il y a plus de filles dans la classe. ◊ *I get more homework than you do.* J'ai plus de devoirs que toi. ◊ *I spent more than 500 euros.* J'ai dépensé plus de cinq cents euros.
*When referring to an additional amount, more than there is already, you usually use **encore**.*
③ <u>encore</u> ◊ *Is there any more?* Est-ce qu'il y a encore? ◊ *Would you like some more?* Vous en voulez encore? ◊ *It'll take a few more days.* Ça prendra encore quelques jours.
④ <u>encore de</u> (*followed by noun*) ◊ *Could I have some more chips?* Est-ce que je pourrais avoir encore des frites? ◊ *Do you want some more tea?* Voulez-vous encore du thé?
♦**more or less** plus ou moins
♦**more than ever** plus que jamais

moreover ADVERB
<u>en outre</u>

morning NOUN
le <u>matin</u> ◊ *this morning* ce matin
◊ *tomorrow morning* demain matin
◊ *every morning* tous les matins
♦**in the morning** le matin ◊ *at 7 o'clock in the morning* à sept heures du matin
♦**a morning paper** un journal du matin

Morocco NOUN
le <u>Maroc</u>
♦**in Morocco** au Maroc

Moscow NOUN
<u>Moscou</u>
♦**in Moscow** à Moscou

Moslem NOUN
le <u>musulman</u>
la <u>musulmane</u>
◊ *He's a Moslem.* Il est musulman.

mosque NOUN
la <u>mosquée</u>

mosquito NOUN
le <u>moustique</u>
♦**a mosquito bite** une piqûre de moustique

most ADVERB, ADJECTIVE, PRONOUN
*Use **la plupart de** when most (of) is followed by a plural noun and **la majeure partie (de)** when most (of) is followed by a singular noun.*
① <u>la plupart de</u> ◊ *most of my friends* la plupart de mes amis
◊ *most people* la plupart des gens

M

◊ *Most cats are affectionate.* La plupart des chats sont affectueux.
♦ **most of them** la plupart d'entre eux
♦ **most of the time** la plupart du temps

2 la majeure partie de ◊ *most of the work* la majeure partie du travail ◊ *most of the class* la majeure partie de la classe ◊ *most of the night* la majeure partie de la nuit
♦ **the most** le plus ◊ *He's the one who talks the most.* C'est lui qui parle le plus.

> When **most** is followed by adjective, the translation depends on whether the noun referred to is masculine, feminine or plural.

♦ **the most ... (1)** le plus ... ◊ *the most expensive restaurant* le restaurant le plus cher
♦ **the most ... (2)** la plus ... ◊ *the most expensive seat* la place la plus chère
♦ **the most ... (3)** les plus ... ◊ *the most expensive restaurants* les restaurants les plus chers ◊ *the most expensive seats* les places les plus chères
♦ **to make the most of something** profiter au maximum de quelque chose
♦ **at the most** au maximum ◊ *Two hours at the most.* Deux heures au maximum.

mostly ADVERB
♦ **The teachers are mostly quite nice.** La plupart des professeurs sont assez gentils.

MOT NOUN
le contrôle technique ◊ *Her car failed its MOT.* Sa voiture n'a pas obtenu le certificat du contrôle technique.

motel NOUN
le motel

moth NOUN
le papillon de nuit

mother NOUN
la mère ◊ *my mother* ma mère
♦ **mother tongue** la langue maternelle

mother-in-law NOUN
la belle-mère
(les belles-mères PL)

Mother's Day NOUN
la fête des Mères

> ⓘ *Mother's Day is usually on the last Sunday of May in France.*

motionless ADJECTIVE
immobile

motivated ADJECTIVE

motivé ◊ *He is highly motivated.* Il est très motivé.

motivation NOUN
la motivation

motive NOUN
le mobile ◊ *the motive for the killing* le mobile du crime

motor NOUN
le moteur ◊ *The boat has a motor.* Le bateau a un moteur.

motorbike NOUN
la moto

motorboat NOUN
le bateau à moteur

motorcycle NOUN
le vélomoteur

motorcyclist NOUN
le motard

motorist NOUN
l' automobiliste MASC/FEM

motor mechanic NOUN
le mécanicien garagiste

motor racing NOUN
la course automobile

motorway NOUN
l' autoroute FEM ◊ *on the motorway* sur l'autoroute

mouldy ADJECTIVE
moisi

to **mount** VERB
1 monter ◊ *They're mounting a publicity campaign.* Ils montent une campagne publicitaire.
2 augmenter ◊ *Tension is mounting.* La tension augmente.

to **mount up** VERB
1 s'accumuler ◊ *Letters had mounted up while we were on holiday.* Les lettres s'étaient accumulées pendant que nous étions en vacances.
2 augmenter ◊ *My savings are mounting up gradually.* Mes économies augmentent progressivement.

mountain NOUN
la montagne
♦ **a mountain bike** un VTT (= vélo tout-terrain)

mountaineer NOUN
l' alpiniste MASC/FEM

mountaineering NOUN
l' alpinisme MASC ◊ *I go mountaineering.* Je fais de l'alpinisme.

mountainous ADJECTIVE
montagneux MASC
montagneuse FEM

mouse NOUN
la <u>souris</u> (*also for computer*) ◊ *white mice* des souris blanches

mouse mat NOUN
le <u>tapis de souris</u>

mousse NOUN
[1] la <u>mousse</u> (*food*) ◊ *chocolate mousse* la mousse au chocolat
[2] la <u>mousse coiffante</u> (*for hair*)

moustache NOUN
la <u>moustache</u> ◊ *He's got a moustache.* Il a une moustache.
♦ **a man with a moustache** un moustachu

mouth NOUN
la <u>bouche</u>

mouthful NOUN
la <u>bouchée</u>

mouth organ NOUN
l' <u>harmonica</u> MASC ◊ *I play the mouth organ.* Je joue de l'harmonica.

mouthwash NOUN
le <u>bain de bouche</u>

move NOUN
see also **move** VERB
[1] le <u>tour</u> ◊ *It's your move.* C'est ton tour.
[2] le <u>déménagement</u> ◊ *Our move from Oxford to Luton ...* Notre déménagement d'Oxford à Luton ...
♦ **to get a move on** se remuer ◊ *Get a move on!* Remue-toi!

to **move** VERB
see also **move** NOUN
[1] <u>bouger</u> ◊ *Don't move!* Ne bouge pas! ◊ *Could you move your stuff please?* Est-ce que tu peux bouger tes affaires s'il te plaît?
[2] <u>avancer</u> ◊ *The car was moving very slowly.* La voiture avançait très lentement.
[3] <u>émouvoir</u> ◊ *I was very moved by the film.* J'ai été très émue par ce film.
♦ **to move house** déménager ◊ *We're moving in July.* Nous allons déménager en juillet.
♦ **to move forward** avancer
♦ **to move in** emménager ◊ *They're moving in next week.* Ils emménagent la semaine prochaine.
♦ **to move over** se pousser ◊ *Could you move over a bit?* Est-ce que vous pouvez vous pousser un peu?

movement NOUN
le <u>mouvement</u>

movie NOUN
le <u>film</u>

♦ **the movies** le cinéma ◊ *Let's go to the movies!* Si on allait au cinéma?

moving ADJECTIVE
[1] <u>en marche</u> (*not stationary*) ◊ *a moving bus* un bus en marche
[2] <u>touchant</u> (*touching*) ◊ *a moving story* une histoire touchante

to **mow** VERB
<u>tondre</u>
♦ **to mow the lawn** tondre le gazon

mower NOUN
la <u>tondeuse à gazon</u>

mown VERB *see* **mow**

MP NOUN
le <u>député</u> ◊ *She's an MP.* Elle est député.

mph ABBREVIATION (= *miles per hour*)
<u>km/h</u> (= *kilomètres-heure*) ◊ *to drive at 50 mph* rouler à 80 km/h

> ⓘ In France, speed is expressed in kilometres per hour. 50 mph is about 80 km/h.

Mr NOUN
[1] <u>Monsieur</u>
(Messieurs PL)
[2] (*in address*)
<u>M.</u>
(MM. PL)

Mrs NOUN
[1] <u>Madame</u>
(Mesdames PL)
[2] (*in address*)
<u>Mme</u>
(Mmes PL)

MS NOUN (= *multiple sclerosis*)
la <u>sclérose en plaques</u> ◊ *She's got MS.* Elle a la sclérose en plaques.

Ms NOUN
[1] <u>Madame</u>
(Mesdames PL)
[2] (*in address*)
<u>Mme</u>
(Mmes PL)

> ⓘ There isn't a direct equivalent of **Ms** in French. If you are writing to somebody and don't know whether she is married, use **Madame**.

much ADJECTIVE, ADVERB, PRONOUN
[1] <u>beaucoup</u> (*with verb*) ◊ *Do you go out much?* Tu sors beaucoup? ◊ *I don't like sport much.* Je n'aime pas beaucoup le sport. ◊ *I feel much better now.* Je me sens beaucoup mieux maintenant.
[2] <u>beaucoup de</u> (*followed by noun*) ◊ *I haven't got much money.* Je n'ai pas

M

☞

beaucoup d'argent. ◊ *I don't want
much rice.* Je ne veux pas beaucoup
de riz.
♦ **very much (1)** (*with verb*) beaucoup ◊ *I
enjoyed the film very much.* J'ai
beaucoup apprécié le film. ◊ *Thank
you very much.* Merci beaucoup.
♦ **very much (2)** (*followed by noun*)
beaucoup de ◊ *I haven't got very
much money.* Je n'ai pas beaucoup
d'argent.
♦ **not much (1)** pas beaucoup ◊ *Have
you got a lot of luggage? – No, not
much.* As-tu beaucoup de bagages? –
Non, pas beaucoup.
♦ **not much (2)** pas grand-chose
◊ *What's on TV? – Not much.* Qu'est-
ce qu'il y a à la télé? – Pas grand-
chose. ◊ *What did you think of it? –
Not much.* Qu'est-ce que tu en as
pensé? – Pas grand-chose.
♦ **How much?** Combien? ◊ *How much
do you want?* Tu en veux combien?
◊ *How much time have you got?* Tu
as combien de temps? ◊ *How much
is it?* (*cost*) Combien est-ce que ça
coûte?
♦ **too much** trop ◊ *That's too much!*
C'est trop! ◊ *It costs too much.* Ça
coûte trop cher. ◊ *They give us too
much homework.* Ils nous donnent
trop de devoirs.
♦ **so much** autant ◊ *I didn't think it
would cost so much.* Je ne pensais
pas que ça coûterait autant. ◊ *I've
never seen so much traffic.* Je n'ai
jamais vu autant de circulation.

mud NOUN
la boue

muddle NOUN
le désordre ◊ *The photos are in a
muddle.* Les photos sont en désordre.

to **muddle up** VERB
confondre (*people*) ◊ *He muddles me
up with my sister.* Il me confond avec
ma sœur.
♦ **to get muddled up** s'embrouiller ◊ *I'm
getting muddled up.* Je m'embrouille.

muddy ADJECTIVE
boueux MASC
boueuse FEM

muesli NOUN
le muesli

muffler NOUN US
le silencieux

mug NOUN
see also **mug** VERB
la grande tasse ◊ *Do you want a
cup or a mug?* Est-ce que vous

voulez une tasse normale ou une
grande tasse?
♦ **a beer mug** une chope à bière

to **mug** VERB
see also **mug** NOUN
agresser ◊ *He was mugged in the
city centre.* Il s'est fait agresser au
centre-ville.

mugger NOUN
l' agresseur MASC

mugging NOUN
l' agression FEM

muggy ADJECTIVE
lourd ◊ *It's muggy today.* Il fait lourd
aujourd'hui.

multiple choice test NOUN
le QCM (= questionnaire à choix
multiples)

multiple sclerosis NOUN
la sclérose en plaques ◊ *She's got
multiple sclerosis.* Elle a la sclérose
en plaques.

multiplication NOUN
la multiplication

to **multiply** VERB
multiplier ◊ *to multiply 6 by 3*
multiplier six par trois

multi-storey car park NOUN
le parking à plusieurs étages

mum NOUN
*You use **maman** only when you are
talking to your mother or using it as
her name; otherwise use **mère**.*
1 la mère ◊ *my mum* ma mère
◊ *her mum* sa mère
2 la maman ◊ *Mum!* Maman! ◊ *I'll
ask Mum.* Je vais demander à
maman.

mummy NOUN
1 la maman (*mum*) ◊ *Mummy says I
can go.* Maman dit que je peux y
aller.
2 la momie (*Egyptian*)

mumps NOUN
les oreillons MASC PL

murder NOUN
see also **murder** VERB
le meurtre

to **murder** VERB
see also **murder** NOUN
assassiner ◊ *He was murdered.* Il a
été assassiné.

murderer NOUN
l' assassin MASC

muscle NOUN
le muscle

muscular ADJECTIVE
musclé

museum NOUN
le musée

mushroom NOUN
le champignon ◊ *mushroom
omelette* l'omelette aux champignons

music NOUN
la musique

musical ADJECTIVE
see also **musical** NOUN
doué pour la musique ◊ *I'm not
musical.* Je ne suis pas doué pour la
musique.
♦**a musical instrument** un instrument
de musique

musical NOUN
see also **musical** ADJECTIVE
la comédie musicale

music centre NOUN
la chaîne stéréo

musician NOUN
le musicien
la musicienne

Muslim NOUN
le musulman
la musulmane
◊ *He's a Muslim.* Il est musulman.

mussel NOUN
la moule

must VERB
*When **must** means that you assume
or suppose something, use **devoir**;
when it means it's necessary to do
something, eg **I must buy some
presents**, use **il faut que …**, which
comes from the verb **falloir** and is
followed by a verb in the
subjunctive.*
[1] devoir *(I suppose)* ◊ *You must be
tired.* Tu dois être fatigué. ◊ *They
must have plenty of money.* Ils
doivent avoir beaucoup d'argent.
◊ *There must be some problem.* Il
doit y avoir un problème.
[2] il faut que ◊ *I must buy some
presents.* Il faut que j'achète des
cadeaux. ◊ *I really must go now.* Il
faut que j'y aille.
♦**You mustn't forget to send her a
card.** N'oublie surtout pas de lui
envoyer une carte.
♦**You must come and see us.**
(invitation) Venez donc nous voir.

mustard NOUN
la moutarde

mustn't VERB = **must not**

to **mutter** VERB
marmonner

mutton NOUN
le mouton

my ADJECTIVE
mon MASC ◊ *my father* mon père
ma FEM ◊ *my aunt* ma tante
mes PL ◊ *my parents* mes parents
*ma becomes **mon** before a vowel
sound.*
♦**my friend (1)** *(male)* mon ami
♦**my friend (2)** *(female)* mon amie
*Do not use **mon/ma/mes** with parts
of the body.*
◊ *I want to wash my hair.* Je voudrais
me laver les cheveux. ◊ *I'm going to
clean my teeth.* Je vais me brosser les
dents. ◊ *I've hurt my foot.* Je me suis
fait mal au pied.

myself PRONOUN
[1] me ◊ *I've hurt myself.* Je me suis
fait mal. ◊ *I really enjoyed myself.* Je
me suis vraiment bien amusé.
◊ *…when I look at myself in the
mirror.* …quand je me regarde dans
la glace.
[2] moi ◊ *I don't like talking about
myself.* Je n'aime pas parler de moi.
[3] moi-même ◊ *I made it myself.* Je
l'ai fait moi-même.
♦**by myself** tout seul ◊ *I don't like
travelling by myself.* Je n'aime pas
voyager tout seul.

mysterious ADJECTIVE
mystérieux MASC
mystérieuse FEM

mystery NOUN
le mystère
♦**a murder mystery** *(novel)* un roman
policier

myth NOUN
[1] le mythe *(legend)* ◊ *a Greek myth*
un mythe grec
[2] l' idée reçue FEM *(untrue idea)*
◊ *That's a myth.* C'est une idée reçue.

mythology NOUN
la mythologie

M

N

naff ADJECTIVE
nul MASC
nulle FEM

to **nag** VERB
harceler (*scold*) ◊ *She's always nagging me.* Elle me harcèle constamment.

nail NOUN
1 l' **ongle** MASC (*on finger, toe*) ◊ *Don't bite your nails!* Ne te ronge pas les ongles!
2 le **clou** (*made of metal*)

nailbrush NOUN
la **brosse à ongles**

nailfile NOUN
la **lime à ongles**

nail scissors PL NOUN
les **ciseaux à ongles** MASC PL

nail varnish NOUN
le **vernis à ongles**
◆ **nail varnish remover** le dissolvant

naked ADJECTIVE
nu

name NOUN
le **nom**
◆ **What's your name?** Comment vous appelez-vous?

nanny NOUN
la **garde d'enfants** ◊ *She's a nanny.* C'est une garde d'enfants.

nap NOUN
le **petit somme**
◆ **to have a nap** faire un petit somme

napkin NOUN
la **serviette**

nappy NOUN
la **couche**

narrow ADJECTIVE
étroit

narrow-minded ADJECTIVE
borné

nasty ADJECTIVE
1 **mauvais** (*bad*) ◊ *a nasty cold* un mauvais rhume ◊ *a nasty smell* une mauvaise odeur
2 **méchant** (*unfriendly*) ◊ *He gave me a nasty look.* Il m'a regardé d'un air méchant.

nation NOUN
la **nation**

national ADJECTIVE
national
(nationaux MASC PL)

◊ *He's the national champion.* C'est le champion national.
◆ **the national elections** les élections législatives FEM

national anthem NOUN
l' **hymne national** MASC

National Health Service NOUN
la **Sécurité sociale**

ⓘ *In France you have to pay for medical treatment when you receive it, and then claim it back from the **Sécurité sociale**.*

---

nationalism NOUN
le **nationalisme** ◊ *Scottish nationalism* le nationalisme écossais

nationalist NOUN
le/la **nationaliste**

nationality NOUN
la **nationalité**

National Lottery NOUN
la **Loterie nationale**

national park NOUN
le **parc national**
(les parcs nationaux PL)

native ADJECTIVE
natal ◊ *my native country* mon pays natal
◆ **native language** la langue maternelle ◊ *English is not their native language.* L'anglais n'est pas leur langue maternelle.

natural ADJECTIVE
naturel MASC
naturelle FEM

naturalist NOUN
le **naturaliste**

naturally ADVERB
naturellement ◊ *Naturally, we were very disappointed.* Nous avons naturellement été très déçus.

nature NOUN
la **nature**

naughty ADJECTIVE
vilain ◊ *Naughty girl!* Vilaine! ◊ *Don't be naughty!* Ne fais pas le vilain!

navy NOUN
la **marine** ◊ *He's in the navy.* Il est dans la marine.

navy-blue ADJECTIVE
bleu marine MASC, FEM, PL ◊ *a navy-blue skirt* une jupe bleu marine

Nazi NOUN

le Nazi
la Nazie
◊ *the Nazis* les Nazis

near ADJECTIVE
| *see also* **near** PREPOSITION |
proche ◊ *It's fairly near.* C'est assez
proche.
♦**It's near enough to walk.** On peut
facilement y aller à pied.
♦**the nearest** le plus proche ◊ *Where's
the nearest service station?* Où est la
station-service la plus proche? ◊ *The
nearest shops were three kilometres
away.* Les magasins les plus proches
étaient à trois kilomètres.

near PREPOSITION, ADVERB
| *see also* **near** ADJECTIVE |
près de ◊ *I live near Liverpool.*
J'habite près de Liverpool. ◊ *near my
house* près de chez moi
♦**near here** près d'ici ◊ *Is there a bank
near here?* Est-ce qu'il y a une
banque près d'ici?
♦**near to** près de ◊ *It's very near to the
school.* C'est tout près de l'école.

nearby ADVERB
| *see also* **nearby** ADJECTIVE |
à proximité ◊ *There's a supermarket
nearby.* Il y a un supermarché à
proximité.

nearby ADJECTIVE
| *see also* **nearby** ADVERB |
① proche (*close*) ◊ *a nearby garage*
un garage proche
② voisin (*neighbouring*) ◊ *We went to
the nearby village of Torrance.* Nous
sommes allés à Torrance, le village
voisin.

nearly ADVERB
presque ◊ *Dinner's nearly ready.* Le
dîner est presque prêt. ◊ *I'm nearly
15.* J'ai presque quinze ans.
♦**I nearly missed the train.** J'ai failli
rater le train.

neat ADJECTIVE
soigné ◊ *She has very neat writing.*
Elle a une écriture très soignée.
♦**a neat whisky** un whisky sec

neatly ADVERB
soigneusement ◊ *neatly folded*
soigneusement plié
♦**neatly dressed** impeccable

necessarily ADVERB
♦**not necessarily** pas forcément

necessary ADJECTIVE
nécessaire

necessity NOUN
la chose nécessaire ◊ *A car is a
necessity, not a luxury.* Une voiture

est une chose nécessaire et non pas
un luxe.

neck NOUN
① le cou (*of body*)
♦**a stiff neck** un torticolis
② l' encolure FEM (*of garment*) ◊ *a V-
neck sweater* un pull avec une
encolure en V

necklace NOUN
le collier

to **need** VERB
| *see also* **need** NOUN |
avoir besoin de ◊ *I need a bigger
size.* J'ai besoin d'une plus grande
taille.
♦**to need to do something** avoir besoin
de faire quelque chose ◊ *I need to
change some money.* J'ai besoin de
changer de l'argent.

need NOUN
| *see also* **need** VERB |
♦**There's no need to book.** Il n'est pas
nécessaire de réserver.

needle NOUN
l' aiguille FEM

needlework NOUN
la couture ◊ *We have needlework
lessons at school.* Nous avons des
cours de couture à l'école.

negative NOUN
| *see also* **negative** ADJECTIVE |
le négatif (*photo*)

negative ADJECTIVE
| *see also* **negative** NOUN |
négatif MASC
négative FEM
◊ *He's got a very negative attitude.* Il
a une attitude très négative.

neglected ADJECTIVE
mal tenu (*untidy*) ◊ *The garden is
neglected.* Le jardin est mal tenu.

negligee NOUN
le déshabillé

to **negotiate** VERB
négocier

negotiations PL NOUN
les négociations FEM PL

neighbour NOUN (US **neighbor**)
le voisin
la voisine
◊ *the neighbours' garden* le jardin
des voisins

neighbourhood NOUN (US
neighborhood)
le quartier

neither PRONOUN, CONJUNCTION, ADVERB
aucun des deux
aucune des deux

N

☞

◊ *Carrots or peas? – Neither, thanks.* Des carottes ou des petits pois? – Aucun des deux merci. ◊ *Neither of them is coming.* Aucun des deux ne vient.

◆**neither ... nor ...** ni ... ni ... ◊ *Neither Sarah nor Tamsin is coming to the party.* Ni Sarah ni Tamsin ne viennent à la soirée.

◆**Neither do I.** Moi non plus. ◊ *I don't like him. – Neither do I!* Je ne l'aime pas. – Moi non plus!

◆**Neither have I.** Moi non plus. ◊ *I've never been to Spain. – Neither have I.* Je ne suis jamais allé en Espagne. – Moi non plus.

neon NOUN
le néon

◆**a neon light** une lampe au néon

nephew NOUN
le neveu
(les neveux PL)
◊ *my nephew* mon neveu

nerve NOUN
[1] le nerf ◊ *She sometimes gets on my nerves.* Elle me tape quelquefois sur les nerfs.
[2] le toupet (*cheek*) ◊ *He's got a nerve!* Il a du toupet!

nerve-racking ADJECTIVE
angoissant

nervous ADJECTIVE
tendu (*tense*) ◊ *I bite my nails when I'm nervous.* Je me ronge les ongles quand je suis tendu.

◆**to be nervous about something** appréhender de faire quelque chose ◊ *I'm a bit nervous about flying to Paris by myself.* J'appréhende un peu d'aller toute seule en avion à Paris.

nest NOUN
le nid

Net NOUN
le Net ◊ *to surf the Net* surfer sur le Net

net NOUN
le filet ◊ *a fishing net* un filet de pêche

netball NOUN

ⓘ Netball is not played in France. Both sexes play basketball or volleyball instead.

◆**Netball is a bit like basketball, but it's normally played by girls.** Le netball ressemble un peu au basket, mais est généralement pratiqué par les filles.

Netherlands PL NOUN

les Pays-Bas MASC PL

◆**in the Netherlands** aux Pays-Bas

network NOUN
le réseau
(les réseaux PL)

neurotic ADJECTIVE
névrosé

never ADVERB
[1] jamais ◊ *Have you ever been to Germany? – No, never.* Est-ce que tu es déjà allé en Allemagne? – Non, jamais. ◊ *When are you going to phone him? – Never!* Quand est-ce que tu vas l'appeler? – Jamais!
Add ne if the sentence contains a verb.
[2] ne ... jamais ◊ *I never write letters.* Je n'écris jamais. ◊ *I have never been camping.* Je n'ai jamais fait de camping. ◊ *Never leave valuables in your car.* Ne laissez jamais d'objets de valeur dans votre voiture.

◆**Never again!** Plus jamais!

◆**Never mind.** Ça ne fait rien.

new ADJECTIVE
[1] nouveau MASC
nouvelle FEM
(nouveaux MASC PL)
◊ *her new boyfriend* son nouveau copain ◊ *I need a new dress.* J'ai besoin d'une nouvelle robe.
[2] (*brand new*)
neuf MASC
neuve FEM
◊ *They've got a new car.* Ils ont une voiture neuve.

newborn ADJECTIVE

◆**a newborn baby** un nouveau-né

newcomer NOUN
le nouveau venu
la nouvelle venue
(les nouveaux venus MASC PL)

news NOUN
[1] les nouvelles FEM PL ◊ *good news* de bonnes nouvelles ◊ *I've had some bad news.* J'ai reçu de mauvaises nouvelles. ◊ *It was nice to have your news.* J'ai été content d'avoir de tes nouvelles.
[2] la nouvelle (*single piece of news*) ◊ *That's wonderful news!* Quelle bonne nouvelle!
[3] le journal télévisé (*on TV*) ◊ *I watch the news every evening.* Je regarde le journal télévisé tous les soirs.
[4] les informations FEM PL (*on radio*) ◊ *I listen to the news every morning.*

J'écoute les informations tous les matins.

newsagent NOUN
le <u>marchand de journaux</u>

newsdealer NOUN US
le <u>marchand de journaux</u>

newspaper NOUN
le <u>journal</u>
(les journaux PL)
◊ *I deliver newspapers.* Je distribue des journaux.

newsreader NOUN
le <u>présentateur</u>
la <u>présentatrice</u>

New Year NOUN
le <u>Nouvel An</u> ◊ *to celebrate New Year* fêter le Nouvel An
♦**Happy New Year!** Bonne Année!
♦**New Year's Day** le premier de l'An
♦**New Year's Eve** la Saint-Sylvestre ◊ *a New Year's Eve party* un réveillon du premier de l'An

New Zealand NOUN
la <u>Nouvelle-Zélande</u>
♦**in New Zealand** en Nouvelle-Zélande

New Zealander NOUN
le <u>Néo-Zélandais</u>
la <u>Néo-Zélandaise</u>

next ADJECTIVE, ADVERB, PREPOSITION
[1] <u>prochain</u> (*in time*) ◊ *next Saturday* samedi prochain ◊ *next year* l'année prochaine ◊ *next summer* l'été prochain
[2] <u>suivant</u> (*in sequence*) ◊ *the next train* le train suivant ◊ *Next please!* Au suivant!
[3] <u>ensuite</u> (*afterwards*) ◊ *What shall I do next?* Qu'est-ce que je fais ensuite? ◊ *What happened next?* Qu'est-ce qui s'est passé ensuite?
♦**next to** à côté de ◊ *next to the bank* à côté de la banque
♦**the next day** le lendemain ◊ *The next day we visited Dublin.* Le lendemain nous avons visité Dublin.
♦**the next time** la prochaine fois ◊ *the next time you see her* la prochaine fois que tu la verras
♦**next door** à côté ◊ *They live next door.* Ils habitent à côté. ◊ *the people next door* les gens d'à côté
♦**the next room** la pièce d'à côté

NHS NOUN
la <u>Sécurité sociale</u>

ⓘ *In France you have to pay for medical treatment when you receive it, and then claim it back from the* ***Sécurité sociale.***
---

nice ADJECTIVE
[1] (*kind*)
<u>gentil</u> MASC
<u>gentille</u> FEM
◊ *Your parents are very nice.* Tes parents sont très gentils. ◊ *It was nice of you to remember my birthday.* C'était gentil de ta part de te souvenir de mon anniversaire.
♦**to be nice to somebody** être gentil avec quelqu'un
[2] (*pretty*)
<u>joli</u> ◊ *That's a nice dress!* Qu'est-ce qu'elle est jolie, cette robe! ◊ *Avignon is a nice town.* Avignon est une jolie ville.
[3] (*food*)
<u>bon</u> MASC
<u>bonne</u> FEM
◊ *It's very nice.* C'est très bon. ◊ *a nice cup of coffee* une bonne tasse de café
♦**Have a nice time!** Amuse-toi bien!
♦**nice weather** le beau temps
♦**It's a nice day.** Il fait beau.

nickname NOUN
le <u>surnom</u>

niece NOUN
la <u>nièce</u> ◊ *my niece* ma nièce

Nigeria NOUN
le <u>Nigéria</u>
♦**in Nigeria** au Nigéria

night NOUN
[1] la <u>nuit</u> ◊ *I want a single room for two nights.* Je veux une chambre à un lit pour deux nuits.
♦**My mother works nights.** Ma mère travaille de nuit.
♦**at night** la nuit
♦**all night** toute la nuit
♦**Goodnight!** Bonne nuit!
♦**a night club** une boîte de nuit
[2] le <u>soir</u> (*evening*) ◊ *last night* hier soir

nightdress NOUN
la <u>chemise de nuit</u>

nightie NOUN
la <u>chemise de nuit</u>

nightlife NOUN
♦**There's plenty of nightlife.** Il y a plein de choses à faire le soir.

nightmare NOUN
le <u>cauchemar</u> ◊ *It was a real nightmare!* Ça a été un vrai cauchemar!
♦**to have a nightmare** faire un cauchemar

nightshirt NOUN
la <u>chemise de nuit</u>

nil NOUN

N

le zéro ◊ *We won one-nil.* Nous avons gagné un à zéro.

nine NUMBER
neuf ◊ *She's nine.* Elle a neuf ans.

nineteen NUMBER
dix-neuf ◊ *She's nineteen.* Elle a dix-neuf ans.

nineteenth ADJECTIVE
dix-neuvième ◊ *her nineteenth birthday* son dix-neuvième anniversaire ◊ *the nineteenth floor* le dix-neuvième étage
♦ **the nineteenth of August** le dix-neuf août

ninety NUMBER
quatre-vingt-dix

ninth ADJECTIVE
neuvième ◊ *the ninth floor* le neuvième étage
♦ **the ninth of August** le neuf août

no ADVERB, ADJECTIVE
1 non ◊ *Are you coming? – No.* Est-ce que vous venez? – Non. ◊ *Would you like some more? – No thank you.* Vous en voulez encore? – Non merci.
2 pas de (*not any*) ◊ *There's no hot water.* Il n'y a pas d'eau chaude.
◊ *There are no trains on Sundays.* Il n'y a pas de trains le dimanche. ◊ *No problem.* Pas de problème.
♦ **I've got no idea.** Je n'en ai aucune idée.
♦ **No way!** Pas question!
♦ **"no smoking"** "défense de fumer"

nobody PRONOUN
1 personne ◊ *Who's going with you? – Nobody.* Qui t'accompagne? – Personne.
*Add **ne** if the sentence contains a verb.*
2 ne ... personne ◊ *There was nobody in the office.* Il n'y avait personne au bureau.
♦ **Nobody likes him.** Personne ne l'aime.

to **nod** VERB
acquiescer d'un signe de tête (*in agreement*)
♦ **to nod at somebody** saluer quelqu'un d'un signe de tête (*as greeting*)

noise NOUN
le bruit ◊ *Please make less noise.* Faites moins de bruit s'il vous plaît.

noisy ADJECTIVE
bruyant

to **nominate** VERB
1 nommer (*appoint*) ◊ *She was nominated as director.* Elle a été

nommée directrice.
2 proposer (*propose*) ◊ *I nominate Ian Alexander as president of the society.* Je propose Ian Alexander comme président de la société.
♦ **He was nominated for an Oscar.** Il a été nominé pour un Oscar.

none PRONOUN
1 aucun MASC
aucune FEM
◊ *How many sisters have you got? – None.* Tu as combien de sœurs? – Aucune. ◊ *What sports do you do? – None.* Qu'est-ce que tu fais comme sport? – Je n'en fais aucun.
*Add **ne** if the sentence contains a verb.*
2 aucun ... ne ◊ *None of my friends wanted to come.* Aucun de mes amis n'a voulu venir.
♦ **There's none left.** Il n'y en a plus.
♦ **There are none left.** Il n'y en a plus.

nonsense NOUN
les bêtises FEM PL ◊ *She talks a lot of nonsense.* Elle dit beaucoup de bêtises. ◊ *Nonsense!* Ne dis pas de bêtises!

non-smoker NOUN
le non-fumeur ◊ *He's a non-smoker.* Il est non-fumeur.

non-smoking ADJECTIVE
non-fumeur ◊ *a non-smoking carriage* une voiture non-fumeurs

non-stop ADJECTIVE, ADVERB
1 direct ◊ *a non-stop flight* un vol direct
2 sans arrêt ◊ *He talks non-stop.* Il parle sans arrêt.

noodles PL NOUN
les nouilles FEM PL

noon NOUN
midi MASC ◊ *at noon* à midi
◊ *before noon* avant midi

no one PRONOUN
1 personne ◊ *Who's going with you? – No one.* Qui t'accompagne? – Personne.
*Add **ne** if the sentence contains a verb.*
2 ne ... personne ◊ *There was no one in the office.* Il n'y avait personne au bureau.
♦ **No one likes Christopher.** Personne n'aime Christopher.

nor CONJUNCTION
♦ **neither ... nor** ni ... ni ◊ *neither the cinema nor the swimming pool* ni le cinéma, ni la piscine

◆**Nor do I.** Moi non plus. ◇ *I didn't like the film. – Nor did I.* Je n'ai pas aimé le film. – Moi non plus.

◆**Nor have I.** Moi non plus. ◇ *I haven't seen him. – Nor have I.* Je ne l'ai pas vu. – Moi non plus.

normal ADJECTIVE
[1] (*usual*)
habituel MASC
habituelle FEM
◇ *at the normal time* à l'heure habituelle
[2] (*standard*)
normal
(normaux MASC PL)
◇ *a normal car* une voiture normale

normally ADVERB
[1] généralement (*usually*) ◇ *I normally arrive at nine o'clock.* J'arrive généralement à neuf heures.
[2] normalement (*as normal*) ◇ *In spite of the strike, the airports are working normally.* Malgré la grève, les aéroports fonctionnent normalement.

Normandy NOUN
la Normandie
◆**in Normandy** en Normandie
◆**to Normandy** en Normandie

north ADJECTIVE, ADVERB
  see also **north** NOUN
[1] nord MASC, FEM, PL ◇ *the north coast* la côte nord
◆**a north wind** un vent du nord
[2] vers le nord ◇ *We were travelling north.* Nous allions vers le nord.
◆**north of** au nord de ◇ *It's north of London.* C'est au nord de Londres.

north NOUN
  see also **north** ADJECTIVE
le nord ◇ *in the north* dans le nord

North America NOUN
l' Amérique du Nord FEM

northbound ADJECTIVE
◇ *The truck was northbound on the M5.* Le camion se trouvait sur la M5 en direction du nord.
◆**Northbound traffic is moving very slowly.** La circulation vers le nord avance très lentement.

northeast NOUN
le nord-est ◇ *in the northeast* au nord-est

northern ADJECTIVE
◆**the northern part of the island** la partie nord de l'île
◆**Northern Europe** l'Europe du Nord

Northern Ireland NOUN
l' Irlande du Nord FEM

◆**in Northern Ireland** en Irlande du Nord
◆**to Northern Ireland** en Irlande du Nord
◆**I'm from Northern Ireland.** Je viens d'Irlande du Nord.

North Pole NOUN
le pôle Nord

North Sea NOUN
la mer du Nord

northwest NOUN
le nord-ouest ◇ *in the northwest* au nord-ouest

Norway NOUN
la Norvège
◆**in Norway** en Norvège

Norwegian ADJECTIVE
  see also **Norwegian** NOUN
norvégien MASC
norvégienne FEM

Norwegian NOUN
  see also **Norwegian** ADJECTIVE
[1] (*person*)
le Norvégien
la Norvégienne
[2] (*language*)
le norvégien

nose NOUN
le nez
(les nez PL)

nosebleed NOUN
◆**to have a nosebleed** saigner du nez
◇ *I often get nosebleeds.* Je saigne souvent du nez.

nosy ADJECTIVE
fouineur MASC
fouineuse FEM

not ADVERB
[1] pas ◇ *Are you coming or not?* Est-ce que tu viens ou pas?
◆**not really** pas vraiment
◆**not at all** pas du tout
◆**not yet** pas encore ◇ *Have you finished? – Not yet.* As-tu fini? – Pas encore.
  Add ne before a verb.
[2] ne ... pas ◇ *I'm not sure.* Je ne suis pas sûr. ◇ *It's not raining.* Il ne pleut pas. ◇ *You shouldn't do that.* Tu ne devrais pas faire ça. ◇ *They haven't arrived yet.* Ils ne sont pas encore arrivés.
[3] non ◇ *I hope not.* J'espère que non. ◇ *Can you lend me £10? – I'm afraid not.* Est-ce que tu peux me prêter dix livres? – Non, désolé.

note NOUN
[1] la note ◇ *to take notes* prendre des notes

N

☞

2 le mot (letter) ◊ I'll write her a note. Je vais lui écrire un mot.

3 le billet (banknote) ◊ a £5 note un billet de cinq livres

to **note down** VERB
noter

notebook NOUN
le carnet

notepad NOUN
le bloc-notes
(les blocs-notes PL)

notepaper NOUN
le papier à lettres

nothing NOUN
1 rien ◊ What's wrong? – Nothing. Qu'est-ce qui ne va pas? – Rien. ◊ nothing special rien de particulier
Add **ne** *if the sentence contains a verb.*
2 ne ... rien ◊ He does nothing. Il ne fait rien. ◊ He ate nothing for breakfast. Il n'a rien mangé au petit-déjeuner.
♦**Nothing is open on Sundays.** Rien n'est ouvert le dimanche.

notice NOUN
see also **notice** VERB
(sign)
le panneau
(les panneaux PL)
♦**to put up a notice** mettre un panneau
♦**a warning notice** un avertissement
♦**Don't take any notice of him!** Ne fais pas attention à lui!

to **notice** VERB
see also **notice** NOUN
remarquer

notice board NOUN
le panneau d'affichage
(les panneaux d'affichage PL)

nought NOUN
le zéro

noun NOUN
le nom

novel NOUN
le roman

novelist NOUN
le romancier
la romancière

November NOUN
novembre MASC
♦**in November** en novembre

now ADVERB, CONJUNCTION
maintenant ◊ What are you doing now? Qu'est-ce que tu fais maintenant?

♦**just now** en ce moment ◊ I'm rather busy just now. Je suis très occupé en ce moment.
♦**I did it just now.** Je viens de le faire.
♦**He should be there by now.** Il doit être arrivé à l'heure qu'il est.
♦**It should be ready by now.** Ça devrait être déjà prêt.
♦**now and then** de temps en temps

nowhere ADVERB
nulle part ◊ nowhere else nulle part ailleurs

nuclear ADJECTIVE
nucléaire ◊ nuclear power l'énergie nucléaire ◊ a nuclear power station une centrale nucléaire

nude ADJECTIVE
see also **nude** NOUN
nu
♦**to sunbathe nude** faire du bronzage intégral

nude NOUN
see also **nude** ADJECTIVE
♦**in the nude** nu

nudist NOUN
le/la nudiste

nuisance NOUN
♦**It's a nuisance.** C'est très embêtant.
♦**Sorry to be a nuisance.** Désolé de vous déranger.

numb ADJECTIVE
engourdi ◊ My legs have gone numb. J'ai les jambes engourdies. ◊ numb with cold engourdi par le froid

number NOUN
1 le nombre (total amount) ◊ a large number of people un grand nombre de gens
2 le numéro (of house, telephone, bank account) ◊ They live at number 5. Ils habitent au numéro cinq. ◊ What's your phone number? Quel est votre numéro de téléphone? ◊ You've got the wrong number. Vous vous êtes trompé de numéro.
3 le chiffre (figure, digit) ◊ I can't read the second number. Je n'arrive pas à lire le deuxième chiffre.

number plate NOUN
la plaque d'immatriculation

nun NOUN
la religieuse ◊ She's a nun. Elle est religieuse.

nurse NOUN
l' infirmier MASC
l' infirmière FEM
◊ She's a nurse. Elle est infirmière.

nursery NOUN
  1 la crèche (*for children*)
  2 la pépinière (*for plants*)
nursery school NOUN
  l' école maternelle FEM

> ⓘ The **école maternelle** is a state school for 2-6 year-olds.

nursery slope NOUN
  la piste pour débutants
nut NOUN
  1 (*peanut*)
  la cacahuète
  2 (*hazelnut*)
  la noisette
  3 (*walnut*)
  la noix
  (les noix PL)
  4 (*made of metal*)
  l' écrou MASC

nutmeg NOUN
  la noix de muscade

nutritious ADJECTIVE
  nourrissant

nuts ADJECTIVE
  ◆He's nuts. Il est dingue.

nutter NOUN
  ◆He's a nutter. Il est complètement cinglé. (*informal*)

nylon NOUN
  le nylon

N

O

oak NOUN
le <u>chêne</u> ◊ *an oak table* une table en chêne

oar NOUN
l' <u>aviron</u> MASC

oats NOUN
l' <u>avoine</u> FEM

obedient ADJECTIVE
<u>obéissant</u>

to **obey** VERB
◆**to obey the rules** respecter le règlement

object NOUN
l' <u>objet</u> MASC ◊ *a familiar object* un objet familier

objection NOUN
l' <u>objection</u> FEM

objective NOUN
l' <u>objectif</u> MASC

oblong ADJECTIVE
<u>rectangulaire</u>

oboe NOUN
le <u>hautbois</u> ◊ *I play the oboe.* Je joue du hautbois.

obscene ADJECTIVE
<u>obscène</u>

observant ADJECTIVE
<u>observateur</u> MASC
<u>observatrice</u> FEM

to **observe** VERB
<u>observer</u>

obsessed ADJECTIVE
<u>obsédé</u> ◊ *He's obsessed with trains.* Il est obsédé par les trains.

obsession NOUN
l' <u>obsession</u> FEM ◊ *It's getting to be an obsession with you.* Ça devient une obsession chez toi.
◆**Football's an obsession of mine.** Le football est une de mes passions.

obsolete ADJECTIVE
<u>dépassé</u>

obstacle NOUN
l' <u>obstacle</u> MASC

obstinate ADJECTIVE
<u>obstiné</u>

to **obstruct** VERB
<u>bloquer</u> ◊ *A lorry was obstructing the traffic.* Un camion bloquait la circulation.

to **obtain** VERB
<u>obtenir</u>

obvious ADJECTIVE
<u>évident</u>

obviously ADVERB
⟦1⟧ <u>évidemment</u> (*of course*) ◊ *Do you want to pass the exam? – Obviously!* Tu veux être reçu à l'examen? – Évidemment!
◆**Obviously not!** Bien sûr que non!
⟦2⟧ <u>manifestement</u> (*visibly*) ◊ *She was obviously exhausted.* Elle était manifestement épuisée.

occasion NOUN
l' <u>occasion</u> FEM ◊ *a special occasion* une occasion spéciale
◆**on several occasions** à plusieurs reprises

occasionally ADVERB
<u>de temps en temps</u>

occupation NOUN
la <u>profession</u>

to **occupy** VERB
<u>occuper</u> ◊ *That seat is occupied.* Cette place est occupée.

to **occur** VERB
<u>avoir lieu</u> (*happen*) ◊ *The accident occurred yesterday.* L'accident a eu lieu hier.
◆**It suddenly occurred to me that ...** Il m'est soudain venu à l'esprit que ...

ocean NOUN
l' <u>océan</u> MASC

o'clock ADVERB
◆**at four o'clock** à quatre heures
◆**It's five o'clock.** Il est cinq heures.

October NOUN
<u>octobre</u> MASC
◆**in October** en octobre

octopus NOUN
la <u>pieuvre</u>

odd ADJECTIVE
⟦1⟧ <u>bizarre</u> ◊ *That's odd!* C'est bizarre!
⟦2⟧ <u>impair</u> ◊ *an odd number* un chiffre impair

of PREPOSITION
⟦1⟧ <u>de</u> ◊ *some photos of my holiday* des photos de mes vacances ◊ *a boy of ten* un garçon de dix ans

de changes to d' before a vowel and most words beginning with "h".

<u>d'</u> ◊ *a kilo of oranges* un kilo d'oranges

de + le changes to du, and de + les changes to des.

<u>du</u> ◊ *the end of the film* la fin du film
<u>des</u> ◊ *the end of the holidays* la fin des vacances

2 (*with quantity, amount*)
en ◊ *He's got four sisters. I've met two of them.* Il a quatre sœurs. J'en ai rencontré deux. ◊ *Can I have half of that?* Je peux en avoir la moitié?
♦**three of us** trois d'entre nous
♦**a friend of mine** un de mes amis
♦**the 14th of September** le quatorze septembre
♦**That's very kind of you.** C'est très gentil de votre part.
♦**It's made of wood.** C'est en bois.

off ADVERB, PREPOSITION, ADJECTIVE
For other expressions with **off,** *see the verbs* **get, take, turn** *etc.*
1 éteint (*heater, light, TV*) ◊ *All the lights are off.* Toutes les lumières sont éteintes.
2 fermé (*tap, gas*) ◊ *Are you sure the tap is off?* Tu es sûr que le robinet est fermé?
3 annulé (*cancelled*) ◊ *The match is off.* Le match est annulé.
♦**to be off sick** être malade
♦**a day off** un jour de congé ◊ *to take a day off work* prendre un jour de congé
♦**She's off school today.** Elle n'est pas à l'école aujourd'hui.
♦**I must be off now.** Je dois m'en aller maintenant.
♦**I'm off.** Je m'en vais.

offence NOUN (US **offense**)
le délit (*crime*)

offensive ADJECTIVE
choquant

offer NOUN
see also **offer** VERB
la proposition ◊ *a good offer* une proposition intéressante
♦**"on special offer"** "en promotion"

to **offer** VERB
see also **offer** NOUN
proposer ◊ *He offered to help me.* Il m'a proposé de m'aider. ◊ *I offered to go with them.* Je leur ai proposé de les accompagner.

office NOUN
le bureau
(les bureaux PL)
◊ *She works in an office.* Elle travaille dans un bureau.

officer NOUN
l' officier MASC

official ADJECTIVE
officiel MASC
officielle FEM

off-licence NOUN
le marchand de vins et spiritueux

off-peak ADVERB
hors saison (*off-season*) ◊ *It's cheaper to go on holiday off-peak.* C'est moins cher de partir en vacances hors saison.
♦**to phone off-peak** appeler pendant les heures creuses

offside ADJECTIVE
hors jeu (*in football*)

often ADVERB
souvent ◊ *It often rains.* Il pleut souvent. ◊ *How often do you go to the gym?* Tu vas souvent à la gym? ◊ *I'd like to go skiing more often.* J'aimerais aller skier plus souvent.

oil NOUN
see also **oil** VERB
1 l' huile FEM (*for lubrication, cooking*)
♦**an oil painting** une peinture à l'huile
2 le pétrole (*crude oil*) ◊ *North Sea oil* le pétrole de la mer du Nord

to **oil** VERB
see also **oil** NOUN
graisser

oil rig NOUN
la plateforme pétrolière ◊ *He works on an oil rig.* Il travaille sur une plateforme pétrolière.

oil slick NOUN
la marée noire

oil well NOUN
le puits de pétrole
(les puits de pétrole PL)

ointment NOUN
la pommade MASC

okay EXCLAMATION, ADJECTIVE
d'accord (*agreed*) ◊ *Could you call back later? – Okay!* Tu peux rappeler plus tard? – D'accord! ◊ *I'll meet you at six o'clock, okay?* Je te retrouve à six heures, d'accord? ◊ *Is that okay?* C'est d'accord?
♦**I'll do it tomorrow, if that's okay with you.** Je le ferai demain, si tu es d'accord.
♦**Are you okay?** Ça va?
♦**How was your holiday? – It was okay.** C'était comment tes vacances? – Pas mal.
♦**What's your teacher like? – He's okay.** Il est comment ton prof? – Il est sympa. (*informal*)

old ADJECTIVE
1 vieux MASC
vieille FEM
◊ *an old dog* un vieux chien ◊ *an old house* une vieille maison
vieux changes to **vieil** *before a vowel and most words beginning with "h".*

O

☞

vieil ◊ *an old man* un vieil homme
When talking about people it is more polite to use âgé instead of vieux.
âgé ◊ *old people* les personnes âgées
[2] (*former*)
ancien MASC
ancienne FEM
◊ *my old English teacher* mon ancien professeur d'anglais
♦**How old are you?** Quel âge as-tu?
♦**He's ten years old.** Il a dix ans.
♦**my older brother** mon frère aîné ◊ *my older sister* ma sœur aînée
♦**She's two years older than me.** Elle a deux ans de plus que moi.
♦**I'm the oldest in the family.** Je suis l'aîné de la famille.

old age pensioner NOUN
le retraité
la retraitée
◊ *She's an old age pensioner.* Elle est retraitée.

old-fashioned ADJECTIVE
[1] démodé ◊ *She wears old-fashioned clothes.* Elle porte des vêtements démodés.
[2] (*person*)
vieux jeu MASC, FEM, PL ◊ *My parents are rather old-fashioned.* Mes parents sont plutôt vieux jeu.

olive NOUN
l' olive FEM

olive oil NOUN
l' huile d'olive FEM

olive tree NOUN
l' olivier MASC

Olympic ADJECTIVE
olympique
♦**the Olympics** les Jeux olympiques MASC

omelette NOUN
l' omelette FEM

on PREPOSITION, ADVERB
see also **on** ADJECTIVE
There are several ways of translating on. Scan the examples to find one that is similar to what you want to say. For other expressions with on, see the verbs go, put, turn etc.
[1] sur ◊ *on the table* sur la table ◊ *on an island* sur une île
[2] à ◊ *on the left* à gauche ◊ *on the 2nd floor* au deuxième étage ◊ *I go to school on my bike.* Je vais à l'école à vélo.
♦**on TV** à la télé ◊ *What's on TV?* Qu'est-ce qu'il y a à la télé?
♦**on the radio** à la radio ◊ *I heard it on the radio.* Je l'ai entendu à la radio.

♦**on the bus (1)** (*by bus*) en bus ◊ *I go into town on the bus.* Je vais en ville en bus.
♦**on the bus (2)** (*inside*) dans le bus ◊ *There were no empty seats on the bus.* Il n'y avait pas de places libres dans le bus.
♦**on holiday** en vacances ◊ *They're on holiday.* Ils sont en vacances.
♦**on strike** en grève
With days and dates on is not translated.
◊ *on Friday* vendredi ◊ *on Fridays* le vendredi ◊ *on Christmas Day* le jour de Noël ◊ *on June 20th* le vingt juin ◊ *on my birthday* le jour de mon anniversaire

on ADJECTIVE
see also **on** PREPOSITION
[1] allumé (*heater, light, TV*) ◊ *I think I left the light on.* Je crois que j'ai laissé la lumière allumée.
[2] ouvert (*tap, gas*) ◊ *Leave the tap on.* Laisse le robinet ouvert.
[3] en marche (*machine*) ◊ *Is the dishwasher on?* Est-ce que le lave-vaisselle est en marche?
♦**What's on at the cinema?** Qu'est-ce qui passe au cinéma?

once ADVERB
une fois ◊ *once a week* une fois par semaine ◊ *once more* encore une fois ◊ *I've been to France once before.* J'ai déjà été une fois en France.
♦**Once upon a time ...** Il était une fois ...
♦**at once** tout de suite
♦**once in a while** de temps en temps
♦**once and for all** une fois pour toutes

one NUMBER, PRONOUN
Use un for masculine nouns and une for feminine nouns.
[1] un ◊ *one day* un jour ◊ *Do you need a stamp? – No thanks, I've got one.* Est-ce que tu as besoin d'un timbre? – Non merci, j'en ai un.
une ◊ *one minute* une minute ◊ *I've got one brother and one sister.* J'ai un frère et une sœur.
[2] on (*impersonal*) ◊ *One never knows.* On ne sait jamais.
♦**this one (1)** celui-ci (*masculine*) ◊ *Which foot is hurting? – This one.* Quel pied te fait mal? – Celui-ci.
♦**this one (2)** celle-ci (*feminine*) ◊ *Which is the best photo? – This one.* Quelle est la meilleure photo? – Celle-ci.
♦**that one (1)** celui-là (*masculine*) ◊ *Which bag is yours? – That one.* Lequel est ton sac? – Celui-là.

◆**that one (2)** celle-là (*feminine*) ◊ *Which seat do you want? – That one.* Quelle place voulez-vous? – Celle-là.

oneself PRONOUN

1 se ◊ *to hurt oneself* se faire mal

2 soi-même ◊ *It's quicker to do it oneself.* C'est plus rapide de le faire soi-même.

one-way ADJECTIVE

◆**a one-way street** une impasse

onion NOUN

l' oignon MASC ◊ *onion soup* la soupe à l'oignon

only ADVERB, ADJECTIVE, CONJUNCTION

1 seul ◊ *Monday is the only day I'm free.* Le lundi est le seul jour où je suis libre. ◊ *French is the only subject I like.* Le français est la seule matière que j'aime.

2 seulement ◊ *How much was it? – Only 10 euros.* Combien c'était? – Seulement dix euros.

3 ne ... que ◊ *We only want to stay for one night.* Nous ne voulons rester qu'une nuit. ◊ *These cassettes are only 3 euros.* Ces cassettes ne coûtent que trois euros.

4 mais ◊ *I'd like the same sweater, only in black.* Je voudrais le même pull, mais en noir.

◆**an only child** un enfant unique

onwards ADVERB

à partir de ◊ *from July onwards* à partir de juillet

open ADJECTIVE

| see also **open** VERB |

ouvert ◊ *The baker's is open on Sunday morning.* La boulangerie est ouverte le dimanche matin.

◆**in the open air** en plein air

to **open** VERB

| see also **open** ADJECTIVE |

1 ouvrir ◊ *Can I open the window?* Est-ce que je peux ouvrir la fenêtre? ◊ *What time do the shops open?* Les magasins ouvrent à quelle heure?

2 s'ouvrir ◊ *The door opens automatically.* La porte s'ouvre automatiquement. ◊ *The door opened and in came the teacher.* La porte s'est ouverte et le professeur est entré.

opening hours PL NOUN

les heures d'ouverture FEM PL

opera NOUN

l' opéra MASC

to **operate** VERB

1 fonctionner ◊ *I don't know how the electoral system operates in*

France. Je ne sais pas comment fonctionne le système électoral en France.

2 faire fonctionner ◊ *How do you operate the video?* Comment fait-on fonctionner le magnétoscope?

3 opérer (*medically*)

◆**to operate on someone** opérer quelqu'un

operation NOUN

l' opération FEM ◊ *a major operation* une grave opération

◆**to have an operation** se faire opérer ◊ *I have never had an operation.* Je ne me suis jamais fait opérer.

operator NOUN

le/la standardiste (*on telephone*)

opinion NOUN

l' avis MASC ◊ *in my opinion* à mon avis ◊ *He asked me my opinion.* Il m'a demandé mon avis.

◆**What's your opinion?** Qu'est-ce que vous en pensez?

opinion poll NOUN

le sondage

opponent NOUN

l' adversaire MASC/FEM

opportunity NOUN

l' occasion FEM

◆**to have the opportunity to do something** avoir l'occasion de faire quelque chose ◊ *I've never had the opportunity to go to France.* Je n'ai jamais eu l'occasion d'aller en France.

opposed ADJECTIVE

◊ *I've always been opposed to violence.* J'ai toujours été contre la violence.

◆**as opposed to** par opposition à

opposing ADJECTIVE

opposé (*team*)

opposite ADJECTIVE, ADVERB, PREPOSITION

1 opposé ◊ *It's in the opposite direction.* C'est dans la direction opposée.

2 en face ◊ *They live opposite.* Ils habitent en face.

3 en face de ◊ *the girl sitting opposite me* la fille assise en face de moi

◆**the opposite sex** l'autre sexe

opposition NOUN

l' opposition FEM

optician NOUN

l' opticien MASC

l' opticienne FEM

◊ *She's an optician.* Elle est opticienne.

O

optimist NOUN
l' optimiste MASC/FEM

optimistic ADJECTIVE
optimiste

option NOUN
1 le choix (choice) ◇ I've got no
option. Je n'ai pas le choix.
2 la matière à option (optional
subject) ◇ I'm doing geology as my
option. La géologie est ma matière à
option.

optional ADJECTIVE
facultatif MASC
facultative FEM

or CONJUNCTION
1 ou ◇ Would you like tea or coffee?
Est-ce que tu veux du thé ou du
café?
Use ni ... ni in negative sentences.
◇ I don't eat meat or fish. Je ne
mange ni viande, ni poisson.
2 sinon (otherwise) ◇ Hurry up or
you'll miss the bus. Dépêche-toi,
sinon tu vas rater le bus.
♦**Give me the money, or else!** Donne-
moi l'argent, sinon tu vas le
regretter!

oral ADJECTIVE
see also **oral** NOUN
oral
(oraux MASC PL)
♦**an oral exam** un oral

oral NOUN
see also **oral** ADJECTIVE
l' oral MASC
(les oraux PL)
◇ I've got my French oral soon. Je
vais bientôt passer mon oral de
français.

orange NOUN
see also **orange** ADJECTIVE
l' orange FEM
♦**an orange juice** un jus d'orange

orange ADJECTIVE
see also **orange** NOUN
orange MASC, FEM, PL

orchard NOUN
le verger

orchestra NOUN
l' orchestre MASC ◇ I play in the school
orchestra. Je joue dans l'orchestre de
l'école.

order NOUN
see also **order** VERB
1 l' ordre MASC (sequence) ◇ in
alphabetical order dans l'ordre
alphabétique

2 la commande (instruction) ◇ The
waiter took our order. Le garçon a
pris notre commande.
♦**in order to** pour ◇ He does it in order
to earn money. Il le fait pour gagner
de l'argent.
♦**"out of order"** "en panne"

to **order** VERB
see also **order** NOUN
commander ◇ We ordered steak and
chips. Nous avons commandé un
steak frites. ◇ Are you ready to order?
Vous êtes prêt à commander?
♦**to order somebody about** donner des
ordres à quelqu'un ◇ She was fed up
with being ordered about. Elle en
avait marre qu'on lui donne des
ordres en permanence.

ordinary ADJECTIVE
1 ordinaire ◇ an ordinary day une
journée ordinaire
2 comme les autres (people) ◇ an
ordinary family une famille comme
les autres ◇ He's just an ordinary
guy. C'est un type comme les autres.

organ NOUN
l' orgue MASC (instrument) ◇ I play the
organ. Je joue de l'orgue.

organic ADJECTIVE
biologique (vegetables, fruit)

organization NOUN
l' organisation FEM

to **organize** VERB
organiser

origin NOUN
l' origine FEM

original ADJECTIVE
original
(originaux MASC PL)
◇ It's a very original idea. C'est une
idée très originale.
♦**Our original plan was to go camping.**
A l'origine nous avions l'intention de
faire du camping.

originally ADVERB
à l'origine

Orkneys PL NOUN
les Orcades FEM PL
♦**in the Orkneys** dans les Orcades

ornament NOUN
le bibelot

orphan NOUN
l' orphelin MASC
l' orpheline FEM

ostrich NOUN
l' autruche FEM

other ADJECTIVE, PRONOUN
autre ◇ Have you got these jeans in
other colours? Est-ce que vous avez

ce jean dans d'autres couleurs? ◊ *on the other side of the street* de l'autre côté de la rue ◊ *the other day* l'autre jour

◆**the other one** l'autre ◊ *This one? – No, the other one.* Celui-ci? – Non, l'autre.

◆**the others** les autres ◊ *The others are going but I'm not.* Les autres y vont mais pas moi.

otherwise ADVERB, CONJUNCTION
    1 sinon (*if not*) ◊ *Note down the number, otherwise you'll forget it.* Note le numéro, sinon tu vas l'oublier. ◊ *Put some sunscreen on, you'll get burned otherwise.* Mets une crème solaire, sinon tu vas attraper des coups de soleil.
    2 à part ça (*in other ways*) ◊ *I'm tired, but otherwise I'm fine.* Je suis fatigué, mais à part ça, ça va.

ought VERB

*To translate **ought to** use the conditional tense of **devoir**.*

◊ *I ought to phone my parents.* Je devrais appeler mes parents. ◊ *You ought not to do that.* Tu ne devrais pas faire ça. ◊ *He ought to win.* Il devrait gagner.

ounce NOUN
    l' once FEM

ⓘ In France measurements are in grammes and kilogrammes. One ounce is about 30 grammes.

◊ *8 ounces of cheese* 250 grammes de fromage

our ADJECTIVE
    notre ◊ *Our house is quite big.* Notre maison est plutôt grande.
    nos PL ◊ *Our neighbours are very nice.* Nos voisins sont très gentils.

ours PRONOUN
    le nôtre + MASC NOUN ◊ *Your garden is very big, ours is much smaller.* Votre jardin est très grand, le nôtre est beaucoup plus petit.
    la nôtre + FEM NOUN ◊ *Your school is very different from ours.* Votre école est très différente de la nôtre.
    les nôtres + PL NOUN ◊ *Our teachers are strict. – Ours are too.* Nos professeurs sont sévères. – Les nôtres aussi.

◆**Is this ours?** C'est à nous? ◊ *This car is ours.* Cette voiture est à nous. ◊ *Whose is this? – It's ours.* C'est à qui? – À nous.

ourselves PRONOUN

    1 nous ◊ *We really enjoyed ourselves.* Nous nous sommes vraiment bien amusés.
    2 nous-mêmes ◊ *We built our garage ourselves.* Nous avons construit notre garage nous-mêmes.

out ADVERB

*There are several ways of translating **out**. Scan the examples to find one that is similar to what you want to say. For other expressions with **out**, see the verbs **go**, **put**, **turn** etc.*

    1 dehors (*outside*) ◊ *It's cold out.* Il fait froid dehors.
    2 éteint (*light, fire*) ◊ *All the lights are out.* Toutes les lumières sont éteintes.
◆**She's out.** Elle est sortie.
◆**She's out shopping.** Elle est sortie faire des courses.
◆**She's out for the afternoon.** Elle ne sera pas là de tout l'après-midi.
◆**out there** dehors ◊ *It's cold out there.* Il fait froid dehors.
◆**to go out** sortir ◊ *I'm going out tonight.* Je sors ce soir.
◆**to go out with somebody** sortir avec quelqu'un ◊ *I've been going out with him for two months.* Je sors avec lui depuis deux mois.
◆**out of (1)** dans ◊ *to drink out of a glass* boire dans un verre
◆**out of (2)** sur ◊ *in 9 cases out of 10* dans neuf cas sur dix
◆**out of (3)** en dehors de ◊ *He lives out of town.* Il habite en dehors de la ville.
◆**3 km out of town** à trois kilomètres de la ville
◆**out of curiosity** par curiosité
◆**out of work** sans emploi
◆**That is out of the question.** C'est hors de question.
◆**You're out!** (*in game*) Tu es éliminé!
◆**"way out"** "sortie"

outbreak NOUN
    1 l' accès MASC (*of disease*) ◊ *a salmonella outbreak* un accès de salmonelle
    2 le début ◊ *the outbreak of war* le début de la guerre

outcome NOUN
    l' issue FEM ◊ *What was the outcome of the negotiations?* Quelle a été l'issue des négociations?

outdoor ADJECTIVE
    en plein air ◊ *an outdoor swimming pool* une piscine en plein air
◆**outdoor activities** les activités de plein air FEM

O

outdoors ADVERB
au grand air

outfit NOUN
la tenue ◊ *She bought a new outfit for the wedding.* Elle a acheté une nouvelle tenue pour le mariage.
♦ **a cowboy outfit** une panoplie de cowboy

outgoing ADJECTIVE
extraverti ◊ *She's very outgoing.* Elle est très extravertie.

outing NOUN
la sortie ◊ *to go on an outing* faire une sortie

outline NOUN
[1] les grandes lignes FEM PL (*summary*) ◊ *This is an outline of the plan.* Voici les grandes lignes du projet.
[2] les contours MASC PL (*shape*) ◊ *We could see the outline of the mountain in the mist.* Nous distinguions les contours de la montagne dans la brume.

outlook NOUN
[1] l' attitude FEM (*attitude*) ◊ *my outlook on life* mon attitude face à la vie
[2] les perspectives FEM PL (*prospects*) ◊ *the economic outlook* les perspectives économiques
♦ **The outlook is poor.** Les choses s'annoncent mal.

outrageous ADJECTIVE
[1] (*behaviour*)
scandaleux MASC
scandaleuse FEM
[2] (*price*)
exorbitant

outset NOUN
le début ◊ *at the outset* dès le début

outside NOUN
| see also **outside** ADJECTIVE |
l' extérieur MASC

outside ADJECTIVE, ADVERB, PREPOSITION
| see also **outside** NOUN |
[1] extérieur ◊ *the outside walls* les murs extérieurs
[2] dehors ◊ *It's very cold outside.* Il fait très froid dehors.
[3] en dehors de ◊ *outside the school* en dehors de l'école ◊ *outside school hours* en dehors des heures de cours

outsize ADJECTIVE
énorme

outskirts PL NOUN
la banlieue ◊ *on the outskirts of the town* dans les banlieues de la ville

outstanding ADJECTIVE
remarquable

oval ADJECTIVE
ovale

oven NOUN
le four

over PREPOSITION, ADVERB, ADJECTIVE
*When there is movement over something, use **par-dessus**; when something is located above something, use **au-dessus de**.*
[1] par-dessus ◊ *The ball went over the wall.* Le ballon est passé par-dessus le mur.
[2] au-dessus de ◊ *There's a mirror over the washbasin.* Il y a une glace au-dessus du lavabo.
[3] plus de (*more than*) ◊ *It's over twenty kilos.* Ça pèse plus de vingt kilos. ◊ *The temperature was over thirty degrees.* Il faisait une température de plus de trente degrés.
[4] pendant (*during*) ◊ *over the holidays* pendant les vacances ◊ *over Christmas* pendant les fêtes de Noël
[5] terminé (*finished*) ◊ *I'll be happy when the exams are over.* Je serai content quand les examens seront terminés.
♦ **over here** ici
♦ **over there** là-bas
♦ **all over Scotland** dans toute l'Écosse
♦ **The baker's is over the road.** La boulangerie est de l'autre côté de la rue.
♦ **I spilled coffee over my shirt.** J'ai renversé du café sur ma chemise.

overall ADVERB
dans l'ensemble (*generally*) ◊ *My results were quite good overall.* Mes résultats étaient assez bons dans l'ensemble.

overalls PL NOUN
les bleus de travail MASC PL

overcast ADJECTIVE
couvert ◊ *The sky was overcast.* Le ciel était couvert.

to **overcharge** VERB
♦ **He overcharged me.** Il m'a fait payer trop cher.
♦ **They overcharged us for the meal.** Ils nous ont fait payer de trop pour le repas.

overcoat NOUN
le pardessus

overdone ADJECTIVE
trop cuit (*food*)

overdose NOUN
l' overdose FEM (*of drugs*) ◊ *to take an overdose* prendre une overdose

overdraft NOUN
le découvert

♦**to have an overdraft** être à découvert

to **overestimate** VERB
surestimer

overhead projector NOUN
le rétroprojecteur

to **overlook** VERB
1 donner sur (*have view of*) ◊ *The hotel overlooked the beach.* L'hôtel donnait sur la plage.
2 négliger (*forget about*) ◊ *He had overlooked one important problem.* Il avait négligé un problème important.

overseas ADVERB
à l'étranger ◊ *I'd like to work overseas.* J'aimerais travailler à l'étranger.

oversight NOUN
l' oubli MASC

to **oversleep** VERB
se réveiller en retard ◊ *I overslept this morning.* Je me suis réveillé en retard ce matin.

to **overtake** VERB
dépasser

overtime NOUN
les heures supplémentaires FEM PL
◊ *to work overtime* faire des heures supplémentaires

overtook VERB *see* **overtake**

overweight ADJECTIVE
trop gros MASC
trop grosse FEM

to **owe** VERB
devoir
♦**to owe somebody something** devoir quelque chose à quelqu'un ◊ *I owe you 50 euros.* Je te dois cinquante euros.

owing to PREPOSITION
en raison de ◊ *owing to bad weather* en raison du mauvais temps

owl NOUN
le hibou
(les hiboux PL)

to **own** VERB
see also **own** ADJECTIVE
posséder

own ADJECTIVE
see also **own** VERB
propre ◊ *I've got my own bathroom.* J'ai ma propre salle de bains.
♦**I'd like a room of my own.** J'aimerais avoir une chambre à moi.
♦**on his own** tout seul ◊ *on her own* toute seule ◊ *on our own* tout seuls

to **own** VERB
see also **own** ADJECTIVE
posséder

to **own up** VERB
avouer
♦**to own up to something** admettre quelque chose

owner NOUN
le/la propriétaire

oxygen NOUN
l' oxygène MASC

oyster NOUN
l' huître FEM

ozone NOUN
l' ozone FEM

ozone layer NOUN
la couche d'ozone

O

P

PA NOUN
la <u>secrétaire de direction</u> (*personal assistant*) ◊ *She's a PA.* Elle est secrétaire de direction.
♦**the PA system** (*public address*) les haut-parleurs MASC PL

pace NOUN
l' <u>allure</u> FEM (*speed*) ◊ *He was walking at a brisk pace.* Il marchait à vive allure.

Pacific NOUN
le <u>Pacifique</u>

pacifier NOUN US
la <u>tétine</u>

to **pack** VERB
see also **pack** NOUN
<u>faire ses bagages</u> ◊ *I'll help you pack.* Je vais t'aider à faire tes bagages.
♦**I've already packed my case.** J'ai déjà fait ma valise.
♦**Pack it in!** (*stop it*) Laisse tomber!

pack NOUN
see also **pack** VERB
[1] le <u>paquet</u> (*packet*) ◊ *a pack of cigarettes* un paquet de cigarettes
[2] le <u>pack</u> (*of yoghurts, cans*) ◊ *a six-pack* un pack de six
♦**a pack of cards** un jeu de cartes

package NOUN
le <u>paquet</u>
♦**a package holiday** un voyage organisé

packed ADJECTIVE
<u>bondé</u> ◊ *The cinema was packed.* Le cinéma était bondé.

packed lunch NOUN
le <u>repas froid</u> ◊ *I take a packed lunch to school.* J'apporte un repas froid à l'école.

packet NOUN
le <u>paquet</u> ◊ *a packet of cigarettes* un paquet de cigarettes

pad NOUN
(*notepad*)
le <u>bloc-notes</u>
(les blocs-notes PL)

to **paddle** VERB
see also **paddle** NOUN
[1] <u>pagayer</u> (*canoe*)
[2] <u>faire trempette</u> (*in water*)

paddle NOUN
see also **paddle** VERB
la <u>pagaie</u> (*for canoe*)
♦**to go for a paddle** faire trempette

padlock NOUN
le <u>cadenas</u>

paedophile NOUN
le <u>pédophile</u>

page NOUN
see also **page** VERB
la <u>page</u> (*of book*)

to **page** VERB
see also **page** NOUN
♦**to page somebody** faire appeler quelqu'un

pager NOUN
le <u>récepteur d'appel</u>

paid VERB see **pay**

paid ADJECTIVE
[1] <u>rémunéré</u> (*work*)
[2] <u>payé</u> ◊ *3 weeks' paid holiday* trois semaines de congés payés

pail NOUN
le <u>seau</u>
(les seaux PL)

pain NOUN
la <u>douleur</u> ◊ *a terrible pain* une douleur insupportable
♦**I've got a pain in my stomach.** J'ai mal à l'estomac.
♦**to be in pain** souffrir ◊ *She's in a lot of pain.* Elle souffre beaucoup.
♦**He's a real pain.** Il est vraiment pénible.

painful ADJECTIVE
<u>douloureux</u> MASC
<u>douloureuse</u> FEM
◊ *to suffer from painful periods* souffrir de règles douloureuses
♦**Is it painful?** Ça te fait mal?

painkiller NOUN
l' <u>analgésique</u> MASC

paint NOUN
see also **paint** VERB
la <u>peinture</u>

to **paint** VERB
see also **paint** NOUN
<u>peindre</u> ◊ *to paint something green* peindre quelque chose en vert

paintbrush NOUN
le <u>pinceau</u>
(les pinceaux PL)

painter NOUN
le <u>peintre</u>

painting NOUN
[1] la <u>peinture</u> ◊ *My hobby is painting.* Je fais de la peinture.
[2] (*picture*)

le <u>tableau</u>
(les tableaux PL)
◊ *a painting by Picasso* un tableau de Picasso

pair NOUN
la <u>paire</u> ◊ *a pair of shoes* une paire de chaussures ◊ *a pair of scissors* une paire de ciseaux
◆ **a pair of trousers** un pantalon
◆ **a pair of jeans** un jean
◆ **a pair of pants (1)** (*briefs*) un slip
◆ **a pair of pants (2)** (*boxer shorts*) un caleçon
◆ **in pairs** deux par deux ◊ *We work in pairs.* On travaille deux par deux.

pajamas PL NOUN US
le <u>pyjama</u> SING ◊ *my pajamas* mon pyjama
◆ **a pair of pajamas** un pyjama
◆ **a pajama top** une veste de pyjama

Pakistan NOUN
le <u>Pakistan</u>
◆ **in Pakistan** au Pakistan
◆ **to Pakistan** au Pakistan
◆ **He's from Pakistan.** Il est pakistanais.

Pakistani NOUN
see also **Pakistani** ADJECTIVE
le <u>Pakistanais</u>
la <u>Pakistanaise</u>

Pakistani ADJECTIVE
see also **Pakistani** NOUN
<u>pakistanais</u> MASC
<u>pakistanaise</u> FEM

pal NOUN
le <u>copain</u>
la <u>copine</u>

palace NOUN
le <u>palais</u>

pale ADJECTIVE
<u>pâle</u> ◊ *a pale blue shirt* une chemise bleu pâle

Palestine NOUN
la <u>Palestine</u>
◆ **in Palestine** en Palestine

Palestinian ADJECTIVE
see also **Palestinian** NOUN
<u>palestinien</u> MASC
<u>palestinienne</u> FEM

Palestinian NOUN
see also **Palestinian** ADJECTIVE
le <u>Palestinien</u>
la <u>Palestinienne</u>

palm NOUN
la <u>paume</u> (*of hand*)
◆ **a palm tree** un palmier

pamphlet NOUN
la <u>brochure</u>

pan NOUN
[1] la <u>casserole</u> (*saucepan*)

[2] la <u>poêle</u> (*frying pan*)

pancake NOUN
la <u>crêpe</u>
◆ **Pancake Day** mardi gras

panic NOUN
see also **panic** VERB
la <u>panique</u>

to **panic** VERB
see also **panic** NOUN
s'<u>affoler</u> ◊ *Don't panic!* Pas de panique!

panther NOUN
la <u>panthère</u>

panties PL NOUN
le <u>slip</u> SING

pantomime NOUN
le <u>spectacle de Noël pour enfants</u>

pants PL NOUN
[1] le <u>slip</u> SING (*briefs*) ◊ *a pair of pants* un slip
[2] le <u>caleçon</u> SING (*boxer shorts*) ◊ *a pair of pants* un caleçon
[3] le <u>pantalon</u> SING (*trousers*) US ◊ *a pair of pants* un pantalon

pantyhose PL NOUN US
le <u>collant</u> SING

paper NOUN
[1] le <u>papier</u> ◊ *a piece of paper* un morceau de papier ◊ *a paper towel* une serviette en papier
[2] (*newspaper*)
le <u>journal</u>
(les journaux PL)
◊ *I saw an advert in the paper.* J'ai vu une annonce dans le journal.
◆ **an exam paper** une épreuve écrite

paperback NOUN
le <u>livre de poche</u>

paper boy NOUN
le <u>livreur de journaux</u>

paper clip NOUN
le <u>trombone</u>

paper girl NOUN
la <u>livreuse de journaux</u>

paper round NOUN
la <u>tournée de distribution de journaux</u>

paperweight NOUN
le <u>presse-papiers</u>

paperwork NOUN
la <u>paperasse</u> ◊ *He had a lot of paperwork to do.* Il avait beaucoup de paperasse à faire.

parachute NOUN
le <u>parachute</u>

parade NOUN
le <u>défilé</u>

paradise NOUN

P

le paradis

paraffin NOUN
le pétrole ◊ *a paraffin lamp* une lampe à pétrole

paragraph NOUN
le paragraphe

parallel ADJECTIVE
parallèle

paralysed ADJECTIVE
paralysé

paramedic NOUN
l' auxiliaire médical MASC
l' auxiliaire médicale FEM

parcel NOUN
le colis

pardon NOUN
♦**Pardon?** Pardon?

parent NOUN
1 le père (*father*)
2 la mère (*mother*)
♦**my parents** mes parents MASC

Paris NOUN
Paris FEM
♦**in Paris** à Paris
♦**to Paris** à Paris
♦**She's from Paris.** Elle est parisienne.

Parisian ADJECTIVE
see also **Parisian** NOUN
parisien MASC
parisienne FEM

Parisian NOUN
see also **Parisian** ADJECTIVE
le Parisien
la Parisienne

park NOUN
see also **park** VERB
le parc
♦**a national park** un parc national
♦**a theme park** un parc à thème
♦**a car park** un parking

to **park** VERB
see also **park** NOUN
1 garer ◊ *Where can I park my car?* Où est-ce que je peux garer ma voiture?
2 se garer ◊ *We couldn't find anywhere to park.* Nous avons eu du mal à nous garer.

parking NOUN
le stationnement ◊ *"no parking"* "stationnement interdit"
*Be careful not to translate **parking** by the French word **parking**.*

parking lot NOUN US
le parking

parking meter NOUN
le parcmètre

parking ticket NOUN

le p.-v. (*informal*)

parliament NOUN
le parlement

parole NOUN
♦**on parole** en liberté conditionnelle

parrot NOUN
le perroquet

parsley NOUN
le persil

part NOUN
1 la partie (*section*) ◊ *The first part of the film was boring.* La première partie du film était ennuyeuse.
2 la pièce (*component*) ◊ *spare parts* les pièces de rechange
3 le rôle (*in play, film*)
♦**to take part in something** participer à quelque chose ◊ *A lot of people took part in the demonstration.* Beaucoup de gens ont participé à la manifestation.

to **part with** VERB
♦**to part with something** se défaire de quelque chose

particular ADJECTIVE
particulier MASC
particulière FEM
◊ *Are you looking for anything particular?* Est-ce que vous voulez quelque chose de particulier?
♦**nothing in particular** rien de particulier

particularly ADVERB
particulièrement
♦**not particularly** pas particulièrement

parting NOUN
la raie (*in hair*)

partly ADVERB
en partie

partner NOUN
1 (*in game*)
le/la partenaire
2 (*in business*)
l' associé MASC
l' associée FEM
3 (*in dance*)
le cavalier
la cavalière
4 le compagnon (*boyfriend*)
la compagne (*girlfriend*)

part-time ADJECTIVE, ADVERB
à temps partiel ◊ *a part-time job* un travail à temps partiel ◊ *She works part-time.* Elle travaille à temps partiel.

party NOUN
1 la fête ◊ *a birthday party* une fête d'anniversaire ◊ *a Christmas party*

une fête de Noël ◊ *a New Year party*
une fête du Nouvel An
[2] la soirée (*more formal*) ◊ *I'm going to a party on Saturday.* Je vais à une soirée samedi.
[3] le parti (*political*) ◊ *the Conservative Party* le Parti conservateur
[4] le groupe (*group*) ◊ *a party of tourists* un groupe de touristes

pass NOUN
see also **pass** VERB
[1] le col (*in mountains*) ◊ *The pass was blocked with snow.* Le col était enneigé.
[2] la passe (*in football*)
♦ **to get a pass** (*in exam*) être reçu ◊ *She got a pass in her piano exam.* Elle a été reçue à son examen de piano. ◊ *I got six passes.* J'ai été reçu dans six matières.
♦ **a bus pass** une carte de bus

to **pass** VERB
see also **pass** NOUN
[1] être reçu (*exam*) ◊ *to pass an exam* être reçu à un examen ◊ *I hope I'll pass the exam.* J'espère que je serai reçu à l'examen. ◊ *Did you pass?* Tu as été reçu?
[2] passer ◊ *Could you pass me the salt, please?* Est-ce que vous pourriez me passer le sel, s'il vous plaît?
◊ *The time has passed quickly.* Le temps a passé rapidement.
[3] passer devant ◊ *I pass his house on my way to school.* Je passe devant chez lui en allant à l'école.

Be careful not to translate **to pass an exam** *by* **passer un examen.**

to **pass out** VERB
s'évanouir (*faint*)

passage NOUN
[1] le passage (*piece of writing*) ◊ *Read the passage carefully.* Lisez attentivement le passage.
[2] le couloir (*corridor*)

passenger NOUN
le passager
la passagère

passion NOUN
la passion

passive ADJECTIVE
passif MASC
passive FEM
♦ **passive smoking** le tabagisme passif

Passover NOUN
la Pâque juive ◊ *at Passover* à la Pâque juive

passport NOUN

le passeport ◊ *passport control* le contrôle des passeports

password NOUN
le mot de passe

past ADVERB, PREPOSITION
see also **past** NOUN
après (*beyond*) ◊ *It's on the right, just past the station.* C'est sur la droite, juste après la gare.
♦ **to go past (1)** passer ◊ *The bus went past without stopping.* Le bus est passé sans s'arrêter.
♦ **to go past (2)** passer devant ◊ *The bus goes past our house.* Le bus passe devant notre maison.
♦ **It's half past ten.** Il est dix heures et demie.
♦ **It's quarter past nine.** Il est neuf heures et quart.
♦ **It's ten past eight.** Il est huit heures dix.
♦ **It's past midnight.** Il est minuit passé.

past NOUN
see also **past** ADVERB
le passé ◊ *She lives in the past.* Elle vit dans le passé.
♦ **in the past** (*previously*) autrefois ◊ *This was common in the past.* C'était courant autrefois.

pasta NOUN
les pâtes FEM PL ◊ *Pasta is easy to cook.* Les pâtes sont faciles à préparer.

paste NOUN
la colle (*glue*)

pasteurized ADJECTIVE
pasteurisé

pastime NOUN
le passe-temps
(les passe-temps PL)
◊ *Her favourite pastime is knitting.* Son passe-temps favori est le tricot.

pastry NOUN
la pâte
♦ **pastries** les pâtisseries FEM

patch NOUN
[1] la pièce ◊ *a patch of material* une pièce de tissu
[2] la rustine (*for flat tyre*)
♦ **He's got a bald patch.** Il a le crâne dégarni.

patched ADJECTIVE
rapiécé ◊ *a pair of patched jeans* un jean rapiécé

pâté NOUN
le pâté

path NOUN
[1] le chemin (*footpath*)
[2] l' allée FEM (*in garden, park*)

P

pathetic ADJECTIVE
lamentable ◊ *Our team was pathetic.*
Notre équipe a été lamentable.

patience NOUN
1 la patience ◊ *He hasn't got much patience.* Il n'a pas beaucoup de patience.
2 la réussite (*card game*) ◊ *to play patience* faire une réussite

patient NOUN
see also **patient** ADJECTIVE
le patient
la patiente

patient ADJECTIVE
see also **patient** NOUN
patient

patio NOUN
le patio

patriotic ADJECTIVE
patriote

patrol NOUN
la patrouille

patrol car NOUN
la voiture de police

pattern NOUN
le motif ◊ *a geometric pattern* un motif géométrique
♦ **a sewing pattern** un patron

pause NOUN
la pause

pavement NOUN
le trottoir

pavilion NOUN
le pavillon

paw NOUN
la patte

pay NOUN
see also **pay** VERB
le salaire

to **pay** VERB
see also **pay** NOUN
1 payer ◊ *They pay me more on Sundays.* Je suis payé davantage le dimanche.
2 régler ◊ *to pay by cheque* régler par chèque ◊ *to pay by credit card* régler par carte de crédit
♦ **to pay for something** payer quelque chose ◊ *I paid for my ticket.* J'ai payé mon billet. ◊ *I paid 50 euros for it.* Je l'ai payé cinquante euros.
♦ **to pay extra for something** payer un supplément pour quelque chose ◊ *You have to pay extra for parking.* Il faut payer un supplément pour le parking.

♦ **to pay attention** faire attention
◊ *Don't pay any attention to him!* Ne fais pas attention à lui!
♦ **to pay somebody a visit** rendre visite à quelqu'un ◊ *Paul paid us a visit last night.* Paul nous a rendu visite hier soir.
♦ **to pay somebody back** rembourser quelqu'un ◊ *I'll pay you back tomorrow.* Je te rembourserai demain.

payable ADJECTIVE
♦ **Make the cheque payable to "ABC Ltd".** Libellez le chèque à l'ordre de "ABC Ltd".

payment NOUN
le paiement

payphone NOUN
le téléphone public

PC NOUN (= *personal computer*)
le PC ◊ *She typed the report on her PC.* Elle a tapé le rapport sur son PC.

PE NOUN
l' EPS FEM ◊ *We do PE twice a week.* Nous avons EPS deux fois par semaine.

pea NOUN
le petit pois

peace NOUN
1 la paix (*after war*)
2 le calme (*quietness*)

peaceful ADJECTIVE
1 paisible (*calm*) ◊ *a peaceful afternoon* un après-midi paisible
2 pacifique (*not violent*) ◊ *a peaceful protest* une manifestation pacifique

peach NOUN
la pêche

peacock NOUN
le paon

peak NOUN
la cime (*of mountain*)
♦ **the peak rate** le plein tarif ◊ *You pay the peak rate for calls at this time of day.* On paie le plein tarif quand on appelle à cette heure-ci.
♦ **in peak season** en haute saison

peanut NOUN
la cacahuète ◊ *a packet of peanuts* un paquet de cacahuètes

peanut butter NOUN
le beurre de cacahuètes ◊ *a peanut-butter sandwich* un sandwich au beurre de cacahuètes

pear NOUN
la poire

pearl NOUN
la perle

pebble NOUN
le galet ◊ *a pebble beach* une plage de galets

peckish ADJECTIVE
- **to feel a bit peckish** avoir un petit creux

peculiar ADJECTIVE
bizarre ◊ *He's a peculiar person.* Il est bizarre. ◊ *It tastes peculiar.* Ça a un goût bizarre.

pedal NOUN
la pédale

pedestrian NOUN
le piéton

pedestrian crossing NOUN
le passage pour piétons

pedestrianized ADJECTIVE
- **a pedestrianized street** une rue piétonne

pedigree ADJECTIVE
de race (*animal*) ◊ *a pedigree dog* un chien de race ◊ *a pedigree labrador.* un labrador de pure race.

pee NOUN
- **to have a pee** faire pipi

peek NOUN
- **to have a peek at something** jeter un coup d'œil à quelque chose
- **No peeking!** On ne regarde pas!

peel NOUN
see also **peel** VERB
l' écorce FEM (*of orange*)

to **peel** VERB
see also **peel** NOUN
1 éplucher ◊ *Shall I peel the potatoes?* J'épluche les pommes de terre?
2 peler ◊ *My nose is peeling.* Mon nez pèle.

peg NOUN
1 (*for coats*)
le portemanteau
(les portemanteaux PL)
2 (*clothes peg*)
la pince à linge
3 (*tent peg*)
le piquet

Pekinese NOUN
le pékinois

pelican crossing NOUN
le passage pour piétons

pellet NOUN
le plomb (*for gun*)

pelvis NOUN
le bassin

pen NOUN
le stylo

to **penalize** VERB
pénaliser

penalty NOUN
1 la peine (*punishment*)

- **the death penalty** la peine de mort
2 le penalty (*in football*)
3 la pénalité (*in rugby*)
- **a penalty shoot-out** les tirs au but MASC PL

pence PL NOUN
les pence MASC PL

pencil NOUN
le crayon
- **in pencil** au crayon

pencil case NOUN
la trousse

pencil sharpener NOUN
le taille-crayon

pendant NOUN
le pendentif

penfriend NOUN
le correspondant
la correspondante

penguin NOUN
le pingouin

penicillin NOUN
la pénicilline

penis NOUN
le pénis

penitentiary NOUN US
la prison

penknife NOUN
le canif

penny NOUN
le penny
(les pence PL)

pension NOUN
la retraite

pensioner NOUN
le retraité
la retraitée

pentathlon NOUN
le pentathlon

people PL NOUN
1 les gens MASC PL ◊ *The people were nice.* Les gens étaient sympathiques.
◊ *a lot of people* beaucoup de gens
2 les personnes FEM PL (*individuals*)
◊ *six people* six personnes ◊ *several people* plusieurs personnes
- **How many people are there in your family?** Vous êtes combien dans votre famille?
- **French people** les Français
- **black people** les Noirs
- **People say that ...** On dit que ...

pepper NOUN
1 le poivre (*spice*) ◊ *Pass the pepper, please.* Passez-moi le poivre, s'il vous plaît.
2 le poivron (*vegetable*) ◊ *a green pepper* un poivron vert

P

peppermill NOUN
le moulin à poivre

peppermint NOUN
la pastille de menthe (*sweet*)

♦ **peppermint chewing gum** le chewing-gum à la menthe

per PREPOSITION
par ◊ *per day* par jour ◊ *per week* par semaine

♦ **30 miles per hour** trente miles à l'heure

per cent ADVERB
pour cent ◊ *fifty per cent* cinquante pour cent

percentage NOUN
le pourcentage

percolator NOUN
la cafetière électrique

percussion NOUN
la percussion ◊ *I play percussion.* Je joue des percussions.

perfect ADJECTIVE
parfait ◊ *Chantal speaks perfect English.* Chantal parle un anglais parfait.

perfectly ADVERB
parfaitement

to **perform** VERB
jouer (*act, play*)

performance NOUN
1️⃣ le spectacle (*show*) ◊ *The performance lasts two hours.* Le spectacle dure deux heures.
2️⃣ l' interprétation FEM (*acting*) ◊ *his performance as Hamlet* son interprétation d'Hamlet
3️⃣ la performance (*results*) ◊ *the team's poor performance* la médiocre performance de l'équipe

perfume NOUN
le parfum

perhaps ADVERB
peut-être ◊ *a bit boring, perhaps* peut-être un peu ennuyeux ◊ *Perhaps he's ill.* Il est peut-être malade.

♦ **perhaps not** peut-être pas

period NOUN
1️⃣ la période ◊ *for a limited period* pour une période limitée
2️⃣ l' époque FEM (*in history*) ◊ *the Victorian period* l'époque victorienne
3️⃣ les règles FEM PL (*menstruation*) ◊ *I'm having my period.* J'ai mes règles.
4️⃣ le cours (*lesson time*) ◊ *Each period lasts forty minutes.* Chaque cours dure quarante minutes.

perm NOUN
la permanente ◊ *She's got a perm.* Elle a une permanente.

♦ **to have a perm** se faire faire une permanente

permanent ADJECTIVE
permanent

permission NOUN
la permission ◊ *Could I have permission to leave early?* Pourrais-je avoir la permission de partir plus tôt?

permit NOUN
le permis ◊ *a fishing permit* un permis de pêche

to **persecute** VERB
persécuter

Persian ADJECTIVE
♦ **a Persian cat** un chat persan

persistent ADJECTIVE
tenace (*person*)

person NOUN
la personne ◊ *She's a very nice person.* C'est une personne très sympathique.

♦ **in person** en personne

personal ADJECTIVE
personnel MASC
personnelle FEM

♦ **personal column** les annonces personnelles FEM PL

personality NOUN
la personnalité

personally ADVERB
personnellement ◊ *I don't know him personally.* Je ne le connais pas personnellement. ◊ *Personally I don't agree.* Personnellement, je ne suis pas d'accord.

personal stereo NOUN
le walkman ®

personnel NOUN
le personnel

perspiration NOUN
la transpiration

to **persuade** VERB
persuader

♦ **to persuade somebody to do something** persuader quelqu'un de faire quelque chose ◊ *She persuaded me to go with her.* Elle m'a persuadé de l'accompagner.

pessimist NOUN
le/la pessimiste ◊ *I'm a pessimist.* Je suis pessimiste.

pessimistic ADJECTIVE
pessimiste

pest NOUN
le/la casse-pieds (*person*) ◊ *He's a real pest!* C'est un vrai casse-pieds!

to **pester** VERB
importuner

pet NOUN
l' animal familier MASC ◊ *Have you got a pet?* Est-ce que tu as un animal familier?
♦**She's the teacher's pet.** C'est la chouchoute de la maîtresse.

petition NOUN
la pétition

petrified ADJECTIVE
pétrifié

petrol NOUN
l' essence FEM
♦**unleaded petrol** l'essence sans plomb
*Be careful not to translate **petrol** by pétrole.*

petrol station NOUN
la station-service
(les stations-service PL)

petrol tank NOUN
le réservoir d'essence

phantom NOUN
le fantôme

pharmacy NOUN
la pharmacie

> ℹ *Pharmacies in France are identified by a special green cross outside the shop.*

pheasant NOUN
le faisan

philosophy NOUN
la philosophie

phobia NOUN
la phobie

phone NOUN
see also **phone** VERB
le téléphone ◊ *Where's the phone?* Où est le téléphone? ◊ *Is there a phone here?* Est-ce qu'il y a un téléphone ici?
♦**by phone** par téléphone
♦**to be on the phone** être au téléphone ◊ *She's on the phone at the moment.* Elle est au téléphone en ce moment.
♦**Can I use the phone, please?** Est-ce que je peux téléphoner, s'il vous plaît?

to **phone** VERB
see also **phone** NOUN
appeler ◊ *I'll phone the station.* Je vais appeler la gare.

phone bill NOUN
la facture de téléphone

phone book NOUN
l' annuaire MASC

phone box NOUN
la cabine téléphonique

phone call NOUN
l' appel MASC ◊ *There's a phone call for you.* Il y a un appel pour vous.
♦**to make a phone call** téléphoner ◊ *Can I make a phone call?* Est-ce que je peux téléphoner?

phonecard NOUN
la carte de téléphone

phone number NOUN
le numéro de téléphone

photo NOUN
la photo
♦**to take a photo** prendre une photo
♦**to take a photo of somebody** prendre quelqu'un en photo

photocopier NOUN
la photocopieuse

photocopy NOUN
see also **photocopy** VERB
la photocopie

to **photocopy** VERB
see also **photocopy** NOUN
photocopier

photograph NOUN
see also **photograph** VERB
la photo
♦**to take a photograph** prendre une photo
♦**to take a photograph of somebody** prendre quelqu'un en photo

to **photograph** VERB
see also **photograph** NOUN
photographier

photographer NOUN
le/la photographe ◊ *She's a photographer.* Elle est photographe.

photography NOUN
la photo ◊ *My hobby is photography.* Je fais de la photo.

phrase NOUN
l' expression FEM

phrase book NOUN
le guide de conversation

physical ADJECTIVE
see also **physical** NOUN
physique

physical NOUN US
see also **physical** ADJECTIVE
l' examen médical MASC

physicist NOUN
le physicien
la physicienne
◊ *He's a physicist.* Il est physicien.

physics NOUN
la physique ◊ *She teaches physics.* Elle enseigne la physique.

physiotherapist NOUN
le/la kinésithérapeute

physiotherapy NOUN

P

☞

la <u>kinésithérapie</u>

pianist NOUN
le/la <u>pianiste</u>

piano NOUN
le <u>piano</u> ◊ *I play the piano.* Je joue du piano. ◊ *I have piano lessons.* Je prends des leçons de piano.

pick NOUN
> *see also* **pick** VERB

◆**Take your pick!** Faites votre choix!

to **pick** VERB
> *see also* **pick** NOUN

1 <u>choisir</u> (*choose*) ◊ *I picked the biggest piece.* J'ai choisi le plus gros morceau.
2 <u>sélectionner</u> (*for team*) ◊ *I've been picked for the team.* J'ai été sélectionné pour faire partie de l'équipe.
3 <u>cueillir</u> (*fruit, flowers*)
◆**to pick on somebody** harceler quelqu'un ◊ *She's always picking on me.* Elle me harcèle constamment.
◆**to pick out** choisir ◊ *I like them all – it's difficult to pick one out.* Ils me plaisent tous – c'est difficile d'en choisir un.
◆**to pick up (1)** (*collect*) venir chercher ◊ *We'll come to the airport to pick you up.* Nous irons vous chercher à l'aéroport.
◆**to pick up (2)** (*from floor*) ramasser ◊ *Could you help me pick up the toys?* Tu peux m'aider à ramasser les jouets?
◆**to pick up (3)** (*learn*) apprendre ◊ *I picked up some Spanish during my holiday.* J'ai appris quelque mots d'espagnol pendant mes vacances.

pickpocket NOUN
le <u>pickpocket</u>

picnic NOUN
le <u>pique-nique</u>
◆**to have a picnic** pique-niquer ◊ *We had a picnic on the beach.* Nous avons pique-niqué sur la plage.

picture NOUN
1 l' <u>illustration</u> FEM ◊ *Children's books have lots of pictures.* Il y a beaucoup d'illustrations dans les livres pour enfants.
2 la <u>photo</u> ◊ *My picture was in the paper.* Ma photo était dans le journal.
3 (*painting*)
le <u>tableau</u>
(les tableaux PL)
◊ *a famous picture* un tableau célèbre
◆**to paint a picture of something** peindre quelque chose
4 (*drawing*)

le <u>dessin</u>
◆**to draw a picture of something** dessiner quelque chose
◆**the pictures** (*cinema*) le cinéma ◊ *Shall we go to the pictures?* On va au cinéma?

picturesque ADJECTIVE
<u>pittoresque</u>

pie NOUN
la <u>tourte</u> ◊ *an apple pie* une tourte aux pommes

piece NOUN
le <u>morceau</u>
(les morceaux PL)
◊ *A small piece, please.* Un petit morceau, s'il vous plaît.
◆**a piece of furniture** un meuble
◆**a piece of advice** un conseil

pier NOUN
la <u>jetée</u>

to **pierce** VERB
<u>percer</u> ◊ *She's going to have her ears pierced.* Elle va se faire percer les oreilles.

pierced ADJECTIVE
<u>percé</u> ◊ *I've got pierced ears.* J'ai les oreilles percées.

piercing NOUN
le <u>piercing</u> ◊ *She has several piercings.* Elle a plusieurs piercings.

pig NOUN
le <u>cochon</u>

pigeon NOUN
le <u>pigeon</u>

piggyback NOUN
◆**to give somebody a piggyback** porter quelqu'un sur son dos ◊ *I can't give you a piggyback, you're too heavy.* Je ne peux pas te porter sur mon dos, tu es trop lourd.

piggy bank NOUN
la <u>tirelire</u>

pigtail NOUN
la <u>natte</u>

pile NOUN
1 le <u>tas</u> (*untidy heap*)
2 la <u>pile</u> (*tidy stack*)

piles PL NOUN
les <u>hémorroïdes</u> FEM PL ◊ *to suffer from piles* avoir des hémorroïdes

pile-up NOUN
le <u>carambolage</u>

pill NOUN
la <u>pilule</u>
◆**to be on the pill** prendre la pilule

pillar NOUN
le <u>pilier</u>

pillar box NOUN

la boîte aux lettres

pillow NOUN
l' oreiller MASC

pilot NOUN
le pilote ◊ *He's a pilot.* Il est pilote.

pimple NOUN
le bouton

pin NOUN
l' épingle FEM
♦**I've got pins and needles.** J'ai des fourmis.

PIN NOUN (= *personal identification number*)
le code confidentiel

pinafore NOUN
le tablier

pinball NOUN
le flipper ◊ *to play pinball* jouer au flipper
♦**a pinball machine** un flipper

to **pinch** VERB
⟦1⟧ pincer ◊ *He pinched me!* Il m'a pincé!
⟦2⟧ piquer (*informal: steal*) ◊ *Who's pinched my pen?* Qui est-ce qui m'a piqué mon stylo?

pine NOUN
le pin ◊ *a pine table* une table en pin

pineapple NOUN
l' ananas MASC

pink ADJECTIVE
rose

pint NOUN
la pinte

> ⓘ *In France measurements are in litres and centilitres. A pint is about 0.6 litres.*

♦**to have a pint** boire une bière ◊ *He's gone out for a pint.* Il est parti boire une bière.
♦**a pint of milk** un demi-litre de lait

pipe NOUN
⟦1⟧ la conduite (*for water, gas*) ◊ *The pipes froze.* Les conduites d'eau ont gelé.
⟦2⟧ la pipe (*for smoking*) ◊ *He smokes a pipe.* Il fume la pipe.
♦**the pipes** (*bagpipes*) la cornemuse ◊ *He plays the pipes.* Il joue de la cornemuse.

pirate NOUN
le pirate

pirated ADJECTIVE
pirate ◊ *a pirated video* une vidéo pirate

Pisces NOUN

les Poissons MASC PL ◊ *I'm Pisces.* Je suis Poissons.

pissed ADJECTIVE
bourré (*informal*)

pistol NOUN
le pistolet

pitch NOUN
> see also **pitch** VERB

le terrain ◊ *a football pitch* un terrain de football

to **pitch** VERB
> see also **pitch** NOUN

dresser (*tent*) ◊ *We pitched our tent near the beach.* Nous avons dressé notre tente près de la plage.

pity NOUN
> see also **pity** VERB

la pitié
♦**What a pity!** Quel dommage!

to **pity** VERB
> see also **pity** NOUN

plaindre

pizza NOUN
la pizza

place NOUN
> see also **place** VERB

⟦1⟧ l' endroit MASC (*location*) ◊ *It's a quiet place.* C'est un endroit tranquille. ◊ *There are a lot of interesting places to visit.* Il y a beaucoup d'endroits intéressants à visiter.
⟦2⟧ la place (*space*) ◊ *a parking place* une place de parking ◊ *a university place* une place à l'université
♦**to change places** changer de place ◊ *Tamsin, change places with Delphine!* Tamsin, change de place avec Delphine!
♦**to take place** avoir lieu
♦**at your place** chez toi ◊ *Shall we meet at your place?* On se retrouve chez toi?
♦**to my place** chez moi ◊ *Do you want to come round to my place?* Tu veux venir chez moi?

to **place** VERB
> see also **place** NOUN

⟦1⟧ poser ◊ *He placed his hand on hers.* Il a posé la main sur la sienne.
⟦2⟧ classer (*in competition, contest*)

placement NOUN
le stage
♦**to do a work placement** faire un stage en entreprise

plaid ADJECTIVE
écossais ◊ *a plaid shirt* une chemise écossaise

plain NOUN

P

☞

see also **plain** ADJECTIVE

la plaine

plain ADJECTIVE, ADVERB

see also **plain** NOUN

[1] uni (not patterned) ◊ a plain carpet un tapis uni

[2] simple (not fancy) ◊ a plain white blouse un chemisier blanc simple

plain chocolate NOUN

le chocolat à croquer

plait NOUN

la natte ◊ She wears her hair in a plait. Elle a une natte.

plan NOUN

see also **plan** VERB

[1] le projet ◊ What are your plans for the holidays? Quels sont tes projets pour les vacances? ◊ to make plans faire des projets

♦Everything went according to plan. Tout s'est passé comme prévu.

[2] le plan (map) ◊ a plan of the campsite un plan du terrain de camping

♦my essay plan le plan de ma dissertation

to **plan** VERB

see also **plan** NOUN

[1] préparer (make plans for) ◊ We're planning a trip to France. Nous préparons un voyage en France.

[2] planifier (make schedule for) ◊ Plan your revision carefully. Planifiez vos révisions avec soin.

♦to plan to do something avoir l'intention de faire quelque chose ◊ I'm planning to get a job in the holidays. J'ai l'intention de trouver un job pour les vacances.

plane NOUN

l' avion MASC ◊ by plane en avion

planet NOUN

la planète

planning NOUN

la préparation ◊ The trip needs careful planning. Le voyage nécessite une préparation méticuleuse.

♦family planning le planning familial

plant NOUN

see also **plant** VERB

[1] la plante ◊ to water the plants arroser les plantes

[2] l' usine FEM (factory)

to **plant** VERB

see also **plant** NOUN

planter

plant pot NOUN

le pot de fleurs

plaque NOUN

la plaque (on wall)

plaster NOUN

[1] le pansement adhésif (sticking plaster) ◊ Have you got a plaster, by any chance? Vous n'auriez pas un pansement adhésif, par hasard?

[2] le plâtre (for fracture) ◊ Her leg's in plaster. Elle a la jambe dans le plâtre.

plastic NOUN

see also **plastic** ADJECTIVE

le plastique ◊ It's made of plastic. C'est en plastique.

plastic ADJECTIVE

see also **plastic** NOUN

en plastique ◊ a plastic bag un sac en plastique ◊ a plastic mac un imperméable en plastique

plate NOUN

l' assiette FEM (for food)

platform NOUN

[1] le quai (at station) ◊ on platform 7 sur le quai numéro sept

[2] l' estrade FEM (for performers)

play NOUN

see also **play** VERB

la pièce ◊ a play by Shakespeare une pièce de Shakespeare

♦to put on a play monter une pièce

to **play** VERB

see also **play** NOUN

[1] jouer ◊ He's playing with his friends. Il joue avec ses amis. ◊ What sort of music do they play? Quel genre de musique jouent-ils?

[2] jouer contre (against person, team) ◊ France will play Scotland next month. La France jouera contre l'Écosse le mois prochain.

[3] jouer à (sport, game) ◊ I play hockey. Je joue au hockey. ◊ Can you play pool? Tu sais jouer au billard américain?

[4] jouer de (instrument) ◊ I play the guitar. Je joue de la guitare.

[5] écouter (record, cassette, music) ◊ She's always playing that record. Elle écoute tout le temps ce disque.

to **play down** VERB

dédramatiser ◊ He tried to play down his illness. Il a essayé de dédramatiser sa maladie.

player NOUN

[1] (of sport)
le joueur
l joueuse
◊ a football player un joueur de football

[2] (of instrument)
le musicien
la musicienne

♦ **a piano player** un pianiste
♦ **a saxophone player** un saxophoniste

playful ADJECTIVE
espiègle

playground NOUN
[1] la cour de récréation (*at school*)
[2] l' aire de jeux FEM (*in park*)

playgroup NOUN
la garderie

playing card NOUN
la carte à jouer
(les cartes à jouer PL)

playing field NOUN
le terrain de sport

playtime NOUN
la récréation

playwright NOUN
le dramaturge

pleasant ADJECTIVE
agréable

please EXCLAMATION
[1] s'il vous plaît (*polite form*) ◊ *Two
coffees, please.* Deux cafés, s'il vous
plaît.
[2] s'il te plaît (*familiar form*) ◊ *Please
write back soon.* Réponds vite, s'il te
plaît.

pleased ADJECTIVE
content ◊ *My mother's not going to
be very pleased.* Ma mère ne va pas
être contente du tout. ◊ *It's beautiful:
she'll be pleased with it.* C'est beau:
elle va être contente.
♦ **Pleased to meet you!** Enchanté!

pleasure NOUN
le plaisir ◊ *I read for pleasure.* Je lis
pour le plaisir.

plenty NOUN
largement assez ◊ *I've got plenty.*
J'en ai largement assez. ◊ *That's
plenty, thanks.* Ça suffit largement,
merci.
♦ **plenty of (1)** (*a lot*) beaucoup de ◊ *I've
got plenty to do.* J'ai beaucoup de
choses à faire.
♦ **plenty of (2)** (*enough*) largement assez
de ◊ *I've got plenty of money.* J'ai
largement assez d'argent. ◊ *We've
got plenty of time.* Nous avons
largement le temps.

pliers PL NOUN
la pince SING
♦ **a pair of pliers** une pince

plot NOUN
see also **plot** VERB
[1] l' intrigue FEM (*of story, play*)
[2] la conspiration (*against somebody*)
◊ *a plot against the president* une
conspiration contre le président

[3] le carré (*of land*) ◊ *a vegetable plot*
un carré de légumes

to **plot** VERB
see also **plot** NOUN
comploter ◊ *They were plotting to
kill him.* Ils complotaient de le tuer.

plough NOUN
see also **plough** VERB
la charrue

to **plough** VERB
see also **plough** NOUN
labourer

plug NOUN
[1] la prise de courant (*electrical*)
◊ *The plug is faulty.* La prise est
défectueuse.
[2] le bouchon (*for sink*)

to **plug in** VERB
brancher ◊ *Is it plugged in?* Est-ce
que c'est branché?

plum NOUN
la prune ◊ *plum jam* la confiture de
prunes

plumber NOUN
le plombier ◊ *He's a plumber.* Il est
plombier.

plump ADJECTIVE
dodu

to **plunge** VERB
plonger

plural NOUN
le pluriel

plus PREPOSITION, ADJECTIVE
plus ◊ *4 plus 3 equals 7.* Quatre plus
trois égalent sept. ◊ *three children
plus a dog* trois enfants plus un
chien
♦ **I got a B plus.** J'ai eu un Bien.

p.m. ABBREVIATION
♦ **at 8 p.m.** à huit heures du soir

> ⓘ *In France times are often given
> using the 24-hour clock.*

♦ **at 2 p.m.** à quatorze heures

pneumonia NOUN
la pneumonie

poached ADJECTIVE
poché ◊ *a poached egg* un œuf
poché

pocket NOUN
la poche
♦ **pocket money** l'argent de poche MASC
◊ *£8 a week pocket money* huit livres
d'argent de poche par semaine

pocket calculator NOUN
la calculette

poem NOUN

P

le poème

poet NOUN
le poète

poetry NOUN
la poésie

point NOUN
see also **point** VERB
1 le point (spot, score) ◊ a point on the horizon un point à l'horizon ◊ They scored 5 points. Ils ont marqué cinq points.
2 la remarque (comment) ◊ He made some interesting points. Il a fait quelque remarques intéressantes.
3 la pointe (tip) ◊ a pencil with a sharp point un crayon à la pointe aiguisée
4 le moment (in time) ◊ At that point, we decided to leave. À ce moment-là, nous avons décidé de partir.
♦ a point of view un point de vue
♦ to get the point comprendre ◊ Sorry, I don't get the point. Désolé, je ne comprends pas.
♦ That's a good point! C'est vrai!
♦ There's no point. Cela ne sert à rien. ◊ There's no point in waiting. Cela ne sert à rien d'attendre.
♦ What's the point? À quoi bon? ◊ What's the point of leaving so early? À quoi bon partir si tôt?
♦ Punctuality isn't my strong point. La ponctualité n'est pas mon fort.
♦ two point five (2.5) deux virgule cinq (2,5)

to **point** VERB
see also **point** NOUN
montrer du doigt ◊ Don't point! Ne montre pas du doigt!
♦ to point at somebody montrer quelqu'un du doigt ◊ She pointed at Anne. Elle a montré Anne du doigt.
♦ to point a gun at somebody braquer un revolver sur quelqu'un
♦ to point something out (1) (show) montrer quelque chose ◊ The guide pointed out Notre-Dame to us. Le guide nous a montré Notre-Dame.
♦ to point something out (2) (mention) signaler quelque chose ◊ I should point out that ... Je dois vous signaler que ...

pointless ADJECTIVE
inutile ◊ It's pointless to argue. Il est inutile de discuter.

poison NOUN
see also **poison** VERB
le poison

to **poison** VERB

see also **poison** NOUN
empoisonner

poisonous ADJECTIVE
1 (snake)
venimeux MASC
venimeuse FEM
2 (plant, mushroom)
vénéneux MASC
vénéneuse FEM
3 (gas)
toxique

to **poke** VERB
♦ He poked the ground with his stick. Il tapotait le sol avec sa canne.
♦ She poked me in the ribs. Elle m'a enfoncé le doigt dans les côtes.

poker NOUN
le poker ◊ I play poker. Je joue au poker.

Poland NOUN
la Pologne
♦ in Poland en Pologne
♦ to Poland en Pologne

polar bear NOUN
l' ours blanc MASC

Pole NOUN
(Polish person)
le Polonais
la Polonaise

pole NOUN
le poteau
(les poteaux PL)
◊ a telegraph pole un poteau télégraphique
♦ a tent pole un montant de tente
♦ a ski pole un bâton de ski
♦ the North Pole le pôle Nord
♦ the South Pole le pôle Sud

pole vault NOUN
le saut à la perche

police PL NOUN
la police ◊ We called the police. Nous avons appelé la police.
♦ a police car une voiture de police
♦ a police station un commissariat de police

policeman NOUN
le policier ◊ He's a policeman. Il est policier.

policewoman NOUN
la femme policier ◊ She's a policewoman. Elle est femme policier.

polio NOUN
la polio

Polish ADJECTIVE
see also **Polish** NOUN
polonais

Polish NOUN
see also **Polish** ADJECTIVE

le <u>polonais</u> (*language*)

polish NOUN
  see also **polish** VERB
  ① le <u>cirage</u> (*for shoes*)
  ② la <u>cire</u> (*for furniture*)

to **polish** VERB
  see also **polish** NOUN
  ① <u>cirer</u> (*shoes, furniture*)
  ② <u>faire briller</u> (*glass*)

polite ADJECTIVE
  <u>poli</u>

politely ADVERB
  <u>poliment</u>

politeness NOUN
  la <u>politesse</u>

political ADJECTIVE
  <u>politique</u>

politician NOUN
  le <u>politicien</u>
  la <u>politicienne</u>

politics PL NOUN
  la <u>politique</u> SING ◊ *I'm not interested in politics.* La politique ne m'intéresse pas.

poll NOUN
  le <u>sondage</u> ◊ *A recent poll revealed that ...* Un sondage récent a révélé que ...

pollen NOUN
  le <u>pollen</u>

to **pollute** VERB
  <u>polluer</u>

polluted ADJECTIVE
  <u>pollué</u>

pollution NOUN
  la <u>pollution</u>

polo-necked sweater NOUN
  le <u>pull à col roulé</u>

polo shirt NOUN
  le <u>polo</u>

polythene bag NOUN
  le <u>sac en plastique</u>

pond NOUN
  ① l' <u>étang</u> MASC (*big*)
  ② la <u>mare</u> (*smaller*)
  ③ le <u>bassin</u> ◊ *We've got a pond in our garden.* Nous avons un bassin dans notre jardin.

pony NOUN
  le <u>poney</u>

ponytail NOUN
  la <u>queue de cheval</u> ◊ *He's got a ponytail.* Il a une queue de cheval.

pony trekking NOUN
  ◆**to go pony trekking** faire une randonnée à dos de poney

poodle NOUN

le <u>caniche</u>

pool NOUN
  ① la <u>flaque</u> (*puddle*)
  ② l' <u>étang</u> MASC (*pond*)
  ③ la <u>piscine</u> (*for swimming*)
  ④ le <u>billard américain</u> (*game*) ◊ *Shall we have a game of pool?* Si on jouait au billard américain?
  ◆**the pools** (*football*) le loto sportif ◊ *to do the pools* jouer au loto sportif

poor ADJECTIVE
  ① <u>pauvre</u> ◊ *a poor family* une famille pauvre ◊ *Poor David, he's very unlucky!* Le pauvre David, il n'a vraiment pas de chance!
  ◆**the poor** les pauvres MASC
  ② <u>médiocre</u> (*bad*) ◊ *a poor mark* une note médiocre

poorly ADJECTIVE
  <u>souffrant</u> ◊ *She's poorly.* Elle est souffrante.

pop ADJECTIVE
  <u>pop</u> ◊ *pop music* la musique pop ◊ *a pop star* une pop star ◊ *a pop group* un groupe pop ◊ *a pop song* une chanson pop

to **pop in** VERB
  <u>passer</u> ◊ *I just popped in to say hello.* Je suis juste passé dire bonjour. ◊ *I need to pop in to the supermarket for some milk.* Je dois passer au supermarché pour chercher du lait.

to **pop out** VERB
  <u>sortir</u> ◊ *He's just popped out to the supermarket.* Il vient de sortir pour aller au supermarché.

to **pop round** VERB
  <u>passer</u> ◊ *I'm just popping round to John's.* Je vais juste passer chez John.

popcorn NOUN
  le <u>pop-corn</u>

pope NOUN
  le <u>pape</u>

poppy NOUN
  le <u>coquelicot</u>

Popsicle ® NOUN US
  la <u>glace à l'eau</u>

popular ADJECTIVE
  <u>populaire</u> ◊ *She's a very popular girl.* C'est une fille très populaire. ◊ *This is a very popular style.* C'est un style très populaire.

population NOUN
  la <u>population</u>

porch NOUN
  le <u>porche</u>

pork NOUN

P

le porc ◊ a pork chop une côtelette de porc ◊ I don't eat pork. Je ne mange pas de porc.

porn NOUN
see also **porn** ADJECTIVE
le porno

porn ADJECTIVE
see also **porn** NOUN
porno MASC, FEM, PL ◊ a porn film un film porno ◊ a porn mag un magazine porno

pornographic ADJECTIVE
pornographique ◊ a pornographic magazine un magazine pornographique

pornography NOUN
la pornographie

porridge NOUN
le porridge

port NOUN
1 le port (harbour)
2 le porto (wine) ◊ a glass of port un verre de porto

portable ADJECTIVE
portable ◊ a portable TV un téléviseur portable

porter NOUN
1 le portier (in hotel)
2 le porteur (at station)

portion NOUN
la portion ◊ a large portion of chips une grosse portion de frites

portrait NOUN
le portrait

Portugal NOUN
le Portugal
◆in Portugal au Portugal
◆We went to Portugal. Nous sommes allés au Portugal.

Portuguese ADJECTIVE
see also **Portuguese** NOUN
portugais

Portuguese NOUN
see also **Portuguese** ADJECTIVE
1 (person)
le Portugais
la Portugaise
2 (language)
le portugais

posh ADJECTIVE
chic MASC, FEM, PL ◊ a posh hotel un hôtel chic

position NOUN
la position ◊ an uncomfortable position une position inconfortable

positive ADJECTIVE
1 (good)
positif MASC

positive FEM
◊ a positive attitude une attitude positive
2 (sure)
certain ◊ I'm positive. J'en suis certain.

to **possess** VERB
posséder

possession NOUN
◆Have you got all your possessions? Est-ce tu as toutes tes affaires?

possibility NOUN
◆It's a possibility. C'est possible.

possible ADJECTIVE
possible ◊ as soon as possible aussitôt que possible

possibly ADVERB
peut-être (perhaps) ◊ Are you coming to the party? – Possibly. Est-ce que tu viens à la soirée? – Peut-être.
◆... if you possibly can ... si cela vous est possible
◆I can't possibly come. Je ne peux vraiment pas venir.

post NOUN
see also **post** VERB
1 (letters)
le courrier ◊ Is there any post for me? Est-ce qu'il y a du courrier pour moi?
2 (pole)
le poteau
(les poteaux PL)
◊ The ball hit the post. Le ballon a heurté le poteau.

to **post** VERB
see also **post** NOUN
poster ◊ I've got some cards to post. J'ai quelques cartes à poster.

postage NOUN
l' affranchissement MASC

postbox NOUN
la boîte aux lettres

postcard NOUN
la carte postale

postcode NOUN
le code postal

poster NOUN
1 le poster ◊ I've got posters on my bedroom walls. J'ai des posters sur les murs de ma chambre.
2 l' affiche FEM (advertising) ◊ There are posters all over town. Il y a des affiches dans toute la ville.

postman NOUN
le facteur ◊ He's a postman. Il est facteur.

postmark NOUN
le cachet de la poste

post office NOUN
la <u>poste</u> ◊ *Where's the post office, please?* Où est la poste, s'il vous plaît? ◊ *She works for the post office.* Elle travaille à la poste.

to **postpone** VERB
<u>remettre à plus tard</u> ◊ *The match has been postponed.* Le match a été remis à plus tard.

postwoman NOUN
la <u>factrice</u> ◊ *She's a postwoman.* Elle est factrice.

pot NOUN
[1] le <u>pot</u> ◊ *a pot of jam* un pot de confiture
[2] la <u>théière</u> (*teapot*)
[3] la <u>cafetière</u> (*coffeepot*)
[4] l' <u>herbe</u> FEM (*marijuana*) ◊ *to smoke pot* fumer de l'herbe
♦ **the pots and pans** les casseroles FEM

potato NOUN
la <u>pomme de terre</u> ◊ *potato salad* la salade de pommes de terre
♦ **mashed potatoes** la purée
♦ **boiled potatoes** les pommes vapeur
♦ **a baked potato** une pomme de terre en robe des champs

potential NOUN
see also **potential** ADJECTIVE
♦ **He has great potential.** Il a de l'avenir.

potential ADJECTIVE
see also **potential** NOUN
<u>possible</u> ◊ *a potential problem* un problème possible

pothole NOUN
le <u>nid de poule</u> (*in road*)

pot plant NOUN
la <u>plante en pot</u>

pottery NOUN
la <u>poterie</u>

pound NOUN
see also **pound** VERB
la <u>livre</u> (*weight, money*) ◊ *How many euros do you get for a pound?* Combien d'euros a-t-on pour une livre? ◊ *a pound coin* une pièce d'une livre

> ⓘ *In France measurements are in grammes and kilogrammes. One pound is about 450 grammes.*

◊ *a pound of carrots* un demi-kilo de carottes

to **pound** VERB
see also **pound** NOUN
<u>battre</u> ◊ *My heart was pounding.* J'avais le cœur qui battait.

to **pour** VERB
[1] <u>verser</u> (*liquid*) ◊ *She poured some water into the pan.* Elle a versé de l'eau dans la casserole.
♦ **She poured him a drink.** Elle lui a servi à boire.
♦ **Shall I pour you a cup of tea?** Je vous sers une tasse de thé?
[2] <u>pleuvoir à verse</u> (*rain*) ◊ *It's pouring.* Il pleut à verse.
♦ **in the pouring rain** sous une pluie torrentielle

poverty NOUN
la <u>pauvreté</u>

powder NOUN
la <u>poudre</u>

power NOUN
[1] le <u>courant</u> (*electricity*) ◊ *The power's off.* Le courant est coupé.
♦ **a power cut** une coupure de courant
♦ **a power point** une prise de courant
♦ **a power station** une centrale électrique
[2] l' <u>énergie</u> FEM (*energy*) ◊ *nuclear power* l'énergie nucléaire ◊ *solar power* l'énergie solaire
[3] le <u>pouvoir</u> (*authority*) ◊ *to be in power* être au pouvoir

powerful ADJECTIVE
<u>puissant</u>

practical ADJECTIVE
<u>pratique</u> ◊ *a practical suggestion* un conseil pratique
♦ **She's very practical.** Elle a l'esprit pratique.

practically ADVERB
<u>pratiquement</u> ◊ *It's practically impossible.* C'est pratiquement impossible.

practice NOUN
l' <u>entraînement</u> MASC (*for sport*) ◊ *football practice* l'entraînement de foot
♦ **I've got to do my piano practice.** Je dois travailler mon piano.
♦ **It's normal practice in our school.** C'est ce qui se fait dans notre école.
♦ **in practice** en pratique
♦ **a medical practice** un cabinet médical

to **practise** VERB (US **practice**)
[1] <u>s'exercer</u> (*music, hobby*) ◊ *I ought to practise more.* Je devrais m'exercer davantage.
[2] <u>travailler</u> (*instrument*) ◊ *I practise the flute every evening.* Je travaille ma flûte tous les soirs.
[3] <u>pratiquer</u> (*language*) ◊ *I practised my French when we were on holiday.* J'ai pratiqué mon français pendant les vacances.

P

4 s'entraîner (*sport*) ◊ *The team practises on Thursdays.* L'équipe s'entraîne le jeudi. ◊ *I don't practise enough.* Je ne m'entraîne pas assez.

practising ADJECTIVE
pratiquant ◊ *She's a practising Catholic.* Elle est catholique pratiquante.

to **praise** VERB
faire l'éloge de ◊ *Everyone praises her cooking.* Tout le monde fait l'éloge de sa cuisine. ◊ *The teachers praised our work.* Les professeurs ont fait l'éloge de notre travail.

pram NOUN
le landau

prawn NOUN
la crevette

prawn cocktail NOUN
le cocktail de crevettes

to **pray** VERB
prier ◊ *to pray for something* prier pour quelque chose

prayer NOUN
la prière

precaution NOUN
la précaution
♦ **to take precautions** prendre ses précautions

preceding ADJECTIVE
précédent

precinct NOUN
♦ **a shopping precinct** un centre commercial
♦ **a pedestrian precinct** une zone piétonnière

precious ADJECTIVE
précieux MASC
précieuse FEM

precise ADJECTIVE
précis ◊ *at that precise moment* à cet instant précis

precisely ADVERB
précisément ◊ *Precisely!* Précisément!
♦ **at 10 a.m. precisely** à dix heures précises

to **predict** VERB
prédire

predictable ADJECTIVE
prévisible

prefect NOUN

> ⓘ *French schools do not have prefects. You could explain what a prefect is using the example given.*

♦ **My sister's a prefect.** Ma sœur est en dernière année et est chargée de maintenir la discipline.

to **prefer** VERB
préférer ◊ *Which would you prefer?* Lequel préfères-tu? ◊ *I prefer French to chemistry.* Je préfère le français à la chimie.

preference NOUN
la préférence

pregnant ADJECTIVE
enceinte ◊ *She's six months pregnant.* Elle est enceinte de six mois.

prehistoric ADJECTIVE
préhistorique

prejudice NOUN
1 le préjugé ◊ *That's just a prejudice.* C'est un préjugé.
2 les préjugés MASC PL ◊ *There's a lot of racial prejudice.* Il y a beaucoup de préjugés raciaux.

prejudiced ADJECTIVE
♦ **to be prejudiced against somebody** avoir des préjugés contre quelqu'un

premature ADJECTIVE
prématuré
♦ **a premature baby** un prématuré

Premier League NOUN
la première division ◊ *in the Premier League* en première division

premises PL NOUN
les locaux MASC PL ◊ *They're moving to new premises.* Ils vont occuper de nouveaux locaux.

premonition NOUN
la prémonition

preoccupied ADJECTIVE
préoccupé

prep NOUN
les devoirs MASC PL (*homework*)
◊ *history prep* les devoirs d'histoire

preparation NOUN
la préparation

to **prepare** VERB
préparer ◊ *She has to prepare lessons in the evening.* Elle doit préparer ses cours le soir.
♦ **to prepare for something** se préparer pour quelque chose ◊ *We're preparing for our skiing holiday.* Nous nous préparons pour nos vacances à la neige.

prepared ADJECTIVE
♦ **to be prepared to do something** être prêt à faire quelque chose ◊ *I'm prepared to help you.* Je suis prêt à t'aider.

prep school NOUN
l' école primaire privée FEM

Presbyterian NOUN
see also **Presbyterian** ADJECTIVE
le presbytérien
la presbytérienne

Presbyterian ADJECTIVE
see also **Presbyterian** NOUN
presbytérien MASC
presbytérienne FEM

to **prescribe** VERB
prescrire

prescription NOUN
l' ordonnance FEM ◊ *You can't get it without a prescription.* On ne peut pas se le procurer sans ordonnance.

presence NOUN
la présence
◆**presence of mind** présence d'esprit

present ADJECTIVE
see also **present** NOUN, VERB
[1] (*in attendance*)
présent ◊ *He wasn't present at the meeting.* Il n'était pas présent à la réunion.
[2] (*current*)
actuel MASC
actuelle FEM
◊ *the present situation* la situation actuelle
◆**the present tense** le présent

present NOUN
see also **present** ADJECTIVE, VERB
[1] (*gift*)
le cadeau
(les cadeaux PL)
◊ *I'm going to buy presents.* Je vais acheter des cadeaux.
◆**to give somebody a present** offrir un cadeau à quelqu'un
[2] (*time*)
le présent ◊ *up to the present* jusqu'à présent
◆**for the present** pour l'instant
◆**at present** en ce moment

to **present** VERB
see also **present** ADJECTIVE, NOUN
◆**to present somebody with something** (*prize, medal*) remettre quelque chose à quelqu'un

presenter NOUN
(*on TV*)
le présentateur
la présentatrice

presently ADVERB
[1] bientôt (*soon*) ◊ *You'll feel better presently.* Tu vas bientôt te sentir mieux.

[2] actuellement (*at present*) ◊ *They're presently on tour.* Ils sont actuellement en tournée.

president NOUN
le président
la présidente

press NOUN
see also **press** VERB
la presse
◆**a press conference** une conférence de presse

to **press** VERB
see also **press** NOUN
[1] appuyer ◊ *Don't press too hard!* N'appuie pas trop fort!
[2] appuyer sur ◊ *He pressed the accelerator.* Il a appuyé sur l'accélérateur.

pressed ADJECTIVE
◆**We are pressed for time.** Le temps nous manque.

press-up NOUN
◆**to do press-ups** faire des pompes ◊ *I do twenty press-ups every morning.* Je fais vingt pompes tous les matins.

pressure NOUN
see also **pressure** VERB
la pression ◊ *He's under a lot of pressure at work.* Il est sous pression au travail.
◆**a pressure group** un groupe de pression

to **pressure** VERB
see also **pressure** NOUN
faire pression sur ◊ *My parents are pressuring me.* Mes parents font pression sur moi.

to **pressurize** VERB
◆**to pressurize somebody to do something** faire pression sur quelqu'un pour qu'il fasse quelque chose ◊ *My parents are pressurizing me to stay on at school.* Mes parents font pression sur moi pour que je reste à l'école.

prestige NOUN
le prestige

prestigious ADJECTIVE
prestigieux MASC
prestigieuse FEM

presumably ADVERB
vraisemblablement

to **presume** VERB
supposer ◊ *I presume so.* Je suppose que oui.

to **pretend** VERB
◆**to pretend to do something** faire semblant de faire quelque chose ◊ *He*

P

☞

pretended to be asleep. Il faisait semblant de dormir.

*Be careful not to translate **to pretend** by **prétendre**.*

pretty ADJECTIVE, ADVERB
[1] joli ◊ *She's very pretty.* Elle est très jolie.
[2] plutôt (*rather*) ◊ *That film was pretty bad.* Ce film était plutôt mauvais.
◆ **The weather was pretty awful.** Il faisait un temps minable.
◆ **It's pretty much the same.** C'est pratiquement la même chose.

to **prevent** VERB
empêcher
◆ **to prevent somebody from doing something** empêcher quelqu'un de faire quelque chose ◊ *They try to prevent us from smoking.* Ils essaient de nous empêcher de fumer.

previous ADJECTIVE
précédent

previously ADVERB
auparavant

prey NOUN
la proie ◊ *a bird of prey* un oiseau de proie

price NOUN
le prix

price list NOUN
la liste des prix

to **prick** VERB
piquer ◊ *I've pricked my finger.* Je me suis piqué le doigt.

pride NOUN
la fierté

priest NOUN
le prêtre ◊ *He's a priest.* Il est prêtre.

primarily ADVERB
principalement

primary ADJECTIVE
principal
(principaux MASC PL)

primary school NOUN
l' école primaire FEM ◊ *She's still at primary school.* Elle est encore à l'école primaire.

prime minister NOUN
le Premier ministre

primitive ADJECTIVE
primitif MASC
primitive FEM

prince NOUN
le prince ◊ *the Prince of Wales* le prince de Galles

princess NOUN
la princesse ◊ *Princess Anne* la princesse Anne

principal ADJECTIVE
| see also **principal** NOUN |
principal
(principaux MASC PL)

principal NOUN
| see also **principal** ADJECTIVE |
le principal (*of college*)

principle NOUN
le principe
(les principaux PL)
◆ **on principle** par principe

print NOUN
[1] le tirage (*photo*) ◊ *colour prints* des tirages en couleur
[2] les caractères MASC PL (*letters*) ◊ *in small print* en petits caractères
[3] l' empreinte digitale FEM (*fingerprint*)
[4] la gravure (*picture*) ◊ *a framed print* une gravure encadrée

printer NOUN
l' imprimante FEM (*machine*)

printout NOUN
le tirage

priority NOUN
la priorité

prison NOUN
la prison
◆ **in prison** en prison

prisoner NOUN
le prisonnier
la prisonnière

prison officer NOUN
le gardien de prison
la gardienne de prison

privacy NOUN
l' intimité FEM

private ADJECTIVE
privé ◊ *a private school* une école privée
◆ **private property** la propriété privée
◆ **"private"** (*on envelope*) "personnel"
◆ **a private bathroom** une salle de bain individuelle
◆ **I have private lessons.** Je prends des cours particuliers.

to **privatize** VERB
privatiser

privilege NOUN
le privilège

prize NOUN
le prix ◊ *to win a prize* gagner un prix

prize-giving NOUN
la distribution des prix

prizewinner NOUN
le gagnant
la gagnante

pro NOUN
- **the pros and cons** le pour et le contre
  ◊ *We weighed up the pros and cons.*
  Nous avons pesé le pour et le contre.

probability NOUN
la <u>probabilité</u>

probable ADJECTIVE
<u>probable</u>

probably ADVERB
<u>probablement</u> ◊ *probably not*
probablement pas

problem NOUN
le <u>problème</u> ◊ *No problem!* Pas de
problème!

proceeds PL NOUN
la <u>recette</u> SING

process NOUN
le <u>processus</u> ◊ *the peace process* le
processus de paix
- **to be in the process of doing
  something** être en train de faire
  quelque chose ◊ *We're in the process
  of painting the kitchen.* Nous sommes
  en train de peindre la cuisine.

procession NOUN
la <u>procession</u> (*religious*)

to **produce** VERB
[1] <u>produire</u> (*manufacture*)
[2] <u>monter</u> (*play, show*)

producer NOUN
(*of play, show*)
le <u>metteur en scène</u>
(les metteurs en scène PL)

product NOUN
le <u>produit</u>

production NOUN
[1] la <u>production</u> ◊ *They're increasing
production of luxury models.* Ils
augmentent la production des
modèles de luxe.
[2] la <u>mise en scène</u> (*play, show*) ◊ *a
production of "Hamlet"* une mise en
scène de "Hamlet"

profession NOUN
la <u>profession</u>

professional NOUN
see also **professional** ADJECTIVE
le <u>professionnel</u>
la <u>professionnelle</u>

professional ADJECTIVE
see also **professional** NOUN
(*player*)
<u>professionnel</u> MASC
<u>professionnelle</u> FEM
◊ *a professional musician* un musicien
professionnel
- **a very professional piece of work** un
vrai travail de professionnel

professionally ADVERB

- **She sings professionally.** C'est une
chanteuse professionnelle.

professor NOUN
le <u>professeur d'université</u>
- **He's the French professor.** Il est
titulaire de la chaire de français.

profit NOUN
le <u>bénéfice</u>

profitable ADJECTIVE
<u>rentable</u>

program NOUN
see also **program** VERB
le <u>programme</u> ◊ *a computer
program* un programme informatique
- **a TV program** US une émission de
télévision

to **program** VERB
see also **program** NOUN
<u>programmer</u> (*computer*)

programme NOUN
[1] l' <u>émission</u> FEM (*on TV, radio*)
[2] le <u>programme</u> (*of events*)

programmer NOUN
le <u>programmeur</u>
la <u>programmeuse</u>
◊ *She's a programmer.* Elle est
programmeuse.

programming NOUN
la <u>programmation</u>

progress NOUN
le <u>progrès</u> ◊ *You're making progress!*
Vous faites des progrès!

to **prohibit** VERB
<u>interdire</u> ◊ *Smoking is prohibited.* Il
est interdit de fumer.

project NOUN
[1] le <u>projet</u> (*plan*) ◊ *a development
project* un projet de développement
[2] le <u>dossier</u> (*research*) ◊ *I'm doing a
project on education in France.* Je
prépare un dossier sur l'éducation en
France.

projector NOUN
le <u>projecteur</u>

promenade NOUN
le <u>front de mer</u>

promise NOUN
see also **promise** VERB
la <u>promesse</u> ◊ *He made me a
promise.* Il m'a fait une promesse.
- **That's a promise!** C'est promis!

to **promise** VERB
see also **promise** NOUN
<u>promettre</u> ◊ *She promised to write.*
Elle a promis d'écrire. ◊ *I'll write, I
promise!* J'écrirai, c'est promis!

promising ADJECTIVE

P

☞

◆**a promising player** un joueur qui a de l'avenir

to **promote** VERB
◆**to be promoted** être promu ◊ *She was promoted after six months.* Elle a été promue au bout de six mois.

promotion NOUN
la promotion

prompt ADJECTIVE, ADVERB
rapide ◊ *a prompt reply* une réponse rapide
◆**at eight o'clock prompt** à huit heures précises

promptly ADVERB
◆**We left promptly at seven.** Nous sommes partis à sept heures précises.

pronoun NOUN
le pronom

to **pronounce** VERB
prononcer ◊ *How do you pronounce that word?* Comment est-ce qu'on prononce ce mot?

pronunciation NOUN
la prononciation

proof NOUN
la preuve

proper ADJECTIVE
[1] vrai (*genuine*) ◊ *proper French bread* du vrai pain français ◊ *We didn't have a proper lunch, just sandwiches.* Nous n'avons pas pris de vrai repas, juste des sandwichs.
◆**It's difficult to get a proper job.** Il est difficile de trouver un travail correct.
[2] adéquat ◊ *You have to have the proper equipment.* Il faut avoir l'équipement adéquat. ◊ *We need proper training.* Il nous faut une formation adéquate.
◆**If you had come at the proper time ...** Si tu étais venu à l'heure dite ...

properly ADVERB
[1] comme il faut (*correctly*) ◊ *You're not doing it properly.* Tu ne t'y prends pas comme il faut.
[2] convenablement (*appropriately*) ◊ *Dress properly for your interview.* Habille-toi convenablement pour ton entretien.

property NOUN
la propriété
◆**"private property"** "propriété privée"
◆**stolen property** les objets volés MASC PL

proportional ADJECTIVE
proportionnel MASC
proportionnelle FEM

◊ *proportional representation* la représentation proportionnelle

proposal NOUN
la proposition (*suggestion*)

to **propose** VERB
proposer ◊ *I propose a new plan.* Je propose un changement de programme.
◆**to propose to do something** avoir l'intention de faire quelque chose ◊ *What do you propose to do?* Qu'est-ce que tu as l'intention de faire?
◆**to propose to somebody** (*for marriage*) demander quelqu'un en mariage ◊ *He proposed to her at the restaurant.* Il l'a demandée en mariage au restaurant.

to **prosecute** VERB
poursuivre en justice ◊ *They were prosecuted for murder.* Ils ont été poursuivis en justice pour meutre.
◆**"Trespassers will be prosecuted"** "Défense d'entrer sous peine de poursuites"

prospect NOUN
la perspective ◊ *It'll improve my career prospects.* Ça va améliorer mes perspectives d'avenir.

prospectus NOUN
le prospectus

prostitute NOUN
la prostituée
◆**a male prostitute** un prostitué

to **protect** VERB
protéger

protection NOUN
la protection

protein NOUN
la protéine

protest NOUN
see also **protest** VERB
la protestation ◊ *He ignored their protests.* Il a ignoré leurs protestations.
◆**a protest march** une manifestation

to **protest** VERB
see also **protest** NOUN
protester

Protestant NOUN
see also **Protestant** ADJECTIVE
le protestant
la protestante
◊ *I'm a Protestant.* Je suis protestant.

Protestant ADJECTIVE
see also **Protestant** NOUN
protestant ◊ *a Protestant church* une église protestante

protester NOUN

le <u>manifestant</u>
la <u>manifestante</u>

proud ADJECTIVE
<u>fier</u> MASC
<u>fière</u> FEM
◊ *Her parents are proud of her.* Ses parents sont fiers d'elle.

to **prove** VERB
<u>prouver</u> ◊ *The police couldn't prove it.* La police n'a pas pu le prouver.

proverb NOUN
le <u>proverbe</u>

to **provide** VERB
<u>fournir</u>
♦ **to provide somebody with something** fournir quelque chose à quelqu'un ◊ *They provided us with maps.* Ils nous ont fourni des cartes.

to **provide for** VERB
<u>subvenir aux besoins de</u> ◊ *He can't provide for his family any more.* Il ne peut plus subvenir aux besoins de sa famille.

provided CONJUNCTION
<u>à condition que</u>

à condition que has to be followed by the subjunctive.

◊ *He'll play in the next match provided he's fit.* Il jouera dans le prochain match, à condition qu'il soit en forme.

provisional ADJECTIVE
<u>provisoire</u>

prowler NOUN
le <u>rôdeur</u>
la <u>rôdeuse</u>

prune NOUN
le <u>pruneau</u>
(les pruneaux PL)

to **pry** VERB
♦ **He's always prying into other people's affairs.** Il met toujours son nez dans les affaires des autres.

pseudonym NOUN
le <u>pseudonyme</u>

psychiatrist NOUN
le/la <u>psychiatre</u> ◊ *She's a psychiatrist.* Elle est psychiatre.

psychoanalyst NOUN
le/la <u>psychanalyste</u>

psychological ADJECTIVE
<u>psychologique</u>

psychologist NOUN
le/la <u>psychologue</u> ◊ *He's a psychologist.* Il est psychologue.

psychology NOUN
la <u>psychologie</u>

PTO ABBREVIATION (= *please turn over*)
<u>T.S.V.P.</u> (= tournez, s'il vous plaît)

pub NOUN
le <u>pub</u>

public NOUN
see also **public** ADJECTIVE
le <u>public</u> ◊ *open to the public* ouvert au public
♦ **in public** en public

public ADJECTIVE
see also **public** NOUN
<u>public</u> MASC
<u>publique</u> FEM
♦ **a public holiday** un jour férié
♦ **public opinion** l'opinion publique FEM
♦ **the public address system** les haut-parleurs MASC PL

publican NOUN
le <u>patron de pub</u>
la <u>patronne de pub</u>
♦ **My uncle's a publican.** Mon oncle tient un pub.

publicity NOUN
la <u>publicité</u>

public school NOUN
l'<u>école privée</u> FEM

public transport NOUN
les <u>transports en commun</u> MASC PL

to **publish** VERB
<u>publier</u>

publisher NOUN
l'<u>éditeur</u> MASC

pudding NOUN
le <u>dessert</u> ◊ *What's for pudding?* Qu'est-ce qu'il y a comme dessert?
♦ **rice pudding** le riz au lait
♦ **black pudding** le boudin noir

puddle NOUN
la <u>flaque</u>

puff pastry NOUN
la <u>pâte feuilletée</u>

to **pull** VERB
<u>tirer</u> ◊ *Pull!* Tirez!
♦ **He pulled the trigger.** Il a appuyé sur la gâchette.
♦ **to pull a muscle** se froisser un muscle ◊ *I pulled a muscle when I was training.* Je me suis froissé un muscle à l'entraînement.
♦ **You're pulling my leg!** Tu me fais marcher!
♦ **to pull down** démolir
♦ **to pull out (1)** arracher (*tooth, weed*)
♦ **to pull out (2)** déboîter (*car*) ◊ *The car pulled out to overtake.* La voiture a déboîté pour doubler.
♦ **to pull out (3)** se retirer (*withdraw*) ◊ *She pulled out of the tournament.* Elle s'est retirée du tournoi.

P

☞

♦**to pull through** s'en sortir ◊ *They think he'll pull through.* Ils pensent qu'il va s'en sortir.

♦**to pull up** s'arrêter (*car*) ◊ *A black car pulled up beside me.* Une voiture noire s'est arrêtée à côté de moi.

pullover NOUN
le pull-over

pulse NOUN
le pouls ◊ *The nurse felt his pulse.* L'infirmière a pris son pouls.

pulses PL NOUN
les légumes secs MASC PL

pump NOUN
  see also **pump** VERB
  [1] la pompe ◊ *a bicycle pump* une pompe à vélo ◊ *a petrol pump* une pompe à essence
  [2] le chausson de gym (*shoe*)

to **pump** VERB
  see also **pump** NOUN
  pomper
♦**to pump up** gonfler (*tyre*)

pumpkin NOUN
le potiron

punch NOUN
  see also **punch** VERB
  [1] le coup de poing (*blow*) ◊ *He gave me a punch.* Il m'a donné un coup de poing.
  [2] le punch (*drink*)

to **punch** VERB
  see also **punch** NOUN
  [1] donner un coup de poing à (*hit*) ◊ *He punched me!* Il m'a donné un coup de poing!
  [2] composter (*in ticket machine*) ◊ *Punch your ticket before you get on the train.* Compostez votre billet avant de monter dans le train.
  [3] poinçonner (*by hand*) ◊ *He forgot to punch my ticket.* Il a oublié de poinçonner mon billet.

punch-up NOUN
la bagarre (*informal*)

punctual ADJECTIVE
ponctuel MASC
ponctuelle FEM

punctuation NOUN
la ponctuation

puncture NOUN
la crevaison ◊ *I had to mend a puncture.* J'ai dû réparer une crevaison.
♦**to have a puncture** crever ◊ *I had a puncture on the motorway.* J'ai crevé sur l'autoroute.

to **punish** VERB
punir

♦**to punish somebody for something** punir quelqu'un de quelque chose

♦**to punish somebody for doing something** punir quelqu'un d'avoir fait quelque chose

punishment NOUN
la punition

punk NOUN
le/la punk (*person*)
♦**a punk rock band** un groupe de punk rock

pupil NOUN
l' élève MASC/FEM

puppet NOUN
la marionnette

puppy NOUN
le chiot

to **purchase** VERB
acheter

pure ADJECTIVE
pur ◊ *pure orange juice* du pur jus d'orange ◊ *He's doing pure maths.* Il fait des maths pures.

purple ADJECTIVE
violet MASC
violette FEM

purpose NOUN
le but ◊ *What is the purpose of these changes?* Quel est le but de ces changements? ◊ *his purpose in life* son but dans la vie
♦**on purpose** exprès ◊ *He did it on purpose.* Il l'a fait exprès.

to **purr** VERB
ronronner

purse NOUN
  [1] le porte-monnaie (les porte-monnaie PL)
  [2] (*handbag*) US
  le sac à main (les sacs à main PL)

to **pursue** VERB
poursuivre

pursuit NOUN
l' activité FEM ◊ *outdoor pursuits* les activités de plein air

push NOUN
  see also **push** VERB
♦**to give somebody a push** pousser quelqu'un ◊ *He gave me a push.* Il m'a poussé.

to **push** VERB
  see also **push** NOUN
  [1] pousser ◊ *Don't push!* Arrêtez de pousser!
  [2] appuyer sur (*button*)
♦**to push somebody to do something** pousser quelqu'un à faire quelque

chose ◊ *My parents are pushing me to go to university.* Mes parents me poussent à entrer à l'université.
♦**to push drugs** revendre de la drogue
♦**Push off!** Dégage!

to **push around** VERB
bousculer ◊ *He likes pushing people around.* Il aime bien bousculer les gens.

to **push through** VERB
se frayer un passage ◊ *The ambulancemen pushed through the crowd.* Les ambulanciers se sont frayé un passage dans la foule.
♦**I pushed my way through.** Je me suis frayé un passage.

pushchair NOUN
la poussette

pusher NOUN
(*of drugs*)
le revendeur
la revendeuse

push-up NOUN
la pompe
♦**to do push-ups** faire des pompes

to **put** VERB
[1] mettre (*place*) ◊ *Where shall I put my things?* Où est-ce que je peux mettre mes affaires? ◊ *She's putting the baby to bed.* Elle met le bébé au lit.
[2] écrire (*write*) ◊ *Don't forget to put your name on the paper.* N'oubliez pas d'écrire votre nom sur la feuille.

to **put across** VERB
communiquer ◊ *He finds it hard to put his ideas across.* Il a du mal à communiquer ses idées.

to **put aside** VERB
mettre de côté ◊ *Can you put this aside for me till tomorrow?* Est-ce que vous pouvez mettre ça de côté pour moi jusqu'à demain?

to **put away** VERB
ranger ◊ *Can you put away the dishes, please?* Tu peux ranger la vaisselle, s'il te plaît?

to **put back** VERB
remettre en place (*replace*) ◊ *Put it back when you've finished with it.* Remets-le en place une fois que tu auras fini.

to **put down** VERB
[1] poser ◊ *I'll put these bags down for a minute.* Je vais poser ces sacs une minute.
[2] noter (*in writing*) ◊ *I've put down a few ideas.* J'ai noté quelques idées.

♦**to have an animal put down** faire piquer un animal ◊ *We had to have our old dog put down.* Nous avons dû faire piquer notre vieux chien.

to **put forward** VERB
[1] avancer (*clock*) ◊ *Next week it'll be time to put the clocks forward an hour.* La semaine prochaine, il sera temps d'avancer les montres d'une heure.
[2] proposer (*idea, argument*) ◊ *to put forward a suggestion* proposer une suggestion

to **put in** VERB
installer (*install*) ◊ *We're going to get central heating put in.* Nous allons faire installer le chauffage central.
♦**He has put in a lot of work on this project.** Il a fourni beaucoup de travail pour ce projet.

to **put off** VERB
[1] éteindre (*switch off*) ◊ *Shall I put the light off?* Est-ce que j'éteins la lumière?
[2] remettre à plus tard (*postpone*) ◊ *I keep putting it off.* Je n'arrête pas de remettre ça à plus tard.
[3] déranger (*distract*) ◊ *Stop putting me off!* Arrête de me déranger!
[4] décourager (*discourage*) ◊ *He's not easily put off.* Il ne se laisse pas facilement décourager.

to **put on** VERB
[1] mettre (*clothes, lipstick, record*) ◊ *I'll put my coat on.* Je vais mettre mon manteau.
[2] allumer (*light, heater, telly*) ◊ *Shall I put the heater on?* J'allume le chauffage?
[3] monter (*play, show*) ◊ *We're putting on "Bugsy Malone".* Nous sommes en train de monter "Bugsy Malone".
[4] mettre à cuire ◊ *I'll put the potatoes on.* Je vais mettre les pommes de terre à cuire.
♦**to put on weight** grossir ◊ *He's put on a lot of weight.* Il a beaucoup grossi.

to **put out** VERB
éteindre (*light, cigarette, fire*) ◊ *It took them five hours to put out the fire.* Ils ont mis cinq heures à éteindre l'incendie.

to **put through** VERB
passer ◊ *Can you put me through to the manager?* Est-ce que vous pouvez me passer le directeur?
♦**I'm putting you through.** Je vous passe la communication.

P

to **put up** VERB

1 mettre (*pin up*) ◊ *The poster's great. I'll put it up on my wall.* Le poster est super. Je vais le mettre au mur.

2 monter (*tent*) ◊ *We put up our tent in a field.* Nous avons monté la tente dans un champ.

3 augmenter (*price*) ◊ *They've put up the price.* Ils ont augmenté le prix.

4 héberger (*accommodate*) ◊ *My friend will put me up for the night.* Mon ami va m'héberger pour la nuit.

♦ **to put one's hand up** lever la main ◊ *If you have any questions, put up your hand.* Si vous avez une question, levez la main.

♦ **to put up with something** supporter quelque chose ◊ *I'm not going to put up with it any longer.* Je ne vais pas supporter ça plus longtemps.

puzzle NOUN
le puzzle (*jigsaw*)

puzzled ADJECTIVE
perplexe ◊ *You look puzzled!* Tu as l'air perplexe!

puzzling ADJECTIVE
déconcertant

pyjamas PL NOUN
le pyjama SING ◊ *my pyjamas* mon pyjama
♦ **a pair of pyjamas** un pyjama
♦ **a pyjama top** un haut de pyjama

pyramid NOUN
la pyramide

Pyrenees PL NOUN
les Pyrénées FEM PL
♦ **in the Pyrenees** dans les Pyrénées
♦ **We went to the Pyrenees.** Nous sommes allés dans les Pyrénées.

Q

quaint ADJECTIVE
  pittoresque (*house, village*)

qualification NOUN
  le diplôme ◊ *to leave school without
  any qualifications* quitter l'école sans
  aucun diplôme
  ♦ **vocational qualifications** des
  qualifications professionnelles

qualified ADJECTIVE
  ⬜1 qualifié (*trained*) ◊ *a qualified
  driving instructor* un moniteur
  d'auto-école qualifié
  ⬜2 diplômé (*nurse, teacher*) ◊ *a
  qualified nurse* une infirmière
  diplômée

to **qualify** VERB
  ⬜1 obtenir son diplôme (*for job*)
  ◊ *She qualified as a teacher last year.*
  Elle a obtenu son diplôme de
  professeur l'année dernière.
  ⬜2 se qualifier (*in competition*) ◊ *Our
  team didn't qualify.* Notre équipe ne
  s'est pas qualifiée.

quality NOUN
  la qualité ◊ *a good quality of life* une
  bonne qualité de vie ◊ *good-quality
  ingredients* des ingrédients de bonne
  qualité ◊ *She's got lots of good
  qualities.* Elle a beaucoup de qualités.

quantity NOUN
  la quantité

quarantine NOUN
  la quarantaine ◊ *in quarantine* en
  quarantaine

quarrel NOUN
  | *see also* **quarrel** VERB |
  la dispute

to **quarrel** VERB
  | *see also* **quarrel** NOUN |
  se disputer

quarry NOUN
  la carrière (*for stone*)

quarter NOUN
  le quart
  ♦ **three quarters** trois quarts
  ♦ **a quarter of an hour** un quart d'heure
  ◊ *three quarters of an hour* trois
  quarts d'heure
  ♦ **a quarter past ten** dix heures et quart
  ♦ **a quarter to eleven** onze heures
  moins le quart

quarter final NOUN
  le quart de finale

quartet NOUN

le quatuor ◊ *a string quartet* un
quatuor à cordes

quay NOUN
  le quai

queasy ADJECTIVE
  ♦ **to feel queasy** avoir mal au cœur
  ◊ *I'm feeling queasy.* J'ai mal au
  cœur.

queen NOUN
  ⬜1 la reine ◊ *Queen Victoria* la reine
  Victoria
  ⬜2 la dame (*playing card*) ◊ *the queen
  of hearts* la dame de cœur
  ♦ **the Queen Mother** la reine mère

query NOUN
  | *see also* **query** VERB |
  la question

to **query** VERB
  | *see also* **query** NOUN |
  mettre en question ◊ *No one
  queried my decision.* Personne n'a
  mis en question ma décision.

question NOUN
  | *see also* **question** VERB |
  la question ◊ *Can I ask a question?*
  Est-ce que je peux poser une
  question? ◊ *That's a difficult question.*
  C'est une question difficile.
  ♦ **It's out of the question.** C'est hors de
  question.

to **question** VERB
  | *see also* **question** NOUN |
  interroger ◊ *He was questioned by
  the police.* Il a été interrogé par la
  police.

question mark NOUN
  le point d'interrogation

questionnaire NOUN
  le questionnaire

queue NOUN
  | *see also* **queue** VERB |
  la queue

to **queue** VERB
  | *see also* **queue** NOUN |
  faire la queue
  ♦ **to queue for something** faire la queue
  pour avoir quelque chose ◊ *We had
  to queue for tickets.* Nous avons dû
  faire la queue pour avoir les billets.

quick ADJECTIVE, ADVERB
  rapide ◊ *a quick lunch* un déjeuner
  rapide ◊ *It's quicker by train.* C'est
  plus rapide en train.
  ♦ **Be quick!** Dépêche-toi!

☞

♦ **She's a quick learner.** Elle apprend vite.

♦ **Quick, phone the police!** Téléphonez vite à la police!

quickly ADVERB
vite ◊ *It was all over very quickly.* Ça s'est passé très vite.

quiet ADJECTIVE
1 (*not talkative or noisy*)
silencieux MASC
silencieuse FEM
◊ *You're very quiet today.* Tu es bien silencieux aujourd'hui. ◊ *The engine's very quiet.* Le moteur est très silencieux.
2 (*peaceful*)
tranquille ◊ *a quiet little town* une petite ville tranquille ◊ *a quiet weekend* un week-end tranquille

♦ **Be quiet!** Tais-toi!

♦ **Quiet!** Silence!

quietly ADVERB
1 doucement (*speak*) ◊ *"She's dead,"
he said quietly.* "Elle est morte" dit-il doucement.
2 silencieusement (*move*) ◊ *He quietly opened the door.* Il a ouvert la porte sans faire de bruit.

quilt NOUN
la couette (*duvet*)

to **quit** VERB
quitter (*place, premises, job*) ◊ *She's decided to quit her job.* Elle a décidé de quitter son emploi.

♦ **I quit!** J'abandonne!

quite ADVERB
1 assez (*rather*) ◊ *It's quite warm*

today. Il fait assez bon aujourd'hui.
◊ *I quite liked the film, but...* J'ai trouvé le film assez bon, mais...
2 tout à fait (*entirely*) ◊ *I'm not quite sure.* Je n'en suis pas tout à fait sûr.
◊ *It's not quite the same.* Ce n'est pas tout à fait la même chose.

♦ **quite good** pas mal

♦ **I've been there quite a lot.** J'y suis allé pas mal de fois.

♦ **quite a lot of money** pas mal d'argent

♦ **It costs quite a lot to go abroad.** Ça coûte assez cher d'aller à l'étranger.

♦ **It's quite a long way.** C'est assez loin.

♦ **It was quite a shock.** Ça a été un sacré choc.

♦ **There were quite a few people there.** Il y avait pas mal de gens.

quiz NOUN
le jeu-concours

quota NOUN
le quota

quotation NOUN
la citation ◊ *a quotation from Shakespeare* une citation de Shakespeare

quote NOUN
see also **quote** VERB
la citation ◊ *a Shakespeare quote* une citation de Shakespeare

♦ **quotes** (*quotation marks*) les guillemets MASC ◊ *in quotes* entre guillemets

to **quote** VERB
see also **quote** NOUN
citer ◊ *He's always quoting Shakespeare.* Il n'arrête pas de citer Shakespeare.

R

rabbi NOUN
le <u>rabbin</u>

rabbit NOUN
le <u>lapin</u>
♦ **a rabbit hutch** un clapier

rabies NOUN
la <u>rage</u>
♦ **a dog with rabies** un chien enragé

race NOUN
see also **race** VERB
1 la <u>course</u> (*sport*) ◊ *a cycle race*
une course cycliste
2 la <u>race</u> (*species*) ◊ *the human race*
la race humaine
♦ **race relations** les relations
interraciales FEM

to **race** VERB
see also **race** NOUN
1 <u>courir</u> ◊ *We raced to catch the*
bus. Nous avons couru pour attraper
le bus.
2 <u>faire la course</u> (*have a race*)
♦ **I'll race you!** On fait la course!

racecourse NOUN
le <u>champ de courses</u>

racehorse NOUN
le <u>cheval de course</u>
(les chevaux de course PL)

racer NOUN
le <u>vélo de course</u> (*bike*)

racetrack NOUN
la <u>piste</u>

racial ADJECTIVE
<u>racial</u>
(raciaux MASC PL)
◊ *racial discrimination* la
discrimination raciale

racing car NOUN
la <u>voiture de course</u>

racing driver NOUN
le <u>pilote de course</u>

racism NOUN
le <u>racisme</u>

racist ADJECTIVE
see also **racist** NOUN
<u>raciste</u>

racist NOUN
see also **racist** ADJECTIVE
le/la <u>raciste</u>

rack NOUN
(*for luggage*)
le <u>porte-bagages</u>
(les porte-bagages PL)

racket NOUN

1 la <u>raquette</u> (*for sport*) ◊ *my tennis*
racket ma raquette de tennis
2 le <u>boucan</u> (*noise*) ◊ *They're making*
a terrible racket. Ils font un boucan
de tous les diables. (*informal*)

racquet NOUN
la <u>raquette</u>

radar NOUN
le <u>radar</u>

radiation NOUN
la <u>radiation</u>

radiator NOUN
le <u>radiateur</u>

radio NOUN
la <u>radio</u>
♦ **on the radio** à la radio
♦ **a radio station** une station de radio

radioactive ADJECTIVE
<u>radioactif</u> MASC
<u>radioactive</u> FEM

radio cassette NOUN
le <u>radiocassette</u>

radio-controlled ADJECTIVE
<u>téléguidé</u> (*model plane, car*)

radish NOUN
le <u>radis</u>

RAF NOUN (= *Royal Air Force*)
la <u>R.A.F.</u> ◊ *He's in the RAF.* Il est
dans la R.A.F.

raffle NOUN
la <u>tombola</u> ◊ *a raffle ticket* un billet
de tombola

raft NOUN
le <u>radeau</u>
(les radeaux PL)

rag NOUN
le <u>chiffon</u> ◊ *a piece of rag* un chiffon
♦ **dressed in rags** en haillons

rage NOUN
la <u>rage</u> ◊ *mad with rage* fou de rage
♦ **to be in a rage** être furieux ◊ *She was*
in a rage. Elle était furieuse.
♦ **It's all the rage.** Ça fait fureur.

raid NOUN
see also **raid** VERB
1 (*burglary*)
le <u>hold-up</u>
(les hold-up PL)
◊ *There was a bank raid near my*
house. Il y a eu un hold-up dans une
banque près de chez moi.
2 la <u>descente</u> ◊ *a police raid* une
descente de police

to **raid** VERB

see also **raid** NOUN

faire une descente dans (*police*)
◊ *The police raided the club.* La police
a fait une descente dans le club.

rail NOUN

[1] la rampe (*on stairs*)
[2] la balustrade (*on bridge, balcony*)
◊ *Don't lean over the rail!* Ne vous
penchez pas sur la balustrade!
[3] le rail (*on railway line*)
♦**by rail** en train

railcard NOUN

la carte de chemin de fer ◊ *a young
person's railcard* une carte de chemin
de fer tarif jeune

railroad NOUN US

le chemin de fer
♦**a railroad line** une ligne de chemin de
fer
♦**a railroad station** une gare

railway NOUN

le chemin de fer ◊ *the privatization
of the railways* la privatisation des
chemins de fer
♦**a railway line** une ligne de chemin de
fer
♦**a railway station** une gare

rain NOUN

see also **rain** VERB

la pluie ◊ *in the rain* sous la pluie

to **rain** VERB

see also **rain** NOUN

pleuvoir ◊ *It rains a lot here.* Il pleut
beaucoup par ici.
♦**It's raining.** Il pleut.

rainbow NOUN

l' arc-en-ciel MASC
(les arcs-en-ciel PL)

raincoat NOUN

l' imperméable MASC

rainforest NOUN

la forêt tropicale humide

rainy ADJECTIVE

pluvieux MASC
pluvieuse FEM

to **raise** VERB

[1] lever (*lift*) ◊ *He raised his hand.* Il
a levé la main.
[2] améliorer (*improve*) ◊ *They want to
raise standards in schools.* Ils veulent
améliorer le niveau dans les écoles.
♦**to raise money** collecter des fonds
◊ *The school is raising money for a
new gym.* L'école collecte des fonds
pour un nouveau gymnase.

raisin NOUN

le raisin sec

rake NOUN

le râteau

(les râteaux PL)

rally NOUN

[1] le rassemblement (*of people*)
[2] le rallye (*sport*) ◊ *a rally driver* un
pilote de rallye
[3] l' échange MASC (*in tennis*)

ram NOUN

see also **ram** VERB

le bélier (*sheep*)

to **ram** VERB

see also **ram** NOUN

emboutir (*vehicle*) ◊ *The thieves
rammed a police car.* Les voleurs ont
embouti une voiture de police.

Ramadan NOUN

le ramadan

ramble NOUN

la randonnée ◊ *to go for a ramble*
faire une randonnée

rambler NOUN

le randonneur
la randonneuse

ramp NOUN

la rampe d'accès (*for wheelchairs*)

ran VERB *see* **run**

ranch NOUN

le ranch

random ADJECTIVE

♦**a random selection** une sélection
effectuée au hasard
♦**at random** au hasard ◊ *We picked the
number at random.* Nous avons
choisi le numéro au hasard.

rang VERB *see* **ring**

range NOUN

see also **range** VERB

le choix ◊ *a wide range of colours*
un grand choix de coloris
♦**a range of subjects** diverses matières
◊ *We study a range of subjects.* Nous
étudions diverses matières.
♦**a mountain range** une chaîne de
montagnes

to **range** VERB

see also **range** NOUN

♦**to range from ... to** se situer entre ...
et ◊ *Temperatures in summer range
from 20 to 35 degrees.* Les
températures estivales se situent
entre vingt et trente-cinq degrés.
♦**Tickets range from £2 to £20.** Les
billets coûtent entre deux et vingt
livres.

rank NOUN

see also **rank** VERB

♦**a taxi rank** une station de taxis

to **rank** VERB

see also **rank** NOUN

♦**He's ranked third in the United States.** Il est classé troisième aux Etats-Unis.

ransom NOUN
la rançon

rap NOUN
le rap (music)

rape NOUN
see also **rape** VERB
le viol

to **rape** VERB
see also **rape** NOUN
violer

rapids PL NOUN
les rapides MASC PL

rapist NOUN
le violeur

rare ADJECTIVE
[1] rare (unusual) ◊ a rare plant une plante rare
[2] saignant (steak)

rash NOUN
l' éruption de boutons FEM ◊ I've got a rash on my chest. J'ai une éruption de boutons sur la poitrine.

rasher NOUN
la tranche ◊ an egg and two rashers of bacon un œuf et deux tranches de bacon

raspberry NOUN
la framboise ◊ raspberry jam la confiture de framboises

rat NOUN
le rat

rate NOUN
see also **rate** VERB
[1] le tarif (price) ◊ There are reduced rates for students. Il y a des tarifs réduits pour les étudiants.
[2] le taux (level) ◊ the divorce rate le taux de divorce ◊ a high rate of interest un taux d'intérêt élevé

to **rate** VERB
see also **rate** NOUN
considérer comme
♦**He is rated the best.** Il est considéré comme le meilleur.
♦**How do you rate him?** Qu'est-ce que vous pensez de lui?

rather ADVERB
plutôt ◊ I was rather disappointed. J'étais plutôt déçu. ◊ £20! That's rather a lot! Vingt livres! C'est plutôt cher!
♦**rather a lot of** pas mal de ◊ I've got rather a lot of homework to do. J'ai pas mal de devoirs à faire.
♦**rather than** plutôt que ◊ We decided to camp, rather than stay at a hotel.

Nous avons décidé de camper plutôt que d'aller à l'hôtel.
♦**I'd rather ...** J'aimerais mieux ... ◊ I'd rather stay in tonight. J'aimerais mieux rester à la maison ce soir. ◊ Would you like a sweet? – I'd rather have an apple. Tu veux un bonbon? – J'aimerais mieux une pomme.

rattle NOUN
le hochet (for baby)

rattlesnake NOUN
le serpent à sonnette

to **rave** VERB
see also **rave** NOUN
s'extasier ◊ They raved about the film. Ils se sont extasiés sur le film.

rave NOUN
see also **rave** VERB
la rave (party)
♦**rave music** le rave

raven NOUN
le corbeau
(les corbeaux PL)

ravenous ADJECTIVE
♦**to be ravenous** avoir une faim de loup ◊ I'm ravenous! J'ai une faim de loup!

raving ADJECTIVE
♦**raving mad** fou à lier ◊ She's raving mad! Elle est folle à lier.

raw ADJECTIVE
cru (food)
♦**raw materials** les matières premières FEM

razor NOUN
le rasoir ◊ some disposable razors des rasoirs jetables
♦**a razor blade** une lame de rasoir

RE NOUN
l' éducation religieuse FEM

reach NOUN
see also **reach** VERB
♦**out of reach** hors de portée ◊ The light switch was out of reach. L'interrupteur était hors de portée.
♦**within easy reach of** à proximité de ◊ The hotel is within easy reach of the town centre. L'hôtel se trouve à proximité du centre-ville.

to **reach** VERB
see also **reach** NOUN
[1] arriver à ◊ We reached the hotel at 7 p.m. Nous sommes arrivés à l'hôtel à sept heures du soir.
♦**We hope to reach the final.** Nous espérons aller en finale.
[2] parvenir à (decision) ◊ Eventually they reached a decision. Ils sont finalement parvenus à une décision.

R

☞

◆**He reached for his gun.** Il a tendu la main pour prendre son revolver.

to **react** VERB
réagir

reaction NOUN
la réaction

reactor NOUN
le réacteur ◊ *a nuclear reactor* un réacteur nucléaire

to **read** VERB
lire ◊ *I don't read much.* Je ne lis pas beaucoup. ◊ *Have you read "Animal Farm"?* Est-ce que tu as lu "La ferme des animaux"? ◊ *Read the text out loud.* Lis le texte à haute voix.

to **read out** VERB
lire ◊ *He read out the article to me.* Il m'a lu l'article.

◆**to read out the results** annoncer les résultats

reader NOUN
(*person*)
le lecteur
la lectrice

readily ADVERB
volontiers ◊ *She readily agreed.* Elle a accepté volontiers.

reading NOUN
la lecture ◊ *Reading is one of my hobbies.* La lecture est l'une de mes activités favorites.

ready ADJECTIVE
prêt ◊ *She's nearly ready.* Elle est presque prête. ◊ *He's always ready to help.* Il est toujours prêt à rendre service.

◆**a ready meal** un plat cuisiné

◆**to get ready** se préparer ◊ *She's getting ready to go out.* Elle est en train de se préparer pour sortir.

◆**to get something ready** préparer quelque chose ◊ *He's getting the dinner ready.* Il est en train de préparer le dîner.

real ADJECTIVE
1 vrai ◊ *He wasn't a real policeman.* Ce n'était pas un vrai policier. ◊ *Her real name is Cordelia.* Son vrai nom est Cordelia.
2 véritable ◊ *It's real leather.* C'est du cuir véritable. ◊ *It was a real nightmare.* C'était un véritable cauchemar.

◆**in real life** dans la réalité

realistic ADJECTIVE
réaliste

reality NOUN
la réalité

to **realize** VERB

◆**to realize that ...** se rendre compte que ... ◊ *We realized that something was wrong.* Nous nous sommes rendu compte que quelque chose n'allait pas.

really ADVERB
vraiment ◊ *She's really nice.* Elle est vraiment sympathique. ◊ *Do you want to go? – Not really.* Tu veux y aller? – Pas vraiment.

◆**I'm learning German. – Really?** J'apprends l'allemand. – Ah bon?

◆**Do you really think so?** Tu es sûr?

realtor NOUN US
l' agent immobilier MASC

rear ADJECTIVE
see also **rear** NOUN
arrière MASC, FEM, PL ◊ *a rear wheel* une roue arrière

rear NOUN
see also **rear** ADJECTIVE
l' arrière MASC ◊ *at the rear of the train* à l'arrière du train

reason NOUN
la raison ◊ *There's no reason to think that ...* Il n'y a aucune raison de penser que ...

◆**for security reasons** pour des raisons de sécurité

◆**That was the main reason I went.** C'est surtout pour ça que j'y suis allé.

reasonable ADJECTIVE
1 raisonnable (*sensible*) ◊ *Be reasonable!* Sois raisonnable!
2 correct (*not bad*) ◊ *He wrote a reasonable essay.* Sa dissertation était correcte.

reasonably ADVERB
raisonnablement ◊ *The team played reasonably well.* L'équipe a joué raisonnablement bien.

◆**reasonably priced accommodation** un logement à un prix raisonnable

to **reassure** VERB
rassurer

reassuring ADJECTIVE
rassurant

rebellious ADJECTIVE
rebelle

receipt NOUN
le reçu

to **receive** VERB
recevoir

receiver NOUN
le combiné (*of phone*)

◆**to pick up the receiver** décrocher

recent ADJECTIVE
récent

recently ADVERB
ces derniers temps ◊ *I've been
doing a lot of training recently.* Je
me suis beaucoup entraîné ces
derniers temps.

reception NOUN
la réception ◊ *Please leave your key
at reception.* Merci de laisser votre
clé à la réception. ◊ *The reception
will be at a big hotel.* La réception
aura lieu dans un grand hôtel.

receptionist NOUN
le/la réceptionniste

recession NOUN
la récession

recipe NOUN
la recette

to **reckon** VERB
penser ◊ *What do you reckon?*
Qu'est-ce que tu en penses?

reclining ADJECTIVE
♦a reclining seat un siège inclinable

recognizable ADJECTIVE
reconnaissable

to **recognize** VERB
reconnaître ◊ *You'll recognize me by
my red hair.* Vous me reconnaîtrez à
mes cheveux roux.

to **recommend** VERB
conseiller ◊ *What do you
recommend?* Qu'est-ce que vous me
conseillez?

to **reconsider** VERB
reconsidérer

record NOUN
  see also **record** VERB
1 le disque (*recording*) ◊ *my
favourite record* mon disque préféré
2 le record (*sport*) ◊ *the world
record* le record du monde
♦in record time en un temps record
◊ *She finished the job in record time.*
Elle a terminé le travail en un temps
record.
♦a criminal record un casier judiciaire
◊ *He's got a criminal record.* Il a un
casier judiciaire.
♦records (*of police, hospital*) les archives
FEM ◊ *I'll check in the records.* Je vais
vérifier dans les archives.
♦There is no record of your booking. Il
n'y a aucune trace de votre
réservation.

to **record** VERB
  see also **record** NOUN
enregistrer (*on film, tape*) ◊ *They've
just recorded their new album.* Ils
viennent d'enregistrer leur nouveau
disque.

recorded delivery NOUN
♦to send something recorded delivery
envoyer quelque chose en
recommandé

recorder NOUN
la flûte à bec (*instrument*) ◊ *She
plays the recorder.* Elle joue de la
flûte à bec.
♦a cassette recorder un magnétophone
à cassettes
♦a video recorder un magnétoscope

recording NOUN
l' enregistrement MASC

record player NOUN
le tourne-disque

to **recover** VERB
se remettre ◊ *He's recovering from a
knee injury.* Il se remet d'une
blessure au genou.

recovery NOUN
le rétablissement
♦Best wishes for a speedy recovery!
Meilleurs vœux de prompt
rétablissement!

rectangle NOUN
le rectangle

rectangular ADJECTIVE
rectangulaire

to **recycle** VERB
recycler

recycling NOUN
le recyclage

red ADJECTIVE
1 rouge ◊ *a red rose* une rose rouge
◊ *red meat* la viande rouge
♦a red light (*traffic light*) un feu rouge
◊ *to go through a red light* brûler un
feu rouge
2 (*hair*)
roux MASC
rousse FEM
◊ *Tamsin's got red hair.* Tamsin a les
cheveux roux.

Red Cross NOUN
la Croix-Rouge

redcurrant NOUN
la groseille

to **redecorate** VERB
1 retapisser (*with wallpaper*)
2 refaire les peintures (*with paint*)

red-haired ADJECTIVE
roux MASC
rousse FEM

red-handed ADJECTIVE
♦to catch somebody red-handed
prendre quelqu'un la main dans le
sac ◊ *He was caught red-handed.* Il a
été pris la main dans le sac.

R

redhead NOUN
le roux
la rousse

to **redo** VERB
refaire

to **reduce** VERB
réduire ◊ *at a reduced price* à prix réduit
♦ **"reduce speed now"** "ralentir"

reduction NOUN
la réduction ◊ *a 5% reduction* une réduction de cinq pour cent
♦ **"huge reductions!"** "prix sacrifiés!"

redundancy NOUN
le licenciement ◊ *There were fifty redundancies.* Il y a eu cinquante licenciements.
♦ **his redundancy payment** ses indemnités de licenciement

redundant ADJECTIVE
♦ **to be made redundant** être licencié ◊ *He was made redundant yesterday.* Il a été licencié hier.

reed NOUN
(*plant*)
le roseau
(les roseaux PL)

reel NOUN
la bobine (*of thread*)

to **refer** VERB
♦ **to refer to** faire allusion à ◊ *What are you referring to?* À quoi faites-vous allusion?

referee NOUN
l' arbitre MASC

reference NOUN
[1] l' allusion FEM ◊ *He made no reference to the murder.* Il n'a fait aucune allusion au meurtre.
[2] les références FEM PL (*for job application*) ◊ *Would you please give me a reference?* Pouvez-vous me fournir des références?
♦ **a reference book** un ouvrage de référence

to **refill** VERB
remplir à nouveau ◊ *He refilled my glass.* Il a rempli mon verre à nouveau.

refinery NOUN
la raffinerie

to **reflect** VERB
refléter (*light, image*)

reflection NOUN
le reflet (*in mirror*)

reflex NOUN
le réflexe

reflexive ADJECTIVE

réfléchi ◊ *a reflexive verb* un verbe réfléchi

refresher course NOUN
le cours de recyclage

refreshing ADJECTIVE
rafraîchissant

refreshments PL NOUN
les rafraîchissements MASC PL

refrigerator NOUN
le réfrigérateur

to **refuel** VERB
se ravitailler en carburant ◊ *The plane stops in Boston to refuel.* L'avion s'arrête à Boston pour se ravitailler en carburant.

refuge NOUN
le refuge

refugee NOUN
le réfugié
la réfugiée

refund NOUN
see also **refund** VERB
le remboursement

to **refund** VERB
see also **refund** NOUN
rembourser

refusal NOUN
le refus

to **refuse** VERB
see also **refuse** NOUN
refuser

refuse NOUN
see also **refuse** VERB
les ordures FEM PL
♦ **refuse collection** le ramassage des ordures

to **regain** VERB
♦ **to regain consciousness** reprendre connaissance

regard NOUN
see also **regard** VERB
♦ **Give my regards to Alice.** Transmettez mon bon souvenir à Alice.
♦ **Louis sends his regards.** Vous avez le bonjour de Louis.
♦ **"with kind regards"** "bien cordialement"

to **regard** VERB
see also **regard** NOUN
♦ **to regard something as** considérer quelque chose comme
♦ **as regards ...** concernant ...

regarding PREPOSITION
relatif à MASC
relative à FEM
◊ *the laws regarding the export of animals* les lois relatives à l'exportation des animaux

♦**Regarding John, ...** Quant à John, ...

regardless ADVERB
♦**regardless of the weather** peu importe le temps
♦**regardless of the consequences** peu importent les conséquences

regiment NOUN
le <u>régiment</u>

region NOUN
la <u>région</u>

regional ADJECTIVE
<u>régional</u>
(régionaux PL)

register NOUN
see also **register** VERB
le <u>registre d'absences</u> (*in school*)

to **register** VERB
see also **register** NOUN
<u>s'inscrire</u> (*at school, college*)

registered ADJECTIVE
♦**a registered letter** une lettre recommandée

registration NOUN
1 l' <u>appel</u> MASC (*roll call*)
2 le <u>numéro d'immatriculation</u> (*of car*)

regret NOUN
see also **regret** VERB
le <u>regret</u>
♦**I've got no regrets.** Je ne regrette rien.

to **regret** VERB
see also **regret** NOUN
<u>regretter</u> ◊ *Give me the money or you'll regret it!* Donne-moi l'argent, sinon tu vas le regretter!
♦**to regret doing something** regretter d'avoir fait quelque chose ◊ *I regret saying that.* Je regrette d'avoir dit ça.

regular ADJECTIVE
1 <u>régulier</u> MASC
<u>régulière</u> FEM
◊ *at regular intervals* à intervalles réguliers ◊ *a regular verb* un verbe régulier
♦**to take regular exercise** faire régulièrement de l'exercice
2 (*average*)
<u>normal</u>
(normaux PL)
◊ *a regular portion of fries* une portion de frites normale

regularly ADVERB
<u>régulièrement</u>

regulation NOUN
le <u>règlement</u>

rehearsal NOUN
la <u>répétition</u>

to **rehearse** VERB
<u>répéter</u>

rein NOUN
la <u>rêne</u> ◊ *the reins* les rênes

reindeer NOUN
le <u>renne</u>

to **reject** VERB
<u>rejeter</u> (*idea, suggestion*) ◊ *We rejected that idea straight away.* Nous avons immédiatement rejeté cette idée.
♦**I applied but they rejected me.** J'ai posé ma candidature mais ils l'ont rejetée.

relapse NOUN
la <u>rechute</u> ◊ *to have a relapse* faire une rechute

related ADJECTIVE
<u>apparenté</u> (*people*) ◊ *We're related.* Nous sommes apparentés.
♦**The two events were not related.** Il n'y avait aucun rapport entre les deux événements.

relation NOUN
1 (*person*)
le <u>parent</u>
la <u>parente</u>
◊ *He's a distant relation.* C'est un parent éloigné. ◊ *my close relations* mes parents proches
♦**my relations** ma famille
♦**I've got relations in London.** J'ai de la famille à Londres.
2 (*connection*)
le <u>rapport</u> ◊ *It has no relation to reality.* Cela n'a aucun rapport avec la réalité.
♦**in relation to** par rapport à

relationship NOUN
les <u>relations</u> FEM PL ◊ *We have a good relationship.* Nous avons de bonnes relations.
♦**I'm not in a relationship at the moment.** Je ne sors avec personne en ce moment.

relative NOUN
le <u>parent</u>
la <u>parente</u>
◊ *my close relatives* mes proches parents
♦**all her relatives** toute sa famille

relatively ADVERB
<u>relativement</u>

to **relax** VERB
<u>se détendre</u> ◊ *I relax listening to music.* Je me détends en écoutant de la musique.
♦**Relax! Everything's fine.** Ne t'en fais pas! Tout va bien.

relaxation NOUN

R

☞

la <u>détente</u> ◊ *I don't have much time for relaxation.* Je n'ai pas beaucoup de moments de détente.

relaxed ADJECTIVE
<u>détendu</u>

relaxing ADJECTIVE
<u>reposant</u>
◆*I find cooking relaxing.* Cela me détend de faire la cuisine.

relay NOUN
◆*a relay race* une course de relais

to **release** VERB
see also **release** NOUN
1 <u>libérer</u> (*prisoner*)
2 <u>divulguer</u> (*report, news*)
3 <u>sortir</u> (*record, video*)

release NOUN
see also **release** VERB
la <u>libération</u> (*from prison*) ◊ *the release of Nelson Mandela* la libération de Nelson Mandela
◆*the band's latest release* le dernier disque du groupe

relegated ADJECTIVE
<u>déclassé</u> (*sport*)

relevant ADJECTIVE
<u>approprié</u> (*documents*)
◆*That's not relevant.* Ça n'a aucun rapport.
◆*to be relevant to something* être en rapport avec quelque chose
◊ *Education should be relevant to real life.* L'enseignement devrait être en rapport avec la réalité.

reliable ADJECTIVE
<u>fiable</u> ◊ *a reliable car* une voiture fiable ◊ *He's not very reliable.* Il n'est pas très fiable.

relief NOUN
le <u>soulagement</u> ◊ *That's a relief!* Quel soulagement!

to **relieve** VERB
<u>soulager</u> ◊ *This injection will relieve the pain.* Cette piqûre va soulager la douleur.

relieved ADJECTIVE
<u>soulagé</u> ◊ *I was relieved to hear ...* J'ai été soulagé d'apprendre ...

religion NOUN
la <u>religion</u> ◊ *What religion are you?* Quelle est votre religion?

religious ADJECTIVE
1 <u>religieux</u> MASC
<u>religieuse</u> FEM
◊ *my religious beliefs* mes croyances religieuses
2 <u>croyant</u> ◊ *I'm not religious.* Je ne suis pas croyant.

reluctant ADJECTIVE

◆*to be reluctant to do something* être peu disposé à faire quelque chose ◊ *They were reluctant to help us.* Ils étaient peu disposés à nous aider.

reluctantly ADVERB
<u>à contrecœur</u> ◊ *She reluctantly accepted.* Elle a accepté à contrecœur.

to **rely on** VERB
<u>compter sur</u> ◊ *I'm relying on you.* Je compte sur toi.

to **remain** VERB
<u>rester</u>
◆*to remain silent* garder le silence

remaining ADJECTIVE
le <u>reste de</u> ◊ *the remaining ingredients* le reste des ingrédients

remains PL NOUN
les <u>restes</u> MASC PL ◊ *the remains of the picnic* les restes du pique-nique
◊ *human remains* des restes humains
◆*Roman remains* les vestiges romains MASC

remake NOUN
le <u>remake</u> (*of film*)

remark NOUN
la <u>remarque</u>

remarkable ADJECTIVE
<u>remarquable</u>

remarkably ADVERB
<u>remarquablement</u>

to **remarry** VERB
<u>se remarier</u> ◊ *She remarried three years ago.* Elle s'est remariée il y a trois ans.

remedy NOUN
le <u>remède</u> ◊ *a good remedy for a sore throat* un bon remède contre le mal de gorge

to **remember** VERB
<u>se souvenir de</u> ◊ *I can't remember his name.* Je ne me souviens pas de son nom. ◊ *I don't remember.* Je ne m'en souviens pas.
In French you often say "don't forget" instead of remember.
◊ *Remember your passport!* N'oublie pas ton passeport! ◊ *Remember to write your name on the form.* N'oubliez pas d'écrire votre nom sur le formulaire.

Remembrance Day NOUN
le <u>jour de l'Armistice</u> ◊ *on Remembrance Day* le jour de l'Armistice

to **remind** VERB
<u>rappeler</u> ◊ *It reminds me of Scotland.* Cela me rappelle l'Écosse. ◊ *I'll remind you tomorrow.* Je te le

rappellerai demain. ◊ *Remind me to speak to Daniel.* Rappelle-moi de parler à Daniel.

remorse NOUN
le remords ◊ *He showed no remorse.* Il a manifesté aucun remords.

remote ADJECTIVE
isolé ◊ *a remote village* un village isolé

remote control NOUN
la télécommande

remotely ADVERB
♦**I'm not remotely interested.** Je ne suis absolument pas intéressé.
♦**Do you think it would be remotely possible?** Pensez-vous que cela serait éventuellement possible?

removable ADJECTIVE
amovible

removal NOUN
le déménagement (*from house*)
♦**a removal van** un camion de déménagement

to **remove** VERB
1 enlever ◊ *Please remove your bag from my seat.* Est-ce que vous pouvez enlever votre sac de mon siège?
2 faire partir (*stain*) ◊ *Did you remove the stain?* Est-ce que tu as fait partir la tache?

rendezvous NOUN
le rendez-vous
(les rendez-vous PL)

to **renew** VERB
renouveler (*passport, licence*)

renewable ADJECTIVE
renouvelable (*energy, resource*)

to **renovate** VERB
rénover ◊ *The building's been renovated.* Le bâtiment a été rénové.

renowned ADJECTIVE
renommé

rent NOUN
see also **rent** VERB
le loyer

to **rent** VERB
see also **rent** NOUN
louer ◊ *We rented a car.* Nous avons loué une voiture.

rental NOUN
la location ◊ *Car rental is included in the price.* Le prix comprend la location d'une voiture.

rental car NOUN
la voiture de location

to **reorganize** VERB
réorganiser

rep NOUN (= *representative*)
le représentant
la représentante

repaid VERB see **repay**

to **repair** VERB
see also **repair** NOUN
réparer
♦**to get something repaired** faire réparer quelque chose ◊ *I got the washing machine repaired.* J'ai fait réparer la machine à laver.

repair NOUN
see also **repair** VERB
la réparation

to **repay** VERB
rembourser (*money*)

repayment NOUN
le remboursement

to **repeat** VERB
see also **repeat** NOUN
répéter

repeat NOUN
see also **repeat** VERB
la reprise ◊ *There are too many repeats on TV.* Il y a trop de reprises à la télé.

repeatedly ADVERB
à plusieurs reprises

repellent NOUN
♦**insect repellent** l'insectifuge MASC

repetitive ADJECTIVE
(*movement, work*)
répétitif MASC
répétitive FEM

to **replace** VERB
remplacer

replay NOUN
see also **replay** VERB
♦**There will be a replay on Friday.** Le match sera rejoué vendredi.

to **replay** VERB
see also **replay** NOUN
rejouer (*match*)

replica NOUN
la réplique

reply NOUN
see also **reply** VERB
la réponse

to **reply** VERB
see also **reply** NOUN
répondre

report NOUN
see also **report** VERB
1 (*of event*)
le compte rendu
(les comptes rendus PL)
2 (*news report*)

R

☞

le reportage ◊ a report in the paper
un reportage dans le journal
3 (at school)
le bulletin scolaire ◊ I got a good
report this term. J'ai un bon bulletin
scolaire ce trimestre.

to report VERB
see also report NOUN
1 signaler ◊ I reported the theft to
the police. J'ai signalé le vol au
commissariat.
2 se présenter ◊ Report to reception
when you arrive. Présentez-vous à la
réception à votre arrivée.

reporter NOUN
le reporter ◊ Charlotte would like to
be a reporter. Charlotte aimerait être
reporter.

to represent VERB
représenter

representative ADJECTIVE
représentatif MASC
représentative FEM

reproduction NOUN
la reproduction

reptile NOUN
le reptile

republic NOUN
la république

repulsive ADJECTIVE
repoussant

reputable ADJECTIVE
de bonne réputation

reputation NOUN
la réputation

request NOUN
see also request VERB
la demande

to request VERB
see also request NOUN
demander

to require VERB
exiger ◊ The job requires a sound
knowledge of classical music. Cet
emploi exige une bonne connaissance
de la musique classique.
♦ What qualifications are required?
Quelles sont les diplômes requis?

requirement NOUN
la condition requise
♦ What are the requirements for the
job? Quelles sont les conditions
requises pour le poste?
♦ entry requirements (for university) les
critères d'entrée MASC

to rescue VERB
see also rescue NOUN
sauver

rescue NOUN
see also rescue VERB
1 le sauvetage ◊ a rescue operation
une opération de sauvetage
♦ a mountain rescue team une équipe
de sauvetage en montagne
2 le secours ◊ the rescue services
les services de secours
♦ to come to somebody's rescue venir
au secours de quelqu'un ◊ He came
to my rescue. Il est venu à mon
secours.

research NOUN
1 la recherche (experimental) ◊ He's
doing research. Il fait de la recherche.
2 les recherches FEM PL (theoretical)
◊ She's doing some research in the
library. Elle fait des recherches à la
bibliothèque.

resemblance NOUN
la ressemblance

to resent VERB
être contrarié par ◊ I really resented
your criticism. J'ai été vraiment
contrarié par tes critiques.

resentful ADJECTIVE
plein de ressentiment
♦ to feel resentful towards somebody
en vouloir à quelqu'un

reservation NOUN
la réservation (booking) ◊ I've got a
reservation for two nights. J'ai une
réservation pour deux nuits. ◊ I'd like
to make a reservation for this evening.
J'aimerais faire une réservation pour
ce soir.

reserve NOUN
see also reserve VERB
1 (place)
la réserve ◊ a nature reserve une
réserve naturelle
2 (person)
le remplaçant
la remplaçante
◊ I was reserve in the game last
Saturday. J'étais remplaçant dans le
match de samedi dernier.

to reserve VERB
see also reserve NOUN
réserver ◊ I'd like to reserve a table
for tomorrow evening. J'aimerais
réserver une table pour demain soir.

reserved ADJECTIVE
réservé ◊ a reserved seat une place
réservée ◊ He's quite reserved. Il est
assez réservé.

reservoir NOUN
le réservoir

resident NOUN

le résident
la résidente

residential ADJECTIVE
résidentiel MASC
résidentielle FEM
◊ *a residential area* un quartier résidentiel

to **resign** VERB
donner sa démission

resistance NOUN
♦ **He was in the resistance.** Il faisait de la résistance.
♦ **the French Resistance** la Résistance

to **resit** VERB
repasser ◊ *I'm resitting the exam in December.* Je vais repasser l'examen en décembre.

resolution NOUN
la résolution
♦ **Have you made any new year's resolutions?** Tu as pris de bonnes résolutions pour l'année nouvelle?

resort NOUN
la station balnéaire (*at seaside*) ◊ *It's a resort on the Costa del Sol.* C'est une station balnéaire sur la Costa del Sol.
♦ **a ski resort** une station de ski
♦ **as a last resort** en dernier recours

resource NOUN
la ressource

respect NOUN
see also **respect** VERB
le respect

to **respect** VERB
see also **respect** NOUN
respecter

respectable ADJECTIVE
1 respectable
2 correct (*standard, marks*)

respectively ADVERB
respectivement

responsibility NOUN
la responsabilité

responsible ADJECTIVE
1 (*in charge*)
responsable
♦ **to be responsible for something** être responsable de quelque chose ◊ *He's responsible for booking the tickets.* Il est responsable de la réservation des billets.
♦ **It's a responsible job.** C'est un poste à responsabilités.
2 (*mature*)
sérieux MASC
sérieuse FEM
◊ *You should be more responsible.* Tu devrais être un peu plus sérieux.

rest NOUN
see also **rest** VERB
1 le repos (*relaxation*) ◊ *five minutes' rest* cinq minutes de repos
♦ **to have a rest** se reposer ◊ *We stopped to have a rest.* Nous nous sommes arrêtés pour nous reposer.
2 le reste (*remainder*) ◊ *I'll do the rest.* Je ferai le reste. ◊ *the rest of the money* le reste de l'argent
♦ **the rest of them** les autres ◊ *The rest of them went swimming.* Les autres sont allés nager.

to **rest** VERB
see also **rest** NOUN
1 se reposer (*relax*) ◊ *She's resting in her room.* Elle se repose dans sa chambre.
2 ménager (*not overstrain*) ◊ *He has to rest his knee.* Il doit ménager son genou.
3 appuyer (*lean*) ◊ *I rested my bike against the window.* J'ai appuyé mon vélo contre la fenêtre.

restaurant NOUN
le restaurant ◊ *We don't often go to restaurants.* Nous n'allons pas souvent au restaurant.
♦ **a restaurant car** un wagon-restaurant

restful ADJECTIVE
reposant

restless ADJECTIVE
agité

restoration NOUN
la restauration

to **restore** VERB
restaurer (*building, picture*)

to **restrict** VERB
limiter

rest room NOUN US
les toilettes FEM PL

result NOUN
see also **result** VERB
le résultat ◊ *my exam results* mes résultats d'examen ◊ *What was the result? – One-nil.* Quel a été le résultat? – Un à zéro.

to **result** VERB
see also **result** NOUN
♦ **to result in** entraîner

to **resume** VERB
reprendre ◊ *They've resumed work.* Ils ont repris le travail.
Be careful not to translate to resume by résumer.

résumé NOUN US
le curriculum vitae

to **retire** VERB

R

☞

prendre sa retraite ◊ *He retired last year.* Il a pris sa retraite l'an dernier.

retired ADJECTIVE
retraité ◊ *She's retired.* Elle est retraitée.
♦ **a retired teacher** un professeur à la retraite

retirement NOUN
la retraite

to **retrace** VERB
♦ **to retrace one's steps** revenir sur ses pas ◊ *I retraced my steps.* Je suis revenu sur mes pas.

return NOUN
see also **return** VERB
1 le retour ◊ *after our return* à notre retour
♦ **the return journey** le voyage de retour
♦ **a return match** un match retour
2 l' aller retour MASC (*ticket*) ◊ *A return to Avignon, please.* Un aller retour pour Avignon, s'il vous plaît.
♦ **in return** en échange ◊ *... and I help her in return* ... et je l'aide en échange
♦ **in return for** en échange de
♦ **Many happy returns!** Bon anniversaire!

to **return** VERB
see also **return** NOUN
1 revenir (*come back*) ◊ *I've just returned from holiday.* Je viens de revenir de vacances.
♦ **to return home** rentrer à la maison
2 retourner (*go back*) ◊ *He returned to France the following year.* Il est retourné en France l'année suivante.
3 rendre (*give back*) ◊ *She borrows my things and doesn't return them.* Elle m'emprunte mes affaires et ne me les rend pas.

reunion NOUN
la réunion

to **reuse** VERB
réutiliser

to **reveal** VERB
révéler

revenge NOUN
la vengeance ◊ *in revenge* par vengeance
♦ **to take revenge** se venger ◊ *They planned to take revenge on him.* Ils voulaient se venger de lui.

to **reverse** VERB
see also **reverse** ADJECTIVE
faire marche arrière (*car*) ◊ *He reversed without looking.* Il a fait marche arrière sans regarder.

♦ **to reverse the charges** (*telephone*) appeler en PCV

> ⓘ *In France, reversing the charges is only possible for international calls.*

◊ *I'd like to make a reverse charge call to Britain.* Je voudrais appeler la Grande-Bretagne en PCV.

reverse ADJECTIVE
see also **reverse** VERB
inverse ◊ *in reverse order* dans l'ordre inverse
♦ **in reverse gear** en marche arrière

review NOUN
la critique (*of book, film, programme*) ◊ *The book had good reviews.* Ce livre a eu de bonnes critiques.

to **revise** VERB
réviser ◊ *I haven't started revising yet.* Je n'ai pas encore commencé à réviser.
♦ **I've revised my opinion.** J'ai changé d'opinion.

revision NOUN
les révisions FEM PL ◊ *Have you done a lot of revision?* Est-ce que tu as fait beaucoup de révisions?

to **revive** VERB
ranimer ◊ *The nurses tried to revive him.* Les infirmières ont essayé de le ranimer.

revolting ADJECTIVE
dégoûtant

revolution NOUN
la révolution
♦ **the French Revolution** la Révolution française

revolutionary ADJECTIVE
révolutionnaire

revolver NOUN
le revolver

reward NOUN
la récompense

rewarding ADJECTIVE
gratifiant ◊ *a rewarding job* un travail gratifiant

to **rewind** VERB
rembobiner ◊ *to rewind a cassette* rembobiner une cassette

rheumatism NOUN
le rhumatisme

Rhine NOUN
le Rhin

rhinoceros NOUN
le rhinocéros

Rhone NOUN
le Rhône

rhubarb NOUN
la rhubarbe ◊ *a rhubarb tart* une tarte à la rhubarbe

rhythm NOUN
le rythme

rib NOUN
la côte

ribbon NOUN
le ruban

rice NOUN
le riz
♦ **rice pudding** le riz au lait

rich ADJECTIVE
riche
♦ **the rich** les riches MASC

to **rid** VERB
♦ **to get rid of** se débarrasser de ◊ *I want to get rid of some old clothes.* Je veux me débarrasser de vieux vêtements.

ridden VERB *see* **ride**

ride NOUN
see also **ride** VERB
♦ **to go for a ride (1)** (*on horse*) monter à cheval
♦ **to go for a ride (2)** (*on bike*) faire un tour en vélo ◊ *We went for a bike ride.* Nous sommes allés faire un tour en vélo.
♦ **It's a short bus ride to the town centre.** Ce n'est pas loin du centre-ville en bus.

to **ride** VERB
see also **ride** NOUN
monter à cheval (*on horse*) ◊ *I'm learning to ride.* J'apprends à monter à cheval.
♦ **to ride a bike** faire du vélo ◊ *Can you ride a bike?* Tu sais faire du vélo?

rider NOUN
1 (*on horse*)
le cavalier
la cavalière
◊ *She's a good rider.* C'est une bonne cavalière.
2 (*on bike*)
le/la cycliste

ridiculous ADJECTIVE
ridicule ◊ *Don't be ridiculous!* Ne sois pas ridicule!

riding NOUN
l' équitation FEM
♦ **to go riding** faire de l'équitation
♦ **a riding school** une école d'équitation

rifle NOUN
le fusil ◊ *a hunting rifle* un fusil de chasse

rig NOUN
♦ **an oil rig** une plate-forme pétrolière

right ADJECTIVE, ADVERB
see also **right** NOUN
There are several ways of translating **right**. *Scan the examples to find one that is similar to what you want to say.*
1 (*factually correct, suitable*)
bon MASC
bonne FEM
◊ *the right answer* la bonne réponse
◊ *It isn't the right size.* Ce n'est pas la bonne taille. ◊ *We're on the right train.* Nous sommes dans le bon train.
♦ **Is this the right road for Arles?** Est-ce que c'est bien la route pour aller à Arles?
2 (*correctly*)
correctement ◊ *Am I pronouncing it right?* Est-ce que je prononce ça correctement?
♦ **to be right (1)** (*person*) avoir raison
◊ *You were right!* Tu avais raison!
♦ **to be right (2)** (*statement, opinion*) être vrai ◊ *That's right!* C'est vrai!
3 (*accurate*)
juste ◊ *Do you have the right time?* Est-ce que vous avez l'heure juste?
4 (*morally correct*)
bien ◊ *It's not right to behave like that.* Ce n'est pas bien d'agir comme ça.
♦ **I think you did the right thing.** Je pense que tu as bien fait.
5 (*not left*)
droit ◊ *my right hand* ma main droite
6 (*turn, look*)
à droite ◊ *Turn right at the traffic lights.* Tournez à droite aux prochains feux.
♦ **Right! Let's get started.** Bon! On commence.
♦ **right away** tout de suite ◊ *I'll do it right away.* Je vais le faire tout de suite.

right NOUN
see also **right** ADJECTIVE
1 le droit
♦ **You've got no right to do that.** Vous n'avez pas le droit de faire ça.
2 la droite (*not left*)
♦ **on the right** à droite ◊ *Remember to drive on the right.* N'oubliez pas de conduire à droite.
♦ **right of way** la priorité ◊ *It was our right of way.* Nous avions la priorité.

right-hand ADJECTIVE
♦ **the right-hand side** la droite ◊ *It's on the right-hand side.* C'est à droite.

right-handed ADJECTIVE
droitier MASC

R

☞

droitière FEM

rightly ADVERB
avec raison ◊ *She rightly decided not to go.* Elle a décidé, avec raison, de ne pas y aller.
♦**if I remember rightly** si je me souviens bien

rim NOUN
la monture ◊ *glasses with wire rims* des lunettes avec une monture métallique

ring NOUN
see also **ring** VERB
1 l' anneau MASC
(les anneaux PL)
◊ *a gold ring* un anneau en or
2 (*with stones*)
la bague ◊ *a diamond ring* une bague de diamants
♦**a wedding ring** une alliance
3 (*circle*)
le cercle ◊ *to stand in a ring* se mettre en cercle
4 (*of bell*)
le coup de sonnette ◊ *I was woken by a ring at the door.* J'ai été réveillé par un coup de sonnette.
♦**to give somebody a ring** appeler quelqu'un ◊ *I'll give you a ring this evening.* Je t'appellerai ce soir.

to **ring** VERB
see also **ring** NOUN
1 téléphoner ◊ *Your mother rang this morning.* Ta mère a téléphoné ce matin.
♦**to ring somebody** appeler quelqu'un ◊ *I'll ring you tomorrow morning.* Je t'appellerai demain matin.
♦**to ring somebody up** donner un coup de fil à quelqu'un
2 sonner ◊ *The phone's ringing.* Le téléphone sonne.
♦**to ring the bell** (*doorbell*) sonner à la porte ◊ *I rang the bell three times.* J'ai sonné trois fois à la porte.
♦**to ring back** rappeler ◊ *I'll ring back later.* Je rappellerai plus tard.

ring binder NOUN
le classeur

ring road NOUN
1 la rocade (*ordinary road*)
2 le périphérique (*motorway*)

rink NOUN
1 la patinoire (*for ice-skating*)
2 la piste (*for roller-skating*)

to **rinse** VERB
rincer

riot NOUN
see also **riot** VERB

l' émeute FEM

to **riot** VERB
see also **riot** NOUN
faire une émeute

to **rip** VERB
1 déchirer ◊ *I've ripped my jeans.* J'ai déchiré mon jean.
2 se déchirer ◊ *My skirt's ripped.* Ma jupe s'est déchirée.

to **rip off** VERB
arnaquer ◊ *The hotel ripped us off.* L'hôtel nous a arnaqués.

to **rip up** VERB
déchirer ◊ *He read the note and then ripped it up.* Il a lu le mot, puis l'a déchiré.

ripe ADJECTIVE
mûr

rip-off NOUN
♦**It's a rip-off!** C'est de l'arnaque! (*informal*)

rise NOUN
see also **rise** VERB
1 la hausse (*in prices, temperature*)
◊ *a sudden rise in temperature* une hausse subite de température
2 l' augmentation FEM (*pay rise*)

to **rise** VERB
see also **rise** NOUN
1 augmenter (*increase*) ◊ *Prices are rising.* Les prix augmentent.
2 se lever ◊ *The sun rises early in June.* Le soleil se lève tôt en juin.

riser NOUN
♦**to be an early riser** être matinal

risk NOUN
see also **risk** VERB
le risque
♦**to take risks** prendre des risques
♦**It's at your own risk.** C'est à vos risques et périls.

to **risk** VERB
see also **risk** NOUN
risquer ◊ *You risk getting a fine.* Vous risquez de recevoir une amende.
♦**I wouldn't risk it if I were you.** À votre place, je ne prendrais pas ce risque.

risky ADJECTIVE
risqué

rival NOUN
see also **rival** ADJECTIVE
le rival
(les rivaux PL)
la rivale

rival ADJECTIVE
see also **rival** NOUN

rival
[1] <u>rival</u> ◊ *a rival gang* une bande
rivale
[2] <u>concurrent</u> ◊ *a rival company* une
société concurrente

rivalry NOUN
la <u>rivalité</u> (*between towns, schools*)

river NOUN
[1] la <u>rivière</u> ◊ *The river runs
alongside the canal.* La rivière longe
le canal.
[2] le <u>fleuve</u> (*major*) ◊ *the rivers of
France* les fleuves de France
♦**the river Seine** la Seine

Riviera NOUN
♦**the French Riviera** la Côte d'Azur
♦**the Italian Riviera** la Riviera italienne

road NOUN
[1] la <u>route</u> ◊ *There's a lot of traffic
on the roads.* Il y a beaucoup de
circulation sur les routes.
[2] la <u>rue</u> (*street*) ◊ *They live across
the road.* Ils habitent de l'autre côté
de la rue.

road map NOUN
la <u>carte routière</u>

road rage NOUN
l' <u>agressivité au volant</u> FEM

road sign NOUN
le <u>panneau de signalisation</u>
(les <u>panneaux de signalisation</u> PL)

roadworks PL NOUN
les <u>travaux</u> MASC PL

roast ADJECTIVE
<u>rôti</u> ◊ *roast chicken* le poulet rôti
◊ *roast potatoes* les pommes de terre
rôties
♦**roast pork** le rôti de porc
♦**roast beef** le rôti de bœuf

to **rob** VERB
♦**to rob somebody** voler quelqu'un
◊ *I've been robbed.* On m'a volé.
♦**to rob somebody of something** voler
quelque chose à quelqu'un ◊ *He was
robbed of his wallet.* On lui a volé
son portefeuille.
♦**to rob a bank** dévaliser une banque

robber NOUN
le <u>voleur</u>
♦**a bank-robber** un cambrioleur de
banques

robbery NOUN
le <u>vol</u>
♦**a bank robbery** un hold-up
♦**armed robbery** le vol à main armée

robin NOUN
le <u>rouge-gorge</u>

robot NOUN
le <u>robot</u>

rock NOUN

| *see also* **rock** VERB |

[1] la <u>roche</u> (*substance*) ◊ *They
tunnelled through the rock.* Ils ont
creusé un tunnel dans la roche.
[2] le <u>rocher</u> (*boulder*) ◊ *I sat on a
rock.* Je me suis assis sur un rocher.
[3] la <u>pierre</u> (*stone*) ◊ *The crowd
started to throw rocks.* La foule s'est
mise à lancer des pierres.
[4] le <u>rock</u> (*music*) ◊ *a rock concert* un
concert de rock ◊ *He's a rock star.*
C'est une rock star.
[5] le <u>sucre d'orge</u> (*sweet*) ◊ *a stick of
rock* un bâton de sucre d'orge
♦**rock and roll** le rock'n'roll

to **rock** VERB

| *see also* **rock** NOUN |

<u>ébranler</u> ◊ *The explosion rocked the
building.* L'explosion a ébranlé le
bâtiment.

rockery NOUN
la <u>rocaille</u>

rocket NOUN
la <u>fusée</u> (*firework, spacecraft*)

rocking chair NOUN
le <u>rocking-chair</u>

rocking horse NOUN
le <u>cheval à bascule</u>

rod NOUN
la <u>canne à pêche</u> (*for fishing*)

rode VERB *see* **ride**

role NOUN
le <u>rôle</u>

role play NOUN
le <u>jeu de rôle</u>
(les <u>jeux de rôles</u> PL)
◊ *to do a role play* faire un jeu de rôle

roll NOUN

| *see also* **roll** VERB |

[1] le <u>rouleau</u>
(les <u>rouleaux</u> PL)
◊ *a roll of tape* un rouleau de ruban
adhésif ◊ *a toilet roll* un rouleau de
papier hygiénique
[2] (*bread*)
le <u>petit pain</u>

to **roll** VERB

| *see also* **roll** NOUN |

<u>rouler</u>
♦**to roll out the pastry** abaisser la pâte

roll call NOUN
l' <u>appel</u> MASC

roller NOUN
le <u>rouleau</u>
(les <u>rouleaux</u> PL)

Rollerblade ® NOUN
le <u>roller</u> ◊ *a pair of Rollerblades* une
paire de rollers

rollercoaster NOUN

R

☞

les <u>montagnes russes</u> FEM PL

roller skates PL NOUN
les <u>patins à roulettes</u> MASC PL

roller-skating NOUN
le <u>patin à roulettes</u>
♦ **to go roller-skating** faire du patin à roulettes

rolling pin NOUN
le <u>rouleau à pâtisserie</u>

Roman ADJECTIVE, NOUN
<u>romain</u> (*ancient*) ◊ *a Roman villa* une villa romaine ◊ *the Roman empire* l'empire romain
♦ **the Romans** les Romains

Roman Catholic NOUN
le/la <u>catholique</u> ◊ *He's a Roman Catholic.* Il est catholique.

romance NOUN
[1] les <u>romans d'amour</u> MASC PL (*novels*) ◊ *I read a lot of romance.* Je lis beaucoup de romans d'amour.
[2] le <u>charme</u> (*glamour*) ◊ *the romance of Paris* le charme de Paris
♦ **a holiday romance** une idylle de vacances

Romania NOUN
la <u>Roumanie</u>
♦ **in Romania** en Roumanie

Romanian ADJECTIVE
<u>roumain</u>

romantic ADJECTIVE
<u>romantique</u>

roof NOUN
le <u>toit</u>

roof rack NOUN
la <u>galerie</u>

room NOUN
[1] la <u>pièce</u> ◊ *the biggest room in the house* la plus grande pièce de la maison
[2] la <u>chambre</u> (*bedroom*) ◊ *She's in her room.* Elle est dans sa chambre.
♦ **a single room** une chambre pour une personne
♦ **a double room** une chambre pour deux personnes
[3] la <u>salle</u> (*in school*) ◊ *the music room* la salle de musique
[4] la <u>place</u> (*space*) ◊ *There's no room for that box.* Il n'y a pas de place pour cette boîte.

roommate NOUN
le/la <u>camarade de chambre</u>

root NOUN
la <u>racine</u>

to **root around** VERB
<u>fouiller</u> ◊ *She started rooting around in her handbag.* Elle a commencé à fouiller dans son sac à main.

to **root out** VERB
<u>traquer</u> ◊ *They are determined to root out corruption.* Ils sont déterminés à traquer la corruption.

rope NOUN
la <u>corde</u>

to **rope in** VERB
<u>enrôler</u> ◊ *I was roped in to help with the refreshments.* J'ai été enrôlé pour servir les rafraîchissements.

rose VERB *see* **rise**

rose NOUN
la <u>rose</u> (*flower*)

to **rot** NOUN
VERB
<u>pourrir</u>

rotten ADJECTIVE
<u>pourri</u> (*decayed*) ◊ *a rotten apple* une pomme pourrie
♦ **rotten weather** un temps pourri
♦ **That's a rotten thing to do.** Ce n'est vraiment pas gentil.
♦ **to feel rotten** être mal fichu (*informal*)

rough ADJECTIVE
[1] (*surface*)
<u>rêche</u> ◊ *My hands are rough.* J'ai les mains rêches.
[2] (*game*)
<u>violent</u> ◊ *Rugby's a rough sport.* Le rugby est un sport violent.
[3] (*place*)
<u>difficile</u> ◊ *It's a rough area.* C'est un quartier difficile.
[4] (*water*)
<u>houleux</u> MASC
<u>houleuse</u> FEM
◊ *The sea was rough.* La mer était houleuse.
[5] <u>approximatif</u> MASC
<u>approximative</u> FEM
♦ **I've got a rough idea.** J'en ai une idée approximative.
♦ **to feel rough** ne pas être dans son assiette ◊ *I feel rough.* Je ne suis pas dans mon assiette.

roughly ADVERB
<u>à peu près</u> ◊ *It weighs roughly 20 kilos.* Ça pèse à peu près vingt kilos.

round ADJECTIVE, ADVERB, PREPOSITION
see also **round** NOUN
[1] <u>rond</u> ◊ *a round table* une table ronde
[2] <u>autour de</u> (*around*) ◊ *We were sitting round the table.* Nous étions assis autour de la table. ◊ *She wore a scarf round her neck.* Elle portait une écharpe autour du cou.
♦ **It's just round the corner.** (*very near*) C'est tout près.

♦ **to go round to somebody's house**
aller chez quelqu'un ◊ *I went round
to my friend's house.* Je suis allé
chez mon ami.

♦ **to have a look round** faire un tour
◊ *We're going to have a look round.*
Nous allons faire un tour.

♦ **to go round a museum** visiter un
musée

♦ **round here** près d'ici ◊ *Is there a
chemist's round here?* Est-ce qu'il y a
une pharmacie près d'ici?

♦ **He lives round here.** Il habite dans les
parages.

♦ **all round** partout ◊ *There were
vineyards all round.* Il y avait des
vignobles partout.

♦ **all year round** toute l'année

♦ **round about** (*roughly*) environ ◊ *It
costs round about £100.* Cela coûte
environ cent livres. ◊ *round about 8
o'clock* à huit heures environ

round NOUN

see also **round** ADJECTIVE

[1] la rangée (*of tournament*)

[2] le round (*of boxing match*)

♦ **a round of golf** une partie de golf

♦ **a round of drinks** une tournée ◊ *He
bought a round of drinks.* Il a offert
une tournée.

to **round off** VERB
terminer ◊ *They rounded off the
meal with liqueurs.* Ils ont terminé le
repas par des liqueurs.

to **round up** VERB

[1] rassembler (*sheep, cattle, suspects*)

[2] arrondir (*figure*)

roundabout NOUN

[1] (*at junction*)
le rond-point
(les ronds-points PL)

[2] (*at funfair*)
le manège

rounders NOUN

ⓘ *Rounders is not played in France.*

♦ **Rounders is a bit like baseball, but
it's mostly played by children.** Le
"rounders" ressemble un peu au
base-ball, mais est surtout pratiqué
par les enfants.

round trip NOUN US
l' aller et retour MASC

♦ **a round-trip ticket** un billet de
aller-retour

route NOUN

[1] l' itinéraire MASC ◊ *We're planning
our route.* Nous établissons notre
itinéraire.

[2] le parcours (*of bus*)

routine NOUN

♦ **my daily routine** mes occupations
quotidiennes

row NOUN

*This word has two pronunciations.
Make sure you choose the right
translation.*

see also **row** VERB

[1] la rangée ◊ *a row of houses* une
rangée de maisons

[2] le rang (*of seats*) ◊ *Our seats are
in the front row.* Nos places se
trouvent au premier rang.

♦ **five times in a row** cinq fois d'affilée

[3] le vacarme (*noise*) ◊ *What's that
terrible row?* qu'est-ce que c'est que
ce vacarme?

[4] la dispute (*quarrel*)

♦ **to have a row** se disputer ◊ *They've
had a row.* Ils se sont disputés.

to **row** VERB

see also **row** NOUN

[1] ramer ◊ *We took turns to row.*
Nous avons ramé à tour de rôle.

[2] faire de l'aviron (*as sport*)

rowboat NOUN US
le bateau à rames

rowing NOUN
l' aviron MASC (*sport*) ◊ *My hobby is
rowing.* Je fais de l'aviron.

♦ **a rowing boat** un bateau à rames

royal ADJECTIVE
royal
(royaux MASC PL)

♦ **the royal family** la famille royale

to **rub** VERB

[1] frotter (*stain*)

[2] se frotter (*part of body*) ◊ *Don't rub
your eyes!* Ne te frotte pas les yeux!

♦ **to rub something out** effacer quelque
chose

rubber NOUN

[1] le caoutchouc ◊ *rubber soles* des
semelles en caoutchouc

[2] la gomme (*eraser*) ◊ *Can I borrow
your rubber?* Je peux emprunter ta
gomme?

♦ **a rubber band** un élastique

rubbish NOUN

see also **rubbish** ADJECTIVE

[1] les ordures FEM PL (*refuse*) ◊ *When
do they collect the rubbish?* Quand
est-ce qu'ils ramassent les ordures?

[2] la camelote (*junk*) ◊ *They sell a lot
of rubbish at the market.* Ils vendent
beaucoup de camelote au marché.

[3] les bêtises FEM PL (*nonsense*) ◊ *Don't
talk rubbish!* Ne dis pas de bêtises!

R

☞

♦ **That's a load of rubbish!** C'est vraiment n'importe quoi! (*informal*)
♦ **a rubbish bin** une poubelle
♦ **a rubbish dump** une décharge

rubbish ADJECTIVE
> *see also* **rubbish** NOUN

nul MASC
nulle FEM
◊ *They're a rubbish team!* Cette équipe est nulle!

rucksack NOUN
le sac à dos

rude ADJECTIVE
[1] (*impolite*)
impoli ◊ *It's rude to interrupt.* C'est impoli de couper la parole aux gens.
[2] (*offensive*)
grossier MASC
grossière FEM
◊ *a rude joke* une plaisanterie grossière ◊ *He was very rude to me.* Il a été très grossier avec moi.
♦ **a rude word** un gros mot

rug NOUN
[1] le tapis ◊ *a Persian rug* un tapis persan
[2] la couverture (*blanket*) ◊ *a tartan rug* une couverture écossaise

rugby NOUN
le rugby ◊ *I play rugby.* Je joue au rugby.

ruin NOUN
> *see also* **ruin** VERB

la ruine ◊ *the ruins of the castle* les ruines du château
♦ **in ruins** en ruine

to **ruin** VERB
> *see also* **ruin** NOUN

[1] abîmer ◊ *You'll ruin your shoes.* Tu vas abîmer tes chaussures.
[2] gâcher ◊ *It ruined our holiday.* Ça a gâché nos vacances.
[3] ruiner (*financially*)

rule NOUN
[1] la règle ◊ *the rules of grammar* les règles de grammaire
♦ **as a rule** en règle générale
[2] le règlement (*regulation*) ◊ *It's against the rules.* C'est contre le règlement.

to **rule out** VERB
écarter (*possibility*) ◊ *I'm not ruling anything out.* Je n'écarte aucune possibilité.

ruler NOUN
la règle ◊ *Can I borrow your ruler?* Je peux emprunter ta règle?

rum NOUN
le rhum

rumour NOUN (US **rumor**)
la rumeur ◊ *It's just a rumour.* Ce n'est qu'une rumeur.

rump steak NOUN
le romsteak

run NOUN
> *see also* **run** VERB

le point (*in cricket*) ◊ *to score a run* marquer un point
♦ **to go for a run** courir ◊ *I go for a run every morning.* Je cours tous les matins.
♦ **I did a ten-kilometre run.** J'ai couru dix kilomètres.
♦ **on the run** en fuite ◊ *The criminals are still on the run.* Les criminels sont toujours en fuite.
♦ **in the long run** à long terme

to **run** VERB
> *see also* **run** NOUN

[1] courir ◊ *I ran five kilometres.* J'ai couru cinq kilomètres.
♦ **to run a marathon** participer à un marathon
[2] diriger (*manage*) ◊ *He runs a large company.* Il dirige une grosse société.
[3] organiser (*organize*) ◊ *They run music courses in the holidays.* Ils organisent des cours de musique pendant les vacances.
[4] couler (*water*) ◊ *Don't leave the tap running.* Ne laisse pas couler le robinet.
♦ **to run a bath** faire couler un bain
[5] conduire (*by car*) ◊ *I can run you to the station.* Je peux te conduire à la gare.
♦ **to run away** s'enfuir ◊ *They ran away before the police came.* Ils se sont enfuis avant l'arrivée de la police.
♦ **Time is running out.** Il ne reste plus beaucoup de temps.
♦ **to run out of something** se trouver à court de quelque chose ◊ *We ran out of money.* Nous nous sommes trouvés à court d'argent.
♦ **to run somebody over** écraser quelqu'un
♦ **to get run over** se faire écraser ◊ *Be careful, or you'll get run over!* Fais attention, sinon tu vas te faire écraser!

rung VERB *see* **ring**

runner NOUN
le coureur
la coureuse

runner beans PL NOUN
les haricots verts MASC PL

runner-up NOUN
le second

la seconde

running NOUN
la course ◊ *Running is my favourite sport.* La course est mon sport préféré.

run-up NOUN
◆**in the run-up to Christmas** pendant la période de préparation de Noël

runway NOUN
la piste

rural ADJECTIVE
rural
(ruraux MASC PL)

rush NOUN
see also **rush** VERB
la hâte
◆**in a rush.** à la hâte

to **rush** VERB
see also **rush** NOUN
1 se précipiter (*run*) ◊ *Everyone rushed outside.* Tout le monde s'est précipité dehors.
2 se dépêcher (*hurry*) ◊ *There's no need to rush.* Ce n'est pas la peine de se dépêcher.

rush hour NOUN
les heures de pointe FEM PL ◊ *in the*

rush hour aux heures de pointe

rusk NOUN
la biscotte

Russia NOUN
la Russie
◆**in Russia** en Russie
◆**to Russia** en Russie

Russian ADJECTIVE
see also **Russian** NOUN
russe

Russian NOUN
see also **Russian** ADJECTIVE
1 le/la Russe (*person*)
2 le russe (*language*)

rust NOUN
la rouille

rusty ADJECTIVE
rouillé ◊ *a rusty bike* un vélo rouillé ◊ *My French is very rusty.* Mon français est très rouillé.

ruthless ADJECTIVE
sans pitié

rye NOUN
le seigle
◆**rye bread** le pain de seigle

R

S

Sabbath NOUN
1. le <u>dimanche</u> (*Christian*)
2. le <u>sabbat</u> (*Jewish*)

sack NOUN
see also **sack** VERB
le <u>sac</u>
♦ **to get the sack** être mis à la porte

to **sack** VERB
see also **sack** NOUN
♦ **to sack somebody** mettre quelqu'un à la porte ◊ *He was sacked.* On l'a mis à la porte.

sacred ADJECTIVE
<u>sacré</u>

sacrifice NOUN
le <u>sacrifice</u>

sad ADJECTIVE
<u>triste</u>

saddle NOUN
la <u>selle</u>

saddlebag NOUN
la <u>sacoche</u>

sadly ADVERB
1. <u>tristement</u> ◊ *"She's gone," he said sadly.* "Elle est partie," a-t-il dit tristement.
2. <u>malheureusement</u> (*unfortunately*) ◊ *Sadly, it was too late.* Malheureusement, il était trop tard.

safe NOUN
see also **safe** ADJECTIVE
le <u>coffre-fort</u>
(les <u>coffres-forts</u> PL)
◊ *She put the money in the safe.* Elle a mis l'argent dans le coffre-fort.

safe ADJECTIVE
see also **safe** NOUN
1. <u>sans danger</u> ◊ *Don't worry, it's perfectly safe.* Ne vous inquiétez pas, c'est absolument sans danger.
♦ **Is it safe?** Ça n'est pas dangereux?
2. <u>sûr</u> (*machine, ladder*) ◊ *This car isn't safe.* Cette voiture n'est pas sûre.
3. <u>hors de danger</u> (*out of danger*) ◊ *You're safe now.* Vous êtes hors de danger maintenant.
♦ **to feel safe** se sentir en sécurité
♦ **safe sex** le sexe sans risques

safety NOUN
la <u>sécurité</u>
♦ **a safety belt** une ceinture de sécurité
♦ **a safety pin** une épingle de nourrice

Sagittarius NOUN

le/la <u>Sagittaire</u> ◊ *I'm Sagittarius.* Je suis Sagittaire.

Sahara NOUN
♦ **the Sahara Desert** le Sahara

said VERB see **say**

sail NOUN
see also **sail** VERB
la <u>voile</u>

to **sail** VERB
see also **sail** NOUN
1. <u>naviguer</u> (*travel*)
2. <u>prendre la mer</u> (*set off*) ◊ *The boat sails at eight o'clock.* Le bateau prend la mer à huit heures.

sailing NOUN
la <u>voile</u> ◊ *His hobby is sailing.* Son passe-temps, c'est la voile.
♦ **to go sailing** faire de la voile
♦ **a sailing boat** un voilier
♦ **a sailing ship** un grand voilier

sailor NOUN
le <u>marin</u> ◊ *He's a sailor.* Il est marin.

saint NOUN
le <u>saint</u>
la <u>sainte</u>

sake NOUN
♦ **for the sake of** dans l'intérêt de

salad NOUN
la <u>salade</u>
♦ **salad cream** la mayonnaise
♦ **salad dressing** la vinaigrette

salami NOUN
le <u>salami</u>

salary NOUN
le <u>salaire</u>

sale NOUN
les <u>soldes</u> MASC PL (*reductions*)
◊ *There's a sale on at Harrods.* Ce sont les soldes chez Harrods.
♦ **on sale** en vente
♦ **The factory's for sale.** L'usine est en vente.
♦ **"for sale"** "à vendre"

sales assistant NOUN
le <u>vendeur</u>
la <u>vendeuse</u>
◊ *She's a sales assistant.* Elle est vendeuse.

salesman NOUN
1. le <u>représentant</u> (*sales rep*) ◊ *He's a salesman.* Il est représentant.
♦ **a double-glazing salesman** un représentant en doubles vitrages
2. le <u>vendeur</u> (*sales assistant*)

sales rep NOUN
le représentant
la représentante

saleswoman NOUN
1 la représentante (*sales rep*)
◊ *She's a saleswoman.* Elle est représentante.
2 la vendeuse (*sales assistant*)

salmon NOUN
le saumon

salon NOUN
le salon ◊ *a hair salon* un salon de coiffure ◊ *a beauty salon* un salon de beauté

saloon car NOUN
la berline

salt NOUN
le sel

salty ADJECTIVE
salé

to **salute** VERB
saluer

Salvation Army NOUN
l' armée du Salut FEM

same ADJECTIVE
même ◊ *the same model* le même modèle ◊ *at the same time* en même temps
♦ **They're exactly the same.** Ils sont exactement pareils.
♦ **It's not the same.** Ça n'est pas pareil.

sample NOUN
l' échantillon MASC

sand NOUN
le sable

sandal NOUN
la sandale ◊ *a pair of sandals* une paire de sandales

sand castle NOUN
le château de sable
(les châteaux de sable PL)

sandwich NOUN
le sandwich ◊ *a cheese sandwich* un sandwich au fromage

sandwich course NOUN
le cours avec stage pratique

sang VERB *see* **sing**

sanitary towel NOUN
la serviette hygiénique

sank VERB *see* **sink**

Santa Claus NOUN
le père Noël

sarcastic ADJECTIVE
sarcastique

sardine NOUN
la sardine

SARS ABBREVIATION

(= *Severe Acute Respiratory Syndrome*)
la pneumonie atypique

sat VERB *see* **sit**

satchel NOUN
le cartable

satellite NOUN
le satellite ◊ *satellite television* la télévision par satellite
♦ **a satellite dish** une antenne parabolique

satisfactory ADJECTIVE
satisfaisant

satisfied ADJECTIVE
satisfait

Saturday NOUN
le samedi ◊ *on Saturday* samedi ◊ *on Saturdays* le samedi ◊ *every Saturday* tous les samedis ◊ *last Saturday* samedi dernier ◊ *next Saturday* samedi prochain
♦ **I've got a Saturday job.** Je travaille le samedi.

sauce NOUN
la sauce

saucepan NOUN
la casserole

saucer NOUN
la soucoupe

Saudi Arabia NOUN
l' Arabie Saoudite FEM
♦ **in Saudi Arabia** en Arabie Saoudite

sauna NOUN
le sauna

sausage NOUN
1 la saucisse
2 le saucisson (*salami*)
♦ **a sausage roll** un friand à la saucisse

to **save** VERB
1 mettre de côté (*save up money*)
◊ *I've saved £50 already.* J'ai déjà mis cinquante livres de côté.
2 économiser (*spend less*) ◊ *I saved £20 by waiting for the sales.* J'ai économisé vingt livres en attendant les soldes.
♦ **to save time** gagner du temps ◊ *We took a taxi to save time.* Nous avons pris un taxi pour gagner du temps.
◊ *It saved us time.* Ça nous a fait gagner du temps.
3 sauver (*rescue*) ◊ *Luckily, all the passengers were saved.* Heureusement, tous les passagers ont été sauvés.
4 sauvegarder (*on computer*) ◊ *I saved the file onto a diskette.* J'ai sauvegardé le fichier sur disquette.
♦ **to save up** mettre de l'argent de côté ◊ *I'm saving up for a new bike.* Je

S

☞

mets de l'argent de côté pour un nouveau vélo.

savings PL NOUN
les économies FEM PL ◊ *She spent all her savings on a computer.* Elle a dépensé toutes ses économies en achetant un ordinateur.

savoury ADJECTIVE
salé ◊ *Is it sweet or savoury?* C'est sucré ou salé?

saw VERB *see* **see**

saw NOUN
la scie

sax NOUN
le saxo (*informal*) ◊ *I play the sax.* Je joue du saxo.

saxophone NOUN
le saxophone ◊ *I play the saxophone.* Je joue du saxophone.

to **say** VERB
dire ◊ *What did he say?* Qu'est-ce qu'il a dit? ◊ *Did you hear what she said?* Tu as entendu ce qu'elle a dit?
- **Could you say that again?** Pourriez-vous répéter s'il vous plaît?
- **That goes without saying.** Cela va sans dire.

saying NOUN
le dicton ◊ *It's just a saying.* C'est juste un dicton.

scale NOUN
1. l' échelle FEM (*of map*) ◊ *a large-scale map* une carte à grande échelle
2. l' ampleur FEM (*size, extent*) ◊ *a disaster on a massive scale* un désastre d'une ampleur incroyable
3. la gamme (*in music*)

scales PL NOUN
la balance SING (*in kitchen, shop*)
- **bathroom scales** le pèse-personne SING

scampi PL NOUN
les scampi MASC PL

scandal NOUN
1. le scandale (*outrage*) ◊ *It caused a scandal.* Ça a fait scandale.
2. les ragots MASC PL (*gossip*) ◊ *It's just scandal.* Ce ne sont que des ragots.

Scandinavia NOUN
la Scandinavie
- **in Scandinavia** en Scandinavie

Scandinavian ADJECTIVE
scandinave

scar NOUN
la cicatrice

scarce ADJECTIVE
limité ◊ *scarce resources* des ressources limitées

- **Jobs are scarce these days.** Il y a peu de travail ces temps-ci.

scarcely ADVERB
à peine ◊ *I scarcely knew him.* Je le connaissais à peine.

scare NOUN
see also **scare** VERB
la panique
- **a bomb scare** une alerte à la bombe

to **scare** VERB
see also **scare** NOUN
- **to scare somebody** faire peur à quelqu'un ◊ *He scares me.* Il me fait peur.

scarecrow NOUN
l' épouvantail MASC

scared ADJECTIVE
- **to be scared** avoir peur ◊ *I was scared stiff.* J'avais terriblement peur.
- **to be scared of** avoir peur de ◊ *Are you scared of him?* Est-ce que tu as peur de lui?

scarf NOUN
1. l' écharpe FEM (*long*)
2. le foulard (*square*)

scary ADJECTIVE
effrayant ◊ *It was really scary.* C'était vraiment effrayant.

scene NOUN
1. les lieux MASC PL (*place*) ◊ *The police were soon on the scene.* La police est vite arrivée sur les lieux. ◊ *the scene of the crime* les lieux du crime
2. le spectacle (*event, sight*) ◊ *It was an amazing scene.* C'était un spectacle étonnant.
- **to make a scene** faire une scène

scenery NOUN
le paysage (*landscape*)

scent NOUN
le parfum (*perfume*)

schedule NOUN
le programme ◊ *a busy schedule* un programme chargé
- **on schedule** comme prévu
- **to be behind schedule** avoir du retard

scheduled flight NOUN
le vol régulier

scheme NOUN
1. le truc (*idea*) ◊ *a crazy scheme he dreamed up* un truc farfelu qu'il a inventé
2. le projet (*project*) ◊ *a council road-widening scheme* un projet municipal d'élargissement des routes

scholarship NOUN
la bourse

school NOUN

l' école FEM
♦to go to school aller à l'école

schoolbag NOUN
le cartable

schoolbook NOUN
le livre scolaire

schoolboy NOUN
l' écolier MASC

schoolchildren PL NOUN
les écoliers MASC PL

schoolgirl NOUN
l' écolière FEM

science NOUN
la science

science fiction NOUN
la science-fiction

scientific ADJECTIVE
scientifique

scientist NOUN
(doing research)
le chercheur
la chercheuse
♦He trained as a scientist. Il a une
formation scientifique.

scissors PL NOUN
les ciseaux MASC PL ◊ a pair of scissors
une paire de ciseaux

to scoff VERB
bouffer (eat) ◊ My brother scoffed all
the sandwiches. Mon frère a bouffé
tous les sandwichs.

scone NOUN
le scone

scooter NOUN
1 le scooter
2 la trottinette (child's toy)

score NOUN
see also **score** VERB
le score ◊ The score was three nil.
Le score était trois à zéro.

to score VERB
see also **score** NOUN
1 marquer (goal, point) ◊ to score a
goal marquer un but
♦to score 6 out of 10 obtenir un score
de six sur dix
2 compter les points (keep score)
◊ Who's going to score? Qui va
compter les points?

Scorpio NOUN
le Scorpion ◊ I'm Scorpio. Je suis
Scorpion.

Scot NOUN
l' Écossais MASC
l' Écossaise FEM

Scotch tape ® NOUN US
le scotch ®

Scotland NOUN
l' Écosse FEM
♦in Scotland en Écosse
♦to Scotland en Écosse
♦I'm from Scotland. Je suis écossais.

Scots ADJECTIVE
écossais ◊ a Scots accent un accent
écossais

Scotsman NOUN
l' Écossais MASC

Scotswoman NOUN
l' Écossaise FEM

Scottish ADJECTIVE
écossais ◊ a Scottish accent un
accent écossais

scout NOUN
le scout ◊ I'm in the Scouts. Je suis
scout.

scrambled eggs PL NOUN
les œufs brouillés MASC PL

scrap NOUN
see also **scrap** VERB
1 le bout ◊ a scrap of paper un bout
de papier
2 la bagarre (fight)
♦scrap iron la ferraille

to scrap VERB
see also **scrap** NOUN
abandonner (plan) ◊ The idea was
scrapped. L'idée a été abandonnée.

scrapbook NOUN
l' album MASC

to scratch VERB
see also **scratch** NOUN
se gratter ◊ Stop scratching! Arrête
de te gratter!

scratch NOUN
see also **scratch** VERB
l' égratignure FEM (on skin)
♦to start from scratch partir de zéro

scream NOUN
see also **scream** VERB
le hurlement

to scream VERB
see also **scream** NOUN
hurler

screen NOUN
l' écran MASC

screen-saver NOUN
l' économiseur d'écran MASC

screw NOUN
la vis

screwdriver NOUN
le tournevis

to scribble VERB
griffonner

to scrub VERB

S

☞

récurer ◊ *to scrub a pan* récurer une casserole

sculpture NOUN
la sculpture

sea NOUN
la mer

seafood NOUN
les fruits de mer MASC PL ◊ *I don't like seafood.* Je n'aime pas les fruits de mer.

seagull NOUN
la mouette

seal NOUN
| see also **seal** VERB |
1 le phoque (*animal*)
2 le cachet (*on letter*)

to **seal** VERB
| see also **seal** NOUN |
1 sceller (*document*)
2 coller (*letter*)

seaman NOUN
le marin

to **search** VERB
| see also **search** NOUN |
fouiller ◊ *They searched the woods for her.* Ils ont fouillé les bois pour la trouver.
♦ **to search for something** chercher quelque chose ◊ *He searched for evidence.* Il cherchait des preuves.

search NOUN
| see also **search** VERB |
la fouille

search engine NOUN
le moteur de recherche

search party NOUN
l' expédition de secours FEM

seashore NOUN
le bord de la mer ◊ *on the seashore* au bord de la mer

seasick ADJECTIVE
♦ **to be seasick** avoir le mal de mer

seaside NOUN
le bord de la mer ◊ *at the seaside* au bord de la mer

season NOUN
la saison ◊ *What's your favourite season?* Quelle est ta saison préférée?
♦ **out of season** hors saison ◊ *It's cheaper to go there out of season.* C'est moins cher d'y aller hors saison.
♦ **during the holiday season** en période de vacances
♦ **a season ticket** une carte d'abonnement

seat NOUN

le siège

seat belt NOUN
la ceinture de sécurité

sea water NOUN
l' eau de mer FEM

seaweed NOUN
les algues FEM PL

second ADJECTIVE
| see also **second** NOUN |
deuxième ◊ *on the second page* à la deuxième page
♦ **to come second** (*in race*) arriver deuxième
♦ **to travel second class** voyager en seconde
♦ **the second of March** le deux mars

second NOUN
| see also **second** ADJECTIVE |
la seconde ◊ *It'll only take a second.* Ça va prendre juste une seconde.

secondary school NOUN
1 le collège
2 le lycée

> ⓘ In France pupils go to a **collège** between the ages of 11 and 15, and then to a **lycée** until the age of 18.

second-class ADJECTIVE, ADVERB
1 de seconde classe (*ticket, compartment*)
♦ **to travel second-class** voyager en seconde
2 à tarif réduit (*stamp, letter*) ◊ *to send something second-class* envoyer quelque chose à tarif réduit

secondhand ADJECTIVE
d'occasion ◊ *a secondhand car* une voiture d'occasion

secondly ADVERB
deuxièmement
♦ **firstly ... secondly ...** d'abord ... ensuite ... ◊ *Firstly, it's too expensive. Secondly, it wouldn't work anyway.* D'abord, c'est trop cher. Ensuite, ça ne marcherait quand même pas.

secret ADJECTIVE
| see also **secret** NOUN |
secret MASC
secrète FEM
◊ *a secret mission* une mission secrète

secret NOUN
| see also **secret** ADJECTIVE |
le secret ◊ *It's a secret.* C'est un secret. ◊ *Can you keep a secret?* Tu sais garder un secret?
♦ **in secret** en secret

secretary NOUN

le/la secrétaire ◊ *She's a secretary.*
Elle est secrétaire.

secretly NOUN
secrètement

section NOUN
la section

security NOUN
1 la sécurité ◊ *a feeling of security*
un sentiment de sécurité ◊ *a*
campaign to improve airport security
une campagne visant à améliorer la
sécurité dans les aéroports
♦ **job security** la sécurité de l'emploi

security guard NOUN
1 le vigile (*on guard*)
2 le convoyeur de fonds
(*transporting money*)

sedan NOUN US
la berline

to **see** VERB
voir ◊ *I can't see.* Je n'y vois rien. ◊ *I*
saw him yesterday. Je l'ai vu hier.
◊ *Have you seen him?* Est-ce que tu
l'as vu?
♦ **See you!** Salut!
♦ **See you soon!** À bientôt!
♦ **to see to something** s'occuper de
quelque chose ◊ *The window's stuck*
again. Can you see to it please? La
fenêtre est encore coincée. Tu peux
t'en occuper s'il te plaît?

seed NOUN
la graine ◊ *sunflower seeds* des
graines de tournesol

to **seek** VERB
chercher
♦ **to seek help** chercher de l'aide

to **seem** VERB
avoir l'air ◊ *She seems tired.* Elle a
l'air fatiguée. ◊ *The shop seemed to*
be closed. Le magasin avait l'air
d'être fermé.
♦ **That seems like a good idea.** Ce n'est
pas une mauvaise idée.
♦ **It seems that ...** Il paraît que ... ◊ *It*
seems she's getting married. Il paraît
qu'elle va se marier.
♦ **There seems to be a problem.** Il
semble y avoir un problème.

seen VERB *see* **see**

seesaw NOUN
le tapecul

see-through ADJECTIVE
transparent

seldom ADVERB
rarement

to **select** VERB
sélectionner

selection NOUN

la sélection

self-assured ADJECTIVE
sûr de soi ◊ *He's very self-assured.* Il
est très sûr de lui.

self-catering ADJECTIVE
♦ **a self-catering apartment** un
appartement de vacances

self-centred ADJECTIVE (US **self-centered**)
égocentrique

self-confidence NOUN
la confiance en soi ◊ *He hasn't got*
much self-confidence. Il n'a pas très
confiance en lui.

self-conscious ADJECTIVE
♦ **to be self-conscious (1)** (*embarrassed*)
être mal à l'aise ◊ *She was really*
self-conscious at first. Elle était
vraiment mal à l'aise au début.
♦ **to be self-conscious (2)** (*shy*) manquer
d'assurance ◊ *He's always been*
rather self-conscious. Il a toujours
manqué un peu d'assurance.

self-contained ADJECTIVE
♦ **a self-contained flat** un appartement
indépendant

self-control NOUN
le sang-froid

self-defence NOUN (US **self-defense**)
l' autodéfense FEM ◊ *self-defence*
classes les cours d'autodéfense
♦ **She killed him in self-defence.** Elle l'a
tué en légitime défense.

self-discipline NOUN
l' autodiscipline FEM

self-disciplined ADJECTIVE
♦ **he is self-disciplined** il fait preuve
d'autodiscipline

self-employed ADJECTIVE
♦ **to be self-employed** travailler à son
compte ◊ *He's self-employed.* Il
travaille à son compte.
♦ **the self-employed** les travailleurs
indépendants MASC PL

selfish ADJECTIVE
égoïste ◊ *Don't be so selfish.* Ne sois
pas si égoïste.

self-respect NOUN
l' amour-propre MASC

self-service ADJECTIVE
♦ **It's self-service.** (*café, shop*) C'est un
self-service.
♦ **a self-service restaurant** un restaurant
self-service

to **sell** VERB
vendre ◊ *He sold it to me.* Il me l'a
vendu.

sell off VERB
liquider

S

to **sell out** VERB
se vendre ◊ *The tickets sold out in three hours.* Les billets se sont tous vendus en trois heures. ◊ *The show didn't quite sell out.* Ce spectacle ne s'est pas très bien vendu.
♦ **The tickets are all sold out.** Il ne reste plus de billets.

to **sell-by date** NOUN
la date limite de vente

selling price NOUN
le prix de vente

Sellotape ® NOUN
le scotch ®

semi NOUN
la maison jumelée ◊ *We live in a semi.* Nous habitons dans une maison jumelée.

semicircle NOUN
le demi-cercle

semicolon NOUN
le point-virgule

semi-detached house NOUN
la maison jumelée ◊ *We live in a semi-detached house.* Nous habitons dans une maison jumelée.

semi-final NOUN
la demi-finale

semi-skimmed milk NOUN
le lait demi-écrémé

to **send** VERB
envoyer ◊ *She sent me a birthday card.* Elle m'a envoyé une carte d'anniversaire.
♦ **to send back** renvoyer
♦ **to send off (1)** (*goods, letter*) envoyer
♦ **to send off (2)** (*in sports match*) renvoyer du terrain ◊ *He was sent off.* On l'a renvoyé du terrain.
♦ **to send off for something (1)** (*free*) se faire envoyer quelque chose ◊ *I've sent off for a brochure.* Je me suis fait envoyer une brochure.
♦ **to send off for something (2)** (*paid for*) commander quelque chose par correspondance ◊ *She sent off for a book.* Elle a commandé un livre par correspondance.
♦ **to send out** envoyer
♦ **to send out for** commander par téléphone ◊ *Shall we send out for a pizza?* Et si on commandait une pizza par téléphone?

sender NOUN
l' expéditeur MASC
l' expéditrice FEM

senior ADJECTIVE
haut placé

♦ **senior management** les cadres supérieurs MASC PL
♦ **senior school** le lycée
♦ **senior pupils** les grandes classes FEM PL

senior citizen NOUN
la personne du troisième âge
(les personnes du troisième âge PL)

sensational ADJECTIVE
sensationnel MASC
sensationnelle FEM

sense NOUN
[1] le bon sens (*wisdom*) ◊ *Use your common sense!* Un peu de bon sens, voyons!
♦ **It makes sense.** C'est logique.
♦ **It doesn't make sense.** Ça n'a pas de sens.
[2] le sens (*faculty*) ◊ *the five senses* les cinq sens
♦ **the sense of touch** le toucher
♦ **the sense of smell** l'odorat MASC
♦ **the sixth sense** le sixième sens
♦ **sense of humour** le sens de l'humour ◊ *He's got no sense of humour.* Il n'a aucun sens de l'humour.

senseless ADJECTIVE
insensé

sensible ADJECTIVE
raisonnable ◊ *Be sensible!* Sois raisonnable!
*Be careful not to translate **sensible** by the French word **sensible**.*

sensitive ADJECTIVE
sensible ◊ *She's very sensitive.* Elle est très sensible.

sensuous ADJECTIVE
sensuel MASC
sensuelle FEM

sent VERB *see* **send**

sentence NOUN
see also **sentence** VERB
[1] la phrase ◊ *What does this sentence mean?* Que veut dire cette phrase?
[2] la condamnation (*judgment*)
[3] la peine (*punishment*) ◊ *the death sentence* la peine de mort
♦ **He got a life sentence.** Il a été condamné à la réclusion à perpétuité.

to **sentence** VERB
see also **sentence** NOUN
♦ **to sentence somebody to life imprisonment** condamner quelqu'un à la réclusion à perpétuité
♦ **to sentence somebody to death** condamner quelqu'un à mort

sentimental ADJECTIVE
sentimental
(sentimentaux MASC PL)

separate ADJECTIVE

see also **separate** VERB

séparé ◊ *I wrote it on a separate sheet.* Je l'ai écrit sur une feuille séparée.

♦ **The children have separate rooms.** Les enfants ont chacun leur chambre.

♦ **on separate occasions** à différentes reprises

to **separate** VERB

see also **separate** ADJECTIVE

1 séparer
2 se séparer (*married couple*)

separately ADVERB

séparément

separation NOUN

la séparation

September NOUN

septembre MASC

♦ **in September** en septembre

sequel NOUN

la suite (*book, film*)

sequence NOUN

1 l' ordre MASC
♦ **in sequence** par ordre
♦ **a sequence of events** une succession d'événements
2 la séquence (*in film*)

sergeant NOUN

1 le sergent (*army*)
2 le brigadier (*police*)

serial NOUN

le feuilleton

series NOUN

1 la série ◊ *a TV series* une série télévisée
2 la suite (*of numbers*)

serious ADJECTIVE

1 sérieux MASC
sérieuse FEM
◊ *You look very serious.* Tu as l'air sérieux.

♦ **Are you serious?** Sérieusement?
2 (*illness, mistake*)
grave

seriously ADVERB

sérieusement ◊ *No, but seriously ...* Non, mais sérieusement ...

♦ **to take somebody seriously** prendre quelqu'un au sérieux
♦ **seriously injured** gravement blessé
♦ **Seriously?** Vraiment?

sermon NOUN

le sermon

servant NOUN

le/la domestique

to **serve** VERB

see also **serve** NOUN

1 servir ◊ *Dinner is served.* Le dîner est servi. ◊ *It's Agassi's turn to serve.* C'est à Agassi de servir.
2 purger (*prison sentence*)
♦ **to serve time** être en prison
♦ **It serves you right.** C'est bien fait pour toi.

serve NOUN

see also **serve** VERB

le service (*tennis*)
♦ **It's your serve.** C'est à toi de servir.

server NOUN

le serveur (*computing*)

to **service** VERB

see also **service** NOUN

réviser (*car, washing machine*)

service NOUN

see also **service** VERB

1 le service ◊ *Service is included.* Le service est compris.
2 la révision (*of car*)
3 l' office MASC (*church service*)
♦ **the Fire Service** les sapeurs-pompiers MASC PL
♦ **the armed services** les forces armées FEM

service area NOUN

l' aire de service FEM

service charge NOUN

le service ◊ *There's no service charge.* Le service est compris.

serviceman NOUN

le militaire ◊ *He's a serviceman.* Il est militaire.

service station NOUN

la station-service
(les stations-service PL)

serviette NOUN

la serviette

session NOUN

la séance

set NOUN

see also **set** VERB

1 le jeu
(les jeux PL)
◊ *a set of keys* un jeu de clés ◊ *a chess set* un jeu d'échecs
♦ **a train set** un train électrique
2 (*in tennis*)
le set

to **set** VERB

see also **set** NOUN

1 mettre à sonner (*alarm clock*) ◊ *I set the alarm for 7 o'clock.* J'ai mis le réveil à sept heures.
2 établir (*record*) ◊ *The world record was set last year.* Le record du monde a été établi l'année dernière.

S

☞

3 se coucher (sun) ◊ The sun was setting. Le soleil se couchait.
♦ **The film is set in Morocco.** L'action du film se déroule au Maroc.
♦ **to set off** partir ◊ We set off for London at 9 o'clock. Nous sommes partis pour Londres à neuf heures.
♦ **to set out** partir ◊ We set out for London at 9 o'clock. Nous sommes partis pour Londres à neuf heures.
♦ **to set sail** prendre la mer
♦ **to set the table** mettre le couvert

settee NOUN
le canapé

to **settle** VERB
1 résoudre (problem)
2 régler (argument, account)
♦ **to settle down** (calm down) se calmer
♦ **Settle down!** Du calme!
♦ **to settle in** s'installer
♦ **to settle on something** opter pour quelque chose

seven NUMBER
sept ◊ She's seven. Elle a sept ans.

seventeen NUMBER
dix-sept ◊ He's seventeen. Il a dix-sept ans.

seventeenth ADJECTIVE
dix-septième ◊ her seventeenth birthday son dix-septième anniversaire ◊ the seventeenth floor le dix-septième étage
♦ **the seventeenth of August** le dix-sept août

seventh ADJECTIVE
septième ◊ the seventh floor le septième étage
♦ **the seventh of August** le sept août

seventy NUMBER
soixante-dix

several ADJECTIVE, PRONOUN
plusieurs ◊ several schools plusieurs écoles
♦ **several of them** plusieurs ◊ I've seen several of them. J'en ai vu plusieurs.

to **sew** VERB
coudre
♦ **to sew up** (tear) recoudre

sewing NOUN
la couture ◊ I like sewing. J'aime faire de la couture.
♦ **a sewing machine** une machine à coudre

sewn VERB see **sew**

sex NOUN
le sexe
♦ **to have sex with somebody** coucher avec quelqu'un
♦ **sex education** l'éducation sexuelle FEM

sexism NOUN
le sexisme

sexist ADJECTIVE
sexiste

sexual ADJECTIVE
sexuel MASC
sexuelle FEM
◊ sexual discrimination la discrimination sexuelle ◊ sexual harassment le harcèlement sexuel

sexuality NOUN
la sexualité

sexy ADJECTIVE
sexy MASC, FEM, PL

shabby ADJECTIVE
miteux MASC
miteuse FEM

shade NOUN
1 l' ombre FEM
♦ **in the shade** à l'ombre ◊ It was 35 degrees in the shade. Il faisait trente-cinq à l'ombre.
2 la nuance (colour) ◊ a shade of blue une nuance de bleu

shadow NOUN
l' ombre FEM

to **shake** VERB
1 secouer ◊ She shook the rug. Elle a secoué le tapis.
2 trembler (tremble) ◊ He was shaking with cold. Il tremblait de froid.
♦ **to shake one's head** (in refusal) faire non de la tête
♦ **to shake hands with somebody** serrer la main à quelqu'un ◊ They shook hands. Ils se sont serré la main.

shaken ADJECTIVE
secoué ◊ I was feeling a bit shaken. J'étais un peu secoué.

shaky ADJECTIVE
tremblant (hand, voice)

shall VERB
♦ **Shall I shut the window?** Vous voulez que je ferme la fenêtre?
♦ **Shall we ask him to come with us?** Si on lui demandait de venir avec nous?

shallow ADJECTIVE
peu profond (water, pool)

shambles NOUN
la pagaille ◊ It's a complete shambles. C'est la pagaille complète.

shame NOUN
la honte ◊ The shame of it! Quelle honte!
♦ **What a shame!** Quel dommage!
♦ **It's a shame that ...** c'est dommage que ...

c'est dommage que has to be
followed by a verb in the
subjunctive.
◊ *It's a shame he isn't here.* C'est
dommage qu'il ne soit pas ici.

shampoo NOUN
le shampooing ◊ *a bottle of
shampoo* une bouteille de
shampooing

shandy NOUN
le panaché

shan't = **shall not**

shape NOUN
la forme

share NOUN
┌─────────────────┐
│ *see also* **share** VERB │
└─────────────────┘
[1] l' action FEM (*in company*) ◊ *They've
got shares in British Gas.* Ils ont des
actions de British Gas.
[2] la part ◊ *Everybody pays their
share.* Tout le monde paie sa part.

to **share** VERB
┌─────────────────┐
│ *see also* **share** NOUN │
└─────────────────┘
partager ◊ *to share a room with
somebody* partager une chambre
avec quelqu'un
♦ **to share out** distribuer ◊ *They shared
the sweets out among the children.*
Ils ont distribué les bonbons aux
enfants.

shark NOUN
le requin

sharp ADJECTIVE
[1] tranchant (*razor, knife*)
[2] pointu (*spike, point*)
[3] intelligent (*clever*) ◊ *She's very
sharp.* Elle est très intelligente.
♦ **at two o'clock sharp** à deux heures
pile

to **shave** VERB
se raser (*have a shave*)
♦ **to shave one's legs** se raser les
jambes

shaver NOUN
♦ **an electric shaver** un rasoir électrique

shaving cream NOUN
la crème à raser

shaving foam NOUN
la mousse à raser

she PRONOUN
elle ◊ *She's very nice.* Elle est très
gentille.

shed NOUN
la remise

she'd = **she had**, = **she would**

sheep NOUN
le mouton

sheepdog NOUN

le chien de berger
(les chiens de berger PL)

sheer ADJECTIVE
pur ◊ *It's sheer greed.* C'est de
l'avidité pure.

sheet NOUN
le drap (*on bed*)
♦ **a sheet of paper** une feuille de papier

shelf NOUN
[1] l' étagère FEM (*in house*)
[2] le rayon (*in shop*)

shell NOUN
[1] le coquillage (*on beach*)
[2] la coquille (*of egg, nut*)
[3] l' obus MASC (*explosive*)

she'll = **she will**

shellfish NOUN
les fruits de mer MASC PL

shell suit NOUN
le survêtement

shelter NOUN
♦ **to take shelter** se mettre à l'abri
♦ **a bus shelter** un arrêt d'autobus

shelves PL NOUN *see* **shelf**

shepherd NOUN
le berger

sheriff NOUN
le shérif

sherry NOUN
le xérès

she's = **she is**, = **she has**

Shetland Islands PL NOUN
les îles Shetland FEM PL

shield NOUN
le bouclier

shift NOUN
┌─────────────────┐
│ *see also* **shift** VERB │
└─────────────────┘
le service ◊ *His shift starts at 8
o'clock.* Il prend son service à huit
heures. ◊ *the night shift* le service de
nuit
♦ **to do shift work** faire les trois-huit

to **shift** VERB
┌─────────────────┐
│ *see also* **shift** NOUN │
└─────────────────┘
déplacer (*move*) ◊ *I couldn't shift the
wardrobe on my own.* Je n'ai pas pu
déplacer l'armoire tout seul.
♦ **Shift yourself!** Pousse-toi de là!
(*informal*)

shifty ADJECTIVE
[1] louche (*person*) ◊ *He looked shifty.*
Il avait l'air louche.
[2] fuyant (*eyes*)

shin NOUN
le tibia

to **shine** VERB
briller ◊ *The sun was shining.* Le
soleil brillait.

S

shiny ADJECTIVE
brillant

ship NOUN
1 le bateau
(les bateaux PL)
2 (warship)
le navire

shipbuilding NOUN
la construction navale

shipwreck NOUN
le naufrage

shipwrecked ADJECTIVE
♦to be shipwrecked faire naufrage

shipyard NOUN
le chantier naval

shirt NOUN
1 la chemise (man's)
2 le chemisier (woman's)

shit EXCLAMATION
Merde! (rude)

to **shiver** VERB
frissonner

shock NOUN
see also **shock** VERB
le choc
♦to get a shock (1) (surprise) avoir un choc
♦to get a shock (2) (electric) recevoir une décharge
♦an electric shock une décharge

to **shock** VERB
see also **shock** NOUN
1 bouleverser (upset) ◊ They were shocked by the tragedy. Ils ont été bouleversés par la tragédie.
2 choquer (scandalize) ◊ I was rather shocked by her attitude. J'ai été assez choqué par son attitude.

shocked ADJECTIVE
choqué ◊ He'll be shocked if you say that. Tu vas le choquer si tu dis ça.

shocking ADJECTIVE
choquant ◊ It's shocking! C'est choquant!
♦a shocking waste un gaspillage épouvantable

shoe NOUN
la chaussure

shoelace NOUN
le lacet

shoe polish NOUN
le cirage

shoe shop NOUN
le magasin de chaussures

shone VERB see **shine**

shook VERB see **shake**

to **shoot** VERB

1 abattre (kill) ◊ He was shot by a sniper. Il a été abattu par un franc-tireur.
2 fusiller (execute) ◊ He was shot at dawn. Il a été fusillé à l'aube.
3 tirer (gun) ◊ Don't shoot! Ne tirez pas!
♦to shoot at somebody tirer sur quelqu'un
♦He shot himself with a revolver. (dead) Il s'est suicidé d'un coup de revolver.
♦He was shot in the leg. (wounded) Il a reçu une balle dans la jambe.
♦to shoot an arrow envoyer une flèche
4 tourner (film) ◊ The film was shot in Prague. Le film a été tourné à Prague.
5 shooter (in football)

shooting NOUN
1 les coups de feu MASC PL ◊ They heard shooting. Ils ont entendu des coups de feu.
♦a shooting une fusillade
2 la chasse (hunting) ◊ to go shooting aller à la chasse

shop NOUN
le magasin ◊ a sports shop un magasin de sports

shop assistant NOUN
le vendeur
la vendeuse
◊ She's a shop assistant. Elle est vendeuse.

shopkeeper NOUN
le commerçant
la commerçante
◊ He's a shopkeeper. Il est commerçant.

shoplifting NOUN
le vol à l'étalage

shopping NOUN
les courses FEM PL (purchases) ◊ Can you get the shopping from the car? Tu peux aller chercher les courses dans la voiture?
♦I love shopping. J'adore faire du shopping.
♦to go shopping (1) (for food) faire des courses
♦to go shopping (2) (for pleasure) faire du shopping
♦a shopping bag un sac à provisions
♦a shopping centre un centre commercial

shop window NOUN
la vitrine

shore NOUN
le rivage
♦on shore à terre

short ADJECTIVE

[1] court ◊ *a short skirt* une jupe courte ◊ *short hair* les cheveux courts

♦**too short** trop court ◊ *It was a great holiday, but too short.* C'étaient des vacances super, mais trop courtes.

[2] petit *(person, period of time)* ◊ *She's quite short.* Elle est assez petite. ◊ *a short break* une petite pause ◊ *a short walk* une petite promenade

♦**to be short of something** être à court de quelque chose ◊ *I'm short of money.* Je suis à court d'argent.

♦**at short notice** au dernier moment

♦**In short, the answer's no.** Bref, la réponse est non.

shortage NOUN

la pénurie ◊ *a water shortage* une pénurie d'eau

short cut NOUN

le raccourci ◊ *I took a short cut.* J'ai pris un raccourci.

shorthand NOUN

la sténo

shortly ADVERB

bientôt

shorts PL NOUN

le short SING

♦**a pair of shorts** un short

short-sighted ADJECTIVE

myope

short story NOUN

la nouvelle

shot VERB *see* **shoot**

shot NOUN

[1] *(gunshot)*
le coup de feu
(les coups de feu PL)

[2] *(photo)*
la photo ◊ *a shot of Edinburgh Castle* une photo du château d'Édimbourg

[3] *(vaccination)*
le vaccin

shotgun NOUN

le fusil de chasse
(les fusils de chasse PL)

should VERB

When should means "ought to", use devoir.

devoir ◊ *You should take more exercise.* Vous devriez faire plus d'exercice. ◊ *He should be there by now.* Il devrait être arrivé maintenant. ◊ *That shouldn't be too hard.* Ça ne devrait pas être trop difficile.

♦**should have** avoir dû ◊ *I should have told you before.* J'aurais dû te le dire avant.

When should means "would", use the conditional tense.

♦**I should go if I were you.** Si j'étais vous, j'irais.

♦**I should be so lucky!** Ça serait trop beau!

shoulder NOUN

l' épaule FEM

♦**a shoulder bag** un sac à bandoulière

shouldn't = **should not**

to **shout** VERB

see also **shout** NOUN

crier ◊ *Don't shout!* Ne criez pas! ◊ *"Go away!" he shouted.* "Allez-vous-en!" a-t-il crié.

shout NOUN

see also **shout** VERB

le cri

shovel NOUN

la pelle

show NOUN

see also **show** VERB

[1] le spectacle *(performance)*

[2] l' émission FEM *(programme)*

[3] le salon *(exhibition)*

to **show** VERB

see also **show** NOUN

[1] montrer

♦**to show somebody something** montrer quelque chose à quelqu'un ◊ *Have I shown you my new trainers?* Je t'ai montré mes nouvelles baskets?

[2] faire preuve de ◊ *She showed great courage.* Elle a fait preuve de beaucoup de courage.

♦**It shows.** Ça se voit. ◊ *I've never been riding before. – It shows.* Je n'ai jamais fait de cheval. – Ça se voit.

♦**to show off** frimer *(informal)*

♦**to show up** *(turn up)* se pointer ◊ *He showed up late as usual.* Il s'est pointé en retard comme d'habitude.

shower NOUN

[1] la douche

♦**to have a shower** prendre une douche

[2] l' averse FEM *(of rain)*

showerproof ADJECTIVE

imperméabilisé

showing NOUN

la projection *(of film)*

shown VERB *see* **show**

show-off NOUN

le frimeur
la frimeuse

shrank VERB *see* **shrink**

to **shriek** VERB

hurler

S

shrimps PL NOUN
les <u>crevettes</u> FEM PL

to **shrink** VERB
<u>rétrécir</u> (clothes, fabric)

Shrove Tuesday NOUN
le <u>mardi gras</u>

to **shrug** VERB
♦ **to shrug one's shoulders** hausser les épaules

shrunk VERB see **shrink**

to **shudder** VERB
<u>frissonner</u>

to **shuffle** VERB
♦ **to shuffle the cards** battre les cartes

to **shut** VERB
<u>fermer</u> ◊ What time do you shut? À quelle heure est-ce que vous fermez? ◊ What time do the shops shut? À quelle heure est-ce que les magasins ferment?
♦ **to shut down** fermer ◊ The cinema shut down last year. Le cinéma a fermé l'année dernière.
♦ **to shut up (1)** (close) fermer
♦ **to shut up (2)** (be quiet) se taire ◊ Shut up! Tais-toi!

shutters PL NOUN
les <u>volets</u> MASC PL

shuttle NOUN
la <u>navette</u>

shuttlecock NOUN
le <u>volant</u> (badminton)

shy ADJECTIVE
<u>timide</u>

Sicily NOUN
la <u>Sicile</u>
♦ **in Sicily** en Sicile
♦ **to Sicily** en Sicile

sick ADJECTIVE
[1] <u>malade</u> (ill) ◊ He was sick for four days. Il a été malade pendant quatre jours.
[2] <u>de mauvais goût</u> (joke, humour) ◊ That's really sick! C'est vraiment de mauvais goût!
♦ **to be sick** (vomit) vomir ◊ I feel sick. J'ai envie de vomir.
♦ **to be sick of something** en avoir assez de quelque chose ◊ I'm sick of your jokes. J'en ai assez de tes plaisanteries.

sickening ADJECTIVE
<u>écœurant</u>

sick leave NOUN
le <u>congé de maladie</u>

sickness NOUN
la <u>maladie</u>

sick note NOUN

[1] le <u>mot d'absence</u> (from parents)
[2] le <u>certificat médical</u> (from doctor)

sick pay NOUN
l' <u>indemnité de maladie</u> FEM

side NOUN
[1] le <u>côté</u> (of object, building, car) ◊ He was driving on the wrong side of the road. Il roulait du mauvais côté de la route.
[2] le <u>bord</u> (of pool, river, road) ◊ by the side of the lake au bord du lac
[3] le <u>flanc</u> (of hill)
[4] l' <u>équipe</u> FEM (team)
♦ **He's on my side. (1)** (on my team) Il est dans mon équipe.
♦ **He's on my side. (2)** (supporting me) Il est de mon côté.
♦ **side by side** côte à côte
♦ **the side entrance** l'entrée latérale
♦ **to take sides** prendre parti ◊ She always takes his side. Elle prend toujours son parti.

sideboard NOUN
le <u>buffet</u>

side-effect NOUN
l' <u>effet secondaire</u> MASC

side street NOUN
la <u>petite rue transversale</u>

sidewalk NOUN US
le <u>trottoir</u>

sideways ADVERB
[1] <u>de côté</u> (look, be facing)
[2] <u>de travers</u> (move)
♦ **sideways on** de profil

sieve NOUN
la <u>passoire</u>

sigh NOUN
see also **sigh** VERB
le <u>soupir</u>

to **sigh** VERB
see also **sigh** NOUN
<u>soupirer</u>

sight NOUN
[1] la <u>vue</u> ◊ to have poor sight avoir une mauvaise vue
♦ **to know somebody by sight** connaître quelqu'un de vue
[2] le <u>spectacle</u> ◊ It was an amazing sight. C'était un spectacle étonnant.
♦ **in sight** visible
♦ **out of sight** hors de vue
♦ **the sights** (tourist spots) les attractions touristiques FEM
♦ **to see the sights of London** visiter Londres

sightseeing NOUN
le <u>tourisme</u>
♦ **to go sightseeing** faire du tourisme

sign NOUN

see also **sign** VERB

1 (*notice*)
le panneau
(les panneaux PL)
◊ *There was a big sign saying
"private".* Il y avait un grand panneau
indiquant "privé".
◆ **a road sign** un panneau
2 (*gesture, indication*)
le signe ◊ *There's no sign of
improvement.* Il n'y a aucun signe
d'amélioration.
◆ **What sign are you?** (*star sign*) Tu es
de quel signe?

to **sign** VERB

see also **sign** NOUN
signer
◆ **to sign on (1)** (*as unemployed*)
s'inscrire au chômage
◆ **to sign on (2)** (*for course*) s'inscrire

signal NOUN

see also **signal** VERB
le signal
(les signaux PL)

to **signal** VERB

see also **signal** NOUN
◆ **to signal to somebody** faire un signe
à quelqu'un

signalman NOUN
l' aiguilleur MASC

signature NOUN
la signature

significance NOUN
l' importance FEM

significant ADJECTIVE
important

sign language NOUN
le langage des signes

signpost NOUN
le poteau indicateur

silence NOUN
le silence

silencer NOUN
le silencieux

silent ADJECTIVE
silencieux MASC
silencieuse FEM

silicon chip NOUN
la puce électronique

silk NOUN

see also **silk** ADJECTIVE
la soie

silk ADJECTIVE

see also **silk** NOUN
en soie ◊ *a silk scarf* un foulard en
soie

silky ADJECTIVE
soyeux MASC

soyeuse FEM

silly ADJECTIVE
bête

silver NOUN
l' argent MASC ◊ *a silver medal* une
médaille d'argent

similar ADJECTIVE
semblable
◆ **similar to** semblable à

simple ADJECTIVE
1 simple ◊ *It's very simple.* C'est
très simple.
2 (*simple-minded*)
simplet MASC
simplette FEM
◊ *He's a bit simple.* Il est un peu
simplet.

simply ADVERB
simplement ◊ *It's simply not
possible.* Ça n'est tout simplement
pas possible.

simultaneous ADJECTIVE
simultané

sin NOUN

see also **sin** VERB
le péché

to **sin** VERB

see also **sin** NOUN
pécher

since PREPOSITION, ADVERB, CONJUNCTION
1 depuis ◊ *since Christmas* depuis
Noël ◊ *since then* depuis ce
moment-là ◊ *I haven't seen him
since.* Je ne l'ai pas vu depuis.
◆ **ever since** depuis ce moment-là
2 depuis que ◊ *I haven't seen her
since she left.* Je ne l'ai pas vue
depuis qu'elle est partie.
3 puisque (*because*) ◊ *Since you're
tired, let's stay at home.* Puisque tu
es fatigué, restons à la maison.

sincere ADJECTIVE
sincère

sincerely ADVERB
◆ **Yours sincerely ... (1)** (*in business
letter*) Veuillez agréer l'expression de
mes sentiments les meilleurs ...
◆ **Yours sincerely ... (2)** (*in personal
letter*) Cordialement ...

to **sing** VERB
chanter ◊ *He sang out of tune.* Il
chantait faux. ◊ *Have you ever sung
this tune before?* Vous avez déjà
chanté cet air-là?

singer NOUN
le chanteur
la chanteuse

singing NOUN
le chant

S

single ADJECTIVE

see also **single** NOUN

célibataire (unmarried)
- **a single room** une chambre pour une personne
- **not a single thing** rien du tout

single NOUN

see also **single** ADJECTIVE

1 l' aller simple MASC (ticket) ◊ A single to Toulouse, please. Un aller simple pour Toulouse, s'il vous plaît.
2 le 45 tours (record)
- **a CD single** un CD single

single parent NOUN
- **She's a single parent.** Elle élève ses enfants toute seule.
- **a single parent family** une famille monoparentale

singles PL NOUN
le simple SING (in tennis) ◊ the women's singles le simple dames

singular NOUN
le singulier ◊ in the singular au singulier

sinister ADJECTIVE
sinistre

sink NOUN

see also **sink** VERB

l' évier MASC

to **sink** VERB

see also **sink** NOUN

couler

sir NOUN
monsieur MASC
- **Yes sir.** Oui, Monsieur.

siren NOUN
la sirène

sister NOUN
1 la sœur ◊ my little sister ma petite sœur
2 l' infirmière en chef FEM (nurse)

sister-in-law NOUN
la belle-sœur
(les belles-sœurs PL)

to **sit** VERB
s'asseoir
- **to sit on something** s'asseoir sur quelque chose ◊ She sat on the chair. Elle s'est assise sur la chaise.
- **to sit down** s'asseoir
- **to be sitting** être assis
- **to sit an exam** passer un examen

sitcom NOUN
la comédie de situation
(les comédies de situation PL)

site NOUN
1 le site ◊ an archaeological site un site archéologique

- **the site of the accident** le lieu de l'accident
2 le camping (campsite)
- **a building site** un chantier

sitting room NOUN
le salon

situated ADJECTIVE
- **to be situated** être situé ◊ The village is situated on a hill. Le village est situé sur une colline.

situation NOUN
la situation

six NUMBER
six ◊ He's six. Il a six ans.

sixteen NUMBER
seize ◊ He's sixteen. Il a seize ans.

sixteenth ADJECTIVE
seizième ◊ the sixteenth floor le seizième étage
- **the sixteenth of August** le seize août

sixth ADJECTIVE
sixième ◊ the sixth floor le sixième étage
- **the sixth of August** le six août

sixth form NOUN
le lycée

sixty NUMBER
soixante

size NOUN

> ℹ️ France uses the European system to show clothing and shoe sizes.

1 la taille (of object, clothing) ◊ What size do you take? Quelle taille est-ce que vous faites?
- **I'm a size ten.** Je fais du trente-huit.
2 la pointure (of shoes)
- **I take size six.** Je fais du trente-neuf.

to **skate** VERB
1 faire du patin à glace (ice-skate)
2 faire du patin à roulettes (roller-skate)

skateboard NOUN
le skateboard

skateboarding NOUN
le skateboard ◊ to go skateboarding faire du skateboard

skates PL NOUN
les patins MASC PL

skating NOUN
le patin à glace ◊ to go skating faire du patin à glace
- **a skating rink** une patinoire

skeleton NOUN
le squelette

sketch NOUN

see also **sketch** VERB

le croquis (*drawing*)

to **sketch** VERB

see also **sketch** NOUN

♦**to sketch something** faire un croquis de quelque chose

ski NOUN

see also **ski** VERB

le ski

♦**ski boots** les chaussures de ski FEM

♦**a ski lift** un remonte-pente

♦**ski pants** le fuseau SING

♦**a ski pole** un bâton de ski

♦**a ski slope** une piste de ski

♦**a ski suit** une combinaison de ski

to **ski** VERB

see also **ski** NOUN

skier ◊ *Can you ski?* Tu sais skier?

to **skid** VERB

déraper

skier NOUN

le skieur

la skieuse

skiing NOUN

le ski ◊ *to go skiing* faire du ski

♦**to go on a skiing holiday** aller aux sports d'hiver

skilful ADJECTIVE

adroit

skill NOUN

le talent ◊ *He played with great skill.* Il a joué avec beaucoup de talent.

skilled ADJECTIVE

♦**a skilled worker** un ouvrier spécialisé

skimmed milk NOUN

le lait écrémé

skimpy ADJECTIVE

1 minuscule (*clothes*)

2 maigre (*meal*)

skin NOUN

la peau

(les peaux PL)

♦**skin cancer** le cancer de la peau

skinhead NOUN

le/la skinhead

skinny ADJECTIVE

maigre

skin-tight ADJECTIVE

collant

skip NOUN

see also **skip** VERB

la benne (*container*)

to **skip** VERB

see also **skip** NOUN

sauter ◊ *to skip a meal* sauter un repas

♦**to skip a lesson** sécher un cours

skirt NOUN

la jupe

skittles NOUN

les quilles FEM PL ◊ *to play skittles* jouer aux quilles

to **skive** VERB

tirer au flanc (*be lazy*)

♦**to skive off** sécher (*informal*) ◊ *to skive off school* sécher les cours

skull NOUN

le crâne

sky NOUN

le ciel

skyscraper NOUN

le gratte-ciel

(les gratte-ciel PL)

slack ADJECTIVE

1 lâche (*rope*)

2 négligent (*person*)

to **slag off** VERB

♦**to slag somebody off** dire du mal de quelqu'un

to **slam** VERB

claquer ◊ *The door slammed.* La porte a claqué. ◊ *She slammed the door.* Elle a claqué la porte.

slang NOUN

l' argot MASC

slap NOUN

see also **slap** VERB

la claque

to **slap** VERB

see also **slap** NOUN

♦**to slap somebody** donner une claque à quelqu'un

slate NOUN

l' ardoise FEM

sledge NOUN

la luge

sledging NOUN

♦**to go sledging** faire de la luge

sleep NOUN

see also **sleep** VERB

le sommeil

♦**I need some sleep.** J'ai besoin de dormir.

♦**to go to sleep** s'endormir

to **sleep** VERB

see also **sleep** NOUN

dormir ◊ *I couldn't sleep last night.* J'ai mal dormi la nuit dernière.

♦**to sleep with somebody** coucher avec quelqu'un

♦**to sleep together** coucher ensemble

to **sleep around** VERB

coucher à droite et à gauche

to **sleep in** VERB

1 ne pas se réveiller (*accidentally*)

◊ *I'm sorry I'm late, I slept in.* Désolé

S

d'être en retard: je ne me suis pas
réveillé.
2 faire la grasse matinée (*on
purpose*)

sleeping bag NOUN
le sac de couchage
(les sacs de couchage PL)

sleeping car NOUN
le wagon-lit
(les wagons-lits PL)

sleeping pill NOUN
le somnifère

sleepy ADJECTIVE
♦**to feel sleepy** avoir sommeil ◊ *I was
feeling sleepy.* J'avais sommeil.
♦**a sleepy little village** un petit village
tranquille

sleet NOUN
see also **sleet** VERB
la neige fondue

to **sleet** VERB
see also **sleet** NOUN
♦**It's sleeting.** Il tombe de la neige
fondue.

sleeve NOUN
1 la manche ◊ *long sleeves* les
manches longues ◊ *short sleeves* les
manches courtes
2 la pochette (*record sleeve*)

sleigh NOUN
le traîneau
(les traîneaux PL)

slept VERB see **sleep**

slice NOUN
see also **slice** VERB
la tranche

to **slice** VERB
see also **slice** NOUN
couper en tranches

slick NOUN
♦**an oil slick** une marée noire

slide NOUN
see also **slide** VERB
1 le toboggan (*in playground*)
2 la diapositive (*photo*)
3 la barrette (*hair slide*)

to **slide** VERB
see also **slide** NOUN
glisser

slight ADJECTIVE
léger MASC
légère FEM
◊ *a slight problem* un léger problème
◊ *a slight improvement* une légère
amélioration

slightly ADVERB
légèrement

slim ADJECTIVE
see also **slim** VERB
mince

to **slim** VERB
see also **slim** ADJECTIVE
faire un régime (*be on a diet*) ◊ *I'm
slimming.* Je fais un régime.

sling NOUN
l' écharpe FEM ◊ *She had her arm in a
sling.* Elle avait le bras en écharpe.

slip NOUN
see also **slip** VERB
1 l' erreur FEM (*mistake*)
2 le jupon (*underskirt*)
3 la combinaison (*full-length
underskirt*)
♦**a slip of paper** un bout de papier
♦**a slip of the tongue** un lapsus

to **slip** VERB
see also **slip** NOUN
glisser ◊ *He slipped on the ice.* Il a
glissé sur le verglas.
♦**to slip up** faire une erreur (*make a
mistake*)

slipper NOUN
le chausson
♦**a pair of slippers** des chaussons

slippery ADJECTIVE
glissant

slip-up NOUN
l' erreur FEM

slope NOUN
la pente

sloppy ADJECTIVE
1 bâclé (*work*)
2 négligé (*person, appearance*)

slot NOUN
la fente

slot machine NOUN
1 la machine à sous (*for gambling*)
2 le distributeur automatique
(*vending machine*)

slow ADJECTIVE, ADVERB
1 lent ◊ *He's a bit slow.* Il est un
peu lent.
2 lentement ◊ *to go slow* (*person,
car*) aller lentement ◊ *Drive slower!*
Conduisez plus lentement!
♦**My watch is slow.** Ma montre
retarde.

to **slow down** VERB
ralentir

slowly ADVERB
lentement

slug NOUN
la limace

slum NOUN
1 le quartier insalubre (*area*)
2 le taudis (*house*)

slush NOUN

la neige fondue

sly ADJECTIVE
rusé (*person*)
♦ **a sly smile** un sourire sournois

smack NOUN
see also **smack** VERB
la tape

to **smack** VERB
see also **smack** NOUN
♦ **to smack somebody** donner une tape à quelqu'un

small ADJECTIVE
petit
♦ **small change** la petite monnaie

smart ADJECTIVE
1 (*elegant*)
chic MASC, FEM, PL
2 (*clever*)
intelligent
♦ **a smart idea** une idée astucieuse

smash NOUN
see also **smash** VERB
l' accident MASC

to **smash** VERB
see also **smash** NOUN
1 casser (*break*) ◊ *I've smashed my watch.* J'ai cassé ma montre.
2 se briser (*get broken*) ◊ *The glass smashed into tiny pieces.* Le verre s'est brisé en mille morceaux.

smashing ADJECTIVE
formidable ◊ *I think he's smashing.* Je le trouve formidable.

smell NOUN
see also **smell** VERB
l' odeur FEM
♦ **the sense of smell** l'odorat MASC

to **smell** VERB
see also **smell** NOUN
1 sentir mauvais ◊ *That old dog really smells!* Qu'est-ce qu'il sent mauvais, ce vieux chien!
♦ **to smell of something** sentir quelque chose ◊ *It smells of petrol.* Ça sent l'essence.
2 sentir (*detect*) ◊ *I can't smell anything.* Je ne sens rien.

smelly ADJECTIVE
qui sent mauvais ◊ *He's got smelly feet.* Il a les pieds qui sentent mauvais.

smelt VERB see **smell**

smile NOUN
see also **smile** VERB
le sourire

to **smile** VERB
see also **smile** NOUN
sourire

smiley NOUN
l' émoticon MASC

smoke NOUN
see also **smoke** VERB
la fumée

to **smoke** VERB
see also **smoke** NOUN
fumer ◊ *I don't smoke.* Je ne fume pas. ◊ *He smokes cigars.* Il fume le cigare.

smoker NOUN
le fumeur
la fumeuse

smoking NOUN
♦ **to give up smoking** arrêter de fumer
♦ **Smoking is bad for you.** Le tabac est mauvais pour la santé.
♦ **"no smoking"** "défense de fumer"

smooth ADJECTIVE
1 (*surface*)
lisse
2 (*person*)
mielleux MASC
mielleuse FEM

smudge NOUN
la bavure

smug ADJECTIVE
suffisant

to **smuggle** VERB
1 passer en fraude (*goods*) ◊ *to smuggle cigarettes into a country* faire passer des cigarettes en fraude dans un pays
2 faire passer clandestinement (*people*)
♦ **They managed to smuggle him out of prison.** Ils ont réussi à le faire sortir de prison clandestinement.

smuggler NOUN
le contrebandier
la contrebandière

smuggling NOUN
la contrebande

smutty ADJECTIVE
cochon MASC
cochonne FEM
◊ *a smutty story* une histoire cochonne

snack NOUN
l' en-cas MASC
(les en-cas PL)
♦ **to have a snack** prendre un en-cas

snack bar NOUN
le snack-bar

snail NOUN
l' escargot MASC

snake NOUN
le serpent

S

to **snap** VERB
casser net (*break*) ◊ *The branch snapped.* La branche a cassé net.
♦**to snap one's fingers** faire claquer ses doigts

snap fastener NOUN
le bouton-pression
(les boutons-pression PL)

snapshot NOUN
la photo

to **snarl** VERB
gronder (*animal*)

to **snatch** VERB
♦**to snatch something from somebody** arracher quelque chose à quelqu'un ◊ *He snatched the keys from my hand.* Il m'a arraché les clés des mains.
♦**My bag was snatched.** On m'a arraché mon sac.

to **sneak** VERB
♦**to sneak in** entrer furtivement
♦**to sneak out** sortir furtivement
♦**to sneak up on somebody** s'approcher de quelqu'un sans faire de bruit

to **sneeze** VERB
éternuer

to **sniff** VERB
1 renifler ◊ *Stop sniffing!* Arrête de renifler!
2 flairer ◊ *The dog sniffed my hand.* Le chien m'a flairé la main.
♦**to sniff glue** sniffer de la colle

snob NOUN
le/la snob

snooker NOUN
le billard ◊ *to play snooker* jouer au billard

snooze NOUN
le petit somme ◊ *to have a snooze* faire un petit somme

to **snore** VERB
ronfler

snow NOUN
see also **snow** VERB
la neige

to **snow** VERB
see also **snow** NOUN
neiger ◊ *It's snowing.* Il neige.

snowball NOUN
la boule de neige
(les boules de neige PL)

snowflake NOUN
le flocon de neige
(les flocons de neige PL)

snowman NOUN
le bonhomme de neige
(les bonshommes de neige PL)

◊ *to build a snowman* faire un bonhomme de neige

SO CONJUNCTION, ADVERB
1 alors ◊ *The shop was closed, so I went home.* Le magasin était fermé, alors je suis rentré chez moi. ◊ *So, have you always lived in London?* Alors, vous avez toujours vécu à Londres?
♦**So what?** Et alors?
2 donc (*so that*) ◊ *It rained, so I got wet.* Il pleuvait, donc j'ai été mouillé.
3 tellement (*very*) ◊ *It was so heavy!* C'était tellement lourd! ◊ *He was talking so fast I couldn't understand.* Il parlait tellement vite que je ne comprenais pas.
♦**It's not so heavy!** Ça n'est pas si lourd que ça!
♦**How's your father? – Not so good.** Comment va ton père? – Pas très bien.
♦**so much** (*a lot*) tellement ◊ *I love you so much.* Je t'aime tellement.
♦**so much ..., so many ...** tellement de ... ◊ *I've got so much work.* J'ai tellement de travail. ◊ *I've got so many things to do today.* J'ai tellement de choses à faire aujourd'hui.
4 aussi (*in comparisons*) ◊ *He's like his sister but not so clever.* Il est comme sa sœur mais pas aussi intelligent.
♦**so do I** moi aussi ◊ *I love horses. – So do I.* J'aime les chevaux. – Moi aussi.
♦**so have we** nous aussi ◊ *I've been to France twice. – So have we.* Je suis allé en France deux fois. – Nous aussi.
♦**I think so.** Je crois.
♦**I hope so.** J'espère bien.
♦**That's not so.** Ça n'est pas le cas.
♦**so far** jusqu'à présent ◊ *It's been easy so far.* Ça a été facile jusqu'à présent.
♦**so far so good** jusqu'ici ça va
♦**ten or so people** environ dix personnes
♦**at five o'clock or so** à environ cinq heures

to **soak** VERB
tremper

soaked ADJECTIVE
trempé ◊ *By the time we got back we were soaked.* Nous sommes rentrés trempés.

soaking ADJECTIVE
trempé ◊ *By the time we got back we were soaking.* Nous sommes rentrés trempés.

♦ **soaking wet** trempé ◊ *Your shoes are soaking wet.* Tes chaussures sont trempées.

soap NOUN
le savon

soap opera NOUN
le feuilleton à l'eau de rose
(les feuilletons à l'eau de rose PL)

soap powder NOUN
la lessive

to **sob** VERB
sangloter ◊ *She was sobbing.* Elle sanglotait.

sober ADJECTIVE
sobre

to **sober up** VERB
dessoûler

soccer NOUN
le football ◊ *to play soccer* jouer au football
♦ **a soccer player** un joueur de football

social ADJECTIVE
social
(sociaux MASC PL)
◊ *a social class* une classe sociale
♦ **I have a good social life.** Je vois beaucoup de monde.

socialism NOUN
le socialisme

socialist ADJECTIVE
see also **socialist** NOUN
socialiste

socialist NOUN
see also **socialist** ADJECTIVE
le/la socialiste

social security NOUN
[1] l' aide sociale FEM (*money*)
♦ **to be on social security** recevoir de l'aide sociale
[2] la sécurité sociale (*organization*)

social worker NOUN
[1] (*woman*)
l' assistante sociale FEM ◊ *She's a social worker.* Elle est assistante sociale.
[2] (*man*)
le travailleur social
(les travailleurs sociaux PL)
◊ *He's a social worker.* Il est travailleur social.

society NOUN
[1] la société ◊ *We live in a multi-cultural society.* Nous vivons dans une société multiculturelle.
[2] le club ◊ *a drama society* un club de théâtre

sociology NOUN
la sociologie

sock NOUN
la chaussette

socket NOUN
la prise de courant
(les prises de courant PL)

soda NOUN
le soda (*soda water*)

soda pop NOUN US
le soda

sofa NOUN
le canapé

soft ADJECTIVE
[1] (*fabric, texture*)
doux MASC
douce FEM
[2] (*pillow, bed*)
mou MASC
molle FEM
♦ **soft cheeses** les fromages à pâte molle MASC
[3] (*hair*)
fin
♦ **to be soft on somebody** (*be kind to*) être indulgent avec quelqu'un
♦ **a soft drink** une boisson non alcoolisée
♦ **soft drugs** les drogues douces FEM
♦ **a soft option** une solution de facilité

software NOUN
le logiciel

soggy ADJECTIVE
[1] (*soaked*)
trempé ◊ *a soggy tissue* un mouchoir trempé
[2] (*not crisp*)
mou MASC
molle FEM
◊ *soggy chips* des frites molles

soil NOUN
la terre

solar ADJECTIVE
solaire
♦ **solar panel** le panneau solaire

solar power NOUN
l' énergie solaire FEM

sold VERB *see* **sell**

soldier NOUN
le soldat ◊ *He's a soldier.* Il est soldat.

solicitor NOUN
[1] (*for lawsuits*)
l' avocat MASC
l' avocate FEM
◊ *He's a solicitor.* Il est avocat.
[2] (*for wills, property*)
le/la notaire
◊ *She's a solicitor.* Elle est notaire.

solid ADJECTIVE
[1] (*not hollow*)

S

☞

massif MASC
massive FEM
◊ *solid gold* l'or massif
[2] solide ◊ *a solid wall* un mur solide
♦ **for three hours solid** pendant trois heures entières

solo NOUN
le solo ◊ *a guitar solo* un solo de guitare

solution NOUN
la solution

to solve VERB
résoudre

some ADJECTIVE, PRONOUN
When some means "a certain amount of", use du, de la or des according to the gender of the French noun that follows it. du and de la become de l' when they are followed by a noun starting with a vowel.

[1] du ◊ *Would you like some bread?* Voulez-vous du pain?
de la ◊ *Would you like some beer?* Voulez-vous de la bière?
de l' ◊ *Have you got some mineral water?* Avez-vous de l'eau minérale?
des ◊ *I've got some Blur albums.* J'ai des albums de Blur.
♦ **Some people say that ...** Il y a des gens qui disent que ...
♦ **some day** un de ces jours
♦ **some day next week** un jour la semaine prochaine
[2] (*some but not all*)
certains ◊ *Are these mushrooms poisonous? – Only some.* Est-ce que ces champignons sont vénéneux? – Certains le sont.
♦ **some of them** quelques-uns ◊ *I only sold some of them.* J'en ai seulement vendu quelques-uns.
♦ **I only took some of it.** J'en ai seulement pris un peu.
♦ **I'm going to buy some stamps. Do you want some too?** Je vais acheter des timbres. Tu en veux aussi?
♦ **Would you like some coffee? – No thanks, I've got some.** Tu veux du café? – Non merci, j'en ai déjà.

somebody PRONOUN
quelqu'un ◊ *Somebody stole my bag.* Quelqu'un a volé mon sac.

somehow ADVERB
♦ **I'll do it somehow.** Je trouverai le moyen de le faire.
♦ **Somehow I don't think he believed me.** Quelque chose me dit qu'il ne m'a pas cru.

someone PRONOUN

quelqu'un ◊ *Someone stole my bag.* Quelqu'un a volé mon sac.

someplace ADVERB US
quelque part

something PRONOUN
quelque chose ◊ *something special* quelque chose de spécial ◊ *Wear something warm.* Mets quelque chose de chaud. ◊ *That's really something!* C'est vraiment quelque chose! ◊ *It cost £100, or something like that.* Ça a coûté cent livres, ou quelque chose comme ça.
♦ **His name is Pierre or something.** Il s'appelle Pierre, ou quelque chose comme ça.

sometime ADVERB
un de ces jours ◊ *You must come and see us sometime.* Passez donc nous voir un de ces jours.
♦ **sometime last month** dans le courant du mois dernier

sometimes ADVERB
quelquefois ◊ *Sometimes I think she hates me.* Quelquefois j'ai l'impression qu'elle me déteste.

somewhere ADVERB
quelque part ◊ *I left my keys somewhere.* J'ai laissé mes clés quelque part. ◊ *I'd like to go on holiday, somewhere sunny.* J'aimerais aller en vacances, quelque part où il fait du soleil.

son NOUN
le fils

song NOUN
la chanson

son-in-law NOUN
le gendre

soon ADVERB
bientôt ◊ *very soon* très bientôt
♦ **soon afterwards** peu après
♦ **as soon as possible** aussitôt que possible

sooner ADVERB
plus tôt ◊ *Can't you come a bit sooner?* Tu ne peux pas venir un peu plus tôt?
♦ **sooner or later** tôt ou tard

soot NOUN
la suie

soppy ADJECTIVE
sentimental
(sentimentaux MASC PL)

soprano NOUN
le/la soprano (*singer*)

sorcerer NOUN
le sorcier

sore ADJECTIVE

sore ... see also **sore** NOUN
- ♦**My feet are sore.** J'ai mal aux pieds.
- ♦**It's sore.** Ça fait mal.
- ♦**That's a sore point.** C'est un point sensible.

sore NOUN
| see also **sore** ADJECTIVE |
la plaie

sorry ADJECTIVE
désolé ◊ *I'm really sorry.* Je suis vraiment désolé. ◊ *I'm sorry, I haven't got any change.* Je suis désolé, je n'ai pas de monnaie. ◊ *I'm sorry I'm late.* Je suis désolé d'être en retard.
- ♦**sorry!** pardon!
- ♦**sorry?** pardon?
- ♦**I'm sorry about the noise.** Je m'excuse pour le bruit.
- ♦**You'll be sorry!** Tu le regretteras!
- ♦**to feel sorry for somebody** plaindre quelqu'un

sort NOUN
la sorte ◊ *What sort of bike have you got?* Quelle sorte de vélo as-tu?

to **sort out** VERB
1 ranger (*objects*)
2 résoudre (*problems*)

so-so ADVERB
comme ci comme ça ◊ *How are you feeling? – So-so.* Comment est-ce que tu te sens? – Comme ci comme ça.

sought VERB *see* **to seek**

soul NOUN
1 l' âme FEM (*spirit*)
2 la soul (*music*)

sound NOUN
| see also **sound** VERB, ADJECTIVE |
1 le bruit (*noise*) ◊ *Don't make a sound!* Pas un bruit! ◊ *the sound of footsteps* des bruits de pas
2 le son ◊ *Can I turn the sound down?* Je peux baisser le son?

to **sound** VERB
| see also **sound** NOUN, ADJECTIVE |
- ♦**That sounds interesting.** Ça a l'air intéressant.
- ♦**It sounds as if she's doing well at school.** Elle a l'air de bien travailler à l'école.
- ♦**That sounds like a good idea.** C'est une bonne idée.

sound ADJECTIVE, ADVERB
| see also **sound** NOUN, VERB |
bon MASC
bonne FEM
◊ *That's sound advice.* C'est un bon conseil.
- ♦**sound asleep** profondément endormi

soundtrack NOUN
la bande sonore

soup NOUN
la soupe ◊ *vegetable soup* la soupe aux légumes

sour ADJECTIVE
aigre

south ADJECTIVE, ADVERB
| see also **south** NOUN |
1 sud MASC, FEM, PL ◊ *the south coast* la côte sud
2 vers le sud ◊ *We were travelling south.* Nous allions vers le sud.
- ♦**south of** au sud de ◊ *It's south of London.* C'est au sud de Londres.

south NOUN
| see also **south** ADJECTIVE |
le sud ◊ *in the south* dans le sud ◊ *the South of France* le sud de la France

South Africa NOUN
l' Afrique du Sud FEM
- ♦**in South Africa** en Afrique du Sud
- ♦**to South Africa** en Afrique du Sud

South America NOUN
l' Amérique du Sud FEM
- ♦**in South America** en Amérique du Sud
- ♦**to South America** en Amérique du Sud

South American ADJECTIVE
| see also **South American** NOUN |
sud-américain

South American NOUN
| see also **South American** ADJECTIVE |
le Sud-Américain
la Sud-Américaine

southbound ADJECTIVE
- ♦**The southbound carriageway is blocked.** La route est bloquée en direction du sud.
- ♦**The suspect vehicle was southbound on the M1.** Le véhicule suspect se trouvait sur la M1 en direction du sud.

southeast NOUN
le sud-est ◊ *southeast England* le sud-est de l'Angleterre

southern ADJECTIVE
- ♦**the southern part of the island** la partie sud de l'île
- ♦**Southern England** le sud de l'Angleterre

South Pole NOUN
le pôle Sud

South Wales NOUN
le sud du Pays de Galles

southwest NOUN

S

le sud-ouest ◊ *southwest France* le sud-ouest de la France

souvenir NOUN
le souvenir
♦ **a souvenir shop** une boutique de souvenirs

Soviet ADJECTIVE
♦ **the former Soviet Union** l'ex-Union Soviétique FEM

soya NOUN
le soja

soy sauce NOUN
la sauce de soja

space NOUN
[1] la place ◊ *There isn't enough space.* Il n'y a pas suffisamment de place.
♦ **a parking space** une place de parking
[2] l' espace MASC (*universe, gap*)
◊ *Leave a space after your answer.* Laissez un espace après votre réponse.

spacecraft NOUN
l' engin spatial MASC

spade NOUN
la pelle
♦ **spades** (*in cards*) le pique SING ◊ *the ace of spades* l'as de pique

Spain NOUN
l' Espagne FEM
♦ **in Spain** en Espagne
♦ **to Spain** en Espagne

Spaniard NOUN
l' Espagnol MASC
l' Espagnole FEM

spaniel NOUN
l' épagneul MASC

Spanish ADJECTIVE
see also **Spanish** NOUN
espagnol ◊ *She's Spanish.* Elle est espagnole.

Spanish NOUN
see also **Spanish** ADJECTIVE
l' espagnol MASC (*language*)
♦ **the Spanish** les Espagnols

to **spank** VERB
♦ **to spank somebody** donner une fessée à quelqu'un

spanner NOUN
la clé anglaise

spare ADJECTIVE
see also **spare** VERB, NOUN
de rechange ◊ *spare batteries* des piles de rechange ◊ *a spare part* une pièce de rechange
♦ **a spare room** une chambre d'amis

♦ **spare time** le temps libre ◊ *What do you do in your spare time?* Qu'est-ce que tu fais pendant ton temps libre?
♦ **spare wheel** une roue de secours

to **spare** VERB
see also **spare** ADJECTIVE, NOUN
♦ **Can you spare a moment?** Vous pouvez m'accorder un instant?
♦ **I can't spare the time.** Je n'ai pas le temps.
♦ **There's no room to spare.** Il n'y a plus de place.
♦ **We arrived with time to spare.** Nous sommes arrivés en avance.

spare NOUN
see also **spare** ADJECTIVE, VERB
♦ **a spare** un autre ◊ *I've lost my key. – Have you got a spare?* J'ai perdu ma clé. – Tu en as une autre?

sparkling ADJECTIVE
pétillant (*water*)
♦ **sparkling wine** le mousseux

sparrow NOUN
le moineau
(les moineaux PL)

spat VERB see **spit**

to **speak** VERB
parler ◊ *Do you speak English?* Est-ce que vous parlez anglais?
♦ **to speak to somebody** parler à quelqu'un ◊ *Have you spoken to him?* Tu lui as parlé? ◊ *She spoke to him about it.* Elle lui en a parlé.
♦ **spoken French** le français parlé

to **speak up** VERB
parler plus fort ◊ *Speak up, we can't hear you.* Parle plus fort, nous ne t'entendons pas.

speaker NOUN
[1] l' enceinte FEM (*loudspeaker*)
[2] l' intervenant MASC (*in debate*)

special ADJECTIVE
spécial
(spéciaux MASC PL)

specialist NOUN
le/la spécialiste

speciality NOUN
la spécialité

to **specialize** VERB
se spécialiser ◊ *We specialize in skiing equipment.* Nous nous spécialisons dans les articles de ski.

specially ADVERB
[1] spécialement ◊ *It's specially designed for teenagers.* C'est spécialement conçu pour les adolescents.

♦ **not specially** pas spécialement ◊ *Do you like opera? – Not specially.* Tu aimes l'opéra? – Pas spécialement.
2 surtout ◊ *It can be very cold here, specially in winter.* Il peut faire très froid ici, surtout en hiver.

species NOUN
l' espèce FEM

specific ADJECTIVE
1 (*particular*)
particulier MASC
particulière FEM
◊ *certain specific issues* certains problèmes particuliers
2 (*precise*)
précis ◊ *Could you be more specific?* Est-ce que vous pourriez être plus précis?

specifically ADVERB
1 spécialement ◊ *It's specifically designed for teenagers.* C'est spécialement conçu pour les adolescents.
2 particulièrement ◊ *in Britain, or more specifically in England* en Grande-Bretagne, ou plus particulièrement en Angleterre
♦ **I specifically said that ...** J'ai clairement dit que ...

specs, spectacles PL NOUN
les lunettes FEM PL

spectacular ADJECTIVE
spectaculaire

spectator NOUN
le spectateur
la spectatrice

speech NOUN
le discours ◊ *to make a speech* faire un discours

speechless ADJECTIVE
muet MASC
muette FEM
◊ *speechless with admiration* muet d'admiration
♦ **I was speechless.** Je suis resté sans voix.

speed NOUN
la vitesse ◊ *a three-speed bike* un vélo à trois vitesses ◊ *at top speed* à toute vitesse

to **speed up** VERB
accélérer

speedboat NOUN
la vedette

speeding NOUN
l' excès de vitesse MASC ◊ *He was fined for speeding.* Il a reçu une contravention pour excès de vitesse.

speed limit NOUN

la limitation de vitesse
♦ **to break the speed limit** faire un excès de vitesse

speedometer NOUN
le compteur

to **spell** VERB
see also **spell** NOUN
1 écrire (*in writing*) ◊ *How do you spell that?* Comment est-ce que ça s'écrit?
2 épeler (*out loud*) ◊ *Can you spell that please?* Est-ce que vous pouvez épeler, s'il vous plaît?
♦ **I can't spell.** Je fais des fautes d'orthographe.

spell NOUN
see also **spell** VERB
♦ **to cast a spell on somebody** jeter un sort à quelqu'un
♦ **to be under somebody's spell** être sous le charme de quelqu'un

spelling NOUN
l' orthographe FEM ◊ *My spelling is terrible.* Je fais beaucoup de fautes d'orthographe.
♦ **a spelling mistake** une faute d'orthographe

spelt VERB *see* **spell**

to **spend** VERB
1 dépenser (*money*)
2 passer (*time*) ◊ *He spent a month in France.* Il a passé un mois en France.

spice NOUN
l' épice FEM

spicy ADJECTIVE
épicé

spider NOUN
l' araignée FEM

to **spill** VERB
1 renverser (*tip over*) ◊ *He spilled his coffee over his trousers.* Il a renversé son café sur son pantalon.
2 se répandre (*get spilt*) ◊ *The soup spilled all over the table.* La soupe s'est répandue sur la table.

spinach NOUN
les épinards MASC PL

spin drier NOUN
l' essoreuse FEM

spine NOUN
la colonne vertébrale

spinster NOUN
la célibataire

spire NOUN
la flèche

spirit NOUN
1 le courage (*courage*)

S

☞

♦**to be in good spirits** être de bonne
humeur
[2] l' <u>énergie</u> FEM (energy)

spirits PL NOUN
les <u>alcools forts</u> MASC PL ◊ I don't drink
spirits. Je ne bois pas d'alcools forts.

spiritual ADJECTIVE
<u>religieux</u> MASC
<u>religieuse</u> FEM
◊ the spiritual leader of Tibet le chef
religieux du Tibet

spit NOUN
> see also **spit** VERB
la <u>salive</u>

to **spit** VERB
> see also **spit** NOUN
<u>cracher</u>
♦**to spit something out** cracher
quelque chose

spite NOUN
> see also **spite** VERB
♦**in spite of** malgré
♦**out of spite** par méchanceté

to **spite** VERB
> see also **spite** NOUN
<u>contrarier</u> ◊ He just did it to spite
me. Il a fait ça juste pour me
contrarier.

spiteful ADJECTIVE
[1] (action)
<u>méchant</u>
[2] (person)
<u>rancunier</u> MASC
<u>rancunière</u> FEM

to **splash** VERB
> see also **splash** NOUN
<u>éclabousser</u> ◊ Careful! Don't splash
me! Attention! Ne m'éclabousse pas!

splash NOUN
> see also **splash** VERB
le <u>plouf</u> ◊ I heard a splash. J'ai
entendu un plouf.
♦**a splash of colour** une touche de
couleur

splendid ADJECTIVE
<u>splendide</u>

splint NOUN
l' <u>attelle</u> FEM

splinter NOUN
l' <u>écharde</u> FEM

to **split** VERB
[1] <u>fendre</u> (break apart) ◊ He split the
wood with an axe. Il a fendu le bois
avec une hache.
[2] <u>se fendre</u> ◊ The ship hit a rock
and split in two. Le bateau a percuté
un rocher et s'est fendu en deux.

[3] <u>partager</u> (divide up) ◊ They decided
to split the profits. Ils ont décidé de
partager les bénéfices.
♦**to split up (1)** (couple) rompre
♦**to split up (2)** (group) se disperser

to **spoil** VERB
[1] <u>abîmer</u> (object)
[2] <u>gâcher</u> (occasion)
[3] <u>gâter</u> (child)

spoiled ADJECTIVE
<u>gâté</u> ◊ a spoiled child un enfant gâté

spoilsport NOUN
le/la <u>trouble-fête</u>

spoilt ADJECTIVE
<u>gâté</u> ◊ a spoilt child un enfant gâté

spoilt VERB see **spoil**

spoke VERB see **speak**

spoke NOUN
le <u>rayon</u> (of wheel)

spoken VERB see **speak**

spokesman NOUN
le <u>porte-parole</u>
(les porte-parole PL)

spokeswoman NOUN
le <u>porte-parole</u>
(les porte-parole PL)

sponge NOUN
l' <u>éponge</u> FEM
♦**a sponge bag** une trousse de toilette
♦**a sponge cake** un biscuit de Savoie

sponsor NOUN
> see also **sponsor** VERB
le <u>donateur</u>
la <u>donatrice</u>

to **sponsor** VERB
> see also **sponsor** NOUN
<u>parrainer</u> ◊ The festival was
sponsored by ... Le festival a été
parrainé par ...

spontaneous ADJECTIVE
<u>spontané</u>

spooky ADJECTIVE
[1] <u>sinistre</u> (eerie)
♦**a spooky story** une histoire qui fait
froid dans le dos
[2] <u>étrange</u> (strange) ◊ a spooky
coincidence une étrange coïncidence

spoon NOUN
la <u>cuiller</u>
♦**a spoonful** une cuillerée

sport NOUN
le <u>sport</u> ◊ What's your favourite
sport? Quel est ton sport préféré?
♦**a sports bag** un sac de sport
♦**a sports car** une voiture de sport
♦**a sports jacket** une veste sport
♦**Go on, be a sport!** Allez, sois sympa!

sportsman NOUN

le <u>sportif</u>

sportswear NOUN
les <u>vêtements de sport</u> MASC PL

sportswoman NOUN
la <u>sportive</u>

sporty ADJECTIVE
<u>sportif</u> MASC
<u>sportive</u> FEM
◊ *I'm not very sporty.* Je ne suis pas très sportif.

spot NOUN
see also **spot** VERB
[1] la <u>tache</u> (*mark*) ◊ *There's a spot on your shirt.* Il y a une tache sur ta chemise.
[2] le <u>pois</u> (*in pattern*) ◊ *a red dress with white spots* une robe rouge à pois blancs
[3] le <u>bouton</u> (*pimple*) ◊ *He's covered in spots.* Il est couvert de boutons.
[4] le <u>coin</u> (*place*) ◊ *It's a lovely spot for a picnic.* C'est un coin agréable pour un pique-nique.
♦ **on the spot (1)** (*immediately*) sur-le-champ ◊ *They gave her the job on the spot.* Ils lui ont offert le poste sur-le-champ.
♦ **on the spot (2)** (*at the same place*) sur place ◊ *Luckily they were able to mend the car on the spot.* Heureusement ils ont pu réparer la voiture sur place.

to **spot** VERB
see also **spot** NOUN
<u>repérer</u> ◊ *I spotted a mistake.* J'ai repéré une faute.

spotless ADJECTIVE
<u>immaculé</u>

spotlight NOUN
le <u>projecteur</u>
♦ **The universities have been in the spotlight recently.** Les universités ont été sous le feu des projecteurs ces derniers temps.

spotty ADJECTIVE
(*pimply*)
<u>boutonneux</u> MASC
<u>boutonneuse</u> FEM

spouse NOUN
l' <u>époux</u> MASC
l' <u>épouse</u> FEM

to **sprain** VERB
see also **sprain** NOUN
♦ **to sprain one's ankle** se faire une entorse à la cheville

sprain NOUN
see also **sprain** VERB
l' <u>entorse</u> FEM ◊ *It's just a sprain.* C'est juste une entorse.

spray NOUN
see also **spray** VERB
la <u>bombe</u> (*spray can*)

to **spray** VERB
see also **spray** NOUN
[1] <u>vaporiser</u> ◊ *to spray perfume on one's hand* se vaporiser du parfum sur la main
[2] <u>traiter</u> (*crops*)
[3] <u>peindre avec une bombe</u> (*graffiti*) ◊ *Somebody had sprayed graffiti on the wall.* Quelqu'un avait peint des graffiti avec une bombe sur le mur.

spread NOUN
see also **spread** VERB
♦ **cheese spread** le fromage à tartiner
♦ **chocolate spread** le chocolat à tartiner

to **spread** VERB
see also **spread** NOUN
[1] <u>étaler</u> ◊ *to spread butter on a slice of bread* étaler du beurre sur une tranche de pain
[2] <u>se propager</u> (*disease, news*) ◊ *The news spread rapidly.* La nouvelle s'est propagée rapidement.
♦ **to spread out** (*people*) se disperser ◊ *The soldiers spread out across the field.* Les soldats se sont dispersés dans le champ.

spreadsheet NOUN
le <u>tableur</u> (*computer program*)

spring NOUN
[1] le <u>printemps</u> (*season*)
♦ **in spring** au printemps
[2] le <u>ressort</u> (*metal coil*)
[3] la <u>source</u> (*water hole*)

spring-cleaning NOUN
le <u>grand nettoyage de printemps</u>

springtime NOUN
le <u>printemps</u>
♦ **in springtime** au printemps

sprinkler NOUN
l' <u>arroseur</u> MASC (*for lawn*)

sprint NOUN
see also **sprint** VERB
le <u>sprint</u>

to **sprint** VERB
see also **sprint** NOUN
<u>courir à toute vitesse</u> ◊ *She sprinted for the bus.* Elle a couru à toute vitesse pour attraper le bus.

sprinter NOUN
le <u>sprinteur</u>
la <u>sprinteuse</u>

sprouts PL NOUN
♦ **Brussels sprouts** les choux de Bruxelles MASC PL

spy NOUN
see also **spy** VERB

S

l' espion MASC
l' espionne FEM

to **spy** VERB

see also **spy** NOUN

♦**to spy on somebody** espionner quelqu'un

spying NOUN
l' espionnage MASC

to **squabble** VERB
se chamailler ◊ *Stop squabbling!* Arrêtez de vous chamailler!

square NOUN

see also **square** ADJECTIVE

[1] le carré ◊ *a square and a triangle* un carré et un triangle
[2] la place ◊ *the town square* la place de l'hôtel de ville

square ADJECTIVE

see also **square** NOUN

carré ◊ *two square metres* deux mètres carrés
♦**It's 2 metres square.** Ça fait deux mètres sur deux.

squash NOUN

see also **squash** VERB

le squash (*sport*) ◊ *I play squash.* Je joue au squash.
♦**a squash court** un court de squash
♦**a squash racket** une raquette de squash
♦**orange squash** l' orangeade FEM
♦**lemon squash** la citronnade

to **squash** VERB

see also **squash** NOUN

écraser ◊ *You're squashing me.* Tu m'écrases.

to **squeak** VERB
[1] pousser un petit cri (*mouse, child*)
[2] grincer (*creak*)

to **squeeze** VERB
[1] presser (*fruit, toothpaste*)
[2] serrer (*hand, arm*)
♦**to squeeze into some tight jeans** rentrer tout juste dans un jean serré

to **squeeze in** VERB
[1] trouver une petite place ◊ *It was a tiny car, but we managed to squeeze in.* La voiture était toute petite, mais nous avons réussi à trouver une petite place.
[2] caser (*for appointment*) ◊ *I can squeeze you in tomorrow at two o'clock.* Je peux vous caser demain à deux heures.

to **squint** VERB

see also **squint** NOUN

loucher

squint NOUN

see also **squint** VERB

♦**He has a squint.** Il louche.

squirrel NOUN
l' écureuil MASC

to **stab** VERB
poignarder

stable NOUN

see also **stable** ADJECTIVE

l' écurie FEM

stable ADJECTIVE

see also **stable** NOUN

stable ◊ *a stable relationship* une relation stable

stack NOUN
la pile ◊ *a stack of books* une pile de livres

stadium NOUN
le stade

staff NOUN
[1] le personnel (*in company*)
[2] les professeurs MASC PL (*in school*)

staffroom NOUN
la salle des professeurs

stage NOUN
[1] la scène (*in plays*)
[2] l' estrade FEM (*for speeches, lectures*)
♦**at this stage (1)** à ce stade ◊ *at this stage in the negotiations* à ce stade des négociations
♦**at this stage (2)** pour l'instant ◊ *At this stage, it's too early to comment.* Pour l'instant, il est trop tôt pour se prononcer.
♦**to do something in stages** faire quelque chose étape par étape

*Be careful not to translate **stage** by the French word **stage**.*

to **stagger** VERB
chanceler

stain NOUN

see also **stain** VERB

la tache

to **stain** VERB

see also **stain** NOUN

tacher

stainless steel NOUN
l' inox MASC

stain remover NOUN
le détachant

stair NOUN
la marche (*step*)

staircase NOUN
l' escalier MASC

stairs PL NOUN
l' escalier MASC SING

stale ADJECTIVE
rassis (*bread*)

stalemate NOUN
le pat (*in chess*)

stall NOUN
le stand MASC ◊ *He's got a market stall.* Il a un stand au marché.
♦ **the stalls** (*in cinema, theatre*) l'orchestre MASC

stamina NOUN
l' endurance FEM

stammer NOUN
le bégaiement
♦ **He's got a stammer.** Il bégaie.

to **stamp** VERB
see also **stamp** NOUN
affranchir (*letter*)
♦ **to stamp one's foot** taper du pied

stamp NOUN
see also **stamp** VERB
[1] le timbre ◊ *My hobby is stamp collecting.* Je collectionne les timbres.
♦ **a stamp album** un album de timbres
♦ **a stamp collection** une collection de timbres
[2] le tampon (*rubber stamp*)

stamped ADJECTIVE
affranchi ◊ *The letter wasn't stamped.* La lettre n'était pas affranchie.
♦ **Enclose a stamped addressed envelope.** Joindre une enveloppe affranchie à vos nom et adresse.

to **stand** VERB
[1] être debout (*be standing*) ◊ *He was standing by the door.* Il était debout à la porte.
[2] se lever (*stand up*)
[3] supporter (*tolerate, withstand*) ◊ *I can't stand all this noise.* Je ne supporte pas tout ce bruit.
♦ **to stand for (1)** (*be short for*) être l'abréviation de ◊ *"BT" stands for "British Telecom".* "BT" est l'abréviation de "British Telecom".
♦ **to stand for (2)** (*tolerate*) supporter ◊ *I won't stand for it!* Je ne supporterai pas ça!
♦ **to stand in for somebody** remplacer quelqu'un
♦ **to stand out** se distinguer ◊ *All the contestants were good, but none of them stood out.* Tous les concurrents étaient bons, mais aucun ne se distinguait.
♦ **She really stands out in that orange coat.** Tout le monde la remarque avec ce manteau orange.
♦ **to stand up** (*get up*) se lever
♦ **to stand up for** défendre ◊ *Stand up for your rights!* Défendez vos droits!

standard ADJECTIVE
see also **standard** NOUN
[1] courant ◊ *standard French* le français courant
[2] ordinaire (*equipment*)
♦ **the standard procedure** la procédure normale

standard NOUN
see also **standard** ADJECTIVE
le niveau
(les niveaux PL)
◊ *The standard is very high.* Le niveau est très haut.
♦ **the standard of living** le niveau de vie
♦ **She's got high standards.** Elle est très exigeante.

stand-by ticket NOUN
le billet stand-by

standpoint NOUN
le point de vue

stands PL NOUN
la tribune SING (*at sports ground*)

stank VERB *see* **stink**

staple NOUN
see also **staple** VERB
l' agrafe FEM

to **staple** VERB
see also **staple** NOUN
agrafer

stapler NOUN
l' agrafeuse FEM

star NOUN
see also **star** VERB
[1] l' étoile FEM (*in sky*)
[2] la vedette (*celebrity*) ◊ *He's a TV star.* C'est une vedette de la télé.
♦ **the stars** (*horoscope*) l' horoscope MASC

to **star** VERB
see also **star** NOUN
être la vedette ◊ *to star in a film* être la vedette d'un film
♦ **The film stars Glenda Jackson.** Le film a pour vedette Glenda Jackson.
♦ **... starring Johnny Depp** ... avec Johnny Depp

to **stare** VERB
♦ **to stare at something** fixer quelque chose

stark ADVERB
♦ **stark naked** complètement nu

start NOUN
see also **start** VERB
[1] le début ◊ *It's not much, but it's a start.* Ce n'est pas grand chose, mais c'est un début.
♦ **Shall we make a start on the washing-up?** On commence à faire la vaisselle?
[2] le départ (*of race*)

to **start** VERB
see also **start** NOUN

S

☞

1 commencer ◊ *What time does it start?* À quelle heure est-ce que ça commence?
♦ **to start doing something** commencer à faire quelque chose ◊ *I started learning French three years ago.* J'ai commencé à apprendre le français il y a trois ans.
2 créer (*organization*) ◊ *He wants to start his own business.* Il veut créer sa propre entreprise.
3 organiser (*campaign*) ◊ *She started a campaign against drugs.* Elle a organisé une campagne contre la drogue.
4 démarrer (*car*) ◊ *He couldn't start the car.* Il n'a pas réussi à démarrer la voiture. ◊ *The car wouldn't start.* La voiture ne voulait pas démarrer.
♦ **to start off** (*leave*) partir ◊ *We started off first thing in the morning.* Nous sommes partis en début de matinée.

starter NOUN
l' entrée FEM (*first course*)

to **starve** VERB
mourir de faim ◊ *People were literally starving.* Les gens mouraient littéralement de faim.
♦ **I'm starving!** Je meurs de faim!

state NOUN
see also **state** VERB
l' état MASC
♦ **he was in a real state** il était dans tous ses états
♦ **the state** (*government*) l'État
♦ **the States** (*USA*) les États-Unis MASC

to **state** VERB
see also **state** NOUN
1 déclarer (*say*) ◊ *He stated his intention to resign.* Il a déclaré son intention de démissionner.
2 donner (*give*) ◊ *Please state your name and address.* Veuillez donner vos nom et adresse.

stately home NOUN
le château
(les châteaux PL)

statement NOUN
la déclaration

station NOUN
la gare (*railway*)
♦ **the bus station** la gare routière
♦ **a police station** un poste de police
♦ **a radio station** une station de radio

stationer's NOUN
la papeterie

station wagon NOUN US
le break

statue NOUN
la statue

to **stay** VERB
see also **stay** NOUN
1 rester (*remain*) ◊ *Stay here!* Reste ici!
♦ **to stay in** (*not go out*) rester à la maison
♦ **to stay up** rester debout ◊ *We stayed up till midnight.* Nous sommes restés debout jusqu'à minuit.
2 loger (*spend the night*) ◊ *to stay with friends* loger chez des amis ◊ *Where are you staying?* Où est-ce que vous logez?
♦ **to stay the night** passer la nuit
♦ **We stayed in Belgium for a few days.** Nous avons passé quelques jours en Belgique.

stay NOUN
see also **stay** VERB
le séjour ◊ *my stay in France* mon séjour en France

steady ADJECTIVE
1 régulier MASC
régulière FEM
◊ *steady progress* des progrès réguliers
2 stable ◊ *a steady job* un emploi stable
3 (*voice, hand*)
ferme
4 (*person*)
calme
♦ **a steady boyfriend** un copain
♦ **a steady girlfriend** une copine
♦ **Steady on!** Doucement!

steak NOUN
le steak (*beef*) ◊ *steak and chips* un steak frites

to **steal** VERB
voler

steam NOUN
la vapeur ◊ *a steam engine* une locomotive à vapeur

steel NOUN
l' acier MASC ◊ *a steel door* une porte en acier

steep ADJECTIVE
raide (*slope*)

steeple NOUN
le clocher

steering wheel NOUN
le volant

step NOUN
see also **step** VERB
1 le pas (*pace*) ◊ *He took a step forward.* Il a fait un pas en avant.
2 la marche (*stair*) ◊ *She tripped over the step.* Elle a trébuché sur la marche.

to **step** VERB

see also **step** NOUN

◆**to step aside** faire un pas de côté
◆**to step back** faire un pas en arrière

stepbrother NOUN
le demi-frère

stepdaughter NOUN
la belle-fille
(les belles-filles PL)

stepfather NOUN
le beau-père
(les beaux-pères PL)

stepladder NOUN
l' escabeau MASC
(les escabeaux PL)

stepmother NOUN
la belle-mère
(les belles-mères PL)

stepsister NOUN
la demi-sœur

stepson NOUN
le beau-fils
(les beaux-fils PL)

stereo NOUN
la chaîne stéréo
(les chaînes stéréo PL)

sterling ADJECTIVE
◆**£5 sterling** cinq livres sterling

stew NOUN
le ragoût

steward NOUN
le steward

stewardess NOUN
l' hôtesse de l'air FEM

stick NOUN

see also **stick** VERB

1 le bâton
2 la canne (walking stick)

to **stick** VERB

see also **stick** NOUN

coller (with adhesive) ◊ Stick the stamps on the envelope. Collez les timbres sur l'enveloppe.

stick insect NOUN
le phasme

to **stick out** VERB
sortir (project) ◊ A pen was sticking out of his pocket. Un stylo sortait de sa poche.
◆**Stick your tongue out and say "ah".** Tirez la langue et dites "ah".

sticker NOUN
l' autocollant MASC

sticky ADJECTIVE
1 poisseux MASC
poisseuse FEM
◊ to have sticky hands avoir les mains poisseuses
2 adhésif MASC

adhésive FEM
◊ a sticky label une étiquette adhésive

stiff ADJECTIVE, ADVERB
rigide (rigid)
◆**to have a stiff back** avoir mal au dos
◆**to feel stiff** avoir des courbatures
◆**to be bored stiff** s'ennuyer à mourir
◆**to be frozen stiff** être mort de froid
◆**to be scared stiff** être mort de peur

still ADVERB

see also **still** ADJECTIVE

1 encore ◊ I still haven't finished. Je n'ai pas encore fini. ◊ Are you still in bed? Tu es encore au lit?
◆**better still** encore mieux
2 quand même (even so) ◊ She knows I don't like it, but she still does it. Elle sait que je n'aime pas ça, mais elle le fait quand même.
3 enfin (after all) ◊ Still, it's the thought that counts. Enfin, c'est l'intention qui compte.

still ADJECTIVE

see also **still** ADVERB

◆**Keep still!** Ne bouge pas!
◆**Sit still!** Reste tranquille!

sting NOUN

see also **sting** VERB

la piqûre ◊ a bee sting une piqûre d'abeille

to **sting** VERB

see also **sting** NOUN

piquer ◊ I've been stung. J'ai été piqué.

stingy ADJECTIVE
pingre

to **stink** VERB

see also **stink** NOUN

puer ◊ It stinks! Ça pue!

stink NOUN

see also **stink** VERB

la puanteur

to **stir** VERB
remuer

to **stitch** VERB

see also **stitch** NOUN

coudre (cloth)

stitch NOUN

see also **stitch** VERB

1 le point (in sewing)
2 le point de suture (in wound) ◊ I had five stitches. J'ai eu cinq points de suture.

stock NOUN

see also **stock** VERB

1 la réserve (supply)
2 le stock (in shop) ◊ in stock en stock
◆**out of stock** épuisé

S

☞

3 le bouillon ◊ *chicken stock* du bouillon de volaille

to **stock** VERB

see also **stock** NOUN

avoir (*have in stock*) ◊ *Do you stock camping stoves?* Vous avez des camping-gaz?

♦**to stock up** s'approvisionner ◊ *to stock up with something* s'approvisionner en quelque chose

stock cube NOUN
le cube de bouillon

stocking NOUN
le bas

stole, stolen VERB see **steal**

stomach NOUN
l' estomac MASC

stomachache NOUN
♦**to have a stomachache** avoir mal au ventre

stone NOUN
1 (*rock*)
la pierre ◊ *a stone wall* un mur en pierre
2 (*in fruit*)
le noyau
(les noyaux PL)
◊ *a peach stone* un noyau de pêche

> *i* In France, weight is expressed in kilos. A stone is about 6.3 kg.

♦**I weigh eight stone.** Je pèse cinquante kilos.

stood VERB see **stand**

stool NOUN
le tabouret

to **stop** VERB

see also **stop** NOUN

1 arrêter ◊ *a campaign to stop whaling* une campagne pour arrêter la chasse à la baleine
2 s'arrêter ◊ *The bus doesn't stop there.* Le bus ne s'arrête pas là. ◊ *I think the rain's going to stop.* Je pense qu'il va s'arrêter de pleuvoir.

♦**to stop doing something** arrêter de faire quelque chose ◊ *to stop smoking* arrêter de fumer

♦**to stop somebody doing something** empêcher quelqu'un de faire quelque chose

♦**Stop!** Stop!

stop NOUN

see also **stop** VERB

l' arrêt MASC ◊ *a bus stop* un arrêt de bus

♦**This is my stop.** Je descends ici.

stopwatch NOUN

le chronomètre

store NOUN

see also **store** VERB

1 le magasin (*shop*) ◊ *a furniture store* un magasin de meubles
2 la réserve (*stock, storeroom*)

to **store** VERB

see also **store** NOUN

1 garder ◊ *They store potatoes in the cellar.* Ils gardent des pommes de terre dans la cave.
2 enregistrer (*information*)

storey NOUN
l' étage MASC ◊ *a three-storey building* un immeuble à trois étages

storm NOUN
1 la tempête (*gale*)
2 l' orage MASC (*thunderstorm*)

stormy ADJECTIVE
orageux MASC
orageuse FEM

story NOUN
l' histoire FEM

stove NOUN
1 la cuisinière (*in kitchen*)
2 le réchaud (*camping stove*)

straight ADJECTIVE
1 droit ◊ *a straight line* une ligne droite
2 raide ◊ *straight hair* les cheveux raides
3 hétéro (*heterosexual*)

♦**straight away** tout de suite

♦**straight on** tout droit

straightforward ADJECTIVE
simple

strain NOUN

see also **strain** VERB

le stress

♦**It was a strain.** C'était éprouvant.

to **strain** VERB

see also **strain** NOUN

se faire mal à ◊ *I strained my back.* Je me suis fait mal au dos.

♦**to strain a muscle** se froisser un muscle

strained ADJECTIVE
froissé (*muscle*)

stranded ADJECTIVE
♦**We were stranded.** Nous étions coincés.

strange ADJECTIVE
bizarre ◊ *That's strange!* C'est bizarre!

stranger NOUN
l' inconnu MASC
l' inconnue FEM

◇ *Don't talk to strangers.* Ne parle pas aux inconnus.
♦ **I'm a stranger here.** Je ne suis pas d'ici.

to **strangle** VERB
étrangler

strap NOUN
[1] la courroie (*of bag, camera, suitcase*)
[2] la bretelle (*of bra, dress*)
[3] la lanière (*on shoe*)
[4] le bracelet (*of watch*)

straw NOUN
la paille
♦ **That's the last straw!** Ça, c'est le comble!

strawberry NOUN
la fraise ◇ *strawberry jam* la confiture de fraises ◇ *a strawberry ice cream* une glace à la fraise

stray NOUN
♦ **a stray cat** un chat perdu

stream NOUN
le ruisseau
(les ruisseaux PL)

street NOUN
la rue ◇ *in the street* dans la rue

streetcar NOUN US
le tramway

streetlamp NOUN
le réverbère

street plan NOUN
le plan de la ville

streetwise ADJECTIVE
dégourdi

strength NOUN
la force

to **stress** VERB
see also **stress** NOUN
souligner ◇ *I would like to stress that ...* J'aimerais souligner que ...

stress NOUN
see also **stress** VERB
le stress

to **stretch** VERB
[1] s'étirer (*person, animal*) ◇ *The dog woke up and stretched.* Le chien s'est réveillé et s'est étiré.
[2] se détendre (*get bigger*) ◇ *My sweater stretched when I washed it.* Mon pull s'est détendu au lavage.
[3] tendre (*stretch out*) ◇ *They stretched a rope between two trees.* Ils ont tendu une corde entre deux arbres.
♦ **to stretch out one's arms** tendre les bras

stretcher NOUN
le brancard

stretchy ADJECTIVE
élastique

strict ADJECTIVE
strict

strike NOUN
see also **strike** VERB
la grève
♦ **to be on strike** être en grève
♦ **to go on strike** faire grève

to **strike** VERB
see also **strike** NOUN
[1] sonner (*clock*) ◇ *The clock struck three.* L'horloge a sonné trois heures.
[2] faire grève (*go on strike*)
[3] frapper (*hit*)
♦ **to strike a match** frotter une allumette

striker NOUN
[1] le/la gréviste (*person on strike*)
[2] le buteur (*footballer*)

striking ADJECTIVE
[1] en grève (*on strike*) ◇ *striking miners* les mineurs en grève
[2] frappant (*noticeable*) ◇ *a striking difference* une différence frappante

string NOUN
[1] la ficelle ◇ *a piece of string* un bout de ficelle
[2] la corde (*of violin, guitar*)

to **strip** VERB
see also **strip** NOUN
se déshabiller (*get undressed*)

strip NOUN
see also **strip** VERB
la bande
♦ **a strip cartoon** une bande dessinée

stripe NOUN
la rayure

striped ADJECTIVE
à rayures ◇ *a striped skirt* une jupe à rayures

stripper NOUN
le strip-teaseur
la strip-teaseuse

stripy ADJECTIVE
rayé ◇ *a stripy shirt* une chemise rayée

to **stroke** VERB
see also **stroke** NOUN
caresser

stroke NOUN
see also **stroke** VERB
l' attaque FEM ◇ *to have a stroke* avoir une attaque

stroll NOUN
♦ **to go for a stroll** aller faire une petite promenade

S

stroller NOUN [US]
la <u>poussette</u>

strong ADJECTIVE
[1] <u>fort</u> ◇ *She's very strong.* Elle est
très forte.
[2] <u>résistant</u> (*material*)

strongly ADVERB
<u>fortement</u> ◇ *We recommend strongly
that ...* Nous recommandons
fortement que ...
◆**He smelt strongly of tobacco.** Il
sentait fort le tabac.
◆**strongly built** solidement bâti
◆**I don't feel strongly about it.** Ça
m'est égal.

struck VERB *see* **strike**

to **struggle** VERB
| *see also* **struggle** NOUN |
se <u>débattre</u> (*physically*) ◇ *He
struggled, but he couldn't escape.* Il
s'est débattu, mais il n'a pas pu
s'échapper.
◆**to struggle to do something (1)** (*fight*)
se battre pour faire quelque chose
◇ *He struggled to get custody of his
daughter.* Il s'est battu pour obtenir
la garde de sa fille.
◆**to struggle to do something (2)** (*have
difficulty*) avoir du mal à faire quelque
chose

struggle NOUN
| *see also* **struggle** VERB |
la <u>lutte</u> (*for independence, equality*)
◆**It was a struggle.** Ça a été laborieux.

stub NOUN
le <u>mégot</u> (*of cigarette*)

to **stub out** VERB
<u>écraser</u> (*cigarette*)

stubborn ADJECTIVE
<u>têtu</u>

stuck VERB *see* **stick**

stuck ADJECTIVE
<u>coincé</u> (*jammed*) ◇ *It's stuck.* C'est
coincé.
◆**to get stuck** rester coincé ◇ *We got
stuck in a traffic jam.* Nous sommes
restés coincés dans un embouteillage.

stuck-up ADJECTIVE
<u>coincé</u> (*informal*)

stud NOUN
[1] la <u>boucle d'oreille</u> (*earring*)
[2] le <u>clou</u> (*on football boots*)

student NOUN
l' <u>étudiant</u> MASC
l' <u>étudiante</u> FEM

studio NOUN
le <u>studio</u> ◇ *a TV studio* un studio de
télévision
◆**a studio flat** un studio

to **study** VERB
[1] <u>faire des études</u> (*at university*) ◇ *I
plan to study biology.* J'ai l'intention
de faire des études de biologie.
[2] <u>travailler</u> (*do homework*) ◇ *I've got
to study tonight.* Je dois travailler ce
soir.

stuff NOUN
[1] le <u>truc</u> (*substance*) ◇ *I need some
stuff for hay fever.* J'ai besoin d'un
truc contre le rhume des foins.
[2] les <u>trucs</u> MASC PL (*things*) ◇ *There's
some stuff on the table for you.* Il y a
des trucs sur la table pour toi.
[3] les <u>affaires</u> FEM PL (*possessions*)
◇ *Have you got all your stuff?* Est-ce
que tu as toutes tes affaires?

stuffy ADJECTIVE
<u>mal aéré</u> (*room*)
◆**It's really stuffy in here.** On étouffe
ici.

to **stumble** VERB
<u>trébucher</u>

stung VERB *see* **sting**

stunk VERB *see* **stink**

stunned ADJECTIVE
<u>sidéré</u> (*amazed*) ◇ *I was stunned.*
J'étais sidéré.

stunning ADJECTIVE
<u>superbe</u>

stunt NOUN
la <u>cascade</u> (*in film*)

stuntman NOUN
le <u>cascadeur</u>

stupid ADJECTIVE
<u>stupide</u> ◇ *a stupid joke* une
plaisanterie stupide
◆**Me, go jogging? Don't be stupid!**
Moi, faire du footing? Ne dis pas de
bêtises!

to **stutter** VERB
| *see also* **stutter** NOUN |
<u>bégayer</u>

stutter NOUN
| *see also* **stutter** VERB |
◆**He's got a stutter.** Il bégaie.

style NOUN
le <u>style</u> ◇ *That's not his style.* Ça
n'est pas son style.

subject NOUN
[1] le <u>sujet</u> ◇ *The subject of my
project was the internet.* Le sujet de
mon projet était l'Internet.
[2] la <u>matière</u> (*at school*) ◇ *What's
your favourite subject?* Quelle est ta
matière préférée?

subjunctive NOUN

le subjonctif ◊ *in the subjunctive* au
subjonctif

submarine NOUN
le sous-marin

subscription NOUN
l' abonnement MASC (*to paper,
magazine*)
♦ **to take out a subscription to**
s'abonner à

subsequently ADVERB
en conséquence

to **subsidize** VERB
subventionner

subsidy NOUN
la subvention

substance NOUN
la substance

substitute NOUN
| see also **substitute** VERB |
(*person*)
le remplaçant
la remplaçante

to **substitute** VERB
| see also **substitute** NOUN |
substituer ◊ *to substitute A for B*
substituer A à B

subtitled ADJECTIVE
sous-titré

subtitles PL NOUN
les sous-titres MASC PL ◊ *a French film
with English subtitles* un film français
avec des sous-titres en anglais

subtle ADJECTIVE
subtil

to **subtract** VERB
retrancher ◊ *to subtract 3 from 5*
retrancher trois de cinq

suburb NOUN
la banlieue ◊ *a suburb of Paris* une
banlieue de Paris ◊ *They live in the
suburbs.* Ils habitent en banlieue.

suburban ADJECTIVE
de banlieue ◊ *a suburban train* un
train de banlieue

subway NOUN
le passage souterrain (*underpass*)

to **succeed** VERB
réussir ◊ *to succeed in doing
something* réussir à faire quelque
chose

success NOUN
le succès ◊ *The play was a great
success.* La pièce a eu beaucoup de
succès.

successful ADJECTIVE
réussi ◊ *a successful attempt* une
tentative réussie

♦ **to be successful in doing something**
réussir à faire quelque chose
♦ **He's a successful businessman.** Ses
affaires marchent bien.

successfully ADVERB
avec succès

successive ADJECTIVE
♦ **on four successive occasions** quatre
fois de suite

such ADJECTIVE, ADVERB
si ◊ *such nice people* des gens si
gentils ◊ *such a long journey* un
voyage si long
♦ **such a lot of** tellement de ◊ *such a lot
of work* tellement de travail
♦ **such as** (*like*) comme ◊ *hot countries,
such as India* les pays chauds,
comme l'Inde
♦ **not as such** pas exactement ◊ *He's
not an expert as such, but ...* Ce n'est
pas exactement un expert, mais ...
♦ **There's no such thing.** Ça n'existe
pas. ◊ *There's no such thing as the
yeti.* Le yéti n'existe pas.

such-and-such ADJECTIVE
tel ou tel MASC
telle ou telle FEM
◊ *such-and-such a place* tel ou tel
endroit

to **suck** VERB
sucer ◊ *to suck one's thumb* sucer
son pouce

sudden ADJECTIVE
soudain ◊ *a sudden change* un
changement soudain
♦ **all of a sudden** tout à coup

suddenly ADVERB
1 brusquement (*stop, leave, change*)
2 subitement (*die*)
3 soudain (*at beginning of sentence*)
◊ *Suddenly, the door opened.*
Soudain, la porte s'est ouverte.

suede NOUN
le daim ◊ *a suede jacket* une veste
en daim

to **suffer** VERB
souffrir ◊ *She was really suffering.*
Elle souffrait beaucoup.
♦ **to suffer from a disease** avoir une
maladie ◊ *I suffer from hay fever.* J'ai
le rhume des foins.

to **suffocate** VERB
suffoquer

sugar NOUN
le sucre ◊ *Do you take sugar?* Est-ce
que vous prenez du sucre?

to **suggest** VERB

S

suggérer ◊ *I suggested they set off early.* Je leur ai suggéré de partir de bonne heure.

suggestion NOUN
la suggestion ◊ *to make a suggestion* faire une suggestion

suicide NOUN
le suicide
♦**to commit suicide** se suicider

suit NOUN
see also **suit** VERB
1 le costume (*man's*)
2 le tailleur (*woman's*)

to **suit** VERB
see also **suit** NOUN
1 convenir à (*be convenient for*)
◊ *What time would suit you?* Quelle heure vous conviendrait?
♦**That suits me fine.** Ça m'arrange.
♦**Suit yourself!** Comme tu veux!
2 aller bien à (*look good on*) ◊ *That dress really suits you.* Cette robe te va vraiment bien.

suitable ADJECTIVE
1 convenable ◊ *a suitable time* une heure convenable
2 approprié (*clothes*) ◊ *suitable clothing* des vêtements appropriés

suitcase NOUN
la valise

suite NOUN
la suite (*of rooms*)
♦**a bedroom suite** une chambre à coucher

to **sulk** VERB
bouder

sulky ADJECTIVE
boudeur MASC
boudeuse FEM

sultana NOUN
le raisin sec
(les raisins secs PL)

sum NOUN
1 le calcul (*calculation*) ◊ *She's good at sums.* Elle est bonne en calcul.
2 la somme (*amount*) ◊ *a sum of money* une somme d'argent

to **sum up** VERB
résumer

to **summarize** VERB
résumer

summary NOUN
le résumé

summer NOUN
l' été MASC
♦**in summer** en été
♦**summer clothes** les vêtements d'été MASC

♦**the summer holidays** les vacances d'été FEM
♦**a summer camp** une colonie de vacances US

summertime NOUN
l' été MASC
♦**in summertime** en été

summit NOUN
le sommet

sun NOUN
le soleil ◊ *in the sun* au soleil

to **sunbathe** VERB
se bronzer

sunblock NOUN
l' écran total MASC

sunburn NOUN
le coup de soleil

sunburnt ADJECTIVE
♦**I got sunburnt.** J'ai attrapé un coup de soleil.

Sunday NOUN
le dimanche ◊ *on Sunday* dimanche ◊ *on Sundays* le dimanche ◊ *every Sunday* tous les dimanches ◊ *last Sunday* dimanche dernier ◊ *next Sunday* dimanche prochain

Sunday school NOUN
le catéchisme

> **ⓘ** *le catéchisme*, the French equivalent of **Sunday school**, takes place during the week after school rather than on a Sunday.

◊ *to go to Sunday school* aller au catéchisme

sunflower NOUN
le tournesol

sung VERB see **sing**

sunglasses PL NOUN
les lunettes de soleil FEM PL

sunk VERB see **sink**

sunlight NOUN
le soleil

sunny ADJECTIVE
ensoleillé ◊ *a sunny morning* une matinée ensoleillée
♦**It's sunny.** Il fait du soleil.
♦**a sunny day** une belle journée

sunrise NOUN
le lever du soleil

sunroof NOUN
le toit ouvrant

sunscreen NOUN
la crème solaire

sunset NOUN
le coucher du soleil

sunshine NOUN

le soleil

sunstroke NOUN
l' insolation FEM ◊ *to get sunstroke*
attraper une insolation

suntan NOUN
le bronzage
♦**suntan lotion** le lait solaire
♦**suntan oil** l'huile solaire FEM

super ADJECTIVE
formidable

superb ADJECTIVE
superbe

supermarket NOUN
le supermarché

supernatural ADJECTIVE
surnaturel MASC
surnaturelle FEM

superstitious ADJECTIVE
superstitieux MASC
superstitieuse FEM

to **supervise** VERB
surveiller

supervisor NOUN
1 (*in factory*)
le surveillant
la surveillante
2 (*in department store*)
le chef de rayon

supper NOUN
le dîner

supplement NOUN
le supplément

supplies PL NOUN
les vivres MASC PL (*food*)

to **supply** VERB
see also **supply** NOUN
fournir (*provide*)
♦**to supply somebody with something**
fournir quelque chose à quelqu'un
◊ *The centre supplied us with all the
equipment.* Le centre nous a fourni
tout l'équipement.

supply NOUN
see also **supply** VERB
la provision ◊ *a supply of paper* une
provision de papier
♦**the water supply** (*to town*)
l'approvisionnement en eau MASC

supply teacher NOUN
le suppléant
la suppléante

to **support** VERB
see also **support** NOUN
1 soutenir ◊ *My mum has always
supported me.* Ma mère m'a toujours
soutenu.

2 être supporter de ◊ *What team
do you support?* Tu es supporter de
quelle équipe?
3 subvenir aux besoins de
(*financially*) ◊ *She had to support five
children on her own.* Elle a dû
subvenir toute seule aux besoins de
cinq enfants.

Be careful not to translate **to support**
by **supporter**.

support NOUN
see also **support** VERB
le soutien (*backing*)

supporter NOUN
1 le supporter ◊ *a Liverpool
supporter* un supporter de Liverpool
2 le sympathisant
la sympathisante
◊ *a supporter of the Labour Party* un
sympathisant du parti travailliste

to **suppose** VERB
imaginer ◊ *I suppose he's late.*
J'imagine qu'il est en retard.
◊ *Suppose you won the lottery.*
Imaginez que vous gagniez à la
loterie.
♦**I suppose so.** J'imagine.
♦**to be supposed to do something** être
censé faire quelque chose ◊ *You're
supposed to show your passport.* On
est censé montrer son passeport.

supposing CONJUNCTION
si ◊ *Supposing you won the lottery ...*
Si tu gagnais à la loterie ...

surcharge NOUN
la surcharge

sure ADJECTIVE
sûr ◊ *Are you sure?* Tu es sûr?
♦**Sure!** Bien sûr!
♦**to make sure that ...** vérifier que ...
◊ *I'm going to make sure the door's
locked.* Je vais vérifier que la porte
est fermée à clé.

surely ADVERB
♦**Surely you've been to London?**
J'imagine que tu es allé à Londres,
non?
♦**The shops are closed on Sundays,
surely?** J'imagine que les magasins
sont fermés le dimanche, non?

surf NOUN
see also **surf** VERB
le ressac

to **surf** VERB
see also **surf** NOUN
surfer
♦**to go surfing** faire du surf
♦**to surf the Net** surfer sur le Net

surface NOUN
la surface

S

surfboard NOUN
la planche de surf
(les planches de surf PL)

surfing NOUN
le surf ◊ *to go surfing* faire du surf

surgeon NOUN
le chirurgien ◊ *She's a surgeon.* Elle
est chirurgien.

surgery NOUN
le cabinet médical (*doctor's surgery*)
♦ **surgery hours** les heures de
consultation FEM

surname NOUN
le nom de famille
(les noms de famille PL)

surprise NOUN
la surprise

surprised ADJECTIVE
surpris ◊ *I was surprised to see him.*
J'ai été surpris de le voir.

surprising ADJECTIVE
surprenant

to **surrender** VERB
capituler

surrogate mother NOUN
la mère porteuse
(les mères porteuses PL)

to **surround** VERB
encercler ◊ *The police surrounded
the house.* La police a encerclé la
maison. ◊ *You're surrounded!* Vous
êtes encerclé!
♦ **surrounded by** entouré de ◊ *The
house is surrounded by trees.* La
maison est entourée d'arbres.

surroundings PL NOUN
le cadre SING ◊ *a hotel in beautiful
surroundings* un hôtel situé dans un
beau cadre

survey NOUN
l' enquête FEM (*research*)

surveyor NOUN
[1] l' expert en bâtiment MASC (*of
buildings*)
[2] le/la géomètre (*of land*)

to **survive** VERB
survivre

survivor NOUN
le survivant
la survivante
◊ *There were no survivors.* Il n'y a
pas eu de survivants.

to **suspect** VERB
see also **suspect** NOUN
soupçonner

suspect NOUN
see also **suspect** VERB
le suspect
la suspecte

to **suspend** VERB
[1] exclure (*from school, team*) ◊ *He's
been suspended.* Il s'est fait exclure.
[2] suspendre (*from job*)

suspenders PL NOUN US
les bretelles FEM PL (*braces*)

suspense NOUN
[1] l' attente FEM (*waiting*) ◊ *The
suspense was terrible.* L'attente a été
terrible.
[2] le suspense (*in story*) ◊ *a film with
lots of suspense* un film avec
beaucoup de suspense

suspension NOUN
[1] l' exclusion FEM (*from school, team*)
[2] la suspension (*from job*)

suspicious ADJECTIVE
[1] méfiant ◊ *He was suspicious at
first.* Il était méfiant au début.
[2] louche (*suspicious-looking*) ◊ *a
suspicious person* un individu louche

to **swallow** VERB
avaler

swam VERB *see* **swim**

swan NOUN
le cygne

to **swap** VERB
échanger ◊ *Do you want to swap?*
Tu veux échanger? ◊ *to swap A for B*
échanger A contre B

to **swat** VERB
écraser

to **sway** VERB
osciller

to **swear** VERB
jurer (*make an oath, curse*)

swearword NOUN
le gros mot

sweat NOUN
see also **sweat** VERB
la transpiration

to **sweat** VERB
see also **sweat** NOUN
transpirer

sweater NOUN
le pull

sweatshirt NOUN
le sweat

sweaty ADJECTIVE
[1] en sueur (*person, face*) ◊ *I'm all
sweaty.* Je suis en sueur.
[2] moite (*hands*)

Swede NOUN
(*person*)
le Suédois
la Suédoise

swede NOUN
le rutabaga (*vegetable*)

Sweden NOUN
la <u>Suède</u>
♦ **in Sweden** en Suède
♦ **to Sweden** en Suède

Swedish ADJECTIVE
see also **Swedish** NOUN
<u>suédois</u> ◊ *She's Swedish.* Elle est
suédoise.

Swedish NOUN
see also **Swedish** ADJECTIVE
le <u>suédois</u> (*language*)

to **sweep** VERB
<u>balayer</u>
♦ **to sweep the floor** balayer

sweet NOUN
see also **sweet** ADJECTIVE
⨕1⨖ le <u>bonbon</u> (*candy*) ◊ *a bag of*
sweets un paquet de bonbons
⨕2⨖ le <u>dessert</u> (*pudding*) ◊ *What sweet*
did you have? Qu'est-ce que vous
avez mangé comme dessert?

sweet ADJECTIVE
see also **sweet** NOUN
⨕1⨖ (*not savoury*)
<u>sucré</u>
⨕2⨖ (*kind*)
<u>gentil</u> MASC
<u>gentille</u> FEM
◊ *That was really sweet of you.*
C'était vraiment gentil de ta part.
⨕3⨖ (*cute*)
<u>mignon</u> MASC
<u>mignonne</u> FEM
◊ *Isn't she sweet?* Comme elle est
mignonne!
♦ **sweet and sour pork** le porc à la
sauce aigre-douce

sweetcorn NOUN
le <u>maïs doux</u>

sweltering ADJECTIVE
♦ **It was sweltering.** Il faisait une
chaleur étouffante.

swept VERB *see* **sweep**

to **swerve** VERB
<u>faire une embardée</u> ◊ *He swerved*
to avoid the cyclist. Il a fait une
embardée pour éviter le cycliste.

swim NOUN
see also **swim** VERB
♦ **to go for a swim** aller se baigner

to **swim** VERB
see also **swim** NOUN
<u>nager</u> ◊ *Can you swim?* Tu sais
nager?
♦ **She swam across the river.** Elle a
traversé la rivière à la nage.

swimmer NOUN
le <u>nageur</u>
la <u>nageuse</u>

◊ *She's a good swimmer.* C'est une
bonne nageuse.

swimming NOUN
la <u>natation</u> ◊ *Do you like swimming?*
Tu aimes la natation?
♦ **to go swimming** (*in a pool*) aller à la
piscine
♦ **a swimming cap** un bonnet de bain
♦ **a swimming costume** un maillot de
bain
♦ **a swimming pool** une piscine
♦ **swimming trunks** le maillot de bain

swimsuit NOUN
le <u>maillot de bain</u>

swing NOUN
see also **swing** VERB
la <u>balançoire</u> (*in playground, garden*)

to **swing** VERB
see also **swing** NOUN
⨕1⨖ <u>se balancer</u> ◊ *A bunch of keys*
swung from his belt. Un trousseau de
clés se balançait à sa ceinture.
♦ **Sam was swinging an umbrella as he**
walked. Sam balançait son parapluie
en marchant.
⨕2⨖ <u>virer</u> ◊ *The canoe swung round*
sharply. Le canoë a viré brusquement.

Swiss ADJECTIVE
see also **Swiss** NOUN
<u>suisse</u> ◊ *Sabine's Swiss.* Sabine est
suisse.

Swiss NOUN
see also **Swiss** ADJECTIVE
le/la <u>Suisse</u> (*person*)
♦ **the Swiss** les Suisses

switch NOUN
see also **switch** VERB
le <u>bouton</u> (*for light, radio etc*)

to **switch** VERB
see also **switch** NOUN
<u>changer de</u> ◊ *We switched partners.*
Nous avons changé de partenaire.

to **switch off** VERB
⨕1⨖ <u>éteindre</u> (*electrical appliance*)
⨕2⨖ <u>arrêter</u> (*engine, machine*)

to **switch on** VERB
⨕1⨖ <u>allumer</u> (*electrical appliance*)
⨕2⨖ <u>mettre en marche</u> (*engine,*
machine)

Switzerland NOUN
la <u>Suisse</u>
♦ **in Switzerland** en Suisse

swollen ADJECTIVE
<u>enflé</u> (*arm, leg*)

to **swop** VERB
<u>échanger</u> ◊ *Do you want to swop?*
Tu veux échanger? ◊ *to swop A for B*
échanger A contre B

S

sword NOUN
l' <u>épée</u> FEM

swore, sworn VERB see **swear**

swot NOUN

see also **swot** VERB

le <u>bûcheur</u>
la <u>bûcheuse</u>

to **swot** VERB

see also **swot** NOUN

<u>bosser dur</u> ◊ *I'll have to swot for my maths exam.* Je vais devoir bosser dur pour mon examen de maths.

swum VERB see **swim**

swung VERB see **swing**

syllabus NOUN
le <u>programme</u> ◊ *on the syllabus* au programme

symbol NOUN

le <u>symbole</u>

sympathetic ADJECTIVE
<u>compréhensif</u> MASC
<u>compréhensive</u> FEM
Be careful not to translate ***sympathetic*** *by* ***sympathique***.

to **sympathize** VERB
♦**to sympathize with somebody** comprendre quelqu'un

sympathy NOUN
la <u>compassion</u>

symptom NOUN
le <u>symptôme</u>

syringe NOUN
la <u>seringue</u>

system NOUN
le <u>système</u>

T

table NOUN
la <u>table</u> ◊ *to lay the table* mettre la table

tablecloth NOUN
la <u>nappe</u>

tablespoon NOUN
la <u>grande cuillère</u>
♦ **a tablespoonful of sugar** une cuillerée à soupe de sucre

tablet NOUN
le <u>comprimé</u>

table tennis NOUN
le <u>ping-pong</u> ◊ *to play table tennis* jouer au ping-pong

tabloid NOUN
le <u>quotidien populaire</u>

tackle NOUN
  see also **tackle** VERB
  1 le <u>tacle</u> (*in football*)
  2 le <u>plaquage</u> (*in rugby*)
♦ **fishing tackle** le matériel de pêche

to **tackle** VERB
  see also **tackle** NOUN
  1 <u>tacler</u> (*in football*)
  2 <u>plaquer</u> (*in rugby*)
♦ **to tackle a problem** s'attaquer à un problème

tact NOUN
le <u>tact</u>

tactful ADJECTIVE
<u>plein de tact</u>

tactics PL NOUN
la <u>tactique</u> SING

tactless ADJECTIVE
♦ **to be tactless** manquer de tact ◊ *a tactless remark* une remarque qui manque de tact

tadpole NOUN
le <u>têtard</u>

tag NOUN
l' <u>étiquette</u> FEM (*label*)

tail NOUN
la <u>queue</u>
♦ **Heads or tails?** Pile ou face?

tailor NOUN
le <u>tailleur</u>

to **take** VERB
  1 <u>prendre</u> ◊ *Are you taking your new camera?* Tu prends ton nouvel appareil photo? ◊ *He took a plate from the cupboard.* Il a pris une assiette dans le placard. ◊ *It takes about an hour.* Ça prend environ une heure.

  2 <u>emmener</u> (*person*) ◊ *He goes to London every week, but he never takes me.* Il va à Londres toutes les semaines, mais il ne m'emmène jamais.
♦ **to take something somewhere** emporter quelque chose quelque part ◊ *Do you take your exercise books home?* Vous emportez vos cahiers chez vous? ◊ *Don't take anything valuable with you.* N'emportez pas d'objets de valeur.
♦ **I'm going to take my coat to the cleaner's.** Je vais donner mon manteau à nettoyer.
  3 <u>demander</u> (*effort, skill*) ◊ *that takes a lot of courage* cela demande beaucoup de courage
♦ **It takes a lot of money to do that.** Il faut beaucoup d'argent pour faire ça.
  4 <u>supporter</u> (*tolerate*) ◊ *He can't take being criticized.* Il ne supporte pas d'être critiqué.
  5 <u>passer</u> (*exam, test*) ◊ *Have you taken your driving test yet?* Est-ce que tu as déjà passé ton permis de conduire?
  6 <u>faire</u> (*subject*) ◊ *I decided to take French instead of German.* J'ai décidé de faire du français au lieu de l'allemand.

to **take after** VERB
<u>ressembler à</u> ◊ *She takes after her mother.* Elle ressemble à sa mère.

to **take apart** VERB
♦ **to take something apart** démonter quelque chose

to **take away** VERB
  1 <u>emporter</u> (*object*)
  2 <u>emmener</u> (*person*)
♦ **to take something away** (*confiscate*) confisquer quelque chose
♦ **hot meals to take away** des plats chauds à emporter

to **take back** VERB
<u>rapporter</u> ◊ *I took it back to the shop.* Je l'ai rapporté au magasin.
♦ **I take it all back!** Je n'ai rien dit!

to **take down** VERB
  1 <u>enlever</u> (*poster, sign*)
  2 <u>décrocher</u> (*painting, curtains*)
  3 <u>démonter</u> (*tent, scaffolding*)
  4 <u>prendre en note</u> (*make a note of*)
  ◊ *He took down the details in his notebook.* Il a pris tous les détails en note dans son carnet.

to **take in** VERB
comprendre (*understand*) ◊ *I didn't really take it in.* Je n'ai pas bien compris.

to **take off** VERB
1 décoller (*plane*) ◊ *The plane took off twenty minutes late.* L'avion a décollé avec vingt minutes de retard.
2 enlever (*clothes*) ◊ *Take your coat off.* Enlevez votre manteau.

to **take out** VERB
sortir (*from container, pocket*)
♦ **He took her out to the theatre.** Il l'a emmenée au théâtre.

to **take over** VERB
prendre la relève ◊ *I'll take over now.* Je vais prendre la relève.
♦ **to take over from somebody** remplacer quelqu'un

takeaway NOUN
1 le plat à emporter (*meal*)
2 le restaurant qui vend des plats à emporter (*shop*) ◊ *a Chinese takeaway* un restaurant chinois qui vend des plats à emporter

taken VERB *see* **take**

takeoff NOUN
le décollage (*of plane*)

talcum powder NOUN
le talc

tale NOUN
le conte (*story*)

talent NOUN
le talent ◊ *She's got lots of talent.* Elle a beaucoup de talent.
♦ **to have a talent for something** être doué pour quelque chose ◊ *He's got a real talent for languages.* Il est vraiment doué pour les langues.

talented ADJECTIVE
♦ **She's a talented pianist.** C'est une pianiste de talent.

talk NOUN
see also **talk** VERB
1 l' exposé MASC (*speech*) ◊ *She gave a talk on rock climbing.* Elle a fait un exposé sur la varappe.
2 la conversation (*conversation*) ◊ *I had a talk with my Mum about it.* J'ai eu une petite conversation avec ma mère à ce sujet.
3 les racontars MASC PL (*gossip*) ◊ *It's just talk.* Ce sont des racontars.

to **talk** VERB
see also **talk** NOUN
parler ◊ *to talk about something* parler de quelque chose

♦ **to talk something over with somebody** discuter de quelque chose avec quelqu'un

talkative ADJECTIVE
bavard

tall ADJECTIVE
1 grand (*person, tree*)
♦ **to be 2 metres tall** mesurer deux mètres
2 haut (*building*)

tame ADJECTIVE
apprivoisé (*animal*) ◊ *They've got a tame hedgehog.* Ils ont un hérisson apprivoisé.

tampon NOUN
le tampon

tan NOUN
le bronzage ◊ *She's got an amazing tan.* Elle a un bronzage superbe.

tangerine NOUN
la mandarine

tangle NOUN
1 l' enchevêtrement MASC (*ropes, cables*)
2 le nœud (*hair*)
♦ **to be in a tangle (1)** être enchevêtré (*ropes, cables*)
♦ **to be in a tangle (2)** être emmêlé (*hair*)

tank NOUN
1 le réservoir (*for water, petrol*)
2 le char d'assaut (*military*)
♦ **a fish tank** un aquarium

tanker NOUN
1 le pétrolier (*ship*)
♦ **an oil tanker** un pétrolier
2 le camion-citerne (*truck*)
♦ **a petrol tanker** un camion-citerne

tap NOUN
1 le robinet (*water tap*)
2 la petite tape (*gentle blow*)

tap-dancing NOUN
les claquettes FEM PL ◊ *I do tap-dancing.* Je fais des claquettes.

to **tape** VERB
see also **tape** NOUN
enregistrer (*record*) ◊ *Did you tape that film last night?* As-tu enregistré le film hier soir?

tape NOUN
see also **tape** VERB
1 la cassette ◊ *a tape of Sinead O'Connor* une cassette de Sinead O'Connor
2 le scotch ® (*sticky tape*)

tape deck NOUN
le magnétophone

tape measure NOUN

le mètre à ruban

tape recorder NOUN
le magnétophone

target NOUN
la cible

tarmac NOUN
le macadam (*on road*)

tart NOUN
la tarte ◊ *an apple tart* une tarte aux pommes

tartan ADJECTIVE
écossais ◊ *a tartan scarf* une écharpe écossaise

task NOUN
la tâche

taste NOUN
see also **taste** VERB
le goût ◊ *It's got a really strange taste.* Ça a un goût vraiment bizarre. ◊ *a joke in bad taste* une plaisanterie de mauvais goût
◆**Would you like a taste?** Tu veux goûter?

to **taste** VERB
see also **taste** NOUN
goûter ◊ *Would you like to taste it?* Vous voulez y goûter?
◆**to taste of something** avoir un goût de quelque chose ◊ *It tastes of fish.* Ça a un goût de poisson.
◆**You can taste the garlic in it.** Ça a bien le goût d'ail.

tasteful ADJECTIVE
de bon goût

tasteless ADJECTIVE
1 fade (*food*)
2 de mauvais goût (*in bad taste*) ◊ *a tasteless remark* une remarque de mauvais goût

tasty ADJECTIVE
savoureux MASC
savoureuse FEM

tattoo NOUN
le tatouage

taught VERB see **teach**

Taurus NOUN
le Taureau ◊ *I'm Taurus.* Je suis Taureau.

tax NOUN
1 les impôts MASC PL (*on income*)
2 la taxe (*on goods, alcohol*)

taxi NOUN
le taxi
◆**a taxi driver** un chauffeur de taxi

taxi rank NOUN
la station de taxis

TB NOUN
la tuberculose

tea NOUN
1 le thé ◊ *a cup of tea* une tasse de thé
◆**a tea bag** un sachet de thé
2 le dîner (*evening meal*)
◆**We were having tea.** Nous étions en train de dîner.

to **teach** VERB
1 apprendre ◊ *My sister taught me to swim.* Ma sœur m'a appris à nager. ◊ *That'll teach you!* Ça t'apprendra!
2 enseigner (*in school*) ◊ *She teaches physics.* Elle enseigne la physique.

teacher NOUN
1 (*in secondary school*)
le professeur ◊ *a maths teacher* un professeur de maths ◊ *She's a teacher.* Elle est professeur.
2 (*in primary school*)
l' instituteur MASC
l' institutrice FEM
◊ *He's a primary school teacher.* Il est instituteur.

teacher's pet NOUN
le chouchou
la chouchoute

tea cloth NOUN
le torchon

team NOUN
l' équipe FEM ◊ *a football team* une équipe de football ◊ *She was in my team.* Elle était dans mon équipe.

teapot NOUN
la théière

tear NOUN
see also **tear** VERB
la larme ◊ *She was in tears.* Elle était en larmes.

to **tear** VERB
see also **tear** NOUN
1 déchirer ◊ *Be careful or you'll tear the page.* Fais attention, tu vas déchirer la page.
2 se déchirer ◊ *It won't tear, it's very strong.* Ça ne se déchire pas, c'est très solide.
◆**to tear up** déchirer ◊ *He tore up the letter.* Il a déchiré la lettre.

tear gas NOUN
le gaz lacrymogène

to **tease** VERB
1 tourmenter (*unkindly*) ◊ *Stop teasing that poor animal!* Arrête de tourmenter cette pauvre bête!
2 taquiner (*jokingly*) ◊ *He's teasing you.* Il te taquine.
◆**I was only teasing.** Je plaisantais.

teaspoon NOUN

T

la petite cuillère
♦ **a teaspoonful of sugar** une cuillerée à café de sucre

teatime NOUN
l' heure du dîner FEM (*in evening*) ◊ *It was nearly teatime.* C'était presque l'heure du dîner.
♦ **Teatime!** À table!

tea towel NOUN
le torchon

technical ADJECTIVE
technique
♦ **a technical college** un lycée technique

technician NOUN
le technicien
la technicienne

technique NOUN
la technique

techno NOUN
la techno (*music*)

technological ADJECTIVE
technologique

technology NOUN
la technologie

teddy bear NOUN
le nounours

teenage ADJECTIVE
1 pour les jeunes ◊ *a teenage magazine* un magazine pour les jeunes
2 adolescent (*boys, girls*) ◊ *She has two teenage daughters.* Elle a deux filles adolescentes.

teenager NOUN
l' adolescent MASC
l' adolescente FEM

teens PL NOUN
♦ **She's in her teens.** C'est une adolescente.

tee-shirt NOUN
le tee-shirt

teeth PL NOUN
les dents FEM PL

to **teethe** VERB
faire ses dents

teetotal ADJECTIVE
♦ **I'm teetotal.** Je ne bois jamais d'alcool.

telecommunications PL NOUN
les télécommunications FEM PL

telephone NOUN
see also **phone** NOUN AND VERB
le téléphone ◊ *on the telephone* au téléphone
♦ **a telephone box** une cabine téléphonique
♦ **a telephone call** un coup de téléphone

♦ **the telephone directory** l'annuaire MASC
♦ **a telephone number** un numéro de téléphone

telesales PL NOUN
la vente par téléphone SING ◊ *She works in telesales.* Elle travaille dans la vente par téléphone.

telescope NOUN
le télescope

television NOUN
la télévision
♦ **on television** à la télévision
♦ **a television licence** une redevance de télévision
♦ **a television programme** une émission de télévision

to **tell** VERB
dire
♦ **to tell somebody something** dire quelque chose à quelqu'un ◊ *Did you tell your mother?* Tu l'as dit à ta mère? ◊ *I told him that I was going on holiday.* Je lui ai dit que je partais en vacances.
♦ **to tell somebody to do something** dire à quelqu'un de faire quelque chose ◊ *He told me to wait a moment.* Il m'a dit d'attendre un moment.
♦ **to tell lies** dire des mensonges
♦ **to tell a story** raconter une histoire
♦ **I can't tell the difference between them.** Je n'arrive pas à les distinguer.

to **tell off** VERB
gronder

telly NOUN
la télé ◊ *to watch telly* regarder la télé
♦ **on telly** à la télé

temper NOUN
le caractère ◊ *He's got a terrible temper.* Il a un sale caractère.
♦ **to be in a temper** être en colère
♦ **to lose one's temper** se mettre en colère ◊ *I lost my temper.* Je me suis mis en colère.

temperature NOUN
la température (*of oven, water, person*)
♦ **The temperature was 30 degrees.** Il faisait trente degrés.
♦ **to have a temperature** avoir de la fièvre

temple NOUN
le temple

temporary ADJECTIVE
temporaire

to **tempt** VERB
tenter ◊ *I'm very tempted!* Je suis très tenté!

♦**to tempt somebody to do something**
persuader quelqu'un de faire quelque
chose

temptation NOUN
la tentation

tempting ADJECTIVE
tentant

ten NUMBER
dix ◊ *She's ten.* Elle a dix ans.

tenant NOUN
le locataire
la locataire

to **tend** VERB
♦**to tend to do something** avoir
tendance à faire quelque chose ◊ *He
tends to arrive late.* Il a tendance à
arriver en retard.

tender ADJECTIVE
1 tendre (*food*)
2 sensible (*part of body*) ◊ *My feet
are really tender.* J'ai les pieds très
sensibles.

tennis NOUN
le tennis ◊ *Do you play tennis?* Vous
jouez au tennis?
♦**a tennis ball** une balle de tennis
♦**a tennis court** un court de tennis
♦**a tennis racket** une raquette de tennis

tennis player NOUN
le joueur de tennis
la joueuse de tennis
◊ *He's a tennis player.* Il est joueur
de tennis.

tenor NOUN
le ténor

tenpin bowling NOUN
le bowling ◊ *to go tenpin bowling*
jouer au bowling

tense ADJECTIVE
see also **tense** NOUN
tendu

tense NOUN
see also **tense** ADJECTIVE
♦**the present tense** le présent
♦**the future tense** le futur

tension NOUN
la tension

tent NOUN
la tente
♦**a tent peg** un piquet de tente
♦**a tent pole** un montant de tente

tenth ADJECTIVE
dixième ◊ *the tenth floor* le dixième
étage
♦**the tenth of August** le dix août

term NOUN
1 le trimestre (*at school*)

2 le terme ◊ *a short-term solution*
une solution à court terme
♦**to come to terms with something**
accepter quelque chose

terminal ADJECTIVE
see also **terminal** NOUN
incurable (*illness, patient*)

terminal NOUN
see also **terminal** ADJECTIVE
le terminal (*of computer*)
♦**an oil terminal** un terminal pétrolier
♦**an air terminal** une aérogare

terminally ADVERB
♦**to be terminally ill** être condamné

terrace NOUN
1 la terrasse (*patio*)
2 la rangée de maisons (*row of
houses*)
♦**the terraces** (*at stadium*) les gradins
MASC

terraced ADJECTIVE
♦**a terraced house** une maison
mitoyenne

terrible ADJECTIVE
épouvantable ◊ *My French is
terrible.* Mon français est
épouvantable.

terribly ADVERB
1 terriblement ◊ *He suffered terribly.*
Il a terriblement souffert.
2 vraiment ◊ *I'm terribly sorry.* Je
suis vraiment désolé.

terrier NOUN
le terrier

terrific ADJECTIVE
super (*wonderful*) ◊ *That's terrific!*
C'est super!
♦**You look terrific!** Tu es superbe!

terrified ADJECTIVE
terrifié ◊ *I was terrified!* J'étais
terrifié!

terrorism NOUN
le terrorisme

terrorist NOUN
le/la terroriste
♦**a terrorist attack** un attentat terroriste

test NOUN
see also **test** VERB
1 l' interrogation FEM (*at school*) ◊ *I've
got a test tomorrow.* J'ai une
interrogation demain.
2 l' essai MASC (*trial, check*) ◊ *nuclear
tests* les essais nucléaires
3 l' analyse FEM (*medical*) ◊ *a blood
test* une analyse de sang ◊ *They're
going to do some more tests.* Ils vont
faire d'autres analyses.
♦**driving test** l'examen du permis de
conduire MASC ◊ *He's got his driving*

T

test tomorrow. Il passe son permis de conduire demain.

to **test** VERB

> see also **test** NOUN

1 essayer ◊ *to test something out* essayer quelque chose
2 interroger (*class*) ◊ *He tested us on the vocabulary.* Il nous a interrogés sur le vocabulaire.

♦**She was tested for drugs.** On lui a fait subir un contrôle antidopage.

test match NOUN
le match international

test tube NOUN
l' éprouvette FEM

tetanus NOUN
le tétanos ◊ *a tetanus injection* un vaccin contre le tétanos

text NOUN

> see also **text** VERB

1 le texte
2 le minimessage (*mobile phone*)

to **text** VERB

> see also **text** NOUN

♦**to text someone** envoyer un minimessage à quelqu'un

textbook NOUN
le manuel ◊ *a French textbook* un manuel de français

Thames NOUN
la Tamise

than CONJUNCTION
que ◊ *She's taller than me.* Elle est plus grande que moi. ◊ *I've got more books than him.* J'ai plus de livres que lui.

♦**more than ten years** plus de dix ans
♦**more than once** plus d'une fois

to **thank** VERB
remercier ◊ *Don't forget to write and thank them.* N'oublie pas de leur écrire pour les remercier.

♦**thank you** merci
♦**thank you very much** merci beaucoup

thanks EXCLAMATION
merci!

♦**thanks to** grâce à ◊ *Thanks to him, everything went OK.* Grâce à lui, tout s'est bien passé.

that ADJECTIVE, PRONOUN, CONJUNCTION

> *Use **ce** when **that** is followed by a masculine noun, and **cette** when that is followed by a feminine noun. **ce** changes to **cet** before a vowel and before most words beginning with "h".*

1 ce ◊ *that book* ce livre
cet ◊ *that man* cet homme
cette ◊ *that woman* cette femme

♦**that road** cette route
♦**THAT road** cette route-là
♦**that one (1)** (*masculine*) celui-là ◊ *This man? – No, that one.* Cet homme-ci? – Non, celui-là.
♦**that one (2)** (*feminine*) celle-là ◊ *Do you like this photo? – No, I prefer that one.* Tu aimes cette photo? – Non, je préfère celle-là.

2 ça ◊ *You see that?* Tu vois ça?

♦**What's that?** Qu'est-ce que c'est?
♦**Who's that?** Qui est-ce?
♦**Is that you?** C'est toi?
♦**That's ...** C'est ... ◊ *That's my teacher.* C'est mon prof. ◊ *That's what he said.* C'est ce qu'il a dit.

> *In relative phrases use **qui** when **that** refers to the subject of the sentence, and **que** when it refers to the object.*

3 qui ◊ *the man that saw us* l'homme qui nous a vus ◊ *the man that spoke to us* l'homme qui nous a parlé
4 que ◊ *the man that we saw* l'homme que nous avons vu ◊ *the man that we spoke to* l'homme à qui nous avons parlé

> ***que** changes to **qu'** before a vowel and before most words beginning with "h".*

◊ *the dog that she bought* le chien qu'elle a acheté ◊ *He thought that Henri was ill.* Il pensait qu'Henri était malade. ◊ *I know that she likes chocolate.* Je sais qu'elle aime le chocolat.

♦**It was that big.** Il était grand comme ça.
♦**It's about that high.** C'est à peu près haut comme ça.
♦**It's not that difficult.** Ça n'est pas si difficile que ça.

thatched ADJECTIVE
♦**a thatched cottage** une chaumière

the ARTICLE

> *Use **le** with a masculine noun, and **la** with a feminine noun. Use **l'** before a vowel and most words beginning with "h". For plural nouns always use **les**.*

le ◊ *the boy* le garçon
l' ◊ *the man* l'homme MASC ◊ *the air* l'air MASC ◊ *the habit* l'habitude FEM
la ◊ *the girl* la fille
les ◊ *the children* les enfants

theatre NOUN (US **theater**)
le théâtre

theft NOUN
le vol

their ADJECTIVE
leur
(leurs PL)
◊ *their house* leur maison ◊ *their parents* leurs parents

theirs PRONOUN
le leur + MASC NOUN ◊ *It's not our garage, it's theirs.* Ce n'est pas notre garage, c'est le leur.
la leur + FEM NOUN ◊ *It's not our car, it's theirs.* Ce n'est pas notre voiture, c'est la leur.
les leurs + PL NOUN ◊ *They're not our ideas, they're theirs.* Ce ne sont pas nos idées, ce sont les leurs.
♦ **Is this theirs? (1)** (*masculine owners*) C'est à eux?
♦ **Is this theirs? (2)** (*feminine owners*) C'est à elles? ◊ *This car is theirs.* Cette voiture est à eux. ◊ *Whose is this? – It's theirs.* C'est à qui? – À eux.

them PRONOUN
⒈ les ◊ *I didn't see them.* Je ne les ai pas vus.
*Use **leur** when **them** means **to them**.*
⒉ leur ◊ *I gave them some brochures.* Je leur ai donné des brochures. ◊ *I told them the truth.* Je leur ai dit la vérité.
*Use **eux** or **elles** after a preposition.*
⒊ eux MASC ◊ *It's for them.* C'est pour eux.
elles FEM ◊ *Ann and Sophie came – Graham was with them.* Ann et Sophie sont venues – Graham était avec elles.

theme NOUN
le thème

theme park NOUN
le parc d'attractions

themselves PRONOUN
⒈ se ◊ *Did they hurt themselves?* Est-ce qu'ils se sont fait mal?
⒉ eux-mêmes MASC
elles-mêmes FEM
◊ *They did it themselves.* Ils l'ont fait eux-mêmes.

then ADVERB, CONJUNCTION
⒈ ensuite (*next*) ◊ *I get dressed. Then I have breakfast.* Je m'habille. Ensuite je prends mon petit déjeuner.
⒉ alors (*in that case*) ◊ *My pen's run out. – Use a pencil then!* Il n'y a plus d'encre dans mon stylo. – Alors utilise un crayon!
⒊ à l'époque (*at that time*) ◊ *There was no electricity then.* Il n'y avait pas l'électricité à l'époque.

♦ **now and then** de temps en temps
◊ *Do you play chess? – Now and then.* Vous jouez aux échecs? – De temps en temps.
♦ **By then it was too late.** Il était déjà trop tard.

therapy NOUN
la thérapie

there ADVERB
⒈ là ◊ *Put it there, on the table.* Mets-le là, sur la table.
♦ **over there** là-bas
♦ **in there** là
♦ **on there** là
♦ **up there** là-haut
♦ **down there** là-bas
♦ **There he is!** Le voilà!
⒉ y ◊ *He went there on Friday.* Il y est allé vendredi. ◊ *Paris? I've never been there.* Paris? Je n'y suis jamais allé.
♦ **There is ...** Il y a ... ◊ *There's a factory near my house.* Il y a une usine près de chez moi.
♦ **There are ...** Il y a ... ◊ *There are five people in my family.* Il y a cinq personnes dans ma famille.
♦ **There has been an accident.** Il y a eu un accident.

therefore ADVERB
donc

there's = there is, = there has

thermometer NOUN
le thermomètre

Thermos ® NOUN
le thermos ®

these ADJECTIVE, PRONOUN
⒈ ces ◊ *these shoes* ces chaussures
♦ **THESE shoes** ces chaussures-là
⒉ ceux-ci MASC ◊ *I want these!* Je veux ceux-ci!
celles-ci FEM ◊ *I'm looking for some sandals. Can I try these?* Je cherche des sandales. Je peux essayer celles-ci?

they PRONOUN
*Check if **they** stands for a masculine or feminine noun.*
ils ◊ *Are there any tickets left? – No, they're all sold.* Est-ce qu'il reste des billets? – Non, ils sont tous vendus.
elles ◊ *Do you like those shoes? – No, they're horrible.* Tu aimes ces chaussures? – Non, elles sont affreuses.
♦ **They say that ...** On dit que ...

they'd = they had, = they would
they'll = they will
they're = they are

they've = **they have**

thick ADJECTIVE
[1] (*not thin*)
épais MASC
épaisse FEM
♦**The walls are one metre thick.** Les murs font un mètre d'épaisseur.
[2] (*stupid*)
bête

thief NOUN
le voleur
la voleuse
♦**Stop thief!** Au voleur!

thigh NOUN
la cuisse

thin ADJECTIVE
[1] mince (*person, slice*)
[2] maigre (*skinny*)

thing NOUN
[1] la chose ◊ *beautiful things* de belles choses
[2] le truc (*thingy*) ◊ *What's that thing called?* Comment s'appelle ce truc?
♦**my things** (*belongings*) mes affaires FEM
♦**You poor thing!** Mon pauvre!

to **think** VERB
[1] penser (*believe*) ◊ *I think you're wrong.* Je pense que vous avez tort.
◊ *What do you think about the war?* Que pensez-vous de la guerre?
[2] réfléchir (*spend time thinking*)
◊ *Think carefully before you reply.* Réfléchis bien avant de répondre.
◊ *I'll think about it.* Je vais y réfléchir.
♦**What are you thinking about?** À quoi tu penses?
[3] imaginer (*imagine*) ◊ *Think what life would be like without cars.* Imaginez la vie sans voitures.
♦**I think so.** Oui, je crois.
♦**I don't think so.** Je ne crois pas.
♦**I'll think it over.** Je vais y réfléchir.

third ADJECTIVE
  see also **third** NOUN
troisième ◊ *the third day* le troisième jour ◊ *the third time* la troisième fois ◊ *I came third.* Je suis arrivé troisième.
♦**the third of March** le trois mars

third NOUN
  see also **third** ADJECTIVE
le tiers ◊ *a third of the population* un tiers de la population

thirdly ADVERB
troisièmement

Third World NOUN
le tiers monde

thirst NOUN

la soif

thirsty ADJECTIVE
♦**to be thirsty** avoir soif

thirteen NUMBER
treize ◊ *I'm thirteen.* J'ai treize ans.

thirteenth ADJECTIVE
treizième ◊ *her thirteenth birthday* son treizième anniversaire ◊ *the thirteenth floor* le treizième étage
♦**the thirteenth of August** le treize août

thirty NUMBER
trente

this ADJECTIVE, PRONOUN
  Use **ce** when **this** is followed by a masculine noun, and **cette** when **this** is followed by a feminine noun. **ce** changes to **cet** before a vowel and before most words beginning with "h".
[1] ce ◊ *this book* ce livre
cet ◊ *this man* cet homme
cette ◊ *this woman* cette femme
♦**this road** cette route
♦**THIS road** cette route-ci
♦**this one (1)** (*masculine*) celui-ci ◊ *Pass me that pen. – This one?* Passe-moi ce stylo. – Celui-ci?
♦**this one (2)** (*feminine*) celle-ci ◊ *Of the two photos, I prefer this one.* Des deux photos, c'est celle-ci que je préfère.
[2] ça ◊ *You see this?* Tu vois ça?
♦**What's this?** Qu'est-ce que c'est?
♦**This is my mother.** (*introduction*) Je te présente ma mère.
♦**This is Gavin speaking.** (*on the phone*) C'est Gavin à l'appareil.

thistle NOUN
le chardon

thorough ADJECTIVE
minutieux MASC
minutieuse FEM
◊ *She's very thorough.* Elle est très minutieuse.

thoroughly ADVERB
à fond (*examine*)

those ADJECTIVE, PRONOUN
[1] ces ◊ *those shoes* ces chaussures
♦**THOSE shoes** ces chaussures-là
[2] ceux-là MASC ◊ *I want those!* Je veux ceux-là!
celles-là FEM ◊ *I'm looking for some sandals. Can I try those?* Je cherche des sandales. Je peux essayer celles-là?

though CONJUNCTION, ADVERB
bien que
  bien que has to be followed by a verb in the subjunctive.

◊ *Though it's raining ...* Bien qu'il pleuve ...

♦ **He's a nice person, though he's not very clever.** Il est sympa, mais pas très malin.

thought VERB *see* **think**

thought NOUN

l' <u>idée</u> FEM (*idea*) ◊ *I've just had a thought.* Je viens d'avoir une idée.

♦ **It was a nice thought, thank you.** C'est gentil de ta part, merci.

thoughtful ADJECTIVE

☐1 (*deep in thought*)

<u>pensif</u> MASC

<u>pensive</u> FEM

◊ *You look thoughtful.* Tu as l'air pensif.

☐2 (*considerate*)

<u>prévenant</u> ◊ *She's very thoughtful.* Elle est très prévenante.

thoughtless ADJECTIVE

♦ **He's completely thoughtless.** Il ne pense absolument pas aux autres.

thousand NUMBER

♦ **a thousand** mille ◊ *a thousand euros* mille euros

♦ **£2000** deux mille livres

♦ **thousands of people** des milliers de personnes

thousandth ADJECTIVE, NOUN

le <u>millième</u>

thread NOUN

le <u>fil</u>

threat NOUN

la <u>menace</u>

to **threaten** VERB

<u>menacer</u> ◊ *to threaten to do something* menacer de faire quelque chose

three NUMBER

<u>trois</u> ◊ *She's three.* Elle a trois ans.

three-dimensional ADJECTIVE

<u>à trois dimensions</u>

threw VERB *see* **throw**

thrifty ADJECTIVE

<u>économe</u>

thrill NOUN

l' <u>émotion</u> FEM (*excitement*)

thrilled ADJECTIVE

♦ **I was thrilled.** (*pleased*) J'étais absolument ravi.

thriller NOUN

le <u>thriller</u>

thrilling ADJECTIVE

<u>palpitant</u>

throat NOUN

la <u>gorge</u> ◊ *to have a sore throat* avoir mal à la gorge

to **throb** VERB

♦ **a throbbing pain** un élancement

♦ **My arm's throbbing.** J'ai des élancements dans le bras.

throne NOUN

le <u>trône</u>

through PREPOSITION, ADJECTIVE, ADVERB

☐1 <u>par</u> ◊ *through the window* par la fenêtre ◊ *I know her through my sister.* Je la connais par ma sœur. ◊ *to go through Birmingham* passer par Birmingham

♦ **to go through a tunnel** traverser un tunnel

☐2 <u>à travers</u> ◊ *through the mist* à travers la brume ◊ *through the crowd* à travers la foule ◊ *The window was dirty and I couldn't see through.* La fenêtre était sale et je n'arrivais pas à voir à travers.

♦ **a through train** un train direct

♦ **"no through road"** "impasse"

throughout PREPOSITION

♦ **throughout Britain** dans toute la Grande-Bretagne

♦ **throughout the year** pendant toute l'année

to **throw** VERB

<u>lancer</u> ◊ *He threw the ball to me.* Il m'a lancé le ballon.

♦ **to throw a party** organiser une soirée

♦ **That really threw him.** Ça l'a décontenancé.

♦ **to throw away (1)** (*rubbish*) jeter

♦ **to throw away (2)** (*chance*) perdre

♦ **to throw out (1)** (*throw away*) jeter

♦ **to throw out (2)** (*person*) mettre à la porte ◊ *I threw him out.* Je l'ai mis à la porte.

♦ **to throw up** vomir

thug NOUN

le <u>voyou</u>

thumb NOUN

le <u>pouce</u>

thumb tack NOUN US

la <u>punaise</u>

to **thump** VERB

♦ **to thump somebody** donner un coup de poing à quelqu'un

thunder NOUN

le <u>tonnerre</u>

thunderstorm NOUN

l' <u>orage</u> MASC

thundery ADJECTIVE

<u>orageux</u> MASC

<u>orageuse</u> FEM

Thursday NOUN

le <u>jeudi</u> ◊ *on Thursday* jeudi ◊ *on Thursdays* le jeudi ◊ *every Thursday*

T

☞

tous les jeudis ◊ *last Thursday* jeudi dernier ◊ *next Thursday* jeudi prochain

thyme NOUN
le thym

tick NOUN
see also **tick** VERB
1 la coche (*mark*)
2 le tic-tac (*of clock*)
◆**I'll be back in a tick.** J'en ai pour une seconde.

to **tick** VERB
see also **tick** NOUN
1 cocher ◊ *Tick the appropriate box.* Cochez la case correspondante.
2 faire tic-tac (*clock*)

to **tick off** VERB
1 cocher (*check*) ◊ *He ticked off our names on the list.* Il a coché nos noms sur la liste.
2 passer un savon à (*tell off*) ◊ *She ticked me off for being late.* Elle m'a passé un savon à cause de mon retard.

ticket NOUN
Be careful to choose correctly between le ticket and le billet.
1 le ticket (*for bus, tube, cinema, museum*) ◊ *an underground ticket* un ticket de métro
2 le billet (*for plane, train, theatre, concert*)
◆**a parking ticket** un p.-v.

ticket inspector NOUN
le contrôleur
la contrôleuse

ticket office NOUN
le guichet

to **tickle** VERB
chatouiller

ticklish ADJECTIVE
chatouilleux MASC
chatouilleuse FEM
◊ *Are you ticklish?* Tu es chatouilleux?

tide NOUN
la marée
◆**high tide** la marée haute
◆**low tide** la marée basse

tidy ADJECTIVE
see also **tidy** VERB
1 bien rangé (*room*) ◊ *Your room's very tidy.* Ta chambre est bien rangée.
2 ordonné (*person*) ◊ *She's very tidy.* Elle est très ordonnée.

to **tidy** VERB
see also **tidy** ADJECTIVE
ranger ◊ *Go and tidy your room.* Va ranger ta chambre.

◆**to tidy up** ranger ◊ *Don't forget to tidy up afterwards.* N'oubliez pas de ranger après.

tie NOUN
see also **tie** VERB
la cravate (*necktie*)
◆**It was a tie.** (*in sport*) Ils ont fait match nul.

to **tie** VERB
see also **tie** NOUN
1 nouer (*ribbon, shoelaces*)
◆**to tie a knot in something** faire un nœud à quelque chose
2 faire match nul (*in sport*) ◊ *They tied three all.* Ils ont fait match nul, trois à trois.
◆**to tie up (1)** (*parcel*) ficeler
◆**to tie up (2)** (*dog, boat*) attacher
◆**to tie up (3)** (*prisoner*) ligoter

tiger NOUN
le tigre

tight ADJECTIVE
1 moulant (*tight-fitting*) ◊ *tight clothes* les vêtements moulants
2 juste (*too tight*) ◊ *This dress is a bit tight.* Cette robe est un peu juste.

to **tighten** VERB
1 tendre (*rope*)
2 resserrer (*screw*)

tightly ADVERB
fort (*hold*)

tights PL NOUN
le collant SING

tile NOUN
1 (*on roof*)
la tuile
2 (*on wall, floor*)
le carreau
(les carreaux PL)

tiled ADJECTIVE
1 en tuiles (*roof*)
2 carrelé (*wall, floor, room*)

till NOUN
see also **till** PREPOSITION
la caisse

till PREPOSITION, CONJUNCTION
see also **till** NOUN
1 jusqu'à ◊ *I waited till ten o'clock.* J'ai attendu jusqu'à dix heures.
◆**till now** jusqu'à présent
◆**till then** jusque-là

Use avant if the sentence you want to translate contains a negative, such as "not" or "never".

2 avant ◊ *It won't be ready till next week.* Ça ne sera pas prêt avant la semaine prochaine. ◊ *Till last year I'd*

never been to France. Avant l'année
dernière, je n'étais jamais allé en
France.

time NOUN
　　① l' heure FEM (*on clock*) ◇ *What time
is it?* Quelle heure est-il? ◇ *What time
do you get up?* À quelle heure te te
lèves? ◇ *It was two o'clock, French
time.* Il était deux heures, heure
française.
　◆ **on time** à l'heure ◇ *He never arrives
on time.* Il n'arrive jamais à l'heure.
　　② le temps (*amount of time*) ◇ *I'm
sorry, I haven't got time.* Je suis
désolé, je n'ai pas le temps.
　◆ **from time to time** de temps en temps
　◆ **in time** à temps ◇ *We arrived in time
for lunch.* Nous sommes arrivés à
temps pour le déjeuner.
　◆ **just in time** juste à temps
　◆ **in no time** en un rien de temps ◇ *It
was ready in no time.* Ça a été prêt
en un rien de temps.
　◆ **It's time to go.** Il est temps de partir.
　　③ le moment (*moment*) ◇ *This isn't a
good time to ask him.* Ce n'est pas le
bon moment pour lui demander.
　◆ **for the time being** pour le moment
　　④ la fois (*occasion*) ◇ *this time* cette
fois-ci ◇ *next time* la prochaine fois
◇ *two at a time* deux à la fois
　◆ **How many times?** Combien de fois?
　◆ **at times** parfois
　◆ **a long time** longtemps ◇ *Have you
lived here for a long time?* Vous
habitez ici depuis longtemps?
　◆ **in a week's time** dans une semaine
◇ *I'll come back in a month's time.* Je
reviendrai dans un mois.
　◆ **Come and see us any time.** Venez
nous voir quand vous voulez.
　◆ **to have a good time** bien s'amuser
◇ *Did you have a good time?* Vous
vous êtes bien amusés?
　◆ **2 times 2 is 4** deux fois deux égalent
quatre

time bomb NOUN
　la bombe à retardement

time off NOUN
　le temps libre

timer NOUN
　le minuteur

time-share NOUN
　l' appartement en multipropriété
　MASC

timetable NOUN
　　① l' horaire MASC (*for train, bus*)
　　② l' emploi du temps MASC (*at school*)

time zone NOUN
　le fuseau horaire

tin NOUN
　　① la boîte ◇ *a tin of soup* une boîte
de soupe ◇ *a biscuit tin* une boîte à
biscuits
　　② la boîte de conserve ◇ *The bin
was full of tins.* La poubelle était
pleine de boîtes de conserve.
　　③ l' étain MASC (*type of metal*)

tinned ADJECTIVE
　en boîte (*food*) ◇ *tinned peaches* des
pêches en boîte

tin opener NOUN
　l' ouvre-boîte MASC

tinsel NOUN
　les guirlandes de Noël FEM PL

tinted ADJECTIVE
　teinté (*spectacles, glass*)

tiny ADJECTIVE
　minuscule

tip NOUN
　　see also **tip** VERB
　　① (*money*)
　le pourboire ◇ *Shall I give him a tip?*
Je lui donne un pourboire?
　　② (*advice*)
　le tuyau
　(les tuyaux PL)
　◇ *a useful tip* un bon tuyau (*informal*)
　　③ (*end*)
　le bout ◇ *It's on the tip of my
tongue.* Je l'ai sur le bout de la
langue.
　◆ **a rubbish tip** une décharge
　◆ **This place is a complete tip!** Quel
fouillis!

to **tip** VERB
　　see also **tip** NOUN
　donner un pourboire à ◇ *Don't
forget to tip the taxi driver.* N'oubliez
pas de donner un pourboire au
chauffeur de taxi.

tipsy ADJECTIVE
　pompette

tiptoe NOUN
　◆ **on tiptoe** sur la pointe des pieds

tired ADJECTIVE
　fatigué ◇ *I'm tired.* Je suis fatigué.
　◆ **to be tired of something** en avoir
assez de quelque chose

tiring ADJECTIVE
　fatigant

tissue NOUN
　le kleenex ® ◇ *Have you got a
tissue?* Tu as un kleenex? ®

title NOUN
　le titre

title role NOUN
　le rôle principal

T

to PREPOSITION
> *à + le changes to au. à + les changes to aux.*

1 à ◊ *to go to Paris* aller à Paris ◊ *to go to school* aller à l'école ◊ *a letter to his mother* une lettre à sa mère ◊ *the answer to the question* la réponse à la question
au ◊ *to go to the theatre* aller au théâtre
aux ◊ *We said goodbye to the neighbours.* Nous avons dit au revoir aux voisins.
♦**ready to go** prêt à partir
♦**ready to eat** prêt à manger
♦**It's easy to do.** C'est facile à faire.
♦**something to drink** quelque chose à boire
♦**I've got things to do.** J'ai des choses à faire.
♦**from ... to ...** de ... à ... ◊ *from nine o'clock to half past three* de neuf heures à trois heures et demie
2 de ◊ *the train to London* le train de Londres ◊ *the road to Edinburgh* la route d'Édimbourg ◊ *the key to the front door* la clé de la porte d'entrée
♦**It's difficult to say.** C'est difficile à dire.
♦**It's easy to criticize.** C'est facile de critiquer.

> *When referring to someone's house, shop or office, use chez.*

3 chez ◊ *to go to the doctor's* aller chez le docteur ◊ *to go to the butcher's* aller chez le boucher ◊ *Let's go to Anne's house.* Si on allait chez Anne?

> *When to refers to a country which is feminine, use en; when the country is masculine, use au.*

4 en ◊ *to go to France* aller en France
au ◊ *to go to Portugal* aller au Portugal
5 (*up to*)
jusqu'à ◊ *to count to ten* compter jusqu'à dix
6 (*in order to*)
pour ◊ *I did it to help you.* Je l'ai fait pour vous aider. ◊ *She's too young to go to school.* Elle est trop jeune pour aller à l'école.

toad NOUN
le crapaud

toadstool NOUN
le champignon vénéneux

toast NOUN
1 le pain grillé ◊ *a piece of toast* une tranche de pain grillé
2 le toast (*speech*) ◊ *to drink a toast to somebody* porter un toast à quelqu'un

toaster NOUN
le grille-pain
(les grille-pain PL)

toastie NOUN
le sandwich chaud ◊ *a cheese and ham toastie* un croque-monsieur

tobacco NOUN
le tabac

tobacconist's NOUN
le bureau de tabac
(les bureaux de tabac PL)

toboggan NOUN
la luge

tobogganing NOUN
♦**to go tobogganing** faire de la luge

today ADVERB
aujourd'hui ◊ *What did you do today?* Qu'est-ce tu as fait aujourd'hui?

toddler NOUN
le bambin

toe NOUN
le doigt de pied

toffee NOUN
le caramel

together ADVERB
1 ensemble ◊ *Are they still together?* Ils sont toujours ensemble?
2 en même temps (*at the same time*) ◊ *Don't all speak together!* Ne parlez pas tous en même temps!
♦**together with** (*with person*) avec

toilet NOUN
les toilettes FEM PL

toilet paper NOUN
le papier hygiénique

toiletries PL NOUN
les articles de toilette MASC PL

toilet roll NOUN
le rouleau de papier hygiénique
(les rouleaux de papier hygiénique PL)

token NOUN
♦**a gift token** un bon-cadeau

told VERB *see* **tell**

tolerant ADJECTIVE
tolérant

toll NOUN
le péage (*on bridge, motorway*)

tomato NOUN
la tomate ◊ *tomato sauce* la sauce tomate ◊ *tomato soup* la soupe à la tomate

tomboy NOUN
le garçon manqué ◊ *She's a real tomboy.* C'est un vrai garçon manqué.

tomorrow ADVERB
demain ◊ *tomorrow morning* demain
matin ◊ *tomorrow night* demain soir
♦ **the day after tomorrow** après-demain

ton NOUN
la tonne ◊ *That old bike weighs a
ton.* Ce vieux vélo pèse une tonne.

> *ⓘ In France measurements are in
> metric tonnes rather than tons. A ton
> is slightly more than a **tonne**.*

tongue NOUN
la langue
♦ **to say something tongue in cheek**
dire quelque chose en plaisantant

tonic NOUN
le Schweppes ® (*tonic water*)
♦ **a gin and tonic** un gin tonic

tonight ADVERB
1 ce soir (*this evening*) ◊ *Are you
going out tonight?* Tu sors ce soir?
2 cette nuit (*during the night*) ◊ *I'll
sleep well tonight.* Je dormirai bien
cette nuit.

tonsillitis NOUN
l' angine FEM

tonsils PL NOUN
les amygdales FEM PL

too ADVERB, ADJECTIVE
1 aussi (*as well*) ◊ *My sister came
too.* Ma sœur est venue aussi.
2 trop (*excessively*) ◊ *The water's too
hot.* L'eau est trop chaude. ◊ *We
arrived too late.* Nous sommes
arrivés trop tard.
♦ **too much (1)** (*with noun*) trop de ◊ *too
much noise* trop de bruit
♦ **too much (2)** (*with verb*) trop ◊ *At
Christmas we always eat too much.* À
Noël nous mangeons toujours trop.
♦ **too much (3)** (*too expensive*) trop cher
◊ *Fifty euros? That's too much.*
Cinquante euros? C'est trop cher.
♦ **too many** trop de ◊ *too many
hamburgers* trop de hamburgers
♦ **too bad!** tant pis!

took VERB *see* **take**

tool NOUN
l' outil MASC
♦ **a tool box** une boîte à outils

tooth NOUN
la dent

toothache NOUN
le mal de dents ◊ *to have toothache*
avoir mal aux dents

toothbrush NOUN
la brosse à dents

toothpaste NOUN
le dentifrice

top NOUN
see also **top** ADJECTIVE
1 le haut (*of page, ladder, garment*)
◊ *at the top of the page* en haut de la
page
♦ **a bikini top** un haut de bikini
2 le sommet (*of mountain*)
3 le dessus (*of table*)
♦ **on top of** (*on*) sur ◊ *on top of the
fridge* sur le frigo
♦ **There's a surcharge on top of that.** Il
a un supplément en plus.
♦ **from top to bottom** de fond en
comble ◊ *I searched the house from
top to bottom.* J'ai fouillé la maison
de fond en comble.
4 le couvercle (*of box, jar*)
5 le bouchon (*of bottle*)

top ADJECTIVE
see also **top** NOUN
grand (*first-class*) ◊ *a top surgeon* un
grand chirurgien
♦ **a top model** un top model
♦ **He always gets top marks in French.**
Il a toujours d'excellentes notes en
français.
♦ **the top floor** le dernier étage ◊ *on the
top floor* au dernier étage

topic NOUN
le sujet ◊ *The essay can be on any
topic.* Cette dissertation peut être sur
n'importe quel sujet.

topical ADJECTIVE
d'actualité ◊ *a topical issue* un sujet
d'actualité

topless ADJECTIVE
aux seins nus (*model*)
♦ **to go topless** enlever le haut

top-secret ADJECTIVE
top secret MASC
top secrète FEM
◊ *top-secret documents* des
documents top secrets

torch NOUN
la lampe de poche

tore, torn VERB *see* **tear**

tortoise NOUN
la tortue

torture NOUN
see also **torture** VERB
la torture ◊ *It was pure torture.*
C'était une vraie torture.

to **torture** VERB
see also **torture** NOUN
torturer ◊ *Stop torturing that poor
animal!* Arrête de torturer cette
pauvre bête!

Tory ADJECTIVE

T

☞

see also **Tory** NOUN
conservateur MASC
conservatrice FEM
◊ *the Tory government* le gouvernement conservateur

Tory NOUN
see also **Tory** ADJECTIVE
le conservateur
la conservatrice
♦ **the Tories** les conservateurs

to **toss** VERB
♦ **to toss pancakes** faire sauter les crêpes
♦ **Shall we toss for it?** On joue à pile ou face?

total ADJECTIVE
see also **total** NOUN
total
(totaux MASC PL)
♦ **the total amount** le total

total NOUN
see also **total** ADJECTIVE
le total
(les totaux PL)
♦ **the grand total** le total

totally ADVERB
complètement ◊ *He's totally useless.* Il est complètement nul.

touch NOUN
see also **touch** VERB
♦ **to get in touch with somebody** prendre contact avec quelqu'un
♦ **to keep in touch with somebody** ne pas perdre contact avec quelqu'un
♦ **Keep in touch!** Donne-moi de tes nouvelles!
♦ **to lose touch** se perdre de vue
♦ **to lose touch with somebody** perdre quelqu'un de vue

to **touch** VERB
see also **touch** NOUN
toucher
♦ **Don't touch that!** N'y touche pas!

touchdown NOUN
l' atterrissage MASC

touched ADJECTIVE
touché ◊ *I was really touched.* Ça m'a beaucoup touché.

touching ADJECTIVE
touchant

touchline NOUN
la ligne de touche

touchpad NOUN
le pavé tactile

touchy ADJECTIVE
susceptible ◊ *She's a bit touchy.* Elle est susceptible.

tough ADJECTIVE

1 dur ◊ *It was tough, but I managed OK.* C'était dur, mais je m'en suis tiré. ◊ *It's a tough job.* C'est dur.
♦ **The meat's tough.** La viande est coriace.
2 (*strong*)
solide ◊ *tough leather gloves* de solides gants en cuir ◊ *She's tough. She can take it.* Elle est solide. Elle tiendra le coup.
3 (*rough, violent*)
dangereux MASC
dangereuse FEM
♦ **He thinks he's a tough guy.** Il se prend pour un gros dur.
♦ **Tough luck!** C'est comme ça!

toupee NOUN
le postiche

tour NOUN
see also **tour** VERB
1 la visite (*of town, museum*) ◊ *We went on a tour of the city.* Nous avons visité la ville.
♦ **a package tour** un voyage organisé
2 la tournée (*by singer, group*) ◊ *on tour* en tournée
♦ **to go on tour** faire une tournée

to **tour** VERB
see also **tour** NOUN
♦ **Paul Weller's touring Europe.** (*singer, artiste*) Paul Weller est en tournée en Europe.

tour guide NOUN
le/la guide

tourism NOUN
le tourisme

tourist NOUN
le/la touriste
♦ **tourist information office** l'office du tourisme MASC

tournament NOUN
le tournoi

tour operator NOUN
le tour-opérateur

towards PREPOSITION
1 vers (*in the direction of*) ◊ *He came towards me.* Il est venu vers moi.
2 envers (*of attitude*) ◊ *my feelings towards him* mes sentiments envers lui

towel NOUN
la serviette

tower NOUN
la tour
♦ **a tower block** une tour

town NOUN
la ville ◊ *a town plan* un plan de ville
♦ **the town centre** le centre-ville
♦ **the town hall** la mairie

tow truck NOUN US
la dépanneuse

toy NOUN
le jouet ◊ *a toy shop* un magasin de
jouets
◆ **a toy car** une petite voiture

trace NOUN

see also **trace** VERB

la trace ◊ *There was no trace of the
robbers.* Il n'y avait pas de trace des
voleurs.

to **trace** VERB

see also **trace** NOUN

décalquer (*draw*)

tracing paper NOUN
le papier calque

track NOUN
[1] le chemin (*dirt road*)
[2] la voie ferrée (*railway line*)
[3] la piste (*in sport*) ◊ *two laps of the
track* deux tours de piste
[4] la chanson (*song*) ◊ *This is my
favourite track.* C'est ma chanson
préférée.
[5] les traces FEM PL (*trail*) ◊ *They
followed the tracks for miles.* Ils
ont suivi les traces pendant des
kilomètres.

to **track down** VERB
◆ **to track somebody down** retrouver
quelqu'un ◊ *The police never tracked
down the killer.* La police n'a jamais
retrouvé l'assassin.

tracksuit NOUN
le jogging

tractor NOUN
le tracteur

trade NOUN
le métier (*skill, job*) ◊ *to learn a trade*
apprendre un métier

trade union NOUN
le syndicat

trade unionist NOUN
le/la syndicaliste

tradition NOUN
la tradition

traditional ADJECTIVE
traditionnel MASC
traditionnelle FEM

traffic NOUN
la circulation ◊ *The traffic was
terrible.* Il y avait une circulation
épouvantable.

traffic circle NOUN US
le rond-point
(les ronds-points PL)

traffic jam NOUN
l' embouteillage MASC

traffic lights PL NOUN
les feux MASC PL

traffic warden NOUN
le contractuel
la contractuelle

tragedy NOUN
la tragédie

tragic ADJECTIVE
tragique

trailer NOUN
[1] la remorque (*vehicle*)
[2] la bande-annonce (*film advert*)

train NOUN

see also **train** VERB

[1] le train
[2] la rame (*on underground*)

to **train** VERB

see also **train** NOUN

s'entraîner (*sport*) ◊ *to train for a
race* s'entraîner pour une course
◆ **to train as a teacher** suivre une
formation d'enseignant
◆ **to train an animal to do something**
dresser un animal à faire quelque
chose

trained ADJECTIVE
◆ **She's a trained nurse.** Elle est
infirmière diplômée.

trainee NOUN
[1] (*in profession*)
le/la stagiaire ◊ *She's a trainee.* Elle
est stagiaire.
[2] (*apprentice*)
l' apprenti MASC
l' apprentie FEM
◊ *a trainee plumber* un apprenti
plombier

trainer NOUN
[1] (*sports coach*)
l' entraîneur MASC
[2] (*of animals*)
le dompteur
la dompteuse

trainers PL NOUN
les baskets FEM PL ◊ *a pair of trainers*
une paire de baskets

training NOUN
[1] la formation ◊ *a training course*
un stage de formation
[2] l' entraînement MASC (*sport*)

tram NOUN
le tramway

tramp NOUN
le clochard
la clocharde

trampoline NOUN
le trampoline

tranquillizer NOUN

T

☞

le tranquillisant ◊ *She's on tranquillizers.* Elle prend des tranquillisants.

transfer NOUN
la décalcomanie (*sticker*)

transfusion NOUN
la transfusion

transistor NOUN
le transistor

transit NOUN
le transit ◊ *in transit* en transit

transit lounge NOUN
la salle de transit

to **translate** VERB
traduire ◊ *to translate something into English* traduire quelque chose en anglais

translation NOUN
la traduction

translator NOUN
le traducteur
la traductrice
◊ *Anita's a translator.* Anita est traductrice.

transparent ADJECTIVE
transparent

transplant NOUN
la greffe ◊ *a heart transplant* une greffe du cardiaque

transport NOUN
| see also **transport** VERB |
le transport ◊ *public transport* les transports en commun

to **transport** VERB
| see also **transport** NOUN |
transporter

trap NOUN
le piège

trash NOUN US
les ordures FEM PL
♦**the trash can** la poubelle

trashy ADJECTIVE
nul MASC
nulle FEM
◊ *a really trashy film* un film vraiment nul

traumatic ADJECTIVE
traumatisant ◊ *It was a traumatic experience.* Ça a été une expérience traumatisante.

travel NOUN
| see also **travel** VERB |
les voyages MASC PL

to **travel** VERB
| see also **travel** NOUN |
voyager ◊ *I prefer to travel by train.* Je préfère voyager en train.

♦**I'd like to travel round the world.** J'aimerais faire le tour du monde.
♦**We travelled over 800 kilometres.** Nous avons fait plus de huit cents kilomètres.
♦**News travels fast!** Les nouvelles circulent vite!

travel agency NOUN
l' agence de voyages FEM

travel agent NOUN
♦**She's a travel agent.** Elle travaille dans une agence de voyages.

traveller NOUN (US **traveler**)
[1] (*on bus, train, plane*)
le voyageur
la voyageuse
[2] (*gypsy*)
le/la nomade

traveller's cheque NOUN (US **traveler's check**)
le chèque de voyage

travelling NOUN (US **traveling**)
♦**I love travelling.** J'adore les voyages.

travel sickness NOUN
le mal des transports

tray NOUN
le plateau
(les plateaux PL)

to **tread** VERB
marcher ◊ *to tread on something* marcher sur quelque chose

treasure NOUN
le trésor

treat NOUN
| see also **treat** VERB |
[1] le petit cadeau (*present*)
[2] la gâterie (*food*)
♦**to give somebody a treat** faire plaisir à quelqu'un

to **treat** VERB
| see also **treat** NOUN |
traiter (*well, badly*)
♦**to treat somebody to something** offrir quelque chose à quelqu'un ◊ *He treated us to an ice cream.* Il nous a offert une glace.

treatment NOUN
le traitement

to **treble** VERB
tripler ◊ *The cost of living there has trebled.* Le coût de la vie y a triplé.

tree NOUN
l' arbre MASC

to **tremble** VERB
trembler

tremendous ADJECTIVE
énorme ◊ *a tremendous success* un succès énorme

trend NOUN
la mode (*fashion*)

trendy ADJECTIVE
branché

trial NOUN
le procès (*in court*)

triangle NOUN
le triangle

tribe NOUN
la tribu

trick NOUN
see also **trick** VERB
[1] le tour ◊ *to play a trick on somebody* jouer un tour à quelqu'un
[2] le truc FEM (*knack*) ◊ *It's not easy: there's a trick to it.* Ce n'est pas facile: il y a un truc.

to **trick** VERB
see also **trick** NOUN
♦**to trick somebody** rouler quelqu'un

tricky ADJECTIVE
délicat

tricycle NOUN
le tricycle

trifle NOUN
le diplomate (*dessert*)

to **trim** VERB
see also **trim** NOUN
[1] égaliser (*hair*)
[2] tondre (*grass*)

trim NOUN
see also **trim** VERB
la coupe d'entretien (*haircut*) ◊ *to have a trim* se faire faire une coupe d'entretien

trip NOUN
see also **trip** VERB
le voyage ◊ *to go on a trip* faire un voyage ◊ *Have a good trip!* Bon voyage!
♦**a day trip** une excursion d'une journée

to **trip** VERB
see also **trip** NOUN
trébucher (*stumble*)

triple ADJECTIVE
triple

triplets PL NOUN
les triplés MASC PL (*boys*)
les triplées FEM PL (*girls*)

trivial ADJECTIVE
insignifiant

trod, trodden VERB see **tread**

trolley NOUN
le chariot

trombone NOUN
le trombone ◊ *I play the trombone.* Je joue du trombone.

troops PL NOUN
les troupes MASC PL ◊ *British troops* les troupes britanniques

trophy NOUN
le trophée ◊ *to win a trophy* gagner un trophée

tropical ADJECTIVE
tropical ◊ *The weather was tropical.* Il faisait une chaleur tropicale.

to **trot** VERB
trotter

trouble NOUN
le problème ◊ *The trouble is, it's too expensive.* Le problème, c'est que c'est trop cher.
♦**to be in trouble** avoir des ennuis
♦**What's the trouble?** Qu'est-ce qui ne va pas?
♦**stomach trouble** troubles gastriques
♦**to take a lot of trouble over something** se donner beaucoup de mal pour quelque chose
♦**Don't worry, it's no trouble.** Mais non, ça ne me dérange pas du tout.

troublemaker NOUN
l' élément perturbateur MASC

trousers PL NOUN
le pantalon SING

trout NOUN
la truite

truant NOUN
♦**to play truant** faire l'école buissonnière

truck NOUN
le camion
♦**a truck driver** un camionneur ◊ *He's a truck driver.* Il est camionneur.

trucker NOUN US
le camionneur

true ADJECTIVE
vrai
♦**That's true.** C'est vrai.
♦**to come true** se réaliser ◊ *I hope my dream will come true.* J'espère que mon rêve se réalisera.
♦**true love** le grand amour

truly ADVERB
vraiment ◊ *It was a truly remarkable victory.* C'était vraiment une victoire remarquable.
♦**Yours truly.** Je vous prie d'agréer mes salutations distinguées.

trumpet NOUN
la trompette ◊ *She plays the trumpet.* Elle joue de la trompette.

trunk NOUN
[1] le tronc (*of tree*)
[2] la trompe (*of elephant*)
[3] la malle (*luggage*)

T

☞

4 le coffre (of car) US

trunks PL NOUN
- **swimming trunks** le maillot de bain

trust NOUN

see also **trust** VERB

la confiance ◇ *to have trust in somebody* avoir confiance en quelqu'un

to **trust** VERB

see also **trust** NOUN

- **to trust somebody** faire confiance à quelqu'un ◇ *Don't you trust me?* Tu ne me fais pas confiance? ◇ *Trust me!* Fais-moi confiance!

trusting ADJECTIVE
confiant

truth NOUN
la vérité

truthful ADJECTIVE
- **She's a very truthful person.** Elle dit toujours la vérité.

try NOUN

see also **try** VERB

l' essai MASC ◇ *his third try* son troisième essai
- **to have a try** essayer
- **It's worth a try.** Ça vaut la peine d'essayer.
- **to give something a try** essayer quelque chose

to **try** VERB

see also **try** NOUN

1 essayer (attempt) ◇ *to try to do something* essayer de faire quelque chose
- **to try again** refaire un essai
2 goûter (taste) ◇ *Would you like to try some?* Voulez-vous goûter?
- **to try on** essayer (clothes)
- **to try something out** essayer quelque chose

T-shirt NOUN
le tee-shirt

tube NOUN
le tube
- **the Tube** (underground) le métro

tuberculosis NOUN
la tuberculose

Tuesday NOUN
le mardi ◇ *on Tuesday* mardi ◇ *on Tuesdays* le mardi ◇ *every Tuesday* tous les mardis ◇ *last Tuesday* mardi dernier ◇ *next Tuesday* mardi prochain
- **Shrove Tuesday, Pancake Tuesday** le mardi gras

tug-of-war NOUN
la lutte à la corde

tuition NOUN

les cours MASC PL
- **private tuition** les cours particuliers

tulip NOUN
la tulipe

tumble dryer NOUN
le sèche-linge
(les sèche-linge PL)

tummy NOUN
le ventre

tuna NOUN
le thon

tune NOUN
l' air MASC (melody)
- **to play in tune** jouer juste
- **to sing out of tune** chanter faux

Tunisia NOUN
la Tunisie
- **in Tunisia** en Tunisie

tunnel NOUN
le tunnel
- **the Tunnel** (Chunnel) le tunnel sous la Manche

Turk NOUN
le Turc
la Turque

Turkey NOUN
la Turquie
- **in Turkey** en Turquie
- **to Turkey** en Turquie

turkey NOUN
1 la dinde (meat)
2 le dindon (live bird)

Turkish ADJECTIVE

see also **Turkish** NOUN

turc MASC
turque FEM

Turkish NOUN

see also **Turkish** ADJECTIVE

le turc (language)

turn NOUN

see also **turn** VERB

1 le tournant (bend in road)
- **"no left turn"** "défense de tourner à gauche"
2 le tour (go) ◇ *It's my turn!* C'est mon tour!

to **turn** VERB

see also **turn** NOUN

1 tourner ◇ *Turn right at the lights.* Tournez à droite aux feux.
2 devenir (become) ◇ *to turn red* devenir rouge
- **to turn into something** se transformer en quelque chose ◇ *The frog turned into a prince.* La grenouille s'est transformée en prince.

to **turn back** VERB
faire demi-tour ◇ *We turned back.* Nous avons fait demi-tour.

to **turn down** VERB
    1 refuser (*offer*)
    2 baisser (*radio, TV, heating*) ◊ *Shall I turn the heating down?* Je baisse le chauffage?

to **turn off** VERB
    1 éteindre (*light, radio*)
    2 fermer (*tap*)
    3 arrêter (*engine*)

to **turn on** VERB
    1 allumer (*light, radio*)
    2 ouvrir (*tap*)
    3 mettre en marche (*engine*)

to **turn out** VERB
    ♦ **It turned out to be a mistake.** Il s'est avéré que c'était une erreur.
    ♦ **It turned out that she was right.** Il s'est avéré qu'elle avait raison.

to **turn round** VERB
    1 faire demi-tour (*car*)
    2 se retourner (*person*)

to **turn up** VERB
    1 arriver (*arrive*)
    2 monter (*heater*)
    ♦ **Could you turn up the radio?** Tu peux monter le son de la radio?

turning NOUN
    ♦ **It's the third turning on the left.** C'est la troisième à gauche.
    ♦ **We took the wrong turning.** Nous n'avons pas tourné au bon endroit.

turnip NOUN
    le navet

turquoise ADJECTIVE
    turquoise MASC, FEM, PL (*colour*)

turtle NOUN
    la tortue

tutor NOUN
    le professeur particulier (*private teacher*)

tuxedo NOUN US
    le smoking

TV NOUN
    la télé

tweezers PL NOUN
    la pince à épiler SING

twelfth ADJECTIVE
    douzième ◊ *the twelfth floor* le douzième étage
    ♦ **the twelfth of August** le douze août

twelve NUMBER
    douze ◊ *She's twelve.* Elle a douze ans.
    ♦ **twelve o'clock (1)** (*midday*) midi
    ♦ **twelve o'clock (2)** (*midnight*) minuit

twentieth ADJECTIVE
    vingtième ◊ *the twentieth time* la vingtième fois
    ♦ **the twentieth of May** le vingt mai

twenty NUMBER
    vingt ◊ *He's twenty.* Il a vingt ans.

twice ADVERB
    deux fois
    ♦ **twice as much** deux fois plus ◊ *He gets twice as much pocket money as me.* Il a deux fois plus d'argent de poche que moi.

twin NOUN
    le jumeau (*boy*)
    la jumelle (*girl*)
    (les jumeaux PL)
    (les jumelles FEM PL)
    ♦ **my twin brother** mon frère jumeau
    ♦ **her twin sister** sa sœur jumelle
    ♦ **identical twins** les vrais jumeaux
    ♦ **a twin room** une chambre à deux lits

twinned ADJECTIVE
    jumelé ◊ *Stroud is twinned with Châteaubriant.* Stroud est jumelée avec Châteaubriant.

to **twist** VERB
    1 tordre (*bend*)
    2 déformer (*distort*) ◊ *You're twisting my words.* Tu déformes ce que j'ai dit.

twit NOUN
    le crétin
    la crétine

two NUMBER
    deux ◊ *She's two.* Elle a deux ans.

type NOUN
    see also **type** VERB
    le type ◊ *What type of camera have you got?* Quel type d'appareil photo as-tu?

to **type** VERB
    see also **type** NOUN
    taper à la machine ◊ *Can you type?* Tu sais taper à la machine?
    ♦ **to type a letter** taper une lettre

typewriter NOUN
    la machine à écrire

typical ADJECTIVE
    typique ◊ *That's just typical!* C'est typique!

tyre NOUN
    le pneu
    ♦ **the tyre pressure** la pression des pneus

T

U

UFO NOUN
l' OVNI MASC (= objet volant non identifié)

ugh EXCLAMATION
pouah!

ugly ADJECTIVE
laid

UK NOUN (= United Kingdom)
le Royaume-Uni
♦**from the UK** du Royaume-Uni
♦**in the UK** au Royaume-Uni
♦**to the UK** au Royaume-Uni

ulcer NOUN
l' ulcère MASC
♦**a mouth ulcer** un aphte

Ulster NOUN
l' Irlande du Nord FEM
♦**in Ulster** en Irlande du Nord

ultimate ADJECTIVE
suprême ◊ *the ultimate challenge* le défi suprême
♦**It was the ultimate adventure.** C'était la grande aventure.

ultimately ADVERB
au bout du compte ◊ *Ultimately, it's your decision.* Au bout du compte, c'est votre décision.

umbrella NOUN
1 le parapluie
2 le parasol (*for sun*)

umpire NOUN
1 l' arbitre MASC (*in cricket*)
2 le juge de chaise (*in tennis*)

UN NOUN
l' ONU FEM (= Organisation des Nations unies)

unable ADJECTIVE
♦**to be unable to do something** ne pas pouvoir faire quelque chose ◊ *I was unable to come.* Je n'ai pas pu venir.

unacceptable ADJECTIVE
inacceptable

unanimous ADJECTIVE
unanime ◊ *a unanimous decision* une décision unanime

unattended ADJECTIVE
♦**to leave something unattended** laisser quelque chose sans surveillance
laissé sans surveillance ◊ *Never leave pets unattended in your car.* Ne laisser jamais d'animaux domestiques sans surveillance dans votre voiture.

unavoidable ADJECTIVE
inévitable

unaware ADJECTIVE
♦**to be unaware (1)** (*not know about*) ignorer ◊ *I was unaware of the regulations.* J'ignorais le règlement.
♦**to be unaware (2)** (*not notice*) ne pas se rendre compte ◊ *She was unaware that she was being filmed.* Elle ne s'était pas rendu compte qu'on la filmait.

unbearable ADJECTIVE
insupportable

unbeatable ADJECTIVE
imbattable

unbelievable ADJECTIVE
incroyable

unborn ADJECTIVE
♦**the unborn child** le fœtus

unbreakable ADJECTIVE
incassable

uncanny ADJECTIVE
étrange ◊ *That's uncanny!* C'est étrange!
♦**an uncanny resemblance** une ressemblance troublante

uncertain ADJECTIVE
incertain ◊ *The future is uncertain.* L'avenir est incertain.
♦**to be uncertain about something** ne pas être sûr de quelque chose

uncivilized ADJECTIVE
barbare

uncle NOUN
l' oncle MASC ◊ *my uncle* mon oncle

uncomfortable ADJECTIVE
pas confortable ◊ *The seats are rather uncomfortable.* Les sièges ne sont pas très confortables.

unconscious ADJECTIVE
sans connaissance

uncontrollable ADJECTIVE
incontrôlable

unconventional ADJECTIVE
peu conventionnel MASC
peu conventionnelle FEM

under PREPOSITION
1 sous ◊ *The cat's under the table.* Le chat est sous la table. ◊ *The tunnel goes under the Channel.* Le tunnel passe sous la Manche.
♦**under there** là-dessous ◊ *What's under there?* Qu'est-ce qu'il y a là-dessous?
2 moins de (*less than*) ◊ *under 20 people* moins de vingt personnes

◊ *children under 10* les enfants de moins de dix ans

underage ADJECTIVE
♦**He's underage.** Il n'a pas l'âge réglementaire.

undercover ADJECTIVE, ADVERB
secret MASC
secrète FEM
◊ *an undercover agent* un agent secret
♦**She was working undercover.** Elle travaillait sous une fausse identité.

to **underestimate** VERB
sous-estimer ◊ *I underestimated her.* Je l'ai sous-estimée.

to **undergo** VERB
subir (*operation, examination, change*)
♦**to be undergoing repairs** être en réparation

underground ADJECTIVE, ADVERB
see also **underground** NOUN
[1] souterrain ◊ *an underground car park* un parking souterrain
[2] sous terre ◊ *Moles live underground.* Les taupes vivent sous terre.

underground NOUN
see also **underground** ADJECTIVE
le métro ◊ *Is there an underground in Lille?* Est-ce qu'il y a un métro à Lille?

to **underline** VERB
souligner

underneath PREPOSITION, ADVERB
[1] sous ◊ *underneath the carpet* sous la moquette
[2] dessous ◊ *I got out of the car and looked underneath.* Je suis descendu de la voiture et j'ai regardé dessous.

underpaid ADJECTIVE
sous-payé ◊ *I'm underpaid.* Je suis sous-payé.

underpants PL NOUN
le slip SING

underpass NOUN
[1] le passage souterrain (*for people*)
[2] le passage inférieur (*for cars*)

undershirt NOUN US
le maillot de corps

underskirt NOUN
le jupon

to **understand** VERB
comprendre ◊ *Do you understand?* Vous comprenez? ◊ *I don't understand this word.* Je ne comprends pas ce mot. ◊ *Is that understood?* C'est compris?

understanding ADJECTIVE
compréhensif MASC
compréhensive FEM
◊ *She's very understanding.* Elle est très compréhensive.

understood VERB *see* **understand**

undertaker NOUN
l' entrepreneur des pompes funèbres MASC

underwater ADJECTIVE, ADVERB
sous l'eau ◊ *This sequence was filmed underwater.* Cette séquence a été filmée sous l'eau.
♦**an underwater camera** un appareil photographique de plongée
♦**underwater photography** la photographie subaquatique

underwear NOUN
les sous-vêtements MASC PL

underwent VERB *see* **undergo**

to **undo** VERB
[1] défaire (*buttons, knot*)
[2] déballer (*parcel*)

to **undress** VERB
se déshabiller (*get undressed*) ◊ *The doctor told me to undress.* Le médecin m'a dit de me déshabiller.

uneconomic ADJECTIVE
pas rentable

unemployed ADJECTIVE
au chômage ◊ *He's unemployed.* Il est au chômage. ◊ *He's been unemployed for a year.* Ça fait un an qu'il est au chômage.
♦**the unemployed** les chômeurs MASC

unemployment NOUN
le chômage

unexpected ADJECTIVE
inattendu ◊ *an unexpected visitor* un visiteur inattendu

unexpectedly ADVERB
à l'improviste ◊ *They arrived unexpectedly.* Ils sont arrivés à l'improviste.

unfair ADJECTIVE
injuste ◊ *It's unfair to girls.* C'est injuste pour les filles.

unfamiliar ADJECTIVE
♦**I heard an unfamiliar voice.** J'ai entendu une voix que je ne connaissais pas.

unfashionable ADJECTIVE
démodé

unfit ADJECTIVE
♦**I'm rather unfit at the moment.** Je ne suis pas en très bonne condition physique en ce moment.

to **unfold** VERB

U

☞

déplier ◊ *She unfolded the map.* Elle a déplié la carte.

unforgettable ADJECTIVE
inoubliable

unfortunately ADVERB
malheureusement ◊ *Unfortunately, I arrived late.* Malheureusement, je suis arrivé en retard.

unfriendly ADJECTIVE
pas aimable ◊ *The waiters are a bit unfriendly.* Les serveurs ne sont pas très aimables.

ungrateful ADJECTIVE
ingrat

unhappy ADJECTIVE
malheureux MASC
malheureuse FEM
◊ *He was very unhappy as a child.* Il était très malheureux quand il était petit.
♦ **to look unhappy** avoir l'air triste

unhealthy ADJECTIVE
1 (*person*)
maladif MASC
maladive FEM
2 (*place, habit*)
malsain
3 (*food*)
pas sain

uni NOUN
la fac (*university*) ◊ *to go to uni* aller à la fac

uniform NOUN
l' uniforme MASC ◊ *the school uniform* l'uniforme scolaire

uninhabited ADJECTIVE
inhabité

union NOUN
le syndicat (*trade union*)

Union Jack NOUN
le drapeau du Royaume-Uni

unique ADJECTIVE
unique

unit NOUN
1 l' unité FEM ◊ *a unit of measurement* une unité de mesure
2 l' élément MASC (*piece of furniture*)
◊ *a kitchen unit* un élément de cuisine

United Kingdom NOUN
le Royaume-Uni

United Nations NOUN
l' O.N.U. FEM (= Organisation des Nations Unies)

United States PL NOUN
les États-Unis MASC PL
♦ **in the United States** aux États-Unis
♦ **to the United States** aux États-Unis

universe NOUN
l' univers MASC

university NOUN
l' université FEM ◊ *She's at university.* Elle va à l'université. ◊ *Do you want to go to university?* Tu veux aller à l'université? ◊ *Lancaster University* l'université de Lancaster

unleaded petrol NOUN
l' essence sans plomb FEM

unless CONJUNCTION
♦ **unless he leaves** à moins qu'il ne parte ◊ *I won't come unless you phone me.* Je ne viendrai pas à moins que tu ne me téléphones.

unlike PREPOSITION
contrairement à ◊ *Unlike him, I really enjoy flying.* Contrairement à lui, j'adore prendre l'avion.

unlikely ADJECTIVE
peu probable ◊ *It's possible, but unlikely.* C'est possible, mais peu probable.

unlisted ADJECTIVE US
♦ **an unlisted number** un numéro qui est sur la liste rouge

to **unload** VERB
décharger ◊ *We unloaded the car.* Nous avons déchargé la voiture.
◊ *The lorries go there to unload.* Les camions y vont pour être déchargés.

to **unlock** VERB
ouvrir ◊ *He unlocked the door of the car.* Il a ouvert la portière de la voiture.

unlucky ADJECTIVE
♦ **to be unlucky (1)** (*number, object*) porter malheur ◊ *They say thirteen is an unlucky number.* On dit que le nombre treize porte malheur.
♦ **to be unlucky (2)** (*person*) ne pas avoir de chance ◊ *Did you win? – No, I was unlucky.* Vous avez gagné? – Non, je n'ai pas eu de chance.

unmarried ADJECTIVE
célibataire (*person*) ◊ *an unmarried mother* une mère célibataire
♦ **an unmarried couple** un couple non marié

unnatural ADJECTIVE
pas naturel MASC
pas naturelle FEM

unnecessary ADJECTIVE
inutile

unofficial ADJECTIVE
1 (*meeting, leader*)
non officiel MASC
non officielle FEM
2 (*strike*)

sauvage

to **unpack** VERB

[1] <u>défaire</u> ◊ *I unpacked my suitcase.* J'ai défait ma valise.

[2] <u>déballer ses affaires</u> ◊ *I went to my room to unpack.* Je suis allé dans ma chambre pour déballer mes affaires. ◊ *I haven't unpacked my clothes yet.* Je n'ai pas encore déballé mes affaires.

unpleasant ADJECTIVE
<u>désagréable</u>

to **unplug** VERB
<u>débrancher</u>

unpopular ADJECTIVE
<u>impopulaire</u>

unpredictable ADJECTIVE
<u>imprévisible</u>

unreal ADJECTIVE
<u>incroyable</u> (*incredible*) ◊ *It was unreal!* C'était incroyable!

unrealistic ADJECTIVE
<u>peu réaliste</u>

unreasonable ADJECTIVE
<u>pas raisonnable</u> ◊ *Her attitude was completely unreasonable.* Son attitude n'était pas du tout raisonnable.

unreliable ADJECTIVE
<u>pas fiable</u> (*car, machine*) ◊ *It's a nice car, but a bit unreliable.* C'est une belle voiture, mais elle n'est pas très fiable.
♦ **He's completely unreliable.** On ne peut pas du tout compter sur lui.

to **unroll** VERB
<u>dérouler</u>

unsatisfactory ADJECTIVE
<u>insatisfaisant</u>

to **unscrew** VERB
<u>dévisser</u> ◊ *She unscrewed the top of the bottle.* Elle a dévissé le bouchon de la bouteille.

unshaven ADJECTIVE
<u>mal rasé</u>

unskilled worker ADJECTIVE
le <u>manœuvre</u>

unstable ADJECTIVE
<u>instable</u>

unsteady ADJECTIVE
<u>mal assuré</u> (*walk, voice*)
♦ **He was unsteady on his feet.** Il marchait d'un pas mal assuré.

unsuccessful ADJECTIVE
<u>vain</u> (*attempt*)
♦ **to be unsuccessful in doing something** ne pas réussir à faire

quelque chose ◊ *an unsuccessful artist* un artiste qui n'a pas réussi

unsuitable ADJECTIVE
<u>inapproprié</u> (*clothes, equipment*)

untidy ADJECTIVE
[1] <u>en désordre</u> ◊ *My bedroom's always untidy.* Ma chambre est toujours en désordre.
[2] <u>débraillé</u> (*appearance, person*) ◊ *He's always untidy.* Il est toujours débraillé.
[3] <u>désordonné</u> (*in character*) ◊ *He's a very untidy person.* Il est très désordonné.

to **untie** VERB
[1] <u>défaire</u> (*knot, parcel*)
[2] <u>détacher</u> (*animal*)

until PREPOSITION, CONJUNCTION
[1] <u>jusqu'à</u> ◊ *I waited until ten o'clock.* J'ai attendu jusqu'à dix heures.
♦ **until now** jusqu'à présent ◊ *It's never been a problem until now.* Ça n'a jamais été un problème jusqu'à présent.
♦ **until then** jusque-là ◊ *Until then I'd never been to France.* Jusque-là je n'étais jamais allé en France.

Use **avant** *if the sentence you want to translate contains a negative, such as "not" or "never".*

[2] <u>avant</u> ◊ *It won't be ready until next week.* Ça ne sera pas prêt avant la semaine prochaine. ◊ *Until last year I'd never been to France.* Avant l'année dernière, je n'étais jamais allé en France.

unusual ADJECTIVE
[1] <u>insolite</u> ◊ *an unusual shape* une forme insolite
[2] <u>rare</u> ◊ *It's unusual to get snow at this time of year.* Il est rare qu'il neige à cette époque de l'année.

unwilling ADJECTIVE
♦ **to be unwilling to do something** ne pas être disposé à faire quelque chose ◊ *He was unwilling to help me.* Il n'était pas disposé à m'aider.

to **unwind** VERB
<u>se détendre</u> (*relax*)

unwise ADJECTIVE
<u>imprudent</u> (*person*) ◊ *That was rather unwise of you.* C'était plutôt imprudent de votre part.

unwound VERB *see* **unwind**

to **unwrap** VERB
<u>déballer</u> ◊ *After the meal we unwrapped the presents.* Après le repas nous avons déballé les cadeaux.

U

up PREPOSITION, ADVERB

> *For other expressions with **up**, see the verbs **go, come, put, turn** etc.*

en haut ◊ *up on the hill* en haut de la colline

♦ **up here** ici
♦ **up there** là-haut
♦ **up north** dans le nord
♦ **to be up** être levé (*out of bed*) ◊ *We were up at 6.* Nous étions levés à six heures. ◊ *He's not up yet.* Il n'est pas encore levé.
♦ **What's up?** Qu'est-ce qu'il y a? ◊ *What's up with her?* Qu'est-ce qu'elle a?
♦ **to get up** (*in the morning*) se lever ◊ *What time do you get up?* À quelle heure est-ce que tu te lèves?
♦ **to go up** monter ◊ *The bus went up the hill.* Le bus a monté la colline.
♦ **to go up to somebody** s'approcher de quelqu'un ◊ *She came up to me.* Elle s'est approchée de moi.
♦ **up to** (*as far as*) jusqu'à ◊ *to count up to fifty* compter jusqu'à cinquante ◊ *up to three hours* jusqu'à trois heures ◊ *up to now* jusqu'à présent
♦ **It's up to you.** C'est à vous de décider.

upbringing NOUN
l' éducation FEM

uphill ADVERB
♦ **to go uphill** monter

upper ADJECTIVE
supérieur ◊ *on the upper floor* à l'étage supérieur

upper sixth NOUN
♦ **the upper sixth** la terminale ◊ *She's in the upper sixth.* Elle est en terminale.

upright ADJECTIVE
♦ **to stand upright** se tenir droit

upset NOUN
> *see also* **upset** ADJECTIVE, VERB

♦ **a stomach upset** une indigestion

upset ADJECTIVE
> *see also* **upset** NOUN, VERB

contrarié ◊ *She's still a bit upset.* Elle est encore un peu contrariée.
♦ **I had an upset stomach.** J'avais l'estomac dérangé.

to **upset** VERB
> *see also* **upset** NOUN, ADJECTIVE

♦ **to upset somebody** contrarier quelqu'un

upside down ADVERB
à l'envers ◊ *That painting is upside down.* Ce tableau est à l'envers.

upstairs ADVERB
en haut ◊ *Where's your coat? – It's upstairs.* Où est ton manteau? – Il est en haut.
♦ **to go upstairs** monter

uptight ADJECTIVE
tendu ◊ *She's really uptight.* Elle est très tendue.

up-to-date ADJECTIVE
1 moderne (*car, stereo*)
2 à jour (*information*) ◊ *an up-to-date timetable* un horaire à jour
♦ **to bring something up to date** moderniser quelque chose

upwards ADVERB
vers le haut ◊ *to look upwards* regarder vers le haut

urgent ADJECTIVE
urgent ◊ *Is it urgent?* C'est urgent?

urine NOUN
l' urine FEM

US NOUN
les USA MASC PL

us PRONOUN
nous ◊ *They helped us.* Ils nous ont aidés. ◊ *They gave us a map.* Ils nous ont donné une carte.

USA NOUN
les USA MASC PL

use NOUN
> *see also* **use** VERB

♦ **It's no use.** Ça ne sert à rien. ◊ *It's no use shouting, she's deaf.* Ça ne sert à rien de crier, elle est sourde.
♦ **It's no use, I can't do it.** Il n'y a rien à faire, je n'y arrive pas.
♦ **to make use of something** utiliser quelque chose

to **use** VERB
> *see also* **use** NOUN

utiliser ◊ *Can we use a dictionary in the exam?* Est-ce qu'on peut utiliser un dictionnaire à l'examen?
♦ **Can I use your phone?** Je peux téléphoner?
♦ **to use the toilet** aller aux W.C.
♦ **to use up (1)** finir ◊ *We've used up all the paint.* Nous avons fini la peinture.
♦ **to use up (2)** (*money*) dépenser
♦ **I used to live in London.** J'habitais à Londres autrefois.
♦ **I used not to like maths, but now ...** Avant, je n'aimais pas les maths, mais maintenant ...
♦ **to be used to something** avoir l'habitude de quelque chose ◊ *He wasn't used to driving on the right.* Il n'avait pas l'habitude de conduire à

droite. ◊ *Don't worry, I'm used to it.*
Ne t'inquiète pas, j'ai l'habitude.
♦ **a used car** une voiture d'occasion

useful ADJECTIVE
    utile

useless ADJECTIVE
    nul MASC
    nulle FEM
    ◊ *This map is just useless.* Cette carte
    est vraiment nulle. ◊ *You're useless!*
    Tu es nul!
♦ **It's useless!** Ça ne sert à rien!

user NOUN
    l' utilisateur MASC
    l' utilisatrice FEM

user-friendly ADJECTIVE
    facile à utiliser

usual ADJECTIVE

habituel MASC
habituelle FEM
♦ **as usual** comme d'habitude

usually ADVERB
    ☐ en général (*generally*) ◊ *I usually*
    get to school at about half past eight.
    En général, j'arrive à l'école vers huit
    heures et demie.
    ☐ d'habitude (*when making a contrast*)
    ◊ *Usually I don't wear make-up, but*
    today is a special occasion.
    D'habitude je ne me maquille pas,
    mais aujourd'hui c'est spécial.

utility room NOUN
    la buanderie

U-turn NOUN
    le demi-tour ◊ *to do a U-turn* faire
    demi-tour

U

V

vacancy NOUN
   1 le poste vacant (*job*)
   2 la chambre disponible (*room in hotel*)
   ♦ **"no vacancies"** (*on sign*) "complet"

vacant ADJECTIVE
   libre

vacation NOUN US
   les vacances FEM PL ◊ *to be on vacation* être en vacances ◊ *to take a vacation* prendre des vacances

to **vaccinate** VERB
   vacciner

to **vacuum** VERB
   passer l'aspirateur ◊ *to vacuum the hall* passer l'aspirateur dans le couloir

vacuum cleaner NOUN
   l' aspirateur MASC

vagina NOUN
   le vagin

vague ADJECTIVE
   vague

vain ADJECTIVE
   vaniteux MASC
   vaniteuse FEM
   ◊ *He's so vain!* Qu'est-ce qu'il est vaniteux!
   ♦ **in vain** en vain

Valentine card NOUN
   la carte de la Saint-Valentin

Valentine's Day NOUN
   la Saint-Valentin

valid ADJECTIVE
   valable ◊ *This ticket is valid for three months.* Ce billet est valable trois mois.

valley NOUN
   la vallée

valuable ADJECTIVE
   1 de valeur ◊ *a valuable picture* un tableau de valeur
   2 précieux MASC
   précieuse FEM
   ◊ *valuable help* une aide précieuse

valuables PL NOUN
   les objets de valeur MASC PL ◊ *Don't take any valuables with you.* N'emportez pas d'objets de valeur.

value NOUN
   la valeur

van NOUN
   la camionnette

vandal NOUN

le/la vandale

vandalism NOUN
   le vandalisme

to **vandalize** VERB
   saccager

vanilla NOUN
   la vanille
   ♦ **vanilla ice cream** la glace à la vanille

to **vanish** VERB
   disparaître

variable ADJECTIVE
   variable

varied ADJECTIVE
   varié

variety NOUN
   la variété

various ADJECTIVE
   plusieurs ◊ *We visited various villages in the area.* Nous avons visité plusieurs villages de la région.

to **vary** VERB
   varier

vase NOUN
   le vase

VAT NOUN (= *value added tax*)
   la TVA (= taxe sur la valeur ajoutée)

VCR NOUN (= *video cassette recorder*)
   le magnétoscope

VDU NOUN (= *visual display unit*)
   la console

veal NOUN
   le veau

vegan NOUN
   le végétalien
   la végétalienne
   ◊ *I'm a vegan.* Je suis végétalien.

vegetable NOUN
   le légume ◊ *vegetable soup* la soupe aux légumes

vegetarian ADJECTIVE
   | *see also* **vegetarian** NOUN |
   végétarien MASC
   végétarienne FEM
   ◊ *I'm vegetarian.* Je suis végétarien.
   ◊ *vegetarian lasagne* les lasagnes végétariennes

vegetarian NOUN
   | *see also* **vegetarian** ADJECTIVE |
   le végétarien
   la végétarienne
   ◊ *I'm a vegetarian.* Je suis végétarien.

vehicle NOUN
   le véhicule

vein NOUN
la veine

velvet NOUN
le velours

vending machine NOUN
le distributeur automatique

Venetian blind NOUN
le store vénitien

verb NOUN
le verbe

verdict NOUN
le verdict

vertical ADJECTIVE
vertical
(verticaux MASC PL)

vertigo NOUN
le vertige ◊ *I get vertigo.* J'ai le vertige.

very ADVERB
très ◊ *very tall* très grand ◊ *not very interesting* pas très intéressant
♦ **very much** beaucoup

vest NOUN
[1] le maillot de corps (*underclothing*)
[2] le gilet (*waistcoat*) [US]

vet NOUN
le/la vétérinaire ◊ *She's a vet.* Elle est vétérinaire.

via PREPOSITION
en passant par ◊ *We went to Paris via Boulogne.* Nous sommes allés à Paris en passant par Boulogne.

vicar NOUN
le pasteur ◊ *He's a vicar.* Il est pasteur.

vice NOUN
l' étau MASC (*for holding things*)

vice versa ADVERB
vice versa

vicious ADJECTIVE
[1] brutal
(brutaux MASC PL)
◊ *a vicious attack* une agression brutale
[2] (*dog, person*)
méchant
♦ **a vicious circle** un cercle vicieux

victim NOUN
la victime ◊ *He was the victim of a mugging.* Il a été victime d'une agression.

victory NOUN
la victoire

to **video** VERB
see also **video** NOUN
[1] enregistrer (*from TV*)
[2] filmer (*with video camera*)

video NOUN

see also **video** VERB
[1] la vidéo (*film*) ◊ *to watch a video* regarder une vidéo ◊ *a video of my family on holiday* une vidéo de ma famille en vacances ◊ *It's out on video.* C'est sorti en vidéo.
[2] la cassette vidéo (*video cassette*)
◊ *She lent me a video.* Elle m'a prêté une cassette vidéo.
[3] le magnétoscope (*video recorder*)
◊ *Have you got a video?* Tu as un magnétoscope?
♦ **a video camera** une caméra vidéo
♦ **a video cassette** une cassette vidéo
♦ **a video game** un jeu vidéo ◊ *He likes playing video games.* Il aime les jeux vidéo.
♦ **a video recorder** un magnétoscope
♦ **a video shop** un vidéoclub

Vietnam NOUN
le Viêt-Nam
♦ **in Vietnam** au Viêt-Nam

Vietnamese ADJECTIVE
vietnamien MASC
vietnamienne FEM

view NOUN
[1] la vue ◊ *There's an amazing view.* Il y a une vue extraordinaire.
[2] l' avis MASC (*opinion*) ◊ *in my view* à mon avis

viewer NOUN
le téléspectateur
la téléspectatrice

viewpoint NOUN
le point de vue

vile ADJECTIVE
dégoûtant (*smell, food*)

villa NOUN
la villa

village NOUN
le village

villain NOUN
[1] le malfrat (*criminal*)
[2] le méchant (*in film*)

vine NOUN
la vigne

vinegar NOUN
le vinaigre

vineyard NOUN
le vignoble

viola NOUN
l' alto MASC ◊ *I play the viola.* Je joue de l'alto.

violence NOUN
la violence

violent ADJECTIVE
violent

violin NOUN

V

☞

le violon ◊ *I play the violin.* Je joue du violon.

violinist NOUN
le/la violoniste

virgin NOUN
la vierge ◊ *to be a virgin* être vierge

Virgo NOUN
la Vierge ◊ *I'm Virgo.* Je suis Vierge.

virtual reality NOUN
la réalité virtuelle

virus NOUN
le virus (*also computing*)

visa NOUN
le visa

visible ADJECTIVE
visible

visit NOUN
see also **visit** VERB
① la visite (*to museum*)
② le séjour (*to country*) ◊ *Did you enjoy your visit to France?* Ton séjour en France s'est bien passé?
♦ **my last visit to my grandmother** la dernière fois que je suis allé voir ma grand-mère

to **visit** VERB
see also **visit** NOUN
① rendre visite à (*person*) ◊ *to visit somebody* rendre visite à quelqu'un
② visiter (*place*) ◊ *We'd like to visit the castle.* Nous voudrions visiter le château.

visitor NOUN
① (*tourist*)
le visiteur
la visiteuse
② (*guest*)
l' invité MASC
l' invitée FEM
♦ **to have a visitor** avoir de la visite

visual ADJECTIVE
visuel MASC
visuelle FEM

to **visualize** VERB
imaginer

vital ADJECTIVE
vital
(vitaux MASC PL)

vitamin NOUN
la vitamine

vivid ADJECTIVE
(*colour*)
vif MASC
vive FEM
♦ **to have a vivid imagination** avoir une imagination débordante

vocabulary NOUN
le vocabulaire

vocational ADJECTIVE
professionnel MASC
professionnelle FEM
♦ **a vocational course** un stage de formation professionnelle

vodka NOUN
la vodka

voice NOUN
la voix
(les voix PL)

voice mail NOUN
la messagerie vocale

volcano NOUN
le volcan

volleyball NOUN
le volley-ball ◊ *to play volleyball* jouer au volley-ball

volt NOUN
le volt

voltage NOUN
le voltage

voluntary ADJECTIVE
volontaire (*contribution, statement*)
♦ **to do voluntary work** travailler bénévolement

volunteer NOUN
see also **volunteer** VERB
le/la volontaire

to **volunteer** VERB
see also **volunteer** NOUN
♦ **to volunteer to do something** se proposer pour faire quelque chose

to **vomit** VERB
vomir

to **vote** VERB
voter

voucher NOUN
le bon ◊ *a gift voucher* un bon d'achat

vowel NOUN
la voyelle

vulgar ADJECTIVE
vulgaire

W

wafer NOUN
la <u>gaufrette</u>

wage NOUN
le <u>salaire</u> ◊ *He collected his wages.* Il a retiré son salaire.

waist NOUN
la <u>taille</u>

waistcoat NOUN
le <u>gilet</u>

to **wait** VERB
<u>attendre</u>
♦ **to wait for something** attendre quelque chose
♦ **to wait for somebody** attendre quelqu'un ◊ *I'll wait for you.* Je t'attendrai.
♦ **Wait for me!** Attends-moi!
♦ **Wait a minute!** Attends!
♦ **to keep somebody waiting** faire attendre quelqu'un ◊ *They kept us waiting for hours.* Ils nous ont fait attendre pendant des heures.
♦ **I can't wait for the holidays.** J'ai hâte d'être en vacances.
♦ **I can't wait to see him again.** J'ai hâte de le revoir.

to **wait up** VERB
<u>attendre pour se coucher</u> ◊ *My mum always waits up till I get in.* Ma mère attend toujours que je rentre pour se coucher.

waiter NOUN
le <u>serveur</u>
♦ **Waiter!** Garçon!

waiting list NOUN
la <u>liste d'attente</u>

waiting room NOUN
la <u>salle d'attente</u>

waitress NOUN
la <u>serveuse</u>

to **wake up** VERB
se <u>réveiller</u> ◊ *I woke up at six o'clock.* Je me suis réveillé à six heures.
♦ **to wake somebody up** réveiller quelqu'un ◊ *Please would you wake me up at seven o'clock?* Pourriez-vous me réveiller à sept heures?

Wales NOUN
le <u>pays de Galles</u>
♦ **in Wales** au pays de Galles
♦ **to Wales** au pays de Galles
♦ **I'm from Wales.** Je suis gallois.
♦ **the Prince of Wales** le prince de Galles

to **walk** VERB
| *see also* **walk** NOUN |
1 <u>marcher</u> ◊ *He walks fast.* Il marche vite.
2 <u>aller à pied</u> (*go on foot*) ◊ *Are you walking or going by bus?* Tu y vas à pied ou en bus? ◊ *We walked 10 kilometres.* Nous avons fait dix kilomètres à pied.
♦ **to walk the dog** promener le chien

walk NOUN
| *see also* **walk** VERB |
la <u>promenade</u> ◊ *to go for a walk* faire une promenade
♦ **It's 10 minutes' walk from here.** C'est à dix minutes d'ici à pied.

walkie-talkie NOUN
le <u>talkie-walkie</u>

walking NOUN
la <u>randonnée</u> ◊ *I did some walking in the Alps last summer.* J'ai fait de la randonnée dans les Alpes l'été dernier.

walking stick NOUN
la <u>canne</u>

Walkman ® NOUN
le <u>baladeur</u>

wall NOUN
le <u>mur</u>

wallet NOUN
le <u>portefeuille</u>

wallpaper NOUN
le <u>papier peint</u>

walnut NOUN
la <u>noix</u>
(les noix PL)

to **wander** VERB
♦ **to wander around** flâner ◊ *I just wandered around for a while.* J'ai flâné un peu.

to **want** VERB
<u>vouloir</u> ◊ *Do you want some cake?* Tu veux du gâteau?
♦ **to want to do something** vouloir faire quelque chose ◊ *I want to go to the cinema.* Je veux aller au cinéma. ◊ *What do you want to do tomorrow?* Qu'est-ce que tu veux faire demain?

war NOUN
la <u>guerre</u>

ward NOUN
la <u>salle</u> (*room in hospital*)

warden NOUN
(*of youth hostel*)

☞

le directeur
la directrice

wardrobe NOUN
l' armoire FEM (*piece of furniture*)

warehouse NOUN
l' entrepôt MASC

warm ADJECTIVE
☐1 (*person*)
chaud ◊ *warm water* l'eau chaude
♦ **It's warm in here.** Il fait chaud ici.
♦ **to be warm** avoir chaud ◊ *I'm too warm.* J'ai trop chaud.
☐2 chaleureux MASC
chaleureuse FEM
◊ *a warm welcome* un accueil chaleureux
♦ **to warm up (1)** (*for sport*) s'échauffer
♦ **to warm up (2)** (*food*) réchauffer ◊ *I'll warm up some lasagne for you.* Je vais te réchauffer des lasagnes.

to **warn** VERB
prévenir ◊ *Well, I warned you!* Je t'avais prévenu!
♦ **to warn somebody to do something** conseiller à quelqu'un de faire quelque chose

warning NOUN
l' avertissement MASC

Warsaw NOUN
Varsovie

wart NOUN
la verrue

was VERB *see* **be**

wash NOUN
see also **wash** VERB
♦ **to have a wash** se laver ◊ *I had a wash.* Je me suis lavé.
♦ **to give something a wash** laver quelque chose ◊ *He gave the car a wash.* Il a lavé la voiture.

to **wash** VERB
see also **wash** NOUN
☐1 laver ◊ *to wash something* laver quelque chose
☐2 se laver (*have a wash*) ◊ *Every morning I get up, wash and get dressed.* Tous les matins je me lève, je me lave et je m'habille.
♦ **to wash one's hands** se laver les mains
♦ **to wash one's hair** se laver les cheveux
♦ **to wash up** faire la vaisselle

washbasin NOUN
le lavabo

washcloth NOUN US
le gant de toilette

washing NOUN
le linge ◊ *dirty washing* du linge sale

♦ **Have you got any washing?** Tu as du linge à laver?
♦ **to do the washing** faire la lessive

washing machine NOUN
la machine à laver

washing powder NOUN
la lessive

washing-up NOUN
♦ **to do the washing-up** faire la vaisselle

washing-up liquid NOUN
le produit à vaisselle

wasn't = **was not**

wasp NOUN
la guêpe

waste NOUN
see also **waste** VERB
☐1 le gaspillage ◊ *It's such a waste!* C'est vraiment du gaspillage!
♦ **It's a waste of time.** C'est une perte de temps.
☐2 les déchets MASC PL (*rubbish*)
◊ *nuclear waste* les déchets nucléaires

to **waste** VERB
see also **waste** NOUN
gaspiller ◊ *I don't like wasting money.* Je n'aime pas gaspiller de l'argent.
♦ **to waste time** perdre du temps ◊ *There's no time to waste.* Il n'y a pas de temps à perdre.

wastepaper basket NOUN
la corbeille à papier

watch NOUN
see also **watch** VERB
la montre

to **watch** VERB
see also **watch** NOUN
☐1 regarder ◊ *to watch television* regarder la télévision ◊ *Watch me!* Regarde-moi!
☐2 surveiller (*keep a watch on*) ◊ *The police were watching the house.* La police surveillait la maison.
♦ **to watch out** faire attention
♦ **Watch out!** Attention!

water NOUN
see also **water** VERB
l' eau FEM

to **water** VERB
see also **water** NOUN
arroser ◊ *He was watering his tulips.* Il arrosait ses tulipes.

waterfall NOUN
la cascade

watering can NOUN
l' arrosoir MASC

watermelon NOUN
la pastèque

waterproof ADJECTIVE
imperméable ◊ *Is this jacket waterproof?* Ce blouson est-il imperméable?
♦**a waterproof watch** une montre étanche

water-skiing NOUN
le ski nautique ◊ *to go water-skiing* faire du ski nautique

wave NOUN
see also **wave** VERB
1 la vague (*in water*)
2 le signe (*of hand*) ◊ *We gave him a wave.* Nous lui avons fait signe.

to **wave** VERB
see also **wave** NOUN
faire un signe de la main ◊ *to wave at somebody* faire un signe de la main à quelqu'un
♦**to wave goodbye** faire au revoir de la main ◊ *I waved her goodbye.* Je lui ai fait au revoir de la main.

wavy ADJECTIVE
ondulé ◊ *wavy hair* les cheveux ondulés

wax NOUN
la cire

way NOUN
1 la façon (*manner*) ◊ *She looked at me in a strange way.* Elle m'a regardé d'une façon étrange.
♦**This book tells you the right way to do it.** Ce livre explique comment il faut faire.
♦**You're doing it the wrong way.** Ce n'est pas comme ça qu'il faut faire.
♦**in a way** ... dans un sens ...
♦**a way of life** un mode de vie
2 le chemin (*route*) ◊ *I don't know the way.* Je ne connais pas le chemin.
♦**on the way** en chemin ◊ *We stopped on the way.* Nous nous sommes arrêtés en chemin.
♦**It's a long way.** C'est loin. ◊ *Paris is a long way from London.* Paris est loin de Londres.
♦**Which way is it?** C'est par où?
♦**The supermarket is this way.** Le supermarché est par ici.
♦**Do you know the way to the station?** Vous savez comment aller à la gare?
♦**He's on his way.** Il arrive.
♦**"way in"** "entrée"
♦**"way out"** "sortie"
♦**by the way** ... au fait ...

we PRONOUN

nous ◊ *We're staying here for a week.* Nous restons une semaine ici.

weak ADJECTIVE
faible

wealthy ADJECTIVE
riche

weapon NOUN
l' arme FEM

to **wear** VERB
porter (*clothes*) ◊ *She was wearing a hat.* Elle portait un chapeau.
♦**She was wearing black.** Elle était en noir.

weather NOUN
le temps ◊ *What was the weather like?* Quel temps a-t-il fait? ◊ *The weather was lovely.* Il a fait un temps magnifique.

weather forecast NOUN
la météo

web NOUN
le web

web browser NOUN
le navigateur

webmaster NOUN
le/la gestionnaire de site

website NOUN
le site web

webzine NOUN
le webzine

we'd = we had, = we would

wedding NOUN
le mariage
♦**wedding anniversary** l'anniversaire de mariage MASC
♦**wedding dress** la robe de mariée

Wednesday NOUN
le mercredi ◊ *on Wednesday* mercredi ◊ *on Wednesdays* le mercredi ◊ *every Wednesday* tous les mercredis ◊ *last Wednesday* mercredi dernier ◊ *next Wednesday* mercredi prochain

weed NOUN
la mauvaise herbe ◊ *The garden's full of weeds.* Le jardin est plein de mauvaises herbes.

week NOUN
la semaine ◊ *last week* la semaine dernière ◊ *every week* toutes les semaines ◊ *next week* la semaine prochaine ◊ *in a week's time* dans une semaine
♦**a week on Friday** vendredi en huit

weekday NOUN
♦**on weekdays** en semaine

weekend NOUN
le week-end ◊ *at weekends* le week-end ◊ *last weekend* le week-end

W

☞

dernier ◊ *next weekend* le week-end prochain

to **weep** VERB
<u>pleurer</u>

to **weigh** VERB
<u>peser</u> ◊ *How much do you weigh?* Combien est-ce que tu pèses? ◊ *First, weigh the flour.* Tout d'abord, pesez la farine.
♦**to weigh oneself** se peser

weight NOUN
le <u>poids</u>
♦**to lose weight** maigrir
♦**to put on weight** grossir

weightlifter NOUN
l' <u>haltérophile</u> MASC

weightlifting NOUN
l' <u>haltérophilie</u> FEM

weird ADJECTIVE
<u>bizarre</u>

welcome NOUN
see also **welcome** VERB
l' <u>accueil</u> MASC ◊ *They gave her a warm welcome.* Ils lui ont fait un accueil chaleureux.
♦**Welcome!** Bienvenue! ◊ *Welcome to France!* Bienvenue en France!

to **welcome** VERB
see also **welcome** NOUN
♦**to welcome somebody** accueillir quelqu'un
♦**Thank you! – You're welcome!** Merci! – De rien!

well ADJECTIVE, ADVERB
see also **well** NOUN
[1] <u>bien</u> ◊ *You did that really well.* Tu as très bien fait ça.
♦**to do well** réussir bien ◊ *She's doing really well at school.* Elle réussit vraiment bien à l'école.
♦**to be well** (*in good health*) aller bien ◊ *I'm not very well at the moment.* Je ne vais pas très bien en ce moment.
♦**get well soon!** remets-toi vite!
♦**well done!** bravo!
[2] <u>enfin</u> ◊ *It's enormous! Well, quite big anyway.* C'est énorme! Enfin, c'est assez grand.
♦**as well** aussi ◊ *We worked hard, but we had some fun as well.* Nous avons travaillé dur, mais nous nous sommes bien amusés aussi. ◊ *We went to Chartres as well as Paris.* Nous sommes allés à Paris et à Chartres aussi.

well NOUN
see also **well** ADJECTIVE
le <u>puits</u>
(les puits PL)

we'll = we will

well-behaved ADJECTIVE
<u>sage</u>

well-dressed ADJECTIVE
<u>bien habillé</u>

wellingtons PL NOUN
les <u>bottes en caoutchouc</u> FEM PL

well-known ADJECTIVE
<u>célèbre</u> ◊ *a well-known film star* une vedette de cinéma célèbre

well-off ADJECTIVE
<u>aisé</u>

Welsh ADJECTIVE
see also **Welsh** NOUN
<u>gallois</u> ◊ *She's Welsh.* Elle est galloise.
♦**Welsh people** les Gallois MASC

Welsh NOUN
see also **Welsh** ADJECTIVE
le <u>gallois</u> (*language*)

Welshman NOUN
le <u>Gallois</u>

Welshwoman NOUN
la <u>Galloise</u>

went VERB see **go**

wept VERB see **weep**

were VERB see **be**

we're = we are

weren't = were not

west NOUN
see also **west** ADJECTIVE
l' <u>ouest</u> MASC ◊ *in the west* dans l'ouest

west ADJECTIVE, ADVERB
see also **west** NOUN
[1] <u>ouest</u> MASC, FEM, PL ◊ *the west coast* la côte ouest
♦**west of** à l'ouest de ◊ *Stroud is west of Oxford.* Stroud est à l'ouest d'Oxford.
[2] <u>vers l'ouest</u> ◊ *We were travelling west.* Nous allions vers l'ouest.
♦**the West Country** le sud-ouest de l'Angleterre

westbound ADJECTIVE
♦**The truck was westbound on the M5.** Le camion roulait sur la M5 en direction de l'ouest.
♦**Westbound traffic is moving very slowly.** La circulation en direction de l'ouest est très ralentie.

western NOUN
see also **western** ADJECTIVE
le <u>western</u> (*film*)

western ADJECTIVE
see also **western** NOUN
♦**the western part of the island** la partie ouest de l'île

♦**Western Europe** l'Europe de l'Ouest

West Indian ADJECTIVE

| see also **West Indian** NOUN |

antillais ◊ *She's West Indian.* Elle est antillaise.

West Indian NOUN

| see also **West Indian** ADJECTIVE |

(*person*)
l' Antillais MASC
l' Antillaise FEM

West Indies PL NOUN
les Antilles FEM PL

♦**in the West Indies** aux Antilles

wet ADJECTIVE
mouillé ◊ *wet clothes* les vêtements mouillés

♦**to get wet** se faire mouiller

♦**dripping wet** trempé

♦**wet weather** le temps pluvieux

♦**It was wet all week.** Il a plu toute la semaine.

wetsuit NOUN
la combinaison de plongée
(les combinaisons de plongée PL)

we've = we have

whale NOUN
la baleine

what ADJECTIVE, PRONOUN
[1] (*which*)
quel MASC
quelle FEM
◊ *What subjects are you studying?* Quelles matières est-ce que tu fais? ◊ *What colour is it?* C'est de quelle couleur? ◊ *What's the capital of Finland?* Quelle est la capitale de la Finlande? ◊ *What a mess!* Quel fouillis!
[2] qu'est-ce que ◊ *What are you doing?* Qu'est-ce que vous faites? ◊ *What did you say?* Qu'est-ce que vous avez dit? ◊ *What is it?* Qu'est-ce que c'est? ◊ *What's the matter?* Qu'est-ce qu'il y a?
[3] qu'est-ce qui ◊ *What happened?* Qu'est-ce qui s'est passé? ◊ *What's bothering you?* Qu'est-ce qui te préoccupe?

*In relative phrases use **ce qui** or **ce que** depending on whether **what** refers to the subject or the object of the sentence.*

[4] (*subject*)
ce qui ◊ *I saw what happened.* J'ai vu ce qui est arrivé. ◊ *I know what's bothering you.* Je sais ce qui te préoccupe.
[5] (*object*)
ce que ◊ *Tell me what you did.* Dites-moi ce que vous avez fait. ◊ *I*

heard what he said. J'ai entendu ce qu'il a dit.

♦**What?** (*what did you say*) Comment?

♦**What!** (*shocked*) Quoi!

wheat NOUN
le blé

wheel NOUN
la roue

♦**the steering wheel** le volant

wheelchair NOUN
le fauteuil roulant

when ADVERB, CONJUNCTION
quand ◊ *When did he go?* Quand est-ce qu'il est parti? ◊ *She was reading when I came in.* Elle lisait quand je suis entré.

where ADVERB, CONJUNCTION
où ◊ *Where's Emma today?* Où est Emma aujourd'hui? ◊ *Where do you live?* Où habites-tu? ◊ *Where are you going?* Où vas-tu? ◊ *a shop where you can buy croissants* un magasin où l'on peut acheter des croissants

whether CONJUNCTION
si ◊ *I don't know whether to go or not.* Je ne sais pas si y aller ou non.

which ADJECTIVE, PRONOUN
[1] quel MASC
quelle FEM
◊ *Which flavour do you want?* Quel parfum est-ce que tu veux?

*When asking **which one** use **lequel** or **laquelle**, depending on whether the noun is masculine or feminine.*

♦**I know his brother. – Which one?** Je connais son frère. – Lequel?

♦**I know his sister. – Which one?** Je connais sa sœur. – Laquelle?

♦**Which would you like?** Lequel est-ce que vous voulez?

♦**Which of these are yours?** Lesquels sont à vous?

*In relative phrases use **qui** or **que** depending on whether **which** refers to the subject or the object of the sentence.*

[2] (*subject*)
qui ◊ *the CD which is playing now* le CD qui passe maintenant
[3] (*object*)
que ◊ *the CD which I bought today* le CD que j'ai acheté hier

while CONJUNCTION

| see also **while** NOUN |

[1] pendant que ◊ *You hold the torch while I look inside.* Tiens la lampe électrique pendant que je regarde à l'intérieur.
[2] alors que ◊ *Isobel is very dynamic, while Kay is more laid-back.*

W

☞

Isobel est très dynamique, alors que Kay est plus relax.

while NOUN
| see also **while** CONJUNCTION |
le moment ◊ *after a while* au bout d'un moment
♦ **a while ago** il y a un moment ◊ *He was here a while ago.* Il était là il y a un moment.
♦ **for a while** pendant quelque temps ◊ *I lived in London for a while.* J'ai vécu à Londres pendant quelque temps.
♦ **quite a while** longtemps ◊ *quite a while ago* il y a longtemps ◊ *I haven't seen him for quite a while.* Ça fait longtemps que je ne l'ai pas vu.

whip NOUN
| see also **whip** VERB |
le fouet

to **whip** VERB
| see also **whip** NOUN |
[1] fouetter (*person, animal*)
[2] battre (*eggs*)

whipped cream NOUN
la crème fouettée

whisk NOUN
le fouet

whiskers PL NOUN
les moustaches FEM PL

whisky NOUN
le whisky
(les whiskies PL)

to **whisper** VERB
chuchoter

whistle NOUN
| see also **whistle** VERB |
le sifflet
♦ **The referee blew his whistle.** L'arbitre a sifflé.

to **whistle** VERB
| see also **whistle** NOUN |
siffler

white ADJECTIVE
blanc MASC
blanche FEM
◊ *He's got white hair.* Il a les cheveux blancs.
♦ **white wine** le vin blanc
♦ **white bread** le pain blanc
♦ **white coffee** le café·au lait
♦ **a white man** un Blanc
♦ **a white woman** une Blanche
♦ **white people** les Blancs

Whitsun NOUN
la Pentecôte

who PRONOUN
[1] qui ◊ *Who said that?* Qui a dit ça? ◊ *Who is Jacques Chirac?* Qui est Jacques Chirac?

*In relative phrases use **qui** or **que** depending on whether **who** refers to the subject or the object of the verb.*
[2] qui (*subject*) ◊ *the man who saw us* l'homme qui nous a vus ◊ *the man who spoke to us* l'homme qui nous a parlé
[3] que (*object*) ◊ *the man who we saw* l'homme que nous avons vu ◊ *the man who she married* l'homme qu'elle a épousé

whole ADJECTIVE
| see also **whole** NOUN |
tout ◊ *the whole class* toute la classe ◊ *the whole afternoon* tout l'après-midi
♦ **a whole box of chocolates** toute une boîte de chocolats
♦ **the whole world** le monde entier

whole NOUN
| see also **whole** ADJECTIVE |
♦ **The whole of Wales was affected.** Le pays de Galles tout entier a été touché.
♦ **on the whole** dans l'ensemble

wholemeal ADJECTIVE
complet MASC
complète FEM
♦ **wholemeal bread** le pain complet

wholewheat ADJECTIVE [US]
complet MASC
complète FEM

whom PRONOUN
qui ◊ *Whom did you see?* Qui avez-vous vu? ◊ *the man to whom I spoke* l'homme à qui j'ai parlé

whose PRONOUN, ADJECTIVE
[1] à qui ◊ *Whose is this?* À qui est-ce? ◊ *I know whose it is.* Je sais à qui c'est. ◊ *Whose book is this?* À qui est ce livre?
[2] dont (*after noun*) ◊ *the girl whose picture was in the paper* la jeune fille dont la photo était dans le journal

why ADVERB
pourquoi ◊ *Why did you do that?* Pourquoi avez-vous fait ça? ◊ *That's why he did it.* Voilà pourquoi il a fait ça. ◊ *Tell me why.* Dis-moi pourquoi.
♦ **I've never been to France. – Why not?** Je ne suis jamais allé en France. – Pourquoi?
♦ **All right, why not?** D'accord, pourquoi pas?

wicked ADJECTIVE
[1] (*evil*)
méchant
[2] (*really great*)
génial
(géniaux MASC PL)

wicket NOUN
le guichet (*stumps*)

wide ADJECTIVE, ADVERB
large ◊ *a wide road* une route large
♦ **wide open** grand ouvert ◊ *The door was wide open.* La porte était grande ouverte. ◊ *The windows were wide open.* Les fenêtres étaient grandes ouvertes.
♦ **wide awake** complètement réveillé

widow NOUN
la veuve ◊ *She's a widow.* Elle est veuve.

widower NOUN
le veuf ◊ *He's a widower.* Il est veuf.

width NOUN
la largeur

wife NOUN
la femme ◊ *She's his wife.* C'est sa femme.

wig NOUN
la perruque

wild ADJECTIVE
1 (*not tame*)
sauvage ◊ *a wild animal* un animal sauvage
2 (*crazy*)
fou MASC
folle FEM
◊ *She's a bit wild.* Elle est un peu folle.

wildlife NOUN
la nature ◊ *I'm interested in wildlife.* Je m'intéresse à la nature.

will NOUN
| see also **will** VERB |
le testament ◊ *He left me some money in his will.* Il m'a laissé de l'argent dans son testament.

will VERB
| see also **will** NOUN |
♦ **I'll show you your room.** Je vais te montrer ta chambre.
♦ **I'll give you a hand.** Je vais t'aider.
Use the French future tense when referring to the more distant future.
♦ **I will finish it tomorrow.** Je le finirai demain.
♦ **It won't take long.** Ça ne prendra pas longtemps.
♦ **Will you wash up? – No, I won't.** Est-ce que tu peux faire la vaisselle? – Non.
♦ **Will you help me?** Est-ce que tu peux m'aider?
♦ **Will you be quiet!** Voulez-vous bien vous taire!
♦ **That will be the postman.** Ça doit être le facteur.

willing ADJECTIVE

♦ **to be willing to do something** être prêt à faire quelque chose

to **win** VERB
| see also **win** NOUN |
gagner ◊ *Did you win?* Est-ce que tu as gagné?
♦ **to win a prize** remporter un prix

win NOUN
| see also **win** VERB |
la victoire

to **wind** VERB
| see also **wind** NOUN |
1 enrouler (*rope, wool, wire*)
2 serpenter (*river, path*) ◊ *The road winds through the valley.* La route serpente à travers la vallée.

wind NOUN
| see also **wind** VERB |
le vent ◊ *There was a strong wind.* Il y avait beaucoup de vent.
♦ **a wind instrument** un instrument à vent
♦ **wind power** l'énergie éolienne FEM

windmill NOUN
le moulin à vent
(les moulins à vent PL)

window NOUN
1 (*of building*)
la fenêtre
2 (*in car, train*)
la vitre
♦ **a shop window** une vitrine
3 (*window pane*)
le carreau
(les carreaux PL)
◊ *to break a window* casser un carreau ◊ *a broken window* un carreau cassé

windscreen NOUN
le pare-brise
(les pare-brise PL)

windscreen wiper NOUN
l' essuie-glace MASC
(les essuie-glace PL)

windshield NOUN US
le pare-brise
(les pare-brise PL)

windshield wiper NOUN US
l' essuie-glace MASC
(les essuie-glace PL)

windy ADJECTIVE
(*place*)
venteux MASC
venteuse FEM
♦ **It's windy.** Il y a du vent.

wine NOUN
le vin ◊ *a bottle of wine* une bouteille de vin ◊ *a glass of wine* un verre de vin

W

☞

◆**white wine** le vin blanc
◆**red wine** le vin rouge
◆**a wine bar** un bar à vin
◆**a wine glass** un verre à vin
◆**the wine list** la carte des vins

wing NOUN
l' <u>aile</u> FEM

to **wink** VERB
◆**to wink at somebody** faire un clin d'œil à quelqu'un ◊ *He winked at me.* Il m'a fait un clin d'œil.

winner NOUN
le <u>gagnant</u>
la <u>gagnante</u>

winning ADJECTIVE
◆**the winning team** l'équipe gagnante
◆**the winning goal** le but décisif

winter NOUN
l' <u>hiver</u> MASC
◆**in winter** en hiver

winter sports PL NOUN
les <u>sports d'hiver</u> MASC PL

to **wipe** VERB
<u>essuyer</u>
◆**to wipe one's feet** s'essuyer les pieds ◊ *Wipe your feet!* Essuie-toi les pieds!
◆**to wipe up** essuyer

wire NOUN
le <u>fil de fer</u>

wisdom tooth NOUN
la <u>dent de sagesse</u>
(les dents de sagesse PL)

wise ADJECTIVE
<u>sage</u>

to **wish** VERB
| see also **wish** NOUN |
◆**to wish for something** souhaiter quelque chose ◊ *What more could you wish for?* Que pourrais-tu souhaiter de plus?
◆**to wish to do something** désirer faire quelque chose ◊ *I wish to make a complaint.* Je désire porter plainte.
◆**I wish you were here!** Si seulement tu étais ici!
◆**I wish you'd told me!** Si seulement tu m'en avais parlé!

wish NOUN
| see also **wish** VERB |
le <u>vœu</u>
(les vœux PL)
◊ *to make a wish* faire un vœu
◆**"best wishes"** (*on greetings card*) "meilleurs vœux"
◆**"with best wishes, Kathy"** "bien amicalement, Kathy"

wit NOUN
l' <u>esprit</u> MASC (*humour*)

with PREPOSITION

[1] <u>avec</u> ◊ *Come with me.* Venez avec moi. ◊ *He walks with a stick.* Il marche avec une canne.
◆**a woman with blue eyes** une femme aux yeux bleus
[2] <u>chez</u> (*at the home of*) ◊ *We stayed with friends.* Nous avons logé chez des amis.
[3] <u>de</u> ◊ *green with envy* vert de jalousie ◊ *to shake with fear* trembler de peur ◊ *Fill the jug with water.* Remplis la carafe d'eau.

within PREPOSITION
◆**The shops are within easy reach.** Les magasins sont à proximité.
◆**within the week** avant la fin de la semaine

without PREPOSITION
<u>sans</u> ◊ *without a coat* sans manteau ◊ *without speaking* sans parler

witness NOUN
le <u>témoin</u> ◊ *There were no witnesses.* Il n'a pas eu de témoins.

witty ADJECTIVE
<u>spirituel</u> MASC
<u>spirituelle</u> FEM

wives PL NOUN *see* **wife**

woke up, woken up VERB *see* **wake up**

wolf NOUN
le <u>loup</u>

woman NOUN
la <u>femme</u> ◊ *a woman doctor* une femme médecin

won VERB *see* **win**

to **wonder** VERB
<u>se demander</u> ◊ *I wonder why she said that.* Je me demande pourquoi elle a dit ça. ◊ *I wonder what that means.* Je me demande ce que ça veut dire. ◊ *I wonder where Caroline is.* Je me demande où est Caroline.

wonderful ADJECTIVE
<u>formidable</u>

won't = **will not**

wood NOUN
le <u>bois</u> (*timber, forest*) ◊ *It's made of wood.* C'est en bois. ◊ *We went for a walk in the wood.* Nous sommes allés nous promener dans le bois.

wooden ADJECTIVE
<u>en bois</u> ◊ *a wooden chair* une chaise en bois

woodwork NOUN
la <u>menuiserie</u> ◊ *My hobby is woodwork.* Je fais de la menuiserie.

wool NOUN

la <u>laine</u> ◊ *It's made of wool.* C'est en laine.

word NOUN
le <u>mot</u> ◊ *a difficult word* un mot difficile
◆**What's the word for "shop" in German?** Comment dit-on "magasin" en allemand?
◆**in other words** en d'autres termes
◆**to have a word with somebody** parler avec quelqu'un
◆**the words** (*lyrics*) les paroles FEM ◊ *I really like the words of this song.* J'adore les paroles de cette chanson.

word processing NOUN
le <u>traitement de texte</u>

word processor NOUN
la <u>machine de traitement de texte</u>

wore VERB *see* **wear**

work NOUN
    | *see also* **work** VERB |
le <u>travail</u>
(les travaux PL)
◊ *She's looking for work.* Elle cherche du travail. ◊ *He's at work at the moment.* Il est au travail en ce moment.
◆**It's hard work.** C'est dur.
◆**to be off work** (*sick*) être malade ◊ *He's been off work for a week.* Il est malade depuis une semaine.
◆**He's out of work.** Il est sans emploi.

to **work** VERB
    | *see also* **work** NOUN |
[1] <u>travailler</u> (*person*) ◊ *She works in a shop.* Elle travaille dans un magasin. ◊ *to work hard* travailler dur
[2] <u>marcher</u> (*machine, plan*) ◊ *The heating isn't working.* Le chauffage ne marche pas. ◊ *My plan worked perfectly.* Mon plan a marché impeccablement.
◆**to work out (1)** (*exercise*) faire de l'exercice ◊ *I work out twice a week.* Je fais de l'exercice deux fois par semaine.
◆**to work out (2)** (*turn out*) marcher ◊ *In the end it worked out really well.* Au bout du compte, ça a très bien marché.
◆**to work out (3)** (*figure out*) arriver à comprendre ◊ *I just couldn't work it out.* Je n'arrivais pas du tout à comprendre.
◆**It works out at £10 each.** Ça fait dix livres chacun.

worker NOUN
(*in factory*)
l' <u>ouvrier</u> MASC

l' <u>ouvrière</u> FEM
◆**He's a factory worker.** Il est ouvrier.
◆**She's a good worker.** Elle travaille bien.

work experience NOUN
le <u>stage</u> ◊ *I'm going to do work experience in a factory.* Je vais faire un stage dans une usine.

working-class ADJECTIVE
<u>ouvrier</u> MASC
<u>ouvrière</u> FEM
◊ *a working-class family* une famille ouvrière

workman NOUN
l' <u>ouvrier</u> MASC

works NOUN
l' <u>usine</u> FEM (*factory*)

worksheet NOUN
la <u>feuille d'exercices</u>

workshop NOUN
l' <u>atelier</u> MASC ◊ *a drama workshop* un atelier de théâtre

workspace NOUN
l' <u>espace de travail</u> MASC (*computing*)

workstation NOUN
le <u>poste de travail</u>
(les postes de travail PL)

world NOUN
le <u>monde</u>
◆**He's the world champion.** Il est champion du monde.

worm NOUN
le <u>ver</u>

worn VERB *see* **wear**

worn ADJECTIVE
<u>usé</u> ◊ *The carpet is a bit worn.* La moquette est un peu usée.
◆**worn out** (*tired*) épuisé

worried ADJECTIVE
<u>inquiet</u> MASC
<u>inquiète</u> FEM
◊ *She's very worried.* Elle est très inquiète.
◆**to be worried about something** s'inquiéter pour quelque chose ◊ *I'm worried about the exams.* Je m'inquiète pour les examens.
◆**to look worried** avoir l'air inquiet ◊ *She looks a bit worried.* Elle a l'air un peu inquiète.

to **worry** VERB
s'<u>inquiéter</u>
◆**Don't worry!** Ne t'inquiète pas!

worse ADJECTIVE, ADVERB
[1] <u>pire</u> ◊ *It was even worse than that.* C'était encore pire que ça. ◊ *My results were bad, but his were even worse.* Mes notes étaient mauvaises, mais les siennes étaient encore pires.

W

☞

2 plus mal ◊ *I'm feeling worse.* Je me sens plus mal.

to **worship** VERB
vénérer (*God*)
♦**He really worships her.** Il est en adoration devant elle.

worst ADJECTIVE
see also **worst** NOUN
♦**the worst** le plus mauvais ◊ *the worst student in the class* le plus mauvais élève de la classe ◊ *He got the worst mark in the whole class.* Il a eu la plus mauvaise note de toute la classe.
♦**my worst enemy** mon pire ennemi
♦**Maths is my worst subject.** Je suis vraiment nul en maths.

worst NOUN
see also **worst** ADJECTIVE
le pire ◊ *The worst of it is that ...* Le pire c'est que ...
♦**at worst** au pire
♦**if the worst comes to the worst** au pire

worth ADJECTIVE
♦**to be worth** valoir ◊ *It's worth a lot of money.* Ça vaut très cher. ◊ *How much is it worth?* Ça vaut combien?
♦**It's worth it.** Ça vaut la peine. ◊ *Is it worth it?* Est-ce que ça vaut la peine? ◊ *It's not worth it.* Ça ne vaut pas la peine.

would VERB
♦**Would you like a biscuit?** Vous voulez un biscuit?
♦**Would you like to go and see a film?** Est-ce que tu veux aller voir un film?
♦**Would you close the door please?** Vous pouvez fermer la porte, s'il vous plaît?
♦**I'd like ...** J'aimerais ... ◊ *I'd like to go to America.* J'aimerais aller en Amérique. ◊ *Shall we go and see a film? – Yes, I'd like that.* Si on allait voir un film? – Oui, j'aimerais bien.
♦**I said I would do it.** J'ai dit que je le ferais.
♦**If you asked him he'd do it.** Si vous le lui demandiez, il le ferait.
♦**If you had asked him he would have done it.** Si vous le lui aviez demandé, il l'aurait fait.

wouldn't = **would not**

wound NOUN
see also **wound** VERB
la blessure

to **wound** VERB
see also **wound** NOUN
blesser ◊ *He was wounded in the leg.* Il a été blessé à la jambe.

to **wrap** VERB
emballer ◊ *She's wrapping her Christmas presents.* Elle est en train d'emballer ses cadeaux de Noël.
♦**Can you wrap it for me please?** (*in shop*) Vous pouvez me faire un papier cadeau, s'il vous plaît?
♦**to wrap up** emballer

wrapping paper NOUN
le papier cadeau

wreck NOUN
see also **wreck** VERB
1 le tas de ferraille (*vehicle, machine*) ◊ *That car is a wreck!* Cette voiture est un tas de ferraille!
2 la loque (*person*) ◊ *After the exams I was a complete wreck.* Après les examens j'étais une véritable loque.

to **wreck** VERB
see also **wreck** NOUN
1 démolir (*building, vehicle*) ◊ *The explosion wrecked the whole house.* L'explosion a démoli toute la maison.
2 ruiner (*plan, holiday*) ◊ *The trip was wrecked by bad weather.* Le voyage a été ruiné par le mauvais temps.

wreckage NOUN
1 les débris MASC PL (*of vehicle*)
2 les décombres MASC PL (*of building*)

wrestler NOUN
le lutteur
la lutteuse

wrestling NOUN
la lutte

wrinkled ADJECTIVE
ridé

wrist NOUN
le poignet

to **write** VERB
écrire ◊ *to write a letter* écrire une lettre
♦**to write to somebody** écrire à quelqu'un ◊ *I'm going to write to her in French.* Je vais lui écrire en français.
♦**to write down** noter ◊ *I wrote down the address.* J'ai noté l'adresse.
♦**Can you write it down for me, please?** Vous pouvez me l'écrire, s'il vous plaît?

writer NOUN
l' écrivain MASC ◊ *She's a writer.* Elle est écrivain.

writing NOUN
l' écriture FEM ◊ *I can't read your writing.* Je n'arrive pas à lire ton écriture.
♦**in writing** par écrit

written VERB *see* **write**

wrong ADJECTIVE, ADVERB

1 (*incorrect*)
faux MASC
fausse FEM
◊ *The information they gave us was wrong.* Les renseignements qu'ils nous ont donnés étaient faux.
♦**the wrong answer** la mauvaise réponse
♦**You've got the wrong number.** Vous vous êtes trompé de numéro.
2 (*morally bad*)
mal ◊ *I think hunting is wrong.* Je trouve que c'est mal de chasser.
♦**to be wrong** (*mistaken*) se tromper

◊ *You're wrong about that.* Tu te trompes.
♦**to do something wrong** se tromper
◊ *You've done it wrong.* Tu t'es trompé.
♦**to go wrong** (*plan*) mal tourner ◊ *The robbery went wrong and they got caught.* Le cambriolage a mal tourné et ils ont été pris.
♦**What's wrong?** Qu'est-ce qu'il y a?
♦**What's wrong with her?** Qu'est-ce qu'elle a?

wrote VERB *see* **write**

WWW NOUN (= *World Wide Web*)
le Web

W

X

Xerox ® NOUN
  see also **xerox** VERB
  la <u>photocopie</u>
to **xerox** VERB
  see also **Xerox** NOUN
  photocopier
Xmas NOUN (= *Christmas*)
  <u>Noël</u>
to **X-ray** VERB

  see also **X-ray** NOUN
♦**to X-ray something** faire une radio de
  quelque chose ◊ *They X-rayed my
  arm.* Ils ont fait une radio de mon
  bras.

X-ray NOUN
  see also **X-ray** VERB
  la <u>radio</u> ◊ *to have an X-ray* passer
  une radio

Y

yacht NOUN
  ① le <u>voilier</u> (*sailing boat*)
  ② le <u>yacht</u> (*luxury motorboat*)

yard NOUN
  ① la <u>cour</u> (*of building*) ◊ *in the yard*
  dans la cour
  ② le <u>mètre</u>

  > *ⓘ In France measurements are in
  metres rather than yards. A yard is
  slightly less than a metre.*

to **yawn** VERB
  <u>bâiller</u>

year NOUN
  l' <u>an</u> MASC ◊ *last year* l'an dernier
  ◊ *next year* l'an prochain
♦**to be 15 years old** avoir quinze ans
♦**an eight-year-old child** un enfant de
  huit ans

  > *ⓘ In French secondary schools,
  years are counted from the **sixième**
  (youngest) to **première** and **terminale**
  (oldest).*

  ◊ *year 7* la sixième ◊ *year 8* la
  cinquième ◊ *year 9* la quatrième
  ◊ *year 10* la troisième ◊ *year 11* la
  seconde
♦**She's in year 11.** Elle est en seconde.
♦**He's a first-year.** Il est en sixième.

to **yell** VERB
  hurler

yellow ADJECTIVE
  jaune

yes ADVERB
  ① <u>oui</u> ◊ *Do you like it? – Yes.* Tu
  aimes ça? – Oui.

♦**Would you like a cup of tea? – Yes
  please.** Voulez-vous une tasse de thé?
  – Je veux bien.

  > *Use **si** when answering negative
  questions.*

  ② <u>si</u> ◊ *Don't you like it? – Yes!* Tu
  n'aimes pas ça? – Si! ◊ *You're not
  Swiss, are you? – Yes I am!* Tu n'es
  pas suisse, si? – Si!

yesterday ADVERB
  <u>hier</u> ◊ *yesterday morning* hier matin
  ◊ *yesterday afternoon* hier après-midi
  ◊ *yesterday evening* hier soir ◊ *all
  day yesterday* toute la journée d'hier

yet ADVERB
  encore
♦**not yet** pas encore ◊ *It's not finished
  yet.* Ce n'est pas encore fini.
♦**not as yet** pas encore ◊ *There's no
  news as yet.* Nous n'avons pas
  encore de nouvelles.
♦**Have you finished yet?** Vous avez
  fini?

to **yield** VERB US
  céder le passage (*on road sign*)

yob NOUN
  le loubard

yoghurt NOUN
  le yaourt

yolk NOUN
  le <u>jaune d'œuf</u>
  (les jaunes d'œuf PL)

you PRONOUN

  > *Only use **tu** when speaking to one
  person of your own age or younger.
  If in doubt use **vous**.*

  ① (*polite form or plural*)
  <u>vous</u> ◊ *Do you like football?* Est-ce
  que vous aimez le football? ◊ *Can I*

help you? Est-ce que je peux vous aider? ◊ *It's for you.* C'est pour vous.
2 (*familiar singular*)
tu ◊ *Do you like football?* Tu aimes le football?

> ***vous** never changes, but **tu** has different forms. When **you** is the object of the sentence use **te** not **tu**. **te** becomes **t'** before a vowel sound.*

3 te ◊ *I know you.* Je te connais. ◊ *I gave it you.* Je te l'ai donné.
t' ◊ *I saw you.* Je t'ai vu. ◊ *I'll help you.* Je vais t'aider.

> ***toi** is used instead of **tu** after a preposition and in comparisons.*

4 toi ◊ *It's for you.* C'est pour toi. ◊ *I'll come with you.* Je viens avec toi. ◊ *She's younger than you.* Elle est plus jeune que toi.

young ADJECTIVE
jeune
◆ **young people** les jeunes

younger ADJECTIVE
plus jeune ◊ *He's younger than me.* Il est plus jeune que moi.
◆ **my younger brother** mon frère cadet
◆ **my younger sister** ma sœur cadette

youngest ADJECTIVE
le plus jeune
la plus jeune
◊ *my youngest brother* mon plus jeune frère ◊ *She's the youngest.* C'est la plus jeune.

your ADJECTIVE

> *Only use **ton/ta/tes** when speaking to one person of your own age or younger. If in doubt use **votre/vos**.*

1 (*polite form or plural*)
votre ◊ *your house* votre maison
vos PL ◊ *your seats* vos places
2 (*familiar singular*)
ton MASC ◊ *your brother* ton frère
ta FEM ◊ *your sister* ta sœur
tes PL ◊ *your parents* tes parents

> ***ta** becomes **ton** before a vowel sound*

◆ **your friend (1)** (*male*) ton ami
◆ **your friend (2)** (*female*) ton amie

> *Do not use **votre/vos** or **ton/ta/tes** with parts of the body.*

◊ *Would you like to wash your hands?* Est-ce que vous voulez vous laver les mains? ◊ *Do you want to wash your hair?* Tu veux te laver les cheveux?

yours PRONOUN

> *Only use **le tien/la tienne/les tiens/ les tiennes** when talking to one person of your own age or younger.*

> *If in doubt use **le vôtre/la vôtre/les vôtres**. The same applies to **à toi** and **à vous**.*

1 le vôtre + MASC NOUN ◊ *I've lost my pen. Can I use yours?* J'ai perdu mon stylo. Je peux utiliser le vôtre?
la vôtre + FEM NOUN ◊ *I like that car. Is it yours?* J'aime cette voiture-là. C'est la vôtre?
les vôtres + PL NOUN ◊ *my parents and yours* mes parents et les vôtres
◆ **Is this yours?** C'est à vous? ◊ *This book is yours.* Ce livre est à vous. ◊ *Whose is this? – It's yours.* C'est à qui? – À vous.
◆ **Yours sincerely** ... Veuillez agréer l'expression de mes sentiments les meilleurs ...
2 le tien + MASC NOUN ◊ *I've lost my pen. Can I use yours?* J'ai perdu mon stylo. Je peux utiliser le tien?
la tienne + FEM NOUN ◊ *I like that car. Is it yours?* J'aime cette voiture-là. C'est la tienne?
les tiens + MASC PL NOUN ◊ *my parents and yours* mes parents et les tiens
les tiennes + FEM PL NOUN ◊ *My hands are dirty, yours are clean.* Mes mains sont sales, les tiennes sont propres.
◆ **Is this yours?** C'est à toi? ◊ *This book is yours.* Ce livre est à toi. ◊ *Whose is this? – It's yours.* C'est à qui? – À toi.

yourself PRONOUN

> *Only use **te** when talking to one person of your own age or younger; use **vous** to everyone else. If in doubt use **vous**.*

1 vous (*polite form*) ◊ *Have you hurt yourself?* Est-ce que vous vous êtes fait mal? ◊ *Tell me about yourself!* Parlez-moi de vous!
2 te (*familiar form*) ◊ *Have you hurt yourself?* Est-ce que tu t'es fait mal?

> *After a preposition, use **toi** instead of **te**.*

3 toi (*familiar form*) ◊ *Tell me about yourself!* Parle-moi de toi!
4 toi-même ◊ *Do it yourself!* Fais-le toi-même!
5 vous-même ◊ *Do it yourself!* Faites-le vous-même!

yourselves PRONOUN
1 vous ◊ *Did you enjoy yourselves?* Vous vous êtes bien amusés?
2 vous-mêmes ◊ *Did you make it yourselves?* Vous l'avez fait vous-mêmes?

youth club NOUN
le centre de jeunes
youth hostel NOUN

☞

Y

l' auberge de jeunesse FEM
(les auberges de jeunesse PL)
Yugoslavia NOUN

la Yougoslavie
♦ **in the former Yugoslavia** en ex-
Yougoslavie

Z

---

zany ADJECTIVE
loufoque
zebra NOUN
le zèbre
zebra crossing NOUN
le passage clouté
zero NOUN
le zéro
Zimbabwe NOUN
le Zimbabwe
♦ **in Zimbabwe** au Zimbabwe
Zimmer frame ® NOUN
le déambulateur
zip NOUN
la fermeture éclair ®
(les fermetures éclair PL)
zip code NOUN US

le code postal
zipper NOUN US
la fermeture éclair ®
(les fermetures éclair PL)
zit NOUN
le bouton
zodiac NOUN
le zodiaque ◊ *the signs of the zodiac*
les signes du zodiaque
zone NOUN
la zone
zoo NOUN
le zoo
zoom lens NOUN
le zoom
zucchini NOUN US
la courgette